THE LONG PARLIAMENT

Memoirs of the

AMERICAN PHILOSOPHICAL SOCIETY

held at Philadelphia

for Promoting Useful Knowledge

Volume 36

THE LONG PARLIAMENT, 1640-1641
A BIOGRAPHICAL STUDY OF ITS MEMBERS

MARY FREAR KEELER

Lecturer in History, Wellesley College

THE AMERICAN PHILOSOPHICAL SOCIETY

INDEPENDENCE SQUARE

PHILADELPHIA

1954

Library of Congress Catalog
Card Number: 54-6118

To the Memory of

J. B. K.

CONTENTS

ACKNOWLEDGMENTS

The encouragement and assistance given by many persons in the course of this study of a parliament I am glad to acknowledge. Scholars and custodians of books and manuscripts, town clerks and shire officials, antiquarians and specialists in local history contributed time and information in generous response to my requests. The privilege which I enjoyed of using the records of counties, towns and boroughs was one for which I find it difficult to express my full appreciation. I am especially grateful also for the courtesies of the staffs of the British Museum, the Public Record Office, the Guildhall Library and Somerset House, the Bodleian and John Rylands libraries, and the Institute of Historical Research. On the American side of the Atlantic my thanks are due to the library staffs at Yale University, the University of Pennsylvania, the Pennsylvania State College, the Library of Congress, and the Martin Library of York, Pennsylvania.

Acknowledgments for special kinds of aid I owe to several groups and institutions. It was in the Graduate School of Yale University that this study was begun, and there a portion of it was presented two decades ago as a doctoral dissertation. The greater part of my research in England was done while I was the holder of one of the National Fellowships awarded by the American Association of University Women. For that aid I am most grateful. To the American Philosophical Society and to its editors I am deeply indebted for making possible the publication of my work. For permissions granted for the use of quotations I express my thanks to the publishers referred to in various footnotes.

With sincere appreciation I acknowledge to Wallace Notestein my obligation for the inspiration that led me to make this study, and for the kindly encouragement which accounts in large measure for its completion. For counsel during various stages of my research and for suggestions regarding parts of my manuscript I am indebted to my friend, Mildred Campbell. To Willson H. Coates, who read my entire manuscript and offered valuable criticisms, I am most grateful. My husband's assistance with the tables in Part I and his understanding and tolerance during the period of writing were of immeasurable value. Other members of my family assisted me with a number of bibliographical details. To them and to the other friends whose interest aided my work I express my gratitude.

M. F. K.

Wellesley College
October, 1953

ABBREVIATIONS

Acts P.C. Acts of the Privy Council.
Add. Ch. British Museum Additional Charters.
Add. MSS. British Museum Additional Manuscripts.
A.H.R. American Historical Review.
Al. Cant. John Venn and J. A. Venn, ed., *Alumni Cantabrigienses . . . to 1751*, 4 v., Cambridge, Univ. Press, 1922–1927.
Al. Oxon. Joseph Foster, ed., *Alumni Oxonienses: The members of the University of Oxford, 1500–1714*, 4 v., Oxford, 1891–1892.
Arch. Camb. Archaeologia Cambrensis: A record of the antiquities of Wales and its marches.
Bean, *Northern Counties.* W. W. Bean, *The parliamentary representation of the six northern counties of England*, Hull, 1890.
Berks. Arch. Jour. The Berks, Bucks & Oxon Archaeological Journal (1895–1929) and *The Berkshire Archaeological Journal* (1930–).
Bibl. Eg. See Eg. MSS.
Bodleian Add. MSS, Carte MSS, etc. Bodleian Library Manuscripts: Additional Manuscripts, Carte Manuscripts, etc.
Brown, *Genesis of the U.S* Alexander Brown, *The genesis of the United States*, 2 v., Boston, 1890.
Burke, *Extinct Peerage.* Sir (John) Bernard Burke, *A genealogical history of the dormant, abeyant, forfeited and extinct peerages of the British Empire*, rev. ed., London, 1866.
Burke, *Landed gentry.* J. Bernard Burke, *A genealogical and heraldic dictionary of the landed gentry of Great Britain and Ireland.*
C. Records of the Chancery, Public Record Office.

C.J. Journals of the House of Commons.
C.S.P.Dom. Calendar of State Papers, Domestic Series.
C.S.P. Col. Calendar of State Papers, Colonial Series.
C.S.P.Ireland. Calendar of State Papers relating to Ireland.
C.S.P. Venetian. Calendar of State Papers relating to English Affairs, existing in the Archives of Venice.
Cal. Com. Adv. Money. Calendar of Proceedings of the Committee for Advance of Money, 1642–1656.
Cal. Com. Comp. Calendar of Proceedings of the Committee for Compounding.
Cal. Inner Temp. Rec. A Calendar of the Inner Temple Records, ed. F. A. Inderwick, London, 1896–1900.
Carlyle, *Cromwell.* Thomas Carlyle, *Oliver Cromwell's Letters and Speeches*, Centenary edition.
Clarendon, *Rebellion.* Edward Hyde, Earl of Clarendon, *The history of the Rebellion and Civil Wars in England*, ed. W. Dunn Macray, 1888.
Coll. Geneal. Collectanea Genealogica.
Commons Debates 1621. Commons Debates 1621, ed. Wallace Notestein, Frances Helen Relf, and Hartley Simpson, 1935.
Commons Debates in 1625. Debates in the House of Commons in 1625, ed. S. R. Gardiner, Camden Society, 1873.
Commons Debates for 1629. Commons Debates for 1629, ed. W. Notestein and F. Relf, 1921.
Complete Baronetage. G. E. Cokayne, *The Complete Baronetage*, 6 v., Exeter, W. Pollard, 1900–1909.
Complete Peerage. G. E. C[okayne], *Complete Peerage of England, Ireland, Great Britain and the United Kingdom*, 1887–1898.

Complete Peerage, Gibbs ed. *The Complete Peerage of England* . . . , by G. E. C., new rev. ed.; ed. by the Hon. Vicary Gibbs, London, St. Catherine Press, 1910–.

D.L.   Deputy Lieutenant.

D.N.B. Dictionary of national biography.

D'Ewes (B).   Helen B. Barber, ed., manuscript edition of the journal of Sir Simonds D'Ewes, July–September, 1641.

D'Ewes (C).   Willson H. Coates, ed., *The journal of Sir Simonds D'Ewes,* New Haven, Yale Univ. Press, 1942.

D'Ewes (N).   Wallace Notestein, ed., *The journal of Sir Simonds D'Ewes,* New Haven, Yale Univ. Press, 1923.

D'Ewes, *Autobiography.*   J. O. Halliwell, ed., *The autobiography and correspondence of Sir Simonds D'Ewes, Bart.,* London, 1845.

E.H.R. English Historical Review.

Eg. MSS.   British Museum Egerton Manuscripts.

English Baronetage (1741).   Thomas Wotton, *The English Baronetage,* London, 1741.

English Baronetage (Kimber ed.).   *The Baronetage of England,* ed. E. Kimber and R. Johnson, London, 1771.

Fairfax correspondence.   George W. Johnson, ed., *The Fairfax correspondence,* London, 1848.

Forster, *Eliot.*   John Forster, *Sir John Eliot,* London, 1864.

Gardiner, *H. of E.*   S. R. Gardiner, *History of England from the accession of James I to the outbreak of the Civil War,* London, 1883–1884.

Gray's Inn Adm. Reg.   Joseph Foster, ed., *The Register of Admissions to Gray's Inn, 1521–1889,* London, 1889.

H.M.C. Historical Manuscripts Commission, Reports.

Harl. MSS.   British Museum Harleian Manuscripts.

H.S.   High Sheriff.

I.P.M. or i.p.m.   Inquisition post mortem.

J.P.   Justice of the Peace.

L.J. Journals of the House of Lords.

Lansd. MSS.   British Museum Lansdowne Manuscripts.

Linc. Inn Rec. Adm.; Linc. Inn Rec., Black Books. The records of the Honorable Society of Lincoln's Inn, Admissions, 2 v.; *Black Books,* 2 v., London, Lincoln's Inn, 1896–1902.

List of Sheriffs.   Public Record Office Lists and Indexes, IX, *List of Sheriffs for England and Wales,* 1898.

Lloyd, *Memoires.*   David Lloyd, *Memoires of the lives . . . of . . . excellent personages,* London, 1668.

Lysons, *Mag. Brit.*   D. and S. Lysons, *Magna Britannia,* 1806–1882.

M. of P.   Return of the names of every member returned to serve in each parliament, Accounts and Papers, Session of 1878.

Marriage Licenses, London.   Allegations of marriage licenses issued by the Bishop of London, Harleian Society, 1887.

May.   Thomas May, *The history of the parliament of England which began November 3, 1640,* 1854 ed., Oxford.

Memoirs of Denzil Holles.   Memoirs of Denzil, Lord Holles, 1699.

M.I.   Monumental inscription.

Mid. Temp. Rec.   C. H. Hopwood, ed., *Middle Temple records,* 4 v., London, Butterworth, 1904–1905.

Misc. Geneal. et Herald.   Miscellanea Genealogica et Heraldica.

M.P.   Member of Parliament.

N. and Q.   Notes and Queries.

Nichols, *Bib. Top.*   J. Nichols, *Bibliotheca Topographica Britannica,* 1774–1795.

Noble, *Regicides.*   Mark Noble, *The lives of the English Regicides,* London, 1798.

Northants MSS.   Northamptonshire Records Society Manuscripts.

O.P.H.   The parliamentary or constitutional history of England, 1751–1761.

P.C.C.   Prerogative Court of Canterbury wills.

Pink MSS.   W. D. Pink's Manuscripts, John Rylands Library, Manchester.

Rec. Soc. Lancs. and Cheshire.   Publications of the Record Society for the publication of original documents relating to Lancashire and Cheshire.

Royal Hist. Soc., *Trans.*   Royal Historical Society, *Transactions.*

Rushworth.   John Rushworth, *Historical Collections of Private Passages of State,* 1721.

S.P.   State Papers, Domestic, Public Record Office.

St. Ch.   Records of the Court of Star Chamber, Public Record Office.

Sanford, *St. and ill.*   John L. Sanford, *Studies and illustrations of the Great Rebellion,* London, 1858.

Shaw, *K. of E.*   W. A. Shaw, *The knights of England,* 2 v., London, Sheratt and Hughes, 1906.

Shrops. Arch. Soc., *Trans.*   Shropshire Archaeological and Natural History Society, *Transactions.*

Sloane MSS.   British Museum Sloane Manuscripts.

Somerset Arch. Proc.   Somersetshire Archaeological and Natural History Society, *Proceedings.*

Somerset and Dorset N. and Q.   Notes and Queries for Somerset and Dorset.

Strafford letters.   The Earl of Strafford's letters and despatches, ed. W. Knowler, London, 1739.

Students admitted to the Inner Temple.   Students admitted to the Inner Temple, 1547–1660, ed. W. H. Cooke.

Verney.   *Verney Papers: Notes of proceedings in the Long Parliament . . . by Sir Ralph Verney,* ed. J. Bruce, Camden Society, 1845.

V.C.H. Bedford, etc.   *The Victoria history of the counties of England,* ed. by William Page and others, London, Constable, 1900–.

Warwick, *Memoires.*   Sir Philip Warwick, *Memoires of the reigne of King Charles I,* 1701.

Williams, *Gloucester.*   W. R. Williams, *The parliamentary history of the county of Gloucester.*   A similar form is used for this author's volumes on Hereford, Oxford and Worcester.

Williams, *Parl. Hist. Wales.*   W. R. Williams, *The parliamentary history of the principality of Wales.*

Willis.   Browne Willis, *Notitia Parliamentaria,* 3 v., London, 1715–1750.

Wilts Arch. Soc. MSS.   Wiltshire Archaeological Society Manuscripts at Devizes.

Wilts. Arch. Mag.   The Wiltshire Archaeological and Natural History Society Magazine.

Winthrop Papers.   Winthrop Papers, revised ed., published by the Massachusetts Historical Society, 1929–1944.

Wood, *Athenae Oxon.*   Anthony à Wood, *Athenae Oxonienses,* ed. P. Bliss, 1813–1820.

Yorks. Arch. Jour.   The Yorkshire Archaeological and Topographical Association Journal.

Y.A.S. Rec. Ser.   Publications of the Yorkshire Archaeological and Topographical Association (later, Yorkshire Archaeological Society), *Record Series.*

INTRODUCTION

The path of one who undertakes the study of a parliament is well marked. Others have travelled it before, and there are companions to journey part of the way with him. In time the paths diverge, for each has a trail to follow to his selected destination, and each may do some trail blazing of his own. But along the course the company travels together are landmarks for all to see, discoveries for them to share with each other, and each has the opportunity, perhaps, to contribute something to the knowledge of the others.

The present study of the personnel of the Long Parliament was begun at the time that English historians were undertaking the history of parliamentary representation in their country, and is finished as that work progresses. The project of the historians will provide the climax for the work of antiquarians and scholars who in earlier decades were exploring the lives of parliament members. To the work of the early searchers, the pioneers of the trail, all later students must turn.

The publication in 1878 by order of parliament itself of the *Return of the Names of Every Member Returned to Serve in Each Parliament* provided a workable guide for such studies. It is not without errors, and there are gaps in the lists when the original records are missing, but its pages must be scanned by all who would delve into parliamentary biography. Replacing earlier and less reliable lists, such as Browne Willis's *Notitia Parliamentaria* (1715–1750), the official return meant that the gates were opened to any who would venture. Increasing numbers of students responded. Dean of them all was William Duncombe Pink, whose notes and queries appeared in local publications all over England, and whose prolific notes have been preserved among the English Manuscripts of the John Rylands Library in Manchester. W. J. R. Williams published before 1900 his parliamentary histories of the English counties of Gloucester, Hereford, Oxford, and Worcester, and of the Principality of Wales. Other workers concentrated on special areas, such as W. W. Bean, G. R. Park, and R. S. Ferguson on the northern regions, W. P. Courtney and others on Cornwall, and A. B. Beaven on Lancashire and also on London. The county historical societies took up the work, printing series of sketches of members in their journals or in separate volumes. Space permits mentioning specifically the work of only a few of the county historians, such as J. J. Alexander (Devon), H. T. Weyman (Shropshire), J. Bean King (Lincolnshire), J. C. Wedgwood (Staffordshire), and more recently A. Gooder (Yorkshire) and S. W. Bates Harbin (Somerset). From the work of those who have preceded me I have drawn extensively for this study of the Long Parliament. W. D. Pink's analyses of committee service and data about careers after 1641 I have used particularly. To a number of the later students

of local history I am indebted for courtesies and encouragement.

Both suggestion and assurance I have found in the publications of several scholars regarding particular parliaments. J. H. Hexter's work on various aspects of the Long Parliament I have used extensively in Part I. The volume on the parliaments of Elizabeth by J. E. Neale, published as my own work neared completion, provided interesting comparisons for my conclusions regarding the later period. And the editors of the parliamentary diaries and journals, especially Wallace Notestein and his colleagues and students, have by their labors greatly enriched the materials for this study.

The explorations of scholars in fields farther removed from parliamentary biography have been of invaluable assistance also. Upon the genealogical studies of Cokayne and Burke pertaining to the titled classes, of Foster and the Venns on the university students, I have leaned heavily. And my coming late upon the scene has enabled me to profit by the publication of large quantities of source material of many types, and by the newer economic and social interpretations to which they are subject. By using the varied sources in print, and by supplementing them with manuscripts of many kinds —court records, wills, rentals and account books, minutes of town councils, diaries and personal correspondence—I have been able to collect a mass of data about the men who were in parliament in 1640. From many details I have tried to select those that reveal most about the members—not merely the record of their pedigrees and the main incidents in their careers—and ones that make comparisons among the members possible. Upon these bases I have attempted also an analysis of the group in terms of their social and economic as well as their political background.

Some explanation is necessary regarding my handling of certain of the vital facts pertaining to the individual members. The vexing matter of dates requires a brief comment. My study of manuscript sources, such as parish registers, wills, and inquisitions post mortem, has shown me that too many of the earlier biographers, and some of the later ones who have made use of their work, have ignored the mode of dating according to the "old style" of the seventeenth century. A death or burial record, for example, which bears the date of January or February, "1649," may be followed by a will drawn up in the summer of the same year. The correct interpretation, of course, is that the death occurred early in 1649/50, new style. I have followed the new style in all dates, and, where there has been need for clarification as to dates between January 1 and March 25 of a year, I have written the year in the manner just cited. Another sort of date correction I have made in numerous instances. A man who died in his seventieth year died, obviously, before he arrived at the age of seventy. But

1

I have discovered that birth dates have sometimes been reckoned on the basis of epitaphs without regard for such a distinction. Heralds' notes about children's ages have been similarly misread, with the result that births have been reckoned a year too early. In my statements of dates for births and deaths, therefore, I have attempted not only to make adjustments according to the new style calendar, but to correct previous misreadings of the latter sort.

A somewhat simpler matter, perhaps, is that of the spelling of proper names. In a period so little orthodox about its spelling there is great lack of uniformity in the treatment of names of more than a syllable or two. I have conformed, in so far as I have been able to discover it, to the style used by a member himself. In other instances I have followed the form which appears in the *Dictionary of National Biography*. In general, although some recent studies, and some branches of the family, have used the older forms of spelling for certain family names (e.g., Wyndham, Vyvyan), I have preferred the simpler forms.

In stating a man's "style" or social rank I have followed the rule of giving in the first instance that to which he was entitled at the time of his election to parliament. I have disregarded in most cases, however, the differentiation made by the heralds between esquires and gentlemen. Those who had been knighted I have designated simply as "Sir So-and-So," and in the cases of baronets or knights of special degrees I have appended the appropriate suffixes. The members who moved up the social ladder during the period of this study—those who became knights or baronets, particularly—are usually found in other biographical collections under the highest title which came to them. But my statements of title have been made for the purpose of designating the ranks which were theirs at the time they became members of the Long Parliament.

My concern has been principally with what the members were like at the time of their election. It has not seemed necessary to go into elaborate detail about aspects of their careers that followed the opening months of 1642, the date I have selected for the end of the period to be studied. Yet this was an evolutionary parliament, as well as a revolutionary one, and the views of many members stand revealed only in terms of the decisions they made in 1642 or 1644 or 1648 or even later. I have, therefore, sketched in, though chiefly from secondary materials, such outlines of their later conduct as seemed essential to rounding out the characterization of the men. Invaluable has been some of the source material of the period after 1642, notably the composition papers of the royalist members, for providing information about their financial affairs at the time the parliament began. Occasional details regarding careers after 1642 have been included for the guidance of those who may seek in this study materials for genealogical research. And I have attempted to establish death dates both for that reason, and because one finds it difficult, after digging so far into the personal history of a man, to ignore the fact of his death, especially when evidence regarding it lies easily at hand. My emphasis throughout my work on the Long Parliament has been, however, on the lives of the members before November, 1640, and on their actions during the first year of the parliament.

The sketches of the careers before 1640 have been written with relatively little attempt to proportion the length of the account to the importance of the member. In some instances conscious curtailment has been unnecessary because of the scarcity of available facts. This is particularly true of men who were very young, or whose origins were in the lower ranks of society. In the case of a man whose role was important I have had to screen my materials further, but I have felt it inadvisable to exclude so much as to minimize the significance of the man. Particularly I have included many details regarding the borough magistrates, details which have escaped the attention of other workers who have not had the time, perhaps, to search the manuscripts of the localities from which such members came. Some of those who sat in the Long Parliament have seemed insignificant because too little has been known of them. By setting forth at some length the accounts of their careers I have attempted to show that many of these were men of influence, locally if not nationally. That fact in itself is important for understanding the nature and work of the parliament, even though on its stage their talents were outshown by those of the more brilliant actors.

As to the latter, the well known figures, I have limited myself chiefly to correcting errors of fact or interpretation. I have added also occasional details that have appeared in recent publications or that my own research has uncovered. Such addenda pertain frequently to economic or social matters concerning which earlier biographers told us too little. I have avoided repeating many of the data about the well known men that are accessible in such works as *D.N.B.* or in the fuller parliamentary histories.. In these cases I have restated only the minimum that seemed necessary to identify the men and, since I have been working with comparisons, to sketch in their backgrounds.

Originally it seemed that I might omit entirely from further investigation the men included in *D.N.B.* or treated in the parliamentary histories of counties, such as those by Williams and Wedgwood. My research was planned accordingly. But it became apparent that numerous corrections were needed, and furthermore, considerable material about those members turned up in my studies of the rest which might well be added to the older accounts of their careers. These additions I have attempted. In the cases, however, of the *D.N.B.* men, whom I have designated in the alphabetical dictionary of members by an asterisk (*), and of the members for the counties of Gloucester, Hereford, Lancaster, Oxford, Stafford, Worcester and Wales, I have not searched thoroughly for all the facts waiting to be reported. Modern biographical studies of the shire members for Somerset and York appeared after I had gone far with my research. In dealing with the members sketched in those volumes, therefore, as with those covered by earlier works, I have greatly shortened my own accounts. And, except where I have discovered errors, I have used for drawing my conclusions about the whole personnel of the parliament the facts presented by my predecessors.

Although the advantages of brevity have been constantly in my mind, I have decided against the wide use of abbreviations within the text itself. The initials for frequently recurring titles of office, such as D.L., J.P., M.P., or even H.S., I have employed extensively. But I have avoided symbols that might have replaced such common words as *married* or *daughter*. In so doing I have chosen to sacrifice brevity for readability.

The three general divisions of the book have been planned with the idea of making it easily usable. A discussion of the whole group of men who made up the House of Commons, 1640–1641, is followed by a section which treats of the members in relation to their constituencies, arranged according to counties. Condensed accounts of elections which aroused special interest are included here, and comments on local influences that affected the returns—influences such as public opinion, the type of electorate, the patrons or leading families. Seventeenth-century elections, lacking the organized party pressure of later periods, have a strongly local flavor. I have attempted to catch that element in some small measure in my report, constituency by constituency. I have followed the alphabetical order of the counties, although there might have been some advantage in arranging the shires according to larger geographical units. The final section of the book, and the longest, consists of the biographical dictionary of the members. Here again I have followed the alphabetical arrangement. Although by this plan the men have been lifted out of their localities, I trust the numerous cross-references and the index, and especially the greater ease for the reader in consulting individual biographies, will make up for the disadvantage of considering a man apart from his constituency.

Because the sources for the biographical sketches are so varied, requiring that facts be pieced together as a mosaic of many fragments, I have been compelled to include more footnote references than might be considered desirable. If other students of parliamentary biography discover through my references some guidance, especially to the manuscript materials available for parallel studies, I trust that the importance of including the footnotes along with the text will be recognized.

Because my footnotes are full I have omitted a formal bibliography. I have felt justified in this decision particularly because of several excellent bibliographical notes that have been published in recent years in connection with many of my sources. I refer especially to the *Interim Report of the Committee on House of Commons Personnel and Politics* (1932), and to the reports of two American historians who have been exploring the sources of seventeenth-century English history. Much of what I might say regarding local collections of manuscripts and about the types of printed sources usable for studying aspects of local and social history has already been said well by Mildred Campbell in *The English Yeoman under Elizabeth and the Early Stuarts* (New Haven, Yale Univ. Press, 1942) and by William B. Willcox in *Gloucestershire, A Study of Local Government, 1590–1640* (New Haven, Yale Univ. Press, 1940). Probably two large groups of sources would in my list be added to those described by Miss Campbell and Mr. Willcox. First would be numerous manuscripts belonging to borough or city corporations, on which I have drawn heavily for material on the merchant members and on elections. And second would be the many sources which I have consulted chiefly for genealogical purposes. These range from such primary material as the inquisitions post mortem at the Public Record Office and wills at various probate registries to the standard works on the peerage and baronetage. I have attempted in rather detailed footnotes to describe the materials I have used on special parts of my study, such as the compiling of the list of members of the parliament or the analysis of their economic position. For those who may be travelling the road of parliamentary biography with me I would add but a single wayside note: The farther one presses from the main travelled paths, the more one learns of the abundance of source materials available. Their richness I have sampled but their depths I have not plumbed.

PART I

PORTRAIT OF A PARLIAMENT

"God hath called a parliament," wrote John Venn of London one spring day in 1640 to his friend, Governor Winthrop, in New England, and "how long it will continue we are not worthy to know, nor what it will bring forth; we are full of fears, and have little ground of comfort or hope of good, save only in the Lord."[1] Eleven years had passed under the rule of King Charles without a parliament, and they had been restless years. For some time before 1640 rumors had run that a parliament would be called.[2] When the king yielded as 1639 was drawing to its close, his writs summoning a parliament to meet in April unleased both hopes and forebodings.

The forebodings were justified by the events that followed. The spring parliament, known in history as the Short Parliament, lasted only long enough to emphasize the issues of the time. The events of the five months after its abrupt closing brought into sharper focus the problems of the nation. The impoverishment of the treasury stood revealed, the unpopularity of the war with the Scots, and the simmering resentment against the men who had advised the king in matters of church and state. When, in the early autumn, another parliament was called to meet on the third of November, John Venn might well have repeated his words of the spring.

It was to a "happy parliament" that some zealots rode in November, confident in their armor of righteousness. Even some less fired with the spirit expressed optimism about the correction of grievances.[3] But to many of the duly elected parliament men[4] from the shires and towns the prospect was simply that of renewing the struggle in which they had contended with indifferent success in earlier parliaments. As for the king's friends, the future was filled with uncertainties.

That such hopes and fears were warranted the course of the parliament soon proved. Grievances came quickly to the fore, followed by attacks upon the king's advisers and upon fundamental features of his administration. For this, the Long Parliament, stopped not with a call for the reform of the recent abuses of Charles' reign. It passed on to demand constitutional change, to establish by legislative process the supremacy of parliament.

This was a revolutionary assembly. In its early months it worked out in practical form the ideas for which those earlier stalwarts, Phelipps, Sir Edward Coke, Sandys, Eliot, and the rest, had labored a decade or two before. As Carlyle viewed it, the Long Parliament "set the whole world upon chase of Parliaments."[5] From its accomplishments came eventually the revolution of 1689.

Significant as the work of the Long Parliament was, comparatively little is known of many of the men who were responsible for its achievements. The story of the years, 1640–1653, the central point in England's political history, has been oversimplified by our labelling succeeding stages in that era by the names of leaders or groups who became dominant in turn. In times when political power was not wielded by organized parties, when unity of leadership was lacking even within factions, and decisions from day to day depended upon the will of scores or even smaller groups of men who might shift their positions, the role of the individual member was much more important that it has since become. Historians, in their concern with the growth of parliamentary government, have too frequently pointed to the work of a few outstanding leaders, overlooking or ignoring the vastly important role of the men on whom the leaders had to depend for majorities. The diaries of this parliament and of the earlier ones of the Stuarts plainly reveal the parts played by dozens of less well known men. In an age when men talked much about the rights of the subject the views of the individual parliament man were significant.

In the Long Parliament the role of the individual members was perhaps the more important because of changes in outlook and in personnel that occurred during the early months of its sitting. As in the case of the revolutionary assemblies of America and France in the following century, internal developments as well as external forces shaped the course of strategy and decision in this revolutionary parliament of England. Especially in the House of Commons the tumults in London and news from the borders or from Ireland affected the temper and the votes of the parliament. The election decisions, furthermore, and the by-elections of the first year, produced a marked change in personnel. Without more detailed knowledge than we have heretofore possessed of the membership of the Commons and of the shifts that were made by individuals and by groups, the work of the Long Parliament cannot be fully interpreted.

Since Carlyle wrote about a century ago, describing the men of the House of Commons of 1640 as "little

---

[1] This letter, now owned by the Massachusetts Historical Society, is printed in *Winthrop Papers* **4**: 221, Mass. Hist. Soc. 1929–1944. I have modernized the spelling in the passage.

[2] One such rumor was circulating in 1638, according to news Bulstrode Whitelocke received from London. Add. MSS, 37,343 (The "Annals" of Bulstrode Whitelocke), fol. 162v.

[3] *The diary of Sir Henry Slingsby, of Scriven, Bart.,* ed. by D. Parsons, 64, London, 1836.

[4] "Parliament man" was the term by which members were most frequently designated at this period. The use of "member of parliament" as a title after a man's name occurred first about 1650, according to S. R. Gardiner. *E.H.R.* **8**: 525, 1893.

[5] Thomas Carlyle, *Oliver Cromwell's letters and speeches* **3**: 316, Centenary edition, London, Chapman and Hall, 1899–1923? (hereafter, Carlyle, *Cromwell*).

more than ticketed shadows," [6] the work of numerous students of parliament has proved that a great deal can be learned about even the obscure members.[7] The biographical approach used in the compilation of the parliamentary history of numerous counties has given perspective for the study of a single parliament. And the work of Mr. Hexter on the strategies of John Pym as he handled a recognizable "middle group" in the first war year of this parliament has called attention to numerous bonds that drew together men of varying interests and backgrounds.[8] But a study of the whole membership, singly and as a group, a survey that cuts across the regional lines of local history, remains to be done. Only by such a study can the proper setting be found for Pym and Hampden, St. John and Selden and Cromwell, for "fiery spirits" like Clotworthy and Hesilrige, and king's men such as Hopton or Grenville or Warwick.

Who were the men who were named to the various committees on grievances, for example, and what had been their personal experiences with the policies of King Charles? To whom was assigned the drawing up of charges against Strafford? Or who were those listed as the earl's defenders in the famous paper posted in Westminster Yard? Who were the wealthy members who pledged their bonds to secure the loans so desperately needed? Who were the servants of the crown whose wealth or official experience so outweighed suspicion of their loyalties that they were permitted to retain their seats even when war came on? Of which members could the king be sure when the parliament opened, and what kind were they who rallied to his cause from the other side when the conflict became one of arms? What personal qualifications had the members to serve as parliament men, or what events in their lives before 1640 can help to explain their decisions? We need to know more of the sufferings that men like William Mallory and Walter Long endured for principles, as well as of the prison terms of Strode and Valentine. The actions of a Denton or a Strangways or a Yelverton regarding ship money, though less famous than Hampden's stand, were significant. We need to know more of Sir Walter Erle, without whom the history of this parliament and of the war in Dorset could not be written. We should know Sir Richard Buller, Carew's colleague in organizing the resistance in Cornwall, and Savile, Strafford's nephew, who flouted his uncle's authority, but died a valued royalist officer. We can learn much from an acquaintance with the city magistrates, men such as Jesson, Allanson, Hooke, or Trelawney from the provincial towns, or Soame of London.

From the personal histories of the individual members must be sought out the answers to a host of questions

about the temper of the parliament and about its work. From the experiences and the backgrounds of the parliament men emerge the details that lend life and color to our picture of the whole. They supply the perspective, the pigments, and the shadings that are needed if we are to have a true picture of the Long Parliament.

To attempt a composite portrait of the membership for the whole period of the parliament, however, would be useless. A series of group portraits would be better. The picture of the Commons of 1640 and 1641 would not be the same as the picture drawn for 1646 or 1649 or 1653. Changes in personnel developed a body quite different from the one that made its bold attack on the structure of absolutism in the early period. Some of the original members died. Many absented themselves for personal or political reasons months before Charles raised his standard at Nottingham and they, with an increasing number who joined them, were in time "disabled" by vote of the House from further serving as members. By 1653 less than a hundred of the parliament men of the first year were still on the rolls, and not all of these were attending. In the places vacated by royalists sat "recruiters" whose views differed greatly from theirs.[9] The representative character of the House was gone and faction ruled.

The date of the attempted arrest of the five members, 4 January 1642, conveniently marks the end of the first stage of the parliament's history. By that time the constitutional work was largely finished and thereafter the problem of arms rather than of laws became uppermost. Already there were changes in the Commons; several men had died, some had been called to the Upper House, and others had been expelled. A few who had been allowed briefly to share in the work of the House had been voted "unduly" returned and had been replaced by men chosen at new elections.[10] New men had come in to occupy the seats concerning which there had been petitions before.

In the following study of the parliament men of 1640 are included therefore all of the Lower House who were recognized as duly elected and returned between the autumn of 1640 and the end of December, 1641, and all who, even if debarred later as their elections were decided, seem to have participated in any business of the parliament. And the elections themselves have been included in the study, for they help to explain the

---

[6] *Ibid.* **3**: 315.

[7] See introduction, p. 1.

[8] J. H. Hexter, *The reign of King Pym,* Cambridge, U.S.A., Harvard Univ. Press, 1941.

[9] R. N. Kershaw points out that the recruiters elected between 1645 and 1648 resembled their predecessors in social types, with possibly a larger proportion of aldermen (The recruiting of the Long Parliament, *History* **8**: 178, 1923–1924). Their politics, however, were certainly less diversified.

[10] The general rule that all those involved in election contests should refrain from sitting until the House decided the case was not always enforced. Some men evidently acted as members until they were actually ordered to withdraw; e.g., Sir Henry Berkeley, Dr. Chaworth, John Craven. A few who died very early, such as Sir Thomas Lucy and Sir John Melton, may never have attended, but they have been included in the group to be studied.

members' relations with their constituencies and sometimes provide the principal clues to a member's politics and later actions.

ATTENDANCE AND ABSENTEEISM, 1640–1642

Had all the members for every constituency been present on the opening day, 3 November 1640, almost five hundred men would have been there, 493, to be exact. The "restoring" of seven boroughs to parliamentary representation during the early months increased to 507 the theoretical membership. But there were 40 others besides, some who were replacements for members who died or left the House, and some who themselves were ousted and replaced. The whole group here considered as the parliament men of 1640 numbers therefore 547.[11]

But the benches of St. Stephen's could not well have accommodated so large a group, nor were they ever so jammed. It was notorious that figures of attendance varied greatly from those of membership. Because of the unusual interest that this parliament aroused, more were present for the opening than had been expected.[12] But there had been delays about some elections. And personal affairs detained various members at home. Perhaps the largest attendance was on 1 March 1641. A division then indicates the presence of 379 voting members. Even at the division on the question of Strafford's attainder on 21 April only 263 voted,[13] and there was an increasing number of leaves of absence granted and of absences taken without leave after that.[14] By mid-August, the plague season in London, both Houses were reported so empty that messages were sent

to the sheriffs to require the members to return,[15] and in the first month after the recess attendance was often so poor in the mornings that business was delayed for lack of a quorum of 40.[16] Although 307 were present at the midnight vote on the Remonstrance in November, the divisions during the remainder of the year indicate an attendance usually smaller than that, sometimes under 200.[17] It was once declared that almost 200 members had failed to return at all after the recess,[18] and the average daily attendance during most of the first year of the parliament was probably below 300. To what extent this fact should modify conclusions based upon a study of the whole membership it is difficult to say. Since absenteeism was probably indulged in more by the very old and the very young, it no doubt emphasizes the importance of the middle-aged members.[19] Although the divisions of 16 June 1641 on the question of fines for unexcused absences suggest some correlation between absenteeism and politics,[20] the members found many reasons besides politics for leaving London in the season of heat and plague. Even after the recess the correlation would be difficult of proof. But after the first month of 1642 the diminishing attendance clearly reflects the political trend,[21] and the realization by many that the major issues concerning church and state were not to be resolved in a parliament.

STRATEGIES FOR THE CONTROL OF THE HOUSE: ELECTIONS AND RETURNS

But fifteen months before, when the elections for the Long Parliament began, there had been more hopefulness, more willingness evident among all groups to assert their strength by votes rather than by resort to arms. After a summer of news and of rumors, of meetings of the Pym group at London and in the country and of the king's negotiations with the Scots and with the peers, the royal order from York on 24 September 1640 for the summoning of a new parliament gave the signal for prospective members to plunge into their canvassing. Friends of the court and workers in the opposition drew up lists of candidates, sought out places

[11] The names of the men in this group were taken first from the official return (M. of P.) and the earlier lists which were printed in Browne Willis, *Notitia Parliamentaria*, 3 v., London, 1716–1750, and in the old *Parliamentary or constitutional history of England* 9, London, 1751–1762 (cited hereafter as *O.P.H.*). The list was then supplemented and corrected by the use of the *Journals of the House of Commons*, the two portions of *The journal of Sir Simonds D'Ewes* which have been edited by Wallace Notestein and Willson H. Coates, New Haven, Yale Univ. Press, 1923 and 1942, a third portion of the same journal edited by Helen B. Barber which is an unpublished thesis at the University of Cornell library, and the published works of other note takers. Several contemporary catalogues of the names of the members at various periods of the parliament have been consulted also. The principal ones are in the collection of Thomason Tracts at the British Museum, one of them being a list printed by Thomas Walkley in 1640 (Thomason Tracts, E. 1091, p. 2), and others printed in 1648, 1659, and 1660 (Thomason Tracts, E. 454, p. 2; 669. f. 21, p. 43; and 669. f. 24, p. 37).

[12] Edward Hyde, Earl of Clarendon, *The history of the Rebellion and civil wars in England*, ed. W. Dunn Macray, 1: 218–220, Oxford, Clarendon Press, 1888 (hereafter, Clarendon, *Rebellion*).

[13] *C.J.* 2: 94, 125.

[14] There had been 16 leaves of absence in December, 1640, 11 in March, 19 or more in April, 20 in June, and 34 in July. They were often for family and business reasons in the earlier months, and repeated leaves were granted to some members. Those of the later months were by no means largely for royalists, though possibly the greater number of departures without leave was by that group.

[15] *C.S.P. Dom., 1641–1643*, 85; D'Ewes (B), 314–315, 467.

[16] D'Ewes (C), 11, 29, 32, *passim*.

[17] *Ibid.*, 186, 275, 374, 386.

[18] Of that number D'Ewes thought that possibly half had not been in attendance for a full month. *Ibid.*, 287.

[19] See the discussion of the age groups below (pp. 19–20).

[20] The tellers for the negatives in the two votes that day were Sir John Strangways, one of the Westons, and one of the Lloyds, all royalists eventually. The tellers for the Yeas were Sir John Evelyn, Pierrepont, and Strode. *C.J.* 2: 626–627.

[21] R. N. Kershaw, The recruiting of the Long Parliament, *History* 8: 169, 1923–1924. Thomas Coke, disturbed by the increasing tumults in London, wrote in March, 1642, of his doubts as to his future course, "Mine own affairs and friends call me back into Derbyshire; the affairs of the Commonwealth call me to London or some other place. I fear that matters grow so fast to a higher period, that before the end of the [spring] circuit London will scarce be a safe place of abode." Dorothea Coke, *The last Elizabethan, Sir John Coke*, 294, 296–297, London, J. Murray, 1937.

for themselves or their relatives, solicited votes, and planned their election strategies. Within three weeks of the order for the issuing of the writs, the elections started,[22] and for another month the polling for the original seats continued. A "great shuffling" for places occurred as at the previous elections, and in numerous instances heated contests developed. In at least 70, probably more, of the 259 original constituencies the men chosen were winners over rival candidates. Sometimes as many as five or six were in the field until the customary pairing of strong candidates for the first and second "voices" reduced the numbers. Thirty-eight of the original elections and at least three of the later ones resulted in challenges which required determination by the House itself.

Many of the elections were confused affairs. Some were near riots. Except in the smaller boroughs and in the towns with extremely limited franchise, election officials had trouble keeping the procedure orderly as large groups of legitimate and pretended electors came in to shout for their candidates. Undoubtedly some sheriffs and bailiffs were guilty of managing the elections in such a way as to favor certain men. Most of them were subject in some degree to pressure by influential men of the town or county, by royal officials or noblemen, and even by the clergy. The county elections especially were noisy, if not turbulent. Freeholders came by hundreds and thousands from the outlying regions to be entertained at their candidates' expense at inns of the county town,[23] often arriving the day before the election. If the number was too great or the vote was too close to be determined by the clamor of the "voice" vote or even by a "view," and individual polling was required, the proceedings sometimes ran for more than a day. Probably more than one harassed sheriff agreed with Suffolk's D'Ewes in resenting as impudent and foolish the charges of unfairness made against them by defeated candidates.[24] Townsmen of the county towns in some instances demanded the right to vote for the knights of the shire as well as for their own borough representatives. In some of the boroughs men appeared from the suburbs and claimed the voting privilege. Excitement was general throughout the country. And in Yorkshire, where nerves had been strained all through the year, there was probably reason for the king's order that the troops be taken out for exercise on election day.[25]

Since questions of the franchise were involved in many of the contested elections of 1640–1641, a brief review of the voters' qualifications may not be out of place. Such questions occurred less frequently regarding shire elections than in the cases of towns because the counties had the long established and uniform qualification of the "forty-shilling freeholder." Occasionally, landlords were reported to have created their tenants "freeholders" just before elections so as to increase their following. But if the results of the vote by "clamor" were challenged and a poll was demanded, any pretenders present among the properly qualified voters ran the risk of discovery by the sheriff's clerks and by the watchers representing the rival candidates.

Lack of uniformity in the matter of the franchise created a major problem in the determining of election controversies of the boroughs. Charters and precedents had to be searched for the answer. Many boroughs limited the vote to their officials, such as the mayor and members of the advisory body or bodies. These were variously called aldermen and councillors, or chief burgesses, sometimes the Four-and-Twenty or the Forty-and-Eight. At other places the "commonalty" assisted in the voting, at least to the extent of "assenting" to the choice made by the officials. The word, "commonalty," seems to have been used with a loose connotation, however. It was applied to a very restricted group at Winchester, for instance, and probably never extended beyond the ranks of the tax payers. In many towns the voters below those of official rank were required to be owners of "burgage" properties, or payers of scot and lot, or pot wallopers. Elsewhere they were called freeholders or freemen. There might be only six or eight of these, quite often less than twenty. A more general franchise, rarer but in increasing demand, included the resident freemen or "inhabitants." But always such voters were expected to be responsible persons, not apprentices, criminals, or paupers who were dependent upon the community.[26] The Welsh custom

---

[22] The earliest county was York (5 October), followed quickly by Staffordshire, home of the Earl of Essex (8 October), Huntingdonshire (10 October), Lincoln, Norfolk, and Somerset (12 October), Bucks and Surrey (14 October). Essex and Oxfordshire, however, home counties of the puritan nobles, Warwick and Say and Sele, did not vote until 28 October, and Warwickshire, Lord Brooke's county, not until 3 November. The towns usually finished their returns within a week or ten days after the county elections but occasionally, as in Wiltshire, voted before the shire. The election dates were of course governed by the "county days," and by the time of the arrival of the writ. Since the writ bearers of the period were often quite unofficial persons, sometimes candidates themselves, it may be suspected that the early elections in so many shires where the opposition was strong was not entirely a coincidence.

[23] Sir John Coke's election expenses of nearly £300 were chiefly for food and lodgings. Sir Robert Harley's expenses, although he was not a new man as was Coke, totaled over £155. H.M.C., Twelfth Report, Cowper MSS (cited hereafter as Coke MSS) 3: 138–141; Fourteenth Report 2 (Portland MSS 3) : 66.

[24] D'Ewes noted fully his conduct of the election and the complaints against him in Harl. MSS, 158, fols. 293v–295v. See below in the section on elections.

[25] H.M.C., Second Report, MSS of the Earl of Spencer, 19.

[26] For a list of the Cornish boroughs and their several types of franchise, see Mary Coate, Cornwall in the great Civil War and interregnum, 1642–1660, 17–19, Oxford, Clarendon Press, 1933 (hereafter, Coate, Cornwall in the great Civil War). In William Bohun's Collection of debates, . . . touching the right of electing members to serve in parliament, London, 1702, several cases from the early part of the seventeenth century appear. I have attempted, in the section on elections which follows this analysis of the parliament as a whole, to report on the electorates of the individual boroughs in 1640.

of extending the borough vote to representatives of neighboring boroughs was peculiar to that region.

The effects of such variations in the extent of the franchise are apparent in the Long Parliament elections. Where the number of voters was very small, control, of course, was easiest, and could be attempted by a manor lord or some neighboring gentleman, or perhaps by some officer of the crown. The small Cornish villages that permitted their officials to write in their own or other names on blank indentures are illustrations of extremely limited franchise. Even more familiar are the towns already recognized as decayed or family boroughs, such as Gatton or Castle Rising, or some of the Wiltshire towns controlled by the Herberts or the Cecils.[27] But the effect of such conditions on the political grouping of the 1640 House should not be exaggerated. Both sides used the opportunities for control that were available to them, just as both complained when any arbitrary limiting of the franchise was attempted. One cannot study the Long Parliament elections, however, without becoming aware of an undercurrent, genuinely democratic and apparently quite independent of the question of the royal prerogative, which was moving townsmen to demand extensions of the voting privilege. In at least ten of the contests of this year the extent of the franchise was an issue of almost equal importance with the national ones, and in ten more it seems to have been the question most interesting of all to the voters.[28]

Before the hour arrived for men to gather at guildhall or castle to cry their candidates' names, much preparatory work had been done by both friends and foes of the king to insure the results they desired. And during the first year that followed the elections both sides used various means to strengthen their positions in the parliament, to reduce the number of their adversaries or to win new adherents to their own cause.

The pre-election tactics employed on behalf of the king were dictated by both tradition and caution. Prudence advised the release of men imprisoned on grounds that might be discussed as grievances when the parliament opened.[29] And according to tradition, numerous official candidates were put into the field. Various royal officials, particularly lawyers, were instructed to try for seats.[30] Boroughs in lands belonging to the crown or connected with the queen's jointure received suggestions about acceptable candidates.[31] And court candidates were proposed for places in the royal duchies of Cornwall and Lancaster and in the principality of Wales. Officialdom everywhere was busy, the lords lieutenant in their counties, Strafford and his military aids in the north and at the border fortresses, the king's cousin, the Duke of Lenox, as Lord Warden of the Cinque Ports, the Prince of Wales's attorney for various places in western England, and commanders of the Channel garrisons. The official patrons were successful particularly in the two duchies and in the Cinque Ports. Noteworthy also were the towns where the Earl of Northumberland as Lord Admiral and as general worked his influence, an influence which in time, however, carried several of his nominees away with him from the king.[32]

In addition to the nominations that were essentially official in character others were proposed personally by noblemen on the king's side. The Duke of Lenox, for example, wrote to many towns outside of his official precincts, and others exerted pressure less as privy councillors or courtiers than as great landlords in their own domains.[33] The nominees of the latter were some-

---

[27] A tabulation of 167 constituencies open to patronage in some form in 1640–1641 discloses that 46 were subject to what was primarily royal or administrative pressure, sometimes to the extent of one assured seat in each place; in 50 others family influence, either of peers or of commoners, and sometimes supplementing royal pressure, was strong; in 35 one seat could usually be counted on by a certain family or nobleman; and 36, including a few one-member towns, were virtually pocket boroughs controlled by a single house. In at least 4 instances, though, the returns from such pocket boroughs were challenged.

The types of borough patronage in 1640 correspond in general with those described by Professor J. E. Neale in *The Elizabethan House of Commons,* chap. VII to XIII, London, Cape, 1949.

[28] A list of decisions in seventeenth century election cases involving the question of the franchise appears in J. C. Wedgwood, *Staffordshire parliamentary history* (2 v., William Salt Archaeological Society, *Staffordshire Historical Collections,* 1917–1920) 2: 37–41 (hereafter, *Staff. parl. hist.*). Wedgwood concludes that in this period the House preferred a broadening franchise. In several of the Long Parliament cases recognition of the larger voting group, usually the "inhabitants at large," benefited the country party, but in others the question of franchise arose in triangular contests between men of the same party, and in at least one instance the decision, out of deference, some thought, to the Earl of Pembroke, went in favor of limited suffrage (D'Ewes [N], 430–432). If there was politics in the decisions, most of them also had a basis in law and tradition (e.g., Great Marlow). One note-taker commented, "I observe the sense of the House to be that no beggar, or man that receives relief, or is not sub[ject] to scot and lot is held capable of giving his voice in election of burgesses." Lansd. MSS, 491, fols. 55v–56.

[29] *C.S.P. Dom., 1640–1641,* 104. This may be compared with the release of the loan refusers before the 1628 parliament.

[30] *Ibid.* A list among the State Papers (S.P. 16, 468/136), probably the basis for these instructions, includes, besides 11 lawyers in the royal employment, one gentleman pensioner, members of the Council at York and of the Council of the Marches, the king's attorneys connected with each, and the judges in Wales. Only three of those listed by name were elected, but several members of the councils were chosen.

[31] *C.S.P., 1640–1641,* 130.

[32] Northumberland tried his patronage with varying success in seaport towns as Lord Admiral, in some northern boroughs as general and also as landowner, and in the southern counties where a number of his estates lay. Three of his agents, Potter, Scawen, and Dowse, were elected, as were also his brother, Henry Percy, and his nephew, Lord Lisle. John Northcote, too, and possibly Campion, may have been assisted by connections with Northumberland.

[33] *C.S.P. Dom., 1640–1641,* 121–122. A form letter prepared for the use of noblemen desiring to nominate M.P.'s for one of King James's parliaments remains among the State Papers (S.P. 14, 135/42). Examples of the peers who acted for the king in 1640 were the Earl of Arundel, landlord in Norfolk and in the

times courtiers who had failed to secure places elsewhere, but were frequently members of the peers' own families or persons in their private employ. The results were not all that the king's friends desired and were in several instances undone by a series of challenges and by-elections.[34] At late as December, 1641, however, members of the opposition party were considering ways to limit the interference by noblemen in elections.[35]

The efforts of the king and his friends to gain a strong position through elections were supplemented by the bestowal of certain royal favors after the parliament had begun its work. Grants of titles, for instance, went not only to supporters of the king but to some of his critics, perhaps in continuation of the policy of placating them. Those who became knights and baronets during 1641 were not only men like Bridgeman and Harrison, who had served the king well, but men so personally interested in grievance cases as Henry Heyman, Martin Lumley, and Sir Christopher Yelverton. Of 21 men of the parliament who were promoted from the ranks of the esquires in 1641, 8 were royalists, 8 were strong parliamentarians, and 5 were moderate or only lukewarm supporters of parliament. There is no indication that the honors caused men actually to change their politics. Several instances, however, suggest not only that there were parliamentarians interested in titles and able to afford them, but also that the titles were sometimes rewards for a course of moderation.

The tactics and strategies employed by the king's opponents both before the original elections and during the course of the parliament can be traced in part. The evidence regarding their work before the elections is more meagre but is sufficient to warrant some surmise. Plans for a parliament and a contest with the king had been on foot at least since 1637.[36] An observer of the Short Parliament elections reported "a kind of cunning, underhand canvass of this nature the greater part of the kingdom over."[37] Groups of the gentry met in Devon and Yorkshire during the summer of 1640 to draw up petitions to the king. Sir Walter Erle's going from Dorset into Devon to assist with the latter county's petition indicates that the work was not confined by county boundaries. From Pym's group meeting in London and in the country that summer there doubtless issued many letters of counsel and instruction. An old story runs that on the eve of the elections Pym and Hampden rode through England to

quicken their partisans,[38] but it is doubtful whether either had time to travel long distances for such a canvass, or whether so personal a touch was needed. Pym and some of his most active lieutenants met again in London just before the parliament opened, readying themselves, no doubt, for the test of strength ahead.[39]

In preparing for the elections, the opposition group used various tactics that resembled those of the king's supporters. They lacked the advantage of having a single head such as the king, but they had their central group which served as a nucleus and which for some years had motivated the actions of its loosely attached adherents. This was the group of which John Pym was leader. It was composed of men, both peers and commoners, who had worked together in the earlier parliaments of Charles, who, as will be explained later, had been associated in many non-political ways in the years between 1629 and 1640, and who emerged as the politicians of their group in the Short Parliament and in the negotiations with the Scots. As the opposition lacked a single head, it lacked also the strength inherent in the king's connection with certain regions like the Cinque Ports, and the advantage of his central position, surrounded by his personal and official servants. But the country faction had available and used widely the patronage of noblemen and even of officials who had sympathy for their cause. If they were lords lieutenant in their shires, especially, elections tended to swing their way. Certainly the power of the earls of Essex, Warwick, Bedford and Pembroke,[40] and of lords Montagu, Say and Sele, and Brooke is reflected in the return of members of their families and of strong puritan groups from the areas where their estates lay. How much organized electioneering or personal canvassing was done by the managers at the center of the faction, it is difficult to say. It seems probable that Pym and his colleagues relied more, as did King Charles, on associations of long standing with men who were familiar with their objectives and who were in strategic positions to influence their own areas.[41]

The country faction succeeded in placing parliament sympathizers in numerous seats that had been occupied

southeast, Lord Mohun in the west, and the earls of Dorset, Newcastle, Chesterfield, and Southampton.

[34] The extent of royalist pressure through these channels is well presented by R. N. Kershaw in an article on The elections for the Long Parliament, *E.H.R.* **38**: 496–508, 1923. Kershaw's findings differ slightly from those presented above.

[35] *C.J.* **2**: 333, 337; D'Ewes (C), 236.

[36] *C.S.P. Venetian, 1636–1639*, 136.

[37] Portion of a letter cited in Willcox, W. B., *Gloucestershire, A study in local government, 1590–1640*, 36, n., New Haven, Yale Univ. Press, 1940 (hereafter, Willcox, *Gloucestershire*).

[38] J. R. Green, *A short history of the English people*, rev. ed., **2**: 98, N. Y., Appleton, 1898.

[39] See Sir Walter Erle.

[40] The Earl of Pembroke may have had less personal influence in 1640 than his family had exercised earlier in Charles's reign, when possibly a dozen seats were connected in some way with them, but his power was still great. Violet A. Rowe, Influence of the Earls of Pembroke on parliamentary elections, 1625–1640, *E.H.R.* **50**: 242–256, 1935.

[41] An indication of what may have occurred in various places before the fall elections is suggested by what happened in Dorchester before the Short Parliament. Even before the election writ arrived, and seven weeks before the election day, the corporation of Dorchester, center of a strong puritan group, selected Bond and Holles to be its members. Charles Herbert Mayo, ed., *The municipal records of the borough of Dorchester*, 435–436. Exeter, W. Pollard, 1908 (hereafter, Mayo, *Municipal records, Dorchester*).

by royalists in the Short Parliament. Not all differences in personnel between the two parliaments can be explained by their efforts, but the trend toward greater numerical strength for the opposition, especially in counties inclined toward puritanism, suggests that there had been effective planning.[42] Possibly the most striking single victory of the faction was in preventing the election of London's recorder, who was the king's choice for the Speaker's chair. Procuring a seat for Sir John Clotworthy of Ireland was another notable achievement.

Having won the first skirmish by gaining a majority of seats in the original elections, the country party, or parliamentarians, as they will usually be described hereafter, found ready for their hands new means for strengthening their position. They possessed now what might be considered a counterpart of the king's historical advantage in the duchies or in Wales. And armed with such power, they used it vigorously. Their overwhelming majority in the Committee of Privileges assured the deciding of election cases to their advantage. Not entirely true is Clarendon's charge that, in the voiding of elections because of irregularities, "no rule of justice was so much as pretended to be observed."[43] The debates on numerous cases show an attempt to apply the law and to interpret local customs. But the decisions favoring royalists were few.[44] The privilege of the House to rule that a man was unfit for membership in their august body was used by the majority as an axe for lopping off of king's men. The early ousting of the "monopolists" gave the dual satisfaction of penalizing offenders against the public good and of purging the House of some of the most loyal followers of King Charles.[45] Likewise satisfying was the decision regarding the "army plotters" late in 1641. Most of the eight by-elections following these expulsions brought in men who favored reforms, although three of the newcomers

afterwards supported the king.[46] Finally, as a source of new recruits, there was the "restoring" of boroughs to representation in parliament. Such restored boroughs in the past had often responded by electing men nominated by the officials or individuals chiefly responsible for securing their restoration. Many became family boroughs.[47] Whether the decisions on reinstatements in 1640–1641 were made with the design of building up the popular majority cannot be proved. But it is not insignificant that of the seven boroughs restored, one in the southeast, where puritanism was strong, three in Devon, and three in the north, all have the earmarks of controlled boroughs and, with the exception of Okehampton, whose lord was a royalist, were plainly open to parliamentary influence. Since both Okehampton men later turned to the popular cause, so offsetting the defection of one Yorkshireman and one from Honiton, the net gain for Pym's party from the restorations was a dozen seats.[48]

Of manipulation of the elections themselves, by either side, or corruption in the sense in which the practice later developed, there is evidence in only a few cases. Officials were at times arbitrary, but they appear to have acted more upon what seemed expedient at the moment than upon instruction. There was carelessness in the sending of the writs to the sheriffs, some being delivered by messengers bearing letters to recommend candidates and some by men who were candidates themselves, but these were old tricks which neither side disdained. Clarendon charged that there was much corruption in the handling of writs so as to prevent the election of London's recorder for any seat,[49] but the abuse, if such it was, seems not to have been general. As to bribery there is evidence only in the case of Bramber, Sussex, and the House showed its disapproval by refusing to seat the man who offered £10 for the place, a decision the more easily made, perhaps, because it barred a royalist and opened the way for a parliamentarian to enter. Instead of the giving of money, there was the time honored custom of supplying entertainment and hospitality. And instruction of the voters, particularly the scores and hundreds who arrived in flocks for the shire elections, was as customary as the provision of meat and drink.

---

[42] Reading, Marlow, Cambridge, Hythe, Sandwich, Harwich, Maldon, and Tewkesbury are examples of changes, the men replaced in several instances being definitely of royalist views. The extent of the change or the real significance of this evidence cannot be determined, however, without a fuller study of the personnel of the Short Parliament.

[43] *Rebellion* 1: 228. Some evidence of the committee's procedure, as well as of the basis for decisions by the House, appears in the account of Bulstrode Whitelocke's election. M. R. Frear, The election at Great Marlow in 1640, *Jour. Mod. Hist.* 14: 433–448, 1942.

[44] Of about 40 election cases mentioned in the diaries and the *Journals*, 1640–1641, decisions favoring royalists over parliamentarians or reformers occurred in not more than 4 cases, and in 14 the reverse was true. In a few instances the issue was settled by other means than a vote, such as by the death of a challenged member or his elevation to the peerage. In the others, such as several where all contestants were apparently of the same politics, the issues are too indefinite for classification.

[45] Again the evidence tends to support Clarendon's comment that the House discriminated even in this matter in favor of such projectors as the majority thought might still be useful (*Rebellion* 1: 228), notably in the cases of Mildmay and John Harrison.

[46] William Smith, Thomas Smith (Bridgewater), and John Coventry.

[47] Wendover in Bucks and Weobly in Herefordshire were recently restored boroughs that were largely controlled by the families that had worked for their restoration. For Professor J. E. Neale's comment on the importance of local interests in the matter of "restoring" boroughs, even in Tudor times, see *The Elizabethan House of Commons*, 141–146.

[48] Sir Gilbert Gerard's erring son, Francis, who was placed for Seaford, was counted a royalist, 1643–1645, but through his father's influence was received again into the fold.

[49] *Rebellion* 1: 220. Some color might be lent to his charge by the speed with which the elections got under way (see note 22 above), but there is basis for no more than a vague conjecture on that point.

Although there were election strategies to which both sides resorted, it would be erroneous to conclude that the results were determined in the majority of cases by the "organization" of either faction. Organization and shrewd politicians each side had, but the influence of a local patron or faction or simply of a tradition more often governed the returns. Personal quarrels and local differences played their part, too, town squabbles and county-wide feuds,[50] and bitter disagreements about religion which turned men's thoughts from what should be reformed to how extreme the reforms should be. In the larger towns where there were business interests also to be considered men were chosen who could lobby best for them. These were men who had succeeded in trade and had held municipal office, rather than gentlemen from the country. To most of the requests for patronage made by noblemen or officials the leading manufacturing and shipping towns had turned a deaf ear. Local interests combined with national issues and with politics on a national scale in determining the political alignments of 1640. The resulting pattern is so complex that it is often impossible to state whether a man was chosen because he was a royalist, because he belonged to a certain family, because he favored puritanism, or simply because he was respected or popular in a community.

POLITICAL FACTIONS, 1640–1641

The election results show how far from being settled public opinion was. In not a few cases a royalist shared a borough or shire with a parliamentarian and from some counties came delegations almost as evenly split. It is misleading, in fact, to consider the members as belonging in 1640 only to the factions known during the Civil War as Roundheads and Cavaliers. Mr. Hexter has shown that as late as 1643 Pym's men included a war group, a peace group, and a more or less fluid middle group on which he could chiefly depend.[51] A similar grouping characterized the Commons of 1640–1641. In one section were the men who from the start were defenders of the king's policies or who came quickly to his side in early debates and divisions. Here were most of the courtiers and many holders of office in the royal administration, as well as lawyers and gentlemen from the areas least affected by religious and social change. Opposing these earliest royalists were the parliamentarians. After working first for the reform of abuses, these followed Pym's leadership into the war and kept their places after the "disabling" of members in 1642–1645. Among them were a few royal officials who had parted from Strafford, more than half of the lawyers, a still larger proportion of the city and town officials,[52] and many gentlemen, especially those from

the regions where puritanism was strong. Between these groups of the right and the left was an active and vociferous element consisting of men who supported the reform efforts of the early period, many of them joining in the proceedings against Strafford, but who eventually swung to the king. They were the moderate reformers, a number of them co-workers with Phelipps or Eliot in earlier years, but they were unwilling to follow the new leadership in the attack on episcopacy and in the resort to arms. When the final lines were drawn they were royalists, but at the time of the elections they undoubtedly represented the country's resentment against personal rule by the king. A few were townsmen from western and northern counties, but they were chiefly gentlemen and lawyers, men such as Henry Belasyse, Sir John Strangways, Capel, Edward Hyde, Falkland, Whistler and Geoffrey Palmer, whose concern for reform was sincere. Of men who swung the other way there were a few, some, for instance, who voted against Strafford's attainder and later became stalwarts of parliament's "cause." There were less than a dozen who vacillated during the war from one side to the other or attempted to straddle the issue. Making these reservations as to parties, and observing that there were three main groups instead of two, we may summarize the results of the elections by counties.

Rare is the county outside of Wales and tiny Rutland which returned a delegation entirely royalist, and even one of Rutland's royalists should be counted a "reformer" at the start. On the parliamentarian side the only "solid" county was Middlesex, half of whose members were the London citizens. But close to it were Northamptonshire and Essex, with majorities of 8 to 1, Lincolnshire, 11 to 1, and Norfolk, 10 to 2. The parliamentarians from Surrey outnumbered the royalists 12 to 2, and of these two one worked with the reform group for a time. The parliamentarians had comfortable majorities from Kent and Hampshire and a smaller one from Sussex. Even among the Cinque Port barons, subject to royal pressure though the ports were, the parliamentarians outnumbered the royalists at the start and gained by replacements. In several counties, notably Lancashire, Hereford, and Shropshire, a large proportion of the boroughs divided their favors evenly between the major factions. Yorkshire's delegation was made up of 13 on each side at the start, 4 men changing afterwards to royalism. Cornwall's large group of 44 included 21 royalists, 5 who became so later, and 18 parliamentarians. The principal divisions among the whole membership of 1640–1641 [53] are shown in table 1 on page 12.

These figures, of course, do not represent the relative strength of the two main groups when parliament opened, for though the figure for the royalists includes those who were expelled during the first year as a result

50 E.g., Leicestershire, Chester, the town and county of Carnarvon, Knaresborough, and others.
51 *The reign of King Pym*, 31–62.
52 For more exact figures regarding the relationship between occupational groups and politics, see p. 23.

53 Several men whose elections were voided or who died too early for their views to be known have been left unclassified.

TABLE 1

CLASSIFICATION OF THE TOTAL MEMBERSHIP, 1640–1641,
ACCORDING TO POLITICS

Parliamentarians	310
Reformers who became royalists	44
Royalists	182
Straddlers and men who turned from king to parliament	6
Others, unclassified	5
	Total 547

of the tactics of their opponents, that for the parliamentarians includes the recruits they gained during the same period.[54] It should be added furthermore that among the ranks of the parliamentarians were many who were far from being ardent in their sympathies. They paid lip service to parliament and declined to take up arms for the king. But their frequent or prolonged absences showed that they were only lukewarm in their attachment to the cause.

VARIATIONS IN VIEWS ON RELIGION

Another aspect of the 1640 parliament men as a group which must be considered is that of division according to religion. Gardiner has said that there was an Episcopalian party in the House before there was a genuine party of royalists.[55] It was differences of opinion about religion and ecclesiastical organization that provided the early lines of cleavage, severing the bonds which had held together the reformers, and turning many into new channels of action. But to trace the threads of the various groups through the maze of religious philosophies is more difficult than to analyze the political pattern, complex though the latter was. The stand of John Pym himself in matters of religion has been variously interpreted.[56] The views of others changed with the passing of time, as in the case of Pickering, who has been described as moving by stages from Presbyterianism to Independency to Brownism to Anabaptism.[57] Men who acted as elders of presbyteries or even

[54] It has been pointed out by Mr. Notestein that Pym's majority, as indicated by such early line-ups as that of 8 February 1641, was not too great. D'Ewes (N), 68, n. For further details on the election results by counties, see the later section on elections, and also Kershaw's figures (*E.H.R.* **38**: 507–508, 1923), which vary somewhat from those above. The map in the last volume of S. R. Gardiner's *History of England from the accession of James I to the outbreak of the Civil War* (10 v., London, 1883–1884 [hereafter, Gardiner, *H. of E.*]) represents the line-up after the first elections fairly well, although it does not take into account the middle or reform group described above, and differs in some areas, such as in the case of Hertfordshire, from the findings of the present study.

[55] *H. of E.* **10**: 2.

[56] Two recent students of Pym reach different conclusions about Pym's feeling toward puritanism. Mr. Hexter pictures him as having a certain amount of puritan zeal without being completely a puritan (*The reign of King Pym*, 195). But S. Reed Brett (*John Pym*, 80–81, London, J. Murray, 1940) describes Pym as an orthodox Anglican, strongly opposed to puritanism.

[57] *D.N.B.*

as lay members of the Westminster Assembly continued to work in parliament after Colonel Pride had presumably rid it of all but the Independents.[58] The terms now used to designate factions or sects were then used loosely enough, often carelessly or maliciously by pamphleteers, even so generic a term as "puritan" not always with the same meaning. It is doubtful whether many a member would have recognized himself in the category to which he has been assigned by contemporary critics or by historians.

Clues to the beliefs of the members appear in speeches and in letters, sometimes in wills. A number of members were serious students of theology, some of them writers on the subject. Most of the M.P.'s could quote at ease from the Scriptures. But amid the fluctuating and shifting currents that mark the course of the Long Parliament's decisions about religion, our judgment of individuals, except for a comparatively small portion of the membership, must be guided by actions rather than by words. And actions were not always dictated by doctrines of sin and salvation. Decisions to work with or to oppose certain religious groups were often governed by expediency rather than by conviction. In many cases influences outside of the sphere of personal belief or inclination, influences which varied in intensity as circumstances changed, help to explain the course that members followed. For some there were considerations of property, since many a parliament man numbered among his estates holdings that were once church rectories and tithes, and with them the rights of advowson. For some there were considerations of family, for several were clergymen's sons or brothers or nephews. A few were fathers or fathers-in-law of divines. And others had relatives who were openly or secretly recusants.[59] There were townsmen in the House who had quarrelled with ecclesiastical authorities regarding the appointment of lecturers or about the dignities claimed by lay and clerical officials. There were gentlemen, too, in whose memories rankled disagreements with parish vicars for causes that were quite mundane. Influences of a secular nature so combined with ecclesiastical ones that the thoughts of many of the parliament men of 1640 on matters of religion were far from fixed.

It is difficult to be sure in every case of why men attached themselves to certain religious groups in 1641 or 1643 or 1648. And it may be questioned whether

[58] For a discussion of the men who managed to combine their Presbyterianism and their Independency, see J. H. Hexter, The problem of the Presbyterian independents, *A.H.R.* **44**: 29–49, 1938–1939.

[59] As in politics, family considerations guided some, but others not at all. To indicate the crossing of lines, a sample list might include Blakiston, the regicide and Independent, who was the son of a pluralist clergyman and brother-in-law of the famed Dr. Cosin; Falkland, the liberal Anglican and son of a Catholic mother; Sir John Holland, a Presbyterian who had a recusant wife; the Coke brothers, Sir John and Thomas, nephews of one of the bishops attainted in 1641, who took opposite sides in the war.

their actions in the later years, affected as they were by so many varying considerations, can safely be used as a guide to division of opinion in the first year of the parliament. For those who died before the crucial years of the war and the Covenant such a test cannot be applied; they must be judged, in the main, by their words or by their actions before 1640. But for the rest of the 547 members here studied, where evidence of other sorts is lacking, the test of action, if used with reservations, may have some value for indicating the relative strength of the major groups.

The split between those willing to accept the established Church of England and the nonconformists was already apparent by the autumn of 1641. Perhaps it may be conceded that most of those who remained loyal to King Charles were loyal also to episcopacy, even though there were among them some who were inclined toward puritanism and some who leaned toward Rome. If this was so, possibly 220 of the total membership may be classified as Anglicans, of whom at least 30 favored modifications of the Laudian system. A small group of 3, perhaps more, were definitely inclined toward Roman Catholicism.[60] Another 35 are so little known that classification cannot be attempted. The remaining 289, including a number who were not parliament men when the issue was first raised early in the session, were nonconformists of some type. They were willing to abolish episcopacy, whether or not they had decided upon the form of church government which should replace it. Included in this group were about 123 who survived Pride's Purge of 1648 and are generally considered Independents, even though at least 25 of them had worked as lay officials in the presbyteries or the Westminster Assembly.[61] The final group of perhaps 166 were those who if only because Colonel Pride secluded them from the House have come to be known as the Presbyterians. Many were genuinely so, but others, though they moved along with the current of the times, had little in common with the Scottish Calvinists.[62]

If the boundary lines of religious groups were then so indefinite, and if their organization, except in so far as it coincided with the shadowy political organization of the period, was so formless, it would be venturing far to state that more than a small percentage of those elected to the Long Parliament in 1640 and 1641 were chosen for religious reasons alone.[63] In some of the counties most affected by dissent, such as those of East Anglia, where a supporter of episcopacy was tolerated at the elections chiefly because of family or royal connection, or in the southeast, some choices were made between advocates of moderate or extreme forms of sectarianism. Occasionally, too, the clergy helped to influence elections. A good many men of anti-Laudian views were chosen from the towns, but more because they stood for the townsmen's developing sense of independence, apparently, than because they were stiff-necked puritans. Religion as one of the great influences of the day undoubtedly had its bearing upon the elections and upon the building of parties. But it seems reasonable to conclude that in most cases the choice of Anglican or Calvinist reflects more the character of religious thought predominating in a constituency than the shadings in the religious views of the individual member, and that the religious influences operating in the Long Parliament were strongest when they combined with forces that were essentially political or economic.

ATTITUDES TOWARD ROYAL POLICIES BEFORE 1640

It was the fortune of the puritan leaders of 1640 that what their following lacked in unity of thought and of plan was compensated for by a general feeling that "It's time for a change." If men in parliament and in the country were undecided about the shape of things to come, they were ready at least to agree that certain things should no longer continue, that some high places needed to be cleansed of their iniquities.[64] Many who were afterwards willing to fight for King Charles shared in this sentiment. The election returns reflected this mood even more strongly that many had

[60] Besides John Belasyse, who had been reared a Catholic by a converted father, Endymion Porter, whose convert wife may have won him over, and perhaps Seaborne, there were possibly a dozen others who had close family ties with the Roman church. Some came of families whose loyalty to Catholicism had simply gone underground for a generation or so, such as the northerners, Danby, the Mallorys, Robert Strickland, or Wentworth of Woolley. There were others with connections at court who had recent converts in their family circles or were themselves inclined, as were Windebank, and possibly the Jermyns, to favor men of that faith.

[61] See note 58 above. By the test of political survival, Sir Richard Wynn, a follower of expediency if any were, might thus be classed an Independent. An intimate of the queen's household, but also of a family long close to Bishop Williams, he retained his seat in parliament after most of the Anglicans and the Presbyterians had departed.

[62] Because the published lists of those secluded by Pride do not name every member turned out in 1648, the figures given here for the Independents and the Presbyterians are not exact.

[63] Sir John Dryden, for example, once reported by the authorities for his encouragement of nonconformist ministers, had gained recognition also as a foe of ship money. William Spurstow, the London merchant who sat for Shrewsbury, was not only the father of the Calvinist divine whose name is entwined in the title of the 1641 pamphlet, *Smectymnuus*, but was among those who had opposed the 1627 loans and was active in the inner circles of London's men of business. Their political actions were perhaps motivated by their religious affiliations, since the resistance movement had strong ties with puritanism (*cf.* Hexter), but with the voters which considerations had most weight it is impossible to say.

[64] The negative frame of mind is well set forth in W. A. Shaw, *A history of the English Church during the civil wars* 1: 2, 7, 2 v., London, Longmans Green, 1900. See also Sanford, John L., *Studies and illustrations of the great rebellion*, 284, London, 1858 (hereafter, Sanford, *St. and ill.*).

feared or anticipated.[65] Yet neither the temper of the times nor the political strategies of court or opposition will suffice for interpreting the 1640 elections. The clues to successful candidacies must be sought also in a study of the members themselves, their qualities of character, their qualifications to serve as parliament men, and the bonds of common interest which had been forged among them before 1640.

One obvious clue to such bonds is suggested both by the restlessness throughout the country and by the eagerness with which the parliament turned to its attack on abuses. Dissatisfaction with the king's devices for collecting revenue, with the plague of monopolies, and with the arbitrary rulings of Laud in matters of the church was widespread. And long before the Scots threatened the northern border signs of concerted resistance had appeared. Loan collectors had been defied. Local officials had ignored orders from Council regarding ship money accounts. Prominent citizens and gentlemen had been willing to go to prison for a principle rather than yield to the royal demands. There were enough examples of resistance between 1625 and 1640, especially in the period after 1629, to suggest that some deliberate planning was back of it. One result certainly was that among those who were willing to be examples a bond of unity was being forged. John Bramston, who was defeated in the 1640 elections by a nephew of Pym, declared that all who had been imprisoned for opposing the loans or the new customs, or who had "any ways appeared obstinate and refractory to the government," or opposed the king on ship money or other matters were elected.[66] Although Bramston's statement is too sweeping, there is considerable truth in his remark, for a large number of the parliament members had indeed dared to oppose the arbitrary policies of Charles and had suffered the consequences. John Hampden was not the only commoner to take a stand against ship money, nor John Rolle alone among the merchants in resisting the payment of tonnage and poundage. The roots of the resistance movement run deep, back as early as James's call for a loan in 1621, and there are echoes of Eliot's voice in the tale of the grievances of the subject and how they were borne.

Nearly 60 of the 1640 parliament men, probably more, had opposed once or oftener the demands of the king for loans, in 1621, 1627, and 1639–1640,[67] and the fathers or close relatives of 30 others; and 18 members

and the relatives of 18 more had been imprisoned in 1627 for their refusals. More than a score of members, most of them different from those in the above group, had suffered imprisonment for other causes, a number on account of their conduct in earlier parliaments— 1621, 1629, and even the Short Parliament—a few for slighter offenses at court. Sir John Jennings and Henry Darley were prisoners at the time the Long Parliament opened. The nature of the charges and the severity of the sentence varied. The eleven-year imprisonment of Strode and Valentine, the sixteen imprisonments within seven years of Vassall, were of a different nature from the locking up of Kirton in his youth for suspected aid to Arabella Stuart's young husband. But the figure of a possible 56 members and relatives of members who had been imprisoned for some cause is probably low for a period when clapping behind bars was a common enough feature of the administration of justice. Others had escaped with fines or warnings for offenses of a different sort. Some forty or more had been warned or reprimanded by the Privy Council or penalized by Star Chamber sentence, some for musters defaults, some for delays in ship money collections, some for staying in London against the royal order.[68] And at least 10, including several who had been consistent offenders in other ways, had experienced the sort of justice meted out by the Court of High Commission. Some few of these had been brought up for morals charges [69] and others for flagrant nonconformity. Still others had quarrelled in their parishes with the emissaries of Laud, or had flouted the authority of their local clergy, or refused to select conforming ministers for the posts for which they held the nomination.

Toward the special exactions devised in the decade preceding 1640 the attitude of many of the members had been hostile. Half a dozen had resisted the knighthood compositions and no doubt the score or more who paid their fines on that account did so grudgingly. Others found in the forest program a grievance that touched them personally. At least 17 members of the 1640 Commons besides Hampden had been reported as ship money refusers; 33 others had opposed or hampered collections in some way; and of the 46 who as county sheriffs had been responsible for collections, 1635–1640, not fewer than 14 had been reprimanded

---

[65] Whitelocke professed astonishment at the spirit of opposition to friends of the court which the people showed. Add. MSS, 37,343, fol. 206v.

[66] *The autobiography of Sir John Bramston,* Lord Braybrooke, ed., 73, Camden Society, 1845. A similar observation about the Short Parliament elections was made by the Venetian ambassador. *C.S.P. Venetian, 1640–1642,* 25.

[67] Rushworth's lists (3: 910–915) for the 1639–1640 loan are quite incomplete, covering not more than eleven counties. At least 14 of those listed as not lending this time had been loan refusers before, and there were doubtless others from the regions not reported by Rushworth.

[68] Among those severely penalized for their offenses were Sir John Corbet, Sir Peter Heyman, and Walter Long. The gap in the Star Chamber records for the critical years makes it impossible to determine how many more of the 1640 members may have felt its lash. It must be recalled, however, that much of the Star Chamber work was with routine legal matters. An examination of the indexes to the cases at the Public Record Office shows that many of the 1640 parliament men had been plaintiffs or defendants there for quite ordinary causes.

[69] Of the latter type Sir Robert Howard's is a well known case. The adultery charge against the elder Bayntun, however, a man whose vigorous opposition to the Stuart program had been about as conspicuous as that of any single member, may well have had politics in it.

by Council for their procrastination and 9 others had required prodding about collecting their own or their predecessors' arrears. City magistrates, also, from London, East Anglia, Devon, and other areas, had worked for relief from the ship money rates laid on their towns, and in their meetings to consider reapportionment had met other townsmen and gentlemen of their counties who were to be their colleagues afterwards in parliament. The grievance list includes musters defaulters, too, critics of coat and conduct money, and those, especially from Yorkshire, who opposed the army plans of 1640. Various representatives from the ports and from the cloth industry areas had protested before 1640 against the trade regulations, the taxes and the "projects" which hampered their interests, and other aspects of royal interference in their personal and local affairs. And over a dozen parliament men had grievances of a more personal nature, either against the king or against Strafford, because of some real or fancied disappointment about office or estate. The case of the father of Denzil Holles illustrates well the effect on a man's attitude toward his sovereign of repeated snubs by creatures of the court. Personal frustrations combined with disapproval of policies to make explosive material by 1640.[70]

The roll of those members who are known to have opposed in some way the policies that resulted in the grievances of the time, or whose close relatives had done so, is long, including 143 of the 547 members involved in this study, slightly more than 1 out of 4.[71] It would be erroneous, however, to place too much emphasis on grievances, for they alone did not govern politics. A third of the men known to have had grievances of some kind supported the king eventually, some very early. Henry Belasyse, for example, twice imprisoned, the second time at the close of the Short Parliament, and a promoter of the Yorkshire petition, was a loyal supporter of the crown by 1642. Sir John Strangways had been removed from the commission of peace for Dorset and had been imprisoned in 1627, but within a few months after the opening of the Long Parliament he swung away from the opposition and became eventually a champion of the royal prerogative. Other striking examples are Manaton of Cornwall, Denton of Bucks, Dutton of Gloucestershire, Capel of Herts, and Palmer of Rutland. It was not the grievances of the eleven years of personal rule by King Charles that made men Roundheads. Rather it was the same forces that

had worked in the parliaments of 1621 to 1629, sharpened now by the experience without parliament, which continued to activate the reforming group. The grievances of 1630 to 1640 had dramatized the issues, had enabled the foes of Laud and of Strafford to build up a resistance movement outside of parliament,[72] and had supplied propaganda for the 1640 elections and for the onslaught by parliament upon the king's ministers. But when the crown itself was threatened, and the church of their fathers, the personal grievances of many yielded to the greater issues.

EXPERIENCE OF THE MEMBERS IN PARLIAMENTS AND PUBLIC LIFE

More important than their feelings about abuses, so far as the constitutional work of the Long Parliament goes, was the wide experience of its members with the general problems of the kingdom. Many had helped the administration to function and had served in previous parliaments. Clarendon remarked that only a few had sat in many parliaments, "the long intermission of Parliaments having worn out most of those who had been acquainted with the rules and orders observed in those conventions."[73] There is some truth in the remark, for more than half of the 1640 parliament men had never served before 1640. For 161 of these the Long Parliament was their first, and 167 had sat for the first time in the spring. About forty per cent, however, had had experience before 1640. The 1621 parliament had included 80 of these men, and more than a hundred had sat in each of the other parliaments of that decade, 156 of them in the critical one of 1628–1629; 148 members had experience in from two to five parliaments before November, 1640, 24 had sat in six, 16 in seven, and 5 elder statesmen counted eight parliaments in their past, with experience dating from the days of Elizabeth. Three, possibly 4, had sat in an Irish parliament.[74] The groups having the longest records of service were of course the perennial M.P.'s, so often chosen to succeed themselves time after time for the same constituency that their elections became

---

[70] Alexander Thomson, John Holles, *Jour. Mod. Hist.* **8**: 145–172, 1936.

[71] Not included in the records on which the above figures are based are the debates of earlier parliaments. Most of the men who had spoken for the opposition before 1640 and lived to serve again in the Long Parliament had gone further than criticism by words in the years that intervened. No doubt the roll of "resisters" would be lengthened if all the speeches were analyzed, just as it would if more records for the 1630–1640 period were studied.

[72] Mr. Hexter asserts that the resistance to the 1627 loan was essentially a puritan resistance (*The reign of King Pym*, 82–84), and so far as it concerns the loan resisters who were elected to the 1640 parliament, the conclusion is justified. There were, however, other loan resisters not chosen in 1640, some of them strong royalists, Wentworth himself being among them; and there were royalists who opposed ship money and Strafford's program in the north—enough to indicate how generally unpopular, regardless of sentiment on other matters, such measures were. The spearhead of resistance to ship money, as symbolized by Hampden and Say and Sele, and by the dilatory sheriffs of 1635–1640, however, was provided by the puritan leadership.

[73] *Rebellion* **3**: 321.

[74] Because many of the returns have been lost and because it has not always been possible to establish the identity between the men of 1640 and those of the same name in earlier parliaments, all of these figures must be considered approximate.

TABLE 2

EXPERIENCE OF THE MEMBERS IN EARLIER PARLIAMENTS

A. Classification of the Membership according to the Number of Previous Elections

English Parliaments before Nov. 1640				Irish Parliament
None	161	Five	32	3 (4?)
One	193[75]	Six	24	
Two	46	Seven	16	
Three	37	Eight	5	
Four	33			

B. Distribution of Experience in Earlier Parliaments

Short Parliament	328 (332?)	1624	106	1601	2
1628–1629	156	1621	80	1597	4
1626	127	1614	42 (36?)	Each of six earlier parliaments	
1625	121	1604	9 (8?)	(1572, etc.) 1 (2?)	

almost a matter of habit.[76] Many who had been in the earlier parliaments of Charles and those of James had worked with the country party, but others had been adherents of Buckingham, and in the years between 1629 and 1640 there was changing of sides between the factions. The organizing of the Long Parliament could not be based entirely upon earlier political affiliations.

The more than three hundred new men, fully three-fifths of the members, who in 1640 filled the seats to which the men of Buckingham's day did not return, present an interesting study in themselves. Among those whose experience began with the Short Parliament the parliamentarians and the royalists were of almost equal number, but if the approximately 17 "reformers" who swung afterwards to the king are counted as potential co-workers with Pym, his advantage among the newcomers of the spring can be reckoned at 101 to 66. He gained a greater advantage among the fresh members elected in the autumn, for the 161 novices included 91 parliamentarians, 59 royalists, and 9 who became royalists after working for a time for reforms.[77] This advantage was gained partly by political strategy after the opening of the parliament, it will be recalled.[78] Nevertheless the increase between May,

1640, and November suggests that the fields had not been left untilled by the reformers during the interval.

Of the newcomers of 1640 almost a third were men not more than thirty years old, inexperienced in a literal sense. Twenty-three, in fact, were not yet of age. The older men, even though new in parliament, usually were experienced in other lines. There were veterans of the court, such as Endymion Porter, Sydenham, Warwick, Windebank, and officials like Harrison and Crispe, royalists all, and some of them casualties of Pym's first attack. Many were merchants, too, and town magistrates, men of the calibre of Cradock, Vassall, and Soame, Spurstow, Bond, and Trelawney,[79] and several lawyers of distinction, Bagshaw, Bridgeman, Geoffrey Palmer, and others. There was the antiquary, D'Ewes, whose knowledge of parliamentary precedent was more profound than that of most of his seniors in experience. And there were more than a score of new men whose local reputations and zeal for reform placed them at once in the front ranks of the opposition.[80]

In addition to experience in parliaments, wide experience with other sorts of public responsibility was among the leading assets of the 1640 personnel. With few exceptions, those who were old enough to be entrusted with office had been called upon to perform some functions in their counties or towns, at court or in mili-

---

[75] Of this group 167 entered parliament first in the Short Parliament. The total without experience before 1640, therefore, was 328.

[76] The 8-parliament men were Sir Arthur Ingram, Sir Thomas Jermyn, Sir Francis Knollys, senior, Sir Oliver Luke, and Sir Henry Wallop; the 7-parliament men were Sir Francis Barnham, Sir Thomas Barrington, Sir Thomas Bowyer, William Cage, Sir Thomas Cheeke, Sir Gervase Clifton, Sir Robert Crane, Sir Walter Erle, Sir Ferdinando Fairfax, Sir Miles Fleetwood, Sir Thomas Lucy, Sir Francis Popham (possibly 8), Sir John Strangways, Sir William Uvedale, Sir Henry Vane, senior, and Sir Thomas Walsingham. Only one man in these two groups, Popham, seems to have missed being chosen for the Short Parliament, but old Sir Francis Knollys, who began his experience under Elizabeth, seems to have missed all but the first parliaments of James I and Charles. He returned with the Short Parliament after an absence of fifteen years.

[77] The group new in the two 1640 parliaments included, therefore, 175 parliamentarians and 151 who in the end were king's men. Two of the total of 328 have not been classified because of lack of sufficient evidence.

[78] See above, p. 10. Pym's net gain was of course greater than is indicated by these figures, which include both royalists

who were expelled and parliamentarians who replaced them. I have found no satisfactory way to state the exact proportions at a single date.

[79] The towns which at this period preferred as M.P.'s their own citizens rather than gentlemen's sons were less affected by the tradition of continuity of service than were the smaller boroughs. Busy merchants apparently regarded serving in parliament, unless it offered the opportunity to lobby for some matter of trade or of town interest, as one of the burdens of civic duty. It was shouldered by aldermen or councillors when their fellows required it of them, as was the office of mayor, and it lacked in their eyes the social prestige which it held for the gentry. There was a less rapid turnover when towns chose their recorders or legal advisers than when they elected men of trade as their M.P.'s.

[80] Examples of such ardent newcomers are John Ashe, Blakiston, Bosevile, Broxholme, Ellis, Nathaniel Fiennes, Glyn, Gurdon, Hesilrige, Heveningham, Cornelius Holland, Maynard (new in the Short Parliament, but chairman of the Committee of Privileges in the Long), Peard, Rigby, Oliver St. John, Tate, Walton, John White (Southwark), and Walter Yonge.

tary commands, even if they had not previously been parliament men. Less than a hundred (94) appear from available records not to have been named for public duties of some type, a figure which would probably be smaller if all the facts of their careers could be discovered.[81] In the case of 69 of these, more than two-thirds, the explanation seems to lie either in their youth, for 34 of them were not over twenty years old, or in the fact that their fathers or elder brothers were living and carrying the responsibilities expected of their families. Of the 25 not so accounted for 15 were merchants, lawyers, agents, or secretaries in private employment, men whose preoccupation with their personal affairs may explain the absence of their names from the lists of public appointees, and 2 others were out of England a great deal of the time before 1640. Of the remaining 8 not known to have held office, less than 2 per cent of the whole membership, 3 are men about whom very few facts are known and the others seem to have been men who preferred lives of retirement to activity.[82] All but a very small minority therefore had been either appointed or elected to some office before the meeting of the Long Parliament.

To enumerate the offices outside of parliament with which its members were familiar would be to list most of the functions which laymen of the wealthier sort were called upon to perform either in their local government or in the king's service (see table 3, on p. 18). Almost half of the members had been named to one or more commissions of local character, such regular ones as those for gaol delivery, oyer and terminer, sewers, or swans, or special ones such as those for martial law in the southern counties in the days of Buckingham, for piracy on the coasts, for investigation of problems connected with soapmaking in the western counties or brickmaking in London, for ecclesiastical causes, or for knighthood compositions. The next largest group consisted of the commissioners of the peace, of whom there were 219, probably more, among the 1640 parliament men.[83] Those who had served as J.P.'s or members of special commissions must have gained a broad understanding of conditions in the country, not only of crimes heinous or small, but of poverty and its causes, of agriculture, of the wool trade and all that touched upon it, and their knowledge was invaluable for the making of laws. Then there were the sheriffs. If several who

had held that office in towns rather than in counties are included, the sheriffs numbered no fewer than 122. Various ones had served in that thankless job more than once and a few in more than one county. The 47 who had been sheriffs in the ship money years had risked incurring their neighbors' displeasure or Council's censure, possibly their own ruin, by the policy of lenience or strictness they followed in regard to rates and collections. Several men had been treasurers for the charities of their counties, and 10 or more had been Vice Admirals. Between 70 and 80 had served as Deputy Lieutenants, the D.L.'s who were responsible for the county militia and who, in the years before 1640, had been concerned with the pressing of troops and with coat and conduct money. Four of the members had been co-Lords Lieutenant of counties, but in three instances they were simply noblemen's sons functioning with their fathers, and the fourth was a privy councillor called upon to act in the absence of others. Concerned with military affairs of a local sort were the 52 who held or had once held commissions in the trained bands, such as captain of a foot company or lieutenant colonel, and the 7 who had been at one time or other commanders of castles or garrisons. There were 7 more who were soldiers by profession, with ranks from captain to colonel, and at least 2 who had held commands in the navy.[84]

Comparable with the offices in the counties in which the knights and gentlemen had served are the town offices in which others had gained their experience. Well over half of the men of trade among the parliament men had been mayors or bailiffs, some of them twice, one of them four times, and Cage of Ipswich six or seven times. Almost all had risen from the ranks, going through the usual stages of chamberlain, sheriff, councilman, and alderman. There were representatives of these varying grades in the local hierarchies among the parliament men, but 4 out of 5 had reached at least the rank of alderman. With the problems of municipal finance, of the poor, of streets and buildings, of relations with the local clergy, of trade and apprentices, and with the administering of local justice these men were familiar. Many had journeyed beyond their towns to consult with officials of other boroughs on common problems, to meet with the county sheriffs or justices on general matters, and even to London on business for their towns as well as for their own affairs. Legal agents of boroughs also were present in the 1640 Commons, including the recorders from more than a score of them, legal counsellors from others, and several town clerks.

Besides men trained in local office were others who had been more directly associated with the crown and the departments of royal administration. More than a score were officers or attorneys connected with the

---

[81] This figure includes about 30 members whose only previous experience seems to have been Short Parliament membership, most of them being in the lower age groups and with fathers living.

[82] Several of these may have served on local commissions or as J.P.'s, but their names are not in the lists for special years which I have consulted. Those most likely to have served were C. Baldwin, W. Drake, H. Killigrew, W. Stanhope, and Z. Tate.

[83] The figures for the commissions have been compiled from the calendared State Papers, from a J.P. list of 1638 (S.P. 16/405), from quarter sessions records, both published and manuscript, some town records, and particularly from several lists among the Chancery MSS at the Public Record Office, C. 181/3, 4, 5 and C. 193/12 and 13.

[84] Not included in these figures are the men who had trailed a pike, chiefly for their own education, in the Netherlands, Germany, or Ireland. (See p. 28.)

courts—Common Pleas, King's Bench, Exchequer, or Chancery—and almost 30 were affiliated with the administration of the duchies of Cornwall and Lancaster or the counties palatine, or with Wales, or the Council of the North, or Ireland. Several agents of the customs service and some of the navy, the ordnance, and the mint can be listed among the public functionaries, and 25 to 30 who held or had held offices pertaining to the royal household and Council, ranging from the high fiscal posts held by Jermyn, Uvedale, and Wynn to the clerkships of Warwick or Lawrence Whitaker or Cornelius Holland. Some held offices known by empty titles but worth hundreds of pounds a year because they opened the way to pensions, projects, and other emoluments. There were a dozen or more who were grooms or gentlemen of the privy chamber, and 7 or 8 who were keepers of royal parks or stewards of manors. Another score or two had attached themselves at one time or other to the court, sometimes in the entourage of favorites or of officials, sometimes even as pensioners, without acquiring title to any particular post. Rarer were the men who had held great offices of state, but two members had represented the king in foreign courts. One of them, Sir Thomas Roe, was actually away during much of the period of this study because of his new mission to the continent. Five privy councillors were in the Commons,[85] including both secretaries of state, and most of them had participated in Star Chamber proceedings of the Council, hearing some of the causes which were on the grievance list of the parliament. At least two who had worked with the Court of High Commission were there, Dr. Eden and Dr. Parry, and they and the other churchman, Dr. Chaworth,[86] had functioned before 1640 as chancellors to bishops. Two other parliament men had been connected in minor ways with ecclesiastical administration.[87] In general, these administrative officers of the crown and of the church were loyal to the king in the struggle with parliament, but there were exceptions, as in the case of the Vanes, Mildmay, Pye, Hippisley, and various others.[88]

A different classification of offices in which the parliament men had gained experience might be by those connected with professions or businesses. Such positions are indicative of the men's proficiency in their occupations and the regard in which they were held by their colleagues. Among the lawyers, for instance, besides

---

[85] Sir Thomas Jermyn, Sir Thomas Roe, Sir William Uvedale, Sir Henry Vane, senior, and Sir Francis Windebank. The last, however, was not long a member.

[86] Chaworth's election was voided early.

[87] Mostyn was long an employee of Bishop Williams, and Wheeler seems to have been associated at least for a time with the offices of Westminster's dean.

[88] The proportion of such officials to the whole membership corresponds perhaps to the lower figure of the estimate by Professor Neale for the last parliament of Queen Elizabeth (*The Elizabethan House of Commons*, 296). For a tabulation of offices in which the Long Parliament members had had experience, see table 3.

TABLE 3

EXPERIENCE OF THE 1640 MEMBERS AS OFFICE HOLDERS*

Local (Counties)		Military Offices (besides D.L.'s)	
Co-Lord Lieutenant	4	Professional in army	7
Deputy Lieutenant	70–77	navy	1 or 2
Vice Admiral	10–11	Garrison commanders	7
Sheriff (town or county)	122	Officers in militia	52
Justice of the peace	219		
Member of local commission	250	Royal Administration and Court	
		Privy Councillor	5
		(Secretary of State	2)
Local (Cities and Boroughs)		Ambassador	2
Mayors or Bailiffs	36	Household officials to king,	
Aldermen	44*	queen or prince	16
Councillor	49*	Clerks and minor officials	9–11
Lower Civic Office	53*	Grooms or Gentlemen of	
Recorder	27	the Privy Chamber	11
Town Clerk	4	Keepers of parks and	
Legal Counsellor	5	manors	7–8
		Officials connected with	
Church		courts of law	24
Chancellor to a bishop	3	Navy and customs officials	6
Secretary to a bishop	1	Mint or ordnance officials	3
Official connected with a deanery	1	Officials connected with duchies, counties palatine, Wales, the North, Jersey, Ireland	27

* The figures in this table include offices formerly held, as well as those still being held in 1640. The men from the towns especially had moved through the lower offices to the higher ones; besides 36 who had been mayors, there were 8 aldermen who had not so served, 5 who were councillors but not aldermen, and 4 who were still in the lower ranks.

those of mainly local reputation, such as the town counsellors and recorders,[89] there were five Masters of Chancery, several Serjeants-at-Law, a counsellor for one of the universities, and the king's counsel for one of the duchies, and the Solicitor General. Several had offices at the inns of court, too, having distinguished themselves sufficiently to be called upon to serve as readers, treasurers, and benchers. Among the soldiers of the House were professionals of the rank of captain, lieutenant colonel, and colonel, and also young lieutenants recently commissioned for the war with the Scots. There were older men, too, whose commissions had long since been surrendered, but whose earlier experience in camp or fleet proved its value in the raising of armies for both sides when civil war drew near. The men of trade, also, were leaders in their fields. Several had been masters or wardens of their companies. Spurstow for years had been his company's agent in London. They had trained apprentices and some had large numbers of men working for them. Several were directors of overseas enterprises, such as the East India Company, and they shared with the lawyers and gentlemen leadership and offices in the undertakings for colonizing America.

---

[89] Clarendon remarked, in connection with the king's need to make a second choice among the lawyers for Speaker, that "there were not found many lawyers of eminent name (though many of them proved eminent men afterwards)." *Rebellion* 1: 221.

The survey of the offices which the parliament men of 1640 had held shows that their background of experience was richly varied. Their positions had given them specialized knowledge in some cases, in others, a comprehension of the general problems of the public economy, and had accustomed them to making decisions. Their official duties, furthermore, particularly if they were in the counties, had provided contacts with other men of their region. J.P.'s who had met and worked together at the quarter sessions were not strangers when they met again at Westminster.

THE AGES OF THE PARLIAMENT MEN

It may be asked whether, if the members were so generally experienced in office, they were seasoned also in years. Some correlation between the lack of experience in office and a member's youth has already been suggested.[90] An examination of the ages of the whole group of the 1640–1641 period reveals that they were men who by modern as well as by seventeenth-century standards would be considered mature. The extremes were the nonogenarian, Sir Francis Knollys, senior, who, despite his age, was more active than some of his juniors, and the lad, Charles Lord Mansfield, who was barely fourteen in 1640. Between them the variation in ages was great.[91] But if the members are grouped by the decades of their birth, the tendency to cluster about the middle years is striking. Of the 84 per cent whose ages were between 26 and 60 years, 139 members had been born in the decade of 1600–1609 and 95 had been born between 1590 and 1599. In other words, 44 per cent, close to half of the total membership whose ages can be reckoned approximately, were between the ages of 30 and 50. The greatest concentration within a 10-year period is found in those born between 1595 and 1604, for 155 members were within the age group of 36 to 45. Since the total number of those aged 41 or more slightly exceeds the total who were but 40 or younger, the median age was probably somewhere in the early forties. Men prominent in the work of the parliament are to be found in all of the age groups except the youngest, but most of the really influential members, whatever their politics, were 35 or over,

TABLE 4

THE AGES OF THE MEMBERS [92]

Aged up to and including 40 years			*Aged over 40 years*		
20 years or under	23	}—54 who were under 26 years	41 to 45	75	}—152 who were aged 41 to 50 years
21 to 25	31		46 to 50	77	
26 to 30	59		51 to 55	49	}—86 who were aged 51 to 60 years
			56 to 60	37	
31 to 35	59	}—139 who were aged 31 to 40			
36 to 40	80		61 to 65	22	}—35 who were over 60 years
			66 to 70	10	
			over 70	3	
indefinite, but not over 40	3		indefinite, but probably over 40	8	
	255			281	

and such leading spirits as Pym, Hampden, Cromwell, Bond, Barrington, Lenthall, Denton, Grenville, Geoffrey Palmer, Denzil Holles, the brothers Ashe and the brothers Rolle, the elder Vane and Spurstow and Soame, were in the age group of 41 to 60. There were, however, men of distinction in the lower age groups, even among those who were under 30.[93]

The fact that about a fifth of the total membership were not over 30 years of age, nearly half of that group being under 26, is one of the interesting features revealed by the age analysis. Earlier parliaments of the century, however, had had their youthful members, some of them minors,[94] and the Long Parliament was probably not unusual in this respect. A good many of its leaders, aged between 40 and 50 now, had begun their parliamentary careers 12, 14, or more years before, when they were relatively young men, and one attempt in this session to exclude a would-be member because he was under age found little favor. Most of the youthful men sent to the Long Parliament, particularly those under 21, were the elder sons of gentlemen, or heirs or younger sons of peers, and were sometimes accompanied by their fathers, a brother, or even a grandfather. They sat

---

[90] See p. 17 above.

[91] Where exact birth or baptismal dates have not been available, I have proposed, on the basis of other evidence, an approximate birth year or a place within a five-year span for all but less than a score of members. For this purpose I have frequently used the data from monumental inscriptions, the age stated at the time of the death of a parent or the admission to a university. Such sources are not too reliable and often show discrepancies. In most cases, a statement of age by the man himself, or one that was given early in his life, is preferable to tombstone data. In the instances in which I have found no reference to age I have assigned members to various decades as the probable ones of their birth, reckoning chiefly from the date of entering a university or inn of court, or, in the case of tradesmen, the admission to the freedom of a town. A dozen or so I have reckoned, on the basis of their activities, simply as born before or after 1600.

[92] This table includes only 536 members. The 11 men whose ages have not been approximated have been omitted.

[93] Examples of those who were aged between 26 and 30 were lords Digby and Falkland, Savile, Nicoll, Knightley, and the younger Vane. Among those of the age group of 31 to 40 were Whitelocke, Pierrepont, Irby, Gervase Holles, Goring, Nathaniel Fiennes, Bridgeman, and Henry Belasyse for the younger half; and Capel, Sir Hugh Cholmley, Colepeper, Glyn, the younger Grimston, Hesilrige, Heveningham, Stawell, and Robert Wallop for the elder half.

[94] In one of the parliaments of King James a count revealed the presence of forty members who were about twenty and several who were not over sixteen (*N. and Q.*, 7th Ser. 11: 501, 1891). Several times in the later parliaments of James proposals were made for prohibiting the election of men under twenty-nine. See D'Ewes (N), 505, n.; E. and A. G. Porritt, *The unreformed House of Commons* 1: 224, Cambridge, Univ. Press, 1903.

chiefly for boroughs rather than as shire knights,[95] and
had evidently been sent to parliament to round out their
education as gentlemen, to learn something of the ways
of London and the court, and to prepare themselves for
the duties in national and local government that were
part of their social heritage. Hesilrige's father, when
he commended his son to Leicester for election in 1625,
wrote that he was "desirous to become a Scholler in
the best Schoole of Cristendome, for knowledge, and
experience (the parliament howse of England)."[96]
Some of the younger members possibly combined their
political education with their training in the law, for
several were enrolled at an inn of court about election
time or even later. Their responsibilities as M.P.'s did
not interfere too much with their studies nor, probably,
with other interests that young men could find at London. Some already were known as wild young blades.
A few hot-headed ones engaged in duels while their
elders debated. The absence of their names from the
records of proceedings for the most part suggests that
they were neither very active in the House nor expected
to be so. They were employed sometimes as messengers
to the House of Lords, particularly if they were noblemen's sons, or on conference committees. Occasionally
one spoke, as when the younger Bayntun boiled up
against Pym or when Pakington offered evidence[97]
against Windebank, and they sometimes offended by
ignoring the customs of the House.[98] But the younger
members in general seem to have caused little trouble
or comment. Those in their later twenties were more
frequently heard from, particularly if their convictions
were already firm. Others, such as Trevanion, were to
make their reputations only when war revealed their
talents.

RELATIONSHIPS TO CONSTITUENCIES: LOCAL MEN OR CARPETBAGGERS

Apparently age was less considered than other qualifications for service in the 1640 parliament. Of more
concern to the voters, besides previous experience in
office or in parliament, was some acquaintance with local
conditions, an understanding of the needs of the constituents, which could come only from living among
them, or nearby. And the great majority of those

chosen that autumn were men who were natives[99] or
residents of the counties in which their constituencies
lay, or of adjacent shires, or were the owners of property in the region, or were connected with it by some
fairly close family tie. About one man of every nine
in the whole membership, however, was a "foreigner"
to the region which chose him and owed his election
to influences outside of his personal bonds with the
locality. Nineteen of the English counties sent none
of these carpetbaggers at all, 10 sent one apiece, and
Wales sent one. The 60 odd members who were carpetbaggers came, in fact, from a relatively small number of
regions, those where opportunities for patronage were
especially strong, whether exercised by the crown in
the Cinque Ports, Cornwall, Lancashire, and other
northern counties, or by powerful lords, both royalist
and parliamentarian, in such counties as Devon, Wilts,
or Oxfordshire.[100] The number of genuine carpetbaggers may be even smaller, for there were possibly
connections with the localities that chose them which
have not yet come to light.

If the region is narrowed to the actual constituency,
however, the situation is different. The shire knights
were gentlemen of their counties, but the M.P.'s for
many boroughs, instead of being permanent "inhabitants" of the towns, were merely gentlemen who lived
nearby or even in a more distant part of the county.
They perhaps had town houses which they occupied
part of the time. Many owned property within the
borough limits, and came to town frequently from their
country seats on personal or public business. Some
were so intimate as to have exchanged with the townsmen the courtesies of a buck for a banquet or gifts of
wine or sugar, and in other cases they were the sons
of such gentlemen. A few were stewards of the principal neighboring lords. Most of the smaller boroughs
sent squires rather than their own burgesses to parliament. Even some larger towns, such as Nottingham,
selected their representatives from the gentry because
their prestige made them more powerful lobbyists for
the town's affairs. Other boroughs assigned one place
to their recorders,[101] who were qualified to speak for
the town, even if they were not residents. Some chose
native sons who had succeeded in trade in London, but

---

[95] Several shire knights, however, belonged to the 26 to 30
age group, including Thomas Lord Wentworth, Chicheley, Lord
Digby, Richard Rogers, Lord Rich, Pickering, and Sir William
Widdrington. Others were still younger, such as Burgoyne of
Bedfordshire, and the minors, William Herbert, who sat for his
family county of Monmouth, and James Lord Compton, whose
father's prestige had won him Warwickshire.

[96] H. Stocks and W. H. Stevenson, *Records of the borough
of Leicester, 1603–1688,* 220, Cambridge, Univ. Press, 1923.
Quoted by permission of the City of Leicester.

[97] D'Ewes (N), 26, 27, 384.

[98] See the case of young Shuttleworth, who refused to move
for a division. D'Ewes (N), 420 and n.

[99] Not all who were "natives" had continued to live in their
counties. Several who were Londoners in 1640 were chosen
for boroughs in the shires of their birth, probably because they
had maintained some connections through trade or through relatives or property.

[100] The distribution of the 64 probable carpetbaggers was as
follows: 1 each from Cumberland, Essex, Herefordshire, Kent,
Norfolk, Somerset, Suffolk, Sussex (early declared void), Warwick, York, Wales; 2 each from Oxford (University), Westmorland; 3 each from Dorset, Northumberland, Staffordshire;
5 from Lancashire; probably 6 each from the Cinque Ports,
Devon, and Hampshire; 8 from Wiltshire; and 9 from Cornwall.

[101] Porritt (*op. cit.* 1: 515) quotes a contemporary comment
on the number of recorders who expected to be chosen "as being
the mouth of the corporation." At least 22 boroughs sent their
own recorders to the Long Parliament.

had retained some local connections.[102] It was principally at the larger towns and cities where there was sufficient business to produce wealth and where there was an increasing independence from the landed classes and a divergence of interest that men from their own population were chosen.[103] They were wealthy magistrates who performed no bowing and scraping before the gentry. They had met the country squires in consultations about local problems, their daughters intermarried with gentlemen's sons, and their civic pride made them bold in dealing with dignitaries of the church and of the crown.

But though the elections of 1640 emphasized the preference for men of local repute, those who were chosen must not be considered provincials. Most of the lawyers and gentlemen had travelled from their homes for their education and for reasons of business and pleasure. A good many retained their connections with their inns of court for some time after their student days, and others had London houses. Even such dutiful sons as Sir John Coke, junior, or Ralph Verney, who stayed in the country most of the time to look after their fathers' estates, made occasional trips to town and visited frequently with the neighboring gentry or with kinsmen in more distant parts.[104] The townsmen, too, had travelled considerably, sometimes to nearby towns for consultations on plague relief or tax rates, sometimes to London concerning law suits or trade. The London connections of dozens of members would of itself make a fascinating study, for there were sons and grandsons and sons-in-law of London aldermen residing in many a shire who doubtless retained some contacts with their city kinsmen. Others had sons or brothers who were tradesmen there.[105] The four citizens who officially represented London in the Long Parliament were outnumbered by M.P.'s of smaller towns who were themselves Londoners or had been trained under London companies.[106] And the streets of Westminster were as familiar to some members as were Cheapside or Coleman Street or Holborn to others. Besides those who were previously acquainted with the houses of parliament, or with offices in the administration or the household, at least forty members had lived for some time in the shadows of Whitehall, where their fathers or stepfathers or brothers had court connections, or where they had tested their own ambitions in an earlier day. The parliament men of 1640 were not unfamiliar with the ways of other parts of England, though their roots were in their shires, the outports, and the county towns.

SOCIAL CLASSES AND OCCUPATIONS OF THE M.P.'S

In choosing representatives who understood their local problems the voters had the advantage also of choosing men who were known to them. Their social position and ability to serve with little or no compensation were items of weight in the lists of the candidates' qualifications. Their ranks, their occupations, their wealth, and their families are important features of the background of the 1640 parliament.

A survey of the members by classes and occupations confirms the traditional view that the majority were country gentlemen who lived out of London most of the time, took an active part in the life of their shires, and drew their incomes chiefly if not solely from lands. Three out of five of the total membership of 1640–1641 (333 or 334) were such gentlemen, bearing variously the title of "Baronet," "Knight," "Esquire," "Gentleman," or courtesy "Lord."[107] The second largest group, the lawyers, included 74 professionally trained men and 5 who were sometimes styled "country solicitors." A third group of 55, which included the greater number of the town magistrates, were the men of trade, the mercers, merchant tailors, clothiers, and "merchants."[108] Other important groups, consisting chiefly of men whom the heralds accounted "gentlemen," were the officials of the royal administration (27), and the courtiers (22). Then there were the men, not all of gentle origin, who were privately employed by prominent persons as business agents or secretaries (13), or who were soldiers (9), or officials of the church (3). And one was a physician, and one a naval officer.

[102] E.g., Bedingfield, Spurstow, and probably Edward Ashe.

[103] At Norwich and Ipswich the honors were divided between townsmen and neighboring gentlemen.

[104] The Yorkshireman, Sir Hugh Cholmley, for example, made long visits with his wife's family in Kent and in Northamptonshire; Lytton of Hertfordshire had visited the Hampshire Wallops; Owfield of Surrey, a Londoner born, had lands and friends in Lincolnshire and lived there for a time; Smith of Chester visited his Somerset kinsmen, as did Napier of Bedford and Northants his in Dorset.

[105] Many a younger son of gentle family, too far down the line to be educated for a profession, had been apprenticed in London and had stayed to prosper there. Other London relatives of the 1640 M.P.'s were of humbler origin.

[106] E.g., Edward Ashe, Bedingfield, Bence, Jenner, Spurstow, and possibly Hooke. If the question of who aroused the apprentices for their mob scenes of this period is to be answered, the links of the members of parliament with the London citizenry should not be overlooked. If Salway's brother and Barnardiston's son, Samuel (D.N.B.), were involved, the relatives of others may have been concerned, even though the M.P.'s themselves avoided complicity. See W. H. Coates's comment on this point (D'Ewes [C], xxxiii).

[107] I have included representatives of the peerage in this category of gentlemen in most cases. Many of them bore the title of lord or viscount because their fathers were peers. Two viscounts, Falkland and Monson, and two barons, Fairfax and Wenman, bore their titles by their own rights, but they were of the Scottish or Irish peerages.

[108] The tradesmen's group, including one or two "gentlemen" whose trade connections may have amounted by 1640 to little more than membership in a city company, can be subdivided as follows: apothecary (1); brewer (1?); chandler (1); clothier (3); draper (4–5); dyer (2); fishmonger (2); goldsmith (1); grocer (2); hosier (1); mercer (2); merchant tailor (1); salter (1); skinner (1); and those known only by the general title of "merchant." The latter men dealt with a great variety of commodities. Some whose interests reached beyond the seas were shipowners, too.

It may be inquired whether any relationship can be shown between the occupations of the members and their politics. The gentlemen, 39 per cent of whom were royalists, were probably moved more strongly by interests that were not primarily of an economic or occupational character. The secretaries or agents of lords tended to follow the politics of their employers. But in the other groups some connection between calling and politics is discernible. The churchmen, the soldiers, the courtiers, were largely royalists. About half of the administrative officials supported the king, two managed to straddle, and ten were parliamentarians. The 74 lawyers divided almost evenly by the time war came, although fully two-thirds of their group had been of the reform element in the early weeks of the parliament. Of the townsmen, including the "country lawyers" as well as the tradesmen, only a fourth were royalists, some belatedly, and most of these were from the strongly royalist areas of the west and north.

Since family background also must have influenced the ideas of the members, some consideration of the classes from which they sprang is of interest. Sons of the newer gentry rubbed shoulders in the Commons of 1640 with the sons of earls or of merchants or of yeomen. Men of obscure origin who were employees of powerful lords crowded for places with squires and baronets whose ancestors had attended parliament two centuries before or who traced their pedigrees back to the conquest. Forty-eight members, slightly less than a tenth of the total, were the sons of earls, viscounts, or barons, 18 being younger sons. Thirty-two were baronets' sons, and more than ten times that figure were sons of gentlemen, albeit some were of the newer gentry removed but a few generations, sometimes a single one, from trade. Twenty-eight were sons of royal officials or courtiers, 22 were lawyers' sons, 4 were sons of clergymen, and one was the son of a doctor. Not a few were sons of distinguished men, and many could boast grandfathers on both sides of their lineage who had been personages of their day. A few had mothers somewhat renowned for their learning,[109] and there can be no doubt that the distinguished father-in-law of more than one M.P. helped to shape his career. The ancestors of 28 members defy labelling. The remaining members, about a tenth of the whole group, came from families below the gentry in rank. Of these the greater number were from merchants' or artisans' families. Some were heirs to great fortunes in London. Probably 6 were of yeoman stock. Two were mariners' sons and one was the son of a musician. Many of this group of humbler stock were by 1640 known as "gentlemen" or "esquires" and several had been knighted.[110] By far the greater number from these various stocks

were the heirs or the heirs apparent of their families, but 2 were of illegitimate birth, and at least 90, about a sixth of the total membership, were younger sons.[111]

THE WEALTH OF THE PARLIAMENT MEN

From the foregoing summary of the social positions of the parliament men it is apparent that the majority were from well known families and were men of importance in their communities. They also were men of substance, men who could afford the costs of election hospitality and could pay their own way, or much of it, at Westminster. To give exact statistics on the elusive question of the purse without benefit of the modern tax return is an impossibility, a statement with which the parliament's Committees for Compounding and for Advance of Money would heartily agree. But enough data and supporting evidence are available to produce certain impressions and to justify some venture into a consideration of the relative size of the members' incomes or the values of their estates.[112] The alacrity with which

---

[109] Lord Wenman's mother is an example.

[110] It would be a mistake to regard the classifications here set up as water-tight compartments, for titles were not always used exactly, and sometimes were interchanged.

[111] See table 5. It will be noted that a third of the lawyers were younger sons and nine of the courtiers, and that many of the other younger sons were distributed among the professions or trades, leaving less than forty who can be classified no more specifically than as gentlemen. Because many of these were of families having ample wealth to provide for them, and others were too young in 1640 to have been marked for a profession, they scarcely fall into the case of the younger son so much pitied by Sir Thomas Wilson in his description of the English classes in 1600. *The state of England*, F. J. Fisher, ed., 24, The Camden Society, 1936.

[112] The sources for the discussion of the wealth of the members range from wills and personal account books to great collections of state papers, from notes taken by travellers as they passed by country houses to lists of those ratable for taxes or loans, or those eligible for titles based partly on wealth. Most helpful for exact figures, besides the family papers which are too few and fragmentary, have been the *Calendars of the Committee for Compounding* and the royalists' "particulars" regarding their pre-war estates. The latter are preserved at the Public Record Office in the series, S.P. 23, and are beginning to appear in the publications of the county societies. Since the tendency of the declarants was to omit holdings from their lists and to under-value them, the evidence they offer has been checked by other data whenever possible. The fines based upon these estate values, however, afford a convenient index for figuring annual incomes, since the most frequent fines of $\frac{1}{10}$ or $\frac{1}{3}$ represent roughly two or five years' annual value. It is more difficult to state correctly the capital values of estates on the basis of the fines, for in some instances the sale value appears to have been figured on a twenty-year rather than the usual fifteen-year term. (See note 129 below.) Less satisfactory because less closely figured are the assessments which appear in the *Calendars of the Committee for Advance of Money* and the property values stated in the inquisitions post mortem which enumerate the lands passing from the deceased to his heir, for they are nominal values only, far below the true ones; but a heavier or lighter assessment, a longer or shorter list of properties and acreages, helps to establish a relative position in the financial scale. The estate values occurring with the names of men proposed after the Restoration for the Knights of the Royal Oak have been accepted in a number of cases. These are estimates only, but they are close enough to the war period to represent values not much higher than they had been in 1640, and in some cases prob-

TABLE 5

	Sons of Peers			Sons of Baronets			Sons of Knights and Gentlemen						Churchmen's Sons	Doctors' Sons	Lawyers' Sons	Sons of Courtiers and Officials	Sons of Non Gentle Family			Musicians Sons	Unknown	Totals
	Elder Sons	Younger Sons	Illegit. Sons	Elder Sons	Heirs Apparent	Younger Sons	Elder Sons	Heirs Apparent	Younger Sons	Illegit. Sons	Sons of New Gentry	Sons of Probable Gentry					Tradesmen	Yeomen	Mariners			
AGENTS or STEWARDS							2		3			2				1	2	1			2	13
ARMY MEN	2				1		3		2			1										9
CHURCH OFFICIALS									2				1									3
COURTIERS	2	2					5		7			1				2	1				2	22
GENTLEMEN	25	15	1	18	7	4	159	36	22	1		6			14	13	8				4	333
LAWYERS		1			1	1	27	1	24		1	4	2		7	3	1				1	74
NAVAL COMMANDER																			1			1
PHYSICIAN														1								1
ROYAL OFFICIALS							7		3			3				9	1	1		1	2	27
TOWN "LAWYERS"																	5					5
TRADESMEN							2		4		3		1		1		27	3	1		13	55
UNKNOWN INDEFINITE																					4	4
TOTALS	29	18	1	18	9	5	205	37	67	1	4	17	4	1	22	28	44	6	2	1	28	547
	48			32			331															

OCCUPATIONS AND FAMILY STATUS OF THE MEMBERS

nearly a hundred members offered in November, 1640, to give their personal security for £1000 apiece in support of a loan to be requested from the city of London is indicative of their wealth. Not all of the wealthy members subscribed,[113] but some were willing to offer their bonds for twice the amount, and before the recess more than a quarter of the total number of members had offered their bonds, a few of them jointly, for sums of £500 or £1000.[114] An even greater proportion of the whole pledged cash for the cause of defense on the eve of the war. The absence of many other names from the subscribers' lists is to be explained by politics rather than by lack of means.[115] There were men who during

ably give truer figures than those reported to the compounding commissioners by the royalists.

The sources for estimates of the incomes of the non-royalists are much less complete. Of considerable help are the lists of their pledges, 1641–1642 (see notes 114 and 115), but these are usable for classifying men as to their relative wealth rather than for exact statements as to their incomes. Another subscription list, that of the "adventurers" for Ireland in 1642, must be used with caution. The volume on the adventurers in the *Calendar of State Papers, Ireland*, makes it clear that the members' subscriptions for lands were not just personal investments. More often they were presented for two or more "compartners," the subscriber's personal share being but half or a much smaller fraction of the sum subscribed. Examples of such multiple subscriptions are Hampden's £1000, Heveningham's £1200, Miles Corbet's £250, to mention several of the better known ones. Aside from these lists, the estimates of the wealth for the popular party men rest on such personal and family records as are available, wills, correspondence, inquisitions post mortem, legal documents, and comments by contemporary writers.

[113] William Heveningham, for example, whose inheritance embraced fifteen manors, was not among the early loan subscribers.

[114] The lists of those offering security for the loans appear in D'Ewes (N), 51–52, 435, n., 438, n., 451, n., 539; and in *C.J.* 2: 222. A comparison of these lists with evidence of wealth from other sources leads to the conclusion that most of the loan subscribers were rich men.

[115] The subscription list of June, 1642, giving the names of those offering to advance horses, money and plate for the de-

the period of this study bought baronetcies, and some who aspired to peerages.[116] Others who could have bought titles because they owned "great and plentiful fortunes" kept the style of "esquire." The index to a member's wealth is not to be found in his politics, nor in the title he bore, nor in the antiquity of his family.

Nor can it be found completely in the sources of his wealth. Real estate was of course the principal basis of wealth for the M.P.'s, as it was for the country at large. Real estate meant not only land used for agriculture, but mines in the north that produced alum and coal, iron furnaces in the Sussex forests, and mills of various sorts. Perhaps the most famous grist mills owned by a member were the Dee Mills in Cheshire that were the chief source of wealth for Francis Gamull. And many of his neighbors supplemented their income from rents with their profit from saltworks. But whatever the nature of their holdings, whether they were "tenements" in villages and towns, or country properties of a manor or two, or great estates of eight, twelve, or even twenty manors, most of the 1640 parliament men, regardless of their social origins, held title to some land.[117] Closely associated with lands were the rectories and tithes, a heritage of the preceding century, that appear in many of the property lists.[118] If a member's land was acquired with money newly gained in trade, it might boast a mansion that outshown in splendor the manor houses of the older gentry.[119] A large number of the M.P.'s had real estate worth £1000 a year or more, and about a tenth counted their income from land at more than £1500. Often their holdings

lay in many different counties, a result of the accumulation of estates through purchase or various lines of inheritance. Not all of the members owned in 1640 the handsome estates that were their family's inheritance, however, for some had fathers still living and in possession, and some were younger sons. But many of these enjoyed liberal allowances from their fathers' properties.[120]

Other important sources of income were businesses and professions. But there are fewer records of these sources left on which to base estimates. The men of trade were apparently well-to-do. They were wealthy clothiers, owners of ships that sailed to distant seas or plied the coastal waters with sea coal for London or woolens from the west, men who in their towns and some in European ports were merchants of great repute. Not all could rival Soame of London, who, a younger son of a lord mayor, had built himself a "great estate," or a Trelawney of Plymouth, who was "a merchant of great reputation" and of a "very good estate," or Humphrey Hooke, one of Bristol's wealthiest citizens, whose real estate, apart from his varied business enterprises, brought him £500 a year. But many had incomes that were comparable with those of country gentlemen of moderate estate, and many had a great deal more.[121] They had been chosen to fill posts of local responsibility, many of them sent their sons to the universities, and they bought lands to which they planned to retire. They gave liberally to charities in their towns and during the war were able to advance considerable sums for the cause of their choice.

The incomes of the lawyers of the House, the principal professional group, were probably lower in average than those of the business men. If they were like their brethren of 1600 who were described as contending among themselves for the crumbs, except for the incredibly rich few who had reached the top,[122] most of the members of the legal profession in 1640 could not count on large returns from their practice. The gentlemen of the gown, however, were often gentlemen of estate as well, and enjoyed profits from their lands in addition to their clients' fees. The distinguished lawyer

---

fense, is in the Bodleian Tanner MSS, 63, fols. 51–61v. A version of the list was published, with a few errors, in *N. and Q.*, 1st Ser., **12**: 338, 358–360, 1855. To this list must be added the names of those who were rounded up for belated subscriptions the following September (*C.J.* 2: 772).

[116] Baronetcies, originally costing £1095 and representing incomes of £1000 a year, were rumored to have been sold for as little as £150 in Buckingham's later years (*The Oglander memoirs*, 48, W. D. Long, ed., London, 1888), and in 1641 were said to cost only £400 (*C.S.P. Dom., 1641–1643*, 38). Peerages were still high. Sir Simonds D'Ewes, who became a baronet in the summer of 1641, made some pointed remarks a few months before about several of the House "of great estate" who were planning to spend £15,000 to £16,000 to be made barons. D'Ewes (N), 392.

[117] In discussing wealth based on lands I have made no attempt in most cases to go into the nature of the tenure. Where rents could be deducted from the total land values of leaseholds, however, I have stated the figure of the net income. I have treated mortgaged lands as if they were in full ownership, but in cases where the interest charges are known I have taken them into account in my conclusions as to a member's financial well-being.

[118] It was stated in 1659 that the tithes of 3845 of 9284 English parishes were in the hands of lay owners. For a discussion of the effect this ownership had on the tithes controversies in the period of the Long Parliament, see Margaret James, The political importance of the Tithe Controversy in the English Revolution, 1640–1660, *History* **26**: 1–18, 1941–1942.

[119] Examples of the homes of the newly rich M.P.'s are Ingram's Temple Newsham in Yorkshire and John Harrison's Ball Park in Hertfordshire.

[120] In my statement of conclusions about the wealth of the members I have chosen the family wealth to which a man was heir apparent, rather than his allowance before his succession, as the figure to represent his comparative financial position. Similarly, when both father and son were members, even when it is known that the father had already settled much of his estate upon the son, I have classified both in the same wealth group. Examples are the Vanes and the Dalstons.

[121] Sir Thomas Wilson, who wrote at the beginning of the century on the various classes in English society, noted that the wealthier townsmen of the county towns might have £300 to £500 a year, or perhaps even £1000. Some of Wilson's figures are stated in terms of capital value rather than of yearly income. A Norwich alderman might be considered wealthy with £10,000 to £20,000, for example, but a Londoner must have not less than £50,000 to be counted rich. (*The state of England*, 12, 20–21, Camden Society, 1936.)

[122] *Ibid.*, 24–25.

and official, Orlando Bridgeman, was said to derive £1000 a year from lands, and Speaker Lenthall owned valuable properties besides having a practice worth £2500 a year. But they were doubtless wealthier than many of their fellows. Ten or eleven lawyers' names appear in the lists of the loan subscribers of 1640 and 1641. Of these several had incomes from offices or from large estates upon which their offers could be based, but the others apparently gave their bonds on the basis of their professional incomes. True estimates of the lawyers' total incomes, however, are almost impossible to find. Such figures as there are pertain chiefly to lands, and as landlords few of the gownsmen had more than a modest position. This was especially true in the cases of those who chose their profession because they were younger sons. On the whole it seems that the available figures underestimate the financial status of the lawyers who were parliament men.[123]

Besides estates, trade, and the practice of law, other sources of revenue drawn upon by the M.P.'s were the royal treasury and the various projects that attracted investment. The courtiers and administrative officials tapped the king's revenues for salaries ranging from a few pounds a year to several hundred. But the pensions they collected for themselves and for their wives, though sometimes appearing in the royal accounts, are often not subject to measurement and probably reach to much higher figures. Many received grants of money owing to the crown from various sources and were permitted to enrich themselves by divers schemes which their fertile brains invented. Endymion Porter and Edmund Windham are good examples of the courtiers who turned to account their intimacy with the king, and John Harrison, whose revenue from his share of the customs farm explains much of his more than £10,000 a year income, illustrates the heights to which a shrewd civil servant might climb. But with these as with the other groups estates counted as the most stable form of wealth. Inherited or purchased lands were both the spring boards and the safety nets for the men who lived their lives in the fickle atmosphere of the court. They did not always suffice, for royal favors had to be requited with generous loans upon demand, and more than one courtier by 1640 had parted with some of his inheritance or mortgaged it heavily.

Among the founts of revenue which were popular with the courtiers were the monopolies and projects of the times. The list of such ventures in which various parliament men had been interested includes projects for soap, alum, coal, saltpetre, gunpowder, and improvements in the Thames and Avon rivers. Those members concerned with the customs farms enjoyed a special advantage in connection with various commodities in trade. Another income of an occasional sort, one which

attracted several shipowners of the House as well as courtiers in the earlier years of Charles's reign, was that from privateering under letters of marque. It was the monopolistic character of many of the projects and patents, however, which made them particularly offensive and these were the ones which came under attack in the Long Parliament. Nevertheless, some men who had gained wealth from such sources were permitted to remain as members.[124]

There were other types of income from investments which did not carry the stigma that was attached to soap or sea coal patents. Investments in projects such as the drainage of the fens in the east or the developing of mines in other areas appealed to many M.P.'s. Not all were lucrative, but an occasional disappointment seemed not to dull the zest with which new enterprises were sought out. Men from all of the social and occupational groups of the 1640 Commons had shown a particular interest in overseas trading ventures and colonizing schemes. The East India and Levant companies, and those for fisheries and settlements in Ireland, numbered more than the merchants of the House among their stockholders.[125] And the projects for colonizing the New World, both the earlier Virginia Company and the more recent ventures in the north and in the Caribbean which had religious as well as profit motives, had interested both the 1640 members and their fathers.[126] The few hundreds of men in the House of Commons reflected the consciousness that was spreading in England of the untapped sources of wealth beyond her shores, and their debates on economic conditions and trade did not depend on tradesmen alone for authorities.

It is apparent from a survey of the sources of their income, from the types of their investments, from their response to requests for the advance of funds, that in the Commons of 1640 were many men of wealth. But not all the members were rich. A number are known to have had but modest estates, and some were perhaps almost entirely dependent upon patrons. There were gradations in wealth as there were degrees in social standing.

---

[123] A number of the members mentioned hereafter as belonging to the group with incomes of less than £500 a year were lawyers.

[124] See Clarendon's comment cited in note 45.

[125] At least 9 members were connected with the East India Company, 2 or 3 with the Levant Company, 1 with the Russian trade, and 2 with trade to Africa. At least 2 were active in Newfoundland ventures, 4 or 5 in the new fisheries company, and 9 or 10, probably more, were interested in Irish lands. If the complete lists of the stockholders of these ventures were available, doubtless even more M.P.'s would be revealed among the "adventurers."

[126] A score or more of the members and the fathers of an even larger number had been interested in the Virginia Company, and some had relatives among its officials. The New England interests were represented by 5 members of the early Dorchester project, 4 who had been concerned with Saybrooke and the sons of several others, and at least 18 who had been connected with the Council for New England or the Massachusetts Bay colony as stockholders, officers, or relatives or close friends of colonists. Others had been concerned with the Maine and Newfoundland developments, and the Providence Island Company counted 11 to 13 who were actively interested in its affairs.

To discover the exact proportions of the several groups classified according to relative wealth is impossible. In the first place, exact figures are lacking. Those we have are often patently incomplete and in some cases were given with the understandable intent of showing a poor financial plight. Indirect evidence must supplement records of profits or rents. A note about the dowry of a daughter, gossip or comment by a man's neighbors or friends, the jottings of travellers who were interested in social comparisons sometimes provide clues. Unreliable for statistical purposes as such materials are—not all men could afford, it is certain, the dowries they hoped they could arrange for their children—they may be combined with factual data to produce some idea of the sort of estate a man enjoyed. In the second place, the criteria by which estates were judged in the seventeenth century to be "great" or "meagre," "fair" or "mean," have not been sufficiently established. What was considered great wealth in Cornwall might be counted but moderate in Suffolk or London, and what would be riches for a man lower in the social order might barely enable a knight or baronet to run his household according to the customs of his kind.[127] By the reckonings of Sir Thomas Wilson at the opening of the century, the incomes of the gentry usually amounted to £500 a year or more, except in the regions far from London, and many of the higher orders of the gentry had over £1000 a year. The incomes of provincial townsmen were somewhat lower, except in the cities, but in London, of course, they were high.[128] It is not certain how accurate Wilson's estimates were for his day, and there is reason to think that if he had been writing in 1640 he would have found some of the corresponding averages lower.[129] But, using Wilson's income scale as a guide, though not

for the most part his social classification, we may attempt to work out a scale of wealth for the period of the Long Parliament and by it group the parliament men.

An income below £500 a year, for example, for men of the types making up this parliament, seems to have been considered hardly more than modest. Oliver Cromwell, for instance, who was considered by himself and by most of his biographers to have had a small fortune, enjoyed probably £300 to £500 a year. His brother-in-law, Walton, was an "obscure" gentleman of about £400 a year.[130] Above £500 annually were the moderate or fair estates. Those men who had incomes of £1000 a year, and apparently there were many such in the 1640 House, were probably considered as having very good estates, verging on the class of the "wealthy."[131] Certainly more than £1500 a year put men into the category of the very wealthy. Of these there are a number of striking examples. John Hampden, reputed to be one of the richest commoners in England, was said to have had an income of more than £1500, and Sir Thomas Fanshawe, a wealthy official of the Exchequer, had over £1600. Superlatives described in their day the extensive lands of Playters and his £2000 a year, Barnardiston's £3000 to £4000, and Capel's £7000. Sir Henry Wallop, who gave a daughter a dowry of £4000, had been called the richest member of the 1628 parliament, and his offer for the defense in 1642 was among the largest. The folly of Sir Francis Popham's sons had despoiled his once "vast estate" worth £8000 to £10,000 a year, but John Harrison, the customs farmer, probably had an income of that size, £1800 of it being from lands alone. The latter, however, seems to have been in a class by himself in the 1640 Commons. Men with much smaller incomes than he were still accounted wealthy.[132] And it should be noted in passing that mortgages and other forms of indebtedness had diminished the net income of several of the wealthiest.[133]

---

[127] An income of £300 to £500 a year was perhaps wealth for a yeoman (Mildred Campbell, *The English yeoman under Elizabeth and the early Stuarts*, 217–219, New Haven, Yale Univ. Press, 1942) but Sir Henry Slingsby's household expenses for his family and twenty-four servants ran to at least £500 in 1638. *The diary of Sir Henry Slingsby, of Scriven, Bart.* Parsons, D., ed., 26, London, 1836.

[128] Wilson estimated the average income for peers to range from £3000 to £5000; for knights, £1000 to £2000; for esquires, £500 to £1000, or possibly as low as £300 in more distant parts. *The state of England*, 12, 20–24. See also note 121.

[129] The records suggest that many of the king's subjects as well as the king suffered a decline in income during the interval between 1600 and 1640. The number of debts and mortgages in many families of the gentry and the turning of their class to new sources of income to supplement their rents are among the indications of this condition. In a recent study of the wealth of 119 peers and 93 baronets, based upon their compounding papers, the conclusion is reached that the average capital value of the peers' estates was £30,290, and of the baronet's estates, £11,114 (E. L. Klotz and Godfrey Davies, The wealth of royalist peers and baronets during the Puritan revolution, *E.H.R.* **58**: 217–219, 1943). Translated into annual incomes, with fifteen years' value being considered the basis for the reckoning of the capital values, the average income of the peers studied was £2,019 and that of the baronets, £741. The order of the baronets of course was begun after Wilson's day, but may be considered as corre-

sponding with the knightly class whose average income he reckoned as £1000 to £2000 a year.

[130] That £500 a year was a more or less basic figure as early as 1626 is suggested by a proposal in Dorset that year that all men having that income be taxed the same amount for a military levy as were the justices of the peace. S.P. 16, 6/59.

[131] Sir Philip Stapleton's £500 a year was referred to by Clarendon as a moderate income; and the £620 a year that Curwen acknowledged to the compounding commissioners was said to represent a diminished estate.

[132] Most of the figures upon which this classification is based are derived from statements of land values, but where loan subscriptions and other evidence provide some real basis for comparisons, I have attempted to fit into the scale a number of men whose chief source of income was not land. It is recognized that a man considered wealthy as a merchant was possibly blessed with an income below that of a wealthy gentleman. But the zeal with which the sons of gentlemen and peers sought marriages with the merchants' daughters, even from towns outside of London, suggests that their standards for judging wealth were not too far apart.

[133] The drain of his eldest son's debts upon Sir Francis Popham's estate has been mentioned. Falkland's case is another

As to where some of the 547 parliament men belong in this rough grouping of fortunes there can be no certainty. About one-fifth of the members cannot be classified because of insufficient evidence, although it may be suspected that a dozen or more of these were at least well-to-do and that others were in the group with moderate incomes or better. Concerning the remaining 439 men more positive statements can be made. At least 55 of them are known to have had incomes above £1500 a year, and almost as many more had incomes ranging between £1000 and £1500. If we add to this number those who by evidence other than figures can be reckoned as wealthy or as the sons of wealthy families, we find that 263, nearly 60 per cent of the 439, close to half of the total membership, were in the category of rich men. A much smaller number, 44, had incomes shown by available figures to be less than £500. But since the figures are based chiefly on real estate values and a good many in this group, such as the lawyers, had other sources of income, it may be presumed that the number to be ranked in the "modest fortune" class is even smaller than it appears. The remaining 132 members, nearly 30 per cent of the 439, and not quite a fourth of the whole membership, were men whose estates ranged from moderate incomes of £500 to £600 a year to the good ones that approached £1000. Close to 90 per cent, therefore, of those about whose income we have some approximate idea, were either moderately well-to-do or wealthy, and the latter class outnumbered the former by about 2 to 1. As to the whole group of 547 men it may be stated, then, that almost three-fourths, probably more, had moderately good incomes or better. If the figures to show incomes from all sources could be found, the fraction might well be higher. It cannot be denied that the parliament men of 1640 were men of substance, and included in their group some of the richest men of England.[134] As a contemporary wrote, "it is against reason that he that hath nothing of his own to give should have power to give away other men's estates, or any part of them, which . . . the Parliament hath."[135]

EDUCATIONAL BACKGROUND OF THE MEMBERS

Since the members were so generally men of means it is not astonishing to find that many of them had been educated in the best fashion of their times. Not only were there 4 doctors of law and one of medicine among them, but at least 3 bachelors of law, 37 masters of arts, and about 70 bachelors of arts. The records of the universities show that of the whole group of members studied 309, possibly 321, had attended either Cambridge or Oxford at least for a time. About 45 more had attended Oxford than Cambridge, a fact accounted for perhaps by the closer proximity of Oxford to the counties having large delegations. But the number who had been bred in Cambridge's "nurseries of puritanism," Emmanuel and Sidney Sussex colleges, was not small. Four or five men had studied also at foreign universities. Even longer than the university list is the roll of those who had attended an inn of court. Perhaps 60 per cent of the total membership had been educated at an inn. With the four inns whose records have been published most fully—Lincoln's Inn, Gray's Inn, the Inner Temple, and the Middle Temple—331 of the M.P.'s had been associated. The records of the other inns would no doubt reveal an even larger total figure. In the admissions registers were the names of many country gentlemen, men who needed some acquaintance with the law for their work as local magistrates. There was an occasional merchant who sought from the inns not only some knowledge of the law but social contacts. And there were the younger sons who had to look beyond their ancestral estates for their livelihood.

The importance of an inn-of-court experience in the background of so large a number of the parliament men of 1640 is not to be overlooked. Not that all of them gained wisdom in the law or drank deeply of revolutionary ideas about politics or religion. Many indulged more in the good times the inns afforded, the gay masques and the novelties of life away from home, than in serious study.[136] But the personal contacts they made at their inns were sometimes of lasting effect. The Middle Temple trained the greatest number, a few more than 100. Gray's Inn trained about 97, and the Inner Temple and Lincoln's Inn between 60 and 70 each. The latter has been described as a shelter for puritanism,[137] and some of the most ardent of Pym's group in the Long Parliament had been contemporaries there of William Prynne. But Pym himself, Hampden, Strode, Whitelocke, and Sir Walter Erle are examples of puritan leaders who were trained in other inns. One cannot turn the pages of the admissions registers without being struck by the fact that the inns even more than

example. Edmund Windham's £3000 a year income was so encumbered by 1640 that only £1000 a year was available for his own use. The Temples of Stowe were another family whose fortunes were on the wane (see Sir Peter Temple).

[134] The study of the wealth of the M.P.'s leads to the conclusion in agreement with G. M. Trevelyan's comment (*English social history*, 233, London, Longsmans Green, 1943) that wealth provides no certain clue to the politics of the time, since every class was itself divided and what predispositions in politics might be attributable to economic and social circumstances were ones of which the men themselves were only half conscious.

[135] Stockdale to Lord Fairfax, *Fairfax correspondence*, George W. Johnson, ed., 2: 261, London, 1848.

[136] Sir Hugh Cholmley regretted afterwards the time he had misspent at the inn (*The memoirs of Sir Hugh Cholmley*, 23-24 [s.l., 1787]). Gervase Holles, older than many of his fellow students, looked askance at their extravagance, but future royalists and future parliamentarians could not forget their common share in the famous masque of 1634.

[137] J. Bruce and S. R. Gardiner, editors, *Documents relating to the proceedings against William Prynne*, xxv, Camden Society, 1877.

the university colleges [138] must have witnessed the meeting and the building of acquaintanceships among the men who were to sit down together to debate the constitution of England in 1640.[139] Some of the friendships formed in the inns did not survive the trying times that followed, but enough of them were acknowledged by parliament men themselves to make their significance worth noting.[140] During the five-year span of 1616 to 1620, for example, although not all of the number were present during the whole period, 76 future members of the Long Parliament were at one or the other of the inns of court as students or as members who kept chambers there.[141] More than 70 of the 1640 M.P.'s who attended an inn stayed to become barristers, and 17 or 18 reached before 1640 the dignity of bencher.

Not all who were admitted to an inn, of course, had previously studied at a university, nor did all university men proceed to an inn. Since the lists of those who had studied at the two different types of institution are by no means identical, it may be estimated that probably four-fifths of the whole body of the 1640 House of Commons had been at some time students at the higher academic centers of England or the continent.[142] Of those whose names do not appear in the student rolls, some of them minor officials, some soldiers, but chiefly the merchants, not a few were by 1640 sending their sons away to be educated and were sponsoring educational institutions in their towns—schools and even an occasional library. As to the sons of wealthy families whose names are missing from the records of the inns and the universities, it may be surmised that a number had been educated abroad.

Education by travel had in fact rounded out the training of a considerable group of the members. Bulstrode Whitelocke began with a tour of his native country, but more started with passes for the continent. Over 60 had travelled to Europe chiefly as students of the languages and customs. Nearly 30 had been sent by their fathers to learn the discipline and the ability to command that only the armies could give, the benefits derived from trailing a pike in the Netherlands for a few months being considered greater than the dangers. A dozen or more had been in Ireland—a few had been born there. Some of the merchants had lived in foreign ports in their early business years. Several members had visited courts of the continent in the trains of ambassadors, or with Charles, the prince, in his youth. A few had themselves been emissaries. And one, Sir Richard Cave, had been for some years in the employ of the Elector Palatine. The states of Europe were the regions best known to the travellers, but the younger Vane had been to America,[143] the elder Knollys had sailed with Drake to the Spanish Main, Rainborow had dealt with the pirates of Sallee, and Sir Thomas Roe's travels had taken him to the Amazon and to the lands of the Great Mogul in India.

The additional polish for a gentleman's career afforded by a sojourn at the English court had been gained by many of the 1640 parliament men. Nearly a sixth of them had danced some attendance at court or had been onlookers there. A dozen or so were Knights of the Bath, and one a Knight of the Garter. But relatively few, less than a tenth of all the members, had become perennials at Whitehall. The rest had turned from the glitter of the court to life in the country, keeping abreast of its gossip and politics by occasional trips to London, by the letters of their friends or of professional purveyors of news, and by meetings among their own kind at the quarter sessions, or at their country houses.

CONNECTIONS BEFORE 1640: TIES OF FRIENDSHIP AND FAMILY

Their familiarity with their countryside, with the questions of wool and corn, of tobacco, butter, fish and iron, their acquaintance with the law and with lawmaking, their language studies, their Bible reading and their ponderings of the problems of the soul, and their bearing of responsibilities for the conduct of their fellow men, all are parts of the background of the men sent to parliament in 1640 and 1641. In the earlier career of almost every member was some experience or

---

[138] Examples of college acquaintances are Slingsby, Yelverton, and Capel, who were fellow commoners under the same tutor at Queen's, Cambridge, in 1619. Capel and Slingsby were intimate friends long afterwards. *The diary of Sir Henry Slingsby, of Scriven, Bart.*, 46, 306.

[139] In an earlier day John Chamberlain wrote to Carleton of "your old schoolefellowes" who had come up to parliament. N. E. McClure, ed., *The letters of John Chamberlain* 1: 212, 243, Phila., *Mem. Amer. Philos. Soc.* 12, 1939.

[140] Whitelocke's friendship with Pyne, whose elopement he helped to plan, did not survive the latter's preference for political extremes, but other companions of his law school days, such as Hyde, Palmer, Bridgeman, and Grimston, continued to be friends in spite of their differences. Among those sharing at one time or other the chamber of Christopher Lewknor at the Middle Temple were Sir Thomas Bowyer, Walter Kyrle, Thomas Leedes, Geoffrey Palmer, Alexander Popham, and Richard Seaborne, all but two of whom were royalists in time. Lewknor and Kyrle entered the Temple in the same month, October, 1627, with Fowell, Gerard Napier, Pyne, and Whitelocke. *Mid. Temp. Rec.* 2: 726.

[141] In an earlier period, 1600–1605, contemporaries of Pym at the Middle Temple were the parliamentarians, Rous, Harley, Dryden, Yonge, Erle, Rudyard, and Nathaniel Stephens, and Pym's friend, William Whitaker, who later deserted parliament; and the royalists, Sir Sydney Montagu and Windebank, and the straddler, Uvedale. Connected with Gray's Inn at the same period were the elder Shuttleworth, Barrington, Fairfax, Masters, all parliamentarians, and Whistler, a reformer who turned eventually to the king.

[142] Information regarding the education of the members in their earlier years is scarce. Some attended Eton, Westminster, the Merchant Taylors' School, some studied at smaller schools under single masters, and others had private tutors. No figures for making comparisons, however, are available.

[143] I have found no evidence from other sources to support Hexter's statement (*The reign of King Pym*, 80) that Darley, too, had been to New England.

position which qualified him in a measure for his task. In the earlier years of the members had been fashioned, also, the links that drew individuals into groups, the bonds of connection that enabled them to accomplish their work in the Long Parliament.

Others have written of the groups and associations that were developing before 1640 among men who were kindred spirits in matters of religion. The nature of the political groups as they took shape has been mentioned at various points in this analysis, groups of which some early ties lay in a university or law school acquaintanceship, or perhaps in previous experience together in parliament, and which had been cemented and strengthened in various ways. For some members there was the bond forged by a common resistance of the Stuart policies of the decade after 1629; and for more, the bond that grew from continuing contacts of many sorts during the same period. The importance of personal contacts—whether within such close-knit groups as the Providence Island Company, to mention but one of the colonial ventures in which the puritans shared,[144] or in the reunions of the literati and humanists with Lord Falkland at Burford or Tew,[145] or the more casual meetings of lawyers on circuit or in London,[146] of business men engaged in a common enterprise, such as Trelawney of Plymouth and Snow of Exeter, of the gentry in their various country occupations and pleasures—can hardly be overemphasized. Not that all such associations had been pleasant. Rivalries and enmities grew out of some contacts.[147] But more frequently there developed bonds of understanding.

The more one studies the pattern of connections among the parliament men, the more he finds himself led inexorably to a consideration of family ties. Connections of almost every degree, by marriage or by blood, existed. The men with no relatives as fellow members of the House are far outnumbered by those who had kinsmen there.[148] An alphabetical list of the members reveals the most obvious relationships, for the 3 Bullers were a father and 2 sons, the 2 Fiennes were brothers, as were 2 of the 3 Cokes and 2 of the 4 Goodwins. Five of the 6 Herberts were descendants of a single distinguished house, and even 2 of the 6 Smiths were kinsmen, albeit brothers-in-law rather than brothers. Sometimes a name held in common means no connection, or at best a distinct relationship between branches of a family separated some generations before. More frequently, though, the connections were close. There were 22 pairs of fathers and sons, 22 pairs of brothers, 2 of half-brothers of the same name and 2 of stepbrothers of different names. Five or more were uncles of members bearing the same family name. Still more had nephews of different surnames, and many were first cousins.[149] Sir Francis Popham was accompanied by a son, 2 grandsons, and 2 grandnephews. Sir Sydney Montagu had 4 nephews present with him. Other men had sons-in-law as their fellows. In fact, when the relationships through mothers, daughters, and wives, the sisters, the cousins and the aunts, are traced, a bewildering maze of connections appears. They reach into the House of Lords, too, for not only were fathers of Commoners there, but also brothers, brothers-in-law, and fathers-in-law.[150]

The familiar proverb quoted by Richard Carew that all Cornish gentlemen were cousins can be applied to almost any district of England at this time, and there existed among the parliament men great family networks that embraced several shires, with occasional threads stretching to very distant points. The classic Hampden-Barrington connection, besides including "the Patriot" and the future Lord Protector and their score or more of kinsmen from the eastern area, had links also in the central regions with the Knightleys and Montagus and in the south with the families of Wallop and Meux.[151] Other mainly puritan groups are those which Hexter describes as the Bedford-Western Gentry connection [152] and the Fiennes-Eastern Gentry group.[153]

[144] For details on the relationships among the puritans, see A. P. Newton, *The colonising activities of the English puritans,* New Haven, Yale Univ. Press, 1914; Frances Rose-Troup, *The Massachusetts Bay Company and its predecessors,* New York, Hitchcock, 1930, and Hexter, *The reign of King Pym.*

[145] Among the Long Parliament members who were of Falkland's circle were Rainsford, Edward Hyde, the poets Waller and Sidney Godolphin, and very probably Selden, Porter, and John Vaughan. Kurt Weber, *Lucius Cary, Second Viscount Falkland,* 82, New York, Columbia Univ. Press, 1940.

[146] Whitelocke's companions on his 1633 circuit included Lenthall, Glyn, and Littleton. R. H. Whitelocke, *Memoirs of Bulstrode Whitelocke,* 85, London, 1860.

[147] Dering and Temple of Stowe, for example, had once been rivals for the hand of a wealthy widow. Little bitterness, however, is known to have resulted from that affair. There were in some counties, though, quarrels which involved whole families and their friends and which lasted sometimes for years.

[148] Probably not more than a quarter of the total membership were without some such link with a fellow member, and well over half of the connections were of fairly close degree.

[149] In four instances these relationships represent replacements, a son or a younger brother succeeding to a place made vacant by his kinsman's death or withdrawal.

[150] The Earl of Warwick had a son, a brother-in-law (Cheeke), and 2 stepsons-in-law (Sir Edward Hungerford and Mildmay) in the Lower House; the Montagus were related to Manchester and his son, Lord Kimbolton; Hesilrige was a brother-in-law of Lord Brooke and Bosvile, a stepbrother. There were brothers of the earls of Hertford, Essex and Northumberland, sons of the earls of Pembroke, Bristol, Dorset and others, and sons-in-law of Bridgwater, Wimbledon, and more.

[151] At least 15 relatives of Cromwell can easily be named, and 16 or more for Barrington, the lists by no means being identical. With the Barrington clan Hexter links that of the Earl of Warwick, which includes, besides Lord Rich and Cheeke, the Wrays and Irby of Lincolnshire (*The reign of King Pym,* 85-87).

[152] Hexter's lists include in family groups men sometimes connected by business affiliation rather than by blood, as when family agents such as Rous and St. John are accounted connections of the Bedford interests (*ibid.,* 84-86). Blood relationships in this group link Rous with his stepbrother, Pym, Pym's son, Charles, and his nephew, Nicoll, his brother-in-law, Upton, and the latter's kinsman by marriage, Clotworthy. Another western

Then there were the north country circles, such as that of east Yorkshire, where Belasyse, Cholmley, Slingsby, Ingram, and Strickland tied in closely with Fairfax, Hotham, Mallory, and Widdrington, or the Lake Country connections linked by the Curwens and the Bellinghams. There were also the connections of the Wynns of north Wales and the borders, and of the Herberts in the south. More distant relationships with these rather strongly localized groups had been formed through inter-regional marriages, the results, perhaps of meetings at London by men from different parts, or of acquaintanceships formed at school or even in parliament.[154] Sir Hugh Cholmley of Yorkshire and Sir Christopher Yelverton of Northants, connected by their marriages with daughters of the Kentish Twysdens, and through them with the Vanes, Derings, and other south country men, were intimate friends who collaborated before 1640, it may be suspected, in politics. Sir Gervase Clifton, by his seven marriages, formed associations extending from Westmorland to Essex and was a brother-in-law once of Cheeke and the Earl of Warwick and again of Wentworth, Earl of Strafford.

Such family ties, though most evident among the gentry and the more readily traced because of the heralds' visitations of this period, are discernible, too, in other social groups and occasionally cross the lines of class. Dennis Bond, the Dorchester draper, was a cousin of the west country clothier, John Ashe, and his brother, Edward, the draper of Canning Street. William Spurstow of St. Stephen's, Coleman Street, agent in London for the Shrewsbury drapers and East India Company director, was related by marriage to Sir Robert Parkhurst of Surrey, John Crew's brother-in-law, and possibly to Cradock and Samuel Owfield.[155] And

the three Pelhams of the House represent well the distribution of the talents of a family noted for its vigor; Sir Thomas, the puritan baronet of Sussex, whose great wealth and power came from the lands and iron furnaces of the older line of the family; Henry Pelham, the lawyer who was Speaker of the House for a brief interval in 1648 and was a younger son of the younger line that had settled in Lincolnshire; and Peregrine Pelham, the regicide, a merchant of Hull by occupation, but sprung likewise from the younger Lincolnshire line and born in Sussex.

Kinship was a basic element in the structure of the Long Parliament. But it was a phenomenon of the class structure of the period, and unless the family tie was supplemented by other types of attachment its effects on conduct were not always great. The strongest associations among the kinsmen who were parliament men were those that resulted from the superimposing upon a family connection of other bonds of interest. The sharing of experiences and of endeavor, the intertwining of many strands of interest among men already connected by blood, makes it difficult sometimes to distinguish which among the ties was of the greatest importance. Since the family groups are more numerous and extensive among the "opposition," it may be assumed that Pym's followers used such connections with greater success at the elections than did the royalists. When other explanations of political allegiance fail, family relations may provide the clue. But such ties did not always hold through the period of political stress, any more than they always prevented disagreements in times of peace.[156] The political differences, earlier for the Vanes, later for the Verneys and for the Earl of Warwick and his son, are familiar. Even the great Hampden-Barrington clan had its black sheep.[157] And the diverging, sometimes wavering, courses of the east Yorkshire kinsmen reveal the tensions and strains that warfare brought to once intimate cousins, brothers, and brothers-in-law.[158]

---

group combining family and colonial interests, which Hexter did not mention in his study, was the Dorset-Devon group associated with the Dorchester colonial scheme. It included such members of the gentry as Sir Walter Erle and his son, their cousin, William Pole, their kinsman by marriage, William Strode, and probably the diarist, Walter Yonge, and also those enterprising men of trade, Dennis Bond of Dorchester, and his cousins, the brothers Ashe.

[153] The Fiennes brothers, James and Nathaniel, were brothers-in-law of Sir Christopher Wray and cousins of Sir Peter Temple, and acquired afterwards two more brothers-in-law among the parliament men, Thomas Erle and Whitehead. Pursuing the links through the Temple connection, one discovers Temple's cousins, Sir Thomas Parker and Sir Alexander Denton, the latter's son-in-law, Francis Drake, and brothers-in-law, the elder Verney, John Trevor, and Lord Wenman, and Wenman's brothers-in-law, Sir Martin Lister and Arthur Goodwin, Hampden's friends. Other appendages could be named, but these are sufficient to indicate the almost endless variations there were on the family theme within the parliament.

[154] Compare A. F. Pollard, The reformation parliament as a matrimonial agency and its national effects, *History* 21: 219–229, 1936–1937.

[155] Other illustrations are Thomas Soame of London, brother-in-law of Sir Nathaniel Barnardiston and uncle of Sir Philip Parker; and John Percival, the merchant of King's Lynn, who was connected by marriage not only with his fellow merchant, Toll, but with Oliver St. John and Cromwell.

[156] Quarrels about property were common, as, for example, between Bassett and Killigrew, who were connections by marriage.

[157] Young Francis Gerard strayed from the fold for a time, to be received into it again only because of the urging of his father, Sir Gilbert; and his cousin, John Meux, offspring of puritans of the Home Counties and of Hampshire and married into a devout family, was one of the swaggering blades of Goring's circle who supported the king in the war. Other royalists of country party families were Warwick's son, Robert, and both sons of the Earl of Bedford. And the younger kin of the Wynns of north Wales upheld the king while their courtier uncle, Sir Richard, hung on the fence.

[158] The bonds of family and friendship, however, remained strong in spite of the war. Sir Hugh Cholmley's desire to surrender his command to his brother, Henry, when he decided to join their cousins, the Hothams, in abandoning the cause of parliament, illustrates Trevelyan's comment regarding the local aspects of the war as waged among gentlemen who had once been friends (*English social history*, 241). In the autumn of 1643 Whitelocke lived for some time with his old friend, Palmer, now

PERSONAL INTERESTS OF THE MEMBERS

Important as their family connections were, the parliament men must be considered as individuals. What can be told of them as personalities, apart from their families and their listings in pedigrees? What were they beyond the types of their day, the hospitable gentlemen, the bustling lawyers, the enterprising men of trade and builders of colonies, the callow heirs to title, and the fawning and ambitious courtiers?

Some insight into the turn of events, or at least into the temper and the grouping of the House, might be gained were the personal interests of the members known, their avocations and their moods. In the majority of cases, unfortunately, most of such details are lacking. A good many men had literary interests, if one may judge by their references to their books and their libraries, and a number were writers themselves. Nine or ten were poets of some recognized ability, among whom the outstanding were Waller, Sidney Godolphin, and Falkland.[159] Others turned to rhyme on occasion and some to serious prose. The tastes of today might find more pleasing Waller's verses to Sacharissa than Fairfax's rhymes of the Psalms or Francis Rous's religious arguments, but the men of 1640 who confessed an interest in the study of religion, history, and philosophy outnumbered those concerned with the arts. The absorption of their times in matters of the soul is reflected by the west country royalists, Vivian and Rodney, and by Richard More in Shropshire and Bagshaw in his Temple chamber, and by Sir Thomas Hutchinson in his Nottinghamshire library that was the Mecca for scholars from the surrounding countryside. Half a dozen members were described by contemporaries as men of great general learning, others as endowed with great "mental talents." There was a fair sprinkling of members besides D'Ewes and Selden and Dering whose legalistic and antiquarian studies had carried them far beyond the contents of their fathers' muniments chests.[160] Mathematics, too, appealed to some, and science to others. Not a few were fond of music. Even among the puritans were gentlemen who were not unfamiliar with dancing and with cards. Sports of the out-of-doors were popular with many. In archery, in the breeding of dogs and horses, or in following the hounds and the falcons they found relief from the monotony of country life. Such avocations knew no political barriers. Sir Samuel Luke was interested in falconry, although, if Luke was the model for Hudibras, Butler ignored that fact. And for many of the squires from the northern counties, whatever their politics, the favorite sport was horse-racing.

The majority of the members were men of family. Most who had reached the age of marrying had taken unto themselves wives, but there were some who remained bachelors all of their years.[161] A few had engaged in the matchmaking for others who were their colleagues—some had even assisted with elopements. A number were widowers by 1640, and several lost their wives during the parliament's first year. Not a few had been married twice or even three times, but the record of the Hothams of five wives for the father and three for the son is unusual, as were the seven marriages of Sir Gervase Clifton, six of them before 1640. They were fathers, too, sometimes of numerous progeny,[162] and were generally anxious to provide well for their daughters and to have their sons educated "in the fear of God and good literature." Not many, however, emulated Slingsby's plan to teach his son according to the principles of Montaigne.[163] They took pride in their houses and their possessions and, if they were financially able, maintained the traditions of hospitality for their friends and for all comers.

The dispositions of the members are as varied as their interests. Foils for the melancholy Hutchinson or pedantic, precedent quoting D'Ewes were gay Sir Frederick Cornwallis, who by his raillery was said to turn many an argument, or the sharp-tongued, impatient Henry Killigrew and the quarrelsome Bayntuns. There were orators, though not all the equal of Rudyard, the "silver trumpet" of the House. And there were men of few words but of great vigor of action, the townsmen and the youths who left the debating to their elders or their betters, or the soldiers with whom the sword was more potent than the tongue. There were the frivolous Noel, who had lost his marriage portion at tennis, and Arthur Jones, who was given to gaming, and Goring's roistering crowd. But there, too, was sober Pierrepont, known for his sound judgment as "Wise William." Among "Saints" and among royalists were those whose lack of morals was the talk of the times.[164] But on both sides, too, were men of keen conscience and of great purity of mind. Tolerant men were there, also, and lovers of peace. The "fiery spirits" of this first year were probably outnumbered by those who chose their sides in the war only after grave searching of soul.

---

turned royalist, at the house of another royalist, Sir Thomas Fanshawe. Add. MSS, 37,343, fol. 258v.

[159] Others in the list might be Porter, Lawrence Whitaker, Pye, Rudyard, and Ralph Goodwin, as well as Coryate's friend, Sir John Strangways. Thomas Coryate, *Coryat's crudities* 1: 34–35, 62, Glasgow, J. MacLehose, 1905.

[160] Edward Bysshe and Gervase Holles are among the better known examples in these fields.

[161] Among the unmarried members was Strode, whose long imprisonment perhaps explains his bachelorhood.

[162] The composition papers of the royalists tell of the "great charge of children" of some of the members, a dozen or sixteen in several cases, and at least Walter Lloyd had eighteen by 1652.

[163] *The diary of Sir Henry Slingsby, of Scriven, Bart.*, 54–55.

[164] Among the royalists were Howard, Lady Purbeck's lover, young Griffith, barred from the House later because of his conduct, rakes of Goring's kind, or men of the type of Benson, who was ousted for selling protections. On the other side were debauchees such as Marten and his crony, Playters, and Sir Peter Temple of Stowe and perhaps the elder Bayntun.

One might try to visualize the scene in the House, looking down perhaps from the gallery where Hesilrige often sat. Near the Speaker's chair usually was D'Ewes, busily jotting his notes, and close to him often were Maynard, Peard, and Barrington and, "across the way," Colepeper, Hyde, and the elder Vane, and sometimes Strode.[165] There when he felt able was Sir Thomas Jermyn, father of the queen's favorite, probably still lame from his accident in France years before. And somewhere sat old Sir Francis Knollys, weighted with his years, and "Crump" Dutton, the wealthy hunchback of Gloucestershire. Towering over the heads of his fellows would be stalwart Sir William Widdrington, one of the "goodliest" persons of his day, and the other north country giant, Richard Barwis. There were handsome and fashionably dressed gentlemen, such as Endymion Porter or Uvedale or the courtly Bevil Grenville. There was Sir Gervase Clifton, hearty and red-haired. And perhaps in the gallery itself was the gentleman whose weight cracked a board one day and sent shivers of a gunpowder plot coursing up men's spines. But appearances after all counted for little, when a shrinking, delicate poet like Sidney Godolphin could become a valiant commander, and a homely country gentleman of moderate means could become ruler of all England.

The men who gathered at Westminster in 1640 and 1641 were well fitted to cope with their task. A few remain unknown except, perhaps, for their locale of counting house or shop, or for their association with a patron, or for a bit of pedigree. The rest, those well known before and the others whom this survey has raised a little from the depths of obscurity, were men in whose backgrounds lay preparation for public service. They had won their elections sometimes by strategy and pressure, but more often because they were local men whose views were known, men who were trusted by their neighbors and who represented local opinion. Of good family for the most part, and educated in the letters or in the law, or else trained in the humbler school of experience, and many of them with long careers in office or in parliament behind them, they were accustomed to power and to making decisions. Some were followers of patrons or of the court, but most were of independent fortunes. Many were wealthy, and even the younger members were generally "of excellent parts and great hopes," the heirs apparent to good estates. As a group they were familiar with all phases of England's life and problems. Theirs was not an assemblage of strangers, but of men who knew each other or each other's families, and who were closely interrelated. In age, the House had the season of years and experience, but youth enough to insure vigorous action. In temper, though extreme conservatives and radicals were present, there were moderate spirits, too, and cool heads to urge the need for delay.

No band of revolutionaries were these, the men of England's revolutionary parliament. Although a considerable number of them had gained prominence in resisting Stuart policies, the views of most on politics and even on religion were in 1640 set on no predetermined goal except the securing of relief from the parts of the king's program which had been most irritating. Loyal to King Charles at the start, and lovers of their homes and countryside, they might have wrought their changes wisely and in a fashion that the majority in any party would have preferred to war. But the blind obstinacy of the king and his intimates, their attempts to halt the progress of the parliament, and the increasing bitterness that developed in the House regarding religion and the means for controlling the king, hastened the break that could not be repaired.

---

[165] D'Ewes (C), 93, 126, 224, 245, *passim.*

PART II

ELECTIONS AND RETURNS

BEDFORDSHIRE

Bedfordshire was noted for its dislike of the Laudian program and for its sympathy with the opposition party.[1] Its members in the Long Parliament were all property holders and residents of the county, and all but one had served in its local administration. And all were puritans, except Thomas Lord Wentworth, who was called to the House of Lords before a month had passed.

The Bedford county knights returned on 19 October 1640 were Thomas Lord Wentworth, a young courtier and son of the Lord Lieutenant of the county, and a man of long experience in the country party, Sir Oliver Luke of Haynes and Woodend; but there had been a close enough contest for Wentworth's place to cause the House to consider seating his opponent, Roger Burgoyne of Sutton, without a new election when Wentworth was called to the Lords on 25 November. An election was ordered eventually, however, and Burgoyne won the place, although opposed this time by another courtier, Sir Lewis Dives, stepson of the Earl of Bristol, and was in the House by March, 1641.[2]

Two returns were made for Bedford borough in November, 1640, each naming Sir Beauchamp St. John of Tillbrook, but one naming with him William Boteler, and the other, Sir Samuel Luke of Cople, just as had been the case in the spring.[3] St. John was seated immediately, but Luke, who was finally recognized, did not sit before 6 August 1641.[4] The contest seems to have turned on the qualifications of the voters. Whereas the indenture naming Boteler declared that the electors were the bailiffs, burgesses, freemen inhabitant and commonalty,[5] Boteler objected that at least a hundred of Luke's voters were ineligible on eighteen different grounds, such as being beggars or receivers of alms, non-resident freemen, excommunicated persons, or felons.[6] Whether politics determined the decision of

the Committee of Privileges in favor of Luke, son of the county member and cousin of St. John, it is impossible to say because of the difficulty in establishing Boteler's identity. William Boteler of Sharnebrook (created a baronet, 1641) was a royalist,[7] but William Boteler of Biddenham worked with the country party during the war.[8] If the former was Luke's rival, a partisan decision favoring Pym's faction is indicated; if the latter, the choice probably lay between the son of a prominent country party member whose views were sure, and a man less well known to the leaders, and represents a decision based on personalities rather than on issues. Boteler had no part in the work of the House.

BERKSHIRE

Berkshire was a county in which the opposition element was growing by 1640. Ship money collections had been increasingly poor since 1638,[9] and there was trouble about collecting coat and conduct money for the Scottish war. At the assizes in July, 1640, the grand jury drew up a petition on grievances which cited, besides the two above mentioned, the grievances of monopolies, the forest laws, and irregularities in the courts.[10] It was natural, therefore, that interest in elections ran high, and that several conflicting returns resulted. The men chosen were chiefly local men, exceptions being Sir Thomas Roe, who was named in a double return for Windsor, and Thomas Howard, son of Wallingford's steward, who was chosen at a by-election in 1641. The opponents of the court carried the county, though one shire representative eventually turned to the king's side. In the original elections, Abingdon was the only clearly royalist borough, but in the by-elections the king gained one supporter each at Wallingford and Windsor, only to lose the latter by a third election before midsummer, 1641.

The Berks county election, which was held at Abingdon on 26 October 1640,[11] seems to have been unevent-

---

[1] *Bedfordshire Notes and Queries* 1: 153, 1886 (hereafter, *Beds. N. and Q.*); *V.C.H. Bedford* 2: 42.

[2] *C.J.* 2: 40, 45, 53, 68; D'Ewes (N), 108 and n.; 480–481. Rumors that Dives was a papist accounted for some of the votes against him.

[3] *M. of P.* 1: 480, 485.

[4] *C.J.* 2: 239.

[5] C. 219/43/Part 1. In 1690 the burgesses, freemen and inhabitant householders not receiving alms were considered the electorate. D. and S. Lysons, *Magna Britannia* 1: 51, London, 1806–1822 (hereafter, Lysons, *Mag. Brit.*).

[6] Notes of Boteler's objections were made on the back of the indenture cited above. Miss Mildred Campbell of Vassar College has informed me that among the Bedford County MSS at the Shire Hall in Bedford (DDTW 8, Nos. 342, 344–347) are Boteler's petition against Luke's election, and several lists of voters with indications of their eligibility. According to the figures given in these documents, which presumably are for this election rather than for that of the spring, Boteler claimed 301

as his total vote and recognized 269 as the legitimate count for Luke, discounting his "voyd voices." It appears, therefore, that 600 or more persons took part in this borough election.

[7] *V.C.H. Bedford* 3: 90; *Beds. N. and Q.*, 2: 254–255, 1889.

[8] *The Bedfordshire Historical Record Society, Publications* 18: 1–42, 1936 (hereafter, *Beds. Hist. Rec.*). As sheriff in 1638 he had collected ship money, though with difficulty (*ibid.*, 43–88; *C.S.P. Dom.*, 1637–1638, 432; 1639, 106–107), and may have lost some favor thereby. In 1654 Cromwell was reported not to favor Boteler's election to parliament. *V.C.H. Bedford* 3: 64.

[9] The county had almost no arrears during the first three years of the levy, but there was a startling jump in the amount of arrears in 1638, and only a small portion of the total was collected in 1639. Royal Hist. Soc., *Trans.*, 3rd Ser., 4: 156, 1910. The sheriff complained in March, 1640, of difficulties greater than those of his predecessors. *C.S.P. Dom.*, 1639–1640, 588–589.

[10] *Ibid.*, 1640, 466–467; 1640–1641, 125.

[11] Berkshire indenture. C. 219/43/Part 1.

ful. The knights elected, John Fettiplace and Henry Marten, both of whom were well known in the county, had been chosen also for the Short Parliament. The latter became a regicide, but the former, though he seems to have opposed the court policies before 1640, became a royalist.

Abingdon was a small borough entitled to a single burgess. Some question of the franchise had arisen in the spring elections, the defeated candidate, Bulstrode Whitelocke, who was the borough recorder, asserting that only the mayor and "principal" and "second" burgesses should vote. The election had at that time gone to Sir George Stonehouse, who lived nearby, and who won with the aid of the "commons," whose votes he had solicited by food and drink and by reminders of the business he gave them.[12] He was re-elected in the autumn, possibly by the same tactics, although there does not seem this time to have been an opponent or a question of the franchise. The town favored parliament during the war. Their choice of a man of court connections, an eventual royalist, was probably occasioned by their familiarity with Stonehouse and his family.[13]

Reading elections in the seventeenth century seem to have been conducted by the corporation, consisting of the mayor, aldermen, and assistants, with a show of assent afterwards by the "commonalty."[14] Frequently the High Steward of the town influenced the vote, as when Lord Wallingford nominated Sir Francis Knollys, junior, 1624–1626.[15] But sentiment in favor of local men and a more general franchise was growing, as the Short Parliament elections indicated. Then six members of the corporation voted against the candidates presented them by their steward, the Earl of Holland, and by Archbishop Laud, on the ground that they were "strangers"; and the commonalty gathered in such numbers for the by-election at the end of April that the corporation took two days to do the work and could finish it only before the assembled crowd.[16] The choice then of the local men, Sir Francis Knollys, senior, and Sir Francis Knollys, junior, without a single vote for the court candidate, may be attributed to this pressure by the inhabitants. In October, 1640, the High Steward nominated his son-in-law, Sir James Thynne, and a committee of the residents asked for a voice in the election. The corporation again acted, selecting the two Knollys men from a list of five;[17] but they first summoned three of the chief commoners into the council

chamber to show them the results and then reported the selection in the open hall, where "a free and general consent of all was given, without any contradiction, but with great alacratye."[18]

The original members for Wallingford elected on 15 October 1640 were Edmund Dunch and Anthony Barker. Their election was declared void on 15 February 1641, however, on the ground that they had not been chosen by "the commonalty." They seem to have been sitting in the House until then, but were required at once to withdraw. Dunch, a neighbor of the town and a parliamentarian, was re-elected promptly and was back in the House within a month. But Barker, the town's recorder and apparently a supporter of parliament, did not return. In his place came the youthful royalist, Thomas Howard, son of Wallingford's High Steward, the Earl of Berkshire.[19]

New Windsor had three different elections before the end of the first session of the Long Parliament. There was first a double return, one indenture of 17 October naming Sir Thomas Roe, the privy councillor, and Thomas Waller, understeward of the town,[20] and the other, dated 22 October, naming Cornelius Holland and William Taylor, both of Windsor and minor officials of the crown. The former pair had been chosen by the corporation. The latter, elected by the inhabitants in general, had not secured the proper officials' signatures for their indenture, and were therefore not duly "returned." This was an instance of the local issues of expanding the electorate and having due notice given before elections. The House of Commons decided on December 8 that "all the men of Windsor had a voice,"[21] but that a new election should be held.[22] Since Sir Thomas Roe was already serving as an M.P. for Oxford University, and Taylor seems to have died before the decision, those affected by it were Holland and Waller. The latter was apparently not popular with the townsmen, for on December 16 a new indenture was made out naming Holland and a William Taylor, presumably the son of the one who had recently died.[23] But in May, 1641, the younger Taylor was expelled from the House for some rash criticisms of its acts, and a third election had to be held. Again there was a contest, this time between Richard Braham of Windsor, a royalist, and Richard Winwood of Denham, Buckinghamshire, a kinsman of Hampden. A complaint by Braham which was presented on 6 July charged the mayor with ignoring majorities which Braham won in three separate elections and with wrongfully returning Winwood as

---

[12] Whitelocke's Annals, Add. MSS, 37, 343, fols. 198–199.

[13] A. E. Preston, *The church and parish of St. Nicholas, Abingdon,* 90, London, Oxford Univ. Press, 1929.

[14] *V.C.H. Berks.* 3: 360–361.

[15] J. M. Guilding, *Reading records* 2: 169, 230–231, 270, 273, London, 1892–1896.

[16] *Ibid.* 3: 488–489, 492–493.

[17] Another of the candidates was Tanfield Vachell of Coley, a relative by marriage of the Knollys family, who was of parliamentarian sympathies and was elected M.P. for Reading in 1645. *Ibid.* 3: 507; *Berks. Arch. Jour.* 40: 84–85, 1936.

[18] Guilding, *Reading records* 3: 507–508.

[19] D'Ewes (N), 361; *C.J.* 2: 85, 105.

[20] Waller was so designated in the fiscal accounts of 1640–1641. R. R. Tighe and J. E. Davis, *Annals of Windsor* 2: 154, London. 1858.

[21] The voters before 1640 had been the corporation, consisting of the mayor, bailiffs, and a group of not over thirty others. *Ibid.* 2: 298.

[22] *M. of P.* 1: 485; *C.J.* 2: 47; D'Ewes (N), 120–121.

[23] Tighe and Davis, *Annals of Windsor* 2: 149.

the member.[24] Winwood had been permitted to take the Protestation, however, on 5 July, and he was sitting in the House at the time of Braham's challenge and was apparently permitted to sit and work as a member thereafter, even though as late as 28 June 1642 a question regarding his election arose.[25] Politics probably accounts for his presence in the House.

BUCKINGHAMSHIRE

The people of Buckinghamshire, years before 1640, evinced their dissatisfaction with royal policies. Their representatives in the parliaments of the 1620's, their justices, their deputy lieutenants and local recorders had been outspoken against the new taxes, the levies of troops, and the ecclesiastical program of the Stuarts. Puritanism was strong in the shire,[26] and a spirit of resistance, of which John Hampden was to become the great example, was quite general. The county was among the most backward in ship money payments,[27] and several of the men sent to the Long Parliament, in addition to Hampden, had opposed the levy. Of the fifteen who served for the county and its boroughs a large proportion are well known figures in the history of the period.[28] Several of them who came in time to be known as Cavaliers must be considered as sympathizing with the opposition in 1640.[29] The majority were of Hampden's faction and remained loyal to parliament, at least passively, during the war. All were of local families or connection.

The Buckinghamshire knights, both parliamentarians, were none other than John Hampden and his intimate friend, Arthur Goodwin of Upper Winchenden. No record of the election proceedings has been found, but there is some indication that the puritan party did not carry the day without contest, for the House resolved on 8 December that "the Election of the Knights of Buckinghamshire should bee not questioned this Parliament." [30]

Amersham's original members were of the local gentry, William Drake of Shardeloes and young William Cheyney of Chesham Bois, a son-in-law of Sir Thomas Barrington. The former owned the manor of Amersham and after Cheyney died early in 1641, he

procured the place for his brother, Francis Drake of Surrey, not a difficult feat, since the right of election rested with the lord's tenants who paid scot and lot.[31] Cheyney was probably considered a protégé of the opposition, and both of the Drakes were puritans, though they were not ardent parliamentarians during the war.

The members for Aylesbury, chosen by the burgesses,[32] were those who served in the spring, both of them sons of prominent families of the county. Sir John Pakington, in fact, owned property in the town itself, although he lived part of the time in Worcestershire. He was a royalist early and his colleague, Ralph Verney, deserted parliament in time.

Buckingham borough selected two country gentlemen of wealth and prominence, Sir Alexander Denton of Hillesden, who virtually owned the town, and his cousin, Sir Peter Temple, Bart., of Stowe. Both had served for Buckingham earlier and were before 1640 members of the opposition element. Denton later abandoned parliament for the king.

Great Marlow was the scene of the principal contest in the county, with court and country factions challenging each other at two successive elections. Since the borough was unincorporated, the voters were the inhabitants, some 150, perhaps nearly 250, persons. The first election, about 21 October, resulted in a double return, one naming two men with royalist connections, John Borlase, whose family owned lands in the parish, and his stepfather, Gabriel Hippesley, a courtier and native of Somerset, who was nominated by the borough lord, Lord Paget. The other return named Borlase and Peregrine Hoby of Bisham, across the Thames in Berkshire, a man well known in the town and a parliamentarian. A fourth name had been entered in the contest, that of Bulstrode Whitelocke, the lawyer, but it was without his knowledge and he was named in neither of the original indentures. The House of Commons considered the case in November, eventually declaring the whole election void, a decision not uninfluenced by Whitelock's friends in the Committee of Privileges and the House. At the by-election, where the same candidates presented themselves, Hoby and Whitelocke won. Their closest contestant, Borlase, challenged them on the ground of irregularity of procedure, of illegal voting by men who were non-freeholders and almsmen,[33] and in Hoby's case, that he had been pricked sheriff of Bucks in the interval between elections and was therefore ineligible to serve as an M.P.[34] The last charge seems to have been the only one on

---

[24] D'Ewes (B), 13–14; Braham's return dated 15 June 1641 (C. 219/43/Part 1); C.J. 2: 200.

[25] C.J. 2: 643.

[26] Some men of the county who had been imprisoned for opposing the collection of coat and conduct money were released in October, by royal order, so as to remove one cause for possible complaints in parliament. C.S.P. Dom., 1640–1641, 128–129, 138. See also V.C.H. Buckingham 4: 530–532.

[27] Royal Hist. Soc., Trans., 3rd Ser., 4: 142, 1910.

[28] Of the thirteen members eight appear in D.N.B., six of them in full articles and two in articles on members of their families.

[29] The royalists include Pakington, Croke, and the elder Verney, who were joined later by Denton and the younger Verney.

[30] D'Ewes (N), 120. This vote preceded Hampden's announcement that he would serve for the county rather than for Wendover.

[31] George Lipscomb, The history and antiquities of the county of Buckingham 3: 161, London, 1847 (hereafter, Lipscomb, Buckingham).

[32] Aylesbury indenture, C. 219/42/Part 1.

[33] The extent of the franchise, whether it was limited to those inhabitants paying scot and lot or whether others, not almsmen, could vote, was one issue in the debate on this case.

[34] The only answer Hoby had for this challenge was to accuse Borlase of having procured his appointment as sheriff so as to make him ineligible for election.

which the popular party men could not fully satisfy the Committee of Privileges, for Whitelocke was named to a committee on 2 January 1641 and his election was declared beyond challenge three days later. No decision between Hoby and Borlase had been reached by 13 January, but since Borlase had in the meantime been returned for Corfe Castle, Dorset, his contest with Hoby seems to have been dropped. The parliamentarians had won the borough, but the absence of Hoby's name as a participant in the proceedings of parliament until 1642 indicates that he served his term as sheriff before entering upon his work as M.P.[35]

Wendover, a borough which had elected John Hampden regularly since its restoration as a parliamentary borough, his family being lords of the manor,[36] chose him again on 22 October 1640, and with him Robert Croke, a lawyer, who had sat for the town in the Short Parliament and whose family lived nearby. Upon Hampden's decision to serve for the county, his place was filled at Wendover by Thomas Fountain of Hulcott, who was a neighbor and probably an acquaintance of Hampden's. Fountain shared the latter's political views, but Croke was a royalist.

Chipping Wycombe, another town with a general electorate,[37] returned its recorder, Thomas Lane of Bucks and Middlesex, who was of the popular party, and Sir Edmund Verney, the courtier, whose estates lay nearby and who had sat for Wycombe in the Short Parliament.

CAMBRIDGESHIRE

Cambridgeshire contributed five of its six members to the parliamentary party, the only royalist being Thomas Chicheley, the young county knight. All were local men in the sense of owning property in the county or having some established connection with it. In a shire where puritanism was strong and where ship money had that year been resisted with some violence,[38] the defeat of the court candidates was not unnatural.

The knights for Cambridgeshire were two sons of old county families, Thomas Chicheley, new to parliament, and a royalist, and Sir Dudley North, heir of Lord North and a somewhat passive supporter of parliament, who had represented the county in the spring. Early in October North's fellow knight of the spring, Sir

John Cutts,[39] had expressed his reluctance to stand again, and in his absence from the county court preceding the arrival of the election writ Chicheley worked to ingratiate himself with the gentry.[40] Because no other county day intervened before Parliament opened, the election did not occur until November 12.[41]

Cambridge University elected on 24 October Dr. Thomas Eden and Henry Lucas, M.P.'s for the university in the Short Parliament. Both were graduates of Cambridge and were affiliated with it at the time of their election. Chosen by polls of 154 and 180 respectively, they defeated by a wide margin two other candidates.[42] Both were supporters of parliament.

The borough of Cambridge probably had the most exciting election in the county, with at least five candidates in the contest. Two were royalists, recommended by the new steward, Lord Keeper Finch; two were local men, an alderman and a councilman; and the fifth was Oliver Cromwell, who had been made a freeman of the borough just before being elected to the Short Parliament. Cambridge had frequently accepted a nominee, sometimes two, of their steward, and as late as April, 1640, chose his candidate, Thomas Meautys, Clerk of the Privy Council, as they had chosen him four times before;[43] but now the court nominees were rejected, and the choice fell among three parliamentary sympathizers. Among them, the consideration was possibly more local politics than national. Although the old election procedure by which the aldermen had held the final power had given way in 1625 to the recognition of the majority vote of the burgesses present in the Guildhall, and it was by this vote that Cromwell and John Lowry, one of the borough councilmen, were elected M.P.'s on 27 October 1640,[44] the mayor and seven aldermen sent up to London an indenture of their own of that date, reporting the election of Richard Foxton, Alderman, as a member.[45] Whether this represents an

---

[35] C.J. 2: 23, 31, 41, 51, 62, 63, 67; D'Ewes (N), 42–43, 88 and n., 102, 105, 107–108, 142 and n., 248; Verney, 2–4; Add. MSS, 34, 343, fols. 208–212; Marlow indentures (C. 219/43/ Part 1). For a more detailed account of this election see M. R. Frear, The election at Great Marlow in 1640, *Jour. Mod. Hist.* 14: 433–448, 1942.

[36] *Records of Buckinghamshire* (published by the Architectural and Archaeological Society for the County of Buckingham) 10: 123, 1910–1916 (hereafter, *Recs. Bucks.*). The electorate seems to have included most of the inhabitants, or burgesses, of the town. Wendover indenture (1647), C. 219/43/Part 1.

[37] *Ibid.*, Wycombe indenture.

[38] Edward Conybeare, *A history of Cambridgeshire*, 222, London, 1897.

[39] *M. of P.* 1: 480.

[40] Henry Smyth of Haldersame to Isaac Appleton, 20 October 1640. Bodleian Tanner MSS, 65, fol. 164.

[41] *C.J.* 2: 21; D'Ewes (N), 2 and n.

[42] Their rivals, Henry Hopkins, Warden of the Fleet, and Sir Henry Spellman, received only 89 and 70 votes, respectively. Spellman later asserted that he had not proposed to stand, but at the same time protested against the methods used to prevent his election. C. H. Cooper and J. W. Cooper, *Annals of Cambridge* 3: 65, 304–305, Cambridge, Warwick (vol. 1–4); Univ. Press (vol. 5), 1842–1908; *Original letters of eminent literary men*, ed. Sir Henry Ellis, 163–164, Camden Society, 1843.

[43] Cooper, *op. cit.* 3: 60–61, 183, 184, 200; *M. of P.* 1: 450, 462, 468, 474, 480. Lord Keeper Finch wrote to the borough on 2 October 1640 to recommend Meautys again and to suggest for the second place, if the borough were willing to choose a "stranger," his own brother, Sir Nathaniel Finch. He sent the letter by the messenger who carried the election writ into the county. Cooper, *op. cit.* 3: 303–304; Cambridge Corporation MSS, Day Book, 1610–1646, fol. 328.

[44] Cooper, *op. cit.* 3: 61, 176; Cambridge Day Book, 1610–1646, fols. 101, 172a, 313, 329.

[45] C. 219/43/Part 1. The indenture purported to be from "the greater part of the burgesses of the borough," but named as

attempt to return to the powers of the closed corporation, or the aldermen's preference for one of their own number to either Lowry or Cromwell, and if so, for what reason, is not clear. No petition against the election of Lowry and Cromwell is recorded, and Foxton, perhaps rejected by the voters at large because younger men than he seemed to be needed for the task ahead, continued to busy himself with local matters, and served afterwards on various parliamentary committees for his region.[46]

CHESHIRE

Cheshire sent four local men to parliament, of whom all but one supported the king when war came, but hardly one of whom in 1640 was definitely a king's man. The county was considerably divided in its religious views, as the petitions and counter-petitions regarding episcopacy in 1641 reveal.[47] It was among the shires that had consistently paid a large proportion of their ship money assessments,[48] but by 1640 such opposition developed, especially among the "great," that the sheriff found his work much impeded, and at the Quarter Sessions just before the Long Parliament met, a petition regarding this and other grievances was planned.[49] Although loyalty to the Crown was to dominate in time, clearly Cheshire was no royalist stronghold in 1640.

Tension was evident in both parliamentary elections for the shire in 1640, the one in the spring being reported one of the bitterest the county had known, with four competitors of the highest rank, each bent on prosecuting his own desires. The issues of justice and religion were to the fore but for the purpose, one observer wrote, of satisfying the ambition of the candidates, "who all joined in their own profit where there was a bare pretence of a public good, and now rend the bowells of it to advance their own interests and popularity."[50] One of those chosen then, Sir William Brereton, puritan and parliamentarian, was re-elected in the autumn. Chosen with him on 19 October was Peter Venables, never before returned to parliament, but a man prominent in local affairs, and brother-in-law of Lord Cholmondeley, a county leader. He had acquiesced in 1640 to his tenants' resistance to ship money collections, but showed his royalist sympathies early in 1641. Sir George Booth and Sir Richard Wilbraham, leading "patriots" and responsible for much of the bitterness of the spring, were probably active again, for they were named as electors on the October return.[51]

The city of Chester chose two aldermen, both former mayors and descendants of magisterial families. In the earlier parliaments of the seventeenth century a courtesy seat had often been given to a man named by the Prince's Attorney, and as late as the spring election of 1640, he had proposed a candidate,[52] but since 1626 the city had preferred Chester men for both places, and if royal influence was so tried in October, it failed. Local as well as national issues had brought forward several candidates in the spring, some of them with followings of tenants as in a county election,[53] and in October Sir Francis Gamull seems to have won on a local matter. Sir Thomas Smith's personal popularity, aside from his politics, probably insured his re-election. Both became royalists later, but before 1640 had criticized the royal program.

CORNWALL

Cornwall was a county where prosperity was declining, but where loyalty to the king was strengthened in the years of 1640 to 1642. There had been complaints against ship money, but as much on the ground of hardship as of principle, and the large delegation Cornwall sent to the Commons, forty-four in all, was at least half royalist at the start and more heavily so as the clash of opinions developed. The shadow of Sir John Eliot was still long in the land, and stanch friends of his went up to Westminster from Cornish boroughs, but their political ties were loosened, particularly as fears for the established church increased, and more than one of them turned eventually to the king.[54] The large number of boroughs, many of them with very few voters, invited patronage. But the efforts of the office of the Duchy of Cornwall, with its list of nominees, were less effective in the 1640 elections than were the persuasions of the local gentry.[55] The uncertainties that characterized the elections there are indicated by the fact that twelve of the constituencies failed to return in the fall the men who had represented them in the parliament of the spring and that five others made a change of one member each. Of the whole group of forty-four chosen for the Long Parliament only fifteen had been in the Short Parliament, and six of these were returned now for different boroughs. Less than half of the constituencies, furthermore, returned both members of the same political views.

Most of the members elected were Cornish men, a few were from Devon, and one or two others, though from more distant parts, were connected with county

---

electors only the mayor and seven aldermen, and seven of that group signed it. The indenture naming Cromwell and Lowry is not among the returns preserved at the Public Record Office.

[46] Cambridge Day Book, 1610–1646, fols. 326, 338, 339, 346, passim; Cooper, op. cit. 3: 355, 356, 384.

[47] C.S.P. Dom., 1640–1641, 529.

[48] Royal Hist. Soc., Trans., 3rd Ser., 4: 142, 1910.

[49] C.S.P. Dom., 1640–1641, 17–18, 145.

[50] Ibid., 1639–1640, 564–565, 590–591; S.P. 16, 450/28.

[51] Cheshire indenture, 19 October, 1640, C. 219/43/Part 1.

[52] S.P. 16, 405/15; Harl. MSS, 2105, fols. 279, 281, 283, 285; M. of P. 1: 456, 463.

[53] C.S.P. Dom., 1639–1640, 168, 341, 538, 564–565, 590. Chester's electorate consisted of the mayor, aldermen and citizens. Harl. MSS, 2105, fols. 279, 281; C. 219/43/Part 1.

[54] Mary Coate, Cornwall in the great Civil War, 28.

[55] For a discussion of the franchise in the boroughs and for the failure of the duchy nominees in the 1640 elections, see ibid., 17–21, 23–24; S.P. 16, 450/15.

families. Those of the group who might be called courtiers or official candidates were west country men, and the popular faction brought in at least as many carpetbaggers as did the royalists, including such figures as Valentine, Yelverton, and Sir Arthur Ingram. Their principal failure was in the case of Sir John Clotworthy, whose false return for Bossiney was voided.

There were several election disputes, two of them based on irregularities in the returns, and at least one on the question of the extent of the franchise, disputes which the popular party were able to turn to their advantage. In each of six instances in which the House chose between disputed returns or in which new elections were ordered the popular faction gained a member. By this means entrance into the parliament was assured for such men as Anthony Nicoll, Sir Richard Buller, Sir Christopher Yelverton, and John Moyle, junior. But at St. Ives the selection of Waller to replace Lord Lisle meant a loss, in time, for their side; and neither faction took advantage of the vacancy John Maynard left at Newport until 1647. Personalities and local differences were probably as important as national issues in the Cornish elections.

The knights for Cornwall were Alexander Carew of Antony and Sir Bevil Grenville of Stowe, both of prominent local families. They typify the fluctuating politics of their shire, for Carew, the ardent foe of the crown, deserted parliament during the war, and Greenville, once Eliot's co-worker, was swinging toward royalism by 1640.

From Bodmin came a double return after the election of 27 October. John Arundell, junior, of Trerice, was seated without question, but Anthony Nicoll of Penvose, Pym's nephew, challenged the election of John Bramston of the Middle Temple, son of the judge, Sir John Bramston, and a royalist.[56] According to Bramston's autobiography, the majority of the Committee of Privileges thought his election good, but Pym prevented the publishing of their report.[57] Nicoll was permitted to sit in the House, being present in early May, 1641,[58] although the case had not been actually determined by July, 1647. Bramston never took his seat. Arundell, who was of a family that had supported the opposition, became a royalist, but Nicoll stayed with the faction of Pym.

The places for Bossiney went undetermined for several months because of irregularities about the returns. On 7 December the House voided two returns of 16 October [59] which named Sir Ralph Sydenham and Sir

John Clotworthy,[60] and another one from the mayor naming Sir Charles Herbert.[61] The reason was that William Coryton, the Vice Warden of the Stannaries and at this time mayor of Bossiney, admitted that he had brought up a blank indenture and inserted the names afterwards.[62] At the ensuing election, 22 December, the ten voters present so divided or withheld their voices as to give three candidates six votes each.[63] Sir Christopher Yelverton, whose return bore the official town seal and arrived first, entered the House and was named to a committee on 30 December.[64] But on 12 January he was ordered to forbear sitting while the House considered two other returns which named Thomas Bond and Sir Ralph Sydenham. The whole election was again voided on 15 February.[65] The men who finally took their places for Bossiney were Sir Ralph Sydenham, who lived at Youlston (Devon), near Barnstaple, and who had court connections and was a royalist, and Sir Christopher Yelverton of Northamptonshire, a parliamentarian.[66] Sydenham probably had court approval in each of the three returns, and Yelverton doubtless had local backers of the popular party to work for him.

Callington, a scot and lot borough,[67] returned by its mayor and five burgesses on 23 October [68] two strangers to the county, George Fane of Northamptonshire and London, a son of the Earl of Westmorland, and Sir Arthur Ingram of London and Yorkshire. Fane was a royalist, but Ingram supported parliament.

The members chosen by Camelford's mayor and burgesses in October [69] were Piers Edgcombe of Mount Edgcombe, who had sat for the borough in the spring, and his brother-in-law, William Glanville of Wiltshire and Devon. Both were royalists.

The borough of Fowey sent in one member who was duly elected, Jonathan Rashleigh, a merchant of the town and several times previously its M.P.[70] But the other representative, Sir Richard Buller of Shillingham, was first seated without having been properly elected, his name having simply been inserted in a blank indenture. When this irregularity was pointed out during the discussion of the Bossiney case, Buller declared

---

[56] Bramston's indenture at the Public Record Office states that he was chosen by the mayor and burgesses (C. 219/43/Part 1); the return naming Nicoll is lost. *M. of P.* 1: 486 and n.; 3: li.

[57] W. P. Courtney, *The parliamentary representation of Cornwall to 1832*, 232–234, London, 1889 (hereafter, Courtney, *Parl. Rep. Corn.*); *D.N.B.* article on Nicoll.

[58] *C.J.* 2: 133, 155; Pink MSS, 307, fols. 155, 163.

[59] The indentures of 16 October were each signed by about fifteen persons (C. 219/43/Part 1), but apparently there had been no regular election.

[60] Clotworthy sat instead for Maldon, Essex.

[61] Pink suggests that this was Sir Charles Harbord of Westminster, the Surveyor General (Pink MSS, 307, fol. 173).

[62] *M. of P.* 1: 486 and n.; D'Ewes (N), 35, 118, 536; *C.J.* 2: 29, 46–47. A candidate from Bossiney in 1609, declaring he had the nomination, sent a sealed indenture to the Earl of Salisbury for him to complete it. *C.S.P. Dom., 1603–1610,* 551.

[63] An analysis of the signatures indicates that the deputy mayor led a group favoring Bond and Sydenham.

[64] *C.J.* 2: 60; D'Ewes (N), 242.

[65] *C.J.* 2: 66, 86; D'Ewes (N), 362.

[66] Yelverton was named on a committee on 27 April and both took the Protestation on 3 May. *C.J.* 2: 129, 133.

[67] Coate, *Cornwall in the great Civil War,* 17.

[68] Indentures, C. 219/43/Part 1.

[69] C. 219/43/Part 1.

[70] Rashleigh's name is given by clerical error as Rainsford in one instance. *C.J.* 2: 32.

that it had occurred without his "privity" and he was therefore spared from punishment, even though the House on 20 November voided the return. Buller was in the House again by 5 December.[71] He was a prominent popular party man. Rashleigh, though earlier a critic of the administration, supported the king.

Three names were sent in for Grampound in October, but William Coryton chose Launceston for his borough instead, and there seems to have developed no question about the other two men.[72] Coryton had served for Grampound in the spring but the others had only family connections with Cornwall. They were James Campbell of London and Essex, son-in-law of Lord Mohun, and Sir John Trevor of Surrey and Wales, whose mother was a Trevanion. Both men supported parliament.

Helston was distinctly a patronage borough in the sway of powerful local families.[73] During most of the seventeenth century the electors chose their burgesses from among the members of the family of Godolphin, who lived in the neighboring parish, or from their nominees.[74] The Long Parliament members were Francis Godolphin of Godolphin, and his brother, Sidney, the poet, both of them royalists.

The original members for Launceston (alias Duncheved) were William Coryton of Coryton, the Vice Warden of the Stannaries, and Ambrose Manaton of Trecarrel, Launceston's recorder.[75] But Coryton was required on 14 November to withdraw because of his management of the election return for Bossiney, and on 18 August 1641 his seat for Launceston was declared vacant.[76] The place was then filled by John Harris of Hayne, Devon, and Kenegie, Cornwall, owner of a manor near Launceston and once before its M.P. He remained loyal to parliament but Manaton, long prominent in the popular party, deserted the cause during the war.

Liskeard's mayor and burgesses [77] returned two royalists as M.P.'s in 1640. They were John Harris of Radford, Devon, who sat for Liskeard in the spring, and Joseph Jane, a former mayor and M.P. for the town.

East Looe selected on 21 October 1640 two Cornish gentlemen, Francis Buller of Shillingham and Tregarrick, and Thomas Lower of St. Winnow. They were said to have been elected unanimously by the mayor and burgesses, but the number of burgesses was small.[78] Buller was a parliamentarian and Lower was a royalist.

The West Looe members returned on 21 October were Thomas Arundell of Duloe, who supported parliament, and the stanch royalist, Henry Killigrew of Lanrack.

Lostwithiel chose by its mayor and burgesses [79] two young royalists, Richard Arundell of the Trerice line, one of the borough's Short Parliament M.P.'s, and John Trevanion of Carhayes.

Michael (St. Michael) was a borough often dominated by the Arundells of Trerice, although in the spring election there had been a dispute about the franchise, with burgesses who were not of the closed corporation apparently attempting to vote.[80] The original members returned for Michael in the autumn were John Arundell, junior, and one of his Lincoln's Inn associates, William Chadwell of Gloucestershire, who had represented Michael in the spring. After young Arundell announced his intention on 9 November to serve for Bodmin, his place at Michael was filled by the distinguished Lincoln's Inn lawyer, Sussex-born Robert Holborne. Both Chadwell and Holborne were sympathetic, as were the Arundells, with the cause of reform, but they swung to the royalist side with the war.

Newport chose as its two members Richard Edgcombe of Mount Edgcombe, a royalist, and John Maynard of Devon, the lawyer who was one of the opposition party leaders. Although Maynard declared his choice of Totnes as his constituency, 8 December 1640, no new election for Newport was ordered until 1647, and between 1644 and that date the town had no representation in the House.[81]

The members for Penryn were of opposing political views, but both came from Devonshire. John Bampfield, junior, of Poltimore, was the parliamentarian. The royalist was Sir Nicholas Slanning of Maristow, a J.P. for Cornwall as well as for Devon, and governor of Pendennis Castle. They were elected by the chief burgess and the burgesses.[82]

St. Germans, the little borough where the Eliot

[71] A Mr. Trefoile was said to have been intended, rather than Buller, when the blank indenture was prepared. *C.J.* 2: 29, 32, 46; D'Ewes (N), 35, 536.

[72] *M. of P.* 1: 486 and notes.

[73] Sir Robert Killigrew nominated a member in 1614. *Liber Familicus of Sir James Whitelocke*, J. Bruce, ed., 41, The Camden Society, 1858.

[74] Courtney, *Parl. Rep. Corn.*, 43; W. T. Lawrance, *Parliamentary representation of Cornwall*, 165, Truro, Netherton and Worth, 1925 (?) (hereafter, Lawrance, *Parl. Rep. Cornwall*).

[75] The electors were the mayor and free burgesses (C. 219/43/Part 1). The town records distinguish between free tenants and free burgesses. Launceston Borough MSS, Mayors' Court Book (1628–1640).

[76] *M. of P.* 1: 486; *C.J.* 2: 29, 261–262.

[77] Liskeard indenture, C. 219/43/Part 1.

[78] East Looe indenture; Coate, *Cornwall in the great Civil War*, 17.

[79] C. 219/43/Part 1. In 1660 the principal patron of Lostwithiel was "Lord M(ohun?)." R. N. Worth, ed., *The Buller Papers*, 117–119, privately printed, 1895 (hereafter, *The Buller Papers*).

[80] *M. of P.* 1: 480, n. Two men had twenty-four votes, but the House recognized those who were chosen by the "true" electors. They had received respectively 13 and 11 votes from the burgesses, the inhabitants consenting (*C.J.* 2: 10). About 20 men besides the mayor signed the Long Parliament indenture. C. 219/43/Part 1.

[81] *M. of P.* 1: 486 and n.; *C.J.* 2: 47; indenture of 1647, returning Maynard's successor (C. 219/43/Part 1). I have found no basis for Carlyle's statement that William Prynne was elected for Newport soon after the Parliament sat (*Cromwell* 3: 334, n.). See *Western Antiquary* 7: 186, 1887–1888.

[82] Penryn indenture, C. 219/43/Part 1.

family had the lordship, had a contest about one place. Benjamin Valentine, whose connection with Cornwall rested entirely, it seems, on Sir John Eliot's friendship and his service in the 1628 parliament for the borough, was granted permission on 5 December and 6 January to keep his seat without question. The contest for the second place, however, was between John Moyle, junior, of Bake, son of another of Eliot's friends, and a Mr. Scawen, probably the William Scawen who had been returned both for St. Germans and for East Looe in the spring.[83] Scawen declared that he had three or four more scot and lot votes than Moyle, but the Moyle family asserted that all the inhabitants who dwelt in the king's borough, regardless of their wealth, were voters, and that even if the franchise were limited, Moyle was ahead.[84] The election was still in question on 6 January, and it was suggested then that Moyle be allowed to sit until his election was voided. Nothing further appears in the records, but Moyle was present in the House in May, 1641,[85] and was not further challenged. Both he and Valentine were parliamentarians, but the Cornish Scawens were royalists.

St. Ives chose by its mayor and burgesses[86] on 22 October Francis Godolphin of Treveneage, whose family often served for the borough,[87] and Philip Lord Lisle. The latter, however, made his choice for Yarmouth, Isle of Wight, on 9 November. He was replaced soon afterwards for the Cornish town by the poet, Edmund Waller, who was a friend of the Godolphins of Godolphin, cousins of the St. Ives member. Godolphin upheld the cause of parliament, but Waller, though sympathetic at the start, turned eventually to the king.

St. Mawes, a little borough which in 1639 had declared itself one of the poorest and able to pay only 30s. for ship money,[88] chose as one member a neighboring country gentleman of opposition views, Richard Erisey of Erisey. The other seat went to a royalist churchman, Dr. George Parry, chancellor of the diocese of Exeter,[89] and M.P. for St. Mawes in the spring. The electors were the mayor and free burgesses.[90]

The mayor and burgesses of Saltash[91] chose for one member George Buller of the Middle Temple, a son of their chief landlords, the Bullers of Shillingham,[92] and a parliamentarian. The other M.P., Edward Hyde of Wiltshire, also a Middle Temple lawyer, may have been aided by the Bullers in the election, but he was not for long of their party.

For Tregony were returned two Cornish royalists. They were John Polwhele of Polewhele and Treworgan, who owned lands near Tregony and had once admired Eliot, and Sir Richard Vivian of Trelowarren. The electors seem to have been the mayor and commonalty.[93]

Truro re-elected its Short Parliament members on 17 October. They were two strong county party men, John Rolle of Devon and London, foe of tonnage and poundage, and Francis Rous of Landrake, the puritan writer and half-brother of Pym.

CUMBERLAND

Cumberland, a county which had supported the Stuart program in ship money and was actively concerned with the border war, was evenly divided between court and parliament in its representation in the Long Parliament. With the exception of Sir John Hippisley, who had spent most of his life near the court, all were northern men, four of them being of old Cumberland families and interrelated.

The county knights, Sir George Dalston of Dalston, and Sir Patrick Curwen, Bart., of Workington, both Cumberland men, had served the county before as M.P.'s and magistrates. Both were royalists.

The Carlisle members, Richard Barwis of Ilekirk and William Dalston, son of the county knight, were men well known in the city. Their families lived nearby and they had both represented the city earlier. They were possibly opposed by a court nominee on this occasion.[94] Barwis was a parliamentarian, and Dalston, a royalist.

Cockermouth was restored as a parliamentary borough on 15 February 1641,[95] possibly in order that the parliamentary cause might be strengthened in the county. The election was nominally by the bailiff and the majority of the resident burgesses.[96] But the manor was owned by the Earl of Northumberland,[97] and the return of Sir John Fenwick, Bart., of Northumberland, a kinsman and more than once an agent of the Percy family, and Sir John Hippisley, a courtier from southern England who had been in the employ of the earl's

---

[83] *M. of P.* 1: 480, 487; Courtney, *Parl. Rep. Corn.*, 286. The name appears as Stowell in D'Ewes (N), 107, 222. Scawen was the antiquarian, brother of Robert Scawen, M.P. (*q.v.*), and head of the family living near St. Germans. J. L. Vivian, *The visitations of Cornwall*, 422, Exeter, 1887 (hereafter, Vivian, *Vis. Cornwall*); Pink MSS, 307, fol. 259.

[84] *The Buller Papers*, 30–31.

[85] *C.J.* 2: 63. The January decision, according to D'Ewes, was that Moyle should be seated. D'Ewes (N), 107, 222.

[86] The 1639 charter had set up a corporation of mayor, twelve capital burgesses, and twenty-four inferior burgesses (Lawrance, *Parl. Rep. Cornwall*, 254). The 1640 indenture bears about a dozen names.

[87] *M. of P.* 1: 457, 463, 474; *Western Antiquary* 5: 34, 36, 1885–1886.

[88] *C.S.P. Dom., 1638–1639*, 429.

[89] *M. of P.* 1: 480, 487. There is no date for Erisey's return, but he was present in the House on 21 November. D'Ewes (N), 52.

[90] Fifteen signed the return. C. 219/43/Part 1.

[91] *Idem.*

[92] The franchise was by burgage tenure. Courtney, *Parl. Rep. Corn.*, 149, 150; Lawrance, *Parl. Rep. Cornwall*, 237.

[93] C. 219/43/Part 1.

[94] *C.S.P. Dom., 1640–1641*, 130.

[95] *C.J.* 2: 61, 86.

[96] Cockermouth indenture for 1642. C. 219/43/Part 1.

[97] R. S. Ferguson, *Cumberland and Westmorland M.P.'s from the Restoration to the Reform Bill of 1867*, 454, London, 1871 (hereafter, Ferguson, *Cumberland and Westmorland M.P.'s*).

predecessor and had sought his patronage elsewhere for the Short Parliament, implies that Northumberland controlled the election. Both of the Cockermouth members supported the cause of parliament.

DERBYSHIRE

Of Derbyshire's four members only one, Allestry, was a royalist, and he seems to have become so after war came. All were local men.

The county members were Sir John Coke of Melbourne and Sir John Curzon of Kedleston, county officials and sons of well known families. Curzon had represented the shire in the spring, but Coke, a newcomer in elections, spent heavily to win his first seat. No records concerning their opponents remain.

Derby borough had four candidates at its October election, and on 25 March 1641, following a protest, the House declared that election void, "in respect the Poll was denied, being legally demanded." [98] The candidates whose return was so voided had been the borough's M.P.'s in the Short Parliament and seem to have had little difficulty in being re-elected in April, 1641. They were borough officials, Alderman Nathaniel Hallowes and Recorder William Allestry. Of their opponents, Thomas Gell and a Mr. Fulwood, [99] the former replaced Allestry both as recorder and as M.P. after he joined the king. [100] Perhaps some distrust of Allestry's views had led to Gell's contesting his seat in 1640, although he seems to have worked with and been trusted by the parliamentary group during the first year and a half of the session.

DEVON

The county of Devon was in 1640 keenly aware of the grievances which M.P.'s from the west country had earlier struggled to right. Economic conditions, with the uncertainties in the wool business, and piracy that threatened shipping, the increasing duties levied on soap manufacture, and the levies of tonnage and poundage, already unsuccessfully opposed by a prominent London merchant of Devonshire birth, John Rolle, made restive a county noted for its trade and industries. The Laudian program met puritan opposition even in Exeter where the city corporation had more than one controversy with the cathedral chapter in the decade of the thirties. [101] Opposition to the Stuart lay program likewise had been shown, whether it was the management of the Stannaries, [102] the ship money assessments, [103] or

the levying of troops for the war in the north. [104] So widespread was the feeling that a petition was prepared at the Exeter assizes and sent to the Council in September, 1640, a petition which the Archbishop considered threatening to the royal prerogative, but which others thought should be forwarded to the King because it bore the names of so many men of importance. [105]

Devonshire was entitled in November, 1640, to twenty seats in the Lower House, but six more were soon added by the restoration of three boroughs. The strong country party majority from the county by this means acquired six more members, only one of whom, William Pole, later deserted them. Of the thirty members who actually served in the House during the period of this study, nineteen were parliamentarians, at least four were known at the time as opposed to abuses in church and state, though they afterwards turned royalist, and only six seem to be classifiable unmistakably as royalists from the early part of the session. Two other parliamentarians and one royalist who figured in Devonshire elections chose to sit for other constituencies. The elections do not seem to have occasioned much controversy, possibly because the royalists were not strong enough. In neither of the two cases, Barnstaple and Okehampton, where questions arose, do national issues seem to have been at stake. In two other boroughs, Beeralston and Plympton Earl, where by-elections occurred, the determination of each side to strengthen its position is evident, but in neither case was the return challenged.

Most of the men chosen in Devon were natives of the county; two came from Somerset but were intimately associated with the patrons of the boroughs which chose them and with the boroughs themselves; two were sons of a nobleman who owned much land and had wide influence in the county; two were lawyers associated with him. Two members, however, of whom one was a courtier and the other probably an employee of a courtier, were carpetbaggers nominated by a borough lord. The larger towns, Exeter, Plymouth, and Barnstaple, returned residents of their own precincts; Dartmouth, one merchant and one neighboring gentleman, and Tiverton likewise. Four of the remaining boroughs, Tavistock, and the three "restored" by this parliament, appear to have been pocket boroughs. The rest selected their candidates from influential families residing nearby. If the country party campaigned vigorously before the elections—and among the Devonshire members were not only Pym himself, but St. John, Maynard, Strode, and the Earl of Bed-

---

[98] *C.J.* 2: 113.

[99] D'Ewes (N), 385.

[100] *M. of P.* 1: 487.

[101] Coate, *Cornwall in the great Civil War*, 39, 56. See below, Exeter, Plymouth, Barnstaple.

[102] A petition against Coryton and the Stannary abuses was presented by one of the shire knights soon after the Long Parliament opened. *The Buller Papers*, 138–139.

[103] Several sheriffs had delayed in their collections, but Devon was not seriously in arrears until 1639 (Royal Hist. Soc., *Trans.*, 3rd Ser., 4: 142, 157, 1910). A Devonshire man wrote to Cot-

tington, 3 February 1640, that, although the county rate was high, "yet there is no grudging; so, as I think, we are the King's best subjects." *C.S.P. Dom., 1639–1640*, xv.

[104] Council was warned by the deputy lieutenants and justices in October, 1640, of the danger of leaving the county open to the pirates by sending their troops north. *C.S.P. Dom., 1640–1641*, 148–149.

[105] *The Buller Papers*, 135–138.

ford's son—their success was with candidates who were known in Devon.

The Devon county members originally returned were Edward Seymour, son of a county leader, and eventually a royalist, and Thomas Wise, native son and former sheriff, a parliamentarian. Upon the death of Wise, Sir Samuel Rolle, wealthy Devonian and puritan, succeeded. Neither the first election, held at Exeter in October, 1640,[106] nor the second, about April, 1641, seems to have been hotly contested.

Ashburton, restored as a parliamentary borough on 26 November 1640,[107] returned Sir Edmund Fowell and John Northcote, both country gentlemen of note and supporters of the country party. Since neither apparently had any direct connections with Ashburton, the influence of a patron, possibly Bedford, a friend of Northcote's, may be suspected.

Barnstaple's members were Richard Ferris, merchant and former mayor, and George Peard, deputy recorder and M.P. for the borough in the Short Parliament. Both men had shared in the town's protests against ship money rates and in the puritanical regulations of town life;[108] but Ferris was eventually disabled as a royalist, while Peard remained a stanch parliamentarian. Possibly suspicion of Ferris's views led to the challenge of his election, and its voiding, 6 August 1641, but he was returned again a few weeks later.

The October election at the town hall was by the mayor, alderman, twenty-four chief burgesses, and the other free burgesses of the town. The mayor proposed to the assemblage three names, Peard, Ferris, and Richard Medford, omitting Peard's colleague of the spring, Thomas Matthews.[109] There were so many shouts for Peard and Matthews in the voice vote that followed, however, that it was impossible to determine the victors. Instead of polling the voters next, the mayor proposed using the procedure customary at municipal elections, meanwhile preventing the disgruntled commoners from leaving the room. The four names were arranged in pairs, the mayor and corporation members made their first choice in each pair, and then the free burgesses were called to do likewise, but individually at the bar. Peard won in the first pair, and Ferris, whom Matthews had preferred to Peard for his closest opponent, won both the corporation and the commonalty vote in the second pair. Matthews petitioned parliament that the election of Peard and Ferris be voided, accusing the mayor of giving preference to a corporation member rather than to one who was not; of electioneering be-

forehand to have the commons vote for anyone of the council he should nominate; and of conducting the election so as to favor Ferris. The mayor's answer was that Matthews had consented both to the new procedure and to being named with Ferris; that Ferris had received 120 votes as against 36 for Matthews; and that the latter had thereupon expressed his approval both of the fairness of the election and of its results. It seems quite clear, however, that the corporation was attempting to control the election, even though the franchise was general, and that Ferris was given a decided advantage, particularly in not being named in the pair with Peard.[110] The voiding of his election by the House resulted possibly from an inclination to combat such a tendency as much as from suspicions as to Ferris's political views. Apparently no contest developed at the by-election.

Beeralston's original members were William Strode, Devonian and puritan of note, and Sir Thomas Cheeke of Essex, another puritan leader, who had been elected by Beeralston to two earlier parliaments. But Cheeke decided to serve for Harwich in his own shire, and on 19 November 1640 Beeralston chose as his successor Hugh Pollard, a Devon army captain, who was expelled from the House slightly more than a year later for his part in the royalist army plot. In his place was next returned young Charles Pym, son of John Pym. Although the "free burgesses" were said to be the electors, they seem to have been swayed largely by the neighboring gentry. Strode had won his place in the spring through a gentlemen's agreement between several candidates and the voters.[111] The country party seems to have hoped to fill Cheeke's place with one of their own number, such as Sir Samuel Rolle,[112] and Pollard's election instead must have been a disappointment, if not a defeat.[113] The choice of none other than Pym's heir as Pollard's successor suggests that others than free burgesses of Beeralston dominated its elections.

From Dartmouth came two local men,[114] both of whom had served the borough in previous parliaments and had worked with the country party. Roger

---

[106] C. 219/43/Part 1.

[107] C.J. 2: 36–37.

[108] Local objections to bands of players, as well as to drunkenness and gaming, are evident in the borough records of the 1630's. Barnstaple Corporation MSS, Receivers' Accounts, 1389–1643, memb. 229; Sessions Court Book, 1581–1631.

[109] The mayor later stated that he considered Matthews less fit than the others to serve. The account of this election, based on Barnstaple MSS 1117, is printed in Joseph B. Gribble, *Memorials of Barnstaple*, 346–350, Barnstaple, 1830.

[110] The arrangement of the pairs in this election is strikingly different from the usual election "pairing" for mutual support; and it was not exactly parallel to the process in municipal voting, where the purpose was to choose one among four for a single office, the winner being selected by an elimination vote from the winners of each pair. *Ibid.*, 350–353.

[111] Involved in that election were five gentlemen of prominent Devon families. The voters numbered 26 on one occasion, and 35 on another. *C.J.* 2: 14.

[112] Among the Buller papers, possibly one of the "blanks" with which Sir Richard Buller (*q.v.*) was accused of dealing, is an indenture of the election of Sir Samuel Rolle, dated 19 November 1640 and bearing the signatures of eight burgesses of Beeralston, but neither signed by the sheriff nor officially returned. *The Buller Papers*, 28–29.

[113] The indenture of Pollard's return bears the names of the mayor and nine others. C. 219/43/Part 1.

[114] The electors at Dartmouth were "the mayor, bailiff, and burgesses." Dartmouth (1646 indenture), C. 219/43/Part 1.

Matthew was a merchant and former mayor of the town; John Upton, a gentleman living at Lupton nearby. After the latter's death in September, 1641, his place was filled by Samuel Browne, a native of Bedfordshire and a prominent lawyer whose intimacy with puritan leaders from the west probably gained him this seat. Upton was an active country party man and Matthew, though eventually disabled as a royalist, had belonged to Eliot's party in the twenties and was cooperating with the parliamentary faction as late as the summer of 1642.

Exeter, according to the custom, sent two prominent citizens to the House. This time they were Robert Walker and Simon Snow, merchants and officers of the corporation. The election was probably by the traditional procedure, the commonalty choosing from a list of four names proposed by the mayor and council.[115] Although the Exeter city government had frequently bickered with the ecclesiastical authorities [116] and royal agents, and was inclined as late as January, 1642, toward the puritan side,[117] both of its M.P.'s by the time the war started had begun to absent themselves from Westminster. Walker was in time disabled as a royalist, but Snow retained his place.

Honiton, one of the boroughs restored in 1640, returned two neighboring gentlemen as its members, Walter Yonge of Colyton and William Pole of Colyton and Colcombe.[118] The former owned property in Honiton and was a strong puritan and parliamentarian; but Pole, probably elected through the influence of his father, another prominent country party man, declared for the king and was disabled in 1643.

Okehampton, another of the restored boroughs, returned on 27 January 1641 two nominees of Lord Mohun, Baron of Okehampton. A third candidate, Sir Shilston Calmady, who was a Devonshire J.P. and parliamentarian, was defeated. Mohun's men, neither of whom seems to have had any connection with the borough or the county, were Edward Thomas, possibly an employee of Mohun's, and Lawrence Whitaker of London, a clerk of the Council. Calmady protested Whitaker's return,[119] and in the spring of 1641 several

Devon men were hoping for the place,[120] but Whitaker seems to have been allowed to sit without fear of losing his seat. Both Whitaker and Thomas, in spite of their previous careers and their patron, supported the popular side in parliament.

Plymouth's members were John Waddon and Robert Trelawney, both members of the corporation and former mayors and Short Parliament members. They were probably elected by vote of the closed corporation.[121] Trelawney was a royalist eventually, but Waddon was a parliamentarian.

Plympton Earl borough went through a series of elections, evidently yielding to strong puritan influences from without. It was a small borough, its property being controlled largely by absentee gentlemen,[122] and its elections by mayor, bailiff and burgesses [123] were undoubtedly controlled. Originally chosen were Sir Nicholas Slanning, the royalist, who was the borough's recorder and had been one of its members in the spring, and Michael Oldisworth, secretary to the Earl of Pembroke and Montgomery, who had no apparent connection with the town and was a country party man. Both had to be replaced promptly, however, for each decided to serve for another constituency. Oldisworth's place was filled by the man who had been the borough's M.P. in the three preceding parliaments, Sir Thomas Hele of Fleet in Devonshire,[124] who at this time was an opponent of abuses ecclesiastical and political, but who was later disabled as a royalist. To fill Slanning's place, the borough chose an agent of the Earl of Northumberland, Hugh Potter of Lincoln's Inn, who was a Devonian by birth but had for many years resided elsewhere. Potter was a parliamentarian.

Tavistock, family borough of the Earl of Bedford,[125] a country party nobleman, named as its members the earl's heir apparent, William Lord Russell, and one of the earl's associates who had several times been M.P. for the borough, John Pym. When Lord Russell succeeded to the earldom in May, 1641, his younger

---

[115] A variation from this procedure had occurred in 1626, but the precedent had been re-established in 1628. Exeter Corporation MSS, Act Book 7, fols. 647, 693.

[116] Exeter Cathedral Library MSS, 3499, No. 173.

[117] Exeter Corporation MSS, Act Book 8, fols. 258, 260.

[118] The election was by the portreeve and burgesses, according to the 1646 indenture. C. 219/43/Part 1.

[119] Exeter City Library MSS, R. Lane's Coll. Devonshire, fols. 119, 244–247, 256–258; W. B. Bridges, *Some account of the barony and town of Okehampton*, 92, rev. ed., Tiverton, 1889 (hereafter, Bridges, *Okehampton*). The returns for Thomas and Whitaker, separately made, but of the same date, list the mayor and 35 others as witnessing Thomas's election, and the mayor and 29 others for Whitaker (C. 219/43/Part 1). The local records state that Thomas was chosen "by general consent," and that Whitaker, named with Calmady, "had most voyces" (Bridges, *loc. cit.*). The mayor, burgesses, and inhabitants were the electors.

[120] E.g., Sir Samuel Rolle, *The Buller Papers*, 34.

[121] In 1659 the freeholders demanded the restoration of their privilege of voting for members of parliament, and their franchise was recognized by parliament, 9 June 1660. *Transactions of the Plymouth Institution and Devon and Cornwall Natural History Society* 5: 563–564, 1873–1876 (hereafter, Plymouth Inst. *Trans.*).

[122] *C.S.P. Dom., 1638–1639*, 232.

[123] C. 219/43/Part 1.

[124] Hele was present in the House on 21 November 1640 (D'Ewes [N], 52), although Slanning's successor was not elected until 20 November (C. 219/43/Part 1). Hele was perhaps so sure of his election that he rode to London without waiting for the formality of the vote and return. The return naming him is no longer extant. This may account for the naming in various places of Sir Richard Strode as Plympton's M.P. Cf. *Western Antiquary* 7: 187, 1887–1888; 8: 47–48, 1888–1889.

[125] *Reports and Transactions of the Devonshire Association* (hereafter, Devon *Trans.*) 43: 371, 1911.

brother, John, was elected to his place.[126] Both of Bedford's sons turned to the king, the younger one by 1642.

Tiverton's mayor and burgesses elected on 20 October 1640 [127] a Devonshire gentleman, Peter Sainthill of Bradninch, and a Tiverton man, George Hartnoll. The latter was a royalist. Sainthill, as a country magistrate, had opposed policies of the crown before 1640, but he eventually sided with the king.

The members for Totness borough were the country party lawyers, Oliver St. John and John Maynard, both members for the borough in the spring. The former had no direct associations with Devonshire and probably owed his 1640 elections to the influence of the Earl of Bedford. Maynard, however, was a Devon man.

DORSET

The county of Dorset sent to Westminster in 1640 several of the outstanding men of the Commons, leaders of both the Roundheads and the Cavaliers. The county which called its own the Reverend John White of Dorchester and the Earl of Bristol naturally supplied men with "causes" both religious and political. Representing religious sectarianism, for example, were such men as Sir Walter Erle, Dennis Bond, or John Browne of Frampton; and speakers for the rights of the subject were Sir John Strangways, Holles, and John Pyne. Of the twenty-two members who between November, 1640, and January, 1642, sat for the county and its boroughs, twelve identified themselves constantly with the cause of parliament, and five or six,[128] who later were ousted as royalists, were probably considered opponents of the court when they were elected. Of the remaining four or five who are classified as royalists from the outset, three gained their places by the nomination of borough patrons, and one of these (Turner) had in an earlier parliament worked with the country party. These three, Borlase, Turner, and Windebank, furthermore, were the only real carpetbaggers in the Dorset group; and the first would not have been elected had a vacancy not been created by the withdrawal of the original carpetbagger, Windebank. Besides these three, five others were not natives of Dorset,[129] but with one possible exception they were residents and property owners there. The county may be said, therefore, to have sent a preponderance of her own sons to the House, and they formed in the early months a powerful force in the opposition group. The scarcity of election con-

tests indicates that there was not much royal interference with the elections. The returns show rather the strength of such local men as the Earl of Bristol, with whom at least three members were closely associated, or the Earl of Pembroke, or such old families as the Trenchards and the Brownes.

The knights for the county of Dorset were George Lord Digby and Richard Rogers of Brianston, both of prominent local families. Both are usually labelled as Cavaliers, but Digby was certainly considered one of the opposition in 1640 and Rogers, who was allied by marriage with the puritan group of the eastern counties, was by no means an unquestioning supporter of the crown. After Digby's call to the Peers, Dorset elected in June, 1641, John Browne of Frampton, who was widely known for his anti-Laudian and anti-court views.

Bridport, a town more than once influenced by the Earl of Bristol-Strangways faction,[130] chose in October, 1640, its recorder, Roger Hill, a parliamentarian, and Giles Strangways. The latter was the heir of a prominent county leader of the opposition group, but both he and his father turned early to the king. The electors were the mayor, bailiffs, and chief burgesses, but in 1645 the commonalty, too, had a share.[131]

At Corfe Castle the electorate consisting of the "mayor, barons and burgesses" [132] usually acted at the pleasure of the lord of the borough, who in 1640 was Sir John Banks, the Attorney-General.[133] They chose on 22 October 1640 Sir Francis Windebank, Secretary of State, who had been disappointed elsewhere, and for whose convenience, by the queen's request, Henry Jermyn stepped aside.[134] With him was returned Giles Green, who lived near the borough and had represented it twice before. Although he was an employee at various times both of the crown and of Sir John Banks, Green in the Long Parliament was a very active member of the puritan faction. After Windebank fled the country under attack a new election was ordered in December, and on 2 January 1641 Corfe Castle chose John Borlase of Buckinghamshire, a son-in-law of Banks. He was involved in the election contest at Great Marlow in his own county, but his election for the Dorset borough resolved his difficulties. He was disabled as a royalist in 1644.

The members for Dorchester, both strong parliamentarians, were Dennis Bond, a business man and magistrate of the town, and Denzil Holles, who lived nearby.

[126] The indenture of 17 June 1641, signed by the bailiff alone, states that the election was made by the bailiff and burgesses. The return for Pym and Lord Russell is missing. C. 219/43/Part 1.

[127] Indenture of 20 October 1640. The electors, according to the indenture of 7 December 1646, were the mayor, capital burgesses, and assistants. C. 219/43/Part 1.

[128] Constantine, Lord Digby, King, Giles and Sir John Strangways, and possibly Richard Rogers.

[129] Hill, Holles, King, Prideaux, Pyne.

[130] The town elected Sir Lewis Dives, stepson of Bristol and son-in-law of Sir John Strangways, in 1626 rather than a nominee of Buckingham (C.S.P. Dom., 1625–1626, 237; M. of P. 1: 463, 469). Dives was not a member for Bridport in the Long Parliament, although his name appears in some lists (e.g., O.P.H. 9: *26; Carlyle 3: 322).

[131] Indentures, C. 219/43/Part 1.

[132] Ibid.

[133] George Bankes, The story of Corfe Castle, 57, London, 1853. Cf. 1614. Liber Familicus of Sir James Whitelocke, 41.

[134] Bull. Inst. Hist. Research 6: 50, 1928–1929.

Both had sat for Dorchester in the spring, and Holles in 1628, too.[135] Their zeal for the cause of puritanism and parliament is a commentary on the state of opinion in Dorchester at this period.

Lyme Regis, a small borough with a general burgess franchise,[136] elected two parliamentarians. Edmund Prideaux, a Devonshire lawyer who may have held some land in Dorset, had served for this borough in the spring. The other member was a leading merchant and former mayor, Richard Rose.

Poole elected its recorder, William Constantine, who lived near the town and who supported the parliamentary cause until 1643, and John Pyne. The latter was a Somerset lawyer of strong opposition views who had represented Poole four times before. The electors were the mayor and burgesses, of whom slightly more than a score were named in the returns.[137] The commonalty may sometimes have voted, however.[138]

Shaftesbury, of which the Earl of Pembroke was lord, seems to have had in 1640 a closed electorate of the mayor and twelve capital burgesses.[139] The earl's influence doubtless accounts for the election both in 1626 and 1640 of Dr. Samuel Turner, the court physician.[140] The other member chosen for the Long Parliament was the town's recorder and resident, William Whitaker, who had served several times before. The latter was a stanch parliamentarian, but Turner, although he was remembered for his earlier attack on Buckingham, worked now with the party of the crown.

Wareham chose in October, 1640, from among at least four candidates, all of whom had some connection with the borough. Edward Pitt, son of Sir William Pitt, who had the patronage of a church there and had sat for the town several times, was willing even to bribe voters to secure the place,[141] but he was unsuccessful. Edward Lawrence, probably the 1626 M.P. for Wareham who was described as of the Grange in the Isle of Purbeck, or his son of the same name,[142] was reported in a return that was sent in either by mistake or by the contrivance of a local official. The Committee of Privileges, urged by Sir Walter Erle, whose son, Thomas, was Lawrence's rival, reported on 1 February 1641 that the return was faulty, and the House decided against Lawrence. The return was corrected on 12 February.[143] The members who sat for Wareham, therefore, were John Trenchard, a neighboring country gentleman who had represented the town four times earlier and was a strong opposition man, and young Thomas Erle, whose father, Sir Walter, was a leader among the puritans of the county. The electorate at Wareham included the mayor, burgesses, and commonalty.[144]

Weymouth and Melcombe Regis, though administered municipally as one borough from the time of Elizabeth, continued to send two burgesses each to parliament.[145] Of the four elected on 21 October 1640 all were Dorset natives who had been at some time in opposition to the crown. They were no doubt elected on that basis, for the town was conscious of its grievances.[146] But only Sir Walter Erle, Weymouth's member, remained with the cause of parliament when war came. Richard King of Sherborne, Recorder of Weymouth and Melcombe Regis, reported as the other Weymouth member, absented himself much after 1641 and was later disabled. Sir John Strangways, one of the Melcombe members, was long a leader in the country party, but followed eventually the line of the Digby family. His colleague was Gerard Napier of More Chrichell and Middlemarsh, who was serving the borough for the first time in this parliament. The electors of this double borough were the mayor, bailiffs, aldermen, and burgesses.[147]

ESSEX

The county of Essex was for many years before 1640 a center for religious and political unrest. It was one of the chief strongholds of puritanism, not only among the lowly but among the great, and many of its leaders had resisted the forced loans of James and Charles as well as the ship money levies; some of its justices declined to aid the Admiralty's saltpetre men or the ministers following Laud's program or the officials who tried to press soldiers.[148] Furthermore the county had been

---

[135] On the earlier occasion the Earl of Suffolk requested that the town elect Sir Dudley Carleton. But the corporation, having anticipated the writ and made their decision on the men to be elected, replied that their constitution required that their burgesses be freemen of the borough (Mayo, *Municipal records, Dorchester*, 435–436). Holles, whose first connection with the town had come with his marrying the heiress of Dorchester's recorder, Sir Francis Ashley, was elected a freeman of the town on the same day that he was first chosen as its M.P., 25 February 1628 (*ibid.*, 395, 425).

[136] The electors were the majority of the chief and other free burgesses, according to the 1640 indenture. C. 219/43/Part 1.

[137] About 22 names appeared on the 1640 indenture, and 26 on that of 1645 (C. 219/43/Part 1).

[138] In 1624 an aspiring candidate wrote that, with the support of the mayor and other leading men, he was sure, "if the Common sorte swaye not." Add. MSS, 29,974, fol. 76.

[139] C. H. Mayo, *The municipal records of the borough of Shaftesbury*, 8, Sherborne, 1889. No general signing by electors appears on the indentures of 1640 and 1645. C. 219/43/Part 1.

[140] *E.H.R.* **50**: 243, 248, 252.

[141] Add. MSS, 29,974, fols. 72, 74, 76, 319; Lansd. MSS, 459, fol. 20v; *M. of P.* **1**: 451, 457, 463.

[142] *Ibid.* **1**: 469; J. P. Rylands, ed., *The visitation of the county of Dorset, taken in the year 1623*, Harleian Society, **20**: 64, 1885 (hereafter, *Vis. Dorset, 1623*).

[143] *C.J.* **2**: 76, 77; D'Ewes (N), 306, 311, 351.

[144] Edward Pitt's letter cited above mentions methods of dealing with the better sort of townsmen or with "the multitude."

[145] Porritt, *The unreformed House of Commons* **1**: 93–94.

[146] A petition of grievances from Weymouth was presented in parliament on 21 December 1640. It mentioned the salt monopoly, ship money, coat and conduct money, and various restrictions on trade. D'Ewes (N), 174; *C.J.* **2**: 55.

[147] Indenture, C. 219/43/Part 1.

[148] See examples in the sketches of the individual members. See also S.P. 16, 60/10; 335/67/i.

aggrieved in 1635 by the declaration that all of it, except one hundred, lay in the Forest of Essex, after four centuries of freedom from the forest laws.[149] But in the 1640 elections grievances were not the only activating force. Here, as in the royalist counties, powerful families wielded their influence. Chief among them was that of Rich, headed by the Earl of Warwick, a mightly landlord and lord lieutenant. Working with the Riches in 1640, as their earlier generations had worked together in the reign of James,[150] was the family of Barrington, which, by its interconnections that extended to many parts of Essex and into the neighboring shires, drew together a great puritan clan of which more than a dozen became parliament men in 1640.

Of the nine men who sat for the county or boroughs of Essex, 1640–1642, only one, the courtier, Sir Henry Mildmay, seemed likely to oppose the reform movement of the time, but he eventually abandoned his royal master's cause. And only one of the nine, Warwick's own son, who was elevated to the peerage soon after the session started, deserted the popular cause. All but one were Essex men by birth or by residence, persons well known to their constituents and familiar with their problems.[151] The only non-Essex man, a carpetbagger from Ireland, was Sir John Clotworthy, who was not unknown to Essex puritans and was a fitting spokesman for the people of the county.

The Essex county election occurred on 26 October 1640[152] at Chelmsford, the shire town, which was not far from the residences of the families of Rich, Barrington, and Masham. It had been the scene of great excitement at the spring election, when men from the puritan boroughs, together with large numbers of county folk who had been stirred up by their ministers, J.P.'s, constables and militia captains, had, under the leadership of their lord lieutenant, Warwick, carried the day against a royalist candidate.[153] Possibly similar tactics were employed in October, but this time without objection afterwards, and the puritans again were the victors, with the election of Warwick's son, Lord Rich, and Sir William Masham, one of the Barrington clan. When Lord Rich was removed to the House of Lords in January, 1641, the by-election was held at Stratford Langthorne, 16 February,[152] and Sir Martin Lumley of Great Bardfield, another Essex puritan, was chosen.

Colchester's members were strong parliamentarians, Sir Thomas Barrington, head of that prominent family, and Harbottle Grimston, a resident of the borough and its recorder. The election was apparently by the members of the corporation and the commonalty, the citizens having in 1628 been recognized in their contention for the right of voting.[154]

The mayor and burgesses of Harwich[155] on 24 October 1640 chose as members two well known puritan gentlemen, both of whom were J.P.'s for the town. Sir Harbottle Grimston, senior, had in his service as a justice for Harwich incurred the rebuke of the Court of High Commission.[156] Sir Thomas Cheeke, brother-in-law of Warwick, had been M.P. for Harwich in the Short Parliament also.

Maldon returned Sir Henry Mildmay, steward of the borough, who had represented it in several earlier parliaments, and Sir John Clotworthy of Ireland and of London, whose election by a Cornish borough and by one in Warwick's county indicates that his presence in parliament was greatly desired by the puritan faction. Both supported parliament, although Mildmay, as a courtier, disagreed at the start with some of the popular program. The electors at Maldon were the bailiffs, aldermen, chief burgesses, and commonalty.[157]

GLOUCESTERSHIRE

Gloucestershire was a county where puritanism had gained a strong foothold, and where resistance had more than once greeted the program of Charles I, whether it was a matter of loans or ship money or of the cloth industry. The great port of Bristol was restive under the royal trade regulations and the private patents that encroached on the business of its merchants. Small wonder is it that the majority of the men sent to parliament in 1640 from the county and its four towns were known as opponents of many of the measures that emanated from London.[158] Yet by 1644 only four of the ten members remained loyal to the cause of parliament.[159] The national issues stand out less clearly in the Gloucestershire elections than in many other shires, although in the Short Parliament elections the rising influence of the puritans was apparent. Only one of the fall elections, that at Tewkesbury, seems to have

---

[149] *The autobiography and correspondence of Sir Simonds D'Ewes, Bart.*, J. O. Halliwell, ed., 2: 136–137, London, 1845 (hereafter D'Ewes, *Autobiography*).

[150] *E.H.R.* **48**: 395–413, 1933.

[151] Family relationships were close in the Essex delegation, for it included the uncle and nephew, Cheeke and Rich, the brothers-in-law, Masham and Barrington, and the Grimstons, father and son.

[152] Indentures, C. 219/43/Part 1.

[153] *C.S.P. Dom., 1639–1640,* 608–609.

[154] The 1640 indenture (C. 219/43/Part 1) mentions only the mayor and burgesses, but the broader franchise had been recognized in the election of Masham (*q.v.*) in 1628. The electors in 1660 were mayor, aldermen, assistants, common council, burgesses, and commonalty. *E.H.R.* **15**: 660, 1900.

[155] C. 219/43/Part 1.

[156] Grimston, who had sat for Essex in the Short Parliament, replaced at Harwich now a courtier who had represented the town in that session.

[157] C. 219/43/Part 1. In 1625 the commonalty had been strong enough to override the choice of the corporation officers. Add. MSS, 12,496, fol. 106.

[158] Henry Brett and Sir Theobald Gorges were probably royalists from the start. Craven and Alford, royalist aspirants at Tewkesbury, were ruled out by election decisions. John George, a suspect because of his court connections, seems not to have become an outright royalist until much later. The majority, 1640–1642, therefore, were opposition men.

[159] Cooke, Pury, and Edward and Nathaniel Stephens.

been severely contested, and there the issue was as much that of the local franchise as it was the choice between puritans and friends of the court.

Few carpetbaggers appear in Gloucestershire's delegation. Two royalists from outside the county who aspired to the Tewkesbury seats were ruled out eventually;[160] Sir Theobald Gorges, courtier, who sat for Cirencester, came from Wiltshire; and the others were all local men by birth or by marriage and residence.

The county members elected for Gloucestershire on 28 October 1640 were of the local gentry, John Dutton of Sherborne, and Nathaniel Stephens, both of whom had large followings in the shire and had more than once opposed the royal administration. Stephens was the more extreme of the two, and had actually been prevented by Dutton's power from being chosen at the spring elections.[161] His strength among the puritan element and the ship money foes, however, carried him in the autumn, and Dutton's personal candidacy may have been necessary to save the other seat from going to another of such views. Dutton, though a supporter of parliament at the start, swung in time to the king; Stephens remained a parliamentarian.[162]

Bristol returned on 12 October 1640 two prominent aldermen and merchants, Humphrey Hooke and Richard Long. The city had complained of its ship money rates, and in the decade before 1640 its merchants had objected to trade monopolies and customs regulations that interfered with the local business. Various merchants had been proceeded against in Star Chamber, and Hooke and Long, who filled the position of master of the Merchant Venturers of the town for all but one year of that decade, were active in their society's efforts to alleviate the burden of regulation and the nuisance of agents from outside.[163] They seemed more parliamentarians than royalists when they were elected as M.P.'s in 1640, but they were expelled in 1642 because their role in the work of the Merchant Venturers was finally interpreted as monopolistic.[164] One may suspect that the tardy expulsion may have been dictated by political reasons as well, for both men were accounted royalists during the war.

The Bristol election was conducted by the usual limited group, consisting chiefly of the corporation and the burgesses who were resident freeholders, despite a petition for extending the franchise to all free burgesses.[165] Hooke and Long represented actually the merchant oligarchy of Bristol.

Cirencester chose on 31 October 1640 John George, a prominent lawyer whose family estate lay in and near the borough, but whose life was associated much with London; and Sir Theobald Gorges, son of a Wiltshire family and something of a courtier, whose connections with Cirencester were probably through his Gloucestershire wife and some properties in the town. Although Cirencester supported parliament at the start of the war,[166] and although George managed to keep his place in parliament until after that time, both he and Gorges were eventually disabled as royalists.

At Gloucester the choice fell on an alderman and city lawyer noted for his puritanism, Thomas Pury, and on Henry Brett, the son-in-law of a former alderman, but a courtier and royalist. Both had been candidates in the spring election with two other men, but though Brett was chosen then, Pury was defeated.[167] And some doubt was thrown on the autumn election when William Lenthall, Gloucester's recorder, who was sitting for Woodstock and was already Speaker, declared in December that he had been nominated for Gloucester but had been denied the poll. The matter was referred to the Committee of Privileges, where it seems to have died.[168] The election was probably conducted within the closed corporation, an attempt in 1624 to have the franchise extended to the general inhabitants having failed.[169]

Tewkesbury's election was confused not only by the number of candidates, all of them from outside of the borough, but also by the question of whether the voting was limited to a closed group or whether it extended to the residents in general, or even to persons living on the outskirts of the town. The two bailiffs rejected before the election one candidate, a son of the Earl of Middlesex,[170] but there are indications that the powerful Worcestershire family of Coventry had some influence in the borough.[171] Three indentures of 22 October 1640 were sent to London naming among them four men, John Craven of London, Sir Edward Alford of

---

[160] One of these, Alford, held some county lands in his wife's right.

[161] C.S.P. Dom., 1639–1640, 580–583; W. B. Willcox, Gloucestershire, A study in local government, 1590–1640, 33–36.

[162] More than 800 were present at the spring election. The October return (C. 219/43/Part 1) gives no indication of the number present.

[163] John Latimer, The history of the Society of Merchant Venturers of the city of Bristol, 111, 118–122, 135–137, Bristol, J. W. Arrowsmith, 1903 (hereafter, Latimer, Merchant Venturers, Bristol).

[164] C.J. 2: 567–568.

[165] C. 219/43/Part 1; Bristol Corporation MSS (hereafter Bristol Corp. MSS), Common Council Book 3 (9 October 1640); John Latimer, The annals of Bristol in the seventeenth century, 147, Bristol, William George's Sons, 1900 (hereafter, Latimer, Annals of Bristol).

[166] W. St. C. Baddeley, A history of Cirencester, 247, Cirencester, Cirencester Newspaper Co., 1924.

[167] C.S.P. Dom., 1639–1640, 582; M. of P. 1: 481.

[168] C.J. 2: 43; D'Ewes (N), 96. Lenthall had been one of the candidates in the spring, but his rumored election for Woodstock perhaps accounts for his not being chosen then by Gloucester. C.S.P. Dom., 1639–1640, 582.

[169] Gloucester indenture, C. 219/43/Part 1; Gloucester Corporation MSS (hereafter Gloucester Corp. MSS), Minute Book, 1565–1632, fols. 253v, 476v, 478v, 497v.

[170] H.M.C., Fourth Report, MSS of Earl De La Warr, 303.

[171] A relative of the Coventrys, Sir Anthony Ashley Cooper, had been returned in the spring, and Craven (q.v.) was a Coventry brother-in-law.

Hertfordshire and Sussex, Sir Robert Cooke of Highnam, Gloucestershire, and Edward Stephens, another county gentleman. The latter two were the choice of the inhabitants and the former were chosen by the bailiffs.[172] The House of Commons on 9 November, upon the recommendation of the Committee of Privileges, ordered all four men to forbear sitting until a decision was reached, and sent for one of the bailiffs as a delinquent. At intervals afterwards there were debates on the issue of the franchise at Tewkesbury, but the order that the would-be members should not sit was apparently not enforced, for it was mentioned again on 11 January without being put to the question, and John Craven at least was present in March.[173] The whole election was declared void on 6 August. In the by-election the old dispute between corporation and freemen recurred. The bailiffs returned on 18 October Alford and Cooke, and the inhabitants on the same date returned Cooke and Stephens. Once more the case was committed, this time for a decision regarding Alford and Stephens, since Cooke's choice by both groups assured him his place. But Alford had been involved also in an election contest for Arundel, Sussex, and after the voiding of the original election of Tewkesbury he declared on 12 November 1641 that he preferred Arundel. Not until 25 December 1643, however, was the final decision of the House made to recognize Alford as a Sussex member and Cooke and Stephens for Tewkesbury.[174] The two candidates who in the proceedings were eliminated, Alford and Craven, were royalists; those recognized as lawful members were stanch parliamentarians.

HAMPSHIRE

Hampshire proved itself in 1640 to be strongly in favor of reforms in spite of the fact that the lieutenants of the county, the Earl of Portland and the Duke of Lenox, expected to have considerable influence over the elections.[175] The county's experience with the billeting of soldiers and martial law in the early years of Charles I had been followed by resistance to the loans[176] and to knighthood composition[177] and by delays in the collection of ship money.[178] The justices protested in 1639 against additional expenses for the repair of St. Paul's.[179] Underlying the discontent was the distress felt by the farmers and clothiers of the region.[180] And accompanying it was the development of a strong group of puritan leaders among the gentry.

The 1640 elections for the county and its twelve boroughs resulted in the choice of a large majority of popular party members, most of them local men. Of the twenty-eight[181] who were returned either originally or in by-elections before January, 1642, all but eight were parliamentarians. Of those eight Vernon was unseated by the voiding of his return; Rainsford, possibly a royalist but definitely interested in the reform of abuses, died before the issues came to extremes; and another, Lord Falkland, was in 1640 scarcely to be counted a partisan of the court. Of the five others, only one of whom, Meux, was a Hampshireman born, possibly three (Davies, Weston, Meux) owed their places to the nomination of borough patrons and one owed his to the office he held (Goring). Among the parliamentarians only two seem to have been unconnected with the county by birth or residence. All but seven of the whole county membership either were born in Hampshire or were residents or office holders there, and one of the seven, Heveningham, had married into a local family.

Relatively few contests developed in the elections in Hampshire. Several boroughs were clearly patronage boroughs, such as Newtown in the Isle of Wight for the royalists, or Whitchurch for the other side. Elsewhere the nominee of a patron was elected side by side with a man who was obviously a local choice. The only election dispute seems to have occurred in the by-election at Andover sometime in the spring of 1641, a case on which the House reached a decision favoring the parliamentary candidate in May, 1642. Although the secretary to one of the lords lieutenant wrote with confidence on 30 September 1640 that most of the places in Hampshire were still free,[182] he must have reckoned without knowledge of the influence of such puritan families as the Wallops, Jervoises, Whiteheads, and Worsleys to control places for their men.

The Hampshire knights who were elected on 26 October were prominent local men, Sir Henry Wallop and Richard Whitehead, both of whom were known as opponents of the royal policies. Both had served for their shire in the Short Parliament and they seem to have been unopposed for re-election.[183]

At Andover, where the right of election lay with twenty-four burgesses and where nominees by out-

---

[172] *M. of P.* 1: 489 and n. One of indentures at the Public Record Office was signed by a single bailiff, Thomas Hale, and the names of the M. P.'s were written in over an erasure. The other bailiff's return mentions Hale as a bailiff but was not signed by him. The original return naming Cooke and Stephens is not extant (C. 219/43/Part 1). Hale's misdemeanor in sending in a third return brought a special rebuke from the House. *C.J.* 2: 23, 44.

[173] *C.J.* 2: 23, 44, 49, 109; D'Ewes (N), 69 and n.; 137–138, 238, 542–543.

[174] *C.J.* 2: 239, 313; 3: 352, 378–379; D'Ewes (C), 69, n., 126–127.

[175] *Archaeologia Cantiana, being Transactions of the Kent Archaeological Society* 12: 81, 1858 (hereafter, *Arch. Cant.*); *C.S.P. Dom., 1640–1641*, 121–122.

[176] Bodleian Rawl. MSS, D 666, fols. 41–43, 103v; Rushworth 3: 912, 914.

[177] Add. MSS, 21,922, fols. 179v–183; S.P. 16, 52/69.

[178] *C.S.P. Dom., 1635–1636*, 392; *1636–1637*, 217–218, 356, 436; *1637*, 21–22, 172, 387.

[179] Rawl. MSS, D 666, fols. 84v–86.

[180] *C.S.P. Dom., 1629–1631*, 403.

[181] These figures include Henry Percy, who **decided on 11** November 1640 to serve for Northumberland.

[182] *C.S.P. Dom., 1640–1641*, 121–122.

[183] *C.S.P. Dom., 1640–1641*, 198.

siders had previously been elected,[184] the voters chose for one seat on 19 October 1640 Robert Wallop, the future regicide and son of the county M.P. The other place went to Sir Henry Rainsford, a Gloucestershire man who had married a Hampshire heiress and lived part of the time in Hampshire. He was said to have been elected without having planned for it himself, and was probably a reformer of Falkland's type, never an extremist. Upon his death in March, 1641, the place was sought by a local gentleman, Sir William Waller, the future parliamentary general, and by Henry Vernon, who was apparently a Shropshireman who was a protégé of the Earl of Southampton. He was eventually a royalist. Eighteen burgesses present divided their votes evenly between the candidates. The bailiff declared three others, one of them a Waller supporter, ineligible to vote because they had not yet taken their oaths as burgesses, and cast his own deciding vote for Vernon. The latter took his place in the House because the bailiff returned him, but after Waller's petition arrived on 30 April 1641 Vernon's name appeared but once more in the *Journals,* and he was probably debarred from sitting. The House decided on 3 May 1642 that Waller should have the seat, the decision being almost a strictly partisan vote of 107 to 102.[185] In the period from May, 1641, until May, 1642, Andover was probably served by Robert Wallop alone.

Christchurch borough was accustomed to accepting the nomination of the manor lord for at least one of its burgesses. It chose on 26 October 1640 a local man, Henry Tulse of Hinton in Christchurch parish, who had been one of its members in the spring, and Matthew Davies, a lawyer from Dorset who had been recommended by Lord Baltimore. Less than a week before the election two other candidates were recommended by the Earl of Pembroke, being proposed in the name of a younger brother of Lord Arundel, who disputed Baltimore's title to be lord of Christchurch manor. Although the mayor wrote to Pembroke on 26 October that the town was already committed to Tulse and Davies, one of the new nominees received 3 votes. Davies received 8, and Tulse had 5.[186] Tulse and Davies accordingly were returned by the mayor and burgesses.[187] The former, a parliamentarian, sat until his death in 1642. Davies, a somewhat moderate royalist, was disabled in 1643.

The mayor and burgesses of New Lymington [188] chose on 20 October their borough lord, Henry Campion of Newton Valence, and a neighboring gentleman, John Button of Buckland in Lymington. Both had represented the town in an earlier parliament, and both were opposition men.

Newport in the Isle of Wight had been restored as a parliamentary borough in Elizabeth's time through the influence of the captain of the island, and for several elections thereafter it accorded to that officer the privilege of naming one or both of its burgesses. In 1628, however, it showed greater independence, expressing preference for local men.[189] The members chosen on 18 October 1640 [190] were Lucius Lord Falkland, who had sat for Newport in the Short Parliament but who otherwise seems to have had no connection with the borough, and an Isle of Wight man, Sir Henry Worsley, Bart. He too had served for the town in the spring. Worsley, a parliamentarian, sat until 1648, but Falkland, turned from his reform work by his distaste for extremes, was disabled in September, 1642.

Newtown in the Isle of Wight seems like Newport to have been accustomed to somewhat formal elections, the mayor and burgesses usually accepting [191] the nomination of the captain or governor of the island. It returned on 19 October 1640 young John Meux, who came of an old family of the island and was an intimate of the governor, the Earl of Portland, and with him Nicholas Weston, a younger brother of the earl who had visited the island several times. Both had sat for Newtown in the Short Parliament, doubtless as Portland's nominees, and both were disabled as royalists in time.

The parliament men for Petersfield, elected on 22 October by the mayor and burgesses,[192] were Sir William Lewis of Wales and of Hampshire, and Sir William Uvedale, a prominent Hampshire courtier. The latter had sat for Petersfield in the spring and several times before, and Lewis had served for it in the spring. He was a strong parliamentarian and a Presbyterian. Uvedale, though suspected of royalism, kept his seat until after 1644 at least.

Portsmouth's election on 25 October 1640 was nominally by the mayor, alderman, and burgesses,[193] but it seems to have been controlled partly by the commander of the garrison [194] and partly by the Lord Admiral of England. One member returned was George Goring, the commander at Portsmouth, who was afterwards expelled from the House for deserting to the king. Originally chosen to serve with him was Henry Percy, brother of the Lord Admiral, the Earl of Northumberland. But upon Percy's decision on 11 November to sit

[184] See the influence of Sir Thomas Jervoise and of Conway in 1628. *C.S.P. Dom., 1627–1628,* 566.

[185] *C.J.* 2: 130, 554, 568. The tellers in the division of 3 May 1642 were two parliamentarians for the Yeas and two royalists for the Nays.

[186] Notes based on Christchurch Borough MSS which were furnished through the courtesy of Herbert Druitt, Esquire, of Christchurch.

[187] Indenture, C. 219/43/Part 2.

[188] New Lymington indenture, C. 219/43/Part 2.

[189] *The Oglander memoirs,* ed. W. H. Long, xiii–xvi, London, 1888; *C.S.P. Dom., 1627–1628,* 540, 568, 576.

[190] The electors were the mayor and burgesses. No signatures appear on the return. C. 219/43/Part 2.

[191] *Ibid.* The Newtown return is a formal indenture in Latin without signatures.

[192] *Ibid.*

[193] *Ibid.*

[194] The Earl of Pembroke as captain of Portsmouth had exercised his control over the elections, 1621–1628. *E.H.R.* 50: 243, 251, 1935.

instead for Northumberland, his place at Portsmouth was filled by an employee of the earl, Edward Dowse. He came of a Hampshire-Wiltshire family and was a parliamentarian.

Southampton, having voted in 1624 to return to the old custom of choosing local men rather than strangers recommended by powerful influences from without,[195] chose on 12 October 1640 two prominent merchants as its M.P.'s. George Gollopp and Edward Exton were aldermen and former mayors and both were parliamentarians. Their electors were the mayor, burgesses, and inhabitants.[196]

The bailiff and burgesses of Stockbridge elected on 27 October two strong parliament supporters, William Heveningham of Norfolk, who was a son-in-law of the influential Sir Henry Wallop, and William Jephson of Froyle, Hampshire. Both had sat for Stockbridge in the spring.

Whitchurch, where the mayor and eight burgesses voted,[197] had by 18 October 1640 been "engrossed" by Sir Thomas Jervoise of Herriard for himself and his son, Richard.[198] They were accordingly returned for the borough on 22 October. The Jervoises were a local family of prominence. Sir Thomas had sat for Whitchurch in each successive parliament from 1621. Both he and his son were strong opponents of the court.

Winchester's members, chosen on 27 October 1640 by the mayor, bailiffs, and "commonalty," or closed mayor's council,[199] were the town's recorder, John Lisle, and the captain of Winchester, Sir William Ogle. The latter lived in or near the city, although he was not a Hampshireman by birth. Lisle was a native of the county, but seems to have become officially connected with Winchester only in 1640, when he was chosen M.P. in the spring and became the recorder. He was a parliamentarian, but Ogle was for the king.

At Yarmouth, Isle of Wight, the mayor and burgesses elected on 27 October 1640 Sir John Leigh, who came of a prominent island family and was a parliamentarian. With him was chosen Philip Lord Lisle, also a supporter of parliament. The latter, scarcely of age at the time of the election and belonging to a family that lived outside of the county, doubtless owed his place at Yarmouth to the Lord Admiral, his uncle.

HEREFORDSHIRE

Herefordshire, a county which knew the abuses of the Court of the Welsh Marches, and where in 1640 there was strong opposition to ship money,[200] divided almost evenly between Roundheads and Cavaliers the delegation it chose in the fall of 1640. The county knights were of opposing views, although they seem to have been paired for the election; and in two of the three towns the same division as to politics occurred. Weobly alone, practically a patronage borough, chose two men who are classed as royalists. Approximately the same relative strength remained after the two by-elections before 1642, for in each case a member who was presumably a royalist was succeeded by a member of his own family who likewise adhered to the king. Few of Hereford's members, however, with the exception of Sir Robert Harley, appear to have been extremists in their factions; several seem to have veered from one side to the other, finally letting force determine whether they should be classed as Roundhead or as Cavalier. This lack of decision may have resulted in part from a certain provincialism in the county, which Harley once termed "the most clownish county of England."[201] Few of its parliament men distinguished themselves in the Commons. Yet Sir Robert Harley, the Presbyterian leader, sat for the county, and Sampson Eure, later to be Speaker at the Oxford parliament, sat for Leominster. With the exception of Arthur Jones, son of Lord Ranelagh of Ireland, all were Herefordshire men and owners of property there. Four of the group were barristers.

The Herefordshire knights elected at the castle at Hereford on 24 October 1640[202] were Sir Robert Harley, the parliamentarian, and Fitzwilliam Coningsby, a prominent country gentleman whose connection with the soap monopoly caused his expulsion from the House a year later. Both were local men who seemed to have the general support of the county gentry; but to safeguard their election they had solicited the backing of the Earl of Essex, and Harley spent some £155, chiefly for wine and lodgings.[203] After Fitzwilliam Coningsby was expelled, his son, Humphrey, also a royalist, was elected on 20 November 1641. He was opposed by a son of Sir Robert Whiting, whom Harley favored.[204]

Hereford city was represented by two local men, Richard Seaborne, a lawyer, and Richard Weaver, alderman and former mayor. The former was disabled eventually as a royalist, although he was by no means an extreme one. Weaver seems to have been of the popular faction. The mayor and citizens were the electors.[205]

At Leominster, where the election was by the bailiff or mayor, with the assent of "the rest of the burgesses,"[206] two lawyers were chosen. Neither seems to have been closely connected with the borough, but

[195] The history and antiquity of Southampton . . . by John Speed, ed. E. R. Aubrey, 95, Southampton Record Society, 1909 (hereafter, Speed, Hist. of Southampton); C.S.P. Dom., 1627–1628, 584.

[196] Indenture, C. 219/43/Part 2.

[197] Ibid.

[198] C.S.P. Dom., 1640–1641, 179.

[199] C. 219/43/Part 2; E.H.R. 41: 444, 1926.

[200] C.S.P. Dom., 1640–1641, 24, 83.

[201] Eg. MSS, 2714, fol. 363.

[202] Indenture, C. 219/43/Part 1.

[203] H.M.C., Fourteenth Report 2, MSS of the Duke of Portland (III), 65, 66.

[204] Ibid., 81–82; indenture, 20 November 1641 (C. 219/43/Part 1).

[205] Indenture of 1642 (C. 219/43/Part 1).

[206] Indenture of 20 October 1640.

each was a Herefordshire man. Sampson Eure, who was prominent in his profession and was long associated with the royal administration, was a royalist; Walter Kyrle was a somewhat lukewarm parliamentarian.

Weobly, a borough restored in 1628 through the efforts of its lord, James Tomkins of Monnington,[207] was practically a patronage borough, although the electors were the mayor and burgesses.[208] One of the M.P.'s chosen was Arthur Jones, of the nobility of Ireland, a royalist who seems to have had no personal connection with the town. Elected with him was William Tomkins, head of the manor family, who had served for the town before and who was probably of royalist sympathies. Following the death of Tomkins before the close of 1640, the seat passed to his brother and successor, Thomas Tomkins, who favored some of the reforms of the early period of the parliament but joined the king before 1644.

HERTFORDSHIRE

Hertfordshire, entitled to six parliament men, was strongly puritanical and reformist in its sentiments in 1640. There had been an increasingly large arrearage in its ship money collections from year to year,[209] with a number of prominent men among the defaulters,[210] and in the home of one of its members, Sir William Lytton, numerous meetings of Pym's strategists were said to have been held. Late in the summer the county prepared a petition of grievances and sent its shire members of the Short Parliament to carry it personally to King Charles at York.[211] Small wonder, then, that all but one of the members chosen in the fall were workers for reform; or that, when one reformer, Capel, turned in time to the king, he was replaced by a parliamentarian. Without exception, the Hertfordshire members were property holders and residents in the county.

Hertfordshire elected at the county court at Hertford on 22 October 1640 two local gentlemen of prominence, the shire M.P.'s of the spring, Sir William Lytton of Knebworth and Arthur Capel of Hadham. Both had worked for the redress of grievances, but the latter was elevated to the peerage in August, 1641, and on 26 August the county replaced him with a stanch parliamentarian, Sir Thomas Dacres of Cheshunt. Four days later there was some question in the House regarding his election, but Dacres was not barred from sitting.[212]

Hertford borough, of which the Earl of Salisbury was chief steward, chose on 26 October 1640, by its mayor, chief burgesses and inhabitants,[213] the earl's heir apparent, Charles Lord Cranborne, and Sir Thomas Fanshawe, K.B., a prominent courtier from the county and often before a member for the borough. The latter was a royalist, but Cranborne supported parliament.

St. Albans had the only election contest of note in the county. Thomas Coningsby, who had served in the Short Parliament for the town, tried to prevent the election of another in his place, and each side accused the other of interference with a free election. According to the reports, violence nearly broke forth, and Coningsby was called up to Westminster to explain his actions. He was eventually released on bail, 18 February 1641, and nothing appears further of the case.[214] The mayor and burgesses elected [215] Sir John Jennings, their other M.P. of the Short Parliament, who lived near St. Albans, and the inexperienced Edward Wingate of Lockley. Both were strong parliamentarians.

HUNTINGDONSHIRE

The little county of Huntingdon, where the land-rich families of Montagu and Cromwell usually influenced appointments and elections,[216] showed in 1640 that issues different from family power were at stake. The county had seen considerable resistance to ship money,[217] and chose as one of its members a relatively obscure man, Valentine Walton of Great Staughton, whose recent imprisonment for underpayment of ship money made him popular enough to defeat the heir of the powerful Cromwells. His colleague, to whom the first seat was assigned, doubtless in deference to his family as well as to his own prominence in the county, was Sir Sydney Montagu of Hinchinbrooke, whose recent removal from his office as Master of Requests may have gained him favor at the polls.[218] The election was held at Huntingdon on 10 October, and was heated enough for swords to be drawn.[219] Both men chosen were county residents, and both seem to have worked with the reform group at the start of the session. Montagu, however, regarded the war as treason, and was expelled in 1642.

The Huntingdon borough members, both of whom supported parliament, were younger sons of the house

[207] W. R. Williams, *The parliamentary history of the County of Hereford,* 126 (hereafter, Williams, *Hereford*).

[208] The indenture of 15 October 1640 was signed by the mayor and about a dozen persons.

[209] Royal Hist. Soc., *Trans.,* 3rd Ser., **4**: 158, 1910.

[210] S.P. 16, 376/106.

[211] Add. MSS, 11,045, fol. 121v; D'Ewes, *Autobiography* **2**: 242.

[212] D'Ewes (B), 581. Dacres's election seems to have been held in St. Albans, for the mayors' accounts record the cost of renting a place for the election. St. Albans Borough MSS, Mayors' Accounts, 1585–1746 (1640–1641),

[213] Hertford indenture, C. 219/43/Part 1.

[214] D'Ewes (N), 370, 496, 508; *C.J.* **2**: 88. For more details on a quarrel at this time between Coningsby and Jennings, see Sir John Jennings.

[215] These were the electors named on the St. Albans indenture. C. 219/43/Part 1. The Earl of Salisbury, steward of the borough, had often influenced its elections. St. Albans Borough MSS, Mayors' Accounts, 1585–1746, accounts for 1624–1625, 1625–1626, 1627–1628, 1641–1642.

[216] *V.C.H. Huntingdonshire* **2**: 14, 24–25; Sanford, *St. and ill.,* 262.

[217] *C.S.P. Dom., 1637–1638,* 246, 420, 565.

[218] Bodleian Tanner MSS, 65, fols. 164, 175.

[219] *Ibid.;* C. 219/43/Part 1.

of Montagu, the cousins Edward and George Montagu. Family influence was even more powerful in the borough than in the county, for since 1630 the corporation had been a closed one and, although the official return formally mentions the burgesses as electors, the popular franchise was gone. The nearest powerful landlord exercised great control,[220] and Sir Sydney Montagu, as the owner of Hinchinbrooke, was no doubt partly responsible for the choice of his nephews, sons of two prominent brothers, to serve for the town.

KENT

Kent sent ten members to parliament, two for the shire and two for each of three boroughs and the city of Canterbury. With one exception all were men from the county, most of them having served as magistrates for some years. Other Kentish men went to the House, too, many of whom had taken part in their shire election, but they represented the separate political entity, the Cinque Ports, and have been considered under that head. There had been objections in Kent to the billeting of soldiers in Buckingham's day, to the levies of ship money and to the pressing of men for the Scottish war. And the movement for ecclesiastical reform had found favor in many prominent families. It is scarcely surprising therefore that of Kent's ten members all but one, the youngest and an outsider, were strong advocates of reform, and that only two of these nine, Colepeper and Dering, remained loyal to episcopacy and the crown. An occasional member who as sheriff or deputy lieutenant had administered the royal measures that were distasteful to the region may have deliberately sought election so as to be present to justify his actions when the expected attack on them came.[221]

The shire was stirred in the spring by an election contest that brought out half a dozen candidates and aroused bitterness among kinsmen and erstwhile friends.[222] One of the chief contestants in the autumn was one who had been defeated in the spring, Sir Edward Dering, Bart., well known J.P. and former lieutenant at Dover. He seems to have arranged for mutual support with Sir John Colepeper, a knight from the western part of the county, but letters from friends before the election indicate that the followers of each were somewhat distrustful of the other. Both expected the parish ministers to campaign for them. All other candidates except a Mr. Browne withdrew from the contest as the voting time approached. Browne, presumably the Richard Browne who served for New

Romney, 1641–1648, was supported principally by Sir Roger Twysden, who had accomplished the defeat of his kinsman, Dering, in the spring.[223] He was spoken of as the candidate of "the precise party."[224] The leading candidates had hoped by pairing to avoid a polling of votes, lest the rivalry among their own followers as to which should have first place might mean the loss of the second seat to a third candidate, and they prepared to strengthen their cause by dispensing wine at the polling place on the heath near Maidstone. As they feared, when the freeholders assembled on 26 October, Browne had enough support to make a poll necessary. He was outnumbered, however, by Dering and Colepeper, and they were accordingly returned.[225] A move to petition against the election, 4 December 1640, was defeated by the simple maneuver of Colepeper, who called on members of the House who had been present at the election to testify that it had been conducted fairly. Their witness that Browne had lost it by many voices satisfied the House.[226] Dering and Colepeper, both representing the reform group in 1640, were alienated from the parliamentary cause by the summer of 1642.

At Canterbury the citizens returned their members of the spring, both parliamentarians, who had in the previous election been chosen in preference to candidates recommended by the Archbishop and the Lord Lieutenant. They were local men, Sir Edward Master, who lived near the town and had been captain of one of its military companies, and his son-in-law, John Nutt of Canterbury, who had been on cordial terms with the city government for some years past. The election in the spring had rested on national as well as local issues, for it was recognized then that the fate of king and country was at stake.[227]

Maidstone, the county town, was excited not only by the shire contests but by its own elections in 1640. Only two candidates seem to have stood in the spring, but a great deal of factionalism was reported there in the fall. The mayor refused to Sir John Sedley, who for years had been captain for the town, the courtesy of being sworn a freeman so that he could stand for election. This refusal Sedley traced to the plan of Sir Francis Barnham, many times M.P. for Maidstone, who wanted to reserve a place there for young Sir Henry Vane, recently returned from New England.[228] On election day, October 28, however, only three candidates were presented. One of them, a Mr. Beale, was

[220] Porritt, *The unreformed House of Commons* 1: 45; W. C. Abbott, ed., *The writings and speeches of Oliver Cromwell* 1: 46, 67–69, Cambridge, Harvard Univ. Press, 1937–1947; C. 219/43/ Part 1.

[221] See Sir Thomas Walsingham.

[222] L. B. Larking, ed., *Proceedings, principally in the County of Kent in connection with the parliaments called in 1640*, 1–8, Camden Society, 1862 (hereafter, Larking, *Proceedings in Kent*); Bodleian Rawl. MSS, D. 141, fol. 4.

[223] Stowe MSS, 184, fols. 15–16. Twysden wrote two days before the election, assuring Dering of his good wishes, but not promising his vote. *Ibid.*, fol. 17.

[224] Stowe MSS, 743, fol. 149.

[225] Larking, *Proceedings in Kent*, 8–12, 15–16; Stowe MSS, 184, fol. 15; 743, fols. 146–158; Bodleian Rawl. MSS, D. 141, fol. 6.

[226] D'Ewes (N), 103, 107.

[227] Add. MSS, 11,045, fol. 99v.

[228] Sedley accused Vane's father of seeking by this means revenge for Sedley's opposition to him in the county election of the spring. Larking, *Proceedings in Kent*, 13.

quickly outvoted. But the successful candidates, each of whom wanted the first place, gave each other the lie and came to blows before the election by the mayor, with the assent of the burgesses, was over. They were both parliamentarians and both were well known in Maidstone. Sir Francis Barnham had a house in the town and Sir Humphrey Tufton lived nearby.[229]

Queenborough, where the election lay with the mayor, jurats, and burgesses,[230] was accustomed to having candidates recommended by noblemen.[231] They chose on 19 October 1640 Sir Edward Hales, Bart., a prominent Kentish gentleman and magistrate, who had been one of their members in the Short Parliament, and with him young William Harrison of Hertfordshire, son of an important customs official who had been chosen in the spring. Harrison was a royalist, but Hales was an active popular party man.

Rochester had sent at least one member of the family of Walsingham to almost every parliament from 1597,[232] and on 24 October 1640 it chose again Sir Thomas Walsingham of Scadbury, who had served for it six times before. The other member this year was a newcomer to parliament, a local man, Richard Lee of Great Delce, nearby. The former, though of a family earlier connected with the court, supported parliament. Lee, too, seems to have done so, but there may have been some suspicion of his loyalty later.

LANCASHIRE

Lancashire was a county restive in matters of religion in the seventeenth century, with strong recusant and puritan elements in its population, but seems to have been less disturbed by such political issues as ship money than were other regions,[233] and was more subject to court influence than some of its neighbors because of the Duchy of Lancaster administration, supplemented by the power of its chief nobleman, the Earl of Derby. Evidence of these influences, as well as of the increasing strength of the puritan faction, appears in the elections of October, 1640, although few details regarding them have been found.[234] The earl's control seems to have had a setback in the county elections,[235] but both Liverpool and Lancaster boroughs conformed to the custom of accepting one nominee of the Chancellor of the Duchy, Clitheroe and Newton were this time family

dominated boroughs, one parliamentarian and one royalist, and both Preston and Wigan re-elected their members of the spring.

Of the fourteen men returned for Lancashire and its towns nine were residents of the county or of nearby Cheshire, two others held offices in the Duchy and owned lands in the county, and another, though long a resident of the London area, was a Lancashire man by birth and owned property there. The only actual carpetbaggers were Sir Richard Wynn of Wales, the queen's treasurer, and Kentish born Sir Roger Palmer, master of the royal household. Probably the five non-residents all owed their places to royal pressure and only one of them kept his seat in the House after the war began.[236] Of the local men, the Cheshire youth who sat for his family borough of Newton is accounted a royalist, and one county member, though active for reforms, 1640–1641, was a royalist by 1642. The rest were all parliamentarians, including such vigorous ones as John Moore and Alexander Rigby who were named judges of the king.

The knights for Lancashire, Roger Kirkby of Kirkby Ireleth, and Ralph Ashton of Middleton, were men well known in the county, and both active in local and national affairs before 1640, although neither had served for the shire in earlier parliaments. Since the Short Parliament members for the county, both royalists and friends of the Earl of Derby,[237] were not re-elected now, it may be suspected that canvassing by the popular party produced this result. Both Ashton and Kirkby worked for the early reforms, and Ashton was a zealous parliamentarian, but Kirkby supported the king at the outbreak of war.

Clitheroe, with some sixty to seventy burgesses and freemen as electors, selected from five candidates the two young men of local families who had been their choice in the spring.[238] Both Ralph Aston of Whalley and Richard Shuttleworth, junior, of Gawthorpe Hall, were parliamentarians.

Lancaster borough, apparently responsive to the Duchy, returned two royalists. Thomas Fanshawe of Jenkins, Essex, a Duchy official and once before M.P. for a Lancashire borough, was a prominent lawyer. John Harrison of Balls, Herts, a Lancastrian by birth, had spent most of his life near London, where he was one of the customs farmers. He was connected with Fanshawe by marriage, and had been M.P. for Lancaster borough in the spring.

Liverpool chose as one member a well-to-do ship

---

[229] Bodleian Rawl. MSS, D. 141, fols. 4, 7; Maidstone indenture, C. 219/43/Part 2.

[230] Indenture, C. 219/43/Part 2.

[231] *Arch. Cant.* 22: 182–183, 1897.

[232] *M. of P., passim.*

[233] Lancashire sheriffs made their ship money returns until 1639 apparently without great complaint. Royal Hist. Soc., *Trans.,* 3rd Ser., 4: 159, 1910; S.P. 16, 364/93; 367/37.

[234] The returns for this election are missing from the Public Record Office, and the only contest which was brought before the House was that concerning Wigan, where a matter of franchise, rather than of candidates, was the issue.

[235] See below. Clarendon (*Rebellion* 2: 342–343, 471) remarked on the earl's loss of influence when war came.

[236] Each outsider served for a different borough, another indication of the custom of accepting one Duchy nomination for each. Only in the shire and the family borough of Clitheroe were both men chosen from the reform group.

[237] W. W. Bean, *The parliamentary representation of the six northern counties of England,* 204, 208, Hull, 1890 (hereafter, Bean, *Northern counties*).

[238] Ashton received 57 votes, Shuttleworth, 52, and 47 votes were scattered among the other three. *Ibid.,* 1191; *Lancashire and Cheshire Antiquarian Notes* 1: 133–134, Leigh, 1885–1886.

owner and former mayor, John Moore, who was strongly parliamentarian in his views. The other member, doubtless a Duchy nominee,[239] was Sir Richard Wynn, the queen's treasurer, who came of a prominent family of north Wales, had spent most of his life at court, and seems to have had no previous connections with Liverpool. Despite his court career and suspicions of him during the war, Wynn retained his seat in the Long Parliament until his death in 1649.

Newton-in-Makerfield, a family-controlled borough during most of its history,[240] returned as one member the seventeen-year-old scion of one of its dominating houses, Peter Legh of Lyme Hall, Cheshire; and as the other, the master of the royal household, Sir Roger Palmer, K.B., who came from Kent. Both were royalists.[241]

The members for Preston-in-Amounderness were the two Lancashire magistrates and parliamentarians chosen in the spring, Thomas Standish of Duxbury Hall, and Richard Shuttleworth, senior, of Gawthorpe Hall.

At Wigan on 26 October 1640 the town burgesses chose by ample margin from among six candidates the two men who had sat for the borough in the spring, Orlando Bridgeman and Alexander Rigby. Although the "inhabitants" demanded to be polled also, and protested the election, the vote by the customary limited franchise was upheld.[242] Both Wigan members were lawyers, the former being king's counsel for the Duchy, and holder of lands in the county, and the latter being a local man. But Bridgeman, supporter of king and Anglicanism, had little in common with the zealous puritan and parliamentarian, Rigby.

LEICESTERSHIRE

In the seventeenth century Leicestershire was divided passionately by the animosities between the families of Hastings and Grey, whose heads were the earls of Huntingdon and Stamford. When the Civil War came the sons of the families, according to Clarendon, "fought the public quarrel with their private spirit and indignation,"[243] the house of Hastings being royalist, and the Greys, parliamentarian. The family feud is more apparent in the Leicester borough elections than in the county, perhaps because the smaller number of

voters gave more opportunity for patronage.[244] Of the four men chosen from Leicestershire in 1640, three were natives and puritans, the only royalist being a lawyer of London and Derbyshire, who had powerful patrons to back him and who had some slight connection himself with the county.

The Leicestershire knights returned on 22 October 1640 were Henry Lord Grey of Ruthin and Sir Arthur Hesilrige of Noseley, both natives of the county, and both strong puritans and supporters of parliament.

At Leicester borough, where the mayor, bailiffs, and burgesses voted,[245] the influence of powerful neighbors played its part. The town's representatives in the Short Parliament had been nominees of the Chancellor of the Duchy of Lancaster and of the Earl and Countess of Devonshire, one of whose manors lay near the town;[246] and in October, in addition to the same nominees, Thomas Lord Grey of Groby was commended to the borough by his father, the Earl of Stamford. Lord Grey, and the countess's nominee, Thomas Coke of Gray's Inn and Derbyshire, were chosen, somewhat to the surprise of the "ancients of the company," who explained afterwards to the Duchy chancellor that their recommendation of his nominee was not "any whit answered, being overswayed by the greater part of voices."[247] Evidently the townsmen were willing to re-elect a man proposed by a powerful neighbor such as the countess, but preferred the puritan, Grey, to the court nominee. Their re-elected member, Coke, though a foe of certain courtiers for his father's sake, was a royalist in the end.

LINCOLNSHIRE

Lincolnshire's twelve members of 1640 included a group of strong puritan leaders. Before the end of 1641 one young member of royalist family had died and been replaced by an active reformer, and another member, a zealous foe of Strafford, had turned to the king, but the rest continued as at the start, one royalist and nine parliamentarians. The popular party had gained at least two seats which had been held by royalists in the spring, but no records remain of election contests.

A doggerel rhyme of the spring had run,[248]

> Choose noe shipp shreiffe, nor Court Athyst,
> Noe fen drayner, nor Church Papist,

and it seems to define as well the issues of the autumn voting. Lincoln men had resisted ship money pay-

---

[239] W. Duncombe Pink and Alfred B. Beaven, *The parliamentary representation of Lancashire*, 178, London, 1889 (hereafter, Pink and Beaven, *Parl. Rep. Lanc.*).

[240] The voters were the resident forty-shilling freeholders. C. 219/43/Part 2 (1645 indenture); Porritt, *The unreformed House of Commons* 1: 97.

[241] William Ashurst, parliamentarian, listed as an original member for Newton by Bean (*Northern counties,* 197, 373), was Legh's successor.

[242] Bean, *Northern counties*, 448, n.; Lancashire and Cheshire Antiquarian Society, *Transactions* 47: 94–99, 1932 (hereafter, Lancs. and Ches. *Trans.*). The inhabitants had agitated for the vote in 1628 also. *Ibid.*, 92.

[243] *Rebellion* 2: 473.

[244] In January, 1640, just before the Short Parliament elections, the Earl of Huntingdon requested the choice of his son by either county or borough. James Thompson, *The history of Leicester,* 359, Leicester, 1849 (hereafter, Thompson, *Leicester*).

[245] Leicester return, C. 219/43/Part 2.

[246] The Earl of Huntingdon's son was rejected. Thompson, *Leicester,* 359; *H.M.C., Eighth Report,* MSS of the Corporation of Leicester, 436, 437.

[247] Thompson, *Leicester,* 361.

[248] Quoted in a newsletter to Lord Scudamore, 2 March 1640, Add. MSS, 11,045, fol. 99v.

ments, and three sheriffs of the ship money period, now elected to the House, had delayed much in their collection duties. Prominent resisters of the 1627 forced loan also were chosen, and the majority leaned toward Presbyterianism or Independency in their religion.

Most of the members were Lincolnshire men by birth and residence, although one man, owner of land in the county, lived over the border in Northamptonshire. With the possible exception of one Lincoln city member, Broxholme, whose family may have been in business there, they were lawyers and country gentlemen.

The Lincolnshire knights, elected on 12 October, were two gentlemen of prominent families, both experienced in earlier parliaments, and in county affairs, and well known for their opposition to the court. They were Sir John Wray, Bart., of Glentworth and Sir Edward Ayscough of South Kelsey. The former had been in the Short Parliament, but Ayscough's place had then been occupied by a royalist sympathizer.

Chosen at the Boston guildhall on 10 October by the mayor and burgesses [249] were two lawyers, both of whom had represented Boston in the spring. Sir Anthony Irby of Boston and Whaplode, and William Ellis, recorder of the town, were both strong parliamentarians.

Grantham was a borough within the queen's dower lands and sometimes subject to her influence.[250] The electorate, which was the assembly comprised of alderman and burgesses,[251] chose on 16 October for its first place a parliamentarian and for the second, the son of a royalist family. The former was Henry Pelham of Gray's Inn and of Belvoir, for some years deputy recorder for Grantham and one of its M.P.'s in the spring. The other was Thomas Hussey of Honington, who had served in no previous parliament, and who died in March, 1641, before his political views became clear. The borough promptly chose in his place, 29 March 1641,[252] a wealthy gentleman, long an opponent of the crown in earlier parliaments, Sir William Armine of Osgodby.

Great Grimsby's members, both of whom had served for the borough before, were Sir Christopher Wray of Ashby and Barlings, a neighbor of the town, and Gervase Holles, a native and periodic resident of Grimsby, and once its mayor. They were of opposite political views, Holles being the royalist, but their election by the mayor and burgesses [253] was more probably influenced by local traditions and friendships than by national politics.

Lincoln city elected on 19 October two active parliamentarians. Thomas Grantham of Goltho, one of the city's members in the spring, was a part time resident

of Lincoln, and John Broxholme was a native and lived there much of the time. He had never before been an M.P., and his election now to the seat filled in the spring by Dr. John Farmerie, the bishop's chancellor,[254] must have been counted a real puritan victory.[255]

The Stamford members were Thomas Hatcher of Careby, who had served for Stamford in the spring and was of the country party, and Geoffrey Palmer of Carlton, Northamptonshire. The latter owned lands near Stamford, but had never before served for this or any other borough. He was probably chosen because of his zeal for reform, although by the end of 1641 he was outspoken in his loyalty to the king.

MIDDLESEX

Middlesex, with its two county members, four for London, and two for Westminster, displayed the independence characteristic of the metropolitan area by electing a solid popular party representation to the Commons, and confirming the decision in the London by-election of 1641 to replace a deceased member. All were residents of the shire or of the city, although their places of birth were as distant as Somerset, Staffordshire, and Wales, and their interests had made them conversant with matters in the Indies and the Levant, Virginia, and Massachusetts. There had been some uncertainties at the spring elections, but those of the autumn, returning in each place the men chosen in the spring, passed without undue excitement. The London region's opposition to the royal prerogative, whether in the form of ship money or new customs duties or abuses of the courts, was mirrored by the members who served for it in the Commons of 1640.

The Middlesex county members chosen were Sir Gilbert Gerard, Bart., of Harrow-on-the-Hill, and Sir John Franklin of Willesden, both well known in the county and both members for their shire in the Short Parliament and previously. They were parliamentarians and were probably elected with little opposition.[256]

The four London members returned in October were wealthy merchants, all of the opposition party, as was the one elected to a place vacated by death in the spring of 1641. The original four had been members in the spring parliament, the aldermen, Thomas Soame and Isaac Penington, councilman Matthew Cradock, and that outspoken merchant and oft-imprisoned foe of the crown, Samuel Vassall. There was probably less excitement at their re-election than there had been at the

---

[249] Boston indenture, C. 219/43/Part 2.

[250] The queen had commended a candidate for the Short Parliament. Grantham Corp. MSS, Court Minute Book, I, fols. 82v, 83.

[251] *Ibid.*; indenture, C. 219/43/Part 2.

[252] Grantham Corp. MSS, Court Minute Book, I, fol. 93.

[253] C. 219/43/Part 2.

[254] *M. of P.* 1: 482; Add. MSS, 11,045 (Scudamore papers), fol. 99v.

[255] According to the return, the electors were the two sheriffs, the mayor, nine aldermen, and some thirty "citizens." C. 219/43/Part 2.

[256] In 1621 Middlesex had declined to elect two royal nominees, arguing that the people could not have free access to privy councillors (*C.S.P. Dom., 1619–1623*, 200), and had emphasized the point in the elections of 1624 and 1625. (See Sir Gilbert Gerard.) The men who had defeated the court candidates in 1625 were chosen in 1640.

mayoralty election a few weeks before.[257] To succeed Cradock, the mayor, aldermen and citizens [258] elected on 1 June 1641 John Venn, a councilman.

Westminster city likewise re-elected on 16 October its members of the spring, John Glyn, the lawyer, who was the city's steward, and William Bell, an apothecary of long residence and activity in St. Margaret's parish. Both were parliamentarians.

MONMOUTHSHIRE

Monmouthshire was a county where family influence, such as that of the Herberts, was strong, but it was swayed also by royal servants in the offices of Wales. Since a dispute about the single seat for Monmouth borough went unsettled for more than three years, only the two county members actually worked in the House before 1642. One of these was a local magistrate, a gentleman of a county family, but his colleague for the shire and the two contestants for the borough seat, although they had connections with Monmouth or neighboring counties, were residents elsewhere. At least three of the four who were claimants to the three seats were probably royalists, although one of the borough candidates may have shifted afterwards. And two royalists had relatives who were active in the cause of parliament.

The county members were William Herbert of Wilton, Wilts, son of the influential Earl of Pembroke and Montgomery, and Sir Charles Williams, a native and resident of Monmouthshire. Herbert had turned toward royalism by 1644, though he seems to have cooperated with parliament as late as 1643; but Williams was probably a royalist at the start.

Monmouth, the only borough of the shire, and entitled to but one seat in the House, sent in two returns. One named Thomas Trevor, who was an auditor of the Duchy of Lancaster and son of a prominent royal official, and who became later a moderate supporter of parliament. The other named a courtier, William Watkins, who officiated for the crown in South Wales but resided at Westminster. Neither seems to have been permitted to serve for the borough on the basis of the 1640 return, although the election was not voided until 29 November 1644. The electorate of mayor, bailiffs, aldermen, and burgesses [259] was doubtless swayed by patrons outside of the town.

NORFOLK

Norfolk was a strongly parliamentarian county, only two of its twelve members returned in 1640 being royalists. With the exception of one of them, who was a nominee for the controlled borough of Castle Rising, all were Norfolk men who resided in or near the con-

stituencies that elected them. The townsmen particularly were ready to protest against ship money and those features of the Stuart program which had adversely affected their trade and industry, and most of the members were puritans, although in several instances moderates rather than extremists in that group were chosen. The issue at the elections seems not to have been that of reform, for that was generally desired, but of how far it should go, and the only case in which there was a double return, although it involved a royalist, was rather a matter of residence qualifications than of politics. There is little evidence of external pressure at any of the elections.

The county members chosen at Norwich on 12 October 1640 were John Potts, afterwards Sir John Potts, of Mannington and Sir Edmund Moundeford of Feltwell, both county magistrates and well known men. Both supported parliament, but Potts, who had been defeated in the spring election for the shire, was more moderate in his religious views than Moundeford.

Castle Rising, a borough of few inhabitants and dominated by the Howards, earls of Arundel,[260] returned originally Sir John Holland, Bart., of Quidenham, who was agent for some of the earl's estates, and Sir Christopher Hatton of Northamptonshire. When the latter preferred the borough of Higham Ferrers instead, the vacancy was filled by his uncle, Sir Robert Hatton of Cambridgeshire and of Kent.[261] Holland was a parliamentarian, but both Hattons were royalists.

King's Lynn's election resembled earlier ones in that the corporation declined to accept a nominee from without, limiting the choice to residents of the borough, but differed from others in that for the first time the voting was thrown open to the freemen.[262] Those selected were two leading aldermen and merchants, John Percival and Thomas Toll. Both were parliamentarians and both reflected their borough's attitude of independence toward the authority of bishops.[263]

Two indentures were sent in for Norwich, both of them naming Richard Harman, a leading hosier and recent mayor of the city, for one place. The others named with Harman in alternate indentures were Richard Catelyn of Lakenham, who resided near Norwich but not within the city limits, and John Toolie, an alderman and one of the Norwich members in the spring.[264] The sheriff explained that he was not sure of Catelyn's eligibility because of his residence outside of the city, and that he sent in his name with the qualifi-

[257] See Thomas Soame. A newsletter of 27 October 1640 mentions a petition of grievances delivered to the newly elected M.P.'s "by the multitude." Add. MSS, 11,045, fol. 128v.

[258] C. 219/43/Part 2, London indenture.

[259] C. 219/43/Part 2.

[260] History and antiquities of the county of Norfolk 5, Freebridge Hundred: 96–97, Norwich, 1781.

[261] The election indentures of 1640, in the name of mayor and burgesses, listed not over 14 voters (C. 219/43/Part 2). In 1673 there were said to be 52 free burgage houses in the town possessed by 30 persons, of whom only 12 lived there. Bodleian Rawl. MSS, A, 172, fol. 149.

[262] H.M.C., Eleventh Report 3, MSS of King's Lynn, 149, 178; King's Lynn MSS, Hall Book 7, fol. 53v; 8, fols. 50, 65v.

[263] Ibid., Hall Book 8, fols. 6v, 9, 54v.

[264] M. of P. 1: 482, 491 and n.

cation that, if the House should find him not duly elected, then Toolie, a resident, should be considered returned instead. The Commons objected to the irregularity in the naming of three men and considered punishing the sheriff for a misdemeanor; however, finding that there seemed to have been no corruption about the management of the election, they decided to inflict no penalty. Harman and Catelyn were declared on 7 November to be duly elected, and the other indenture was ordered off the file.[264a] The Norwich assembly voted soon after the election, however, that thereafter none but a freeman of the city at the time of election should be chosen, and censured also the action of the county sheriff for his refusal to count in the shire election the voices of Norwich freeholders.[265] Harman was a popular party man, having worked in the city's interests against ship money and probably in the quarrels with the cathedral clergy. Catelyn, though favoring some of the early reforms, was leaning toward royalism by the end of 1642.

Thetford elected again on 16 October [266] its members of the spring, Sir Thomas Wodehouse, Bart., of Kimberley, and Framlingham Gawdy, Esq., of West Harling. The former, more moderate in his views than Gawdy, was opposed by the zealous puritan, Tobias Frere,[267] but both members were supporters of the parliamentary cause. It was to the approaching "happy parliament" that Gawdy had asked to be sent for his seventh time as Thetford's M.P.[268]

Elections at Great Yarmouth were in the hands of the corporation and afforded opportunity for attempts at patronage. The earls of Dorset and Northumberland, Steward of Yarmouth and Lord High Admiral, respectively, had recommended candidates for the Short Parliament and they doubtless wrote again in the autumn. The old rule requiring that a man be a freeman of the borough to be eligible for election had been abolished at the beginning of the reign of Charles, but no candidate proposed from without was elected on either occasion in 1640.[269] In both instances the borough chose two of its own men, Miles Corbet, their recorder, and Edward Owner, merchant and for many years champion of the town's rights. Both were parliamentarians.

[264a] C.J. 2: 22; D'Ewes (N), 5 and n. According to the returns, Harman received 1089 votes, Toolie, 275, and Catelyn, 906. C. 219/43/Part 2. Toolie was afterwards a royalist, but the records do not show what stand he took in 1640.

[265] Norwich Corporation MSS, Folio Assembly Book, 1613–1642, fols. 353v, 354. At the adoption of the resolution about future M.P.'s for the city it was stated that a group of voters "for some private ends" had voted for a non-freeman.

[266] The return of 16 October names as electors the mayor, burgesses and commonalty. C. 219/43/Part 2.

[267] V.C.H. Norfolk 2: 507.

[268] R. H. Mason, The history of Norfolk, 279, London, 1884.

[269] C. J. Palmer, ed., The history of Great Yarmouth, by Henry Manship 2: 202–207, Great Yarmouth, 1854–1856 (hereafter, Manship's Yarmouth).

NORTHAMPTONSHIRE

Puritanism and opposition to the crown had long been prevalent in Northamptonshire [270] and the elections of 1640 reflect the widespread discontent there. Resistance to the forced loans, clamor by "turbulent spirits" against the deputy lieutenants, and a general opposition to ship money [271] so strong that the 1640 sheriff, himself not impartial, described the county as "a great body charged with humors apt to be inflamed," [272] were the shire's response to the Stuart program; and a strongly parliamentarian group was returned in the October elections. Of the nine men only one was a royalist, and in the two instances of challenged returns, the issue was more that of the local franchise than of the king's prerogative. But the county had its men of royalist leaning, too, whose position became clearer as war approached, men such as the Earl of Manchester and Lord Northampton. It may not be insignificant that at least three county men who took the king's side in 1642 found their seats for the 1640 parliament in boroughs outside the county.[273] Those who sat for Northamptonshire and its boroughs were almost all residents of the county or of places nearby.

The members for Northamptonshire, elected 29 October 1640, were Sir Gilbert Pickering, Bart., of Titchmarsh, and his uncle, Sir John Dryden, Bart., of Canons Ashby. Their fathers had been active in county affairs and leaders in resistance to the Stuart policies, and both were themselves strong parliament men.

The mayor and burgesses of Brackley [274] returned on 28 October John Crew of Stene, who had been a county member in the spring and owned land near the town, and Sir Martin Lister of Bucks and Leicestershire, owner of land in the county and in the previous session M.P. for Brackley. Both were popular party men.

Higham Ferrers, a borough in the queen's jointure,[275] chose as its single member Sir Christopher Hatton, K.B., of the prominent county family, and steward of the town.[276] He was the only royalist in the county's delegation.

Northampton, where Strafford's policies were dis-

---

[270] Dr. Sibthorpe wrote in June, 1638, of the widespread nonconformity there. C.S.P. Dom., 1637–1638, 535.

[271] Ibid., 1639–1640, 587; Royal Hist. Soc., Trans., 3rd Ser., 4: 159, 1910; and sketches of the Northamptonshire members.

[272] Yelverton to Nicholas, 17 February 1640, S.P. 16, 445/54.

[273] Geoffrey Palmer, M.P. for Stamford, Lincolnshire; Sir Robert Hatton, M.P. for the controlled borough of Castle Rising, Norfolk; Sir Edward Griffin, M.P. for Downton, Wilts. All were named in the Northamptonshire commission of array in 1642. Brit. Mus. Bibl. Eg., 1048, fol. 16.

[274] Brackley indenture, C. 219/43/Part 2.

[275] V.C.H. Northampton 3: 271.

[276] Hatton's successor was chosen by the mayor, aldermen and burgesses (C. 219/43/Part 2), and possibly Hatton was chosen likewise, for after the Short Parliament election a committee had given its opinion that the borough's new charter sanctioned not a closed electorate but one of all resident freeholders. Opinions of Sir Robert Heath, Geoffrey Palmer and Mr. St. John, Northants MSS, F.H. 3467, 3500.

liked, and where the franchise was regularly limited to the members of the borough council, had a contest and resulting petition because a hundred or two of the freemen had attempted to vote.[277]   The case was unlike that of the spring,[278] for the men chosen now by the closed group were both parliamentarians, and one of them was the choice also of the excluded freemen, an evidence of the strength of the opposition sentiment in the borough which had been built up in the era of ship money.   Both returns sent by the corporation were irregular because they lacked the mayor's signature, but the Committee of Privileges recommended on 6 January 1641 the temporary seating of the men so returned, and no further reference to the case appears in the records.[279] Both had sat for Northampton in the spring.   The family of Richard Knightley of Fawsley had frequently represented the borough, regularly since 1621, but Zouch Tate of Delapré may have been helped to his place by his father's friend, Edward Lord Montagu of Boughton, whose influence in the town was great.[280]

Peterborough had at least three candidates and sent in a double return.   Both indentures named William Fitzwilliam of Milton, son of Lord Fitzwilliam, whose family were influential in the town and who had sat for it in the spring.   Contestants for the other seat were Sir Robert Napier, Bart., of Luton Hoo, Bedfordshire, and Anthony Fane, a younger son of the Earl of Westmorland.   The House voted on 9 November and 6 January to seat Fitzwilliam, since he was named on both returns, and on 4 February to recognize Napier as the second member.[281]   Since all three were supporters of parliament, the issue at the election seems to have been that of the franchise rather than of the political views of the candidates.

NORTHUMBERLAND

Northumberland's group of eight representatives reveals the divergent influences, military, political, religious, and economic, at work in that harassed border county.   Two friends of the court sat for the shire, although one of them, Henry Percy, probably owed his place as much to his brother, the Earl of Northumberland, as to royal influence.   Two royalists sat for Morpeth.   But in the two principal towns, Berwick and Newcastle, the member of the Council of the North

nominated for each by Strafford [282] found his election contested both locally and in parliament, and was replaced in each case by a man willing to work for reform. One of these owed his place to the Earl of Northumberland, but a group of puritan townsmen probably accounted for the Newcastle member.   According to the final division, five of those seated were royalists, but the records show that another of the group, Sir Henry Anderson of Newcastle and Yorkshire, was a vigorous foe of Strafford and Laud in 1640.   Six of the members were natives of the county, the outsiders being Percy and Scawen, Northumberland's nominees.   The disappointed candidates of Strafford, Melton and Osborne, came from York.

The shire knights for Northumberland were men who had of recent months been active in military affairs on the border.   Henry Percy, though of the old northern family, had previously been more familiar with the southern counties and the court.   But Sir William Widdrington of Widdrington had for some time been prominent in Northumberland.   Both were friends of the court and were expelled early as royalists.

Berwick-on-Tweed saw the intervention in its election on 3 October not only of the Earl of Northumberland but of the military governor of the town, Sir John Conyers, acting by power of his office and as agent for Strafford.   The townsmen rejected for first place both Northumberland's nominee, his secretary, Hugh Potter, who had served for Berwick in the Short Parliament, and Conyers's candidate.   For that seat they chose instead their other Short Parliament member, their recorder, Sir Thomas Widdrington of Cheesebourne Grange, who was said to have had Strafford's support. Conyers succeeded in getting the less desirable second seat for Strafford's nominee, Sir Edward Osborne, Vice President of the Council of the North.[283]   The Committee of Privileges reported unfavorably on Osborne's case, however, probably on the basis of complaints from Northumberland's friends, and on 7 December 1640 the House voided Osborne's election and ordered a new one.[284]   Two weeks later the Berwick electors chose another of Northumberland's secretaries, Robert Scawen of Cornwall and London,[285] and he entered promptly upon his duties.   Both he and Widdrington were strong parliamentarians.

The Morpeth members were two local men, both royalists.   Sir William Carnaby of Thernham had served for the town in two parliaments of the 1620's,

[277] *Ibid.*, F.H. 3501; *Records of the borough of Northampton,* edited by C. A. Markham and J. C. Cox, 2: 435–437, 496, London, 1898 (hereafter, *Records of Northampton*).

[278] D'Ewes (N), 222, n.

[279] *Ibid.; C.J.* 2: 63.

[280] Sir Philip Warwick, *Memoires of the reigne of King Charles I,* 222, 1701 (hereafter, Warwick, *Memoires*); H.M.C., *MSS of Lord Montagu of Beaulieu,* 87, 88–89.

[281] *C.J.* 2: 23, 63, 78; D'Ewes (N), 222–223, 326. D'Ewes mentions the right of election in this case but does not explain the circumstances. The lists of signatures on the two indentures at the Public Record Office (C. 219/43/Part 2) are distinctly different, suggesting that the extent of the franchise may have been the issue.

[282] Four of the Northumberland group, however, voted against Strafford's attainder: Carnaby, Fenwick, Scawen (a parliamentarian in other respects), and Sir William Widdrington. Verney, 58.

[283] *C.S.P. Dom., 1640–1641,* 258, 404. The Berwick indenture of 3 October was signed by the mayor and four bailiffs in full court. C. 219/43/Part 2. Widdrington and Osborne had been rejected at York five days before.

[284] D'Ewes (N), 119 and n.

[285] Indenture of 22 December, reporting the election of 21 December. C. 219/43/Part 2.

but John Fenwick, heir apparent to the Fenwicks of Wallington, was a newcomer to civic office.[286]

At Newcastle-on-Tyne the restlessness which was an outgrowth of the spread of puritanism, the monopolies in the soap and coal trades, and the levies of ship money and tonnage and poundage was in evidence at the choice of a new lecturer in the winter of 1639–1640 and at the elections for the Short Parliament.[287] It is not surprising that the October elections produced a double return. One seems to have named Sir Henry Anderson and Sir John Melton, and another to have named John Blakiston.[288] Anderson, who in 1640 was living at Long Cowton in Yorkshire, but was a former Newcastle mayor with interests in the coal trade, was present in parliament early in November, and his seat was apparently not challenged. He was zealous for reforms, but was eventually disabled as a royalist. Sir John Melton, courtier and Secretary of the Council of the North, probably never took his seat in the House, for the election case had not been determined when he died on 16 December. The next day the House voted to await the report on the original election instead of ordering a new one at once, and on 30 January 1641 Blakiston's election was declared good and the sheriff was notified to come to amend the return.[289] Melton was doubtless Strafford's nominee. Blakiston, a Newcastle mercer who was already known for his views on the church, was a strong parliamentarian.

NOTTINGHAMSHIRE

Nottinghamshire, on whose soil the king's standard was raised in 1642, was a county where resistance to ship money had not been flagrant,[290] and where the 1640 elections went off without undue excitement. No results were challenged, and all those selected were of county families and residence. Four of the six were royalists, although one of the most devoted of these, Robert Sutton, seems to have been interested in the early reform measures of the Long Parliament. The other two were outstanding as puritan and parliament leaders, one being the father of Colonel John Hutchinson and the other, Millington, a regicide.

The county members elected at Nottingham shire hall on 2 November 1640[291] were Sir Thomas Hutchinson of Owthorpe and Robert Sutton of Averham, both county men of prominence, and both members for the shire in the Short Parliament. They worked together for reforms in the early months, but Sutton was an acknowledged royalist by 1642.

The East Retford bailiffs and burgesses[292] returned the youthful heir apparent of William Cavendish, Earl of Newcastle, Charles Lord Mansfield, and the town's high steward and M.P. of the spring, Sir Gilbert Clifton, Bart., of Clifton. Both were royalists.

Nottingham borough, which for the 1628 parliament had elected "strangers" from the neighboring gentry for the admitted purpose of saving expense and gaining powerful support for the town's interests,[293] chose in 1640 two men who were outside of the corporation. William Stanhope of Linbey, who had lived in Nottingham most of the preceding decade, was a half-brother of the Earl of Chesterfield, as well as brother-in-law of Sir Thomas Hutchinson, and became a royalist eventually. The other member, Gilbert Millington of Felley Abbey, lawyer, county magistrate, and later regicide, probably owed his election less to family influence than to his reputation as an active public official.

OXFORDSHIRE

Oxfordshire had displayed before November, 1640, considerable opposition to the crown, especially in the matter of ship money and the pressing of troops.[294] Its delegation to the Long Parliament was made up largely of men interested in reforms, both administrative and ecclesiastical. Four sons of noblemen were in the original group returned, but two of them, royalists, vacated their seats early and were replaced by commoners. Two prominent courtiers served, the privy councillor, Sir Thomas Roe, and the Exchequer official, Sir Robert Pye, but neither was ousted from parliament for royalism, although the former's absences abroad may have been what spared him. Three lawyers elected in Oxfordshire played important roles in the House, Speaker Lenthall, John Selden, and John Whistler, of whom the latter turned royalist in time. John Smith, former mayor of Oxford, lacked distinction either of birth or by profession, but he was a royalist. The delegation was almost evenly divided in their final choice of sides, most of them being moderate members of their respective factions. And most of them were county men or from neighboring shires, though Selden and Roe hailed from more distant parts. The pressure at the elections, except at the university, was chiefly that of noblemen powerful in the shire, such as Lord Say and Sele, the Earl of Pembroke and Montgomery, and the Earl of Berkshire. The elections seem to have occurred without undue excitement or more than the usual efforts at control.

The county knights, elected 28 October 1640, were Thomas Lord Wenman of Thame Park and James Fiennes, elder son of Viscount Say and Sele, one of the

---

[286] The electors were the two bailiffs and the burgesses of the town. C. 219/43/Part 2.

[287] C.S.P. Dom., 1639, 450; 1639–1640, 384, 402, 600–603; S.P. 16, 439/76.

[288] The original returns are missing. The editors of M. of P. (1: 491 and n.) were uncertain as to the order of the elections.

[289] C.J. 2: 53, 76, 90, 93; D'Ewes (N), 385; Bean, Northern counties, 564.

[290] C.S.P. Dom., 1637, 410.

[291] Nottinghamshire indenture, C. 219/43/Part 2.

[292] These were the electors, according to a 1644 indenture, C. 219/43/Part 2.

[293] Nottingham Corporation MSS, Hall Book 1627–1628, fol. 57.

[294] C.S.P. Dom., 1637–1638, 566; 1639, 246; 1640–1641, 70, 125; Royal Hist. Soc., Trans., 3rd Ser., 4: 160, 1910.

leaders in the opposition movement. Both were county men and parliamentarians. According to Bulstrode Whitelocke, he and Sir William Waller had been urged by friends to try for the election, too. When they learned, however, that Wenman and Fiennes were joining their forces to secure both seats, "the usual course for menambira Magistratum, though not so honourable as a free election," and recalled that both were noblemen of "great fortunes, interest & dependency," [295] they decided not to make the attempt.

Banbury, where the electors were the mayor, aldermen, and burgesses,[296] returned for its single member Nathaniel Fiennes, the younger son of its High Steward, Viscount Say and Sele. He had been elected there in the spring also, and was a parliamentarian.

The Oxford city members were chosen on 12 October 1640 by the mayor, bailiffs, and "commonalty," the latter group having a choice only from those nominated by the mayor and council. The city recorder, John Whistler, won the first place, defeating by 340 to 317 Charles Lord Andover. But the latter, son of the town's High Steward, the Earl of Berkshire, then gained the second seat by defeating, 463–296, the former mayor of Oxford, John Smith. When the young nobleman left the House of Commons to go to the Peers on 18 November, Smith was promptly elected to the vacancy.[297] Lord Andover and Smith were both royalists and Whistler, though an active worker for reforms, especially of the church, was eventually disabled as a royalist.

Oxford University was represented by two famous gentlemen, Sir Thomas Roe, diplomat and privy councillor, and John Selden, the lawyer and foe of abuses. Secretary Windebank's nephew, writing after his uncle had failed to regain the university seat he had held in the Short Parliament, commented on the influence of "some higher power," but rejoiced that "the Puritan faction prevailed not." [298] Both men had studied at Oxford, but neither resided in the county in 1640.

Woodstock was a town long influenced by the Herbert family, the stewardship of the royal manor there carrying considerable patronage over elections.[299] But in 1640 there was perhaps some objection to their control, for two returns were filed. One, dated October 23, and purporting to be by the "burgesses and freemen," named Sir William Fleetwood and Benjamin Mericke, gent.; the other, dated October 27, reported the election by the unanimous vote of the mayor and commonalty of William Lenthall, who was the town's recorder, and William Herbert, a younger son of the Earl of Pembroke.[300] The earlier return was not recognized by the House, perhaps because of its irregularity. But young Herbert, having been elected by two other constituencies, decided not to serve for Woodstock. A new return, dated 2 December, named in his place Sir Robert Pye, Auditor of the Exchequer, and it may be surmised that he, too, owed the place to Pembroke.[301] Lenthall was an Oxfordshire man. Pye lived nearby in Berkshire when he was not at court, but seems to have had no connection personally with Woodstock. Both upheld parliament, although Pye had begun his court career under the wing of Buckingham.

RUTLAND

The Rutland county members chosen in October, 1640, at Okeham, were the men who had served also in the Short Parliament, both of them county residents. Sir Guy Palmes of Ashwell, an active worker in the popular faction in his younger days, absented himself from the House as the rift with the king widened, but his younger colleague, Baptist Noel of Exton, a nobleman's son, was a royalist from the start.

SHROPSHIRE

The Shropshire group in the 1640 Commons were all men connected with the county, either by birth, business, or marriage. There is no evidence of external influences in the elections, although one or two of the boroughs were practically family boroughs, and Ludlow was intimately associated with the Council of the Marches of Wales. There seems to have been little concerted resistance to the ship money collections in the county, despite a petition from one area in 1639 for a revision of the rates,[302] nor widespread dissatisfaction with the Council of the Marches.[303] Yet it is interesting to note that of the six constituencies sending members four, including the county, split their votes to return a royalist paired with a parliamentarian, and that the two boroughs which returned both members of the same party, royalists in each case, were the family owned borough of Bridgnorth and Ludlow, seat of the royal administration for the border.

---

[295] Whitelocke's "Annals," Add. MSS, 37,343, fols. 206v–207.
[296] Banbury indenture, C. 219/43/Part 2.
[297] Oxford Corporation MSS, A.5.7, Council Book, 1629–1663, fols. 104v–105, 110; C.J. 2: 30; Oxford indenture, C. 219/43/Part 2.
[298] Dr. Thomas Read to his brother, Robert, 26 October 1640. C.S.P. Dom., 1640–1641, 197. The Earl of Pembroke, as chancellor of the university, had several times influenced its elections (E.H.R. 50: 250, 251, 1935). The chancellor who succeeded him was Laud.
[299] Ibid.; Liber Famicus of Sir James Whitelocke, 19, 40.

[300] The latter indenture was worded briefly and formally in Latin and was attested by the town seal but no signature. The other, written in English and declaring that the sheriff's warrant had been directed "to us, the Burgesses and Freemen," was signed personally by over fifty men (C. 219/43/Part 2). The Latin return may well have come from the pocket of the Herberts.
[301] The new return follows the same form as that naming Lenthall and Herbert. Woodstock indentures, C. 219/43/Part 2.
[302] Add. MSS, 25,040, fols. 107v–108. A large proportion of the assessments until the last year was paid. Royal Hist. Soc., Trans., 3rd Ser., 4: 161, 1910.
[303] For politics in Shropshire, 1640–1642, see Shropshire Archaeological and Natural History Society, Transactions, 4th Ser., 18: 11–39, 1941–1943 (hereafter, Shrops. Arch. Soc., Trans.).

The economic interests of the county are reflected more clearly, perhaps, than its political or religious views. Of the twelve members one was a royal official, a good many were country gentlemen of established families, but two were the sons of families connected also with Londoners in the wool trade (Whitmore and Acton), and one, William Spurstow, who had been brought up in the woolen business in Shrewsbury, was a prominent London merchant with an experience of nearly four decades in handling relations between London and the counties and foreign ports.

The Shropshire knights were Sir John Corbet of Stoke-upon-Terne and his cousin, Sir Richard Lee, Bart., of Langley and Acton Burnell. Both had been active in county affairs, but they differed in politics, Corbet being a parliamentarian and Lee, a royalist.

Bishop's Castle, part of the honor of Clun, elected [304] on 24 October 1640 Sir Robert Howard, lord of the manor [305] and frequently M.P. for the borough, and a neighboring gentleman who likewise had represented the town earlier, Richard More of Linley. Howard, whose morals were notorious, was a royalist. His colleague was strongly puritanical and a parliamentarian.

Bridgnorth, by unanimous vote of its bailiffs and burgesses, returned on 12 October 1640,[306] as it had the preceding spring, two men who were related to the owner of Bridgnorth Castle, both of them royalists. They were Edward Acton of Aldenham Hall and his kinsman, Thomas Whitmore of Apley, son of the borough's chief landlord.

Ludlow, a closed corporation under its charter issued by James I,[307] returned on 10 October 1640 the two men who had been elected there in the spring. They were local men, Charles Baldwin of Elsich, and Ralph Goodwin, an official connected with the Council of the Marches who had been M.P. for Ludlow several times before. They were said to have had to labor much with purses and feasts for the burgesses to win the spring election against Sir Robert Napier (q.v.), son-in-law of the Earl of Bridgwater,[308] but there is no record of a contest in October. Both men were royalists.

At Shrewsbury there had been more agitation against ship money than elsewhere in the county, and there was dissatisfaction, also, about a Laudian curate at one of

the churches.[309] But the town in the Long Parliament election [310] chose a royalist as one of its parliament men. He was Francis Newport of High Ercall, son of one of the wealthiest gentlemen of the county and of a family influential for several generations in Shrewsbury. The other member, representative of the town's business interests and of the newer thought in religion and politics, was William Spurstow. Once a draper of Shrewsbury, Spurstow was by 1640 a Londoner and a leader in overseas mercantile enterprises.

The Great Wenlock members chosen on 26 October 1640 by the bailiff and burgesses [311] were Thomas Littleton of Stoke Milburgh, a law student whose father was Wenlock's recorder, and William Pierrepont, whose principal residence was outside the county, but who by marriage had gained Shropshire lands and offices. The latter was a moderate parliamentarian. Littleton was a royalist.

SOMERSET

Somerset had had vigorous spokesmen for the liberties of the subject in the earlier Stuart parliaments, and several of those who were returned in October, 1640, had been of that number, or were sons of such leaders. Ship money had been protested more than once in the county, and in 1639–1640, when the sheriff was of opposition views, the collections were poor.[312] The principal church dignitary of the county, the Bishop of Bath and Wells, was among those most vigorously attacked after parliament opened.[313] But when the test of war came, the majority of the Somerset parliament men took the side of the king. Of the eighteen men who served for John Pym's native county before January, 1642, excluding Lord Digby, who decided not to occupy the seat offered him by one of the Somerset boroughs, only five were parliamentarians from start to finish. But at least five others, though royalists in the end, must have been reckoned as popular party supporters at the time of their election.[314] The two disputed elections, those of the shire and Ilchester, perhaps had family rivalries as much as national issues involved, for there had been feuds in Somerset before between such royalists as Stawell and the opposition Phelipps family, and the latter's part-time partisans, the Pouletts. Although the political complexion of the delegation was not permanently changed by the three by-elections (Bridgwater, Ilchester, and Milborne Port), two of the three men so elected were probably sympathetic with the opposition before they turned to the king. One of them replaced a courtier-monopolist.

The group were country gentlemen, principally, but

---

[304] The bailiff and burgesses were the electors, according to the indenture. C. 219/43/Part 2.

[305] The borough had been in the hands of the earls of Suffolk and Northampton, temp. James I, and the town consulted Northampton regarding their choice of a member for a by-election in 1610. Shrops. Arch. Soc., Trans., 2nd Ser., 10: 43, 1898; 1st Ser., 10: 133, 1887.

[306] Bridgnorth indenture, C. 219/43/Part 2.

[307] Its electors, consisting of 12 aldermen and 25 common councillors (Harl. MSS, 6806, fol. 257), were described in the return as the bailiffs and burgesses. C. 219/43/Part 2.

[308] Shrops. Arch. Soc., Trans., 2nd Ser., 7: 25, 26, 1895; Willis, 3: 235. Napier's election to the Long Parliament for Peterborough, Northamptonshire, did not occur until nearly two weeks after the Ludlow election.

[309] Shrops. Arch. Soc., Trans., 4th Ser., 16: 30–36, 1937–1938.

[310] The electors were the mayor, aldermen, and burgesses. C. 219/43/Part 2.

[311] Wenlock indenture, C. 219/43/Part 2.

[312] C.S.P. Dom., 1639–1640, 569, 580; Royal Hist. Soc., Trans., 3rd Ser., 4: 160, 1910.

[313] D'Ewes (N), 542.

[314] J. Digby, E. Kirton, Phelipps, Poulett, T. Smith.

there was a lawyer, Hunt, a courtier, Windham, and a Taunton citizen, Searle, who was probably a merchant. The two Pophams lived chiefly in Wiltshire, but owned Somerset lands and had family connections there; the Digbys were from Dorset. Sir Peter Wroth, a resident of Kent and London, was the only one who might be called a carpetbagger, but he probably had lands in the county, was present at the shire election, and seems to have been chosen as virtually a proxy for his brother, Sir Thomas Wroth, who was active in county affairs. Noble families whose influence undoubtedly played a part behind the scenes in the election were those of Digby, Seymour, and Poulett.

The Somerset knights elected on 12 October 1640 at Ilchester were Sir John Poulett of Hinton St. George and Sir John Stawell, K.B., of Cothelstone. Both were of prominent local families, but neither had sat in the Short Parliament. Both were royalists in the war, but the Pouletts were of the popular side before 1640. A petition about the election was referred on 9 November to the Committee of Privileges, but it was never reported out of committee.[315] Possibly it was a protest of Poulett's brother-in-law, Thomas Smith, who had been county M.P. in the spring.[316] The other Short Parliament member, Hopton, who was elected four days later at Wells, had probably not sought re-election by the shire.

The members for Bath returned on 21 October were William Bassett of Claverton and Alexander Popham of Littlecote, Wilts. The latter, who had sat for Bath in the spring and doubtless owed his seat to his father's influence in the county, was a strong parliamentarian. Bassett, although he showed some coolness toward the royal administration in the 1630's, was a royalist.

Bridgwater elected on 16 October, by its mayor, aldermen, and chief burgesses,[317] as one member Sir Peter Wroth of Kent, who was a brother of their recorder and sometime M.P. Wroth supported parliament until his death in 1644. The other member was Edmund Windham of Kentsford, a courtier, who was disabled in January, 1641, because he was a monopolist. He was replaced by Thomas Smith of Long Ashton, who had sat for the borough in 1628 and for the county in the spring, and as Lord Poulett's son-in-law was doubtless regarded as of the popular side. He was fighting for the king in 1642.

The Ilchester election of 14 October was voided by vote of the Commons on 15 February 1641 on the ground that due notice of the election had not been given. Sir Henry Berkeley of Yarlington and Robert Hunt of Speckington therefore withdrew, although both had already participated in the work of the House.[318]

Hunt was re-elected, but Berkeley was replaced by Edward Phelipps of Montacute, son of a prominent popular leader of earlier years. There may have been politics in the voiding of the election, since the Berkeleys were friends of the court, and both Hunt and Phelipps were connected with opposition circles in Somerset and Dorset. But both of the Ilchester members in time deserted to the king.

The bailiff and burgesses of Milborne Port elected [319] on 17 October George Lord Digby, eldest son of the Earl of Bristol, and Edward Kirton of Castle Cary, agent of the Seymour family in the county. After Lord Digby decided to serve for his home county of Dorset, 9 November 1640,[320] his place at Milborne Port was given to his younger brother, John Digby. All the Milborne members favored reform at the start of the parliament, but all eventually turned to the king.

Minehead seems to have been controlled in this period partly by the Luttrells of Dunster Castle.[321] A kinsman of the family had sat in the Short Parliament, and both of the Long Parliament members were related to the head of the family, Thomas Luttrell. They were his father-in-law, Sir Francis Popham of Littlecote, Wilts, and his eldest son, Alexander Luttrell. The former was a parliamentarian, and the latter was probably accounted of that party, although he was too young to have weight in politics and died before the war began.

Taunton, a town that suffered severely from the plague in 1640, returned its mayor, George Searle, and a neighboring gentleman, Sir William Portman, Bart., of Orchard Portman, who had been its representative in the spring. The latter was a royalist, but Searle sat in parliament until the end.

The city of Wells elected on 16 October Sir Ralph Hopton of Witham, who had served as its M.P. in 1628, and Sir Edward Rodney of Stoke Rodney, elected many times before for Wells. Both were prominent in the county then and were as prominent afterwards for their royalism.

STAFFORDSHIRE

Staffordshire, home county of the Earl of Essex, reflected his influence in its 1640 elections. But there are indications also of pressure from powerful royalist families within the county and nearby. There are signs too of a desire among the local gentry for relief from the annoyances of the king's personal rule, but a desire not strong enough to countenance rebellion. No election contests in the shire are recorded. The county and Stafford borough re-elected their members of the spring, and the other boroughs, which, with the possible exception of Lichfield, were more or less closed, were influenced according to tradition by big

---

315 *C.J.* 2: 22.

316 Smith's finding a place for Bridgwater after a vacancy occurred early there may explain the dropping of the matter. Smith was a royalist by 1642.

317 Indenture, C. 219/43/Part 2.

318 *C.J.* 2: 34, 85; D'Ewes (N), 361.

319 Indenture, C. 219/43/Part 2.

320 *M. of P.* 1: 493 and n.; *C.J.* 2: 25.

321 H. C. Maxwell Lyte, *A history of Dunster and the families of Mohun and Luttrell* 1: 179, London, St. Catherine Press, 1909; *M. of P.*

land owners nearby. An unusually large number of by-elections occurred in Staffordshire before 1642, both the county and Lichfield losing by death members who were inclined toward the opposition, and Tamworth having to fill one of its places three times. The royalists gained in the by-elections of the county and Lichfield and in the second, but not the third, at Tamworth. As to the other members, both of those for Stafford and one for Newcastle were consistent royalists, and the survivor of the original county knights, Littleton, became so in time. The only continuously country party men who sat from the start were a puritan newcomer from Lichfield and a Welsh-born soldier returned by Newcastle. Of the fourteen men named in the returns, 1640–1642, only seven were really Staffordshire men, but four others came from neighboring counties and probably had family connections with the shire.

The Staffordshire members, elected at Stafford [322] on 8 October 1640, were Sir William Bowyer of Knypersley and Sir Edward Littleton, Bart., of Pillaton. Both had sat in the Short Parliament and sympathized with the reform movement. Bowyer died early in 1641, however, and in his place was chosen Sir Harvey Bagot of Blithfield, another prominent man of the county. He was disabled as a royalist less than two years afterwards and Littleton, too, went over to the king in time.

The original members for Lichfield, elected on 8 October 1640, were Sir Walter Devereux, stepbrother of the Earl of Essex, who had been chosen in the spring also, and Michael Noble. The latter was a newcomer to parliament, and was a resident of the cathedral close and Town Clerk of Lichfield. Both men were parliamentarians, but when Devereux died in the summer of 1641, a friend of the court was chosen (12 August) in his place. The latter was Sir Richard Cave, who was currently in the service of the Elector Palatine. [323]

Newcastle-under-Lyme was a borough that was frequently controlled by the owners of Trentham manor. [324] The electors, probably few more than a hundred, [325] seem to have included the principal officials, the twenty-four chief burgesses, and various "common" burgesses, and their choice of 13 October 1640 was reported as unanimous. [326] One of the men so returned was the owner of Trentham manor, Sir Richard Leveson, a royalist. The other, who was probably nominated for both of the 1640 elections by the Earl of Essex, was Sir John Meyrick,

a professional soldier who was born in Wales and was a parliamentarian.

Stafford re-elected the members chosen [327] in the spring, two young sons of local gentlemen, Ralph Sneyde, junior, of Keele, and Richard Weston, junior, of Rugeley. Both were royalists.

The Tamworth members, returned 12 October 1640, were entirely different from those chosen in the spring. There had been an attempt then to secure a broader franchise, [328] but the results in the autumn suggest that powerful lords still exerted considerable pressure. Ferdinando Stanhope, a royalist, son of the Earl of Chesterfield, probably owed his seat to his father, who had married the widow of Sir Humphrey Ferrers of Tamworth Castle. But the return of William Strode, the popular party leader from Devon, indicates pressure from the other side, possibly the hand of Essex. [329] The choice a month later of Henry Wilmot, an army man, when Strode decided to serve for a Devon borough, may have resulted from the influence of Essex, also. Wilmot's desertion to the king before the next summer again opened the place, and this time (18 December 1641) a genuine foe of the crown was chosen, Sir Peter Wentworth of Lillingston Lovell, Bucks. Ferdinando Stanhope had had little connection with Tamworth or the county, and the three men who were chosen in succession for the other seat were all foreign to the shire.

SUFFOLK

In Suffolk, where puritanism was widespread, where the wool trade was declining, and where there had been grumbling and even rioting against the impressment of soldiers, the Long Parliament elections produced a delegation predominantly Roundhead. Twelve of the sixteen members were parliamentarians, although several of those so labelled had before the parliament seemed inclined to support the crown and were only lukewarm toward parliament during the war; [330] and only a minority, chiefly from the seaport towns, became active partisans for the rebellion. The royalists, including the Comptroller of the Household and his son, were all of Suffolk families and probably gained their places as much by family influence as by royal pressure. Most of the members were Suffolk men by birth or residence, but one Orford member lived chiefly in Norfolk, and the seacoast town of Aldeburgh chose a Londoner, a

[322] Staffordshire indenture, C. 219/43/Part 2. Sir Harvey Bagot was one of the first signers of the return for Bowyer and Littleton.

[323] Cave's election in the full county court of the city was by some forty citizens. Michael Noble was present and signed the return. C. 219/43/Part 2.

[324] Wedgwood, *Staff. Parl. Hist.* 2: xix.

[325] Slightly over 100 inhabitants gathered to take the Protestation in May, 1641. *H.M.C., Fifth Report,* MSS of the Duke of Sutherland, 141.

[326] Indenture, C. 219/43/Part 2; Newcastle Corporation MSS, Order Book I; Red Book (1590–1669), fols. 123, 125.

[327] The mayor, burgesses and some others of the town residents were the electors. C. 219/43/Part 2.

[328] In Palmer's collections for Tamworth (Add. MSS, 28,175, fol. 109) is a transcript of a petition signed by 85 men who protested limiting the vote in a town of at least 300 householders to the bailiffs and chief burgesses alone. The indentures for the successive Tamworth elections, 1640–1641, however, appear in the simplest of forms and were signed by the bailiffs only. C. 219/43/Part 2.

[329] Essex may have been influential in the spring, also. His mother owned Drayton, whose proprietors often controlled the borough. Wedgwood, *Staff. Parl. Hist.* 2: 53, 57, 143.

[330] E.g., Crane, North, and Playters.

sea captain, as one of its M.P.'s. Only three elections seem to have been vigorously contested, and only two of those to have turned on national issues. A royalist was defeated at the county polls, but a moderate man, inclined in 1640 to cooperate with the court, defeated a well known puritan at Sudbury.

The Suffolk shire election occurred at Ipswich on 19 October 1640 with the two puritan knights of the preceding parliament, Sir Nathaniel Barnardiston of Ketton and Sir Philip Parker of Erwarton, being opposed by a court sympathizer, Henry North of Mildenhall, son of Sir Roger North, M.P. for Eye. Although North protested against the confusion during the whole time of the election, the accounts left by Sir Simonds D'Ewes, the sheriff, leave no doubt that North was defeated by about seven hundred votes.[331]

The bailiffs and burgesses of Aldeburgh returned on 22 October 1640 [332] the well known Captain William Rainborow of London, who had sat for the town in the Short Parliament and was a friend of local families, and one of their borough merchants, Alexander Bence. Both were parliamentarians.

Bury St. Edmunds, which usually gave at least one of its seats to a Jermyn of Rushbrook, returned two of that family, Sir Thomas Jermyn, privy councillor, and his son, Thomas. Both were royalists.

The Dunwich bailiffs and burgesses [333] elected on 23 October the two men who had represented the borough in the spring, Henry Coke, Esq., of Thorington and Dunwich, and Anthony Bedingfield, Gent., a Suffolk born merchant of London whose family were connected with Dunwich affairs. The latter was a parliamentarian but Coke, by 1642, had turned to the king.

The borough of Eye, at this time part of the lands of the queen, returned by its bailiffs and burgesses [334] two local men of royalist inclination. Sir Frederick Cornwallis, Bart., of Bromehall, of a family of courtiers, remained loyal to the crown, but his colleague, Sir Roger North of Great Finborough, though a supporter

of his son, the royalist candidate for the shire, joined the parliamentarians in the end.

Ipswich was the scene not only of the tumultuous county election but of excitement regarding its own members. The town had been reported by the metropolitical visitors of 1635 as "very factious," and more than once had shown disrespect toward its bishop.[335] It was suffering also from the decline of trade.[336] But personalities and local rivalries seem to have weighed as heavily as either of the above circumstances in the election squabbles of 1640. William Cage, many times before a member for the town, had won in the spring, apparently without contest, but another townsman and former member had then been defeated by 104 to 95 votes by John Gurdon of Great Wenham, who was neither a freeman nor a resident.[337] Before the next election, great preparations were made, as the peace-loving sheriff, D'Ewes, reported, by factions that made old friends and allies antagonists, and Cage and Gurdon were again returned. D'Ewes doubted somewhat the legality of Cage's being elected while he was still in office as bailiff,[338] but no petition against the return appears in the records. Both men were strong opposition members.

The Orford members returned on 22 October 1640 were Sir William Playters, Bart., of Sotterley, a newcomer to parliament but long active in county affairs, and Sir Charles Le Groos of Crostwight, Norfolk, who had served for Orford three times before. Both continued to be members until 1648, but were of moderate views.

At least three men stood for election at Sudbury on 26 October,[339] Sir Robert Crane, Bart., of Chilton, Sir Simonds D'Ewes of Stowe Langstoft, the county sheriff, and Brampton Gurdon of Assington, a gentleman of more extreme puritan views, and father of the Ipswich member. The election of D'Ewes was unquestioned, but Gurdon's son challenged Crane's return and on December 7 urged the House to send for the mayor. Those who favored Gurdon's cause were the more aggressive members, such as Hesilrige and Pym, whereas some of the reformers who were to turn royalist, Whistler, Bagshaw, and others, were for Crane. Inasmuch as Crane had supported the royalist candidate at the shire election, and was connected by family tie with the Jermyns, it is evident that he was considered a possible friend of the court. A hot debate in the Commons on 8

---

[331] The figures showed at least 2,240 for Parker, 2,140 for Barnardiston, and 1,422 for North. Both puritan candidates were missing when the polling began, and the sheriff and the Ipswich constables were bitterly criticized by the North faction for their handling of the election. Several women who held 40 shilling freeholds voted for Barnardiston and Parker, but their votes were ruled out. A riot occurred at one time. J. J. Raven, *The history of Suffolk*, 205–206, London, 1895. This election is included among those discussed by R. N. Kershaw in The elections for the long parliament, *E.H.R.* **38**: 503, 1923, and one version of D'Ewes's narrative appears in full in Thomas Carlyle's *Critical and miscellaneous essays* **4**: 400–426, 1860. There are a few supplementary details in Harl. MSS, 158, fols. 293v–295v, and D'Ewes, *Autobiography* **2**: 255. Nothing about the case appears in *C.J.*

[332] *M. of P.* **1**: 494; C. 219/43/Part 2.

[333] A larger proportion of the electorate appeared on this occasion than in the spring, including 30 of the 36 corporation members and 16 freemen. Dunwich Borough MSS, Minute Book, 1627–1653, fols. 115v, 118–119.

[334] W. A. Copinger, ed., *The manors of Suffolk* **3**: 259, London, T. F. Unwin, 1905–1911; C. 219/43/Part 2.

[335] *C.S.P. Dom.*, 1635, xxxii; *1639–1640*, 221.

[336] *The humble petition from the bailiffs, portsmen and other inhabitants of Ipswich*, London, 1641.

[337] Nathaniel Bacon, *The annalls of Ipswich*, W. H. Richardson, ed., 522, Ipswich, 1884; Ipswich Corporation MSS, General Courts Book, 7 James I–18 Charles I, fol. 89.

[338] D'Ewes, *Autobiography* **2**: 247; D'Ewes (C), 242–243. The voters were bailiffs, burgesses and commonalty. C. 219/43/Part 2.

[339] The mayor, aldermen and burgesses were the electors. C. 219/43/Part 2.

December ended, however, with a vote that Crane's election was good.[340]

SURREY

Surrey sent to the Long Parliament a delegation strongly favoring reform, only one of the fourteen members being inclined toward royalism at the start. One other, an outspoken critic of Laud's ecclesiastical program in 1640, joined the king later. The trend toward puritanism in the county and the opposition to such measures as the attempt to extend the forest of Windsor there[341] help to explain the political uniformity. Ship money does not seem to have met with so much opposition here as elsewhere, but a considerable part of the 1639 assessment was not collected.[342]

The elections were not eventful. In three instances, each of them a borough largely dominated by the family of one of the candidates returned, there were double returns, but local or personal differences rather than national issues seem to have been involved, and none of them reveals any particular pressure on behalf of or against the crown. In fact, the only Surrey election which bears unmistakably the impress of 1640 trends was that of Southwark, the least typical of the Surrey constituencies. The two lawyers who were selected there, neither of them connected with Surrey or with Southwark, had come into prominence as opponents of Laud's program. Elsewhere the members chosen were of the local gentry, most of them living in or near their boroughs, a considerable proportion having served them before as parliament men.

The proximity to London no doubt accounts for the inclusion of four[343] out of fourteen members who were closely associated with business interests in the city, either tradesmen themselves or the sons of wealthy citizens who were now living as gentlemen on Surrey estates.

The county members elected on 14 October 1640 were two country gentlemen of prominence, Sir Richard Onslow and Sir Ambrose Browne. They had served together for the shire in 1628 and in the Short Parliament, and had been J.P.'s and active in county affairs for some years. Both were parliamentarians and seem to have won their seats without contest.

The Blechingley members, also Surrey men and parliamentarians, were John (afterwards Sir John) Evelyn of Godstone and Edward Bysshe of Smallfield. The former had represented the borough in 1628 and the latter's father had been its member at least four times. The franchise rested, according to a 1624 ruling, with the burgageholders, not with the residents at large.[344]

Gatton, though notorious as a rotten borough from the fifteenth century, had a disputed election in October, 1640.[345] In 1621 and 1628 the "freeholders" had contested the return made by the owner of most of the town.[346] On 23 October 1640 eighteen "burgesses of the borough" returned Samuel Owfield, owner of Gatton manor and four times previously M.P. for the borough, and his claim to the first seat was unquestioned. But two other returns of the same date were sent in, one naming Edmund Saunder, who had sat with Owfield in the Short Parliament, and the other, Thomas Sandys, who probably lived at Little Pattensham in Leatherhead. Although Saunder ostensibly had fourteen votes to Sandys's eight, the latter was recognized by the House on 3 November 1641 because his voters were residents in the town, whereas Saunder's backers included too many who, though freeholders, were not residents. Others whose franchise was questioned were a minister, a parish clerk, and a convicted recusant, but the main issue seems to have been the definition of "burgess of the borough."[347] Both Owfield and Sandys supported parliament.

Guildford returned as its members Sir Robert Parkhurst of nearby Pirford, descendant of an old Guildford family, and George Abbot of London, whose family likewise had many Guildford connections. Both had sat for the town before and both were country party men. They were returned by the mayor and "probes homines" of the borough.[348]

Three returns for Haslemere were filed, indicating a double election, but no record remains of the circumstances. Sir John Jaques, Bart., of Middlesex and Surrey, a gentleman pensioner who had been one of the town's M.P.'s in the spring,[349] failed to gain the recognition of the House in the fall. Those who were seated were Poynings Moore of Loseley, whose family had often controlled elections at Haslemere, since the borough was a parcel of their manor of Godalming,[350] and John Goodwin of Blechingley and the Inner Temple, whose family was seated on the Surrey-Sussex border not far from Haslemere. Both members, especially Goodwin, were parliamentarians.

Reigate also sent in three names on separate returns, 21 October 1640, but no reference to the case appears in the records of the parliament. Although the town was

---

[340] D'Ewes (N), 119, 120; *C.J.* **2**: 47; Raven, *The history of Suffolk*, 206.

[341] Owen Manning and William Bray, *The history and antiquities of the county of Surrey* **1**: Intro., xii–xiii, London, 1804–1814 (hereafter, Manning and Bray, *Surrey*).

[342] Royal Hist. Soc., *Trans.*, 3rd Ser., **4**: 160, 1910.

[343] Abbot, Bludder, Owfield, Parkhurst.

[344] A. U. M. Lambert, *Blechingley: A parish history* **1**: 328; **2**: 424–425, London, Mitchell, Hughes and Clarke, 1921; Manning and Bray, *Surrey*, **2**: 295–296.

[345] *Surrey Archaeological Collections* (published by the Surrey Archaeological Society) **39**: 59, 1931 (hereafter, *Surrey Arch. Coll.*); E. W. Brayley, *A topographical history of Surrey* **4**: 314, London, 1850 (hereafter, Brayley, *Surrey*).

[346] *C.S.P. Dom., 1619–1623*, 221–222; *M. of P.* **1**: 478 and n.

[347] Gatton indentures, C. 219/43/Part 2; *C.J.* **2**: 303.

[348] Guildford Indenture, C. 219/43/Part 2.

[349] *M. of P.* **1**: 483, 494; *Complete Baronetage* **2**: 55.

[350] Manning and Bray, *Surrey* **1**: 657.

almost a pocket borough of the Howard family,[351] Sir Francis Howard of Great Bookham, one of the three named in the indentures, was not seated.[352] Those who served were Howard's relative, William Viscount Monson, who owned the manor of Reigate and had been its M.P. before, and Sir Thomas Bludder of Flanchford in Reigate, who had served for the town since 1624. Monson was a parliamentarian, but Bludder was a royalist, though not markedly so in the early months of the session.

Southwark, by contrast with the rural boroughs of Surrey, elected two London lawyers without Surrey connection as its M.P.'s. Edward Bagshaw, who came of a Derbyshire family, and John White, who was Welsh by birth, no doubt owed their election for this, their first parliament, to their reputations as enemies of the Laudian program. Bagshaw eventually joined the king, but White was a prominent worker wtih Pym in the Commons.

SUSSEX

The county and towns of Sussex, aside from the Cinque Ports located within its borders, were entitled to twenty men in parliament. Before January, 1642, however, because of double returns and the replacement of original members who died, three more were added to the number of parliament men from that shire. Nearly all were Sussex men by birth or by residence, three came from the Surrey or Kent side of the borders, and only Dr. Chaworth, whose election was soon declared void, seems to have been completely an outsider. Most of them, too, were country gentlemen who lived near the towns that chose them, a few being from families that had transferred their wealth from London to Sussex a generation or two before, but others being of very old families. Only Cawley, the Chichester brewer's son who sat for Midhurst, and possibly Marlott of Shoreham, can be considered as having some connection with town occupations.

In politics the county was rather sharply divided between east and west,[353] with Chichester as the center for a royalist group, as the developments of 1642 were to show. Ship money seems to have occasioned less discontent here [354] than in other counties not so near the sea, but people recalled the martial law of Buckingham's day and the later encroachments of royal power upon the liberties of the subject. Puritanism was a strong influence, especially in east Sussex. A number of the men elected in 1640 had already attempted to curb Laud's program. The fact that three of the Sussex men became regicides indicates the strength of feeling

in their county. Of the Sussex members twelve of those originally chosen and two "recruiters" were supporters of parliament. At least one other, Sir Thomas Bowyer, must be accounted a worker for reforms at least until 1642, although he is usually classified as a royalist. The remaining eight, who were king's men, included the churchman, Chaworth, who sat for only a few weeks. Four of these seem to have had fairly close connections with the court, Buckhurst, Farnefold, Sir William Morley, and Lewknor, and two others were friends or relatives of the last named.[355]

The shire members chosen at Lewes on 21 October 1640 [356] were prominent gentlemen of the county, both residents of the eastern area, both puritans, and both members of the Short Parliament. They were Anthony Stapley of Patcham, the future regicide, and his good friend, Sir Thomas Pelham, Bart., of Halland, a great landowner.

Arundel held two elections before January, 1642, both of which show the influence of neighboring lords and were contested. Originally returned in 1640 were Henry Garton, a Sussex man by birth and property who lived chiefly at the Temple in London, and Sir Edward Alford, also Sussex born, but identified for most of the preceding decade with Hertfordshire and London. Their election was challenged by one of the Sackville family, a younger son of the powerful Earl of Dorset, but after he had twice failed to appear to explain his case, the Committee of Privileges in January, 1641, dismissed his plea. Although the House did not decide until November, 1641, that their election was good, Garton was active in the work of the Commons before the end of March, and Alford, though he did not declare until after August that he wished to serve for Arundel rather than for Tewkesbury, was present at the vote on Strafford's attainder.[357] He was a royalist. After the death in October of Henry Garton, who seems to have been of the popular party, the House resolved on 12 November that their election was good, and ordered that a new one be held for filling Garton's place.[358] Word reached the Commons in December that the Earl of Arundel had commended his secretary, Harman, to the town, and Cromwell and others of his side, probably fearing the return of a second royalist, procured the appointment of a committee to consider the influence of noblemen at elections at Arundel and elsewhere. There followed the Commons' vote on 10 December that letters from peers should not be allowed to influence free elections.[359] The mayor and burgesses of Arundel officially returned John Downes of Bulberough as their

[351] *Surrey Arch. Coll.* 39: 59, 1931.

[352] The indenture naming Howard bears a slightly shorter list of names of electing "burgesses" than the others. C. 219/43/Part 2.

[353] Charles Thomas-Stanford, *Sussex in the great Civil War and the interregnum, 1642–1660,* 5, London, Chiswick Press, 1910 (hereafter, Thomas-Stanford, *Sussex in the great Civil War*).

[354] Royal Hist. Soc., *Trans.,* 3rd Ser., 4: 160, 1910.

[355] The puritan leaders of east Sussex show a similar grouping by kinship and association, with Pelham and Stapley in the center, and around them at least Rivers and Shelley.

[356] Sussex indenture, C. 219/43/Part 2.

[357] Verney, 58; *C.J.* 2: 114.

[358] *C.J.* 2: 302, 313; D'Ewes (C), 126.

[359] *C.J.* 2: 333, 337; D'Ewes (C), 236, 260.

new member,[360] but a second indenture sent by "some others of that Burrough," possibly naming Harman, was called to the attention of the House on 28 December. Downes was granted permission on 15 January 1642 to sit until the election should be determined, but a decision seems not to have been reached by 17 June 1642.[361] Downes, however, retained his place and eventually sat in judgment on the king. He was "of Sussex" at the time of his election, but he may not have been a native of the county and seems to have had no previous connection with Arundel.

The Bramber election resulted in the uncontested return of one member, Sir Thomas Bowyer, Bart., of Leythorne, who had served for the borough many times before. But the second place was contested by Sir Edward Bishop of Parham, a royalist, and Arthur Onslow, scion of a prominent parliamentarian family of Surrey. Upon evidence that Bishop had offered a bribe of £10 for his election, the House declared both his and Onslow's return void and debarred Bishop from seeking the office again. Onslow was successful at the new election and was in the House by spring.[362] Bowyer, though generally listed among the royalists, seems to have worked with the reform group during the first year of the parliament.

The Chichester members were Sir William Morley, a country gentleman who lived at Halnaker, not far from the city, and whose father had several times been M.P. for Chichester, and the town's recorder, Christopher Lewknor, who had been its member in the Short Parliament. Both men were royalists. Whether others sought election does not appear.[363] One prominent citizen of the opposite views, William Cawley, got his seat in the parliament for the smaller borough of Midhurst.

East Grinstead, on the borders of Surrey and Kent, was represented by the royalist, Richard Lord Buckhurst, son of the Earl of Dorset, whose family usually controlled at least one seat for the borough, and by the parliamentarian, Robert Goodwin of Horne, Surrey, whose family had for many years been associated with this Sussex borough and who had been its M.P. several times before. Goodwin's place was contested by Sir William Colepeper, Bart., of Wakehurst, but on 24 December 1640 the House decided in favor of the former.[364] He had won his place in the spring in competition with one of Dorset's two nominees, parliament recognizing his poll of the votes of the inhabitants rather

than just those holding by burgage tenure;[365] and the autumn contest may have involved the same question. The indenture returned for Colepeper was apparently that of the mayor and burgesses alone,[366] and as late as 1679 Goodwin spoke for the right of the inhabitants to vote.[367]

At Horsham not only was the franchise limited to the burgage tenements, of which there were 54 in 1611,[368] but the men selected were from the borough. Thomas Middleton and Hall Ravenscroft had both sat for the town before and both supported the popular party. But the former was suspected somewhat of royalist sympathy during the war.

Lewes, where the inhabitants as well as the burgage holders voted, had a strong puritan faction which in the spring elections had overridden the suggestions of neighboring lords.[369] Two strong puritans and parliamentarians were elected there in October, James Rivers of Combe, who had been one of the successful candidates in the spring, and Herbert Morley of Glynde. The latter may have been chosen late in the spring, also, to fill a vacancy. After Rivers died in 1641 his place was taken by Henry Shelley of Southover, near Lewes, another opposition man.

Midhurst, an unincorporated borough in the Chichester end of Sussex, returned by its public official, the bailiff, two royalists. Thomas May of Rawmere, a neighbor of the town, had served for it in the previous parliament. Dr. Richard Chaworth of Oxford, who afterwards became Chancellor of Chichester, possibly had had some connections with the region before 1640. His election was challenged, however, by William Cawley, a prominent citizen of Chichester. On 6 January 1641 the Commons voted that May and Chaworth, because the bailiff returned them, should sit as members until their election should be voided and that Cawley, returned without sanction of the bailiff, should not be admitted until the election was determined. On 15 February, however, May and Cawley were pronounced duly elected and the bailiff was sent for to correct the return in favor of the latter. A parliamentarian layman thereupon replaced the ecclesiastic whom the bailiff had returned. Possibly Chaworth was the nominee of the borough lord, Viscount Montague.[370]

---

[360] C. 219/43/Part 2. In the 1623 election about 66 electors had gathered for the voting. T. W. Horsfield, *The history, antiquities, and topography of Sussex* 2: App., 29, Lewes, 1835 (hereafter, Horsfield, *Hist. Sussex*).

[361] *C.J.* 2: 380, 628, 630; D'Ewes (C), 355.

[362] *C.J.* 2: 51, 133; D'Ewes (N), 160.

[363] The city administration was divided in its political views as late as August, 1642, many of the councillors favoring parliament rather than the king. *V.C.H. Sussex* 3: 87.

[364] *C.J.* 2: 30, 58; Pink MSS, 311, fol. 495c. For Buckhurst's choice of constituency, see the paragraph on Steyning below.

[365] *C.J.* 2: 10; *Sussex Archaeological Collections* (Publication of the Sussex Archaeological Society) 20: 153–154, 1868 (hereafter, *Sussex Arch. Coll.*).

[366] C. 219/43/Part 2.

[367] *C.J.* 9: 587. The inhabitants participated in electing Buckhurst's successor in 1645 (C. 219/43/Part 2), but it was decided in 1689 that the burgage-holders only should thereafter be electors. Many burgage tenements belonged to the Sackville family. *Sussex Arch. Coll.* 20: 154–155, 1868.

[368] William Albery, *A parliamentary history of Horsham*, 11–12, London, Longmans Green, 1927; W. D. Cooper's Parliamentary history of Sussex, Horsfield, *Hist. Sussex* 2: App., 42.

[369] *C.S.P. Dom., 1639–1640*, 387; Horsfield, *Hist. Sussex* 2: App., 46; indenture, C. 219/43/Part 2.

[370] *C.J.* 2: 63, 86, 89. The electors were the free burgesses. *Sussex Arch. Coll.* 20: 20, 1868.

The members for Shoreham were two who had served for it several times before. John Alford of Offington, not far from the town, was a parliamentarian of a sort, and the son of a stronger one. His colleague, William Marlott, was a resident of Shoreham and was more active for the popular cause.

From Steyning came three returns dated 12 October 1640 which named separately Thomas Leedes of nearby Wappingthorne, Richard Lord Buckhurst, son of the Earl of Dorset, and Sir Thomas Farnefold of Gatewick in Steyning.[371] In parliament it was decided on 15 February 1641 that Leedes should be admitted as a member, pending a final decision.[372] According to D'Ewes, Buckhurst was at the same time seated without question,[373] although he appears to have been sitting already for East Grinstead. Farnefold was no doubt admitted when Buckhurst's preference for the latter borough was made clear. He had served for Steyning several times before, but Leedes was a newcomer on the scene. All three of the candidates were royalists.

WARWICKSHIRE

Warwickshire was the scene of a struggle for power between the royalist family of Compton, led by the Earl of Northampton, and the puritan family of Greville, headed by Lord Brooke. The undercurrents of feeling against ship money and of the puritans' rebellion against the Laudian program are likewise evident, particularly in the case of Coventry, where the rich men of the wool trade had more power than the nobles. Warwick borough was controlled principally by Lord Brooke, but the county, where the sheriff sought to manage the elections of both spring[374] and fall to secure royalist candidates, showed the power of the Comptons. Two of the three constituencies[375] had contests followed by petitions. In the case of the county there was a new election, and the royalists remained in control. But in each of the two boroughs where deaths made by-elections necessary before the summer of 1641, strong parliamentarians who had served for those boroughs in the Short Parliament were returned to the House. The royalists were clearly outnumbered. With the exception of one borough member, Lord Brooke's half-brother, who lived chiefly in Yorkshire, and those of Tamworth, the border borough, all of the Warwickshire delegation were county residents.

Warwickshire had a contested election, but the sheriff returned on 2 November 1640 the names of James Lord Compton, heir apparent of the royalist Earl of North-

ampton, who had demanded his son's election,[376] and William Combes, one of the county magistrates.[377] The latter seems to have been sympathetic with the reform group.[378] The House of Commons considered allowing Combes to sit, unseating Compton alone, and he was present in November, testifying about the election,[379] but was unseated when the whole election was voided. The third candidate for the shire seat was the puritan, William Purefoy of Caldecote, a close friend of Lord Brooke and already burgess-elect for Warwick borough. Although it was afterwards declared that Purefoy's following would have given him a victory by three to one, the sheriff prevented it by moving the county court from one place to another and by breaking off the polling which he had consented under pressure to conduct. These misdemeanors were admitted by the sheriff on 2 December and the House thereupon declared the election void. But the sheriff, evidently the tool of the royalist faction, managed the by-election also, making possible the return of Lord Compton once more and with him another royalist, Richard Shuckburgh of Over Shuckburgh. Purefoy had apparently decided to content himself with his borough seat. Combes was again a candidate, and his friends petitioned on his behalf, but the case does not seem to have been reopened for consideration in parliament.[380]

Coventry was in the center of a region which had been troubled in the decade or so preceding the Long Parliament by a decline in trade and by the effects of increasing enclosures. The citizens had worked for lower ship money rates and had given William Prynne a warm welcome when he passed through on his way to prison at Carnarvon. Sentiment against the administration and against Laud's program was strong, and may have been stirred further by a visit which John Pym is said to have made to the city shortly before the election, ostensibly to look after some property which he owned nearby. The power of the crown to control elections through the closed corporation had been successfully challenged in 1627 and, though the Earl of Northampton had become Coventry's recorder in 1640, he seems to have had little influence over its elections.[381] The town was listed for a court nomina-

---

[371] C. 219/43/Part 2. The indentures for Leedes and Buckhurst were signed by more burgesses than was that of Farnefold.

[372] C.J. 2: 86.

[373] D'Ewes (N), 361.

[374] A newsletter of 28 February 1640 reported that the sheriff took the election writ to the county himself and planned to hold the election speedily before the majority of the freeholders could assemble. Add. MSS, 11,045, fol. 96.

[375] Tamworth, on the border of Staffordshire, has been considered in the section on the latter county.

[376] C.S.P. Dom., 1640–1641, 113.

[377] C. 193/13; S.P. 16/405.

[378] He was described in 1642 as of the same strain as Purefoy when the latter was declared a traitor to the king. D.N.B., "William Purefoy."

[379] Combes spoke against the sheriff's stand regarding the third candidate, Purefoy. C.J. 2: 23; D'Ewes (N), 95, 306. Since Combes took no other part in the work of the parliament I have not attempted further to identify him. It was possibly his son who was nominated for the Knights of the Royal Oak in 1660. English Baronetage 4: 376, 1741.

[380] D'Ewes (N), 133; C.J. 2: 69.

[381] C.S.P. Dom., 1640–1641, 371; T. W. Whitley, The parliamentary representation of the city of Coventry, 77, 79–80, Coventry, 1894 (hereafter, Whitley, Parl. Rep. Coventry); Benjamin Poole, Coventry: Its history and antiquities, 369, London, 1870 (hereafter, Poole, Hist. Coventry).

tion prior to the Short Parliament election,[382] but there was little chance in 1640 for that procedure to be successful.[383] The members chosen in the autumn were two aldermen and former mayors, John Barker and Simon Norton. When the latter died in July, 1641, his place was filled by another of similar experience, William Jesson. Both Barker and Jesson were strong puritans and parliamentarians; Norton was probably less ardent. Jesson, who had served in the Short Parliament, had some difficulties with the Earl of Northampton the following summer, but the city records give no indication that the earl prevented his re-election in the fall. Since Jesson presented a petition concerning the election in February, 1641, however, it seems that he probably had wished to be chosen again.[384]

Tamworth is considered with the boroughs of Staffordshire (q.v.).

The original members for Warwick borough were Sir Thomas Lucy of Charlecote, many times previously its M.P., and William Purefoy of Caldecote, the puritan factionary. Upon Lucy's death in early December, a new election was ordered, and in February the House dealt with a controversy regarding two indentures which had come in. One was sent by the bailiffs and the other by some residents at large. It was ordered on 18 February that the man named in the bailiffs' indenture should sit until his election should be found illegal.[385] By this means a seat was assured to Godfrey Bosvile of Gunthwaite, Yorkshire, and Wroxhall, Warwickshire, who had been Warwick's M.P. in the Short Parliament. He was a strong parliamentarian and doubtless owed his election to the influence of his stepbrother, Lord Brooke.

WESTMORLAND

Westmorland's delegation of four members, two for the county and two for Appleby, were all royalists by 1644, but one of the shire knights and one borough member cooperated during the first part of the Long Parliament with the reform party. Family and personal experiences, rather than constitutional principles, possibly explain their politics. The group was evenly divided also as to connections with the county. Of the two outsiders, however, one had the bond of marriage with the powerful county family of Clifford and had sat for his Westmorland borough in the Short Parliament.

The only carpetbagger seems to have been the courtier, Sir John Brooke.

The county members, elected at Appleby on 22 October 1640,[386] were baronets of prominent local families, Sir Philip Musgrave of Hartley, and Sir Henry Bellingham of Helsington. The former was a consistent royalist. Bellingham's section of the county had shown some opposition to ship money,[387] and he cooperated for a time with the reform party, but became a royalist in the end. Both had represented Westmorland in the spring.

The Appleby members, chosen by mayor, aldermen, and freemen,[388] were both foreign to the section. The wife of Richard (Boyle) Lord Dungarvan, however, was a Clifford, and he doubtless profited by her family's influence at both 1640 elections. His colleague, Sir John Brooke of Heckington, Lincolnshire, was an elderly courtier and projector who was probably a royal nominee. He seems to have had no previous connection with Appleby. Dungarvan worked with Pym's faction for some months before siding with the king. Brooke was a steady royalist.

WILTSHIRE

Wiltshire was a county entitled in 1640 to thirty-four seats in the Commons. Three new members entered belatedly to fill vacancies before 1642, but one borough, Downton, was served by a single burgess because the House failed to determine a contested by-election. Of the thirty-seven parliament men who represented Wiltshire all but eleven were residents or property owners of the county;[389] and three of the eleven came from nearby shires, one of them having intermarried with a Wiltshire family. Of the remaining eight who might be called carpetbaggers five had in earlier parliaments represented some Wiltshire constituency and were men of considerable national prominence.[390] Several of the sixteen boroughs, notably Downton, Old Sarum, Wilton, and possibly Hindon, were virtually pocket boroughs of the Herberts, though their power was shared sometimes with another family, as it apparently was with the Cecils at Old Sarum. The Herberts seem to have controlled one seat at Salisbury, too.[391] The Seymours were powerful at Marlborough and Bedwin. The controlled boroughs were used for some of the outsiders. Four of the boroughs, on the other hand (Calne, Devizes, Marlborough, Salisbury), sent one member

---

[382] It was listed with other boroughs to which nominations had been sent in 1623. S.P. 16, 450/15.

[383] The voters in October 1640, in the "full county" court of the city (Coventry indenture, C. 219/43/Part 3), were probably the freemen as well as the corporation members.

[384] C.J. 2: 78.

[385] C.J. 2: 87, 88; D'Ewes (N), 364 and n., 369, 407. A controversy between the corporation and the freeholders who sought the franchise had developed at the 1620 election (The Black Book of Warwick, ed. Thomas Kemp, 409–411, Warwick, 1898; Warwick Corporation MSS, The Black Book, fols. 271–273). The indenture for the original election, 27 October 1640, specified as the electors, however, the bailiffs, burgesses and inhabitants, and was signed by about eighteen men. C. 219/43/Part 3.

[386] Indenture, C. 219/143/Part 3.

[387] C.S.P. Dom., 1637, 469.

[388] Indenture, C. 219/143/Part 3.

[389] Non-native property holders were Ashburnham, Wheeler, and Cecil. Jenner possibly belongs in this group, but he may have come from a Wiltshire family.

[390] Fleetwood, Edward Herbert, Oldisworth, Rudyard, and Vane.

[391] The original election at Downton shows the influence of the Herberts and possibly of the Hampshire courtier, Uvedale. The contest in the by-election, however, indicates that Downton was not absolutely in the Herberts' pocket. See E.H.R. 50: 244–256, 1935.

each who was an actual inhabitant if not an official of the town. And most of the others made their selection from families of prominence in the neighborhood. Even the three members who were London men, Edward Ashe, Jenner, and Wheeler, had some county connection. The second was living on his Wiltshire property at the time of his election, Wheeler owned property in or near the town which chose him, and Ashe had enough connections with Wilts and Somerset through his family and his woolen business to have been known to his electors.

As to politics, only thirteen [392] of Wiltshire's thirty-seven parliament men were royalists. The parliamentarians included such vigorous men as the brothers Ashe, Sir Edward Hungerford, Ludlow, Poole, and Rudyard, and that sufferer for parliamentary privilege, Walter Long, who entered just at the close of the period of this study. The forces of unrest had troubled Wiltshire ship money collectors and loan commissioners. The tide of puritanism was rising in the county. And concern about the state of the county's great clothing trade, known to J.P's, land owners, clothiers, and London businessmen, was reflected in the attacks of the Wilts members against the abuses of the administration.

The shire election at Wilton on 3 November [393] seems to have been a calm one, even though the candidates were not those who in the spring had been elected without opposition. [394] Lord Andover, for whom some men were prepared to vote, sent word in October that he would not stand against the combination in the field, [395] the strong parliamentarian, Sir Henry Ludlow of Maiden Bradley, and the wealthy courtier, Sir James Thynne.

Great Bedwin returned two royalists on 23 October. Sir Walter Smith lived in or near the borough, but Richard Harding, though Wiltshire born and owning property not far from Bedwin, was probably at court much of the time. He perhaps owed his election to the Seymour family, whose influence at Bedwin was strong. The electors there were the portreeve and burgesses. [396]

Calne was virtually a closed corporation and was dominated often by the royalist Duckett family, owners of the hundred. [397] The electors on 26 October 1640 were the borough constable and sixteen burgesses. [398] They chose a royalist of a Calne family, George Lowe,

who may have served them in previous parliaments, and a parliamentarian, Hugh Rogers of Somerset, youthful son-in-law of the borough's powerful neighbor, Sir Edward Bayntun.

Chippenham had a contest, the matter of the franchise possibly being one of the issues. In 1624 it had been the scene of a dispute in which John Pym and Sir Francis Popham were the rivals, one of the questions being the right of the inhabitants, in addition to the regular burgesses, to vote. Precedent then seemed to be on the side of the closed corporation. [399] The existing indenture of 26 October 1640 declared that the election of Sir Edward Bayntun and Sir Edward Hungerford was by the bailiff with the assent of the burgesses inhabitant and freemen burgesses. [400] Both were parliamentarians, but in the early months of 1641 Bayntun's election was before the Committee of Privileges, the challenger being Sir Francis Popham. Since Bayntun was at the time unpopular because of the way he had levied ship money in the county, it appears that the attack on his election was perhaps part of a plan to drive him out of the House. [401] But Popham was a member for another borough, and Bayntun had already done committee work and continued to be active in the House. [402] Since no further reference to the Chippenham case occurs, it was apparently dropped. Bayntun lived not far from Chippenham and had been its M.P. in the spring and once before. Hungerford, too, had been its member in the spring and owned property in the town.

Cricklade chose by its bailiff and burgesses [403] on 26 October two non-residents who had represented the borough in the Short Parliament. Robert Jenner, once of London, lived not far away, and Thomas Hodges of Gloucestershire was a relatively close neighbor. Both were parliamentarians.

The mayor and burgesses of Devizes re-elected one of their Short Parliament M.P.'s, Edward Bayntun, son of the Chippenham member, who resided near the town and whose family had served it before in parliament and in local government. With him was returned now the borough's recorder, Robert Nicholas. [404] Both were of the popular party.

Downton was a burgage tenure borough often dominated by the earls of Pembroke, who were lords of the manor. [405] William Herbert, son of Pembroke, was elected in October, but chose afterwards to serve for

[392] The figure does not include the elder Sir Henry Vane, although he was probably considered loyal to the king at the time of his election.

[393] M. of P. 1: 495; Wiltshire indenture, C. 219/43/Part 3.

[394] Lord Herbert and Sir Francis Seymour. C.S.P. Dom., 1639–1640, 604.

[395] Calendar of the Clarendon State Papers preserved in the Bodleian Library, Rev. O. Ogle and W. H. Bliss, ed., 1: 209, Oxford, 1872 (hereafter, Calendar of Clarendon State Papers).

[396] C. 219/43/Part 3.

[397] A. E. W. Marsh, A history of the borough and town of Calne, 29–31, 38, 50, Calne, Robert S. Heath, 1903 (hereafter, Marsh, Hist. of Calne).

[398] Calne indenture, C. 219/43/Part 3.

[399] M. of P. 1: 461, n.; Harl. MSS, 6806, fol. 262; C.J. 1: 735; John Glanville, Reports of certain cases . . . , ed. Topham, 47–62, London, 1775.

[400] C. 219/43/Part 3. The freemen participated also in 1648.

[401] C.J. 2: 68, 80, 81; D'Ewes (N), 330, n., 334.

[402] C.J. 2: 64, passim.

[403] C. 219/43/Part 3.

[404] M. of P. 1: 495; Devizes indenture, C. 219/43/Part 3.

[405] W. Albery, A parliamentary history of the ancient borough of Horsham, 10, n.; Sir Richard Colt Hoare, The history of modern Wiltshire 3 (4): 19, London, 1822–1843 (hereafter, Hoare, Wilts.); E.H.R. 50: 244, 251, 252, 1935.

Monmouth. His colleague, Sir Edward Griffin of Northamptonshire, a courtier, doubtless owed his election either to the Herberts or to his Hampshire father-in-law. But the by-election for William Herbert's successor produced a contest unusual in a controlled borough. The two returns sent in December reported the election by somewhat different groups of electors of two young men of court connection, Sir Anthony Ashley Cooper and Richard Gorges.[406] Whereas the original return had named as electors the bailiff and eighteen burgesses, the new returns, both of which were sent in by the deputy bailiff, showed a larger number of voters present. The Gorges indenture stated that the electors were the deputy bailiff and about thirty-three burgesses. The electors according to the Cooper return were of about the same number, but were different in identity, and were said to be the bailiff, the burgesses named, and other burgesses and inhabitants.[407] Perhaps the absence of the bailiff accounts for the seeming irregularity. The House seems to have been inclined to favor Cooper but for some reason, possibly the objections of Denzil Holles, the case was not reported out of committee. The decision to recognize Cooper was not taken, in fact, until 1660.[408]

Heytesbury elected by its bailiff and less than a score of burgesses [409] two men who were associated with the manor of Heytesbury. Thomas Moore's family had owned the manor for some years back, and were apparently still the owners in 1640. Edward Ashe, a London draper of a Somerset family, afterwards owner of the manor, perhaps had some connections with the town by 1640, but the influence of his brother and friends more probably explains his election. Both M.P.'s were of the popular party. Moore had sat in the Short Parliament, but his colleague then was one of the Berkeleys,[410] and the choice of Ashe now probably resulted from work by the opposition strategists.

Hindon seems to have been accustomed to accepting the nominees of a patron. Thirty-five of the inhabitants even wrote before the Short Parliament election asking a nobleman to recommend men to them, since no one living in the borough was fit to discharge the office.[411] Perhaps the same thing occurred in the autumn, although the return of two men different from those elected in the spring suggests that a different nobleman, possibly Pembroke, did the nominating. Sir Miles Fleetwood of Northamptonshire and London, and Robert Reynolds, a London lawyer, were both of the popular party. Upon Fleetwood's death in 1641, however,

the town chose in his place a man of local connections, Thomas Bennett of Pythouse, whose family were royalists. One Mr. Howe, who opposed Bennett, never succeeded in gaining recognition from the House, even though Bennett's early death shortly before 13 August 1641 again vacated the seat. The vacancy lasted until 1645.[412]

Ludgershall's members who were chosen by the mayor and the burgesses, some forty of whom signed the return, were of opposing factions, but had been chosen together in the spring. Sir John Evelyn of West Deane was a Wiltshire country gentleman of strong opposition views. William Ashburnham, an army officer and courtier, held various Wiltshire estates by right of his wife. After his expulson from the House late in 1641 the town chose as his successor Walter Long of Whaddon, a leader in the cause of parliament.

Of Malmesbury's members, Sir Neville Poole had twice before served the borough and was well known in the county as a critic of the crown. His colleague in both parliaments of 1640, Anthony Hungerford, lived chiefly in Oxfordshire, but came of an old Wiltshire family and owned land there. He became a royalist eventually. Their electors were the aldermen and twelve capital burgesses.[413]

Marlborough, a town which Clarendon said was notorious for its disaffection toward crown and church,[414] elected two men who in 1640 shared the views of the opposition. Sir Francis Seymour came of a family that was often resident in the town and frequently provided it with parliament men. His colleague was the borough's town clerk, John Franklin. When Seymour became a peer, his place was filled by Philip Smith, who seems to have belonged to a family residing near the town, and who, too, was of the opposition. The mayor and burgesses were the electors.[415]

Old Sarum was a rotten borough controlled chiefly by the earls of Pembroke and Salisbury who respectively owned the manor and the castle. A half dozen so-called burgesses returned in October, 1640,[416] a member of each earl's family. Edward Herbert, member for Old Sarum in the spring and a royalist, surrendered his seat when he was appointed Attorney General, but Salisbury's son, Robert Cecil, supported parliament. Herbert's successor in 1641, Sir William Savile, Bart., of Yorkshire, though Strafford's nephew, and in time an ardent royalist, possibly owed his seat to the Earl of

---

[406] For their identities see *D.N.B.* and *Complete Peerage* (Gibbs ed.; **6**: 16–17).

[407] C. 219/43/Part 3.

[408] D'Ewes (N), 344, 504–505; Pink MSS, 311, fol. 496b; Louise Fargo Brown, *The first Earl of Shaftesbury*, 39, New York, Appleton-Century, 1933.

[409] C. 219/43/Part 3.

[410] *M. of P.* **1**: 484.

[411] *C.S.P. Dom., 1639–1640,* 155. The name of the nobleman addressed does not appear.

[412] D'Ewes (B), 419, 454–455. No return for the original election exists. The April return of Bennett declares that the electors were the sub-bailiff and the burgesses, about twenty-six of whom were named and witnessed the indenture. C. 219/43/Part 3.

[413] *Ibid.; The Wiltshire Archaeological and Natural History Magazine* 47: 500, 1935–1937 (hereafter, *Wilts. Arch. Mag.*).

[414] James Waylen, *A history of the town of Marlborough,* 148–149, London, 1854 (hereafter, Waylen, *Hist. of Marlborough*).

[415] C. 219/43/Part 3.

[416] *Ibid.; E.H.R.* **50**: 244, 1935.

Pembroke, whom he knew both at court and in business relationships.

Salisbury sent in two election returns. One from the closed corporation renamed the Short Parliament representatives, Robert Hyde, the town's recorder, and Michael Oldisworth, secretary to the Earl of Pembroke, whose family had long been influential there.[417] The other, purporting to come from the citizens at large, named two local men, one of whom was an alderman and afterwards M.P. A popular petition to parliament attacked Hyde for his promoting ship money collections, suppressing preaching, discouraging the education of poor children, and for his effort to intimidate various chief burgesses who had voted against him at the spring election. Although in the ensuing debate in the House Hyde's conduct and election were challenged by the more extreme reformers, such as Erle, Holles, and Hotham, with Strangways and Falkland being his defenders, the decision was at last made on 3 March 1641 not on the queston of Hyde's politics but on the extent of the franchise at Salisbury. By a vote of 216 to 133 the House upheld the election by the closed corporation. D'Ewes suggested that this decision against the trend toward a broader franchise was the result in part of the previous acquaintance the House had with Hyde and Oldisworth and particularly because of its regard for Oldisworth's noble patron.[418] Hyde was of course a royalist and Oldisworth a parliamentarian.

Westbury's members, elected by the mayor and burgesses,[419] were not borough residents. William Wheeler of Westminster, however, owned property in the parish. And John Ashe, who had served for Westbury in the Short Parliament, was a widely known clothier whose native county was Somerset.

Wilton, home of the Earl of Pembroke and Montgomery, naturally returned at least one Herbert nominee to the House. It simply re-elected in October its members of the spring, Benjamin Rudyard, lawyer and official, who had often owed a place to the earl, and Secretary of State Vane.[420] Both were carpetbaggers whom the mayor and burgesses elected,[421] and both supported parliament.

The Wooton Bassett members were different from those of the spring. The town had frequently chosen non-residents, even men from outside the county,[422] but its mayor and burgesses on 21 October 1640 [423] chose two men from neighboring county families. William Pleydell, the royalist lawyer, probably lived more in London than in Wiltshire, but his colleague, Edward

Poole of the Oaksey family, was from nearby and was a parliamentarian.

WORCESTERSHIRE

Worcestershire was entitled to nine members, the borough of Bewdley having but one seat. A tenth man came in, however, after one Evesham place was vacated early in 1641. The county knights and the Worcester city members were parliamentarians, those of the shire having won their victory under the eye of a not unfriendly sheriff. There were Worcestershire men, including this sheriff, who had opposed ship money,[424] and the triumph of vigorous foes of the court was in keeping with their sentiment. With the exception of one other member, Evesham's recorder, Cresheld, the others from Worcestershire were royalists.[425] Two were prominent courtiers and probably nominees of the crown, Herbert and Porter, and another was the son of the former Lord Keeper, Coventry, who had died less than a year before. All of the members except Porter, who came of a Gloucestershire family, had some connections with the county by birth, family, possessions, or office.

The Worcester county election occurred on 21 October 1640 at the castle at Worcester, and the sheriff returned as the duly elected members John Wilde, a prominent lawyer of the county who had frequently sat for Droitwich and was now Recorder of Worcester, and Humphrey Salway, a county J.P. Both were parliamentarians. They had been opposed by Sir Thomas Littleton, Bart.,[426] one of the shire knights in the Short Parliament, and a Mr. Dingle. Littleton challenged the return. He argued that on the first voice vote he had been clearly chosen for the first seat, but that the sheriff had twice changed the place of the election, had accepted names written beforehand for the polls, and had denied the vote to some who were entitled to it. His opponents declared that Littleton's seeming victory by voice at first had occurred because the space was too small for all the voters to get in and that many of his supporters were boys, women, and poor people, that he had agreed to each change of place, and had withdrawn his followers at last only because he was already outnumbered by Wilde and Salway.[427] The contentions of Littleton,

---

[417] The city chose local men instead of the earl's nominees, however, in 1626. *Ibid.* **50**: 250, 1935.

[418] D'Ewes (N), 83, 98–99, 344, 430–432, 544–545; *C.J.* **2**: 82, 95–96.

[419] C. 219/43/Part 3.

[420] *E.H.R.* **50**: 244–245, 252, 1935.

[421] Wilton indenture, C. 219/43/Part 3.

[422] One or both members came from outside in the parliaments of 1624–1640. *M. of P.*

[423] Indenture, C. 219/43/Part 3.

[424] Much of the ship money was uncollected in 1637 and 1639 (Royal Hist. Soc., *Trans.*, 3rd Ser., **4**: 161, 1910), and the sheriff in 1640 made excuses concerning his difficulties in collecting and distraining (*C.S.P. Dom., 1638–1639*, 391; *1640–1641*, 41, 59).

[425] The parliamentarians outnumbered the royalists; 5 to 4, even after the Evesham by-election, where a royalist replaced a royalist. Perhaps the refusal of the House to accept the proffered resignation of one aged member from the city of Worcester came from a desire to avoid shifting the balance.

[426] *M. of P.* **1**: 484. The other Short Parliament knight, Sir John Pakington, also a royalist, was elected the day before at Aylesbury.

[427] The figures given were 170 for him, about 500 for Wilde, and over 600 for Salway. D'Ewes (N), 463.

who was a royalist,[428] were supported in the House by Sir Henry Herbert, the Bewdley member, and, before the case was decided, he and Wilde at one time came to blows. But eventually Littleton's petition was dropped.[429]

Bewdley, a one member borough, had been listed for a royal nominee in 1623 and in the spring of 1640.[430] The return in October, 1640, of the man chosen in the spring, Sir Henry Herbert, a distinguished courtier, indicates that royal influence, as well as his ownership of lands in the county, gained him the place. Another return, sent by a larger number of electors, who seem to represent the freeholders rather than the bailiff and chief burgesses, named Sir Ralph Clare, K.B., a courtier from the neighborhood who had sat for Bewdley in four parliaments of the 1620's.[431] Perhaps those outside of the borough officers preferred their old member to Herbert, a new royal nominee. No challenge by Clare, however, seems to have reached the House.

Droitwich, a town which for some previous parliaments had named as one of its members the lawyer, Wilde, foe of the court, chose [432] in his place in October, 1640, none other than the professional courtier, Endymion Porter. He was a Gloucestershire man by birth and seems to have had no Droitwich or Worcestershire connections. With him was named Samuel Sandys of Ombersley, head of a prominent county family and M.P. for Droitwich in the spring. Both were royalists.

The Evesham election was contested, although the seat of Richard Cresheld, Serjeant at Law, recorder of the borough, and several times previously its M.P., was not in question. Named with him in the official return by mayor and corporation was William Sandys from nearby Fladbury, who had sat for Evesham in the Short Parliament. Another return of the same date, but irregular in form, named Cresheld and John Coventry.[433] The latter lived in Somerset, but came of a distinguished Worcestershire family. His return was not recognized by the House, but Sandys was first suspended and then expelled, 21 January 1641, as a monopolist, the charge having been brought, Sandys told one diarist, by Coventry. The new election, 2 February 1641, gave the place to Coventry.[434] Since both he and Sandys were

royalists, the choice between them seems to have been on personal rather than on political grounds.

At Worcester there had been considerable feeling against ship money,[435] and some resentment against the Avon River project of William Sandys (q.v.) which had been sanctioned by the crown, but the choice of its parliament men in 1640 followed traditional lines.[436] In the full county court of the city in session at the guildhall,[437] two aldermen of the town were elected, the aged John Cowcher and the younger John Nash. Both were members for Worcester in the spring, and both were parliamentarians.

YORKSHIRE

The Yorkshire members reflect the wide difference of opinion on national and local issues that characterized their county in 1640. A shire whose ship money had been fairly well collected until that year [438] but which petitioned that summer against the burden of soldiery brought on it by the Scottish war was perhaps naturally divided. The growing annoyance of the Council of the North and of Strafford's heavy hand, the wider spread of puritanism, particularly in the south and east and in the larger towns, and the concern in the cities about the future of their trade, all had their bearing on the elections. There were relatively few heated contests aside from those for the shire and the city of York, at both of which Strafford's candidates were beaten, and none of the returns was challenged. Most of the men elected were neighbors or residents of their constituencies, the chief exception being Sir Henry Vane, junior, who had been acepted at Hull in the spring after some persuading by his father and was returned again now. Family influence rather than public issues dictated the choice in many of the smaller boroughs, and men closely allied with the Catholic faith rubbed shoulders with Presbyterians and puritans.

To classify the Yorkshire parliament men by their politics is difficult, if not misleading. This was the county whose Hothams and Sir Hugh Cholmley fought for parliament and then turned to the king, whose William Mallory and Henry Belasyse were earlier and later spokesmen for the liberty of the subject before they became royalists in the summer of 1642. There was a considerable number of members, furthermore, who were attending their first parliament and whose opinions, aside from those of their families, are difficult to judge. It appears, however, if the members for two restored boroughs are not counted, or the parliamentarian from Hull who replaced the one of similar views

[428] Littleton was named in the king's commission of array in September, 1642. Birmingham Reference Library, Calendar of Worcester MSS, 206 (No. 351507).

[429] The hearings occurred during March, 1641, but no record of a decision remains. D'Ewes (N), 440–442, 461–463, 481–482, 492; C.J., 62, 75, 105.

[430] S.P. 16, 450/15.

[431] Bewdley indentures, C. 219/43/Part 3; W. R. Williams, The parliamentary history of the county of Worcester, 164, 166, Hereford, 1897 (hereafter, Williams, Worcester).

[432] The franchise seems to have been limited to the two bailiffs and a small number of burgesses. C. 219/43/Part 3.

[433] Evesham returns (ibid.). The final indenture naming Coventry, 2 February 1641, corresponds in form with the first one naming Cresheld and Sandys.

[434] M. of P. 1: 496; C.J. 2: 22, 26, 27, 71; D'Ewes (N), 23, n., 267, 268.

[435] Less than half of its 1636 assessment had been paid in by the end of 1638. C.S.P. Dom., 1638–1639, 391. These arrears were used later by royal consent for relief work. Worcester Corporation MSS, Order Book II, fol. 188; Audit Book II, 215.

[436] In 1625 and 1626 the city had yielded to external pressure in selecting outsiders for one or both places (ibid., Order Book II, fols. 91, 97), but usually both places went to citizens.

[437] Worcester indenture, C. 219/43/Part 3.

[438] Royal Hist. Soc., Trans., 3rd Ser., 4: 161, 1910.

who died, and if Belasyse, Cholmley, and the Hothams are considered as parliament supporters in 1640, that of the group of twenty-six chosen in the fall elections thirteen were parliamentarians and thirteen were royalists. The death of Lister of Hull in December made no change, for his successor, Pelham, held similar views. But the early restoration of the boroughs of Malton and North Allerton, bringing an increase of three to the side of parliament and a fourth, the lawyer, Heblethwaite, who worked at first with the dominant faction before he deserted the cause, can scarcely escape the interpretation of being accomplished by Pym's party as a means of strengthening their forces. And the change at Knaresborough, sanctioned if not connived in by Fairfax, whereby a henchman of the queen was ousted from his seat in 1641, to be replaced in 1642 by a member of the Fairfax clan, leads to the conclusion that the king's party had no monopoly on election management.

The county elections in Yorkshire had in the 1620's been hotly contested affairs, manifestations usually of the Savile-Wentworth feud.[439] Wentworth's power was tested again at York Castle in October, 1640, but this time he lost. In spite of the king's taking his army out to exercise, allegedly to help keep order at the election, and of the sheriff's efforts,[440] Wentworth's candidates, his nephew, Sir William Savile, and Sir Richard Hutton, were beaten by his critics, Ferdinando Lord Fairfax and Henry Belasyse of Coxwold. But though the latter was in 1640 no follower of Strafford, he joined the king's party at the start of the war.

Aldborough was a town which was practically controlled by the owner of the manor,[441] since the electorate at this time consisted of fewer than a dozen burgesses. Richard Aldborough of Ellingthorpe Hall, son of the owner of the manor, and Robert Strickland of Thornton Bridge, who was a J.P. in the East Riding, were the members chosen on 7 October 1640.[442] Both were royalists.

Beverley, a closed corporation, returned two men of families which frequently supplied its M.P.'s at this period.[443] Occasionally there were attempts at control

from outside,[444] and there was a third candidate at each of the 1640 elections,[445] but those chosen for the Long Parliament were Sir John Hotham, Bart., of Scorborough, and Michael Warton of Beverley. The latter was a royalist by 1643, but his course may have been, like Hotham's, with parliament at the start.

Boroughbridge returned two strong parliamentarians, the burgage holders who elected numbering a score or more on this occasion.[446] Sir Philip Stapleton of Warter and Thomas Mauleverer of Allerton Mauleverer, both county J.P.'s, but new as representatives for Boroughbridge, were selected.[447]

The Hedon members likewise were parliamentarians, Sir William Strickland of Boynton and John Alured of the Charterhouse, near Hull. The latter had served for Hedon in the spring. The freemen of the town were the electors.[448]

Hull chose country party men for its members. The decay of its woolen trade and the scarcity of money had led the town government as early as 1621 to a study of causes. A report was submitted to the Privy Council with recommendations of means to cope with the competition of both Europeans and Londoners.[449] The failure of the royal administration to alleviate those troubles and the growing sympathy for puritanism at Hull help to explain the election returns of 1640. At elections before 1640, one seat had often been assigned to a nominee of the Steward of Hull,[450] but there was reluctance this year to accept a nominated candidate from any source. The persuasions of Secretary Vane in the spring, however, won the town's second seat for his son, Sir Henry Vane, junior,[451] and he was reelected in the autumn. Re-elected with him was Sir John Lister, one of Hull's most prominent citizens. But Lister died before the parliament had been sitting for two months, and he was replaced by another citizen and parliamentarian, Peregrine Pelham. The elections were conducted first in the Council House by the mayor

[439] V.C.H. York 3: 417; Arthur Gooder, The parliamentary representation of the county of York 2 (Y.A.S. Rec. Ser. 96, 1937): 121-135 (hereafter, Gooder, Parl. Rep. York). Mr. Gooder kindly let me use some of his notes and his manuscript while it was being prepared for publication.

[440] H.M.C., Second Report, MSS of the Right Honourable Earl Spencer, 19; Various Collections 8: MSS of the Hon. F. L. Wood, 54.

[441] G. R. Park, Parliamentary representation of Yorkshire, 220, Hull, 1886.

[442] Richard Aldborough's father and eight other burgesses signed the return (C. 219/43/Part 3). The number of burgage holders who voted was usually 7-11 in the seventeenth century, but there was an attempt after the Restoration to extend the franchise to all inhabitants paying scot and lot. Yorks. Arch. Jour. 34: 25-34, 1939.

[443] Beverley Borough Records, ed. J. Dennett (Y.A.S. Rec. Ser. 84, 1933), xv.

[444] Beverley Borough MSS, Minute Book 1597-1660, fol. 15.

[445] Ibid., fol. 66. The candidate defeated in October 1640, Sir Thomas Metham, was a royalist. Bean, Northern Counties, 740, 756, 763.

[446] Yorks. Arch. Jour. 27: 326, 1924; indenture, C. 219/43/ Part 3.

[447] Strafford had nominated a relative of Windebank's in the spring (C.S.P. Dom., 1639-1640, 347), but I have found no record of his intervention in the Long Parliament election.

[448] Park, Parliamentary representaiton of Yorkshire, 251.

[449] Hull Corporation MSS, Bench Book V, fols. 45-48.

[450] The Archbishop of Canterbury, as steward, and some royal officials had made successful nominations for some of the parliaments of James, but Strafford, who had become steward in July, 1640, does not seem to have tried to control the election (ibid., fols. 60v, 61, 70v, 262v, 264).

[451] Vane was nominated in the spring of 1640 by the Lord Admiral, and the town, though unwilling to recognize the nomination by virtue of that office, bowed to the wishes of Vane's father, the Secretary. C.S.P. Dom., 1639-1640, 568; Hull Corporation MSS, Letters, December, 1639.

and aldermen, the burgesses afterwards giving their assent in the Common Hall.[452]

Knaresborough, a town lying within the lands assigned to the queen, had in it some eighty-eight burgage houses which entitled their owners to vote. The number of actual electors was usually below that figure.[453] These burgesses elected to the Long Parliament Sir Henry Slingsby, Bart., of Scriven, and Henry Benson of Knaresborough, whose father was a leading property owner and whose stepson was bailiff and deputy steward of the manor. At both of the 1640 elections Slingsby and Benson defeated Sir Richard Hutton. They do not seem to have collaborated for the purpose, but each was supported by his own friends and workers, and in the autumn Slingsby supplied £16 worth of wine for the voters.[454] All three men were royalists. Benson, however, was evicted from parliament on 2 November 1641 for the sale of protections, his ousting being accomplished, it was said, by a local enemy, Thomas Stockdale, with the knowledge and perhaps the connivance of Lord Fairfax.[455] There followed an election on 12 November 1641, at which Fairfax's brother-in-law, Sir William Constable, won thirteen votes and Benson's stepson, William Dearlove, the bailiff, thirty-three. The Fairfax-Constable group declared that the burgesses had been intimidated because of Dearlove's position and challenged the election on that ground and on the argument that he, as bailiff, could not also be M.P.[456] After some debate the House on 7 December 1641 referred the case to a committee, but seemed less concerned about the election procedures than about Dearlove's character and his collaboration with Benson in the sale of protections. Not until 17 August 1642 was his election declared void. Constable's entry into the House then and the replacement of Slingsby later by Stockdale show the way the political tide had turned.[457]

New Malton was restored as a parliamentary borough on 11 December 1640.[458] The following month the freemen of the town [459] elected two lawyers of the East Riding as their representatives, Thomas Heblethwaite of Norton, owner of some property in Malton, and Henry Cholmley of Barley. The former was eventually a royalist, but Cholmely was a parliamentarian.

North Allerton, similarly restored, elected by its bailiff and burgesses on 15 January 1641 [460] a prominent puritan and foe of Strafford, Henry Darley of Buttercrambe, and John Wastell of Scorton, a lawyer of similar views.

Pontefract, a borough for which Sir Thomas Wentworth had sat in 1624,[461] elected two of his family in 1640.[462] Sir George Wentworth of Wentworth Woodhouse, Strafford's brother, had been elected in the spring also. With him in the fall was a cousin, Sir George Wentworth of Woolley. Both were royalists.

The resident burgesses of Richmond [463] chose as their M.P.'s two stanch royalists, Sir William Pennyman, Bart., of Marske, who had served for Richmond in the Short Parliament, and Sir Thomas Danby of Farnley, a cousin of Strafford's.

Members for Ripon were William Mallory of Studley, Ripon, who had long been influential in Ripon's affairs and many times its M.P., and his son, John Mallory. Both were royalists, although the elder Mallory had been of the country party in earlier parliaments.[464] The voters were the burgage holders, subject largely to the landlord, either the Archbishop of York or the Mallorys.[465]

Scarborough re-elected its members of the spring, Sir Hugh Cholmley of Whitby, who had sat for the borough several times, and his cousin, John Hotham, Esquire, of Scorborough. Both were prominent among the critics of Strafford in 1640, but both deserted parliament later. The electors here were the bailiffs, burgesses and commonalty.[466]

Thirsk, a borough several times before 1640 served by the family of Belasyse, chose again two members of that house. The electors were some two dozen burgesses, the burgage holders.[467] John Belasyse of Worlaby, Lincoln, who had sat for Ripon in April, was a younger son of Lord Fauconberg; and Sir Thomas Ingram of Sheriff Hutton was Fauconberg's son-in-law. Both were royalists.

York was restive at this period because of declining trade and was irked by the rule of the Council of the North, especially during Wentworth's presidency. There was a growing number of puritans and Presbyterians among its citizenry, also.[468] As early as 1632

[452] Hull Corporation MSS, Bench Book V, fols. 60v, 70v.
[453] Park, *Parliamentary representation of Yorkshire*, 112; Bodleian MSS Top. Yorks. c. 4, fol. 4; *Yorks. Arch. Jour.* 34: 213–216, 1939.
[454] *The diary of Sir Henry Slingsby, of Scriven, Bart.,* 50–51, 63–64.
[455] See Benson. In a letter to Fairfax, 12 November 1641, Stockdale wrote, "Your lordship and I do divide the blame and malice of putting out Henry Benson and opposing William Dearlove's coming in." *Fairfax correspondence* 2: 261–262.
[456] *Ibid.* The indenture at the Public Record Office (C. 219/43/Part 3), however, shows twenty-six signers for Constable.
[457] D'Ewes (C), 242–243; *C.J.* 2: 334, 724, 725; Pink MSS, 299, fols. 577–578; *M. of P.* 1: 497.
[458] *C.J.* 2: 49.
[459] Indenture, 8 January 1641. C. 219/43/Part 3.
[460] Indenture, C. 219/43/Part 3.
[461] *M. of P.* 1: 461.
[462] The mayor, aldermen and burgesses, apparently a closed group, were the electors. C. 219/43/Part 3.
[463] Richmond indenture. C. 219/43/Part 3.
[464] The second seat had gone in the spring to a relative of the Archbishop of York, owner of Ripon manor, and frequently before to his nominees. *Ripon Millenary Record* 2: App., xiv, 1886–1891; Ripon Corporation MSS, Old Towne Book, 1607–1666, fols. 218, 356.
[465] *Yorks. Arch. Jour.* 32: 79–81, 1935.
[466] C. 219/43/Part 3.
[467] *Ibid.;* Park, *Parliamentary representation of Yorkshire,* 204.
[468] *The life of Marmaduke Rawdon of York,* ed. R. Davies, 125, n. (126–127), Camden Society, 1863; Francis Drake, *Ebo-*

the corporation adopted a rule against the choosing of "strangers" recommended to them as M.P.'s.[469] Two friends of Strafford, residents of the city, managed to carry the election for the Short Parliament. But on 28 September the voters refused re-election to Sir Edward Osborne, Vice President of the Council of the North, and Sir Thomas Widdrington, York's own recorder. The election, which was described by the latter as troublesome and disorderly,[470] went against them chiefly because Strafford had commended them and was present in York at the time, one observer reported.[471] Two prominent aldermen, Sir William Allanson and Thomas Hoyle, were elected instead.[472] Both were parliamentarians.

CINQUE PORTS

The Cinque Ports, numbering eight after the Long Parliament restored Seaford, and traditionally patron-controlled, sent twenty-one men as their "barons" to the House before January, 1642. The extra number is accounted for by replacements for vacancies caused by death or by the choice of another constituency, but especially by the expulsion of three court sympathizers as "monopolists." The Duke of Lenox seems to have exercised the Lord Warden's usual privilege of naming at least one baron in each port except in the restored borough of Seaford and at Sandwich, where the local freemen defied the attempt of their magistrates to follow his counsel. His nominees included officials at Dover and in the customs service, at least one courtier of a prominent Sussex family, and others who enjoyed some personal connection by kinship or service with himself.[473] Most of them were royalists. Other royalists who owed their seats to patronage were a secretary of the Sussex nobleman, the Earl of Dorset, and a son of the Finch family which controlled both the earldom and the port of Winchelsea.

Despite the shadow of patronage in the port elections, here as elsewhere in 1640 the trend was to the electing of local men. Few were actually residents of the towns that chose them, but most of them, even some of the "nominated" candidates, were of Kent or Sussex families and some lived near the towns. The chief carpet-baggers were two customs farmers, a secretary of the Lord Warden, a connection of his by marriage and another possibly in the employ of his family and, by contrast, the son of one of the puritan leaders of parliament. At least two of the ports, Sandwich and Hastings, illustrate another current trend in the attempt of the commonalty to override the decisions of their magistrates regarding elections.

In politics the Cinque Ports were divided, the country party men outnumbering the royalists nine to seven in the original group. Even two who owed their places to the patronage of Lenox adhered to parliament at least until 1648. The by-elections, chiefly to replace royalists, gave the country party a wider margin, for one royalist so returned, Webb, was ousted almost as soon as he was elected, and another who eventually joined the king, William Smith, seems to have favored moderate reform until some time in 1642. The other "recruiters" were parliamentarians.[474]

Dover, accustomed to receiving nominations from the Lord Warden for one or both of its barons, one place frequently going to an official of the castle,[475] chose for both of the 1640 parliaments two Kentish men of parliamentary views who had been associated with Cinque Port affairs, Sir Peter Heyman of Somerfield and Sir Edward Boys of Fredville, deputy constable of the castle. When Heyman died early in 1641 Benjamin Weston, younger brother of the Earl of Portland, was named in his place. He seems to have had no previous connection with the town, and may have been the nominee of Lenox, a brother-in-law of Portland. He espoused the side of parliament, however, keeping his seat until the end. The voters at Dover included the mayor, jurats, and "commonalty." [476]

At Hastings the Short Parliament election had aroused considerable feeling between the corporation and the freemen of the town, the former supporting candidates backed by various noblemen, including the Lord Warden, and the freemen supporting a Sussex puritan gentleman who owned property there, and declaring that the corporation's candidates had offered bribes of money and supplies to secure their election.[477] In the autumn two of the court candidates again presented themselves, Secretary Windebank's nephew and secretary, Robert Read, whom the corporation had upheld in the spring, and John Ashburnham, the well known courtier from Sussex, who had served for Hastings in 1628 and had failed of election in the spring be-

---

racum: or the history and antiquities of the city of York, 230–231, London, 1736 (hereafter, Drake, York).

[469] York Corporation MSS, House Book 35, fol. 180. This was during the mayoralty of Thomas Hoyle (q.v.), who in 1628 successfully challenged the return of Sir Thomas Savile as one of York's members. M. of P. 1: 479; Add. MSS, 33,595, fol. 46v.

[470] H.M.C., Twelfth Report 4, MSS of the Duke of Rutland (I), 523.

[471] C.S.P. Dom., 1640–1641, 158.

[472] The York indenture (C. 219/43/Part 3) declares that the election was unanimous. The way to unanimity had been prepared in 1620 by the adoption of a rule of election procedure which carefully limited the group representing the "commonalty" who, with the mayor, aldermen and upper council, acted as electors. York Corporation MSS, House Book 34, fols. 208v–209.

[473] The following were probably nominees of the Lord Warden: Weston and possibly Boys (Dover); Ashburnham (Hastings); Harvey (Hythe); Warwick and Webb (New Romney); Jacob (Rye); Crispe and probably Smith (Winchelsea).

[474] The parliamentarians eventually outnumbered the royalists by 11 to 5.

[475] J. Bavington Jones, Annals of Dover, 379–382, Dover, "Dover Express" Works, 1916; C.S.P. Dom., 1619–1623, 192; 1625–1626, 217; 1627–1628, 583.

[476] C. 219/43/Part 3; C.S.P. Dom., 1628–1629, 7.

[477] Ibid., 1639–1640, 565–566, 607; 1640, 3, 12, 17, 28, 56; S.P. 16, 405/39.

cause he had started his race too late.[478] This time, however, the rank and file of the freemen were better organized to oppose the mayor and jurats and, though Ashburnham's election must be traced to the rulers' and the Lord Warden's support, the defeat of Read by the puritan gentleman, Thomas Eversfield of Grove, Sussex, must be attributed to the freemen.[479] Rumors that Read was a papist contributed to his defeat, and his attempt to prove priority over his opponent as a freeman of the town was of no avail.[480]

Hythe, a borough accustomed to choosing one or two nominees of the Lord Warden, had as its electors in 1640 the mayor, jurats, commonalty, and freemen, the total number present on 20 October 1640 being thirty-two.[481] The choice fell on a stanch parliamentarian and neighbor of the town, Henry Heyman, son of a former member for Hythe and himself its representative in the Short Parliament, and on John Harvey of London. The latter was a native of Folkstone, but seems to have concerned himself little with Hythe before this time. He was probably the Lord Warden's nominee.[482] The Duke of Lenox was later charged in parliament with having interfered in the Hythe elections.[483] Harvey supported parliament, however, rather than the king.

New Romney held three elections to fill its seats. Although local men had been sent to the preceding session, the assembly of the corporation sent word to the Lord Warden four days before the election that they approved his nominee, Philip Warwick, the royalist, and on 18 October, with twenty-one present, the mayor, jurats, and commonalty elected Warwick and Norton Knatchbull as their burgesses. Both were Kentish men, but neither had been previously a freeman of New Romney. Warwick presently sent the corporation a gift of £20 and asked permission to take his freeman's oath by commission in London instead of appearing at Romney; but soon after parliament opened he decided to make the Welsh borough of Radnor his constituency and a new election had to be held at Romney. On 13 November, with twenty-two present, the town chose in his place the Lord Warden's secretary, Thomas Webb, another royalist who had no connection with the borough. But he was expelled from parliament as a monopolist, 21 January 1641. After considerable delay, the voters of New Romney, with twenty-two present, chose on 26 April a Kentish gentleman who had been disappointed in the county election, Richard Browne of Great

Chart.[484] With his election, the port now had as its members two supporters of parliament.

Rye elected, by its mayor, jurats, and commonalty,[485] two royalists and non-residents as its first members for the Long Parliament. One was John White, probably of a Sussex family, who as the Earl of Dorset's secretary had secured a seat for Rye in the spring; and the other was Sir John Jacob of London, farmer of the customs, and probably the Lord Warden's nominee. Jacob was expelled as a monopolist, however, on 21 January 1641, and Rye then elected in his place William Hay of Horsted Parva, Sussex, member of a local puritan and parliamentary family, and brother-in-law of a Rye resident.

Sandwich had had a confused election in the spring, when the commonalty, tricked as they felt themselves to have been by the officials, declined to vote for their candidates who were nominees of the Lord Warden and the Lord Admiral, and petitioned parliament to recognize their own candidates, two Kentish gentlemen, Sir Thomas Peyton, Bart., of Knowlton, and Edward Partridge of Bridge.[486] In early October, when plans for the new parliament were in the making, the mayor and jurats reported with chagrin to the Lord Warden that they doubted whether his nominee, Lord Grandison, could be elected, since many of the commons were refractory and even the more reserved commoners seemed to be pledged to Mr. Partridge. Peyton, too, was in the field, but was so much less certain of his ground that he had to forego attending the shire election in order to look after his interests in Sandwich.[487] On 28 October the mayor, jurats and commonalty gathered at the guildhall at the sound of the horn and, by common consent, admitted as freemen of the port four candidates; namely Lord Grandison, Nathaniel Finch, one of the candidates of the spring, and Partridge and Peyton. With the customary procedure of "pricking" the votes of those present, the election resulted in a majority for Peyton and Partridge. The former was present and took his oath, but Partridge, so sure of himself as to be absent from the election, entered upon his service without taking the oath of either freeman or baron.[488] As the mayor reported to Lenox, Grandison received 87 voices "of the better sort," but the unruly multitude, worked upon by agents from some of the castles, gave 106 votes to Partridge and 179 to Peyton.[489] Both of the men so

[478] C.S.P. Dom., 1639–1640, 607; 1640–1641, 158, 160–161.

[479] Read seems to have had the Lord Warden's support this time only for the second seat, but was backed as before by the Earl of Dorset and another.

[480] Ibid., 172, 198; S.P. 16, 450/39/i. One allegation against Eversfield in the spring was that he was neither freeman nor resident, although various freemen were tenants of his.

[481] George Wilks, The barons of the Cinque Ports, 68–75, 77, Folkstone, 1892?; Hythe Borough MSS, Assembly Book, 1608–1624, 1635–1645, fol. 240.

[482] See sketch of John Harvey below.

[483] Arch. Cant. 12: 84–85, 1878.

[484] New Romney Borough MSS, Common Assembly Book, 1622–1701, fols. 257–265, 282–283, 293; C.J. 2: 71.

[485] These were the voters named in the 1645 indenture. C. 219/43/Part 3.

[486] Sandwich Borough MSS, 5.M.7 (Year Book C and D), fols. 364v–367v; 5.N.5 (Letters, 1639–1644), fols. 11–14; Add. MSS, 33,512, fols. 30, 36; C.S.P. Dom., 1639–1640, 561, 568–569; Add. MSS, 44,846, Peyton letters of 23 and 24 March 1640.

[487] Sandwich Borough MSS, 5.N.5, fols. 37v–38; Add. MSS, 44,846, Peyton letters of 19 and 25 October 1640.

[488] Sandwich Borough MSS, 5.M.7, fols. 376v–377.

[489] Ibid., 5.N.5, fol. 38. The Lord Warden's request for a record of the voting by name could not be acceded to because

chosen were interested in reforms and Partridge especially had some knowledge of Sandwich's local problems. He was a stanch puritan and parliamentarian, but Peyton was loyal to the king personally and turned to his side in time.

Seaford was restored as a parliamentary borough on 4 February 1641, in spite of the fears of some of the puritan leaders that the lord of the town would at once cause papists to be chosen as its parliament men. Others reassured them, asserting that "wee would take care hee should not send papists to bee members heere,"[490] and their measures were effective, for the two men returned were Sir Thomas Parker of Ratton, Sussex, a strong parliamentarian, and Francis Gerard of Middlesex, heir of Sir Gilbert Gerard, a prominent puritan leader, and kinsman of Hampden. The conversion of young Gerard to the king's side, 1642–1645, was scarcely in accord with the plan, but he was afterwards allowed to repent and return to the Commons.

Winchelsea, though its electors were described as mayor, jurats, and freemen,[491] was a much impoverished borough,[492] and for some years had been largely influenced by the Finch family, some one of whom had sat for the town in most of the parliaments since 1620. The family member in both 1640 parliaments was John Finch, who seems to have supported parliament mildly until his death in 1642. The other seat went first to Sir Nicholas Crispe, Londoner and royalist customs farmer, who too had served in the Short Parliament, possibly as the Lord Warden's nominee. On Crispe's expulsion as a monopolist, 2 February 1641, Winchelsea replaced him with another outsider, a Middle Temple lawyer, William Smith of Buckinghamshire, who had possibly some slight connection with the Lord Warden. Smith was a moderate parliamentarian at the start, but was eventually expelled as a royalist in 1644.

WALES

The principality of Wales, with its twelve counties and twelve boroughs that were entitled to a single seat each, returned to Westminster in the autumn of 1640 a group who were largely royalists and for the most part Welshmen. There were few contests, the principal ones occurring in Carnarvonshire. The loyalty to the crown which James I had cultivated was bearing fruit, and feeling against the current abuses in church and state seems not to have been widespread. The mild puritanism that had filtered into some of the eastern and commercial areas by the 1620's had developed no strong political force, and such voices as had been raised in the 1621 parliament against monopolies were generally quiet

now.[493] Even the ship money collections appear to have gone smoothly until the year before the Long Parliament, and no close correlation can be shown between the arrears of certain counties then [494] and the politics of their M.P.'s. Welsh descent, family connection, pressure through officials of the crown, and by such noble families as the Herberts were the chief influences at work at the elections. Court pressure may possibly account for the choice of six members, although all but one of them were Welshmen born. The family of the Earl of Pembroke and Montgomery filled four of the Welsh seats, in addition to others in neighboring counties. The feuding families of the north, Wynn of Gwydir and Griffith of Llyn, won two seats each, with three other places going to men usually associated with the house of Wynn. And men of other prominent families in their respective counties filled the remaining seats.

The elections were in most instances uneventful. Of the Brecon contest we know only that the court candidate was allowed to take his seat before a decision was reached and that he continued to hold it. And in Carnarvonshire, where the family quarrels of Wynn and Griffith colored both shire and borough elections, there was injected another issue that was peculiar to Wales, the rights of the "out boroughs" who participated with the chief county town in choosing the single borough M.P.[495] The lack of emphasis on national issues accounts somewhat for the difficulty in classifying all the Welsh members as to their politics, and for the trouble several had in deciding on their roles and in playing them consistently. Three-fourths of the twenty-four members may be called royalists, though at least three of these vacillated for some time and were not unseated until the war was far advanced. And one man of the six who are considered as parliamentarians was not continuously in the trust of the popular party. The distance from Westminster and the concern with local rather than with English politics must be taken into account in the analysis of the Welsh elections.[496]

The Anglesey members represented factions that in local affairs were ancient enemies. John Bodvel of Llanigrad was returned for the county, and John Griffith, the elder, of Llyn, Carnarvonshire, sat for Beaumaris. Both elections were held at Beaumaris on 15

---

the tally was kept only for the names of the candidates, not showing who cast each vote.

[490] D'Ewes (N), 321–322; *C.J.* **2**: 78.

[491] W. D. Cooper, Parliamentary history of Sussex, Horsfield, *History of Sussex* **2**: Appendix iii, 72.

[492] See Evelyn's description of it in 1652, cited in *Sussex Arch. Coll.* **8**: 211, 1856.

[493] G. H. Dodd, Wales's parliamentary apprenticeship (1536–1625), *Transactions of the Honourable Society of Cymmrodorion*, 53, 1942 (hereafter, *Trans. of the Hon. Soc. of Cymmrodorion*).

[494] Royal Hist. Soc., *Trans.*, 3rd Ser., **4**: 142, 162, 1910.

[495] For a discussion of the rights of the burgesses of the "out boroughs" in another Welsh county in the seventeenth century, see the evidence brought up in the Montgomery election of 1728. *Collections historical and archaeological relating to Montgomeryshire*, by the Welshpool-Powysland Club, **22**: 204–205, 1888 (hereafter, *Montgomeryshire Collections*).

[496] See A. H. Dodd's study of the part the Welsh members played in the English parliaments, 1536–1625 (*Trans. of the Hon. Soc. of Cymmrodorion*, 8–72, 1942). Many of his conclusions are appropriate for the 1640 group of M.P.'s.

October 1640, the borough electors being the mayor, bailiffs, and burgesses.[497] Bodvel had sat for Anglesey in the spring and supported the reforming faction for a time, but turned to the king when war came. Griffith, a new incumbent for Beaumaris, was a royalist from the start.

The county of Brecon returned as its member a lawyer and royal official of the region, William Morgan of Ddrew, who had served for the shire in the spring. He steered a middle course in politics, managing to keep his seat, but being several times suspected of royalism. Brecon borough had a double return, but the House seems never to have determined the case in its entirety. It simply followed the recommendation of the Committee of Privileges in ordering on 6 January 1641 that Herbert Price should sit, and that Robert Williams should not sit, until the election could be determined.[498] Possibly Price's service for Brecon in the Short Parliament gave him his advantage. He was a Brecon man, but a courtier and royalist.[499]

The Cardigan county member, though a newcomer to parliament, was a well known local magistrate of royalist views, Walter Lloyd of Llanfair Clydogan and Llaney. Returned for Cardigan borough was the distinguished lawyer, John Vaughan of Trawscoed, Cardiganshire, who had sat for the town in two preceding parliaments. He kept in favor with the parliamentarians through 1644, but was eventually classified as a royalist. Both men from Cardiganshire arrived at Westminster more than a month late because the sheriff had receved the writs too late to conduct the elections at the appointed time.[500]

Carmarthen county re-elected on 5 November its Short Parliament M.P., Henry Vaughan of Derwydd, a royalist whose family had wide influence in the county. Chosen by the mayor and burgesses of Carmarthen town on 19 October[501] was Francis Lloyd of Maesyfelin, county Cardigan, a courtier and royalist, who had served for the borough in the spring.

Carnarvon witnessed the most heated election contests, both for the county and for the borough, of any of those in Wales in 1640. The issues were more local than national, representing feuds betwen local families, although the old struggle of the Wynns of Gwdir and the Griffiths of Llyn was less evident than on previous occasions.[502] Both elections were delayed by the late

arrival of the writs, but protests eventually reached parliament against the return of John Griffith, junior, for the county and of William Thomas for the borough.[503] The Griffith candidates had carried the elections, largely through the management of John Griffith, the elder, but one of the Wynn family, backers of Thomas Glyn in both cases, rejoiced that the victory had cost Griffith a great deal of money.[504] William Thomas of Aber was supported by the Griffiths this time, although his father had previously assisted the Wynns against the Griffith faction.

In the case of the county, it was charged by Thomas Glyn, who was probably the county's member in the spring, and elder brother of John Glyn, the lawyer (q.v.), that the sheriff delayed the poll for several hours and afterwards moved it to a meadow outside the town, upon the request of Griffith's father. According to Glyn, a voice vote favoring him had already been taken, and many of his supporters departed, thinking the poll had been adjourned until the next county day. On Griffith's side it was declared that the Glyn faction had got possession of the writ, failing to deliver it to the sheriff until the morning of the election; but they declared that all the other proceedings were regular and that more than 500 voted for Griffith. Committee hearings on the case were ordered as late as 13 May 1641,[505] and it was rumored in July that only the pressure of business had prevented a report to the House recommending a new election.[506] No such report seems to have been made.

As to Carnarvon borough, the Griffiths were involved because the elder John Griffith was mayor there and responsible for the election. It was held on December 3, the day after the county election,[507] as the custom was, so that men from the "out boroughs," such as Conway, could vote for their collective borough representative while they were in town on county business. Thomas Glyn, the challenger for this seat as well as for that of the shire, asserted that Griffith refused to give the proper notice to the "out boroughs,"[508] letting the word of the election reach those who had come for the county voting only informally or by hearsay, and refusing to grant an extension of time so that more men might be summoned.[509] The committee on elections seems at

[497] Indentures, C. 219/43/Part 3.

[498] C.J. 2: 63; D'Ewes (N), 223.

[499] The original returns for Brecon are missing. According to that of 1647, the electors were the aldermen, capital burgesses, and other burgesses. C. 219/43/Part 3.

[500] M. of P. 1: 498 and n. The borough electors were the mayor and burgesses. C. 219/43/Part 3.

[501] Indentures, C. 219/43/Part 3.

[502] For the scheming by both sides in the 1621 election, see the Calendar of Wynn (of Gwydir) Papers, 1515–1690, 144–148, 155–157, Aberystwith, National Library of Wales, 1926 (hereafter, Cal. Wynn Papers). The Wynn papers contain many references to later elections of this period also.

[503] C.J. 2: 25, 86–87.

[504] Cal. Wynn Papers, 272.

[505] C.J. 2: 123, 143, 144, 145; D'Ewes (N), 455, n., 490; W. R. Williams, The parliamentary history of the principality of Wales, 60, Brecknock, 1895 (hereafter, Williams, Parl. Hist. Wales).

[506] Cal. Wynn Papers, 274.

[507] C. 219/43/Part 3.

[508] The Carnarvon indenture of 3 December 1640, made in the name of John Griffith as mayor, was endorsed by about 57 men, including several who described themselves as mayors, aldermen, and bailiffs of neighboring villages. C. 219/43/Part 3.

[509] At the committee hearings on 8 March the witnesses differed as to the number of Conway men present. It seems, however, that of perhaps forty Conway burgesses slightly under thirty had come to the shire election, and possibly a few more

one time to have planned to report Thomas's election as void, but as in the case of the shire, the report was never given.[510] The consequence was that both John Griffith the younger of Llyn and William Thomas of Aber kept their seats until they were disabled for other reasons—Griffith for charges of immoral conduct, and Thomas for royalism.

Two men of prominent Denbigh families, both parliamentarians, sat for the county and borough. Sir Thomas Middleton of Chirk Castle was the shire member. He had represented the shire twice before, though not since 1625, and replaced a man of royalist views who had sat in the spring.[511] The borough member was Simon Thelwell of Plas-y-Ward, a newcomer to parliament.

The Flint members, both disabled as royalists in 1644, and both of local families, were John Mostyn of the Inner Temple and of Tregarneth, Anglesey, who had sat for the county in the spring, and John Salisbury, junior, of Bachegraig. The latter had not served for Flint borough before, but he seems to have been chosen without opposition by the "burgesses" of that town and of other boroughs within the county. The electors included several prominent country gentlemen.[512]

Two Herberts occupied the Glamorgan seats, but they were not closely akin and were different in their politics. The county member, Philip Lord Herbert, a Somerset magistrate, doubtless owed his place to his father, the Earl of Pembroke and Montgomery, who was Vice Admiral of South Wales, and whom he followed in politics. The M.P. for Cardiff borough was William Herbert of Cogan Pill and Cardiff. Although he had possibly been an official in local administration under the earl, this Herbert was a royalist.

The single place for Merioneth county was filled by William Price of Rhiwlas, Merioneth, a young man who had but recently come into his estates in this and nearby counties, and had never served before in parliament. He was the grandson of a prominent royal official and supported the king.

Montgomeryshire, home of the Herberts of Cherbury and their kin, had usually chosen in the previous century Herberts or their nominees, sometimes dividing the honors with the family of Price.[513] The county member elected in the autumn of 1640 was Sir John Price, Bart., of Newton, a kinsman of the Herberts. He was apparently an anti-court man when he was elected and was a stranger to parliament, but late in 1645 he was counted a royalist. The Montgomery borough member, elected by the two bailiffs and the burgesses,[514] was Richard Herbert, heir of the Earl of Cherbury, who had sat for the shire in the spring and was a royalist.

Pembroke county and its two boroughs returned the men who had served in the Short Parliament. The shire knight, a veteran of many parliaments for his county, was John Wogan, the elder, of Wiston, a parliamentarian. From Haverfordwest came Sir John Stepney, Bart., of Prendergast, who was a royalist, although his town favored parliament.[515] Pembroke borough re-elected Hugh Owen of Orielton, a wealthy gentleman and magistrate, who supported parliament.

Radnor's members were both royalists. The county member, Captain Charles Price of Pilleth, a friend of Strafford, had represented the borough often and had sat for the county in the spring. The Radnor borough member, who was chosen by the burgesses of the various boroughs in the county,[516] was the only non-Welshman returned by a Welsh constituency to this parliament. He was Philip Warwick of Westminster, a court nominee who had never before been a parliament man.

---

[510] Ibid.; Cal. Wynn Papers, 274.
[511] Sir Thomas Salisbury, Bart. Willis 3: 239.
[512] C. 219/43/Part 3.

than half of that number voted in the borough election. D'Ewes (N), 455–456, n., 475, n. (475–476).

[513] E.H.R. 46: 227–228, 1931.
[514] C. 219/43/Part 3.
[515] Archaeologia Cambrensis, 6th Ser., 15: 1–4, 1915 (hereafter, Arch. Camb.).
[516] Those were the electors, according to the 1647 indenture. C. 219/43/Part 3.

PART III

BIOGRAPHICAL DICTIONARY OF THE PARLIAMENT MEN

An asterisk (*) before any name in the following biographical dictionary indicates that material on that person appears in *D.N.B.* Full accounts of such lives are not included here.

George Abbot (1601–1645), of London, merchant, was M.P. for Guildford, Surrey, 1640–1645.[1] He was the third but eldest surviving son of the great London merchant, lord mayor, and M.P., Sir Maurice Abbot (d. 1642), by his second wife, Margaret Barnes, and a nephew of Laud's predecessor in the archbishopric of Canterbury.[2] He was baptized at St. Stephen's, Coleman Street, 14 June 1601,[3] and until he was about thirty pursued an academic career. He matriculated at Balliol, Oxford, in 1619, was graduated B.A. (1621–1622), M.A. (1625), and B.C.L. (1630), became a fellow at Merton College in 1622, and in 1627 was incorporated at Cambridge.[4] Probably the deaths of his older brothers, whereby he became his father's heir,[5] called him from the cloisters to trade, for he was afterwards described as a merchant and of London.[6]

The earlier generation of the Abbot family had been born at Guildford, and Sir Maurice was a Surrey J.P.,[7] but George seems to have had no public relations with the borough or the county before 1640. He was elected to both of the 1640 parliaments by Guildford, but he was not anxious for the seat. Not only is his name missing from committee lists and debates and the list of the members who took the Protestation of 1641,[8] but on 6 July 1641 it was moved at Abbot's request that he be permitted to decline his election and be replaced. His indebtedness for £150,000 was the reason he gave for his plea. The House denied the request,[9] but Abbot was probably absent much of the time. He was summoned to attend on 22 January 1644 and 29 September 1645, but was probably out of the country on business on the latter occasion, for he died soon afterwards at Salamanca. He was buried on 12 or 14 November 1645 at St. Stephen's.[10] He left a widow, Mary, daughter and coheir of Sir John Windham.[11]

Abbot was in 1640 the heir to a large fortune and business. Whether the debts referred to in his plea to be dismissed from parliament were actually embarrassing, or whether they represented business so great that they required all his attention, is uncertain. No figures estimating the value of his father's business and his have been found. Abbot seems not to have taken enough interest in the affairs of parliament to pledge support for the loans of 1640–1641, but he must have been considered at least tolerant of the parliamentary party since he kept his seat nominally until his death. He should not be confused with George Abbott, "the puritan," who was M.P. for Tamworth, 1645–1649.[12]

Edward Acton (1600–1659), of Aldenham Hall and Acton, Shropshire, was M.P. for Bridgnorth, 1640–5 February 1644.[13] He was the son and heir of Walter Acton of Aldenham Hall and his wife, Frances, daughter and heiress of Edward Acton of Acton Scott. His family was well known in the county, and his father was active in county affairs, serving as sheriff in 1630, and being long a J.P.[14] Edward was baptized at Morville, 20 July 1600, and about 1620 he married Sarah, daughter of Richard Mytton of Halston, Shropshire.[15] He seems to have held no public office before 1640, probably because his father was still active. Possibly he owed his seat for Bridgnorth in both parliaments of 1640 to the Whitmore family, owners of much of the town, with whom his London kinsman, Sir William Acton, was intimate.[16]

In the Long Parliament Acton offered his bond for £1000 for the loan of March, 1641,[17] but otherwise played no important part in its affairs. He took the king's side when war came, was disabled 5 February 1644, and sat in the Oxford parliament. The king created him a baronet as a reward for his loyalty, 17 January 1644.

---

[1] *M. of P.* **1**: 494.

[2] Abbot is mentioned briefly in *D.N.B.*, "Sir Maurice Abbot." See also *Surrey Arch. Coll.* **3**: 257, 1865.

[3] Pink MSS, 296, fol. 2.

[4] *Al. Oxon.; Al. Cant.*

[5] He was called so in 1630. *Surrey Arch. Coll.* **3**: 257, 1865.

[6] He was identified as of London when he was elected M.P. in March, 1640 (*M. of P.* **1**: 483). One George Abbot was living in All Hallowes Barking in 1638 and a Mr. Abbot was living near Sir Maurice Abbot in St. Michael, Cornhill. T. C. Dale, *The inhabitants of London in 1638,* 4, 145, The Society of Genealogists, London, 1931 (hereafter, Dale, *Inhabitants of London*).

[7] C. 193/13; S.P. 16/405.

[8] *C.J.* **2**: 132–133, *passim;* Pink MSS, 296, fol. 2.

[9] *C.J.* **2**: 201; D'Ewes (B), 20.

[10] *C.J.* **3**: 374; Pink MSS, 296, fol. 2; Joseph Foster, Members of Parliament, *Collectanea Genealogica* **2**: 1, 1883 (hereafter, *Coll. Geneal.*).

[11] *N. and Q.,* 1st Ser., **10**: 384, 1854.

[12] *Coll. Geneal.* **2**: 2, 1883; *Al. Cant.*

[13] *M. of P.* **1**: 492; *C.J.* **3**: 389.

[14] C. 193/13; S.P. 16/405.

[15] *Complete Baronetage* **2**: 217; Foster, Members of Parliament, England, 11 (*Coll. Geneal.* **2**, 1883).

[16] Shrops. Arch. Soc., *Trans.,* 4th Ser., **4**: 281, 1914.

[17] D'Ewes gives the name as Sir William Acton, but Sir William was not a member. D'Ewes (N), 438, n.

Eventually he compounded for his estates. Acton died at the age of fifty-nine and was buried on 29 June 1659.

Apparently Acton had an ample estate. His fine as a delinquent at two-thirds was £5242, reduced later to a third, £2000. In his will, dated 20 March 1651/2, he listed a manor and other lands in the county for his four younger children and set aside £500 as a legacy for one of them.[18]

Richard Aldborough, or **Aldeburgh** (1607–1649), of Ellingthorpe Hall, Aldborough, sat for the Yorkshire town of Aldborough from 1640 until he was disabled, 6 September 1642. He was the eldest son and heir apparent of Arthur Aldborough (living in 1654) by his wife, Elizabeth, daughter of Richard Holland of Heaton, Lancashire,[19] and was born in 1607.[20] He matriculated at Magdalene College, Cambridge, at Easter, 1624.[21] He represented Aldborough in the parliaments of 1625 and 1626, owing his election no doubt to his father, who owned the manor.[22] He married Alice, daughter of William Mallory of Studley (q.v.), at Ripon Cathedral on 22 November 1627.[23] No more is known on him until 1640, when he was elected by Aldborough to the Short Parliament. He and his father were present at the county election in October, and when Richard was elected again at his old constituency that month, his father was the principal burgess there and as such signed the return.[24]

Aldborough was not active in the Long Parliament, but voted against the attainder of Strafford.[25] He was absent at call on 16 June 1642, was disabled the following September 6, and sat in the Oxford parliament.[26] He finally left the country and died beyond seas at Michaelmas, 1649. His father, who had been in arms for the king, and Richard's son, William, afterwards compounded for his sequestered estates. His possessions seem to have consisted mainly of Humberton manor and Kirby rectory, which had been settled on him at the time of his marriage, his father having reserved to himself then a life interest in the Ellingthorpe property of a declared value of £160 a year. Aldborough became joint owner with his father-in-law in 1641 of another Yorkshire manor.[27]

His father-in-law and his brother-in-law, John Mallory, were M.P.'s in 1640 for Ripon. One of his sisters married the brother and heir of Sir George Wentworth of Woolley,[28] another colleague.

Sir Edward Alford (c. 1592–1653), of Cashiobery, Hertfordshire, member for Arundel, Sussex, until his disablement, 22 January 1644, was definitely seated for Arundel after a return naming him also for Tewkesbury was voided, 6 August 1641. He was in the House before that date, taking the Protestation on 3 May.[29] The second son of Edward Alford of Offington, Sussex (d. 1631), and younger brother of John Alford, M.P. for Shoreham (q.v.), he was born about 1592. He matriculated at Christ Church, Oxford, in 1612 and in 1614 entered Lincoln's Inn.[30] His father, M.P. for Colchester in 1625 and a contestant there in 1628, was an ardent champion of reforms, and Edward, who was elected for Steyning in 1628,[31] may have followed his lead then. But after his father's death Edward formed connections which perhaps explain his forsaking the views his father held. He was knighted at Whitehall on 8 December 1632 and that month he married Mary, daughter of Baptist Hicks, Viscount Camden, who was twice a widow[32] and a coheiress of her father. She brought to Alford an interest in numerous properties in the shires of Gloucester, Warwick, and Hertford.[33] Their chief residence seems to have been at Cashiobery in Hertfordshire, an estate which had been left to Lady Alford by her first husband. Sir Edward was named to several local commissions in that county and was a J.P. for St. Albans in 1639.[34] He received in 1636 a warrant for using his dogs at Cashiobery,[35] but he also had a town house in Holborn.[36] After his wife's death in 1639, probably after 1640, Alford married Ann Corbett, daughter of the Chancellor of Norwich.[37]

Of Alford's politics during the 1630's little is known. He sent no answer to the request for contributions to the crown in 1639,[38] was elected by Tewkesbury to the

---

[18] Pink MSS, 296, fol. 13. Acton's will, dated 20 March 1651/2, was proved 24 December 1659. P.C.C., 520 Pell.

[19] *Visitation of Yorkshire in 1584/5 and 1612,* 279, ed. Joseph Foster, London, 1875.

[20] His parents were married shortly after 25 January 1606, and he was aged slightly over six in January 1613/4. I.P.M. of Richard Aldborough, C. 142/669/5.

[21] *Al. Cant.*

[22] *M. of P.* **1**: 467, 473; Lawson-Tancred, Parliamentary History of Aldborough and Boroughbridge, *Yorks. Arch. Jour.* **27**: 326, 1924.

[23] *Yorks. Arch. Jour.* **17**: 180 and n., 1902–03.

[24] *M. of P.;* Yorkshire and Aldborough indentures, C. 219/43/ Part 3.

[25] "Mr. Albro." Verney, 58.

[26] *C.J.* **2**: 626, 754; *O.P.H.* **9**: 12.

[27] *Cal. Com. Comp.,* 1958, 1986–1987; *Yorkshire royalist composition papers,* ed. J. W. Clay, *Y.A.S. Rec. Ser.* **18**: 217, 1895.

[28] *The visitation of the county of York, 1665 and 1666, by William Dugdale,* Surtees Society **36**: 10, 1859 (hereafter, Dugdale, *Vis. York*).

[29] *C.J.* **2**: 133, 239; **3**: 352, 374, 378–379.

[30] *Rec. Linc. Inn Adm.* **1**: 164.

[31] *M. of P.* **1**: 475, 478; *Debates in the House of Commons in 1625,* ed. S. R. Gardiner, 8, 69–70, 121, Camden Society, 1873 (hereafter, *Commons Debates in 1625*); *Essex Review* **5**: 193–196, 1896; John Forster, *Sir John Eliot* **1**: 128, 339; **2**: 99, London, 1864 (hereafter, Forster, *Eliot*). See William Masham.

[32] Her previous husbands were Sir Charles Morrison of Cashiobery (d. 1628) and Sir John Cooper of Dorset (d. 1631), father of Anthony Ashley Cooper.

[33] *Cal. Com. Comp.,* 85, 1009; S.P. 16, 534/120–122; *C.S.P. Dom., 1635–1636,* 323; *1636–1637,* 377; *1637–1638,* 495–496.

[34] C. 181/5, fols. 243, 260, 269, 270, 272.

[35] *C.S.P. Dom., 1635–1636,* 315.

[36] Dale, *Inhabitants of London,* 190.

[37] A son and a daughter of this union were baptized at Offington in 1645 and 1648. Foster, Members of Parliament, *Coll. Geneal.* **2**: 30; Add. MSS, 5698, fol. 187.

[38] Rushworth **3**: 913.

Short Parliament,[39] and in the autumn of 1640 was a candidate both there and at Arundel. Opposition by country party men in Gloucestershire led to a double return, which was the apparent reason for his choosing Arundel as his constituency. There was some question of his right to that seat, also, but the House confirmed his possession of it on 12 November 1641.[40] By this time he had voted against Strafford's attainder.[41] He served on no committees and before the summer of 1642 absented himself from parliament. He was active for the king during the war, and was afterwards fined heavily. He died intestate in 1653, aged sixty-one.

Sir Edward's estates, lying in five counties, were valued at considerably more than £1200 a year before the war. These did not include the Alford inheritance in Sussex to which he later succeeded.

Relatives of his in the 1640 House were his brother, John, a cousin, Fettiplace, Arthur Capel, who married his stepdaughter, and Baptist Noel, a nephew by marriage.[42]

John Alford (*c*. 1590–1649), of Offington in Broadwater, Sussex, M.P. for Shoreham, 1640–1648, was a brother of Edward Alford, the M.P. for Arundel (*q.v.*). He was the eldest son and heir of Edward Alford of London and Offington (d. 1631) by his wife, Judith, daughter and heiress of Edmund Downing of Suffolk. His grandfather, Roger Alford, was secretary to Sir William Cecil, *temp.* Elizabeth, and his father, besides serving long in county affairs in Sussex, was an active worker against the Stuart policies in the parliaments of the 1620's.[43] John, who was born about 1590, matriculated at St. John's College, Oxford, 13 February 1607, aged sixteen, being described then as of London. He married in 1620 Frances, daughter of Sir Thomas Bishop, Bart., of Parham, Sussex. He had settled on him then the manor of Hamsey near Lewes, and when his father died in 1631 came into possession of the family's chief manor of Offington.[44]

Alford sat for Shoreham in the 1626 parliament, for Arundel in 1628, and for Shoreham again in the spring of 1640. He served meanwhile as a J.P. in Sussex and a commissioner for various local matters, including the

collecting of the 1640 subsidy.[45] Although he served his parliamentary apprenticeship under his father, Alford showed but a lukewarm attitude toward the Long Parliament after the opening months. He was a Strafford sympathizer, was named to one committee concerning the case, and voted against the earl's attainder. He obtained leave to go into the country on 31 July 1641,[46] and was probably out of the House often thereafter. Although he voted to support Essex and agreed to lend £100 for the cause in 1642, the records show that he was summoned to attend at various times that year and later and that his loyalty was in doubt. He was named but once more to a committee before his seclusion in December, 1648.[47] Poor health may have accounted for some of his inactivity, for in 1643 he was ill enough to draw up his will.[48] He died on 5 January 1648/9 and was buried at Broadwater. An inscription there terms him "truly honorable and religious." [49]

Alford had an ample estate. He inherited from his father various Sussex and London properties and the arrears, at least, of a small pension.[50] Two of his Sussex manors were worth £690 a year, and he told the House in 1642 that he had an estate consisting of debts in Ireland to the value of £10,000.[51] He married furthermore into a wealthy family.[52] His proposal in his will in 1643 of £3000 for an unmarried daughter and his assessment at £1000 for the twentieth in 1644 [53] are other indications of his means.

Relatives who sat with Alford in the 1640 parliament were his brother, Edward, a cousin, Fettiplace, and a son-in-law, Eversfield. These and his brother-in-law, Sir Edward Bishop, who was defeated at the Bramber election, were Cavaliers. But on the Roundhead side he had at least one intimate friend, Sir Thomas Pelham.[54]

Sir William Allanson (*d.* 1656), draper and alderman of York, was M.P. for the city of York, 1640–1653. He was the second son of Christopher Allanson, yeoman (d. 1612), of Ampleforth in the North Riding,[55] and he learned the draper's trade at York as apprentice to Robert Askwith, twice mayor of the city, three times master

[39] *M. of P.* **1** : 481.

[40] *C.J.* **2** : 302, 313; D'Ewes (C), 126.

[41] Verney, 58.

[42] References in addition to those cited above are: Pink MSS, 296, fols. 45–46; W. R. Williams, *The parliamentary history of the county of Gloucester*, 236–237, Hereford, 1898 (hereafter, Williams, *Gloucester*); J. G. Alford and W. P. W. Phillimore, *Alford family notes*, 38–39, London, Phillimore, 1908. Both of the latter works contain some errors, partly as a result of the confusing of the older and the younger Edward Alford.

[43] C. 181/3 and 4, *passim;* S.P. 16, 521/170; Forster, *Eliot* **1** : 128, 339; **2** : 472, n.; *Commons Debates 1621*, ed. Wallace Notestein, Frances Helen Relf, and Hartley Simpson, **2** : 120, 403, *passim*, New Haven, Yale Univ. Press, 1935; *C.S.P. Dom., 1628–1629*, 204, 563. See also Edward Alford, M.P. for Arundel.

[44] I.P.M., Edward Alford, C. 142/509/17.

[45] C. 193/13; S.P. 16/405; C. 181/4, fol. 326; 181/5, fol. 289; *Sussex Arch. Coll.* **9** : 105, 1857.

[46] *C.J.* **2** : 39, 230; Verney, 58.

[47] Pink MSS, 296, fol. 49; *C.J.* **3** : 389; *Sussex Arch. Coll.* **5** : 102, 1852.

[48] P.C.C., 70 Fairfax.

[49] Add. MSS, 5698, fol. 186.

[50] I.P.M. cited above; *C.S.P. Dom., 1637–1638*, 245.

[51] *Sussex Arch. Coll.* **17** : 82, 1865; *C.J.* **2** : 838.

[52] His royalist brother-in-law was said to be worth £2500 a year. Thomas-Stanford, *Sussex in the Great Civil War*, 124–125.

[53] *Cal. Com. Adv. Money*, 420.

[54] Alford's will. References in addition to those cited above are *M. of P.* **1** : *passim*; Alford and Phillimore, *Alford family notes*, 25–28, 33–35; Pink MSS, 296, fol. 44.

[55] His mother was probably the Margery who was named as Christopher's wife in his will. York Registry **32**, fol. 20.

of the Merchant Tailors' Company, and several times M.P.[56] Allanson became a freeman of York on 28 September 1611,[57] entered the Merchant Tailors' Company on 7 August 1612, and prospered sufficiently in his business to be chosen as master of the company in 1620 and 1628.[58] He entered the city government as chamberlain in 1617, was sheriff in 1623, one of the "Four and Twenty" from 1624 to 1632, and alderman thereafter. He was mayor in 1633.[59] Allanson married three times, (1) at St. Michael le Belfrey in York, 6 June 1615, Hester, daughter of William Sunley (Lunley?), tailor and official of York, who died in 1620;[60] (2) on 12 June 1621 at St. Crux, York, Lucy, daughter of Alexander Orracke, who died in 1631; and (3) on 19 June 1632 Anne, daughter of Charles Tancred, Esq., of Whixley. He had issue by each marriage, and his first son by his third wife, his eventual heir, Charles, was named for the king, who visited York while Allanson was mayor and consented to be his child's godfather.[61]

The year of 1633 was a significant one in Allanson's career. As mayor and host to the king he was knighted at the time of Charles's visit,[62] but he showed also that year that he was a stubborn defender of the city's dignities against pretensions of clerical and lay officials. He quarrelled with the Vice President of the Council of the North regarding his right as mayor to occupy the President's place in St. Michael's church, and with the Archdeacon of York for his daring to sit higher than the mayor in services at the cathedral.[63]

After his term in the mayoralty Allanson continued to work for the city's welfare and privileges. He was named to committees to go to London several times, 1636–1639, regarding the city's disagreements with the clergy and about its charter and other matters, and to attend the Council of the North to question York's assessments. He was concerned also with routine matters and with the local trained bands. And in February 1640, having opposed the choosing of Strafford to be High Steward of York, he refused to be on the committee that was to present Strafford with his patent of office.[64] He probably opposed the election to the Short Parliament of a nominee of Strafford's and a royalist

alderman, and his faction, that of the puritans, gained the upper hand in the autumn. Late in September, amidst some disorder, the city rejected Strafford's nominees and chose as their parliament men Allanson and a fellow alderman of similar views, Thomas Hoyle.[65]

This was Allanson's first experience in parliament, but he was early named to committees, including those on monopolies, tonnage and poundage, and the clergy.[66] With Hoyle he pledged £500 for the loan of March, 1641.[67] He was one of the York commission for scandalous ministers in 1642,[68] was at Hull at the time of the uprising there against the Hothams, and was named then to the temporary committee for defense.[69] During the remainder of the Long Parliament he was active for the parliamentary cause both in London and in his county. He became Clerk of the Hanaper and was added to the Committee at Goldsmiths' Hall, but he declined to sit in judgment on the king after being appointed to the trial commission.[70] He was mayor of York again in 1655 and died there on 6 December 1656. He was buried the next day at St. Michael le Belfrey.[71]

According to Noble,[72] Allanson found his employment for parliament during the war so lucrative that he could buy several former church properties in and near York, but probably died in poverty. Holles, too, noted in his *Memoirs*[73] that Allanson was among those who profited financially during this period. But Allanson doubtless had wealth in other forms than land in 1640, his pledges for the loan and his personal share of £150 for the Irish venture[74] suggest that he had means, and not all of the lands referred to in his will in 1656 were recent acquisitions. He left by it at least £50 for charities.[75] Allanson's marriages indicate an ascent on the social scale that was possible as his wealth increased, and his widow, Anne, re-married into the gentry. She was a kinswoman of one of Sir John Hotham's wives.[76]

William Allestry (*c.* 1598–1655), of Alvaston, Derbyshire, Recorder of Derby, was M.P. for Derby, 1640–1643. The grandson of an innholder, bailiff of Derby and M.P., who had acquired Alvaston Grange, about three miles from the town,[77] he was the eldest son of

[56] Biographical data on Askwith in the Yorkshire Archaeological Society's MSS at Leeds, Skaife MSS, **9**, fol. 12.

[57] York Corporation MSS, Chamberlain's Account Book, **14**, 1611, fol. 58.

[58] Skaife MSS, cited above, **9**, fol. 6.

[59] York Corporation MSS, House Book 34, fols. 107, 248, 274, 302, 315; House Book 35, fols. 163, 164, 189.

[60] *Register of St. Michael le Belfrey, York*, Part I, pp. 128, 130, 143, Yorkshire Parish Register Society, 1897.

[61] *Ibid.*, 173, *passim; The life of Marmaduke Rawdon*, 126, n., Camden Society, 1863.

[62] York Corporation MSS, House Book 35, fol. 210v.

[63] *Ibid.*, fols. 203, 214, 218–220; *C.S.P. Dom., 1633–1634*, 72, 105–106. The question of precedence had started with an earlier mayor. Bodleian Firth MSS, b. 2, fol. 183.

[64] York Corporation MSS, House Book 35, fols. 241, 303, 324v, 350; House Book 36, fols. 26, 27, 31, 32, 36v, 39v, 40, 42.

[65] *The life of Marmaduke Rawdon*, 125, n. (126–127).

[66] *C.J.* **2**: 31, 99, 107.

[67] D'Ewes (N), 439, n.

[68] Pink MSS, 296, fols. 57–58.

[69] Add. MSS, 19,398, fol. 146; T. T. Wildridge, ed., *The Hull letters*, 39–41, 151–152, Hull, 1886 (?).

[70] Noble, *Regicides* **1**: 73; *Cal. Com. Comp.*, 137; *O.P.H.* **9**: 10.

[71] *The life of Marmaduke Rawdon, loc. cit.*; Foster, *Members of Parliament, Coll. Geneal.* **2**: 32, 1883.

[72] Mark Noble, *The lives of the English regicides* **1**: 73, London, 1798.

[73] Page 134.

[74] *C.S.P. Ireland, Adventurers*, 81.

[75] *The life of Marmaduke Rawdon, loc. cit.*; Drake, *York*, 222.

[76] Add. MSS, 19,398, fol. 146.

[77] Foster, *Members of Parliament, England, Coll. Geneal.* **2**: 34–35, 1883; Daniel and Samuel Lysons, *Magna Britannia* **5**,

Thomas Allestry of Alvaston, "gentleman" (d. 1630),[78] by his wife Anne, daughter of Roger Barker of Alvaston, or Constance (Isley), and was born about 1598.[79] After attending Derby grammar school and St. John's, Cambridge, for a short time, Allestry entered Gray's Inn in 1618. He was called to the bar in 1625, was associated with that inn for some time afterwards, and by 1638 was a reader at Barnard's Inn.[80] By the latter date also he was Recorder of Derby, and a member of the borough's commission for gaol delivery.[81] He served for a time as feodary of Derbyshire, but was succeeded in that post by a brother, George, in November, 1640.[82] Allestry married twice, (1) at Derby in 1629, Sarah, daughter of Thomas Smith, who died in 1638, and (2) at Alvaston, 8 March 1641, Mary, daughter of William Agard and widow of Edward Smith.[83]

Allestry sat for Derby in both parliaments of 1640 and, though his original election to the Long Parliament was voided in March, 1641, was promptly re-elected.[84] He was sent into his county in August to see that the ordinance against recusants was enforced, but he took little active part in the work of the House, and was absent for some time in 1642. He returned in December of that year upon summons, but was disabled for non-attendance, 19 October 1643 and 22 January 1644, and removed from his recordership.[85] He eventually compounded for his estates and, dying 4 September 1655, was buried at Derby.[86]

Allestry's landed possessions were not large, consisting chiefly of the house and lands at Alvaston, with certain others in the county by which he had augmented his inheritance. His will refers further to some leases worth about £100 a year,[87] and when he compounded he asserted that his real estate was small, charged with

debts of £1000, and that his fine of £737 was more than a third of his estate. The Committee for Advance of Money, in consideration of his payment of that fine and the loss of his practice, released him from most of their £600 assessment upon him.[88]

John Alured (1607–1659), of the Charterhouse in Sculcoates, near Hull, regicide, was a member for Hedon, Yorkshire, 1640–1653. He was the son and heir of Henry Alured (1581–1628), once an M.P., by Frances, daughter of Francis Vaughan of Sutton upon Derwent. His grandfather, John, and his great-grandfather, Thomas, had been M.P.'s for Hull in Elizabeth's reign.[89] His uncle, Thomas Alured (d. 1638), M.P. for Hedon in 1628 and a co-worker with Eliot, was afterwards secretary to Lord Keeper Coventry.[90] John was born in March, 1607, and christened at Preston on April 4.[91] He was admitted to Gray's Inn, 11 August 1628, but he probably returned to Yorkshire without attaining the bar. On 17 November 1631 he married, at Bossall, Mary, daughter of Sir Richard Darley of Buttercrambe and sister of Pym's friend, Henry Darley (q.v.). A second marriage, possibly after 1640, was with a Mary Arnold of London.[92] He was a sewers commissioner for the East Riding in 1634, and a J.P. there.[93]

In July, 1638, Alured was again in London and staying at a house in Blackfriars. He was reported then to Council for some remarks commending the Scots and their methods of settling their disagreements with the king. At a preliminary hearing Alured denied any traitorous implications in his words or friendship for the Scots, but he was required to give his bond for £2000 for further appearance. Sir Frederick Cornwallis (q.v.) was one of his sureties. There seem to have been no further developments. Windebank noted in his minutes that Alured lived near the Scottish border and had £400 to £500 a year.[94]

Alured was elected for Hedon to the Short Parliament,[95] and in the following July was a signer of the Yorkshire petition.[96] He was present at the shire election on 5 October[97] and was re-elected himself by Hedon. He was not a leader in debates or committees, but was sent into Yorkshire in July, 1641, with the committee for disarming recusants,[98] and he interfered

"Derbyshire," 124, London, 1806–1822 (hereafter, Lysons, *Mag. Brit.*); Add. MSS, 6705 (J. Reynolds, Derbyshire Collection), fol. 95v.

[78] The heralds listed Mr. Allestry in 1611 among those who had assumed the title of gentlemen without proof of arms. Add. MSS, 6669 (Wolley's Derbyshire Collection), fol. 121.

[79] Pink MSS, 296, fol. 68; 307, fol. 330. According to the i.p.m. of Thomas Allestry (C. 142/474/67), William was aged 31 and more in 1630; he was "aged 57" at his death in 1655.

[80] B. Tacchella, ed., *The Derby school register, 1570–1901*, 20, London, Bemrose, 1902; *Al. Cant.*; J. Foster, Register of Admissions to Gray's Inn, *Coll. Geneal.* 2: 8, 1883.

[81] Notes supplied me by Mr. F. Williamson, Director and Curator of the Derby Museum and Art Gallery. The name of the recorder was written erroneously as John in the gaol delivery list, C. 181/5, fol. 237.

[82] *C.S.P. Dom., 1640–1641*, 223.

[83] W. P. W. Phillimore and LL. LL. Simpson, *Derbyshire parish registers, marriages* 6: 113; 9: 21, London, Phillimore, 1906–1912; Stephen Glover, *The history, gazetteer and directory of the county of Derby*, ed. Thomas Noble, 2: 468, Derby, 1829–1833 (hereafter, Glover, *Derbyshire*).

[84] *C.J.* 2: 113; D'Ewes (N), 385.

[85] *C.J.* 2: 267, 845, 881; 3: 374; Pink MSS, 307, fol. 330.

[86] Glover, *Derbyshire* 2: 468.

[87] I.P.M. cited above; Add. MSS, 6705, fols. 11v, 24–26; 6672, fol. 274; Allestry's will, dated 2 July 1655 and proved 8 August 1657, P.C.C., 303 Ruthen.

[88] *Cal. Com. Comp.*, 991; *Cal. Com. Adv. Money*, 420.

[89] Bean, *Northern Counties*, 824.

[90] Pink MSS, 296, fol. 81; *H.M.C., Twelfth Report* 2: Coke MSS, 350, 420; Hull Corporation MSS, Bench Book V, fol. 223v; Wildridge, *Hull Letters*, 17; *C.S.P. Dom., 1637–1638*, 441; Forster, *Eliot* 2: 241.

[91] I.P.M. of Henry Alured, 1628, C. 142/452/42; *Yorkshire Genealogist* 1: 7, 1888.

[92] *Yorkshire Genealogist* 1: 3, 1888.

[93] C. 181/4, fol. 190; C. 193/13; S.P. 16/405.

[94] *C.S.P. Dom., 1637–1638*, 558, 574.

[95] Willis 3: 238.

[96] *C.S.P. Dom., 1640*, 524.

[97] Yorkshire indenture, C. 219/43/Part 3.

[98] *C.J.* 2: 267.

with the raising of royalist troops near Hull in 1642.[99] He served afterwards with the parliamentary armies and as a civilian committeeman in his county. He was named a king's judge and signed the death warrant.[100] He died shortly before 18 March 1653/4,[101] and was buried at Sculcoates.

Not a great landholder, Alured had for his principal possession Sculcoates manor with its appendages. Some of them had belonged to the church until Tudor times.[102] He owned also some properties near Hedon,[103] and he may have inherited some lands from his mother's family [104] in the North Riding.[105]

Sir Henry Anderson (c. 1583–1659), of Long Cowton, Yorkshire, was M.P. for Newcastle-on-Tyne from 1640 until he was disabled on 4 September 1643 for deserting to the royal cause.[106] His family was prominent in business and in public affairs in Newcastle and Durham from the early sixteenth century, and was particularly interested in the coal trade. He was the son and heir of the greatest of the Newcastle merchants of Elizabeth's time,[107] Henry Anderson (1545–1605) of Newcastle and Durham (sheriff, mayor, four times M.P., governor of the Merchants' Company). His mother was that magistrate's second wife, Fortune, daughter of Sir Cuthbert Collingwood. Anderson was born about 1583,[108] matriculated at Christ's Church, Oxford, in 1599, and was admitted at Gray's Inn, 11 February 1602. About 1605 he married Mary, daughter of Richard Remington of Lockington, Archdeacon of the East Riding,[109] and prepared to follow in his father's steps as a business man and public official. He was admitted

as a hostman in the coal trade in 1606, and was knighted at Sir Thomas Heselrige's house in 1608.[110]

Sir Henry was mayor of Newcastle, 1613–1614, interrupting his term to serve the town in the 1614 parliament.[111] In 1615–1616 he was sheriff of Northumberland, and was particularly concerned with the growing problem of the recusants.[112] In 1619 council ordered the arrest of Anderson and other Newcastle merchants, but no statement of the reason or the result appears.[113] He was a J.P. in Durham from 1620, if not earlier, as well as a member of other commissions for that county,[114] and in 1623 was complained of in Chancery for abusing his prestige as a J.P. and "a great man in the country" by enclosing more than his share of some commons.[115] In the same year he and a brother-in-law and other prominent men of Newcastle were charged with having combined to restrain the free trade in coal there.[116] Anderson wrote in 1629 to thank Secretary Coke for saving him from being Northumberland's sheriff again, and to promise his aid in raising funds in Durham, northern Yorkshire, and Newcastle by "good, lawful and honest means." [117]

Meanwhile Anderson was returned for Newcastle to the parliaments of 1621–1626. He was interested in reforms within the church and in securing parliamentary representation for Durham.[118] And in 1624 he showed himself somewhat opposed to the crown, but aware of the danger of not granting funds for use in Ireland and Bohemia. He did not sit in the 1628 parliament, perhaps because of a change of residence, for by 1630 he had disposed of his Durham estates and established himself at Long Cowton in Yorkshire. He had a prolonged quarrel with a neighbor about the control of a rectory, and was as a result a defendant in recurring Star Chamber suits.[119] And he continued to be interested in searching out recusants.[120]

In the autumn of 1640 Sir Henry was again attracting attention by his disaffection toward the king's service in Northumberland and his contemptuous remarks about the training of soldiers there, but he was punished only with a sharp reproof.[121] He was an active member of the Long Parliament in its early months, and was named to such important committees as those on the Star

---

99 Bodleian Clarendon MSS, 21, No. 1615.

100 Noble, *Regicides* 1: 75; Pink MSS, 296, fol. 78.

101 His son stated on that date that Alured had recently died. *C.S.P. Ireland, Adventurers*, 313.

102 I.P.M. of Henry Alured; Hull Library MSS, copy of De la Pryme's "Annals of Hull," fols. 435–436; T. T. Wildridge, *Old and New Hull*, 128–136, Hull, 1884.

103 John Rylands Library English MSS, Peacock MSS, 236, fols. 169–170.

104 *V.C.H. York, North Riding* 2: 113, n.

105 Other references used for this sketch: *Yorks. Arch. Jour.* 10: 456, 1889; Joseph Hunter, *Familiae Minorum Gentium*, ed. Clay, Harleian Society 37–40: 992, 1894–1896 (hereafter, *Fam. Min. Gent.*).

106 It is suggested in *M. of P.* (1: 491, n.) that Anderson was elected to replace Sir John Melton, but the latter's death did not occur until December 16, and Anderson was present on November 11 (D'Ewes [N], 25).

107 J. U. Nef, *The rise of the British coal industry* 2: 285 and n., London, G. Routledge, 1932.

108 His birth date sometimes appears as 1583. He was "aged 17" on entering Oxford in November, 1599 (*Al. Oxon.*), and was aged 21 and more on 5 August 1605, according to his father's i.p.m. C. 142/643/8.

109 Pink MSS, 296, fol. 95. Their son, Henry, was aged 9 in 1615. G. W. Marshall, ed., *The visitation of Northumberland in 1615*, 59, London, 1878 (hereafter, Marshall, *Vis. Northumberland*). His second wife, living in 1658, was Elizabeth, daughter of Mrs. Constance Hopkins (Anderson's will, P.C.C., 354 Pell).

110 *Archaeologia Aeliana* (Publications of the Society of Antiquaries of Newcastle upon Tyne), 4th Ser., 18: 52, 1940 (hereafter, *Arch. Ael.*).

111 *M. of P.* 3: xxxix; *The letters of John Chamberlain* 1: 525.

112 S.P. 14, 86/125.

113 *Acts P.C., 1618–1619*, 444; *1619–1621*, 85, 87.

114 C. 181/3, fol. 9v; 181/4, fols. 6, 52, *passim*; C. 193/12, 13; *C.S.P. Dom., 1629–1631*, 301. He was a loan commissioner in 1626 (*Acts P.C., 1625–1626*, 445).

115 C. 3/333/3.

116 S.P. 14, 145/24.

117 *H.M.C., Twelfth Report* 1, Coke MSS, 379.

118 *Commons Debates 1621* 2: 82, n., 322, 396; 7: 639.

119 Anderson and his son were fined £300 each, reduced later to £60 each. *C.S.P. Dom., 1631–1632*, 519, 536; S.P. 16, 231/46, 47; 232/43; 372/16, 17, 32; *V.C.H. York, North Riding* 1: 161.

120 *C.S.P. Dom., 1637–1638*, 76.

121 *Ibid., 1640–1641*, 75; Add. MSS, 11,045, fol. 145.

Chamber, the Lords Lieutenant, and scandalous ministers.[122] He attacked Strafford and Laud in debate as traitors.[123] In the summer of 1641 when the army was being disbanded he was sent north, and in 1642 was named to the committee on scandalous ministers for Durham and to one of the defense committees.[124] He was absent a good deal after that, being concerned with northern developments, and in September, 1642, was ready to confer with Fairfax on military plans but was still hoping for some peaceful arrangements with the king.[125] He was readmitted to the House in April, 1643, after explaining an absence of some months, but became involved in the Hotham affair at Hull. The younger Hotham had married Anderson's daughter and Sir Henry was under growing suspicion and was at last disabled on 4 September 1643 for joining the king. He lost heavily during the war and was held a prisoner for a time.[126] He died in 1659. His will, dated in July, 1658, was proved on 20 June 1659.[127]

Before the war Anderson was probably a wealthy man, although he had sold his Durham inheritance, and some of his property had diminishing value for coal production.[128] His manor of Long Cowton in Yorkshire alone was lucrative enough to provide his daughter's portion of at least £1300, or £100 a year.[129] He declared in 1654 that his sequestered estates had been rented out by the compounding officials for £1700 annually, which was probably less than their earlier value, and that his loss in personal property by seizure at Hull totalled £2500.[130]

* Sir William Armine, or Armyne, Bart. (1593–1651), of Osgodby, Lincolnshire, and Orton Longville, Hunts, was elected for Grantham, 29 March 1641, *vice* Hussey,[131] and sat until his death in 1651. The son and heir of Sir William Armine of Osgodby, M.P., H.S. (d. 1621), by his first wife, Martha, daughter of William

Lord Eure,[132] he was educated at Sidney Sussex, Cambridge,[133] and by 1621, when he was first returned an M.P., was already "a gentleman of note in the county." [134] During the next two decades Armine opposed the policies of Buckingham and the crown in parliament and outside, served three times as sheriff, twice in Huntingdonshire and once in Lincolnshire, was an active J.P. and member of various commissions,[135] and was one of the D.L.'s for his county in 1639.[136] His third term as sheriff, 1639–1640, accounts for his absence from the Short Parliament, and probably for his not being elected originally in the fall of 1640.

Armine was apparently very well-to-do, although his absence from the House at the time of the early loan subscriptions eliminates one source of information about his wealth. He was enjoying in 1640 not only his family estates in Lincolnshire and elsewhere, but also the properties his second wife, a granddaughter of the Earl of Shrewsbury, had inherited in Derbyshire, Huntingdonshire, and Yorkshire.[137]

Through his second wife Armine was related to several of his fellow members. They included her nephew, William Pierrepont, and the more distant kinsmen, Savile, Cavendish, and the Herberts.[138] Armine was described by Whitelocke as "a gentleman of good understanding and conversation, who could give his opinion upon good reason." [139]

John Arundell (1614–1644), of Trerice in Newlyn, Cornwall, was elected in October, 1640, for both Bodmin and St. Michael's, and chose to sit for the former.[140] He was disabled for royalism in 1644. Known usually as John Arundell, junior, he was the heir apparent of the wealthy Trerice branch of a famous old Cornish family, being the eldest son of John Arundell (1576–1654),[141] J.P. and M.P., by his wife, Mary, daughter of George Cary of Clovelly. He was a nephew of Thomas

122 *C.J.* 2: 44, 50, 52, 54, *passim.*

123 A. H. A. Hamilton, ed., *Note book of Sir John Northcote,* 73, London, 1877 (hereafter, *Note book of Sir John Northcote*).

124 *C.J.* 2: 372, 626; Pink MSS, 296, fol. 94.

125 Anderson and others to Fairfax, 24 September 1642. Add. MSS, 15,858, fol. 215.

126 *C.J.* 3: 227; *H.M.C., Fifth Report,* House of Lords MSS, 107–108, 115.

127 P.C.C. 354 Pell. An abstract of the will is printed in *Y.A.S. Rec. Ser.* 9: 148, 1890.

128 I.P.M. cited in note 3; *History of Northumberland* (Northumberland County History Committee) 13: 244, Newcastle upon Tyne, Andrew Reid, 1893–1935.

129 Will of Isabel Hotham, abstracted in *Y.A.S. Rec. Ser.* 9: 42–43, 1890; *Cal. Com. Comp.,* 2334.

130 *Cal. Com. Comp.,* 2336, 3162. References in addition to those cited specifically are: Bean, *Northern Counties,* 577; C. H. Hunter Blair, *Members of Parliament for Northumberland and Newcastle upon Tyne, Arch. Ael.,* 4th Ser., 23: 134, 137–138, 1945; Foster, Members of Parliament, England, *Coll. Geneal.* 2: 44–45, 1883; Richard Welford, *Men of Mark 'Twixt Tyne and Tweed* (3 v.), 47–51, 67–79, Newcastle, 1895.

131 *M. of P.* 1: 490; Grantham Corporation MSS, Court Minute Book, 1, fol. 93.

132 A. R. Maddison, *Lincolnshire pedigrees* 1: 40–41, London, Harleian Society, 1902–1906 (hereafter, Maddison, *Lincs. Ped.*).

133 *Al. Cant.*

134 Quotation from the corporation records in P. Thompson, *The history and antiquities of Boston,* 450, n., Boston, 1856 (hereafter, Thompson, *Boston*).

135 C. 193/12, 13; S.P. 16/405; C. 181/4, fol. 29v; 181/5, fols. 18, 361; *C.S.P. Dom., 1633–1634,* 408.

136 S.P. 16, 426/39.

137 *V.C.H. Lincoln* 2: 282; West Riding Sessions Records, *Y.A.S. Rec. Ser.* 54: 274, n., 1915; Add. MSS, 6671 (Wolley's Derbyshire Collections), fol. 137; 6675, fol. 14; 6670, fols. 86v, 87v. Armine's son and heir, when making his will in 1657, mentioned his wife's jointure of £618 a year, and proposed portions of £8000 and £6000 for his two daughters. P.C.C., 54 Wotton.

138 *Fenland N. and Q.* 2: 104, 1894; Add. MSS, 6674, fols. 137v–138.

139 Add. MSS, 37,343, fol. 268.

140 *M. of P.* 1: 486 and n.; 3: li. The election dispute at Bodmin between Bramston and Nicoll (*q.v.*) does not seem to have concerned Arundell.

141 The elder Arundell seems to have died in 1654 (see note 143 below) rather than in 1656, as in *D.N.B.,* and was still not called "Sir John" in 1651. *Cal. Com. Comp.,* 2238.

Arundell and a brother of Richard Arundell, fellow M.P.'s (q.v.).[142] John was baptized at Newlyn on 3 March 1614,[143] was subscribed at Oxford, 9 December 1631, and was admitted to Lincoln's Inn two years later.[144] He was probably the John Arundell who was licensed in 1637 to travel for three years,[145] and he seems to have taken no part in public affairs before 1640. It was probably he rather than his father who was elected to the Short Parliament for Tregony. His brother, Richard, made his parliamentary debut at the same time.[146] Their father, a friend of Eliot and co-worker with him in the attacks on Buckingham in earlier parliaments, had resisted the knighthood compositions and as late as 1638 had been a musters defaulter in Devon.[147] The election of his heir to the Long Parliament was doubtless expected to strengthen the popular cause.

Young John Arundell, however, was never prominent in the House and seems to have been named to few committees.[148] Most of the appointments of "Mr. Arundell" were probably those of the elder member of the family, John's uncle. But either John or his brother, Richard, was the Arundell who voted against the attainder of Strafford.[149] He was absent at call on 16 June 1642,[150] joined his father and Grenville in executing the Commission of Array in Cornwall, and after being summoned several times to attend was disabled on 22 January 1644. He assisted his father at Pendennis Castle and lost his life in the king's service shortly before November, 1644.[151] He was buried on 14 July 1646 at Newlyn.[152]

Since John was unmarried in 1640 he probably had not had any of the family estates settled on him. His father was reputedly one of the wealthiest men in the county, however,[153] and with his second son paid a heavy fine for royalism.[154]

* **Richard Arundell** (d. 1687), of Trerice, Cornwall, and of Lincoln's Inn, was M.P. for Lostwithiel, 1640–

22 January 1644. The second son of John Arundell of Trerice (1576–1654), and younger brother of John Arundell (1614–1644), the Bodmin M.P. (q.v.), he was admitted with the latter to Lincoln's Inn, 16 November 1633. He was called to the bar there on 18 November 1640, and kept his chambers until he was suspended on account of his royalism in 1646.[155] He sat for Lostwithiel in both parliaments of 1640, but left when the war began. Unmarried at the time of his election, he eventually took to wife the widow of his royalist colleague, Sir Nicholas Slanning.[156] His work in the Long Parliament can scarcely be distinguished from that of his brother and their uncle, and Richard was probably the least active of the three. He or John was a Straffordian.[157]

A younger son, Richard probably had but little property of his own in 1640. Before his father's death, however, he owned some properties in Devonshire worth £145 a year.[158] For his family's wealth, see John Arundell.

Thomas Arundell (1577–1648), of Duloe, Cornwall, M.P. for West Looe, 1640–1648, was one of the Arundells of Trerice, being a younger brother of the royalist defender of Pendennis Castle and uncle of the two others of the family who served in the Long Parliament. Unlike those relatives, he supported parliament against the king, although his family connections led to some suspicion of him by the parliamentarians during the war.[159] The second son of John Arundell of Trerice (d. 1580), by his second wife, Gertrude, daughter of Robert Denny's of Holcombe, he was baptized at Newlyn on 12 November 1577. While his elder brother stayed in Cornwall, Thomas went to fight in the Netherlands and, according to Carew, behaved "with so wel-liked a cariage" that he was promoted far more rapidly than was usual for one of his age and experience.[160] He married (1) before 1620 Mary, daughter of Sir Gamaliel Capel, and (2), sometime between 1623 and 1629, Julian, daughter of George Cary of Clovelly, a sister of his brother John's wife. He was living at Duloe in 1621 and was then engaged in some lawsuits about lands he had purchased.[161] He may have been a J.P. in Cornwall in 1622,[162] although the presence of others of his name in the county makes the identity of the person listed in the commission uncertain.

The Long Parliament was the first one in which Arundell served. He may have been the "Mr. Arundell" who was named on 14 November to the

[142] Vivian, *Vis. Cornwall*, 12, 14. Trevanion became the younger John's brother-in-law, but probably not before 1640.

[143] C. E. H. Chadwyck Healey, *The history of part of West Somerset*, 96–97, London, H. Sotheren, 1901 (hereafter, Chadwyck Healey, *West Somerset*).

[144] *Al. Oxon.; Linc. Inn Rec. Adm.* **1**: 222.

[145] *C.S.P. Dom., 1637*, 359.

[146] *M. of P.* **1**: 480. There was possibly a disputed election on this occasion. Willis **3**: 230; Rushworth **3**: 1106; Courtney, *Parl. Rep. Corn.*, 170.

[147] *C.S.P. Dom., 1628–1629*, 24; *1633–1634*, 139; S.P. 16, 409/46; 410/163.

[148] Pink MSS, 296, fol. 163.

[149] Verney, 58.

[150] *C.J.* **2**: 626.

[151] *C.J.* **2**: 772; **3**: 374; *H.M.C., Fourth Report*, MSS of Earl De la Warr, 307; Pink MSS, 307, fol. 158; Clarendon, *Rebellion* **3**: 103, n.

[152] Chadwyck Healey, *loc. cit.*

[153] *Ibid.;* Clarendon, *Rebellion* **2**: 452; **4**: 215.

[154] The fine of £10,000 was set for father and son. *Cal. Com. Comp.*, 223, 2238.

[155] *Linc. Inn Rec. Adm.* **1**: 222; *Black Books* **2**: 356, 368, 371.

[156] Vivian, *Vis. Cornwall*, 12, 14.

[157] Verney, 58.

[158] *Cal. Com. Comp.*, 153.

[159] Courtney, *Parl. Rep. Corn.*, 132.

[160] Carew's *Survey of Cornwall* cited in Chadwyck Healey, *West Somerset*, 88.

[161] Chancery Proceedings, C. 3/299/23; 330/35.

[162] C. 193/13.

committee to consider the Bossiney election, and to several other committees of the early months,[163] but he did not play an important part in the work of the House. When war came he was more in his element. He promised to furnish a horse for the defense in 1642,[164] and two months later joined Carew and Buller against his relatives to prevent the execution of the Commission of Array in Cornwall.[165] He was named to some of the wartime committees for the western counties. Absent at call on 26 September 1648, Arundell died a few weeks later. He was buried at Westminster Abbey on 7 November.[166] His will, dated 3 November, was proved on 17 November 1648 by his son, John. One of the witnesses to his will was his friend and colleague, Francis Godolpin of Treveneage (q.v.).[167]

Arundell's will mentioned various properties he held in Duloe parish, several in the towns of East Looe and West Looe, and some in Devon. To a daughter who was already married he left £300 in addition to what had been provided for her, as well as £100 for her children.[168]

* **John Ashburnham** (1603–1671), courtier and royalist from Sussex, was a member for Hastings from 1640 until May, 1642.[169] He was educated at Peterhouse, Cambridge, and Gray's Inn,[170] and in 1628 was rumored to be about to marry the daughter and heiress of Lord Lumley.[171] Instead he married the next year another lady of fortune, Frances, only child of William Holland of West Burton, Sussex, indirect heir of a Chichester alderman, thereby easing his work of repairing his family's financial position.[172] Ashburnham derived other income from his connections at court, such as the grant in 1628 of 500 marks a year from the farmers of wine licenses,[173] and his various transactions with secretary Nicholas.[174]

Ashburnham seems to have held no local offices in Sussex, but he was chosen M.P. for Hastings in 1628, and spoke in that parliament in defense of Buckingham.[175] He was a fellow member then of Walter Long (q.v.), whose Star Chamber fine was granted afterwards to him, a fact which the Long Parliament was not to overlook.[176] He was named a commissioner for collecting the subsidy in Sussex in 1640,[177] and with the backing of the Lord Warden of the Cinque Ports was a candidate for election at Hastings for the Short Parliament. He failed then, partly through lack of exertion and partly because he was to go to Scotland with the army and would therefore be unable to serve.[178]

Ashburnham's financial position permitted him to offer £1000 for the loan in 1640,[179] but his income is difficult to estimate. His landed estates, some of recent acquisition, were probably more extensive than he reported afterwards to the compounding commissioners, for his fine, set at the large proportion of half of his estate, was £1270.[180]

Fellow members of the 1640 parliament were Ashburnham's brother, William, and two brothers-in-law, Sir Frederick Cornwallis and Sir Edward Dering.

* **William Ashburnham** (c. 1604–1679), courtier and soldier, was M.P. for Ludgershall, Wilts, from 1640 until his expulsion for complicity in the army plot, 9 December 1641. He had sat for Ludgershall in the spring also.[181] He was a younger brother of John Ashburnham (q.v.) and came of a Sussex family. He was in the Low Countries as a soldier in 1625.[182] He married (1627?) Jane, daughter of Lord Butler of Hertfordshire, who was the young and rich widow of James, Earl of Marlborough, Lord High Treasurer.[183] He was named to local commissions for Hampshire and Bedfordshire, 1636 and 1640, and was a J.P. in Hampshire and Wiltshire.[184] At some time, too, he was cofferer to King Charles.[185] He continued to be active in the army and was a lieutenant colonel with Conway on

---

[163] The name, "Sir Robert Arundell," which appears once, may have been intended for any one of the three Arundells in the House, although none of them was a knight. *C.J.* **2**: 29, 31, 61.

[164] *N. and Q.*, 1st Ser., **12**: 359, 1855.

[165] *H.M.C., Fourth Report*, MSS of Earl De La Warr, 307.

[166] Pink MSS, 307, fol. 228.

[167] P.C.C., 168 Essex.

[168] Authorities in addition to those cited above are Chadwyck Healey, *West Somerset*, 96–97; Vivian, *Vis. Cornwall*, 12.

[169] He had absented himself before 2 May 1642, but was not finally "disabled" until 5 February 1644. *C.J.* **2**: 560; **3**: 389.

[170] *Al. Cant.*

[171] D'Ewes, *Autobiography* **2**: 206. Lord Lumley in 1640 was listed as a patron for Ashburnham's candidacy for election. S.P. 16, 450/15.

[172] *Sussex Arch. Coll.* **48**: 8, n., 1905; Thomas-Stanford, *Sussex in the great Civil War*, 189. He married a second time, also, though his first wife was living in 1642 (*Sussex Arch. Coll.* **33**: 56, 1883; Horsfield, *Hist. Sussex* **1**: 559).

[173] *C.S.P. Dom., 1628–1629*, 197. An Elizabeth Ashburnham, perhaps his mother, was enjoying a court pension of £300 a year in 1630. S.P. 16, 180/16, fol. 41.

[174] *D.N.B.; C.S.P. Dom., 1635*, 472–473; *1638–1639*, 186, 480; *1639*, 276; *1640–1641*, 554.

[175] *M. of P.* **1**: 479; *O.P.H.* **8**: 196. Forster (*Eliot* **2**: 263) indicates that none of Buckingham's friends dared come to his defense.

[176] *C.S.P. Dom., 1637–1638*, 409; D'Ewes (N), 496.

[177] *Sussex Arch. Coll.* **9**: 105, 1857.

[178] *C.S.P. Dom., 1639–1640*, 607.

[179] D'Ewes (N), 52. He probably ventured some money in the Irish fisheries project in 1633. S.P. 16, 231/15/i; 325/43.

[180] *Cal. Com. Comp.*, 1863; S.P. 23/207, 135. In 1648 Ashburnham listed as his pre-war properties only two Sussex manors and some property in Dorset, totalling little more than £315 in yearly value, and mentioned £1900 as owing to him and his own debts of £3500.

[181] *M. of P.* **1**: 484, 496; *C.J.* **2**: 337.

[182] *C.S.P. Ireland, 1647–1660, Addenda*, 49, 53.

[183] *Sussex Arch. Coll.* **33**: 60, 1883; Horsfield, *Hist. Sussex* **1**: 558.

[184] C. 181/5, fols. 115, 359; C. 193/13; S.P. 16/405.

[185] Most authors state that he was cofferer after the Restoration, but Horsfield (*op. cit.* **1**: 558) asserts that he was cofferer to both Charles I and Charles II.

the northern border in 1639 and 1640.[186] His election to parliament for Ludgershall both times in 1640 was the result probably of royal influence and that of his wife, through whom Ashburnham had come to enjoy numerous Wiltshire estates. His politics were very different from those of his colleague, Sir John Evelyn, but the election apparently occurred without contest. Ashburnham seems to have left to his brother the burden of speaking in parliament, preferring to devote most of his time to matters military.

It was stated in later years that Ashburnham was not born to a farthing,[187] but his marriage greatly improved his condition. He was probably the "Mr. Ashburnham" who offered £1000 as security for the loan in 1640.[188] Afterwards his wife declared that her losses caused by the war amounted to £20,000. Estates in Hampshire as well as Wiltshire were mentioned.[189]

Ashburnham was probably related through his wife's family to Endymion Porter and John Belasyse, fellow M.P.'s.

Edward Ashe (1599–1656), of London, M.P. for Heytesbury, Wiltshire, 1640–1653, was a brother of the more celebrated John Ashe, the member for Westbury (q.v.). He was the second son of James Ashe of Somerset, by Grace, daughter of Richard Pitt of Weymouth.[190] His father, a well-to-do clothier, whose personal estate alone was estimated as worth £15,000 in 1637, opposed ship money, refusing to serve as assessor and resisting payment himself until Council in Star Chamber ordered him to pay.[191] Born in 1599,[192] Edward was apprenticed in 1616 to the Drapers' Company of London. He lived in the city for most of the remainder of his life. He became a successful draper, rivalling in the number of his apprentices such a well known merchant as Sir Maurice Abbot. He was one of the livery men of the company assessed for the poll tax in 1641, but he paid a fine instead of serving as warden five years later.[193] Before 1631 Ashe married

Elizabeth, daughter of Christopher Woodward of Lambeth, sometime an alderman of London, and by her had two sons and a daughter.[194] They lived in the parish of St. Michael's Crooked Lane in Candlewick ward. Ashe at various times audited the churchwardens' accounts of the parish, but paid a fine in 1632 rather than serve as a churchwarden himself.[195] From his residence on Canning (i.e. Cannon?) Street Ashe was conducting some overseas trade in 1635.[196] His wife died in St. Michael's parish about 1638.[197] Ashe seems to have married a second time, for his will of 1656 mentioned his wife, Elizabeth, who survived him.[198]

Presumably Ashe had been too much absorbed in his business affairs before 1640 to desire office. But the experience of his father and his brother at the hands of King Charles's administration perhaps made him feel that the time had come for action. He may have been persuaded also by the group of London puritans, such as Spurstow and Soame, with whom he could scarcely not have been acquainted, or by his mother's relatives in Dorchester. Probably it was the influence of his family which secured the Heytesbury seat for him. He was afterwards the owner of Heytesbury manor, but does not seem to have purchased it until 1644.[199] His election there for the Long Parliament brought him for the first time to the House of Commons.

Edward Ashe was an active member of the Long Parliament throughout its history. He was named early to committees and had served on seventy-four different ones by the end of 1652. They included some on matters of the church, on providing troops for Ireland in 1642, and the Committee for Compounding. He was also a member of the wartime committee for Wiltshire.[200] He was living at his house in Fenchurch Street in 1651,[201] and when he died in 1656 was buried at All Hallowes Staining in London. The memorial to him at Heytesbury described him as of Halstead, Kent, as well as lord of the manor of Heytesbury.[202]

---

[186] C.S.P. Dom., 1639, 224, 276; 1640, 609; Add. MSS, 26,781, fol. 91.

[187] Lansd. MSS, 805, 1, fol. 88.

[188] His brother was listed separately. D'Ewes (N), 52.

[189] Cal. Com. Comp., 77, 105, 1282.

[190] Pink MSS, 296, fol. 172; Somerset and Dorset N. and Q. 3: 179, 1892–1893; Frederick Brown, Abstracts of Somerset Wills 3: 46, privately printed, 1887–1890 (hereafter, Brown, Somerset Wills); The visitation of London, 1633, 1634, 1635 (Harleian Society, 15, 17) 1: 26, 1880–1883 (hereafter, Vis. London [Harleian Society]).

[191] S.P. 16, 356/103. James Ashe's will dated in 1642 (P.C.C., 56 Twisse) mentioned various properties and assigned legacies amounting to over £3000.

[192] The year was noted in the diary of his kinsman, William Whiteway of Dorchester. Proceedings of the Dorset Natural History and Antiquarian Field Club 16: 66, 1895 (hereafter, Dorset N.H. Proceedings).

[193] Percival Boyd, The roll of the Drapers' Company of London, 6, Croydon, Andreas Press, 1934; A. H. Johnson, The history of the Worshipful Company of the Drapers of London 4: 138, 139, 172, n., Oxford, Clarendon Press, 1914–1922; The mem-

bers of the City Companies in 1641, comp. by T. C. Dale, 9, London, Society of Genealogists, 1934 (hereafter, Members of the City Companies, 1641).

[194] Hoare, Wilts. 1 (2): 118, 150; Alfred B. Beaven, The aldermen of the city of London 2: 185, London, E. Fisher, 1908–1913; Vis. London, loc. cit. Ashe's sons, Edward and James, entered the Merchant Taylors' School in 1644. C. J. Robinson, ed., Merchant Taylors' school register 1: 165, Lewes, 1882–1883.

[195] Guildhall Library MSS, 1188, Churchwardens' Accounts, St. Michael's Crooked Lane, 1, fols. 173, 186, 213, 231v, 253v.

[196] S.P. 16, 318/21; Sussex Arch. Coll. 18: 175, 1866.

[197] St. Michael's Churchwardens' Accounts cited above (1, fol. 239v) refer to the funeral expenses of Mistress Elizabeth Ashe.

[198] Ashe's widow, apparently confused by Hoare with his first wife, was said to have died in 1698, aged 78 (Hoare, loc. cit.).

[199] Ibid.

[200] C.J. 2: 50, 54, passim; Pink MSS, 296, fol. 172; Wilts. Arch. Mag. 26: 344, 1892; O.P.H. 9: 7.

[201] Arch. Cant. 4: 189, 1861.

[202] His age of 47 as quoted from the M.I. by Hoare (Wilts. 1 (2): 150) should probably have been read as 57. Hoare and

That Ashe had prospered in his business is evident not only from the records of his company but from his purchases of land. His purchase of a manor in Wiltshire and one in Kent during the war [203] was not entirely a result of his being on the side of the victors. His pledge for the defense in 1642 of four horses with maintenance, and of £500 in money, if needed, within an hour's warning,[204] indicates that he had ample means at his disposal. He paid a fine of £1000 to be discharged from serving as a London alderman in 1653.[205] His will of 1656 mentioned various houses and properties in London, Wiltshire, Oxfordshire, and Ireland, referred to dowries of £1000 each for two daughters, and noted legacies amounting to more than £7300.[206]

Not only did Ashe have a brother working closely with him in the Long Parliament, but he was related through his mother's family to Denis Bond.

John Ashe (1597–1659), of Freshford, Somerset, was M.P. for Westbury, Wilts, 1640–1653. He was the eldest son of the wealthy clothier, James Ashe of Westcombe in Batcombe (d. 1642), by his wife, Grace Pitt,[207] and was born in 1597.[208] While his younger brothers, Edward (q.v.) and Jonathan, became cloth merchants in London, John followed his father's trade in the western counties, prospered, and secured numerous landed estates. In 1637 he was described as "the greatest clothier in England." [209] He married Elizabeth, daughter of Henry Davison of Freshford, and had by her several children, of whom the eldest son, James, was M.P. for Bath, 1643–1653.[210]

Ashe was a collector for the 1627 loan, but he was himself reported as defaulting on the whole amount assessed him, so setting an example for resistance in his region.[211] About ten years later, while his father was taking a stand against ship money,[212] John Ashe was summoned by the Attorney General to answer for his share in attacking the ecclesiastical abuses of the time. He was charged with being a confederate of William Prynne, John Bastwick, and Henry Burton in the publication and distribution of such libellous works as *News from Ipswich* and *A Divine Tragedy Lately Enacted.*

His part was that, knowing the contents of the volumes, he had in the latter part of 1636 distributed them in Somerset and elsewhere. Ashe was summoned to London in January, 1637, but was presently allowed to return under bond to Somerset because of the thousands of his work people who were dependent upon him there. The full hearings on the conspiracy charge were scheduled for the following April in Star Chamber. The further records of the case, however, tell only of the trial and the punishment meted out to the principals in it.[213] Later that year John Ashe joined with five other west country clothiers in attacking the soap monopoly, certifying that they needed imported soaps for their fine fabrics and warning of the damage to their trade which would follow the restrictions on foreign soaps.[214] He supported the protests against the ship money assessments, 1639–1640.[215]

Although Ashe had not served in parliament before 1640, he was elected both times that year for Westbury.[216] He was a very active member of the Commons, serving on the committee concerning scandalous ministers and more than a hundred others during the course of the parliament. Among the important ones were those on the Admiralty, on trade, and the celebrated Committee of Goldsmiths' Hall, of which he was chairman from 1643.[217] He promised considerable sums for the Irish venture in 1642, and in June pledged £10 weekly for the duration of the war. By 1646 he was said to have spent nearly £11,000 in the service of the state.[218] Although Ashe incurred the hatred of the royalists by his work in dealing with sequestered estates, he seems to have managed his task with an attempt at reasonableness,[219] and even Sir Roger Twysden found him moderate in his treatment of royalists in so far as the orders of the House permitted.[220] Ashe was a Presbyterian elder [221] and was secluded by Pride's Purge in 1648, but was soon readmitted to the House, and sat until the end. He served in each parliament thereafter until his death in 1659. He is said to have favored making Cromwell king.[222]

Pink differ in their statements as to whether Ashe died in July or in October, 1656.

[203] Hoare, *loc. cit.*

[204] *N. and Q.*, 1st Ser., **12**: 338, 1855.

[205] Beaven, *op. cit.* **1**: 211, 234.

[206] Pink MSS, 296, fol. 172v.

[207] Pink MSS, 296, fol. 177; Hoare, *Wilts.* **3** (1): 41. A brief sketch of Ashe's life appears in S. W. Bates Harbin, *Members of parliament for the county of Somerset*, Somersetshire Archaeological and Natural History Society *Proceedings* **83**: Appendix, 158–159, Taunton, 1939 (hereafter, Bates Harbin, *Members of parliament, Somerset*).

[208] William Whiteway's Commonplace Book, Dorset N.H. *Proceedings* **16**: 66, 1895.

[209] *Winthrop Papers* **3**: 400, 1929.

[210] *Somerset and Dorset N. and Q.* **4**: 78–79, 1894–1895.

[211] S.P. 16, 68/82.

[212] See Edward Ashe.

[213] S.P. 16, 354/180; 362/103; Harl. MSS, 6867, fols. 136–143; *Winthrop Papers* **3**: 400–401, 1929; *C.S.P. Dom., 1636–1637*, 393–394; *1637*, 49.

[214] *Ibid., 1637*, 397.

[215] *Ibid., 1639–1640*, 588.

[216] *M. of P.* **1**: 484, 496.

[217] *C.J.* **2**: 50, 54, *passim;* Pink MSS, 296, fol. 177.

[218] Pink MSS, *loc. cit.; Somerset Arch. Proc.* **14**: 53, 1867; *N. and Q.*, 1st Ser., **12**: 338, 1855.

[219] He wrote to Norwich in 1644, for example, explaining the procedures. Add. MSS, 15,903, fol. 40. *The mystery of the good old cause* (7, London, 1669; reprinted by J. C. Hotten, London, 1863), however, attributes most of Ashe's wealth to what he gained from the royalists.

[220] *Arch. Cant.* **4**: 147, 1861. In 1648 Cromwell remonstrated with Ashe for permitting a former royalist to make his composition too easily (Sloane MSS, 1519, fol. 186). In 1650 Ashe expressed to his kinsman, Denis Bond, disapproval of too much severity. *Cal. Com. Comp.*, 226.

[221] *A.H.R.* **44**: 31, n., 1938–1939.

[222] *E.H.R.* **17**: 429, 1902.

Ashe's estate in Somerset and Wiltshire included at least two manors, that of Beckington perhaps coming to him only after his father's death in 1642, and much of the parish of Freshford.[223] His will, dated in March, 1656/7, mentions other Wiltshire manors and lands in Ireland, the latter doubtless being acquisitions of the war period. His will assigned £2500 to two daughters and £500 to each of his five sons, and mentioned particularly the materials of his trade in the possession of his wife and son at Freshford.[224]

Denis Bond and Edward Ashe were his relatives in the 1640 House.

Ralph Ashton, or **Assheton** (1596–1651?), of Middleton, Lancashire, was M.P. for his county, 1640–1648.[225] The eldest son of Richard Ashton of Middleton (d. 1618), by Mary, daughter of Thomas Venables of Kinderton, Cheshire, he was baptized at Middleton in January, 1595/6. He was educated possibly at Sidney Sussex College, Cambridge (M.A., 1615), and at Gray's Inn,[226] where he became a barrister and by 1639 a bencher. Ashton married Elizabeth, daughter of John Kaye of Woodsom, Yorkshire, was H.S., Lancashire, 1632–1633,[227] and a member of the sewers commission.[228] He may have been M.P. for Clitheroe, 1625 and 1626, but was chosen for the county for the first time in October, 1640. Ashton was somewhat in arrears for the loan of 1627,[229] but does not seem to have been penalized.

Ashton worked with the popular party in the House, was named to several early committees, including that on ship money,[230] and in 1642 was named to the commissions on scandalous ministers and on executing the militia ordinances in his county. His military career as Colonel Ashton, commander-in-chief of the parliamentary army in Lancashire, followed. He was a Presbyterian,[231] and was probably secluded from the House in

1648. Dying on 17 February 1650/1, he was buried 25 February at Middleton.[232]

The extent of Ashton's estate is not known, but it may be presumed that he had considerable means. His grandfather had owned various lands in Yorkshire and Lancashire, some of which were Ralph's in the 1630's,[233] and his mother's portion had been £1000.[234] He was probably the Ashton who pledged £250 for the defense in 1642.[235] When he made his will he planned £1000 portions for his daughters and enumerated a dozen "manors and lordships" in Lancashire, although part of his estate had already been settled.

Among Ashton's relatives in the House were the other Ashton, Peter Venables, who was a half-uncle, Peter Legh, and John Moore.[236]

Ralph Ashton, or **Assheton** (c. 1605–1680), of Whalley Abbey and of Downham, Lancashire, M.P. for Clitheroe, 1640–1648,[237] was the eldest son and heir apparent of Sir Ralph Ashton, Bart., of Great Lever and Whalley (d. 1644), by his first wife, Dorothy, daughter of Sir James Bellingham of Westmorland. Sir Ralph was a J.P and D.L. for some years, as well as a receiver of part of the revenues of the Duchy of Lancaster,[238] but he seems to have been outlawed for some offence about 1630, and in 1636 was found guilty by the Court of High Commission on a morals charge, although in deference to his age and his family the usual public penalty was commuted to a donation of £300 toward the repair of St. Paul's.[239] His eldest son Ralph was born about 1605,[240] matriculated at University College, Oxford, 21 February 1623, and was admitted at Gray's Inn, 7 May 1624. He married in 1630 Dorothy, daugh-

[223] J. Collinson, *The history and antiquities of the county of Somerset* 1: 126; 2: 200, Bath, 1791 (hereafter, Collinson, *Somerset*); Add. MSS, 30,989.

[224] P.C.C., 387 Pell.

[225] Pink and Beaven, *Parl. Rep. Lanc.*, 71. Occasionally the Ralph Ashton who sat for Clitheroe has been identified as the county member (Carlyle 3: 317; Bean, *Northern Counties*, 179, *Complete Baronetage* 1: 150); but a 1648 list of members styles the shire member "esquire," whereas his younger kinsman was by then a baronet (Thomason Tracts, E. 454, 17), and most of the Lancashire historians agree that the county member was of the Middleton line.

[226] *Al. Cant.* The Cambridge student, however, may have been an uncle, Ralph Ashton of Kirby, Yorkshire, who was mentioned in 1617 as having the degree of M.A., and desiring to become a divine. Will of Sir Richard Ashton (senior) of Middleton, 1617, Chester Probate Registry.

[227] *List of Sheriffs*, 73.

[228] C. 181/4, fol. 130v.

[229] S.P. 16, 70/72.

[230] *C.J.* 2: 42, 45, 51. The "Mr. Ashton" of the *Journals* was more probably the shire knight than the younger Clitheroe member.

[231] *A.H.R.* **44**: 36, n., 1938–1939.

[232] Pink MSS, 296, fol. 199; Bean, *op. cit.*, 197. The date sometimes appears as 1650, but Ashton declared himself in good health late in January, 1650. His will, dated 24 January, 1649/50, was proved in London, 10 May 1651. P.C.C., 80 Grey.

[233] Will of Sir Richard Ashton, Chester Probate Registry; *Lancashire and Cheshire Antiquarian Notes* 1: 93, 1885; Add. MSS, 33,935 (Moreton Correspondence), fol. 314.

[234] J. P. Earwaker, ed., *Lancashire and Cheshire Wills and Inventories* (Chetham Society, N.S., **28**) 2: 167, 1893.

[235] *N. and Q.*, 1st Ser., **12**: 360, 1855.

[236] Moore addressed Ashton as "uncle" in 1645. *A calendar of . . . the . . . papers of the Moore family*, ed. by J. Brownbill, Record Society for the Publication of Original Documents relating to Lancashire and Cheshire 67: 51, 1913 (hereafter, *Moore Papers*).
Additional references are: *The visitation of the county palatine of Lancaster made in the year 1664–5*, ed. by F. R. Raines, Chetham Society, 1st Ser., **84, 85, 88**: 14–15, 1872–1873 (hereafter, *Vis. Lanc., 1664–5*); *M. of P.* 1: 464, 470, 490.

[237] *M. of P.* 1: 490; 1648 list of members, Thomason Tracts, E. 454, 17.

[238] C. 193/12; S.P. 14, 131/48, i; *C.S.P. Dom., 1603–1610*, 197, 519.

[239] *Ibid., 1629–1631*, 298–299; *1635–1636*, 104, 126, 500–501.

[240] He was aged 8 at the 1613 visitation and 17 when he entered Oxford. Several authors give 1617 as his birth year, confusing him with a half-brother, Radcliffe, who was born then (*The Parish Register of Whalley*, published by the Lancashire Parish Register Society, 19, Preston, 1936).

ter of Nicholas (Tufton), Earl of Thanet, who died early in 1635 and was buried at Downham, the residence with which Ashton seems to have been identified during his father's lifetime. Ashton took a second wife in 1644.

Ashton may have been a J.P in his county in 1638,[241] but was probably not an M.P. before his election to the Short Parliament for Clitheroe.[242] He was a parliamentarian, as was his kinsman, the county member, but it is difficult because of the identity of names to distinguish his service in the House.[243] He was probably active in disarming recusants in Lancashire in 1641, promised at least two horses for the defense in June, 1642,[244] and was named to various parliamentary committees for his county during the war. By 1643 he had taken over his father's work connected with the Duchy revenues, and was called to account by parliament for not having turned in the money properly, but he gave a satisfactory answer, and kept his seat in the Commons until 1648. He was an elder in his county presbytery.[245] Ashton succeeded to his father's baronetcy in 1644, and died on 30 January 1679/80.

His family properties, of which he was not in control in 1640, included Yorkshire lands, one manor of which was worth £2300, as well as extensive holdings in Lancashire.[246] His tastes seem to have led him to religious studies, and he compiled before his death three folio books of notes on divinity which he considered publishing.[247]

Ashton numbered among his relatives in the 1640 House, besides the shire member, an uncle, Sir Henry Bellingham, a cousin, Thomas Standish, and kinsmen by marriage, the Mallorys of Yorkshire and Sir Humphrey Tufton.

Sir Edward Ayscough (1596–1654?), of South Kelsey, Lincolnshire, sat for his county, 1640–1648.[248] The head of a great county family, connected with many others there and in Yorkshire,[249] he was the eldest surviving son of William Ayscough (d. 1611), by his wife, Katherine, daughter of William Heneage of Hainton, and the heir of his grandfather, Sir Edward Ayscough of South Kelsey (d. 1612). He was baptized at Stallingborough, 24 August 1596,[250] probably studied at Sidney Sussex, Cambridge, and was knighted in 1613.[251] Before 1618 he married Frances, daughter of Sir Nicholas Clifford, and stepdaughter of Sir William Wray.[252]

Ayscough was M.P. for Lincoln in 1621 and 1628,[253] became a friend of John Eliot and worked with the country party men from his own county, such as Hatcher and Armine.[254] He was among those put under restraint for refusing the 1627 forced loan.[255] In Lincolnshire he served as J.P., was named to various commissions,[256] and was sheriff, 1631–1632.[257] He was a candidate at both shire elections in 1640, but was defeated in the spring by the royalist, Sir Edward Hussey.[258]

An active member of the Long Parliament, Ayscough was named to the Committee of Privileges, and to others on ship money, the Star Chamber, and the breach of parliamentary privileges. He pledged £1000 toward the loan in 1640,[259] and when war came served on various parliamentary committees for his county and was among the Lincolnshire men denounced as traitors by the king. He was secluded from the House by Pride's purge in 1648, seems to have been alive in 1652, but died before 1 July 1654.[260] His will, dated 9 November 1648, was proved 1 July 1654.[261]

Ayscough was the owner by inheritance of at least five manors in Stallingborough and vicinity,[262] and by purchase of other properties. His will indicates that he had more than an absentee's interest in tillage and in country sports.

---

[241] S.P. 16, 385/13.

[242] *M. of P.* 1: 482. See Ralph Ashton, of Middleton.

[243] Occasionally he was identified as of Downham (*C.J.* 2: 825). W. D. Pink believed he served on 37 committees, 1640–1648. Pink MSS, 296, fol. 201.

[244] "Mr. Ashton" promised the horses; "Mr. Ralph Ashton," £250. *N. and Q.*, 1st Ser., 12: 360, 1855.

[245] *A.H.R.* 44: 36, n., 1938–1939.

[246] T. D. Whitaker, *The history and antiquities of the deanery of Craven*, 265–266, 3rd ed., London, 1878; Lancs. and Ches. Antiq. Soc., *Trans.* 41: 55, 1926. His father sold properties worth over £200 a year for £9500 in 1629. Shrops. Arch. Soc., *Trans.*, 3rd Ser., 2: 26, n., 1902.

[247] T. D. Whitaker, *An history of the original parish of Whalley* 2: opp. p. 2, 4th ed., London, 1876. Additional references: *Complete Baronetage* 1: 150; *The visitation of the county palatine of Lancaster, 1613*, Chetham Society, 1st Ser., 82: 46, 1871 (hereafter, *Vis. Lanc., 1613*); *Al. Oxon.*; Bean, *Northern Counties*, 250, n.; Pink and Beaven, *Parl. Rep. Lanc.*, 253.

[248] *M. of P.* 1: 490; *Lincolnshire Notes and Queries* 11: 55, 1910–1911 (hereafter, *Lincs. N. and Q.*).

[249] His paternal grandmother was a Grantham, his father's sister married into the Savile family of Yorkshire, and his own sister married Thomas Hatcher (*q.v.*). *Complete Baronetage* 1: 49; *Lincs. N. and Q.* 1: 31, 1888–1889.

[250] Maddison, *Lincs. Ped.* 1: 64–66.

[251] *Al. Cant.*

[252] Charles Dalton, *History of the Wrays of Glentworth* 1, pedigree, London, 1880–1881.

[253] *M. of P.* 1: 452, 476. The 1614 member of his name (Willis 3: 170) was probably his father's younger brother, Edward Ayscough of Lincoln's Inn (Maddison, *Lincs. Ped.* 1: 65), for the 1640 member did not become a freeman of Lincoln until 1621 (Lincoln Corporation MSS, Entries of Common Council, 1599–1638, fol. 173).

[254] Forster, *Eliot* 2: 654, 656.

[255] S.P. 16, 89/2; *C.S.P. Dom., 1627–1628*, 81.

[256] *Lincs. N. and Q.* 1: 137, 1888–1889; 4: 182, 1894–1895; C. 181/3; 181/4, fols. 30, 170; 181/5, fols. 19, 27, 53.

[257] *List of Sheriffs*, 80.

[258] *Lincs. N. and Q.* 22: 21, 1932–1933; *M. of P.* 1: 482.

[259] *C.J.* 2: 21, 45, 53, 75; D'Ewes (N), 52.

[260] Pink MSS, 296, fol. 254; Thompson, *Boston*, 773.

[261] P.C.C., 107 Alchin.

[262] I.P.M. of William Ayscough, 1611 (C. 142/325/192); abstract of i.p.m. of Sir Edward Ayscough, 1612 (S.P. 14, 79/211).

Two brothers-in-law, Thomas Hatcher and Sir Christopher Wray, were fellow members of the 1640 House, as well as a cousin, Thomas Grantham.

Sir Harvey Bagot, Bart. (1591–1660), of Blithfield, Straffordshire, was M.P. for his county from March, 1641, after Sir William Bowyer's death, until he was disabled as a royalist, 24 November 1642. He had been M.P. for Staffordshire in 1628 and in the county had served as sheriff, J.P.,[1] D.L.,[2] and a member of various commissions, including one in 1639 to deal with the rioters against the enclosure of forests near Uttoxeter.[3] He compounded for knighthood at £25 in 1631.[4]

Bagot's estate by inheritance and by marriage included six or seven manors and other lands in the counties of Stafford and Warwick with an income of perhaps £540. But he settled most of it on his heir in May, 1641, retaining only a small income of less than £350 a year.[5] He had reason to complain later that his assessments, such as that for £2000 in 1644, were more than his estate was worth.[6]

* Edward Bagshaw (d. 1662), of the Middle Temple and of Northamptonshire, was M.P. for Southwark from 1640 until he was disabled, 22 January 1644.[7] He came of a Derbyshire family and was the second son of Edward Bagshaw, gentleman, of London (d. before 25 November 1608).[8] His mother was probably Mary Heming, who married as her second husband Sir Augustine Nicholls, Justice of Common Pleas.[9] Edward was educated at Oxford and the Middle Temple. One of his good friends at his inn was Bulstrode Whitelocke. It was there in 1640 that his Lenten lectures attacking the temporal power of the clergy brought him the disfavor of king and archbishop, but the high approval of many of his fellows.[10] One result was his election to the Long Parliament for Southwark, although he had not sat in parliament previously, nor held office in Surrey.

Bagshaw worked closely with Pym and his group in their early attacks on grievances, administrative, economic, and ecclesiastical.[11] But he was disabled early in 1644 after he had joined the king at Oxford.

Little is known of his estate. He held some land in Northamptonshire,[12] and in June, 1642, pledged for the defense £50 in plate without interest, although he specified that it be used for king and parliament conjunctively and not divided.[13]

Charles Baldwin (1598?–1675), of Elsich and Stokesay, Shropshire, was a member for Ludlow, 1640–5 February 1644.[14] He was the son and heir of William Baldwin of Elsich in Diddlebury (d. 1614), by his wife, Barbara, daughter of Richard Brooke of Whitchurch, Hants.[15] He was born in November, 1598, and was baptized at Ludlow on November 26.[16] He married in June, 1617, Mary, daughter of Francis Holland of Burwarton, widow of Robert Lutley of Bromcroft.[17]

Baldwin seems to have led a quiet life, his first major public service being that of member for Ludlow in the Short Parliament.[18] He was not active as a member of the Long Parliament and was named to no committees. When war came he joined the king at Oxford[19] and was disabled in 1644. During the war he was assessed in turn £1000 and £400 by the Committee for Advance of Money, and was fined £586 when he compounded for his royalism.[20] He died in February, 1674/5, and was buried at Diddlebury on February 17.[21]

[1] C. 193/12, 13.

[2] S.P. 16, 412/9.

[3] *C.S.P. Dom., 1639–1640*, 172; C. 181/4, fol. 189; 181/5, fol. 180.

[4] The William Salt Archaeological Society, *Collections for a history of Staffordshire*, 1st Ser., 2 (2): 22, 1881 (hereafter, *Staff. Hist. Coll.*).

[5] S.P. 23/201/481–483.

[6] Bagot proved by 1648 that his estate was worth only £1745, and that he had debts of £3120. He protested again in 1655 at the assessment of a tenth on an estate estimated to be £424 a year. *Cal. Com. Adv. Money*, 420; Wedgwood, *Staff. Parl. Hist.* 2: 54–55. See also G. Wrottesley, A history of the Bagot family, *Staff. Hist. Coll.*, N.S., 11: 94–104, 1908.

[7] *M. of P.* 1: 494; *C.J.* 3: 374.

[8] *Mid. Temp. Rec.* 2: 499. It is suggested by A. R. Ingpen (*The Middle Temple bench book*, 193, London, Chiswick Press, 1912) that he was born about 1584, but the date of his entering Oxford, 1604, makes it seem probable that he was born nearer to 1590.

[9] The name of Edward's elder brother, but not his own, appears in the Nicholls pedigree. W. C. Metcalfe, ed., *The visitations of Northamptonshire*, 119, London, 1887.

[10] *C.S.P. Dom., 1639–1640*, 521, 522–523; B. Whitelocke, *Memorials of the English affairs* 1: 95–97, 1853.

[11] D'Ewes (N), 11–12, 425; *C.J.* 2: *passim*.

[12] G. Baker, *The history and antiquities of the county of Northampton* 2: 57, London, 1822–1841.

[13] *N. and Q.*, 1st Ser., 12: 359, 1855.

[14] *M. of P.* 1: 492; *C.J.* 3: 389.

[15] Shrops. Arch. Soc., *Trans.*, 1st Ser., 9: 303–304, 1886; 4th Ser., 2: 327, 1912.

[16] According to the i.p.m. of his father (C. 142/346/184), Charles was aged 16 (17?) years, 2 months, and 4 days on 25 January 1614/5. The manuscript is badly faded. The birth date appears as 1593, however, in the articles on Baldwin by H. T. Weyman and Evelyn H. Martin in Shrops. Arch. Soc., *Trans.*, 2nd Ser., 7: 26, 1895, and 4th Ser., 2: 327, 1912. The latter writer calls attention to the baptismal date and to the fact that Baldwin's M.I. states that he died in his 71st year, in February, 1674 (*sic*).

[17] *Ibid.*, 4th Ser., 2: 327–328, 1912.

[18] Willis 3: 235. Baldwin was a member in 1631 of a commission to inquire concerning certain public works at Bridgnorth (Add. MSS, 30,345, fol. 13). A contemporary letter reported him "importunately" laboring with his friends and his purse with the burgesses to secure his election for the first time. Shrops. Arch. Soc., *Trans.*, 2nd Ser., 7: 26, 1895.

[19] Pink MSS, 297, fol. 53.

[20] *Cal. Com. Comp.*, 1227; Shrops. Arch. Soc., *Trans.*, 2nd Ser., 7: 26, 1895.

[21] *Shropshire Parish Registers*, Shropshire Parish Register Society, Hereford Diocese, 15: 67, 1912. His will was dated 1 October 1674 and proved 31 May 1675. In it he mentioned "my parish of Diddlebury" and "my parsonage and rectories

Baldwin's father had held properties in five or more parishes in Shropshire,[22] and his wife was a coheiress of her family. Little else is known of his estate.

John Bampfield (*c.* 1610–1650), of Poltimore, near Exeter, was M.P. for Penryn in Cornwall, 1640–1650. He was the third but eldest surviving son of John Bampfield of Poltimore (living in 1650) by Elizabeth, daughter of Thomas Drake of Buckland, Devon. His grandfather, Sir Amias Bampfield (d. 1625/6), and his father had been M.P.'s and taken an active part in public affairs in Devon. The elder John Bampfield was a J.P., D.L., and sheriff,[23] and was one of the opposition group in his region. He was in arrears in his ship money in 1637,[24] and signed the Devonshire petition against abuses in the Stannaries in 1640.[25] John Bampfield, junior, was born about 1610 and was possibly a lieutenant in the army in Ireland in 1626.[26] He matriculated at Wadham College, Oxford, 30 October 1629, aged nineteen, and entered the Middle Temple early in 1631. He was "bound" there with John Maynard.[27] In 1632 Bampfield married[28] Gertrude, daughter and coheir of Amias Coplestone of Coplestone and Warleigh, Devon, acquiring with her considerable wealth.

The younger Bampfield seems to have held no civic office before 1640, but he was a friend and neighbor of John Northcote,[29] whose politics his resembled. He was named to a committee on preaching ministers and to several on matters of secondary importance in the early period of the parliament. Although he was created a baronet in July, 1641, he brought in £100 the next year for the service of parliament in his county.[30] He afterwards contributed toward the expenses of Plymouth's siege,[31] and fought for parliament. Bampfield was an Independent by 1647 and kept his seat until his death. He died in his fortieth year, 24 April 1650,

and was buried at Poltimore.[32] His father seems to have outlived him at least by some months.[33]

Bampfield's family were wealthy, their chief manor of Poltimore alone comprising a whole parish. They owned at least two other manors in Devon, and from his wife's family came other holdings. His son, who was considered as of great wealth in his student days,[34] was estimated to be worth £1900 a year in 1660.[35]

Anthony Barker (*c.* 1604–*c.* 1667), of Sunning, Berkshire, and recorder of Wallingford, was returned for that borough, 15 October 1640, and appears to have sat in the House until his election was declared void on 15 February 1641. He was not re-elected in the by-election, Thomas Howard, royalist younger son of the Earl of Berkshire, replacing him.[36] Barker was the fourth but second surviving son of Sir Anthony Barker of Sunning, J.P., H.S., M.P. (d. 1630), by Jane, daughter of Edward Eldrington of Beech Hall, Essex.[37] He matriculated at Oxford (Trinity College), 5 December 1623, "aged nineteen," and was graduated B.A. in 1626.[38] He entered the Middle Temple immediately afterwards, and was bound there for a time with George Buller. He became a barrister in 1633, and in his later years was reader (1654), bencher (1656), and treasurer (1666).[39] Barker was named one of the sewers commissioners of Berkshire in 1638,[40] and by 1640 was Wallingford's recorder. He married, probably about that time or before, Frances, daughter of Richard Knight of Chawton in Hampshire.[41]

Barker's election to the Long Parliament was his first. There are no indications as to the reason for his being chosen except that he was the town's recorder. He seems to have been on good terms with the government under the Commonwealth, but was probably not conspicuous in political matters, distinguishing himself

---

of Diddlebury and Long Stanton." Shrops. Arch. Soc., *Trans.*, 4th Ser., **2**: 332–333, 1912.

[22] I.P.M., C. 142/346/184.

[23] C. 193/13; *C.S.P. Dom., 1638–1639*, 496; *1633–1634*, 402; Devon *Trans.* **10**: 310, 1878; **32**: 94, 1900; **48**: 322, 331, 1916; *Devon and Cornwall N. and Q.* **6** (i): 225, 1911; Pink MSS, 297, fol. 62.

[24] S.P. 16, 435/33/i.

[25] *The Buller Papers*, 137, 139.

[26] *C.S.P. Ireland, 1625–1632*, 146. One Bampfield, possibly the colonel of the Civil War period (Clarendon, *Rebellion* **4**: 327), was recommended for a captaincy under Mansfeld in 1624. S.P. 14, 174/45.

[27] *Mid. Temp. Rec.* **2**: 772.

[28] The marriage license was dated 30 April 1632 (Harding MSS, 18 [North Devon Athenaeum], fol. 92). The marriage date in *Complete Baronetage* (**2**: 101), 3 May 1637, is possibly a misprint for 1632.

[29] Bampfield's father wrote to Edward Seymour (*q.v.*) on 9 January 1641 to say that his son had stayed to help with Northcote's affairs. *H.M.C., Fifteenth Report*, 7, MSS of the Duke of Somerset, 64.

[30] *C.J.* **2**: 54, 94, 205, 783.

[31] Plymouth Inst. *Trans.* **5**: 304, 1873–1876.

[32] M.I. in Poltimore church.

[33] John Bampfield of Poltimore, Esquire, assigned certain lands to trustees on 12 September 1650. Somerset County Record Office MSS, Hobhouse Gift, 1931, No. 19.

[34] T. L. Pridham, *Devonshire celebrities*, 6–7, Exeter, 1869; Sir William Pole, *Collections towards a description of the county of Devon*, 166, 171–172, 231, London, 1791 (hereafter, Pole, *Descr. of Devon*).

[35] *English Baronetage* **4**: 366, 1741. In addition to the authorities cited above see *Note book of Sir John Northcote*, xxv; F. T. Colby, ed., *The visitation of the county of Devon in the year 1620*, Harleian Society, **6**: 17, London, 1872 (hereafter, *Vis. Devon, 1620*).

[36] *M. of P.* **1**: 485 and n.; **3**: App., xliv; Willis **3**: 241, 312; D'Ewes (N), 361; *C.J.* **2**: 85.

[37] W. Berry, *County genealogies: Pedigrees of Berkshire families*, vi, London, 1837 (hereafter, Berry, *Ped. of Berks. fam.*); W. Harry Rylands, ed., *The four visitations of Berkshire* (Harleian Society, **56–57**) **1**: 163–164, 1907–1908 (hereafter, *Vis. Berks.*); *M. of P.* **1**: 450; I.P.M., Sir Anthony Barker, C. 142/497/144; C. 193/13.

[38] *Al. Oxon.*

[39] *Mid. Temp. Rec.* **2**: 703, 775, 813–814; **3**: 1069, 1103, 1210.

[40] C. 181/5, fol. 198.

[41] *Vis. Berks.* **1**: 164; Pink MSS, 307, fol. 41.

more in his profession. He died about 25 January 1667.[42]

Barker's estate was probably not large, since he was a younger son and his father's lands were apparently not extensive.[43]

John Barker (fl. 1624–1670), alderman of Coventry, was a member for his town from 1640 until 1653 (?). A draper by trade, he came presumably of a family of drapers who had owned properties in Much Park Street and been city officials from Tudor times. He was probably a grandson of Richard Barker, mayor (1572) and benefactor (d. 1604), and son of either Richard's son, Thomas, draper (mayor, 1600–1601), or of John Barker, draper, mayor (1614), and for many years alderman (d. 1634).[44] John Barker, frequently styled "junior" in the city records to distinguish him from the alderman and former mayor of the same name, was a member of the common council and sheriff of Coventry in 1624, was mayor, 1634–1635, and an alderman after that time until he resigned in 1655.[45] While he was mayor he got for himself the business of selling to the city the woolen goods for the uniforms of some servants and almsfolk.[46] But of greater importance was his work, supported by William Jesson (q.v.) and Simon Norton (q.v.), in dealing with the county sheriff and representatives of other Warwickshire towns concerning the ship money rate of 1635. By persistent appeals to Council and with the support of the bishop and of several of the local gentry, Barker and his colleagues secured a reduction of Coventry's rate to about half of the figure originally demanded.[47]

Barker had never been an M.P. before the Long Parliament, but he proved himself a stanch parliamentarian. He gave his bond jointly with his colleague, Norton, for £1000 for the loan in November, 1640, and in June, 1642, promised to supply £50 for the defense.[48] He was in Coventry much of the time during the summer and autumn of 1642, preparing for its defense, and be-

came a colonel and governor of the city during the war.[49] He was secluded by the purge of 1648, but was re-admitted in October, 1649.[50] Barker and his wife were living in greatly reduced circumstances for at least a decade after the Restoration, and several times the city granted him funds.[51]

In 1640 Barker was probably a prosperous draper. Besides his business he may have had an interest in the city coal lands,[52] and he held leases on several other city properties.[53] He was one of the chief rate payers in his ward.[54]

Barker was related to William Jesson by marriage, being probably a brother-in-law or a cousin.

* Sir Nathaniel Barnardiston (1588–1653?), of Ketton, Suffolk, one of his county's knights, 1640–1653, was the head of a very old and wealthy family of Suffolk, enjoying an income of possibly £4000 a year.[55] He had sat in four parliaments before the session of November, 1640, although when he was returned in 1628 it was said that he was less popular in the county at large than with the deeply religious men whose efforts chiefly accounted for his election.[56] He had been sheriff and a D.L. and had served the county for many years as a J.P.[57]

A close friend of John Winthrop, Barnardiston was probably a stockholder of the Massachusetts Bay Company, and was interested in its affairs when he was returned to the 1640 parliaments.[58] He counted among his fellow members of the Long Parliaments his brother-in-law, Thomas Soame of London, several cousins through the Knightley connections, such as Richard Knightley and the Lukes, and as fairly close relatives by marriage, Gurdon, D'Ewes, and Sir Philip Parker.[59]

---

[42] He was still treasurer at the Temple on 28 November 1666, but had died before 25 January 1667. *Mid. Temp. Rec.* **3**: 1213.

[43] I.P.M. cited above.

[44] John Barker (mayor 1614) was possibly a younger son of Richard (mayor 1572), for he, too, was associated with Much Park Street. A younger Richard Barker does not seem to have gone far with municipal offices. The relationships to John Barker, M.P., that I have suggested above are based upon the frequent occurrence of the names in the Coventry Corporation MSS; for example, A 25 (Leases and Rentals), fol. 85; A 14 a (Council Minutes), fols. 561–563, 634; Birmingham Reference Library MSS, 335,861; Add. MSS, 11,634 ("Annals of the City of Coventry"), fols. 11–18. See also Poole, *Hist. Coventry*, 371, 372; *History, gazetteer and directory of Warwickshire*, 516, Sheffield, Francis White & Co., 1850.

[45] Coventry Corporation MSS, A 14 a (Council Minutes), fols. 514, 533–536, 576, 599, 631, *passim;* A 14 b, fols. 42, 49, 118v.

[46] Coventry Corporation MSS, A 22 (Accounts), fols. 274, 281, 282.

[47] Coventry Corporation MSS, A 35 (Ship Money Accounts).

[48] D'Ewes (N), 52; *N. and Q.*, 1st Ser., **12**: 360, 1855.

[49] Coventry Corporation MSS, A 14 b, fols. 28v, 29, *passim;* Add. MSS, 11,364, fol. 18v; *C.J.* **3**: 390.

[50] Whitley, *Parl. Rep. Coventry,* 82, 90, 93; *H.M.C., Tenth Report* **6**, MSS of Mr. P. P. Bouverie, 95.

[51] Coventry Corporation MSS, A 14 b, fols. 145v, 177v. He requested a life allowance, 4 December 1670. Poole, *Hist. Coventry*, 375.

[52] One Mr. John Barker was a lessee of those lands in 1622. Coventry Corporation MSS, A 14 a, fol. 472.

[53] *Ibid.*, A 14 a, fols. 629, 653; A 14 b, fols. 46v, 57; A 29 (Leases and Rentals, 1613–1808), *passim.*

[54] At one time Barker's assessment on the basis of goods was the same as that of Jesson and Norton and equal to that of the elder John Barker. Coventry Corporation MSS, 75, fols. 1–3.

[55] His estate was reputedly worth £4000 a year about 1620 (*D.N.B.*), and at least £3000 a year in 1658. *Suffolk Institute of Archaeology and Natural History* **8**: 132, 1894 (hereafter, *Suff. Inst. Arch.*). He does not seem to have pledged his bond for the loans, but in June, 1642, promised for the defense two horses and the continuance of the £500 he had formerly lent. *N. and Q.*, 1st Ser., **12**: 338, 1855.

[56] *C.S.P. Dom., 1628–1629,* 6; Suffolk Church Notes, 1655–1665, Add. MSS, 15,520, fol. 65.

[57] C. 193/12 and 13; S.P. 16/405.

[58] *Winthrop Papers* (1929–1944) **1**: 325, 336; **2**: 230, 264, n.: **4**: 217.

[59] His brother married into the Gurdon connection (*East Anglian*, N.S., **4**: 338, 1891–1892); one of his cousins married

Barnardiston was affiliated with the Suffolk presbytery during the war, but seems not to have been among the "secluded" members of 1648.[60]

* Sir Francis Barnham (c. 1577–1646?), of Hollingbourne, Kent, member for Maidstone, 1640–1646, had sat in every parliament since 1603, except that of 1625, and from 1621 his constituency was Maidstone. He was born about 1577,[61] being the eldest son and heir of Martin (later Sir Martin) Barnham of London and Hollingbourne (H.S. Kent, d. 1610), by his first wife, Ursula, daughter of Robert Rudston of Boughton, Monchelsea.[62] He was educated at Trinity College, Cambridge (matriculated c. 1592), and Gray's Inn,[63] but seems to have taken no degree. His marriage to Elizabeth Lennard was in 1599.[64]

In Kent, Sir Francis was a captain of the trained bands by 1621,[65] and he was a J.P.[66] and a member of various local commissions.[67] From 1626 to 1639 or longer he was a D.L.[68] His house at Maidstone was used in 1634 as headquarters for the visiting Vicar General.[69] His prestige in the town was great, and in the 1640 elections his influence was apparent.[70] Although a parliamentarian, Barnham was somewhat lukewarm when war came, and was in danger of expulsion and sequestration on account of absences in September, 1643.[71]

Barnham's inherited lands were worth something over £400 when his father died, and his wife's dowry was not great.[72] He doubtless followed his father's example in increasing his estates, however, and by 1640 was apparently well-to-do. He owned numerous properties in Kent,[73] and was at one time a stockholder in the Virginia Company.[74] His offer for the defense in 1642 was a free loan of £100.[75]

Sir Thomas Barrington, Bart. (c. 1589–1644), of Barrington Hall in Hatfield Broadoak, Essex, sat for Colchester from 1640 until he died in 1644. The heir of an old Essex family of wealth and influence, being the son of Sir Francis Barrington, the first baronet (d. 1628), by his wife, Joan, daughter of Sir Henry Cromwell, he was born in or before 1589.[76] He was admitted to Gray's Inn on 5 November 1602.[77] Before 1615 Barrington married Frances, daughter and co-heiress of well-to-do John Gobert of Coventry;[78] and in October, 1624, having been for a time a widower, he married Judith, daughter of Sir Rowland Lytton and widow of Sir George Smith of Hertfordshire. The match was described by John Chamberlain as one very fit "for yeares, bloud, estate, conformity of studies (somewhat poeticall)," and it established important family connections, for Barrington was now a brother-in-law of Sir William Lytton (q.v.) and of Sir Henry Wallop (q.v.), with the latter of whom he was already intimate, and a cousin of several other 1640 parliament men through the St. John line of his wife's ancestry.[79] Barrington was knighted before 1621,[80] and in 1628 succeeded to his father's baronetcy.

Barrington's father, active as a J.P., and M.P. seven times for his county, 1601–1628,[81] was a prominent member of the puritan element in his shire. He opposed the court program in the decade before his death, was several times summoned by Council to answer for his actions, and was among those imprisoned, 1626–

D'Ewes (D'Ewes, Autobiography 1: 249; 2: 89); Parker was his wife's nephew.

[60] J. H. Hexter lists Barnardiston among the Presbyterians who were not regicides or rumpers (A.H.R. 44: 36, n., 1938–1939), but ill health probably accounted for most of his absences from the House in the later period. His name does not appear among the lists of secluded members printed in Rushworth (7: 1355) or the London tract printed in 1649 for M. Spark, entitled, A vindication of the imprisoned and secluded members of the House of Commons.

[61] The Ancestor 9: 195–196, 1904.

[62] The visitation of Kent, . . . 1619–1621, ed. Hovenden, Harleian Society, 42: 168, 1898 (hereafter, Vis. Kent, 1619); A visitation of Kent, 1663–1668, ed. Armytage, Harleian Society, 54: 8, 1906 (hereafter, Vis. Kent, 1663–1668). D.N.B. errs in terming him the son of Sir Martin's second wife, an error which Hasted made and corrected (Edward Hasted, The history and topographical survey of the county of Kent 5: 340; 6: 563, 2nd ed., Canterbury, 1797–1801 [hereafter, Hasted, Kent]). An indenture of 18 January 1580, preceding Sir Martin's second marriage, mentioned Francis (I.P.M., Sir Martin Barnham, C. 142/319/198). See also Barnham's biography of his father in The Ancestor 9: 191–209, 1904.

[63] Al. Cant.

[64] Complete Baronetage 3: 285.

[65] H.M.C., MSS of A. G. Finch 1: 42.

[66] C. 193/12.

[67] C. 181/4, fols. 18v, 32, passim; 181/5, fols. 258, 288.

[68] Acts P.C., 1625–1626, 448; S.P. 16, 160/10; 417/112.

[69] C.S.P. Dom., 1634–1635, 366.

[70] Larking, Proceedings in Kent, 12–14; Bodleian Rawl. MSS, D. 141, fol. 7.

[71] C.J. 3: 256.

[72] The Ancestor 9: 196–197, 204, 1904.

[73] Hasted, Kent 4: 297, 411; 5: 469; 6: 567–568.

[74] Alexander Brown, The genesis of the United States 2: 544, 825, Boston, 1890 (hereafter, Brown, Genesis of the U.S.).

[75] N. and Q., 1st Ser., 12: 360, 1855.

[76] Complete Baronetage 1: 28. He was aged 40 or more in 1629. I.P.M., Sir Francis Barrington, C. 142/450/72.

[77] Foster, Register of Admissions to Gray's Inn, Coll. Geneal. 2: 45, 1883.

[78] His son and heir, John, was born in 1615 (Essex Archaeological Society, Transactions, N.S., 12: 204, 1913 [hereafter, Essex Arch. Soc., Trans.]); The visitations of Essex (Harleian Society, 13–14) 1: 343, 1878–1879 (hereafter, Vis. Essex); I.P.M., C. 142/777/100. The marriage date is given as in or before 1605 in Complete Baronetage.

[79] The letters of John Chamberlain 2: 572, 587; Eg. MSS, 2644 (Barrington Papers), fols. 182, 209, 214, 215, 219. Among the new connections were Judith Lytton's first cousins, Sir Beauchamp St. John and Sir Oliver Luke, her cousins, once removed, Oliver St. John and Samuel Luke, a cousin by marriage, Sir Miles Fleetwood; and Robert Wallop was nephew as well as cousin.

[80] He was styled knight in January, 1621. M. of P. 1: 453.

[81] Complete Baronetage 1: 28; M. of P.

1628, for refusing the loan.[82] Sir Francis's son, Thomas, was groomed for a similar career. He may have been a member of the 1614 parliament, and sat for Newtown in the Isle of Wight, one of his family's boroughs, in the five parliaments of 1621 to 1629.[83] In the parliaments of 1621 and 1626 he kept notes.[84] He was sympathetic with his father's party but, by the end of 1628, he began to doubt the wisdom of pushing too rapidly for total reform, preferring some reasonable satisfaction from the king and ministers to the risk of accomplishing nothing or bringing catastrophe by overhaste, and considered going abroad either as a traveller or a soldier for a time. He was still in London, however, in February, 1629,[85] and probably did not carry out the intention. Outside of parliament Sir Thomas was an active J.P.[86] and a member of local commissions in Essex, Middlesex, and Hampshire.[87] He avoided the burden of being sheriff, possibly through the intercession of his wife's relative, Secretary of State Dorchester,[88] but he was one of the D.L.'s of Essex under the lieutenancy of his kinsman, the Earl of Warwick.[89]

Barrington was in London often, 1630–1634, and occasionally at the court, where he seems to have had business matters to arrange with the Lord Treasurer and the Earl of Holland.[90] He showed his position during the period of personal rule by supporting his brother-in-law, Masham, a fellow J.P., in refusing to assist the saltpetre work for the Admiralty in their county, and by joining Warwick in objecting to the application of the forest laws there.[91] He seems to have been lenient as a justice toward ship money refusers,[92] but not to have followed his kinsmen, Hampden and

Gerard, in resisting payment himself.[93] A stanch puritan of Presbyterian leaning, a friend of Roger Williams and other divines,[94] Barrington was interested in America and became a prominent member of the Providence Island Company, of which Pym was treasurer. He invested more than £1100 in the venture between 1631 and 1635.[95] The lecturer of the parish in London where he was living, 1636–1637, was reported for non-conformity.[96]

When 1640 came, Barrington, with the powerful backing of Warwick, and assisted by puritan divines, justices, and men from the boroughs, and his own outlay of some £42, secured a seat as knight for his shire in the Short Parliament.[97] He exchanged constituencies with his brother-in-law, Masham, in the autumn, being returned for Colchester, and in the Long Parliament was one of the most active members. He belonged to Pym's group, becoming one of his principal lieutenants in managing his strategy.[98] He acted as a witness in Strafford's trial and was a member of most of the important committees, being named to over a hundred between November, 1640, and April, 1644.[99] He lent his wealth also for the cause, offering to be bound for £1000 for the 1640 loan, for £500 in March and again in July, 1641,[100] and in June, 1642, promising another £500 and the maintenance of four horses.[101] He was a parliamentary committeeman in Essex during the war and a lay member of the Westminster Assembly,[102] but outlived Pym by less than a year. Barrington died at Hatfield Broadoak on 18 September 1644, and was succeeded by his son, John.[103]

Although Sir Thomas left an estate that in 1644 was heavily encumbered through his colonial ventures and his advances for the "cause," [104] he was one of the wealthy men of the 1640 Commons. The family manors lay in Yorkshire and Hampshire, as well as in Herts and Essex, and there were various buildings of theirs in

---

[82] S.P. 14, 127/82; S.P. 16, 522/120, 60/10.

[83] Willis 3: 172; M. of P. 1: 453, 459, passim.

[84] Commons Debates 1621 3; C.S.P. Dom., 1625–1626, 347; S.P. 16, 29/12.

[85] H.M.C., Seventh Report, MSS of G. A. Lowndes, Esq., 544; Eg. MSS, 2645, fols. 11, 13. One Capt. Barrington was listed in July, 1628, as lately of Colonel Rich's regiment. S.P. 16, 3/62.

[86] H.M.C., Tenth Report, County of Essex MSS, 4: 502–507; C. 193/13; S.P. 16, 190/174; C.S.P. Dom., 1629–1631, 476, 532.

[87] C. 181/4, fols. 1v, 72, 89; 181/5, fols. 16, 71, passim.

[88] She wrote to Dorchester about 1631 begging his aid against her husband's nomination. Dorchester had been a guest in their home early in 1630. C.S.P. Dom., 1629–1631, 207; 1631–1633, 229.

[89] Eg. MSS, 2646, fol. 64.

[90] According to family letters, he seems to have advanced money to Holland and to the Lord Treasurer in order to purchase a park or an office, and according to the state papers, the sum of £1084 was noted as owing to him from the revenues in 1634–1635. His name was coupled with that of Burlamachi and others, to whom £6084 were to be paid. S.P. 16, 284/75, 294/62; Eg. MSS, 2646, fols. 2, 29, 30, 34, 46, 62. He seems to have advanced some money for the Earl of Warwick in 1631 and in his correspondence of 1642 was mentioned a debt "wherein we are engaged for my Lord of Holland" (ibid., fol. 175; 2645, fol. 299).

[91] C.S.P. Dom., 1633–1634, 281, passim; Essex Arch. Soc., Trans., N.S., 19: 292, 1930; Gardiner, H. of E. 7: 365.

[92] C.S.P. Dom., 1638–1639, 231.

[93] He and his mother in one year paid £15 for their chief manor and 7 s. on another property. S.P. 16, 358/12, 14.

[94] Eg. MSS, 2643, fols. 1, 3, 76.

[95] H.M.C., Seventh Report, MSS of G. A. Lowndes, Esq., 538, 589; Newton, The colonising activities of the English puritans, 65. His father had had Virginia Company interests. Susan M. Kingsbury, ed., The records of the Virginia Company of London 3: 318, Washington, Govt. Print. Off., 1906–1935.

[96] C.S.P. Dom., 1636–1637, 260.

[97] Ibid., 1639–1640, 609; Essex Arch. Soc., Trans., N.S., 12: 211, 1913.

[98] Hexter, The reign of King Pym, 89.

[99] C.J. 2: 20, passim; Pink MSS, 297, fols. 119–120.

[100] D'Ewes (N), 52, 435, n.; C.J. 2: 222.

[101] N. and Q., 1st Ser., 12: 360, 1855.

[102] Essex Review 5: 201, 1896; Stowe MSS, 189, fol. 5; Pink MSS, loc. cit.

[103] I.P.M., Sir Thomas Barrington, C. 142/777/100.

[104] Some 2000 ounces of his plate were delivered to the Guildhall committee before he died (Essex Review 5: 202, 1896). His son was said in 1645 to be left burdened with debts of £10,000 (Essex Arch. Soc., Trans., N.S., 23: 282, 1942).

London.[105] One of his Isle of Wight manors was described by a neighbor as the best one in the island, and it alone seems to have brought in several hundred pounds a year.[106]

Barrington was a man of wide experience and of varied interests. A gentleman "generally well approved of," [107] his literary tastes led him in 1638 to purchase Rider's translation of Horace's odes,[108] but he was fond also of hunting with dogs and hawks.[109] He preferred moderate measures to extremes, but by the time of the Long Parliament seems to have concluded that only strong measures could solve the political and religious difficulties.

Sir Thomas affords one of the best examples of the network of family connections that tied together the 1640 parliament men. He was a first cousin of Hampden, Cromwell, and Dunch; a brother-in-law of Masham, Lytton, Sir Henry Wallop, and Sir Gilbert Gerard, and uncle of Meux, Francis Gerard, and of Oliver St. John's first wife. By his second marriage other connections were established,[110] and by his daughter's marriage to William Cheyney in 1639 he acquired a son-in-law who was with him in the parliament. With the exception of a few of the youngest, all of his kinsmen in the House were of the popular party.[111]

Richard Barwis (1602–1649), of Ilekirk (Hildekirk), Cumberland, was M.P. for Carlisle, 1640–1649.[112] His family had been seated at Ilekirk for more than a century, had intermarried with prominent families of the region, and had held many county offices. His grandfather, Richard (d. 1599), was steward of Wigton. His father, Anthony Barwis (1580–1616), married Grace, daughter of William Fleming of Rydal and sister-in-law of Sir John Lowther, member of the Council of the North. Richard, the only surviving son of Anthony, was born in the spring of 1602,[113] and was doubly or-

phaned in July, 1616.[114] As soon as he came of age he entered into lawsuits to gain possession of his inheritance.[115] He was probably the Richard Barwis who was admitted to Gray's Inn in March, 1641,[116] but nothing is known of his schooling.

Barwis held various offices from early in the reign of Charles, serving as a J.P. in Cumberland and a member of local commissions such as those for piracy or for collecting the 1627 loan.[117] He was sent to parliament for Carlisle in 1628.[118] He seems to have been a D.L. soon afterwards,[119] and as sheriff, 1634–1635, he collected ship money.[120] He may have held also municipal offices in Carlisle, although the presence of a Barwick family there at the same period has led to some confusion of identities.[121]

Returned as a member for Carlisle to both parliaments of 1640, Barwis supported the popular side. He was not active in the work of the House, but in 1642 promised £50 for the defense,[122] and was named to the committee for scandalous ministers for his county. Later he served on other local committees, was one of the commissioners to Scotland in 1644,[123] and was instrumental in bringing Leslie's forces to terminate the siege of Carlisle.[124] He served as mayor of Carlisle in 1648, with the consent of parliament, and was buried in Westward parish church there on 13 February 1649.[125]

Sometime before 1640 Barwis married Frances, daughter of Sir Edward Musgrave of Hayton Castle, but he left no direct heirs.[126] He was known as an "excellently accomplisht gentleman," and one of wisdom and piety.[127] Even a writer of royalist sympathy remarked that his family was of very good esteem.[128]

[105] At least ten manors and various other large possessions were enumerated in the i.p.m.'s cited above. See also Essex Arch. Soc., *Trans.*, N.S., **1**: 78, 1878; **2**: 11, 1884; *C.S.P. Dom., 1629–1631*, 281.

[106] Oglander, *A royalist's notebook*, 137. From two of the Hants manors Barrington planned in 1644 to provide £446 a year for a younger son. When his elder son married, other lands were mentioned as the source of £3000 to £4000 for a daughter of the union. I.P.M., C. 142/777/100.

[107] S.P. 16, 170/54.

[108] Essex Arch. Soc., *Trans.*, N.S., **12**: 223, 1913.

[109] Eg. MSS, 2646, fol. 115.

[110] See note 79 above.

[111] More distantly related were D'Ewes (*Autobiography* **2**: 223) and Cheeke (*H.M.C., Seventh Report*, MSS of G. A. Lowndes, Esq., 558).

[112] *M. of P.* **1**: 487, 498, n.

[113] I.P.M., Anthony Barwis, C. 142/354/101; Cumberland and Westmoreland Antiquarian and Archaeological Society, *Transactions*, N.S., **37**: 113–117, 1937 (hereafter, *Cumb. and Westm. Trans.*); *The memoirs of Sir Daniel Fleming*, Cumb. and Westm. A. and A. Soc., Tract Series, **11**: 53, 1928.

[114] *Cumb. and Westm. Trans.*, 1st Ser., **13**: 112, 1913; i.p.m. above.

[115] C. 3/334/2.

[116] Richard Barwis of Islekirk, Esquire. *Gray's Inn Adm. Reg.*, 230.

[117] C. 193/12, 13; C. 181/4, fols. 25, 81; S.P. 16, 56/34; *C.S.P. Dom., 1637–1638*, 172.

[118] *M. of P.* **1**: 475.

[119] S.P. 16, 152/46/i.

[120] *C.S.P. Dom., 1635–1636*, 13.

[121] The name of the Carlisle family appears sometimes as Barwis. One Richard Barwis was a member of the Carlisle Merchant Guild in 1635 (R. S. Ferguson and W. Nanson, *Some municipal records of the city of Carlisle*, 90, Carlisle, 1887). The M.P. himself was mayor in 1648. He may have been mayor in 1627. *Cumb. and Westm. Trans.*, N.S., **37**: 118, 119, 1937.

[122] Bodleian Tanner MSS, 63, fol. 58. The name appears incorrectly in *N. and Q.*, 1st Ser., **12**: 360, 1855.

[123] Pink MSS, 307, fol. 311; *Cal. Com. Comp.*, 3.

[124] Isaac Tullie, *Narrative of the siege of Carlisle*, ed. Samuel Jefferson, 2, Carlisle, 1840.

[125] *Cumb. and Westm. Trans.*, 1st Ser., **13**: 112, 150, 1913.

[126] *Ibid.*, N.S., **37**: 117, 1937; Barwis's will (P.C.C., 34 Fairfax). A Frances Barwis, possibly his daughter, was buried in Westward church in 1623. *Cumb. and Westm. Trans.*, 1st Ser., **13**: 112, 1913.

[127] *Ibid.*, 150–151.

[128] E. Sandford, *A cursory relation of all the antiquities & familyes in Cumberland*, Cumb. and Westm. A. and A. Soc.,

He was nicknamed Giant Richard, or Great Barwis, because of his physical stature and the tales that were told of his strength.[129]

In estate Barwis was amply provided for. His father had died possessed of seven or eight manors, including over 1,300 acres, and of houses in Carlisle and other important towns of the region. Richard sold some of his properties before 1649, whether because he had trifled away his inheritance, as the royalists said,[130] or because of other reasons, such as the war. But he still owned at the time he made his will four or five manors, with mines, quarries, and coal holes, and had an interest in the salt works at Cannonby.[131]

Barwis was related through his paternal grandmother to his fellow M.P.'s, the Dalstons,[132] and Sir Patrick Curwen, the latter of whom was one of the overseers of his will. He was related by marriage also to Roger Kirkby.

William Bassett (1602–1656), of Claverton, near Bath, and of Ewley, Gloucestershire, was M.P. for Bath, 1640–5 February 1644. He was the son and heir of William Bassett of Claverton (d. 1613) by his wife, a daughter of Rice Davies of Backwell, Somerset, was born in 1602, and became a ward of the king upon his father's death.[133] He entered Lincoln's Inn on 1 June 1622,[134] but returned to Somerset without having been called to the bar. He married (1) Mary, daughter of Moses Tryon of Harringworth, Northamptonshire,[135] and (2) in January, 1630, Elizabeth, daughter and heiress of Sir Joseph Killigrew. She was a niece of Henry Killigrew (q.v.), and stepdaughter of Sir John Stawell of Cothelstone (q.v.).[136] In 1632 Bassett and his wife brought suit against Henry Killigrew and others regarding a portion of his wife's inheritance in Cornwall to which Killigrew had laid claim.[137]

By this time Bassett was taking part in public affairs. He was treasurer for the hospitals in his part of Somerset in 1630, and throughout the following decade was a J.P. and a member of other commissions.[138] He was one of the twenty-five justices who in 1633 requested an interpretation of the new rules about the Sabbath and professed alarm at the growing contempt of authority in the county.[139] As sheriff of Somerset in 1637 he had trouble collecting ship money. His frequent letters to Council indicate that he tried to execute orders, though with some delays. He even advanced £800 of his own money at one time. But he was summoned before Council with other sheriffs still in arrears in September, 1637, and was required to resume his activity. He was in London to make a payment in January, 1638, and in the following May he asked Council's support in a suit brought against his constables by John Pyne (q.v.).[140] But he was not always zealous in the king's affairs. He had paid an unusually large fine to the knighthood commissioners in 1631,[141] and in 1639 he sent excuses instead of money in reply to the king's request for funds.[142]

Bassett had not served in parliament before 1640. He was present at the county election when his wife's stepfather, Stawell, was chosen for the shire, and he signed the indenture.[143] He worked for a time in parliament with the popular party, but was seldom named to committees. He was appointed in 1642 to the county committee on scandalous ministers, took the oath and Covenant in 1643, but was disabled in February, 1644, for having joined the king.[144] He compounded in time for his estate, and died in 1656. He was still living on 25 March 1656, but had died by the following 6 August.[145]

Bassett owned a large estate, some parts of which had been in his family from early times. Others, such as Claverton, were of recent purchase.[146] His properties and some claimed in his wife's right were declared in his petition to the compounding commissioners to be worth only some £435 a year.[147] His fine at a third, set first at £2512, was later reduced to £1935.[148] But in

---

Tract Series, **4**: 27, 1890 (hereafter, Sandford, *Antiq. & Fam. Cumberland*).

[129] Cumb. and Westm. *Trans.*, N.S., **37**: 118, 1937.

[130] Sandford, *op. cit.*, 27; Anthony Barwis's i.p.m. cited above.

[131] The will of Richard Barwis, dated 22 January 1648/9, and proved by his widow, 12 March 1648/9. P.C.C., 34 Fairfax.

[132] Barwis was mentioned as a cousin in the will of Sir George Dalston's father, Sir John Dalston. P.C.C., 44 Seager.

[133] I.P.M. of William Bassett, 1614, C. 142/340/200. His maternal grandfather is called William Davy in *The visitation of the county of Gloucester, taken in the year 1623*, Harleian Society, **21**: 206 and n., 1885 (hereafter, *Vis. Glouc.*). See also *Somerset and Dorset N. and Q.* **3**: 62, 1892–1893; Collinson, *Somerset* **1**: 148.

[134] *Linc. Inn Rec. Adm.* **1**: 190.

[135] A deed of 31 December 1627, Bassett to Tryon, was possibly part of the marriage settlement. Somerset County Record Office MSS (Taunton), Skrine Collection, 1931, Parcel V (hereafter, Somerset Rec. Off. MSS).

[136] *Somerset and Dorset N. and Q.* **3**: 62, 1892–1893; Collinson, *op. cit.* **1**: 148. An indenture of 20 March 1629/30 refers to the marriage settlement on 20 January 1630. *A calendar of the charters . . . in the muniment room at Sherborne House*, 191–192, privately printed, 1900 (hereafter, *Calendar of Sherborne muniments*).

[137] Chancery suit, C. 3/395/103.

[138] *Quarter sessions records for the county of Somerset*, ed. E. H. Bates and E. H. Bates Harbin (Somerset Record Society, 23–24) **2**: 127, *passim*, 1907, 1908; Somerset Rec. Off. MSS, Quarter Sessions Rolls, Nos. 74–78, *passim*; C. 193/13; S.P. 16/405; C. 181/5, fol. 366.

[139] *C.S.P. Dom., 1633–1634*, 350.

[140] *Ibid., 1636–1637, 1637, 1637–1638, passim*.

[141] *Somerset and Dorset N. and Q.* **4**: 114, 118, 1894–1895.

[142] Rushworth **3**: 912.

[143] C. 219/43/Part 2.

[144] Pink MSS, 297, fol. 140.

[145] Somerset Rec. Off. MSS, Skrine Collection, 1931, Parcel V.

[146] Collinson, *op. cit.* **1**: 146; **2**: 109.

[147] S.P. 23/208/515.

[148] *Cal. Com. Comp.*, 1181–1182. His assessment by the Committee for the Advance of Money was changed in 1645 from £1000 to £1500 but was afterwards respited because his personal

1660 his son's estate was reported to be worth £1800 a year.[149]

Sir Edward Bayntun, or **Bainton** (1593–1657), of Bromham, Wiltshire, was M.P. for Chippenham, 1640–1653. He was the heir of a family long prominent in local and national affairs. One ancestor was vice-chamberlain to three queens of Henry VIII, and his grandfather, Sir Edward Bayntun, was a member of two Elizabethan parliaments. His father, Sir Henry Bayntun of Bromham (d. 1616), was sheriff, colonel of the trained bands, and M.P. (1584–1611).[150] His mother was Lucy, daughter of Sir John Danvers of Dauntsey, and granddaughter of John Nevil, fourth Lord Latimer. From her Bayntun inherited lands in Northamptonshire and Yorkshire.[151] Edward was baptized at Bromham, 5 September 1593, and matriculated at Christ Church, Oxford, in 1610. He was knighted in 1613, and the next year took his father's former seat as M.P. for Devizes.[152] He succeeded to the family estates in 1616. He married (1) Elizabeth (d. 1635), daughter of Sir Henry Maynard of Easton, Essex, secretary to Lord Burleigh;[153] and (2) Mary Bowell.[154]

Bayntun followed the family tradition of serving often in parliament. He was M.P. for Wiltshire (1621), Devizes (1624, 1625), Chippenham (1626 and both parliaments of 1640).[155] He was listed as one of the chief burgesses and councillors of Devizes in 1623;[156] and was a J.P.[157] in the county and a D.L.[158] He was sheriff of Wilts, 1637–1638, and incurred the animosity of several powerful neighbors, including Sir Francis Seymour (q.v.), by his harsh tactics in securing ship money. His actions were later discussed in parliament.[159]

Neither in his public nor in his private life was Sir Edward always moved by high principles. And he had a disposition which led him into frequent quarrels and lawsuits. Early in 1620 a quarrel with one Duns produced the rumor that he was going beyond seas for a duel.[160] In 1623 a London poulterer complained in Chancery that Bayntun and an agent were using him to dispose of "corrupt" coneys for the London market and were quarrelling with him about the financial side of the bargain.[161] Six years later Bayntun was charged before the Court of High Commission with neglecting a woman of Salisbury by whom he had had two illegitimate children, but the king pardoned him for those adulteries and any others.[162] In 1627 Bayntun yielded to the demands for a loan to the king by deducting the sum from £100 which he said was due him from the king.[163] The county sheriff complained in 1632 that Bayntun was neglecting his duties as a D.L.[164] And in that year and the next Bayntun and Nathaniel Stephens (q.v.), with some other Wiltshire men interested in the cloth trade, were summoned to answer in Star Chamber for having obstructed the work of a royal commissioner sent to investigate frauds in the clothing business. Bayntun was accused of having encouraged his tenants at Bromham who were weavers to disobedience and violence. Star Chamber proceedings in the case were still pending early in 1637,[165] but the outcome is not known. Two years later Bayntun was having trouble with his assistants about the ship money collecting and he was being required by Council to explain his accounts.[166] He declined in 1639 to lend money to the king.[167]

In both parliaments of 1640 Sir Edward espoused the popular cause, and he was assigned to some early committee work. But his conduct regarding ship money collecting had not been forgotten, and he was required to answer before the committee studying such abuses, and early in 1641 even the legality of his election was challenged. He made his peace with the opposition leaders, however, and between 1641 and 1643 worked with them, although he was not active on committees or as a speaker. He was among the earliest to take the Protestation of May, 1641.[168] The following August he was dangerously wounded in a duel with a fellow member, Richard Rogers of Dorset.[169] He took command of the parliamentary forces in his county when the war began,[170] but was not long in agreement with his co-workers there. He quarrelled violently with his neighbor, Sir Edward Hungerford, in January, 1643,[171] and in the summer fled to the Isle of Wight and began moves

estate to the value of £3000 had all been taken (*Cal. Com. Adv. Money*, 420–421).

[149] *English Baronetage* 4: 374, 1741.

[150] MSS of the Wiltshire Archaeological Society Library at Devizes (hereafter, Wilts. Arch. Soc. MSS), Bayntun Commonplace Book, pedigree; Pink MSS, 297, fol. 167; Add. MSS, 5496, fols. 73, 776.

[151] Pedigree cited above; Pink MSS, *loc. cit.*; Bayntun Commonplace Book, fols. 24–25; abstract of the will of Lady Lucy Bayntun (Brown, *Somerset Wills* 4: 119).

[152] *Al. Oxon.*; Pink MSS, 297, fol. 164.

[153] Hoare, *Wilts.* 3 (4): 7; Noble, *Regicides* 1: 86.

[154] Pink MSS, 297, fol. 164.

[155] *M. of P.*

[156] G. W. Marshall, ed., *The visitation of Wiltshire, 1623*, 88, London, 1882 (hereafter, Marshall, *Vis. Wilts.*).

[157] C. 193/12, 13; S.P. 16/405.

[158] *C.S.P. Dom., 1631–1633*, 67.

[159] *Wilts. Arch. Mag.* 3: 220, 1857; D'Ewes (N), 141–142, 176–177.

[160] S.P. 14, 112/26.

[161] Chancery suit, C. 3/335/73.

[162] *C.S.P. Dom., 1629–1631*, 92, 116. It was a standing order at Bayntun's house that the servants of his visitors be made drunk, a practice which John Evelyn termed barbarous and unbecoming to a knight. Marsh, *Hist. of Calne*, 233.

[163] S.P. 16, 55/89.

[164] *C.S.P. Dom., 1631–1633*, 193.

[165] S.P. 16, 346/68; *C.S.P. Dom., 1631–1633*, 312, 326–327; *1633–1634*, 136–137.

[166] *Ibid., 1639*, 253, 254, 536.

[167] Rushworth 3: 912.

[168] *C.J.* 2: 64, 68, 80, 81; D'Ewes (N), 330 and n., 334; Noble, *Regicides* 1: 85.

[169] *The Nicholas Papers*, 5, Camden Society, 1886.

[170] Add. MSS, 18,980, fol. 6; Pink MSS, 297, fol. 164.

[171] *D.N.B.*, "Sir Edward Hungerford."

to secure the king's pardon. He was brought up to London and held a prisoner of parliament for a time, but by June, 1644, had recovered his seat in the Commons.[172] He was named one of the king's judges, but did not act. He kept his seat in the House, however, until the end. He died on 8 December 1657.[173]

Bayntun's father owned three Wiltshire manors in addition to that of Bromham near Calne,[174] and from his mother's family some north country properties came to him. Both his father and he added to their Wiltshire holdings by purchase, and the properties, by the time they passed to Sir Edward's son, produced an income of between £1800 and £2000 a year.[175] Sir Edward, when he made his will in 1657, settled £200 a year from Bromham on a younger son, and assigned a legacy of £500 to another.[176]

Bayntun was the father of the M.P. of the same name who sat for Devizes. And a daughter was the wife of Hugh Rogers, M.P. for Calne. John Dutton of Gloucestershire was a brother-in-law.

Edward Bayntun (1618–1679), of Bromham, Wiltshire, was M.P. for Devizes, 1640–1648 (?).

He was the eldest son of Sir Edward Bayntun, the Chippenham member (q.v.) by his first wife, and was baptized at Bromham on 2 December 1618. He matriculated at St. John's College, Oxford, 15 January 1635/6, and entered Lincoln's Inn on 28 April 1638.[177] In the spring of 1640 he was chosen for the place often occupied by one of his family as M.P. for Devizes. He was re-elected in the autumn, and sat in the Long Parliament until Pride's Purge or later. He was chosen again by the borough in 1654 and in 1675 and 1679. In 1659 and 1660 he sat for Calne.[178]

The younger Bayntun somewhat resembled his father in temperament and apparently followed his lead in politics. He dared to call even John Pym to task during the debate of 20 February 1641 on Pym's proposals regarding the London loan, and desired that Pym give the House satisfaction for suggesting arbitrary proceedings.[179] He served as his father's aid with the army and in committee work after the war began,[180] and his coolness toward the extreme element brought an accusation in 1647 that he was of royalist sympathy. He was suspended, but was presently reinstated, and remained a member until 1648 or 1653.[181] A royalist by 1660, he served in the Convention Parliament, and was created a Knight of the Bath at the coronation in 1661.[182] He died in the summer of 1679.[183]

Apparently a bachelor during the Long Parliament and the Civil War, Bayntun was licensed on 29 May 1661 to marry Stuarta, daughter of Sir Thomas Thynne of Richmond.[184]

Anthony Bedingfield (1602–1652 ?), of London, mercer, was M.P. for Dunwich, Suffolk, 1640–1652 (?).[185]

He came of the old family connected with Ditchingham, Norfolk, and Darsham, Suffolk, being the fifth surviving son of Thomas Bedingfield, Esq. (d. 1636), by his wife, Dorothy, daughter of John Southwell of Darsham.[186] He was baptized in the family parish of Bedingfield, 9 September 1602,[187] and as a younger son was sent early to London to learn a trade. His eldest brother, Philip, became head of the family and a parliamentarian in politics, and his second brother, Sir Thomas, of Gray's Inn and Darsham, was for some time legal counsellor for Dunwich, M.P. from there in 1621 and 1626, Attorney General for the Duchy of Lancaster in 1638, and afterwards Justice of Common Pleas.[188] Another brother was John Bedingfield of Halesworth, also a lawyer, who was for some years steward and counsellor for Dunwich, as well as steward for one of the manors of the Coke family.[189]

Anthony became a member of the Mercers' Company of London by apprenticeship in 1628, and continued to be an active member of the company, serving as its master in 1651.[190] He was interested in trade with

[172] Calendar of Clarendon State Papers 1: 244; Whitelocke, Memorials of the English Affairs 1: 210, 263, 1853; H.M.C., Seventh Report, MSS of Sir H. Verney, Bart., 445.

[173] O.P.H. 9: 8; Wilts. Arch. Soc. MSS, Sadler's "Wiltshire Genealogy," Bromham Parish.

[174] St. Ch. 8/75/12.

[175] Wilts. Arch. Soc. MSS, Sadler, Rodney Cheney and Avebury Parishes; Bayntun Commonplace Book, fols. 19–25. The family's Wiltshire estates were near Devizes and Chippenham. See F. H. Goldney, ed., Records of Chippenham, 44, Chippenham, 1889.

[176] His will was dated 31 October 1657 and proved 4 January 1657/8. P.C.C., 19 Wotton.

[177] Pink MSS, 297, fol. 165; Al. Oxon.; Linc. Inn Rec. Adm. 1: 235.

[178] M. of P. 1: 484, 495, 502, 510, 516, 530, 538.

[179] D'Ewes (N), 384.

[180] May, 301; Pink MSS, loc. cit.

[181] Noble, Regicides 1: 86. According to some authorities (e.g. Pink and Al. Oxon.) Bayntun was secluded by the purge in 1648, but he is listed as sitting until the end in O.P.H. (9: 8).

[182] Pink MSS, loc. cit.; Wilts. Arch. Soc. MSS, Bayntun Commonplace Book, fol. 23.

[183] Pink MSS, loc. cit.; Brown, Somerset Wills 4: 119; pedigree in the Bayntun Commonplace Book; Wilts. Arch. Soc. MSS, Sadler's "Wiltshire Genealogy," Bromham Parish. Bayntun's will was proved 26 December 1679. P.C.C., 187 King.

[184] Pink MSS, loc. cit.

[185] M. of P. 1: 494.

[186] Burke, Landed Gentry 1: 79, 1850; Suff. Inst. Arch. 8: 133, 1894; a contemporary pedigree in the Norwich Public Library MSS, 3, L 2723, fol. 70.

[187] Add. MSS, 19,091 (Davy collection), fol. 99.

[188] Their father had been M.P. for Eye in 1586. Pink MSS, 297, fols. 194, 195, 196; D.N.B., Sir Thomas Bedingfield (1593–1661); Dunwich Borough MSS, Minute Book, 1595–1619, fols. 311, 315v.

[189] Ibid., Minute Book, 1627–1653, fols. 41, 50, 70, 117, 134; Add. MSS, 15,520, fol. 134v; 19,082, fol. 365; Alfred Suckling, The history and antiquities of the county of Suffolk 2: 337, London, 1846–1848. John was the father of another Chief Justice, Sir Henry Bedingfield.

[190] Information supplied from the records of the Mercers' Company by Frank D. Watney, Esq., Clerk of the Company.

Europe and seems to have spent some time in Hamburg and Antwerp.[191] His interest in the cloth trade led him to Yorkshire connections also and by 1635 he and his partners were interested not only in woolens but in coal and land investments there.[192] He was in 1638 a referee in the case of a shipowner engaged in the coal business between Newcastle and London,[193] and his residence then was probably in the region of Foster Lane and Cheapside.[194] He kept up his Suffolk interests, however, having inherited and bought lands there, and had friends and relatives in Ipswich, Stowmarket and Dunwich, as well as in the smaller towns.[195]

Bedingfield seems to have held no public office before 1640, but he was elected to both parliaments that year for Dunwich, having been made a freeman there upon the nomination of his brother, John, the borough's steward, on the day of his election in March.[196] He was not conspicuous at the start of the Long Parliament, but between 1641 and 1648 was named to many committees, including that of the recess, and several on financial matters, on lay preachers, and on grievances.[197] With Cage of Ipswich he pledged £700 toward reducing Ireland in 1642,[198] and kept his seat in the House until his death. He used his parliamentary privilege to avoid having to serve as a London alderman in 1650,[199] and died, unmarried, about 1652. He was buried at Gislingham,[200] and his will, dated 20 September 1650, was proved 9 August 1652.

A wealthy man at his death, owning in addition to his London business lands in Suffolk and Yorkshire, he enumerated in his will gifts to various parishes and to his relatives and apprentices which amounted to over £12,000. His expressed concern for "orthodox" ministers,[201] and his executors' description of him as a "Catholic-Christian" [201a] suggest that although he was probably a puritan, he was not one of the most extreme sort.

Henry Belasyse, or **Bellasis** (1604?–1647), of Coxwold, Yorkshire, was M.P. for his county, 1640–6 September 1642. He came of an old and wealthy Yorkshire family, being the eldest son of Sir Thomas Belasyse, Bart., first Lord Fauconberg (M.P., d. 1652).[202] He was educated at Cambridge and Lincoln's Inn, and was M.P. for Thirsk, his father's old constituency, 1625 and 1626, and for the county of York in 1628. At the close of the session in 1629 Belasyse favored the reading of Eliot's articles and the choosing of a Speaker who would comply with the wishes of the House.[203] Two years later he was imprisoned in the Fleet for a few weeks for an affront to Wentworth, the Lord President of the Council of the North.

During the 1630's Belasyse was a J.P. in the North Riding and Durham and a member of several other commissions for the northern counties.[204] He sat for Yorkshire again in the Short Parliament, and was questioned by Council afterwards, with his cousin, Sir Hugh Cholmley, and Sir John Hotham, for their remarks about the county's grievances. Belasyse returned to the north after his brief imprisonment to plan the Yorkshire petitions and to work for another parliament.[205] His victory in the October shire election with his cousin and good friend, Lord Fairfax, against Sir Richard Hutton and Wentworth's nephew, Savile,[206] who had been one of the informers against him in the spring, illustrates both his popularity in the county and the anti-Wentworth feeling there. The violation of his parliamentary privilege was duly noted in the House in February, 1641.[207]

Henry Belasyse was a prominent member of the Long Parliament. He was named to the Committee of Privileges and to others of importance, such as that for the declaration on the state of the kingdom and some on army matters. He spoke frequently on army affairs.[208] In March, 1641, he may have pledged £500 to secure the loan,[209] and was one of the committee sent with the Remonstrance to the king in December.[210] But with the imminence of war, he parted company

---

[191] His name appears in a list of merchants interested in overseas ventures in January, 1627 (S.P. 16, 147/41), and his will refers to a number of acquaintants in Hamburg and Antwerp. P.C.C., 215 Bowyer.

[192] With his partner, Robert Lowther, and backed by the City, he was engaged in lawsuits with the magistrates of Leeds in 1635 regarding tolls on goods purchased by Londoners at fairs (London Corporation MSS, Rep. 49, fols. 163v–164). In his will Bedingfield mentioned his coal business, some Yorkshire properties he had bought, and some charitable gifts for Leeds and Hull.

[193] S.P. 16, 390/167.

[194] Mr. Bedingfield was one of the large rent payers in this area in 1638, living near Mr. James Ashe (Dale, *Inhabitants of London, 1638,* 60). The London parishes remembered in his will were Lothbury and Coleman Street.

[195] Bedingfield's will, and i.p.m. of Thomas Bedingfield, 1637, C. 142/544/56.

[196] Dunwich Borough MSS, Minute Book, 1627–1653, fols. 115v, 119.

[197] *C.J.* 2: 288, *passim;* Pink MSS, 297, fol. 190.

[198] £400 was Bedingfield's personal share. *C.S.P. Ireland, Adventurers,* 241.

[199] London Corp. MSS, Rep. 60, fol. 245v; Beaven, *The aldermen of the City of London* 1: 170, 317.

[200] M.I. without date cited in the Davy collection, Add. MSS, 19,089, fol. 271.

[201] P.C.C., 215 Bowyer.

[201a] M.I. at Gislingham, as cited in note 200.

[202] Various authorities (e.g., *Al. Cant.*) give his baptismal date as 20 May 1604. It appears as 20 May 1602, however, in the article on Belasyse in Gooder, *Parl. Rep. York* 2: 46–47.

[203] *Commons Debates for 1629,* 240, 255.

[204] C. 193/13; S.P. 16/405; C. 181/5, fols. 114, 192, *passim.*

[205] *C.S.P. Dom., 1640,* 130, *passim; The memoirs of Sir Hugh Cholmley,* 63–64, 1787; Gooder, *loc. cit.*

[206] *C.S.P. Dom., 1640–1641,* 158.

[207] D'Ewes (N), 322–323.

[208] *Ibid.,* 335; *C.J.* 2: 20, 25, 109, *passim;* D'Ewes (C), 44, 114, 256, 341.

[209] "Mr. Bellasis" may, however, have been his brother. D'Ewes (N), 439, n.

[210] D'Ewes (C), 219–220.

with his cousin, Lord Fairfax,[211] and his party, and from the spring of 1642 was a worker for the king. He died during his father's lifetime in May, 1647.[212]

Because his father was alive, Belasyse had in 1640 only a part of the fortune to which he was heir. The family's estates in Yorkshire, Cumberland, and Durham, in which his father retained a life interest, were worth about £2000 a year before the war, and the lands Henry had in possession seem to have been worth £1000 or more yearly. His fine at compounding was set at a third, £3429.[213] His widow declared in 1651 that her jointure had been small.[214]

Because his family had intermarried with many others of the north country, Belasyse had numerous relatives among the 1640 parliament men. They included his brother, John, his brother-in-law, Slingsby, his first cousins, the Cholmleys, his father's cousin, Lord Fairfax, and a cousin by marriage, Sir William Strickland.

* **John Belasyse**, or **Bellasis** (1615–1689), of Worlaby, Lincolnshire, afterward Baron Belasyse, was a member for Thirsk, Yorkshire, 1640–6 September 1642. The second son of Lord Fauconberg,[215] and brother of Henry Belasyse (q.v.), he was born on 24 June 1615 [216] at his father's home in Yorkshire. He was educated there until he was twelve, and was the only one of Fauconberg's children to be reared in the Roman faith to which he had recently been converted. He was sent next to Cambridge and afterwards to France, where he spent about two years. He returned then to be maintained by his father at the English court until his marriage. His admission to Gray's Inn in March, 1641, was probably for social rather than for educational purposes.[217] Belasyse married clandestinely on 8 March 1636 the fifteen- or sixteen-year-old daughter and sole heir of Sir Robert Boteler of Walton Woodhall, Herts. He and his bride, Jane, were fined £150 for their action by the Court of High Commission.[218] Since Jane after her father's death had had several guardians, one of whom was Endymion Porter (q.v.), the next few years were filled with business regarding her inheritance in Hertfordshire and Bedfordshire.[219] The couple made their home at Worlaby, Lincolnshire, but spent long periods visiting with Belasyse's brother-in-law, Sir Henry Slingsby (q.v.).[220]

In 1638 Belasyse petitioned against the plans of the Lincolnshire sewers commissioners for draining his lands,[221] but he seems to have held no public responsibilities in that county. He may have been with the army in the north in 1639,[222] and in the summer of 1640 he carried messages to the Scots in preparation for the meeting at Ripon.[223] He was elected to both [224] of the parliaments of 1640 for Thirsk, a borough which had several times chosen his father and his brother.

In the Long Parliament John Belasyse was less active than Henry and it is sometimes difficult to distinguish them because the records frequently omit the given names. John was named, however, to a committee dealing with the fens,[225] and he pledged £1000 for the loan in November, 1640.[226] Late in 1641 he was several times teller on the royalist side at divisions,[227] and in the following year plunged into royalist activities for the army. He was absent from the House on 16 June and was disabled 6 September 1642.[228]

Belasyse was the younger son of a wealthy father and had married well. Although his father and brother were still living when he compounded in 1646, the fine for his estate, reckoned at a moiety, was £7500. It was set, however, at £2073.[229]

For the relatives of Belasyse in the Long Parliament, see Henry Belasyse.[230]

William Bell (fl. 1617–1660), of St. Margaret's, Westminster, an apothecary, sat for his city, 1640–1648. He was probably of a north country family, Yorkshire

---

[211] Clarendon, *Rebellion* 2: 461–462; Gooder, *loc. cit.*

[212] The date is given as 20 May by Gooder. It was 1 May, according to the church register. *Y.A.S. Rec. Ser.* 18: 169, 1895.

[213] *Y.A.S. Rec. Ser.* 18: 167–170, 1895.

[214] *Cal. Com. Adv. Money*, 421. She was the only child, however, of a father who was said to be wealthy. *Transactions of the Thoroton Society* 40: 9, 1936 (hereafter, Thoroton Soc., *Trans.*).

[215] Because the *D.N.B.* article on Belasyse contains several errors and omits most of the period before 1644, I have rewritten the early part completely. Some of the details are based upon the memoir compiled by Belasyse's secretary, Joshua Moone (Brit. Mus. Birch MSS, 4162, fols. 74–84; *H.M.C., Cal. of MSS of the Marquis of Ormonde*, N.S., 2: 376–399).

[216] *Ibid.* The date appears as 1614 in *Complete Peerage* (Gibbs ed.) 2: 89. John was aged "about 6," however, according to a deed of 9 October 1621, and 16 in 1631. *Proceedings of the Society of Antiquaries of Newcastle upon Tyne*, 4th Ser., 1: 133, 1923–1924. He was probably not the John Belasyse of Durham who was admitted to Peterhouse, Cambridge, in 1638, aged 17, although that has been suggested. *Al. Cant.*

[217] Foster, Register of Admissions to Gray's Inn, *Coll. Geneal.* 2: 57, 1883.

[218] *Complete Peerage* (Gibbs ed.) 2: 90; *C.S.P. Dom., 1636–1637*, 264.

[219] Her properties were valued at £430 a year in possession and £370 a year in reversion at this time. One Hertfordshire manor was sold about 1647 for £2560. Add. MSS, 33,575, fols. 27–28; *C.S.P. Dom., 1637*, 576; *1637–1638*, 19, 78.

[220] *The diary of Sir Henry Slingsby, of Scriven, Bart.*, 3, 19, 30, 58.

[221] S.P. 16, 378/75.

[222] He supplied six horses at least. *H.M.C., Cal. of MSS of the Marquis of Ormonde*, N.S., 2: 377; S.P. 16, 427/38/ii, v.

[223] *C.S.P. Dom., 1640–1641*, 89, 91, 93.

[224] *M. of P.* 1: 484, 497.

[225] *C.J.* 2: 99.

[226] D'Ewes (N), 52. He or his brother was the "Mr. Bellasis" who pledged £500 in March. *Ibid.*, 439, n.

[227] D'Ewes (C), 105, 304.

[228] *C.J.* 2: 626, 754.

[229] Bean, *Northern Counties*, 1081, n.

[230] Some further corrections and additions to the *D.N.B.* article appear in *The Bulletin of the Institute of Historical Research* 4: 48, 1926–1927.

or Lincolnshire,[231] and was a member of the London Apothecaries' Company, of which in 1636 he was warden.[232] He lived in St. Margaret's parish in Westminster, however, for some time before 1617, for he was one of the overseers of the parish, 1617–1618, and two of his children were buried there in 1618 and 1620. His name appears regularly among the parish records thereafter as overseer and as churchwarden.[233] Little is known of his business, but his residence on King Street doubtless acquainted him with some of the prominent men of the court, among them Sir Robert Pye and Edward Nicholas. He sometimes looked after the latter's house during his absences from Westminster, and in 1637 sought his help and that of other friends at court in an effort to be excused from serving on some commission, possibly that of the peace.[234] He was, however, a member of the local sewers commissions for several years,[235] and in May of 1640 was apparently a J.P.[236] In the confused Westminster election of March of that year Bell won his first seat in parliament, and although there had been some doubt regarding his return then,[237] he was chosen in October with the same colleague.

Bell was not a leader in the House and his early committee appointments were chiefly for activities in the Westminster area, including the arranging for religious services in his parish of St. Margaret's.[238] He was named to the committee for scandalous ministers in Middlesex in 1642 and served on the parliamentary committees of the county during the war years. He was also a member of the committees for army supplies, medical as well as monetary,[239] but was secluded by the purge of 1648. He returned in 1660[240] and died sometime before 23 May 1664, the date on which his will was proved.[241]

According to Bell's will, he owned several properties in London, his residence and other houses in Westminster and two in Kingsbury, Middlesex, with pastures and woods, and another group of four houses in Westminster worth £100 a year which he assigned to his younger son. He left some small legacies to servants and to a parish in Lincolnshire and to St. Margaret's. But the contemporary royalist comment was that Bell, "the apothecary to the body politique, hath as little given him as hee deserves in honest times," and was protected by parliamentary privilege from accounting for some parish funds with which he was entrusted.[242]

Sir Henry Bellingham, Bart. (d. 1650), of Helsington and Levens, Westmorland, was one of his county's M.P.'s, 1640–11 October 1645.[243] He was the eldest surviving son and heir apparent[244] of Sir James Bellingham of Helsington, J.P., D.L. (d. 1642),[245] by his wife, Agnes, daughter of Sir Henry Curwen of Workington. He was born probably about 1595, was admitted a fellow commoner at Queen's College, Cambridge, in November, 1609, and entered the Middle Temple in 1611.[246] He married, about 1613, Dorothy, daughter of Sir Francis Boynton of Yorkshire,[247] and in 1620 he was created a baronet and was knighted. In June, 1625, Sir Henry and his father were present in the Star Chamber with other tenants of the barony of Kendal regarding a dispute between the tenants and the agents of the crown.[248]

Bellingham was chosen M.P. for Westmorland in 1625 and 1626, and was a J.P. in his county from about that period.[249] He served also on the commission of oyer and terminer, 1639–1640.[250] He was returned for his county again to both of the parliaments of 1640, and seems for a time to have cooperated with the country party leaders. He pledged £500 in support of the loan in March, 1641,[251] and was named to several important committees of the early period, including those on ship money and army supply.[252] He was one of the commissioners for scandalous ministers in Westmorland in 1642 and after the outbreak of war was named to the parliamentary committees there.[253] He

---

[231] Bell named a Lincolnshire parish in his will (P.C.C., 88 Bruce). His brother, Thomas, whom he named overseer of the will, was probably the Fleet Street apothecary (S.P. 16, 539/71/i) for whom he bore witness in 1640 when Thomas asked to be excused from serving as one of the London sheriffs (London Corporation MSS, Rep. 54, fol. 180). This may have been the same Thomas Bell, merchant, who described himself in the 1634 visitation as the son of Thomas Bell of Runnoll, Yorkshire. *Vis. London* 1: 63. That Thomas Bell, like the one named in the will, had a son William.

[232] Pink MSS, 297, fol. 209; list of the company members in 1641 in S.P. 16, 539/71/i.

[233] Records of the Parish of St. Margaret's, Westminster, **151, 153, 154** (Overseers' Accounts, 1617–1624, 1630–1642), *passim;* **16–21** (Churchwardens' Accounts, 1628–1639), *passim.*

[234] *C.S.P. Dom., 1636–1637*, 75; *1637*, 372–373; *1638–1639*, 26.

[235] C. 181/4, fol. 191; 181/5, fols. 162, 229.

[236] *C.S.P. Dom., 1640*, 226, 227, 240.

[237] S.P. 16, 447/30/i; *M. of P.* 1: 482.

[238] Others dealt with the disarming of recusants, searching the neighborhood of parliament for ill-affected persons, and considering the case of John James, the alleged papist. *C.J.* 2: 24, 31, 128, 141, 348.

[239] Add. MSS, 22,619, fol. 181; B. Whitelocke, *Memorials of the English Affairs* 1: 318; *Cal. Com. Comp.*, 55.

[240] Thomason Tracts, 669. f. 24, p. 37.

[241] The will, dated 19 September 1653 (P.C.C., 88 Bruce), had named two sons, but it was proved in 1664 with two nephews

as the administrators. Bell was evidently a widower when he wrote his will.

[242] Quoted in Bankes, *The story of Corfe Castle*, 232.

[243] *C.J.* 4: 304.

[244] An elder brother died in 1611 (*Y.A.S. Rec. Ser.* **34**: 214, 1904).

[245] *H.M.C., Twelfth Report* 7, MSS of S. H. le Fleming, 14; *Y.A.S. Rec. Ser.* **4**: 94, 1888; **54**: 15 and n., 1915.

[246] *Al. Cant.; Mid. Temp. Rec.* 2: 534.

[247] Cumb. and Westm. *Trans.*, N.S., **4**: 133, 1904.

[248] J. Nicolson and R. Burn, *The history and antiquities of the counties of Westmorland and Cumberland* 1: 57, London, 1777 (hereafter, Nicolson and Burn, *Hist. of Westmorland and Cumberland*).

[249] C. 193/12, 13; S.P. 16/405.

[250] C. 181/5, fols. 274, 348.

[251] D'Ewes (N), 439, n.

[252] *C.J.* 2: 45, 69.

[253] Pink MSS, 297, fol. 221.

was respited on 5 February 1644 for being absent on call, but by the end of the year had joined the king at Oxford, and was disabled for his desertion, 11 October 1645.[254] With his son, Sir James, Bellingham petitioned in 1646 to compound for their sequestered estates, but he offended further during the northern uprising of 1648 and had his fine increased. He died in October, 1650, before his case had been settled.[255]

The Bellingham properties were extensive, lying in several of the northern counties. Sir Henry's income as originally reported when he compounded was £800 a year but the report was corrected by an addition of nearly £500 a year. Because a large part had already been settled on his son, Bellingham's original fine at ⅓, over £3200, was less than it would otherwise have been.[256] His successor was reputedly worth £1500 a year in 1660.[257] A dowry of £2000 for one daughter was mentioned in Sir Henry's will.

Bellingham was related through his mother to his fellow M.P., Sir Patrick Curwen, and he was a brother-in-law of Sir William Mallory and uncle of Ralph Ashton [258] of Whalley.[259]

Alexander Bence (born *c.* 1590), merchant of Aldeburgh, Suffolk, and of London, sat for Aldeburgh, 1640–1648. He was a younger son of Alexander Bence (*d.* 1612), an Aldeburgh merchant and bailiff, by his first wife, Mary, daughter of Thomas Squire, and was born about 1589 or 1590.[260] He inherited from his father and from his maternal grandfather several properties in and near Aldeburgh and shares in ships,[261] and in 1613 was apprenticed in London to John Bence, possibly his elder brother, and was admitted to the London Grocers' Company in 1621. He retained some connections with that company, as its records of 1649 and later show,[262] but apparently returned to Aldeburgh to live and carry on his business. He was one of the

Suffolk men discharged from his obligations under the privy seals, 1625–1626,[263] and was described as of Aldeburgh in 1627,[264] the year in which his brother, John, was reported as a loan refuser.[265] Alexander married Ann Allet of Rendham in 1620,[266] and probably Elizabeth Fowle at Knodishall in 1633.[267] With his brothers and a nephew Bence was co-owner of several ships sailing from Aldeburgh and London,[268] and he may have been a member of the Society of Saltmakers of Great Yarmouth.[269] Possibly he was livng in a house belonging to his naval friend, Captain Rainborow (*q.v.*), at Wapping in 1638.[270]

Bence was elected to parliament for the first time in October, 1640, replacing his brother, Squire, who had served for their town in the spring.[271] He was not prominent during the early months, but was named to the recess committee in 1641 and by 1642 was being recognized, judging by his committee appointments, as an authority on naval and fiscal matters. He was named to the wartime committee on scandalous ministers for Suffolk and became one of the Commissioners of the Admiralty.[272] With his brother, Squire, who was again a member, he contributed more than £600 toward the Irish venture in 1642, and his own promise for the defense that year was one horse.[273] He was a Presbyterian and was secluded from the House in 1648,[274] but was active during the Cromwellian period. He was elected an alderman of London in 1653, but was excused when he pleaded insufficiency of estate.[275] A contemporary wrote about 1655, however, that his income was about £1200 a year, with at least £300

[254] *C.J.* 3: 390; 4: 304.

[255] His will, dated 15 October 1650, was proved on 27 May 1651 (P.C.C., 78 Grey), but he was referred to on 26 October 1650 as recently dead (*Cal. Com. Comp.*, 1137).

[256] *Cal. Com. Comp.*, 1136–1137; S.P. 23/197/431–435; S.P. 23/230/97.

[257] *English Baronetage* 4: 377, 1741.

[258] Nicolson and Burn, *op. cit.* 1: 205.

[259] References in addition to those cited above are *Complete Baronetage* 1: 145; *M. of P.* 1: 466, 472, 484, 495.

[260] Burke, *Landed Gentry* 1: 81, 1850; pedigrees in Muskett's Suffolk collections, Add. MSS, 33,857, fols. 18v–19, 42. Alexander was under 24 years of age in 1613. I.P.M. of Alexander Bence, 1613, C. 142/335/21.

[261] Add. MSS, 33,857, fol. 137.

[262] MSS of the Grocers' Company of London, Quire of Warden's Accounts, 1611–1622, 105v, 422. In 1649 Bence was summoned by the company to be made of the livery, but did not appear. In 1658, however, because he had been fined for alderman and was an "ancient member," he was granted admission to the Court of Assistants with exemption from serving first in the lower offices. *Ibid.*, Calendars of the Orders of the Court of Assistants 4: 309, 659, 680.

[263] S.P. 16, 523/80.

[264] Add. MSS, 19,080 (Davy collection), fol. 142v.

[265] *East Anglian*, N.S., 13: 7, 1909–1910.

[266] C. Partridge, Suffolk Marriages (transcripts from registers, Ipswich City Library) 7: 145. John and Alexander Bence, sons of "Mr. Alexander" and Anne, were baptized at Carlton, Suffolk, in 1622 and 1625. Add. MSS, 19,091, fol. 169.

[267] A. T. Winn, ed., *The register of the Parish Church of Knodishall*, 58, London, Bemrose, 1909. According to Muskett (Add. MSS, 33,857, fol. 42), Bence's second wife was a sister of Samuel Vassall (*q.v.*), but I have found no proof of that point.

[268] *C.S.P. Dom., 1628–1629*, 296; *1635*, 329, 384.

[269] C. T. Carr, *Select charters of trading companies*, 150, London, Selden Society, 1913.

[270] J. J. Muskett, *Suffolk manorial families* 1: 157, Exeter, W. Pollard, 1900–1914.

[271] Squire, a sea captain (*C.S.P. Dom., 1628–1629*, 296) and merchant, was elected again *vice* Rainborow in 1642. *M. of P.* 1: 483, 494; *H.M.C., Various Collections* 4, Aldeburgh, MSS, 307.

[272] *C.J.* 2: 152, 271, 288, *passim;* Pink MSS, 297, fol. 228. He was one of the admiralty commissioners disliked by John Moore (*q.v.*) and his family. *H.M.C., Tenth Report* 4, Capt. Stewart's MSS, 97.

[273] *C.S.P. Ireland, Adv.,* 231; Bodleian Tanner MSS, 63, fol. 60.

[274] *A.H.R.* 44: 36, n., 1938–1939.

[275] London Corp. MSS, Rep. 62, fol. 374; Beaven, *The aldermen of the city of London* 1: 222, 317.

more from lands, and that he had a great estate in Irish lands.[276] Bence was still alive in 1660.[277]

Thomas Bennett (1620–1641), of Pythouse, Wiltshire, was probably the M.P. for Hindon from April, 1641, following the death of Sir Miles Fleetwood, until early August 1641.[278] His death of smallpox occurred shortly before 13 August.[279] He was the eldest son and heir apparent of Thomas Bennett of Pythouse (c. 1588–1663), by Melior, daughter of Richard Thomas, and the grandson of Thomas Bennett (1563–1635).[280] The family owned several properties in Tisbury parish besides their principal seat there, several buildings in Hindon, and some lands and leases in Dorset and Somerset. Their income in 1646 was estimated to be £668 a year.[281] The younger Thomas was born in 1620, and matriculated from Hart Hall, Oxford, on 13 October 1637.[282] He may have been serving under the Earl of Northumberland in the army in 1640.[283] Apparently he never married.

Elected to parliament at twenty-one, Bennett had little part in the work of the House during his short period of service. He was named to no committees. He was allowed to take the Protestation though a question regarding his election had not been determined even at the time of his death.[284] Not until 1645 was a writ issued for the choosing of his successor.[285] No evidence concerning Bennett's politics has been found, but his father and his brother, John, were royalists,[286] and he possibly shared their views. Another Thomas Bennett of Norton Bavent and Westbury, son of William Bennett (d. 1617), was a parliamentarian, and lived until 1654.[287]

Henry Benson (1579–1643), of Knaresborough, Yorkshire, was returned for that borough on 13 October 1640, but was expelled by House vote on 2 November 1641. He was the son and heir of Peter Benson of Knaresborough (d. 1640), by his wife, Jane Denison, and was baptized in 1579.[288] His father, who described himself as late as 1615 as a yeoman,[289] was an important man in Knaresborough and owned many properties there and nearby, including the largest number of burgage houses in the town. His land purchases and claims to titles involved him in various lawsuits, in one of which he was referred to as a man of great wealth but one who paid only a niggardly stipend to the vicar of a rectory he owned.[290] He was an agent or friend of Sir William Craven, the Yorkshireman who became Lord Mayor of London,[291] and in 1630 was reported as qualified by wealth for knighthood.[292] Sir Henry Slingsby, with whose family the Bensons had more than one disagreement, wrote in 1630 that Peter Benson was the mover of disputes in the town.[293] He was at one time under-bailiff and rent collector there.[294]

Henry Benson, who seems to have been outshone locally by his father, was M.P. for Knaresborough in 1626 and 1628. He won his seat in the latter year by defeating Slingsby.[295] A bachelor until the age of fifty-four, he married in 1633 Elizabeth (Bullock), widow of John Dearlove of Pannal. Through this marriage he acquired three stepsons who later assisted him with his affairs. By 1641, perhaps earlier, one of them, William Dearlove, was bailiff and steward of the manor of Knaresborough for its owner, the queen. The family's hold on the borough was described then as corrupt and "an insufferable bondage" by Thomas Stockdale, a local man whose enmity they had incurred.[296] Although there were triangular contests involving two prominent knights of the county when the 1640 elections came around, Benson was elected to both of the parliaments of that year.[297]

He was not an active member of the House, however. In April, 1641,[298] he obtained leave of absence and was reported by a neighbor in mid-June to have been in Yorkshire for the past eight weeks. Meanwhile Lord Fairfax, with whom Benson had had some earlier

[276] Add. MSS, 15,520, fol. 125v.

[277] Pink MSS cited above; Thomason Tracts, 669. f. 24, p. 37.

[278] M. of P. 1: 496.

[279] D'Ewes (B), 419. The evidence of his death in 1641 establishes the identity of the M.P. as the younger Thomas Bennett of Pythouse.

[280] Hoare, Wilts. 4 (1): 132; Cal. Com. Comp., 941.

[281] I.P.M., Thomas Bennett (d. 1635), C. 142/151/116; S.P. 23/174/563–572.

[282] Al. Oxon.

[283] Pink MSS, 297, fol. 244. Pink's notes on the Bennetts are contradictory (fols. 240 and 244) because he was not certain that the M.P. was the younger man of the name.

[284] The House declined on 13 and 18 August to order a new election because the case of a rival's claim to Bennett's seat had not been heard. D'Ewes (B), 419, 454–455.

[285] O.P.H. 9: 7.

[286] Cal. Com. Comp., 76, 941.

[287] Hoare, op. cit. 3 (2): 78; Wilts. Arch. Mag. 26: 344, 1892; will, P.C.C., 414 Alchin.

[288] Mr. W. A. Atkinson of Knaresborough kindly supplied some of the data about Benson and called my attention to other sources. See his articles on local history at Knaresborough in which the Bensons were involved, Yorks. Arch. Jour. 33: 175–195, 1938; 34: 213–221, 1939.

[289] St. Ch. 8/67/10.

[290] Y.A.S. Rec. Ser. 53: 40, 216, 1915; Bodleian MSS Top. Yorks., C. 4, fols. 4–14, 20–28, 79–80, 102; Chancery case, C. 3/318/30.

[291] Craven remembered him in his will. Yorks. Arch. Jour. 13: 443, 1895.

[292] Y.A.S. Rec. Ser. 61: 107, 1920.

[293] Bodleian Firth MSS, b. 2, fol. 181v.

[294] Yorks. Arch. Jour. 34: 217, 1939.

[295] Ibid.; M. of P. 1: 473, 479.

[296] Fairfax correspondence 2: 265; Knaresborough wills, Surtees Society, 104: x, 1902; Pink MSS, 322. Benson mentioned in his will having had a transaction in 1636 with Stockdale, then of London but afterwards of Bilton Park near Knaresborough, in the course of which that "cunning patch" sought to defeat the Bensons.

[297] The diary of Sir Henry Slingsby, of Scriven, Bart., 50, 63.

[298] C.J. 2: 115.

quarrel, and of whose plans for paying the soldiers raised in the town Benson disapproved, seems to have lent his ear to Thomas Stockdale's plans for challenging Benson's right to continue as a member.[299]   It may be suspected that there was politics as well as local rivalry in the matter.   Soon after the summer recess, Benson was charged in parliament with having abused his privileges as a member by selling protections to persons not his servants in and about London and even in more distant parts.   Benson did not deny the charges, protesting merely that he thought his actions legal, but the House voted on 2 November 1641 to expel him as "unworthy and unfit" to be a member.[300]   An attempt to have his stepson, Dearlove, replace him failed.[301]   Shortly afterwards Benson was rumored to be favoring recusants.[302] He was sent for several times as a delinquent, but he eluded the messenger, and was probably never arrested on those grounds or on those of royalism until May, 1643.[303]   He probably died soon afterwards, for his will, dated 8 March 1642/3, was proved at York the following October 7.[304]

Benson's will gives little indication that he was a man of means, but he complained when he wrote it that his properties had been much damaged by the parliamentary party.   His holdings, as his father's, were chiefly in and near Knaresborough.   Some of them, probably only a part, were reported as in 1648 worth £70 a year.[305]

Despite his politics and his shortcomings, Benson was said to have been a great friend of one fellow M.P., Sir Henry Ludlow,[306] the parliamentarian.

Sir Henry Berkeley (c. 1579–c. 1667), of Yarlington, Somerset, was returned for Ilchester in a double return in October, 1640, and sat for some time in the House before a new election was ordered, 15 February 1641.   He lost his place then to Edward Phelipps.[307] He was the second son of Sir Henry Berkeley of Bruton (d. 1601) and a younger brother of Sir Maurice Berkeley.   Born about 1579, he matriculated at Queen's College, Oxford, in February, 1590, aged eleven, went to

Ireland with his elder brother in 1600, and was knighted at Whitehall in 1609.[308]   He had been assigned the Yarlington properties of the family before his father's death,[309] and settled there after his marriage with Elizabeth, daughter of Sir Henry Nevill of Billingbeare, Berks.[310]   He was an active magistrate in his county, and was an M.P. in 1626, 1628, and 1640 (Short Parliament).   Sir Henry joined the other justices in requesting relief from the 1627 loan, and his brother, Sir Maurice, was imprisoned for resisting it.[311]   Berkeley objected also to some of the ship money rates,[312] and in 1639 he promised only a nominal £5 toward the king's expenses in the north.[313]

Perhaps suspicion of Berkeley's politics led to his being unseated on a technicality in 1641.[314]   He became an active royalist with the coming of war, and suffered heavily for the king's cause.   He died sometime between 21 September 1666 and 27 September 1667.   His request was that he be buried according to the rites of the Church of England.[315]

Sir Henry's properties, mostly in the vicinity of Ilchester, were worth before the war, according to the compounding papers, about £500 a year, and he was fined £1187.[316]   But when he made his will he mentioned lands that were not included in the declaration to the commissioners, and planned portions for his children which imply a larger income than £500 a year.[317] Berkeley's character was sketched by Lloyd as follows:

This Gentleman was well known for his Ancient and Honourable Family, his good Education, his great Observations and Experience, his famous Hospitality, his rich and happy Tenants and Dependents, whereof he carried 500 to the Kings side; the orderly Government of his Family . . . ; the exemplariness of his Devotion, honouring God as sincerely, as God had graciously honoured him; the plainness of his temper, his word being parchment, and his very yea, an obligation; the humility of spirit, which made him like a fixed Star, the higher he was, the less he seemed; his Zeal for the Church . . . ; his serviceableness in the Countrey in all publick Capacity that found him out, de-

---

[299] Various letters from Stockdale to Fairfax refer to their local disagreements, and Stockdale had by June, 1641, secured copies of some of Benson's letters which he thought might be used against him. *Fairfax correspondence* 2: 107–108, 112–113, 288, 290.

[300] *C.J.* 2: 301; D'Ewes (C), 66.

[301] *Ibid.*, 242–243.

[302] Stockdale wrote to Fairfax in November and December, 1641, that Benson's faction was encouraging recusants, possibly to win favor with the queen. *Fairfax correspondence* 2: 264, 288, 290, 376.

[303] *Fairfax correspondence* 2: 323, 346, 376, 392; *C.J.* 2: 800; Pink MSS, 297, fol. 248.

[304] York Registry, 1643–1644.

[305] *Cal. Com. Comp.*, 1448; S.P. 23/80/123.

[306] *Fairfax correspondence* 2: 290.   Additional references used for Benson are: *Genealogical history of the family of the late Bishop William Stubbs*, ed. F. Collins, *Y.A.S. Rec. Ser.* 55: ix–x, 204, 1915; *Yorkshire County Magazine* 2: 231–233, 1892.

[307] *M. of P.* 1: 493; *C.J.* 2: 34, 85; D'Ewes (N), 361.

[308] Pink MSS, 297, fol. 261; Shaw, *K. of E.* 2: 148.

[309] I.P.M., Sir Henry Berkeley, 1602, C. 142/270/148.

[310] *The visitation of the county of Somerset in the year 1623*, ed. F. H. Colby, Harleian Society, 11: 7, 1876 (hereafter, *Vis. Somerset*).   One of Berkeley's daughters by this marriage became the wife of Francis Godolphin (Helston M.P.).   *Complete Baronetage* 3: 188.

[311] S.P. 16, 60/32; Rushworth 1: 473.

[312] *C.S.P. Dom., 1636–1637*, 18; *1638–1639*, 232; S.P. 16, 376/136.

[313] Rushworth 3: 911.

[314] He had already been named to one committee.   *C.J.* 2: 34.

[315] A codicil to his will of 1663 was added at the former date, and it was proved on the latter one.   Brown, *Somerset Wills* 6: 102–103; Harl. MSS, 1228, fol. 11.

[316] S.P. 23/190/193–194; *Cal. Com. Comp.*, 240, 1405–1406.

[317] A portion of £2000 for an unmarried daughter and additions of £100 each for two daughters already married are mentioned in his will.   Possibly the compounding declaration excluded properties which had already been settled on Berkeley's son.

ciding an hundred controversies at a cheaper rate in his Hall, than one is ended at Westminster.[318]

Berkeley was related through his wife to Henry Killigrew.[319]

* John Blakiston (1603–1649), mercer of Newcastle-on-Tyne, the regicide, was a member for his town from 1641 until his death. He seems to have been a candidate in opposition to Sir John Melton and protested the latter's return. On 17 December 1640 the House voted, though Melton had died, that the original case should be decided instead of a new election *vice* Melton being ordered; and on 30 January 1641 Blakiston's election was declared good.[320]

A younger son of a clergyman, Blakiston was probably apprenticed in 1613 to Christopher Shafto, boothman.[321] He married a merchant's widow and became a free burgess of Newcastle as a mercer in 1627. He was a hostman or colliery owner there also,[322] and travelled to London and elsewhere on his business. He was probably a chamberlain of Newcastle in 1632,[323] but had not served in parliament before 1641.

Blakiston's offer for the defense in 1642 was not large, £50,[324] but he subscribed £450 or £750 for the Irish lands venture, in addition to an amount which he pledged for his town.[325]

Sir Thomas Bludder (*c.* 1597–1655), of Flanchford in Reigate, Surrey, was M.P. for Reigate from 1640 until he was disabled for going to the Oxford parliament.[326] He was the eldest son and heir of Sir Thomas Bludder of Flanchford and Mile End (d. 1618) by his wife, Mary, daughter of Christopher Harris of Essex.[327] His father was a successful merchant of London, a victualler of the navy, who was interested in various mining ventures and in the Virginia Company. He was one of the farmers of the imposition on sea coals

and a contractor in Ingram's alum business.[328] The younger Thomas was born about 1597 or a few years earlier.[329] He matriculated at Christ's College, Cambridge, in 1614 (B.A. 1616/7), and was probably admitted to the Inner Temple in 1616. He was knighted at Whitehall in 1618,[330] and had by that time or shortly after established himself in court circles. Bludder married three times, but the name of only his third wife, who survived him, is known. She was Elizabeth, or Jane, daughter of Robert Brett of Rotherby, Leicestershire, a kinswoman of Buckingham's lady, and cousin of the courtier, Arthur Brett. Sir Thomas's daughter, Anne, by her or by an earlier wife, was born in January, 1620, and buried at Flanchford in 1621. His son and heir, George, his third wife's child and Buckingham's namesake, was born at Denmark House in 1622, and had as his godparents Lord Treasurer Cranfield as well as Buckingham and his countess.[331]

When his father died in 1618 Sir Thomas inherited his lands and his ventures. He renewed at intervals the farm of the tax on sea coal, from which each farmer had received as much as £1000 over expenses in 1617, but which was somewhat less valuable when the agreements of 1620 and 1629 specified the exact income to be assured the crown.[332] He continued to be interested in the early 1620's in the alum business also and in the Virginia Company.[333] He was a gentleman of the privy chamber in 1625 and joined with another of his wife's relatives, Sir Alexander Brett, in the office of surveyor of the ordnance in the Tower, an office which he took over alone for a short period after Brett's death in 1627.[334] Even Buckingham's death did not sever his court connections. In 1633 and 1636 Bludder petitioned for a share of certain money due the crown, and received in 1635 a grant of certain fines. His wife, too, enjoyed a royal grant of a moiety of the office of king's printer, but both petitioned in 1636 for compensation for damages done them by the interference of

[318] *Memoires,* 114–116.
[319] References in addition to those cited above are: Bates Harbin, *Members of Parliament, Somerset,* 144–145; *Somerset and Dorset N. and Q.* 3: 102, 1892–1893; *Vis. Berks.* 2: 181.
[320] *C.J.* 2: 53, 76, 90, 93; D'Ewes (N), 385. *Cf.* Sir Henry Anderson.
[321] C. H. Hunter Blair, *The Mayors of Newcastle upon Tyne, 1216–1940, Arch. Ael.,* 4th Ser., 18: 67, 1940. The statement of parentage and the death date given in this article disagree with the commonly accepted ones and with the same author's note on Blakiston in his Members of Parliament for Northumberland and Newcastle upon Tyne, *Arch. Ael.,* 4th Ser., 23: 139, 1945.
[322] Nef, *The rise of the British coal industry* 2: 291.
[323] Welford, *Men of Mark 'Twixt Tyne and Tweed* 1: 334–335.
[324] *N. and Q.,* 1st Ser., 12: 360, 1855.
[325] *C.S.P. Ireland, Adventurers,* 76. His total £900 pledge represents the town's share as well as his own. He did not advance £900 himself, as is suggested in *D.N.B.*
[326] *M. of P.* 1: 494; *O.P.H.* 9: 4.
[327] Bludder pedigree, *Surrey Arch. Coll.* 3, 1865.

[328] Brown, *Genesis of the U.S.,* 830; Nef, *The rise of the British coal industry* 2: 270; Manning and Bray, *Surrey* 1: 306; Lansd. MSS, 152, fol. 68; *C.S.P. Dom., 1611–1618,* 91, 114; *1623–1625,* 204.
[329] He was aged 21 "and more" at his father's death, 2 November 1618. I.P.M., Sir Thomas Bludder, C. 142/380/114.
[330] *Al. Cant.*
[331] Manning and Bray, *Surrey* 1: 306; *The letters of John Chamberlain* 2: 429; *The visitations of Surrey . . . 1623,* ed. Bannerman, Harleian Society, 43: 111, 126, 1899 (hereafter, *Vis. Surrey, 1623*).
[332] Brown, *Somerset Wills* 5: 89–90; *C.S.P. Dom., 1619–1623,* 114; *1628–1629,* 497; Nef, *The rise of the British coal industry* 2: 270–271.
[333] S. M. Kingsbury, *The records of the Virginia Company of London* 3: 318; *H.M.C., Various Collections* 8, MSS of the Hon. F. L. Wood, 19, 28.
[334] *C.S.P. Dom., 1625–1626,* 94, 201; *1627–1628,* 448; *1628–1629,* 110; *1625–1649,* 267; Shrops. Arch. Soc., *Trans.,* 2nd Ser., 10: 88, 1897–1898.

others.[335] Bludder was asked to lend £500 to King Charles early in his reign.[336]

Meanwhile Sir Thomas was a J.P. in London, and was named for nearly two decades as one of the Surrey justices.[337] He sat regularly also in parliament, beginning with that of 1621. He was chosen by the freeholders of Gatton in that year in preference to a nominee of the borough lord.[338] From 1624 to 1640 Reigate was his constituency. The contest there in October, 1640, probably concerned the other member, Monson, rather than Bludder.[339] In 1639 Bludder seems to have promised to attend the king in the north, but for some reason he failed to go.[340]

Although he was a follower of the court, Bludder was not an outspoken royalist in the Long Parliament. He was not listed among the Straffordians, but neither was he named to any committee or in the list of those taking the 1641 Protestation. His appointment, however, to the Surrey committee on scandalous ministers in 1642 [341] suggests that he was not considered yet as disloyal to parliament. Before the end of May, 1643, however, his properties were under sequestration,[342] for he had joined the king, and he was afterwards disabled for having sat in the Oxford parliament. A writ for the choosing of his successor was issued, 3 September 1645.[343] He died on 29 September 1655, and was buried at Reigate.[344]

Bludder's father had left him considerable wealth in lands and in enterprises. These included three manors in Surrey, for one of which he had paid more than £3000 in 1601.[345] Bludder owned land in Essex also, but when he compounded he declared his income from lands as only £218 a year and from the sea coal tax £280 a year at one time and £500 a year at another. His fine at a tenth, £407 (1646), was increased in 1648 to £937, and another fine of £600 was assessed in 1650.[346] An inventory of his goods in 1643 included a considerable library containing the classics, works on religion and on travel, some law books and some of contemporary literature, and a collection of maps.[347] His epitaph

mentioned his "noble hospitality" and his "ingenious sweetness." [348]

John Bodvel, or **Bodville,** or **Bodevile** (1617–1663), of Llanigrad, Anglesey, and Bodvill Castle, county Carnarvon, was M.P. for Anglesey, 1640–5 February 1644.[349] He was the son and heir of Sir John Bodvel of Llanigrad, J.P., H.S.[350] (d. 1631), by his wife, Elizabeth, daughter of Sir John Wynn of Gwydir, and was born in 1617.[351] He was admitted to the Inner Temple in 1633.[352] He may have married before 1640 Anne, daughter of Sir William Russell, Bart., the wife who deserted him in 1646 and to whom he paid alimony afterwards.[353] His public life seems to have begun with the Short Parliament.

Bodvel's father had at least once run into trouble with the Council of the Marches of Wales and with the higher clergy,[354] and during the first year of the Long Parliament Bodvel worked with the popular party. In this course he was advised, perhaps, by his uncle, Sir Richard Wynn (q.v.). He pledged £1000 in support of the loan in November, 1640, and was named to a score of committees, including one to collect materials for the debate on the new canons, one on Virginia, and one on raising funds.[355] He was one of the diarists from whom D'Ewes occasionally borrowed notes to cover times of his own absence.[356] He disliked papists,[357] and in the summer of 1641 wrote to a relative that the passage of the bills to abolish Star Chamber and High Commission was a blessing that should encourage men to pay their poll money cheerfully.[358] He was in the House on 27 December 1641,[359] but with the outbreak of war deserted to the king. He lived to see the Restoration, and died about April, 1663.[360]

Bodvel inherited extensive possessions in the counties of Carnarvon, Merioneth, and Anglesey, and was reputed in 1644 to be worth about £1800 a year. The parliamentarians therefore assessed him £2500.[361] In 1651 he declared his estate worth only £1200 a year, however, and subject to annuities of £1000 to relatives.[362]

[335] H.M.C., *Twelfth Report* 2, Coke MSS, 37; *C.S.P. Dom., 1636–1637*, 267, 273, 291.
[336] S.P. 16, 90/70/i. His assessment in the county was £30. Brayley, *Surrey*, App. ii, 25.
[337] C. 193/12, 13; S.P. 16/405; *C.S.P. Dom., 1637*, 110.
[338] *Ibid., 1619–1623*, 221–222; *Commons Debates 1621* 4: 24.
[339] *M. of P.* 1: 453, *passim; Surrey Arch. Coll.* 39: 59, 1931.
[340] S.P. 16, 427/38/vi.
[341] Pink MSS, 297, fol. 292.
[342] Add. MSS, 28,191A.
[343] *O.P.H.* 9: 4.
[344] *Surrey Arch. Coll.* 11: 197, 1893.
[345] Manning and Bray, *Surrey* 1: 305; I.P.M. cited above. Portions of £1000 each were planned for four of the elder Bludder's daughters. Brown, *Somerset Wills* 5: 89–90.
[346] S.P. 23/208/387–400; *Cal. Com. Comp.*, 1498. An assessment of £400 in 1645 was reduced, however, to £300 in 1647. *Cal. Com. Adv. Money*, 633.
[347] Add. MSS, 28,191A.

[348] Manning and Bray, *Surrey* 1: 316.
[349] *M. of P.* 1: 497; *C.J.* 3: 389.
[350] C. 193/12, 13; *List of Sheriffs*, 236.
[351] I.P.M., Sir John Bodvel, C. 142/475/131. The father and son are confused by W. R. Williams in *Parl. Hist. Wales*, 3.
[352] *Students admitted to the Inner Temple*, 278.
[353] *Cal. Wynn Papers*, 297, 300; *Cal. Com. Comp.*, 1599.
[354] *Cal. Wynn Papers*, 166, 170–172, 177, 179.
[355] *C.J.* 2: 48, 64, 107, *passim;* Pink MSS, 297, fol. 309; D'Ewes (N), 539.
[356] D'Ewes (C), 220, n.
[357] D'Ewes (N), 301.
[358] *Cal. Wynn Papers*, 273.
[359] D'Ewes (C), 355.
[360] Williams, *loc. cit.; Cal. Wynn Papers*, 374.
[361] I.P.M. cited above; *Cal. Com. Adv. Money*, 434.
[362] *Cal. Com. Comp.*, 1600.

* **Dennis Bond** (1588–1658), woolen-draper and magistrate of Dorchester, was a member for his borough, 1640–1653. He had represented Dorchester in his first parliament the preceding spring,[363] and was a leader in the attacks on Anglicanism and the court. The son and heir of John Bond, gentleman, of Lutton in Steple, Dorset (d. 1633), by Margaret, daughter of Richard Pitt of Weymouth, he was born 30 August and baptized at Melcombe Regis 1 September 1588.[364] Having become established in the woolen business in Dorchester and married there, Bond was a constable of the town in 1619[365] and a capital burgess by 1621. He served afterwards as bailiff, mayor, and alderman.[366] He was among those of Dorchester who backed the Reverend John White's New England project.[367] He refused in 1636 to pay ship money on two properties he owned in the Isle of Purbeck,[368] and was doubtless in agreement before 1640 with the Ashe brothers, John and Edward (*q.v.*), who were apparently his first cousins.[369]

Bond does not seem to have had great wealth,[370] and did not join in the pledges for the loans in 1640 and 1641. He excused himself on 19 September 1642 from a new promise for the defense, however, declaring that he had paid £100 already and had lost his horse in the service.[371]

John Borlase (1619–1672), of Bockmer in Medmenham, Bucks, sat for Corfe Castle, Dorset, from January, 1641, succeeding Windebank, until he was disabled, 4 March 1644.[372] The descendant of an old Buckinghamshire family, many of whom had been magistrates and M.P.'s, Borlase was the eldest son and heir of Sir William Borlase of Marlow and Bockmer (d. 1630) by his wife, Amy, daughter of Sir Francis Popham of Littlecote, Wiltshire. He was born at the Popham home on 21 August 1619, and matriculated at Magdalen Hall, Oxford, 30 April 1635.[373] He entered the Inner Temple in January, 1637, and, on 4 December of that year, married at St. Giles in the Fields, Alice, eldest daughter of Sir John Banks. Probably that marriage explains his political affiliation with the court party, for various members of his own family were parliamentarians. His mother's second husband, too, may have

been influential, for he was a courtier, Gabriel Hippisley.[374]

In the spring of 1640 Borlase was elected by Great Marlow, Bucks, for his first service as M.P. He failed to secure that seat in the autumn, although he and his stepfather were candidates in two successive elections there.[375] After the failure in his own neighborhood Borlase was then assisted by his father-in-law, Chief Justice Banks, to the seat for Corfe Castle, a borough which he controlled.[376] He was named to no committees in the House, either because of his youth or because his politics were suspected. On 4 May 1642 he was created a baronet. But at the outbreak of the war he was named to the parliamentary committees in the midland counties, and in December, 1642, he voted to support the Earl of Essex and lent £200 for the use of parliament.[377] But his support was only nominal. He was granted a respite from disablement on 22 January 1644, but was disabled on the following March 4.[378] He afterwards denied having sat in the Oxford parliament, although he was in Oxford when it met, and in 1645 he compounded for his estates.[379] He survived to sit in the 1661 parliament. Dying on 8 August 1672, he was buried four days later at Little Marlow. His will, dated 7 August, was proved on 19 August 1672 by his son and heir, Sir John Borlase.[380]

The Borlase family inheritance in Bucks and Oxfordshire was large. It included in 1629 ten manors and various farms, vicarages, and advowsons of churches.[381] When Sir John compounded he declared that his estates suffered £3000 damage during the war. His fine, reckoned at eight years' purchase, was set in 1646 at a third, £6800. His income must have been considered as over £2500 a year.[382]

Borlase was a grandson of one fellow member, Sir Francis Popham, a nephew of Alexander Popham, and a first cousin of Alexander Luttrell. A more distant kinsman was Sir William Lytton, who had been an intimate of his father's.[383]

Godfrey Bosvile, Bosevile, or **Boswell** (1596–1658), of Gunthwaite, Yorkshire, and Wroxhall, Warwickshire, was returned for Warwick borough after Sir Thomas Lucy's death, and sat from 18 February 1641

---

[363] *M. of P.* **1**: 481, 488.

[364] I.P.M., John Bond, 1633, C. 142/498/181; Pink MSS, 297, fol. 322. Burke (*Landed Gentry* **1**: 117, 1851) identifies Pitt as of North Crichett, Somerset. *D.N.B.* omits parentage and birth date.

[365] Dorset N.H. *Proceedings* **13**: 59, 1892.

[366] *D.N.B.;* Mayo, *Municipal records, Dorchester,* 390, 715.

[367] *Somerset and Dorset N. and Q.* **17**: 108, 1921–1923.

[368] He owed 3 *l.* 11 *s.* 10 *d.* on them. S.P. 16, 319/89.

[369] Their mothers were both daughters of Richard Pitt.

[370] The estate left by his father at his death (i.p.m. above) was not large, but doubtless Bond had had some part of it settled on him before that date.

[371] *C.J.* **2**: 772.

[372] *M. of P.* **1**: 488; *C.J.* **3**: 415.

[373] *Al. Oxon.*

[374] *V.C.H. Buckingham* **3**: 80.

[375] See Great Marlow election.

[376] G. Bankes, *The story of Corfe Castle,* 57.

[377] *V.C.H. Buckingham* **4**: 536; *C.J.* **2**: 889.

[378] *C.J.* **3**: 374, 415.

[379] *Cal. Com. Comp.,* 919.

[380] P.C.C., 98 Eure.

[381] I.P.M. of William Borlase, senior (grandfather of John), 1629, C. 142/451/107; *V.C.H. Buckingham* **3**: 80, 82, 83.

[382] *Cal. Com. Comp.,* 919–920.

[383] *The letters of John Chamberlain* **1**: 254, n. Additional references used for Borlase are: Pink MSS, 298, fol. 348; *Complete Baronetage* **2**: 169; *Genealogist,* N.S., **2**: 229–235, 283–287, 1885.

until 1653.[384] He came of an old Yorkshire family, being the son and heir of Ralph Bosvile of Gunthwaite, who died while he was in Ireland with the army in 1600. His mother was Mary, daughter of Christopher Copley of Wadworth, and he succeeded to the York estates of the main branch of the Bosvile family in 1615. Godfrey was born on 10 April 1596,[385] and by his mother's second marriage in 1602 became a stepson of Fulke Greville of Thorpe Latimer, Lincolnshire, and half-brother of Robert, second Lord Brooke, the puritan.[386] On 4 May 1614 Godfrey married at Gunthwaite Margaret, daughter of Sir Edward Greville of Harold Park, Essex, and a descendant of the Grey family,[387] and seems to have lived thereafter chiefly in the West Riding of Yorkshire. He was treasurer for the lame soldiers there about 1621, and for many years was a J.P.[388] He was assessed £10 for the privy seals there in 1626.[389] He is sometimes identified also as of Wroxhall, Warwickshire, and possibly held other lands in that county too.[390] At least one of his relatives, possibly a cousin, was in New England in 1638 and married Herbert Pelham, a leader in Massachusetts Bay affairs.[391]

Bosvile was elected to his first parliament for Warwick in the spring of 1640, doubtless through the influence of his stepbrother, Lord Brooke, but his place was taken by Sir Thomas Lucy in the fall. Back at Westminster after Lucy's death, Bosvile was named to committee work in April, 1641,[392] but he was less active then than he became in the later years of the parliament. He promised either a horse or £100 for the defense in June, 1642,[393] served as a committeeman for Yorkshire and Warwickshire during the war, and was a colonel in the parliamentary army. He was a member also of the Committee for Compounding,[394] and was named a

commissioner for the trial of King Charles, but in the latter capacity did not function.[395] He died in 1658.[396]

Little is known of Bosvile's wealth. Besides his Warwickshire properties, his family inheritance in Yorkshire included three manors in the West Riding, totalling some 800 acres.

Bosvile was a brother-in-law of Sir Arthur Hesilrige (q.v.).

Sir Thomas Bowyer, Bart. (1586–1650), of Leythorne in North Mundham, Sussex, was a member for Bramber, 1640–23 November 1642.[397] Born on 28 November 1586, he was the eldest son and heir of Thomas Bowyer of Leythorne and of the Middle Temple, a distinguished lawyer and M.P. (d. 1595), by his second wife, Jane, daughter of John Birch, Baron of the Exchequer.[398] His family had been in Sussex for some generations, but his grandfather, Thomas Bowyer, who was a well-to-do grocer of London, extended the family's holdings in the county.[399] The third Thomas was possibly a student at the Middle Temple in 1606,[400] but he seems to have pursued his father's profession no further, devoting himself rather to family and county affairs and to serving in parliament. He was created a baronet in 1627. Bowyer married (1) Ann, daughter and heiress of Adrian Stoughton (married 1608; d. 1623); (2) Jane, daughter and heiress of Emery Cranley, already twice a widow (married 1624; d. April, 1640); and (3) Anne (married before 1642; d. 1683).[401] With his eldest son, the fourth Thomas, Bowyer had a violent quarrel about 1637 because the son had married a wife with too small a portion, and the son's appeal against his threatened disinheritance was listed for consideration before the king late in 1638. No record of the outcome has been found.[402] The daughter-in-law does not seem to have been entirely forgiven, but her children were provided for in Sir Thomas's will.[403]

Bowyer began his parliamentary career in 1614, when he sat for Midhurst. He served in seven successive parliaments, 1621–1640, for Bramber, but never seems to have been a very articulate member.[404] He was a

[384] It was ordered on 18 February that Bosvile be allowed to take his seat, about which there was some question, until his election was declared illegal. *C.J.* 2: 87, 88; D'Ewes (N), 369.

[385] I.P.M. of Ralph Bosvile, 1616. C. 142/354/114; *Yorks. Arch. Jour.* 7: 298, 1882.

[386] J. Foster, *Pedigrees of the county families of Yorkshire* 1, Bosvile, London, 1874 (hereafter, Foster, *Yorkshire families*); *Complete peerage* (Gibbs ed.) 2: 333; Bodleian Dodsworth MSS, 139, fols. 85–86. Pink errs in identifying Bosvile with the Kent branch of his family (Pink MSS, 298, fol. 361).

[387] I.P.M. cited above.

[388] C. 193/12, 13; S.P. 16/405; Foster, *Yorkshire families*, loc. cit.

[389] *Acts P.C., 1625–1626*, 428.

[390] Foster, *loc. cit.* Bosvile and Jesson were granted in 1641 the parliamentary privilege of freedom from suit against freeholds of theirs. *C.J.* 2: 236.

[391] *Winthrop Papers* 2: 315, n., 1929.

[392] *C.J.* 2: 126.

[393] *N. and Q.*, 1st Ser., 12: 360, 1855.

[394] Pink MSS, 298, fols. 361–362; *Cal. Com. Comp.*, 180; *H.M.C., Various Collections* 7: MSS of Sir Harvey Bruce, 296. Noble (*Regicides* 1: 119) stated that Bosvile became extremely popular in parliament because of his "prodigious prejudice against the court."

[395] Noble, *loc. cit.*

[396] Foster, *Yorkshire families*, *loc. cit.* Noble thought that Bosvile survived the Restoration.

[397] *M. of P.* 1: 494; *C.J.* 2: 860.

[398] *Complete Baronetage* 2: 31; Pink MSS, 298, fol. 410; *Sussex Records Society Publications* 14: 35, 1912 (hereafter, *Sussex Rec. Soc.*).

[399] *Sussex Arch. Coll.* 42: 21–23, 27–28, 1899.

[400] *Mid. Temp. Rec.* 2: 461.

[401] *Complete Baronetage* 2: 31. A child of the third marriage was baptized at North Mundham on 14 February "1641." Add. MSS, 5699, fol. 271.

[402] *C.S.P. Dom., 1637*, 238–239; *1638–1639*, 46–47.

[403] P.C.C., 69 Bowyer.

[404] *M. of P., passim;* Willis 3: 236. He spoke in the 1621 parliament on the encouragement of shipping. *Commons Debates 1621* 3: 341.

J.P. in Sussex by 1622,[405] sheriff in 1626,[406] and afterwards a Vice Admiral.[407] He served also on various local commissions, including that for the first subsidy of 1640.[408] Bowyer was assessed an unusually heavy sum, £70, for knighthood composition in 1630,[409] and at the start of the Long Parliament was probably willing to work with the reform group.

Sir Thomas was named to twenty-three committees between 6 November 1640 and 21 June 1642, including one on monopolists, one on Strafford's case, and that on the recess.[410] And he offered his bond for £1000 for the 1640 loan.[411] By June, 1642, however, events were moving in a direction which did not please him. He was then absent, attended in September after a summons and pledged £50 in money or plate for the defense, but was already working for the king in Sussex. He was active in the attempt to secure the magazine at Chichester for the king and on November 23, with three other Sussex M.P.'s, was disabled and sent for as a delinquent.[412] He was afterwards assessed heavily, but died before his fine for royalism had been fixed. He was buried at Mundham, 28 February 1650. Lloyd's tribute to him was that his "soul was enriched by many virtues, whereof the most orient was his humility, which took all men's affections without resistance."[413]

That Bowyer's estate was ample is manifest. He inherited his father's properties in central and west Sussex and in London, and in 1637 his heir declared the estate was worth £1200 a year.[414] Although Bowyer's executors in 1650 alleged that the lands would have to be sold to pay debts of £8000 and care for his widow and thirteen children, he had directed in his will of the year before the raising of portions of £600 each for two granddaughters and annuities of over £200 for his widow and heir. His fine was set in 1652 at a third, £2033.[415]

Sir Thomas was probably related distantly to Sir William Bowyer, the Staffordshire member.[416]

Sir William Bowyer (1588–1641), of Knypersley, Staffordshire, was M.P. for his shire from 1640 until his death shortly before 15 March 1641.[417] He was possibly a student at Cambridge in 1601,[418] and was long active in public affairs in Staffordshire. Besides

being a J.P. and sheriff, he was a knighthood commissioner in 1631,[419] and a D.L.[420] And four times before the Long Parliament he was M.P. for the county. Bowyer was named to several important committees dealing with abuses of the subject and with church reform, 1640–1641.[421]

Sir William was evidently well-to-do. He owned extensive properties in the county,[422] and was among those who pledged £1000 as security for the loan in 1640.[423]

Bowyer was a first cousin of his fellow member, Sir Christopher Yelverton (q.v.).[424]

* Richard Boyle, Viscount Dungarvan, afterwards Earl of Burlington and Earl of Cork (1612–1698), was M.P. for Appleby, Westmorland, 1640–10 November 1643.[425] The second son but heir apparent of Richard, the wealthy first Earl of Cork (d. 1643), he spent a short time at Oxford,[426] and was travelling abroad in 1633.[427] His marriage with Elizabeth, daughter of Lord Clifford and kinswoman of Strafford, occurred at Skipton, Yorkshire, on 3 July 1634.[428] With her Boyle acquired lands worth £930 a year and the prospect of some £600 more annually,[429] and he was promised about £6000 a year by his father.[430] He may have lived at his father's Dorset estates for a time, since his name appears on a list of J.P.'s for that county about 1634,[431] but he was a parishioner of St. Margaret's, Westminster, 1637–1638,[432] and was sent in the latter year to head the court delegation that greeted the Venetian ambassador.[433]

Dungarvan was elected to the Short Parliament for Appleby, doubtless through the influence of the Cliffords.[434] In the Long Parliament he cooperated for the first year with Pym's party, offering his support for the loan of March, 1641, and being named to at least

[405] C. 193/12, 13.
[406] List of Sheriffs, 138.
[407] C.S.P. Dom., 1635, 565; 1635-1636, 151.
[408] C. 181/4, fol. 46v; 181/5, passim; Sussex Arch. Coll. 9: 104, 1857.
[409] Sussex Arch. Coll. 16: 50, 1864.
[410] C.J. 2: 31, 39, 288; Pink MSS, 298, fol. 411.
[411] D'Ewes (N), 52.
[412] C.J. 2: 772, 860; Pink MSS, 298, fol. 411.
[413] Quoted in Sussex Arch. Coll. 19: 94 and n., 1867.
[414] Ibid. 42: 28-29, 1899; C.S.P. Dom., 1637, 238.
[415] Cal. Com. Comp., 833; will, P.C.C., 69 Bowyer.
[416] The Sussex Bowyers were said to be an offshoot of the Staffordshire family. Sussex Arch. Coll. 42: opp. p. 20, 1899.
[417] M. of P. 1: 493; C.J. 2: 104.
[418] Al. Cant.

[419] Staff. Hist. Coll. 2 (2): 10, 1881.
[420] S.P. 16, 201/57/i; 412/9.
[421] C.J. 2: 39, 43, 84.
[422] Staff. Hist. Coll., N.S., 4: 41, 60, 68, 1901; 6 (1): 9, 19, 1903.
[423] D'Ewes (N), 52.
[424] For Bowyer's life, see Wedgwood, Staff. Parl. Hist. 2: 20–21.
[425] C.J. 3: 307.
[426] Dorothea Townshend, The life and letters of the great Earl of Cork, 248, New York, Duckworth, 1904.
[427] Add. MSS, 33,936 (Moreton correspondence), fol. 79.
[428] Yorks. Arch. Jour. 18: 400, n., 1904-1905. D.N.B. dates the marriage as 5 July 1635.
[429] S.P. 23/192/215–219. Boyle's fine at compounding, apparently reckoned on his English estates, was set at a tenth, £1631. Cal. Com. Comp., 1474.
[430] The Earl of Birkenhead, Strafford, 166, London, Hutchinson, 1938.
[431] C. 193/13.
[432] The Records of St. Margaret's Parish, Overseers Accounts, 154.
[433] C.S.P., Venetian, 1636-1639, 472.
[434] M. of P. 1: 484; Bean, Northern Counties, 616.

one committee on the merchants' grievances.[435] He was not listed among those opposing Strafford's attainder. Probably his wife's connection with the former Lord Deputy was outweighed by the recollection of his father's experiences with him. In the summer of 1641 Dungarvan attended a conference with Pym and others of his party while the king was in Scotland.[436] On 25 August 1641 he was granted leave of absence to go to Ireland after the recess, and in November was authorized to take a command there.[437] He was disabled on 10 November 1643, however, for having turned to the king.

Lord Dungarvan was the heir apparent to enormous wealth in 1640 and, besides the income from his wife's properties, had an allowance of £1500 a year from his father.[438]

Relatives of Dungarvan among the parliament men were his brothers-in-law, Goring and Arthur Jones.

Sir Edward Boys (1579–1646), of Fredville in Nonington, Kent, member for Dover, 1640–1646, came of a widespread Kentish family, of which his was the Nonington branch. His grandfather, Edward Boys, Esq., of Nonington (d. 1599), had been sheriff of Kent, and his great-uncle, Sir John Boys of St. Gregory's, Canterbury (d. 1612), was the eminent lawyer, steward to five archbishops, judge, and M.P.[439] His parents were Sir Edward Boys of Fredville (d. 1635) and Mary, daughter of Sir Peter Wentworth of Lillinston Dayrell, Oxfordshire, a niece of Sir Francis Walsingham. Through his mother, therefore, Boys was a grandson of the celebrated puritan M.P. of Elizabeth's day, Peter Wentworth, and a cousin of his fellow member of the Long Parliament, Sir Peter Wentworth (q.v.). His own father was a foe of the crown, was warned by the Council for his opposition to the loans of 1621 and 1627, and in 1624 was called to appear before Council for some cause unstated.[440] Edward, his parents' eldest son and heir, was baptized on 19 July 1579,[441] may have been graduated B.A. at Cambridge (Corpus Christi) in 1597, and in November, 1599, was admitted to the Middle Temple, where his uncle John was a bencher, and where he was "bound" with his father.[442] He married Elizabeth, daughter and co-

heiress of Alexander Hamon of Acris and Bishopsbourne, in 1603 or 1604, was knighted before 1625, and early in 1635 succeeded his father.[443]

He succeeded him in office as well as in estate, for he served as a J.P. in Kent and a member of the commissions on sewers, piracy, and other local matters.[444] Even before his father's death he had entered into public life, however, for he was M.P. for Christchurch, Hants, in 1625, and for Sandwich in 1626, replacing in the latter instance a court nominee.[445] He was named to a commission dealing with Sandwich school in 1633,[446] and by 1640 was acting constable of Dover Castle under the Lord Warden.[447] In the spring elections of 1640, he supported Dering, but not Colepeper, for the county knight and was himself returned for Dover then and in the autumn, although he was not popular with all factions there.[448]

Boys was an active supporter of the reform movement both in the House [449] and in his county after war came. In 1642 he promised two horses and £50 for the defense,[450] was named a D.L. for Kent, and a member of the parliamentary committees there, and succeeded in keeping Dover Castle out of royalist hands.[451] He died about August, 1646, a writ for choosing his successor being ordered 11 August.[452]

Sir Edward seems to have owned part of a manor near Sandwich left him by his grandfather and parts of three others in Kent and several farms. He had settled part of his estate on his heir, John, however, about 1626.[453] He and that son, also known as of Nonington, are to be distinguished from their royalist relatives, Edward and John Boys of Bonnington in Goodneston, and from the other pair of parliamentarians, Edward (d. 1649) and John Boys of Betshanger.[454]

* Sir William Brereton, Bart. (1604–1661), of Handforth, the parliamentary general, represented Cheshire, 1640–1653. He matriculated at Brasenose College, Oxford, in 1621 and entered Gray's Inn in 1623.[455] He was a J.P. for both county and city of Chester, as well

---

[435] D'Ewes (N), 451, n.; C.J. 2: 43.

[436] D'Ewes (C), 353.

[437] C.J. 2: 271; D'Ewes (C), 127, n., 189.

[438] His father's household expenses were running in 1639 to £200 a week, and his provision for his younger children was generous. Townshend, op. cit., 260, 290, 470–505; Add. MSS. 18,023, fols. 7–19.

[439] Vis. Kent, 1619, 40; Arch. Cant. 30: 81, 1914; Add. MSS. 33,896, fol. 54v; W. Boys, Collections for an history of Sandwich, 423, n., Canterbury, 1792 (hereafter, Boys, Sandwich).

[440] Acts P.C., 1623–1625, 453, 471; S.P. 14, 127/82; S.P. 16, 89/5.

[441] Lillian B. Behrens, Under thirty-seven kings, 44, London, St. Catherine Press, 1926; Pink MSS, 298, fol. 429.

[442] Al. Cant.; Mid. Temp. Rec. 1: 397.

[443] Add. MSS. 34,106, fol. 49v; I.P.M. of Sir Edward Boys, sen., C. 142/526/150.

[444] C. 193/12, 13; S.P. 16/405; C. 181/4, fols. 75, 101; 181/5, fols. 80, 262, 292.

[445] M. of P. 1: 465, 473, n.; Boys, Sandwich, 411, n.; C.S.P. Dom., 1625–1626, 230.

[446] Boys, Sandwich, 203; Add. MSS. 33,896, fol. 54v.

[447] C.S.P. Dom., 1640–1641, 373.

[448] Larking, Proceedings in Kent, 10–11, 24. One writer declared that the rabble were the "best men in the repute of Sir B."

[449] He served on some 16 committees, 1641–1646.

[450] N. and Q., 1st Ser., 12: 359, 1855.

[451] Arch. Cant. 2: 182, 1859; 11: 32, 1874; C.J. 2: 724.

[452] C.J. 4: 642. His will was proved at Canterbury in 1646. Kent Archaeological Society, Records Branch 6: 548, 1920 (hereafter, Kent. Arch. Soc., Records Branch).

[453] I.P.M. cited above; Hasted, Kent 9: 456; 10: 68.

[454] Behrens, op. cit., 48; Vis. Kent, 1619, 39; Arch. Cant. 3: 183, 1860; 30: 80–82, 1914; Pink MSS, 298, fol. 432.

[455] Al. Oxon.

as a member of other local commissions,[456] and had been M.P. for Cheshire twice before. The owner of property in Chester and elsewhere in the county and in Lancashire, Brereton was engaged in the decade before 1640 in a lawsuit with the city government regarding some of them.[457] He delayed paying his ship money rates there on the ground of an inequality in the assessment, and was accused of encouraging others to refuse, but by April, 1637, had made his payment.[458] He was among those interested in the New England settlements of that period,[459] and during the war was a Presbyterian elder, although an Independent in his religious views.[460] His stand in these matters as well as his politics seems to have helped him win the unusually heated county election of the spring of 1640, but personal rivalries among prominent families also played their part.[461]

Described by Clarendon as "a gentleman of competent fortune,"[462] Brereton had before December, 1641, contributed toward the maintenance of troops in Ireland, and in June, 1642, pledged £100 as well as the maintenance of four horses for the defense.[463] Although he received grants of land from parliament in compensation for losses during the war, most of the manors which he named in 1661 as the source of £1000 portions for his three daughters had been his before the war.[464]

Henry Brett (c. 1587–1674), of Hatherley, Gloucestershire, and of Westminster, was M.P. for Gloucester, 1640–1 February 1644. He came of a Leicestershire family, being the eldest son and heir of William (or James ?) Brett of Rotherby by his wife, Anna, daughter of Anthony Beaumont and sister of Mary, Countess of Buckingham. He was, therefore, a first cousin of the Duke of Buckingham.[465] But he does not seem to have aspired to such heights at court through the latter's favor as did his sister, Anne, who married Lionel Cranfield, or his younger brothers, Alexander and Arthur.[466] He was born about 1587,[467] possibly studied at Trinity, Cambridge,[468] and eventually established some connections at court. But though he held an office for a time under the Lord Chancellor,[469] and for at least ten years before 1640, perhaps as early as 1623, had a residence in Westminster,[470] he married before 1622 the daughter of an alderman of Gloucester. His wife was Margaret, daughter of alderman Thomas Seames, and widow of Anthony Rudd. Their first child, significantly named George, was a year old in 1622. And perhaps it is as significant that, by virtue of his marriage, Brett was made a burgess of the city of Gloucester on 16 March 1629, a few months after Buckingham's assassination.[471] In 1635 the city granted Brett new leases on his dwelling house in East Gate Street and another property he rented from the city.[472] But the absence of his name from the lists of J.P's and other commissions for the county suggests that he spent most of his time at London.

Brett was elected to both parliaments of 1640 for Gloucester, but he did not become an active member. He was granted various leaves of absence as war approached, and although he agreed to support the Earl of Essex and subscribed £50 for the cause in September, 1642, he later deserted to the king at Oxford. He was granted a respite in January, 1644, but was disabled on 1 February.[473] After compounding in time for his delinquency, Brett seems to have spent his later years at Gloucester. He died on 31 March 1674. His will of 23 March 1674 was proved the following June.[474]

Brett's financial standing is best revealed by his composition papers. They enumerated four manors or large estates in Gloucestershire and town properties in Gloucester, Tewkesbury, and Westminster. Their pre-war valuation was £400 a year, according to Brett, or £510, by another reckoning. His fine at a tenth was slightly above £873.[475]

* Orlando Bridgeman (1609–1674), of the Inner Temple, King's Counsel of the Duchy of Lancaster and

[456] C. 193/12 and 13; S.P. 16/405; C. 181/3; 181/4, fol. 192v.

[457] Chester Corporation MSS, Assembly Book, 1624–1684, fols. 12, 25; Harl. MSS, 2101, fol. 37; *C.S.P. Dom., 1637*, 5, 116. Brereton's house in Chester was searched by the royalists in 1642. *Cheshire Sheaf*, 1st Ser., 3: 1, 1885.

[458] Rupert H. Morriss, *The siege of Chester, 1643–1646*, ed. by P. H. Lawson, 16–17, Chester, G. R. Griffith, 1924; *C.S.P. Dom., 1637*, 1.

[459] *Winthrop Papers* 2: 13, n., 1929; F. Rose-Troup, *The Massachusetts Bay Company and its predecessors*, 135.

[460] *A.H.R.* 44: 31, n., 1938–1939.

[461] Brereton seems to have been supported by Lord Savage, Lord Cholmondeley and Lord Strange, and opposed by Sir George Booth, although his wife was related to the latter and had died in the Booth mansion in 1636. *C.S.P. Dom., 1639–1640*, 564–565, 590–591; Harl. MSS, 2129, fol. 90.

[462] *Rebellion* 2: 469.

[463] *C.J.* 2: 362; *N. and Q.*, 1st Ser., 12: 358, 1855.

[464] *Cheshire Sheaf*, 3rd Ser., 18: 54, 1921; J. P. Earwaker, *East Cheshire: past and present* 1: 259, London, 1877–1880 (hereafter, Earwaker, *East Cheshire*).

[465] His father's name appears as William in a 1619 pedigree (*The visitation of the county of Leicester, 1619*, Harleian Society, 2: 206, 1870 [hereafter, *Vis. Leic., 1619*]), but several authors refer to him as James. Williams, *Gloucester*, 194; Pink MSS, 298, fol. 484; Sir John Oglander, *A royalist's notebook*, 16, n., ed. F. Bamford, London, Constable, 1936.

[466] Oglander, *loc. cit.*; *The letters of John Chamberlain* 2: 442, 571; *D.N.B.*, "Lionel Cranfield, Earl of Middlesex."

[467] He was aged 87 at his death in 1674 (Williams, *loc. cit.*); but his next younger brother, Alexander, was reported to be aged 32 in 1619 (*Vis. Leic., 1619, loc. cit.*).

[468] *Al. Cant.*

[469] Williams, *loc. cit.*

[470] Records of St. Margaret's Parish, Overseers' Accounts, 153, 154. One of his close neighbors at Westminster was Edmund Windham, the courtier and M.P. (*q.v.*).

[471] *The visitation of the county of Leicester, loc. cit.*; Williams, *loc. cit.*; Gloucester Corp. MSS, Minute Book, 1565–1632, fol. 532.

[472] *Ibid.*, Minute Book, 1632–1656, fol. 42.

[473] *C.J.* 2: 772; 3: 374, 384; Pink MSS, 298, fol. 484.

[474] Brown, *Somerset Wills* 5: 6.

[475] S.P. 23/192/855–859; *Cal. Com. Comp.*, 1447–1448.

Vice-Chamberlain of the County Palatine of Chester, was M.P. for Wigan from 1640 until his disablement as a royalist, 29 August 1642. Born at Exeter, 30 January 1608/9,[476] he was the eldest son of John, Bishop of Chester (d. 1652), and nephew of the Edward Bridgeman who had twice served Wigan as M.P. After an education at Cambridge and Gray's Inn he had become well known in his profession and as an official in the Lancaster-Chester region. He had found a seat in the Short Parliament for Wigan after learning that he could not sit for Chester, where a local man was preferred.[477]

Although a Straffordian [478] and outspoken in defense of king and episcopacy,[479] Bridgeman was named to the important recess committee, 9 September 1641. He was warned by a friend at the time of the attempted arrest of the five members, however, that it might be wise for him to leave the city for a while, and he was absent on 16 June 1642, and disabled soon after.[480]

Bridgeman married a Shropshire heiress and owned lands in Lancashire and several nearby counties. His income from lands alone was probably £1000 a year or more.[481] Clarendon states that Bridgeman's credit and estate, both "very good," materially assisted in supplying Chester for its defense.[482]

Sir John Brooke (1575–1660?), of Heckington, Lincolnshire, and of the court, was M.P. for Appleby, Westmorland, 1640–1643.[483] A grandson of George Lord Cobham, and cousin of Henry Lord Cobham, who was attainted in 1603, he was the second but eldest surviving son of Sir Henry Brooke, alias Cobham (d. 1592), of Sutton at Home, Kent, and in 1645 succeeded to the forfeited barony of Cobham. His mother was Anne, daughter of Sir Henry Sutton of Nottinghamshire.[484] John was born on 15 August 1575,[485] and followed his elder brother, Sir Calisthenes Brooke, in a military career. He was a protégé of the Cecils for some years. He was a captain at Amiens in 1597, and

between that time and 1600 was employed with commands in Ireland and in the Netherlands.[486] He was knighted before 30 October 1597, probably with his brother, Calisthenes, in May.[487] As late as June, 1600, Sir John was in Ireland, but the next February he was a colonel commanding the Middlesex forces assigned to protect London and guard the prisoners involved in the Essex conspiracy.[488] He was described by this time as one of the queen's servants.[489] Brooke travelled to the continent in 1601 and 1610,[490] and became interested in various commercial projects. He had journeyed with Sir Thomas Roe to Guiana early in 1610, and in 1614 the East India Company considered sending him to the east, but selected Roe instead.[491] Brooke was a member of the king's council for New England, was a patentee of lands in Virginia, and was for some years active in the affairs of that colony and of other American developments.[492]

In the meantime, escaping the difficulties of the senior branch of his family, Sir John was progressing at court. He was granted a life pension of £100 in 1607 and by 1630 had accumulated others which entitled him to a total of £800 yearly.[493] He had some office connected with Dover Castle in 1615, and the next year was one of the partners who succeeded to Ingram's alum contract.[494] He was interested in such later enterprises as soap making, the new saltpetre process, and the fen drainage project. He was named a commissioner in 1630 to compound for lands previously granted by the crown at undervalues, and in 1639 for reforming abuses in the drapery business.[495] As Sir John Brooke of Kent he was admitted in 1614 to the Society of Lincoln's Inn, and upon paying £30 in 1626 he became an associate of the bench.[496] He was a member of the Council of War in 1628,[497] was a parishioner of St. Margaret's, Westminster, during the 1630's,[498] and was with the army in the north in 1639.[499] Before 1640 Brooke served in three parliaments, for Gatton in 1614, Oxford City in 1621, and Great Bedwin in 1625, probably being

[476] E. R. O. Bridgeman and Charles G. O. Bridgeman, *The sequestration papers of Sir Orlando Bridgeman*, Shrops. Arch. Soc. *Trans.*, 3rd Ser., 2: 1, 1902. This corrects the date of 1605 or 1606 that appears in *D.N.B.* and elsewhere.

[477] *M. of P.* 1: 482; *C.S.P. Dom., 1639–1640*, 341. Bridgeman does not seem to have been a J.P. locally, although his father was a J.P. in Cheshire and Wales in 1638. S.P. 16/405.

[478] Verney, 58.

[479] D'Ewes (N), 175, 337, 427–428.

[480] *C.J.* 2: 288, 369, 626, 742.

[481] Shrops. Arch. Soc., *Trans.*, 3rd Ser., 2: 14–35, 64, 1902; *Cal. Com. Comp.*, 61, 104, 1430.

[482] *Rebellion* 2: 470.

Other references are *D.N.B.*; Pink and Beaven, *Parl. Rep. Lanc.*, 225.

[483] The sketch of Brooke by W. R. Williams in *The parliamentary history of the county of Oxford*, 114, Brecknock, 1899 (hereafter, Williams, *Oxford*) is so faulty as to require rewriting.

[484] *Complete Peerage* (Gibbs ed.) 3: 338–339.

[485] I.P.M., Sir Henry Brooke alias Cobham, C. 142/235/89. In 1646, however, Brooke gave his age as 74. S.P. 23/193/514.

[486] *C.S.P. Dom., 1595–1597*, 445, 525, 548; *1598–1601*, 51, 149; *C.S.P. Ireland, 1598–1599*, 452, 497; *1599–1600*, 78.

[487] *C.S.P. Dom., 1595–1597*, 525; Pink MSS, 298, fol. 560.

[488] *C.S.P. Ireland, 1600–1601*, 278; *Acts P.C., 1600–1601*, 156, 172.

[489] *Acts P.C., 1601–1604*, 190.

[490] *C.S.P. Dom., 1601–1603*, 111; *1603–1610*, 596.

[491] *H.M.C., MSS of the Marquess of Downshire* 2: 251, 390.

[492] Brown, *Genesis of the U.S.* 2: 834.

[493] *C.S.P. Dom., 1603–1610*, 361; *1611–1618*, 33; S.P. 16, 180/18/67.

[494] *C.S.P. Dom., 1611–1618*, 298; St. Ch. 8/158/3.

[495] Pink MSS, 298, fol. 560; *C.S.P. Dom., 1627–1628*, 2; *1629–1631*, 186; S.P. 16, 378/49. Sir John was not a teller of the Exchequer as Williams states (*Oxford*, 114); that official was Mr. John Brooke of Suffolk (Add. MSS, 15,520, fol. 129v).

[496] *Linc. Inn Rec. Adm.* 1: 167; *Black Books* 2: 261.

[497] Pink MSS, *loc. cit.*

[498] Records of St. Margaret's Parish, Overseers' Accounts, 153.

[499] *C.S.P. Dom., 1639*, 99; S.P. 16, 427/38/v.

a court nominee each time.[500] He was never an outstanding member, but he was chosen among the courtiers of the 1621 parliament to carry the remonstrance and petition to the king, and spoke once against a monopoly patent.[501]

Sir John's connections with Lincolnshire, where he had the estate of Heckington, involved him in some local offices in that county. He was named a sewers commissioner there in 1631· and during the following decade was named to various local commissions of that county and those adjoining.[502] He was also a J.P.[503]

Brooke did not sit in the Short Parliament. His election for Appleby, Westmorland, was doubtless the result of his court connections, for he seems to have had no previous relations with that borough. He was named to a committee on Virginia in December, 1640, but was not otherwise active. He was summoned to attend, 23 August 1642, but was working to raise support for the king in Lincolnshire, and was therefore disabled, 15 March 1643.[504] Sir John sat in the Oxford parliament, was created Baron Cobham in 1645, and compounded for his royalism, 1646–1647. He died in 1659 or 1660, and was buried, 20 May 1660, at Wakerly, Northamptonshire.[505]

Sir John had married twice. His first wife, Anne, whom he married before 21 January 1609, died in London in 1625. Sometime before October, 1636, he married Frances, daughter of Sir William Bamfield of Middlesex and of Dame Anne Lyster.[506]

Brooke inherited some lands in Kent worth about £550 a year. These he afterwards sold to the Duke of Richmond with most of the Cobham inheritance which became his in 1643.[507] His Lincolnshire manor of Heckington, valued at £850 a year before the war, was mortgaged in 1638 for £7000 and was otherwise encumbered. He enjoyed a royal pension of £300 until the coming of the Civil War, but seemed to have been living beyond his means. His assessment in 1644 was £2000, and his fine at compounding was £1300.[508]

Sir Ambrose Browne, Bart. (c. 1591–1661), of Bettsworth Castle near Dorking, Surrey, was one of his county's knights from 1640 until the purge of 1648. The descendant of a line settled at Bettsworth from the time of Henry VI, he was the son and heir of Sir Matthew Browne (M.P. 1601) by his wife, Jane, daughter of Sir Thomas Vincent of Stoke D'Abernon. He was born about 1591 and at twelve succeeded his father, who was killed in a duel on 4 August 1603.[509] He matriculated at Jesus College, Cambridge, in 1606. His admission to Gray's Inn in 1625 was perhaps more for social than for academic reasons.[510] In October, 1607, he married Elizabeth, daughter and heiress of William Adam of Saffron Walden, Essex. He became a baronet in 1627.

Public responsibilities came early to Browne. He was a J.P. in Surrey before the end of the reign of James I, and was still a magistrate in 1638.[511] He was regularly a member of the commission of oyer and terminer, also,[512] and was sheriff for Surrey and Sussex, 1624–1625.[513] He was a D.L. there in 1628 and 1638.[514] And in the parliaments of 1628 and the spring of 1640 he represented his shire.[515] He opposed the forced loans of 1621 and 1627, each time being listed among those summoned to attend Council to explain their reluctance.[516] In 1639 he sent no answer to the king's request for further contributions toward his expenses.[517]

Browne was probably a puritan. He was a useful but not an outstanding member of the country party during the early months of the Long Parliament. He was named to committees on army supply and on the lords lieutenant [518] and in November, 1640, offered his bond for £1000 for the loan.[519] His pledge for the defense in June, 1642, was two horses.[520] He was a parliamentary committeeman in Surrey during the war and in 1643 his house was garrisoned for parliament.[521] He was secluded in December, 1648, however, and was under some suspicion of delinquency, 1650–1651.[522] He died on 16 August 1661 and was buried at Dorking.

[500] M. of P. 1: 452, 466; 3: xl.

[501] Commons Debates 1621 2: 499; 5: 88, n.

[502] C. 181/4, fol. 83v; 181/5, fols. 27, 32, passim.

[503] C. 193/13; S.P. 16/405.

[504] C.J. 2: 54, 733; 3: 1. He was greatly incensed at the plundering of his London house in his absence in April, 1643. John Rylands Library English MSS, 234, fols. 61–62.

[505] Complete Peerage (Gibbs ed.) 2: 338–339. According to the M.I. of his widow, she died in December, 1676, having been a widow for 17 years, 3 months (T. Allen, The history of the county of Lincoln 1: 347, London, 1834). This would place Brooke's death in 1659.

[506] Complete Peerage loc. cit.; Allen, loc. cit. His wife's mother was buried at Wakerly in 1657. Arch. Cant. 11: 207, 1877; Northamptonshire Notes and Queries 3: 211, 1890.

[507] S.P. 23/193/509; Hasted, Kent, 3: 459, 461, 479, 504; Add. MSS, 21,426, fols. 76–77. Brooke's difficulties in managing his estate in his later years were probably because of his advanced age rather than because of weakness of character, as suggested in Arch. Cant. (11: 206, 1877; 12: 96, 1878).

[508] Cal. Com. Comp., 1, 1230–1231; S.P. 23/193/509–517; Cal. Com. Adv. Money, 422; Pink MSS, 298, fol. 560

[509] Manning and Bray, Surrey 1: 557–558; W. Berry, County genealogies; pedigrees of Surrey families, 80, London, 1837 (hereafter, Berry, Surrey families).

[510] Al. Cant.

[511] C. 193/13; S.P. 16/405; C.S.P. Dom., 1637, 110.

[512] C. 181/4, fol. 72; 181/5, passim.

[513] List of Sheriffs, 138.

[514] H.M.C., Seventh Report, MSS of W. M. Molyneux, Esq., 677; C.S.P. Dom., 1638–1639, 50.

[515] M. of P. 1: 478, 483.

[516] S.P. 14, 127/80; S.P. 16, 89/5.

[517] Rushworth 3: 914.

[518] C.J. 2: 31, 50. Pink notes, however, that Browne was named to only five committees, 1640–1645. Pink MSS, 298, fol. 582.

[519] D'Ewes (N), 52.

[520] N. and Q., 1st Ser., 12: 360; 1855.

[521] H.M.C., Fourth Report, MSS of Earl De la Warr, 279.

[522] Cal. Com. Comp., 304, 393, 398.

Sir Ambrose owned considerable property in Surrey,[523] and was apparently a wealthy man. The estate of his son, Sir Adam Browne, was valued about 1660 at £1600 a year.[524]

Browne was related somewhat distantly to another parliament man of the same surname, Richard Browne of Great Chart.[525]

John Browne (1580–1659), of Frampton, Dorset, puritan, was a knight for his county from 28 June 1641, being elected after Digby was elevated to the peerage, until 1653. Born late in 1580,[526] he was the son and heir of Sir John Browne of Frampton, twice sheriff of Dorset, D.L. and Vice Admiral, who died in 1627 on the expedition to the Isle of Rhé. The family was one of wealth and influence in the county. Through his mother, Jane (d. 1634), daughter of Sir Henry Portman of Orchard, Somerset,[527] Browne was connected with another prominent family, and was a first cousin of Sir William Portman, M.P. for Taunton (*q.v.*). After studying at Oxford (matriculated Magdalen, 1598) and the Middle Temple (admitted 1599) without taking degrees,[528] Browne married in 1607 at Charminster Elizabeth, daughter of Sir George Trenchard of Wolveton.[529] This alliance with a strong puritan family foreshadows Browne's later career.

Browne's political activity began with his election to the 1621 parliament for Bridport. He stood unsuccessfully for the shire in 1626. Although the townsmen of Dorchester, where the election was held, and where he was a property owner and popular, gave him their support, he was defeated in a close vote (511–498) by the court candidate who had the backing not only of the election officials but of Browne's own brother-in-law, Sir John Strangways (*q.v.*). He was returned for Bridport in 1628, but his election was declared void.[530] He concerned himself thereafter with local duties, being a J.P.,[531] a sewers commissioner,[532] and, in 1632–1633, sheriff.[533]

A friend of the Reverend John White of Dorchester, Browne subscribed £20 toward his New England colonial venture. He served on one of the committees for it in 1624.[534] In 1635 Browne was under investigation with White by Sir John Lambe and other agents of Laud regarding the relation between the religious leaders of Dorset and Dr. Stoughton. Browne was possibly included in the investigation because Stoughton was his son-in-law, but only the examination of White remains among the State Papers.[535] But not only was Browne associated with the religious nonconformists. He brushed with the king's civil servants, too. He was summoned in 1632 to compound for knighthood.[536] He was reported as a ship money refuser in 1636, having declined to pay in four places. The sheriff so reporting him was his brother-in-law, Sir Thomas Trenchard.[537] By September of the following year Browne and other leading opponents of the levy had been forced by distraints to conform, the distraining sheriff being another of Browne's relatives by marriage, Richard Rogers, his royalist fellow knight of the Long Parliament.[538]

In that parliament and in the war John Browne worked against the king. He served on numerous committees, many of them being concerned with ecclesiastical matters. Eventually he was named a commissioner for the trial of King Charles. He attended some of the sessions of the trial but did not sign the warrant for execution.[539] He died on 16 March 1659 and was buried on 7 April at Frampton.[540] His will, dated 1 November 1658, was proved on 7 May 1659.[541]

Although a royalist writer minimized Browne's position, calling him a "petty committee-man" who seized delinquents' goods for his own benefit,[542] he was well-to-do even before the war. His father's properties, including several manors and other holdings of over five thousand acres in Somerset and Dorset,[543] were worth about £1000 a year. Browne's own acquisitions, some of them no doubt added as a result of the war, enabled him before his death to give £2300 to a daughter and over £450 to assist two sons in business, and to provide for his other children. He left also £40 a year for Frampton parish and maintenance funds for a school he had built "for a publique good."[544] His pledge for

---

[523] Manning and Bray, *Surrey* 1: 554, 558; 2: 182.

[524] *English Baronetage* 4: 376, 1741.

[525] References in addition to those above are: *Complete Baronetage* 2: 29; Pink MSS, 298, fol. 582.

[526] I.P.M., Sir John Browne, 1628, C. 142/439/56.

[527] *H.M.C., Fifth Report*, Weymouth and Melcome Regis MSS, 581; John Hutchins, *The history and antiquities of the county of Dorset* 2: 298 and n., 3rd ed., Westminster, 1861–1870 (hereafter, Hutchins, *Dorset*); *Somerset and Dorset N. and Q.* 3: 214, 1892–1893.

[528] *Al. Oxon.; Mid. Temp. Rec.* 1: 395.

[529] Hutchins, *loc. cit.*

[530] *M. of P.* 1: 451, 475; *Somerset and Dorset N. and Q.* 4: 23–24, 1894–1895.

[531] C. 193/13; S.P. 16, 188/53/142; S.P. 16/405.

[532] C. 181/4, fol. 173; 181/5, fol. 226.

[533] *List of Sheriffs*, 39.

[534] *Somerset and Dorset N. and Q.* 7: 37, 1898–1899; 17: 109, 1921–1923; Dorset N.H. *Proceedings* 13: 65, 1892.

[535] *C.S.P. Dom., 1635*, 435, 459; *Somerset and Dorset N. and Q.* 7: 37, 1898–1899.

[536] *Ibid.* 4: 19, 1894–1895.

[537] S.P. 16, 319/89. Browne owed £13 for Frampton and £4.16.0 for each of the other places.

[538] S.P. 16, 367/2.

[539] Pink MSS, 298, fols. 593–594; Noble, *Regicides* 1: 121.

[540] Hutchins, *Dorset* 2: 298. Noble's statement that Browne survived the Restoration doubtless resulted from confusing him with his son of the same name who died in 1670. The son was sheriff in 1642 and could not have been the M.P.

[541] P.C.C., 266 Pell.

[542] *The mystery of the good old cause*, 11.

[543] I.P.M. cited above.

[544] Browne's will. A rectory and a vicarage of which he had been patron were evaluated at slightly more than £94 a year in

the defense in 1642, a horse and £100, was somewhat higher than the average.[545]

Besides the kinsmen of Brown mentioned above, others of the Long Parliament who were relatives were another brother-in-law, John Trenchard, a nephew, Giles Strangways, and several more who were connections by marriage.

Richard Browne (d. c. 1649), of Shingleton in Great Chart, Kent, elected M.P. for New Romney, *vice* Webb, on 26 April 1641, seems to have held his seat until 1648.[546] A descendant of the Brownes of Betchworth, Surrey, he was a younger son of Sir Thomas Browne of that place by his second wife, Helena, daughter and heiress of William Harding, and widow of Richard Knevett of Wiltshire. He was his mother's heir, and was a half-brother of Sir Matthew Browne of Betchworth, father of the 1640 M.P., Sir Ambrose Brown (*q.v.*).[547] Said to have been a barrister of Lincoln's Inn, he was possibly the Richard Browne of Surrey who was admitted there in 1585, or the one "of Southants" who entered in 1601.[548] Early in James's reign he purchased his estate in Great Chart and continued to live there with his wife, Margaret, daughter and heiress of James Aston of Westerham.[549] A near neighbor and friend was Sir Roger Twysden.[550]

Browne was listed among the Kentish gentlemen delinquent about paying their promised loans early in Charles's reign.[551] He was sheriff of the county, 1629–1630, and a sewers commissioner,[552] but does not seem to have tried for a place in parliament before 1640. He was probably the "Mr. Browne" who was backed by Twysden and "the precise party" for one of the county seats in the contest with Colepeper and Dering that autumn,[553] but was defeated. He turned next to the vacancy in the port of New Romney created by

the dismissal of Webb, the royalist, and on 26 April 1641 was elected to the House.[554]

Browne supported the parliamentary cause, promised £100 for the defense in June, 1642, and in the following summer was named a D.L. in Kent and a member of the committees to deal with the justices, with scandalous ministers, and with other county matters. His deep concern about reforms in the church is indicated by his fear that the Lords would bury in "a Lawne wynding sheete" the bill regarding episcopacy.[555] He served on a dozen or more committees in parliament between 1641 and 1648, but was absent several times in the later years because of illness.[556] He may have been secluded by Pride's Purge, but died within a few years afterwards. His will, dated 23 August 1647, was proved by his grandson, Richard Browne, 9 June 1653.[557]

Browne's estate was considerable, though he was a younger son, for both his mother and his wife were heiresses. He referred in his will to several properties purchased before 1640, enumerated lands and manors in some seven Kentish parishes, and others in Bedfordshire, and directed raising to £500 the portions for each of his four married daughters.

* Samuel Browne (c. 1598–1668), of Arlesey, Bedfordshire, was M.P. for Dartmouth, Devon, from October, 1641, until 1653, filling a place vacated by death. The eldest son of a Northamptonshire vicar, Nicholas Browne of Polebrook, and related through his mother to the lords St. John of Bletsoe, Browne was educated at Cambridge and Lincoln's Inn for the law. He was called to the bench in July, 1641, shortly before his election.[558] His first cousin, Oliver St. John, with whom he had been associated at the Inn,[559] was M.P. for Totness, and possibly helped secure Browne his place. His political and religious views were appropriate for a successor of Upton (*q.v.*). Browne seems to have had no previous connection with Dartmouth or the county, nor had he sat in any earlier parliament. He had probably served as a J.P. in Essex, his wife's county, however, and had been named in 1630 for the sewers commission in Bedfordshire.[560]

As to his estate, Browne inherited from his father various small properties lying in Bedfordshire, Herts, Kent, Surrey and London.[561] His offer of £100 for the defense in June, 1642, was not a large one.[562] By

---

an ecclesiastical survey of about 1654. Lansd. MSS, 459, fols. 29v, 30.

[545] *N. and Q.,* 1st Ser., **12**: 338, 1855.

[546] New Romney Borough MSS, Common Assembly Book, 1622–1701, fol. 293; *O.P.H.* **9**: 13.

[547] Add. MSS, 14,311, fol. 57; 33,919, fol. 254. Pink (Pink MSS, 298, fol. 601) identifies the member as the grandson of this Richard Browne, but the elder Browne lived long enough to have been the member and the one who was a candidate for Kent was referred to as old. His half-brother, Matthew, was born about 1563. Manning and Bray, *Hist. Surrey* **1**: 557.

[548] One was called to the bar in 1609. *Linc. Inn Rec. Adm.* **1**: 103, 131; *Black Books* **2**: 121. In 1613 a John Browne, son and heir apparent of Richard Browne of Great Chart, Kent, was admitted to the Inn (*ibid., Adm.* **1**: 164).

[549] Hasted, *Kent* **7**: 502; Add. MSS, 33,919, fol. 254.

[550] *Arch. Cant.* **27**: 54, 1905.

[551] His promise had been £16. S.P. 16, 73/30/i.

[552] *C.S.P. Dom., 1629–1631,* 307; C. 181/4, fol. 32v; 181/5, fol. 334.

[553] A friend wrote to Dering, 21 October 1640, that "old Browne" had been set up by Twysden against Dering when his own hopes for re-election failed. Stowe MSS, 184, fols. 15–16; 743, fol. 149; Larking, *Proceedings in Kent,* 16 and n.

[554] New Romney Borough MSS, Common Assembly Book, 1622–1701, fol. 293.

[555] *N. and Q.,* 1st Ser., **12**: 359, 1855; *C.J.* **2**: 724; *Arch. Cant.* **2**: 175–176, 182, 1859; Pink MSS cited above.

[556] The last date of such an absence in the records was 28 September 1648. Pink MSS, *loc. cit.*

[557] P.C.C., 275 Brent.

[558] *Linc. Inn Rec., Black Books* **2**: 359.

[559] Sanford, *St. and ill.,* 389.

[560] C. 181/4, fol. 174; C. 181/5, fol. 75.

[561] *Beds. Hist. Rec. Soc.* **2**: 138, 1914.

[562] *N. and Q.,* 1st Ser., **12**: 359, 1855.

the time of his death Browne had become wealthy,[563] but he was probably not so in 1641.

John Broxholme (1583–1647), of Broxholme Place, Lincoln city, and of Barrow, Lincolnshire, was M.P. for Lincoln from 1640 until his death in 1647. He came of a family connected with both Lincoln and Grimsby, being the eldest son and heir of William Broxholme of those places (d. 1619),[564] by his second wife, Anne, daughter of William Marbury of Girsly. He was born on 20 May and baptized on 26 May 1583 at St. Peter at Gowts in Lincoln.[565] He was described as of Lincoln in the license, dated 23 September 1619, for his marriage with Troth Fowkes, widow of Sir Henry Fowkes and daughter of Richard Gedney,[566] but in 1622 he was described as of Barrow.[567] He was living at Barrow in 1627, when he was summoned to appear before Council as one of the refusers of the loan,[568] but seems to have taken up residence in Lincoln again by the time of the heralds' visitation in 1634.[569] Between 1627 and 1640 he was appointed regularly to the sewers commissions for the city and county, and in 1638 was concerned with a special drainage project, the "level" of Ancholme.[570] Broxholme seems to have held no other public office before his election to parliament in the autumn of 1640. He was styled "esquire," however, and was on intimate terms with prominent families such as the Pelhams of Brocklesby, his kinsmen.[571]

In spite of his inexperience in parliament, Broxholme was named at once to the Committee of Privileges in November, 1640, and shortly afterwards to such other important ones as those on the courts, the customs farmers and grievances of the ports, superstition and idolatry, and Strafford's trial. He was sent into his county for the disarming of recusants in August, 1641,[572] and during the war was a member of the militia and sequestration committees there. He died about March, 1647, and was buried in Westminster Abbey, 5 March

of that year.[573] His will, dated 10 April 1645, was proved 20 November 1647.[574]

Broxholme inherited from his father four manors and appurtenances in Lincolnshire and the family residence and an inn in the city,[575] and added to these holdings during his lifetime. The legacies provided by his will were modest, but his elder son, William, was reputedly worth £1000 a year in 1660.[576]

Francis Buller (c. 1603–1677), of Shillingham, sat for East Looe, Cornwall, 1640–1648. He was the eldest son and heir apparent of Sir Richard Buller of Shillingham (q.v.). Born about 1603, he was admitted and matriculated at Sidney Sussex, Cambridge, in 1620. In 1622 he entered the Middle Temple, where he was bound for a time with his father and John Maynard (q.v.). It is not known that he was summoned to the bar, but he still held a chamber at the Temple in 1646 when his eldest son was admitted.[577] On 21 November 1625 at St. Stephen's by Saltash, Buller married Thomasine, daughter of Sir Thomas Honeywood of Elmsted, Kent.[578]

Barely of age when he entered parliament for the family borough of Saltash in 1624, Buller was re-elected by the borough in 1625, but was defeated when he tried for Michael in 1628.[579] In 1633 and 1637 he was captain of the company of trained bands from his region.[580] He served for Saltash in the Short Parliament and when he was chosen by East Looe in the autumn was careful to ask the town for a list of its grievances.[581] Francis Buller and his younger brother, George, were named occasionally to committees before 1642, but their father was the prominent member of the family in the work of the House. Francis followed Sir Richard in working for the popular cause, was an active committeeman in the west during the war, but was secluded in 1648.[582] One of his friends wrote that his seclusion was not because the army or parliament distrusted him, but because it was known he "had not heart" for the justice that was to be done to the king.[583] Despite his friends' urging that he return to the House, Buller seems to have lived thereafter in retirement. He died

[563] See his will, *Beds. Hist. Rec.* **2**: 141–142, 1914.

[564] I.P.M., William Broxholme, C. 142/379/65.

[565] *The parish register of St. Peter at Gowts*, Lincoln Record Society, Parish Register Section, **8**: 7, 1923; Pink MSS, 298, fol. 621; manuscript notes supplied from his studies of Lincolnshire M.P.'s by Mr. J. Bean King.

[566] A. Gibbons, *Lincoln marriage licenses*, 87, London, 1888; A. Gibbons, *Notes on the visitation of Lincolnshire, 1634*, 7, 9, Lincoln, 1898.

[567] Letters of administration for the estate of John Broxholme of Lincoln, Esq., 4 April 1622, Lincoln Consistory Court, Administrations, 1622.

[568] S.P. 16, 56/39, fol. 76; *Acts P.C., 1627*, 241.

[569] *Lincs. N. and Q.* **2**: 9, 1890–1891.

[570] C. 181/3; 181/4, fols. 40v, 84v, 155v; 181/5, fols. 133, 300; S.P. 16, 178/75.

[571] He was once a bondsman for Sir William Pelham for a loan, and was named a trustee of his will in July, 1643 (P.C.C., 32 Essex). He had been a commissioner for the i.p.m. of Sir William Pelham, Senior, in 1629. C. 142/453/73.

[572] *C.J.* **2**: 21, 34, 55, 84, 98, 267.

[573] *Lincs. N. and Q.* **8**: 104, 1904–1905; *Fenland N. and Q.* **2**: 107, 1892–1894; Pink MSS, 298, fol. 621.

[574] P.C.C., 230 Fines.

[575] I.P.M. cited above, n. 564.

[576] *English Baronetage* **4**: 368, 1741. The son, who was listed for the proposed Knights of the Royal Oak, was described at his death in 1684 as loyal to the Church of England and to the king. *Lincolnshire Church notes made by William John Monson*, Lincoln Record Society, **31**: 19, 1936.

[577] *Al. Cant.; Mid. Temp. Rec.* **2**: 678, 937.

[578] Vivian, *Vis. Cornwall*, 57.

[579] *M. of P.* **1**: 457, 463, 474 and n.

[580] *The Buller Papers*, 15, 17.

[581] *Ibid.*, 29.

[582] Pink MSS, 307, fol. 222; Coate, *Cornwall in the great Civil War*, 224, n.

[583] *The Buller Papers*, 109–111.

in 1677. His will, with a codicil of 12 June 1677, was proved 22 November that year.[584]

Buller's chief estate, his paternal inheritance, was still in his father's hands in 1640. He had a town house at Plymouth, however, where his wife was living in 1642.[585] The family estate was said to be worth £3000 a year in 1660.[586]

Francis Buller was a cousin and a friend of Thomas Wise, the Devonshire member (*q.v.*), and became guardian of his children.

George Buller (*c.* 1607–1646), a lawyer of the Middle Temple, M.P. for his family's borough of Saltash in Cornwall, 1640–1646, was one of three members of his family who sat in the Long Parliament. He was the second son of Sir Richard Buller of Shillingham and a younger brother of Francis Buller (*c.* 1603–1677). Born sometime between 1603 and 1609,[587] he was admitted in 1627 to the Middle Temple. He was called to the bar there ten years later and probably remained in London to practice, for he had a chamber at the Temple until his death.[588] He represented his cousin, Thomas Wise (*q.v.*), in some of his dealings with Council regarding his ship money collections in 1639.[589] While the Long Parliament was in session (1643), he married Mary, daughter of George Hanger, a London merchant.[590]

Buller represented Saltash in both parliaments of 1640, was named to the commission on scandalous ministers in Cornwall in 1642, and joined his father and brother in working for the parliamentary cause. He subscribed £600, apparently his personal investment, for the reducing of Ireland, and in June, 1642, offered to provide a horse for the defense.[591] He died in the spring of 1646. His will, dated 29 March 1646, was proved by his widow on 13 May,[592] and his chamber at the Temple had a new occupant by 8 May 1646.[593] Although he was a younger son, Buller assigned portions of £1000 for each of two young children when he made his will.

Sir Richard Buller (*c.* 1579–1642) of Shillingham, near Saltash, was M.P. for Fowey, Cornwall, 1640–1642. His original return was invalidated by the House on 20 November 1640, since it appeared that he had been irregularly returned by means of a blank indenture, but Buller himself was not blamed, since it "appeared not to be with his Privity." He was back in the House by 5 December, following a legitimate election.[594]

Sir Richard was the elder son of Francis Buller of Tregarrick and Shillingham (H. S., d. 1616) by his wife, Thomasine, daughter of Thomas Williams of Stowford, Devon, Speaker of the House of Commons, and was something over thirty-seven years of age at his father's death.[595] He was admitted to the Middle Temple in December, 1597, and kept a chamber there long afterwards.[596] He may have been a barrister, for he served for a time as recorder for Saltash.[597] About 1601 he married Alice, daughter of Sir Rowland Hayward, an alderman and Lord Mayor of London.[598] He was knighted at Greenwich in 1608,[599] was undersheriff in Cornwall for the Prince of Wales in 1611–1612,[600] and may possibly have been connected with Buckingham in his early years at court,[601] though by 1627 he had travelled far in the opposite direction. Buller may have paid a fine rather than serve as sheriff in 1616,[602] but within a few years he was engaged in numerous activities in his county. Besides serving Saltash as recorder he worked with Sir John Eliot, the Vice Admiral, on a commission for improving the harbor at Plymouth and Saltash.[603] He was long a commissioner on piracy,[604] and was an active J.P. and D.L.[605] He served also in parliament, sitting for St. Germans in 1621, and for Saltash, 1625–1628. In his first parliament he spoke for the correction of grievances.[606]

In 1627 Buller's opposition to the policies of Buckingham came to a crisis. He had been threatened by Council in 1625 for not paying in full the county composition demanded of him,[607] and in June, 1627, was

---

[584] *Western Antiquary* 11: 82, 1891–1892; Pink MSS, 307, fol. 222.

[585] *The Buller Papers*, 87, 91.

[586] *Western Antiquary* 7: 39, 1887–1888.

[587] His elder brother was born about 1603 and a younger brother, the third son, was baptized in 1609. Vivian, *Vis. Cornwall*, 57. He gave his age as 33, however, at the time he married in 1643. Pink suggests 1607 as approximate for his birth year. Pink MSS, 307, fol. 286.

[588] *Mid. Temp. Rec.* 2: 719, 855, 939.

[589] *C.S.P. Dom., 1638–1639*, 306; *1639–1640*, 147.

[590] Pink MSS, *loc. cit.*

[591] *Ibid.; C.S.P. Ireland, Adventurers*, 12–13; *N. and Q.*, 1st Ser., 11: 359, 1855.

[592] P.C.C., 73 Twisse.

[593] *Mid. Temp. Rec.* 2: 939.

[594] *C.J.* 2: 29, 32, 46; D'Ewes (N), 35, 536.

[595] Vivian, *Vis. Cornwall*, 56–57; Pink MSS, 307, fol. 191.

[596] *Mid. Temp. Rec.* 1: 380, 408; 2: 719.

[597] *C.S.P. Dom., 1628–1629*, 65.

[598] A marriage settlement was made in 1601. I.P.M., Francis Buller, C. 142/356/108. His wife, through her mother, was related to the Smith family of Ostenhanger, Kent (Pink MSS, 307, fol. 191), and to several persons of prominence at court. *Cf.* Sir Thomas Fanshawe, K.B.

[599] Shaw, *K. of E.* 2: 145.

[600] Pink MSS, *loc. cit.*

[601] Sir John Hippisley, one of Buckingham's henchmen, wrote in 1627 to Nicholas to recommend Buller for some employment in Cornwall, saying, "He was a servant to my Lord 'when time was.'" *C.S.P. Dom., 1627–1628*, 219. This was about the time that Buller was removed from the commission of the peace. See below.

[602] S.P. 14, 135/41.

[603] *C.S.P. Dom., 1628–1629*, 65; Forster, *Eliot* 1: 186.

[604] C. 181/3, fol. 113; 181/5, fol. 165.

[605] C. 193/12, 13; S.P. 16, 72/57; *The Buller Papers*, 9, 14, 17, 24.

[606] *M. of P.; Commons Debates 1621* 2: 59, n., 130.

[607] *The Buller Papers*, 10, 11.

reported as a loan refuser, although he had been a member of the loan commission. Buckingham and his agent in Cornwall, Sir James Bagg, procured the king's consent for the removal of Buller and another loan refuser from the commission of the peace and for their summons before Council. Buller had apparently acted with Eliot and Coryton in the matter, but unlike them, he avoided imprisonment and satisfied Council by the end of the summer that he had paid his personal assessment of £25. He was acting again as a J.P. in 1628.[608] He was unsuccessful, however, in preventing Bagg from nominating his co-member for parliament from Saltash that year.[609]

Sir Richard was sheriff of Cornwall, 1636–1637, and managed to have his full quota of ship money paid by the end of his term, although not without difficulty.[610] He showed some indifference toward his task as a D.L. in raising troops for the Scottish War,[611] and in 1639 sent no reply when he was asked to advance money personally for that cause.[612] He was chosen by his county for the Short Parliament. In the autumn he procured the election of two of his sons for Cornish boroughs, and contented himself with one of the Fowey places. Doubtless his personal record made the Committee of Privileges, headed by his friend, John Maynard,[613] and the House itself lenient regarding the irregularities in the Fowey returns.

Sir Richard Buller was an active member of the Long Parliament. He was permitted to talk with Strafford on some private matter in December, and was named to a score of committees, 1640–1642. They included several on church reforms and the correction of grievances.[614] In June, 1642, he promised for himself and his elder son, Francis, to contribute three horses for the defense.[615] He joined with Carew to secure eastern Cornwall for parliament when war began,[616] but died before 20 November 1642. He was buried at Plymouth on 1 December.[617] His will, dated 30 March 1640, was proved 1 March 1646/7.[618]

Sir Richard owned a large estate, including Shillingham manor with its mansion and grist mills near Saltash, halves of four other manors, and scattered properties lying in a dozen Cornish parishes. Other holdings lay in Montgomeryshire and Devon.[619] When he made his will four daughters had already been provided for, but he assigned £1000 as a portion for one still unmarried. His widow declared in 1645 that she had lost "a great estate" through her affection for parliament.[620] Buller's income was probably several thousand pounds a year before the war.[621]

Roger Burgoyne (1618–1677), of Sutton, Bedfordshire, and Wroxhall, Warwickshire, sat for the former county from early in 1641 [622] until the purge of 1648. His family's connections with Bedfordshire date from the fifteenth century and with Warwickshire from the dissolution of the monasteries. They maintained residences in both counties.[623] His grandfather was sheriff of Bedfordshire, 1616–1617, and his father, 1640–1641.[624] The son and heir of John Burgoyne, Esq. (baronet, 1641; M.P. Warwickshire, 1645), by his wife, Jane, daughter and heiress of William Kempe of Spain's Hall in Finchingfield, Essex, Roger was baptized at Wroxhall, 10 March 1618, and was admitted to Emmanuel College, Cambridge, in 1634. He entered Lincoln's Inn three years later,[625] and in May, 1638, was granted a pass for three years of foreign travel.[626]

Although young and without previous experience in office,[627] Burgoyne was a candidate in the Bedfordshire election of October, 1640, opposing Thomas Lord Wentworth (q.v.), and, when the latter's seat was vacated on 25 November, Burgoyne again sought the place.[628] In spite of efforts by Sir Lewis Dives, stepson of the Earl of Bristol and a royalist and alleged "papist," to delay the new election, if not to secure it for himself, Burgoyne, the sheriff's son, was elected in December or January and was participating in the work of the House early in March, even before a disposition had been made of the charges against Dives.[629]

[608] S.P. 16, 72/57; C.S.P. Dom., 1627–1628, 231 and passim; 1628–1629, 346.

[609] Ibid., 65.

[610] Ibid., 1636–1637, 435, 490; 1637, 577.

[611] Ibid., 1640, 264; The Buller Papers, 23.

[612] Rushworth, 913.

[613] M. of P. His son, Francis, was bound with Buller and Maynard when he entered the Middle Temple. See Fowey election.

[614] C.J. 2: 46, 49, 84, 91, 107, passim.

[615] N. and Q., 1st Ser., 12: 358, 1855.

[616] R. Polwhele, The history of Cornwall 4: 97, rev. ed., Falmouth, 1803–1816 (hereafter, Polwhele, Cornwall); Clarendon, Rebellion 2: 448–450.

[617] Vivian, Vis. Cornwall, 638; The Buller Papers, 86.

[618] P.C.C., 48 Fines.

[619] I.P.M. cited above; Chancery proceedings, C. 3/301/55, 68; 302/12; 334/9; The Buller Papers, 94–97; C. S. Gilbert, An historical survey of the county of Cornwall 2: 39, London, 1817–1820 (hereafter, Gilbert, Hist. survey of Cornwall).

[620] Courtney, Parl. Rep. Corn. 103.

[621] See Francis Buller.

[622] He is styled "Sir Roger Burgoyne, Bart." in the official list (M. of P. 1: 485), but his father was created the first baronet of the family in 1641.

[623] The estates included at least four manors in Bedfordshire. Lysons, Mag. Brit. 1: 124, 139; V.C.H. Bedford 2: 238, 239, 244, 248; F. L. Covile, The worthies of Warwickshire, 74–75, Warwick, 1870.

[624] List of Sheriffs, 3.

[625] Al. Cant.; Linc. Inn Rec. Adm. 1: 233.

[626] C.S.P. Dom., 1637–1638, 423.

[627] He was not a member of the Short Parliament, as stated in Complete Baronetage 2: 104.

[628] The House ordered on 1 December 1640 that a warrant for filling Wentworth's place should not be issued until "Mr. Burgin's" election should be determined. C.J. 2: 40. There is no record of a decision regarding this first attempt.

[629] C.J. 2: 53, 68; D'Ewes (N), 480, n., 481.

Burgoyne offered his bond for £500 for securing the loan in March, 1641,[630] and, despite a baronetcy for his father and knighthood for himself in July of that year, worked with the opposition group. He seems to have taken some part in the work against innovations in the churches,[631] and with the coming of war became even more active for the cause of parliament. In June, 1642, he promised to provide two horses for the defense,[632] and he joined with his father in organizing Bedfordshire for the war.[633] He was secluded in 1648, sat again in the 1656 parliament, but was able to make his peace with Charles II and continue in public life after the Restoration.[634]

Burgoyne was not married during the time he was a member of the Long Parliament. He lived until 16 September 1677,[635] and was known in his later years as a man of piety, prudence and learning.[636]

John Button (c. 1596–1665), of Buckland in Lymington, Hampshire, was M.P. for New Lymington, 1640–1648 or 1653.[637] He was the eldest son of John Button of Buckland by his wife, Eleanor, daughter of Sir Bernard Drake of Ash, Devon, and was a grandson of William Button of Alton Priory, Wilts, and a first cousin of the Wiltshire royalist, Sir William Button, Bart.[638] He probably matriculated at Exeter College, Oxford, in 1611, aged fifteen, and he entered the Middle Temple in 1613.[639] By 1624 he had succeeded to the Buckland property through the deaths without male issue of his father's younger brothers.[640] He married (1) Eleanor, daughter of Thomas South of Badesley, Hants,[641] and (2) in 1631 Amy, daughter of Sir William Oglander

of Nunwell, sister of the diarist, Sir John Oglander, and widow of William Thorne, Dean of Chichester.[642]

Button was active in Hampshire affairs throughout the reign of King Charles. He was M.P. for Lymington in 1625,[643] and later in the year was reported as able to lend £15 to the king.[644] He was a J.P. by this time and for many years afterwards was a member of the commission of the peace and of other local commissions.[645] He served as a captain at the musters in 1625 and from 1626 to 1637 was a serjeant major.[646] In 1636–1637 he was sheriff. It was evident now, however, that Button was not prepared to conform with all of the royal program. He had paid £10 for the 1627 loan only after asking to be excused from it.[647] He paid a knighthood composition of £25 in 1630.[648] While he was sheriff, he managed to collect by the end of his year most of the £6000 levy on his county, but wrote frequently to Council about the effort it required. He was still concerned with collecting the small remainder in January, 1638, under threat of being forced to appear before Council regarding the money.[649] In 1639 Button was a lieutenant colonel of the New Forest regiment, and was occupied with the levy of coat and conduct money and the assembling of troops to be sent out of the county.[650]

Elected to the Long Parliament in 1640, Button joined the side of the opponents of the crown and was particularly active when the war began. He was named to various committees in his shire, and was a colonel in the parliamentary army and active in military operations in 1643 and 1644.[651] He was ill in 1647 and 1648 and excused from attending the House, but seems to have returned when the parliament re-assembled in 1660. He died on 7 March 1665, and was buried at Lymington.[652]

Little is known of Button's financial standing. His assessment for the 1627 loan was not large, and he is not known to have contributed in a monetary way to the parliamentary cause. He belonged to the younger branch of his family, and may not have owned much land beyond his moiety of the manor of Buckland. Parliament in 1645 was granting him a weekly allowance of £4.[653]

[630] Ibid., 439.

[631] D'Ewes (C), 17, 98, 335.

[632] N. and Q., 1st Ser., 12: 360, 1855.

[633] V.C.H. Bedford 2: 44.

[634] Beds. N. and Q. 1: 154, 1886. Burgoyne's friendship with Ralph Verney (q.v.) may have helped his return to favor. Several letters written by Burgoyne to Verney are calendared in H.M.C., Seventh Report, MSS of Sir Harry Verney, Bart., 444–450, 453, 464.

[635] Ibid., 494; F.A. Blaydes, Genealogia Bedfordiensis, 283, London, 1890.

[636] Shillingfleet dedicated the 1662 edition of his Origines Sacra to Burgoyne as his patron. Add. MSS, 21,067 (Marsh's collection), fol. 100.
Other references used are Pink MSS, 307, fol. 5; F. A. Blaydes, ed., The visitations of Bedfordshire, 1566, 1582, and 1634, Harleian Society, 19: 88, 1884 (hereafter, Vis. Beds.).

[637] According to O.P.H. 9: 1, he was not secluded. Pink, however (Pink MSS, 298, fol. 709), states that he was secluded in 1648.

[638] Pink MSS, 298, fols. 707, 709, 711; Pedigrees from the visitation of Hampshire, ed. Rylands, Harleian Society, 64: 212, 1913 (hereafter, Vis. Hants.); W. Berry, County genealogies. Pedigrees of the families of the county of Hants, 34–35, London, 1833 (hereafter, Berry, Ped. Hants.).

[639] Al. Oxon.; Mid. Temp. Rec. 2: 565. He was described as the son and heir of John Button of Upavon, Wilts, Esquire, deceased.

[640] V.C.H. Hampshire 4: 647.

[641] Berry, loc. cit. Their only son, John, entered the Inner Temple in 1641. Students admitted to the Inner Temple, 311.

[642] A royalist's notebook, ed. F. Bamford, 107 and n., pedigree.

[643] M. of P. 1: 465.

[644] S.P. 16, 521/177/i; Add. MSS, 21,922, fol. 16v.

[645] C. 193/12, 13; S.P. 16/405; C. 181/4, fols. 17v, 49v; 181/5, fol. 230; C.S.P. Dom., 1636–1637, 139, 163.

[646] Add. MSS, 21,922, fols. 5, 62, 110, 151v, 166, 188, 201.

[647] Bodleian Rawl. MSS, D 666, fol. 103v.

[648] Add. MSS, 21,922, fol. 176v.

[649] Ibid., fol. 199; C.S.P. Dom., 1636–1637, 436, 469; 1637, 21–22, 172, 429; 1637–1638, 5, 166.

[650] Add. MSS, 26,781, fols. 66, 72, 89.

[651] Add. MSS, 24,860, fol. 145; H.M.C., Tenth Report 6, MSS of P. P. Bouverie, Esq., 91; G. N. Godwin, The Civil War in Hampshire, 76, 104, 218, rev. ed., Southampton, H. M. Gilbert, 1904.

[652] Pink MSS, 298, fol. 709.

[653] Pink, loc. cit.; V.C.H. Hampshire 4: 647.

Among his fellow parliament men of 1640 was John Mewes, the son of a first cousin, and Button's intimate friend, Richard Whitehead.[654]

* Edward Bysshe (c. 1615–1679), of Smallfield in Burstow, Surrey, sat for Blechingley, 1640–1653. His father, Edward Bysshe of Lincoln's Inn and of Burstow (d. between 1649 and 1656),[655] was said to have made his fortune chiefly from his practice in the Court of Wards,[656] and had been feodary in Surrey.[657] He represented Blechingley four or five times before his son stepped into his place in the Long Parliament.[658] Edward, junior, was a Lincoln's Inn barrister also (1634). In 1635 he married a sister of one of his associates there, a daughter of John Green of Essex, a Serjeant-at-Law.[659] He seems, however, to have been little known before 1640 or not to have engaged in public affairs. He was already interested in heraldry, apparently, by 1640. One of his early appointments was to the committee concerned with the earl-marshal's court and heralds' fees.[660] Bysshe was, however, an inconspicuous member of the House. He was absent for a time in January, 1644,[661] but retained his place until the end.

Practically nothing is known of his wealth. His father was still living in 1640, and Bysshe's name does not appear in the lists of loan subscribers, 1640–1642.

William Cage (1575–1656), alderman or portman of Ipswich, sat for Ipswich, 1640–1645. He was the son and heir of Edward Cage of Burstall and Ipswich, twice bailiff of the town (d. 1607), by his wife, Mary, and was christened at St. Matthew's, Ipswich, 11 August 1575.[1] He married (1), in 1597, Rabedge, daughter of Thomas Wood, whose widow was by this time Cage's stepmother, and (2), in 1636, Alice, daughter of John Lea of Coddenham and widow of Simon Bloomfield.[2] Cage at some time studied law, although apparently not at any inn of court, for he frequently acted as an

attorney for Ipswich [3] and was described by Sir Simonds D'Ewes as a "country gown man" of "reasonable abilities." [4]

Cage became a burgess of Ipswich by patrimony in 1605 and was active in town affairs from that time. He served in most of the municipal offices, chamberlain, claviger, portman, governor of the hospital, and was six or seven times bailiff.[5] He was also a J.P. and member of local commissions, and for some years captain of the Ipswich trained bands.[6] Frequently he travelled to London on town business about the renewal of its charter, the relations with the London clothworkers, the military levies, or the ship money rates and other taxes,[7] and he represented Ipswich at a meeting of Suffolk borough delegates to apportion their ship money in 1638.[8] Cage was concerned also about religious matters in the town, opposing stricter control of parishes by the bishop, and in 1637 was among the justices accused of failing to quell the riots that damaged the bishop's property in Ipswich.[9]

Parliaments had been in Cage's experience, also, for he was returned to that of 1614 at an Ipswich by-election, and served in each one thereafter until his death.[10] He spoke in 1626 for increasing the coastal defenses,[11] and in the 1628–1629 session took notes which were referred to at least once in 1640.[12] He encountered some opposition in the Long Parliament elections, but his reputation for wisdom and his puritan sympathies gained him his place.[13] He was named to the Committee of Privileges in the 1640 House, to that on recusancy and to many others,[14] and during the war, despite his

---

[654] He was an overseer of Whitehead's will. P.C.C., 24 Bruce.
[655] *Linc. Inn Rec., Black Books* **2**: 380, 411.
[656] Manning and Bray, *Surrey* **2**: 285. Aubrey asserts that the neighbors considered the Bysshe family as an upstart one, only a generation or two removed from millers and yeomen. John Aubrey, *The natural history and antiquities of the county of Surrey* **3**: 73, London, 1718–1719 (hereafter, Aubrey, *Surrey*).
[657] *C.S.P. Dom., 1637*, 193.
[658] *M. of P.* **1**: 466, 471, 478, 483; *Surrey Arch. Coll.* **39**: 60, 1931.
[659] *E.H.R.* **43**: 387–389, 1928.
[660] *C.J.* **2**: 34.
[661] *C.J.* **3**: 374.
[1] F. Haslewood's transcriptions from the register of St. Matthew's, Ipswich City Library. Cage referred in his will to his birth in this parish.
[2] Transcript of Burstall Parish Registers, Ipswich City Library; *East Anglian*, N.S., **13**: 68, 1909–1910.

[3] Bacon, *The Annalls of Ipswich*, 432; manuscript notes of the late Mr. V. B. Redstone from the Ipswich Treasurer's Accounts and Chamberlain's Accounts. Cage referred in his will to various executorships he had managed.
[4] *Autobiography* **2**: 247.
[5] Bacon, *op. cit.*, 423, 425, 434, 446, *passim;* Ipswich Corporation MSS, Assembly Book **4**, fols. 1, 4, 5; **5**, fols. 1, 5, *passim.*
[6] *Ibid.*, General Courts Book, 7 James–18 Charles I, fols. 6, 21, 60; Pink MSS, 299, fol. 378; C. 181/3, fol. 18; 181/4, fols. 102v, 151, 187v.
[7] Ipswich Corporation MSS, Assembly Book **4**, fol. 481; **5**, fols. 6, 212, 249, 257; Chamberlain's Accounts, 1627–1628, 1633–1634; Treasurer's Accounts, 1635–1637.
[8] Dunwich Corporation MSS, Minute Book, 1627–1653, fol. 96.
[9] Ipswich Corporation MSS, Assembly Book **5**, fols. 267, 277, 293; *East Anglian*, N.S., **2**: 209–210, 316–317, 1887–1888; Raven, *The history of Suffolk*, 210–211.
[10] Add. MSS, 19,093 (Davy collection), fol. 92v; *M. of P.* **1**: 453, 460, *passim.* Willis (**3**: 173) gives the names of two other members, doubtless the original ones, for the 1614 session, and *M. of P.* (**3**: App., xl) gives but one name. Cage's M.I. states that he served in eight parliaments.
[11] *E.H.R.* **17**: 736, 1902.
[12] *C.J.* **2**: 7.
[13] D'Ewes, who apparently favored Cage's opponent, perhaps because he doubted Cage's eligibility to be returned while he was serving as bailiff (D'Ewes [C], 242), remarked that, although Cage had abilities, "sure he is not the only wise man in Ipswich." *Autobiography* **2**: 247.
[14] *C.J.* **2**: 21, 29, 113; D'Ewes (N), 397; Pink MSS, 299, fol. 378.

years, worked actively for the cause of parliament. He died on 4 November 1645, and was buried at Burstall.[15]

Cage was a well-to-do townsman, owning property in Ipswich and the county, including a country house at Burstall, and was reputed to enjoy, with his wives' estates, an income of between £400 and £500 yearly.[16] His pledge of £300 for the Irish venture in 1642, however, was largely an investment for his son-in-law.[17]

James Campbell (1615–1659), of London and Essex, was M.P. for Grampound, Cornwall, 1640–1648. He came of a family of ironmongers who had made their fortune in London and had filled high offices there. His grandfather, Sir Thomas, was Lord Mayor in 1609–1610; his uncle, Sir James (1576–1642), was Lord Mayor twenty years later, was a master of the Ironmongers' Company, and a member of the East India, Virginia, French and Eastland Companies. The M.P.'s father was Robert Campbell (d. 1638), second son of Sir Thomas, who was a master of the Ironmongers' Company, and alderman and sheriff of London. Robert's wife, Alice, daughter of William Willington of Clehanger, Herefordshire,[18] married after his death the courtier, Sir Edward Savage. When she died in October, 1640, Savage brought suit against her executors for a greater share of the estate than she had assigned him by her will.[19] James, eldest son of Robert and Alice, and one of his mother's executors, was born in 1615,[20] matriculated at Christ's College, Oxford, 24 February 1632, and was student at Lincoln's Inn in 1634.[21] On 8 November 1638 he married Theophila, daughter of John, first Baron Mohun of Okehampton, Devon,[22] and two days later succeeded to his father's estate. Afterwards he resided in London and at Woodford, Essex.

Campbell served in none but the Long Parliament, and no doubt owed his election in Cornwall to his father-in-law. He was not a prominent member, but made use of his parliamentary privilege to gain a stay in the lawsuit started that year by his stepfather.[23]

He offered his security for the loan in March, 1641,[24] and remained loyal to parliament even though Mohun was a Cavalier. He was named to various parliamentary committees for Essex during the war, and held his seat in the House until the purge of 1648.[25] He died in December, 1659, and was buried on 23 December at Barking, Essex.[26] Letters of administration were granted on 18 July 1660 to his widow.[27]

Campbell's family was very wealthy. Robert was not only his father's heir, but was the recipient also of part of the estate of his uncle, Sir James Campbell. The latter, willed him at his death in 1642 £2000 and a manor.[28] His father's lands included a manor in Essex and one in Surrey.[29] And there was no doubt considerably more estate in money value, for the portion left to James' five sisters came to at least £4000.[30]

Henry Campion (born *c.* 1586), of Newton Valence, Hampshire, and of Putney, Surrey, sat for the borough of Lymington, Hants, of which he was lord, from 1640 until 1648 or 1653.[31] He was a grandson of a prominent London citizen, Henry Campion (d. 1588), and the eldest son and heir of the latter's second son, Abraham (d. 1611), who was a wealthy clothworker of the city. His mother was Helen, daughter of the London merchant, Richard Duffield. He was a cousin of the royalist Campions of Combwell, Kent.[32] Henry was born about 1586, and at the death of his father in 1611 inherited the manors of Newton Valence and Old and New Lymington in Hampshire, some properties in Surrey and Kent, and £3000 in money.[33] He was admitted to the Middle Temple in 1605 and held a chamber there until about 1613.[34] Although he and his younger brothers and sisters seem to have been well

---

[15] Bacon, *op. cit.*, 443, 540. Cage's will, dated 15 September 1645, with a codicil of 1 October, was proved 4 March 1645/6. P.C.C., 37 Twisse.

[16] According to his will, Cage's second wife's lands were worth £100 a year. One estimate of the rentals from his own estate alone was £300, but others make it higher. Add. MSS, 33,858 (Muskett's collection), fols. 44v–45; 15,520 (Davy), fols. 12v, 39.

[17] With Bedingfield Cage pledged £700, of which £400 was the former's, and £250 was for Cage's son-in-law. *C.S.P. Ireland, Adventurers*, 241.

[18] G. E. Cokayne, *The lord mayors and sheriffs of the city of London, 1601–1625*, 41–43, London, 1897 (hereafter, Cokayne, *Lord Mayors*); Brown, *Genesis of the U.S.* 2: 842.

[19] *C.S.P. Dom.*, *1640–1641*, 190.

[20] I.P.M., Robert Campbell, C. 142/580/100; *Complete Baronetage* 3: 184.

[21] *Al. Oxon.*; *Linc. Inn Rec. Adm.* 1: 223.

[22] Cokayne, *loc. cit.*; Vivian, *Vis. Cornwall*, 326.

[23] *C.J.* 2: 53, 57.

[24] D'Ewes (N), 435, n., 438, n. (439). The name appears in one list as "Sir James Cauldell," doubtless because a diarist confused the nephew with the uncle. In September, 1642, "Mr. Cambell" promised to lend £500 gratis for the defense. *C.J.* 2: 778.

[25] Pink MSS, 307, fol. 197; *O.P.H.* 9: * 20.

[26] Cokayne, *loc. cit.*

[27] P.C.C., Act Book, 1660, fol. 81v.

[28] Abstract of the will of Sir James Campbell. J. Nicoll, *Some account of the worshipful company of ironmongers*, 539–542, London, 1866.

[29] I.P.M. cited above.

[30] Of this James received part on account of the deaths of two unmarried sisters before 1645. London Corporation MSS, Orphans' Leger 1627–1647, fol. 279; Rep. 52, fols. 126v–127.

[31] *M. of P.* 1: 493; Pink MSS, 299, fol. 384.

[32] J. Comber, *Sussex Genealogies* 3, Lewes: 33–34, Cambridge, Heffer, 1931–1933; *Vis. Kent, 1619*, 95–96; Pink MSS, *loc. cit.*

[33] I.P.M., Abraham Campion, C. 142/321/102; will of Abraham Campion, P.C.C., 28 Wood. Abraham Campion had been one of twenty-one Londoners assessed £60 each for a subsidy shortly before his death (Lansd. MSS, 165, fol. 229v), and about the year of his death he petitioned Council for the payment of more than £7200 due him from the king and the prince. *C.S.P. Dom., 1611–1618*, 106.

[34] *Mid. Temp. Rec.* 2: 453, 463, 560; London Corporation MSS, Common Serjeants' Book, 1, fol. 423.

provided for by their father, Henry before long became deeply involved in accounts with the Aldermen's Court of London concerning the portions for the younger children and the debts of a brother to the city. From 1624 until 1632 most of Henry's Hampshire lands were under the control of trustees for the city for the collection of interest owed by his brother. Henry was reduced, according to the London records, to "great poverty," and "bereft of his whole patrimony and means of maintenance of himself, his wife, and many children." At length with the aid of relatives Henry made a settlement with the city in 1632 and recovered at least partial control over his properties.[35] The wife to whom the reports refer was Anne, daughter of John Willet of London.[36]

Henry Campion was elected to the 1621 parliament for Lymington,[37] but doubtless his financial difficulties prevented further service of that kind for some years. He may have been an agent of some sort for the Earl of Northumberland later.[38] His name does not appear among the lists of local commissions. But by 1640 his fortunes seem to have improved, and in 1642 he promised to furnish one horse for the defense.[39] He was a parliamentarian, but was not active in the Commons. During the war he was named to several parliamentary committees for Surrey and Hampshire, and he kept his seat in the Commons until 1648, or possibly 1653.[40] He seems to have died in or before 1659.[41]

* Arthur Capel (1604–1649), of Hadham, Hertfordshire, was M.P. for his county from 1640 until he was raised to the peerage, 6 August 1641. He was the only son of Sir Henry Capel of Raines Hall, Essex, by Theodosia, daughter of Sir Edward Montagu of Boughton, Northamptonshire, and was born 20 February and baptized 11 March 1604 at Hadham Parva.[42] He matriculated at Queen's College, Cambridge, during Lent, 1619,[43] having as a fellow student there Sir Henry Slingsby (q.v.), and in 1632 succeeded to his family estates.[44] He succeeded also to responsi-

bilities, being a member of the local commissions of oyer and terminer and of the peace.[45] He seems not to have been among the resisters of ship money,[46] but he excused himself in 1639 from contributing towards the king's northern journey.[47] He went with his colleague, Lytton, in September, 1640, to carry to the king at York their county's petition against grievances,[48] and was evidently accounted one of the reform group when he was elected to the Long Parliament. Soon after the opening it was Capel's initiative which led to the pledging by the wealthy members of their securities for the loan.[49]

Capel himself was one of the wealthiest members of the House, indeed, one of the wealthiest commoners of England, holding "a very noble fortune of his own by descent, and a fair addition to it by his marriage." [50] His lands lay in at least ten counties from East Anglia to Somerset, and their total rents were estimated about 1650 to be above £7000.[51] He promised to furnish 100 horses for the king in June, 1642,[52] and is said to have incurred debts amounting to £20,000 for the royalist cause.[53]

Capel was through his mother a nephew of Sir Sydney Montagu and a cousin of Edward and George Montagu and Sir John Wray. He was a kinsman and friend of Sir Thomas Barrington,[54] and through his wife was connected with Sir Edward Alford.

* Alexander Carew (1609–1644), of Antony, Cornwall, was M.P. for his county from 1640 until he was disabled for planning to desert the cause, 4 September 1643.[55] He was among those created baronet in 1641. The only surviving son of Richard Carew of Antony (d. 1643), he was admitted to the Middle Temple on 18 March 1628, and was still there in May, 1629.[56] He married in 1631 Jane, daughter of Robert Rolle of Heanton, Devon, becoming a brother-in-law of Sir Samuel Rolle (q.v.) and of John Rolle, the merchant

---

[35] London Corporation MSS, Rep. 38, fols. 188v–190; Rep. 43, fol. 292v; Rep. 44, fols. 65, 99; Rep. 47, fols. 33v–35v.

[36] *Surrey Arch. Coll.* 10, Campion pedigree, 1887–1891.

[37] *M. of P.* 1: 453.

[38] Hugh Potter (q.v.), an agent of the earl's before 1640, referred in his will of January, 1659, to a fellow servant, Henry Campion. P.C.C., 53 Laud.

[39] *N. and Q.*, 1st Ser., 12: 360, 1855.

[40] Add. MSS, 24,860, fol. 145; Godwin, *The Civil War in Hampshire,* 104; Pink MSS, 299, fol. 384. Pink thought that Campion was secluded in 1648, but it is indicated in *O.P.H.* (9: 1) that he sat until 1653.

[41] Pink, *loc. cit.*

[42] Robert Clutterbuck, *The history and antiquities of the county of Hertford* 1: 244, London, 1815–1827 (hereafter, Clutterbuck, *Herts*). Clutterbuck used parish registers for his dates. *D.N.B.* dates Capel's birth, however, as "1610?."

[43] *Al. Cant.*

[44] His father died in 1622, and his grandfather, whose heir he then became, died in 1632. Clutterbuck, *Herts* 1: 243.

[45] C. 181/5, fols. 17, 72, *passim;* C. 193/13; S.P. 16/405.

[46] He paid on several estates in Essex, 1635–1636 (S.P. 16, 358/11, 30).

[47] Rushworth 3: 912.

[48] Add. MSS, 11,045, fol. 121v; D'Ewes, *Autobiography* 2: 242.

[49] D'Ewes (N), 51 and n.

[50] Clarendon, *Rebellion* 4: 510 and n. The compounding commissioners allowed Lady Capel £1,000 a year as her jointure from her husband's sequestered estates.

[51] Clutterbuck, *Herts* 1: 228, 237, 335; 3: 411, *passim;* H.M.C., *Various collections* 7, MSS of the Earl of Essex, 346–347; D. Warrand, *Hertfordshire families,* 93, London, Constable, 1907; *Cal. Com. Comp.,* 1931–1934.

[52] *Somerset Arch. Proc.* 14 (2): 53, 1867.

[53] Alfred Kingston, *Hertfordshire during the great Civil War,* 111 and n., London, 1894 (hereafter, Kingston, *Herts. during the Civil War*).

[54] Eg. MSS, 2646, fol. 140.

[55] *C.J.* 3: 227.

[56] *Mid. Temp. Rec.* 2: 730, 748. Clarendon (*Rebellion* 3: 236) referred to Carew's good education and his knowledge of the law.

(*q.v.*).[57] Although his father was still alive, Carew must in 1640 have been in possession of certain parts of the family estates, for he offered his bond for £1000 for the loan in March, 1641.[58] When he made his will in December, 1644, he mentioned lands in Cornwall from which he hoped to have portions of £500 raised for each of his children.[59] He was a man of means, apparently, although Clarendon asserted that Carew's policy of early cooperation with parliament was followed for "no other motives than of popularity and interests."[60]

Richard Erisey was a cousin of Carew, and Hele was a relative by marriage.

Sir William Carnaby (*c.* 1593–1645), of Thernham, Northumberland, was M.P. for Morpeth, 1640–26 August 1642. The descendant of a family located in Northumberland in the mid-fourteenth century, he was born about 1593, the elder son of William Carnaby of Langley and Thernham (d. 1622 or 1623), by his wife, Mabel, daughter of Cuthbert Carnaby of the Aydon line of the family. He was knighted on 10 August 1619, and sometime before 1636 married Jane, daughter of Sir Robert Bindloss of Barwick Hall, Lancastershire.[61] Carnaby was a D.L. in his county by 1625,[62] and served many years as a justice and a member of various commissions in the northern counties.[63] He was sheriff of Northumberland in 1636, and seems to have collected his quota of ship money[64] vigorously. Several suits were brought against him in Exchequer later for distresses he had levied upon the lands of those who were slow to pay.[65] He had sat, meanwhile, in several parliaments, in 1624 for Morpeth, in 1628 for Northumberland, and in the spring of 1640 for Marlborough, Wiltshire.[66] He was active in the summer of 1640 in plans for the defense of his castle.[67]

Sir William was not a prominent member of the Long Parliament, but was named fairly frequently to committee work on such lesser matters as the postmasters or the law concerning salt marshes, and to the committee on the Court of Wards, and certain aspects of the charges against Strafford.[68] In March, 1641, Carnaby joined with his colleague, Fenwick, to pledge £500 for the new loan,[69] but he voted against Strafford's attainder,[70] and when war threatened was among the first to ride away to the north to prepare for it.[71] He was disabled on 26 August 1642,[72] served under Newcastle in the royalist army, and withdrew to France after Marston Moor. Carnaby died in Paris in October, 1645, and was buried near there.

Carnaby owned numerous properties in Northumberland, having added to his family inheritance by purchase. Those listed by his heiress at compounding were declared to be worth some £365 annually before the war.[73] Carnaby was assessed £2000 in 1644,[74] but the fine on his estate, set first at $\frac{1}{6}$, £750, then increased to £1490, was confirmed in 1650 at the original figure.[75]

Carnaby was a kinsman through his maternal grandmother of the Widdringtons. Sir Thomas Widdrington, though his politics differed from Carnaby's, was his daughter's guardian.[76]

* Lucius Cary, second **Viscount Falkland** (1610?–1643), of Great Tew, Oxfordshire, was M.P. for Newport, Isle of Wight, 1640–22 September, 1642. He was Newport's member in the Short Parliament, also.[77] Having been educated in the universities of Ireland and England, Cary was admitted to Lincoln's Inn after he returned to live in England. His admission was granted on 18 January 1638 at the request of William Lenthall (*q.v.*).[78] He was reported as a ship money defaulter on three properties in Hertfordshire in 1637, the bailiffs declaring that they dared not distrain for fear of being sued.[79] He seems to have had little direct connection with Hampshire, his properties lying chiefly in the counties of Hertford, Oxford, and Kent.[80] His father's estates, which in 1630 were estimated to be worth nearly £57,500, with some £2700 a year income, were encumbered with debts said to be over £3000 a

---

[57] *Complete Baronetage* 2: 126.

[58] D'Ewes (N), 439. The name is spelled "Cary," as it frequently appears in the *Journals*.

[59] Will dated 20 December and proved 28 December 1644. P.C.C., 12 Rivers.

[60] *Rebellion* 3: 236.

[61] *History of Northumberland*, Northumberland County History Committee, 10: opp. p. 408; Marshall, *Vis. Northumberland*, 18–19.

[62] S.P. 16, 7/74; 66/86.

[63] C. 193/12, 13; S.P. 16/405; *C.S.P. Dom., 1635*, 370, 510; C. 181/5, fols. 275, 324.

[64] Royal Hist. Soc., *Trans.*, 3rd Ser., 4: 159, 1910; *C.S.P. Dom., 1635–1636*, 461.

[65] *Arch. Ael.*, 3rd Ser., 4: 32, 1908.

[66] *M. of P.* 1: 459, 476; Bean, *Northern Counties*, 552. A representative of the Scottish Covenanters admitted having talked with Carnaby at a London theatre in the spring of 1640, though not about parliament. *C.S.P. Dom., 1640*, 140.

[67] *Ibid.*, 579.

[68] *C.J.* 2: 73, 79, 82, 87.

[69] D'Ewes (N), 439, n.

[70] Verney, 58. His quarrel with Peard, referred to on 23 March (*C.J.* 2: 111–112), possibly arose out of their disagreement about Strafford.

[71] *Yorks. Arch. Jour.* 7: 370, 1882.

[72] *C.J.* 2: 738.

[73] S.P. 23/214/760. Mrs. Jane Carnaby was rated in 1663 for £416 on most of these properties. *History of Northumberland* 5: 333, n.

[74] Estates in Yorkshire and Durham, as well as in Northumberland, were included in the assessment. *Cal. Com. Adv. Money*, 422.

[75] *Cal. Com. Comp.*, 2046.

[76] *Ibid.*

[77] *M. of P.* 1: 483, 493; *C.J.* 2: 777.

[78] *Rec. Linc. Inn Adm.* 1: 234.

[79] S.P. 16, 376/106.

[80] Clutterbuck, *Herts.* 1: 127; Hasted, *Kent* 10: 278; Add. MSS, 29,974, fols. 144, 148; *D.N.B.*

year.[81] It seems reasonable to accept his statement that from the "noble fortune" of perhaps £2000 a year which he inherited from his maternal grandfather, he had by 1638 paid as much for the support of his mother and to his father's creditors as he had for his own family's maintenance.[82] His assessment of only £300 by parliament in 1643 indicates that his wealth was not then considered great. Yet he was reported to have lent to king £1500 by 1648.[83]

Falkland's famous coterie at Burford and Tew in the period before 1640 included such fellow parliament men as Hyde, Sidney Godolphin, Waller, and Rainsford.[84]

Richard Catelyn, or **Cateline** (*c.* 1584–1662), of Lakenham and Kirby Cane, Norfolk, was M.P. for Norwich, 1640–22 January 1644. A grandson of Richard Catelyn, Serjeant-at-Law, M.P., and commissioner for trying the rebels in the time of Mary Tudor, he was the son and heir of Thomas Catelyn of Lakenham (d. 1636) by Judith, daughter of Edward Ellington of Theydon Bois, Essex. One of his great-grandfathers had been a Norwich alderman. Richard was born about 1584 and in 1602 entered Lincoln's Inn.[85] He married first Mary, daughter of Sir Robert Houghton, who died in March, 1629/30, and second, in 1631, Dorothy, daughter of Sir Henry Neville of Billingsbere, Berkshire.[86]

Catelyn's residence near Norwich kept him in touch with local affairs. He had been interested in the county election held at Norwich in January, 1624,[87] but had never been elected to parliament before 1640. About 1630 he was an associate of Miles Corbet in a group of trustees for a small Norwich church with allegedly nonconformist ministers,[88] and in 1631 he was named a commissioner, possibly as a J.P., to secure the city's answer to complaints exhibited against certain aldermen by Sir Robert Heath.[89] His election to parliament in October, 1640, however, was contrary to the Norwich custom of choosing only resident freemen as their members, and was accomplished by a special group anxious to have his services. The perplexed sheriff returned a prominent alderman as alternate, should the House not

recognize Catelyn's election, but the Committee of Privileges decided promptly that he should be seated.[90]

Catelyn was named to some minor committees in the early weeks, and offered his bond for £1000 for the loan in November, 1640.[91] He was at his home in July, 1641, however,[92] and though he was named to the county committee on scandalous ministers in 1642, he was probably absent much of the time during that year and the next, and was disabled for deserting the House, 22 January 1644.[93] Pleading ill health and family cares as his excuse, Catelyn petitioned in 1645 to compound, and was discharged from sequestration in April, 1647.[94] He died in his seventy-ninth year and was buried at Kirby Cane, 24 October 1662.

He was probably a wealthy man, having inherited various large properties and acquired others by marriage.[95] His composition papers, listing only part of his lands with rents totalling some £453 a year,[96] do not present a true picture of his position.[97]

Sir Richard Cave (d. 1645), courtier, agent for the Queen of Bohemia, was elected for Lichfield, Staffordshire, 12 August 1641, after Devereux died, and was disabled as a royalist, 30 August 1642.[98] He has been identified as the son of Thomas Cave of St. Helen's, Worcestershire, who came of yeoman stock.[99] But he may have had some connection with the old Cave family of Stanford, Northamptonshire, and of Leicestershire, who were intermarried with families in Staffordshire and Worcestershire. Cave was an intimate of Sir Thomas Roe, who was connected by marriage with the Caves of Stanford and was said to have been elected once at Tamworth in Staffordshire through their influence.[100] Cave's origins were not necessarily hum-

[81] Add. MSS, 29,974, fols. 144, 148; Clarendon, *Rebellion* 3: 181.

[82] *Ibid.* 3: 179; *C.S.P. Dom., 1636–1637,* xli–xlii, 230.

[83] *Cal. Com. Adv. Money,* 190, 999.

[84] For a recent discussion of Falkland and his circle, see Kurt Weber, *Lucius Cary, second Viscount Falkland,* New York, Columbia Univ. Press, 1940.

[85] *Linc. Inn Rec. Adm.* 1: 134.

[86] Norwich Public Library MSS, Cokayne's Norfolk Parish Registers, 2: 164. Sir Henry Berkeley (*q.v.*) married a sister of Dorothy.

[87] *The official papers of Sir Nathaniel Bacon,* 39–41, Camden Soc., 1915.

[88] S.P. 16, 531/134.

[89] Norwich Corp. MSS, Folio Assembly Book, 1613–1642, fol. 265.

[90] *C.J.* 2: 22; D'Ewes (N), 5 and n. Norwich passed an ordinance on 28 October, following the election, making it a punishable offense at future parliamentary elections to vote for any one not a freeman at the time of election. Norwich Corp. MSS, Folio Assembly Book, 1613–1642, fol. 354.

[91] *C.J.* 2: 44, 61; D'Ewes (N), 52.

[92] Norwich Corp. MSS, Folio Assembly Book, 1613–1642, fol. 363.

[93] *C.J.* 2: 763, 845, 918; 3: 374. The Norwich officials wrote to him about June, 1643, reminding him of his public duties, even though they might be tedious and prejudicial to his private affairs. Add. MSS, 22,619 (papers relating to Norwich), fol. 76.

[94] *Cal. Com. Comp.,* 113, 942.

[95] F. Blomefield, *Topographical history of the county of Norfolk* 8: 31, London, 1805–1810 (hereafter, Blomefield, *Norfolk*); Add. MSS, 19,092 (Davy's collection), fols. 382v, 383v; *H.M.C., Fourth Report,* House of Lords MSS, 34.

[96] S.P. 23/72/606. His Lakenham estate, unlisted there, was valued at over £1000 in 1657. Norwich Public Library MSS, Clayton MSS, 101.

[97] Other references on Catelyn are Pink MSS, 299, fol. 421; *East Anglian,* N.S., **10**: 361–363, 1903–1904.

[98] *M. of P.* 1: 493; *C.J.* 2: 744.

[99] W. C. Metcalfe, ed., *The visitation of the county of Worcester, 1682–1683,* 29, Exeter, 1883; Wedgwood, *Staff. Parl. Hist.* 2: 85.

[100] Wedgwood, *op. cit.* 2: 19.

ble.[101] Of his early career nothing is known, but he was probably in the service of the Elector Palatine before 1636, for on the occasion of the latter's visit to Cambridge that year one Richard Cave was created M.A. by the university.[102] He was a knight by 1637, and between that time and 1640 was acting as the Elector's agent sometimes at Westminster and sometimes abroad.[103] D'Ewes described him on the occasion of his maiden speech on 28 August 1641 as the agent of the Queen of Bohemia.[104] Lloyd later termed him a "hardy courtier." [105]

Cave was disappointed in plans to get a seat, possibly for Windsor, for the opening of the Long Parliament.[106] Seated for Lichfield by 28 August, he spoke several times before the recess on matters of foreign policy. His speech on 31 August introduced a plan for organizing a new stock company for the West Indies, to be headed by the Prince Elector, as a means of attacking the King of Spain.[107] Cave was interested in August and September in the possibility of succeeding Sir William Berkeley as ambassador to Constantinople, but he seems to have stayed in England. He married during the recess.[108] Sir Richard served on the recess committee,[109] and during the winter months of 1641–1642 was named to several committees concerned with defense plans.[110] With the coming of war, however, he joined the king and was promptly disabled.[111]

Charles Cavendish, Lord Mansfield (c. 1626–1659), heir apparent of the Earl of Newcastle, was M.P. for East Retford, 1640–22 January 1644, and probably the youngest member of the House, having been born possibly as late as 1626.[112] He was the third but eldest surviving son of William Cavendish, Earl (later Duke) of Newcastle and privy councillor, the royalist commander, by his first wife, Elizabeth, daughter and sole heir of William Bassett of Blore, Staffordshire, and was the heir apparent to great wealth.[113] He was admitted to Gray's Inn, 18 May 1641,[114] being already an M.P.

With several of noble blood Mansfield was named to attend one conference with the Lords, 10 November 1640, but no other note of his activity in the House remains. He was granted leave of absence, 10 August 1641, was not permitted by his father to return again to Westminster, and was formally disabled as a royalist, 22 January 1644.[115] According to his petition to the compounding commissioners in 1647, Mansfield was in his father's company during the war and in his later sojourn in Europe, but was in the care of tutors and did no fighting.[116] He was cleared of the charges of delinquency in 1654,[117] and died in 1659. He was unmarried in 1640.

* **William Cawley** (1602–1666?), M.P. for Midhurst, 1640–1653, the regicide, was the son and heir of a well-to-do brewer and mayor of Chichester, John Cawley (d. 1621), by his second wife.[118] As his father had wished, he studied at Oxford (Hart Hall) and Gray's Inn (entered 1622).[119] Whether he turned again to his father's business as a brewer is not clear, although various writers, following Noble, have called him a brewer.[120] When he paid his knighthood fine in 1630 he was listed as "of Chichester, gent." [121] Before 1640 he added to the lands outside of Chichester which his

[101] The pedigrees of Cave of Stanford, however (Harl. MSS, 1233, fol. 114v; *Vis. Leic., 1619*, 126–128), reveal no Richard Cave living in 1640. One Worcestershire connection of the family was Sir Rowland Berkeley, a royalist (*V.C.H. Worcestershire* 4: 257, 259).

[102] *Al. Cant.*

[103] The *Calendars of State Papers* covering the years 1637–1640; Harl. MSS, 6988, fol. 107.

[104] D'Ewes (B), 573.

[105] *Memoires*, 671.

[106] *C.S.P. Dom., 1640–1641*, 121, 248.

[107] D'Ewes (B), 573, 586, 604, 644.

[108] *C.S.P. Dom., 1641–1643*, 99, 127, 134.

[109] *Ibid., 1641–1643*, 135; *C.J.* 2: 288.

[110] *C.J.* 2: 361; Pink MSS, 299, fol. 423.

[111] For his later career, see Wedgwood, *op. cit.* 2: 85.

[112] He declared he was only fifteen in 1642, and still in the care of tutors (*Cal. Com. Comp.*, 1799). The accuracy of his statement has been doubted (W. D. Pink in *N. and Q.*, 7th Ser., 11: 501–502, 1891), but 1626 is accepted as the approximate date of his birth by Cokayne (*Complete Peerage* 6: 23 and n.). His parents were married in 1618 (*The letters of John Chamberlain* 2: 174), an elder brother, Charles, died in infancy about April, 1620, and another, William, died in March, 1637 (1637/8?). A younger brother, Henry, was born in 1630 or 1631. Glover, *Derbyshire* 2: 122; *H.M.C., Thirteenth Report* 2, MSS of the Duke of Portland, 118, 122, 124; Arthur Collins, *Historical collections of the noble families of Cavendish, . . . ,* 45, London, 1752; *N. and Q.*, cited above.

[113] Newcastle was reputedly one of the wealthiest peers in England, owning large estates in Notts, Derbyshire and Yorkshire worth £22,000 a year, and having acquired with his wife lands said to be worth £2400 a year, as well as a jointure of £800 yearly and over £6000 in money. His rents for a third of the year, 1640–1641, were almost £5000, and his losses during the war were stated to be over £733,000. Collins, *op. cit.*, 25; *Derbyshire Archaeological and Natural History Society Journal* 11: 47, n., 1887; 13: 2–7, 165–166, 1891 (hereafter, *Derbys. Arch. Jour.*); *Yorks. Arch. Jour.* 23: 354, 1915; *H.M.C., Thirteenth Report* 2, MSS of the Duke of Portland, 133.

[114] *Gray's Inn Adm. Reg.*, 230.

[115] *C.J.* 2: 25, 249; 3: 374.

[116] *Cal. Com. Comp.*, 1799; *N. and Q.*, 7th Ser., 7: 501, 1889. Lloyd's comment (*Memoires*, 672, n.) that Mansfield held "an eminent command" under his father seems to be erroneous.

[117] *H.M.C., Thirteenth Report* 2, MSS of the Duke of Portland, 141–142; *C.S.P. Dom., 1653–1654*, 385.

[118] W. Berry, *County genealogies: Pedigrees of the families of the county of Sussex*, 284, London, 1830 (hereafter, Berry, *Sussex Genealogies*). Cawley's death occurred on "6 Jan. 1666," according to an inscription (*Sussex Arch. Coll.* 34: 36, 1886). It should probably be read as 1666/7. It appears as 1666 in *D.N.B.*

[119] *Sussex Arch. Coll.* 34: 24, 1886; *Al. Oxon.*; *Gray's Inn Adm. Reg.*, 165.

[120] *Regicides* 1: 136; Thomas-Stanford, *Sussex in the great Civil War*, 16; *Sussex Arch. Coll.* 5: 31, 1852.

[121] *Ibid.* 16: 50, 1864. He was termed "esquire" in 1628. *M. of P.* 1: 478.

father had left him, some of them being bought from Sir Thomas Bowyer (q.v.).[122] Not all of his enlarged estate, therefore, can be traced to sequestration proceedings. He does not seem to have been wealthy, enough, however, to offer security for the loans, 1640–1641. His estate brought £2100 when it was sold in 1663.[123]

Except for his service as M.P. for Chichester in 1628 and as a commissioner for the second subsidy of 1640,[124] nothing is known of Cawley's political experience before the Long Parliament. He won his seat there after a contest with the learned churchman, Dr. Richard Chaworth, Chancellor of the Diocese of London and later of Chichester.[125] The early reports on the contest threatened a decision against Cawley, but on 15 February 1641 he was declared duly elected.[126]

Of Cawley's wife, Catherine, married sometime before 1640,[127] we know only that she died in 1650.[128] A William Cawley, Esquire, and his wife, Mary, were living in 1655.[129]

Charles Cecil, Viscount Cranborne (1619–1660), M.P. for Hertford, 1640–1653, was the eldest surviving son and heir apparent of William Cecil, second Earl of Salisbury (d. 1668), by his wife, Catherine, daughter of Thomas Howard, Earl of Suffolk. He was born in 1619, was created K.B. at the coronation of King Charles,[130] and was admitted in 1634 to St. John's, Cambridge.[131] On 2 April 1639 young Lord Cranborne married at St. Martin's in the Fields Diana, younger daughter and coheiress of James (Maxwell), Earl of Dirletoun, a marriage which greatly increased his fortune but brought the charge of avarice upon both his father and him.[132] The next year Cranborne was holding his first public offices, being named a J.P. for St. Albans,[133] and sharing with his father the lord lieutenancy of Hertfordshire. He journeyed with others of the court in April, 1640, to greet the Spanish ambassador at Greenwich.[134]

Cranborne's election to both parliaments of 1640 for

Hertford[135] was the result doubtless of his father's position as chief steward of the borough and lord of the manor.[136] In the Long Parliament he worked with the opposition forces and in 1642, when his father hesitated to execute the militia ordinance, was named sole lieutenant for his county. He served in the shire part of the time during the war, but eventually returned to work in parliament.[137] He died during his father's lifetime, early in December, 1660.[138]

Although he was the heir apparent in 1640 to numerous properties in Hertfordshire, Dorset, Wilts, and other counties, and entitled through his wife to many more,[139] Lord Cranborne was being sued by creditors in 1641, chiefly for his wife's extravagances.[140]

Relatives of Cranborne's among the 1640 parliament men were his younger brother, Robert, an uncle, Sir Robert Howard, a brother-in-law, Lord Lisle, and his first cousins, Lord Andover and Thomas Howard.[141]

Robert Cecil (fl. 1634–1660), of Hertfordshire, younger son of the Earl of Salisbury, was M.P. for Old Sarum, 1640–1653.[142] Born some time after 1619, he was the second surviving son of William, Earl of Salisbury, and a younger brother of Lord Cranborne (born 1619), the Hertford M.P. (q.v.). With the latter he was admitted to St. John's, Cambridge, in October, 1634,[143] but nothing else is known of him before his election to the Long Parliament. Since his father owned many Wiltshire properties, including Old Sarum Castle and an interest in its rotten borough,[144] his return for that constituency was a matter of family politics. He was a parliamentarian like his father and brother, and served in the army and in wartime committees for Hertfordshire.[145] He probably did not marry until after 1640. His wife, Catherine Hopton, was buried at Hatfield on 7 August 1657.[146] He survived

[122] Sussex Rec. Soc. **14**: 47, 1912; Cal. Com. Comp., 834.

[123] Sussex Arch. Coll. **34**: 37, 1886.

[124] Ibid. **9**: 105, 1857.

[125] Al. Oxon.

[126] C.J. **2**: 63, 86.

[127] Cawley's son, William, entered the Inner Temple in 1645. Students admitted to the Inner Temple, 317.

[128] Berry, loc. cit.; Add. MSS, 5699, fol. 181.

[129] This may, however, have been the M.P.'s son. Sussex Rec. Soc. **19**: 43, 1914.

[130] Clutterbuck, Herts **2**: 341; Warrand, Hertfordshire Families, 117.

[131] Al. Cant.

[132] Her dower was said to be £18,000, £4000 in jewels and £800 a year in English lands, with others in Scotland. C.S.P. Dom., 1638–1639, 622.

[133] C. 181/5, fol. 370.

[134] C.S.P. Dom., 1640, 6, 658; H.M.C., Fourth Report, House of Lords MSS, 27.

[135] M. of P. **1**: 481, n., 489; Willis **3**: 232.

[136] Clutterbuck, Herts **2**: 141, 146.

[137] Kingston, Herts. during the Civil War, 11, 15, 28, 152.

[138] H.M.C., Fifth Report, MSS of the Duke of Sutherland, 158.

[139] Clutterbuck, Herts **1**: 134; **2**: 141, passim; **3**: 503; Lysons, Mag. Brit. **1**: 499; C.S.P. Dom., 1611–1618, 412; Cal. Com. Comp., 2427. The Exchequer receipts indicate that his father had lent to the king £9000 between December, 1639, and June, 1640. S.P. 16, 453/74.

[140] The House considered on 31 August 1641 lifting Cranborne's protection as an M.P. on account of his creditors' claims. He sought to show, however, that the debts were chiefly his wife's; in spite of an allowance of £400 a year for her personal expenses, she had in a year and a half incurred a debt of £5000 or £6000. The sympathies of the House seemed to lie with the husband. Add. MSS, 11,045, fol. 140.

[141] In addition to the above references, see Complete Peerage **7**: 41.

[142] M. of P. **1**: 496; O.P.H. **9**: 8.

[143] Al. Cant. See also Charles Cecil, Lord Cranborne.

[144] Hoare, Wilts. **4** (2): 50; **6**: 603.

[145] Pink MSS, 299, fol. 463; Kingston, Herts. during the Civil War, 11, 28.

[146] T. Blore, The history and antiquities of the county of Rutland **1**: 25, Stanford, 1811 (hereafter, Blore, Rutland).

to return with the Rump just before the Restoration,[147] but the date of his death is not known. It was sometime before 20 November 1707.[148]

Cecil probably had no independent income in 1640, since his father and elder brother were living then.

William Chadwell (1614–1680), a lawyer of Lincoln's Inn and of Bradwell (Broadwell), Gloucestershire, sat for Michael, Cornwall, 1640–22 January 1644. He was the son and heir apparent of William Chadwell of Bradwell by his wife, Dorothy Hodge, and was born on 12 March and baptized on 20 March 1614 at Bradwell. His father was said by one authority to have been a yeoman,[149] but his father's older brother was described in 1613 as a gentleman,[150] and the M.P. was admitted to Oxford as a gentleman's son. He matriculated at Exeter College, Oxford, 2 December 1631, and was graduated B.A. in 1632. During the Civil War the university conferred on him the degree of D.C.L.[151] Chadwell was admitted to Lincoln's Inn in January, 1632, and he was called to the bar there in February, 1640.[152] He was probably a friend of the Arundell family, two of whom entered Lincoln's Inn when he did, and quite possibly he owed his two elections of 1640 at Michael, which was often an Arundell borough, to their influence. The Short Parliament return was challenged, but his election by the limited franchise of the borough was approved by parliament.[153] He may have married sometime before 1640, and have been the father of the Edward Chadwell who entered Oxford in 1650.[154]

Although Chadwell was inexperienced in parliament before 1640, he was named to a few committees, 1640–1641. His knowledge of the law probably explains his being named in company with Maynard, Selden, and four other lawyers to a committee involving the rights of members of the Irish parliament, 12 November 1640. He spoke several times in debates regarding points of law, and in the discussion of the new canons seems to have condemned the bishops' action rather because it violated the common law than because parliament had not been consulted.[155] With his lawyer colleagues, Edward Hyde and Robert Holborne, Chadwell went to join the king in Yorkshire in the summer of 1642.[156] He was suspended in September for not attending the House, and ordered to be brought up in custody in November. After sitting in the Oxford parliament, he was finally disabled, 22 January 1644.[157] Chadwell petitioned in 1646 to compound, stating that his father was living and was displeased with his delinquency. His fine at a tenth was only £30,[158] indicating that his landed estate was small. He seems to have lived quietly thereafter, and was buried at Bradwell on 6 December 1680.[159]

Richard Chaworth (1603 ?–1672), of the University of Oxford, D.C.L., and Chancellor of the Diocese of London, was one of the few ecclesiastics in the House. He was named in a double return for Midhurst, Sussex, and was recognized as a member between 6 January and 15 February 1641. He has been included in this study because he was present part of the time, although on 15 February his election was voided in favor of William Cawley.[160]

Chaworth came of a distinguished Nottinghamshire family, being a younger son of John Chaworth (H.S.; d. 1638) by Jane, daughter of David Vincent of Stoke Dabernon, Surrey, and a brother of George, Viscount Chaworth of Armagh (d. 1639).[161] Born in 1599 or 1603,[162] he matriculated in 1621 at Christ's Church, Oxford. He was associated with that college for many years, being awarded the degrees of B.A., M.A., B.C.L. and D.C.L. (1640), and serving there as proctor in 1632. He became chancellor of the London diocese in 1637 and held the post until 1663.[163] He retained his connections with Oxford as late as 1646, probably longer.[164] He married Sophia, a younger daughter of Robert, Earl of Lindsey, and a relative of the Montagus of Boughton.[165]

There is no indication that Richard Chaworth was active in lay politics before 1640, his brother having inherited their father's responsibilities as sheriff and J.P. and having sat once in parliament (Notts, 1621), and tried in 1624 for Arundel, Sussex.[166] Perhaps his brother's death in 1639 spurred Richard to political activity, or possibly his concern for the established church was the cause. Why Midhurst was chosen for his constituency is not clear, though he probably had strong friends in Sussex and at the Restoration he be-

---

[147] Thomason Tracts, 669. f. 24, p. 37. In *Al. Cant.* Cecil's death is given as in 1657, his wife's burial date perhaps being mistaken for his.

[148] D. Warrand, *Hertfordshire families,* 115.

[149] Pink MSS, 307, fol. 281.

[150] I.P.M. of the M.P.'s grandfather, William Chadwell, senior, C. 142/335/28.

[151] *Al. Oxon.*

[152] *Linc. Inn Rec. Adm.* 1: 219; *Black Books* 2: 354.

[153] *M. of P.* 1: 480 and n.; *C.J.* 2: 10.

[154] Edward was then described as the third son of William Chadwell, gent. (Pink MSS, 307, fol. 281), and may have been a younger brother rather than a son of the M.P.

[155] *C.J.* 2: 27, 276; D'Ewes (N), 71 and n., 338; *Note book of Sir John Northcote,* 101 and n.

[156] *Yorks. Arch. Jour.* 7: 66–67, 1882.

[157] *C.J.* 2: 750, 845; 3: 374.

[158] *Cal. Com. Comp.,* 1565.

[159] Pink MSS, 307, fol. 281.

[160] *M. of P.* 1: 495, n.; *C.J.* 2: 63, 86.

[161] Add. MSS, 6705, fol. 29; I.P.M. of John, Viscount Chaworth, C. 142/664/1; Pink MSS, 299, fol. 457. Pink errs in terming Richard a son rather than a brother of George.

[162] According to his M.I., he died in 1672 in his 74th year (Manning and Bray, *Surrey* 1: 426); but he was "aged 18" when he matriculated at Oxford in 1621.

[163] *Al. Oxon.*; Bodleian Tanner MSS, 69, fol. 141.

[164] Bayntun Commonplace Book (Wiltshire Archaeological Society Library), fols. 42–43; *Cal. Com. Comp.,* 1529.

[165] Manning and Bray, *Surrey* 1: 424.

[166] Pink MSS, 299, fol. 457; C. 193/13; Horsfield, *Hist. Sussex* 2: App., 29.

came Chancellor of Chichester. His 1640 return was drawn up by the borough officials, doubtless in response to a patron's request, but it was challenged by William Cawley, the elect of "the burgesses." During his brief period as a member of the Long Parliament Chaworth was present at some of the debates on church government,[167] but we have no record of other activity. When he died in 1672, Dr. Chaworth was buried at Richmond, Surrey.[168]

Of Chaworth's financial standing no evidence has been found beyond a reference to his leasing a Wiltshire manor in 1646 from the Bishop of Salisbury for a yearly rental of £180.[169]

Sir Thomas Cheeke (d. 1659), of Pirgo, Essex, was M.P. for Harwich, 1640–1648 (1653 ?).[170] He was the grandson of Sir John Cheeke, the celebrated tutor of Edward VI, and the eldest son of Henry Cheeke (d. 1586), sometime secretary to the Council of the North. His mother was Frances, daughter of Sir Humphrey Ratcliffe, and sister of Edward Ratcliffe, Baron Fitzwalter and last Earl of Sussex.[171] The Cheeke family came originally from Mostyn in the Isle of Wight, and owned lands in several of the western and midland counties, but Thomas Cheeke is identified chiefly with London and Essex, where he purchased the Pirgo estate.[172] He was born probably between 1570 and 1575,[173] and after his father's death may have made his home with his stepmother's family, the Constables. He was doubtless the Thomas Cheeke of Yorkshire who entered Lincoln's Inn in 1590.[174] Years later (1629) he was created M.A. at Cambridge.[175] At the opening of James's reign he was knighted at the Charterhouse,[176] and possibly aspired to a place at court. His first marriage with a daughter of Peter Osborne connected him with a powerful family, and Lady Cheeke's death through the carelessness of a surgeon was an item of

court gossip in 1615.[177] By October, 1617, Cheeke had made another important connection by marrying Essex, daughter of Robert, first Earl of Warwick.[178] With his new brother-in-law, the second earl, Cheeke shared many interests. He was concerned with Virginia Company affairs, for instance, as early as 1612, and was active as a member of the council, 1619–1620. Later he became a stockholder in the puritans' Providence Island Company.[179]

Sir Thomas was long a public official in Essex. He served on various local commissions there,[180] and was for many years a J.P., being named for Malden and Harwich as well as for the county.[181] He joined the Essex J.P.'s in protesting against the money requested from the county for setting forth a ship in 1627,[182] but seems to have acted as a loan commissioner that year and to have reported defaulters and paid £25 himself.[183] About six years later, after he had spent the winter in London, he was threatened with Star Chamber proceedings for violating the rules about eating flesh in Lent.[184] Meanwhile he had sat in numerous parliaments. He served for Newport, Cornwall (1614), for Harwich, having been chosen also for Boston (1621), for Essex (1624), Beeralston (1625), Maldon (1626), Colchester (1628), and Harwich (Short Parliament).[185] From 1621, probably from 1614, Cheeke was closely associated with the country party.[186]

Sir Thomas was chosen by both Beeralston and Harwich for the Long Parliament, but preferred the Essex town.[187] He was one of the active members of Pym's faction, and was named among others to the committee on the Virginia plantation, and to several of the wartime committees in his county.[188] He was a Presbyterian elder, 1646–1648, and may have been secluded from parliament by Pride's Purge.[189] He died on 25 March 1659, and was buried at St. Alban's, Wood Street. His will, dated 30 April and 22 September 1658, was proved 18 April 1659.[190]

In keeping with his ancestry and marriages, Cheeke

[167] D'Ewes (N), 307, n.

[168] Manning and Bray, *Surrey* 1: 426, 431.

[169] Bayntun Commonplace Book cited above.

[170] According to Pink (Pink MSS, 299, fol. 460), he was secluded in 1648, but he may have been a member until 1653.

[171] Berry, *Ped. of Berks. Fam.*, 42–43; *Vis. Hants*, 54. In 1640, upon the prospect of the death of the earl without issue, Cheeke put in a claim for the barony of Fitzwalter, but nothing came of it. *H.M.C., Fourth Report,* House of Lords MSS, 31.

[172] Philip Morant, *The history and antiquities of the county of Essex* 1: 61, London, 1768 (hereafter, Morant, *Essex*); Thomas Wright, *The history and topography of the county of Essex* 2: 430 and n., London, 1836 (hereafter, Wright, *Essex*). Cheeke was living in Middlesex in 1617 and then sold some rents in Bedfordshire (*Beds. Hist. Rec.* 2: 100–101, 1914). The M.P.'s for Hampshire constituencies in 1604 and 1614 (*M. of P.*) were doubtless relatives.

[173] His parents were married in 1569, and his father married again in 1585. Thomas was old enough in 1586 to write a letter to Lord Burghley requesting his father's books. Lansd. MSS, 51, fol. 29.

[174] *Linc. Inn Rec. Adm.* 1: 111.

[175] *Al. Cant.*

[176] Courtney, *Parl. Rep. Corn.*, 376–377.

[177] Brown, *Genesis of the U.S.* 2: 853; *The letters of John Chamberlain* 1: 578.

[178] *Vis. Essex* 1: 278. An indenture of 22 October 1617 names Sir Thomas Cheeke of St. Martin's in the Fields, Middlesex, and his wife, Dame Essex. *Beds. Hist. Rec.* 2: 100, 1914.

[179] Brown, *loc. cit.*; Kingsbury, *Records of the Virginia Company* 1: 211, 224, *passim*; Newton, *The colonising activities of the English puritans*, 126.

[180] C. 181/3, fol. 120; 181/4, fols. 72v, 76; 181/5, fol. 55.

[181] C. 191/12, 13; *C.S.P. Dom., 1634–1635*, 227; *H.M.C., Tenth Report* 4: County of Essex MSS, 503.

[182] S.P. 16, 59/52.

[183] S.P. 16, 44/8, 52/64, 67/49.

[184] Add. MSS, 11,056, fol. 64v.

[185] *M. of P.* 3: App., xxxvii; 1: 451, *passim*.

[186] He was named, for instance, with Erle, Jephson, and others to the committee on Fleet prison in 1621. *Commons Debates 1621* 6: 455.

[187] *M. of P.* 1: 487, 489.

[188] *C.J.* 2: 54, 60; Pink MSS, 299, fol. 460.

[189] *Essex Review* 28: 16, 1919. See note 170 above.

[190] Pink MSS, 318; P.C.C., 212 Pell.

seems to have owned numerous lands, some being in Northamptonshire and Somerset.[191] By the time he wrote his will, most of his estate had probably been settled, but he still held three Somerset manors, specified a trust fund of £8000 for his younger children, and legacies of over £300.

Among Cheeke's relatives in the Long Parliament, besides his brother-in-law, the Earl of Warwick, and his nephew, Lord Rich, were Sir Gervase Clifton, related by one of his marriages, a son-in-law, Richard Rogers, and two who became so eventually, Francis Gerard and Lord Mandeville.

William Cheyney, or **Cheyne** (1622–1641), of Chesham Bois, Bucks, was M.P. for Amersham from 1640 until his death in April, 1641.[192] The heir of a wealthy old county family that had settled near Amersham in the fourteenth century, he was the son of Frances Cheyney (H.S. 1634; d. 1644) and Anne, daughter of Sir William Fleetwood of Missenden. William was born in London on 29 December 1622 and was christened there on 22 January following. In the month that he was seventeen he married Lucy, only daughter of Sir Thomas Barrington of Essex, the well known puritan leader (q.v.).[193] He was possibly an officer in Colonel Lunsford's regiment the following summer,[194] but was well under age when he was elected to the Long Parliament in the autumn. The prestige of his wife's connections as well as of his own family probably accounts for his election, and he was doubtless considered an ally of the popular faction, although a younger brother was afterwards a royalist.[195] Cheyney died in London, 20 April 1641, and was buried two days later at Chesham Bois.[196]

Cheyney's family owned extensive properties and both he and his brother married into wealthy families. A younger brother's portion of £1000 was mentioned in their father's will.[197]

* Thomas Chicheley (1614–1699), of Wimpole, Cambridgeshire, was knight for his county from 12 November 1640 [198] until his disablement as a royalist, 16

December 1642. The son and heir of Sir Thomas Chicheley (d. 1616), by his wife, Dorothy, daughter and coheir of Sir Thomas Kempe of Kent, he was born in 1614.[199] His family was wealthy, and his father had served as a J.P. and M.P. for his county.[200] Thomas entered the Inner Temple in November, 1632, and was granted the degree of M.A. from Cambridge in 1636.[201] From about the time he came of age, Chicheley took up responsibilities in Cambridgeshire, being named to several local commissions, 1635–1640,[202] and acting as sheriff, 1637–1638. He was conscientious about setting the ship money rates, but had difficulty with his collections, and in July, 1638, his father-in-law, Sir William Russell, Treasurer of the Navy, made his excuses to Council for Chicheley's delays and his failure to appear in person to explain.[203] The following April, as a D.L. for Cambridgeshire, Chicheley signed a request for a lighter military levy on the county because of the poverty there.[204]

Chicheley's first wife, whom he married before 28 July 1638, was Sarah, daughter of Sir William Russell of Chippenham, Cambridgeshire.[205] His mother seems to have resided in Westminster part of the time,[206] and his family connections were with court circles. He was a zealous royalist himself, voted against Strafford's attainder, and by 16 June 1642 had absented himself from the House, his disablement following quickly.[207] Surviving the war and the Restoration, Chicheley died on 1 February 1698/9.[208]

One of the wealthy members of the House, Chicheley offered to be bound for £1000 to support the loan in November, 1640,[209] and when he petitioned to compound for his delinquency in 1646 he estimated the value of four manors and other lands in Kent and Cambridgeshire as £1000 to £1100 a year clear. His fine was set at a tenth, 1985 l. 10 s. 8 d., but despite this penalty, and his claims of debts totalling £5000 and damages of £3500,[210] Chicheley's estate was said to be

[191] Morant, *Essex* **1**: 61, *passim;* Nichols, *Bib. Top. Brit.* **4** (vi): 30; Northants MSS, Finch Hatton 2719; S.P. 16, 89/30; St. Ch. 8/86/23.
[192] *M. of P.* **1**: 485 and n.
[193] *The visitation of the county of Buckingham made in 1634,* Harleian Society, **58**: 27–28, 1909 (hereafter, *Vis. Bucks.*); *Recs. Bucks.* **6**: 206, 1887.
[194] *C.S.P. Dom., 1640,* 648.
[195] Pink designated Cheyney as a royalist (Pink MSS, 307, fol. 66), possibly because his younger brother, Charles, afterwards Viscount Newhaven, married a daughter of the Duke of Newcastle.
[196] *Recs. Bucks.* **6**: 208, 1887.
[197] P.C.C., 9 Rivers. The family of Cheyney was a leading one in Buckinghamshire and held numerous estates there (*V.C.H. Buckingham* **3**: 219, 220, 342; Lysons, *Mag. Brit.* **1**: 468, 539, 552). One of the properties was worth £210–250 a year in 1620. Bodleian Willis MSS, 30, fols. 14v, 16.
[198] D'Ewes (N), 2 and n.

[199] I.P.M. of Sir Thomas Chicheley, C. 142/358/98; W. H. Challen, Transcript of the Register of Marriages of St. Michael's Crooked Lane, London (Guildhall Library), 11; Hasted, *Kent* **7**: 274. *D.N.B.* errs as to the dates of Chicheley's life and omits the names of his parents.
[200] Cooper, *Annals of Cambridge* **3**: 62, 102.
[201] *Al. Cant.*
[202] C. 181/5, fols. 2, 353.
[203] *C.S.P. Dom., 1635–1636,* 149, where the letter is incorrectly placed in January, 1635/6; *ibid., 1637–1638,* 577; *List of Sheriffs,* 14.
[204] S.P. 16, 417/64.
[205] *C.S.P. Dom., 1637–1638,* 577. His second wife was Anne Coventry, widow of Sir William Savile (q.v.). *Bull. Inst. Hist. Research* **2**: 94, 1924–1925.
[206] Overseers' Accounts, St. Margaret's, Westminster, **151** (1619–1620); S.P. 16, 441/7.
[207] Verney, 58; C.J. **2**: 626, 769.
[208] *Al. Cant. D.N.B.* gives 1694 as the date.
[209] D'Ewes (N), 539.
[210] S.P. 23, 192/869; *Cal. Com. Comp.,* 1437. His "particular" does not list, however, all the lands listed in his father's i.p.m. as his inheritance.

worth £2000 [211] a year in 1660, and his style of living was that of a wealthy man.

Henry Cholmley (1609–1666), a lawyer, of Barley and West Newton Grange, Yorkshire, was returned M.P. for the restored borough of New Malton, 8 January 1641, and kept his seat until 1648.[212] A brother of Sir Hugh Cholmley (q.v.), and second son of Sir Richard Cholmley of Whitby (d. 1631) by his first wife, Susan Legard, he was baptized at Whitby, 2 February 1608/9.[213] He was educated for the law, entering Gray's Inn, 10 August 1618, and the Inner Temple in 1628.[214] He was still at his inn when his father died in 1631, but was possibly expelled in 1635 for having led in some disorder considered scandalous to the society. He seems to have been reinstated afterwards.[215] His father provided him with only £50 a year from his estate, but, as his brother afterwards wrote, he amended this by marrying Katherine, daughter of Henry Stapleton of Wighill, widow of Sir George Twisleton of Barley, Bart. By this marriage Cholmley became a brother-in-law of Sir Philip Stapleton, the Presbyterian leader, and he probably took up residence at his wife's home, for he described himself as late as 1650 as of Barley.[216] According to his brother, Cholmley was tall and well built, "a kind, well-natured man, and loving true friend, valiant and ingenious, a good solicitor in his business, and diligent in all his affairs."

Cholmley probably held no civic office before 1640, but he was lieutenant colonel under his brother in a Yorkshire regiment, and when Sir Hugh's commission as colonel was withdrawn by Strafford's orders after his stand against ship money, 1639–1640, Henry was proposed by Sir Hugh to be his successor. Both were with the king's guard at North Allerton in 1640, both signed the Yorkshire petition of July, and Henry was still with the army in November.[217] After his election as a parliament man, Henry was named on 2 April 1641 to be present at Strafford's trial, and in May he was sent in his brother's place to bear instructions from parliament to the army in York.[218] He was knighted on 27 December 1641.[219] With his brother he supported the cause of parliament against the king, was present at York in May, 1642,[220] and continued to be a parliamentarian throughout the war, even after Sir Hugh Cholm-

ley changed sides.[221] He was secluded from the House in 1648.[222] Afterwards he assisted Fairfax with plans for the Restoration,[223] but left England and died at Tangier in 1666. He was buried at Newton Grange, 30 June 1666.[224]

Relatives of Cholmley in the 1640 House included his brother and two brothers-in-law, Sir Philip Stapleton and Sir William Strickland.[225]

* Sir Hugh Cholmley (1600–1657), of Whitby, Yorkshire (created baronet in 1641), was M.P. for Scarborough from 1640 until he was disabled for going over to the king, 3 April 1643.[226] He had represented the borough four times previously. Between 1618, when he went to Gray's Inn, and 1626, Cholmley lived chiefly in London and Kent, especially after his marriage with Elizabeth Twysden, and in later years he was a frequent visitor with his wife's relatives. But after the 1626 parliament and his knighting, 19 May 1626,[227] his concern for his estate caused him to return to Yorkshire. Having improved his affairs by more rigid economies than his father and he had previously practiced, he was ready after his father's death in 1631 to "condescend" to enter again into public office. He served as a J.P and a D.L., and from 1636 was colonel of the trained bands in his part of the county.[228] He was also a member of various local commissions.[229] His extensive lands, estimated to be worth £2700 or even £3000 a year before his father's difficulties, and as worth at least £1600 yearly even when they were most encumbered, in addition to his wife's portion of £3000, enabled him to live "in as handsome and plentiful fashion at home as any gentleman in all the country" of his rank, with an ordinary household of some thirty to forty persons, and to appear at public meetings "in a very gentlemanly equipage."

One may suspect that the family visits of Cholmley with his brother-in-law, Sir Christopher Yelverton (q.v.), in 1639 were not unconnected with the stand which both men took regarding ship money that year. For Cholmley's leadership in resistance in his region Strafford presently made him suffer.[230] Sir Hugh's attack on ship money in the Short Parliament and his summons before Council afterwards with his cousin, Henry

[211] *East Anglian*, N.S., **2**: 115, 1887–1888.

[212] *M. of P.* **1**: 497. His name appears in some earlier lists for North Allerton, the members for the two newly restored boroughs being confused.

[213] *Parish Register of Whitby*, Part 1: 2, Yorkshire Parish Register Society, 1928.

[214] *Gray's Inn Adm. Reg.*, 152; *Students admitted to the Inner Temple*, 253.

[215] *Cal. Inner Temp. Rec.* **2**: 221, 335.

[216] *Y.A.S. Rec. Ser.* **9**: 126, 1890; **18**: 222, 1895.

[217] *C.S.P. Dom.*, *1640*, 524; *1640–1641*, 269.

[218] *Ibid.*, *1640–1641*, 577; *C.J.* **2**: 115, 138.

[219] *Bull. Inst. Hist. Research* **3**: 189, 1925–1926.

[220] Drake, *York*, 149.

[221] *Y.A.S. Rec. Ser.* **54**: 363, 370–373, 1915; *Yorks. Arch. Jour.* **7**: 67, 1882; *E.H.R.* **32**: 578, 1917.

[222] *O.P.H.* **9**: 13.

[223] *Bull. Inst. Hist. Research*, loc. cit.

[224] *Yorks. Arch. Jour.* **23**: 384, 1915.

[225] References in addition to those cited above are: Foster, *Yorkshire families* **3**, Cholmley; *The memoirs of Sir Hugh Cholmley, Knt. and Bart.* (s.l., 1787), 18, 29, 60–63; Pink MSS, 299, fol. 478.

[226] *C.J.* **3**: 28.

[227] For corrections on several facts about Cholmley's career, see *Bull. Inst. Hist. Research* **3**: 189, 1925–1926.

[228] C. 193/13; S.P. 16/405; *C.S.P. Dom.*, *1635–1636*, 252.

[229] C. 181/4, fol. 114; 181/5, fols. 15, 99, 128, 275.

[230] Strafford, a friend of Cholmley's father, was a kinsman by marriage.

Belasyse, and his old friend, Hotham, are well known.[231] The following year he joined with Sir William Strickland to pledge £1000 to secure the loan,[232] and was an active member of the Commons in the first period of the Long Parliament. He seems to have been loyal to the Anglican Church, with no leaning toward Presbyterianism.

When he compounded for his estates Sir Hugh declared lands worth some £1170 a year, most of which, in anticipation of "these troubles," he had settled in 1640 on his eldest son. His properties included alum works, parts of which he rented as late as 1649 at £200 a year, and various manors and farms near Whitby. His fine of £850, a third, was based upon only part of the estate.[233]

Relatives of Cholmley in the 1640 parliament were his brother, Henry, two brothers-in-law, Yelverton and Sir William Strickland, and his cousins, Henry and John Belasyse. The Hothams were relatives also and close family friends, and he was connected with Sir John Poulett, whose sister, Margaret, married his royalist half-brother, Sir Richard Cholmley.[234] Sir Hugh's family stayed during part of his Long Parliament service in Lord Poulett's house in Chiswick.[235]

Sir Gervase Clifton, Bart. (1587–1666), of Clifton, Nottinghamshire, M.P. for East Retford from 1640 until his disablement during the war, was born about September, 1587, being the posthumous son of George Clifton by his wife, Winifred, daughter of Sir Anthony Thorold of Marston, Lincolnshire. He was the successor at the age of four months of his grandfather, "Sir Gervase the Gentle" (d. 20 January 1588).[236] He was made K.B. at James's coronation, and that year matriculated at St. John's, Cambridge, where he received his M.A. on the occasion of the prince's visit in 1612. He was admitted to the Inner Temple in 1607,[237] and was created a baronet at the institution of the order in 1611. Not only was his own family prominent and well-to-do, but Clifton acquired connections with many others, as well as additions to his estates, by his seven matrimonial ventures, six of which occurred before 1640. His wives were (1) Penelope Rich (d. 1613), daughter of the first Earl of Warwick; (2) Frances Clifford (d. 1627), daughter of the fourth Earl of Cumberland and sister of Strafford's first wife; (3) Mary (d. 1631), widow of Sir Francis Leke and daughter of John Egioke of Egioke, Worcestershire; (4) Isabel (d. 1637), widow of John Hodges, a London alderman, and daughter of Thomas Meeke of Wolverhampton; (5) Anne (d. 1639), daughter of Sir Francis South of Kelsterne, Lincolnshire; and (6) Jane, daughter of Anthony Eyre of Rampton, Notts.[238]

Sir Gervase performed many public duties, beginning at an early age. He was sheriff of Notts, 1610–1611, an active J.P. from 1618 at least,[239] a member of numerous local commissions,[240] a D.L. and assistant in the collections of loans by privy seals in 1625–1626.[241] He was Steward of East Retford from 1616 until his death,[242] was M.P. for his shire, 1614, 1621, 1624, 1625, and 1628, for Nottingham in 1626, and for East Retford both times in 1640.[243] In the Long Parliament Clifton was named to one important early committee, that on the lieutenancies, and pledged £1000 to support the loan in November, 1640, and £500 for that of 1641.[244] He voted against the attainder of Strafford, his brother-in-law and friend,[245] and deserted parliament for the king. He declared afterwards, however, that he had never borne arms, and compounded for his estates in 1646. He died on 28 June 1666, and was buried on 2 August at Clifton.

Clifton's large estate, including mills near Nottingham,[246] was said before the war to have brought him an annual income of about £3000,[247] and his compounding papers reveal a declared income of some £2804 a year. His fine, set first at ⅔, £12,120, was reduced and paid at £7625.[248]

Clifton's friend, Dr. Thoroton, wrote of him that he was "certainly more gentle than his Grandfather, being generally the most noted Person of his Time for Courtesy, he was very prosperous, and beloved of all. He generously, hospitably and charitably entertained all, from the King to the poorest Beggar." [249] He was an intimate of men of the highest social position, such

---

[231] C.S.P. Dom., 1640, 154. The D.N.B. article does not make it clear that this incident was connected with the parliament.

[232] D'Ewes (N), 439, n.

[233] Cal. Com. Comp., 2062; Y.A.S. Rec. Ser. 58: 201, 1917; Bull. Inst. Hist. Research 3: 189, 1925–1926.

[234] Yorks. Arch. Jour. 23: 355, 1915.

[235] In addition to the above references, see The memoirs of Sir Hugh Cholmley, Knt. and Bart. (1787), 23–24, 38–56, 58–61, 65, 73, 89–90.

[236] Complete Baronetage 1: 19; Thoroton Soc., Trans. 15: 162–163, 1911; O.P.H. 9: *36.

[237] Al. Cant.; Cal. Inner Temp. Rec. 2: 29.

[238] His seventh wife, married after 1655, was a daughter of the Earl of Huntingdon.

[239] Robert Thoroton, The antiquities of Nottinghamshire 2: 141, 2nd ed., Nottingham and London, 1790–1797 (hereafter, Thoroton, Notts.); C. 181/3, fols. 10v, 23v; C. 193/12, 13; Nottinghamshire Quarter Sessions Minute Books (MSS at the office of the Clerk of the Peace, Nottingham), 10 and 11, passim.

[240] C. 181/3, fols. 5, 117; 181/4, fols. 23v, 32; 181/5, fols. 8, 76, 190, 319.

[241] He seems to have been careful in his collections, but made some excuses because of his county's smallness and declining prosperity. S.P. 16, 10/61; 381/73; C.S.P. Dom., 1625–1626, 231; H.M.C., Various Collections 7: 395.

[242] Ibid., 390.

[243] M. of P. 1: 452, passim; 3: App., xxxix.

[244] C.J. 2: 50; D'Ewes (N), 52, 435, n., 451, n.

[245] Verney, 58.

[246] Thoroton Soc., Trans. 15: 162, 1911; Thoroton, Notts. 1: 112, 115, 117, 141; Robert White, The Dukery Records, 111, 112, 375, Nottingham, Thornton Press, 1904; Nottingham Corporation MSS, 3393, Hall Book, 1617–1618, fol. 36.

[247] C.S.P. Dom., 1635–1636, xviii, 11.

[248] S.P. 23/195/927–928; Cal. Com. Comp., 1318; C.J. 5: 429.

[249] Notts., 108. See also H.M.C., Various Collections 7: 402.

as the earls of Newcastle, Kingston, Carlisle, and Exeter, was a friend of his fellow member, Hutchinson, and connected by his marriages with leaders in both political factions, and included Thomas Hobbes among his correspondents.[250] He seems to have preferred country life to the court, although he had been educated for a possible career there, and was said to be sincere and "conformable" in his religion.[251]

* Sir John Clotworthy (d. 1665), of Ireland and of London, sat for Maldon, Essex, from 1640 until 1648. The son of a Devonshire family, but chiefly of Irish residence and interests, Clotworthy was a newcomer to the English parliament in 1640 and seems to have had no previous connection with Maldon. He had been a member of the Irish parliament of 1634, however,[252] and was connected by marriage and by friendship with such English puritans as John Upton[253] of Devonshire, friend and brother-in-law of Pym, and John Winthrop, junior. He was interested in the Massachusetts settlements.[254] Clotworthy's collisions in Ireland with both Strafford[255] and the established church made him a candidate of importance in the 1640 elections, as his return for two places some distance apart implies. Clarendon wrote that powerful influences secured his return for a Devon borough, by which he probably meant the indenture for Bossiney, Cornwall, which was voided;[256] and doubtless the same sort of influence, probably that of Warwick himself, secured his place for Maldon in the room of the borough's own recorder who had been its member in the spring.[257] Clotworthy was identified as of St. Andrew's, Holborn, in his return.[258]

Clotworthy owned lands in north Ireland,[259] but his name does not appear in the lists of contributors to the parliamentary cause in the early years. Through his wife, Mary, daughter of Viscount Ranelagh,[260] he was a brother-in-law of young Arthur Jones, a fellow M.P. in 1640.

Henry Coke (1591–1661), of Thorington, Suffolk, was M.P. for Dunwich, 1640–7 September 1642. He was the fourth surviving son of Chief Justice Sir Edward Coke (d. 1634) by his first wife, Bridget, daughter and coheiress of John Paston of Huntingfield Hall. He was born at the latter place on 27 August 1591, and baptized there four days later.[261] He was admitted to Queen's College, Cambridge, in 1607, and to the Inner Temple in 1610.[262] He married Margaret, daughter and heiress of Richard Lovelace of Kingsdowne, Kent, on 24 August 1619, and lived for a time thereafter at his father's home at Stoke in Buckinghamshire.[263] In June, 1620, however, his father settled some of his estate, assigning to Henry and his wife Thorington manor and adjoining lands in Suffolk, two Cambridgeshire manors and some Essex lands,[264] and they presently took up residence at Thorington.[265] He was probably the Henry Coke, Esq., who was called before Council as a loan refuser from Suffolk in December, 1626, but was released upon his promise to pay.[266] Through his father's influence, no doubt, he was elected to the three parliaments of 1624–1626 for Chipping Wycombe in Bucks.[267]

Coke was a J.P. in Suffolk from 1634, and a member of other commissions for the county.[268] He paid his ship money rates apparently without protest,[269] and sought election to parliament again in 1640. By this time he had leased some property from Dunwich, which was not far from Thorington and within his family's circle of influence, and in March secured his title as freeman of the borough and his election to the Short Parliament.[270]

In the Long Parliament Coke was active from the start. He was named to the Committee of Privileges,

[250] Ibid., 294, 295, 401, 402, passim. There are copies of various letters to Clifton also in Lansd. MSS, 238, fols. 144–158.

[251] His friend, Francis Chigwell of Merton College, once congratulated him upon leaving London, since his religion esteemed as vicious some of the practices of the court (Lansd. MSS, 238, fol. 148). See also Harl. MSS, 6803, fol. 50. For a brief sketch of Clifton's career, see Thoroton Soc., Trans. 37: 36–40, 1933.

[252] C.S.P. Ireland, 1633–1647, 63.

[253] His sister married before 1623 a brother of John Upton who had settled in county Antrim. Burke, Landed Gentry 2: 1458, 1851.

[254] Winthrop Papers 3: 187, 1929; Winthrop's Journal 1: 164 (Hosmer), New York, Scribner's, 1908. Governor Winthrop's son visited Clotworthy in Ireland in 1635 and gave advice to a group who were interested in going to New England.

[255] Among various grievances he had against Strafford was the repeated postponement of the assigning of a company to his command. C.S.P. Ireland, 1647–1660, Addenda, 180.

[256] Rebellion 1: 224; M. of P. 1: 486 and n.; D'Ewes (N), 35, 118, 536; E.H.R. 50: 253, 1935. See Bossiney election.

[257] M. of P. 1: 481.

[258] C. 219/43/Part 1.

[259] D'Ewes (C), 119.

[260] Bull. Inst. Hist. Research 4: 50, 1926–1927.

[261] G. A. Carthew, The hundred of Launditch 3: 109–112, Norwich, 1877–1879.

[262] Al. Cant.; Cal. Inner Temp. Rec. 2: 48.

[263] Carthew, op. cit. 3: 112; Copinger, The manors of Suffolk 2: 165; Arch. Cant. 20: 61, 1893.

[264] Carthew, op. cit. 3: 115–116. Fuller declared that Sir Edward Coke's estate was so great that all his sons might seem elder brothers by the large possessions left to them. (Article on Sir Edward Coke, D.N.B.) Although Sir Edward was reported in 1623 to be "cracked" by his own debts and those of his sons (C.S.P. Dom., 1619–1623, 517), Henry seems not to have shared his brothers' responsibility for that condition. C. W. James, Chief Justice Coke, 80, London, Country Life, 1929.

[265] He was living at Thorington by 1628, and after his father's death had full possession. Add. MSS, 19,082 (Davy collection), fol. 397.

[266] Acts P.C., 1626, 426, 427.

[267] M. of P. 1: 456, 462, 468.

[268] C. 193/13; S.P. 16/405; C. 181/5, fols. 205, 351.

[269] His Thorington rate one year was over £2. V. B. Redstone, ed., The ship-money returns for the county of Suffolk, 1639–1640, xiii, Suff. Inst. Arch., Ipswich, 1904.

[270] Dunwich Borough MSS, Minute Book, 1595–1616, fols. 38v, 305v; 1627–1653, fols. 74, 97v, 115v; H.M.C., Various Collections 7, Dunwich MSS, 88, 93; M. of P. 1: 453, 483, 528.

and in December spoke in regard to the confiscation of his father's books. When the final break with the king arrived, however, Coke deserted the House and was among the first to be disabled, 7 September 1642.[271] He sheltered at his home for one period during the war an Anglican divine who was wanted by the parliamentarians, was himself a prisoner for a time, and refused to pay an assessment of £300 as a twenty-fifth part of his estate.[272] He died in 1661 and was buried at Thorington, 19 November 1661.[273]

Coke's estate, besides his inheritance of Thorington and his interest in other manors of Suffolk and nearby counties, included his wife's share of her family's Kentish possessions.[274] Despite the effects of the war, his annual income was reported in 1655 to be £1500 to £2000.[275]

Sir John Coke, Junior (c. 1608–1650), of Melbourne, Derbyshire, sat for his county, 1640–1650. He was the eldest surviving son of Sir John Coke, Secretary of State (d. 1644), by his first wife, Mary, daughter of John Powell of Preston (or Presteign), Herefordshire, and brother of Thomas Coke (q.v.). Born about 1608,[276] and educated at Cambridge (Trinity College) and at Gray's Inn, which he entered in 1627,[277] he was knighted at Innerwick in 1633.[278] About the same time he married Elizabeth, daughter of Thomas (or Timothy) Pusey of Selston, Notts, widow of William Willoughby, who was the heiress to a "great fortune." By the next year he had joined his father as J.P. in Derbyshire. He became a D.L. shortly afterwards, and was one of the commissioners for gaol delivery in 1638.[279] During this period in the country, Sir John looked after his father's estates, living partly at Melbourne and partly at Selston. Sir Gervase Clifton, his neighbor, was among his good friends.[280]

Coke was interested in the Short Parliament elections, though more for others than for himself,[281] and

his first candidacy was in the autumn. Having spent nearly £300 to entertain the more than 1100 voters who came to Derby to vote for him,[282] Sir John was chosen one of the Derbyshire knights, 5 November 1640, and became very active on the popular side. In the early months of the Long Parliament Coke spoke against the clergy who had made the new canons and against Strafford, and offered his bond as security for £1000 for the loan.[283] He promised two horses for the defense of king and parliament on 8 November 1642 and, although his brother, Thomas, was a royalist and he himself was under some suspicion in 1643, he supported parliament during most of the war, serving on several local committees, and sitting in the Westminster Assembly in 1645.[284] Retiring to the continent after the execution of King Charles, Coke was in Geneva in the winter of 1649–1650,[285] and died in Paris before 20 August 1650.

Although his father was living in 1640, Coke had doubtless had a settlement of some of the family estates made on him at the time of his marriage. By the time the Coke inheritance had passed to his royalist brother, it was considered worth more than £850 a year, and his brother's fine at a third, chiefly on this estate, was £2,700.[286]

Thomas Coke (1614–1656), of Gray's Inn and of Derbyshire, M.P. for Leicester borough, 1640–22 January 1644, was the second surviving son of Sir John Coke, secretary of state, by his first wife, Mary Powell, and a younger brother of the Derbyshire member, Sir John Coke, junior. Born in 1614 and educated at Trinity College, Cambridge, and Gray's Inn (entered 1630),[287] he had a legal practice in London by 1640. He seems to have made his chief residence there, occasionally visiting Derbyshire,[288] but after 1635 was several times named to the sewers commissions in Lincoln and Leicester shires,[289] probably because he was interested in Sir William Killigrew's fen drainage there.[290] In 1637 Coke acquired an interest in the crown's profits from lead mines at Worksworth in

271 C.J. 2: 21, 756; Note book of Sir John Northcote, 88.
272 James, Chief Justice Coke, 113; Manship's Yarmouth 2: 208, n.
273 Suff. Inst. Arch. 9: 24, 1897.
274 Add. MSS, 19,080 (Davy collection), fol. 235v; 19,082, fols. 328, 385, 386v; Hasted, Kent 2: 479; Arch. Cant. 20: 60, 1893.
275 Add. MSS, 19,082, fol. 359. He was planning a £2000 marriage portion for a daughter in 1649. Bodleian Tanner MSS, 98, fol. 43.
276 Derbys. Arch. Jour. 11: 63, n., 1889; Dorothea Coke, The last Elizabethan, 39. His elder brother Joseph seems to have been an only child in April, 1608. H.M.C., Twelfth Report 1, Coke MSS, 64.
277 Ibid., vi; Al. Cant.; Gray's Inn Adm. Reg., 182.
278 Shaw, K. of E. 2: 201.
279 C. 193/13; S.P. 16/405; C. 181/5, fol. 237; V.C.H. Derby 2: 136; H.M.C., Twelfth Report 1, Coke MSS, 459; 2: 252.
280 Ibid. 2: 29; 3: 136–137; Ninth Report 2, MSS of H. C. Pole-Gell, Esq., 390.
281 His support was sought by a county candidate (ibid., Twelfth Report 2, Coke MSS, 246), and he seems to have acted as his brother's agent at Leicester.

282 H.M.C., Twelfth Report 3, Coke MSS, 138–141.
283 Add. MSS, 11,045, fol. 144; D'Ewes (N), 52, 412. The name appears in one list as Sir John Croke, but there was no such member. Numerous letters that Coke wrote to his father attest his interest in the House proceedings. H.M.C., Twelfth Report 2, Coke MSS, 271, passim.
284 C.J. 2: 840; Pink MSS, 307, fols. 327–328.
285 H.M.C., Seventh Report, MSS of Sir H. Verney, Bart., 457.
286 S.P. 23, 219, fols. 787–788; Cal. Com. Comp., 1844. Other references, in addition to those cited, are John Talbot Coke, Coke of Trusley (privately printed, 1880), 58–66; G. Baker, The history and antiquities of the county of Northampton 1: 141, London, 1822–1841 (hereafter, Baker, Northampton). Sir John is mentioned briefly in the article on his father in the D.N.B.
287 Gray's Inn Adm. Reg. 190; Pink MSS, 299, fol. 524.
288 H.M.C., Twelfth Report 2, Coke MSS, 102, 248; Dale, Inhabitants of London, 1638, 187.
289 C. 181/5, fols. 84, 132, 362; S.P. 16, 437/13.
290 C.S.P. Dom., 1640–1641, 309.

Derbyshire and from the office of barmaster, from which he derived a net income of £200 to £300 a year.[291]

Coke seems to have been little known in the borough of Leicester before his election there for the Short Parliament, upon the recommendation of his father's friends, the Earl and Countess of Devonshire, as "a man without exception, whether you consider his ability or his affection to his country, most worthy of the place." [292] His elder brother assisted also, interviewing the borough officials and arranging for Thomas to appear at the proper time to take his freeman's oath.[293] Coke won attention in this parliament by his defense of the bishops, possibly out of consideration for his uncle, George Coke, Bishop of Hereford, whereby he aroused much feeling in the House, but gained in other quarters respect for his wise and generous carriage.[294] Elected to the Long Parliament through the same influences as in the spring, Coke won early favor with the reform element by supplying information against Secretary Windebank.[295] He voted against the attainder of Strafford,[296] however, protested later against ecclesiastical innovations proposed by parliament, and spoke so vehemently against the militia bill on 7 December 1641 that the Speaker censured him.[297] Letters to his father the following January and March expressed great concern about the affairs of the commonwealth, his fears that matters were moving fast "to a higher period," and his uncertainties as to the course he should take.[298] He was named an assessment commissioner for Leicestershire in 1643, but joined the king's parliament at Oxford and was disabled, 22 January 1644.[299]

Coke compounded as a royalist in 1648, being fined £500, was under arrest for alleged treason in 1650, and the following year, having succeeded to his brother's estates, was fined an additional £2,200, one of the largest amounts in his county.[300] He died at Tottenham High Cross in August, 1656, and was buried at Melbourne. He was survived by his wife, whom he married possibly after 1640, Mary Pope of Wostaton, Shropshire, and a three-year-old son, John. Although his family were well-to-do, Coke seems to have owned little real estate during the lifetime of his father and brother, living chiefly on the income from his legal practice and from the crown lead mines.[301]

* **Sir John Colepeper** (1600–1660), of Hollingbourne, Kent, M.P. for his shire, 1640–22 January 1644, came of a family prominent in Kent and Sussex. He was the second but eldest surviving son of Thomas Colepeper of Wigsell, Sussex (d. 1613), by his first wife, Anne, daughter of Sir Stephen Slaney, Lord Mayor of London. He was born in 1600, was baptized at Saleshurt, Sussex, 17 August 1600,[302] and in 1618 succeeded his elder brother as head of his family. He may have studied at Cambridge,[303] going later to the armies abroad. He was knighted in 1621. After his marriage in London in 1628 to Philippa, daughter of George Snelling of West Grinstead, he made his residence at Hollingbourne rather than at Wigsell.[304] He married again in 1631, his second wife being his cousin, Judith.

Colepeper was a J.P. in Kent at least by 1638,[305] and was sent to the Short Parliament by Rye.[306] He was paired with Sir Edward Dering in the heated contest for the county seats in October.[307] A supporter of reform in the early part of the Long Parliament, Colepeper pledged his security for £1000 in November, 1640, and in the following March.[308] He was a member of the committee for the 1641 recess, but had absented himself by June, 1642. He was not formally disabled as a royalist, however, until 22 January 1644.[309] He died on 11 July 1660.[310]

Colepeper's wealth consisted chiefly of lands in Kent, especially in the western part. He held some in Sussex and had scattered holdings also in Lincolnshire and Warwickshire.[311] His loan pledges suggest that he was one of the wealthier members of the House.

James Lord Compton (1622–1681), of Compton Wyniates, Warwickshire, afterwards third Earl of Northampton, was elected for his county through his

[291] Add. MSS, 6681, fols. 231–232; Cal. Com. Comp., 1844, 2775.

[292] H.M.C., Eighth Report, MSS of the Corporation of Leicester, 436; Thompson, Leicester, 359.

[293] H.M.C., Twelfth Report 2, Coke MSS, 252; H. Hartropp, Register of the Freemen of Leicester 1: 126, Leicester, E. Backus, 1927–1933.

[294] J. T. Coke, Coke of Trusley, 67; H.M.C., Twelfth Report 2, Coke MSS, 261.

[295] Neither of Secretary Coke's sons was friendly to Windebank and both were suspicious of Vane, their father's successor. Ibid., 264–265; D'Ewes (N), 26.

[296] Verney, 57.

[297] D'Ewes (C), 25, n.; 246–248. D'Ewes thought young Coke deserved censure less for his remarks than for his misquoting of a precedent.

[298] D. Coke, The last Elizabethan, 294, 297.

[299] C.J. 3: 374; Pink MSS, 299, fol. 524.

[300] Cal. Com. Comp., 1844–1849; V.C.H. Derbyshire 2: 136; Coke, Coke of Trusley, 68.

[301] The family estates included various manors in Derbyshire and Northamptonshire. Derbys. Arch. Jour. 13: 144–147, 1891; Baker, Northampton 1: 141.

[302] Errors regarding Colepeper's parentage in D.N.B. and Hasted (Kent 5: 486) are corrected in the article on The Sussex Colepepers by F. W. Attree and J. H. L. Booker in Sussex Arch. Coll. 47: 65–68, 1904.

[303] Al. Cant.

[304] Sussex Arch. Coll. 47: 67–68, 1904. D.N.B. identifies this wife incorrectly.

[305] S.P. 16/405.

[306] M. of P. 3: App., xliii.

[307] Larking, Proceedings in Kent, 11, 15; Stowe MSS, 743, fols. 149, 156, 157; D'Ewes (N), 107.

[308] D'Ewes (N), 52, 438, n.

[309] C.J. 2: 288, 626; 3: 374.

[310] Sussex Arch. Coll. 47: 68, 1904. The date was 11 June 1660, according to D.N.B.

[311] Add. MSS, 18,471, fol. 109; Arch. Cant. 14: 58, 1882; Cal. Com. Comp., 1058, 1289, 3276–3277.

father's influence on 2 November 1640, and was re-elected promptly after the voiding of the original return.[312] He was disabled in 1643. The son and heir of Spencer, second Earl of Northampton (d. 1643), by his wife, Mary, daughter of Sir Francis Beaumont, he was born 19 August 1622. From the time of his father's succession to his earldom in 1630 he was styled Lord Compton.[313] He was admitted to Queen's College, Cambridge, 21 January 1637, having received the degree of M.A. there the year before.[314] On the eve of the Long Parliament elections he was travelling or in military service in the Netherlands, whence his father summoned him home in September.[315] Young though he was, Lord Compton joined in the vote against Strafford's attainder,[316] and when the war began he took up arms for the king and was accordingly disabled. He succeeded to his father's peerage in 1643, and after the royalist cause was lost compounded heavily for his estates[317] and was permitted to leave the country. He died at Castle Ashby in Northamptonshire, 15 December 1681, and was buried with his ancestors in Warwickshire.[318]

Lord Compton was the heir apparent in 1640 to one of the largest fortunes in England. His father's estates lay in eleven counties, and in 1636 he had settled £20,000 for his younger children's portions. The Compounding Committee, reckoning Compton's fine after he had succeeded his father, set it first at a third, £5,738, but altered it quickly to £20,820, and reduced it later to £14,153. An additional £500 was levied in 1650–1651.[319]

Fitzwilliam Coningsby (c. 1595–1666), of Hampton Court, Herefordshire, was a member for his county from 1640 until he was expelled on 30 October 1641 for his connection with the soap monopoly. The descendant of an ancient family, he was the only surviving son and heir of Sir Thomas Coningsby, the soldier (J.P., M.P., H.S., d. 1625), by Philippa, daughter of Sir William Fitzwilliam, Lord Deputy of Ireland. He was born probably about 1595,[320] and was graduated

B.A. from Oxford in 1613. Four years later he married in London Cecilia, eldest daughter of Lord Abergavenny.[321] He was a loan commissioner in Hertfordshire in 1620 and 1627,[322] M.P. for his county, 1621, and sheriff there in 1626. For many years he was a J.P.[323] and was a member of numerous special commissions for the western counties and Wales.[324] He succeeded his father as High Steward of Leominster, and in 1633 was a member of the Council of the Marches of Wales.[325] Through some of his connections at court Coningsby was named as one of the beneficiaries of the soap project under the second patent, 12 April 1636. Afterwards he tried to prove that he had not been an active promoter of the scheme.[326]

Coningsby joined with his friend, Sir Robert Harley, to win the shire election of October, 1640, having the backing of the local gentry and having solicited the support of the powerful Earl of Essex.[327] When the report on the soap business was brought into the Commons after the recess of 1641, however, even Harley's influence could not save Coningsby from expulsion as a monopolist, and his membership in the House was abruptly terminated.[328] He served the king actively during the war, compounded in time for his estates, and lived until 1666.

The Coningsby family had been described in 1614 as one of "note, quality, and authority,"[329] and from his father Fitzwilliam inherited more than thirteen manors, some advowsons, and other properties that extended to several thousands of acres in the counties of Hereford, Worcester, and Salop. A sister had had a portion of £2000.[330] His income about the time of the Long Parliament was over £2100 a year,[331] possibly as much as £4000.[332] But he seems to have lived extravagantly and to have been forced before 1640 to mortgage his lands heavily to meet his obligations. One of his creditors termed Coningsby "powerful and dilatory."

[312] M. of P. 1: 495 and notes; C.S.P. Dom., 1640–1641, 113.

[313] Complete Peerage 6: 72.

[314] He had probably been a student at Eton before going to Cambridge (Townshend, The life and letters of the great Earl of Cork, 310), and was created D.C.L. at Oxford in 1642. Al. Cant.

[315] C.S.P. Dom., 1640–1641, 113.

[316] Verney, 57.

[317] His plea then that his royalism was dictated during his minority by his father is belied by the letter he wrote to Prince Rupert just after his father's death, volunteering to serve the king with life and fortune. Add. MSS, 18,980, fol. 28.

[318] Compton did not marry until 1647. Complete Peerage 6: 72.

[319] One Northamptonshire property was worth £500 a year, another in Bucks, £100 annually, three other manors totalled £600 a year, and another, alone, was considered worth £1810 a year. Cal. Com. Comp., 67, 94, 102, 233, 1247–1249.

[320] He and an elder brother were named in a document of 1596. Add. MSS, 6693, fols. 335, 336.

[321] Add. MSS, 6693, fol. 14v; C. 142/424/93 (I.P.M. of Sir Thomas Coningsby).

[322] H.M.C., Fourteenth Report 2, MSS of the Duke of Portland (III), 12; S.P. 16, 54/2.

[323] C. 193/12, 13; S.P. 16/405.

[324] C. 181/3; 181/4, fols. 162v, 186v; 181/5, fols. 13, 66, 124.

[325] Pink MSS, 299, fol. 548; Arch. Camb., 6th Ser., 17: 196, 1917.

[326] D'Ewes (C), 56–57.

[327] H.M.C., Fourteenth Report 2: 65.

[328] C.J. 2: 299; D'Ewes (C), loc. cit.

[329] St. Ch. 8/77/20.

[330] I.P.M. cited above; H.M.C., Fourteenth Report 2: 1; Birmingham Reference Library MSS, 402476, 397534. Another manor of Coningsby's lay in Leicestershire. Cal. Com. Comp., 111.

[331] S.P. 23/221/329–338. His income was given as £2000 a year in 1660. English Baronetage 4: 367, 1741.

[332] Richard Symonds noted in 1645 that the Coningsby of Hampton Court who was governor of Hereford had £4000 a year. Richard Symonds, Diary of the marches of the royal army, ed. C. E. Long, 195, Camden Society, 1859 (hereafter, Symonds, Diary).

His fine at compounding, set at a third, was £4243.[333] He seems to have been in seriously straightened circumstances during the war.[334]

Coningsby was a kinsman of William Fitzwilliam, M.P. for Peterborough.[335]

Humphrey Coningsby (born 1622), of Hampton Court, eldest son of Fitzwilliam Coningsby (q.v.), replaced his father as M.P. for Herefordshire, 20 November 1641.[336] He won the election against a candidate favored by Sir Robert Harley,[337] although the latter had been his father's friend. Humphrey was only nineteen at the time. He had started his education at Oxford and the Middle Temple, but his service in parliament and his royalist activity during the war cut short his studies. He was disabled for deserting parliament, 8 May 1643, and 22 January 1644.[338] He seems to have married sometime after 1641, and outlived his father only a short time. He died between 1666 and 1675.[339] Coningsby's son, Thomas (1656 ?–1729), became Earl Coningsby.[340]

William Constantine (1612–1670), Recorder of Poole, Dorset, was M.P. for that borough, 1640–4 September 1643.[341] His family came originally from Shropshire, settling first at Poole and then at Merly-Romford a few miles distant. His great-grandfather was three times mayor of the town. The M.P.'s father, Henry Constantine of Merly, married in 1605 Elizabeth, daughter of Thomas Evelyn of Ditton, Surrey, and died in 1613 when his only son, William, was but six months old.[342] The latter was a second cousin of Sir John Evelyn of Wiltshire (q.v.) and a generation closer to John Evelyn of Surrey (q.v.). Constantine entered Emmanuel College, Cambridge, in 1627, removed apparently to Queen's, Oxford, in 1628, and in 1630 entered the Middle Temple, his father's and his grandfather's inn. He was bound there with George Evelyn, one of his mother's relatives.[343] He was called to the bar in 1637 and continued his connection with the Temple for many years, becoming a Bencher (1659), Reader (1664), and Treasurer (1668).[344]

Constantine was admitted a burgess of Poole in

1631,[345] but was apparently absent most of the time during the years of his law studies. He had to answer the knighthood commissioners by agent in 1632.[346] But he returned after he became a barrister, was named to the Dorset sewers commission in 1638,[347] and in December of the following year was appointed Poole's recorder.[348] As such he was a gaol delivery commissioner in 1640,[349] and was elected both in the spring and the fall as M.P.[350] He married (1) before 1642, Jane, daughter of Thomas Hanham of Dean's Court in Winbourne (d. 1654), and (2) in 1655 Anne, daughter of William Collyer.[351]

In the Long Parliament Constantine was active, speaking against Strafford, and helping to manage the trial of Justice Berkeley in the spring of 1642. He served on some committees in the House and on that for scandalous ministers in Dorset.[352] In June, 1642, he promised a horse for the defense,[353] but the next summer he wrote to Poole advising its surrender to the king, and he was accordingly disabled by parliament, 4 September 1643, and deprived of his recordership.[354] He afterwards declared that he wrote the letter under compulsion while a prisoner of the royalists, and that his attendance at Oxford afterwards was not of his choice.[355] He was prisoner of parliament, too, for a period,[356] and eventually was allowed to compound for his estates, 1645–1646. He survived the Restoration to be restored as Poole's recorder. He became recorder at Dorchester, also, and was knighted in 1668. He died in 1670, his will of 2 October being proved 7 November 1670.[357]

A man under thirty at the time of his election, and newly started in his profession, Constantine was not wealthy in 1640. He had lands worth slightly over £143 a year in Dorset, with others in reversion that were worth £140 a year, according to his statement when he compounded. What the income from his practice was he did not declare. By the time he made his will he had accumulated additional wealth. He seems to have been a deeply religious man, one who

[333] S.P. 23/221/336; *Cal. Com. Comp.*, 351, 2064–2069.

[334] Add. MSS, 11,047, fols. 221, 223, 225.

[335] In addition to the authorities cited above see *M. of P.*; Williams, *Hereford*, 41, 44; *D.N.B.*, "Sir Thomas Coningsby."

[336] *M. of P.* **1**: 489.

[337] *H.M.C., Fourteenth Report* 2, MSS of the Duke of Portland, 81–82.

[338] *C.J.* **3**: 75, 374.

[339] Pink MSS, 299, fol. 549. See also Williams, *Hereford*, 46.

[340] *D.N.B.*

[341] *M. of P.* **3**: xliv; *C.J.* **3**: 227.

[342] Hutchins, *Dorset* **3**: 304, n.; Manning and Bray, *Surrey* **3**: 14.

[343] *Al. Cant.; Al. Oxon.; Mid. Temp. Rec.* **1**: 279; **2**: 453, 762.

[344] *Ibid.* **2**: 855, *passim*; **3**: *passim; Al. Oxon.*

[345] J. Sydenham, *The history of the town and county of Poole,* 240 and n., Poole, 1839.

[346] *Somerset and Dorset N. and Q.* **4**: 19, 1894–1895.

[347] C. 181/5, fol. 226.

[348] Sydenham, *loc. cit.*

[349] C. 181/5, fol. 333.

[350] *M. of P.* **1**: 481; **3**: xliv.

[351] Hutchins, *loc. cit.*

[352] *C.J.* **2**: 94; D'Ewes (N), 415, n. (416); Pink MSS, 299, fol. 559.

[353] *N. and Q.*, 1st Ser., **12**: 360, 1855.

[354] *C.J.* **3**: 227; Sydenham, *loc. cit.*; A. R. Bayley, *The great Civil War in Dorset*, 108–110, Taunton, Wessex Press, 1910.

[355] *Cal. Com. Comp.*, 940.

[356] Whitelocke, *Memorials of the English affairs* **1**: 280, 284, 1853.

[357] *Al. Oxon.*; Sydenham, *loc. cit.*; Mayo, *Municipal records, Dorchester*, 455–456.

sympathized with a reformed and purified Anglican church.[358]

Constantine was related through his first wife to John Pyne, his colleague for Poole in parliament.

Sir Robert Cooke (1598–1643), of Highnam, Gloucestershire, was elected for Tewkesbury in 1640, and after that election was voided on 6 August 1641, was re-elected in October, 1641. He held his seat until his death in 1643. Born in 1598,[359] he was the son and heir of Sir William Cooke of Highnam (M.P., d. 1619), by Joyce, only daughter of Sir Thomas Lucy of Charlcote, Warwickshire. He was educated at Oxford and Gray's Inn, was knighted in 1621, and probably about that time married Dorothy, daughter of Sir Miles Fleetwood of Aldwinkle, Northamptonshire, Receiver of the Court of Wards.[360] He may have been M.P. for Fowey, Cornwall, in 1624,[361] and perhaps held some place under his father-in-law in the Court of Wards for a time. His connections with the court were referred to at a later date,[362] and his residence in London in 1624 and 1625 was his excuse for defaulting from the Gloucester musters.[363] Sometime after 1633, his first wife having died, Cooke married Jane (Danvers), widow of George Herbert, the poet.[364]

Cooke and his family were on friendly terms with the city government of Gloucester, and he was named a J.P there in 1624.[365] He was afterwards one of the city's agents in negotiations about ship money and in procuring money for plague relief.[366] He was a county J.P. also, and a sewers commissioner,[367] and in 1635 was a D.L. and a captain of horse in the trained bands.[368] A puritan in religion, Cooke was compelled shortly before 1640 to answer before the High Commission regarding the church at Tetbury. And apparently as such he was the choice of the gentry to be one of the shire knights in the Short Parliament. But he antagonized many of his original supporters by instructing his followers to vote for a man of even stronger opposition views for the second place, instead of for the more moderate man with whom he had at first been paired.[369] Perhaps this accounts for Cooke's seeking

a seat for a borough rather than for the county the next time, although he was present at the shire election and signed the return.[370] He seems to have been popular enough at Tewkesbury to be named in both of the indentures sent from there at the 1641 by-election.[371]

Although Cooke was not sure of his seat until the autumn of 1641, he may have sat for a time during the early weeks of the parliament, for the order debarring the men involved in the election dispute was apparently not enforced,[372] but he was not named among those taking the Protestation of May, and was busy in February and March as a J.P. in Gloucestershire.[373] He became an active member, however, as soon as the by-election made his position sure, and showed himself interested in Irish affairs, in the Remonstrance, and in planning for the defense.[374] In June, 1642, he promised two horses and maintenance for the cause, as well as £100,[375] and he served in the army and as governor of Tewkesbury early in the war. His death occurred sometime between 8 June and 16 December 1643.[376]

Cooke was a man of means, as his subscription of 1642 and his bonds later for military expenses indicate.[377] The properties he inherited included several manors in and about the city of Gloucester, and he was among those most heavily burdened for the city's trained bands.[378] His marriages brought him lands in other counties, and his investments included even an interest in a Gloucester ship. His will mentioned annuities, aside from rents, of £460, and his provision for the younger sons by his first wife was a portion of £500 each. But in arranging for his twelve children, Cooke mentioned in his will the heavy losses the war had brought him and expressed the hope that parliament might reimburse his survivors out of the estates of delinquents, particularly those of the popish religion.

Relatives of Sir Robert Cooke in the Long Parliament were his father-in-law, Fleetwood, and Fleetwood's kinsmen, Sir Oliver and Sir Samuel Luke. For the latter Cooke spoke in announcing their pledges for the defense in 1642. Thomas Hodges was a brother-in-law, and Sir Robert Harley was a cousin of some degree.[379]

[358] In his will (P.C.C., 145 Penn), Constantine referred to himself as in title knight but in truth a sinner, to his membership in the Church of England, and to the need for the clergy to be reduced to their primitive spiritual state.

[359] I.P.M., Sir William Cooke, C. 142/378/146.

[360] *Vis. Glouc.*, 45 and n.

[361] *M. of P.* 1: 456. His father had once served for a Cornish borough, and his father-in-law was influential.

[362] S.P. 16, 472/55.

[363] Gloucester Corp. MSS, Letter Book 1619–1639, fols. 21, 60.

[364] Three younger children, apparently by this marriage, were mentioned in Cooke's will of 8 June 1643. P.C.C., 142 Rivers.

[365] Gloucester Corp. MSS, Minute Book, 1565–1632, fols. 474v, 520; Accounts, 1635–1653, fols. 7, 9, 27v, 66, *passim*.

[366] *Ibid.*, Accounts, 1635–1653, fols. 42v, 100v, 124.

[367] C. 193/13; S.P. 16/405; C. 181/5, fol. 26.

[368] Gloucester Corp. MSS, Letter Book, 1619–1639, fol. 201.

[369] *C.S.P. Dom., 1639–1640*, 580–582; *M. of P.* 1: 481.

[370] Gloucestershire indenture, C. 219/43/Part 1.

[371] *M. of P.* 1: 489 and n.; *C.J.* 2: 23, 239; D'Ewes (C), 107, n.

[372] See Tewkesbury election.

[373] *H.M.C., Fourth Report*, House of Lords MSS, 53.

[374] *C.J.* 2: 347; Verney, 127; Pink MSS, 299, fol. 569; D'Ewes (C), 107, 197, 360.

[375] *N. and Q.*, 1st Ser., 12: 338, 1855.

[376] His will (proved 1645) was dated 6 June 1643. P.C.C., 142 Rivers. On 16 December 1643 his widow petitioned parliament regarding his estate. *C.J.* 3: 342.

[377] Bristol Museum and Art Gallery MSS, Ellacombe Collection, 216; *Cal. Com. Comp.*, 28.

[378] I.P.M. cited above; Gloucester Corp. MSS, Letter Book, 1619–1639, fol. 208; Accounts, 1635–1653, fol. 26.

[379] *H.M.C., Fourteenth Report* 2, MSS of the Duke of Portland (III), 49. Cooke seems not to have been related to the family of Coke, of which several members sat in the House.

In addition to the authorities cited above, see Williams, *Gloucester*, 53.

* Sir John Corbet, Bart. (1594–1662), of Stoke-upon-Terne, and Adderley, Shropshire, was a member for his county from 1640 to 1648.[380] He is not to be confused with his distant kinsman, Sir John Corbet of Sprowston, Norfolk, brother of Miles Corbet (q.v.), who was imprisoned for refusing the 1627 loan and died in 1628.[381] The Shropshire Corbet was a student at Lincoln's Inn in 1615,[382] and in his county was a J.P., sheriff, and member of various commissions.[383] He is known chiefly for the Council and Star Chamber proceedings and ensuing imprisonments that resulted from his protests at the quarter sessions against the levy of muster-master's fees by the Lord Lieutenant of the county.[384] He protested also against the ship money rates there in 1638,[385] and at some time before 1640 quarrelled with a neighbor, who had Laud's backing, about the type of chapel for his church of Adderley.[386] Sir John was a Presbyterian elder later.[387]

Sir John, who seems to have been well-to-do, offered his bond for £1000 for the loan in November, 1640, and in March, 1641.[388]

Corbet was a first cousin of Sir Richard Lee, his colleague for Shropshire.

* Miles Corbet (d. 1662), of Lincoln's Inn and Yarmouth, the regicide, sat for Yarmouth, 1640–1653. He studied at Christ's College, Cambridge, before entering Lincoln's Inn.[389] His elder brother, Sir John Corbet, who died in 1628, aged thirty-seven, was one of the loan resisters imprisoned in 1627 for their action.[390] Miles was named recorder at Yarmouth in 1625 and was also town clerk for a time, but in 1640 the local council reproached him for neglecting the latter office since he had moved his residence into the country.[391]

He was a county J.P., also, and in 1628, a commissioner for sea breaches.[392] John Winthrop was one of his friends.[393]

Corbet's estate was probably not large, since he was a younger son, but it is doubtful that he was so lacking in worldly goods as some royalists assumed.[394] He was a joint purchaser of some lands while he was Yarmouth's recorder,[395] and subscribed £50 for the defense in June, 1642.[396] When he was executed he is said to have declared that he had come to parliament with an estate, but had spent all of it.[397]

Sir Frederick Cornwallis, Bart. (1610–1662), of Bromehall, Suffolk, and of the court, was M.P. for Eye, 1640–23 September 1642. He was a younger son of Sir William Cornwallis, K.B., M.P. (d. 1611), by his second wife, Jane, daughter of Hercules Mewtas, was born on 14 March 1610, and in 1626 succeeded his half-brother, Thomas, in possession of the family estates. His was a very old Suffolk family, and for several generations had been prominent at court, his grandfather, Sir Thomas Cornwallis, having been a privy councillor for Mary Tudor, and his uncle, Sir Charles, and his father, courtiers of Elizabeth and James. Frederick was introduced when young into the household of the Prince of Wales and probably accompanied the prince on his journey to Spain in 1623. He was created a baronet in 1627 and knighted in 1630. About the latter year Cornwallis married Elizabeth, daughter of Sir John Ashburnham of Sussex, sister of the king's favorite, John Ashburnham (q.v.), and again, before 1641, Elizabeth, daughter of Sir Henry Crofts of Saxham, half-sister of William, Baron Crofts.[398]

Sir Frederick probably spent much of his time at court. Early in 1633 he accompanied Lord Arundel on his mission to Bohemia,[399] and both he and his lady were in the service of the royal household and recipients of income from royal sources.[400] He was named second

---

[380] M. of P. 1: 492. Corbet was the original member, being in the House as early as 30 November 1640 (C.J. 2: 39), not the successor to the royalist, Sir Richard Newport, as indicated in O.P.H. (9: *37) and Carlyle (3: 332). Compare Shrops. Arch. Soc., Trans., 4th Ser., 11: 162–163, 171, 1927–1928.

[381] Doubt as to the identity of the two Corbets was expressed by the author of the article on Sir John in D.N.B. The identity of the loan refuser as the Norfolk man is made clear by a newsletter of 1628 (T. Birch, The court and times of Charles the first, ed. R. F. Williams, 1: 315, London, 1849) and by his son's petition in 1647 (Cal. Com. Adv. Money, 784).

[382] Linc. Inn Rec. Adm. 1: 170.

[383] C. 181/3; 181/4, fol. 185v.

[384] D.N.B.

[385] C.S.P. Dom., 1639, 252.

[386] Shrops. Arch. Soc., Trans., 4th Ser., 13: 123–124, 1931–1932.

[387] A.H.R. 44: 36, n., 1938–1939.

[388] D'Ewes (N), 52, 439, n. Corbet's royalist son, John, of St. James's, London, fined £1000 in 1650, was enjoying a rent charge of £500 from his father's estates at that time (Cal. Com. Comp., 205, 735, 2221). D.N.B. errs in stating the amount of the fine.

[389] Al. Cant.

[390] Complete Baronetage 1: 219 and n.; Cal. Com. Adv. Money, 784. Miles was probably born sometime between 1591 and 1600.

[391] Great Yarmouth Corporation MSS, Assembly Book 6, fols. 7, 467.

[392] S.P. 16, 192/79; C. 193/13; C. 181/5, fol. 206.

[393] Winthrop Papers 1: 408, 1929–1944.

[394] The mystery of the good old cause, 14; Mason, Norfolk, 306.

[395] Norfolk Archaeology 13: 152, 177, 1898 (hereafter, Norf. Arch.).

[396] N. and Q., 1st Ser., 12: 360, 1855. Corbet's subscription of £250 for Ireland, however, was less than the average, and the money belonged to his merchant brother, Thomas. C.S.P. Ireland, Adventurers, 66.

[397] Mason, Norfolk, 330.

[398] Complete Baronetage 2: 13; Copinger, The manors of Suffolk 3: 237–238; Lloyd, Memoires, 662; Pink MSS, 299, fols. 604, 605, 607; Add. MSS, 19,079 (Davy collection), fol. 96v, and 19,089, fol. 82v. He married his second wife against her father's wishes, losing thereby half of her £4000 inheritance (Cal. Com. Adv. Money, 696).

[399] Birch, The court and times of Charles the First 2: 212, 271.

[400] C.S.P. Dom., 1635–1636, 433; 1636–1637, 303; S.P. 16, 284/75. Lady Cornwallis was a resident in St. Margaret's parish, Westminster, 1632–1633 (St. Margaret's Parish Overseers' Accounts 153).

for a duel Henry Jermyn proposed to fight in 1637,[401] and in 1639–1640 was with the army in the north as a lieutenant in the king's bodyguard.[402] He had been named to the Suffolk commission for piracy in 1627,[403] but otherwise seems to have been aloof from public affairs there until 1640. His election at Eye for both parliaments of that year was owing in part to royal influence, since the borough was then crown property.[404]

Cornwallis was a stanch royalist in the 1640 House. He was named early to the committee on the Star Chamber,[405] but was soon arguing against the disbanding of the Irish army because of the "enemy in our bosome," and voted against the attainder of Strafford.[406] He was disabled on 23 September 1642, charged with recruiting foreign officers for the king's cause,[407] and was identified thereafter entirely with royalism. He followed Charles II into exile, and survived the Restoration to become Baron Cornwallis of Eye, Treasurer of the Household, and privy councillor. He died 31 January 1662, and was buried at Brome. Lloyd[408] describes Sir Frederick as,

a Man of so chearful a spirit, that no sorrow came near his heart: and of so resolved a mind, that no fear came into his thoughts; so perfect a Master of Courtly and becoming Raillery, that he could do more with one word in Jest, than others could do with whole Harangues in Earnest; a well-spoken man, competently keen in modern Languages, of a comely and goodly Personage.

Sir Frederick inherited most of his family's properties lying in Suffolk, Norfolk, and Yorkshire, and received others from the estate of his mother's second husband, Sir Nathaniel Bacon.[409] He declared in his compounding petition that his lands were worth some £800 a year, but that they were encumbered by mortgages of over £6000 and debts of more than £1200. His fine, set at a tenth, was £800.[410]

* **William Coryton** (1580–1651), of Coryton and Newton Ferrars on the Devon-Cornwall border, Vice Warden of the Stannaries and mayor of Bossiney, was returned in October, 1640, for both Grampound and Launceston. He made his choice for the latter, but was required on 14 November to withdraw because of his management of the Bossiney returns, and on 18 August 1641 was deprived of his seat.[411] Because he participated, however, in the debate on supply on 13 November, he must be included in the list of Long Parliament members.[412]

Born in 1580,[413] and long active in affairs in Cornwall, Coryton was an official and M.P. whose career is well known. Besides being connected with the Stannaries and the duchy and being a D.L. in the county, Coryton was sheriff in 1613 and was for many years a J.P.[414] He considered standing for the county in the 1621 elections, but yielded to one of his kinsmen instead,[415] and he probably influenced more of the subsequent elections than that of Bossiney which put an end to his career as an M.P.[416] Although a strong opponent of the king in the 1620's, and as late as 1639–1640 so reluctant about lending money to the crown that Council summoned him for an explanation,[417] Coryton seems to have been considered untrustworthy by his former friends when parliament met.

Coryton's royalism during the war cost him a considerable fine. His family inheritance included nine manors in Devon and Cornwall,[418] and his income from lands alone was about £700 a year. His fine of a tenth, £1244, was reduced to £828 on account of annuities to be paid out of that income.[419]

John Coventry (born c. 1610), of Barton, Somerset, was M.P. for Evesham, Worcestershire, from 2 February 1641 until he was disabled, 12 August 1642.[420] The second son of Thomas Lord Coventry, the Lord Keeper (d. 1640), he was born probably about 1610 or 1611, matriculated at St. John's, Cambridge, in 1625, and was admitted to the Inner Temple in 1626.[421]

[401] Birch, op. cit. 2: 271.

[402] S.P. 16, 538/91/ii; Add. MSS, 11,045 (Scudamore papers), fol. 127v.

[403] C. 181/3.

[404] M. of P. 1: 483, 494. The honor of Eye did not pass to the Cornwallis family until 1698. Copinger, op. cit. 3: 259, 263; Add. MSS, 19,089, fols. 132, 134v.

[405] C.J. 2: 44. Cornwallis had been a suitor in the court in 1635. S.P. 16, 291/123.

[406] D'Ewes (N), 484, n.; Verney, 58.

[407] C.J. 2: 779.

[408] Memoires, 663.

[409] Add. MSS, 19,089 (Davy), fols. 63, 69, 320v; 19,090, fols. 22, 138–140; 19,079, fols. 94, 218; S.P. 14, 79/270–271, 299; V.C.H. York, North Riding 2: 377.

[410] S.P. 23/204/599; Cal. Com. Comp., 1390. Cornwallis's declaration does not seem, however, to include his Yorkshire properties. A 1663 list of the values of estates of peers in the North Riding reports for Lord Cornwallis, £800 (H.M.C., Various Collections 2: 119), although it is not clear that this refers to the Yorkshire holdings alone.

[411] M. of P. 1: 486; C.J. 2: 29, 261–262.

[412] D'Ewes (N), 535. He was appointed to a committee the same day. C.J. 2: 28.

[413] I.P.M. of Peter Coryton, 1605, C. 142/662/101; statement by Coryton's daughter in 1647. Cal. Com. Comp., 1678.

[414] List of Sheriffs, 23; C. 193/13; S.P. 16/405.

[415] S.P. 14, 117/55.

[416] E.H.R. 50: 246–247, 1935.

[417] Rushworth (3: 913) listed him as sending no reply to the request in 1639, and the 1640 summons was for his delay in paying an assessment of £500 requested as one of the king's "servants." S.P. 16, 447/36, 37, 94.

[418] I.P.M. cited above.

[419] S.P. 23/200/623–629; Cal. Com. Comp., 387, 398, 1678.

[420] He was first named in a double return, 16 October 1640, but was apparently not recognized, although his competitor, William Sandys, was threatened with losing his seat because of being a monopolist. When Sandys was expelled in January, Coventry replaced him. M. of P. 1: 496; C.J. 2: 22, 26; D'Ewes (N), 267–268.

[421] Al. Cant. Francis, Lord Coventry's third son (born 1612), was admitted there in 1628 (ibid.). John, the Lord Keeper's first son by his second marriage, is mentioned in D.N.B. under "Sir Thomas Coventry" and "Sir John Coventry (d. 1682)."

Coventry married, probably before 1634, a Somerset-shire heiress, and thereafter had his principal residence near Taunton. He was a J.P. there in 1634 and keeper of the rolls in 1637.[422] With his brother-in-law, Sir William Portman (q.v.), Coventry signed a statement that Taunton's ship money rate was too heavy.[423] He was also on the commission of oyer and terminer for several neighboring counties and for Somerset.[424] In 1639 he contributed £100 toward the king's expenses in the north,[425] but the Long Parliament was his first. He doubtless owed his seat for a Worcestershire borough partly to his elder brother, since the principal estates of his family lay in that county.[426]

In the 1640 parliament Coventry voted against Strafford's attainder,[427] and was commended once by Sir Henry Mildmay for his grasp of parliamentary procedure.[428] He spoke on the side of king and church during the debate on the Remonstrance,[429] and was disabled in August, 1642, for taking up arms for King Charles.[430] He was living in 1656, but apparently died before the Restoration.[431]

When Coventry compounded as a royalist, he was fined at a tenth, £4000. His estates, including those he enjoyed by right of his wife, were distributed among seven counties, from Somerset and Monmouthshire to Hants and Lincoln and Derby, and had a yearly value of at least £2135.[432]

John Cowcher, or **Coucher** (c. 1562–1653?), weaver and alderman of Worcester, was M.P. for his city from 1640 until nearly the end, although his advanced age probably prevented his attending after the early summer of 1641.[433] He was the son and heir of John Cowcher, twice bailiff of Worcester, and was born about 1562.[434] He was probably the John Cowcher who married Mary Fleet at St. Helen's, Worcester, on 20 November 1581.[435] He was by 1590 an important member of the clothiers' company of his city, and he held offices in the city government from the time he was chamberlain (1585) until his death. He was bailiff in 1593 and 1595 and an alderman from 1594.[436] Cowcher worked for a new charter for the town from 1603 until it was secured in 1621,[437] and he was called upon for other services, ranging from a study of the pollution of the River Severn by water from the dyers' vats to collections for the loans in 1612 and 1627.[438] He was elected one of the Worcester M.P.'s to all but two of the parliaments from the accession of James. In that of 1621 he spoke several times on the problems of the wool trade and of the clothiers.[439] The knighthood commissioners in 1631 required a fine from him in the city and from either him or his son, John, in a country parish.[440]

Despite Cowcher's age, there seems to have been no hesitation in Worcester about sending him once more to parliament late in 1640. He may not have been present regularly, but he took the Protestation in May, 1641. Twice that year, in August and in December, he requested the House to relieve him of the burden of attending and to arrange for a new election,[441] but his request was not granted. He died sometime between 13 August 1652 and 29 August 1653.[442]

Cowcher was probably a prosperous clothier when he was in his prime. He complained in his old age of having paid off the debts of his eldest son twice and of being brought low in his estate. Nevertheless, he held, besides a country place his father had purchased in Clifton-upon-Teame parish, a number of other houses and farms in the counties of Worcester, Hereford, and Gloucester, and several leases within the city itself.[443]

Cowcher was probably an uncle by marriage of his colleague, John Nash.

* **Matthew Cradock** (d. 1641), of the Skinners' Company of London, a wealthy merchant, sat for London from 1640 until his death, 27 May 1641. Probably the grandson of the Matthew Cradock, Stafford merchant at the time of the heralds' visitation of 1583,[444] but not to be

[422] C. 193/13; S.P. 16/405; Add. MSS, 28, 273, fol. 82v.
[423] C.S.P. Dom., 1636–1637, 536.
[424] C. 181/5, fols. 10, 93, passim.
[425] Rushworth, 3: 911.
[426] I.P.M. of Thomas Lord Coventry at Evesham. C. 142/594/68. His brother was a Worcestershire J.P. in 1638. S.P. 16/405.
[427] Verney, 58.
[428] D'Ewes (N), 497, n. Coventry's brother-in-law, Anthony Ashley Cooper, described him as an extraordinary man in every way, of great mental talents. D.N.B., "Sir John Coventry."
[429] D'Ewes (C), 185, n., 205.
[430] C.J. 2: 716.
[431] Pink MSS, 299, fol. 633. A sketch of Coventry's life appears in Williams, Worcester, 144–145.
[432] Cal. Com. Comp., 1382; L.J. 9: 629; S.P. 23/183/476–477.
[433] He was still a member in 1648 (Thomason Tracts, E. 454, p. 17), and died sometime between 13 August 1652, the last time he was sworn an alderman at Worcester, and 29 August 1653, the first year in many that his name was not on the rolls there. Worcester Corporation MSS, Order Book 3, fols. 8, 12. His will, dated 20 May 1652, was proved 5 May 1654. P.C.C., 150 Alchin.
[434] According to his will he was ninety years old in 1652.
[435] She was presumably a daughter of Thomas Walsgrove, alias Fleet, of that parish. J. B. Wilson, ed., The parish book of

St. Helen's Church in Worcester 1: 15, 16, 22; 2: 7, London, Chiswick Press, 1900. In the pedigree of Twitty, a family into which his daughter married, Cowcher's name appears erroneously as Thomas. W. C. Metcalfe, ed., The visitation of the county of Worcester, 1682–1683, 94, Exeter, 1883 (hereafter, Vis. Worc.).
[436] Worcester Corporation MSS, Order Book 1, fols. 161, 196, passim; 2, fol. 62, passim.
[437] Ibid. 2, fols. 7v, 12v, 71v–75.
[438] Ibid. 2: fols. 30v, 82; S.P. 16, 77/33.
[439] Commons Debates 1621 3: 189, 317; 5: 503.
[440] Williams, Worcester, 94. The son was living in that parish in 1652, according to Cowcher's will.
[441] C.J. 2: 133, 262; H.M.C., Fourth Report, House of Lords MSS, 99; D'Ewes (C), 349.
[442] See note 433.
[443] Cowcher's will; Worcester Corporation MSS, Order Book 1, fol. 194; 2, fol. 59.
[444] Staff. Hist. Coll. 3 (2): 4, 113, 1882. Mrs. F. Rose-Troup identifies him as the son of Matthew Cradock of Stafford by

confused with a cousin, Matthew Cradock of Stafford and Caverswall (d. 1636),[445] he was probably a member of the Skinners' Company by apprenticeship, and in 1640 was one of its wardens.[446] He married (1) Damaris, daughter of Richard Wyn of Shrewsbury, and (2) Rebecca, daughter of Thomas Jordan of London. Through his first wife he was connected with his fellow M.P.'s of 1640, Spurstow, Parkhurst, and Owfield.[447] Cradock was a resident of Walbroke Ward at the time of his election to the Long Parliament.[448] His mercantile interests had ranged from an early venture in the wool trade in 1615 to the great colonial enterprises for which he is famous.[449] He was the owner of ships, for at least one of which he secured letters of marque in 1627.[450]

In city affairs, too, Cradock was a leader. He was in 1633 one of the commissioners of the London court of requests, and in 1640 a member of the council and auditor of accounts. As one of the aldermen he was chosen to represent London in the Short Parliament,[451] and by his early death the Long Parliament lost a zealous reformer.[452]

Sir Robert Crane, Bart. (1586–1643), of Chilton, near Sudbury, was M.P. for Sudbury, 1640–1643. He was the only son and heir of Henry Crane (d. 1586), by his second wife, Catherine, daughter of John Jernegan of Somerley, and the heir of his grandfather, Sir Robert Crane of Chilton (d. 1591). He was born in 1586 and was reared under the guardianship of his grandfather and of his grandmother's family, the Jermyns of Rushbrook. He was knighted in 1605 and in January, 1607, married at Blackfriars Dorothy, daughter of Lord Chief Justice Hobart.[453] Perhaps in deference to the latter

Crane was granted special admission successively to the Inner Temple and Lincoln's Inn in 1607 and 1608.[454] His first wife dying in 1624, Crane married later in that year Susan, one of the daughters of Sir Giles Allington of Cambridgeshire. He became a baronet in 1627.[455]

The heir of an old and influential family, Crane was one of the big landholders of Suffolk, owning properties in numerous parishes there, and also in Essex and Norfolk. He was interested before 1634 in some Irish lands, but without great success.[456] Several benefactions to Sudbury attest his friendship for that town, as well as his wealth.[457] Crane was proud of the antiquity of his family, and took some interest in antiquarian pursuits.[458] Another of his avocations as a country gentleman was the breeding of hunting dogs.[459]

In keeping with his wealth and position, Crane was prominent in public affairs long before 1640. He was a J.P. from the time of James I, a member of many local commissions,[460] a D.L. for most of the time from 1619 until his death,[461] and in 1631–1632 was sheriff. He was elected to his first parliament in 1614, sitting for Sudbury, won a county seat in 1620 by some vigorous campaigning, sat for Sudbury again 1624, 1625, and 1628, and for the county in 1626 and the Short Parliament.[462] In the 1621 debates Crane showed great concern for the wool trade and for action upon what parliament wanted as well as upon what the king requested.[463] He was more amenable to Buckingham's will by 1625,[464] yielding perhaps to advice from his

---

Dorothy Greenham, and brother of Samuel Cradock of Thiselton, Rutland (*The Massachusetts Bay Company and its predecessors*, 139).

[445] Wedgwood, *Staff. Parl. Hist.* 2: 22; Beaven, *The aldermen of the city of London* 1: 290. *D.N.B.* suggests their identity.

[446] London Corporation MSS, Rep. 54, fol. 237v.

[447] F. Rose-Troup, *loc. cit.*

[448] S.P. 16, 453/75.

[449] He was a member of the new wool dyeing group of 1615, one of the cloth traders of the Eastland Company in 1633, and a member of the East India, Virginia, and Massachusetts Bay companies. C. T. Carr, ed., *Select charters of trading companies*, 80, London, Selden Society, 1913; *C.S.P. Dom., 1631–1633*, 546; E. B. Sainsbury, ed., *A calendar of the court minutes, &c. of the East India Company, 1635–1639*, vi, 73, *passim*, Oxford, Clarendon Press, 1907– ; Kingsbury, *Records of the Virginia Company* 3: 63.

[450] *C.S.P. Dom., 1628–1629*, 293, 299; *1636–1637*, 376.

[451] *M. of P.* 1: 482; London Corporation MSS, Rep. 39, fols. 68, 99; Rep. 47, fol. 384.

[452] Committees of the Long Parliament to which he was named included those on monopolists and on Emmanuel College. He was present to take the Protestation on 5 May 1641. *C.J.* 2: 30, 40, 95, 135.

[453] He was not the son of Sir Robert Crane, as is stated in *Complete Baronetage* (2: 15) and elsewhere. The corrections regarding his parentage appear in Copinger, *The manors of Suffolk* (2: 291, n.), and W. S. Appleton, *The Cranes of Chilton*,

66–87, Cambridge, U.S.A., 1868. Henry's son was not born before 20 June 1586, but was mentioned in family papers of 20 December 1586, as well as in his grandfather's will of 1590. Add. MSS, 33,858 (Muskett's collections), fol. 132; P.C.C., 16 Harrington.

[454] *Cal. Inner Temp. Rec.* 2: 29; *Linc. Inn Rec. Adm.* 1: 147.

[455] *Complete Baronetage* 2: 15. By his second marriage Crane became a brother-in-law of the wives of Sir Thomas Fanshawe, K.B. (*q.v.*), and Zouch Tate (*q.v.*). Through his grandmother he was a kinsman of Sir Thomas Jermyn and his son (*q.v.*).

[456] Copinger, *op. cit.* 3: 273, 284; *Suff. Inst. Arch.* 8: 149–150, 1894; I.P.M. of Sir Robert Crane, 1645 (C. 142/706/32); Add. MSS, 19,078, fols. 338v, 392v; 19,084, fol. 247; Bodleian Tanner MSS, 69, fols. 11, 135, 152; 70, fol. 29.

[457] *Suff. Inst. Arch.* 13: 272, 291, 1909.

[458] Robert Reyce dedicated to Crane his *Breviary of Suffolk* (*Suffolk in the XVIIth century: The breviary of Suffolk, by Robert Reyce, 1618*, ed. Lord F. Harvey, London, J. Murray, 1902 [hereafter, Reyce, *Breviary of Suffolk*]). Sir Robert granted D'Ewes permission in 1640 to make use of his family charters. D'Ewes, *Autobiography* 2: 238–239.

[459] Bodleian Tanner MSS, 69, fol. 149, *passim*.

[460] C. 193/12, 13; C. 181/3, fol. 117; 181/4, fols. 9v, 67; 181/5, fols. 62, 120, 144, 317.

[461] Add. MSS, 39, 245 (Suffolk official letters), fols. 43, 179v; H.M.C., *Thirteenth Report* 4, MSS of E. R. Wodehouse, Esq., pp. 441, 457; S.P. 16, 149/228v; Tanner MSS, 70, fol. 81.

[462] Tanner MSS, 69, fols. 150, 151; 290, fols. 28, 37; *M. of P.* 1: 453, 460, 466, 471, 477, 483; 3: App., xl.

[463] *Commons Debates 1621* 2: 410; 3: 289, n., 320, 355, 400; 5: 386.

[464] Forster, *Eliot* 1: 425.

kinsmen, the Jermyns, and in 1626 was willing to join John Winthrop in urging the election of Sir Robert Naunton of the court as a shire knight.[465] His desire to keep on good terms with the popular leaders as well as with the court caused him to refuse to sign the musters warrants for 1628, lest he embroil himself with parliament, although he urged the other deputy lieutenants to sign,[466] and in 1639 or 1640 he asked the help of his cousin, Jermyn, in seeking to be excused from a contribution toward the costs of the Scottish war.[467]

Crane sought the middle of the road in the 1640 elections and in the House. He supported the royalist candidate in both county elections,[468] and won his own place for Sudbury in the autumn in competition with the puritan gentleman, Brampton Gurdon. Although Gurdon's charge of misdealing by the officials was not accepted, the discussion of Crane's case shows that the opposition men such as Pym and Hesilrige preferred Gurdon to Crane, and that his supporters were moderate reformers such as Whistler, Bagshaw, and Strangways.[469] Sir Robert pledged his support for the loan of November, 1640, and in June, 1642, promised four horses for the defense of "king and parliament not divided."[470] He had been absent part of the preceding winter,[471] but did not break with the House leadership, and was named in the spring to the committee on the defense of the kingdom. He served on the Suffolk committee for scandalous ministers,[472] and was in command of a company of foot until his death.[473] He died in London, 17 February 1643, and was buried at Chilton.[474]

* **John Craven** (1610–1648), of London, was returned in a contested election for Tewkesbury in October, 1640, and sat for a time during the early months of the session. Following the voiding of the whole election on 6 August 1641, however, he was not re-elected.[475] The younger son of Sir William Craven, Lord Mayor of London, he became a student at the Middle Temple, where he was "bound" with Bulstrode Whitelocke.[476] He married a daughter of Lord Spencer of Wormleighton in 1634, and in 1637, after a quarrel with Sir John Maynard in London, went to live for a time with his

wife's family.[477] He was possibly the Lieutenant John Craven who was listed for a company to be raised in county Leinster, Ireland, in April, 1640.[478] Craven seems to have had no direct connection with Tewkesbury, and probably owed his election there to a powerful friend, perhaps his sister's husband, Thomas Lord Coventry.[479] His offer to lend £1000 toward army expenses in March, 1641, may have been one reason for parliament's delay in voiding his return.[480]

Craven's wealth was perhaps his best claim to fame at that time as it was afterwards. With an intention expressed as early as 1636 to have an estate large enough to enable him to bequeath £10,000, Craven acquired lands in several counties. He had received £5000 or more from his father's estate.[481] His assessment by parliament in 1644 was £3000.[482] The bequests enumerated in his will, besides the famous £100 for the Craven Scholarships, total more than £9000. The date of his will and that of its proving show that Craven died between 25 June 1647 and 27 February 1647/8.[483]

Thomas Whitmore, another 1640 M.P., was a cousin of Craven.

Richard Cresheld, or **Creswell** (d. 1652), Serjeant-at-Law, was M.P. for Evesham, Worcestershire, from 1640 until he was named a Justice of the Common Bench in 1648.[484] Norfolk born and educated in the law at Lincoln's Inn, Cresheld probably owed his early connections with Evesham to a family tie with Sir Francis Egiock, an Exchequer official from Worcestershire, whom he succeeded as recorder at Evesham in 1622.[485] Chesheld served in three parliaments for that borough before 1630. He was a J.P. for Evesham in 1626 and later for Worcestershire,[486] and a member of several local commissions.[487]

---

[465] Tanner MSS, 72, fol. 69; *Winthrop Papers* 1: 326, 1929–1944.

[466] *V.C.H. Suffolk* 2: 188.

[467] Tanner MSS, 65, fols. 35–36.

[468] *Ibid.*, fol. 124; Raven, *The history of Suffolk*, 206.

[469] *C.J.* 2: 47; D'Ewes (N), 119, 120.

[470] *Ibid.*, 51; *N. and Q.*, 1st Ser., 12: 360, 1855.

[471] Tanner MSS, 66, fols. 298–299.

[472] *C.J.* 2: 589; Pink MSS, 299, fol. 645.

[473] *East Anglian*, N.S., 4: 337, 1891–1892.

[474] His will, dated 13 February 1642/3, is abstracted in Add. MSS, 12,518, fols. 7–8. Among its terms were instructions for paying £3000 to each of his five daughters, since he left no son.

[475] *C.J.* 2: 23, 109; D'Ewes (N), 238, 515.

[476] *Mid. Temp. Rec.* 2: 740.

[477] S.P. 16, 362/31; *C.S.P. Dom., 1637,* 391.

[478] Bodleian Carte MSS, 1, fol. 182v. His brother, Lord Craven, was a close friend of Captain Charles Price (*q.v.*), the soldier who served long in Ireland. Price's will, P.C.C. 101 Twisse.

[479] Sir Anthony Ashley Cooper, husband of one of Lord Coventry's sisters, had represented Tewkesbury in the Short Parliament. For the Coventry-Craven relationship, see I.P.M., Thomas Lord Coventry, C. 142/594/68.

[480] D'Ewes (N), 515; *C.J.* 2: 109.

[481] *Yorks. Arch. Jour.* 13: 443, 1895; London Corporation MSS, Rep. 51, fols. 243–247.

[482] He was then described as of Drury Lane and Ryton, Salop. *Cal. Com. Adv. Money*, 299.

[483] *Yorks. Arch. Jour.* 13: 445–446, 1895. The date of his death appears in *D.N.B.* as 1649. Craven is briefly mentioned in Williams, *Gloucester*, 237.

[484] Williams, *Worcester*, 142. A sketch of Cresheld's life appears in Edward Foss, *Judges of England* 6: 287–288, London, 1857.

[485] *The letters of John Chamberlain* 2: 466 and n. Cresheld's will (P.C.C., 67 Bowyer) mentioned two cousins Egiock. The town chose him as Egiock's successor, despite Sir Thomas Coventry's recommendation of another man. S.P. 14, 134/74.

[486] C. 193/12, 13; S.P. 16/405.

[487] C. 181/4, fols. 18, 64v; 181/5, fol. 149, *passim*; Add. MSS, 15,857, fol. 211v.

Cresheld is said to have battled in the courts and in the 1628 parliament against the prerogative doctrine,[488] but he was one of the lawyers on the king's side during the ship money trials of 1637.[489] In 1640 he promised to lend £50 toward the king's expenses, having been solicited as a royal official.[490] In the early period of the Long Parliament Cresheld was not a prominent member either in committee work or in debate, but his knowledge of the law seems to have been regarded highly.[491] He subscribed £100 for the defense in 1642.[492]

Cresheld married, probably sometime before 1615,[493] and left at his death several married daughters. Almost nothing is known of his estate, but quite possibly much of it had been settled before 1640. He described himself in 1650 as aged and infirm.[494]

* John Crew (1598–1679), of Stene, Northamptonshire, was M.P. for Brackley, 1640–1648. The eldest son of the noted lawyer and Speaker of the House, Sir Thomas Crew of Stene (d. 1634), he was educated at Magdalen College, Oxford (B.A. 1618), and Gray's Inn, where he was called to the bar in 1624,[495] and sat in his first parliament for Amersham that year.[496] He was a J.P and member of other commissions in Northamptonshire,[497] and held various properties in that county, including some near Brackley. His wife was the coheiress of an Essex family.[498] With his fellow members, Sir Christopher Hatton and Dryden, Crew proffered £1000 toward the loans in 1641,[499] and his pledge for the defense in 1642 was substantial.[500] He was a brother-in-law of Sir John Curzon and Sir Robert Parkhurst, and a connection by marriage of Sir Simonds D'Ewes.[501]

* Nicholas Crispe (c. 1599–1666), London merchant and customs farmer, was elected for Winchelsea to both parliaments of 1640, but was attacked as a monopolist early in the Long Parliament and expelled 2 February 1641. A member of the Salters' Company of London as his father had been, Crispe for some years before 1638 held a captaincy in the city trained bands,[502] and seems to have had little connection with local matters outside of the city before the 1640 elections.[503] His merchandising ventures, however, were far flung, including, besides his lucrative trade in gold and slaves from Guinea, an interest in the East India Company and in the Barbary Company.[504] For several of his ships he had secured letters of marque, and the post of customs farmer he acquired in 1640.[505] Crispe is said to have absented himself from the House soon after the opening attack, 21 November 1640, on his exclusive patent for the importation of redwood and copperas,[506] for which he was eventually disabled.

Crispe was probably one of the wealthiest of the 1640 parliament men. Although he lost heavily during the years that followed, in fines and in business and shipping losses and in loans to the king, he stated at the time of compounding, 1648–1649, that he held real estate in London and Essex worth about £594 yearly. He estimated his Guinea trade interest as worth some £140,000, but declared his losses were £200,000 and his debts £300,000.[507]

Robert Croke (c. 1611–1680/1), lawyer, of Checkers, Buckinghamshire, and of Hampton Poyle, Oxfordshire, sat for Wendover, 1640–15 November 1643. He was the descendant of a prominent family, being a grandson of Sir John Croke, the judge, a grand-nephew of Sir George Croke, the judge of ship money case fame, and a nephew of Dr. Charles Croke, the divine.[508] His father, Sir Henry Croke, was Clerk of the Pipe in the Exchequer from 1615 until his death in 1659, and by his marriage with Bridget, one of the coheiresses of Sir William Hawtrey of Checkers, had acquired that estate and others in Buckinghamshire. Sir Henry was a J.P. there and in Oxfordshire [509] and M.P., 1614, 1628.[510]

---

[488] Forster, *Eliot* 2 : 102.

[489] Birch, *The court and times of Charles the First* 2 : 275.

[490] S.P. 16, 538/84.

[491] Some of his committee appointments were concerned with points of law (*C.J.* 2 : 87, 217), and in 1643 parliament attempted to have him named a judge (Clarendon, *Rebellion* 2 : 442).

[492] *N. and Q.,* 1st Ser., 12 : 360, 1855.

[493] He was called to the bar that year. A son, William, was admitted to Lincoln's Inn in 1627. Pink MSS, 318.

[494] His will, dated 1 August 1650, was proved 3 February 1651/2.

[495] *Al. Oxon.; Gray's Inn Adm. Reg.,* 136.

[496] Addenda collected by the History of Parliament Committee. The Amersham return for this year is missing from *M. of P.*

[497] C. 193/13; S.P. 16/405; C. 181/4, fols. 140v, 180v.

[498] I.P.M. of Sir Thomas Crew, C. 142/515/88; Baker, *Northampton* 1 : 299, 584–585, 684, 688, 748; 2 : 51.

[499] D'Ewes (N), 439, n.; *Cal. Com. Comp.,* 28.

[500] £200 and 4 horses. *N. and Q.,* 1st Ser., 12 : 338, 1855.

[501] Harl. MSS, 165, fol. 4; D'Ewes, *Autobiography* 1 : 361.

[502] London Corporation MSS, Rep. 47, fol. 131v; 49, fol. 206v; 52, fol. 240.

[503] Crispe does not seem to have been a member of the Kentish family of the name located at Quekes in the Isle of Thanet at this period (*Vis. Kent, 1619,* 74; Hasted, *Kent* 10 : 298–299; *Arch. Cant.* 12 : 406–407, 416–418, 1878). Winchelsea, however, was notorious already as a rotten borough (*Sussex Arch. Coll.* 8 : 211, 1856).

[504] Sainsbury, *A calendar of the court minutes &c. of the East India Company, 1640–1643,* 360; *C.S.P. Dom.,* 1640, 654; S.P. 16, 400/81.

[505] *C.S.P. Dom., 1629–1631,* 156; *1631–1633,* 237; *1640,* 149; D'Ewes (N), 197.

[506] *C.J.* 2 : 33; D'Ewes (N), 312, 540; Lansd. MSS, 491, fol. 56.

[507] *Cal. Com. Comp.,* 1651; S.P. 23/206/907–909, 913–915. See also *M. of P.; Complete Baronetage* 4 : 11.

[508] Lipscomb, *Buckingham* 2 : 189; Lysons, *Mag. Brit.* 1 : 541; *D.N.B.* articles on Sir John Croke and Sir George Croke.

[509] S.P. 16, 405.

[510] *Al. Oxon.* Sir Henry's name appears once in the records of the Long Parliament, but there is no indication that he was a member. The man named as "Sir Henry" in the list of the

Robert, his eldest son, was born about 1611, studied for a time at Amersham under Dr. Charles Croke, and matriculated at Balliol College, Oxford, 31 October 1629, aged eighteen. He received no degree until he was created M.D. in 1644,[511] but was admitted to the Inner Temple on 9 June 1627 and called to the bar in 1635.[512] Before April, 1639, he received a grant in reversion of his father's office of Clerk of the Pipe, but did not step into it until his father's death.[513] He married at St. Andrew's, Holborne, on 29 June 1634, Susanna, daughter and coheiress of Sir Peter Van Lore, Bart., of Tilehurst, Berkshire, the wealthy merchant.[514] On 9 August 1641 he was knighted at Whitehall.[515]

Croke was elected for Wendover to both parliaments of 1640.[516] He played but a minor role there, not often being named to committees. He was not listed among the "Straffordians," but when the war began, joined his father in support of the king. He was accordingly disabled, 15 November 1643.[517] After compounding for his estates, 1646–1647, he seems to have abstained from active politics. Following the Restoration, he still held his office in the Exchequer and became an associate and bencher of Gray's Inn.[518] He died on 8 February 1680/1, and was buried at Ellesborough.[519]

At the time of his election as a parliament man Croke was not yet in possession of his inheritance, and seems to have resided in Oxfordshire and London rather than at his father's place near Wendover. He doubtless benefited from his wife's properties, although lawsuits regarding Van Lore's estates continued for nearly three decades.[520] The parliamentary assessment in 1644 of £2000 indicates that he was considered wealthy, but his compounding fine, at a tenth, was £772.[521]

Relatives of Croke in the 1640 House were Bulstrode Whitelocke and his cousins by marriage, Harbottle Grimston and Richard Jervoise.

* Oliver Cromwell (1599–1658) sat for the borough of Cambridge, having been made a freeman there just before the Short Parliament elections. He had been

an M.P. twice before November, 1640, a J.P. in Huntingdonshire and the Isle of Ely,[522] member of other local commissions,[523] and an opponent of the knighthood compositions of 1630,[524] as well as of the fen drainage. His estate, though moderate in comparison with those of many of his colleagues, enabled him to advance more than £1000 for the parliamentary cause before September, 1643,[525] and included lands inherited from his maternal uncle in addition to the estate of £300 a year or more which his father had enjoyed. His income was possibly £400 to £500 a year.[526]

Cromwell had numerous relatives in the House,[527] as well as associates of his Inn of Court days.[528]

Sir Patrick Curwen, Bart. (c. 1602–1664), of Workington, Cumberland, was knight for his shire, 1640 to 1643 or 1644. He had represented his county in the four preceding parliaments, having stepped in 1625 into the place his father had occupied in 1621.[529] His family was one of the oldest in England, and lived in a Tudor mansion that was transformed from the border fortress where Curwen's great-grandfather had received Mary Queen of Scots in 1568. His grandfather, Sir Nicholas Curwen (d. 1604), and his father, Sir Henry Curwen (d. 1623), had served their county as M.P. and sheriff. The latter married on 1 January 1601 Katherine, daughter of Sir John Dalston of Dalston Hall, Cumberland, and their first son, Patrick, was born early in 1602.[530] When he was barely eighteen (28 February 1619/20), Patrick married Isabella, daughter and coheir of Sir George Selby of Whitehouse, Durham. At Easter of that year he matriculated at Queen's College, Cambridge,[531] but he stayed for no degree. His only child, Henry (d. 1636), was born the following year.

Shortly after his father's death in 1623, Patrick took up his family's official responsibilities, and apparently followed their pattern of loyalty to the crown. He was probably a supporter of Buckingham in the parliaments of 1625–1628, for it was by the Duke's influence that

---

Committee of Privileges (*C.J.* 2: 21) was probably Mr. Henry Coke.

[511] *Al. Oxon.*; Wood, *Fasti Oxon.* 2: 77–78.

[512] *Cal. Inner Temp. Rec.* 2: 163, 226.

[513] *C.S.P. Dom.*, 1639, 1.

[514] Pink MSS, 307, fol. 98; Sir Alexander Croke, *The genealogical history of the Croke Family* 1: 501–503, Oxford, 1823.

[515] Shaw, *K. of E.* 2: 210.

[516] *M. of P.* 1: 480, 485.

[517] *C.J.* 2: 108; 3: 311.

[518] *Gray's Inn Adm. Reg.*, 289.

[519] Both Croke and Lipscomb give the date of his death as 8 February 1680, but since their accounts were based on the parish register and the monumental inscription, the correct reading of the date is probably 1680/1.

[520] *Arch. Cant.* 16: 52, 1886. One manor of Croke's mother's inheritance (*V.C.H. Buckingham* 4: 75) was valued in 1620 at nearly £400 a year (Bodleian Willis MSS, 30, fols. 6, 9v).

[521] *Cal. Com. Comp.*, 1471; Pink MSS, 307, fol. 97.

[522] *V.C.H. Huntingdonshire* 2: 15; C. 193/13 (1634, Isle of Ely).

[523] C. 181/5, fols. 235, 294.

[524] S.P. 16, 189/46, i, fol. 135; Abbott, *The writings and speeches of Oliver Cromwell* 1: 71 (hereafter, Abbott, *Cromwell*).

[525] So Cromwell stated in a letter to St. John, 11 September 1643, remarking at the same time that he could not well do more, because "my estate is little." Brit. Mus. Stowe MSS, 184, fol. 55.

[526] Sanford, *St. and Ill.*, 210, 216, 246; Abbott, *Cromwell* 1: 12, 82–83.

[527] They included Hampden, Dunch, Percival and others. See S. J. Weyman, Oliver Cromwell's kinsfolk, *E.H.R.* 6: 48–60, 1891.

[528] Abbott suggests (*Cromwell* 1: 33–34), on the basis of Cromwell's friends, that Gray's Inn, rather than Lincoln's Inn, may have been the place of his supposed legal studies.

[529] *M. of P.* 1: 450, 463, 468, 475, 480.

[530] I.P.M. of Sir John Dalston (C. 142/514/44) and of Sir Henry Curwen (C. 142/404/119).

[531] *Al. Cant.*

he was created a baronet in 1627.[532] He was a loan commissioner for his county that year,[533] and as an army captain and a D.L.[534] was engaged in levying soldiers for the Rochelle expedition. He served also as a J.P. and member of other commissions, as one of the county's escheators,[535] and in 1636–1637 was sheriff. He collected most of the ship money required of Cumberland during his term and without difficulty.[536] He was concerned in 1639 and 1640 with military affairs on the border and as a colonel was active in arranging for more troops for the defense of the county.[537]

As Cumberland's member in both of the 1640 parliaments Curwen supported the king. He promised his security for the loan in 1640, giving his pledge with his fellow knight for £1000.[538] But he was sworn one of the witnesses for Strafford's cause and voted later against his attainder.[539] He was appointed to various committees, some of them dealing with army affairs, and others with irregularities among the clergy, and was named in 1642 as one of the commissioners for scandalous ministers in Cumberland.[540] He went back to his county that year, joined the king, and was twice disabled by the House, 15 March 1643 and 22 January 1644.[541] Sir Patrick later compounded for his estates and was heavily fined. After sitting in parliament again in 1661,[542] he died on 15 December 1664 and was buried at Workington.

The Curwen family estates had declined from the time when they had been enriched by lands of the church in the preceding century. But though Sir Patrick's father had alienated some of his properties, he still owned at his death four manors and parts of others, which included 6000 or more acres,[543] and a daughter of the house had a dowry of £1000 in 1639. Sir Patrick's marriage helped him to rebuild his fortunes considerably, probably by several thousand pounds,[544] and before the war damaged the business he collected, in addition to his rents, certain profits from coal, salt making and salmon fishing interests. His declaration to the compounding commissioners of four manors as his chief property, with an income of £620, out of which £360 were payable as annuities, seems to have been an underestimate. His original fine of £2700 was reduced

to £2000, but a fine for second offence was set in 1649 at a sixth, £1392, with later abatements of £240–£300. In spite of losses amounting to possibly £23,000, his heir's estate was reported after 1664 as worth £1000 a year.[545]

In his leisure time Curwen indulged in horse racing, the chief amusement of his part of the country. His will indicates that he abhorred extremes in religion, preferring the middle way of the Church of England. He was interested in education.[546] Lloyd described him as "a pious and peaceful man, . . . master of a great wit and a vigorous discourse, outdoing most in action," and of a "clear and heroic mind."[547]

As might be expected of the head of one of the dominant families of the north, Curwen was related to various parliament men of 1640, including the Dalstons, Barwis, Sir William Widdrington, Sir Henry Bellingham, the Mallorys, and the younger Fenwick.[548]

Sir John Curzon, or **Curson, Bart.** (1598–1686), of Kedleston, Derbyshire, was a member for his shire, 1640–1648. His old county family, famed for their riches and hospitality, had been "Knights when the Crown wanted money, and Esquires when it did not,"[549] and had filled local offices and sent knights to parliament since the fifteenth century.[550] The Long Parliament member was the son and heir of John Curzon, esquire (H.S. 1609, d. 1632), by his wife, Millicent, daughter of Sir Ralph Sacheverell of Stanton, Derbyshire, and of Barton, Notts, and was born on 13 November 1598. He matriculated at Oxford in 1618 (Magdalen College), possibly travelled to the continent later that year, and in 1620 entered the Inner Temple.[551] Three years later, on 26 August 1623, he married Patience, daughter of Thomas Crew of Stene, sister of John Crew (q.v.), his father settling on him at that time the estate of Kedleston and other properties.[552]

In Derbyshire Curzon followed his family tradition by serving on the commission of the peace and of gaol delivery,[553] and either he or his father was a loan com-

[532] The fee of £1095 usually charged for a baronetcy was waived. C.S.P. Dom., 1627–1628, 85.
[533] S.P. 16, 56/34.
[534] S.P. 16, 73/41/i.
[535] C. 193/12, 13; C. 181/4, fols. 25, 81; C. 142/507/162.
[536] C.S.P. Dom., 1636–1637, 485; Royal Hist. Soc., Trans., 3rd Ser., 4: 157, 1910.
[537] Strafford Letters, 315.
[538] D'Ewes (N), 52.
[539] L.J. 4: 115; Verney, 58.
[540] C.J. 2: 61, 152; Pink MSS. 307, fol. 306.
[541] C.J. 3: 1, 374; Cal. Com. Comp., 985.
[542] M. of P. 1: 521.
[543] Will of Sir Henry Curwen (proved 1597), York Probate Registry, vol. 27, fols. 151–153; Chancery proceedings, C. 3/326/5; I.P.M. of Sir Henry Curwen, C. 142/404/119.
[544] The dowry of his wife's sister and coheir was £7000.

[545] Cal. Com. Comp., 985–986; S.P. 23/179/596; Pink MSS. 307, fol. 306; English Baronetage 4: 364, 1741.
[546] H.M.C., Fourth Report, Queen's College MSS., 458.
[547] Memoires, 692–693.
[548] Additional references used for this sketch are: Complete Baronetage 2: 10; J. F. Curwen, A pedigree of the family of Curwen, 46–51, Kendal, T. Wilson, 1904?; J. F. Curwen, A history of the ancient house of Curwen, 125–149, Kendal, T. Wilson, 1928; R. S. Ferguson, Cumberland and Westmorland M.P.'s, 11, 344; W. Jackson, The Curwens of Workington Hall, Cumb. and Westm. Trans., 1st Ser. 5: 182–204, 1879–1880; Nicolson and Burn, Hist. of Westmorland and Cumberland 1: 205; Sandford, Antiq. & Fam. Cumberland, 19–20.
[549] W. Hutton, The history of Derby, 262, 2nd ed., London, 1817 (hereafter, Hutton, Derby).
[550] Derbys. Arch. Jour., N.S. 2: 40, 1926–1927; Glover, Derbyshire 1: App., 20.
[551] Al. Oxon.; Bodleian Tanner MSS. 74, fol. 115.
[552] I.P.M. of John Curzon, 1632, C. 142/485/100.
[553] C. 193/13; S.P. 16/405; C. 181/3, fol. 237.

missioner in 1627, lending £12 himself to the king.[554] Succeeding his father in 1632, Curzon became the first baronet of his line, being created as of Nova Scotia in 1636 and of England in 1641. He obtained a grant in 1636 of the reversion of the office of Receiver-General of the Duchy of Lancaster, but did not enter upon the office before 1649.[555] In 1637–1638 Curzon was sheriff of Derbyshire and, although he experienced the current difficulties in collecting ship money, managed to gather in most of that year's assessment as well as much of the arrears. He appeared twice before Council before his accounts were complete, and declared in 1640 that he had incurred expenses of at least £150 in the work. During the same period he was busy also as a D.L.[556]

Curzon entered parliament first in 1628, sitting then for Brackley, and in the spring of 1640 represented Derbyshire.[557] He was an active member of the Long Parliament, working with the popular leaders, was named to numerous committees, and offered his bond for £1000 toward the loan in November, 1640.[558] Although his second baronetcy was granted by the king personally as he passed through Derbyshire in August, 1641,[559] Curzon stayed with the opposition, promised two horses for the defense in June, 1642,[560] and remained in parliament until he was secluded in December, 1648. He long survived the Restoration, died in his eighty-ninth year, 13 December 1686, and was buried at Kedleston.

That Curzon was a well-to-do member is indicated by his baronetcies as well as by his bond of November, 1640. His inheritance included several manors in Derbyshire and other property in Hampshire, to which he added later by purchases.[561] He should not be confused with the Oxfordshire royalist of the same name.[562]

Sir Thomas Dacres (1587–1668), of Cheshunt, Hertfordshire, elected to replace Capel as a member for his county, 26 August 1641, sat until Pride's Purge in 1648. Born on 19 October 1587, he was the eldest surviving son of Sir Thomas Dacres (d. 1615) by his second wife, Dorothy, daughter of Thomas (Francis ?)

Pigot of Dodershall, Bucks, and a descendant of Robert Dacres, privy councillor to Henry VIII.[1] He probably studied at Cambridge, matriculating at St. John's in 1603,[2] and about 1609 married Martha, daughter of Thomas Elmes of Lilford, Northamptonshire.[3] He completed his father's term as sheriff of Hertfordshire after the latter's death in July, 1615,[4] and was knighted at Theobalds, 22 February 1617.[5] He served as a captain in Mansfeld's expedition, and was rumored to have been lost at the fall of Breda in 1625,[6] but his friends' mourning for him was premature. He was a D.L. in Hertfordshire in 1627,[7] and by 1640 had been for nearly twenty years a J.P. and a member of various local commissions.[8] Dacres had some influence outside of his county, too, probably through his being a cousin by marriage of Secretary Dorchester, for in 1629 he arranged for his eldest son to travel abroad with one of the royal ambassadors, and the following year was seeking some other favor from the secretary.[9]

Sir Thomas was elected to the parliament of 1626 by his county and also by the borough of Higham Ferrers, near which he owned property, but he served for his own shire. He was re-elected in 1628[10] and probably worked with the country party. His wife's father or brother was presumably the Thomas Elmes who was among the gentlemen imprisoned for having refused the 1627 loan.[11] Dacres himself seems to have acquiesced in the ship money collections of the next decade, but in 1639 he declined to contribute toward the king's journey north,[12] and in the spring of that year and of 1640 he was summoned to attend Council as a musters defaulter.[13] He was present in October, 1640, when Capel and Lytton were elected as shire knights[14] and, after he had been chosen as Capel's successor in 1641, was named on the important recess committee[15] and quickly stepped into active work with the opposition. In June, 1642, he generously offered two horses and £200 for the defense,[16] and during the war served on

---

[554] *Derbys. Arch. Jour.*, 1st Ser. **21**: 74, 81, 1899.

[555] W. R. Williams, *Official lists of the duchy and county of Lancaster*, 23, London, privately printed, 1901.

[556] *C.S.P. Dom.*, *1637–1638*, 327, 412, 597; *1638–1639*, 29, 297; *1639–1640*, 454; Royal Hist. Soc., *Trans.*, 3rd Ser., **4**: 157, 1910.

[557] *M. of P.* **1**: 476, 481.

[558] *C.J.* **2**: 44, 50, 267, *passim;* Pink MSS, 307, fol. 326v; D'Ewes (N), 52.

[559] *V.C.H. Derbyshire* **2**: 126.

[560] *N. and Q.*, 1st Ser. **12**: 360, 1855.

[561] C. 142/485/100; *V.C.H. Hampshire* **4**: 348; *Derbys. Arch. Jour.*, 1st Ser. **11**: 5–7, 1889.

[562] Lloyd, *Memoires*, 700. The Sir John Curzon, listed as a proposed Knight of the Royal Oak, with an estate of £500 a year, and sometimes indentified as of Kedleston (Wotton, *English Baronetage* **4**: 372, 1741), was probably the Oxfordshire man. Besides the authorities cited above, see, for Curzon of Kedleston, *Complete Baronetage* **2**: 132–133; Glover, *Derbyshire* **2**: 566.

[1] I.P.M., Sir Thomas Dacres, 1616, C. 142/359/119; Clutterbuck, *Herts* **2**: 100, 101; Lipscomb, *Buckingham* **1**: 406.

[2] *Al. Cant.*

[3] Several deeds concerning the marriage settlement are mentioned in his father's I.P.M. Dacres's eldest son, Thomas, entered Oxford in October, 1629, "aged 20." *Al. Oxon.*

[4] *The letters of John Chamberlain* **1**: 612.

[5] Clutterbuck, *Herts* **2**: 101; Pink MSS, 300, fol. 697. Shaw (*K. of E.* **2**: 161) identifies the 1617 knight as of Cumberland, but the Hertfordshire Dacres was referred to as "Sir" in April, 1617. *C.S.P. Dom.*, *1611–1618*, 461.

[6] *The letters of John Chamberlain* **2**: 618, 620 and n.

[7] S.P. 16, 63/76.

[8] C. 193/12, 13; S.P. 16/405; C. 181/4, fol. 178v; 181/5, fol. 40.

[9] *Al. Oxon.; C.S.P. Dom.*, *1629–1631*, 365, 392.

[10] *M. of P.* **1**: 469, 470, 475; *C.S.P. Dom.*, *1635*, xxxiv.

[11] Rushworth, **1**: 473.

[12] *Ibid.* **3**: 914. His name occurs in the list of Hampshire men.

[13] *C.S.P. Dom.*, *1639*, 193; *1640*, 186; S.P. 16, 420/10.

[14] Hertfordshire indenture, C. 219/43/Part 1.

[15] *C.J.* **2**: 288.

[16] *N. and Q.*, 1st Ser., **12**: 338, 1855.

various county committees and was particularly active as a speaker to arouse enthusiasm for the cause.[17] Dacres was secluded in 1648, survived the Restoration, and died late in 1668, being buried at Cheshunt on 26 December.

Sir Thomas was a man of means, his inherited estates including four manors and numerous other properties in Hertfordshire and Essex, several of the midland counties, and London. His wife's jointure had been no less than £2000.[18] In 1660 the family estates, which had by that time apparently passed to his son, were valued at £1000 a year.[19]

Dacres was somewhat distantly related to Alexander Carew (q.v.) [20] and connected through his wife with Hesilrige.[21]

Sir George Dalston (d. 1657), of Dalston, Cumberland, was M.P. for his county, 1640 to 1643 or 1644. His family was old and wealthy, having been enriched by monastery lands after the dissolution, and having increased their estates by fortunate marriages. His parents were Sir John Dalston (D.L. and several times sheriff, d. 1633) and his second wife, Frances, daughter and coheir of Thomas Warcop of Smardale in Westmorland. Sir John was said to have an income of £3000 a year.[22] George, his father's eldest son, was born before 1593,[23] but later than 1580, and matriculated at Cambridge (Queen's), about 1596.[24] He afterwards spent some time at the court of Queen Elizabeth, but returned to the north county to marry and live as a squire. On 11 February 1603/4 he married a rich heiress, Catherine, daughter of John Tamworth of Halsted, Leicestershire. She was coheiress to a third of her father's possessions in the latter county, Nottingham, Dorset and Radnor, valued at £3600 a year.[25] Dalston was knighted in 1607,[26] and by February, 1608, was a captain at the fort of Carlisle.[27] His wife died in 1614, leaving him a son, William (q.v.), and four daughters.[28]

Sir George filled many offices in his county. He was a D.L. in 1616,[29] sheriff of Cumberland, 1618–1619,[30] and was a J.P. in Cumberland, Westmorland, and Durham for many years.[31] He served on commissions for piracy and oyer and terminer in his own and neighboring counties,[32] and in 1633 was captain of Carlisle citadel.[33] He was one of the Carlisle aldermen in 1634.[34] He was engaged frequently in lawsuits concerning his family estates and those of his wife,[35] but was said to have gained a reputation for great justice and integrity in office. He represented Cumberland regularly in parliament, beginning with that of 1621,[36] and seems in his earlier parliaments to have taken a moderate course on the relations between king and subject.

Dalston's course in the Long Parliament, too, avoided extremes. He subscribed £1000 jointly with Curwen for the 1640 loan,[37] and seems to have acquiesced in the attainder of Strafford. He was named to nearly a dozen committees before the recess, including those on army supply, and on the Star Chamber and the Court of High Commission. He was probably absent by June, 1642, although he was that year named a commissioner for scandalous ministers,[38] and was disabled on 15 March 1643 for having executed the commission of array. He was named to two parliamentary committees for his county after that, but was disabled again, 22 January 1644.[39] He compounded for his estates in 1645. Dalston made his will on 9 September 1657 and probably died soon afterwards.[40] His funeral sermon was preached on September 28 by Jeremy Taylor.

Sir George's wealth, estimated at one time as over £3000 a year, came from six or more manors lying in the northern counties and some in the south.[41] He settled the larger part of his estate in 1635 on his son, William, and when he compounded for his delinquency he listed properties with a total income of but £707 a year.[42] He planned a portion of £1000 for an unmarried daughter when he made his will. Both he and

[17] Pink MSS, 300, fol. 697; Kingston, *Herts. during the Civil War*, 152.

[18] I.P.M. cited above; Clutterbuck, *Herts* 2: 100.

[19] The son seems to have been a royalist, for this estimate was given at his nomination for the Knights of the Royal Oak. *English Baronetage* 4: 370, 1741.

[20] Dacres's paternal grandmother was one of the Carews of Anthony, Cornwall. Pink MSS, 300, fol. 697.

[21] Hesilrige's first wife was a sister of Dacres's wife.

[22] Sandford, *Antiq. & Fam. Cumberland*, 29.

[23] He was aged forty and more at his father's death in December, 1633. I.P.M.'s of Sir John Dalston, C. 142/507/162, C. 142/514/44.

[24] *Al Cant.*

[25] Cumb. and Westm. *Trans.*, 1st Ser., 7: 204, 1884; N.S. 10: 218, 1910.

[26] *Al. Cant.*

[27] *C.S.P. Dom., 1603–1610*, 406.

[28] Cumb. and Westm. *Trans.*, N.S. 10: 218, 1910; John Fetherston, ed., *The visitation of the county of Cumberland in the year 1615*, Harleian Society 7: 5, 1872 (hereafter, *Vis. Cumberland, 1615*).

[29] *H.M.C., Twelfth Report 7*, MSS of Mr. S. H. Le Fleming, 14.

[30] *List of Sheriffs*, 28.

[31] C. 193/12, 13; S.P. 16/405; *C.S.P. Dom., 1638–1639*, 312.

[32] C. 181/4, fols. 25, 81; 181/5, fols. 14, 70, *passim; C.S.P. Dom., 1635*, 510.

[33] Pink MSS, 307, fol. 305.

[34] *Reprints of rare tracts . . . illustrative of the history of Carlisle*, Miscellaneous, 30, Newcastle, 1844–1849.

[35] St. Ch. 8/70/11; *Winthrop Papers* 2: 12 and n., 1929.

[36] *M. of P.* 1: 450, *passim.*

[37] D'Ewes (N), 52.

[38] Pink MSS, 307, fol. 305; *C.J.* 2: 66, 75, *passim.*

[39] *C.J.* 3: 1, 374.

[40] P.C.C., 466 Ruthen.

[41] I.P.M.'s cited above; Chancery Proceedings, C. 3/343/7, C. 3/345/12; *Y.A.S. Rec. Ser.* 58: 33, 183, 1917; *C.S.P. Dom., 1631–1633*, 165; *V.C.H. Hampshire* 4: 105.

[42] *Cal. Com. Comp.*, 960; S.P. 23/192/509–510, 517, 547.

his father enjoyed horse racing and were described as "great gamsters never without two or three Roning horses the best in england & venter the 100 pounds frely," and as being "brave" housekeepers.[43] He was said, however, to have cared little for money itself, but to have managed his estates wisely and given much to the poor.

He may have had a leaning toward Roman Catholicism,[44] but in religion as in politics he disliked controversy. He was fond of sermons, respected ministers who clung to their principles, and opposed persecution. Jeremy Taylor, who preached Dalston's funeral sermon, characterized him as "of a meek and gentle spirit, but not too soft," one who loved God and the church, and was "a lover of his country's liberties, and yet an observer of the laws of his king."[45]

Dalston was an uncle of his fellow member, Sir Patrick Curwen, and father of Carlisle's M.P., William Dalston.[46]

William Dalston (d. 1683), of Smardale, Westmorland, and of Dalston, Cumberland, was M.P. for Carlisle, 1640–22 January 1644. He was the son and heir apparent of Sir George Dalston (q.v.), member for the county. He was born at Smardale between 1604 and 1614,[47] was admitted to St. John's, Cambridge, 6 July 1631, and to Gray's Inn five months later.[48] Shortly after 11 December 1635 he married Anne, daughter of Thomas Bolles of Osberton, Notts, and of Mary Lady Bolles, acquiring with her manors in that county and in Yorkshire which brought his family's already numerous estates to their greatest extent. His wife died in April, 1639.[49]

The younger Dalston appears to have held no public office before 1640, but was elected to the Short Parliament for Carlisle.[50] He was named to few committees of the Long Parliament but while he was in attendance there was created a baronet (15 February 1641) and was knighted at Whitehall, 31 July 1641.[51] With the

outbreak of war he took up a colonelcy in Cumberland under the Earl of Newcastle, and was disabled from sitting in the House, 22 January 1644.[52] With his father he petitioned in 1645 to compound for their estates, and he succeeded Sir George in 1657. He spent his later years at Heath Hall, Yorkshire, and died on 13 January 1683. He seems to have been listed as a "papist" in 1648.[53]

Although Dalston's father was still in possession of some of the family estates in 1640, William held in his own right a number of the properties inherited from his mother's family in the southern counties, and some from his wife's family.[54] He seems to have had an annual income, independent of his father's approximately £700 a year, of at least £437–£500 a year. He was fined more heavily than his father by the compounding committee, perhaps because of his greater activity during the war. His fine was set first at a third, £3600, and reduced later and paid at £3000.[55]

Sir Thomas Danby (1610–1660), of Farnley and Thorpe Perrow, Yorkshire, served for Richmond from 1640 until he was disabled, 6 September 1642. He came of an old family which had been settled at Farnley early in the sixteenth century and owned extensive lands and coal pits in "Mashamshire." His maternal grandmother, a Roman Catholic as late as 1627, was a Wentworth, aunt of Thomas, Earl of Strafford. Danby's parents, Christopher Danby of Leighton (d. 1624) and his wife, Frances, daughter of Edward Parker Lord Morley,[56] were recusants, also, and were accused at one time of harboring priests. They did not get along well, partly because of Christopher's inability to manage his estate and his temper, and at least twice during Thomas's childhood were separated.[57] Their eldest son, Thomas, was born in 1610 and in 1627 matriculated at St. John's, Cambridge. Three years later he married Katherine, daughter of Christopher Wandesford of Kirklington,[58] a kinsman of Wentworth and official under him in Ireland, and afterwards his successor as Lord Deputy.[59] Danby was living with or visiting his father-in-law in 1633 when he was knighted at Dublin by Wentworth along with the latter's younger brother, George,[60] who was a friend of Danby and afterwards his colleague in parliament. Two of Danby's children were living with their grand-

[43] Sandford, *Antiq. & Fam. Cumberland*, 29.
[44] *Cal. Com. Comp.*, 99.
[45] Portions of the sermon are printed in Cumb. and Westm. *Trans.*, 1st Ser., **7** : 203, 1884, and in William Hutchinson, *The history of the county of Cumberland* **2**: 454–456, Carlisle, 1794 (hereafter, Hutchinson, *Hist. Cumberland*).
[46] References in addition to those cited above are *V.C.H. Cumberland* **2** : 317; F. Haswell, The family of Dalston, Cumb. and Westm. *Trans.*, N.S., **10** : 201–270, 1910; Ferguson, *Cumberland and Westmorland M.P.'s*, 347.
[47] His age was given as seventeen at his matriculation at Cambridge in 1631, but a brother younger than he seems to have been baptized in 1610. His parents married in 1604, and his mother died in 1614. Cumb. and Westm. *Trans.*, N.S. **10** : 218, 221, 1910.
[48] *Al Cant.*
[49] Cumb. and Westm. *Trans.*, 1st Ser., **7** : 205, 1884; N.S., **10** : 221, 224, 1910; S.P. 23/192, fols. 517, 527–528, 547.
[50] *M. of P.* **1** : 480.
[51] *Complete Baronetage* **2** : 81.

[52] *C.J.* **3** : 374; Pink MSS, 307, fol. 310.
[53] *Cal. Com. Comp.*, 99.
[54] Dorset N. H. *Proceedings* **56** : 57, 1934.
[55] *Cal. Com. Comp.*, 960–961; S.P. 23/192/527–529, 533–541.
[56] I.P.M., Christopher Danby of Leighton, C. 142/404/118; *Y.A.S. Rec. Ser.* **34** : 57–58, 1904; *Yorkshire County Magazine* **3** : 62, 1893.
[57] *Thoresby Society Publications* **37** : 1–28, 1946; St. Ch. 8/120/2.
[58] *Al. Cant.*; *Yorks. Arch. Jour.* **1** : 240, 1870.
[59] *D.N.B.*
[60] Shaw, *K. of E.* **2** : 202.

parents in Ireland as late as 1639,[61] but Danby himself had become by then active in the affairs of his county. He was a J.P. in the North Riding, a member of the sewers commission,[62] and in 1635 became a D.L.[63] He was sheriff, 1637–1638, and collected ship money with some severity.[64] As an officer in the trained bands in 1639 Sir Thomas was one of the group who addressed the king in January, questioning the wisdom of sending all of the county's forces away at the same time.[65] He returned the following summer from a trip to London much disturbed by the news of the king and of the north that he had heard while he was away.[66]

Danby had not served in parliament before he was elected in October, 1640, for Richmond, a town which had once chosen his father-in-law.[67] His principal activities in the Long Parliament were as a supporter of his cousin, Strafford. He gave evidence for him at his trial, voted against his attainder,[68] and had to defend himself for a time because he had followed Strafford's orders about court martialling men under his command.[69] He left eventually to raise troops for the king in Yorkshire and was disabled, 6 September 1642.[70] He compounded with a heavy fine, 1645–1650, and lived until 1660. He died in London on 5 August 1660, and was buried on August 18 at York Minster.[71]

Danby inherited from his father some ten manors of over 2000 acres in Yorkshire, which his father had estimated in 1610 to be worth at least £1550 a year.[72] When he compounded for his estates in 1645, he declared values of £1500 a year, but asked allowance for annuities and rents of £420 and debts of £5000 and some mortgages. His fine was set at £4780.[73] Even though he sold some of his lands to pay his fine, Danby still held enough when he made his will late in 1659 to plan for portions totalling £6000 for five of his children. He referred in his will also to several plantations in Virginia which were to go to a younger son who had already spent some time in the colony.[74]

Although Danby's grandmother and his parents favored Romanism, I have found no indication that he himself was not a conforming Anglican.[75]

Henry Darley (born c. 1596), of Buttercrambe, Yorkshire, was returned for the restored borough of North Allerton, 15 January 1641, and continued to sit, except for an interval in 1649, until 1653.[76] He was born about 1596, the son and heir apparent of Sir Richard Darley, J.P. (d. c. 1654),[77] and was educated at Cambridge and Gray's Inn. In 1619 he married Marjory Hungate of York, who died in 1624;[78] and about 1630 he married Elizabeth, daughter of William Watts of London, granddaughter of a Lord Mayor. He was M.P. for Aldborough in the 1628 parliament,[79] and in his own county was a sewers commissioner for some years.[80]

Darley's family were puritans and he became interested in the colonial ventures in which the puritans were active. He was acquainted with Winthrop and Pym, and was a stockholder in the Massachusetts Bay Company, the Saybrooke enterprise, and the Providence Island Company.[81] He may have been in the Netherlands in 1634,[82] but was in Yorkshire in 1639. His protests against the soldiery in the county and particularly his work in negotiating with the Covenanters led to Strafford's order for his imprisonment without bail at York early in the autumn of 1640. He was released sometime after 30 November.

By 16 February 1641 Darley was present in the parliament. He was named to such early committees as those on the Court of Wards and on the powers of the clergy.[83] In 1642 he was active in the plans for the army and pledged £200 for the defense.[84] He continued to play an important role during the war years, and was living late in 1665. He died, however, before 12 August 1671.[85]

Darley's father was still in possession of the family estates in 1640, but as early as 1622 Henry was associated with him in some of his business affairs. Their principal holdings were Buttercrambe manor and two

---

[61] *The autobiography of Mrs. Alice Thornton,* Surtees Society 62: 13, 1875.
[62] C. 193/13; S.P. 16/405; C. 181/5, fols. 106, 173.
[63] Bean, *Northern Counties,* 1011.
[64] Add. MSS, 6672, fol. 222; Hull Corporation MSS, Danby's letter of 21 October 1637 to Hull.
[65] S.P. 16, 409/53; Sloane MSS, 650, fol. 92.
[66] *C.S.P. Dom., 1639,* 410.
[67] Bean, *Northern Counties,* 1203.
[68] *Ibid.,* 1011; Verney, 57.
[69] D'Ewes (N), 326, 329; *C.J.* **2**: 79.
[70] *C.J.* **2**: 754.
[71] *Yorks. Arch. Jour.* **1**: 240, 1870.
[72] I.P.M. cited above; St. Ch. 8/120/2; *Thoresby Society Publications* 37: 8–9, 1946.
[73] *Cal. Com. Comp.,* 1014–1015; *Y.A.S. Rec. Ser.* **20**: 86, 1896.
[74] Danby's will (dated 11 November 1659), York Registry, **54**, fol. 97.
[75] *Cf.* his kinsman, Sir George Wentworth of Woolley.

[76] *M. of P.* **1**: 497 and n. In several lists Darley has been confused with his brother, Richard, a "recruiter" for Malton.
[77] *Y.A.S. Rec. Ser.* **1**: 109, 1885; Gooder, *Parl. Rep. York* **2**: 74.
[78] He was described in the license as of "Screyingham," the name of one of his family's manors. *Yorks. Arch. Jour.* **14**: 497, 1898; *Y.A.S. Rec. Ser.* **32**: 25, 1902; will of Richard Darley of Buttercrambe, 1599, York Registry **27**, fol. 689.
[79] *M. of P.* **1**: 479.
[80] C. 181/3; 181/4, fol. 114.
[81] F. Rose-Troup, *The Massachusetts Bay Company and its predecessors,* 141; *Winthrop Papers* **3**: 198–199, 1929; **4**: 268. I have found no evidence to support Hexter's statement (*The reign of King Pym,* 80) that Darley had been to New England.
[82] Pym, writing in November, 1634, to his son, Alexander, then with the States' army, spoke of having talked earlier with "Mr. Darley" about Alexander's conduct. Add. MSS, 11,692, fol. 1.
[83] *C.J.* **2**: 87, 99, 105.
[84] *N. and Q.,* 1st Ser., **12**: 338, 1855.
[85] Gooder, *op. cit.* **2**: 78.

others,[86] but they had bought additional properties in the same region before 1640 and some in Durham.[87]

Darley was a brother-in-law of John Alured (q.v.).

Matthew Davies (1595–1678), of the Middle Temple and of Shaftesbury, Dorset, sat for Christchurch, Hants, 1640–16 March 1643.[88] He was the eldest son and heir of Edward Davies of Chicksgrove, Wiltshire, by Joan, daughter of Robert Cave of Bagley, near Gillingham, Dorset, and was baptized at Tisbury, Wilts, in April, 1595. He was a nephew of Sir John Davies (d. 1626), who was Attorney-General in Ireland.[89] On 4 April 1614 he was admitted to the Middle Temple, and was called to the bar there in 1623 in the company of two future colleagues of the 1640 parliament, Sir Simonds D'Ewes and John George. He retained his connection with the Temple as late as February, 1645.[90] He married Anne, daughter of Edward Mervyn of Fonthill, Wilts,[91] and in 1624 served as M.P. for Hindon. The Matthew Davies who was M.P. for Cardiff in 1604 and 1614[92] was probably a cousin.[93]

Between 1624 and 1640 Davies must have been concerned chiefly with his legal practice. He was recommended for Christchurch in September, 1640, by Lord Baltimore, the lord of the borough and manor. He was described then as of Shaftesbury.[94] He was not an active member of the Long Parliament, however, and by the spring of 1642 had begun to absent himself from the House. On 28 April 1642 it was reported that he, with William Whitaker and another Dorset M.P., had returned after some absence without leave. And he was sent for with them on 15 February 1643 as an absentee.[95] He was disabled on March 16 for not appearing on summons. After sitting in the Oxford parliament he compounded, 1645–1646, for his delinquency. He seems to have retired to private life after that. He died in 1678, aged eighty-three, and was buried at Tisbury.[96]

Davies's income probably came chiefly from his practice. The landed estates which he reported when he compounded were chiefly some leases in Dorset, valued above rents at £58 a year. At least one of his holdings was mortgaged in 1642 to make provision for some of his

five children. His fine was set by the committee at £300 and was paid promptly.[97]

Sir Alexander Denton (1596–1645), of Hillesden, near Buckingham, was a member for Buckingham borough from 1640 until 22 January 1644. His family were virtually lords of the borough[98] and his father, Sir Thomas Denton (d. 1633), had been a prominent county leader, serving as J.P., M.P., sheriff, and deputy lieutenant.[99] His mother was Susan, daughter of John Temple of Stowe, and Alexander was probably born at that celebrated estate. He was baptized on 21 March 1596,[100] and entered Oxford (Christ's Church) in 1612. On 2 September 1617 he married Mary, daughter and coheiress of Edmund Hampden of Hartwell, a cousin of John Hampden and of Winwood (q.v.), and two weeks later was knighted.[101] Sometime previously his sister married Sir Edmund Verney (q.v.), with whom he was on terms of intimacy for years.[102]

Denton was elected to parliament for Buckingham borough in 1625 and 1626.[103] His father opposed the 1621 loan and in 1627 was threatened with Council action for his further reluctance to lend.[104] And when Sir Alexander succeeded him in 1633, he, too, showed himself in opposition to various policies of the crown. During the decade before 1640 he was a J.P. and member of several commissions for the borough and county of Buckingham and for Oxfordshire,[105] but it was his term as sheriff, 1637–1638, which best showed his politics. He was reported as lax in his ship money collections, partly because of the influence of his friends and kinsmen, and for a time in 1638 and in 1639 was under custody of agents appointed by Council to see that he collected over £700 of the arrears.[106] He refused to pay the fees of the pursuivants or to advance money for the arrears from his own purse, but avoided the leading question as to whether he thought the levy illegal by declaring that he was no lawyer.[107] He seems to have been ordered to appear before Council regarding the

86 I.P.M. cited above; will of Richard Darley, 1599.
87 Y.A.S. Rec. Ser. 58: 197, 203, 1917; Cal. Com. Comp., 3215; Chancery proceedings, C. 3/343/38.
88 M. of P. 1: 493; C.J. 3: 4.
89 Pink MSS, 300, fol. 729; Hoare, Wilts., 4 (ii): 36.
90 Mid. Temp. Rec. 2: 578, 682, 938.
91 Hoare, loc. cit.
92 M. of P. 1: 448, 461; 3: xli.
93 Pink MSS, 300, fol. 729. The M.P.'s of 1614 and 1624 are treated as the same man by A. H. Dodd in Wales's Parliamentary Apprenticeship (1536–1625), Transactions of the Honourable Society of Cymmrodorion, 35–36, 70–71, 1942.
94 A copy of the letter from the manuscripts of the old corporation was supplied through the courtesy of the town clerk and Mr. Herbert Druitt, Esq.
95 C.J. 2: 545, 966.
96 Pink MSS, 300, fol. 729.

97 S.P. 23/175/69; Cal. Com. Comp., 959.
98 Symonds, Diary, 20; I.P.M., Sir Thomas Denton, C. 142/543/11.
99 Lipscomb, Buckingham 1: xvii; 2: 560; S.P. 16, 187/1/1, 203/51/109.
100 Lipscomb, op. cit. 2: 576; 3: 17. Denton was a first cousin of Sir Peter Temple, M.P. (q.v.).
101 W. P. W. Phillimore, ed., Buckinghamshire parish registers, marriages 3: 64, London, Phillimore, 1902–; Al. Oxon. Denton's wife was a sister of the wife of Lord Wenman (q.v.).
102 J. Bruce, ed., Letters and papers of the Verney family, 105, passim, Camden Society, 1853 (hereafter, Verney Papers).
103 M. of P. 1: 462, 468.
104 S.P. 14, 127/82; S.P. 16, 89/5.
105 C. 181/4, fols. 68, 179; 181/5, fols. 240, 338; C. 193/13.
106 C.S.P. Dom., 1637–1638, 337; 1638–1639, 137; 1639, 491, 502; V.C.H. Buckingham 4: 532. His arrears were over £852. Royal Hist. Soc., Trans., 3rd Ser., 4: 156, 1910.
107 Add. MSS, 11,045 (Scudamore Papers), fol. 67v.

same matter in January, 1640, and in the following September to have objected to the orders for the gathering of the trained bands.[108]

As a member for Buckingham in the Short Parliament and in the next, Denton must have been regarded as a co-worker with Hampden and his other kinsmen of the opposition. But after supporting their proceedings in the early weeks, giving his bond for £1000 toward the loan in November and being named to the committee on the lords lieutenant, Denton opposed the attainder of Strafford,[109] and in 1642 was frequently absent. His brother-in-law, Sir Edmund Verney, may have had some influence on his conduct. In the autumn of 1642 Denton attended parliament upon summons and promised two horses for the cause. He was named the next year to the parliamentary committee for his county. Repeated absences from Westminster and attendance at the Oxford parliament, however, led to his being disabled, 22 January 1644.[110] Shortly afterwards his house was besieged and taken by the parliamentarians and he was made a prisoner. He died on 1 January 1645, before plans for effecting his exchange had been completed.[111]

His later years brought Denton a decline in wealth as well as in political fortunes. Having inherited from his father at least three manors in Bucks and Oxfordshire, the parsonage and other properties in Buckingham borough, and having married a wife who shared with two sisters an inheritance of £2000 a year,[112] Denton had before his year as sheriff been well-to-do. Contemporary comments put his income at £1000 to £2750 a year, and his pledge for the loan in 1640 and the £1500 assessment[113] put on him later indicate that he was among the wealthy parliament men. In 1639, however, perhaps as a consequence of his troubles as sheriff, Denton was in financial difficulties, and by 1641 he had arranged to sell part of his lands and to place the rest in the hands of trustees for settling his debts.[114] His son declared in 1651 that the debts against Denton's lands before the outbreak of war exceeded their total annual value.[115]

Sir Alexander was related to ten or more of his fellow members of the 1640 House, most of them being members of the popular faction. In addition to those mentioned previously, there were kinsmen on his

mother's side, such as the Fiennes brothers and Sir Thomas Parker, and his daughter's husband, Francis Drake.

* **Sir Edward Dering, Bart.** (1599–1644), of Surrenden, Kent, M.P. for his shire from 1640 until he was disabled, 2 February 1642, for having printed his speeches,[116] was a well known antiquary who had more than once had political aspirations. Born on 28 January 1599,[117] and educated at Cambridge and the Middle Temple,[118] he travelled on the continent in 1620 and the next year spent some weeks in Ireland, looking after some family leases.[119] He married three times between 1618 and 1629. Besides being lieutenant at Dover, Dering served in various local offices, being a J.P.[120] and a member of several commissions, including that for the knighthood compositions.[121] In the latter work he seems to have exerted himself strenuously, as he did with ship money in its early years,[122] activity which was used as an argument against his election in 1640.[123] Some unpleasant relations with churchmen, ranging from the local parson to Archbishop Laud, probably affected his ideas regarding church reform.[124] Dering was among the gentlemen summoned to attend the king at York in 1639 but, pleading ill health and the importance of his work in the county, he refrained from going.[125]

Sir Edward was elected M.P. for Hythe in 1625 upon the recommendation of his friend, Sir Norton Knatchbull.[126] He was defeated in the county elections for the Short Parliament after a bitter contest with his kinsman, Sir Roger Twysden,[127] but he contrived to defeat the plans of the latter and of other local politicians in the fall.[128] His work in the parliament for lay and ecclesiastical reforms, 1640–1641, and his subsequent career are well known.

As heir apparent to his father's estates in Kent worth £1000 a year, Dering had been granted at his first marriage in 1619 £700 a year for maintenance. His wife's portion was £3000. But he does not seem to have en-

---

[108] S.P. 16, 441, 29/63; C.S.P. Dom., 1640–1641, 57.

[109] C.J. 2: 50; D'Ewes (N), 52; Verney, 59.

[110] Pink MSS, 307, fol. 82; C.J. 3: 374.

[111] Lipscomb, op. cit. 3: 17; V.C.H. Buckingham 4: 173–174, 539; Pink MSS, loc. cit.

[112] Lipscomb, op. cit. 2: 304; V.C.H. Buckingham 2: 257; I.P.M. of Sir Thomas Denton; The letters of John Chamberlain 1: 558. His sister Verney's dowry was £2300 (Verney Papers, 105).

[113] Symonds, Diary, 20; Cal. Com. Comp., 67; Pink MSS, 307, fol. 82v.

[114] Verney Papers, 274; Cal. Com. Comp., 2878; C.J. 2: 160–161, 164.

[115] Cal Com. Comp., 2269, 2878.

[116] M. of P. 1: 490; C.J. 2: 411.

[117] Bodleian Gough Kent MSS, 20, fol. 1. D.N.B. gives 1598 as the date.

[118] Ibid., fols. 2–3; Mid. Temp. Rec. 2: 621, 627.

[119] Gough Kent MSS, 20, fols. 7, 23, 25.

[120] C. 193/13; C.S.P. Dom., 1633–1634, 88.

[121] C. 181/3; 181/4, fols. 18v, 88; 181/5, fols. 80, 287; Boys, Sandwich, 216; Stowe MSS, 743, fol. 85.

[122] Stowe MSS, 743, fols. 106, 132.

[123] Ibid., fol. 140.

[124] C.S.P. Dom., 1633–1634, 568–569; 1636–1637, 447–448; Arch. Cant. 22: 90, 1897; 23: 189, 1898.

[125] Stowe MSS, 743, fols. 128, 132; S.P. 16, 427/38/vi.

[126] Wilks, The barons of the Cinque Ports, 75, 76.

[127] Larking, Proceedings in Kent, 1–8; Stowe MSS, 184, fol. 10; 743, fols. 136–142.

[128] Larking, Proceedings in Kent, 8–19; Stowe MSS, 184, fols. 15–16; 743, fols. 146–158; Bodleian Rawl. MSS, D. 141, fol. 6; Add. MSS, 44,846.

joyed more than £400 a year for some time, and in 1632, with £100 coming from his Dover lieutenancy, his income appears to have totalled £600. Heavy official expenses and the need to settle his father's estate led him to sell some properties and to arrange for new leases, 1636–1638.[129] He complained in 1639 of his expenses and debts.[130] Although he was reported just before his death in 1644 to have an estate of £800 yearly, the fine of £1000 imposed by the compounding committee was not enforced,[131] and he is said to have died in comparative poverty.[132]

Dering had several relatives in the 1640 Commons. He was related through the Twysdens to the Vanes, Yelverton and Sir Hugh Cholmley,[133] but he sometimes opposed them politically.[134] Through his first wife he was a nephew of Sir Humphrey Tufton and through his second, a brother-in-law of John and William Ashburnham. Peard, the lawyer, was an intimate friend.[135]

Sir Walter Devereux (1591–1641), natural son of the second Earl of Essex and half-brother of the third earl, the parliamentary general, was M.P. for Lichfield from 1640 until his death shortly before 26 July 1641.[136] In 1608 his grandmother, Lettice, Countess of Leicester, was considering a marriage for him with a daughter of Lady Stallenge.[137] He seems to have been closely associated during much of his life with his half-brother, in whose cause he was always ready to act. He was examined by Council and incarcerated for a fortnight in the Fleet in 1613 for having been the earl's second in a proposed duel,[138] and served with him in the Palatinate in 1625–1626.[139] He possibly served afterwards in Ireland.[140] Aside from his frequent elections as M.P. for Tamworth and Lichfield, doubtless through the influence of his grandmother and his brother, Sir Walter seems to have taken little personal part in Staffordshire affairs, and probably spent much of his time at court.[141]

* Sir Simonds D'Ewes (1602–1650), of Stow Langstoft, Suffolk, the antiquary, and diarist of this parliament, sat for Sudbury, 1640–1648. He enjoyed a good estate, having had a settlement of £500 a year from his father's lands arranged upon his marriage with an heiress in 1626, with the prospect of possibly £1000 a year in reversion,[142] and his rentals of 1635 indicate that his income was probably nearer to £1300 or £1500.[143]

The decade of 1630 to 1640 had not been an entirely happy one for D'Ewes. His father had died in 1631 with an investigation by Star Chamber impending,[144] and D'Ewes himself was threatened with action by the same court in February, 1633, for having stayed in London contrary to royal order.[145] He thereafter lived in Suffolk. He had followed with interest the settling of New England and the plans for the Providence Island Company, and in 1636, moved by both family tragedy and public events, had some thought of going to America.[146] With the cause of Protestanism in Europe also he was in touch, being on friendly terms with the Netherlands ambassador.[147] He seems to have avoided public duties, however, until the "unwelcome preferment" to the shrievalty of Suffolk came to him in 1639. His experiences in seeking lower ship money rates and in avoiding both Council censure and financial ruin [148] may well have caused him to seek a place in the Long Parliament.

Sir Simonds had some doubts as to his eligibility because his term as sheriff would not end until after the elections were held, and he wrote to the Earl of Worcester to inquire whether a western constituency might be found for him.[149] But Sudbury voted for him, apparently without challenge, and, as he wrote, "I was elected and by myselfe returned," [150] and the House seems not to have questioned the irregularity. To the study of the Star Chamber and ship money he turned his zeal,[151] and his wealth also he placed at the service of parliament, offering his bond for £1000 in November, 1640, and proposing that the figure be doubled.[152] He

---

[129] Gough Kent MSS, 20, fols. 4, 9–12, 15, 27, 31, 34, 98–103; Sir Edward Dering's I.P.M., C. 142/777/99; Hasted, *Kent 7*: 467–475.
[130] Stowe MSS, 743, fol. 132.
[131] *Cal. Com. Comp.*, 831, 832.
[132] Add. MSS, 18,471, fol. 203; Larking, *Proceedings in Kent*, l–li.
[133] *Vis. Kent, 1619*, 136.
[134] Vane and Dering were opponents at the Short Parliament elections.
[135] Add. MSS, 34,195, fol. 30.
[136] *M. of P.* 1: 493; D'Ewes (B), 189.
[137] *C.S.P. Dom., 1603–1610*, 478.
[138] *The letters of John Chamberlain* 1: 475, 478; *Acts P.C., 1613–1614*, 231, 244. Other instances of his concern about his brother's family affairs and gossip connected with them appear in the *Verney Papers*, 168–169.
[139] *C.S.P. Dom., 1625–1626*, 26, 383; *The letters of John Chamberlain* 2: 618.
[140] *C.S.P. Ireland, 1647–1660, Addenda, 1625–1660*, 47.
[141] Sketches of Devereux's life appear in Wedgwood, *Staff. Parl. Hist.* 2: 52–53, and Williams, *Parl. Hist. Wales*, 161.

[142] D'Ewes, *Autobiography* 1: 146, 321; 2: 153. By his will D'Ewes provided that his lands should go to his male heir, and set aside £4000 for his daughters. *Ibid.* 2: 155.
[143] Harl. MSS, 7659, fol. 7v–8.
[144] His fees from Chancery were the field of investigation. Birch, *The court and times of Charles the First* 2: 100, 102.
[145] It was more than fright at Palmer's censure (*D.N.B.*) that led to D'Ewes's withdrawal from London. A Star Chamber proclamation concerning D'Ewes was issued in 1633. Add. MSS, 11,056, fol. 64.
[146] Harl. MSS, 167, fol. 105; 287, fol. 265; D'Ewes, *Autobiography* 2: 145.
[147] *Ibid.* 1: 361, 421.
[148] Harl. MSS, 99, fols. 9, 10; 379, fols. 60, 71, 109; *C.S.P. Dom., 1639–1640*, 376; *1640*, 59, 269–270, 274.
[149] *Autobiography* 2: 243–246.
[150] D'Ewes (N), 1.
[151] On a day of meeting with the committee on Prynne's case D'Ewes wrote to his wife, "last Monday . . . we utterlie damned shipp-monie." Harl. MSS, 379, fol. 75.
[152] D'Ewes (N), 52, 539.

was an elder in the Suffolk presbytery during the war.[153]

D'Ewes was related to Dering and Barnardiston, and was an old friend of at least two other 1640 M.P.'s, Palmer and Crew.[154]

* **George Lord Digby** (1611?–1676?), of Sherborne Castle, Dorset, eldest son of the Earl of Bristol, was M.P. for his county from 1640 until he was called to the Lords on 10 June 1641. He was elected for Milborne Part in Somerset, too, and when he chose to serve for Dorset, his brother, John, was quickly elected to replace him in the other seat.[155] Digby was baptized in 1612 at Madrid while his father was ambassador there, but he seems to have been born in England shortly before 22 February 1610/11, and to have been taken to Spain as an infant.[156] He was well educated and widely travelled, and about 1632 married the Earl of Bedford's daughter, Anne.[157] He spent part of his time at court, and in 1634 was for a brief period a prisoner in the Fleet and was prosecuted in Star Chamber as a result of a quarrel at court.[158] In 1637 he was reported to the London magistrates for having spent Christmas at Essex House instead of in the country.[159] But he was more often at his father's seat, Sherborne Castle, and was a J.P. in Dorset and member of the sewers commission.[160] He was commended by Council in 1640 for his efforts in training men for the Scottish war.[161] His own experiences and his father's had prejudiced him somewhat against the court, and his relationship with the Earl of Bedford had probably influenced his views also. When he was elected to the Long Parliament he was doubtless considered a supporter of the opposition.

A brother-in-law of William Lord Russell and his younger brother, both 1640 parliament men, Lord Digby was no doubt well provided for by both his own and his wife's family. Clarendon mentioned the "ease and plenty" of his father's fortune.[162] Sherborne alone was reputedly worth £800 a year in the poorest times, and double that figure at others.[163]

The date of Digby's death was probably 20 May 1676.[164]

John Digby (1618–166–), second son of the Earl of Bristol, was elected M.P. for Milborne Port, Somerset, after his brother, Lord Digby, decided on 9 November to serve for Dorset. John was disabled as a royalist on 5 August 1642.[165] He was born in London about March, 1618,[166] matriculated at Magdalen College, Oxford, in 1634,[167] and early in 1639 rode up from Sherborne to London to offer his service to the Earl of Northumberland for the border war. He was captain of a troop of horse in the north in 1640,[168] and was a newcomer to parliament when he entered late that year. He was named to the committee on the Star Chamber in December,[169] joined his brother in voting against Strafford's attainder,[170] and was among the first to leave London to raise forces for the king in 1642. He served as a general of horse under Hopton during the war, afterwards retiring to the continent. He followed his brother's example in his later years and died as a secular priest at Pontoise sometime after 15 March 1663.[171]

* **John Downes** (fl. 1635–1664), of Bulberough, Sussex, the regicide, was returned for Arundel, 20 December 1641, following Henry Garton's death. Although there was some question on December 28 whether he or the Earl of Arundel's nominee should sit, the House ordered on 15 January 1642 that Downes should be admitted until the election was determined. As late as 17 June no decision had been reached, but Downes was evidently sitting, for he was listed that month among those making pledges for the defense.[172] Since his election and return occurred within the period of this study, Downes is briefly considered here.

The regicide's identity is not certain, but he was probably the barrister of the Inner Temple who was

---

[153] *A.H.R.* **44**: 36, n., 1938–1939.

[154] Stowe MSS, 743, fol. 95; Harl. MSS, 165, fol. 4; D'Ewes (C), 193.

[155] *M. of P.* **1**: 488, 493 and n.; *C.J.* **2**: 25.

[156] 1612 is commonly given as the year of his birth, on the basis, no doubt, of the record of his baptism (*D.N.B.*; Dorothea Townshend, *George Digby, second earl of Bristol*, 10, London, H. W. Wilson, 1924). But in a letter of 22 February 1610/11 concerning Sir John Digby's plans to leave for Spain, it was stated that he was taking with him his wife and their young son, the last of his name and the only heir. The same correspondent reported to a friend on 7 November 1612 that Digby had had his son baptized on Gunpowder Treason day. *H.M.C., Report on the MSS of the Marquess of Downshire* **3**: 27, 400.

[157] Early in 1632 it was reported that Digby was to marry Anne Russell as soon as he returned from his travels. Egerton MSS, 2646, fol. 21.

[158] *D.N.B.*; Clarendon, *Rebellion* **1**: 461 and n.; *C.S.P. Dom.,* 1635–1636, 523.

[159] S.P. 16, 378/94.

[160] C. 193/13; C. 181/5, fol. 225; *C.S.P. Dom.,* 1638–1639, 306.

[161] *Ibid.,* 1640–1641, 104, 106.

[162] *Rebellion* **2**: 532.

[163] *The letters of John Chamberlain* **2**: 25.

[164] *D.N.B.* dates his death on 20 March 1677 in his 65th year. H. M. Digby, however, writing in *The Ancestor* (**11**: 71–88, 1904) dates it on 20 May 1676 in his 65th year. Perhaps a misreading of the latter date as "20 Mar. 1676," or 1676/7, new style, accounts for the discrepancy.

[165] *M. of P.* **1**: 493 and n.; *C.J.* **2**: 25, 704.

[166] The birth of a son to the Earl of Bristol was noted in a letter of 7 March 1618. *C.S.P. Dom.,* 1611–1618, 526; *The letters of John Chamberlain* **2**: 147.

[167] *Al. Oxon.*

[168] *C.S.P. Dom.,* 1638–1639, 306; 1640–1641, 80.

[169] *C.J.* **2**: 44.

[170] Verney, 58.

[171] Burke, *Extinct Peerage*, 170; Pink MSS, 300, fol. 761.

[172] *M. of P.* **3**: xliv; *C.J.* **2**: 333, 380, 628, 630; *N. and Q.,* 1st Ser., **12**: 359, 1855; D'Ewes (C), 236, 355.

excused for absences in June, 1642, "in regard he is a parliament man." [173] He may possibly have been the John Downes of Manby, Lincolnshire, who was admitted to the Temple in 1631.[174] If so, he was perhaps an early acquaintance of Cromwell, whose concern about the Arundel election was voiced in the House in December, and whose tool Downes was afterwards said to be. However, Downes was appointed as early as 1633 to the auditorship for the Duchy of Cornwall,[175] and is listed by Noble as a Londoner.[176] He had some Sussex connections by 1640, for he was named that year as a commissioner for collecting the subsidy,[177] and he was identified as of Bulberough in the election return of 1641.[178] He was appointed in 1642 to the sequestration committee for that county.[179] His acquisitions of Sussex royalists' lands [180] were not the first properties he owned in the region. He was sufficiently well-to-do to dispense with any parliamentary wages from his constituency.[181]

Downes's wife, Hannah, was living in 1653,[182] but nothing else is known of her. Downes was a prisoner in the Tower in 1660, but was released before 17 January 1662 and was pardoned in 1664. He may have gone to America to die.[183]

Edward Dowse, or **Douce** (*c.* 1582–1648), of Petworth, Sussex, was M.P. for Portsmouth, Hants, from late in November, 1640, *vice* Percy, until 1648.[184] Born about 1582, he was the second son of Thomas Dowse (d. 1602) of Salisbury and of Broughton, Hants, by his wife, Blanche (d. 1608), daughter of John Covert of Slaugham, Sussex. He was a younger brother of Sir Francis Dowse (born *c.* 1578) of Wallop and Broughton.[185] He matriculated at Hart Hall, Oxford, in 1597, aged fifteen, and was graduated B.A. in 1601 and M.A. in 1604.[186] By 1615 he had been appointed to the service of the man who was long to be his patron, being named in October of that year to

attend young Lord Percy at Cambridge.[187] He received his M.A. from Cambridge in 1616,[188] and probably remained in Percy's household afterwards. A younger brother, Sir Edmund Dowse, became a courtier and was cupbearer to Queen Henrietta Maria.[189] Edward Dowse was M.P. for Cricklade in 1625 and for Chichester in the Short Parliament.[190] He seems to have married late in life. His employer, the Earl of Northumberland, referred in June, 1640, to Dowse's going to visit his "mistress" in the country, but stated that the marriage might have to be deferred until Northumberland returned with victory from the north.[191] The identity of the lady is unknown beyond the mention of her in Dowse's will as Mistress Gresham Dowse.[192] There seem to have been no children.

Probably in anticipation of his election, Dowse was made a burgess of Portsmouth by the corporation on 3 November 1640.[193] His patron's brother, Henry Percy, did not announce in the House until 11 November his decision to serve for the county of Northumberland rather than for Portsmouth, and the writ for the new election was not ordered until two days later.[194] On 28 November Dowse was permitted to take the communion with the House, although his official return had not yet come in, and he probably took his place regularly soon afterwards. One diarist spoke of him as Northumberland's steward when he noted that Dowse was given permission of 10 March 1641 to go into the country on some urgent business.[195] Although his brother, Sir Francis, was a royalist,[196] Edward Dowse followed his patron's lead and supported parliament. He promised £50 for the defense in 1642,[197] and was a parliamentary committeeman in Hampshire and Sussex during the war. Illness prevented him from attending at Westminster in October, 1647, and he died shortly afterwards.[198] His will, dated 12 October 1647, was proved on 29 April 1648. A writ for a new election was ordered the following November.[199]

Dowse was probably a man of no great wealth. His father had left him £100 [200] but probably little else. Yet in his long employment by the Earl of Northumberland, most of the time unmarried, he accumulated enough

[173] *Cal. Inner Temp. Rec.* **2**: 267. Downes was called to the bar in May, 1642. *Ibid.* **2**: 265.

[174] *Students admitted to the Inner Temple,* 267.

[175] Coate, *Cornwall in the great Civil War,* 167.

[176] "A Londoner, of mean family." *Regicides* 1: 184. He was styled of Hampstead, Middlesex, in a deed of 1654. *Sussex Rec. Soc.* **29**: 61, 1924.

[177] *Sussex Arch. Coll.* **9**: 105, 1857.

[178] Arundel indenture, C. 219/43/Part 2.

[179] Thomas-Stanford, *Sussex in the great Civil War,* 120.

[180] For the palace and manor of the Bishop of Chichester Downes paid over £1300. Thomas-Stanford, *op. cit.,* 56.

[181] Horsfield, *Hist. Sussex* **2**: App., 29.

[182] *Sussex Rec. Soc.* **19**: 43, 1914.

[183] *C.S.P. Dom., 1661–1662,* 245; J. G. Muddiman, *The trial of King Charles the First,* 112 and n., London, W. Hodge, 1928. This is a correction to *D.N.B.*

[184] *M. of P.* **1**: 493.

[185] *Vis. Hants.,* 58; *Sussex Arch. Coll.* **47**: 125 and n., 1904; I.P.M., Thomas Dowse, C. 142/270/105.

[186] *Al. Oxon.*

[187] *H.M.C., Sixth Report,* MSS of the Duke of Northumberland, p. 230.

[188] *Al. Cant.*

[189] *Sussex Arch. Coll.* **47**: 125 and n., 1904.

[190] *M. of P.* **1**: 466, 483.

[191] *C.S.P. Dom., 1640,* 260.

[192] P.C.C., 60 Essex.

[193] Robert East, *Extracts from records . . . of Portsmouth,* 352, new ed., Portsmouth, 1891.

[194] *C.J.* **2**: 26; *M. of P.* **1**: 493; **3**: xliv.

[195] *Note book of Sir John Northcote,* 13 and n.; D'Ewes (N), 464, n.; *C.J.* **2**: 100.

[196] *Cal. Com. Comp.,* 77, 1177.

[197] *N. and Q.,* 1st Ser., **12**: 360, 1855.

[198] Add. MSS, 24,860, fol. 145; Pink MSS, 300, fol. 790.

[199] *C.J.* **6**: 80.

[200] P.C.C., 70 Woodhall.

to leave some £170 to £200 in legacies besides the provision he made for his wife. His will mentioned his books in his study at Northumberland's house at Petworth and a farm which he had bought from his patron.[201]

Francis Drake (fl. 1627–1659), of Walton-on-Thames, Surrey, was M.P. for Amersham, Bucks, from May, 1641, replacing Cheyney, until 1648.[202] A descendant of the Devonshire Drakes, he was a younger brother of William Drake (q.v.), his colleague for Amersham, and the second son of Francis Drake of Esher and Walton-on-Thames, a gentleman of the privy chamber to King James and M.P. (d. 1633). His earliest connection with Buckinghamshire came through his mother, Joan, who was the eldest daughter and coheir of William Tothill of Shardeloes, Bucks, one of the Six Clerks of Chancery, whose properties near Amersham passed to Francis's brother, William.[203] Both Francis and William seem to have been influenced by their mother's melancholy religious nature.[204] And their father, though attached earlier to the court of James, had by 1627 become a critic of crown policies and been summoned before Council for his reluctance regarding the forced loan.[205]

Francis Drake was born after 1606, probably around 1610,[206] and may have attended Emmanuel College, Cambridge (matric. 1627), graduating B.A. in 1630/1 and M.A. in 1634.[207] On his father's death he succeeded to the estate of Walton-on-Thames. He married twice. Authorities differ as to which was the earlier marriage, but the evidence indicates that the first wife was Dorothy, daughter of Sir William Spring of Pakenham Hall, Suffolk, whose son, Sir William Drake (d. 1690), eventually succeeded to the Amersham properties of the family. On 23 April 1637 Francis Drake married at Claydon, home of the bride's aunt, Lady Verney, Elizabeth, daughter of Sir Alexander Denton of Hillesden (q.v.).[208]

Although Drake's father had served as a J.P. in Surrey,[209] the first office which Francis held seems to

have been that of M.P., and he owed his place for Amersham in the Long Parliament no doubt to his brother's influence. He worked with the parliamentarians, and at the outbreak of war promised to supply £100 in plate and to have a horse in readiness.[210] He was named to various parliamentary committees for Surrey, but, sharing probably his brother's dislike for extremes, or influenced by the conduct of his father-in-law, Denton, Drake was absent beyond seas for a time in 1644. He returned to the House, however, and remained a member until the purge of 1648. Under the Protectorate he was not only a member of parliament, but favored making Cromwell king in 1657.[211] He seems to have been alive in 1660,[212] but had died before 1669.[213]

Since Drake was a younger son, his fortune could not be compared with his brother's, and his Buckinghamshire connections were through his brother and his wife. His father left him some of his Surrey estates, however, and his brother, William, whose lands passed in time to Francis's son, was said to have been very liberal toward him.[214]

William Drake (1606–1669), of Shardeloes, near Amersham (cr. Bart., 1641), was M.P. for Amersham, 1640–1648. He was the elder brother of Francis Drake (q.v.), and the inheritor of most of the wealth of his maternal grandfather, William Tothill, one of the Six Clerks of Chancery (d. 1626).[215] Both of his parents seem to have been puritans.[216] William was baptized on 28 September 1606, and, after studying at Amersham under Dr. Charles Croke, entered Christ's Church, Oxford, about 1624. His companionship there with his servant and fellow student, John Gregory, who was described by Wood as "the miracle of his age for critical and curious learning," [217] helped to cultivate similar interests in Drake and he later became a great collector of books, particularly of the Latin authors, and gained a considerable reputation as a scholar and a patron of learning. Early in 1626 he entered the Middle Temple, where he was bound with Simonds D'Ewes (q.v.) and John White, the puritan lawyer (q.v.), the latter being

---

[201] P.C.C., 60 Essex.

[202] M. of P. **1**: 485 and n.; C.J. **2**: 130, 144.

[203] Lipscomb, Buckingham **3**: 154.

[204] Manning and Bray, Surrey **2**: 746–747, n.

[205] S.P. 16, 89/5.

[206] His elder brother was baptized in 1606. Francis was old enough to act as executor of his father's will in 1634. P.C.C., 43 Seager.

[207] Although Drake's father and brother were Oxford men, it seems probable that Francis went to Cambridge. His son, Francis, entered St. John's, Cambridge, in 1658. Al. Cant.

[208] Francis Drake, son of Francis and Elizabeth (died 1701, aged sixty), took over at the Middle Temple in 1673 the chambers of his elder brother, Sir William (Mid. Temp. Rec. **3**: 1275). Since the latter was the son of Francis Drake by Dorothy Spring (Burke, Landed Gentry **1**: 348, 1851), his mother was evidently Drake's first wife. Pink MSS, 307, fol. 67; Lipscomb, Buckingham **3**: 21.

[209] S.P. 14, 97/51; C. 193/12, 13; S.P. 16, 192/66.

[210] N. and Q., 1st Ser., **12**: 358, 1855.

[211] Pink MSS, loc. cit.; Surrey Arch. Coll. **36**: 71, 1925.

[212] Thomason Tracts, 669. f. 24, p. 37.

[213] When his brother died in 1669, his heir was not Francis, but Francis's son. Complete Baronetage **2**: 108, n.

[214] Surrey Arch. Coll. **7**: 211–213, 1880; Lipscomb, Buckingham **3**: 168.

[215] V.C.H. Buckingham **2**: 357.

[216] His mother's religion seems to have run to emotional extremes (Manning and Bray, Surrey **2**: 746–747, n.); and his father spoke in the 1625 parliament about the dangers of Arminianism. Commons Debates in 1625, 71.

[217] Wood, Athenae Oxon. **3**: 205. No Oxford degree until that of M.A. in 1669 is recorded (Al. Oxon.), but Drake's studies at Christ's in his youth are mentioned in his epitaph. Lipscomb, Buckingham **3**: 168.

a cousin.[218] Afterwards he transferred to Gray's Inn,[219] and may have spent much of his time in London, for he seems to have taken little part in the usual activities of a country squire in Bucks. He never married.

Drake's father had been M.P. for Amersham in 1625 and 1626, and in 1637 William purchased the manor which included most of the borough. For many years thereafter his family dominated the elections. He was returned for Amersham to both of the 1640 parliaments and his brother was elected to the second place for the borough in 1641.[220]

In the Long Parliament Drake was named to several important committees[221] and offered his security for the loan of March, 1641.[222] But he was not entirely hostile to the court, and his elevation to knighthood and a baronetcy in July, 1641, was perhaps a reward for his moderation. A speech purporting to be by him during the debate on the Grand Remonstrance urged the adoption of some means to curb the growing confusion, and the steering of a moderate course in religious matters as in Elizabeth's day.[223] His subscription in 1642 of £200 and the maintenance of two horses was for the use of king and parliament "conjunctively."[224] When war came he was named to the Committee of the Associated Counties, but, with the assent of parliament, absented himself "for his health" beyond the seas from February, 1643, to October, 1644, and again from 1647 to 1648. He was secluded by Pride, but in 1652 he became Chirographer of the Court of Common Pleas under Chief Justice St. John.[225] He rejoined the Rump in 1660 and sat in the 1661 parliament for Amersham until his death on 28 August 1669.

According to contemporary comment, Drake was very well-to-do. His grandfather had been able to lend the king £1000,[226] and Drake's inheritance from him was ample.[227] He was reported to have dealt liberally with his family and neighbors, and before his death founded some almshouses at Amersham.[228]

Drake's principal interests seem to have been in literature. He was reported to have been an omniverous reader, and seems to have been a man little inclined to activity in politics or in war. Small wonder is it that he shunned the decisions of warfare by going abroad even though his religious views and his kinship and connection with some of the leaders had prompted him to support the early work of the parliament.[229]

Sir John Dryden, Bart. (*c.* 1580–1658?), of Canons Ashby, Northamptonshire, was M.P. for his shire, 1640–1653. Born about 1580, he was the son and heir of Sir Erasmus Dryden, Bart. (d. 1632), by Frances, daughter and coheir of William Wilkes of Hodnell, Warwickshire. Sir Erasmus, J.P., M.P., twice sheriff, signed the petition on behalf of the nonconformist ministers in James's reign and was imprisoned in 1627 for resisting the forced loan.[230] John Dryden matriculated from Broadgates Hall, Oxford, 29 October 1596, aged sixteen, and entered the Middle Temple in 1602. He married three times, (1) about 1605, Priscilla, daughter of James Quarles of Romford, Essex;[231] (2) Anna, daughter of Henry Parvis of Ruckholts in Low Layton, Essex, who died early in 1631; and (3) by license of 2 July 1632, he aged fifty and she twenty-two, Honor, daughter and coheiress of Sir Robert Bevill, K.B., of Chesterton, Hunts.[232] He succeeded this year to his family estates and baronetcy, and presently assumed his father's leadership likewise in the resistance movement.

Sir John was a J.P. for Northamptonshire in 1634 and a sewers commissioner,[233] but in 1635 was reported for negligence in other duties by both ecclesiastical and lay authorities. The metropolitical visitors, having been instructed by Laud to investigate the parishes of which Dryden was patron, reported him responsible for the absence of conformist ministers and churchwardens, and Sir John promised to rectify that matter.[234] As sheriff of Northamptonshire this year his actions in assessing ship money brought protests from some parts of the county,[235] and his failure to collect more than about half of the allotment involved him in difficulties with the Council for several years afterwards. He was accused, with the backing of such prominent neighbors as Rich-

---

[218] *Mid. Temp. Rec.* **2**: 703, 733. "Cousin" John White of the Middle Temple was named one of the executors of Drake's father's will in 1633. P.C.C., 43 Seager.

[219] *Gray's Inn Adm. Reg.*, 188.

[220] *V.C.H. Buckingham* **3**: 145, 147; *M. of P.* **1**: 462, 468, 480, 485.

[221] These included the Committee of Privileges ("Mr. Duke"), several on religious matters, and that for the recess. *C.J.* **2**: 21, 288, *passim*.

[222] D'Ewes (N), 452, n.

[223] D'Ewes (C), 117, n.; *Sir William Drake his speech* (1641), Davidson Pamphlet Collection of the Plymouth Institution.

[224] *N. and Q.*, 1st Ser. **12**: 358, 1855.

[225] *H.M.C., Tenth Report* **4**: Boycott's MSS, 217.

[226] S.P. 16, 52/61.

[227] Drake's own father settled only part of his estate on him because he had been so well provided for otherwise. Tothill had left £1000 to Drake's sister, Joan. Will of Francis Drake. P.C.C., 43 Seager.

[228] Lipscomb, *Buckingham* **3**: 168; *V.C.H. Buckingham* **3**: 141, 155.

[229] References in addition to the ones cited above are Pink MSS, 307, fol. 65; *Complete Baronetage* **2**: 108; *Recs. Bucks.* **2**: 350, 1863.

[230] C. 193/13; *C.S.P. Dom.*, 1603–1610, 200; 1627–1628, 310; Rushworth **1**: 473.

[231] An indenture dated 10 October 1605, apparently connected with the marriage settlement, is mentioned in the I.P.M. of Dryden's mother, C. 142/497/135.

[232] *Marriage licenses, London* **2**: 207, Harleian Society **26**, 1887.

[233] C. 193/13; S.P. 16, 405; C. 181/4, fol. 180.

[234] *C.S.P. Dom.*, 1634–1635, 601; 1635, xxxv. In 1640 Dryden was a party with others in some case before the Court of High Commission. *Ibid.*, 1640, 385, 392, 429; 1640–1641, 384, 392, 395.

[235] *Ibid.*, 1635, 442, 446, 482, 560.

ard Knightley and Edward Bagshaw, of aiding a ship money foe to avoid payment, and it was rumored early in 1637 that he and his successor were to be made examples in Star Chamber proceedings. Both made some efforts under pressure to collect the arrears, but his successor complained in June, 1637, that Dryden considered himself relieved of the task and unwilling to do more. Not until January, 1639, however, did Council notify them that the remainder of the arrears would thereafter be left to Exchequer process.[236]

The Long Parliament was Dryden's first, but his election for the shire without having previously sat indicates the prestige he enjoyed in his county. He was an enthusiastic member, and wrote once to an uncle of his pleasure in being a carrier of straw and stubble for the skillful builders of the great work.[237] He advanced money for the cause,[238] served on his county sequestration committee during the war,[239] and was appointed Keeper of the Rolls of Northamptonshire before 1650. He died about 1658, his will being dated 20 January 1657 and proved 11 November 1658.

Dryden was a man of considerable wealth, having inherited lands and church interests in Northamptonshire, Warwickshire and Cumberland,[240] and acquired others by marriage, one of the latter being worth over £400 yearly. His will of 1657 directed the payment of £2500 to each of two daughters, £3000 to another, and £2000 to each of his four younger sons.[241]

Sir John was an uncle of the Restoration poet, his namesake. His colleagues in the Long Parliament included his kinsman, Richard Knightley, and his friend, Edward Bagshaw.[242]

Edmund Dunch (1603–1678), of Little Wittenham, near Wallingford, Berkshire, sat for Wallingford from November, 1640, until the election was declared void, 15 February 1641, and, promptly re-elected, served until 1653.[243] He came of a wealthy family which had frequently represented the borough.[244] His grandfather, Edmund Dunch (d. 1623), who was a J.P. and sheriff

of the county,[245] seems to have refused the 1621 loan.[246] Sir William Dunch, father of the 1640 member, sat in the 1603 parliament, and died in 1611. His wife was Mary, daughter of Sir Henry Cromwell, and aunt of the Protector and of John Hampden.[247] The latter became administrator of Lady Mary's estate in 1624, with the consent of her son, Edmund.[248]

Dunch was born in February, 1602/3,[249] entered Gray's Inn, 2 November 1621,[250] and began his public career while he was still a ward. He was elected by Berkshire to the parliaments of 1624, 1625, and 1626, and by Wallingford in 1628.[251] His name was on the 1629 list of nominees for sheriff of Berkshire, but he did not serve until 1633.[252] He was named on the sewers commissions for Berks, Oxford, Wilts, and Gloucestershire in 1633 and 1635.[253] Sometime before 20 May 1636 he married Bridget, only daughter of Sir Anthony Hungerford of Down Ampney, Gloucestershire, who inherited a fortune of over £60,000 after her father's death in 1637.[254] This addition to his own large possessions, consisting of at least twelve manors in Berks, Wilts, Hants, and Oxfordshire,[255] must have made Dunch very well-to-do.

It became apparent early that Dunch's political views resembled those of his cousin, John Hampden. He refused to compound for knighthood in 1630, for example, declaring that he had no land of the specified value three years before the king's coronation,[256] an argument derived, perhaps, from the fact that he was then a minor. And in 1639, although he furnished several horses for the army in the north,[257] possibly his quota

[236] *Ibid., 1635–1636,* 166, 348; *1636–1637,* 196 and *passim; 1637,* 256; *1638–1639,* 192–193, 373; S.P. 16, 343/17; Birch, *Court and times of Charles the First* 2: 284.

[237] *H.M.C., Second Report,* MSS of Sir Henry Dryden, Bart., p. 63.

[238] *Ibid., Sixth Report,* House of Lords MSS, 174.

[239] *Northamptonshire Notes and Queries* 4: 250, 1892.

[240] Baker, *Northampton* 1: 538, 653; I.P.M., C. 142/487/31, 135; Cumb. and Westm., *Trans.,* 1st Ser., 14: 223, 1897.

[241] P.C.C., 595 Wotton.

[242] Other authorities used for this sketch are *Complete Baronetage* 1: 128; *Al. Oxon;* J. Wake ed., *Quarter Sessions records of the county of Northampton,* Northamptonshire Record Society 1: 251, 1924 (hereafter, *Quarter Sess., Northants*).

[243] *M. of P.* 1: 485 and n.; 3: App., xliv; Willis 3: 241, 242; *C.J.* 2: 85, 105.

[244] J. K. Hedges, *The history of Wallingford* 2: 103, London, 1881; Mark Noble, *Memoirs of the protectoral-house of Cromwell* 2: 159, 2nd ed., Birmingham, 1787 (hereafter, Noble, *House of Cromwell*).

[245] *Ibid.* 2: 157; Berry, *Ped. of Berks. Fam.,* vi; C. 193/13.

[246] S.P. 14, 127/82.

[247] *Vis. Berks.* 1: 87–88; *Berks. Arch. Jour.* 14: 84, 1908.

[248] She had died before her father-in-law. Brown, *Somerset Wills* 5: 24.

[249] *V.C.H. Berks.* 4: 382. The date appears occasionally as 1602. Dunch's age was twenty at the time of the 1623 visitation and sixty-two at that of 16 March 1664/5. *Vis. Berks.* 1: 88, 197.

[250] *Gray's Inn Adm. Reg.,* 164.

[251] *M. of P.* 1: 456, 462, 468, 474. The 1624 member was not the grandfather, as Noble thought (*House of Cromwell* 2: 157), for he had died the preceding year. Chamberlain wrote of the election of Dunch for Berkshire in January, 1624, while he was still a ward. *The letters of John Chamberlain* 2: 543.

[252] Harl. MSS, 7000, fol. 271v; *V.C.H. Berks.* 4: 382.

[253] C. 181/4, fol. 147v; 181/5, fol. 42.

[254] *Berks. Arch. Jour.* 35: 139, 1931; *Vis. Berks.* 1: 197. On 20 May 1636 Dunch and his wife sued Dame Anne Hungerford for possession of some plate that had belonged to his wife's grandmother, Dame Constance Lucy. Wilts. Arch. Soc. MSS, Sadler's "Wiltshire Genealogy," Avebury Parish.

[255] His family inheritance included eleven manors before he came into possession (S.P. 14, 79/11–12, 273, 281, 353; *V.C.H. Berks.* 3: 494, 504, n.; 4: 24, 31). He purchased another manor in Wiltshire in 1630 for £2310 (*Wilts. Arch. Mag.* 42: 13, 1922–1924; Wilts. Arch. Soc. MSS, Sadler's "Wiltshire Genealogy," Cricklade Parish). He sold a Hampshire manor in 1661 for £5600 (*Ibid.,* Avebury).

[256] S.P. 16, 180/24, fol. 93.

[257] S.P. 16, 427/38/ii, iv.

for the trained bands, he made no reply when asked for a contribution of cash toward the king's expenses there.[258] Some post at court or in the army seems to have been his by this time, for in March, 1640, he was termed one of the king's servants in a list of men to be summoned for a new loan. Dunch was out of town, however, on the first day set for him to appear before Council, and whether he consented to pay the £500 assessment is not known.[259]

Elected to both of the 1640 parliaments for Wallingford, Dunch was named to various important committees. He was appointed to that on ship money before his original election was voided, and later ones were concerned with ecclesiastical and military affairs.[260] In June, 1642, he promised four horses for the defense,[261] and during the war he served as a captain and a county committeeman. Noble wrote that "he was a strenuous advocate for the liberty of the subject, which occasioned him to suffer very great and severe hardships from the court," and that his "acrimony was great" against the king who, during the war, "had taken all" from him.[262] He supported his cousin Cromwell's government, and was created Baron Burnell of East Wittenham in 1658 as a reward. He upheld the restoration of the Stuarts in 1660, though, and lived until 1678. He was buried on 4 August 1678, aged seventy-six, at Little Wittenham.[263]

Dunch's relatives in the Long Parliament included, besides those of the Cromwell connection, his wife's kinsman, Sir Thomas Lucy.

John Dutton (1594–1657), of Sherborne, Gloucestershire, was one of his county's knights, 1640–1 January 1644. The eldest surviving son of William Dutton of Sherborne by Anne, daughter of Sir Ambrose Nicholas, once Lord Mayor of London, he succeeded in 1618 to great wealth and an important place in his county.[264] He had been educated at Oxford and the Inner Temple,[265] and shortly after his father's death married Elizabeth, daughter of Sir Henry Bayntun of Wiltshire.[266] He became a county magistrate, serving for many years as a J.P. and a member of various local commissions in his own and neighboring counties.[267]

He was a D.L. in Gloucestershire in 1624 and was named a commissioner for the 1627 loan. He was among the group of half of the twenty-five commissioners who refused to serve or to subscribe themselves, and who were summoned before Council. Dutton was committed to the Gatehouse following his hearing in March, 1627, having as an additional charge against him the failure to report a letter that urged resistance, and he was kept a prisoner until early the next year.[268] But though he had sat for his county in the parliaments of 1624 and 1625, he was not elected to that of 1628 as were so many others among the loan resisters.

Dutton was not without friends at court, however. His brother, Ralph, was a gentleman of the privy chamber and Endymion Porter was a friend. To the latter Dutton appealed in 1629 when a quarrel with the vicar of his parish threatened to bring him into disfavor with the archbishop himself.[269] Possibly through Porter also Dutton and his wife arranged in 1635 to purchase from another courtier the wardship of the young Earl of Downe and the control of his estates that were worth some £2000 a year. The ward was brought to live at Sherborne and in 1638 was married to Dutton's younger daughter, Lucy.

In 1640 Dutton was active in planning the county election for the Short Parliament, but even his great influence was offset by the strength of the more extreme faction.[270] Possibly his exasperation at that time led to his decision in the autumn to be a candidate in person. He seems to have had no trouble in carrying the day. He was probably considered a friend of reform, but no sympathizer with advanced puritanism. His great wealth he willingly placed at the service of the state, promising his bond for twice the amount requested as security for the 1640 loan. And in February, 1641, he was named to the committee on the bill for abolishing superstition and idolatry and for considering the case of Dr. Montagu. By the summer of 1642, however, he was absenting himself from the House, and although he returned in September to pledge support to Essex and to promise ten, or possibly twenty, horses for the cause,[271] he was voted out of the House on 1 January 1644. He sat in the Oxford parliament, was a prisoner in July, 1644,[272] and later compounded and paid a heavy fine. He seems afterwards to have been on friendly terms with Cromwell and to have been at peace with the government long before his death on 14 January 1657.[273]

[258] Rushworth 3: 913.

[259] S.P. 16, 447/36, 37, 94.

[260] C.J. 2: 45, 105, passim; Pink MSS, 307, fols. 39–40.

[261] N. and Q., 1st Ser., 12: 360, 1855.

[262] House of Cromwell 2: 161. Parliament voted Dunch a weekly allowance in 1645 (Pink, loc. cit.).

[263] Complete Peerage 2: 83–84.

[264] Dutton's father was described as great "in ability, fame, and alliance" in the county. Chancery case, C. 3/357/20.

[265] Students admitted to the Inner Temple, 605.

[266] The marriage settlement was dated 5 July 1619 (Calendar of Sherborne Muniments, 11). Mrs. Dutton died about May, 1638 (Vis. Glouc., 55), and Dutton married again probably at some date between 1647 and 1651 (Calendar of Sherborne Muniments, 13–14).

[267] C. 193/12, 13; S.P. 16/405; C. 181/4, 5, passim; 181/5, passim.

[268] S.P. 16, 54/28, 28/i, v; Acts P.C., 1627, 125, 374, 449; Willcox, Gloucestershire, 119 and n.; Birch, The court and times of Charles the First 1: 212.

[269] C.S.P. Dom., 1628–1629, 586.

[270] Ibid., 1639–1640, 580–582; Willcox, Gloucestershire, 34–36.

[271] D'Ewes (N), 52; C.J. 2: 84, 91, 772.

[272] Whitelocke, Memorials of the English affairs 1: 280, 1853.

[273] He even proposed a marriage between his family and Cromwell's. The date of Dutton's death appears as 18 February 1656/7 in one collection of family papers, and as 14 January in another.

The wealth of the Duttons is mentioned in all accounts of the family. John Dutton was spoken of as one of the richest men in England, both his mother and his paternal grandmother having brought additional funds from London into the family. His mother's jointure of £3000 was matched by a similar amount allotted to one of his sisters, and his own estates numbered at least nine manors in Gloucestershire and Worcestershire. One of them alone was said to be worth £1000 a year,[274] and the lands he settled on his wife when he married were worth £500 a year.[275] His assessment by parliament was £3000, increased afterwards to £4000,[276] and his compounding fine at a tenth, more than £5216, was reckoned on his own statement that his estates were worth before the war some £2524 a year.[277] He is said to have offered during the war to lend £50,000 to the king.

But Dutton was spoken of in his day as one who enjoyed his fortune with humility, being noted for his meekness as well as for his riches, and for his learning, his prudence, and his good works.[278] He was known as "Crump Dutton" because of his humped back, and in his own household he was a stern disciplinarian.

Through his first wife Dutton was brother-in-law and uncle of the two members of the Bayntun family who were fellow M.P.'s.[279]

* Thomas Eden, LL.D. (d. 1645), long associated with Cambridge University, and its member in earlier parliaments, sat for the University, 1640–1645. Besides holding offices in the Church and the University, Dr. Eden was for many years named a J.P. in Suffolk, the Isle of Ely, and Cambridge, as well as a member of other local commissions.[1] His connection with the Court of High Commission led to some talk of including him in the proceedings against Laud in the early months of the session,[2] but the charges were not pressed, and he retained his seat.

Eden was a man of wealth, and from 1640 to 1642 he lent generous sums for the public cause.[3] When

he drew up his will in 1643 he planned to leave £4000 each to his two nieces and named other legacies of considerable size.[4]

Piers Edgcombe (1609–1667), of Mount Edgcombe, Cornwall, near Plymouth, was a member for Camelford, 1640–22 January 1644. He was the head of an ancient and distinguished house. His grandfather, Piers (1536–1607), son of Richard Edgcombe, had been sheriff and M.P., and had been interested in Sir Richard Grenville's projects for exploring the distant seas and in developing the mines of western Britain and Ireland. Sir Richard Edgcombe (d. 1639), father of the M.P., was a member of the Council for New England, a J.P., sheriff, and D.L. in Cornwall,[5] and M.P. for Grampound and Bossiney. He was one of the royalists who supported the cause of Buckingham against the attacks of Eliot's faction in the early years of King Charles.[6] Piers, the eldest son of Sir Richard by his second wife, Mary, daughter of Sir Thomas Coteeles of London, was aged eleven in 1620. He studied at St. John's, Cambridge, matriculating in 1626, and was probably the "Perseus Edsgaimb" who was admitted to study at Leyden University in June, 1629.[7] In the preceding year, while still under age, he was successful among five candidates at the parliamentary election at Newport, Cornwall.[8] In 1636 he married Mary, daughter of John Glanville of Broad Hinton, Wilts, receiving with her a portion of £3000, and three years later succeeded to the Edgcombe estate.[9] He had some responsibilities for the defenses of Plymouth in 1639.[10]

In 1640 Edgcombe was elected in the spring and the fall as M.P. for Camelford. He voted against the attainder of Strafford,[11] and absented himself upon the outbreak of hostilities. The House ordered that he be brought up in custody in November, 1642, but did not vote for his disablement until January, 1644.[12] After fighting for the king, he surrendered his command and in 1647 arranged to compound for his estates. He served again in parliament after the Restoration, and

[274] I.P.M., C. 142/378/107; Chancery suit, C. 3/357/20.
[275] *Calendar of Sherborne Muniments*, 11.
[276] *Cal. Com. Adv. Money*, 424–426.
[277] S.P. 23/197/9–11, 17; *Cal. Com. Comp.*, 1273.
[278] Wood, *Fasti Oxon.* 2: 42.
[279] In addition to the authorities cited above see: *Historical and genealogical memoirs of the Dutton family, of Sherborne in Gloucestershire*, 70–76, 103–124, *passim*, privately printed, 1899; *Memorials of the Duttons of Dutton in Cheshire*, xxiv, 102, London, privately printed, 1901; *M. of P.*; Williams, *Gloucester*, 51–52.

[1] C. 193/12, 13; S.P. 16/405; C. 181/5, fols. 20, 39, 73, 130, *passim*.
[2] *C.S.P. Dom.*, 1640–1641, 447–448, 479; *C.J.* 2: 93; D'Ewes (N), 38–39, 163. In 1636 Eden had advocated moderation in the enforcing of the new church regulations (Bodleian Tanner MSS, 68, fol. 52). Some of his 1640 colleagues had come under his ecclesiastical jurisdiction in parts of Suffolk. *C.S.P. Dom.*, 1639–1640, 562; 1640–1641, 195.
[3] Eden lent £500 to the king early in 1640 (S.P. 16, 446/42) and, though he did not give his bond for the loan of November,

1640, he pledged £1000 for that purpose in March, 1641, and the next year promised £800 more (D'Ewes [N], 438, n., 539; Pink MSS, 307, fol. 128). In September, 1642, Eden stated that he had lent £1000 for the parliament, £500 for Ireland, and would lend £200 more. *C.J.* 2: 757.
[4] J. J. Howard, ed., *The visitation of Suffolk, 1561* 1: 13–15, Lowestoft, 1866.
[5] C. 193/12, 13; Pink MSS, 300, fol. 13; *E.H.R.* 50: 249, 1935; Brown, *Genesis of the U. S.* 2: 883; *Devon and Cornwall Notes and Queries* 9: 78–79, 1916–1917 (hereafter, *Devon and Cornwall N. and Q.*).
[6] Lawrance, *Parl. Rep. Cornwall*, 94; Forster, *Eliot* 1: 472; 2: 106–109; Coate, *Cornwall in the great Civil War*, 22.
[7] *Al. Cant.* He was created D.C.L. at Oxford in 1644. Wood, *Fasti Oxon.* 2: 66.
[8] Courtney, *Parl. Rep. Corn.*, 378.
[9] I.P.M., Sir Richard Edgcombe, C. 142/579/52.
[10] *C.S.P. Dom.*, 1638–1639, 293, 469.
[11] "Mr. Edgcombe." Verney, 58.
[12] *C.J.* 2: 845; 3: 374.

died on 6 January 1666/7.[13] Edgcombe's will, dated 12 May 1666, was proved 14 May 1667. His epitaph describes him as "a pattern to posterity, and an honour to the age he lived in; a master of languages and sciences, and a lover of the king and church, which he endeavoured to support to the utmost of his power and fortune."[14]

Of Edgcombe's fortune there are numerous evidences. Carew commented on the excellence of his mansion at Mount Edgcombe.[15] His father's properties at the time of his death included thirteen manors and other holdings in Devon and Cornwall.[16] Piers owned furthermore some Hampshire properties inherited from his mother's family,[17] and he bought a Sussex manor in 1641.[18] His compounding papers reveal a yearly income of over £1200,[19] but it may have been nearer £2000,[20] and one observer reported it to be £3000.[21] His fine, set first at a tenth, £2513, was afterwards changed because of an undervaluation and also because of the intercession of Lord Fairfax on his behalf.[22] Edgcombe planned a portion of £5000 for his eldest daughter when he made his will in 1666.[23]

Piers Edgcombe was a brother of Richard Edgcombe, a brother-in-law of William Glanville, and a relative through his grandmother of Alexander Luttrell, all fellow parliament men of 1640.[24]

Richard Edgcombe (1612–1655), of Bodrigan in Gorran, Cornwall, was a member for the Cornish borough of Newport from 1640 until he was disabled for royalism in 1644. The second son of Sir Richard Edgcombe of Mount Edgcombe, and younger brother of Piers, M.P. for Camelford, he was born in 1612. He matriculated at St. John's, Cambridge, at Easter, 1627.[25] Elected to his first parliament in the fall of 1640, he was never active in the House, but was a stanch supporter of the king. He was disabled and sat in the Oxford parliament in 1644.[26] He served

under his brother's command during the war and surrendered and made his composition with him. His fine, set in 1647 at a tenth, £589, was reduced by half; but a later tenth, £157, to cover earlier omissions, he paid in 1651.[27] According to his will, he inherited some Hampshire properties from his mother's family as well as Cornish ones from his father.[28] He died unmarried on 5 November 1655, and was buried at Gorran.[29]

* William Ellis (1607–1680), a lawyer of Gray's Inn and Recorder of Boston, sat for that town in both parliaments of 1640, and was a strong parliamentarian. He was the second son of Sir Thomas Ellis of Grantham (d. 1627), by his wife, Jane, daughter of Gabriel Armstrong of Wishall, Nottinghamshire, and was baptized at Grantham, 19 July 1607.[30] He was graduated B.A. from Christ's College, Cambridge, in 1627, and became a barrister at Gray's Inn eight years later.[31] He probably returned to Lincolnshire soon afterwards, for he was named to the sewers commissions there in 1638 and 1639,[32] and in the latter year became Recorder of Boston.[33]

Ellis owned property near Boston,[34] and was considered in 1643 a person of good estate.[35] His pledge for the defense in 1642 was £100.[36] He was a Presbyterian elder in his county, and was apparently secluded in 1648,[37] but readmitted in 1649.

Richard Erisey (1590–1668), of Erisey, Cornwall, was M.P. for St. Mawes, 1640–1648. He was a grandson of Richard Erisey, the friend of Martin Frobisher,[38] and son of James Erisey (M.P. 1584), a sea captain who sailed for America under Drake in 1585 and died in 1601. His mother was Elizabeth, daughter of Thomas Carew of Antony,[39] and two of the Carews

---

[13] The date sometimes appears as 1666, old style. His successor in parliament was chosen on 25 March 1667.

[14] Gilbert, *Hist. Survey of Cornwall* 1: 31; Pink MSS, 307, fol. 184.

[15] Richard Carew, *Survey of Cornwall*, 239, rev. ed., London, 1811.

[16] I.P.M. cited above.

[17] *The Oglander Memoirs* (Long), 83 and n.; *V.C.H. Hampshire* 5: 179, 180, 187, 244; 4: 200.

[18] Add. MSS, 5686, fol. 71.

[19] He originally reported about £700 a year, later admitting over £500 more. S.P. 23/199/441–443.

[20] So it was valued in 1660. *Western Antiquary* 7: 39, 1887–1888.

[21] Richard Symonds, *Diary*, 61. He was assessed £3000 by the parliamentarians in 1644. *Cal. Com. Adv. Money*, 423.

[22] *Cal. Com. Comp.*, 1082–1083.

[23] P.C.C. 61 Carr.

[24] In addition to the authorities cited above, see *M. of P.;* Vivian, *Vis. Cornwall*, 142.

[25] *Al. Cant.*

[26] *O.P.H.* 9: *22. A writ for electing his successor was ordered on 9 February 1646/7. *C.J.* 5: 79.

[27] *Cal. Com. Comp.*, 1082–1083.

[28] His will, dated 5 March 1654/5, was proved on 23 April 1656. P.C.C., 112 Berkeley.

[29] Vivian, *Vis. Cornwall*, 142; Gilbert, *Hist. Survey of Cornwall* 2: 847.

[30] *The parish registers of Grantham in the county of Lincoln* 1: 44, Lincoln Record Society, Parish Register Series, 4, 1916; Maddison, *Lincs. Ped.* 1: 326. *D.N.B.* gives 1609 as his birth year.

[31] *Al. Cant.* The details of Ellis's career at Cambridge are wrong as they appear in *D.N.B.*

[32] C. 181/5, fols. 222, 300.

[33] Thompson, *Boston*, 458.

[34] *Ibid.*, 542. His father had settled some property on him in 1624. I.P.M. of Sir Thomas Ellis. C. 142/452/62.

[35] Thompson, *Boston*, 84, n.

[36] *N. and Q.*, 1st Ser., 12: 360, 1855.

[37] *A vindication of the imprisoned and secluded members of the House of Commons*, London (printed for Michael Spark, 1649). He is listed as one of the Independents who worked with the presbyteries by J. H. Hexter in *A.H.R.* 44: 31, n., 1938–1939.

[38] *E.H.R.* 21: 539–540, 1906.

[39] Brown, *Genesis of the U. S.* 2: 886; Pink MSS, 300, fol. 75; *Devon and Cornwall N. and Q.* 21: 255–257, 1940–1941.

were his guardians during his minority.[40] Born on 19 May 1590,[41] he was a student at Leyden University in 1606, and was at the Middle Temple from 1610 to 1614.[42] He married (1) at Bickley, Devon, in 1615 Elizabeth, daughter of Peter Carew of Bickley; and (2) about 1619 or 1620, Mary, daughter of Sir James Ley, Bart., of Westbury, Wilts.[43] He lived most of the time at his large estate of Erisey near St. Mawes.[44] He was a J.P. by 1626 and for many years afterwards,[45] and may have been concerned with the coastal defenses also.[46] In 1628 he was one of the commissioners for assessing the subsidy.[47]

Erisey did not serve as an M.P. until the Long Parliament. In 1639 he declined to contribute to the king,[48] and was of the popular party, as was his cousin, Alexander Carew (q.v.). He offered his bond for £1000 for securing the loan in November, 1640,[49] and though he took no great part in debates or committee work and was absent part of the time in 1642, he stayed with parliament after Carew deserted the cause. He was named to various wartime committees for his county, but was secluded in 1648. He died in 1668. His will, dated 7 October 1667, was proved at Exeter, 31 July 1668.[50]

The value of Erisey's estate is unknown. It included an area of more than 1800 acres in over a score of parishes in Cornwall.[51] Erisey or his son had an interest in the Cornish mines in 1656[52] and probably before. His pledge for the loan in 1640 suggests that he was one of the well-to-do members.

Thomas Erle, or **Earle** (c. 1621–1650), of Charborough, Dorset, was M.P. for Wareham, 1640–1648. His election was challenged, but the Commons, urged by his father and his friends, decided on 1 February 1641 in his favor. With the correcting of the return on 12 February young Erle became a legitimate member.[53] The eldest son of Sir Walter Erle, the puritan M.P. for Weymouth (q.v.), Thomas was born about 1621, being aged two at the 1623 visitation, and matriculated at Magdalen Hall, Oxford, in February, 1636, aged fourteen.[54] He entered the Middle Temple, his father's inn, early in 1638, and was bound there with Edward Bagshaw (q.v.). Nine years afterwards he was called to the bar.[55]

Erle was elected to the Short Parliament for Milborne Port, Somerset,[56] but he was probably inactive because of his youth. Even in the Long Parliament he was not named to a committee until 20 October 1642. During the war he was a captain of horse for the parliamentary army.[57] He was secluded by the purge of 1648,[58] and died during his father's lifetime, 1 June 1650.[59] Sometime during the course of the Long Parliament Erle married Susan, fourth daughter of William Lord Say and Sele, and sister of James and Nathaniel Fiennes, his fellow M.P.'s.[60]

Sir Walter Erle, or **Earle** (1586–1665), of Charborough, Dorset, sat for Weymouth, 1640–1648. He was one of the most active leaders of the puritan group and was ranked by Clarendon among the "ephori."[61] He was born on 22 November 1586, the eldest son of Thomas Erle of Charborough (d. 1597) and his wife, Dorothy, daughter of William Pole of Colyton, Devon. His mother's second husband, Walter Vaughan of Fallersden, Wiltshire (later Sir Walter), seems to have been the children's guardian during their minority.[62] Erle was educated at Oxford (matriculated at Queen's, 1602) and at the Middle Temple (admitted 1604),[63] but did not take degrees. His later concern with military matters suggests that he may have spent some of his early years with the armies abroad—he referred to himself once as a sword man rather than a gown man—but no record of such experience has been discovered. He was knighted at Thetford on 4 May 1616. Before 1 April 1617 he married Anne, daughter of Francis Dymoke, who was heiress of her father and her cousin, Sir Henry Dymoke. With her Erle acquired some valuable properties in Warwickshire.[64]

Erle began in 1614 what was to be a long and somewhat turbulent public career. He sat in parliament for Poole that year and in 1621 and 1624. He was Sheriff of Dorset, 1618–1619,[65] and was probably already a J.P., for he was accused in 1622 of using his authority as a justice to arrest unfairly persons suspected of

---

[40] St. Ch. 8/130/7.

[41] I.P.M., Richard Erisey, C. 142/662/107.

[42] *Western Antiquary* 4: 253, 1884–1885; *Mid. Temp. Rec.* 2: 522, 582.

[43] Vivian, *Vis. Cornwall*, 155.

[44] Gilbert, *Hist. Survey of Cornwall* 2: 99; Lysons, *Mag. Brit.* 4: 125.

[45] C. 193/12, 13; S.P. 16/405; *C.S.P. Dom., 1628–1629*, 221.

[46] *Ibid., 1634–1635*, 130.

[47] *H.M.C., Fourth Report*, MSS of J. J. Rogers, Esq., 405.

[48] Rushworth 3: 913.

[49] "Mr. Erskin." D'Ewes (N), 52.

[50] Pink MSS, 300, fol. 75; Vivian, *loc. cit.*

[51] I.P.M. cited above; St. Ch. 8/130/7.

[52] *Devon and Cornwall N. and Q.* 10: 153, 1918–1919.

[53] *M. of P.* 1: 488; *C.J.* 2: 76, 77; D'Ewes (N), 306, 311, 351.

[54] *Vis. Dorset, 1623*, 37; *Al. Oxon.*

[55] *Mid. Temp. Rec.* 2: 864, 947.

[56] *M. of P.* 1: 483.

[57] Pink MSS, 300, fol. 78.

[58] *A vindication of the imprisoned and secluded members of the House of Commons*, 28, London, 1649.

[59] *Al. Oxon.*

[60] Burke, *Landed Gentry* 1: 350, 1851; *D.N.B.* article on Erle's son, General Thomas Erle.

[61] *Rebellion* 2: 299.

[62] Hutchins, *Dorset* 3: 498; Burke, *Landed Gentry* 1: 350, 1851; *Somerset and Dorset N. and Q.* 4: 68–69, 1894–1895.

[63] *Al. Oxon.; Mid. Temp. Rec.* 2: 448.

[64] Several indentures relating to these properties (1617–1626), to which Erle and his wife were parties, are among the Birmingham Reference Library MSS, Nos. 348116, 348118, 348121–348124, 348127, 348131.

[65] *List of Sheriffs*, 39.

poaching on his property.[66] He was greatly interested in American colonial projects about this time. He bought in 1620 five shares of Virginia Company stock and was present afterwards at several meetings of the company court.[67] He was active also in the New England project of the Reverend John White of Dorchester, and in March, 1624, was chosen governor of the company.[68]

In the parliaments of the 1620's Erle played an active role. He showed himself interested in 1621 in matters of trade, of religion, and of administration. He attacked monopolies and other grievances and urged action regarding recusancy, scandalous ministers, and the observance of the Sabbath. It was the strong puritanical spirit of his speech of 15 February 1621 that led to the attack on him by his fellow member, Shepherd, an attack which produced in Erle's defense the maiden speech of John Pym.[69] In the 1624 parliament Erle was named to the committee on simony at the universities.[70] Sitting for Dorset in 1625, he complained of the release from prison of various convicted recusants and proposed an ingenious scheme for assisting the justices in dealing with recusancy. He urged also the limiting of tonnage and poundage.[71] He served for Lyme Regis in 1626 and was so vigorous in his attacks on Buckingham and on Dr. Montagu[72] that, a month after the dissolution, he was removed from the commission of peace.[73] He was one of the Dorset D.L.'s by this time and seems to have been excused from having to contribute on the privy seals that year,[74] but in 1627 he was reported to Council as a loan refuser and was imprisoned for some months in the Fleet. He was one of the five gentlemen who tried unsuccessfully to secure release under writ of habeas corpus, but was freed with the others in time for the new parliamentary elections.[75] He was promptly elected for Dorset, and was again a leader in the popular faction.[76]

During the interim of the king's personal rule, Erle continued to be active in his county. He had been restored by this time to the peace commission, and served on others also.[77] His concern about ecclesiastical affairs continued.[78] When ship money was levied in 1636 he was reported a defaulter in several parishes, but through distraints he was made by the following year to comply.[79] Two years later Sir Walter ignored the king's request for a new contribution for his expenses.[80] He was sent to the Short Parliament for Lyme Regis, and was among the members who were arrested and searched at the close of that session.[81] Undaunted, he continued to agitate for reforms. He was evidently present at Exeter to assist with the framing of the Devonshire petition on grievances in September.[82] He seems to have had no difficulty securing one of the Weymouth seats in October,[83] and went up to London ahead of time to aid Pym with plans for the parliament.[84]

Sir Walter was naturally a leader in the more extreme group of the Long Parliament. He spoke frequently and worked on many committees.[85] He was especially active in the attack on Strafford and from November, 1640, worked with the committee that planned his trial. Somewhat officiously he demanded that as a "sword man," rather than a lawyer, he be given the management of the twenty-fourth article. His inability to prove the point at the trial invited the remark attributed to the queen that "that water-dog did bark, but not bite, but the rest did bite close."[86] Erle was among the first to point out the advantage to be gained in using for the state the fortunes of persons who were disloyal.[87] He supported the London petition against episcopacy, and worked on the plans for the Remonstrance. Although officious in his manner in the House, and a quibbler on points of order, Erle spoke with authority on military matters. During the excitement aroused by the first army plot he was sent down to look after the safety of his county, and when war came he was commissioned a colonel in the par-

---

[66] St. Ch. 8/138/14.

[67] Kingsbury, *Records of the Virginia Company* 1: 345, 415; 3: 61; Brown, *Genesis of the U. S.*, 1069.

[68] *Somerset and Dorset N. and Q.* 17: 109, 1921–1923; Dorset N.H. Proceedings 13: 65, 1892; *Acts P.C., 1625–1626,* 376.

[69] *Commons Debates 1621* 1: 150, n.; 2: 26, n.; 34, n.; 82 and n.; 95; 3: 221, 362; 5: 353, *passim.*

[70] *C.J.* 1: 762.

[71] Forster, *Eliot* 1: 386; *C.S.P. Dom., 1625–1626,* 189; S.P. 16, 6/59; *Commons Debates in 1625,* 43, 118.

[72] Forster, *Eliot* 1: 534, 578; *E.H.R.* 17: 732, 735, 1902; *C.S.P. Dom., 1625–1626,* 354, 355; *H.M.C., Various Collections* 4: MSS of F. H. T. Jervoise, 171.

[73] *Somerset Arch. Proc.,* 1st Ser., 16 (ii): 26, 1870.

[74] *Acts P.C., 1625–1626,* 305.

[75] *C.S.P. Dom., 1627–1628,* 16, 299, 336; S.P. 16, 85/53; Rushworth 1: 473; Birch, *The court and times of Charles the First* 1: 189, 280; *Fairfax Correspondence* 1: 70, n.; Forster, *Eliot* 2: 61, 83 and n.

[76] *Commons Debates for 1629,* ed. W. Notestein and Frances H. Relf, 18–19, 35, 47, 254, 257, Minneapolis, Univ. of Minnesota, 1921.

[77] C. 193/13; S.P. 16, 189/230/83; C. 181/5, fol. 226.

[78] *C.S.P. Dom., 1631–1633,* 402; *1637–1638,* 396.

[79] S.P. 16, 319/89; *C.S.P. Dom., 1637,* 400.

[80] Rushworth 3: 913.

[81] *C.S.P. Dom., 1640,* 152–154.

[82] *The Buller Papers,* 135–138.

[83] He was made a freeman of the town the day after his election as M.P., probably to insure himself against any challenge. H. T. Moule, *Catalogue of the . . . documents of the borough of Weymouth and Melcombe Regis,* 113, Weymouth, 1883.

[84] He and Pym were said to have insisted on the search for arms in some papists' lodgings in Chancery Lane on November 1. Add. MSS, 11,045, fol. 131.

[85] Pink found that he was named to over 260 committees between 6 November 1640 and 5 December 1648. The Committee of Privileges was the first. *C.J.* 2: 21.

[86] D'Ewes (N), 514, 546; Whitelocke's "Annals," Add. MSS, 37,343, fols. 221, 222v.

[87] D'Ewes (N), 35, n.

liamentary army and governor of Dorchester. He offered to supply four horses for the defense for himself and his son, Thomas (*q.v.*), in June, 1642,[88] and in 1643 took Pym's place as lieutenant of the ordnance.[89] As the war went on Erle acquired a reputation of attempting more than he was able to do, as in the failure of the siege of Corfe Castle,[90] but his loyalty to the cause until Pride's Purge was unquestionable. After his seclusion in 1648, he returned as a member for Dorset in 1654. He survived until 1665, outliving his son, Thomas, and was buried on 1 September of that year at Charborough.

Contemporary comment pictures Erle as one of the wealthy men of his county. The estate he inherited from his father included at least four manors with over 7000 acres of land, and several rectories and vicarages in Dorset and Devon.[91] By his marriage he acquired some Warwickshire properties, parts of which he sold before 1640 for £3250.[92] And he purchased additional lands in his own county.[93]

Among Erle's relatives in the 1640 Commons, besides his son, was Sir William Pole, who was a kinsman of Erle's mother. The marriage of his son with the sister of James and Nathaniel Fiennes occurred during the parliament, but probably not until after 1640. But Sir Walter was connected by marriage and by friendship with William Strode, whose brother, Sir Richard, had married one of Erle's sisters.[94] It was Erle who forced Strode to leave the House in time to avoid arrest in January, 1642.[95]

Sampson Eure, or **Evre** (d. 1659?), Serjeant-at-Law, of Gatley Park, Herefordshire, was M.P. for Leominster in that county, 1640–22 January 1644.[96] He was a younger son of Sir Francis Eure, M.P. and Chief Justice of North Wales, by his first wife, Elizabeth Lennard of Kent. Called to the bar at Gray's Inn in 1617, Eure advanced steadily in the legal profession, gaining the post of King's Attorney in Wales for life in 1622. He was a bencher of his inn in 1638. With Ralph Goodwin (*q.v.*) he became in 1625 an examiner in the Court of the Marches of Wales, and in 1635 he sought an appointment as king's serjeant or at least as queen's serjeant or solicitor for the prince. He was disappointed in these plans, however,[97] as he was in 1636 and 1637 when he was talked of as Sir Walter Pye's successor as Attorney

of the Court of Wards or Bridgeman's as Justice of Wales.[98] But he became a Serjeant-at-Law in 1640, and eventually king's serjeant. Throughout the reign of Charles I, Eure served as a J.P. in the Welsh counties,[99] and in 1640, with his new title, was named to the commission of gaol delivery of London.[100] He attended one parliament before 1640, serving in 1621 for Beaumaris.[101] In the early plans for the Long Parliament he was among the court candidates who were to be proposed for election.[102]

As a member of the 1640 Commons Eure offered his bond for £1000 for securing the loan in November, and was named to a half-dozen committees before the end of 1641. These included the Committee of Privileges, one on the bill for disarming recusants, and others that involved legal questions.[103] Eure was knighted at Whitehall on 7 August 1641.[104] He was absent frequently after 1641, finally joined the king, and became Speaker of the Oxford Parliament. He lived until 1659 and letters of administration were granted on 5 December 1659 to a creditor.[105] His wife, who was Martha, daughter of Anthony Cage of Longston, Cambridgeshire (married about 1633),[106] lived until about 1672.[107]

Eure's income was probably a good one, far beyond his fee of £40 a year as Serjeant-at-Law. His real estate in Herefordshire was worth at least £130 a year, and he had other lands in the counties of Carnarvon and Carmarthen.[108] In addition to those sources was his legal practice. He seems to have been occupying a town house in St. Andrew's, Holborn, in 1638.[109] His fine at compounding, however, was only £185 when originally set at a tenth, and was afterwards reduced to £110.[110]

Although he was not closely related to many of his fellow parliament men, Eure had been associated in office with Ralph Goodwin. He was close enough in kinship to Sir Robert Harley, although not always in agreement,[111] to call him cousin and to ask him in 1635 to stand as godfather [112] for one of his children.[113]

---

[88] *N. and Q.*, 1st Ser., **12**: 360, 1855.
[89] Whitelocke, *Memorials of the English affairs* **1**: 229, 1853.
[90] Bankes, *The story of Corfe Castle*, 59.
[91] Hutchins, *Dorset* **3**: 498.
[92] Birmingham Reference Library MSS cited above.
[93] *Somerset and Dorset N. and Q.* **1**: 255, 1889–1890.
[94] *Western Antiquary* **1**: 56, 1881–1882.
[95] Sources in addition to those cited above are Pink MSS, 300, fols. 80–82; *M. of P.*; D'Ewes (N) and D'Ewes (C), *passim; Fairfax Correspondence* **1**: 88, n.
[96] *M. of P.* **1**: 489; *C.J.* **3**: 374.
[97] S.P. 16, 257/51/i; Add. MSS, 37,343, fol. 132.

[98] *Strafford Letters* **1**: 506; **2**: 152.
[99] C. 193/12, 13; S.P. 16/405.
[100] C. 181/5, fol. 371.
[101] *M. of P.* **3**: iii, n.; S.P. 14, 119/28.
[102] S.P. 16, 468/136.
[103] *C.J.* **2**: 21, 160, 350, *passim;* D'Ewes (N), 52.
[104] Shaw, *K. of E.* **2**: 210.
[105] P.C.C., Act Book, 1659, fol. 365.
[106] Their marriage settlement was dated 22 June 1633. S.P. 23/192/557.
[107] Pink MSS, 300, fol. 103.
[108] S.P. 23/192/557.
[109] Dale, *Inhabitants of London*, 190.
[110] *Cal. Com. Comp.*, 1510–1511.
[111] *C.S.P. Dom., 1629–1631*, 383, 400–401.
[112] *H.M.C., Fourteenth Report* **2**: MSS of the Duke of Portland **3**: 33, 34, 52.
[113] In addition to the authorities cited above see Williams, *Parl. Hist. Wales*, 10.

John Evelyn (1591–1664), of Lee Place, Godstone, Surrey, was a member for Blechingley, 1640–1648. He was a grandson of George Evelyn (d. 1603), founder of the Surrey line of gunpowder patentees, and the second son of John Evelyn of Kingston and Godstone (d. 1627) by his wife, Elizabeth, daughter of William Stevens of Kingston.[114] His father, sometimes described as one of the Six Clerks of Chancery,[115] was a partner in the family gunpowder monopoly, was a Surrey J.P.,[116] and in 1621 he or his son, the M.P., opposed the forced loan.[117] John, the younger, was baptized at Kingston on 20 October 1591, was probably admitted at Emmanuel College, Cambridge, in March, 1606, and in 1610 entered the Middle Temple.[118] He married Thomasine, daughter and coheir of William Heynes of Chessington, on 24 November 1618,[119] and lived afterwards in the parish of Godstone. His handsome residence there is said to have cost £9000.[120] He was a J.P in Surrey from early in the reign of Charles I,[121] and served Blechingley in the 1628 parliament.[122]

John was early associated with his father in business matters. His elder brother, George, became an administrative official and lived in London and in Wiltshire. John and his father were members of the Virginia Company in 1612.[123] By 1621 the son was a partner in the gunpowder business, and after his father's death took complete charge. By contracts renewed periodically with the government until 1636 Evelyn was the official powder maker of the kingdom, supplying for a fixed price per pound a certain proportion of powder from all the saltpetre delivered to him.[124] He experienced difficulties in the early years of King Charles because he had made large investments in new mills and then lost the business of the East India Company through the grant of a separate patent to them, and because Charles's treasury failed to pay its bills. He held up deliveries at one time in 1625 because £2550 were owing to him, and in the 1628 parliament he introduced a bill which would have improved his business at the expense of the saltpetre men. The ordnance officer of the Tower prudently suggested this year that an investigation of Evelyn's supplies in his storehouses in the country be postponed until parliament ended.[125] Disappointed in the price the government offered him and in his effort to keep the business as an absolute monopoly, his contract in 1635 being renewed for one year only, Evelyn finally petitioned for reimbursement for losses of £2000 and for the £5000 he had spent on the mills. From 1635 to 1639 he was the object of investigations regarding the fulfilment of his part of the contract and his alleged sales of powder that had been in his hands when the contract ended. No doubt the occasional gifts Evelyn made to the king and to the ordnance officers [126] were more than covered by the profits he enjoyed while his monopoly lasted.

Meanwhile Evelyn had come to disagree with the royal administration in other ways. He sent no answer to the request for £20 under a privy seal in 1625,[127] and in 1627 was listed as attending Council for his reluctance regarding the loan.[128] He refused again to lend in 1639.[129] He was not a member of the Short Parliament, but when he returned in the autumn of 1640 he was prepared to work with the opposition.

Evelyn was interested in religious matters, being one of the Presbyterians of the House. In his earlier experience in parliament he had been named to a committee dealing with ministers and the sacrament,[130] and in the Long Parliament he spoke against recusancy and was appointed to several committees on ecclesiastical affairs. He was named also to the committee on tonnage and poundage, but he resented the discussion of his family's business as a monopoly,[131] and his desire for reforms seems not to have reached to feeling against the king personally. Perhaps his knighting at Whitehall on 25 June 1641 was in recognition of this fact,[132] and as late as December he urged consultation with the king before measures touching Ireland were decided upon.[133] He pledged £1000 as security for the 1640 loan, promised in June, 1642, to supply two horses, and in October, to bring in £200 for the defense. But, less ardent than his nephew from Wiltshire, he hesitated about supporting Essex and consented only after the Tower had been proposed for him. He promised then

---

[114] *Vis. Surrey, 1623*, 44; Helen Evelyn, *History of the Evelyn family*, 202, London, Eveleigh Nash, 1915; Manning and Bray, *Surrey* **2**: 327.

[115] Aubrey, *Surrey* **3**: 90. George, elder brother of the Blechingley M.P., followed their father in this office.

[116] *Surrey Arch. Coll.* **5**: Evelyn pedigree, 1871.

[117] S.P. 14, 127/80.

[118] *Al. Cant.; Mid. Temp. Rec.* **2**: 530.

[119] Evelyn, *History of the Evelyn family*, 202.

[120] A. U. M. Lambert, *Godstone, A parish history*, 267, 274, privately printed, 1929 (hereafter, Lambert, *Godstone*); Aubrey, *Surrey* **3**: 88.

[121] C. 193/12, 13; S.P. 16/405; S.P. 16, 185/6/10v.

[122] *M. of P.* **1**: 478.

[123] Brown, *Genesis of the U. S.*, 546, 547, 887.

[124] An outline of Evelyn's contracts was prepared by him in 1637 (S.P. 16, 361/9). References to the contracts are scattered through the *Calendars of State Papers, Domestic*, from 1620 until 1639. One outline of his contracts appears in *C.S.P. Dom.*, 1635, 90. See also J. U. Nef, *Industry and government in France and England, 1540–1640*, Philadelphia, *Mem. Amer. Philos. Soc.* **15**: 89–96, 1940.

[125] S.P 16, 95/80; *C.S.P. Dom., 1628–1629*, 176.

[126] *Ibid., 1635–1636*, 143; *1639–1640*, 294–295.

[127] Brayley, *Surrey* **5**: App. 2, p. 25.

[128] S.P. 16, 89/5.

[129] Rushworth **3**: 914.

[130] Manning and Bray, *Surrey* **3**: App., cxxii.

[131] D'Ewes (N), 300, 494, n.; *C.J.* **2**: 65, 84, 107.

[132] Pink MSS, 300, fol. 115.

[133] D'Ewes (C), 223. In his will, written in 1663, Evelyn referred to the misfortunes of his "soveraigne Lord and Master King Charles, the best of men." Evelyn, *History of the Evelyn family*, 204–206.

another £100 loan.[134] Suspicion arose against him once more in 1643, but he remained a member of parliament until 1648. He was a parliamentary committeeman in Surrey, and an elder in his presbytery during the war years. He died early in 1664 and was buried at Godstone on 18 January 1663/4.[135]

Evelyn had wealth in lands as well as in industry. By inheritance and by arrangements with several of his brothers, he was the owner of three manors and other lands, chiefly in Surrey, totalling some thousands of acres,[136] and said at one time to be worth more than £1400 yearly.[137] When his son, Sir John, was to be married in 1653, land worth at least £500 a year was settled on him, and the son's estate was estimated in 1660 to be worth £1800 a year.[138]

Evelyn was an uncle of Sir John Evelyn, who sat for Ludgershall, Wiltshire, and a somewhat more distant kinsman of John Evelyn, the diarist.

Sir John Evelyn (1601–1685), of West Deane, Wiltshire, was M.P. for Ludgershall, 1640–1648.[139] He came from the Surrey family whose fortune was made in the gunpowder monopoly, and was a nephew of John Evelyn of Godstone (1591–1664), the Blechingley M.P. (q.v.). He was the eldest son of George Evelyn of Everley and West Deane, one of the Six Clerks of Chancery (d. 1636), by his wife, Elizabeth, daughter and heiress of Sir John Rivers. He was born on 11 August and baptized on 20 August 1601 at Kingston on Thames. He was admitted to the Merchant Taylors' School in London in 1612/3,[140] and may have studied at Emmanuel College, Cambridge (B.A. 1618/9).[141] In April, 1622, he married Elizabeth, daughter of Robert Cox of London, and was granted then in settlement most of his father's inheritance consisting of at least five manors and other properties in Wiltshire, Hampshire, and Surrey. He was knighted at Salisbury the following August.[142] Evelyn was recommended to Salisbury for the first parliament of Charles I by Attorney General Heath, but was rejected because the corporation preferred local men. He was returned for Wilton in 1626.[143]

Between 1629 and 1640 he was a member of various local commissions for Wiltshire and neighboring counties,[144] and he served also as a J.P.[145] He was concerned in 1634–1635 about the defense of his father and others of the Six Clerks in a case brought against them in Star Chamber because of alleged exactions in office, and was in London part of the time while the answers to the charge were being prepared.[146] When his father died in January, 1636, the family were disappointed to have his office granted to another, and not to his younger son, for whom he had tried to purchase the reversion. Their challenge of the new appointee, however, was unsuccessful.[147] It was reported at this time by a neighbor and intimate of the family, Dr. Matthew Nicholas, a brother of Secretary Nicholas, that George Evelyn left to his son, Sir John, an estate of about £2000 a year, from which some £700 were payable to his mother and brother, but that there were large debts of at least £7000.[148] Some of the family properties in Surrey had been mortgaged or sold before this, and apparently some of those in Wiltshire, too, were being considered for sale.[149]

It may have been for business reasons that Evelyn entertained in his home in 1637 William Ashburnham and his brother, John (q.v.).[150] But though he had contacts with the court, Evelyn did not refrain from criticizing royal policies. With other J.P.'s of Wiltshire he was reproved in 1637 for obstructing the work of the royal purveyors of timber for the navy and was threatened with summons before Council for contempt.[151] In 1639 he refused to make a contribution to the crown.[152] His election to both of the parliaments of 1640 for Ludgershall insured the presence of an opposition man to balance the royalist, William Ashburnham, who held the other seat for the borough.[153]

Sir John was an active worker with the popular party from the early days of the Long Parliament. He served on committees for reforms in the church, on the subsidy, and on Irish affairs, and was a leader in his county when war came.[154] He was probably the Evelyn who offered his bond for £1000 to secure the loan in 1640, and who promised in 1642 to furnish four horses and £200 for the defense.[155] He was in fact one of the

[134] D'Ewes (N), 52; N. and Q., 1st Ser., 12: 360, 1855; C.J. 2: 801, 822.

[135] C.J. 3: 374. Whitelocke, Memorials of the English affairs 1: 208, 241, 1853; Pink MSS, 300, fol. 116; A.H.R. 44: 36, n., 1938–1939.

[136] Lambert, Godstone, 265, 277, 278.

[137] This was the estimate made by one son in a lawsuit in 1669. Evelyn, History of the Evelyn family, 208–209.

[138] English Baronetage 4: 376, 1741; Manning and Bray, Surrey 2: 328.

[139] M. of P. 1: 496.

[140] Robinson, Merchant Taylors' School Register 1: 74 and n.; H. Evelyn, The history of the Evelyn family, 499; Pink MSS, 300, fol. 112.

[141] His father was an Emmanuel man also. Al. Cant.

[142] I.P.M., George Evelyn, C. 142/551/107; Pink MSS, loc. cit.

[143] Hoare, Wilts. 6: 349; M. of P. 1: 472.

[144] C. 181/4, fol. 17v; 181/5, fols. 187, 210, 317.

[145] C. 193/13; S.P. 16/405.

[146] C.S.P. Dom., 1634–1635, 464–465, 585.

[147] Ibid., 1635, 148, 251; Strafford Letters 1: 511; Evelyn, History of the Evelyn family, 490, 496.

[148] S.P. 16, 312/34. George Evelyn had been asked for £1000 as a loan in 1627, in view of his great estate and the many favors he owed the king. S.P. 16, 52/61. He was listed in 1633 as an adventurer in the Guinea Company. Bodleian Tanner MSS, 71, fol. 161v.

[149] Lambert, Godstone, 274; S.P. 16, 241/51, 79.

[150] C.S.P. Dom., 1636–1637, 488.

[151] Ibid., 1637, 137.

[152] Rushworth 3: 912.

[153] M. of P. 1: 484, 496.

[154] C.J. 2: 28, 99, 130; Pink MSS, 300, fol. 112.

[155] D'Ewes (N), 52; N. and Q., 1st Ser., 12: 338, 1855.

most active in urging military preparations in the summer of 1642, and was proclaimed a traitor in November for his work against the king's cause. He was refused access to King Charles when he went with five other members to negotiate for a settlement that month.[156] He was a lay member of the Westminster Assembly from the start until 12 June 1643. With his uncle, the Blechingley M.P., he incurred some suspicion in the latter year, but was exonerated and readmitted to the House in 1644. He sat thereafter until the purge of 1648. Returning with the Rump in 1660 and sitting in the Convention Parliament, Sir John so made his peace with the king as to receive a royal pardon at the Restoration. He died in his eighty-fourth year on 26 June 1685, and was buried at West Deane.[157]

Besides being a nephew of one fellow parliament man, Evelyn was probably related through his mother to two Sussex members, James Rivers and Robert Goodwin.

Thomas Eversfield (1614–1649), of Grove in Hollington, Sussex, member for Hastings, 1640 to 5 February 1644, was the descendant of the younger branch of his family, and is to be distinguished from his second cousin, Sir Thomas Eversfield of Denn in Horsham (1599–c. 1654), sometimes referred to as "the elder." Thomas, the M.P., was born in July, 1614, the eldest son and heir of Nicholas Eversfield of Grove (J.P., H.S. for Sussex, M.P. for Hastings, 1624–1628, d. 1629), by his first wife, Dorothy, daughter of Edward Goring of Okehurst.[158] He entered the Inner Temple in 1632,[159] and on 10 May 1638 was married at St. Bartholomew's the Great in London to Jane, daughter of John Alford of Offington (q.v.).[160]

Young Eversfield seems to have been named to no offices in his county until 1640, when he was appointed to the commission on the subsidy,[161] and first gained political prominence during the spring elections of that year. He was active then in the Hastings election, through agents and tenants, opposing the court candidate, Robert Read, and, when he threatened to challenge the latter's return on the ground of bribery, was himself accused by the town magistrates of attempting to set the populace against their officials in order to

win the seat.[162] Unsuccessful at that time, his victory in the autumn was probably considered that of a foe of the crown. His father had opposed the 1621 loan, had quarrelled with a vicar concerning tithes and had been summoned to Star Chamber about the matter,[163] and in the 1626 parliament had collaborated with members of the popular party.[164] Among Thomas's own friends in the 1640 House were such prominent parliamentarians as Sir Thomas and Henry Pelham [165] and his father-in-law, Alford.

But Eversfield was not to play his father's role. He obtained leave of absence on 21 April 1641, was knighted the following July at Whitehall, and seems to have been named only once on a committee. He was probably absent at the time of the pledging for the defense in June, 1642, but in October promised to support the Earl of Essex and to provide £100.[166] He was summoned in May, 1643, to attend or be fined, and though named soon afterwards to some of the parliamentary committees for Sussex, was discharged from them and threatened with sequestration in the autumn. Disabled from sitting in the House, 5 February 1644,[167] he secured release from sequestration in June by paying in £800 for the cause. He died about five years later, being buried at Hollington, 24 November 1649. His will, dated in July, 1644, was proved by two brothers in May, 1650.[168]

Eversfield's estate probably consisted of most of the six manors and other properties, including iron works, which had been his grandfather's in 1612, and his father's in 1629.[169] Some of the properties were in Hastings. In his will Eversfield mentioned other estates in Kent which were to come to him from the Alfords, his wife's family, and proposed portions totalling £4000 to £4500 for his two daughters. His only son, John, succeeded him.

Edward Exton (died c. 1664), merchant and alderman of Southampton, was M.P. for his town from 1640 until 1648, possibly 1653.[170] He was the eldest son of John Exton (mayor, 1588–1589, 1594–1595), and was admitted to burgess-ship in 1611.[171] He was already showing business enterprise, being listed that

---

[156] Sanford, St. and ill., 497; Clarendon, Rebellion 2: 391; May, 273; Diary of John Rous, 127, Camden Society, 1856.

[157] Pink MSS, 300, fols. 112–114; Evelyn, History of the Evelyn family, 499–500.

[158] Comber, Sussex Genealogies, Horsham, 90–94; Pink MSS, 300, fols. 124, 125.

[159] Students admitted to the Inner Temple, 271.

[160] Comber, loc. cit. Their children's baptisms were recorded at Offington (Add. MSS, 5698, fol. 187). Eversfield may have had an earlier marriage in April, 1635, at Buddington, Sussex, to Elizabeth Goring. Both she and an infant son died in 1636. Add. MSS, 5699, fol. 34.

[161] Sussex Arch. Coll. 9: 104, 1857. He was named a sewers commissioner in 1641. C. 181/5, fol. 411.

[162] C.S.P. Dom., 1639–1640, 565–566; 1640, 3, 12, passim; S.P. 16, 448/45; 450/39.

[163] S.P. 14, 127/79; St. Ch. 8/195/28.

[164] C.S.P. Dom., 1625–1626, 354, 355.

[165] Both were named overseers of his will.

[166] C.J. 2: 124, 804; Pink MSS, cited above.

[167] C.J. 3: 389; Thomas-Stanford, Sussex in the great Civil War, 120.

[168] P.C.C., 65 Pembroke; Pink MSS.

[169] Inquisitions post mortem, 1485–1649, Sussex Record Society 14: 84, 1912; I.P.M. of Nicholas Eversfield, C. 142/448/86.

[170] M. of P. 1: 493. He sat until 1653, according to O.P.H. 9: *40; according to Pink (Pink MSS, 300, fol. 128), he was secluded in 1648.

[171] The assembly books of Southampton, ed. J. W. Horrocks, Southampton Record Society 4: 65, n., 1917–1925.

year as one of the original subscribers of the Company of Merchants of London Trading to France.[172] He offended the city authorities two years later by refusing to serve as juror for the king's court leet there and by "presumptively and contemptuously" refusing to appear before the mayor and aldermen on special summons to take his oath as a common burgess. A fine was levied on him lest other young burgesses of his rank likewise show disrespect for their duties. The same year he offended the regular wharf porters by hiring his own speedier men to land his shipments of Newfoundland fish, but he placated them by arranging to pay to the regular porters a percentage of the cost of the work. In 1615 he was in arrears for his rent for the Woollen Hall. But he seems to have conformed more with custom as the years passed, for from 1615 to 1621 he served the town in various capacities, as juror of the court leet, constable, steward, bailiff, and sheriff, and he was mayor, 1623–1624 and 1636–1637.[173] As an alderman Exton was named in 1629 to the local commission of gaol delivery and in 1636 to the commission on piracy.[174] He was named a justice of the town under the new charter of 1640.[175]

Experienced as Exton was in local affairs, the Long Parliament was the first to which he was elected. He seems to have been irregular in attendance there, having numerous leaves of absence, one of them as early as 17 December 1640, and he was named to no committees of the House. Late in 1642 and again in the spring of 1643 he was ordered to return to explain his absences, but was each time admitted to his seat.[176] He was named to the wartime parliamentary committees for Hampshire, and may have sat until the end of the parliament. He was among those present when the remnants of the parliament reassembled in the spring of 1660, but seems to have been inactive after the Restoration.[177] He died in 1663 or 1664. His will, dated 17 January 1662/3, was proved by his widow, 12 July 1664. He was probably buried in St. Lawrence's Church in Southampton.[178]

Alderman Exton was a man of prominence in his town. He was evidently a prosperous merchant with varied overseas interests and was the holder of several important properties in Southampton and in the Isle of Wight.[179] In his will he referred to a former wife and to several daughters and grandchildren by her, as well as to his "present" wife, Frances. He assigned small legacies to his numerous relatives, and left remembrances, too, to two ministers of Southampton and to the poor of several parishes. To a daughter still unmarried he assigned a portion of £500.

* **Sir Ferdinando Fairfax** (1584–1648), of Denton, Yorkshire, second Baron Fairfax of Cameron, was a knight for Yorkshire from 1640 until his death in 1648. He was admitted to Gray's Inn, 3 May 1602,[1] and gained his military education in the Netherlands. He was a J.P in the West Riding by 1611, and was active as a county magistrate until the Civil War.[2] He served also on other local commissions, including that for the loan on privy seals in 1626,[3] and sat in every parliament from 1614 until his death. Until October, 1640, his constituency was Boroughbridge.[4] His military leadership in the border war as well as in the matter of the Yorkshire petition of July, 1640,[5] probably explains his elevation to the shire seat then. He wielded political influence in the Knaresborough neighborhood, too, for he and his friends were instrumental in the unseating of Benson there and in getting Fairfax's brother-in-law, Sir William Constable, into the place.[6]

A widower at the time of his election,[7] Lord Fairfax was the father-in-law of Sir Thomas Widdrington, a brother-in-law of Sir George Wentworth of Woolley,[8] and a relative and friend of Bulstrode Whitelocke,[9] all fellow members of the Long Parliament. He was a man of wealth, having in the spring of 1640 succeeded to his inheritance. Although he had complained during his early widowerhood of the inadequacy of his father's allowance of £300 a year for him and his children,[10] portions of £1000 to £1500 apiece had been arranged for four of his daughters between 1636 and

---

[172] *Ibid.* 3: 59, n.; Carr, *Select charters of trading companies*, 66.

[173] *The assembly books of Southampton* 3: 59 and n., 61, 75; *Southampton court leet records*, ed. F. J. C. Hearnshaw and D. M. Hearnshaw (Southampton Record Society, 2, 4), 1 (3): 467–468, 1906–1907; *The book of examinations and depositions, 1622–1644*, ed. R. C. Anderson (*Southampton Record Society*, 29, 31, 34), 1: 22, n., 1929, 1931, 1934; B. B. Woodward, T. C. Wilks, and C. Lockhart, *A general history of Hampshire* 2: 317, n., London, 1861–1869.

[174] C. 181/4, fol. 23; 181/5, fol. 86.

[175] Woodward, Wilks, and Lockhart, *A general history of Hampshire* 2: 312.

[176] *C.J.* 2: 52; Pink MSS, 300, fol. 128.

[177] *Ibid.;* Godwin, *The Civil War in Hampshire*, 104; Add. MSS, 24,860, fol. 145; *H.M.C., Tenth Report* 6, MSS of P. P. Bouverie, 91.

[178] P.C.C., 80 Bruce.

[179] Brit. Mus. Add. Charters, 17,449; *The assembly books of Southampton* 4: 49; Exton's will.

[1] Gray's Inn Adm. Reg., 103.

[2] *West Riding Sessions Records* (*Y.A.S. Rec. Ser.* **54**: 2, 7, *passim*, 1915); C. 193/12, 13; *Yorks. Arch. Jour.* **5**: 379, 400, 1879.

[3] C. 181/3, fols. 8, 121; 181/4, *passim*; 181/5, *passim*; S.P. 16, 44/4.

[4] *M. of P.* 1: 454, 461, *passim;* 3: xli. The 1614 and 1621 parliaments are not mentioned in *D.N.B.*

[5] *C.S.P. Dom., 1640*, 524.

[6] See Henry Benson. Various letters from Fairfax dated from Knaresborough, 1636–1637, are among the Bodleian Fairfax MSS, 31, fols. 74, 85v, 86, 92.

[7] His first wife died in 1619 (*Bull. Inst. Hist. Research* **4**: 54, 1926–1927), and his second wife was in 1640 still the wife of Thomas Hussey (*q.v.*).

[8] Wentworth's first wife (d. 1624) was a sister of Fairfax.

[9] Whitelocke, *Memorials* 1: 194, 1853.

[10] *Fairfax correspondence* 1: xxxiv–xxxv.

1640.[11] For his peerage his father had paid £1500, and he had spent a large sum to add the manor of Bolton Percy to his possessions.[12] In November, 1640, Lord Fairfax gave his security for £1000 toward the loan.[13]

Fairfax was interested in horse breeding.[14] Other avocations were said to have been mathematics and the rhyming of the Psalms.[15]

George Fane (1616–1663), of St. Andrew's, Holborn, and of Northamptonshire, was M.P. for Callington, Cornwall, 1640–16 January 1643. He was the fifth son of Francis Fane, first Earl of Westmorland (d. 1629), and godson of George Manners, Earl of Rutland. His mother was Mary, daughter and sole heiress of Sir Anthony Mildmay and granddaughter of Sir Walter Mildmay, founder of Emmanuel College, Cambridge. He was born in 1616,[16] and was admitted in 1632 to that college as "of Northamptonshire." He was awarded the degree of M.A. as a nobleman's son in 1635,[17] and later in the same year sailed with his brother, Anthony, for Dieppe.[18] With two of his brothers, Fane was with the army in the north in 1639,[19] but his election to the Long Parliament brought his first experience in civic office.

George Fane was named to several committees of the Long Parliament, including that on ship money and some on church government and the Jesuits, and he spoke occasionally.[20] But he joined the king when war came, was disabled by parliament in 1643, and served as a colonel in the royal army. It is doubtful whether he was the George Fane of Chelsea who compounded in 1649, acknowledging a total estate, real and personal, of only £60.[21] He was chosen M.P. again in 1661 for Wallingford, and died two years later. His burial from Hatton Garden, 25 April 1663, is recorded in the register of St. Bartholomew the Great, and administration of his goods was granted to a creditor.[22]

Fane was probably unmarried in 1640.[23] He was a cousin of at least one other member of the Long Parliament, Sir Henry Mildmay.

* **Sir Thomas Fanshawe**, K.B. (1596–1665), of Ware Park, Hertfordshire, Remembrancer of the Exchequer,

was a member for Hertford borough from 1640 until his disablement, 7 September 1642.[24] He probably travelled abroad in 1618,[25] and was a member of each successive parliament, beginning with that of 1624, and sitting for Hertford each time except in 1626.[26] In his county he was a J.P., D.L., and member of various local commissions,[27] and in 1628 seems to have performed some functions under the Receiver General of the Duchy of Cornwall.[28]

In the Long Parliament, Fanshawe voted against the attainder of Strafford, was named to several committees of minor importance,[29] and was expelled in September, 1642, for his royalist actions.

Sir Thomas was a wealthy man, owning extensive properties in Hertfordshire and others in Derbyshire. His father's income had been estimated as £4000 a year[30] and his own marriages had no doubt added materially to his income. Both he and his father had been interested in the Virginia Company,[31] and he may have held stock in the East India Company also.[32] His wealth led to frequent calls for loans to the crown,[33] and in the Long Parliament he offered his bond for £1000 for the 1640 loan.[34] He had settled most of his estate by 1642, partly to care for debts of £14,000, and partly to provide £11,000 as portions for five daughters, but the income from his chief properties then was over £1600 a year.[35] His losses during the war and his heavy fine deprived him of most of his riches.

Fanshawe was a cousin of Thomas Fanshawe, the member for Lancaster, and Sir Christopher Hatton of Northamptonshire, and was related by marriage to Sir Robert Crane and Zouch Tate.[36]

Thomas Fanshawe (1607–1652), of Jenkins in Barking, Essex, Esquire, sat for Lancaster borough from 1640 until 25 November 1643. His father, Sir Thomas Fanshawe of Jenkins and London (1580–1631), barrister, Clerk of the Crown and Surveyor-General to

[11] Bodleian Fairfax MSS, 31, fols. 66–70, 131, 135.
[12] *Fairfax Correspondence* 1: xxvi–xxvii, lxx–lxxi.
[13] D'Ewes (N), 52.
[14] *Y.A.S. Rec. Ser.* 9: 5–8, 1890.
[15] *Fairfax Correspondence* 1: lxxxiii.
[16] O. Barron, ed., *Northamptonshire families*, 97, 112; Courtney, *Parl. Rep. Corn.*, 271.
[17] *Al. Cant.*
[18] Barron, *op. cit.*, 97. His brother, Anthony (born 1614), was an unsuccessful candidate for election at Peterborough in 1640.
[19] S.P. 16, 427/38/ii, iv; *C.S.P. Dom., 1639*, 272.
[20] *C.J.* 2: 45, 73, 105; D'Ewes (C), 333, 342.
[21] *Cal. Com. Comp.*, 2099; S.P. 23/217/473.
[22] Barron, *op. cit.*, 112.
[23] His wife was born in 1630. *Ibid.*

[24] *M. of P.* 1: 489; *C.J.* 2: 756.
[25] *The letters of John Chamberlain* 2: 149, 171.
[26] *M. of P.* 1: 458, *passim.*
[27] Clutterbuck, *Herts* 3: 296; *C.S.P. Dom., 1637*, 126; S.P. 16/405; C. 181/4, fol. 76; 181/5, fols. 4, 257, 350.
[28] S.P. 16, 528/32.
[29] Verney, 57; *C.J.* 2: 52, 60.
[30] Add. MSS, 27,929, fols. 1–5; *Derbys. Arch. Jour.* 20: 126, 1898; Clutterbuck, *Herts* 2: 28; *The memoirs of Ann Lady Fanshawe*, C. H. Fanshaw, ed., 11, London, John Lane, 1907.
[31] His maternal grandfather was Sir Thomas Smyth, treasurer of the Virginia Company. Brown, *Genesis of the U. S.*, 888–889.
[32] India Office MSS, Home Ser., Misc., 39, fol. 69.
[33] He had been accounted able to lend £1000 in 1627 and in 1639–1640 he lent at least £1000 (S.P. 16, 52/61, 453/74). Lloyd declared Fanshawe advanced £2000 toward the Scottish expedition (*Memoires*, 684).
[34] D'Ewes (N), 52.
[35] S.P. 23/208/685–687; Add. MSS, 27,979, fol. 5.
[36] Clutterbuck, *Herts* 3: 294. Crane, Tate, and Fanshawe married sisters.

James I, had represented Lancaster, 1604–1629; he was a younger son of Sir Thomas Fanshawe of Ware and Jenkins (d. 1601), Remembrancer of the Exchequer, and half-brother of Sir Henry Fanshawe of Ware, to whom the office of remembrancer passed. Thomas, the eldest son of the surveyor-general by his wife, Anne, daughter of Urias Babington, a London draper, was baptized at Barking, 22 November 1607,[37] matriculated at Trinity College, Cambridge, 1622 (M.A. by royal order, 1624), and studied at the Inner Temple.[38] He married about 1626 Susan, daughter and coheir of Matthew Otten of Putney and Walthamstow, Surrey,[39] and made his residence at Barking.

Under Charles I Fanshawe became coroner and attorney of King's Bench.[40] He served also on the Essex sewers commission,[41] and was probably M.P. for Preston, 1626. In June, 1641, he was a partner in the auditorship of the northern parts of the Duchy of Lancaster, an office in which he had been preceded by his father and his uncle.

A strong royalist, Fanshawe was not active in the Long Parliament, and by the autumn of 1642 was an absentee. He refused to attend, upon summons, and was accordingly disabled, 25 November 1643.[42] Fanshawe sat in the Oxford parliament, later compounded for his estate, and died in 1652. His will, dated 22 January 1651/2, was proved on 3 February of that year.[43]

Fanshawe had a good yearly income, but seems to have been considerably in debt before the war added to his troubles. His debts of 1635–1639, for which his friend, Sir Christopher Hatton (q.v.), stood bond, amounted to over £3800,[44] and by the time he made his composition, he declared his debts and bonds for others totalled £12,000. The value of his several Essex estates he put at over £700 a year, and his salary from his King's Bench office was £200. His fine, reckoned at a tenth, was set at £1300, with a reduction if he made certain settlements on the ministry.[45]

Sir Thomas Fanshawe, K.B., his fellow member, was a cousin, and John Harrison a kinsman by marriage.

Sir Thomas Farnefold (1599–1643), of Gatewick in Steyning, Sussex, was one of three men named in returns for Steyning, 12 October 1640, and seems to have been recognized as one of its members until his death in March, 1643.[46] He came of a family seated in Sussex for over two centuries, several of his ancestors having been M.P.'s for Steyning, and was the second son of Richard Farnefold of Gatewick (1548–1609) by his wife, Dorothy, daughter and coheiress of a well-to-do yeoman, Thomas Parson of Steyning. Born in 1599, he became heir to the family properties upon his elder brother's death in 1611.[47] During his minority he was the ward in turn of Sir Thomas Leedes, Sir Edward Sackville, and Bartholomew Rogers, Usher of the Court of Wards. The latter matched his ward at seventeen with his daughter, Dorothy, and proceeded, as Farnefold afterwards complained, to devastate and mismanage his inheritance to the extent of some thousands of pounds of damage.[48] Farnefold's education may have included service in arms in Europe, for he mentioned in his will in 1639 that he had "lost" his life in the king's service.[49] His father-in-law's connections probably brought him some attachment to the royal court, for he was listed among the residents of St. Margaret's parish, Westminster, 1620–1621,[50] and was knighted at Theobalds on 22 December 1621.[51] He was committed to the Marshalsea in 1622 for having had some quarrel with Viscount Wallingford,[52] and retained some of his Westminster connections as late as 1641.[53] Either because of the expenses of life at court or because of losses incurred during his wardship Farnefold sold or mortgaged a number of his properties in Steyning. His wife died in 1636, leaving him with eight young children. He married in London about a year later Elizabeth Cudmore, widow, of Kelvedon.[54] In 1638 he spent about a fortnight as a prisoner in the Fleet, both his incarceration and his release being ordered by Council.[55]

---

[37] Pink MSS, 301, fol. 36; *Misc. Geneal. et Herald.*, N.S., 2: 8, 1876; Clutterbuck, *Herts* 3: 294.

[38] *Al. Cant.*

[39] Clutterbuck confuses Fanshawe with his son, Thomas, in giving the name of his wife (*Herts* 3: 294). An indenture made about the time of his marriage was dated 15 February 1625/6. S.P. 23, 205/589.

[40] Norwich Corporation MSS, Folio Assembly Book, 1613–1642, fol. 206; *C.S.P. Dom.*, 1629–1631, 97.

[41] C. 181/4, fol. 76.

[42] *C.J.* 2: 845, 955; 3: 319.

[43] J. Matthews and G. F. Matthews, *Abstracts of probate acts in the prerogative court of Canterbury* 6: 62, London, 1902–.

[44] Northamptonshire Record Society MSS, F.H. 3381 (hereafter, Northants. MSS). Numerous papers in this Hatton collection show that Fanshawe and Hatton were close friends.

[45] S.P. 23/205, 589–596; *Cal. Com. Comp.*, 1661. Other references, besides those cited above, are: *Al. Cant.*; *M. of P.* 1: 444, 458, 464, 470, 476; 3: App., iii, n.; xxxviii; W. R. Williams, *Official lists of the duchy and county palatine of Lancaster*, 53, Brecon, 1901; *Memoirs of Ann Lady Fanshawe*, 15, 312, and Appendix, pedigrees A and B.

---

[46] *M. of P.* 1: 495 and n. See also Richard Sackville, Lord Buckhurst. Farnefold was referred to as deceased, not as disabled, when a new election was ordered for Steyning in 1645. *C.J.* 4: 272.

[47] W. Powell Breach, Farnefold of Steyning, *Sussex Arch. Coll.* 59: 84–112, 1918; I.P.M.'s of Richard Farnefold and Walter Farnefold, C. 142/311/115 and 325/196.

[48] *H.M.C., Fourth Report*, House of Lords MSS, 124; Harl. MSS, 6803, fol. 14.

[49] P.C.C., 11 Rivers.

[50] Records of St. Margaret's Parish, Overseers' Accounts, **151**.

[51] Pink MSS, 301, fol. 48.

[52] *Acts P.C.*, 1621–1623, 254, 271.

[53] St. Margaret's Overseers Accounts, **154**.

[54] *Sussex Rec. Soc.* **19**: 179, 1914; *Sussex Arch. Coll.* 59: 102–103, 1918.

[55] *C.S.P. Dom.*, 1637–1638, 156, 185.

Farnefold had kept his family's principal seat at Gatewick and was named a J.P. in Sussex in the 1630's and a sewers commissioner.[56] He represented Steyning in the parliaments of 1624, 1625, and 1628 and in the Short Parliament.[57] His return in the autumn of 1640 might have been unchallenged had Lord Buckhurst not appeared as a candidate, but the latter's choice for East Grinstead made it possible for Farnefold to retain the Steyning seat. There is no evidence, however, that Farnefold actually sat in the Long Parliament, for he was named neither for committee nor in debate, and his name is missing from the role of Straffordians, where it might have been expected to appear, and from the more inclusive list of those taking the Protestation of 1641.[58] He was apparently in poor health when he made his will in June, 1639, and perhaps never attended the parliament. He died in March, 1643, and was buried at Steyning.[59] His will was proved 17 December 1644.

Farnefold was undoubtedly royalist in his sympathies, and quite possibly lost most of his living, as well as his life, in his master's service. His will directed that more of his diminished estate be sold to provide portions of £200 each for five younger children.

* Sir John Fenwick, Bart. (c. 1579–1658), of Fenwick and Wallington, Northumberland, represented Cockermouth, Cumberland, from its restoration (15 February 1641) until 6 January 1642, when he chose to occupy a seat for his native county that had been vacated. He was disabled 22 January 1644,[60] reinstated in June, 1646, and finally secluded in 1648. He was born about 1579,[61] and led an active life in the northern counties, where he was wealthy and influential. Besides sitting for Northumberland in the five parliaments before the Long Parliament, he was for a time in command at Tynemouth Castle for the Earl of Northumberland, was possibly sheriff of his county in 1619,[62] and was a D.L. there.[63] He was a J.P. there and in Durham for many years,[64] and a member of various commissions in Yorkshire and the other northern counties.[65] He does not seem to have had any special connection with Cumberland or Cockermouth, but probably owed his election

in 1641 for the latter borough to the Earl of Northumberland, owner of the manor of Cockermouth.[66]

Fenwick inherited many estates in the north from his father, Sir William Fenwick, and from his maternal grandfather, Sir John Forster, including interests in various coal and lead mines.[67] He purchased other properties, too, and by 1640 had some interest in the salt business.[68] He promised two horses for the defense in 1642.[69] The rentals of the properties of his son and successor in 1663 came to more than £1500.[70] One of Sir John's special avocations was horse breeding.[71]

Fenwick had numerous relatives in the 1640 House, including his eldest son, the Morpeth member. Sir Henry Slingsby was a brother of Sir John's first wife.[72] Sir John died in 1658, aged seventy-nine.[73]

John Fenwick (c. 1612–1644), of Wallington, Northumberland, was M.P. for Morpeth, 1640–22 January 1644.[74] He was the son and heir apparent of Sir John Fenwick, Bart. (q.v.), by his first wife, Catherine Slingsby, and was aged three at the 1615 visitation.[75] He is described in one family pedigree as of Hexham Abbey.[76] Fenwick matriculated at Trinity College, Cambridge, in 1628, and was admitted to Gray's Inn in 1630. He married Mary, daughter of Sir George Selby of Whitehouse, Durham,[77] and in 1639–1640 served under Conway as captain of a troop of horse.[78] He seems to have held no county offices before his election to the Long Parliament.

The younger Fenwick joined Carnaby in pledging £500 for the loan in March, 1641,[79] and voted against Strafford's attainder.[80] Otherwise he did not distinguish himself in the House. He was appointed to several parliamentary committees for his county in 1642,[81] but after he became a colonel of dragoons for the king he was disabled, 22 January 1644. He was killed at Marston Moor the following July.

---

[56] C. 193/13; S.P. 16/405; C. 181/5, fol. 138.

[57] M. of P. 1: 460, 466, 478, 483.

[58] Pink remarked that he had in no way traced Farnefold as present. Pink MSS, 310, fol. 48.

[59] Sussex Arch. Coll. 59: 103, 1918; Add. MSS, 5698, fol. 248v; Sir Thomas's I.P.M., C. 142/774/11.

[60] M. of P. 1: 487, n., 491; C.J. 2: 86; 3: 374.

[61] He was aged thirty-five and more in September, 1614, according to the I.P.M. of Sir William Fenwick (C. 142/346/163). He stated in 1651, however, that he was very aged and infirm, being eighty-five years old. Cal. Com. Comp., 2487.

[62] Bean, Northern Counties, 489.

[63] C.S.P. Dom., 1638–1639, 310.

[64] C. 193/12, 13; S.P. 16/405.

[65] C. 181/3, fols. 8, 121; 181/4, fols. 36, 61; 181/5, fols. 14, 98, passim.

[66] Cf. Sir John Hippisley.

[67] History of Northumberland, Northumberland County Historical Commission 3: 10, 57–59.

[68] Cal. Com. Comp., 2487; C.S.P. Dom., 1640, 15.

[69] N. and Q., 1st Ser., 12: 360, 1855.

[70] John Hodgson, A history of Northumberland, Part 3, vol. 1: 328–329, Newcastle upon Tyne, 1820–1858.

[71] E.H.R. 5: 352, 1890.

[72] D.N.B. errs in naming her the daughter of Sir Ralph Slingsby instead of Sir Henry Slingsby the elder. Complete Baronetage 2: 40; Vis. Northumberland, 1615, 32.

[73] Complete Baronetage 2: 40.

[74] M. of P. 1: 491; C.J. 3: 374.

[75] Marshall, Vis. Northumberland, 32. Fenwick is mentioned in the D.N.B. article on his father.

[76] J. H. Hill, The history of the parish of Langton, 218, Leicester, 1867.

[77] Al. Cant.

[78] C.S.P. Dom., 1640, 496, 559.

[79] D'Ewes (N), 439, n.

[80] Verney, 58.

[81] Pink MSS, 301, fol. 80.

Among Fenwick's colleagues in the 1640 House were his father, his uncle, Sir Henry Slingsby, and his relative by marriage, Sir Patrick Curwen, who seems to have been a brother-in-law of Fenwick's wife.

Richard Ferris (1580–1649), a merchant of Barnstaple, Devon, originally returned for that borough in October, 1640, and re-elected after the House on 6 August 1641 voided his first election,[82] was a member until his disablement early in 1644.[83]

Ferris came of a family active in Barnstaple affairs in the previous century, his father being Philip Ferris, merchant, deputy receiver in 1600.[84] His mother was Thomasine Cade.[85] Born in 1580,[86] he probably spent his early years in Barnstaple in training for business. He may have been away for a time, for one Richard Ferris was readmitted to the freedom of the borough, as if after an absence, about 1607,[87] and in 1611 Richard Ferris was one of the Barnstaple men named in the patent for the company of Merchants of London trading into France.[88] And from 1611 until 1617, at least, he was an aide to the English consul in Lisbon.[89] He married (1) Mary Beaple of Barnstaple in 1625; and (2) after 1627, Elizabeth, daughter of Dr. John Downe of Instow.[90]

From 1632 to 1633, Ferris was mayor of Barnstaple, being by then a leading merchant there.[91] During his term of office a speedier postal service to London was inaugurated, local measures to curb gaming in the alehouses and to restrict the eating of flesh in Lent were insisted upon, and Ferris took the initiative in urging common action by the Devon port towns for defense against the pirates.[92] Later in the decade, he served as alderman, burgess of the council,[93] as collector for money for the repair of St. Paul's,[94] as committeeman for arranging with the county sheriff for easing the ship money assessment on his town,[95] and in 1638 he was named on the county commission on exacted fees.[96]

Whether Ferris sought a place in the Short Parliament does not appear, but, as one of four candidates in the autumn, he defeated a fellow merchant who had been elected in the spring. The defeated man challenged the election,[97] and, although Ferris had sat in the House and had taken the Protestation in May, 1641,[98] his election was declared void on 6 August. Promptly re-elected, Ferris returned to Westminster in the autumn, but did not become an active member either in debate or in committees. In June, 1642, he promised a free loan of £50 for the defense,[99] later assisted with measures for defending Barnstaple, and in 1643 was named on one of the parliamentary committees for Devon.[100] By January, 1644, however, as an alleged member of the royalist parliament at Oxford, he was disabled.[101] Ferris seems never to have been an ardent royalist. He died in 1649,[102] and was buried in Barnstaple parish church, where an ornate monument commemmorates his services and benefactions.

In estate Ferris was prosperous, being probably one of the wealthiest merchants of his town. In his will of 19 June 1646 he mentioned properties in Barnstaple and in nearby parishes, but stated that a great part of his estate was in the form of goods then in others' hands and beyond seas. His bequests included not only £2500 in money to be paid to his wife after the settlement of his overseas estate, and perpetual endowments for a school in Barnstaple and for apprenticing poor children, but numerous other legacies amounting to some £1970. References to several London merchants who were friends, and to a cousin dwelling in Ireland, confirm the other evidences that Ferris was more than a provincial tradesman. His epitaph proclaims his interest in learning, his prudence and justice, his religious faith and zeal; "not stones but deeds build up his monument." [103]

John Fettiplace (*c.* 1583–1658), of Childrey, Berkshire, and Swinbrooke, Oxfordshire, sat for Berkshire, 1640–22 January 1644. The descendant of several old Berkshire lines, he was the eldest son of the large family of Sir Edmund Fettiplace of Childrey and Swinbrooke

[82] *C.J.* 2 : 239; *M. of P.* 1 : 487 and n.

[83] Pink MSS, 307, fol. 351.

[84] Manuscripts of the Corporation of Barnstaple (hereafter, Barnstaple MSS), Receivers' Accounts, 1389–1643, membrane 131.

[85] Devon *Trans.* 72 : 260, 1940.

[86] Richard, son of Philip, was baptized on 4 August 1580 (Thomas Wainwright, ed., *Barnstaple parish register*, 25, Exeter, J. G. Commin, 1903). According to his M.I. in Barnstaple, Richard, the M.P., was "aet. 67" at his death in 1649.

[87] Barnstaple MSS, Receivers' Accounts, 1398–1643, accounts for 1606–07, membrane 170.

[88] Carr, *Select charters of trading companies*, 67.

[89] *H.M.C., MSS of the Duke of Buccleugh and Queensbury* 1 : 180–181.

[90] Wainwright, *Barnstaple parish register*, 21; Devon *Trans.* 72 : 260, 1940.

[91] Barnstaple MSS, Sessions Court Book, 1631–1642.

[92] Barnstaple MSS, Nos. 2200, 2202, 2203, 680; Plymouth Corporation MSS, No. 360.

[93] Barnstaple MSS, Sessions Court Book 1631–1642 (1633 and 1638); J. R. Chanter and T. Wainwright, *Barnstaple records* 1 : 35, 103, Barnstaple, A. E. Barnes, 1900.

[94] Gribble, *Memorials of Barnstaple*, 630.

[95] Barnstaple MSS, Receivers' Accounts 1389–1643, membrane 229.

[96] C. 181/5, fol. 218.

[97] Barnstaple MSS, No. 1117, printed in full in Gribble, op. cit., 346–350.

[98] *C.J.* 2 : 133. Perhaps he was the "Mr. Perryn" named on committees, 17 and 30 December, 1640. *Ibid.* 2 : 52, 60.

[99] *N. and Q.*, 1st Ser., 12 : 360, 1855.

[100] Pink MSS, 307, fol. 351.

[101] *Ibid.;* R. W. Cotton, *Barnstaple during the great Civil War*, 39, 79, London, 1889.

[102] His will was proved 3 January 1649/50 (P.C.C., 5 Pembroke). He seems to have had no children.

[103] M.I., St. Peter's Church, Barnstaple, under an effigy of a recumbent figure clad in magisterial robes.

(d. 1613), by Anne, daughter of Roger Alford.[104] He was born about 1583,[105] and matriculated at Queen's College, Oxford, early in 1594. He may have graduated B.A. from Hart Hall in 1600,[106] and probably entered Lincoln's Inn the next year.[107] He succeeded his father in 1613, becoming head of his family, but he never married.

Fettiplace sat for Berkshire in the parliaments of 1626 and 1628,[108] and by this time was a J.P. in Oxfordshire. He served as a magistrate there and in Berkshire for many years, was named also to other local commissions,[109] and was sheriff of the latter county in 1631.[110] He was among those who refused to compound with the knighthood commissioners in 1630, but eventually he paid a fine of £30.[111] He was reported six years later among the Oxfordshire officials who refused to pay ship money,[112] and in 1639 excused himself from contributing towards the king's expenses in the north.[113] Certainly Fettiplace might have been expected to work with the opposition forces when he was elected to both of the 1640 parliaments for Berkshire.[114]

But Fettiplace was not one of Pym's stalwarts in the Long Parliament. He supported them to the extent of offering his security for £1000 for the loan in November,[115] but was named to no important committees, and in the spring of 1641 voted against Strafford's attainder.[116] The attacks on the established church as well as upon the king's advisers probably influenced Fettiplace, for he seems to have been a devout Anglican. His pledge of four horses for the defense in 1642 was given in September instead of in June,[117] and he delayed some time before taking the Covenant in 1643. Absenting himself from the House by September of that year, he finally joined the king at Oxford and was therefore secluded, 22 January 1644.[118] Fettiplace compounded for his delinquency in 1646, and seems to have lived in retirement thereafter until his death, 20 March 1658. His will, dated 9 July 1656, with a codicil of 15 March 1657/8, was proved 20 May 1658. His heir was his nephew, John, who became a baronet in 1661.[119]

The family of Fettiplace held numerous lands, and those of John of Childrey embraced five or six manors with appurtenances in Berkshire, Bedfordshire, Wilts and Oxfordshire, over 2000 acres in extent. He declared their worth when he compounded as slightly more than £1000 a year, above all annuities payable out of them. His fine, set at a tenth, was £1,943.[120] By his will Fettiplace left legacies totalling over £1,930, and before that, in 1652, had founded a school at Dorchester, Oxfordshire. The instructions he drew up for the school give some idea of the founder's religion and also of his views about education. He specified that the masters should be a pattern of godliness, that the books be without taint of atheism, epicurism, or popish superstition, and that the daily prayers be in accord with the former Anglican confession. He desired that good learning and manners, with a proper emphasis upon the classics, be taught, but he warned against violence in discipline and directed that play periods be not overlooked.[121]

Fettiplace was a generous man and interested in his relatives and friends. Among the latter was Sir Robert Pye, 1640 M.P. A kinsman was possibly William Pleydell.[122]

James Fiennes (*c.* 1601–1674), of Broughton, M.P. for Oxfordshire, 1640–1648, was the eldest son and heir apparent of William, Viscount Say and Sele. He was educated at Cambridge and Lincoln's Inn,[123] and was named occasionally to local commissions for the Oxford region between 1634 and 1641.[124] He was M.P. four times, three of them for Oxfordshire, before the autumn of 1640, and it was not strange that "Squire Fiennes," son of the county's prominent puritan leader, should be chosen again for the Long Parliament.[125]

Although he was a stockholder in the Providence

[104] *Vis. Berks.* 1: 206; W. N. Clarke, *Parochial topography of the hundred of Wanting,* 68, Oxford, 1824 (hereafter, Clarke, *Wanting*).

[105] He was aged thirty and over in June, 1613 (I.P.M., Sir Edmund Fettiplace, C. 142/333/42), was said to be thirteen when he matriculated at Oxford (January, 1594), and was in his seventy-sixth year when he died, 20 March 1657/8 (M.I., cited in F. N. Davis, ed., *Parochial collections made by Wood and Rawlinson* [Oxfordshire Record Society, 11] 3: 298, 1929).

[106] *Al. Oxon.* References to Queen's College occur several times in the statutes for Fettiplace's endowed school (see below).

[107] *Linc. Inn Rec. Adm.* 1: 133. His younger brother, Edward, became a lawyer there. *Vis. Berks.* 1: 206.

[108] *M. of P.* 1: 468, 474.

[109] C. 193/12, 13; *C.S.P. Dom., 1629–1631,* 278; *1640,* 528; S.P. 16/405; C. 181/4, fol. 147v; 181/5, fols. 280, *passim.*

[110] *C.S.P. Dom., 1631–1633,* 45.

[111] S.P. 16, 180/24, fols. 91v–94.

[112] S.P. 16, 336/5/i.

[113] Rushworth 3: 912.

[114] *M. of P.* 1: 480, n., 485; *C.S.P. Dom., 1639–1640,* 162.

[115] D'Ewes (N), 52.

[116] Verney, 58.

[117] *C.J.* 2: 772.

[118] *C.J.* 3: 374; Pink MSS, 307, fol. 12; Clarke, *Wanting,* 69–70.

[119] P.C.C., 323 Wotton; Davis, *loc. cit.; Complete Baronetage* 3: 182.

[120] Most of the lands mentioned in his father's inquisition post mortem were listed by Fettiplace in his compounding papers (S.P. 23/192/370; *Cal. Com. Comp.,* 1542). Another manor which he bought in 1629 (*V.C.H. Berks* 4: 290) was mentioned in his will.

[121] Add. MSS, 25,426, fols. 4–17.

[122] Pye was named in his will, as was one William Pleydell. Several others of the latter family were described as cousins.

[123] *Al. Cant.; Linc. Inn Rec. Adm.* 1: 205.

[124] C. 181/4, fol. 179; 181/5, fol. 400.

[125] *H.M.C., Fourteenth Report* 2, MSS of the Duke of Portland (III), 66; Add. MSS, 37,343, fols. 206v–207; *M. of P.* 1: 492, *passim.*

Island Company,[126] James Fiennes seems to have been less zealous in public affairs and in the puritan cause than his father and his brother, Nathaniel (q.v.). He promised two horses for the defense in 1642,[127] but was named to but few committees of the House, 1640–1647.[128]

Relatives of Fiennes who were fellow parliament men in 1640, besides his brother, were his brother-in-law, Sir Christopher Wray, and his cousin, Sir Peter Temple, and others of more distant connection.

* Nathaniel Fiennes (1608–1669), the single M.P. for Banbury, Oxfordshire, 1640–1648, was the second son of Lord Say and Sele, and brother of the county member, James Fiennes (q.v.). He had possibly studied at the Middle Temple [129] as well as at Oxford and Geneva. His absence from the country much of the time before 1639 prevented him from taking part in local affairs and holding offices.[130] Fiennes owed his seat for both of the 1640 parliaments for Banbury to his father, who was High Steward of the town.[131]

John Finch (d. 1642), of the Inner Temple (?), was M.P. for Winchelsea from 1640 until his death about November, 1642.[132] He was a member of the wealthy and distinguished Kentish family seated near Winchelsea, being apparently a son of one of the younger sons of Sir Moyle Finch of Eastwell (d. 1615), and a nephew of Thomas, first Earl of Winchelsea, and of Sir Heneage Finch, Recorder of London and one time Speaker of the House of Commons.[133] His father was possibly Sir Moyle's third son, John (1579–1624), a barrister of the Inner Temple, who married Anne, daughter of Thomas Walker,[134] or Sir Moyle's sixth

son, Robert, who was alive in 1622.[135] He may have been the John Finch "of London" who entered the Inner Temple in 1631,[136] but otherwise nothing is known of him until his appearance as M.P. for Winchelsea in both parliaments of 1640.[137] The town was virtually a family borough, at least one of its representatives, 1621–1629, having been either a Finch or one of their relatives. Sir Roger Twysden, a Finch son-in-law, had hoped in the spring of 1640 to procure the place for his brother, Thomas,[138] but it went instead to his cousin, John Finch. The latter was knighted sometime between 18 December 1641 and 11 June 1642.[139]

As a kinsman of Lord Keeper Finch, the Long Parliament member interceded with the House to grant Sir John a hearing before the vote against him was taken,[140] and he was appointed on 2 April 1641 to the committee to be present throughout the trial of Strafford. He was named to no other committee of importance, however, and twice in 1641 was granted leave of absence.[141] He seems to have been less concerned than his cousin, Sir Roger Twysden, about the problem of episcopacy,[142] and in 1642 not only promised to provide two horses for the defense,[143] but was named in August to help to enforce the militia ordinance in Northamptonshire,[144] and on 28 October was appointed to the committee to handle reports from the members working in their counties. He had opposed the first vote for disabling Colepeper,[145] however, and in September confided to his cousin, Twysden, that he would gladly travel with him. He died not long afterwards at Farningham, Kent, as a result of a fall from a horse, and administration of his estate was granted on 10 December 1642 to his kinsman, Thomas Twysden, and his uncle, Francis Finch.[146] Apparently he died unmarried and without direct heirs. Through the Twysdens he was related to two fellow members, Yelverton and Sir Hugh Cholmley.

William Fitzwilliam (c. 1609–1659), of Milton, Northamptonshire, M.P. for Peterborough, 1640–1648,

---

[126] Newton, *The colonising activities of the English puritans,* 126.

[127] *N. and Q.,* 1st Ser., **12**: 360, 1855.

[128] Pink MSS, 301, fols. 103–104. A sketch of his life appears in Williams, *Oxford,* 53.

[129] He was made a bencher there in 1655, although there is no record of his being admitted or being called to the bar. *Mid. Temp. Rec.* **3**: 1087, 1105.

[130] The royalist comment was that Fiennes was very little known in England before he appeared in parliament. Add. MSS, 27,990, fol. 38.

[131] *Berks. Arch. Jour.* **4**: 62, 1898. See also Williams, *Oxford,* 59.

[132] *M. of P.* **1**: 497. He was named to a committee, 28 October 1642 (*C.J.* **2**: 825), but had died by 10 December.

[133] He was a nephew of Francis Finch, according to the administration of his estate, and kinsman of Thomas Twysden (*Arch. Cant.* **20**: 34, 1893). Francis, one of Sir Moyle Finch's sons, was living in 1641, and is said to have died without children (Hasted, *Kent* **7**: 406). John was not a son of Francis, as Pink suggested (Pink MSS, 301, fol. 122). He could not have been Sir Heneage's son, John, for the latter lived until 1682 (*D.N.B.*).

[134] Bryan I'Anson, *The history of the Finch family,* 55, London, Janson & Co., 1933; *Students admitted to the Inner Temple* (1878 ed.), 148. The 1619 pedigree, however, shows no children for John (*Vis. Kent, 1619,* 68).

[135] *Ibid.; Sussex manors* (Sussex Record Society, **19**) **1**: 237, 1914.

[136] *Students admitted to the Inner Temple* (1878 ed.), 268.

[137] One John Finch, Esq., was a sewers commissioner for Kent in 1627 (C. 181/5), but there is no certainty that he was the M.P.

[138] *M. of P.* **1**: 455, *passim;* Larking, *Proceedings in Kent,* 4.

[139] *C.J.* **2**: 348; *N. and Q.,* 1st Ser., **12**: 360, 1855.

[140] D'Ewes (N), 168, 172, 174; *Note book of Sir John Northcote,* 84, n.

[141] *C.J.* **2**: 115, 214, 348; D'Ewes (C), 310 and n.

[142] *Arch. Cant.* **1**: 197, 1858.

[143] *N. and Q., 1st Ser.,* **12**: 360, 1855.

[144] *C.J.* **2**: 711. The other members of the committee were Northamptonshire men. *Northamptonshire Notes & Queries* **5**: 145, 1894.

[145] *C.J.* **2**: 739, 825.

[146] *Arch. Cant.* **2**: 193, 1859; **20**: 34, 1893. A writ for replacing him was ordered 3 September 1645 (*O.P.H.* **9**: 14).

was the son and heir apparent of William, first Baron Fitzwilliam of Lifford, Donegal, by his wife Catherine, daughter of William Hide of Berkshire, and succeeded as second baron, 6 January 1644. His family were influential landowners near Peterborough,[147] and his father opposed the fen drainage undertakings in 1629, and ship money in 1637, and was reported also as a musters defaulter.[148] William, who was born between 1603 and 1609,[149] studied at Emmanuel College, Cambridge, where he was admitted, 23 August 1621, and in 1638 married Jane, widow of Robert Perry, and daughter and coheiress of a London alderman, Hugh Perry (or Hunter).

Fitzwilliam was named in 1640 on the Northamptonshire commission of oyer and terminer, and with his father on several other commissions, including that of the peace, for Peterborough.[150] His election to the Short Parliament for that town was a natural consequence of his family's position there, and his re-election in October occurred almost without challenge, since he was named in each of two returns, and was recognized by the House on 6 January 1641.[151] Although he kept his seat until 1648, Fitzwilliam was named only for minor committee work, 1640–1643, and seems to have been concerned thereafter chiefly with county committees.[152] In September, 1644, the Committee for Advance of Money assessed him at £800, but there are no other indications of leanings toward royalism.[153] He died at his London house, 21 February 1659, and was buried at Marholm.

Through his paternal grandmother, a daughter of Sir Walter Mildmay, Fitzwilliam was related to his fellow M.P.'s, Sir Henry Mildmay and George Fane, as well as to Anthony Fane, a disappointed candidate in the Peterborough election.[154]

Sir Miles Fleetwood (d. 1641), of Aldwinkle, Northamptonshire, and of London, Receiver General of the Court of Wards and Liveries, was M.P. for Hindon, Wilts, from 1640 until his death in 1641. He was the

eldest son of Sir William Fleetwood of Middlesex and of Cardington, Bedfordshire, Receiver General before him, by his wife, Joan, sister of Gervase Lord Clifton.[155] He was admitted to Gray's Inn, 9 January 1588,[156] and was knighted in Ireland by the Lord Deputy in 1602.[157] By 1610 he was serving as under-steward of the honor of Grafton, and he succeeded his father about that time, certainly before 1618, in the receivership of the Court of Wards.[158] He held the management of Grafton manor at least until 1636,[159] and the receivership until his death. He married about 1598 Anne, daughter of Nicholas Luke of Bedfordshire, sister of Sir Oliver Luke (q.v.), and for the remainder of his life was on intimate terms with members of that puritan family and their connection.[160]

Fleetwood served on various local commissions, including that of the peace, for Bedfordshire and Northamptonshire, and was a D.L. in the latter county.[161] In 1627 and 1628 he exerted himself in disafforesting work, receiving £950 as a remuneration.[162] He had been granted £5000 in 1625 in recognition of his work in increasing the royal revenues under King James, but in 1628 he requested that his salary and pensions be put on a more regular basis.[163] His remuneration from both of his administrative offices was considerable.[164]

In the meantime, Sir Miles sat in parliament in 1614 for Huntingdon, and in every parliament thereafter until his death, though for varying constituencies. Most of them were in counties where he had little personal connection.[165] His official position doubtless helped him to win elections, but it did not assure the king of his support in the parliaments. In fact, Fleetwood made it clear fairly early that he sympathized with the growing movement of the opposition. In 1621 he urged that help be sent to the Palatinate and was one of the com-

[147] *V.C.H. Northampton* 2: 474, 476, 487; *Fenland Notes and Queries* 2: 389, 1892–1894; I.P.M. of Sir William Fitzwilliam, 1620, in the Bridges Collection, Bodleian MS Top. Northants c. 27, fols. 520–522.

[148] *C.S.P. Dom., 1629–1631*, 111; *1635*, 524; *1636–1637*, 480; S.P. 16, 376/113.

[149] His parents were married, 11 April 1603 (F. A. Blaydes, *Genealogia Bedfordiensis*, 158, London, 1890), and the baptisms of three sisters were recorded at Castor, Northants, 29 May 1608, 15 November 1609, and 13 January 1610/11 (Bishop Kennett's Collection, Lansd. MSS, 991, fols. 168v–169). His age was "about 29" at the time of his own marriage in July, 1638.

[150] C. 181/5, fols. 364, 365.

[151] *M. of P.* 1: 482, 491, and n.; *C.J.* 2: 63; D'Ewes (N), 222–223.

[152] *C.J.* 2: 160, 825; Pink MSS, 301, fol., 161.

[153] *Cal. Com. Adv. Money*, 248.

[154] In addition to the references cited above, see *Complete Peerage* (Gibbs ed.) 5: 520–521; *Al. Cant.*

[155] Lipscomb, *Buckingham* 3: 227; Pink MSS, 301, fol. 174. A biographical sketch of Fleetwood appears in Williams, *Oxford*, 200.

[156] *Gray's Inn Adm. Reg.*, 72.

[157] Add. MSS, 4784, fol. 95.

[158] *C.S.P. Dom., 1603–1610*, 149, 595; *1611–1618*, 558.

[159] *Strafford letters* 1: 524; *C.S.P. Dom., 1635*, 7, 141.

[160] Fleetwood's daughter, Dorothy, afterwards the wife of Sir Robert Cooke (q.v.), was baptized at the Luke home in 1599. F. A. Blaydes, *Genealogia Bedfordiensis*, 367.

[161] C. 193/12, 13; S.P. 16/405; *Quarter Sessions records of the county of Northampton*, ed. J. Wake, Northamptonshire Record Society 1: 1, 37, 1924; C. 181/3; 181/4, fol. 180; Williams, *loc. cit.*

[162] *C.S.P. Dom., 1627–1628*, 214, 372; *1628–1629*, 223.

[163] *Ibid., 1628–1629*, 188, 344, 345; Williams, *op. cit.*, 201.

[164] In 1634, for example, report had it that Sir Miles had received £18,000 for letting leases of thirty-one years in the manor of Grafton (Bodleian Firth MSS, 12, fol. 244v). And from the Court of Wards office he probably received much more than the fee of 200 marks a year that was listed as his salary in 1616. Stowe MSS, 575, fol. 9.

[165] He sat for Westbury (1621), Launceston (1624, preferring it to Blechingley), Newton in Lancashire (1625, 1626), Woodstock (1628), and Hindon (both parliaments of 1640). *M. of P.*

mittee to carry the petition and remonstrance to the king.[166] In 1624 he brought in some of the charges against the Lord Treasurer,[167] and in 1629 he denounced recusancy and upheld the cause of the merchant, John Rolle.[168] He seems not to have joined his kinsmen in resisting the loan of 1627, however, and paid £30 from his Northamptonshire estates.[169] And perhaps he paid a £1000 loan requested of him in 1639–1640.[170]

As a parliament man of experience, one who was intimate with leaders in the puritan group, Fleetwood was a prominent member in the early weeks of the Long Parliament. He spoke out against the financial burdens of the people, and showed himself much interested in matters of the church. His committee appointments included the Committee of Privileges, and those on monopolies, Star Chamber, ship money, the charges against Strafford and against Laud, and various others on ecclesiastical abuses.[171] He was among those offering security of £1000 for the November, 1640, loan,[172] but he died before he could contribute further for the cause. His death on 8 March 1641 deprived the popular party of a very active senior member. It remained for his son, Charles, to carry on the family's support of parliament by his military leadership.[173]

Thomas Fountain (d. 1646), of Hulcott and Walton, Bucks, sat for Wendover from early in the Long Parliament (chosen *vice* Hampden, after 8 December 1640) until his death in 1646.[174] He came of a family which had several branches in the county, his line having settled at Walton shortly after 1538. His grandfather, John Fountain (d. 1596), who was variously described as "gentleman" or "esquire," was probably escheator of Bedfordshire and Bucks about 1570.[175] John owned Hulcott manor, with some 700 acres and a mill, and several properties in Walton and other places, all near Aylesbury, and most of them passed to his heir, Thomas Fountain, "esquire" (d. 1623), and then to the latter's nephew, Thomas, eldest son of his brother, John.[176]

The nephew was the 1640 M.P. Thomas, the uncle, appears to have been an intimate friend of Sir Alexander Hampden of Hartwell, whose kinswoman, Joyce Ashfield, he married at Hartwell in 1597.[177] It is conceivable that Thomas Fountain, the nephew, visited sometimes in the home of Sir Alexander Hampden while he lived at Hampden House and made the acquaintance of the latter's cousin, the patriot.

The date of the younger Fountain's birth is unknown, but it was probably around 1600. He and two younger brothers were mentioned in a property settlement of 1615 [178] and he was married in 1628. His father owned some property near Aylesbury about 1600,[179] and he may have been the Thomas Fountain of Aylesbury who in 1622 engaged in a suit in Chancery regarding a bond he had given in behalf of a young kinsman.[180] He did not gain possession of his uncle's estate at Hulcott immediately after the latter's death, for his aunt was still living there in 1628 and he seems to have been residing at Walton, but he had possession at both places by 1640.[181] Meanwhile, he married at Stone on 23 October 1628 Alice, daughter of William Claydon of Bishopstone.[182] By her he had at least six children, including his heir, Thomas (born about 1630), who was sent for his education to Cambridge and the Inner Temple.[183]

Of Fountain's politics before 1640 there is no evidence, but he doubtless agreed with the stand taken by Hampden and other puritans of his neighborhood. When a vacancy in the Short Parliament for Aylesbury occurred in April, 1640, he was one of two candidates returned for the place, but it is doubtful whether a decision on the case was reached before the dissolution.[184] His election to Hampden's seat for Wendover late in 1640 or early in 1641 may have been the result of Hampden's influence there. Fountain became increasingly active in the House, paid £200 for the venture in Irish lands in 1642, and promised to supply a horse for the defense.[185] He was named on several parliamentary committees for Bucks during the war and in 1645 was receiving a weekly allowance because his property was in the royalists' hands.[186] Late that year Fountain played an aggressive role in the county's elec-

[166] *Commons Debates 1621* **3**: 447; Forster, *Eliot* **1**: 97; Bodleian Tanner MSS, 265, fol. 21v.
[167] *H.M.C., MSS of R. R. Hastings* **2**: 65.
[168] *Commons Debates for 1629*, 114, 140, 235.
[169] S.P. 16, 58/109.
[170] £1500 was the figure considered in 1639, but it may have been reduced to £1000. S.P. 16, 453/42, 74, 75; *C.S.P. Dom., 1638–1639*, 605.
[171] *C.J.* **2**: 21, 40, *passim;* D'Ewes (N), 33, 139, 534; Pink MSS, 301, fol. 174.
[172] D'Ewes (N), 52.
[173] *D.N.B.; Al. Oxon.*
[174] *M. of P.* **1**: 485 and n.; Willis **3**: 241; *C.J.* **2**: 101.
[175] *V.C.H. Buckingham* **2**: 343, 344; **3**: 13. To Mr. Frederick G. Gurney of Egginton, Leighton Buzzard, I am indebted for many useful notes on the Fountain family and for suggestions regarding the identity of the M.P.
[176] Gurney notes; I.P.M.'s of John Fountain, gentleman (C. 142/246/119), and Thomas Fountain, esquire (C. 142/430/187).

[177] *Vis. Bucks.,* 4; Phillimore, *Buckinghamshire parish registers, marriages* **3**: 63. He was frequently named as if a relative of Hampden in family deeds. Gurney notes; I.P.M. of Thomas Fountain.
[178] *Ibid.*
[179] Bodleian Willis MSS, 30, fols. 23v, 25.
[180] C. 3/348/43.
[181] Gurney notes; *V.C.H. Buckingham* **2**: 343; S.P. 16, 539/74.
[182] Phillimore, *op. cit.* **3**: 46.
[183] Gurney notes; Fountain's will; *Al. Cant.*
[184] *M. of P.* **1**: 480; Pink MSS, 307, fol. 68.
[185] *C.S.P. Ireland, Adventurers,* 6; *N. and Q.,* 1st Ser., **12**: 359, 1855.
[186] *Berks. Arch. Jour.* **31**: 175, 178, 1927; *C.J.* **3**: 452; Pink MSS, 307, fol. 99.

tion of Colonel Fleetwood.[187]   He died before 15 September 1646,[188] and his will, dated 18 January 1643/4, was registered in 1646.[189]

Few definite facts are known of Fountain's estate. He represents a family which was rising in wealth and in social position, but, as compared with his neighbors and colleagues, he had probably not more than a moderate estate.   One of his uncle's smaller properties had been worth £100 or more a year in 1620, however,[190] and his income was doubtless several times that figure. He seems to have settled the chief estate of his inheritance by 1640, and neither his pledge for the defense nor his will indicates any pretense to wealth.[191]

Sir Edmund Fowell (1593–1674), of Fowellscombe in Ugborough, Devon, sat for Ashburton in that county from the time it was restored as a parliamentary borough late in 1640[192] until 1648 or 1653. A younger son of Arthur Fowell of Fowellscombe (d. about 1606), by Mary, daughter of Richard Reynell of East Ogwell, Devon, he was born on 6 June and baptized on 15 August 1593 at Ugborough.   In June, 1612, he succeeded his brother, Arthur, as heir to the family estates.[193]   In 1614 he married Margaret, daughter of Sir Anthony Poulett of Hinton St. George and governor of Jersey, and sister of John, first Baron Poulett. Probably this family connection led to his being knighted at Greenwich, 3 November 1619.   Fowell resided part of the time in Cornwall.[194]

Sir Edmund was an active J.P. in Devon in the 1630's, and between 1624 and 1640 was named to commissions dealing with piracy, soap manufacturing and other problems of the western counties.[195]   He had never served in parliament, however, before his election late in 1640.

In the Long Parliament Fowell supported Pym's group, and was named to several of the early committees regarding recusants and church reforms.[196]   He gave his bond for £1000 for the loan in March, 1641,[197] but in June, 1642, his promise of two horses was "for King, Kingdom and Parliament conjunctively." [198]   During the war he headed the Devonshire sequestration committee and was otherwise active for the cause of parliament, but seems to have dropped out of politics after 1648.[199]   He returned to vote for the Restoration in 1660, was made a baronet in 1661, and died shortly before 9 October 1674.

Fowell's estate was ample, including lands in Devon and Cornwall.[200]   His marriage into the Poulett family, the dowry of £1050 arranged for one of his daughters in 1633,[201] and his contributions for parliament, 1641–1642, are indications of his wealth.

Fowell should be distinguished from his first cousin, Edmund Fowell, Esq., lawyer and town clerk of Plymouth, who was M.P. for Tavistock, 1646 and 1659.[202] Sir Edmund was related by marriage to Sir John Poulett (q.v.), and others of his connection, and had served in the county sessions with many of his other colleagues.[203]

John Franklin (d. 1643?), town clerk of Marlborough, was M.P. for his town from 1640 until his death, probably in 1643.   He came of the Franklins of Sherston, where some of the family were lessees of Sherston manor under the Earl of Hertford in 1612.[204]   He was the only surviving son of William Franklin, a Marlborough woolendraper (d. 1630–1631), who seems to have been active in the borough government from about 1585, and was mayor in 1613 and 1619.[205]   John was probably just about of age when he took the oath of allegiance, apparently for the trained bands, in October, 1611,[206] and he was admitted on 4 December 1612 to the freedom of the borough as the son of one who had been a burgess before his child's birth.[207]   The next reference

[187] Bulstrode Whitelocke, *Memorials of the English affairs* 1: 530–534, 550, later ed., Oxford, 1853 (hereafter, Whitelocke, *Memorials* [1853]).

[188] A new election for Wendover was ordered then.   *C.J.* 4: 668.

[189] Somerset House, Archdeaconry Bucks, 1646, No. 73.

[190] Bodleian Willis MSS, 30, fols. 6, 9v. This property was valued at not more than a fourth of the value assigned to Hulcott and its appurtenances in the list of properties in the I.P.M. of John Fountain.

[191] Gurney notes; will of Thomas Fountain (1646), cited above; will of Thomas Fountain of "Huckett," esquire, his son (1656), P.C.C., 137 Berkeley.

[192] Ashburton was restored by vote of the House on 26 November 1640, and Fowell was named to a committee on 29 January 1641.   *C.J.* 2: 37, 75.

[193] I.P.M. of Arthur Fowell (d. 1612), 1617, Wards 7/58/125.

[194] *Note book of Tristram Risdon,* ed. J. Dallas and H. C. Porter, 183, London, 1897.

[195] S.P. 16/405; C. 181/3, fol. 130; 181/4, fol. 52v; 181/5, fols. 167, 183, 264.   Fowell's name appears frequently in the Devonshire Quarter Sessions Minute Books, 1625–1640 (Devonshire MSS at Exeter).

[196] Pink MSS, 307, fol 343; *C.J.* 2: 113, 129.

[197] D'Ewes (N), 438, n.   The name appears as Powell.

[198] *N. and Q.,* 1st Ser., 12: 338, 1855.

[199] Pink MSS, 307, fols. 342–343.   *O.P.H.* (9: *25), however, indicates that he sat until 1653.

[200] I.P.M., Arthur Fowell; Exeter City Library MSS, Exeter Deeds and Documents, Nos. 30,295 and 40,657.

[201] S.P. 16, 246/24.

[202] Devon *Trans.* 48: 336, 1916; *Vis. Devon, 1620,* 114; Ingpen, *The Middle Temple bench book,* 197.

[203] In addition to the above authorities, see *Complete Baronetage* 3: 189.

[204] St. Ch. 8/140/13.   Franklin's will of 1642 mentions some copyhold lands at Sherston, and his father by his will left a legacy to the poor of Sherston (P.C.C., 74 St. John).   His kinsman, Captain John Franklin, son of Richard Franklin of Sherston, who shared his captivity in 1643 (*Cal. Com. Comp.,* 1329), has sometimes been confused with the M.P.   (Pink MSS, 301, fol. 343).

[205] Marlborough Corporation MSS, 5, "C 100," fols. 4, 5, 13, *passim;* Chamberlains' Accounts, 1572–1771; extracts from the borough records by B. H. Cunington, *Wilts, Berks & Hants County Paper* (21 Dec. 1928).

[206] Marlborough MSS, 5, fols. 88, 99.

[207] *Ibid.,* Chamberlains' Accounts, 1572–1771, year 1612.

to him in the town records is the note that 26s.8d. were paid to him for his services as town clerk in 1618.[208] Where he studied law is not known, but from this time he was engaged in much legal business for the borough, and his widow stated in 1651 that the war had resulted in the loss of £300 a year from her husband's practice.[209] Besides acting as town clerk regularly, Franklin was chamberlain in 1622, constable in 1624, and after his father's death served as one of the chief burgesses. He made several trips to London and to Salisbury on the town's legal business,[210] and in 1625 was concerned with raising troops in Marlborough. He was probably the John Franklin who was arrested in May, 1625, with others of the region on the charge that they had accepted bribes from men seeking to evade impressment for Mansfeld's expedition. Franklin resisted the Council order that he repay the money, and was accordingly summoned a second time and instructed to obey and to make a public acknowledgment before the county D.L.'s.[211] He was afterwards concerned with raising troops for the Isle of Rhé expedition. He managed a suit in Exchequer for the town in 1632, receiving for his services that year nearly £115. After he became one of the chief burgesses he sometimes advanced money for the town's use and showed himself interested in the local schools.[212]

Franklin was chosen for the first time as an M.P. in the autumn of 1640. He was not active in the House, but was of the popular side. In June, 1642, he promised to contribute £50 for the defense,[213] and in November brought the matter of the defending of Marlborough to the attention of parliament. He went there himself to participate in its resistance, and at its fall on 4 December was captured and carried away to Oxford. With his kinsman of the same name, Captain John Franklin, he was held a prisoner there, and negotiations for his exchange in July, 1643, were unsuccessful.[214] His death occurred while he was still a captive,[215] and a writ for choosing his successor was ordered by parliament on 12 November 1645. Parliament voted his widow a pension in 1646.[216]

Franklin was probably not a wealthy man, as compared with the country gentlemen, but he owned lands in Marlborough and in the county in addition to having his legal practice. Besides losing a substantial income from that, he lost by plundering during the war, according to his widow's statement, some £500 and lands worth £40 a year. She declared that he laid out £80 of his own money for his men. By his will, which was dated 19 September 1642, he assigned legacies of over £1600. The figure excluded, apparently, the portions previously arranged for married daughters.[217]

Franklin's wife, Deborah, by whom he had nine children, six of whom were named in his father's will in 1629, survived until late in 1657. One son served as a major in the parliamentary army and was killed in the war. Another entered the clergy and had the charge at Bromham at the time of his mother's death.[218]

Sir John Franklin, or **Francklyn,** knight (1600–1648), of Willesden, Middlesex, was a member for his shire from 1640 until his death in March, 1648. The son and heir of Richard Franklin of Willesden (d. 1615), by his wife, Frances, daughter of Francis Roberts of that parish,[219] he was baptized there on 27 April 1600. He was knighted at Theobalds in 1614 and in July, 1615, succeeded his father.[220] It was probably he who matriculated at Peterhouse, Cambridge, at Easter, 1614, and entered Gray's Inn in 1615.[221] Before 1630 he married Elizabeth, daughter of George Purefoy of Wadley, Berkshire, by whom he had a large family. His family accounts indicate that he had numerous friends among the nobility and gentry in the vicinity of London, as well as in more distant counties where he owned lands, that he was fond of dress and entertainment, and was a devotee of sports.[222]

In 1624 and 1625 Sir John was a candidate in the parliamentary elections. Defeated for Middlesex in 1624, he was recommended by Buckingham, then Lord Warden, for Rye the next time, but was chosen in his

---

[208] *Ibid.*, year 1618.

[209] *Cal. Com. Comp.*, 1540. The borough's copy of the Statutes at Large, purchased in 1618, was placed in Franklin's custody. Notes of B. H. Cunington, *Wilts, Berks & Hauts County Paper* (5 Oct. 1928). He was probably too young to have been the John Franklin of Wilts who matriculated at Oxford in 1582, aged 18 (*Al. Oxon.*), but he sent his own son, William, to the Middle Temple in 1640. *Mid. Temp. Rec.* 2: 892.

[210] Marlborough MSS, Chamberlains' Accounts, 1572–1771, years 1619–1640.

[211] *Acts P.C., 1625–' 26,* 54, 68, 76, 111, 130, 131.

[212] Marlborough MSS, Chamberlains' Accounts, years 1634–1640.

[213] *M. of P.* 1: 496; *N. and Q.,* 1st Ser., 12: 360, 1855.

[214] Waylen, *Hist. of Marlborough,* 159–164, 181–204; Sanford, *St. and ill.,* 527–528; *Cal. Com. Comp.,* 1329.

[215] Waylen (*loc. cit.*) gives July, 1643, as the date of Franklin's death, but he may have confused the member with the other John Franklin who was a prisoner with him. The

latter, a younger man, died that summer after a half year's imprisonment. *Cal. Com. Comp.,* 1329.

[216] *O.P.H.* 9: 9; Waylen, *op. cit.,* 204; *Cal. Com. Comp.,* 1539.

[217] *Ibid.,* 1540; will, P.C.C., 93 Twisse. Letters of administration were granted on 27 June 1646 and again on 10 June 1655.

[218] *Cal. Com. Comp.,* 1539; will of Deborah Franklin, P.C.C., 17 Wotton.

[219] No evidence of kinship with the Marlborough M.P. of the same name has been found.

[220] I.P.M. of Richard Franklin, C. 142/349/166.

[221] *Al. Cant.; Gray's Inn Adm. Reg.,* 138. In the latter, the name appears as John Franckling of Wilseen, county Westmorland, knight.

[222] Excerpts from Sir John's account book are found in Add. MSS, 6316 (a collection of items on archery), fol. 30, and *Archaeologia* 15: 157–163, 1806.

own county of Middlesex, defeating there Sir John Suckling, the Comptroller of the Household.[223] In 1626 and 1628 he sat for Wootton Bassett, Wilts, and in the Short Parliament for Middlesex.[224] He was a J.P. in Middlesex, and in 1637 was named on a royal commission for executing an old ordnance for the training of men in archery.[225] He refused a contribution to the king in 1639, however,[226] collected with some reluctance the coat and conduct money in 1640,[227] and in the parliaments of 1640 was one of the popular party.

Franklin was named in the Long Parliament to committees on the ministry and on petitions and to the recess committee of September, 1641. He promised £500 toward the loan in March, 1641, continued his pledge in July,[228] and in 1642 promised 4 horses and maintenance for the defense.[229] He served on the various parliamentary committees for Middlesex, 1642–1645, but hesitated somewhat about taking the Covenant. He died on 24 March 1647/8, and was buried at Willesden, where it was inscribed on his tombstone that "to publicke services no man brought more of integrity, of zeal, lesse of himselfe. To the publicke sins and calamities of the state, no man lesse of fuell, more of sorrow." [230]

Sir John was a wealthy man, having inherited from his father five manors and numerous other holdings in various parts of Middlesex, Herts, Bucks, and Bedfordshire, as well as in the counties of Warwick, Worcester, Gloucester, and Wilts,[231] and having acquired more by purchase, especially in Hertfordshire. Among the monetary provisions of his will were portions totalling £4000 for three daughters, a £450 annuity for his wife in addition to £500, gifts of £85 a year for various charities and public works, and other legacies amounting to over £700. The references to his library of books at Willesden, to a fund for increasing the library at All Souls', Oxford, and to the building of a new parish church at St. Andrew's, Holborn, show that his interests were not limited to sports and good living. Affectionately remembered in his will were several yeoman kinsmen, but mentioned among his friends were Dr.

Harvey and the widow of Sir John Banks.[232] His son and heir, Richard, became a baronet in 1660.[233]

Francis Gamull (1606–1654), of Chester and of Buerton Hall, Cheshire, was M.P. for Chester from 1640 until 22 January 1644. Baptized at St. Oswald's, Chester, 25 November 1606, Gamull was the descendant of city mayors on both sides of his house, his father's family in particular having been prominent in city affairs, and was the only surviving son of Thomas Gamull, Recorder of Chester (M.P. 1601, d. 1613), by Alice, daughter of Richard Bavand, alderman, mayor, and M.P.[1] He was reared after his father's death in the home of his stepfather, Edward Whitby, recorder of the city,[2] entered the Inner Temple in 1622 and was still a member there in 1624, but does not seem to have become a barrister.[3] In October, 1624, he married at Eccleston Christian, daughter of Sir Richard Grosvenor, Bart., to whom he had been betrothed when only a child.[4] After her death in June 1640, Gamull married Elizabeth, widow of Robert Ravenscroft and daughter of Sir Randle Mainwaring of Over Peover, a kinswoman of Sir Thomas Smith (q.v.). His career lay, however, in Chester, where his uncle, William Gamull, was mayor, 1620–1621, and later master of the Merchants' Company.[5] Francis became a freeman in September, 1625, an alderman in 1630, and mayor, 1634–1635.[6] During his mayoralty Gamull helped survey the boundaries, some of which were involved in the suit between Sir William Brereton (q.v.) and the city, and, as the officer responsible for the ship money assess-

---

[223] H.M.C., Thirteenth Report 4, Rye MSS, 73; The letters of John Chamberlain 2: 543, 614; Birch, The court and times of Charles the First 1: 18.

[224] M. of P. 1: 464, 472, 478; 3: App., xliii.

[225] C. 193/13; S.P. 16/405; C.S.P. Dom., 1637, 66.

[226] Rushworth 3: 914.

[227] C.S.P. Dom., 1640, 543.

[228] C.J. 2: 54, 61, 222, 288; D'Ewes (N), 435, n.

[229] N. and Q., 1st Ser., 12: 338, 1855.

[230] Archaeologia 15: 157, n., 1806.

[231] I.P.M. cited above. It was possibly his sister, described simply as the daughter of "one Franklin of Middlesex," who at her marriage into the well known Smith family of Leeds Castle, Kent, in 1617 was said to have a portion of £4000. The letters of John Chamberlain 2: 62.

[232] P.C.C., 90 Essex. At least two of his father's uncles were yeomen in 1608 (I.P.M. cited above), and one of the various John Franklins mentioned in Sir John's will (1640) was a yeoman. His father, styled "esquire" when he died, was probably but one generation removed from yeoman status.

[233] Additional references: Complete Baronetage 3: 126; Middlesex Pedigrees, G. J. Armytage, ed., Harleian Society 65: 3, 1914 (hereafter, Middlesex Ped.); Pink MSS, 301, fol. 342.

[1] George Ormerod, The history of the county palatine and city of Chester 1: 196–197, 2nd ed., London, 1882 (hereafter, Ormerod, Chester); Chester Corporation MSS, Assembly Book, 1539–1624, fols. 269v, 270, 272, 280v.

[2] Whitby was Alice Gamull's third husband, her first one having been David Lloyd, D.D. Cheshire Sheaf, 1st Ser., 2: 218, 1880–1882; Harl. MSS, 2093, fol. 202.

[3] Students admitted to the Inner Temple, 236; Harl. MSS, 2093, fol. 190.

[4] Arrangements for the marriage had been made in 1613, but the wedding did not occur until 1624. Harl. MSS, 2039, fol. 140; Pink MSS, 302, fol. 8. See also I.P.M. of Thomas Gamull, Cheshire inquisitions post mortem, 1630–1660 2: 36, Record Society for the Publication of Original Documents relating to Lancashire and Cheshire, 1935 (hereafter Rec. Soc. Lancs. and Cheshire).

[5] Chester Corporation MSS, Assembly Book, 1539–1624, fols. 354–361, 370v; 1624–1684, fols. 26, 48; Harl. MSS, 1191, fol. 131; 2004, fols. 133, 153; 1991, fol. 125.

[6] J. H. E. Bennett, The rolls of the freemen of the city of Chester, Rec. Soc. Lancs. and Cheshire, 51: 111, 1906; Chester Corporation MSS, Assembly Book, 1624–1684, fol. 25; Mayor's Court Files, 1634–1635.

ments, was sharply rebuked by the royal council for upholding the argument of Sir Thomas Smith (*q.v.*) that the levy should fall only on the property which was his residence.[7] In April, 1638, Gamull joined with other city officials in collecting ship money and in consulting about the respective rights of the county and the city in that matter.[8] He opposed the city recorder as candidate for the Short Parliament, fearing an adverse decision regarding certain property he held near Chester would follow the recorder's election, but received only a scattered vote.[9] In the period before the next election Gamull accepted the captaincy of the city's trained bands.[10]

Gamull was not a conspicuous member of the Long Parliament, was named to no committees, but seems to have attended regularly.[11] He wrote to his first wife's father in May, 1641, reporting the progress made in the House, and commenting, regarding news from France, that Richelieu was much like Strafford in his policy of reducing the subjects of the country to a most servile condition. His comments on the increasing zeal evident in the debates on episcopacy indicate that though he probably approved of the attack on the king's ministers, Gamull favored less rigorous measures in matters of the church.[12] He supported the king when war came, was in Chester in October, 1642, to raise troops for his army, and was thereafter active in military affairs in the city, and disabled for his royalism on 22 January 1644. He received a knighthood and baronetcy the following April and entertained King Charles in his Chester house during the siege. Afterwards he fled the kingdom for a time, but returned by 1649, and upon his death, 27 November 1654, was buried at St. Mary's in Chester.

Gamull was a man of means, his paternal inheritance including lands in Cheshire, Staffordshire and Shropshire, and especially the celebrated Dee Mills, with their fishing rights and other privileges at Chester.[13] His income from these properties and lands that came to him from his mother's family amounted to between £773 and £1064 a year, of which £500–£800 came from the mills.[14] These, the most valuable, were also the most

troublesome of his assets, for they included a causeway or weir in the river by which Gamull attempted to maintain a monopoly on all milling business there and later to control the city works. As a consequence, from the time of his minority until 1640 Gamull was engaged in almost continuous lawsuits with would-be competitors, journeying often to London for hearings in Exchequer or Star Chamber, and as a city official guarding carefully his control of the city water supply.[15] Fear that the election of Chester's recorder to parliament would result in new attacks on his causeway had led Gamull to stand for election himself in the spring of 1640, and probably explains also his candidacy in the autumn. That his fears were justified is indicated by the fact that after Chester fell to the Roundheads parliament in 1646 permitted the city to destroy the causeway and move the mills.[16] This action, together with losses directly traceable to the war, was stated by Gamull's heirs to have cost his estate nearly £24,000.

Lloyd described Gamull as a man of good hand and heart, of exact life "as well as great parts," in nothing redundant or defective, and abhorring sin.[17]

Henry Garton (*c.* 1600–1641), of the Middle Temple and of Wollavington, Sussex, returned for Arundel on 22 October 1640 and recognized early in 1641,[18] was M.P. until his death in October, 1641. Born about 1600, a younger son of Sir Peter Garton of Wollavington (d. 1606) by his wife, Judith, daughter of Sir Thomas (or Sir John) Shirley of Isfield, he succeeded his older brothers in 1633. His family's estates had been built up in Sussex chiefly by a grandfather who had made his fortune in London in Elizabeth's time.[19] Garton was educated at Queen's College, Oxford, matriculating in 1615, aged fifteen, and receiving his B.A.

---

[7] Chester Corporation MSS, Assembly Book 1624–1684, fol. 33; *C.S.P. Dom.*, *1634–1635*, 488; Harl. MSS, 2093 (Holme's Collections), fol. 135.

[8] S.P. 16, 388/31.

[9] *C.S.P. Dom.*, *1639–1640*, 564–565, 590.

[10] Chester Corporation MSS, Assembly Book, 1624–1684, fol. 53.

[11] The Chester records indicate Gamull's absence from the city during the early months, and the sending of letters to him in London. Chester Corporation MSS, A2, Assembly Orders, 1639–1642, *passim;* F5, Accounts and Rentals, 1622–1656, 1641 rentals.

[12] Harl. MSS, 2081, fol. 93.

[13] Harl. MSS, 1991, fols. 123–126, 130–137.

[14] The lower figures were those given by Gamull in his compounding papers, quite possibly underestimates, and he declared his estate was charged with £3560 for portions and debts (S.P. 23/216, pp. 211–213). The higher figures are based upon

reports by his guardian during his minority and upon claims by his daughters afterwards when they sought recovery of their inheritance (Harl. MSS, 2039, fols. 17–18, 89–92, 140–141; *Cheshire Sheaf,* 3rd Ser., **5**: 57–58, 1903). Gamull's fine, set at ⅛, was £940, and his mills, even after their most lucrative part had been destroyed, were rented in 1651 for £226 a year. *Cal. Com. Comp.*, 455, 1874.

[15] Harl. MSS, 2081, fols. 1–91, 121–152, 189–190; 2082, fol. 140; 2083, fols. 29–91, 208; *C.S.P. Dom.*, *1633–1634*, 380; *1634–1635*, 226, 488; *1637*, 455; Chester Corporation MSS, Assembly Book, 1539–1624, fols. 355, 358v; 1624–1684, fols. 26, 28.

[16] *Cal. Com. Comp.*, 330; S.P. 23/216, p. 212.

[17] *Memoirs*, 692. Other references, in addition to those cited, are *Complete Baronetage* **2**: 456–457; Pink MSS, 307, fol. 146; Thomas Malbon, *Memorials of the Civil War in Cheshire*, ed. James Hall, Rec. Soc. Lancs. and Cheshire, **19**: 181, n., London, 1889.

[18] Although the House took formal action only after his death, 12 November 1641, Garton was named for committee work on 30 March 1641. *C.J.* **2**: 114, 313; D'Ewes (C), 126.

[19] I.P.M.'s, C. 142/292/165; 720/7; *Sussex Arch. Col.* **65**: 211, 1924; **29**: 60, 1869; *The visitations of the county of Sussex . . . 1530 . . . and 1633-4*, Harleian Society **53**: 132 (hereafter, *Vis. Sussex, 1633-4*).

in 1618,[20] and was associated with the Middle Temple from his admission in 1618 until his burial in the Temple Church, 30 October 1641. He was called to the bar in 1626,[21] and probably spent most of his time in London. He may have had a house in the parish of All Hallows on the Wall in 1638.[22] A good deal of his practice may have been with the Court of Wards, for in 1641 a petition was sent to the House of Lords by two persons who declared his prosecutions of them in the Court of Wards and elsewhere had ruined them.[23] Garton does not seem to have been active in the affairs of his native county and his first association with parliament came with his return in May, 1640, for Arundel, replacing Lord Maltravers.[24]

Garton, if he followed his mother's kinsmen, probably belonged to the puritan and parliamentarian group in Sussex. His appointment to the committee to consider reforms in elections in March, 1641,[25] suggests that he was an advocate of change. His early death of the plague in the autumn of 1641, however, prevents us from learning more of his political views.

Garton married twice, (1) Mary, daughter and heir of Sir John Lake (or Luke) of Hertfordshire; and (2) about April, 1640, Dorothy, daughter of Sir William Whitmore of Apley, Salop, and sister of Thomas Whitmore, royalist M.P. for Bridgnorth, 1640 (q.v.).[26] The parliamentarian members to whom he was related were James Rivers and possibly Robert Goodwin.

Of Garton's fortune only the evidences of inquisitions post mortem and a few deeds remain. The principal estate at Wollavington, said to have been bought in 1586 for £4000, was supplemented by at least three other manors and a number of smaller holdings in Sussex.[27] Both of his marriages were with ladies of dower, and his lawyer's fees must have augmented a comfortable income.

* Framlingham Gawdy (1589–1655), of West Harling, Norfolk, sat for Thetford, 1640–1653, as he had six times before.[28] His education was probably private, and his admission to Gray's Inn in 1624[29] was doubt-

less for social reasons. He was a J.P. for Norfolk and for Thetford borough,[30] a loan commissioner, 1621–1622 and 1627,[31] and also a D.L. and sheriff.

As heir of the Framlinghams as well as of the Gawdys, he inherited at least ten manors in Norfolk and Suffolk, and before 1640 increased his possessions.[32] His father intended that he should have an income of £1000 a year, but the family accounts of 1633–1634 indicate that it was something above that figure.[33] Gawdy died in February, 1654/5.[34]

Among Gawdy's fellow members who were fairly close kinsmen were Moundeford, Sir Francis Knollys and his son,[35] and Sir Philip Parker.

John George (1594–1678?), of London and of Cirencester and Baunton, Gloucestershire, was M.P. for Cirencester, 1640–1645. He was the grandson or grandnephew of Christopher George of Cirencester and the Middle Temple (d. 1598),[36] and the eldest surviving son of Robert George, gentleman, of Cirencester, by Margaret, daughter of Edward Oldsworth. He was baptized on 15 September 1594,[37] may have studied at Oxford (B.A. 1614),[38] and eventually became a barrister at the Middle Temple. He was Reader of the New Inn in 1637 and was later bencher and treasurer at the Temple.[39] He married in London in 1627 Elizabeth, daughter of John Tirrell of St. Ives, Hunts.,[40] and was probably the Mr. John George who had a house on King Street in Westminster at least as early as 1632.[41] About October, 1637, he secured a court post as Clerk of the Wardrobe, an office which he surrendered in March, 1639.[42] It was probably during this period that George acquired an interest in patents

---

[20] Al. Oxon.

[21] Mid. Temp. Rec. 2: 632, 714; Cal. Inner Temp. Rec. 2: 359.

[22] Dale, Inhabitants of London, 20.

[23] H.M.C., Fourth Report, MSS of the House of Lords, 40.

[24] M. of P. 1: 483.

[25] C.J. 2: 114. Possibly he had experienced the opposition of the Earl of Arundel in his election, as did his successor, John Downes.

[26] Pink MSS, 302, fol. 29; Vis. Sussex, 1633-4, 132; Henry Garton's I.P.M., C. 142/616/24; will of Dorothy Garton, 1649, P.C.C., 166 Fairfax.

[27] Sussex Rec. Soc. 20: 342, 502, 1915; Sussex Arch. Coll. 65: 211, 1924; I.P.M. cited above.

[28] He sat until 1653, according to D.N.B. According to O.P.H. (9: *33), he was secluded in 1648. His first parliament was that of 1614 (M. of P. 3: xxxix), not 1621, as in D.N.B.

[29] Gray's Inn Adm. Reg., 171.

[30] C. 193/12 and 13; C. 181/4, fols. 4, 68, 428.

[31] Bodleian Tanner MSS, 243, fols. 22v, 24; S.P. 16, 76/25.

[32] H.M.C., Tenth Report, Gawdy MSS, 54, 106; Blomefield, Norfolk 1: 257, 259, 306, 438. Gawdy's contribution toward the defense in 1642, however, was £50, not above the average. N. and Q., 1st Ser., 12: 360, 1855.

[33] Notes from the Gawdy papers, Add. MSS, 27,400, fols. 228v–229; 36,989, fol. 19.

[34] Add. MSS, 27,400, fol. 163v. His age was given as sixty-five and the year as "1654," but also as 7 Charles II. A note at a manorial court, 3 April 1655, mentioned his death since the last court, and at the court of 12 October 1655 his will was mentioned. Add. MSS, 19,092 (Davy's collection), fol. 25.

[35] His wife was a daughter of Sir Robert Knollys, and Gawdy had spent part of his early life in the latter's guardianship. Blomefield, Norfolk 1: 306.

[36] Mid. Temp. Rec. 1: 317, 391, 349.

[37] Vis. Glouc., 248–249; I.P.M., Robert George, junior, 1626, C. 142/430/166.

[38] Al. Oxon.

[39] Mid. Temp. Rec. 2: 860; Ingpen, The Middle Temple bench book, 200.

[40] J. Foster, ed., London marriage licenses, 1521–1869, 537.

[41] Records of St. Margaret's Parish, Overseers' Accounts, 151, 153, 154.

[42] Mid. Temp. Rec. 2: 860; C.S.P. Dom., 1638–1639, 617. He received £14 from the royal revenues as fee in February, 1639. S.P. 16, 412/149.

governing part of the waters of the Thames, with various fines appertaining, an interest which led to complaints against him in 1640.[43] Meanwhile he retained connections with Gloucestershire. He was listed for a large contribution for the loan of 1626 on the basis of lands there,[44] and in 1639 he was present at the sessions as a J.P.[45] He was a D.L. for the county also, and represented Cirencester in the parliaments of 1626 and 1628, and both times in 1640.

George's place in the Long Parliament was in doubt for some weeks after the opening, not because of an election dispute, but because petitions had come in charging him with extreme abuses and the extortion of heavy fines under the patent pertaining to the Thames waters. His case was referred to the committee on monopolies, and George's excuses barely saved him from being expelled as a monopolist.[46] By March of 1641, however, he was named to a committee and was afterwards appointed to a few others. He seems to have been regarded as a parliamentarian in the early years, and in 1642 promised to provide one horse for the defense[47] and helped to garrison Cirencester for parliament. He was accounted lost to the cause only when, after he had been captured and his life had been spared by the royalists, he ventured to sit in the Oxford parliament.[48] He survived the Restoration, sat again in parliament (1661), and was buried at Baunton on 6 January 1678 (1678/9?).[49]

Of wealth George had certainly a moderate amount. He inherited at least part of the estate of three manors and other properties that Christopher George had owned in and near Cirencester and in Wilts.[50] And he had doubtless improved his fortunes by his practice of law and his connections at court. His pledge for the cause in 1642, however, was comparatively small.[51]

Francis Gerard (c. 1620–1681–5), of Flambards, Harrow-on-the-Hill, M.P. for Seaford from its restoration in February, 1641, until 1648, was the son and heir of Sir Gilbert Gerard, Bart. (q.v.), and a kinsman of Cromwell and Hampden. Born about 1620, he was granted admission with a younger brother to Gray's Inn in 1625, and probably matriculated at St. Catherine's, Cambridge, in 1632.[52] Before May, 1636, he had been granted the reversion of the "filazer's" office,[53]

and in July, 1638, he took the oath of allegiance before a Middlesex official, possibly in preparation for foreign travel.[54] He was probably unmarried[55] and without experience in county office or in parliament when he was chosen for Seaford in 1641, his election having doubtless been arranged by friends of his family.[56]

Young Gerard was little active in his early years in the Long Parliament, rarely being named to committees, and he was absent on 16 June 1642 and 5 February 1644.[57] In fact, he was said for a time during the war to have been in arms for the king, and was in France just before it was arranged through his father's influence that he be allowed to return to the House in 1645.[58] He was more active thereafter, and was secluded with his father in the purge of 1648. He succeeded to his father's baronetcy in 1670 and died between 1681 and 1685.[59]

Sir Gilbert Gerard, Bart. (1587–1670), of Flambards, Harrow-on-the-Hill, Middlesex, sat for Middlesex, 1640–1648(?). Descended from the Gerards of Lancashire, he was a grandson of William Gerard of Harrow (d. 1584), a brother of Elizabeth's Master of the Rolls,[60] and the son and heir of William Gerard of Harrow (c. 1551–1609), Clerk of the Council of the Duchy of Lancaster under Elizabeth and James, by his wife Dorothy, daughter of Anthony Radcliffe, a London alderman.[61] He was born late in 1587,[62] was granted admission to Gray's Inn apparently in 1592,[63] and may have been a student at Trinity College, Cambridge, in 1602.[64] Succeeding his father in 1609, he married about five years later Mary, daughter of Sir Francis Barrington of Essex, establishing thereby a connection which was to be of great importance in his later career. Through his wife he acquired not only the manor of Aston Clinton, Bucks,[65] but a group of

---

[43] D'Ewes (N), 76, 544.
[44] S.P. 16, 19/116.
[45] Gloucester Corp. MSS, Letter Book, 1640–1660, fol. 3.
[46] C.J. 2: 38, 39, 51; D'Ewes (N), 76, 83, 159, 543–544.
[47] N. and Q., 1st Ser., 12: 360, 1855.
[48] Pink MSS, 302, fol. 66; Clarendon, *Rebellion* 2: 447; Sanford, *St. and ill.*, 527–528.
[49] *Vis. Glouc.*, 248.
[50] I.P.M. cited above. One of his properties was listed in 1626 at £100 a year. S.P. 16, 19/116.
[51] In addition to the above authorities see *M. of P.*; Williams, *Gloucester*, 157.
[52] *Gray's Inn Adm. Reg.*, 176; *Al. Cant.*
[53] C.S.P. Dom., 1635–1636, 451. He seems to have been in possession of the office in 1645. Pink MSS, 302, fol. 72.

[54] *C.S.P. Dom., 1637–1638,* 560.
[55] He afterwards married a daughter of Sir Thomas Cheeke (q.v.).
[56] *M. of P.* 1: 497 and n. D'Ewes's report of the debate on the restoring of Seaford indicates some fears by members of the puritan party that the lord of the town would have "papists" chosen, and that measures were taken to prevent such an occurrence. D'Ewes (N), 321–322.
[57] *C.J.* 2: 102, 626; 3: 390.
[58] *H.M.C., Seventh Report,* MSS of Sir H. Verney, Bart., 450.
[59] *O.P.H.* 9: 14; *Complete Baronetage* 1: 142.
[60] Pink and Beaven, *Parl. Rep. Lanc.*, 66–67, 220. From the Master of the Rolls the barons Gerard descended.
[61] *Middlesex Ped.*, 19–20; I.P.M.'s of the two William Gerards, C. 142/204/102 and 308/156; M.I.'s in the Harrow church.
[62] He was aged twenty-two at his father's death in August, 1609 (I.P.M.).
[63] *Gray's Inn Adm. Reg.*, 83. Two of Sir Gilbert's sons were admitted in 1625 (*ibid.*, 176), and in his will he referred to his chambers there (P.C.C., 37 Penn).
[64] *Al. Cant.*
[65] *V.C.H. Buckingham* 2: 313.

puritan leaders as kinsmen, and presently was numbered among the active partisans of their cause. He was created a baronet in 1620.

Gerard's experience in parliament began with his election for Middlesex in 1621, and he sat afterwards for the county in 1624, 1625, and 1626. He had been chosen in 1624 for Newtown in the Isle of Wight, doubtless through the Barrington influence, and possibly to assure him a seat should his candidacy in his own shire fail. But his victory by popular acclaim in Middlesex against the court candidates was overwhelming, a victory which he repeated in 1625 against one of the same opponents.[66] With his kinsmen, the Barringtons, he resisted the 1621 loan [67] and supported in parliament Eliot's attacks on the king's ministers.[68] He was not, however, a member of the session of 1628. As sheriff of Buckinghamshire, 1626–1627, he again affronted the Duke of Buckingham by failing to be present when the favorite visited Aylesbury, conduct for which he was required to answer at the next assize.[69] And he was summoned before Council about the same time, probably for having opposed the new forced loan,[70] but seems to have managed to avoid imprisonment. One of the ship money foes in 1636, Gerard set an example in Middlesex apparently by the simple expedient of absenting himself from the shire at the time the collectors came for his £12, and the local authorities proposed having him "sent for" by Council as a warning to others.[71] Meanwhile he served for many years as a J.P. in that county and a member of lesser commissions.[72]

Sir Gilbert was an intimate of Oliver St. John, whose wife was a niece of his lady,[73] and he was one of Pym's colleagues in the Providence Island Company.[74] He may have been serving in February, 1639, in his father's old office of clerk to the council of the Duchy of Lancaster,[75] but was certainly reckoned as one of Pym's group when parliament met again.

Elected by Middlesex to both of the 1640 parliaments, Sir Gilbert was an active member. His committee appointments were numerous and varied, including those on privileges, several petitions on grievances, ecclesiastical reforms, the state of the army, questions of the Virginia plantation and the wool trade,

as well as for arranging the trial of Strafford and correcting administrative abuses and for the recess.[76] He pledged £1000 to secure the loan in November, 1640, lent £500 in 1641, subscribed toward the reducing of Ireland, and in June, 1642, promised to furnish and maintain four horses for the defense.[77] In July, 1642, Gerard was appointed treasurer for the army, and during the war was an active committeeman for Middlesex as well as prominent in the councils of war. By 1648 he was said to have advanced nearly £9000 of his own money for the cause, a statement which, in combination with the several pledges listed above, belies the royalist charge that he had been much in debt before his parliamentary offices and opportunities enriched him.[78] He was inclined somewhat toward presbyterianism, for he was among those secluded and imprisoned in December, 1648. But he was released soon afterwards, and, although he may not have returned to sit in the House, held an office in the gift of parliament.[79] He assisted with the Restoration in 1660, but retired soon afterwards. He died on 6 January 1669/70, and was buried at Harrow.[80]

Relatives of Gerard's in the 1640 parliament, besides his son, Sir Francis, of doubtful loyalty, and his brother-in-law, Barrington, included Cromwell, Hampden, the Lukes and the Wallops, and some eight other fellow members.

William Glanville (c. 1616–1680), of Broad Hinton, Wiltshire, was a member for Camelford, Cornwall, 1640–22 January 1644. He was the son and heir apparent of Sir John Glanville, king's serjeant, Speaker of the House of Commons in the Short Parliament (d. 1661), by his wife Winifred Bourchier. He was born about 1616 [81] and was admitted to Lincoln's Inn on 3 April 1633.[82] His father owned lands in Devon as well as in Wiltshire, but Glanville's election for Camelford probably resulted from the influence of his sister's husband, Piers Edgcombe, who was chosen there at the same time. Glanville was named to the committee on subsidies, 30 April 1641, and took the oath and Covenant in 1643,[83] but he eventually joined his brother-in-law and his father on the king's side and was disabled in 1644.[84] He retired to Oxford, where he was created D. Med. in March, 1644, and sat in the king's parliament there.[85] Eventually he made his composition with

[66] M. of P. 1: 452, passim; Birch, The court and times of Charles the First 1: 18; The letters of John Chamberlain 2: 543, 614.
[67] S.P. 14, 127/83.
[68] Forster, Eliot 1: 341.
[69] Birch, op. cit. 1: 197.
[70] Acts P.C., 1627, 53, 54.
[71] C.S.P. Dom., 1636–1637, 155.
[72] C. 193/13; S.P. 16, 181/20, fols. 59–60; C. 181/5, fol. 114.
[73] Eg. MSS, 2645, fols. 283, 341.
[74] C.S.P. Dom., 1629–1631, 552.
[75] Pink MSS, 302, fol. 70. In a list of "Parliament men" drawn up in 1640, apparently in anticipation of the elections, Gerard is listed as having an office in the duchy granted him for three lives (S.P. 16, 472/55), and during the interregnum he functioned for a time as chancellor of the duchy.

[76] C.J. 2: 20, 24, 33, 34, 44, passim.
[77] Ibid. 2: 222; D'Ewes (N), 52, 435, n.; N. and Q., 1st Ser., 12: 338, 1855.
[78] Add. MSS, 27,990 (Sir John Percival's notes), fol. 38v.
[79] See note 75. Hexter (A.H.R. 44: 36, n., 1938–1939) accounts Gerard an Independent, but his name has been linked with the Presbyterians by other authors, according to Pink.
[80] Pink MSS, 302, fols. 70–80; Complete Baronetage 1: 142.
[81] His parents were married about 1615. D.N.B.
[82] Linc. Inn. Rec. Adm. 1: 220.
[83] C.J. 2: 130; Pink MSS, 307, fol. 182.
[84] C.J. 3: 374.
[85] Al. Oxon.; Wood, Fasti Oxon. 2: 68.

the parliamentarians at two years' value. No records of his estate value have been found, but his father, as head of the family, paid the principal fine of £2320, with £1350 settled for a rectory.[86] Glanville married Frances Gibbs in 1653, succeeded his father in 1661, and died on 4 October 1680.[87]

* **John Glyn, or Glynne** (1603–1666), of Lincoln's Inn, Steward of Westminster, was M.P. for Westminster, 1640–1648.[88] The son of a prominent Carnarvonshire family,[89] he had spent most of his life after 1624 in London, and had aspired to positions at or near the court in his early career.[90] The father of his first wife was a teller of the Exchequer and Glyn was Steward of Westminster by 1639. He had already been a J.P. there and a member of the sewers commission for Middlesex for some years.[91] He was elected to both parliaments of 1640 for Westminster, having been chosen in the spring at Carnarvon also.[92]

Generally described as one of the Presbyterian leaders, it has been suggested in a recent study that he probably inclined more toward the Independents;[93] and in his politics in the early years of the Long Parliament, he was one of the "middle group" between the war and the peace factions of the parliamentarians.[94]

Glyn was related through his mother to the two John Griffiths of the 1640 House, and perhaps shared some of their antipathy toward their Carnarvonshire neighbors, the Wynns.[95]

Francis Godolphin (c. 1588–1652), of Treveneage, Cornwall, sat for St. Ives, 1640–1648. The son and heir of William Godolphin of Treveneage (M.P., d. 1611?), by Jane, daughter and coheiress of Walter Gaverigan (married 11 December 1587), he was a first cousin of Sir William Godolphin of Godolphin, father of the brothers who represented Helston in the Long Parliament. At the age of sixteen he matriculated at Exeter College, Oxford, 7 December 1604. He was admitted to the Middle Temple early in 1607,[96] and in November, 1616, married Ann, daughter of Richard Carew of Antony, Cornwall.[97] He or his cousin, Francis Godolphin of Godolphin (q.v.), was a member of several local commissions, 1629–1638,[98] and he was sheriff of the county, 1638–1639.[99] Despite considerable poverty in the county and the delays he encountered in the towns, Godolphin managed by the end of his shrievalty to send in most of his ship money allotment.[100]

A newcomer to parliament in November, 1640, he was a member of the popular side, following in politics his wife's family rather than his own. But he took little part in debates, and was absent from the House a number of times before the war began, partly on account of ill health.[101] It was probably his cousin rather than he who offered to back the loan in November, 1640.[102] Godolphin, the St. Ives member, was named to several parliamentary committees for Cornwall during the war, was still a member in September, 1648, but was probably secluded at the end of the year.[103] He died a few years later and was buried at Crowan, 4 February 1652.

Practically nothing is known of Godolphin's financial standing. Although he came of the younger branch of his family, the fact that he was pricked for sheriff indicates that he was a man of substance. At one time during his term of office he feared that he might have to make up the ship money arrears out of his own purse.[104]

Francis Godolphin (1605–1667?), of Godolphin, near Helston, Cornwall, was M.P. for Helston, 1640–1644. The first son and heir of Sir William Godolphin of Godolphin (d. 1613), by his wife, Thomasine, daughter and heiress of Thomas Sidney of Wrighton, Norfolk,

---

[86] *Cal. Com. Comp.*, 1661; Waylen, *Hist. of Marlborough*, 239. His sister's portion when she married Edgcombe was £3000.

[87] Pink MSS, 307, fol. 182; Wilts. Arch. Soc. MSS, Sadler's "Wiltshire Genealogy," Broad Hinton Parish.

[88] In *M. of P.*, 1641 appears as the date, but Glyn was active in the House from November, 1640. By most authorities he has been considered as purged with the Presbyterians, although his name does not appear in the lists of Pride's Purge, but Hexter (*The reign of King Pym*, 41) thinks he was a member until the king's execution.

[89] He is identified as the second son of Sir William Glyn by Williams (*Parl. Hist. Wales*, 60) and by W. E. Whittaker (*The Glyns of Hawarden*, Flintshire Historical Society Publications, 7, 1906), rather than the eldest son as in *D.N.B.* The elder brother was probably the Thomas Glyn who was more active in Carnarvonshire affairs, several times M.P. for that county, and even an unsuccessful candidate in the Long Parliament elections there.

[90] His father tried to place one son, probably Thomas, in Buckingham's retinue in 1617. *Cal. Wynn Papers*, 128.

[91] C. 193/13; S.P. 16/405; C. 181/5, fols. 162, 229.

[92] *M. of P.* 1: 482, 484.

[93] *A.H.R.* 44: 36, n., 1938–1939.

[94] Hexter, *The reign of King Pym*, 40.

[95] In the Long Parliament elections, however, Thomas Glyn was a rival of the Griffiths. See both shire and borough of Carnarvon.

[96] *Al. Oxon.; Mid. Temp. Rec.* 2: 474. According to the admission record, Godolphin's father died before 1607, but 1611 is elsewhere given as the date of his death.

[97] Since Alexander Carew (q.v.) was a son of Richard, presumably Ann was his sister. But Ann, wife of Godolphin, does not appear in all of the Carew pedigrees.

[98] C. 181/4, fol. 3v; 181/5, fols. 183, 204.

[99] S.P. 16, 401/10; *C.S.P. Dom.*, 1639, 338.

[100] *Ibid.*, 62–63, 339; *1639–1640*, 432.

[101] Pink MSS, 307, fol. 268.

[102] D'Ewes (N), 539.

[103] Pink MSS, *loc. cit.* The St. Ives member has sometimes been confused with his cousin, the Helston member (e.g., *O.P.H.*, 9: *21). Pink clarified that point in *Western Antiquary* 9: 132–133, 1889–1890.

[104] *C.S.P. Dom.*, 1639, 63. In addition to the references cited above, see *M. of P.*; Vivian, *Vis. Cornwall*, 184.

he was born on 25 December and baptized at St. Margaret's, Westminster, 27 December 1605.[105] His father was granted for life in 1608 the receivership of the counties of Devon and Cornwall, with the survey of the Exchequer, as his own father had held it before.[106] Francis matriculated at Exeter College, Oxford, 25 June 1624,[107] and was elected to parliament for Helston in 1626. He sat for St. Ives in 1628.[108] He was for some years one of the commission for piracy,[109] and was vice admiral for the Scilly Isles as his ancestors had been before him.[110] As sheriff of Cornwall, 1637–1638, he collected his full amount of ship money.[111]

Godolphin sat in the Short Parliament for Cornwall.[112] Returned for a borough constituency in the autumn, he was probably the Francis Godolphin who offered his bond for £1000 for the first loan,[113] but he was a royalist in sentiment and was probably absent most of the time after July, 1641. He was disabled for his desertion and his work for the king on 22 January 1644.[114] After the Restoration Godolphin sat again in parliament and was created a Knight of the Bath. He died about 1667.[115]

Godolphin had shown some literary talent while he was in college, but he did not attain the fame of his brother, Sidney (q.v.). Both brothers were friends of Hobbes.[116] Sometime before 1635 Francis Godolphin married Dorothy, second daughter of Sir Henry Berkeley of Yarlington, Somerset (q.v.). His third son, Sidney, became the first Earl of Godolphin.[117]

Godolphin's estate, said in 1660 to be worth £1000 a year,[118] included several manors and tin mines in Cornwall and some lands in Norfolk, where his father's purchases had added to his mother's family inheritance.[119]

The Helston M.P. is to be distinguished from the member of the same name, a kinsman, who sat for St. Ives.

* Sidney Godolphin (1610–1643), of Godolphin, poet, was M.P. for his family's borough of Helston, Cornwall, 1640–1643. The second son of Sir William Godolphin (d. 1613), and younger brother of Francis Godolphin, his colleague for Helston, he was educated at Oxford and one of the inns of court and by travel abroad. After his sojourn in France and the Netherlands, and a journey to Denmark with the Earl of Leicester, he took up some office and life at court, "where his excellent disposition and manners, and extraordinary qualifications made him very acceptable." [120] He became a member also of Lord Falkland's set at Tew.[121] He was M.P. for Helston in 1628 and in both parliaments of 1640. He seems to have been with Hopton's troop on the northern border in 1639,[122] and when he was elected to parliament was possibly willing, as were his friends, Falkland and Hyde, to work for some reforms.

Either he or his brother was a "Straffordian" who voted against the earl's attainder,[123] and in December, 1641, Sidney offended the popular faction in the House by proposing a plan which would have defeated part of Pym's strategy in dealing with the peers.[124] With the outbreak of the war, he plunged into action with the royalist forces in the west, and lost his life at Chagford early in February, 1643.

Although small of body and of a sensitive and retiring disposition, Godolphin's courage ranked him with the stalwarts in the often-quoted rhyme:

> The four wheels of Charles's wain,
> Grenville, Godolphin, Trevanion, Slanning, slain.

His mind, according to his friend, Hobbes, was characterized by "clearness of judgment . . . largeness of fancy, [and] strength of reason." [125]

Godolphin married not long before his death, and is said to have left a daughter, Margaret.[126] The chief beneficiaries mentioned in his will of June, 1643, however, were his brother, Francis, and his "dear cousin, Mrs. Jane Berkeley." To the latter he bequeathed £1000, and to Thomas Hobbes he left £200.[127] Although Godolphin was a younger son, his means were sufficient "for a cheerful subsistence in any course of Life he proposed to himself." [128] His inheritance included especially some Norfolk properties from his mother's family and some in Cornwall that came to him on the death of a younger brother.[129]

---

[105] I.P.M., Sir William Godolphin, 1614, C. 142/346/172; Lipscomb, *Buckingham* 4: 560.

[106] *C.S.P. Dom., 1603–1610*, 427.

[107] *Al. Oxon.*

[108] *M. of P.* 1: 468, 474.

[109] C. 181/3, fol. 113; 181/5, fols. 166, 374.

[110] *C.S.P. Dom., 1635–1636*, 423; *1637–1638*, 362.

[111] *List of Sheriffs*, 23; Royal Hist. Soc., *Trans.*, 3rd Ser., 4: 156, 1910.

[112] *M. of P.* 1: 480.

[113] D'Ewes (N), 539.

[114] *C.J.* 3: 374; Pink MSS, 307, fol. 203.

[115] Vivian, *Vis. Cornwall*, 184; *Complete Baronetage* 3: 188.

[116] To Francis Godolphin Hobbes dedicated his *Leviathan* in 1651, apparently in recognition of the two hundred pounds which Godolphin had sent him, possibly as a legacy left by his brother. Thomas Hobbes, *Leviathan*, iii–iv, London, George Routledge & Sons, Ltd., 1907.

[117] *Complete Baronetage* 3: 188.

[118] *Western Antiquary* 7: 39, 1887–1888.

[119] I.P.M. cited above.

---

[120] *The life of Edward Earl of Clarendon* (1759 ed.) 1: 46.

[121] K. Weber, *Lucius Cary, second Viscount Falkland*, 131–135; Coate, *Cornwall in the great Civil War*, 48–49.

[122] S.P. 16, 427/38/ii, v.

[123] Verney, 58.

[124] D'Ewes (C), 228 and n.

[125] Thomas Hobbes, *Leviathan*, 493.

[126] Vivian, *Vis. Cornwall*, 184; Pink MSS, 307, fol. 202.

[127] P.C.C., 6 Fines. Godolphin's brother, Francis, married one of the daughters of Sir Henry Berkeley (q.v.).

[128] *The life of Edward Earl of Clarendon* (1759 ed.) 1: 46.

[129] I.P.M., Sir William Godolphin, C. 142/346/172, and Sidney Godolphin's will.

George Gollopp, or **Gallop** (*d.* 1650), merchant and alderman of Southampton, was M.P. for his borough, 1640–1650 (1648?). He came of a Dorset family, but had lived for many years in Southampton and had been its M.P. in 1625, 1626, and 1628.[130] He was the fifth son of Thomas Gollopp (d. 1610) of North Bowood and Strode, Dorset, "gent.," by his wife, Agnes, daughter of Humphrey Watkins of Holwell. He was born in the parish of Abbott Stoke, Dorset,[131] and was named in the marriage settlement of his next older brother, Thomas, junior, in 1588. Thomas married a daughter of George Paulet of Southampton,[132] and his brother, George, may have been with him in the town then, for in 1596 George Gollopp was a suitor in the borough's court leet as the successor to Paulet in the possession of some property.[133] He seems to have been in charge of some of the borough funds in 1604, and from 1606 served in a series of offices—constable, steward, bailiff, sheriff, mayor (1621–1622, 1632–1633), and alderman. He tried to avoid the shrievalty and later offices, paying fines and refusing once to buy his robe of office, but eventually he yielded.[134] He was a churchwarden at one time,[135] and was named to the commissions of gaol delivery and piracy, and was a J.P.[136]

In his business Gollopp was interested in trade with France in salt and woolens, and with Newfoundland for fish. In 1621 and 1624 he experienced shipping losses to the French and to pirates. He and two fellow townsmen negotiated in 1630 an agreement with some Londoners regarding the Newfoundland trade. And in 1639 he was shipping linens to Spain.[137] He was considered wealthy enough to be put on the loan lists of 1626–1627, but he refused either to subscribe or to pay to the county commissioners and was notified in January, 1627, that he must appear before Council. Lord Conway was particularly anxious that Gollopp seem not to be spared, lest the military activities then going on in the county be prejudiced. The local deputy lieutenants, such as Sir Thomas Jervoise (*q.v.*), however, were reluctant to be too harsh with their "loving friend," Gollopp,[138] and he apparently escaped arrest.

In the Long Parliament Gollopp was not an active member. He was frequently absent, as was his colleague, Exton, though sometimes on parliamentary business. He was summoned several times, 1642–1643, on account of absences, but was named to parliamentary committees for his region, and in the later years was excused a number of times from attending because of illness.[139] He may have continued to be a member after 1648,[140] but died in the early summer of 1650. His will, dated 22 April, was proved on 3 July 1650.[141]

Gollopp married and had at least one son who died early.[142] At his death a nephew, Roger Gollopp, succeeded him. He owned various properties in Southampton and in 1625 was described also as "of Stanbridge" (near Romsey). He erected a mansion on the site of the old castle of Southampton which he had held from 1619.[143] In his will he directed his burial in the chancel of All Hallowes' church in the town and left £200 for a borough charity, as well as small gifts to ministers and schoolmasters. His will enumerated legacies totalling more than £650.

* Arthur Goodwin (1593 ?–1643), of Upper Winchendon, Bucks, one of the knights for Buckinghamshire, 1640–1643, was John Hampden's intimate friend from boyhood and was a leader in puritan circles. His father, Sir Francis (d. 1634), had distinguished himself as an advocate of parliamentary privilege and reform, opposing the policies of the Stuarts and their favorites both within parliament and without, and being summoned at least once before Council for his opposition to the loans.[144] And Arthur, in his first parliament (1621), ventured to propose that the court nominee for Speaker be taken at his word when he protested his unfitness to serve and that another man be chosen.[145] Arthur sat in three other parliaments before the Long Parliament (1624, 1626, and the Short Parliament),[146] and at some time before 1625 was an officer with the armies in the Palatinate. He may have missed the parliament of the latter year because of serving again under the Elector Palatine.[147] As to local activities before 1640, although his father had been a J.P. and D.L., the son is not known to have been named to any but the sewers commission.[148]

---

[130] *M. of P.* 1: 465, 471, 477, 493.

[131] *Vis. Dorset, 1623*, 43; will of George Gollopp, P.C.C., 112 Pembroke. His oldest brother was born about 1552. I.P.M. of Thomas Gollopp, senior, C. 142/662/126.

[132] I.P.M. cited above.

[133] *Southampton court leet records* 1 (2): 304; *The book of examinations and depositions, 1622–1644*, Southampton Record Society 1: 3, n.

[134] *Southampton court leet records* 1 (3): 416; *The book of examinations and depositions, 1622–1644* 1: 3, n.; *The assembly books of Southampton* 4: 17, 60, 72; Woodward, Wilks, and Lockhart, *A general history of Hampshire* 2: 312 and n.

[135] *The assembly books of Southampton* 3: 69.

[136] C. 181/4, fol. 23; 181/5, fol. 86; *The book of examinations and depositions, 1622–1644* 1: 39, 54; 2: *passim*.

[137] *Ibid.* 1: 45–46; 2: 73; 3: 84; *Acts P.C., 1621–1623*, 147.

[138] Add. MSS, 21,922, fols. 86v–88v; S.P. 16, 52/69.

[139] *C.J.* 2: 869, 872; Pink MSS; *H.M.C., Tenth Report* 6, MSS of P. P. Bouverie, 91; Godwin, *The Civil War in Hampshire*, 104; Add MSS, 24,860, fol. 145.

[140] *O.P.H.* 9: *40.

[141] P.C.C., 112 Pembroke.

[142] *Vis. Dorset, 1623*, 43.

[143] *The book of examinations and depositions, 1622–1644* 1: 3, n.; Brit. Mus. Add. Charters, 17,449; *V.C.H. Hampshire* 3: 499.

[144] Gardiner, *H. of E.* 1: 167–170; *Commons Debates 1621* 2: 73, 82, n., *passim*; S.P. 14, 127/82, 148/29.

[145] *C.S.P. Dom., 1619–1623*, 220; *Commons Debates 1621* 5: 430, n.

[146] *M. of P.* 1: 450, *passim*.

[147] *C.S.P. Ireland, 1647–1660, Addenda, 1625–1660*, 49.

[148] C. 181/5, fols. 244, 272; S.P. 16, 187/1, 203/51/109.

Goodwin was a man of substance, as was his friend, Hampden. He was heir to his father's manors, of which there were at least five, two of them alone being worth some £700–£800 a year.[149] He inherited also some of his maternal grandfather's lands, but it was alleged that the Duke of Buckingham had prevented his enjoyment of them.[150] His wife's portion in 1618 had been £1500, and the dower proposed in 1634 for Goodwin's only child was £2000.[151] Goodwin pledged £1000 toward the 1640 loan, joined with Hampden the following July to lend £1000 for the army, and in 1642 subscribed for the defense £100 and the maintenance of four horses.[152]

Goodwin died at Clerkenwell on 16 August 1643,[153] less than two months after he had written to his daughter the letter containing his touching eulogy of his friend, Hampden.[154] He was buried 19 August at Woburn.[155] His will, dated 6 February 1638/9, with a codicil of 30 August 1642, was proved on 11 November 1644.[156]

Goodwin's colleagues in the 1640 parliament included his brother-in-law, Wenman, as well as his friends of the Hampden-Cromwell connection.

John Goodwin (c. 1603–1674), of Blechingley, Surrey, and of the Inner Temple, was a member for Haslemere, 1640–1653. He was one of three claiming the seats for that borough. No record remains of the decisions of the House, but Goodwin spoke in debate as early as 8 February 1641, and was unquestioned thereafter.[157] He was the second son of Edward Goodwin of Horne, Surrey, and East Grinstead, and a younger brother of Robert Goodwin (q.v.), M.P. for East Grinstead.[158] Born about 1603, he entered the Inner Temple in November, 1622, and was admitted to the bar in 1630. He was called to the bench in 1649.[159] He married Katherine, daughter and coheiress of Sir Richard Deane, alderman and Lord Mayor of London, and in 1635 was executor of his father-in-law's estate.[160] He may have

lived in London much of the time,[161] for he seems not to have had responsibilities of a public nature in Surrey before 1640. He sat in no parliament before that of November, although he may have been a candidate for Reigate in the spring.[162]

Both Goodwin and his brother, Robert, were active members of the country faction. They opposed in 1641 the extension of the forests in their county,[163] and in the Long Parliament John was named to many committees, including those on tonnage and poundage and on the recess. He advocated the committing of the London petition against episcopacy,[164] and in his religious views seems to have stepped easily from being a Presbyterian elder into the fold of the Independents.[165] When war approached he pledged one horse and £50 for the defense,[166] and during the war he was a committeeman in Surrey. He assisted with the plans for bringing the king to trial but was not one of his judges. He continued to be active during the Cromwellian period and survived the Restoration. Goodwin died on 18 February 1673/4 and was buried at Worth, Sussex.[167] His will, dated 21 December 1672, was proved by his brother on 6 March 1673/4.[168]

Of Goodwin's wealth before 1640 little has been learned. He was a younger son but had married well, and doubtless had an income from his profession. His marriage brought him some stock in East India Company which he still held in 1672.[169] During the war he acquired some lands from the church and from royalists and an office in Chancery said to be worth £700 a year, but he lost them with the Restoration.[170]

Ralph Goodwin (d. 1658), of Ludlow, an under official in the government of the Welsh Marches, was M.P. for Ludlow, 1640–5 February 1644.[171] He was the son of Ralph Goodwin, probably of Bristol, and may have studied at Trinity, Cambridge (matric. 1608), and graduated B.A. in 1611–12 and M.A. in 1615, and been incorporated at Oxford, 11 July 1615. He is said to have been a learned author and an excellent poet. He was a burgess of Ludlow, and either he or his father was

---

[149] Bodleian Willis MSS, 30, fols. 7, 10v; I.P.M.'s of Sir Francis and Arthur Goodwin (C. 142/525/128; C. 142/777/104); Lysons, *Mag. Brit.* 1: 532, 664, 669, 655, 671; *V.C.H. Buckingham* 3: 111; 4: 123.

[150] Bodleian Carte MSS, 77, fol. 80v.

[151] I.P.M.'s cited above; F. F. Starr, *English Goodwin family papers* 1: 203, Hartford, privately printed, 1921.

[152] D'Ewes (N), 52; *C.J.* 2: 222; *N. and Q.*, 1st Ser., 12: 338, 1855.

[153] I.P.M., C. 142/777/104.

[154] Bodleian Carte MSS, 103, fol. 92; printed in *Berks. Arch. Jour.*, N.S., 1: 19, 1895.

[155] Bodleian Willis MSS, 1, fol. 647.

[156] P.C.C., 1 Rivers. *D.N.B.* gives the date of the will in the old style, 1638.

[157] D'Ewes (N), 337; Willis, 3: 250; Pink MSS, 311, fol. 495b. He is suggested as a recruiter in *M. of P.* (1: 494, n.).

[158] Add. MSS, 12,478, fol. 22v; *Vis. Surrey, 1623*, 124.

[159] *Students admitted to the Inner Temple*, 235; *Cal. Inner Temp. Rec.* 2: 187, 289; Pink MSS, 302, fol. 208.

[160] *A visitation of the county of Surrey, 1662–1668*, Harleian Society 60: 51 (hereafter, *Vis. Surrey, 1662*); Pink MSS, 302,

fol. 209; Sainsbury, *A calendar of the court minutes, &c. of the East India Company, 1635–1639*, 135.

[161] Several of his name were London residents in 1638. Dale, *Inhabitants of London*, 3, 47.

[162] Willis 3: 236; Add. MSS, 27,990, fol. 38v.

[163] Manning and Bray, *Surrey* 1: xiii, n.

[164] *C.J.* 2: 107, 288, *passim*; D'Ewes (N), 337.

[165] *A.H.R.* 44: 31, n., 1938–1939.

[166] Bodleian Tanner MSS, 63, fol. 56.

[167] Pink MSS, 302, fol. 209; Manning and Bray, *Surrey* 3: 675; Add. MSS, 5698, fol. 166v.

[168] Abstract, *English Goodwin family papers* 1: 272.

[169] Sainsbury, *op. cit.*, 1635–1639, 135; *English Goodwin family papers* 1: 272.

[170] *Surrey Arch. Coll.* 39: 62, 1931; Manning and Bray, *Surrey* 3: cxli; *Archaeologia* 10: 444, 1792; *Mystery of the good old cause*, 17.

[171] *C.J.* 3: 389.

muster-master of the county in 1621.[172] In 1625 the office of Examiner of the Court of the Marches was granted to him and to Sampson Eure.[173] He became a protégé of Conway, Lord President of the Marches,[174] and upon Conway's recommendation in 1628 became deputy to Sir Adam Newton, the secretary and clerk of the Council of the Marches.[175] This office he held for at least sixteen years.[176] In 1639 he was summoned to join the army in the north, but Lord Goring arranged for him to be excused.[177]

Beginning with 1624, Goodwin was elected to six successive parliaments for Ludlow.[178] In the early period of the Long Parliament he was named to various committees, one concerning Cambridge and others concerning the laws against the Jesuits and other religious matters, but his committee work seems to have ended with the leave of absence which he was granted in December, 1641.[179] He was probably absent most of the time after that, became Prince Rupert's secretary,[180] and was disabled for his royalism in 1644. He may have been at the siege of Bristol, and in 1646 compounded, paying a fine of some £412. He died in May, 1658, and was buried at Ludlow.[181]

Goodwin was reported at one time to have an estate which included lands worth £300 a year and personal property worth £6000 to £8000.[182] Among the lands he reported to the Compounding Committee were some in Herefordshire and Montgomeryshire that were worth £85 yearly.[183]

Goodwin's first wife, Dorothy, who died in 1643, was a daughter of Walter Long of Wroxhall, Wilts, who was elected M.P. for Ludgershall late in 1641.

Robert Goodwin (*c*. 1601–*c*. 1681), of Horne, Surrey, was M.P. for East Grinstead, Sussex, from 24 December 1640, when his election was declared good, until 1653.[184] His family had been identified with both East Grinstead and Horne for some generations. His grandfather, John, was granted arms in 1597. Robert was the eldest son of Edwin Goodwin (d. 1627) by his wife, Susan, daughter of Richard Wallop of Bugbrooke, Northamptonshire.[185] His father was among those who opposed the forced loans of 1621 and 1625–1626,[186] and the family were part of the puritan element in their county. Robert was born about 1601, and entered the Inner Temple in 1620.[187] He succeeded his father in 1627 and in 1634 married Mary, daughter of Sir John Rivers, Bart., of Chafford, Kent.[188] He was a trustee for William Lord Monson in some land transactions in 1628,[189] and was a J.P. in Surrey from as early as 1631.[190]

According to his own statement when he was a very old man, Goodwin sat for East Grinstead in the 1621 parliament, but he may have meant that he was a contestant for the place, since the records indicate that two others were East Grinstead's members that year.[191] He served for that borough in 1626 and 1628, however, as well as in both parliaments of 1640.[192] In the 1628 parliament Goodwin showed an interest in London affairs.[193] It is possible that some connections with the London companies took him occasionally to Ireland, for one Robert Goodwin, Esquire, was elected to the Irish parliament of 1634 for Londonderry,[194] and during the Civil War and Commonwealth Goodwin was very active in Irish matters.

Goodwin won his place for East Grinstead in the Short Parliament, although it was sought by the Earl of Dorset's secretary, John White (*q.v.*). His victory was based on a broader franchise than White contended was customary, but the House recognized Goodwin's arguments supporting the vote by the general inhabitants.[195] In the autumn Goodwin was opposed by Sir William Colepeper, Bart., of Wakehurst, and though the House on November 16 ordered both men to forbear sitting, Goodwin's title to the place was approved on December 24,[196] and thus a strong parliamentarian was seated. Robert Goodwin, who is not to be confused with the other parliamentarians, his brother, John, and Arthur, or with the royalist, Ralph Goodwin, who sat for Ludlow, was named to many important committees in 1641. They included those on tonnage

---

[172] Shrops, Arch. Soc., *Trans.*, 2nd Ser., 7: 24–25, 1895; *Al. Cant.; Al. Oxon.*

[173] Williams, *Hereford*, 127.

[174] Goodwin wrote to Endymion Porter early in 1630, commenting that his loss by Conway's death was more than the loss of a father. *C.S.P. Dom., 1629–1631*, 495.

[175] Various letters concerning Goodwin's employment as the deputy secretary are included in Harl. MSS, 7000, fols. 228–230v. In one of them Goodwin was described to Newton as one of whom "nothing but well" was known.

[176] Goodwin's statement in 1646, when he was being questioned regarding money that might be owing to Lord Goring from officials of the Court of the Marches. *Cal. Com. Adv. Money*, 703.

[177] S.P. 16, 427/38/vi.

[178] *M. of P.* 1: 459, 465, 471, 477; *Willis* 3: 235.

[179] *C.J.* 2: 52, 73, 119, 340.

[180] *Cal. Com. Adv. Money*, 704.

[181] Shrops. Arch. Soc., *Trans.*, 2nd Ser., 7: 24–25, 1895.

[182] Part of the money was said to have come with his second wife. *Cal. Com. Adv. Money*, 704.

[183] These are the only lands listed in his "particular." S.P. 23/206/589.

[184] *M. of P.* 1: 494; *C.J.* 2: 58; D'Ewes (N), 188.

[185] *Vis. Sussex, 1633–4*, 1; *Sussex Rec. Soc.* 24: 161 and n., 1917.

[186] S.P. 14, 127/80; S.P. 16, 19/70/i.

[187] *Students admitted to the Inner Temple*, 230.

[188] Manning and Bray, *Surrey* 2: 330.

[189] Brayley, *Surrey* 4: 222, n.

[190] C. 193/13; S.P. 16, 191/99; *C.S.P. Dom., 1637*, 110.

[191] *M. of P.* 1: 453. Goodwin made his statement on 7 April 1679. *C.J.* 9: 587.

[192] *M. of P.* 1: 472, 478, 483.

[193] *Commons Debates for 1629*, 53, 134, 181, and index.

[194] *C.S.P. Ireland, 1633–1647*, 65.

[195] *C.J.* 2: 10. Goodwin seems to have been a candidate for Reigate also. *Ibid.* 2: 7.

[196] Pink MSS, 311, fol. 495c; *C.J.* 2: 30, 58.

and poundage, the lay activities of the clergy, subsidies, Secretary Windebank, and the recess. He favored the London petition against episcopacy, and in October, 1641, led the attack on the "evil counsellors" of the crown.[197] After the war began his responsibilities increased. He was sent to Ireland in 1642 to promote the cause of parliament there, and was subsequently appointed agent for Londonerry and a member of the joint committee for Irish affairs (1645). He was one of the commissioners to the Scots, too, and to King Charles, and served on the compounding committee and on the Council of State.[198] He was a Presbyterian elder in his county, but stayed with the Independents after 1648.[199] He was knighted by Henry Cromwell in Dublin in 1658.[200]

Goodwin retired to private life with the Restoration and died about 1681. His will, dated in 1672, was published before witnesses, 29 July 1680, and was proved by his widow on 11 May 1681.[201]

Goodwin was probably in comfortable circumstances, although not wealthy. From his father he inherited in 1627 a number of small holdings and one manor in or near East Grinstead, and his two sisters had dowries of £400 apiece.[202] About that time he and his brother, John, acquired an interest in a Warwickshire manor.[203] He pledged a horse and £50 for the defense in 1642,[204] and ventured some funds in Irish lands.[205]

Goodwin's brother-in-law, James Rivers, was for a time a fellow M.P.

Sir Theobald Gorges

Sir Theobald Gorges (c. 1594–c. 1647), of Ashley, Wilts, was M.P. for Cirencester in Gloucestershire, 1640–22 January 1644. A younger son of Sir Thomas Gorges of Ashley (d. 1610), and brother of Edward, first Baron Dundalk, he was born about 1594.[206] He entered the Middle Temple in 1611,[207] and in 1616 was knighted at Greenwich. As early as 1603 he had been granted with two brothers an office connected with certain Chancery writs, and he was for some years after his knighting an usher of the privy chamber.[208] Before 1623 he married Anne, daughter of Sir Henry Poole of Saperton, Gloucestershire,[209] a prominent country party man. Gorges was living in St. Margaret's parish, Westminster, 1619–1620,[210] but before the next decade ended was a J.P. in Wiltshire,[211] and one of the commissioners for Braden Forest.[212]

Gorges owned some quit rents at Cirencester,[213] but his first official connection with the town seems to have been his election as M.P. late in October 1640. It was his first parliament, and he never became an important member. He was seldom named to committees, obtained a leave of absence in August, 1641, and probably absented himself without leave as the extremists gained in strength. He was warned in September, 1643, about neglecting the service of the House, and was disabled for his desertion in 1644.[214] He equipped his son to fight for parliament, but was himself taken prisoner and held until his compounding, 1645–1646. He died about the end of 1647. His will, dated 3 December 1647, was proved 13 April 1648.[215]

Sir Theobald inherited from his wealthy father the manor of Ashley. When he compounded he declared his income from that manor and other properties to be about £188 a year. But he seems to have owned also a London property worth £50, and his plan, according to his will, to provide portions of £1000 for each of three daughters suggests that his income was more than his "particular" shows. His fine must have been reckoned according to the declared value, for it was £209 (a tenth) or £520 (a third), the latter figure being the one required of him.[216]

Gorges was related to at least four of his fellow parliament men of 1640. Edward Phelipps and Thomas Smith were his nephews, and Sir Neville Poole and Edward Poole were, respectively, a brother-in-law and a nephew by marriage.[217]

George Goring

* George Goring (1608–1657), of Hurst Pierpoint, Sussex, courtier, colonel in the army and governor of Portsmouth, was a member for Portsmouth, 1640–16 August 1642. The prodigal son of a wealthy privy councillor, Lord Goring, an honorary M.A. from Cam-

[197] C.J. 2: 107, 115, 130, 205, 288, 297; D'Ewes (N), 338; D'Ewes (C), 44.

[198] Pink MSS, 302, fols. 213–215; C.J. 4: 191, 198; R. Dunlop, *Ireland under the Commonwealth* 2: 438 and n., Manchester, Univ. Press., 1913.

[199] A.H.R., 44: 31, n., 1938–1939.

[200] Shaw, K .of E. 2: 224.

[201] J. J. Goodwin, *English Goodwin family papers* 1: 281–282.

[202] I.P.M., Edward Goodwin, C. 142/568/122.

[203] Cal. Com. Comp., 2947.

[204] N. and Q., 1st Ser., 12: 359, 1855.

[205] Part of his venture was subscribed by relatives (C.S.P. Ireland, Adventurers, 100), but his lands in Leinster were referred to in his will. Goodwin, loc. cit.

[206] At the time of his second marriage in 1646 Gorges gave his age as fifty-two (*Marriage licenses, London* 2: 277). His brother, Lord Dundalk, was born about 1583 (ibid. 1: 297; I.P.M. of Sir Thomas Gorges, C. 142/315/180).

[207] Mid. Temp. Rec. 2: 535.

[208] Hoare, *Wilts.* 3 (V): 30; St. Ch. 8/130/10.

[209] Vis. Glouc., 126.

[210] Records of St. Margaret's Parish, Overseers' Accounts, 1617–1624, fols. 5v, 11.

[211] C. 193/12, 13; S.P. 16/405; C.S.P. Dom., 1637, 137.

[212] Calendar of Treasury Papers, 1556–7–1696, 3.

[213] S.P. 23/175/132.

[214] Pink MSS, 302, fol. 231; C.J. 2: 233; 3: 374.

[215] P.C.C., 59 Essex. Gorges was survived by his second wife, Anne, daughter of John Gage, whom he married in 1646.

[216] I.P.M. cited above; Wilts. Arch. Mag. 46: 16–34, 1932–1934; S.P. 23/175/130–132; S.P. 16, 61/100; Cal. Com. Comp., 1045.

[217] In addition to the authorities cited above see Williams, *Gloucester*, 158.

bridge,[218] and experienced in numerous military and diplomatic expeditions abroad,[219] he was a newcomer to the House of Commons in November, 1640.

Goring's lavish spending and heavy debts had been a feature of his earlier career. He was named in 1628 as a co-farmer of wine licenses with his father,[220] but when he was questioned in 1641 as a participant in his father's monopolies, he convinced the committee that he was not himself a monopolist.[221] Although his father's and his wife's fortunes were large, the landed estates in Goring's possession before the war—his father was still alive—were said to have an income of only £390 a year, and these he soon mortgaged on account of debts of over £4000.[222]

Goring was a brother-in-law of his fellow M.P.'s, Lord Dungarvan, and Arthur Jones.

Thomas Grantham (1612–165–), of Goltho, Lincolnshire, was M.P. for Lincoln city throughout the Long Parliament.[223] He was the eldest surviving son of Sir Thomas Grantham of Goltho and St. Katherine's (d. 1630), J.P., M.P., who had been one of Eliot's supporters in parliament and had suffered restraint for resisting the forced loan of 1627.[224] His mother was Frances, daughter of Sir John Puckering, the Lord Keeper.[225] Thomas was baptized at St. Botolph's, Lincoln, 5 November 1612, and was reared in a household which kept up the old traditions of hospitality, entertaining the nobility and gentry of the region and in 1617 the king himself. He was educated "beyond seas," [226] a pass for him to travel for three years, attended by three servants, having been issued in February, 1625/6,[227] and even after his father's death he was soldiering in the Netherlands in 1631.[228] The following year, however, he married Dorothy, daughter of Sir

William Alford of Bilton and Meaux, Yorkshire,[229] and moved into life after his father's pattern.

From 1634 Grantham was a J.P. in Lincolnshire, and a member of local commissions there and in Yorkshire.[230] As sheriff of his county, 1638–1639, he had difficulty collecting ship money, but seems not to have fallen greatly into arrears. His explanation to Council for some shortcomings was the condition of the county and the demands there for money for other royal needs.[231] He represented Lincoln in both parliaments of 1640 and showed himself again to be of his father's views. He was named to the Committee of Privileges of the Long Parliament, and to the committee on the Bishop of Bath and Wells, but was not active in later committee work. In the summer of 1641 he was sent to Lincolnshire to assist with the disarming of recusants,[232] and, when war broke out, not only promised to furnish two horses for the defense,[233] but became colonel of a regiment which was accounted one of the best in the armies of parliament.[234] His military duties caused him to be absent frequently from the House thereafter. He died on 22 November 1655 or 1656.[235]

Grantham inherited from his father four or five manors near Lincoln and several large properties within the city,[236] and by his marriage gained some Yorkshire estates. He does not, however, seems to have been one of the wealthiest members of the House.

Giles Green (d. 1656), of Allington and Motcombe in the Isle of Purbeck, Dorset, was M.P. for Corfe Castle, 1640–1648. In a varied career he seems to have been something of a merchant, a lawyer, a civil servant, and the manager of estates, emerging with the Civil War as a vigorous director of maritime affairs. As the son of John Green of Dorchester, merchant, he was admitted to the Middle Temple, 24 June 1614,[237] but he returned to Dorset without reaching the bar. Taking up residence at Weymouth, where he was a property holder by 1617, he seems to have been both a merchant and a legal counsellor for the town, possibly acting as Town Clerk. He was ordered to proceed in 1621, for example, against agents of the sheriff for violating the liberties of the borough, and the next year he was re-

[218] *Al. Cant.*

[219] Cadiz, 1625 (S.P. 16, 522/16, 17); France, 1627 (Add. MSS, 21,922, fol. 104); courtesy missions to the Netherlands, 1627 and 1639. *C.S.P. Venetian, 1636–1639,* 148, 606.

[220] *C.S.P. Dom., 1628–1629,* 197.

[221] D'Ewes (N), 312 and n.

[222] S.P. 23/214/727–729.

[223] *M. of P.* 1: 490. He seems not to have attended regularly after 1647. Pink MSS, 302, fol. 381.

[224] Maddison, *Lincs. Ped.* 2: 423; C. 193/12, 13; *M. of P.* 1: 444, *passim;* Forster, *Eliot* 1: 304; Rushworth 1: 473; S. P. 16, 89/2.

[225] Through his father's second wife, Lucy (Boughton) Sacheverell, Grantham was linked with the Hutchinson family of Civil War fame. Maddison, cited above; *The genealogie of the severall branches of the . . . family of Grantham of Goltho* (privately printed, London). The second Lady Grantham and a clergyman were defendants in a case before the Court of High Commission in 1635, evidently regarding their religious views. *C.S.P. Dom., 1635,* 193, 199, 215.

[226] Lucy Hutchinson, *Memoirs of the life of Colonel Hutchinson,* 48, London, G. Bell, 1902.

[227] *Acts P.C., 1625–1626,* 348.

[228] Letter of Grantham to his uncle and guardian, Sir Thomas Puckering, Bart., dated Bergen op Zoom, 24 September 1631. Harl. MSS, 7000, fol. 414.

[229] *Paver's marriage licenses, Y.A.S., Rec. Ser.* **40**: 17, 1909.

[230] C. 193/13; S.P. 16/405; C. 181/4, fol. 189v; 181/5, fols. 29, 82, 331.

[231] *C.S.P. Dom., 1638–1639,* 430, 603; *1639,* 28, 235.

[232] *C.J.* 2: 20, 50, 267; Pink MSS, 302, fol. 381.

[233] *N. and Q.*, 1st Ser., **12**: 359, 1855.

[234] Clarendon, *Rebellion* 2: 364.

[235] Pink, cited above. The year of his death appears only as 165– on the M.I. at Goltho. Lincolnshire Parish Registers (Lincoln Library MSS), 2: 183.

[236] I.P.M. of Sir Thomas Grantham, C. 142/457/91; will of Sir Thomas Grantham, Consistory Court of Lincoln, 1630, fols. 487–489.

[237] *Mid. Temp. Rec.* 2: 581. His eldest son, doubtless named for his grandfather, was John Green of Enfield, Middlesex, who became clerk of the New River Company. *Somerset and Dorset N. and Q.* 2: 288, 1891; 3: 78, 1892–1893.

imbursed for expenses in delivering letters from the Privy Council and in some town lawsuits.[238] He may have acted also as counsellor for the office of alnager in Somerset at this period, and by 1625 was referred to as a clerk of the Crown Office.[239] His familiarity with Edward Nicholas and with legal procedure a few years later suggests that his work had brought him into contact more than once with the royal officials of Westminster.[240] He was still listed as a merchant of Weymouth in 1628 when he was named one of a commission to investigate certain imposts on shipping,[241] but his activities had expanded beyond those of business enterprise.

His associations with the Isle of Purbeck region apparently date from his lease in 1620 from Lady Hatton of the old manor and hamlet of Allington or Alflington near Corfe Castle. He eventually established his residence there, functioned occasionally as agent for Lady Hatton in her management of the castle, and later became agent for Sir John Banks in his lordship of the Isle of Purbeck.[242] But he retained also his interest in his native town of Dorchester. He subscribed £20 toward the Reverend John White's New England project that originated there and was in 1624 named to the governing committee of the Dorchester Company.[243] Sometime before 1631 he donated a set of Melancthon's works to that town.[244]

Green was sent to his earliest parliaments, those of 1621, 1625, and 1626, for Weymouth and Melcombe Regis. He sat for Corfe Castle in 1628.[245] He spoke briefly in the 1621 Commons in the discussion of the composition required of the London victuallers,[246] and in 1626 spoke regarding funds for an adequate navy.[247] During the interval between 1629 and 1640 he was concerned chiefly with local affairs, such as piracy or shipping in Weymouth harbor, or the Dorset sewers commission.[248] He apparently made use of his contacts in London, for in April, 1636, he secured a royal appointment as surveyor of the saltworks set up under the new patent, and in 1637 he paid Secretary Windebank £5 for some favor.[249] But Green was not loyal in every way to the authorities at Westminster. He seems to have been excused from a £10 loan by privy seal in

1626,[250] and in 1637 he was reported as a ship money defaulter for one of his farms in the Isle of Purbeck.[251]

A member for Corfe Castle in both parliaments of 1640, Giles Green showed himself to be busy and useful, working steadily with the reform group. His committee appointments, of which there were not less than ten before the recess of 1641, ranged from those on various aspects of ecclesiastical administration to those on breaches of parliamentary privilege, on subsidies, and on ship money. He made several reports on matters of trade and imposts, and after the recess became increasingly important. He attacked monopolies, was named in January, 1642, to assist with defense plans, and was chairman of the committee for salt, soap, leather, and wine.[252] Before the year ended he was named to the select committee on Ireland, and was a member of the parliamentary committees for Dorset, and a Commissioner of the Customs. He served during the war as chairman of the committee on the navy and customs, by 1645[253] was a commissioner of the Admiralty,[254] and by 1646 was chairman of the committee on foreign affairs.[255] He was secluded in 1648,[256] but continued to live for at least part of the time thereafter at London, for he was buried on 5 January 1656 at St. Benet Fink.[257]

Green's wife, Elizabeth—, survived him,[258] as well as two sons and several married daughters. One of his daughters (d. 1638) was the first wife of Roger Hill, the Bridport M.P. (q.v.), who was a nephew by marriage of one of Green's sisters.[259] Another daughter married a Walter Yonge, probably a son of the M.P. of that name.[260]

[238] Moule, Catalogue of the . . . documents of the borough of Weymouth and Melcombe Regis, 107, 110, 140; Pink MSS, 302, fol. 388.
[239] St. Ch. 8/295/30.
[240] S.P. 16, 142/27; C.S.P. Dom., 1631–1633, 320.
[241] Ibid., 1627–1628, 567.
[242] Hutchins, Dorset 1: 529; C.S.P. Dom., 1631–1633, 568; S.P. 16, 266/23.
[243] Somerset and Dorset N. and Q. 17: 109, 1921–1923; Dorset N.H. Proceedings 13: 65, 1892.
[244] Mayo, Municipal records, Dorchester, 581.
[245] M. of P.
[246] Commons Debates 1621 3: 84, n.
[247] E.H.R. 17: 736, 1902.
[248] C.S.P. Dom., 1631–1633, 320, 568, 570; C. 181/5, fol. 226.
[249] C.S.P. Dom., 1635–1636, 360; S.P. 16, 371/60.

[250] Acts P.C., 1625–1626, 372.
[251] S.P. 16, 319/89.
[252] C.J. 2: 33, 56, 91, 107, 181, 265, 378, passim; D'Ewes (C), 191, 257 and n., 284.
[253] C.J. 2: 750; Bayley, The great Civil War in Dorset, 390, 415; H.M.C., Fifth Report, House of Lords MSS, 54; Sainsbury, A calendar of the court minutes, &c. of the East India Company, 1640–1643, 307, 364. His conduct on the navy committee displeased some of his colleagues, such as John Moore, whose wife once wrote that all of the members of the committee were "base rogues," of whom Green seemed to be the greatest. H.M.C., Tenth Report 4, Captain Stewart's MSS, 97–98. In 1647 Green had printed in London a Declaration in vindication of the honour of parliament and of the Navy and Customs (printed by Laurence Blacklock).
[254] Somerset and Dorset N. and Q. 2: 288, 1891.
[255] Brit. Mus. Birch MSS, 4200, fols. 12, 13, 15, 70.
[256] Add. MSS, 27,990, fol. 38v; Pink MSS, 302, fol. 388.
[257] Somerset and Dorset N. and Q. 2: 288, 1891. Green's will, dated 21 December 1655, with a codicil later, was proved on 20 May 1656. P.C.C., 30 Berkeley.
[258] His wife married again in 1660, describing herself then as 50. Somerset and Dorset N. and Q. 3: 78–79, 1892–1893.
[259] Brown, Somerset Wills 3: 82; Vis. Dorset, 1623, 55. Green's will named as executor his "brother-in-law," John Hill, and as overseer Roger Hill, Serjeant-at-law.
[260] Green's son-in-law, Walter Yonge, who was named in his will, may have been the one who entered Oxford in 1626 (Al. Oxon.).

Green accumulated during his lifetime, and probably by 1640, a comfortable estate, although he was hardly to be termed wealthy. He owned several farms in Dorset, from two of which by 1644 goods to the value of £350 had been taken as supplies for the Wareham garrison.[261] His pledge of a horse and £50 for the defense in 1642 [262] was a considerable one. The Motcombe estate, by which he identified himself when he made his will in 1656, was a recent acquisition. At that time he was able to add £200 to the portion of the daughter who had received the smallest one earlier, and to provide an annuity of £100 for his wife.

* **Sir Bevil Grenville** (1596–1643), of Stowe, was a member for Cornwall, 1640–19 September 1642. He came of an old Cornish family and, as Clarendon put it, "was a gallant and sprightly gentleman, of the greatest reputation and interest in Cornwall," and was "the generally most loved man of that county." [263] He held lands of considerable value from his own family and his wife's,[264] and took an interest also in the industries of the region, experimenting with the use of coal instead of wood for the melting of tin.[265] During the Civil War he maintained the men of his command at his own expense.[266]

Grenville spent some time at court after his Oxford years, his father having some interest there,[267] and he was granted a pass for travelling abroad in 1623.[268] He was a member of every parliament from 1621 until the Civil War, and was a J.P. in Cornwall.[269] He was named also to numerous commissions,[270] including that for the loan in 1626, although he opposed the loan himself.[271] He seems to have renewed his court contacts by 1639. He was one of the "king's servants above stairs" who were with the army then, being attached to the bodyguard troop commanded by Philip Lord Herbert.[272] He was knighted in July of that year.[273] Already he had settled his affairs in Cornwall, mortgaging some of his holdings in 1638 for £20,000 and others within the next three years for perhaps £7000 more, and preparing to devote himself to the king's cause.[274] By the time of the 1640 elections, Grenville felt that he had

lost much of his political popularity in his county,[275] but he was strong enough still to carry a borough in the spring and the shire election in the autumn apparently without difficulty.[276] And he was wealthy enough to offer his bond for £1000 to secure the loan in November, 1640.[277]Otherwise he was not an active member of the House and turned to action in the field when war came.

Grenville's interests, besides politics and the management of his properties, included the reading of poetry and history.[278]

* **Henry Lord Grey of Ruthin** (1594–1651), M.P. for Leicestershire from 1640 until he succeeded as the ninth Earl of Kent in 1643, was the son and heir of the Leicestershire clergyman, Anthony Grey, who became Earl of Kent in his old age in 1639. Through his mother he was a relative of Purefoy, the puritan member for Warwickshire. Grey studied at Cambridge,[279] was admitted to Gray's Inn, 31 January 1616,[280] and as Lord Ruthin represented the county of Leicester in the Short Parliament.[281] He seems, however, to have held no local offices.

Lord Grey's wealth is difficult to estimate. His father's estate was probably not large, even the earldom having brought him no more than £500 a year,[282] but Grey's first marriage, with Mary, daughter of Sir William Courteen, must have improved his circumstances. He was probably the Lord Grey who was reported among the property owners of London able to advance money for a loan in May, 1640.[283]

* **Thomas Lord Grey of Groby** (1623 ?–1657), the regicide, M.P. for Leicester, 1640–1653, was the son of the wealthy puritan Earl of Stamford, and was chosen upon his father's recommendation to the borough.[284] Under eighteen at the time of his election, young Grey was admitted to Gray's Inn, 16 March 1641.[285] His

[261] C. H. Mayo, ed., *The minute books of the Dorset Standing Committee*, 21–22, Exeter, W. Pollard, 1902. A different farm was the one on which he had failed to pay ship money.

[262] *N. and Q.*, 1st Ser., **12** : 359, 1855.

[263] *Rebellion* **2** : 452; **3** : 82, n.

[264] Gilbert, *Hist. survey of Cornwall* **1** : 509; Lysons, *Mag. Brit.* **4** : 163; Forster, *Eliot* **2** : 624–625.

[265] Gilbert, *loc. cit.*

[266] Coate, *Cornwall in the great Civil War*, 38.

[267] *Ibid.*, 85.

[268] *Acts P.C., 1623–1625*, 47.

[269] C. 193/12; *C.S.P. Dom., 1637*, 9

[270] C. 181/3, fols. 113, 130; 181/5, *passim*; S.P. 16, 54/20.

[271] S.P. 16, 54/20; Coate, *op. cit.*, 22.

[272] S.P. 16, 427/38/v; 538/91/ii.

[273] *C.S.P. Dom., 1639*, 384.

[274] *Cal. Com. Comp.*, 2214–2215; Coate, *op. cit.*, 23.

[275] He wrote in 1640 to Sir Edward Seymour that he was not sure of a single borough for himself or for those he might nominate, although two had offered to choose him if he would serve personally. Coate, *op. cit.*, 24–25.

[276] Grenville's Short Parliament service for Launceston is not mentioned in *D.N.B.*, perhaps because the return is lacking from *M. of P.* See Willis **3** : 230; Rushworth **3** : 1105.

[277] D'Ewes gives the name as Sir Edward Greenfield (D'Ewes [N], 52), but there was no such M.P.

[278] Coate, *op. cit.*, 86–87.

[279] He was probably the Henry Grey who was admitted to Sidney Sussex College, 31 March 1611 (B.A. 1615). Another Henry Grey matriculated at Jesus College in 1602. *Al. Cant.*

[280] *Gray's Inn Adm. Reg.*, 138.

[281] *M. of P.* **1** : 482.

[282] *C.S.P. Dom., 1639–1640*, 158.

[283] S.P. 16, 453/75. Certain Kentish properties came to Grey by this marriage, also. Hasted, *Kent* **1** : 166; **9** : 207.

[284] He was made a freeman, 23 October 1640. Helen Stocks and W. H. Stevenson, *Records of the borough of Leicester, 1603–1688*, 311; Hartropp, *Register of the freemen of Leicester*, 126.

[285] *Gray's Inn Adm. Reg.*, 229.

role in the early period of the Long Parliament was unimportant, even his assignment to the committee to wait on the king with the remonstrance [286] being traceable probably to noble birth rather than to political precocity. Through his mother, Lord Grey was related to his fellow members, Lord Andover and Thomas Howard.

Sir Edward Griffin (c. 1605–1681), of Dingley and Braybrook, Northamptonshire, a gentleman of the privy chamber, was M.P. for Downton, Wilts, 1640–5 February 1644. The descendant of a family prominent at court in the previous century and active in county affairs,[287] he was the heir of his grandfather, Sir Edward Griffin of Dingley, K.B. (d. 1620). The latter's elder son, known as Sir Thomas Griffin of Braybrooke (d. 1615), married as his second wife in 1604 Elizabeth, daughter of George Touchet, Lord Audley, and widow of Sir John Stawell of Cothelstone in Somerset. By Lady Elizabeth, whose son by her first marriage was the royalist Sir John Stawell of the Long Parliament (q.v.), Sir Thomas had his son, Edward Griffin, the M.P.[288] The latter should not be confused with his uncle of the same name, a younger son of Sir Edward Griffin, K.B.[289]

Griffin was born about 1605, and matriculated at Queen's College, Oxford, 25 October 1616, aged eleven.[290] He seems to have remained after his father's death in the care of his mother, although by 1622 his guardian was the influential courtier, Sir William Uvedale of Hampshire (q.v.). The latter obtained in that year a license for the marriage of his seventeen-year-old ward and his thirteen-year-old daughter, Frances Uvedale.[291] By this marriage young Griffin's ties with the court were established. He was knighted at Whitehall, 20 May 1625,[292] and by a letter patent of December, 1626, was granted special livery of his grandfather's extensive estates in Northamptonshire and Leicester-

shire.[293] He probably spent more of his time at court than in the country, for he does not seem to have been named to local office. He may have assisted with preparations for the Isle of Rhe expedition, and by 1638 was a gentleman of the privy chamber. In the latter year, when the attention of Laud and the Council was drawn to Griffin's alleged encroachment on the rights of the church on one of his properties, considerable lenience toward him was displayed in the instructions for settlement.[294] He was notified in the summer of 1639, as were most officials and persons connected with the court, that a loan for the king was expected of him—in his case, £1000—and he may have been serving with the army in the north at that time.[295] The following January his father-in-law, Uvedale, secured for him the reversion of his own office of Treasurer of the Chamber.[296]

Sir Edward had not served in parliament before 1640. His election in the spring and the fall of that year for Downton, a borough near the Hampshire border that was frequently controlled by the Herbert family, doubtless resulted from the influence of his Hampshire father-in-law or of Pembroke, the Lord Chamberlain.[297] He was not an active member of the Commons, and was apparently more loyal to the king than was his father-in-law. Griffin followed rather the example of his stepbrother, Stawell. As a member of the royal household Griffin joined King Charles at Oxford and sat in the assembly there. He was consequently expelled from the Long Parliament on 5 February 1644.[298] When he petitioned to compound in 1646 he declared that he had not borne arms. With the Restoration he again became a gentleman of the privy chamber, and was eventually Treasurer of the Chamber. He died on 5 May 1681, and his son and successor was created Baron Griffin of Braybrooke in 1688.[299]

The Griffin family was well-to-do. It was stated that when his parents married £1000 a year had been allowed as his mother's jointure and that she brought £12,000 to her husband. But the properties had been somewhat encumbered before Sir Edward came into possession, and a prolonged suit in regard to his title was waged by his mother against her husband's relatives.[300] Sir Edward himself seems to have mortgaged some of them in 1640, and when he made his composition as a royalist he asserted that from a total gross

---

[286] D'Ewes (C), 212.

[287] One ancestor was Attorney-General under Edward VI and Mary (Brit. Mus. Add. Ch., 6018–1623); one was H.S. Northamptonshire, 1582 (Add. Ch., 6069).

[288] The statement of relationships above is based upon various legal papers pertaining to the family, such as those connected with Lady Griffin's lawsuit regarding the estate (C.S.P. Dom., 1635–1636, 454; Add. Ch., 6124), Sir Edward's compounding papers (Cal. Com. Comp.), and some of the Stawell family papers. (See George D. Stawell, A Quantock family, the Stawells of Cothelstone and their descendants, 80, Taunton, Wessex Press, 1910 [hereafter, Stawell, The Stawells of Cothelstone].) There are errors regarding Griffin's parentage in Pink MSS, 302, fol. 449; Burke, Extinct Peerages, 255; and Al. Oxon.

[289] He studied at Oxford and the Middle Temple, was knighted before 1617, and was commonly styled "of Gumley." Al. Oxon.; Mid. Temp. Rec. 2: 444; St. Ch. 8/125/6; will of Sir Edward Griffin, K.B. (dated 1619, proved 1625), P.C.C., 128 Clarke.

[290] Pink MSS, 302, fol. 449.

[291] Marriage licenses, London, Harleian Society, 2: 113, 1887.

[292] Shaw, K. of E. 2: 188.

[293] He entered upon them as kinsman and nearest heir. Add. Ch., 6022. His grandfather's I.P.M. of 11 August 1621 likewise so described him, and gave his age as 16. Bodleian MSS Top. Northants, C. 27, fols. 533–535.

[294] C.S.P. Dom., 1627–1628, 434; 1637–1638, 206; Pink MSS, loc. cit.

[295] S.P. 16, 427/38/ii, iv; 447/36, 37, 94.

[296] C.S.P. Dom., 1639–1640, 389, 474.

[297] See Downton election.

[298] C.J. 3: 389.

[299] Pink MSS, loc. cit.; Burke, Extinct Peerages, loc. cit.

[300] Add. Ch., 6124; C.S.P. Dom., 1635–1636, 454; 1636–1637, 384. Griffin held at least one Hampshire manor in right of his wife. V.C.H. Hampshire 4: 153.

income of about £1200 a year he received, after deductions for annuities, interest, and other obligations, only £564. A subsequent report placed his gross income some £550 higher. His fine at a tenth was £1700.[301]

Related by marriage to Uvedale, and by blood to Sir John Stawell and to Sir James Thynne, a cousin, Griffin had other connections among the 1640 parliament men, such as Sir Guy Palmes, possibly Geoffrey Palmer, and even the parliamentarians, Hesilrige and Cromwell.[302]

John Griffith (c. 1591–1642 ?), of Cefnamlwch in Llyn, Carnarvonshire, was M.P. for Beaumaris, Anglesey, 1640–1642. The heir of his father, John Griffith, H.S., M.P., he was widely known in north Wales for his feud with such families as the Bodvels, Wynns, and Thomases, and was their rival both in matters of property and local offices and in seeking places at court. He received part of his education at Lincoln's Inn. His pursuit of law cases was with such zeal that criticism was voiced in Star Chamber that, though "neither counsellor, solicitor, or attorney allowed," he was agent or solicitor in all suits involving people in the counties of Carnarvon, Anglesey, Denbigh, and Chester, and sometimes on both sides, with the result that he accumulated a very great estate by legal chicanery.[303] Griffith for some time aspired without great success to a court career. He was aided in his early period by his wife's family, the Trevors, and made his home when he was in London with Sir Thomas Trevor, Baron of the Exchequer.[304] But he earned an unenviable reputation for bribery, and in 1621 found himself out of a place at court. He managed presently with the assistance of Buckingham to secure the constableship of Carnarvon,[305] but a year or two later failed to obtain a Council clerkship which he desired.[306] And shortly before Buckingham's death Griffith was reported to be so discouraged about a court career that he talked of going abroad.[307] The assassination of the favorite caused him to forsake Westminster almost entirely, except as his employment in legal cases took him there.[308]

Meanwhile in Carnarvonshire Griffith and his father, "a great man of command in those parts,"[309] had not been inactive. The father was sheriff in 1618,[310] and their faction so managed the county election of 1620 as to secure the return of the son to parliament, defeating their rival, Sir Richard Wynn (q.v.).[311] A member again in 1626, Griffith used his place in the House to curry favor with Buckingham[312] and to blend a personal quarrel with the public attack on the Bishop of Bangor.[313] He probably served in the Isle of Rhé expedition in 1627,[314] and after representing his county again in 1628, turned his attentions chiefly to Welsh affairs. He was a vice admiral in north Wales and a J.P. and a member of various commissions.[315]

Griffith was not chosen for the Short Parliament, and in the Long Parliament was not a prominent member. He supported the court faction, both he and his son (M.P. for Carnarvonshire) voting against the attainder of Strafford.[316] He was named to an occasional committee,[317] but he is said to have died about the time the war began, 10 August 1642. His death occurred certainly before 7 December 1646.[318]

John Griffith (fl. 1633–1648), of Llyn, was M.P. for Carnarvonshire, 1640–10 August 1642. There were delays and disagreements about his election as late as May, 1641, and it was rumored in July that an adverse report from the committee was impending, but that the House had no time to receive it.[319] But both he and his father had been sitting as members before that, and there seems to have been no further questioning of his

---

[301] Cal. Com. Comp., 1206; S.P. 23/195/621–622.

[302] Palmes's sister seems to have married into the Griffin family (S.P. 23/195/161; Foster, Yorkshire families 3, Palmes); Add. Ch., 6124.

[303] St. Ch. 8/31/3. The comment was made during the course of a bitter and prolonged lawsuit involving a kinsman of the Wynns of Gwydir and of Lord Keeper Williams. Cal. Wynn Papers, xvii, 148, 149, 152, passim.

[304] Ibid., 148, 206. The John Griffith who was secretary to the Earl of Northampton (d. 1614) during his wardenship of the Cinque Ports, and who was M.P. in 1614 and possibly in 1608, was probably not John Griffith of Llyn (Ibid., 94, 95; C.S.P. Dom., 1611–1618, 110, 317; M. of P.; Pink MSS, 302, fol. 452; Trans. of the Hon. Soc. of Cymmrodorion, 69, 1942.

[305] Cal. Wynn Papers, 153, 155, 159, 164–167, 172.

[306] Ibid., 172, 183, 209.

[307] Ibid., 203, 207, 221, 223.

[308] C.S.P. Dom., 1635–1636, 337; 1637–1638, 602.

[309] St. Ch. 8/31/3.

[310] Williams (Parl. Hist. Wales, 60) assigns the post of sheriff to Griffith, the son, since he thought the father had died in 1609. But the father was still living in 1624 (Cal. Wynn Papers, 200), and the List of Sheriffs (248) does not distinguish the official as the son. Since the son was at court during much of this period, it seems probable that his father was then sheriff (Cal. Wynn Papers, 138). The father died before March, 1628. Cheshire Sheaf, 2nd Ser., 1: 182, 1891.

[311] The younger Griffith and his wife were said to have gone into the county a short time before the election, lest a question of non-residence be raised, and their faction worked vigorously with the freeholders in the canvass. Cal. Wynn Papers, 144–147.

[312] Ibid., 226–227.

[313] C.S.P. Dom., 1625–1626, 355; S.P. 16, 30/8.

[314] C.S.P. Dom., 1627–1628, 229, 373, 423.

[315] Ibid., 1628–1629, 364; 1631–1633 and succeeding volumes; C. 193/13; S.P. 16/405; C. 181/4, fol. 95v; 181/5, fol. 369.

[316] Verney, 58.

[317] Pink MSS, 302, fol. 454.

[318] The writ for choosing his successor was issued on the latter date, and according to O.P.H. (9: 14), Griffith died on the 1642 date. Since that was also the date of his son's expulsion from the House, it seems possible that there may have been some confusion as to the events that occurred on that day. The son was still referred to as "the younger" in October, 1642 (C.J. 2: 816). Williams, however, accepts 10 August 1642 as the date of the elder Griffith's death.

[319] M. of P. 1: 498 and n.; C.J. 2: 25, 61, 115, 145–146; D'Ewes (N), 208, 454–456, 490; Cal. Wynn Papers, 274.

right to the seat.[320]   The son and heir apparent of John Griffith, "the elder" (*c.* 1591–1642 ?), who was M.P. for Beaumaris, he was admitted to Lincoln's Inn on 18 May 1633.[321]   He may have served as a lieutenant under the Earl of Northumberland in 1640.[322]

In 1640–1641 Griffith was a member of the court party, joining with his father in voting against Strafford's attainder.[323]   Clarendon stated that he was following the court to gain preferment and that in the early period he "always opposed (as far as not consenting) all the undutiful acts towards the King."   But a rebuff from the queen early in 1642 led him to turn informer as to her plans and he was said to have been welcomed to the side of parliament by no less a man than Hampden.[324]   But Griffith was a man of moods and passions that were not easily reconciled with the sedate party.   He was questioned early in 1642 regarding challenges he was reported to have given, and although he escaped arrest at that time,[325] he was placed in the custody of Black Rod the following June because of an attack he was alleged to have made on Lady Elizabeth Sedley.   The House voted on 10 August 1642 to expel him for his misconduct.[326]   He was reported later that year to be serving in the army under Essex, but there is no record that he had to answer further for the complaints made against him.[327]   And there is reason to doubt a statement sometimes made that he sat in the Oxford parliament.[328]   Some years later he reported a Cheshire man to parliament as a papist and a royalist, and in 1648 he fled to Scotland because a coroner's jury had found him guilty on a murder charge arising from attentions Griffith was paying to a neighbor's lady.   He was said to have died afterwards in Paris.[329]

Sir Harbottle Grimston, Bart. (1578–1648), of Bradfield, Essex, M.P. for Harwich from 1640 until his death in February, 1648, was the descendant of an old and distinguished family originally of Yorkshire.   His grandfather, Edward Grimston (d. 1599), had been comptroller of Calais, and his parents were Edward Grimston, a Master of Chancery and M.P. (d. 1610), and Joan, daughter and coheiress of Thomas Risby, a wealthy Suffolk clothier.[330]   He was born about 1578,[331] and was admitted to Gray's Inn, 1 November 1594.[332] In or before 1599 he married Elizabeth, daughter of Ralph Coppinger of Stoke, Kent, who brought to him lands and a dowry of £1000.[333]   Grimston was knighted at the Tower, 14 March 1604, succeeded his father in 1610, and the next year was created a baronet.

Now the head of his family, Sir Harbottle entered soon upon public service.   He was returned to the 1614 parliament for Harwich, but served as sheriff of Essex, 1614–1615.[334]   He became a J.P in his county before the end of James's reign, and afterwards acted also for Maldon and Colchester and on other commissions.[335] By 1621 he had joined forces with the puritan element in his section, and was summoned with Sir Francis Barrington and Masham (*q.v.*) to attend Council for opposing the 1621 loan.   He was warned again to attend in 1625.[336]   He was concerned that year and the next with military affairs and defense problems on the coast,[337] and in 1626 sat for Essex in parliament, having been chosen also for Colchester.[338]   He was named a commissioner for the forced loan that followed, but was himself a defaulter, and was summoned before Council and imprisoned until illness brought him release under bond.[339]   It is small wonder that his election with Barrington as knight of the shire in 1628 was accomplished with the open support of the J.P.'s and the constables, being a veritable triumph over the court.[340]   In 1632 Sir Harbottle incurred the displeasure of the Court of High Commission by a judgment he and others returned regarding a Harwich minister and some religious practices, a judgment which the court regarded as greatly biased.[341]   He does not, however, appear to have de-

---

[320] Both he and his father were referred to as members on 26 August 1641 (*C.J.* 2: 273), and there seems to have been no doubt about his place at the time of his expulsion the next year.

[321] *Linc. Inn Rec. Adm.* 1: 221.

[322] Pink MSS, 302, fol. 454.

[323] Verney, 58.

[324] *Rebellion* 1: 576–577.

[325] *C.J.* 2: 404; Add. MSS, 14,827, fol. 22v.

[326] *H.M.C., Fifth Report,* House of Lords MSS, 28; *C.J.* 2: 613, 626, 712; Harl. MSS, 378, fol. 1.

[327] *C.J.* 2: 804, 816.

[328] *O.P.H.* 9: 15; Pink MSS, 302, fol. 454.

[329] *Cheshire Sheaf,* 3rd Ser., 32: 14–42, 1937.   See also Williams, *Parl. Hist. Wales,* 60.

[330] Grimston is mentioned briefly in the article on his son (*q.v.*) in *D.N.B.*   For more details, see *Archaeologia* 40: 451–470, 1866; *Complete Baronetage* 1: 106; *Essex Review* 5: 202–203, 1896; Add. MSS, 19,090, fol. 97.

[331] He was aged about thirty-two in August, 1609 (I.P.M., Edward Grimston, C. 142/316/18), but in his seventieth year when he died in February, 1647/8.   M.I., cited in *Essex Review* 39: 122, n., 1930.

[332] *Gray's Inn Adm. Reg.,* 86.

[333] Their first son was born in August, 1600 (Add. MSS, 19,090, fol. 161v).   Lady Grimston's portion was referred to in a lawsuit brought against her and her husband by some stepbrothers.   C. 3/340/29.

[334] *M. of P.* 3: xxxviii; *List of Sheriffs,* 46.   During his shrievalty Grimston was fined 100 *s.* in the Office of Pleas. S.P. 14, 135/41.

[335] C. 193/12, 13; C. 181/3; S.P. 16, 188/92, fol. 235v; H.M.C., *Tenth Report* 4: County of Essex MSS, 502–507; C. 181/4, fols. 1, 72; 181/5, fols. 16, 55, *passim.*

[336] S.P. 14, 127/82; S.P. 16, 522/120.

[337] *C.S.P. Dom., 1625–1626,* 96, 566.

[338] *M. of P.* 1: 469.

[339] S.P. 16, 54/47; *C.S.P. Dom., 1627–1628,* 204.

[340] Birch, *The court and times of Charles the First* 1: 323, 329; *C.S.P. Dom., 1628–1629,* 6.

[341] Their judgment was criticized as insolent and angry. *Ibid., 1631–1633,* 125, 145, 256, 276.

faulted on ship money, for he paid £10 for Bradfield alone on the 1636 writ.[342]

Grimston was elected to the Short Parliament for the county, he and Barrington (q.v.) winning with aid of the Earl of Warwick. As a member for Harwich in the Long Parliament, he worked with the puritan group, but either because of his age or some moderation in his views, or because his son, Harbottle, junior, was present to share his load, was less prominent in House affairs than his earlier career seems to warrant.[343] In June, 1642, he pledged one horse for the defense, and £20 as a gift,[344] and during the war was a committeeman and a Presbyterian elder in Essex. He died in his seventieth year, 19 February 1647/8,[345] and was succeeded by his son, the Colchester M.P. His will, dated 16 August 1641, was proved 6 March 1648.[346]

Grimston's estate was a good one.[347] From his father he had inherited seven manors in Essex and Suffolk, with numerous town properties in both counties,[348] and by his marriage he acquired an interest in some Kentish lands.[349] He increased his Essex holdings by purchase also.[350] He was not a heavy contributor toward the parliamentary cause, however, possibly because much of his estate had been settled before 1640.[351]

* **Harbottle Grimston** (1603–1685), recorder of Colchester, Essex, sat for that town, 1640–1648.[352] He was the second but eldest surviving son of Sir Harbottle Grimston (1578–1648), M.P. for Harwich (q.v.), and studied at Cambridge (Emmanuel) and at Lincoln's Inn. At the latter place he became a friend of Bulstrode Whitelocke (q.v.), who helped bring about Grimston's marriage in 1629 with Mary, daughter of Sir George Croke, the judge.[353] By this time Grimston

had become a barrister and had taken his place for the first time in parliament.[354]

For the next few years Grimston probably lived much of the time in London, where he kept his chambers at his inn.[355] He was among those who were ordered summoned before Star Chamber in February, 1633, for violating the rules about eating flesh on Fridays,[356] but the outcome of the order is not known. For a number of years he was a J.P. and member of local commissions for Middlesex.[357] Following his appointment as recorder at Harwich and Colchester he was named to several local commissions in Essex, also, and seems to have been a J.P. there in 1639.[358] In the year that he became recorder for Colchester, the town, probably counselled by him, paid none of its ship money levy.[359]

A member for Colchester in both parliaments of 1640, Grimston worked for the removal of grievances in church and state.[360] He was an elder in the Presbyterian classis in Essex, 1646–1648.[361] Although his father was living in 1640, Grimston was probably enjoying a part of his inheritance. His estate, considered good at the time of his first marriage,[362] and increased after 1640 by his second marriage (before 1652) and by various purchases,[363] was estimated in 1655 as worth between £3000 and £4000 a year.[364]

Grimston had several relatives among the 1640 parliament men, in addition to his father. Robert Croke was a cousin by marriage and his wife's sister had married Richard Jervoise, who, with his father, Sir Thomas, served for Whitchurch, Hants.[365] His friend, Whitelocke, was also a relative by marriage.

* **John Gurdon** (1595–1679), of Great Wenham, Suffolk, sat for Ipswich, 1640–1653. He had won his seat for the same borough in the spring by defeating a local man by a narrow margin.[366] Gurdon was born on 3 July 1595, and educated at Emmanuel College, Cambridge (matriculated 1611) and Gray's Inn, where he

---

[342] S.P. 16, 358/82.

[343] Pink states (Pink MSS, 302, fol. 462) that he was named to only ten committees between 1640 and December, 1646. Among them were, however, such important ones as those on Vassall's case, on ship money, and on popish recusants. C.J. 2: 43, 45, 113.

[344] N. and Q., 1st Ser., 12: 358, 1855.

[345] Essex Review 28: 16, 1919; V.C.H. Essex 2: 233; Pink MSS cited above.

[346] P.C.C., 50 Essex.

[347] Whitelocke, Memoirs of Bulstrode Whitelocke, 41–42.

[348] I.P.M., Edward Grimston, C. 142/316/18. Several of these were mentioned in Sir Harbottle's will as settled for his wife's jointure. He lived sometimes in Suffolk as well as at Bradfield.

[349] Hasted, Kent 4: 29; C. 3/340/29.

[350] Essex Arch. Soc., Trans., N.S., 13: 141, 1915; Add. MSS, 19,083, fol. 159.

[351] By his will he left £30 for the poor and various small legacies, but his children seem already to have been provided for.

[352] There is no record of the original return (M. of P. 1: 488, 489, n.), but he was named to the Committee of Privileges, 6 November. C.J. 2: 21.

[353] R. H. Whitelocke, Memoirs of Bulstrode Whitelocke, 41–42.

[354] Linc. Inn Rec., Black Books 2: 282; M. of P. 1: 475.

[355] Linc. Inn Rec., Black Books 2: 297, 379. He was probably the "Mr. Grimston" listed in St. Andrew's parish, Middlesex, in 1638 (Dale, Inhabitants of London, 1638, 192), but seems to have resided later in St. Bartholomew by the Exchange (Archaeologia 45: 81, 1880).

[356] Add. MSS, 11,056, fol. 64v.

[357] C. 193/13; S.P. 16/405; C.S.P. Dom., 1637–1638, 507; C. 181/5, fols. 114, 426.

[358] C. 181/5, fols. 170, 239, 366; C.S.P. Dom., 1639, 57.

[359] Ibid., 1637–1638, 419.

[360] An example is his speech of 7 November 1640. D'Ewes (N), 5–6.

[361] Essex Review 28: 16, 1919.

[362] Whitelocke, loc. cit.

[363] Morant, Essex 2: 229, 261, 262.

[364] Add. MSS, 19,090, fol. 92; 15,520, fol. 81v.

[365] Lipscomb, Bucks 1: 132; Pink MSS, 305, fols. 64, 65; Complete Baronetage 1: 106.

[366] Gurdon was the first non-resident chosen by Ipswich for many years. He defeated Edmund Day, a former member for the town, by a vote of 104-95. Bacon, The annalls of Ipswich, 522; M. of P. 1: 483.

was admitted in 1614.[367] He lived at Great Wenham during the lifetime of his father, Brampton Gurdon (d. 1649), and apparently took little part in Suffolk affairs, although his father was a J.P. and sheriff. He was, however, named to the sewers commission in 1634.[368] He enjoyed an ample estate, including lands in Suffolk and Essex left him by his grandfather,[369] his annual income being estimated in 1655 at £1400.[370] He personally subscribed £600 for reducing Ireland in 1642,[371] and on the eve of the war offered to lend £100 freely for the defense.[372] He served as a Presbyterian elder, but is usually considered an Independent.[373]

Gurdon was a brother-in-law of his colleague, Sir Philip Parker.

Sir Edward Hales, Bart. (1576–1654), of Woodchurch and Tunstall, Kent, was M.P. for Queenborough, 1640–18 April 1648, but was not active in the House after the early weeks of 1643.[1] His family was one of the most prominent in Kent, his ancestors having held in Tudor times several important offices at court.[2] Edward was the son and heir of William Hales of Tenterden by Elizabeth, daughter of Paul Johnson of Fordwich, and was born in 1576. In May, 1602, he married Deborah, only child of Martin Harlakenden of Woodchurch, receiving with her a considerable estate, and taking up residence thereafter at Woodchurch.[3] He was knighted in 1603 and created a baronet in 1611. Hales married a second time in 1616, his new wife being Martha, wealthy widow of Sir James Cromer of Tunstall and daughter of Sir Matthew Carew. His new father-in-law was pleased at his daughter's match with "a fine and learned gentleman, of an exceeding good carriage," with an income of £4000 a year.[4] The marriage of Hales's eldest son by his first wife with Lady Cromer's daughter insured the passing of Tunstall with other Carew and Cromer lands to his family.[5]

Hales's public career was long, and included many activities in his county and in parliament. As early as 1600 he was named as a deputy for the Lords of Romney Marsh,[6] and he was sheriff, 1608–1609. In 1621 he was a captain of the Kentish trained bands and was

soon afterwards a D.L.[7] As such he was concerned with the billeting of soldiers, as well as with the 1627 loan,[8] and he was still listed as a D.L. in 1639.[9] The local commissions to which he was named were numerous, ranging from those for oyer and terminer to that for knighthood compositions,[10] and he was a J.P. for Kent and for Rochester from late in the reign of James until the Long Parliament.[11] He sat for Hastings in parliament, 1605–1611 and 1614. He served for Queenborough in 1625, and for the county in 1626, winning against a candidate backed by Buckingham, and for Queenborough again in the Short Parliament.[12] In his earlier years in politics Hales probably leaned toward the opposition group, for he was one of sixty Kentish gentlemen summoned before Council regarding the 1621 loan,[13] but he seems to have served the king faithfully in later years and in the spring of 1640, having been summoned to Council with other rich gentlemen regarding a loan, was said to have lent £2000.[14] He may have had some controversy with Archbishop Laud, since he was one of the leading landowners complained of in 1636 by the ministers of Romney Marsh for their tactics in forcing the ministers to accept a low money payment per acre in lieu of the tithes of wool and pasturage.[15] And his support of Dering in the 1640 elections may have resulted not only from neighborliness but from views held in common.[16] Hales's personal experiences with the Court of Wards in 1638 and 1640, in the latter year regarding his own grandson,[17] may account in a measure for his manifest desire in the Long Parliament for the reform of that court.

In the Commons of 1640 Hales was an active member at the outset, working for the liberty of the subject and serving, by September, 1642, on eighteen committees. They included those on privileges, the Court of Wards, pluralities, and the recess.[18] He promised his security for £1000 for the loans in 1640 and 1641,[19] and on 23 July 1641 joined four others in offering £2000 for the cause.[20] He was named to several parliamentary com-

---

[367] *Winthrop Papers* 1: 64, 1929–1944; *Al. Cant.* Only an approximate date of his birth appears in *D.N.B.*

[368] C. 181/4, fol. 173v; C. 193/12; Suckling, *The history and antiquities of the county of Suffolk* 1: xliii.

[369] Muskett, *Suffolk manorial families* 1: 282; will of Brampton Gurdon, 1647, P.C.C., 68 Pembroke.

[370] Add. MSS, 19,077 (Davy collection), fol. 70.

[371] *C.S.P. Ireland, Adventurers*, 173.

[372] *N. and Q.*, 1st Ser., 12: 360, 1855.

[373] *A.H.R.* 44: 31, n., 1938–1939.

[1] *M. of P.* 1: 490; *C.J.* 5: 556; Pink MSS, 303, fol. 15.

[2] *Arch. Cant.* 5: 27–28, 1863; *Vis. Kent, 1619*, 59.

[3] *Arch. Cant.* 14: 64, 359, 1882.

[4] *C.S.P. Dom., 1611–1618*, 412, 416–417.

[5] Hasted, *Kent* 6: 88–90; *Arch. Cant.* 14: 65, 1882.

[6] Add. MSS, 24,798, fol. 192.

[7] *H.M.C., MSS of A. G. Finch* 1: 43; *C.S.P. Dom., 1619–1623*, 614.

[8] Egerton MSS, 2087, fols. 22, 35, 38, 39, 43; *C.S.P. Dom., 1627–1628*, 275.

[9] S.P. 16, 409/7; 417/112.

[10] C. 181/3; 181/4, fol. 18v, *passim*; 181/5, fol. 16, *passim*; S.P. 16, 173/30/55; 180/25/95; Stowe MSS, 743, fols. 85–86.

[11] C. 193/12, 13; S.P. 16/405; *C.S.P. Dom., 1635*, 459.

[12] *M. of P.* 1: 447, 464, 469, 481; 3: App., xli; *Arch. Cant.* 22: 183, 1897; *C.S.P. Dom., 1625–1626*, 217, 221.

[13] S.P. 14, 127/82.

[14] Add. MSS, 11,045, fol. 116.

[15] *C.S.P. Dom., 1635–1636*, 195.

[16] Larking, *Proceedings in Kent*, 18.

[17] *C.S.P. Dom., 1637–1638*, 598; *1640–1641*, 214, 224; *Arch. Cant.* 14: 82, 1882.

[18] Pink MSS, 303, fol. 16; *C.J.* 2: 21, 87, 101, 288.

[19] D'Ewes (N), 52, n., 438, n.

[20] *C.J.* 2: 222. It is not clear whether this was £2000 each or jointly.

mittees in his county when the war began,[21] but by February, 1643, had incurred distrust on account of absences. He was summoned on February 15 to attend, and in June was sent to the Tower for a suspected part in the Kentish uprising. He recovered his estate by paying a £6000 fine, but seems to have remained a prisoner of the House until 18 April 1648. A new election was not ordered, however, until 10 May 1648.[22] Shortly afterwards his name was involved in the royalist plot in Kent, in which his grandson and heir, Edward, was a leader, but he disavowed any connection with the scheme and threatened, according to Clarendon, to disown his heir.[23] He died in September or October, 1654, aged seventy-eight, and was buried at Tunstall.

Sir Edward was undoubtedly one of the wealthy parliament men of 1640. His lands lay in many parts of Kent,[24] and Clarendon referred to him as having the "greatest fortune of that country." [25] He seems about 1634 to have been interested to the extent of £8000 in some financial venture in which Lord Wentworth was interested,[26] but the nature of it is unknown. When Hales made his will in 1651, most of his estate had been settled, but he left bequests amounting to over £1770. His will directed that his funeral be simple, without pomp or vanity, and that his grandchildren be reared "in the fear of God and good literature." [27]

Nathaniel Hallowes (1582?–1661), alderman of Derby, was M.P. for Derby borough, 1640–1653.[28] He seems to have been the son of Thomas Hallowes who was baptized at St. Werburgh's, Derby, 25 November 1582, but has sometimes been identified as the son of Samuel Hallowes of Dronefield.[29] Possibly he was the "Mr. Hallowes of Norton" who was reported by the heralds in 1611 as having without warrant assumed the title of gentleman,[30] but his career was identified closely with the town of Derby, where he was one of the two major bailiffs in 1622 and in 1630, and where he was an alderman by the time of his first elec-

tion to parliament in April, 1640.[31] He was married in or before 1621, and his wife, Eleanor, survived him.[32]

Hallowes spoke seldom in the early period of the Long Parliament, and was named on few committees except those dealing with his county before 1644. During the war he supported parliament, was active on numerous local committees, and was among the members granted a weekly allowance in 1645, as well some royalists' lands.[33] He was Mayor of Derby, 1657–1658, returned with the Rump in 1659, and was buried 12 March 1660/1 at All Saints' in Derby.[34]

Although Hallowes does not appear to have been wealthy, he was purchasing properties in and near Derby in 1636 and 1638,[35] and in 1642 pledged £50 for the defense, in addition to advancing personally £300 of the £1400 he subscribed for himself and others for reducing Ireland.[36]

* **John Hampden** (1594–1643), of Great Hampden, "the patriot," elected for both Wendover and Buckinghamshire, decided to serve for the county.[37] He had been a member of each consecutive parliament after his first in 1621. Wendover, whose representation he had helped to restore, was virtually a pocket borough of the Hampdens.[38] His resistance to policies of the Stuarts dates back to 1621, for he was among the men of his county warned in 1622 to attend Council regarding the 1621 loan. He apparently yielded that time, promising £30,[39] but his resistance was repeated in 1625 and 1627, the prelude to his stand on ship money.

By 1640 Hampden had a national reputation as a puritan leader and foe of ship money. He had long been known in his county as a gentleman of an old and wealthy family, one who served on the commission of the peace and of sewers, who was fond of country amusements and was also a lover of books and of learning.[40] The estates that came to him from his family and by

---

[21] *Arch. Cant.* 2: 181, 1859; 9: 32, n., 1874.

[22] *C.J.* 2: 968; 3: 258; 5: 536, 556; Pink MSS, *loc. cit.*

[23] *Arch. Cant.* 14: 68–71, 1882; Clarendon, *Rebellion* 4: 333, 342–343.

[24] *Arch. Cant.* 14: 58, 1882; 31: 257, 1915; Hasted, *Kent* 4: 7, 257; 5: 360, 370, *passim.*

[25] *Rebellion* 4: 333.

[26] *Strafford letters* 1: 293.

[27] *Arch. Cant.* 14: 77–84, 1882. In addition to the references cited above, see also *Complete Baronetage* 1: 76.

[28] The November election was declared void in March, 1641, but Hallowes was re-elected in April.

[29] Pink MSS, 307, ff. 331–332, and notes by Pink in *Notts and Derbyshire Notes and Queries* 1: 33, 1892–1893; 3: 141–142, 1895 (hereafter, *Notts and Derbys. N. and Q.*). The member's second son, Samuel, known as of Norton, was aged eighteen in 1653. *Ibid.;* G. F. Russell Barker and Alan H. Stenning, *The record of old Westminsters* 1: 415, London, Chiswick Press, 1928.

[30] Add. MSS, 6669, fol. 122.

[31] Glover, *Derbyshire* 1: App., 30; Hutton, *Derby*, 83; *M. of P.* 1: 481.

[32] Nathaniel, said to be the son of Nathaniel Hallowes, the M.P., was baptized at St. Werburgh's, 13 November 1621. *Notts and Derbys. N. and Q.* 1: 33, 1892–1893.

[33] Pink MSS, 307, fol. 331; Glover, *Derbyshire* 1: App., 75; *Cal. Com. Comp.*, 1732, 1735, 2301.

[34] Glover, *op. cit.* 1: App., 30; Thomason Tracts, 669. f. 24, p. 37; notes supplied by Mr. F. Williamson, Director of The Derby Museum and Art Gallery.

[35] Add. MSS, 6672, fols. 277v, 279v. The estate of Mugginton with which he was identified in his later years seems to have been a wartime acquisition. *Derbys. Arch. Jour.* 35: 177, 1913; *Cal. Com. Comp.*, 1735.

[36] *N. and Q.*, 1st Ser., 12: 360, 1855; *C.S.P. Ireland, Adventurers*, 144, 148.

[37] *C.J.* 2: 47.

[38] *M. of P.* 1: 450, 462, *passim; Recs. Bucks.* 10: 123, 1910–1916.

[39] S.P. 14, 127/82.

[40] *V.C.H. Buckingham* 2: 288; C. 193/12, 13; C. 181/3, fol. 116v; S.P. 16, 191/76; Lord Nugent, *Memorials of John Hampden* 1: 148, 2nd ed., London 1832.

his marriage with an Oxfordshire heiress had made him one of the richest gentlemen in England, according to Clarendon, with an income of more than £1500 a year.[41] His pledges of 1640–1642 are indicative of his financial standing. He offered his bond for £1000 for the loan in November, 1640, joined with his intimate friend, Arthur Goodwin, in pledging a loan of £1000 a few months later, and in June, 1642, subscribed for the defense £200 in plate and three horses, with maintenance.[42] The £1000 sum he subscribed for reducing Ireland that year was chiefly for other "adventurers."[43]

Hampden was related to many of his fellow parliament men of 1640, including, besides those of the Cromwell connection, his cousin, Waller, his son-in-law, Knightley, his second wife's father and brother of the house of Knollys, and his daughter's father-in-law, Sir Robert Pye.

Richard Harding (*c.* 1593–1657?), courtier, of Pewsey, Wiltshire, was a member for Great Bedwin, Wilts, 1640–1644. He came of a family of seemingly good connection but modest estate, being probably the third son of John Harding of Salisbury and of Pewsey, Esquire (d. 1609), and his wife, Honor.[44] He matriculated at St. Edmund Hall, Oxford, in 1609, aged sixteen, and perhaps entered Lincoln's Inn two years later.[45] Except for his work in 1619 and 1632 as a trustee in connection with the marriage settlement of his brother, Thomas, who lived in Salisbury,[46] Harding's name disappears from Wiltshire annals for nearly three decades. It seems probable that he became a protégé of the Seymour family, earls of Hertford, whose tenant and neighbor his father had been, and that under their guidance he established his court connections. One Richard Harding was a resident of St. Margaret's parish in Westminster, 1617–1624.[47] He was among those associates of the court who were either with the army in the north or were supplying horses in the summer of 1639.[48] And in July, 1641, after he had been chosen to parliament, he was appointed through the influence of the prince's governor, the Marquis of Hertford, as a groom of the bedchamber of the prince. At that time he was described by Edward Nicholas as the Richard Harding, who married Mrs. Clare, an acquaintance of the last Lord Warden [49] (i.e., Theophilus Howard, Earl of Suffolk).

Richard Harding was named for the Short Parliament by Great Bedwin, having been elected after a contest there, and was returned again in the autumn. He is not known to have had any personal connection with the borough. The Seymours' power which had been evident in the naming of one of their family as his colleague for the Short Parliament probably accounts for his election.[50] And Harding seems to have followed their lead in politics. He voted against the attainder of Strafford,[51] and though he was named to two committees, and took the Protestation of May, 1641,[52] he was never an active member of the House. He was in York in March, 1642,[53] joined the king and the prince at Oxford, and was disabled for his desertion of parliament, 5 February 1644.[54] In August of that year the king chose Harding to carry a message to Essex, since he was "a gentleman who had been before of much conversation with the earl and much loved by him."[55] He followed his royal master into exile [56] and probably died abroad about 1657. His will, written at Bruges, with a codicil of 10 November 1657, was proved by his only child, Honora Harding, on 6 June 1662. She had been commended by her father's wish to the guardianship of Sir Edward Hyde.[57]

Harding was probably not a man of wealth. He had inherited a Wiltshire farm, out of which were charged by his father's will annuities of £80 a year that by 1640 may have reverted to him. He was assessed £1000 by parliament in 1644, however.[58] His property at Westminster was still under sequestration in 1648,[59] and he seems to have made no attempt to compound. His possessions at the time he made his will were chiefly clothing, some jewels and some books. His wife had already been buried at Pewsey when he wrote his

[41] *Rebellion* 3: 59–60. Among his several Buckinghamshire manors, that of Dunton, by no means the principal one, was reported in a 1620 survey as worth £270–£300 a year (Bodleian Willis MSS, 30, fols. 12v, 14v, 16). The names of four or five other manors he owned in Buckinghamshire appear in *V.C.H. Buckingham* 2: 288–289, 360; Lysons, *Mag. Brit.* 1: 570–571, *passim.*

[42] D'Ewes (N), 52; *C.J.* 2: 222; *N. and Q.,* 1st Ser., 12: 338, 1855.

[43] *C.S.P. Ireland, Adventurers,* 46.

[44] Will of John Harding (1609), P.C.C., 55 Dorset; I.P.M. (1609), C. 142/310/7; Pink MSS, 303, fol. 92.

[45] *Al. Oxon.; Linc. Inn Rec. Adm.* 1: 156. He was listed at the Inn in 1611 as the son of John Harding of Salisbury, gent.

[46] Wilts. Arch. Soc. MSS, J. W. Taylor's notes on the Broncker Family, 2, 1632; Marshall, *Vis. Wilts,* 50.

[47] St. Margaret's Overseers Accounts, **151.**

[48] S.P. 16, 427/38/v.

[49] *C.S.P. Dom., 1641–1643, 63.*

[50] *M. of P.* 1: 484, 495; *Wilts. Arch. Mag.* 6: 299–300, 1860; *C.J.* 2: 15. Sir Francis Seymour, brother of the second earl, was buried in Great Bedwin church. *D.N.B.*

[51] Verney, 59.

[52] *C.J.* 2: 103, 133, 253. One committee was that on the court of the Welsh Marches.

[53] *Calendar of Clarendon State Papers* 1: 226.

[54] *C.J.* 2: 626; 3: 389.

[55] Clarendon, *Rebellion* 3: 395; H.M.C., *Sixth Report,* House of Lords MSS, 21.

[56] *The Nicholas Papers* 1: 126 and n., 208, 237, 261; 2: 93, Camden Society, 1886 and 1892.

[57] P.C.C., 84 Laud. This will, in which he described himself as Richard Harding of Pewsey, Wiltshire, and referred frequently to his intimacy with members of the royal family and the court circle, provides the most certain identification of Harding with the son of John and Honora Harding of Pewsey as mentioned in the documents in note 44.

[58] *Cal. Com. Adv. Money,* 435.

[59] *Cal. Com. Comp.,* 92.

will, but he was willing to die in exile, confirmed in his devotion to the cause of Anglicanism and the crown.

* Sir Robert Harley, K.B. (1579–1656), of Brampton Castle, Herefordshire, M.P. for his county, 1640–1648, was a well-known puritan gentleman and Master of the Mint (1626–1635, 1643–1649). Educated at Oxford and the Middle Temple, allied by his marriages with the families of Corbet, Newport, Herbert, and Conway, Harley was in public life from the time he held his first royal office and was elected to his first parliament in 1604. He served in five parliaments before November, 1640,[60] was long a J.P. for both the city and the county of Hereford,[61] and a member of other local commissions for various border counties and Wales.[62] Before 1640 he had held offices in the forests and the mint, and was a member of the Council of the Marches of Wales. In his county he had served also as a captain of the trained bands and D.L.[63] He seems to have avoided a shrievalty, although he was listed among the possibilities for nomination as sheriff in 1625.[64] His interest in the enterprises of his day is evident from his purchase of a share of stock in the Virginia Company in 1623.[65] And Harley's leaning toward Presbyterianism had gained him some notoriety before the days of the Long Parliament. In 1638 he was under accusation, presumably by High Commission, for countenancing a non-conforming rector and schoolmaster.[66]

Harley was a man of means as well as of influence. His offer in the Long Parliament of security of £1000 for the November loan [67] and his pledge of two horses for the defense in 1642 [68] were preliminaries to larger contributions for the cause of parliament.[69] He was somewhat financially embarrassed about 1616, when he was considering the sale of land worth £400 a year to satisfy his creditors; [70] but in 1623, when he married Brilliana Conway, he had £400 a year in possession, was practically free of debt, and soon afterwards received the remainder of his father's estates.[71] He was not satisfied about 1628 with the additional £500 a year he was receiving as Master of the Mint,[72] but he was hardly to be considered as greatly in debt and very poor [73] at the time he entered the Long Parliament.

A contemporary observer noted that in 1645 his estate was worth £1500 a year.[74]

Harley had various relatives in the 1640 House of Commons. Among the royalists were his second wife's cousin, Sir Henry Herbert, and her nephew, Francis Newport, and a "cousin," Sampson Eure. His mother's relatives included Sir Henry Wallop and other parliamentarians.[75]

Richard Harman (d. 1646), hosier and alderman of Norwich, served for his city, 1640–1646. He was probably the son of Edward Harman of Norwich,[76] and the Richard Harman who was admitted a freeman of the city in 1613 after serving an apprenticeship to Robert Garsett, merchant and alderman. As a master hosier his name appears in the records of admission of his own apprentices as freemen, 1625–1639,[77] and he was among the hosiers able to keep their full number of workers employed during the hard winter of 1630–1631.[78] Some time before 1618 he married Cicely, daughter of Richard Skottow, a Norwich alderman, and lived with her in St. Andrew's parish until her death in 1636.[79] In 1637 he married Mary, daughter of Edward Everard and widow of another hosier of the city, Nathaniel Remington.[80]

Harman became a member of the Norwich council in 1619, was sheriff, 1626–1627, and was chosen an alderman in April, 1631.[81] He was sent to London in 1634 with others of the town on "the business of the ship," and in 1636 was the chief collector of ship money in Norwich. During his mayoralty, 1639–1640, Harman met with men from other Norfolk towns to arrange their shares of ship money costs,[82] and he was

[60] Harley's service for Herefordshire in 1626 and for Evesham in 1628 is omitted in *D.N.B.* See *M. of P.* 1: 469, 479.

[61] C. 193/12, 13; S.P. 16/405.

[62] C. 181/3, 4, and 5, *passim.*

[63] Add. MSS, 11,050, fols. 102, 103, 103v; S.P. 16, 408/73.

[64] S.P. 16, 9/43.

[65] Kingsbury, *Records of the Virginia Company* 3: 66.

[66] *C.S.P. Dom.,* 1637–1638, 249.

[67] D'Ewes (N), 52.

[68] *N. and Q.,* 1st Ser., 12: 359, 1855.

[69] He later declared that he suffered losses to the amount of £20,000. Shrops. Arch. Soc., *Trans.,* 3rd Ser., 8: 292, 1908.

[70] *Montgomeryshire Collections* 20: 88, 1886.

[71] *C.S.P. Dom.,* 1619–1623, 587, 608, 622; S.P. 14, 146/82.

[72] *C.S.P. Dom.,* 1625–1626, 577; 1628–1629, 11.

[73] Bankes, *The story of Corfe Castle,* 232.

[74] Symonds, *Diary* (Camden Society), 195.

[75] In addition to the authorities cited above, see Williams, *Parl. Hist. Wales,* 178–179.

[76] *East Anglian Pedigrees,* ed. by Arthur Campling, Norfolk Record Society, 13: 98, 1940. He was not the son of Edmund Harman, worsted weaver, who became a freeman in 1623, for that Richard Harman was a skinner by trade (P. Millican, *The register of the freemen of Norwich, 1548–1773,* 121, 227, Norwich, Jarrold, 1934; *Eastern Counties Collectanea,* 214, 1872–1873), although he has been so identified by B. Cozens-Hardy and E. A. Kent in their *Mayors of Norwich, 1403–1835,* 80, Norwich, Jarrold, 1938. The alderman Richard Harman, afterwards the M.P., was a hosier. Millican, *The register of the freemen of Norwich,* 87.

[77] *Ibid.,* 86–87, 104.

[78] W. L. Sachse, ed., *Minutes of the Norwich court of mayoralty, 1630–1631,* Norfolk Record Society, 15: 132, 1942.

[79] *East Anglian pedigrees,* 98. Several of their children were baptized in that parish, according to the St. Andrew's parish registers, which I was permitted to see.

[80] *East Anglian pedigrees,* 98; Millican, *The register of the freemen of Norwich,* 86–87; Add. MSS, 22,619, fol. 136.

[81] Norwich Corp. MSS, Folio Assembly Book, 1613–1642, fols. 90, 102v, 216v, 261; *Minutes of the Norwich court of mayoralty, 1630–1631,* 149.

[82] Norwich Corp. MSS, Folio Assembly Book, 1613–1642, fols. 301, 341–350; Mayor's Court Book, 1634–1646, fol. 95; Yarmouth Corp. MSS, Assembly Book 6, fol. 452.

named in July, 1640, to the Norwich commission of oyer and terminer.[83]

The Long Parliament was Harman's first,[84] and he was never conspicuous in the House, but by the time war came, was named to several committees there as well as for his county. He joined with Moundeford in pledging £600 for reducing Ireland in the spring of 1642, and in June promised to supply a horse for the defense.[85] He was an active worker for his city's interests and for puritanism and parliament from 1643 to 1645,[86] but died the next year. He was buried at St. Andrew's, Norwich, 2 December 1646.[87]

Harman was a wealthy man at the time of his death, and probably at the time of his election to parliament. His will referred to properties in several places outside of Norwich and to some handsome furnishings in his residence in St. Peter Hungate parish, and directed the payment of £1000 each to five of his children.[88] His eldest son, Richard, afterwards known as of Woodalling, went to Cambridge and Gray's Inn, and married a daughter of Sir Charles Le Groos (q.v.).[89]

John Harris (c. 1586–1657), of Hayne, Devon, not far from the Cornish border, and of Kenegie, Cornwall, sat for Launceston, Cornwall, from 1641, after Coryton's election was voided (18 August 1641), until 1648.[90] He was a great-grandson of John Harris, an eminent lawyer of the mid-sixteenth century, and was connected with the Grevilles of Warwickshire through his paternal grandmother. He was the eldest son and heir of Arthur Harris of Hayne and Kenegie (d. 1628), who was a magistrate in Devon, sheriff in Cornwall and captain for the king at St. Michael's Mount, near which his Kenegie seat was located. His mother was Margaret, daughter and sole heiress of John Davilles of Devon. Harris was born about 1586.[91] He may have been a student at Lincoln's Inn in 1607.[92] He married (1) Florence, daughter of Sir John Windham of Somerset, and (2) in 1631 Cordelia, daughter of John Baron Mohun.[93] By his second marriage he became a brother-in-law of James Campbell (q.v.).

Harris sat in the 1621 parliament for Launceston, a town not far from Hayne.[94] He was a member of various local commissions for Devon and Cornwall, 1624–1629,[95] but was anxious to be relieved in 1628 of the responsibilities of the fort at the Mount which had fallen into his charge upon his father's death that year.[96] Although both of his marriages allied him with royalist families, and his kinsman, the Harris who sat for Liskeard in 1640, supported the king, Harris of Hayne was a puritan and a parliamentarian. With William Strode he was victorious in a contested election at Beeralston in the spring of 1640,[97] and he signed the Devonshire petition against Coryton and the Stannaries that year.[98] As a free burgess of Launceston [99] he may have helped to elect Coryton to the Long Parliament, but when the latter was expelled on account of his conduct elsewhere, Harris quickly succeeded him. He never became prominent in the parliament, but he pledged £50 for the defense in 1642,[100] and remained a member until the purge of 1648.[101] He died on 6 March 1657 and was buried the following day at Lifton.[102] His will, dated 5 February 1657, was proved by his widow, 16 June 1657.[103]

Harris inherited at his father's death five manors in Devon and Cornwall and other properties in those counties and in Somerset, and some buildings in London.[104] His estate was said to be worth £1000 a year at the time of the war,[105] and when he died his lands included seven manors.[106]

John Harris (c. 1597–1648), of Radford, near Plymouth, was M.P. for Liskeard, Cornwall, 1640–22 January 1644. He was a kinsman of the member of the same name who sat for Launceston, though their lines had branched apart some generations back. The Liskeard member's family lived before 1625 principally in the neighborhood of Liskeard and had interests in the borough, but they also had connections at court early in the reign of King James.[107] John Harris, the

---

[83] C. 181/5, fol. 364.

[84] He has been confused, however, by Pink (Pink MSS, 303, fol. 117) and H. LeStrange (Norfolk official lists, 252, Norwich, 1890) with the Nicholas Harman who sat for Castle Rising in the Short Parliament. Willis, **3**: 234.

[85] Pink MSS, 303, fol. 117; C.S.P. Ireland, Adventurers, 314; N. and Q., 1st Ser., **12**: 360, 1855.

[86] Add. MSS, 22,619, fols. 23, 31, 161, 181; 22,620, fol. 22.

[87] St. Andrew's parish register.

[88] His will was dated 20 September 1646 and signed 17 November. P.C.C., 49 Fines.

[89] Al. Cant.; East Anglian pedigrees, 98.

[90] M. of P. **1**, 486; C.J. **2**: 29, 261–262.

[91] Burke, Landed Gentry **1**: 540, 1851; Vivian, Vis. Cornwall, 206–207; Courtney, Parl. Rep. Corn., 363.

[92] A John Harris of Devon, gentleman, was admitted on 10 February 1607. Linc. Inn Rec. Adm. **1**: 145.

[93] Vivian, loc. cit.; Complete Baronetage **4**: 58.

[94] M. of P. **1**: 450.

[95] C. 181/3, fols. 113v, 130v; 181/4, fol. 3; Acts. P.C., 1612–1623, 437.

[96] Secretary Conway, "a near kinsman" of Harris, arranged for his relief. C.S.P. Dom., 1628–1629, 218, 220.

[97] M. of P. **1**: 481 and n.; Devon Trans. **41**: 158, 1909; C.J. **2**: 14.

[98] The Buller Papers, 137.

[99] Launceston Borough MSS, Mayors' Court Books, 1639–1641.

[100] N. and Q., 1st Ser., **12**: 359, 1855.

[101] O.P.H. **9**: *18.

[102] Pink MSS, 307, fol. 210.

[103] P.C.C. 235 Ruthen.

[104] I.P.M., Arthur Harris, 1628, C. 142/440/85.

[105] Richard Symonds, Diary (Camden Society, 1859), 44.

[106] Harris's will.

[107] A Liskeard burgess brought suit in Star Chamber (1611 and 1613) against John Harris, senior, for his alleged attempt to secure all the milling business from the town. St. Ch. 8/181/6; 166/10.

M.P., was the second son of John Harris of Lanrest, Cornwall (d. 1623), by his wife, Joan, daughter and heiress of Robert Hart of Plimston in Stoke Climsland, Cornwall. When his elder brother died without issue in November, 1623, John inherited the Lanrest estate. Early in 1625, then aged about twenty-eight, he inherited the Radford property through the death of his father's uncle, Sir Christopher Harris. His father had been a J.P., D.L., and M.P., and his elder brother, who married a sister of Sir Bevil Grenville (q.v.), was M.P. in 1621.[108] As John Harris of Radford, the new head of the house was reported for not sending his horses to the Devonshire musters in 1629.[109] He was named with Thomas Wise, Sir Nicholas Slanning, and others who lived in or near Plymouth as commissioners for the repair and maintenance of Catwater in 1635.[110] And in 1637 Harris was one of the commissioners for piracy in Cornwall.[111] He married about 1630 Elizabeth Johnson (born Champernowne), who died in 1637;[112] and in 1641 he married Mary, daughter of Arthur Chichester, a few months after the death of her first husband, Harris's neighbor and colleague in the Long Parliament, Thomas Wise.[113]

Harris sat for Liskeard in the parliament of 1628 and in both that were called in 1640.[114] He was never active in the Commons, and after the war began was absent frequently. He was eventually disabled, 22 January 1644.[115] He garrisoned his house for the king,[116] and died in the spring of 1648. He was ill when he wrote his will on 24 March, and had died before 24 April.[117]

In addition to his father's holdings in Liskeard parish, Harris inherited the properties of his great-uncle, Sir Christopher Harris, which included three manors in Devon, parts of two in Cornwall, and numerous properties in towns of both counties.[118] His will mentioned briefly his personal estates, the lands having been previously settled. Harris was assessed £600 by parliament in 1646, a reduction from the original demand for £1000.[119]

John Harrison (c. 1589–1669), of Balls Park, Hertfordshire, and Aldcliffe Hall, Lancashire, a customs farmer, was M.P. for Lancaster borough, 1640–4 September 1643. The twelfth son of William Harrison of Aldcliffe Hall by Margaret, daughter of Christopher Gardiner of Urswick, he was born at Beamond about 1589. When he was about twenty-two he was sent to London, first to Lord Treasurer Salisbury and then to John (later Sir John) Wolstenholme, under whose supervision he was launched upon his career as a customs official.[120] He married in 1616 Margaret, daughter of Robert Fanshawe of Fanshawe Gate, a kinswoman of the Fanshawes of the Exchequer and a member at that time in the Wolstenholme household,[121] and thereafter took up residence nearby in the parish of St. Olave, Hart Street.[122]

During the next quarter century Harrison was important in the affairs of trade and royal finance. He was interested in the Virginia Company and the East India Company, and was possibly treasurer of the fisheries company in 1637.[123] One of the farmers of the customs by the beginning of Charles's reign, Harrison became interested in ways of improving the revenue system, and for some years advocated, for the sake of efficiency, the creation of a customs commission to replace the farmers. But his plans were not approved by such patronage dispensers as Buckingham, Lord Treasurer Weston, and their successors, and eventually, perceiving the hopelessness of his efforts, and having amassed an ample fortune for himself, Harrison retired a few years before 1640 from the Customs House to live in his splendid new mansion at Balls in Hertfordshire.[124] To the king's request for a loan for his expenses in the north in 1639 Harrison made no reply,[125] but in the summer of 1640, upon the urgent pleas from the king and Lord Cottington, Harrison joined with the other "old farmers" in a new contract whereby they were to advance on account, from their personal and joint bonds, some £250,000 for the Scottish war. To relieve further the distressed treasury, especially in view of the rising sentiment against ship money, Harrison next proposed the sale of most of the royal forests and parks, but before the officials had considered his plan parliament had become the leading authority on revenue.[126]

Harrison was elected to the Short Parliament for Queenborough and Lancaster, but preferred the latter, and in the autumn secured that place for himself and the Queenborough seat for his son William (q.v.). He

[108] Vivian, *Vis. Cornwall*, 209; *Vis. Devon, 1620*, 140; Gilbert, *Hist. Survey of Cornwall* 2: 135–137.

[109] S.P. 16, 150/76/iii.

[110] *Devon and Cornwall N. and Q.* 12 (i) : 239, 1922–1923.

[111] C. 181/5, fol. 166.

[112] Vivian, *loc. cit.* The marriage occurred in the sixth year of Charles's reign, according to their son's compounding papers. *Cal. Com. Comp.*, 2893.

[113] *Cal. Com. Comp.*, 2894. Several authorities (e.g., Vivian, Devon *Trans.* 41: 137, 138, 1909) have confused the marriages of Harris and his son. The latter's wife was Mary Rashleigh.

[114] *M. of P.* 1: 474, 486; Willis, 3: 230.

[115] *C.J.* 3: 374.

[116] Courtney, *Parl. Rep. Corn.*, 253.

[117] P.C.C., 175 Fairfax; *Cal. Com. Comp.*, 117, 2893.

[118] I.P.M., Sir Christopher Harris, C. 142/688/38.

[119] *Cal. Com. Adv. Money*, 718.

[120] *Vis. London* (Harl. Soc., **15**) 1: 354, 1880; *Memoirs of Ann Lady Fanshawe*, 21.

[121] *Marriage licenses, London* (Harl. Soc., **26**) 2: 43, 1887.

[122] *The registers of St. Olave, Hart Street, London*, ed. by W. Bruce Bannerman, Harleian Society, Register Series **46**: 31, 32, *passim*, 1916.

[123] Brown, *Genesis of the U. S.*, 913–914; *C.S.P., Colonial, East Indies, 1574–1660*, 186, 492; *C.S.P. Dom., 1636–1637*, 489.

[124] Harrison's own account of his plan is found in Brit. Mus. Stowe MSS, 326, fols. 33–52, 89.

[125] Rushworth 3: 913.

[126] Stowe MSS, 326, fols. 71–73, 77, 89–90.

withdrew from the House temporarily during the investigation of monopolies, with some of which he was connected,[127] but he was too valuable a member to be unseated so early. The Commons was seeking £50,000 to be borrowed in advance of a subsidy and secured by the bonds of fifty members, and in Harrison's absence persuaded his son William to offer in Harrison's name to procure that sum. Surprised by his son's action, Harrison consulted with Lord Cottington before consenting to undertake the task, but was rewarded by being summoned to return to his seat in the House on 25 November and soon afterwards by being knighted at Whitehall.[128] Thereafter he was named to various committees of parliament, including one on Virginia and one on pluralities, as well as that on army pay, and when on 1 June 1641 the House voted its condemnation of the customs farmers, it was specifically without prejudice to his seat in the Commons.[129] Harrison continued to underwrite the finance measures, pledging his bond for the loan in March, 1641,[130] offering in May to advance £150,000,[131] in April of 1642 subscribing £1200 for the reducing of Ireland,[132] and in June promising to supply four horses for himself and his son for the defense.[133] He was named on some of the early war committees for Hertfordshire, but by midsummer, 1643, had joined the king and was on 4 September 1643 "disabled" from sitting. He was held a prisoner for a time and heavily fined. Recovering somewhat in fortune with the Restoration, Harrison lived until 28 September 1669. He was buried in All Saints, Hertford, 4 October 1669.

A man of great wealth before the war, owning properties in several eastern counties and in Lancashire and having an interest in the alum business as well as in the customs farm, Harrison's yearly income about 1640 was possibly over £10,000.[134] His fine, set first at a moiety, £10,745, was finally discharged in 1648 upon his paying £1,000.[135] Harrison's daughter described

him as "a handsome gentleman, of great natural parts, a great accountant, of vast memory." He was a kinsman by marriage of both of the Fanshawes who sat in the 1640 House, and possibly of other members.[136]

William Harrison (1619–1643), M.P. for Queenborough, Kent, 1640–24 June 1643,[137] was not a Kentish man and seems to have had no connection with the county or the borough prior to his election. He was the second but eldest surviving son of the wealthy customs farmer, John Harrison of London and Hertfordshire (q.v.), who had been elected by Queenborough in the spring, but had sat for another constituency. William's mother was Margaret, daughter of Robert Fanshawe.[138] He was baptized at St. Olave's Hart Street, London, 24 September 1619, matriculated at St. Catherine's, Cambridge, in 1637 (B.A. 1637–1638), and was admitted at Gray's Inn the same year.[139] Entering parliament for the first time in November, 1640, young Harrison's most active part was his promise in his father's name to secure the £50,000 needed for the loan. He spoke once against Laud, and afterwards defended his father when he was accused of being a monopolist.[140] In the spring of 1642 he promised £600 for the reducing of Ireland, but with the start of war he joined the king and was disabled, 24 June 1643.[141] He died at Oxford that year as a result of an injury during a skirmish with the Roundheads, and was buried at Exeter College Chapel. The king is said to have praised Harrison as a "very good and gallant young man." [142]

George Hartnoll (died c. 1662), "gentleman," of Tiverton, Devon, was M.P. for Tiverton from October, 1640, until his disablement sometime between 22 January 1644 and 5 October 1646.[143] A member of a family having several branches in and near Tiverton, and apparently below the rank of gentry at the opening of the century,[144] he was possibly the son of George or

---

[127] D'Ewes (N), 540; C.J. 2: 34.

[128] Stowe MSS, 326, fols. 90v–91; D'Ewes (N), 66–67; C.J. 2: 36.

[129] C.J. 2: 64, 88, 101, 164.

[130] D'Ewes (N), 452, n.

[131] Kingston, Herts. during the Civil War, 122; S. R. Gardiner, The fall of the monarchy of Charles I, 2: 166, London, 1882.

[132] C.S.P. Ireland, Adventurers, 302.

[133] N. and Q., 1st Ser., 12: 358, 1855.

[134] In his own estimate of losses sustained between 1643 and 1649 Harrison valued his lands at over £1800 yearly, and the loss from being deprived of his alum and customs profits at £50,000. He estimated his losses of all sorts at £97,574. Stowe MSS, 184, fols. 161–162. His daughter afterwards estimated his losses at over £130,000, stating "we were as poor as Job" (Memoirs of Ann Lady Fanshawe, 22, 24–25). Harrison's share in the fine laid on the former customs farmers by the act of 1641 was some £10,800. Stowe MSS, 326, fol. 92.

[135] Cal. Com. Comp., 95, 114, 808; The royalist composition papers . . . of Lancaster, ed. by J. H. Stanning (Rec. Soc. Lancs. and Cheshire, 29), 3: 165 and n., 1896.

[136] His daughter said his relatives included the families of "Aston," Sandys, and Curwen. Memoirs of Ann Lady Fanshawe, 21.

Additional references concerning Harrison are: M. of P. 1: 481, 482, 490; Kingston, Herts. during the Civil War, 28, 122–123; Pink MSS, 303, fol. 141.

[137] M. of P. 1: 490; C.J. 3: 143.

[138] Pink MSS, 303, fol. 150.

[139] Al. Cant.; Gray's Inn Adm. Reg., 213.

[140] D'Ewes (N), 66–67, 169, 540.

[141] Pink MSS, 303, fol. 150.

[142] Memoirs of Ann Lady Fanshawe, xviii, 20, 25.

[143] His disablement was respited in 1644, but a new election was ordered, 5 October 1646. C.J. 3: 374; 4: 683.

[144] E. S. Chalk, "Notes on the Members for Tiverton, 1621–1832," Devon Trans. 67: 323, 1935. Various members of his family appear in Exeter Deeds and Documents (Exeter City Library MSS), Nos. 1380, 34,575, 1171, 1172, 1177. An improvement in his social position is indicated by Hartnoll's reference in his will to a son-in-law who was a Mr. Joshua Northcott. P.C.C., 82 Bruce.

John Hartnoll of Tiverton and brother of the James Hartnoll who was rector there, 1631–1635.[145] A Thomas Hartnoll of Tiverton was in the royalist army.[146] George was probably a merchant or tradesman of Tiverton, was married before 1623,[147] and doubtless prospered and participated in borough affairs. He entered the 1640 parliament, however, without earlier experience in the House, and was never an active member. He was summoned as an absentee several times between 16 June 1642 and 9 May 1643,[148] and was allowed a respite on 22 January 1644.[149] No further reference to him appears after 1646. He made his will on 5 June 1662, describing himself then as "George Hartnoll the elder" and aged and infirm. He probably died soon afterwards, and the will was proved by his son on 8 July 1664.[150]

Almost no evidence of Hartnoll's financial standing in 1640 remains, for he seems to have subscribed to none of the loans and contribution lists of that period. But he was probably in comfortable circumstances, for in his will he referred to a temporal estate "farre above my deserts" and enumerated various properties, including a fulling mill and others which he had bought, in Tiverton and nearby. He left legacies of over £340, including one of £50 for charities in Tiverton for honest poor husbandmen.

John Harvey (1582–1645), of London and Westminster, M.P. for Hythe, 1640–1645, was a brother of Dr. William Harvey, the physician, being the second son of Thomas Harvey of Folkstone, a former Kentish yeoman, by his second wife, Joane, daughter of Thomas Halke. He was born at Folkstone, 12 November 1582,[151] and although several of his younger brothers became wealthy London merchants, he seems to have turned, as did their elder brother, to a professional career. He may have acted sometimes as a business agent for his brothers, Daniel and Eliab, grocers,[152] for

early in 1623 his absence beyond seas delayed his assuming the executorship of the estate of another brother, Thomas, also a well-to-do merchant,[153] and with them he had a prolonged accounting with the London Court of Aldermen regarding the management of the estate and the affairs of their nephew, John.[154] His own career lay, however, in the royal administration, in which he was assisted doubtless by his elder brother and the latter's patron, the Duke of Lenox. He was probably the John Harvey, then a serjeant in ordinary to the king, who was admitted to Gray's Inn in 1625,[155] and the one who, as one of the king's "servants," was sent on a brief mission to France in 1626.[156] That year, jointly with his brother, Daniel, he became king's receiver for Lincolnshire, a position similar to that of John Pym for Hants and Wiltshire, and was still holding the post in 1637.[157] He may have been named one of the commissioners for the London court of requests in 1637,[158] and probably had a lease on a property in Paternoster Row in 1640.[159] His connections with his native county seem to have been slight, but he may have been the one of his name listed on the commission of oyer and terminer there in 1641.[160]

Harvey's election to the Long Parliament, his first, was probably upon the recommendation sent to Hythe by the Lord Warden of the Cinque Ports, the Duke of Lenox.[161] Though not a leader in the House, nor often appointed to committees, he supported the reform party in its early work and was still in attendance in February, 1642.[162] His loyalty may have been questioned later, for in 1643 and 1644 he was asked for £500 by the parliament and his grocer brothers were heavily assessed,[163] but he was named in 1644 as one of the original Grocers' Hall committee. He died about July, 1645, unmarried, having named as the sole executor of his will his fellow M.P., Harbottle Grimston, junior.[164]

Harvey seems not to have left a large estate, but he bequeathed £80 to Hythe and left other legacies totalling

[145] *Al. Oxon.* Pink (MS 303, fol. 156) suggests that the George Hartnoll whose will was proved at Exeter in 1634 may have been his father, but the original will of George Hartnoll of "Movette Howe" at the Exeter Probate Registry indicates that he had no son. W. Harding (*The history of Tiverton* 2: Bk. 4: 39 Tiverton, 1845–1847) states that James's father was John Hartnoll, a Tiverton merchant.

[146] *Cal. Com. Adv. Money*, 1283.

[147] A son was baptized in May, 1623 (Chalk, *loc. cit.*). Hartnoll's son, George, was admitted to Cambridge in 1646, aged twenty-one. *Al. Cant.*

[148] *C.J.* 2: 626; Pink MSS, 303, fol. 156.

[149] *C.J.* 3: 374.

[150] P.C.C., 82 Bruce.

[151] *Vis. London* (Harleian Society) 1: 359; *D.N.B.*, "Dr. William Harvey"; Pink MSS, 303, fol. 172.

[152] W. W. Grantham, ed., *List of the wardens of the Grocers' Company*, 26, London, Metcalfe & Cooper, 1907; MSS of the Grocers' Company, Quire of Wardens' Accounts, 1601–1611, *passim*, and Calendar of Orders of the Court of Assistants 4; S.P. 16, 453/75.

[153] Will of Thomas Harvey, P.C.C., 27 Swann.

[154] London Corporation MSS, Rep. 43, fols. 163v, 175–178; Rep. 49, fols. 53–54; Rep. 51, fols. 180, 316–319; Rep. 52, fols. 16, 377. At no time do the records refer to John, uncle of the heir, as a merchant.

[155] He was styled also as "of Kent, gent." *Gray's Inn Adm. Reg.*, 176.

[156] *Acts P. C., 1625–1626*, 451.

[157] Pink MSS, cited above; *C.S.P. Dom., 1625–1649*, 462, 568.

[158] London Corporation MSS, Rep. 51, fol. 278v.

[159] "John Harvey of London, Esq." (*ibid.*, Rep. 54, fol. 62). A "Mr. Harvey of Paternoster Row" was handling the money for one of Secretary Nicholas's transactions in 1639. *C.S.P. Dom., 1639*, 224. There were several of the name resident in London at this period, however.

[160] C. 181/5, fol. 386.

[161] Hythe Borough MSS, Assembly Book, 1608–1645, fol. 240.

[162] Hythe Borough MSS, 291, letter from H. Heyman.

[163] *Cal. Com. Adv. Money*, 138–140, 301.

[164] The will, dated 20 June 1645, was proved, 28 July. P.C.C., 93 Rivers.

over £500.[165]   He was somewhat distantly connected with his fellow M.P.'s, Parkhurst and Spurstow.[166]

* Thomas Hatcher (1589?–1677), of Careby, Lincolnshire, M.P. for Stamford, 1640–1653, was the son and heir of Sir John Hatcher of Careby (d. 1640), and was probably a student at Emmanuel College, Cambridge, in 1603, and at Lincoln's Inn in 1607.[167]   He was named to various commissions in his county and Rutland from 1627, on,[168] and was a J.P. from about 1634.[169]   He was a brother-in-law of Sir Edward Ayscough (q.v.), and in his earlier parliaments, a friend of Sir John Eliot.[170]   His father was reported as a ship money defaulter in 1636.[171]

Hatcher seems to have inherited an ample estate when his father died in 1640, although the extent of his wealth is not known.[172]

* Sir Christopher Hatton, K.B. (1605–1670), of Kirby, Northamptonshire, the single member for Higham Ferrers, 1640–October 1645, was the son of Sir Christopher Hatton, K.B. (d. 1619), and successor to many of the properties of Elizabeth's Lord Chancellor of the same name.   He was a nephew of Sir Robert Hatton, 1640 M.P., a cousin of both of the Fanshawes, and related by marriage to the Montagus and Sir Dudley North (q.v.).   Born on 28 June 1605, Sir Christopher was educated at Cambridge and Gray's Inn.[173]   During the 1630's he was a J.P. in his county and member of various commissions.[174]   He was probably M.P. for Peterborough, 1624 and 1625,[175] may have sat for Clitheroe during part of the next parliament,[176] and was elected for Higham Ferrers, whose steward he had been since 1636, to both parliaments of 1640.[177]   Chosen by Castle Rising also in the October elections, he preferred Higham Ferrers.

Hatton owned a large estate in Northamptonshire, one manor of which alone brought in over £500 annually.[178]   He joined two fellow countians in pledging £1000 for the loan in 1641.[179]   According to his compounding papers, his income above rents was over £2200 a year, though subject to annuities of some £1160.   His fine, set first at £4156, was reduced upon review to £3226.[180]

Sir Robert Hatton (d. 1653), of Bishopsbourne, Kent, and of Clinton and Oakington, Cambridgeshire, was elected for Castle Rising, Norfolk, 20 November 1640, replacing his nephew, Sir Christopher Hatton (q.v.), who had decided to sit for Higham Ferrers.   Sir Robert was disabled for royalism, 7 September 1642.[181]   The second son of John Hatton of Long Stanton, Cambridgeshire, by Jane, daughter of Robert Shute, Baron of the Exchequer and Justice of Common Pleas, he entered Gray's Inn in 1602 and was knighted at Whitehall in 1617.   He married May, daughter of Sir Robert Leigh of Baguley, Cheshire.   His parliamentary career, which began in 1614, was assisted by various borough patrons.   He sat for Queenborough, 1614, for Sandwich in 1621 until the House voided his place, owing his election this time to Lord Zouch, and for Sandwich in 1624 and 1625, preferring it to Stafford.   He seems to have made some effort for Kent in the 1626 election,[182] but afterwards associated himself with the Cambridge-Northamptonshire area.   He was a sewers commissioner in Kent in 1624, but during the 1630's was a member of various local commissions for the counties of Cambridge and Northampton, and a J.P. there,[183] and possibly a D.L.   He was living at Beningfield, Northants, in 1640,[184] and in February renewed his oath as freeman at Cambridge, possibly hoping to be elected there for the Short Parliament.[185]   He was not returned, however, until after the opening of the Long Parliament, when he obtained the vacant seat for Castle Rising through the influence of the Howard family, lords of the borough.

Hatton was named to several committees of the 1640 parliament,[186] but he was a strong royalist and was

---

165 *Ibid.;* Hythe Borough MSS, 291, letter from Grimston, 15 September 1645.

166 Harvey's brother, Thomas, married into that connection.

167 *Al. Cant.*

168 C. 181/3; 181/4, fols. 40, 159; 181/5, fols. 84, 133; *C.S.P. Dom., 1638–1639,* 425.

169 C. 193/13; S.P. 16/405.

170 Forster, *Eliot* 2: 653–655 and n.

171 *C.S.P. Dom., 1635–1636,* 361; *1636–1637,* 397.

172 Most of his father's estate seems to have been settled on Thomas sometime before 1640, but Sir John provided in his will of that year for 1000 marks toward the dowry of one of Thomas's daughters, and enumerated a quantity of plate and furniture for his son. Will of Sir John Hatcher, Consistory Court of Lincoln, 1640, fols. 408–409.

173 *Al. Cant.* The uncertainty as to his birth date (*D.N.B.*) is corrected here on the basis of his father's I.P.M. (C. 142/376/100), wherein his age was given as exactly 14 years on 28 June 1619.

174 C. 193/13; S.P. 16/405; C. 181/4, fol. 180; 181/5, fols. 8, 68, 97, *passim.*

175 As Christopher Hatton, Esq. *M. of P.* 1: 459, 465.

176 Addenda collected by the History of Parliament Committee.

177 *Ibid.; V.C.H. Northampton* 3: 271; *C.J.* 2: 4.

178 Baker, *Northampton* 1: 84, 88, 164, *passim;* Add. MSS, 28,571 (Finch-Hatton papers), fol. 6.

179 D'Ewes (N), 451, n.; *Cal. Com. Comp.,* 28.

180 *Ibid., 1579–1582;* S.P. 23/200/129–142. £2530 is the value listed elsewhere (*Cal. Com. Adv. Money,* 1209). Numerous papers relating to his properties and those of his mother's family are among the Northants MSS, e.g., Finch-Hatton 1174, 3009–3011, 3018, 3381.

181 *M. of P.* 1: 491; *C.J.* 2: 755.

182 *M. of P.* 1: 455, 461, 465, 476; 3: App., xxxviii; *C.S.P. Dom., 1619–1623,* 212, 213; *1625–1626,* 217.

183 C. 181/3, fol. 115; 181/4, fol. 154; 181/5, fols. 39, 130, 196, 364; C. 193/13; S.P. 16/405; *C.S.P. Dom., 1637,* 350.

184 *C.S.P. Dom., 1640,* 242; *1640–1641,* 177.

185 He was made a freeman first in 1613. Cambridge Corporation MSS, Cambridge Day Book, 1610–1646, fol. 310.

186 *C.J.* 2: 60, 98, 101.

called to answer in April, 1641, for words he spoke in defense of Digby, and he voted against Strafford's attainder. He was disabled on 7 September 1642 for having helped to execute the commission of array, and refusing to attend upon summons.[187] He was imprisoned for a time, sat in the Oxford parliament, eventually compounded for his estate and, after having been overseas in 1652, died on 10 January 1653.[188]

Hatton compounded for properties in Cambridgeshire and Northamptonshire having a declared value of £250 a year, but he may have owned other lands in 1640 as well. His fine was set provisionally at £1000, but his estates were afterwards ordered to be sold.[189]

William Hay (1594–1664), of Horsted Parva, Sussex, was M.P. for Rye, 1641–1653, replacing Sir John Jacob, who was expelled as a monopolist.[190] He was a grandson of a former mayor of Hastings, being a younger son of John Hay of Hurstmonceau and Gray's Inn (d. 1605) by his wife, Mary, daughter of William Morley of Glynde. He was a younger brother of the puritan, Herbert Hay, who opposed the 1627 loan, was removed from the commission of the peace for venturing too far into ecclasiastical matters, and was later M.P. for Arundel and a parliamentarian.[191] William, born in December, 1594,[192] may have matriculated at Cambridge (Pembroke or Clare) in 1612,[193] and sometime after 1615 married Susan or Lucan, daughter of Barnaby Hodgson (Hudson) of Framfield. Several of his children were baptized at Horsted Parva, 1632–1639, and his wife was buried there, 14 December 1640. His eldest son, William, entered Gray's Inn in 1644.[194]

As a younger brother, Hay seems to have held no offices before 1640,[195] and doubtless owed his election to the vacant place at Rye to the influence of his brother, his mother's relative, Herbert Morley of Glynde (q.v.), and possibly a brother-in-law, who was a Rye resident.[196] He was not named often to committees in the early period of the parliament, but was sent into his county in 1641 to help enforce the regulations against recusants.[197] He offered £100 for the defense in June,

1642,[198] was an active committeeman during the war, and retained his seat until the end of the session. He sat also in the parliaments of 1654 and 1656 and with the returned Rump in 1659.[199] Dying in 1664, Hay was buried on 26 December at Horsted Parva.[200] His will, dated 3 October 1663, was proved 3 February 1665.[201]

Hay's landed estates were probably not extensive, the manor of Horsted Parva being his chief possession,[202] but his offer for the defense in 1642 was at least an average one. His fortunes perhaps improved during the war, for his will mentions provision for some £1250 in legacies for three younger children.

Thomas Heblethwaite (d. 1647), of the Middle Temple and of Norton, near Malton, Yorkshire, was elected for Malton on 8 January 1641, following its restoration as a parliamentary borough on 11 December, and was disabled late in 1644.[203] He may have matriculated sizar at St. John's, Cambridge, about 1594,[204] and as the third son of John Heblethwaite of Wisbitch, Cambridgeshire, gentleman, was admitted to the Middle Temple, 23 June 1598. He was called to the bar in 1605, and retained a chamber at the Temple for some years.[205] Soon after he became a barrister, however, he seems to have gone to live with a cousin, James Heblethwaite of Norton, near Malton, who eventually left him his property. As "Thomas Heblethwaite of New Malton, gent.," he was licensed in 1605 to marry Anne Hildyard of Butterwick. She was a daughter of Richard Hildyard and a sister of Sir Christopher Hildyard of Wynstead in Holderness. She died about 1609, having borne Heblethwaite's son, James, and several daughters.[206] In 1614 Heblethwaite, now styled "esquire," married Mary (Sutheby), widow of Thomas Hungate of North Allerton.[207]

Heblethwaite was probably a shrewd lawyer who managed to improve his fortunes considerably. With his cousin, James, he bought several pieces of property in and near Norton, 1612–1613, and continued to buy others for himself for some years.[208] His cousin's death in 1616 brought him, besides a mill in Acklam and a

[187] C.S.P. Dom., 1640–1641, 560; Verney, 57; C.J. 2: 755.

[188] C.J. 3: 373; Mason, Norfolk, 289; Cal. Com. Comp., 593.

[189] Hatton's "particular" (S.P. 23/214/599) is apparently incomplete. Cal. Com. Comp., 379, 593, 1649–1650; Northants MSS, F.H., 2536.

Hatton's life is sketched in Wedgwood, Staff. Parl. Hist. 2: 45.

[190] M. of P. 1: 497.

[191] Pink MSS, 303, fol. 234; S.P. 16, 89/5; C.S.P. Dom., 1639–1640, 387.

[192] Pink MSS, 303, fol. 236; Comber, Sussex Genealogies, Ardingley, 237; Lansd. MSS, 873, fols. 58–60; Berry, Sussex Genealogies, 118.

[193] Al. Cant.

[194] Add. MSS, 5697, fol. 252; Gray's Inn Adm. Reg., 238.

[195] He was named a sewers commissioner in 1641. C. 181/5, fol. 412.

[196] John Fagge or Flagg, Esq. of Rye, mentioned in his will.

[197] C.J. 2: 267.

[198] N. and Q., 1st Ser., 12: 360, 1855.

[199] Pink MSS, cited above; Thomason Tracts, 669. f. 24, p. 37.

[200] Add. MSS, 5697, fol. 252.

[201] P.C.C., 16 Hyde.

[202] Sussex manors (Sussex Record Society, 19) 1: 227, 1914; Sussex Arch. Coll. 24: 217, 1872.

[203] M. of P. 1: 497, n.; Cal. Com. Comp., 874.

[204] Al. Cant.

[205] Mid. Temp. Rec. 1: 385; 2: 456, 532. He was still connected with the Temple when his son entered Cambridge in 1626. Al. Cant.

[206] Yorks. Arch. Jour. 11: 213 and n., 1891; Dugdale, Vis. York, 205.

[207] Ibid.; Yorks. Arch. Jour. 13: 372 and n., 1895. Heblethwaite's grandson, Sir Thomas, of Norton, has sometimes been confused with the M.P.

[208] Y.A.S. Rec. Ser. 53: 187, 192, 197, 1915; 58: 11, 111, 156, 169, 221–223, 1917.

smithy in Malton, scattered properties in the counties of York, Westmorland, and Lancaster, and even in London.[209] He paid £25 about 1630 as composition for not being knighted.[210] And he was active in county affairs. He was a commissioner for compounding with recusants in 1628,[211] was a J.P. in the North and East Ridings from early in the reign of Charles,[212] and from 1630 he was on the commission of oyer and terminer for York and the nearby counties.[213] He was also a D.L. in Yorkshire in 1639.[214] But he had never been sent to parliament. Perhaps his signing the Yorkshire petition of July, 1640,[215] prepared the way for his election for Malton as soon as the borough was restored to representation.

Despite his inexperience in the House, Heblethwaite was named to eight or nine committees in 1641, some of them on legal matters, one on the ship money bill, and one on the Bishop of Ely. He seems to have been working with the popular party, and in August, 1641, was sent into his county to enforce the disarming of recusants.[216] That his legal skill was valued is indicated by his being assigned with one of the Serjeants-at-Law on 18 December 1641 to draft a special bill.[217] But by 1642 events had turned beyond his inclinations. He was absent on 16 June 1642, and, though he was present in October to pledge £40 for the cause, did not attend much after that. He was listed in September, 1643, as one who had been absent for some time, and on 29 November 1644 he was disabled, it being reported that he had been absent for two years. It was stated that he had excused himself from attending the Oxford parliament because of infirmities, but that he had served the royalist cause as a J.P. and with a contribution of £300. Within a month parliament voted that he should be fined £500 for his defection.[218] A new assessment of the fine was made on 11 May 1647,[219] but Heblethwaite had already died at Hull. He was buried on 27 March 1647 at Norton.[220]

Sir Thomas Hele, or **Heale,** Bart. (1595?–1670), of Fleet in Holberton, Devon, was elected for Plympton, Devon, shortly after 9 November 1640, *vice* Oldisworth,[221] but was disabled for deserting the House, 22 January 1644. The descendant of a prominent west country family, Hele was the second son of Thomas Hele, Esq., of Fleet (H.S. Devon 1617; d. 1624), by Bridget, daughter of Sir Henry Champernowne of Modbury. He was born about 1595,[222] possibly matriculated at Oxford (Exeter) in 1608, aged sixteen, graduating B.A. in 1612 and M.A. in 1615,[223] and in 1614 was admitted to the Inner Temple.[224] When his father died Thomas succeeded to the family estates by his father's direction, although his elder brother was living.[225] He was created a baronet in May, 1627, the usual fee being dispensed with,[226] and a year or two later married Penelope, daughter and coheir of Emorbe Johnson of Wigborow, Somerset.[227] A second wife, married at Kensington in 1632, was Elizabeth, daughter of Edward Elwayes.[228]

Meanwhile Hele had become active in local affairs. He was named regularly from 1626 as a Devonshire[229] J.P., was one of the 1627 loan commissioners,[230] and was named to numerous other local commissions.[231] Pricked as sheriff of Devon in January, 1636,[232] Sir Thomas seems to have collected his full rate of ship money,[233] but in 1639 he declined to contribute toward the king's northern journey.[234] He served in the parliaments of 1626 and 1628 for Plympton, near which some of his property lay, and was elected there again in the spring of 1640. He was present at the county election in the fall and signed the return.[235]

In the early months of the Long Parliament Hele was an active member, working with his cousins, John and Sir Samuel Rolle, in the country party. He was named to such committees as those on superstition and idolatry and on the subsidies, served as a witness in Strafford's trial,[236] and offered his bond for £1000 for the loan in November, 1640.[237] By the summer of 1642, however, he had begun to absent himself from the House. He was excused and readmitted, 12 July 1642, was absent and sent for in November, and in January, 1643, was ordered to lend £200. Actively

[209] Will of James Heblethwaite (1611) proved at York, 1616. York Probate Registry 34: fol. 108.

[210] *Y.A.S. Rec. Ser* **61**: 106, 1920.

[211] *C.S.P. Dom., 1628–1629,* 205.

[212] C. 193/12, 13; S.P. 16, 189/8/i, fol. 17; 189/8/vii, fol. 27.

[213] C. 181/4, fols. 36v, 61; 181/5, fol. 15, *passim.*

[214] *H.M.C., Twelfth Report* **2**: Coke MSS, 208.

[215] *C.S.P. Dom., 1640,* 524.

[216] *C.J.* **2**: 75, 85, 143, 181, 267, 298; Pink MSS, 303, fol. 262.

[217] D'Ewes (C), 312 and n.

[218] *C.J.* **2**: 626, 792, 802; **3**: 256, 708; *Cal. Com. Comp.,* 874.

[219] *Cal. Com. Adv. Money,* 809.

[220] *Al. Cant.*

[221] Hele was present on 21 November 1640. D'Ewes (N), 52.

[222] His elder brother, Samuel, aged thirty and over in 1624, survived until 1661, but Thomas and his other brothers were provided for by their father's settlement of 1623. I.P.M. of Thomas Hele, C. 142/423/79; Pink MSS, 303, fol. 271.

[223] *Al. Oxon.*

[224] *Students admitted to the Inner Temple,* 210.

[225] I.P.M., cited above.

[226] *C.S.P. Dom., 1627–1628,* 193.

[227] A son by this marriage died in 1665, aged thirty-six. Pink MSS, *loc. cit.*

[228] *Kensington parish registers,* Harleian Society, Registers Series **16**: 70, 1890. Hele seems to have married a third time after 1646.

[229] C. 193/12 and 13; S.P. 16/405; Devonshire MSS, Quarter Sessions Minute Books, 1633–1640.

[230] S.P. 16, 53/96.

[231] C. 181/4, fol. 52v; 181/5, fols. 187, 209, 218, *passim.*

[232] S.P. 16, 311/89.

[233] Royal Hist. Soc., *Trans.,* 3rd Ser., **4**: 157, 1910.

[234] Rushworth **3**: 913.

[235] Devon indenture, C. 219/43/Part 1.

[236] *C.J.* **2**: 84, 115, 130.

[237] D'Ewes (N), 52.

serving the king thereafter, he was disabled in January, 1644.[238] He made great contributions to the royal cause,[239] but later compounded for his estates. Sir Thomas died on 7 March 1670 and was buried at Holberton.

Hele, who was described by Lloyd as a gentleman of great estate and repute,[240] had inherited from his father four manors and other possessions, comprising some 1200 acres in Devon and Cornwall.[241] His composition papers of 1646–1649 show an admitted pre-war income of over £1165 a year, and his fine for royalism was reckoned at ⅔, £14,176, or 1/10, £2834.[242]

Sir Thomas had numerous associates and relatives as fellow M.P.'s. The Rolle brothers were his first cousins, and Carew was a cousin by marriage. That Hele met with criticism in his county when he decided for the king appears from the lines of his friend, Robert Herrick:[243]

> Stand by the *Magick* of my powerfull Rhymes
> 'Gainst all the indignation of the Times.
> Age shall not wrong Thee; or one jot abate
> Of thy both Great, and everlasting fate.

* Edward Herbert (*c.* 1591–1657), of Aston, the Solicitor General, was M.P. for Old Sarum from 1640 until his appointment as Attorney-General removed him to the Upper House in January, 1641.[244] Educated at Queen's College, Oxford, and at the Inner Temple,[245] his career in parliament and in his profession before 1640 is well known. He was supported by Laud for one of the two Short Parliament seats for which he was returned,[246] and in the Long Parliament elections he was a court nominee.[247] Family influence, too, probably accounted for his election to his first parliament (1621) for Montgomery borough, to three later ones for Downton, and to both of the 1640 parliaments for Old Sarum.[248]

Herbert was an active member of the Virginia Company, 1619–1624,[249] and appears to have held more offices in and near London than in Wiltshire. He was long a J.P. in Westminster and was appointed to numerous local commissions for Middlesex, Kent, Sussex, Lincolnshire, and Northamptonshire.[250] He was probably occupying a pretentious house in St. Andrew's, Holborn, in 1638,[251] and he offered as his excuse for violating the rule against spending Christmas in London that he had no country house.[252] He was asked in 1640 to advance £500 for the king's expenses, a figure somewhat lower than that asked of many of the court officials, but he seems to have escaped with paying only £200 after some delay.[253] His wife was an heiress and he presumably had a substantial income.

To the others of the Herbert name among the parliament men of 1640 he was related. His nearest kinsman among them was his first cousin, Henry Herbert, who was likewise a courtier and royalist.

* Sir Henry Herbert (1595–1673), of Ribbesford, Worcestershire, Master of the Revels, was M.P. for Bewdley, Worcestershire, 1640–20 August 1642. He was a J.P. for the county,[254] a commissioner of oyer and terminer for Wales and the Marches, and a member in 1633 of the Council of Wales.[255] In the Long Parliament he was a member, sometimes chairman, of the committee on Sir Lewis Dives, dealing with election contests, and he made a speech in December, 1640, against the oppressions of one deputy lieutenant in Worcestershire. On another occasion he was reproached in the House for his abusive words toward Serjeant Wilde and others.[256] He was disabled in 1642 for royalism.

Herbert was reputedly well-to-do. When he compounded, 1646–1648, he enumerated properties in the counties of Middlesex, Essex, Montgomery, and Worcester, several of the latter being near Bewdley. He stated that they were worth £415 a year and that his office at court was worth £500 yearly. Later he was said to have underestimated his Worcestershire holdings by nearly forty-five per cent, but there is no record that his earlier fine of a third, £1330, was altered.[257]

Herbert was an uncle of the Montgomeryshire member, Richard Herbert, and related through his mother to Francis Newport.[258]

* Philip Lord Herbert (1621–1669), M.P. for Glamorganshire, 1640–1653, was the fourth but eldest surviving son of the Welsh magnate and Lord Chamberlain,

[238] Pink MSS, 303, fol. 271; *C.J.* **3**: 374.
[239] Wood, *Fasti Oxon.* **2**: 43.
[240] *Memoires,* 691.
[241] I.P.M. cited above. Two of his sisters had dowries of £1000, and £500 were assigned for each of his younger brothers, according to his father's settlement. S.P. 23/189/494. Properties of Hele in Exeter are referred to in Exeter Corporation MSS, Act Book VII, fol. 848, and in *Cal. Com. Comp.,* 1239.
[242] S.P. 23/189/492–499; *Cal. Com. Comp.,* 1239. In 1650 it was reported that he had undervalued his estate by ⅓ to ½. *Ibid.,* 336.
[243] *The poetical works of Robert Herrick,* ed. by F. W. Moorman, 280, Oxford, Clarendon Press, 1915. Besides the references cited above, see *M. of P.; Complete Baronetage* **2**: 19.
[244] *M. of P.* **1**: 496.
[245] *Al. Oxon.* Williams (*Parl. Hist. Wales,* 148) names Cambridge by mistake.
[246] Guilding, *Reading records* **3**: 488, 492–493.
[247] S.P. 16, 468/136.
[248] *C.S.P. Dom., 1640,* 42; *E.H.R.* **45**: 109, 1930; **50**: 254, 1935.
[249] Brown, *Genesis of the U. S.,* 919.

[250] C. 193/13; S.P. 16/405; C. 181/4, fol. 191; 181/5, *passim.*
[251] Dale, *Inhabitants of London* **1**: 189.
[252] S.P. 16, 378/94.
[253] S.P. 16, 446/42, 43; 447/37, 94; 538/84.
[254] C. 193/13; S.P. 16/405.
[255] C. 181/5, fol. 369; *Arch. Camb.,* 6th Ser., **17**: 195, 1917.
[256] *C.J.* **2**: 60, 94; D'Ewes (N), 145, 415, 455, n.
[257] *C.J.* **5**: 516; *Cal. Com. Comp.,* 236, 1072; S.P. 23/186/526–532.
[258] A sketch of Herbert's career appears in Williams, *Worcester,* 165–166.

Philip, Earl of Pembroke and Montgomery (d. 1650). He was baptized on 20 February 1621 and on the death of his elder brother, Charles, in 1635 became his father's heir.[259] After studying at Westminster School and Oxford, he travelled on the continent, returning in 1637.[260] The family fortunes had declined by 1639, and his marriage that year with Sir Robert Naunton's daughter, Lady Banning, was intended to repair them. The gossips of the day reported that his family planned a series of matches by which all of the estates of the lady's first husband would pass to the Herberts.[261] Lord Herbert was with the king in the north as a captain in 1639,[262] and by 1640 was one of the joint lieutenants of Somersetshire, and a J.P. there.[263] He sat for Wilts in the Short Parliament.

The heir apparent to estates lying in numerous counties from Kent to Wales,[264] Lord Herbert pledged £1000 for the 1640 loan.[265] He supported the cause of parliament in numerous other ways and remained a member until 1653. He was a brother of William Herbert, who sat for Monmouthshire, and through his first wife was connected with Thomas Lower of Cornwall (q.v.).[266]

* Richard Herbert (1600 ?–1655), of Montgomery and of St. Julian's, county Monmouth, was M.P. for Montgomery borough from 1640 until his disablement for royalism, 12 September 1642.[267] His family virtually controlled both shire and borough, and he had sat in the spring for the shire of Montgomery.[268] The son and heir of Edward, first Lord Herbert of Cherbury, by his wife, Mary, daughter and heiress of Sir William Herbert of Julians,[269] he received in 1625 a pass to travel for three years.[270] He was a J.P. in Shropshire

by June, 1631,[271] and afterwards served both in that county and in Montgomeryshire,[272] and as a commissioner for the Welsh Marches.[273] He was listed as a member of the Council of the Marches in 1633.[274]

Herbert married well and even while his father lived had an income of £500 or £600 from the Herbert estates, but he annoyed his father by running into debt.[275] His composition papers declared that he had an income of some £500 or more, with an additional £1120 a year expected in reversion after his father, but that his debts were at least £7000.[276]

An army officer by 1639, Captain Herbert was among those whose troops were ordered to be disbanded in July, 1641,[277] at the same time as Henry Percy's, probably because of the army plot fears.

Richard Herbert was a kinsman of the other Herberts of the 1640 House, being a nephew of Sir Henry Herbert and a cousin, in various degrees, of the others. Francis Newport, too, was a relative.

William Herbert (1609–1642), of Cogan Pill near Cardiff, Glamorganshire, was M.P. for Cardiff, 1640–1642. Although there has been some confusion about his identity because of the frequency with which the name occurs in the Cardiff area, the 1640 M.P. seems to have been the son and heir of William Herbert of Cogan and Cardiff (d. 1628) and the grandson of Nicholas Herbert, sheriff and M.P.[278] He was also heir male of William Herbert of White Friars, Cardiff (d. 1645), his father's cousin, who was probably M.P. for Cardiff in 1621 and afterwards was deputy vice admiral for the Earl of Pembroke in South Wales.[279] The younger William was born in May, 1609,[280] was a J.P. for Glamorganshire in 1638, and with his cousin of White Friars was a member of the sewers commission the next year.[281] He sat in both parliaments of 1640, being identified in the indenture of the spring as "of Cardiff." [282]

A Straffordian and royalist, Herbert left the House

[259] D.N.B. dates his birth in 1619. But of the Earl of Montgomery's first three sons (born 1616, 1618, 1619), the first two died in infancy, and the third, Charles, who was aged seven in 1626, died in 1635. C.S.P. Dom., 1611–1618, 392, 487, 528, 533; 1619–1623, 71; Birch, The court and times of Charles the First 1: 132 and n. For the baptismal date of Philip see Barker and Stenning, The record of old Westminsters 1: 450.

[260] C.S.P. Dom., 1637, 55.

[261] E.H.R. 50: 256, 1935; C.S.P. Dom., 1638–1639, 605, 621–622. Herbert and his wife petitioned the Court of Wards about income from land assigned to her daughters in 1641. Ibid., 1640–1641, 235.

[262] S.P. 16, 538/91/ii.

[263] C.S.P. Dom., 1640, 641; C. 181/5, fol. 365.

[264] Hasted, Kent 6: 175, passim; Hoare, Wilts. 6: 574; Lansd. MSS, 459, fols. 155v, 156v, 157v, 158.

[265] D'Ewes (N), 539.

[266] In addition to D.N.B. and the above authorities see Williams, Parl. Hist. Wales, 97.

[267] M. of P. 1: 498; C.J. 2: 762.

[268] J. E. Neale, Three Elizabethan elections, E.H.R. 46: 227, 228, 1931.

[269] Montgomeryshire Collections 6: 416–417, 1873; Williams, Parl. Hist. Wales, 143.

[270] Acts P.C., 1625–1626, 104. He was referred to then as the son of Lord Herbert of Castle Island, which was the title his father held in the Irish peerage before he was created Lord Cherbury.

[271] S.P. 16, 194/57.

[272] C. 193/13; S.P. 16/405.

[273] C. 181/4, fols. 162, 368.

[274] Arch. Camb., 6th Ser., 17: 195, 1917.

[275] Huntingdon Library Quarterly 5: 317–332, 1941–1942.

[276] Cal. Com. Comp., 1682; S.P. 23/206/175–179; Montgomeryshire Collections 18: 276–280, 1885.

[277] C.J. 2: 220.

[278] I.P.M. of William Herbert (son of Nicholas Herbert), C. 142/447/57; Williams, Parl. Hist. Wales, 106; Cardiff records, ed. J. H. Matthews 2: 15, 34; 5: 490, Cardiff, by order of the Corporation, 1898–1911; Thomas Nicholas, Annals and antiquities of the counties and county families of Wales 2: 609, London, 1872.

[279] Pink, in identifying the 1640 M.P. with the M.P. of 1621, has confused the three William Herberts (Pink MSS, 303, fol. 330). It was doubtless the Herbert "of White Friars" who was acting for the Earl of Pembroke in 1635. C.S.P. Dom., 1635, 248; Cardiff Records 5: 489.

[280] I.P.M. cited above.

[281] S.P. 16/405; C. 181/5, fol. 295.

[282] H.M.C., Fourth Report, House of Lords MSS, 24.

with the start of the war, and he was killed fighting at Edgehill.[283] The combined estates of the two branches of the family which passed afterwards to his son, William Herbert "of St. Fagans," [284] were said to be worth £1000 a year in 1660.[285]

William Herbert (*c.* 1622–1646 ?), of Wilton, Wiltshire, was M.P. for Monmouthshire, 1640–1644.[286] The fifth son of Philip, Earl of Pembroke and Montgomery, he was born about 1622, and was educated at Westminster School and at Exeter College, Oxford, where he was created M.A. in 1636.[287] He had not previously been in parliament, but in the autumn of 1640 was chosen for three constituencies, Downton, Woodstock, and Monmouthshire, his family's county. He announced on 20 November his decision to serve for the county.[288] He was not often mentioned in the affairs of the House and had several leaves of absence. He was a member of the assessment commission for county Monmouth in 1643,[289] but he seems to have been disabled as a royalist on 5 February 1644.[290] The writ for the election of his successor was not ordered, however, until 11 September 1646, following his death.[291]

Herbert was the next younger brother of Philip Lord Herbert, M.P. for Glamorganshire.

* Sir Arthur Hesilrige, or Haselrig, Bart. (d. 1661), of Noseley, Leicestershire, was a member for his county, 1640–1653. The son and heir of Sir Thomas Hesilrige, Bart., of Noseley and of Alderton, Northamptonshire (H.S., J.P., D.L., M.P.,[292] d. 1630), Arthur was born before 1608,[293] and was educated at Westminster School, Magdalene College, Cambridge, and Gray's Inn.[294] About 1624 he married well, receiving a portion of £3000 with his bride.[295] By this time he was a

captain of horse in Leicestershire,[296] but in 1625, when he aspired with his father's support to a seat in parliament, was defeated at Leicester borough.[297] After his father's death Sir Arthur served on several local commissions for his county, and as a J.P.[298]

Hesilrige's father opposed the loans of 1621 and 1627,[299] and his first wife's father, Thomas Elmes, was probably arrested for similar refusals.[300] Inspired by such action, as well as influenced presently by Pym and by his second wife's brother, Lord Brooke, young Hesilrige was himself summoned before both Council and the Court of High Commission during the decade of the 1630's for both criticizing and defying the authorities, and was imprisoned by Council order in the Fleet for a time in 1635.[301] He was one of the proprietors of Saybrooke that year and may possibly have been considering a New England residence in 1636.[302] By the time of his election to the parliaments of 1640, Hesilrige was prepared to work with his friends and kinsmen, leaders in the opposition party, and in spite of his inexperience in the House to take a prominent part.

Having inherited a considerable estate in the counties of Leicester, Northampton, and Northumberland,[303] and augmented it by two marriages into well-known families, Hesilrige was considered well-to-do, and his subscriptions to the loans in 1640 and 1641 bear out the reputation.[304] He was said to have been "of a morose and haughty temper," [305] but a criticism from his county that he was "but a flash," with "more will than wit," [306] seems hardly to have been justified.

* William Heveningham (1604–1678), of Ketteringham, Norfolk, the regicide, sat for Stockbridge, Hampshire, 1640–1653. He owed his election there to both of the 1640 parliaments [307] no doubt to his influential father-in-law, Sir Henry Wallop (*q.v.*). Of old East Anglian ancestry, he was the holder of extensive prop-

---

[283] Verney, 58; Pink, *loc. cit.;* Williams, *loc. cit.;* O.P.H. **9**: 15; *C.J.* **4**: 366, 412.

[284] *Cardiff records* **5**: 489.

[285] *English Baronetage* **4**: 379, 1741.

[286] *M. of P.* **1**: 491; *C.J.* **3**: 389.

[287] Williams, *Parl. Hist. Wales,* 123; Barker and Stenning, *The record of old Westminsters* **1**: 450.

[288] *M. of P.* **1**: 492, 495; *C.J.* **2**: 33.

[289] Pink MSS, 303, fol. 332.

[290] *C.J.* **3**: 389. The other William Herbert, M.P. for Cardiff, had been killed at Edgehill. The confusing of identities probably explains why some authors have stated that the Monmouthshire M.P. was disabled in 1642 and why others have considered him a member until the time of his death.

[291] Williams, *loc. cit.*

[292] C. 193/12; S.P. 16, 70/70; Leicestershire Architectural and Archaeological Society, *Transactions* **2**: 268–269, 1870.

[293] At his father's death in January 1629/30, not 1629, as in *D.N.B.,* Arthur was aged 22 and more (I.P.M. of Sir Thomas Hesilrige, C. 142/454/33). A brother, Donald (baptized 1600, d. 1629), and a brother, John (baptized 1602), matriculated at Cambridge with Arthur in 1617. *Al. Cant.*

[294] Barker and Stenning, *The record of old Westminsters* **1**: 452.

[295] *Arch. Ael.,* 3rd Ser., **6**: 22, 1909. By this marriage Hesilrige became a brother-in-law of Sir Thomas Dacres (*q.v.*).

[296] S.P. 16, 70/70.

[297] Stocks and Stevenson, *Records of the borough of Leicester, 1603–1688,* 220.

[298] C. 181/4, fols. 100, 118, 146, 166; 181/5, fol. 383; S.P. 16, 190/10, no. 4.

[299] S.P. 14, 127/82; S.P. 16, 89/5.

[300] Rushworth **1**: 473.

[301] He had critized the deputy lieutenants and defaulted from musters payments. The charges against him in ecclesiastical matters are not stated. *C.S.P. Dom., 1631–1633,* 445–446, 521; *1634–1635,* 494, 532; *1635,* 192, 199, 604; *1635–1636,* 83, 92.

[302] *Winthrop Papers* **3**: 198–199, 209, 233, 1929.

[303] I.P.M. cited above; *Arch. Ael.,* 3rd Ser., **6**: 20–22, 1909; Sanford, *St. and ill.,* 395; *Complete Baronetage* **1**: 202. Portions of Hesilrige's properties were mortgaged for £1800 in 1630, but redeemed in 1637. Leicestershire Archaeological Society, *Transactions* **12**: 262–264, 1921–1922. The manor of Noseley alone apparently was worth £600 or more a year in 1659. *Ibid.* **17**: 90, 1932–1933; **19**: 36, 1935–1936.

[304] D'Ewes (N), 52, 435, n.; Add. MSS, 27,990, fol. 42.

[305] *Ibid.*

[306] D'Ewes (N), 3, n.; 95, n.

[307] *M. of P.* **1**: 483, 493.

erties in Norfolk and Suffolk.[308] He was educated in part at Cambridge (admitted at Pembroke, 1621).[309] He served as a J.P.[310] and sheriff of Norfolk and as a member of various local commissions for that area.[311] With his father and others of his family he refused the forced loan of 1627, but he does not seem to have undergone the several months' imprisonment which his father suffered.[312] In 1636 he had to permit two royal patentees to enter upon some of his marsh lands for the purpose of making salt.[313] He is not known, however, to have defaulted in ship money payments. He paid, at least in 1640.[314]

Heveningham was a man of substance, although his name does not appear in the loan lists of the parliament, 1640–1641. His manors were numerous, and in 1639 he arranged to pay £1000 at the marriage of a sister.[315] He pledged £600 for the reducing of Ireland in 1642, and later promised to provide three horses and £100 for the defense.[316] He was a Presbyterian elder[317] during the war, but sat with the "Independents" after 1648.

Heveningham had various relatives among the opposition members of the 1640 House of Commons. The Wallops were his father-in-law and brother-in-law, and through them he was connected with Sir Henry Worsley, Sir William Lytton, and the Barrington group. From East Anglia came such kinsmen as Framlingham Gawdy, Moundeford, and Wodehouse.[318]

Henry Heyman (1610–1658), of Somerfield in Selling, Kent, was a member for Rye, 1640–1653. He was the son and heir of Sir Peter Heyman (q.v.), well known for his opposition stand in earlier parliaments and M.P. for Dover until his death in 1641. His mother was Sir Peter's first wife, Sarah Collet. Henry was baptized at Selling, 20 November 1610, was admitted to Gray's Inn, 3 February 1626,[319] and probably about 1640 or 1641 married Mary, daughter and heir of Daniel Holford of West Thurrock, Essex.[320] He seems to have taken little part in public life before 1640, probably because his father was still living, but he was elected to the Short

Parliament for Hythe, a borough for which his father had formerly sat, and near which he resided. His re-election on 20 October seems to have been without question.[321]

A stanch parliamentarian like his father, Henry became increasingly active in the House after Sir Peter's death in February, 1641.[322] Although he was knighted at Whitehall on 7 July 1641 and created a baronet the next month, he was not turned from his course. He wrote to his constituency in 1642, strongly condemning the attack on the five members and the plans of the malignants,[323] and in June pledged, for the defense of the king, kingdom, privileges of parliament and liberties of the subject, two horses and £100 in plate.[324] He was named a D.L. for Kent and a member of various county committees, 1642–1645,[325] and, though absent for some time, 1647–1648, kept his seat in the House until 1653. He died at Gray's, Essex, in 1658, and was buried at Selling, administration of his estate being granted in December of that year.

Heyman inherited considerable wealth from his father and by his marriage gained several Essex properties.[326] He must be considered a man of good estate.[327]

* **Sir Peter Heyman** (1580–1641), of Somerfield, Selling, Kent, M.P. for Dover from November, 1640, until his death early in February, 1641,[328] was a leader in the popular faction. He had been educated at Emmanuel College, Cambridge,[329] and had been an active member of five parliaments before the Long Parliament, gaining a reputation not only as a foe of the royal program but as a sufferer, by fines and imprisonment, for his resistance. He was a J.P for the Cinque Ports as early as 1618, and afterwards a member of numerous commissions in Kent.[330] His election to his first parliament in 1621 had been with the commendation of Lord Zouch, who wrote to Hythe describing him as "a very sufficient noble gent," who was high in his esteem.[331] He spoke frequently in that parliament,[332] and opposed the loans of 1621 and 1627.[333] He had travelled both in Ireland and on the continent, and would probably

[308] *Suff. Inst. Arch.* 8: 170, 1894; Add. MSS, 19,082, fol. 16v; 19,083, fols. 10v, 51. The I.P.M. of his father, Sir John Heveningham (C. 142/515/68), mentions more than fifteen manors in his possession in 1634.
[309] *Al. Cant.*
[310] S.P. 16/405.
[311] C. 181/5, fols. 205, 284, 342.
[312] S.P. 16, 77/3/ii; *C.S.P. Dom., 1627–1628, 327, 445, 448.*
[313] *Ibid., 1636–1637, 371–372.*
[314] *The ship-money returns for the county of Suffolk, 1639–1640,* ed. Redstone, 85, Suffolk Institute of Archaeology, 1904.
[315] *H.M.C., Tenth Report* 2: MSS of the Gawdy Family, 174.
[316] *C.S.P. Ireland, Adventurers, 3; N. and Q.,* 1st Ser., 12: 358, 1855.
[317] *A.H.R.* 44: 31, n. (32), 1938–1939.
[318] *H.M.C., Tenth Report* 2, MSS of the Gawdy Family, 174; Bodleian Tanner MSS, 67, fol. 189.
[319] *Gray's Inn Adm. Reg.,* 177.
[320] She died in 1643, leaving two sons. Add. MSS, 18,477, fol. 342.

[321] *M. of P.* 1: 497; 3: App. xliii; Hythe Borough MSS, Assembly Book, 1608–1645, fols. 238, 240.
[322] From 25 February 1641 to the end of 1651 he served on nearly eighty committees, including important ones dealing with recusancy and the defense. Pink MSS, 303, fol. 241.
[323] Wilks, *The barons of the Cinque Ports,* 81–82.
[324] *N. and Q.,* 1st Ser., 12: 359, 1855.
[325] *C.J.* 2: 724; *Arch. Cant.* 2: 181, 1859; 9: 32, n., 1874.
[326] He held the patronage of a vicarage there in 1654. Lansd. MSS, 459, fol. 120.
[327] In addition to the above references, see *Complete Baronetage* 2: 135.
[328] *M. of P.* 1: 497; *C.J.* 2: 82; D'Ewes (N), 334.
[329] *Al. Cant.*
[330] S.P., 14, 97/51; C. 181/3, fol. 3v; 181/4, fols. 18v, 48v, 88; 181/5, fols. 262, 288; Boys, *Sandwich,* 216.
[331] Wilks, *The barons of the Cinque Ports,* 70.
[332] *Commons Debates 1621* 2: 209; 3: 201, 221, *passim.*
[333] S.P. 14, 127/82; S.P. 16, 89/5.

have been one of the leaders in the struggle with the crown, 1641–1642, had not death ended his career and passed his responsibilities on to his son, Henry (*q.v.*).

Heyman was probably one of the wealthier members of the House, despite the financial distress from which he complained that his wife and ten children were suffering during his imprisonment in 1629.[334] He had inherited more than six manors in Kent, had acquired some Irish estates before 1640, and by two marriages with daughters of London merchants had further improved his circumstances. He was one who offered to be bound for £1000 for the loan in 1640.[335]

* **Roger Hill** (1605–1667), of the Inner Temple, Recorder of Bridport, Dorset, was M.P. for that borough, 1640–1653.[336] He became in time Serjeant-at-law and Baron of the Exchequer. The heir of an old Somerset family seated at Poundsford near Taunton, and nephew of Walter Yonge, the Honiton M.P. (*q.v.*),[337] he may have studied at St. John's, Cambridge (matriculated sizar, 1622),[338] before entering the Inner Temple (1624). Having been called to the bar there in 1632, he apparently returned to his native region to practice. In 1635 he married Katherine (d. 1638), daughter of Giles Green of Allington (*q.v.*), with whose family his own had been connected through an earlier marriage.[339] By October, 1640, Hill was Recorder of Bridport, and in 1641 he was a reader at one of the inns of chancery.[340] He was possibly the "Roger Hill, gent., of Taunton" who was Taunton's M.P. in the Short Parliament, but he had an uncle of the same name, usually designated as of Taunton, who had been mayor of the town and who later worked with his nephew, the Bridport member, on parliamentary committees during the war. The uncle was perhaps the Short Parliament member.[341]

In the Long Parliament Hill, though with little or no experience in the House, was named as early as 13 November 1640 to the committee on Leighton's petition, and he served on more than sixty committees before the parliament ended.[342] He was outspoken in his attacks on the ecclesiastical hierarchy.[343] His second marriage

in 1641 with a half-sister of John Gurdon (*q.v.*)[344] suggests the group in the parliament in which he moved. He was an elder in his presbytery, but worked afterwards as an Independent.[345]

As to Hill's estate there is little evidence beyond the royalist comment that until he acquired properties through the war time sequestrations he was "of no considerable estate."[346] He had inherited the family property at Poundsford, however,[347] and in June, 1642, promised £100 for the defense,[348] a sum larger than that offered by many.

Sir John Hippisley (d. 1655 ?), courtier, of Bushey Park, Middlesex, was M.P. for Cockermouth, Cumberland, from its restoration in February, 1641, until 1653.[349] He came of a Somerset family, being the grandson of John Hippisley of Stone Easton, who had a large estate, and a younger son of William Hippisley of Marston (d. 1630) by his wife, who was of the Burley family of the Isle of Wight.[350] As a young man he entered the service of Henry, Earl of Northumberland, and was in his employ during the earl's imprisonment, at least from 1611 to 1614.[351] He was knighted at York, 14 April 1617,[352] and had probably attached himself by that time to Buckingham. He was referred to early in 1618 as Buckingham's principal favorite,[353] and during the latter's ascendancy was loath neither to give him advice nor to ask him for favors. By this time, probably, Hippisley had married Catherine, daughter of Sir Roger Norton of Rotherfield, Hampshire.[354]

Sir John's influence at court had procured for him before 1619 an interest in the royal customs on butter exported from certain western ports.[355] He sat in the parliament of 1621 for Petersfield,[356] elected no doubt with the aid of his father-in-law. He travelled to Spain with Buckingham and the prince in 1623, and in the controversy that developed with Bristol urged his patron to show patience, for all the eyes of the world were on

---

[334] *C.S.P. Dom., 1628–1629,* 551. The House voted £5000 for his heirs in 1646 in recompense for his losses.

[335] *I.P.M.,* Henry Heyman, 1614 (C. 142/362/167); Hasted, *Kent* **8**: 106, 307–309, 431; *C.S.P. Dom., 1623–1625,* 278; Add. MSS, 18,472, fol. 342; D'Ewes (N), 52.

[336] *D.N.B.* errs in dating his entry into the House in 1645. The return (*M. of P.* **1**: 488; C. 219/43/Part 1) assigned him to the Middle Temple instead of to the Inner Temple.

[337] *Vis. Devon, 1620,* 325; Brown, *Somerset Wills* **1**: 35–36.

[338] *Al. Cant.* His son, Roger, was admitted at Jesus, Cambridge, in 1658.

[339] *Vis. Dorset,* 55.

[340] *C.J.* **2**: 107.

[341] *M. of P.* **1**: 483; *Somerset and Dorset N. and Q.* **4**: 79, 1894–1895; **12**: 259, 1910–1911; *Cal. Com. Comp.,* 289, 315; Brown, *Somerset Wills* **3**: 81.

[342] *C.J.* **2**: 28; Pink MSS, 304, fol. 401.

[343] D'Ewes (N), 426; D'Ewes (C), 371 and n.

[344] *D.N.B.;* Copinger, *The manors of Suffolk* **1**: 18.

[345] *A.H.R.* **44**: 31, n. (32), 1938–1939.

[346] *The mystery of the good old cause,* 22; Add. MSS, 27,990, fol. 39.

[347] Roger Hill's will, P.C.C., 44 Carr.

[348] *N. and Q.,* 1st Ser., **12**: 360, 1855.

[349] *O.P.H.* **9**: *23.

[350] Pink MSS, 307, fol. 318; Burke, *Landed gentry,* 1851; *Middlesex pedigrees,* Harleian Society **65**: 82, 1914.

[351] *The letters of John Chamberlain* **1**: 318, 513; *Acts P.C., 1613–1614,* 269.

[352] *Somerset and Dorset N. and Q.* **2**: 248, 1891.

[353] *The letters of John Chamberlain* **2**: 152, 200.

[354] Pink MSS, 307, fol. 319. Hippisley's daughter, Elizabeth Hugessen, had five children when she died in December, 1642. *Arch. Cant.* **23**: 129, 1898.

[355] He complained in a Chancery suit in 1619 against some attempts to defraud him of the profit from this grant which he had earned by his "long and good service" to the king. C. 3/313/47.

[356] *M. of P.* **1**: 453.

him and this was the time to win honor and fame.[357] He failed to win a seat for Middlesex, even with the duke's support, in the elections for the 1624 parliament, but sat again for Petersfield.[358] When Buckingham became Lord Warden of the Cinque Ports that year Hippisley was made Lieutenant of Dover Castle. It was rumored in 1628 that he was to be made a lord,[359] but the keepership of Bushey Park seems to have been the only other special favor which he received through Buckingham.[360] He used his powers over shipping and travellers at Dover with such lack of scruple that complaints came in from many persons, including the Netherlands ambassador, and foreign and English merchants and captains, and early in 1625 and in 1626 his conduct was brought to the attention of parliament.[361] He and his sea-captain brother profited further by the hostilities of 1626 to 1628, when they did a flourishing business of preying upon French shipping. Hippisley wrote to his patron and Nicholas, offering to share the profits with them, saying, "This is the way to put you out of debt."[362] He assisted Buckingham with the Cinque Port elections for the first three parliaments of Charles, obtaining for himself one of Dover's places each time.[363] Early in 1628 he was aspiring to a place nearer the king as Lieutenant of the Pensioners,[364] but the favorite's death brought him a change of fortune. Although he retained his Bushey Park keepership and indulged in a little more privateering,[365] he was presently replaced at Dover by Sir Edward Dering, and as late as 1637 was involved in cases in the Admiralty and the Exchequer regarding goods which he had confiscated during his lieutenancy.[366] He continued, however, to be a J.P. in Kent and Middlesex,[367] and maintained his residence near the court at the Mewes.[368] He was appointed to the commission to investigate the depopulation of several of the western counties, work in which John Pym was a colleague,[369] but in 1640, his elder brother having died, he sold the family estate of Marston in Somerset,[370] severing his principal tie with his native county.

With the word of a new parliament, Hippisley aspired to return to national politics. He persuaded the Earl of Northumberland, successor of his first patron, to commend him to Dover late in 1639,[371] but the town would not have him. His election for Cockermouth sometime after 15 February 1641 is doubtless to be explained by the fact that Northumberland was lord of the castle and manor there. And Hippisley was loyal to his new patron. He supported parliament and, though most of his early committee appointments were concerned only with matters in and near Westminster, he was named in January, 1642, to the Committee of Safety at the Guildhall,[372] and during the war was named to most of the parliamentary committees for Middlesex. He was appointed in 1642, 1646, and 1648 on commissions to treat with the king,[373] was a member of the committee for abolishing the kingship in 1649, and from then until the end of the session was increasingly active in the work of the House.[374] He continued to live at Bushey Park much of the time, made his will as "of Richmond, Surrey," on 25 January 1655, and probably died soon afterwards. His will was proved 14 February 1656.[375]

Of Sir John's worldly estate few evidences remain. That he was an opportunist his career and his official correspondence show. His fortunes had doubtless ebbed after Buckingham's death, but he could still lend the king £1000 for a loan at 8 per cent in 1631. He received warrants in 1632 for the repayment of part of his lieutenancy, and the next year invested £200 in the fisheries venture.[376] He received at least a share of the £10,350 for which he sold the Somerset property in 1640, and in 1642 he promised to provide three horses for the defense.[377] It was typical of him that he used the opportunities of the war to profit by the losses of the royalists. Not only did he get parliament in 1652 to vote him £1250 in recompense for the arrears due him from Bushey Park, but he refused at the same time to surrender to the Compounding Committee certain money they claimed on goods he had bought from them.[378]

---

[357] C.S.P. Dom., 1619–1623, 541, 582; Harl. MSS, 1681, fols. 370–371.

[358] The letters of John Chamberlain 2: 543; M. of P. 1: 459.

[359] C.S.P. Dom., 1623–1625, 333, 352, 386; D'Ewes, Autobiography 2: 205.

[360] He held it first for the duke's life and then was issued a lifetime grant of his own. C.S.P. Dom., 1628–1629, 272, 344.

[361] Ibid., 1625–1626, 84, passim; 1627–1628, 184; 1629–1631, 136; S.P. 16, 40/36; H.M.C., Fourth Report, MSS of the Earl of De la Warr, 289.

[362] C.S.P. Dom., 1627–1628, 78, 83, 161, passim. He received letters of marque for four ships between January, 1626, and June, 1627. Ibid., 1628–1629, 286, passim.

[363] M. of P. 1: 467, 473, 479; C.S.P. Dom., 1625–1626, 217, 218, 221; 1627–1628, 537, 541, 543; 1628–1629, 7.

[264] Ibid., 1627–1628, 541.

[365] Ibid., 1628–1629, 594; 1629–1631, 155.

[366] Ibid., 1629–1631, 136, 212; 1631–1633, 144. S.P. 16, 362/31.

[367] C. 193/12, 13; S.P. 16/405.

[368] C.S.P. Dom., 1628–1629, 33; 1633–1634, 428.

[369] C. 181/5, fols. 1, 43, 44; S.P. 16, 229/12/252.

[370] Burke, Landed gentry, 1851; D. Townshend, The life and letters of the great Earl of Cork, 350.

[371] C.S.P. Dom., 1639–1640, 400; Add. MSS, 18,016, fol. 1, v.

[372] C.J. 2: 197, 317, 318, 369.

[373] May, 273; Pink MSS, 307, fols. 318–319.

[374] Ibid. Of the 72 committees to which he was named throughout the parliament, 50 were in the period after the king's death.

[375] P.C.C., 65 Berkeley.

[376] C.S.P. Dom., 1629–1631, 536, 559; Stowe MSS, 743, fol. 89; S.P. 16, 231/15/i, fols. 31–32.

[377] N. and Q., 1st Ser., 12: 360, 1855.

[378] Somerset and Dorset N. and Q. 2: 248, 1891; Cal. Com. Comp., 523, 581.

Peregrine Hoby (1602–1678), of Bisham, Berkshire, was elected for Great Marlow, Bucks, on 21 October 1640 and again on 23 November, after the House had ordered a new election. He lived near Marlow, though in a different county, and seems to have been the most popular of all the candidates in a complicated election. His second election was challenged, partly because he had been pricked sheriff just before it occurred, and a decision had not been reached by 13 January 1641.[379] Hoby was apparently required to serve his term as sheriff, and during most of 1641 he was occupied with his duties in Berkshire, though still being counted a member of the House.[380] His name is missing from the *Journals,* even from the list of those taking the Protestation, but he was present by June, 1642, and from 1643 to 1648 was fairly active.[381]

Hoby was the natural son of a wealthy and learned father, Sir Edward Hoby of Bisham (1560–1617), the diplomat and controversialist, who made Peregrine, despite his illegitimacy, his heir.[382] Born about 1602, and reared under the care of Archbishop Abbott, he was possibly an officer in the Cadiz expedition of 1625 and in that to Rochelle.[383] He resisted the knighthood composition of 1630, but eventually made his peace with the commissioners and promised to pay £30.[384] The following year, 14 April, he married Katherine, daughter of Sir William Dodington of Breamore, Hampshire.[385] He either supplied a horse for the Lieutenant-General's troop in the north in August, 1639, or was present with it as an officer.[386] He was named that year to the sewers commission for Berkshire and Wiltshire, but does not seem to have been a J.P until later.[387]

In the Long Parliament, his first, Hoby worked with the popular party, and was active on various county committees for Berkshire until his seclusion in December, 1648. He was returned again for Marlow after the Restoration and died in May, 1678.[388]

Hoby seems to have been a man of means. Besides his principal manor of Bisham near Marlow he had properties in Hants and Kent, and his wife was heir to certain lands of her family.[389] His pledge for the defense in 1642 was two horses.[390] When new arms were granted to him in 1664 he was described as "well deserving not only for his good conversation and discreet demeanor, but also for a prudent discharge of his duty to his country." [391]

Thomas Hodges (died *c.* 1675), of Shipton Moyne, Gloucestershire, and of the Middle Temple, was M.P. for Cricklade in Wiltshire, 1640–1648. His family owned various properties nearby in Wiltshire, some formerly the possessions of the church,[392] but their activities were chiefly in the affairs of Gloucestershire. He was the eldest son and heir of Thomas Hodges of Shipton (J.P., H.S., d. 1638) by his wife, Joyce, daughter of Sir George Snigge, Recorder of Bristol and Baron of the Exchequer.[393] A number of important Bristol properties that had belonged to Snigge passed to Hodges's father and eventually came into his hands.[394] The younger Thomas was admitted to the Middle Temple in 1622, and he was still described as of the Temple when his own son, Thomas, was admitted there in 1646.[395] He was identified as of Shipton Moyne, however, when in 1633 he sold his grandfather's Bristol mansion for £820.[396] He married (1) Dulsabella, daughter of John Syms of Poundsford, Somerset (d. 1628), and (2) Mary, daughter of Sir William Cooke of Highnam, Gloucestershire.[397] She was a sister of Sir Robert Cooke (*q.v.*), and was connected by marriage with such puritan families as the Fleetwoods and the Lukes.[398]

Hodges was a J.P in Gloucestershire, as was his father before him,[399] and was possibly the Mr. Hodges of Somerset who refused to contribute to the king in 1639.[400] He was elected to the Short Parliament for

---

[379] Whitelocke, who was Hoby's colleague for Marlow and was permitted by 2 January to take his seat, noted that "Mr. Hoby & I tooke our places," omitting any comment about Hoby's duties as sheriff (Add. MSS, 37,343, fol. 212v). See Great Marlow election.

[380] *List of Sheriffs,* 6; D'Ewes (B), 571.

[381] *N. and Q.,* 1st Ser., **12**: 359, 1855; Pink MSS, 307, fol. 88.

[382] His father's executors objected in 1619 to Peregrine's being described in a lawsuit as a bastard (C. 3/312/73), but the records of the visitation of 1665 indicate that Hoby himself acknowledged his illegitimacy. *Vis. Berks.* **1**: 228; **2**: 148–149.

[383] "Ensign Hobbie," 1625; "Lieutenant Hobby," 1628. S.P. 16, 522/16; 111/62.

[384] S.P. 16, 180/24/86.

[385] *Vis. Berks.* **1**: 228; *The parish registers of Bisham,* 22, The Parish Register Society, 1898.

[386] S.P. 16, 427/38/iii.

[387] C. 181/5, fol. 271.

[388] Pink MSS, 307, fol. 88; *Berks. Arch. Jour.* **31**: 178, 1927; *M. of P.* **1**: 519.

[389] Hasted, *Kent* **6**: 262; Nichols, *Bib. Top.* **4**: 10–11; Bodleian Tanner MSS, 63, fol. 57.

[390] *N. and Q.,* 1st Ser., **12**: 359, 1855.

[391] *Vis. Berks.* **2**: 151, n. Hoby is mentioned briefly in *D.N.B.,* "Sir Edward Hoby."

[392] *Gloucestershire N. and Q.* **1**: 362, 455, 1881; Lansd. MSS, 459, fol. 161v; *Wilts. Arch. Mag.* **41**: 29, 1920–1921.

[393] Pink MSS, 304, fol. 441; *List of Sheriffs,* 51; Brown, *Somerset Wills* **1**: 21–22.

[394] St. Ch. 8/175/24; Bristol Corporation MSS, Audit Books, **19–21,** entries of 1627, 1630, 1640.

[395] *Mid. Temp. Rec.* **2**: 677, 942. He probably had a London house in 1638. Dale, *Inhabitants of London,* 193.

[396] He was called Thomas Hodges, the younger, since his father was then living. Bristol Library MSS, Bristol Coll., 10160, fols. 252–255.

[397] Pink MSS, *loc. cit.*

[398] See Cooke.

[399] C. 193/13; Gloucester Corporation MSS, Letter Book, 1640–1660, fol. 3.

[400] Rushworth **3**: 914. Pink thought the loan refuser of 1639 was more probably this Thomas Hodges than the one who was elected as a recruiter from Somerset in 1646. Pink MSS, 304, fol. 441.

Cricklade, and again in the autumn.[401] He was not a conspicuous member of the Long Parliament in its early period, but worked with the country party.[402] In June, 1642, he promised to supply two horses for the defense,[403] and was active in organizing his county's resistance to the royal forces. With another Gloucestershire member, Stephens, he advanced £720 for their county's defense before February, 1643,[404] and he continued to work for the popular cause there and in Wiltshire until his expulsion in 1648. He survived the Restoration but died sometime before 3 August 1675. Administration of his estate was granted at that time to his daughter, Joyce.[405]

Besides owning properties in Wiltshire and Gloucestershire, Hodges had also some Somerset lands. One portion of his father's holdings had been valued in 1626 at £200 a year.[406] He must be distinguished, however, from the Thomas Hodges (c. 1604–1649), son of George Hodges of Wedmore, who sat for Ilchester after January, 1646,[407] and from the London merchant, Thomas Hodges, who was interested in the Virginia Company.[408]

* Robert Holborne (d. 1647), of Lincoln's Inn, was elected for Michael, Cornwall, after John Arundell chose Bodmin for his constituency (9 November 1640), but he was disabled as a royalist, 22 January 1644.[409] A native of Sussex and known for his defense of Hampden in the ship money case, Holborne had late in 1639 attacked tonnage and poundage also, on behalf of a merchant's widow. He was elected to the Short Parliament for Southwark on the basis of his reputation as foe of the king and of oppression.[410] His election for the Cornish borough of the Arundells in the fall resulted possibly from his association at Lincoln's Inn with some of that family, as well as with Chadwell, the other lawyer member for Michael. But he was not named often to committees, his principal appointments being to those concerned with the authority of the convocation.[411] Not only did he vote against Strafford's attainder, but in November, 1641, he made a learned, legalistic argu-

ment on behalf of the bishops.[412] His last committee appointment was on 29 March 1642, and he probably left the House soon afterwards. He was absent the following June.[413] And the next February he was created D.C.L. at Oxford.[414]

Holborne was the steward for a Sussex manor in 1622 and engaged in some legal transactions involving other Sussex lands in 1628 and 1636.[415] His composition papers indicate that his chief real estate, worth £80 a year, was some land in Warwickshire which he held in right of his wife, Anne. His fine at a tenth, before the Warwickshire property was reported, was but £95.[416]

* Cornelius Holland (born 1599 ?), a clerk in the royal household, sat for Windsor, Berkshire, for most of the Long Parliament. Although his original return was voided, he was re-elected within eight days, and remained a member until the end.[417] He was described in the return as "of New Windsor," but most of his connections were with London and the royal residences.[418] The first Berkshire commission on which he was named seems to have been that for the perambulation of Windsor Forest in 1641.[419]

Holland was the son of Ralph Holland, who lived in St. Lawrence Pountney parish, London, and may have held a minor post in the royal household under King James.[420] Cornelius, born in March, 1599 (1599/1600 ?),[421] was educated at Cambridge, and had a wife and a son by February, 1628. In 1630 he was on the king's pension lists for £160 a year, half of the sum being the pension which under King James had been assigned to his father, Ralph, and half being his own return for a clerkship at the court.[422] By that year also he had taken up residence on Millbank, Westminster.[423] His advancement under Sir Henry Vane in the royal household, where he became clerk comptroller for the Prince of Wales, was accompanied in 1635 by the keepership of

---

[401] M. of P. 1: 484, 495.

[402] Pink estimated that he served on possibly thirty committees of the House between 1640 and 1648. Pink MSS, loc. cit. One of them was that on the Bishop of Ely. C.J. 2: 56.

[403] N. and Q., 1st Ser., 12: 360, 1855.

[404] H.M.C., Fifth Report, House of Lords MSS, 73; Calendar of Clarendon State Papers 1: 242.

[405] Gloucestershire N. and Q. 1: 455, 1881.

[406] S.P. 16, 19/116. Holles (Memoirs, 132) declared that Mr. Hodges of Gloucestershire was one of the members who lined their pockets with a thousand pounds at least during the war. He was assigned in 1647 as reparations £1000 from the estates of the Earl of Worcester (Pink MSS, loc. cit.). But he was by no means a poor man when he entered the parliament.

[407] M. of P. 1: 493; Pink MSS, 304, fol. 442.

[408] Brown, Genesis of the U. S., 924; S.P. 16, 453/75.

[409] C.J. 2: 23; 3: 374.

[410] Add. MSS 11,045, fols. 73v, 97, 101v.

[411] C.J. 2: 48, 81, 129.

[412] Verney, 58; D'Ewes (C), 134–135.

[413] C.J. 2: 504, 626.

[414] Wood, Fasti Oxon. 2: 45.

[415] Sussex Rec. Soc. 20: 302, 1915; 29: 17, 1924.

[416] S.P. 23/196/686; Cal. Com. Comp., 1586.

[417] M. of P. 1: 485, and n.; Tighe and Davis, Annals of Windsor 2: 149.

[418] He was a parishioner of St. Margaret's, Westminster, from 1630 to 1639 (Records of the Parish of St. Margaret's, Overseers' Accounts, vols. 153–154), and was grouped with others from Middlesex in a list of 1639 (Rushworth 3, 914). He was with the royal children at Richmond in June, 1640. C.S.P. Dom., 1640, 301.

[419] C. 181/5, fol. 421.

[420] Proof that Cornelius was Ralph's son appears in a 1630 list of pensions (S.P. 16, 180/16, fol. 34). The somewhat dubious authority, The mystery of the good old cause (p. 20), states that Cornelius's father died in the Fleet, a prisoner for debt.

[421] 1599 is the date given in D.N.B. Other authorities suggest it was more probably 1600, new style.

[422] S.P. 16, 180/16, fol. 34; 180/18, fol. 69.

[423] Records of the Parish of St. Margaret's, cited above.

the royal pastures of Creslow, Bucks,[424] probably as a part of his eighteen-year lease of the manor house and pastures there. His salary seems to have been at least £827 a year, and the rental for the property was only £200.[425] A contemporary comment placed the value of Holland's controls at Creslow at £1800 to £2000 a year. His employment included a post on the board of the Green Cloth, and he was said to have increased his fortunes by other offices and by participation in patents and monopolies.[426] The fact that he was asked for a loan in 1639, along with other civil servants and men of wealth, suggests that he was then far from poor.[427]

Holland was named on the Middlesex commission of the peace (1634),[428] but he seems to have had no particular associations with Berkshire. His official connections perhaps had made him somewhat familiar to the residents of Windsor, however, and when his first election was voided, there appears to have been no opposition to his re-election. In the parliament he served on numerous committees, especially those concerned with the church, and was an active member.[429] His subscription for the defense in June, 1642, was two horses.[430]

Holland has come in for scathing comments by those who disagreed with his politics, ranging from derogatory remarks about his birth and early service in the household to charges of fraudulent practices in office and of voting for the king's death in order to secure royal lands.[431] Much of the opprobrium can probably be traced to the bitterness of the times. His puritan zeal, his obvious ambition before 1640 as well as after, and the fact that, after having served in the royal household so intimately, he became a regicide, undoubtedly made him a mark for such attacks. But it appears that Holland's birth and early offices were less obscure than his enemies hinted, that the tactics he used for improving his fortunes were similar to those employed by other servants of the crown, regardless of party, and that before the Long Parliament began he enjoyed a more than comfortable income.

Sir John Holland, Bart. (1603–1701), of Quidenham, Norfolk, M.P. for Castle Rising, 1640–1648, and a diarist of the parliament, owed his election no doubt to the Earl of Arundel, patron of the borough, whose agent he had been for some years. He was the son and heir of Sir Thomas Holland of Quidenham and Wortwell Hall, M.P. and J.P., by his wife, Mary, daughter of Sir Thomas Knyvet of Ashwell Thorpe, and was born at the latter place in October, 1603.[432] He was educated at Christ's College, Cambridge, and the Middle Temple,[433] succeeded his father in 1626,[434] and in 1629 became a baronet without fee.[435] Before December, 1632, he married Alathea, widow of William Lord Sandys of the Vine, and daughter and coheir of John Panton of county Denbigh, a lady of considerable estate, whose adherence to the Catholic faith seems not to have disturbed her Presbyterian husband, although he found it necessary to allay the suspicions of parliament on this point in 1640.[436]

Holland took an active part in Norfolk affairs, held commands as captain and colonel in the county militia, and served as a J.P. and a D.L.[437] He was elected to the Short Parliament for his county,[438] and aspired to the same place in the autumn. But, in order to avoid "sidings and faction" among the gentry, he yielded the contest to John Potts (q.v.), and turned to Castle Rising for his own place.[439]

Sir John was a man of conviction, favoring reforms, but the achieving of them by moderate means if possible. He spoke out in November against grievances, ecclesiastical, administrative, and economic,[440] and was named to numerous committees, especially those concerned with reforms in the church.[441] He was a Norfolk committeeman during the war,[442] but hoped for an early peace and was one of the commissioners for negotiating with the king at Oxford in 1643.[443] He was secluded with other Presbyterians in 1648, but was a member of the council of state appointed in 1660 just before the return of Charles II. He served in the Cavalier parliament, where again he was not afraid to speak. He died, aged ninety-eight, on 19 January 1701.

---

[424] C.S.P. Dom., 1631–1633, 250; 1635–1636, 1.

[425] The lease was renewed with parliament's consent in 1645, and Holland eventually bought the property. C.J. 4: 270; V.C.H. Buckingham 3: 335, 337.

[426] The mystery of the good old cause, 20–21. According to this source, Holland was turned out of the Green Cloth post for fraud, but on 11 September 1645 the House of Commons resolved that the self-denying ordinance should not prevent his holding his place as paymaster and clerk of the Green Cloth to the Prince. C.J. 4: 270.

[427] He failed, however, to answer the request. Rushworth 3: 914.

[428] C. 193/13.

[429] According to Pink's figures, he was named to 272 committees, 1640–1653. Pink MSS, 307, fol. 48.

[430] N. and Q., 1st Ser., 12: 359, 1855.

[431] Memoirs of Denzil Holles, 135–136; The mystery of the good old cause, loc. cit.; citations from Cole's MSS in Lipscomb, Buckingham 1: 250–251; Noble, Regicides 1: 360.

[432] Complete Baronetage 2: 74; Blomefield, Norfolk 1: opp. 344. A sketch of his father and family appears in Commons Debates 1621 1: 90–94, and of Sir John Holland, in D'Ewes (C), Introduction, xxxv–xxxvii.

[433] Al. Cant.; Mid. Temp. Rec. 2: 679, 731.

[434] I.P.M. of Sir Thomas Holland. C. 142/429/129.

[435] C.S.P. Dom., 1628–1629, 574.

[436] D'Ewes (N), 58; C.J. 2: 35, 119, 126; Bodleian Tanner MSS, 239, fols. 12, 15.

[437] C. 193/13; S.P. 16/405, 421/137.

[438] The return is not in M. of P., but see Willis 3: 233, and H.M.C., Tenth Report 2, Gawdy MSS, 176.

[439] H.M.C., Tenth Report 2, Gawdy MSS, 176.

[440] D'Ewes (N), 15–16.

[441] C.J. 2: 39, 91, 99, 101, 119.

[442] Mason, Norfolk, 281; Pink MSS, 304, fol. 458.

[443] Bodleian Tanner MSS, 63, fols. 121, 126; May, 277, 278.

Holland was a man of ample means, having inherited seven manors and other lands in Norfolk and Suffolk, and having married well.[444] He offered his bond for £1000 in November, 1640, and in 1642 promised to supply two horses and £100 for the defense.[445] Whitelocke described him as "a person of excellent parts as well as [a] person [who] showed a very good judgement & testimony of his abilities." [446]

* Denzil Holles (1599–1680), of Dorchester and of Damerham South, Wiltshire,[447] was a member for Dorchester from 1640 until his impeachment in 1647. Although of bourgeois ancestry, Holles represented high social position in his period, for he was the second son of an earl, the brother and brother-in-law of two others, and the cousin of another.[448] His kinsman, Gervase Holles (q.v.), wrote that his education was equal to the best and beyond that of most of the nobility.[449] He was created B.A. on the occasion of Prince Charles's visit to Cambridge in 1613, and was a resident at Christ's College there and graduated M.A. in 1616. He was admitted in 1615 to Gray's Inn.[450]

After Holles's experiences in the early parliaments of King Charles, his imprisonment and the costly proceedings in the courts that grew out of his conduct in 1629,[451] he continued to be a part of the movement of resistance. He absolutely refused to pay ship money in Wiltshire in 1635, and encouraged his mother-in-law, Lady Ashley, to resist payment in Dorset.[452] He opposed the saltpetre men who were sent to work on his property in 1637. In 1638 he had to appear before Council in a suit brought against him on some charge of damage done to the property of his landlord, the Earl of Salisbury, at Damerham.[453] And the next year he ignored the request for a loan for royal expenses in the north.[454] He was named to the Dorset sewers commission in 1638, and to the commission of oyer and terminer in Wilts and Hertfordshire in 1641.[455] He won his seat for the Short Parliament by the decision

of Dorchester to return "townsmen" rather than such a court nominee as Sir Dudley Carleton.[456]

Holles came of a wealthy family, and at his first marriage with the heiress of Sir Francis Ashley acquired various properties near Dorchester.[457] His father settled on him then some Cornish lands valued at about £2500, with the expectation of a further settlement that would bring his estate to possibly £1000 a year. The year after his father's death, however, his mother-in-law sued his mother and his elder brother, charging them with preventing the earl from making such a final settlement on his younger son.[458] In spite of that disappointment, however, Holles seems to have had ample resources. He was able in June, 1642, to subscribe £300 and the maintenance of four horses for the defense.[459]

Holles was related to several of his fellow parliament men of 1640. His second cousin, Gervase, his first cousin, William Stanhope, and Ferdinando Stanhope, a cousin's son, were among the royalists. But on the other side was Sir Thomas Hutchinson, the husband of another cousin. And after his first wife died in 1641,[460] his marriage with a daughter of Sir John Shirley of Isfield, Sussex, connected him with several of the Sussex puritans.

* Gervase Holles (1607–1675,) of Great Grimsby, Lincolnshire, and of the Middle Temple, the antiquary and royalist, was a member for Grimsby from October, 1640, until his disablement, 22 August 1642. He was suspended for a time in April, 1641, but was apparently attending as late as January, 1642.[461] Holles was born at Grimsby, 9 March 1606/7,[462] and was a second cousin of Denzil Holles, the Presbyterian leader, in whose father's home he received part of his education. He was called to the bar at the Middle Temple in 1639,[463] and was elected by Grimsby to both parliaments of the following year.

Holles owned some lands near Grimsby, most of which had come to him from his maternal grandfather, and rented other properties there. Neither his father's nor his own estate was large, however, and his income

---

[444] I.P.M. cited above; Blomefield, *Norfolk* 5: 220.

[445] D'Ewes (N), 52; *N. and Q.,* 1st Ser., 12: 359, 1855. His pledge was given in the latter instance for the defense of the true protestant religion, the king's person and authority, and "our laws, liberties and privileges, conjunctively."

[446] Whitelocke's Annals, Add. MSS, 37,343, fol. 268.

[447] *Wilts. Arch. Mag.* 26: 343, 1892; *Mid. Temp. Rec.* 2: 960.

[448] He was the son and brother of two earls of Clare, a brother-in-law of Strafford, and a cousin of the first Earl of Chesterfield. See Alexander Thomson, "John Holles," *Jour. Mod. Hist.* 8: 145–172, 1936.

[449] *Memorials of the Holles family*, 109, Camden Society, 1937.

[450] *Al. Cant.;* Add. MSS, 32,464, fols. 121–122.

[451] He afterwards estimated his losses on this account at some £13,000. *D.N.B.*

[452] S.P. 16, 319/89; *C.S.P. Dom.,* 1635, 523; *1640*, 57–58.

[453] *Ibid., 1636–1637,* 437, 449; *1638–1639,* 44–45, 84–85.

[454] Rushworth 3: 913.

[455] C. 181/5, fols. 225, 377.

[456] Mayo, *Municipal records, Dorchester,* 436. He had been admitted a freeman of Dorchester the day before he was first elected as its M.P. in 1628. *Ibid.,* 395.

[457] Hutchins, *Dorset* 2: 410, 412; Exeter City Library MSS, Exeter Deeds and Documents, No. 2715.

[458] *C.S.P. Dom., 1637–1638,* 353, 455; *Calendar of Clarendon State Papers* 1: 154.

[459] *N. and Q.,* 1st Ser., 12: 338, 1855.

[460] Her death was given as in June, 1640, in *D.N.B.,* but the Dorchester parish register cited in Manning and Bray (*Surrey* 2: 31) dates her burial on 19 February 1641.

[461] *M. of P.* 1: 490; *C.J.* 2: 128, 329, 404, 730.

[462] Gervase Holles, *Memorials of the Holles family,* Camden Society, 3rd Ser., 55: 227, 1937. He was baptized on 13 March 1606/7. *Lincolnshire Church Notes made by Gervase Holles,* Lincoln Record Society 1: v, 1911. 1606 is the year given in *D.N.B.*

[463] *Mid. Temp. Rec.* 2: 881.

from lands in 1640 was probably not more than £150–£175 a year.[464]

Humphrey Hooke (*c.* 1580–1659), alderman of Bristol, sat for his town, 1640–12 May 1642.[465] He was born about 1580 in Chichester, Hampshire, being related perhaps to the Bramshott Hookes near there,[466] and seems in his early life to have been connected with the Ironmongers' Company of London, possibly for his apprenticeship.[467] But as a young merchant he sought his fortune in the west, and on 4 February 1606/7 was granted the freedom of Bristol by virtue of his marriage with Cicely, daughter of Thomas Young, merchant.[468] Allied thus with a family of prominence, and equipped with a good measure of ability and shrewdness, Hooke embarked on a business career that brought him wealth and distinction. In the records of the corporation and of the Society of Merchant Venturers from 1610 until 1645 Hooke's name is associated with most matters of importance in Bristol. He was one of its commercial magnates, 1630–1640.

Hooke served in the usual town offices, as sheriff (1614–1615), councillor (1614–1632), alderman (1632–1645), and twice as mayor (1629–1630, 1643–1644). In performing civic duties he was concerned not only with matters of the quays and the streets, of finances and the schools or the preachers' salaries, but he treated with agents of the crown and more than once rode to London in the interest of Bristol's trade or to secure a more favorable ruling on the burdens of purveyance or ship money.[469] He had a personal interest in most of the maritime or mercantile projects in which Bristol men were then engaged, whether as a patentee for the Newfoundland plantation in 1610 or the backer of a new voyage in search of a northwest passage in 1631.[470] And his younger son, William, migrated to New England and was for a time on Gorges's council for Maine.[471] Hooke subscribed toward an expedition sent against the Algerine pirates in 1620,[472] and, although he opposed the requisitioning of ships for Buckingham's fleet in 1628, he and his partners between 1626 and 1630 took out letters of marque on several ships. One of them was said in 1630 to have brought in prizes worth at least £40,000.[473]

In Bristol's Society of Merchant Venturers Hooke was particularly active. He was treasurer, 1616–1617, and was master for eight terms (1621–22, 1630–35, 1638–39). He was a leader in the company's venture on the export of hides, in their attempt to break the Levant Company's monopoly on the importation of currants, and in their agreements on the soap trade.[474] But in his zeal for those enterprises, he eventually became involved in the antagonism developing against the Society among the smaller merchants of Bristol. With Richard Long (*q.v.*) he opposed the investigations of the company's accounts by royal officials in 1637,[475] and in 1639–1640 he was criticized locally for having become one of the farmers of Sir Henry Hungate's patent for the export of Welsh butter, and for his part in the company's contract with the London vintners for collecting their new wine duty. With the Londoners, too, there was trouble, and just before the Long Parliament was called Hooke was preparing to go to London regarding the matter. He was still concerned with it in 1642.[476]

Hooke was elected by Bristol to the Short Parliament[477] and again in the fall. He joined with his colleague, Long, in pledging £1000 to secure the loan in November,[478] but in spite of his long experience in commercial matters he was named to few committees. His connections with patentees and projectors in Bristol may have led to distrust of him in a House opposed to monopolies. Although he was named on 13 and 28

[464] Holles, *Memorials of the Holles family*, 203, 221. His own declaration to the compounding commissioners indicates a net income of slightly over £110 a year from lands, but his fine, set at a third, £738, in 1646, and at £860 in 1653, indicates a somewhat higher valuation by the commissioners. S.P. 23/185/950; *Cal. Com. Comp.*, 1056.

[465] *M. of P.* 1: 489; *C.J.* 2: 567–568. Williams (*Gloucester*, 114) gives but a brief note on Hooke.

[466] In his will Hooke referred to his age and his birthplace. Bristol Museum and Art Gallery, Ellacombe MSS, 491 (abstracted in H. E. Nott, ed., *The deposition books of Bristol*, The Bristol Record Society's Publication 6: 249–250, 1935). A pedigree of the Hookes of Bramshott appears in *Vis. Sussex, 1633–4*, 162–163.

[467] After he became a merchant in Bristol Hooke seems to have been assessed about 1626 or 1627 for a share in the subsidy or loan required of the London Ironmongers. Bristol Municipal Library MSS, Bristol Collection, 10160, fol. 163. No reference to Hooke appears in the printed history of the Ironmongers' Company.

[468] Bristol Corp. MSS, Audit Book **15**, 1605–1609.

[469] Nott, *The deposition books of Bristol*, 248; Bristol Corp. MSS, Common Council Book **3**: various entries, 17 March 1629–1 January 1638.

[470] Latimer, *Merchant venturers, Bristol*, 149, 158.

[471] Pink MSS, 304, fol. 510; *Province and court records of Maine* 1: 31, Maine Historical Society, 1928. The puritan divine, William Hooke (1600–1677), who was in New England, 1640–1645 (*D.N.B.*), was possibly a relative.

[472] MSS of the Society of Merchant Venturers of Bristol, Book of Trade, 1598–1693, fol. 2.

[473] *C.S.P. Dom., 1628–1629*, 9, 288, 300, *passim; 1629–1631*, 470; Latimer, *Annals of Bristol*, 105, 109.

[474] Nott, *The deposition books of Bristol*, 248; Bristol Municipal Library MSS, Bristol Collection, 10160, fols. 201–204; MSS of The Society of Merchant Venturers of Bristol, Book of Trade, 1598–1693, fols. 2v, 51–55; Bristol Corp. MSS, Common Council Book **3**: 25 April 1634.

[475] S.P. 16, 378/14. Cf. Richard Long.

[476] *C.S.P. Dom., 1639–1640*, 39–40; *1640–1641*, 108; MSS of the Society of Merchant Venturers of Bristol, Book of Trade, 1598–1693, fols. 242, 244, 245, 249; Hall Book of Proceedings 1: fols. 3, 25–29, *passim*; Latimer, *Merchant venturers, Bristol*, 116–119. In the matter of the wine duties, at least, one object of the Merchant Venturers was to spare the town from a plague of "foreign" collectors.

[477] Latimer, *Annals of Bristol*, 147; Bristol Corp. MSS, Audit Book **21**, 1640 accounts.

[478] D'Ewes (N), 52.

January 1642 to committees regarding the disposition of certain ships,[479] his work with the wine duties in Bristol was being investigated by the following month. On 12 May 1642 both he and Long were expelled from the House as monopolists because, as Merchant Venturers, they were considered beneficiaries from the wine business.[480] But the next month he pledged £200 toward Bristol's £1000 subscription for maintaining the army in Ireland.[481] During the war he was involved in financial transactions with each party that took over the town. He has usually been considered a royalist, but some service to the parliamentary cause shortly before the surrender of Bristol to Fairfax won him a favor later from Cromwell. He compounded as a delinquent, 1647–1650, but his fine of £669 was reduced to £125 and afterwards may have been cancelled entirely.[482] Hooke lived until 1659, and was buried at St. Stephen's, Bristol, on 31 March 1659.[483]

Alderman Hooke was one of Bristol's wealthiest men. In lists of subscriptions and subsidies his name was usually among those listed for the largest amounts. He occupied a fine house and other buildings near the river,[484] and in his compounding papers declared that he held properties in Bristol worth £201 a year and five manors and other properties in other parts of Gloucestershire which were worth £300 a year. The ownership of real estate worth £500 a year, in addition to the income he must have had from trade, meant that Hooke was prosperous indeed. Even after his loan of over £340 to the parliamentarians and of considerable sums to the royalists,[485] he was able when he wrote his will to plan legacies for his children and grandchildren totalling more than £4100. The income of his grandson and heir, Sir Humphrey Hooke, was said to be £1500 a year in 1660.[486]

* Sir Ralph Hopton, K.B. (1596–1652), of Witham, Somerset, was a member for Wells, 1640–5 August 1642. He was born in March 1595/6,[487] and studied at Oxford and the Middle Temple.[488] In addition to serving with the armies on the continent, Hopton was a member of the parliaments of 1621 and 1628, and was also a J.P. in his county. He apparently held some place at court, for he was listed among the "king's servants" in 1639 and 1640, and he was captain of a troop of the royal bodyguard in the north in May, 1639.[489] Perhaps this explains his failure to contribute money to the king from his own county in the latter year.[490]

Hopton inherited properties from his father and from an uncle, Sir Thomas, sometime a court pensioner,[491] and his estates at the time of his compounding included, besides his home near Wells and other county properties,[492] lands in Essex, Kent, Monmouth, Herefordshire, and Wilts. His rents from one Somerset estate and those in Herefordshire were said to be £920 before the war.[493] He was one of the loan subscribers for £1000 in 1640.[494]

Hopton's wife was a relative of Arthur Capel (*q.v.*), and her daughter was Richard Rogers's first wife.[495]

* Sir John Hotham, Bart. (1589–1645), of Scorborough, Yorkshire, M.P. for Beverley, 1640–7 September 1643, was well known as a soldier, M.P., sheriff, and politician. Born about July, 1589,[496] he had fought in the armies on the continent and then turned to politics at home. He was elected M.P. for two boroughs, Beverley and Appleby, in 1625,[497] and sat thereafter so regularly for Beverley that it seems to have been virtually a family borough, at least for one seat.[498] Sir John was named a commissioner for the loans on privy seals in 1627, but he refused to attend meetings, ignoring the warrants sent for him,[499] and was among those imprisoned for their opposition and released just in time for the 1628 parliament.[500] He was a J.P. for the East Riding, the North Riding, Beverley, and Hull,[501] and was active in military matters of the county as a colonel or a D.L. in 1638 and 1639.[502]

[479] *C.J.* **2** : 375, 401.

[480] MSS of the Society of Merchant Venturers of Bristol, Book of Trade, 1598–1693, fols. 253–254. It is perhaps not insignificant that George Peard of Barnstaple was chairman of the committee on monopolies which was revived for the purpose of investigating the role of the Bristol Merchant Venturers. *C.J.* **2** : 415, 567–568.

[481] Bristol Corp. MSS, Common Council Book **3** (letter of 14 June 1642).

[482] Latimer, *Annals of Bristol*, 202; *Cal. Com. Comp.*, 1629–1630.

[483] Pink MSS, 304, fol. 510. Hooke's will, dated 25 June and 17 November 1658, was proved 20 April 1659.

[484] Add. MSS, 5496, fol. 110; Bristol Corp. MSS, Common Council Book **3**, *passim*; Audit Book **20, 21,** *passim*.

[485] S.P. 23/91/977–978; *Cal. Com. Comp.*, 1629–1630.

[486] *English Baronetage* **4** : 366, 1741.

[487] Somerset Rec. Off. MSS, Genealogical Notes of H. Hobhouse, Hopton pedigree. 1598, or even 1601, usually appears as Hopton's birth year, probably on the basis of the statement (e.g., Blore, *History of Rutland* **1** : 133, n.) that he was about fifty-four when he died in 1652.

[488] *Mid. Temp. Rec.* **2** : 577, 600.

[489] S.P. 16, 427/38/v ; 447/36 ; 538/91/ii.

[490] Rushworth **3** : 914.

[491] Brown, *Somerset Wills* **6** : 52.

[492] Collinson, *Somerset* **3** : 414.

[493] *Cal. Com. Comp.* **1** : 94, 102, 205, 208, 302, 611, 699.

[494] D'Ewes (N), 52.

[495] See Rogers. In addition to the authorities cited above see Bates Harbin, *Members of Parliament, Somerset* (147–149), for the latest sketch of Hopton's career.

[496] He was aged nineteen years and eleven months when his father died on 15 June 1609. I.P.M., C. 142/319/179.

[497] *M. of P.* **1** : 466, 467.

[498] Bean, *Northern Counties*, 740, 756, 763; *Y.A.S. Rec. Ser.* **84** : xv, 100, 102, 1933; Beverley Borough MSS, Minute Book, 1597–1660, fol. 66.

[499] *C.S.P. Dom., 1627–1628*, 140; S.P. 16, 60/52.

[500] Rushworth **1** : 473.

[501] C. 193/13; S.P. 16/405; C. 181/5, fols. 159, 286.

[502] *H.M.C., Twelfth Report* **2** : Coke MSS, 205; *C.S.P. Dom., 1638–1639*, 305.

Hotham inherited from his father four Yorkshire manors with some other properties in Beverley,[503] and by his five successive marriages and by purchase increased his holdings.[504] He promised £500 or more to secure the loan in March, 1641.[505] The personal property which was seized at his Hull house after he deserted parliament included £1680 worth of plate and a library of books. Of the total of £6200 that was taken, part belonged to his daughter-in-law and part was money collected for paying his men.[506]

Relatives of Sir John in the 1640 parliament were his son, a son-in-law, Stapleton, and his cousins, the Cholmleys.

* **John Hotham** (1610–1645), of Scorborough, member for Scarborough, 1640–8 September 1643, is well known. He was born in 1610, was admitted to Gray's Inn in 1628,[507] and served as a soldier abroad. By the end of 1635 he was a widower and the father of three children, and before his death in 1645 had married twice more.[508] Hotham had two fathers-in-law in the Long Parliament, Sir John Wray and Sir Henry Anderson, in addition to his father, Sir John Hotham, and several other members were close of kin. He was present with his father at the Yorkshire election in October, 1640,[509] and was named to several committees in 1641.[510] He is better known for his brief military career that followed.

Little can be said as to Hotham's finances in 1640, since his father was then living. He had married well, however, and his third wife, Isabel Anderson, mentioned the loss of at least £7000 of her husband's personal estate following his arrest at Hull.[511]

Charles Howard, Viscount Andover, K.B. (c. 1615–1679), of Oxfordshire and Wilts, was M.P. for Oxford until 18 November 1640, when he left the House to enter the upper chamber as a peer.[512] He was the eldest son of Thomas, first Earl of Berkshire, was named a J.P. in Wilts before 1640,[513] and was joint high steward of Ampthill manor early that year.[514] He owed his elections at Oxford to both of the 1640 parliaments to the influence of his father, who was steward

there.[515] Andover was named to the Committee of Privileges,[516] but to no other before he left the Commons. He was a royalist in his politics. When he compounded as such in 1649, he declared that his settled income in 1640 was only £250 a year, his father still being in possession of the estates worth more than £2000 a year.[517] Thomas Howard (q.v.) was his brother.

* **Sir Robert Howard,** K.B. (1585?–1653), of Clun, Shropshire, was M.P. for Bishop's Castle, 1640–6 September 1642. The fifth son of Thomas Howard, Earl of Suffolk, he was the owner for life of the honor of Clun and the lord of Bishop's Castle.[518] He was a J.P. in Shropshire for some years,[519] and was six times M.P. for his borough of Bishop's Castle. But his intrigues with Lady Purbeck seem to have been Howard's chief claim to notoriety. He owned lands worth, according to his composition papers, £295 a year.[520]

Howard was an uncle of Thomas and Charles Howard, for brief periods his fellow members in the Long Parliament.

Thomas Howard (1619–1706), M.P. for Wallingford, Berkshire, was chosen after the original election was declared void on 15 February 1641, and remained a member until 22 January 1644.[521] He was the second son of Thomas, first Earl of Berkshire (d. 1669), and his wife, Elizabeth, daughter of William Cecil, Earl of Exeter. His brother, Charles Lord Howard (q.v.), was a member for a few days for Oxford. Thomas was baptized at St. Martin's in the Fields, 14 November 1619,[522] and when he was about fourteen set out with his brother for three years of foreign travel. In May, 1638, he was licensed again to travel for three years,[523] and his trips may have included some army experience, for early in 1642 he was referred to as Captain Thomas Howard.

Howard was in England early in 1640, and in January was said to have been challenged to a duel by Lord Broghill for paying attention to the latter's lady-love, Mrs. Harrison. In June, 1641, he married Frances, daughter of Sir Richard Harrison of Hurst, Berkshire,

[503] I.P.M. cited above.
[504] East Riding Antiquarian Society, *Transactions* 2: 26, 1894; *Yorks. Arch. Jour.* 28: 52, 1926.
[505] D'Ewes (N), 439, n.; 451, n. (452).
[506] Wildridge, *Hull letters*, 32–34, 162–163.
[507] *Gray's Inn Adm. Reg.*, 184.
[508] C. Dalton, *History of the Wrays of Glentworth* 2: 26, 61, Aberdeen, 1880–1881.
[509] York county indenture, C. 219/43/Part 3.
[510] *C.J.* 2: 113, 145, 206.
[511] Her dowry was to be £1300 at her father's death, and £100 a year until then. *Y.A.S. Rec. Ser.* 9: 42–44, 1890.
[512] *M. of P.* 1: 492; *C.J.* 2: 30. A sketch of Lord Howard's life appears in Williams, *Oxford*, 115–116.
[513] C. 193/13.
[514] Pink MSS, 304, fol. 575.

[515] Oxford Corporation MSS, A.5.7, Council Book, 1629–1663, fols. 33, 104v–105, 110.
[516] *C.J.* 2: 21.
[517] *Cal. Com. Comp.*, 1967–1971. Clarendon wrote of Lord Howard's father that, while his affection toward the crown was good, "his interest and reputation were less than anything but his understanding." *Rebellion* 2: 533.
[518] Shrops. Arch. Soc., *Trans.*, 2nd Ser., 10: 43–45, 1897–1898.
[519] C. 193/13; S.P. 16/405.
[520] S.P. 23/205/446–449. His compounding fine, reckoned at a third, was £737, or at two-thirds, £1475. He seems to have been able to secure a reduction of the larger proportion to £942. *Cal. Com. Comp.*, 1292–1293.
[521] *M. of P.* 1: 485 and n.; 3: App., xliv; *C.J.* 2: 85.
[522] *Complete Peerage* 1: 343.
[523] *C.S.P. Dom., 1625–1649*, 461; *1637–1638*, 454.

a maid of honor to the queen.[524] His election to par-liament in 1641 was doubtless the result of his father's influence as steward of Wallingford.[525]

Never an active member of the Commons, Howard was reported on 12 January 1642 as helping to or-ganize a troop of horse for the king. He was sum-moned to attend, but was absent at call, 16 June 1642, and finally, on 22 January 1644, was "disabled." [526] He eventually succeeded his brother, Charles, becoming the third Earl of Berkshire in 1679, and lived until 12 April 1706.[527]

Thomas Hoyle, or **Hoile** (d. 1650), merchant and alderman of York, was M.P. for his city, 1640–1650. He was the son of Thomas Hoyle of Slaithwaite in Huddersfield,[528] and served an apprenticeship to Mathew Topham, a York merchant and alderman. Hoyle was admitted a freeman of the city on 20 January 1611/12, the Merchant Adventurers at the same time fining him 40 s. "for trading before he was free." [529] He rose in the ranks of his company, however, and was its governor, 1629–1631.[530] His particular trade was probably that of ironmonger, for he was elected "for the Ironmongers" to the Common Council in 1619.[531] In 1611 Hoyle married Elizabeth, daughter of William Maskew, an inn holder and city official. She died on 9 December 1639. His second wife, Susanna, survived him.[532]

Hoyle served in most of the city offices of York, beginning with that of chamberlain in 1614. He was a councillor (1619), sheriff (1621–1622), alderman (from 1626), and mayor (1632–1633).[533] But though he went through the routine offices, he did not always do things in a routine way. He and his co-sheriff, for instance, notified the corporation that they would make less sump-tuous the customary sheriffs' feast, and would contribute £50 each to the city's poor fund.[534] He was several times a member of committees to prepare instructions for the city M.P.'s, and for agents going to Westminster

to lobby for the city's interests. In 1636 he went to London once or twice regarding the city's controversy with the cathedral dean and about the new charter. He helped also to manage the York trained bands, and joined his colleague, Allanson (q.v.), in preparing a letter to Strafford in January, 1639, urging the wisdom of keeping part of the forces within the city.[535] Hoyle was elected by York to the 1628 parliament, winning recognition after a contest with Sir Thomas Savile.[536]

In his relations with the king's officials in the north Hoyle was perhaps less quarrelsome than Allanson. He assisted with the protest against the privy seals in 1626,[537] but when Wentworth was about to visit York as President of the Council of the North, and his friends feared a clash with the mayor over the matter of prece-dence, Sir Henry Slingsby approached Alderman Hoyle, as a person both honored and loved by Wentworth, to ask him to pave the way. The visit, however, had to be postponed.[538] By 1640 Hoyle's disapproval of Straf-ford's program in the north apparently outweighed any earlier sympathy. He was a member of a committee that planned a new protest to the Lord Deputy in October, 1639;[539] and his election to the Long Parlia-ment was in a contest with nominees of Strafford,[540] a somewhat delayed response to the resolution adopted during Hoyle's mayoralty against external influences at parliamentary elections.[541]

Alderman Hoyle was active in committee work in the 1640 Commons from the start.[542] He joined Allan-son in pledging £500 for the loan in March, 1641,[543] and subscribed £450 of his own for the Irish venture in 1642.[544] A zealous supporter of parliament, he was added in 1643 to the Committee at Goldsmiths' Hall,[545] succeeded the royalist mayor of York by order of par-liament in 1644, and for a time held an office in the Exchequer, a post which was said to be worth £1000 to £1200 a year. His suicide in Westminster on the first anniversary of the king's death, 30 January 1650, was attributed by the royalists to remorse, but since Hoyle had had no share in the king's trial, his state of being "non compos mentis" perhaps had other causes.[546] The Reverend John Shaw, who knew Hoyle and his family well, wrote in his diary that Hoyle "was generally accounted a very good man," but that he had grown

[524] Ibid., 1639–1640, 365; 1641–1643, 27.
[525] J. K. Hedges, The history of Wallingford 2: 121, London, 1881.
[526] C.J. 2: 372, 373, 626; 3: 374.
[527] Complete Peerage 1: 343.
[528] Yorkshire Genealogist 2: 250, 1890. Thomas Hoyle, clothier, and his wife, Isabel, who were buried at Huddersfield, about 1580–1581, were possibly his grandparents. Y.A.S. Rec. Ser. 19: 80, 1895.
[529] York Corporation MSS, Freemen's Roll, I, C/Y, fol. 250; Chamberlains' Account Book, 14, Part 2, fol. 53; York Merchant Adventurers' MSS, Book A, fols. 8, 147v.
[530] Ibid., Book A, fols. 149–149v.
[531] York Corporation MSS, House Book 34, fols. 159v, 247v. The membership of the Common Council was allotted among the several trades. Drake, York, 184.
[532] Yorks. Arch. Jour. 5: 61, n., 1879; 12: 158, 1893.
[533] Yorks. Arch. Jour. 5: 61, n., 1879; York Corporation MSS, House Books 34 and 35, passim.
[534] Ibid., House Book 34, fol. 232.

[535] Ibid., House Book 34, fols. 209v, 210v; House Book 35, fols. 4v, 5, 6, 303, 313, 314; House Book 36, fol. 18.
[536] M. of P. 1: 479; Bean, Northern Counties, 1108; Add. MSS, 33,595, fol. 46v.
[537] York Corporation MSS, House Book 35, fol. 6.
[538] Bodleian Firth MSS, b. 2, fol. 183, passim.
[539] York Corporation MSS, House Book 36, fol. 31v.
[540] C.S.P. Dom., 1640–1641, 158.
[541] York Corporation MSS, House Book 35, fol. 180.
[542] C.J. 2: 30, 43, 49, 61; Pink MSS, 322.
[543] D'Ewes (N), 439, n.
[544] C.S.P. Ireland, Adventurers, 295.
[545] Cal. Com. Comp., 2.
[546] Yorks. Arch. Jour. 5: 61, n., 1879; The life of Marmaduke Rawdon, 125, n. (127); Add. MSS, 27,990, fol. 39.

excessively melancholy before his death, although he was not even near London at the time of the king's trial.[547]

Distorted views of the personal profit Hoyle collected during the war period have lived along with the remorse legend.[548] He seems to have inherited some lands in Wakefield from his father,[549] and before 1640 he was evidently a man of substance in York.[550] He leased various properties there, and declared losses of as much as £200 in goods from his house at one time during the war.[551]

* Anthony Hungerford (c. 1608–1657), of Black Bourton, Oxfordshire, was M.P. for Malmesbury, Wilts, from 1640 until he was disabled as a royalist in 1644. The younger son of a family prominent in Wiltshire and the neighboring counties, he was a half-brother of Sir Edward Hungerford, the parliamentarian (q.v.). He entered Oxford in 1623, aged fifteen, and went to the Middle Temple in 1625.[552] Besides his marriage (before 1632) and his service on the sewers commission for Berkshire and Oxfordshire in 1634,[553] little else is known of his life before his election by Malmesbury to both of the 1640 parliaments.

Hungerford was left by his father (d. 1627) his Oxfordshire estate and certain leases in Wiltshire.[554] His promise of two horses for the defense in 1642 [555] was much less than his elder and wealthier brother pledged, but was more than the poorer members offered. When he compounded for his delinquency in 1646 he listed estates worth some £333 a year, but the local committees found his lands in Wilts, Oxford, Berks, and Gloucestershire worth annually £450 to £500, and his fine, set at a tenth in 1646, was £2532.[556] The amount of the fine, suggesting an income of possibly £1250 a year, may have taken into account the fact that he was later to own his brother's larger estate.[557]

A life-long acquaintance described Hungerford in 1652 as a most honest and religious man, not given to swearing or drunkenness, and valiant and faithful in all services he performed for the parliament.[558]

* Sir Edward Hungerford, K.B. (1596–1648), of Corsham, Wilts, sat for Chippenham, 1640–1648. He was a graduate of Oxford (B.A. 1611), and had studied at the Middle Temple.[559] He was a member of every parliament from 1614 on, except that of 1626, serving for Wiltshire constituencies on all but one occasion. Bath elected him in 1625.[560] He served in his own county as J.P.,[561] sheriff (1632) and D.L., and was a member of various local commissions there. In 1628 he had some connection with the office of Receiver General of the Duchy of Cornwall.[562]

Hungerford, a puritan, came to the Long Parliament with a personal grievance against Archbishop Laud on account of a book written by his father. His own appearance before Laud and others in the inner Star Chamber in 1638 regarding the salary of a curate of whom he was part patron, seems to have displeased him less.[563] His stand regarding ecclesiastical matters was manifest early in the parliament and he was a leader in proposing that Laud be charged with treason.[564]

Sir Edward was one of the wealthier members of the House. He was the heir of a maternal uncle as well as of his father, and had married the coheiress of a London alderman.[565] He owned some property in Chippenham,[566] had town houses in London and Bath,[567] and held lands in various parts of Berks, Somerset, and Wiltshire.[568] He ignored the king's request for a loan in 1639,[569] but in 1640 and 1641 offered his security for £1000 for the loans parliament planned, and in July, 1641, promised a loan of £2000.[570] His pledge of six horses for the defense in 1642 was one of the larger offers.[571] His father's will in 1627 had referred to Sir Edward's "competent measure of earthly blessings," and his own will of 1648, which assigned various large bequests and ample dowries for his nieces, despite his monetary losses brought by the war,[572] gives further indication of his wealth.

Among Hungerford's relatives in the 1640 House,

[547] *Yorkshire diaries and autobiographies,* Surtees Society, **65**: 146, 1877.
[548] Cf. *Memoirs of Denzil Holles,* 134.
[549] *Yorkshire Genealogist* **2**: 251, 1890.
[550] His privy seal assessment in 1626 was not in the highest bracket, however. *Acts P.C., 1625–1626,* 431.
[551] York Corporation MSS, House Books 34 and 36; *H.M.C., Sixth Report,* House of Lords MSS, 205.
[552] *Al. Oxon.; Mid. Temp. Rec.* **2**: 700.
[553] C. 181/4, fol. 179v.
[554] Add. MSS, 33,412, fol. 76–77.
[555] *N. and Q.,* 1st Ser., **12**: 360, 1855.
[556] *Cal. Com. Comp.,* 867; S.P. 23/175/461, 467.
[557] In spite of his losses and fines during the war, Hungerford's will of 1654 mentioned dowries of £3000 for each of his six daughters and named some ten or more manors as then in his possession. P.C.C., 57 Wotton.
[558] Add. MSS, 33,412, fol. 81v.

[559] *Al. Oxon.; Mid. Temp. Rec.* **2**: 562. His widow left a scholarship fund for her husband's college, Queen's, at Oxford. Add. MSS, 33,412, fols. 78–79.
[560] *M. of P.* **3**: xl; **1**: 454, 461, 465, 478, 484, 495.
[561] C. 193/12; S.P. 16/405.
[562] C. 181/5, fols. 10, 64, *passim;* S.P. 16, 528/32.
[563] *D.N.B.; E.H.R.* **16**: 292–307, 1901; *C.S.P. Dom., 1637–1638,* 205.
[564] D'Ewes (N), 160, 162–163.
[565] His widow listed in her will of 1673 legacies of nearly £18,000, after her husband's estate had already passed to his heir. Add. MSS, 33,412, fols. 77–79.
[566] Goldney, *Records of Chippenham,* 2, 3.
[567] London Corporation MSS, Rep. 50, fol. 123; J. F. Meehan, *Famous houses of Bath,* 5, Bath, B. & J. F. Meehan, 1901.
[568] Lysons, *Mag. Brit.* **1**: 297; Add. MSS, 34,566, fol. 21–32.
[569] Rushworth **3**: 915.
[570] D'Ewes (N), 52, n., 452, n.; *C.J.* **2**: 222. The latter was possibly a joint offer.
[571] *N. and Q.,* 1st Ser., **12**: 358, 1855.
[572] Add. MSS, 33,412, fols. 77, 104. See also the composition papers of his brother, Anthony.

besides his stepbrother and heir, Anthony Hungerford, were Sir Henry Mildmay, whose wife was a sister of Lady Hungerford, and Sir Thomas Hutchinson, whose son married Hungerford's niece, Lucy Apsley.[573] He was connected also with the Earl of Warwick, who married in his later years Lady Hungerford's widowed mother, Susan Halliday.[574]

Robert Hunt (c. 1609–1680), of the Middle Temple and of Speckington in Compton Pauncefote, Somerset, was returned for Ilchester in a double return in 1640, and was re-elected after the original return had been voided on 15 February 1641. He was disabled on 5 February 1644.[575] He was the son and heir of John Hunt of the Temple and of Speckington (d. 1660), by his wife, Katherine, daughter of Alexander Popham of Huntworth. His father, who moved into the county from Dorset before 1625,[576] signed the petition regarding ship money rates in Somerset in 1637.[577] Robert was born at Forstone, Charminster, Dorset, about 1609, and was admitted in May, 1625, to the Middle Temple and bound with his father. He probably matriculated at Caius College, Cambridge, later that year, but his education seems to have been principally at the Temple. Among others who were bound with him there were Giles Strangways and a son of John Browne of Frampton (q.v.). Hunt was called to the bar in 1633, and still held a chamber at his inn in 1642.[578] He was styled "Serjeant Hunt" on one occasion,[579] but I have found no other record of the title. In 1635 he married the sister of one of his fellow students, Elizabeth, daughter of John Browne of Frampton, the Dorset puritan.[580] The match seems to have affected his politics but little.

By 1640 Hunt was a J.P. in Somerset,[581] and he was elected that autumn for the first time as M.P. He had some quarrel early in the session with Grimston which was referred to the Speaker for settlement.[582] He was named various times to committees, though chiefly to those of secondary importance.[583] In 1642 he promised to supply one horse for the defense,[584] but after the

war started he deserted. He was disabled on 5 February 1644.[585] His father was possibly the royalist John Hunt who was nominated for the Knights of the Royal Oak in 1660,[586] but Robert reconciled himself sufficiently with the Cromwellians to be a county official by 1654. He was returned M.P. for Somerset in 1659 and for Ilchester in 1660.[587] He died on 20 February 1679/80, "aged about 71." [588]

When Hunt compounded for his estates he reported his income from land before the war as only 117 l. 17 s. 11 d., but this was while his father was living, and did not take into account income from his legal practice.[589] John Hunt's estate was reported worth £1500 yearly in 1660.[590] Hunt's match with the Brownes of Dorset had doubtless been a good one.[591]

Thomas Hussey (c. 1613–1641), of Honington, Lincolnshire, served for Grantham from 1640 until he died in March, 1641.[592] He was the son and heir apparent of a prominent Lincolnshire gentleman, J.P. and twice sheriff, Sir Edward Hussey of Honington, Bart. (d. 1648), by his wife, Elizabeth, daughter and heiress of George Anton of Lincoln and heiress of her uncle, Thomas Taylor of Lincoln.[593] Born about 1613,[594] Thomas entered Gray's Inn on 11 March 1631,[595] and in December, 1633, married Rhoda, daughter and coheiress of Thomas Chapman of London.[596] His father settled on him then lands worth £600 yearly, and he probably stayed thereafter in the country, preparing to succeed his father as an active leader in county affairs. He was named a sewers commissioner in 1635,[597] became a burgess of Grantham in February, 1639,[598] and may have sought election there for the Short Parliament,[599] though without success. Although the Long Parliament was his first, Hussey was named to several

---

[573] Hungerford was a party to the marriage settlement of John and Lucy Hutchinson in 1638 (C.S.P. Dom., 1634–1635, 97; Hutchinson MSS, 1, at the Nottingham Public Library). John Hutchinson was later a trustee for some of Hungerford's lands (Add. MSS, 34,566, fol. 21).

[574] Somerset and Dorset N. and Q. 7: 10, 1898–1899; D.N.B.

[575] C.J. 2: 34, 85; D'Ewes (N), 361.

[576] T. Gerard, The particular description of the county of Somerset, ed. Bates, Somerset Record Society Publications, 15: 183, 1900 (hereafter, Gerard, Partic. Descr. Somerset).

[577] S.P. 16, 357/140; Somerset Arch. Proc. 16 (ii): 19, 1870.

[578] Al. Cant.; Mid. Temp. Rec. 2: 700, 728, 813, 917.

[579] C.J. 2: 26.

[580] Collinson, Somerset 2: 77.

[581] Somerset and Dorset N. and Q. 1: 70, 1889–1890; 9: 175, 1904–1905.

[582] C.J. 2: 26.

[583] C.J. 2: 102, 164, passim. Pink counted nine committees for Hunt before he was disabled. Pink MSS, 304, fol. 657.

[584] N. and Q., 1st Ser., 12: 360, 1855.

[585] C.J. 3: 389.

[586] English Baronetage 4: 374, 1741.

[587] M. of P. 1: 509, 515; Pink MSS, loc. cit.

[588] Inscription cited by Collinson, Somerset 2: 77.

[589] Somerset Arch. Proc. 16 (ii): 19, 1870. Hunt and his father sold a Dorset farm in 1655 for £2700. Dorset N. H. Proceedings 54: 111, 1932.

[590] English Baronetage, loc. cit.

[591] A sketch of Hunt's political career in greater detail appears in Bates Harbin, Members of Parliament, Somerset, 171.

[592] M. of P. 1: 490 and n.

[593] Maddison, Lincs. Ped. 2: 529–530; Complete Baronetage 1: 60; S.P. 16/405.

[594] He was said to be aged twenty-two in 1634, but, according to his marriage license of 4 December 1633, was then only twenty. Pink MSS, 304, fol. 673.

[595] Gray's Inn Adm. Reg., 192.

[596] After Hussey's death, his widow married Ferdinando Lord Fairfax (q.v.). T. Blore, The history and antiquities of the county of Rutland 1: 108.

[597] C. 181/5, fol. 53.

[598] Grantham Corporation MSS, Court Minute Book 1, fol. 71.

[599] A letter from another candidate to the corporation in February, 1640, cautioned against the election of immature and inexperienced men of only thirty. C.S.P. Dom., 1639–1640, 491–492.

important committees, including that on petitions, and three bearing on high church tendencies. The final committee to which he was named was that on the popish hierarchy, 16 March 1641. He died soon afterwards, apparently after only a brief illness, for the writ for the choosing of his successor was ordered on 25 March.[600]

Besides enjoying at least £600 yearly, Hussey was the heir apparent to a large estate.[601] If he inherited his father's political views, he would probably have become a royalist with the war, but in the winter of 1640–1641, he seemed to be interested at least in ecclesiastical reforms.

Sir Thomas Hutchinson (1589–1643), of Owthorpe, Notts, M.P. for Nottinghamshire, 1640–1643, was the only son of Thomas Hutchinson (d. 1599) of Owthorpe, and Jane, daughter of Henry Sacheverell of Radcliffe upon Sore, and the heir of both sides of his house.[602] He was related to most of the "eminent and noble" families of the region, and, though his own family's fortunes had declined somewhat because of frequent wardships of the heirs, as his daughter-in-law wrote, their reputation for hospitality and generosity was still high.[603] Hutchinson was born in 1589 and after his father's death became the ward of Sir Germaine Poole, with whom he had many suits about his properties after he came of age.[604] He was admitted to Gray's Inn, 10 February 1609,[605] but returned before long to the country, where by his private studies in place of formal education he gained in time the reputation as an authority on "school divinity."[606] He was knighted in March, 1617.[607] His first wife, mother of the parliamentary colonel, was Margaret, daughter of Sir John Byron,[608] and his second, whom he married in 1631, was Katherine, daughter of John Stanhope, half-sister of the Earl of Chesterfield, and sister of William Stanhope (q.v.). Sir Thomas lived in London for a time after his second marriage, but returned eventually to his country house at Owthorpe and his town house in Nottingham.[609]

In the affairs of his county Sir Thomas was active. He was a J.P. from as early as 1618,[610] a member of numerous commissions for Notts and nearby shires,[611] and sheriff, 1620–1621. He was a member for Notts in the 1626 parliament, and early in the following year was arrested in Lincolnshire and called before Council for having declined to act as a loan commissioner. He seems to have been imprisoned with his friend, Sir Thomas Grantham, long enough to prevent his re-election in 1628, for he did not return to parliament again until 1640.[612] He was a D.L. in 1637 and 1638,[613] and chosen for his shire for the Short Parliament.

A respected member of the Long Parliament, Sir Thomas pledged his support for the loans of 1640 and 1641,[614] and was named to various committees, including that on ship money and several on matters of the church. He promised £100 for the defense in September, 1642,[615] but died within a year, 18 August 1643, and was buried at London.[616]

Hutchinson's paternal estate included over 3000 acres in Nottinghamshire, and to these were added lands from his mother's family and of his own purchase, the latter including particularly properties in Nottingham borough. His chief estate at Owthorpe was valued at some £390 a year in 1638, and he enjoyed at least £100 more from others.[617] His daughter-in-law wrote of him that:

[He was] ever faithful to his trust and his country's interest, though never approving violence and faction. . . . He was a person of great beauty and comeliness in all ages, of a bounteous and noble nature, of clear courage, sweet and affable conversation, of a public spirit, . . . a true lover of all pious learned persons, and no less of honest plain people, of a most tender conscience, and therefore much for and endeavouring moderation.[618]

---

[600] C.J. 2: 61, 84, 101, 105, 112.

[601] His father's yearly income before the war, exclusive of the £600 already settled on Thomas, was estimated to be some £1900, including wealth from wool growing. His fine for royalism, set at a third in 1648, was nearly £9000. S.P. 23/184/435–436; Cal. Com. Comp., 1022–1023.

[602] Hutchinson shared part of the Sacheverell estates, however, "out of tenderness" for his cousin Eleanor. Thoroton Soc., Trans. 14: 20, 1910.

[603] Memoirs of the life of Colonel Hutchinson, 57.

[604] Ibid.; I.P.M. of Thomas Hutchinson, 1599, C. 142/256/16.

[605] Gray's Inn Adm. Reg., 120.

[606] His private library, worth some £1000, attracted to his home most of the learned and religious men of the region, and his membership on committees on religion in parliament is evidence of his interests. Memoirs of the life of Colonel Hutchinson, 39.

[607] Shaw, K. of E. 2: 161.

[608] She was well educated and had once been in the household of Lady Arabella Stuart. She was a kinswoman of William Fitzwilliam (q.v.). Memoirs of the life of Colonel Hutchinson, 41–44.

[609] Ibid., 46; Records of the borough of Nottingham 5: 179, London, Quaritch, 1882–1914; Overseers Accounts, Parish of St. Margaret's, Westminster, 53, 1632–1633. Sir Thomas was summoned before Star Chamber this year for violating the orders on eating flesh on Fridays, and was among those refused the king's permission to spend the Christmas season in London. Add. MSS, 11,056, fol. 64; C.S.P. Dom., 1631–1633, 529.

[610] Thoroton, Notts. 2: 141; Thoroton Soc., Trans. 15: 170–172, 1911; 19: 79–80, 1915; Nottinghamshire Quarter Sessions Minute Books (MSS), 11, fols. 1, 95; C. 193/12 and 13.

[611] C. 181/4, fols. 40, 83v, 159; 181/5, fols. 9, 97, 191.

[612] S.P. 16, 55/1; Acts P.C., 1627, 74, 123; Memoirs of the life of Colonel Hutchinson, 48 and n. His name is not in Rushworth's list (1: 473), nor in those showing Grantham's imprisonment (Acts P.C., 1627, 395, 430). Grantham was father of the 1640 member of his name.

[613] C.S.P. Dom., 1637, 250; S.P. 16, 381/73.

[614] D'Ewes (N), 52, n., 435, n.

[615] C.J. 2: 39, 45, 50, 155, 772.

[616] Memoirs of the life of Colonel Hutchinson, 167, n.

[617] I.P.M. cited above, note 604; Nottingham Public Library Hutchinson MSS, 1, marriage articles, 1638, and a deed of 1 August 1619; Nottingham Corporation MSS, Hall Books, 3408, fol. 19; 3411, fol. 33.

[618] Memoirs of the life of Colonel Hutchinson, 39–40.

Hutchinson's relatives in the House, besides his wives' kinsmen, Fitzwilliam and Stanhope, Denzil Holles and Pennyman, included Ellis and Grantham from Lincolnshire.[619]

* **Edward Hyde** (1609–1674), of Pirton, Wiltshire, and of the Middle Temple, afterwards Earl of Clarendon, was M.P. for Saltash, Cornwall, 1640–11 August 1642. The third but eldest surviving son of Henry Hyde of Dinton, Wilts, nephew of Sir Nicholas Hyde,[620] the judge, and first cousin of his fellow M.P., Serjeant Robert Hyde, Edward, too, was a lawyer who had built up a substantial practice by 1640. He had enjoyed the king's favor as early as his Oxford days,[621] and during his travels on the continent, about 1634 or 1635, was anxious to keep in the favor of persons prominent at court.[622] Hyde's first marriage occurred in the winter of 1631–1632;[623] and his second, by a license of 10 July 1634, occurred on 20 July at Westminster.[624] Hyde was a J.P. in Wiltshire for some years,[625] and was elected to the Short Parliament for both Wootton Bassett and Shaftesbury, choosing to sit for the former.[626] His election for Saltash in October was probably a result of the Buller influence,[627] since he was at that time known to be in favor of many administrative reforms. He was appointed to a committee as late as 2 November 1641,[628] but had begun to absent himself from the House by the following March.[629]

Hyde was a man of means, though not of great landed estate, in 1640. His father seems to have relied on his brothers to care for part of his son's maintenance during his student days,[630] and the £800 set aside for portions of Edward's younger brother and sister went long unpaid after their father's death.[631] At the time of Edward's second marriage some properties in Pirton, Wilts, were settled on him by his father, and his principal other inheritance was the manor of Cricklade, with certain lesser holdings in that county and in Somerset.[632] Hyde apparently subscribed £1000 for the loan in 1641, however.[633] His real estate was estimated to be worth £600 a year in 1660.[634]

* **Robert Hyde** (1595–1665), of Dinton, Wiltshire, Serjeant-at-Law and Recorder of Salisbury, sat for the latter city from 1640 until he was disabled for royalism, 4 August 1642.[635] A younger son of Sir Lawrence Hyde, an eminent lawyer and official at court, who was still living in 1640, Robert Hyde had by that date won considerable recognition of his own ability in the legal profession. He was educated at Magdalen Hall, Oxford,[636] and at the Middle Temple. One of his companions at the Temple for a time was Henry Campion, M.P. for Lymington in 1640.[637] In Wiltshire Hyde was named to various offices. He may have been a D.L. in 1625,[638] and was a loan commissioner in 1627 and a sewers commissioner later.[639] With his father he was a J.P. for the county for many years, and in 1634 he was a justice in Salisbury.[640] Although he and his father as J.P.'s were accused in 1638 of negligence with regard to the securing of timber for ships, so incurring the threat of Star Chamber proceedings, the charge seems to have been dropped.[641] But in Salisbury Hyde antagonized a part of the population by supporting the ship money collectors and by attempting to discourage certain puritanical practices in the town. His conduct led to attempts to defeat him at both parliamentary elections in 1640.[642] One of Hyde's distinguished clients in the county was the Earl of Hertford.[643]

Robert Hyde was more positive in his support of the crown than was his cousin, Edward, at the beginning of the Long Parliament. Although he agreed with Salway to pledge £1000 as security for the loan in March, 1641,[644] he voted soon afterwards against the attainder of Strafford. And in August, 1642, he was sent to the Tower and disabled "for concealing some words that were spoken against the parliament."[645]

Hyde probably did not enjoy in 1640 much income from land, since he was a younger son and his father

[619] Hutchinson MSS, deed of 1 August 1619, cited above; the will of Thomas Hutchinson, York Probate Registry 27, fols. 709–711.

Further authorities used are: *The visitations of the county of Nottingham*, G. W. Marshall, ed., Harleian Society Publications 4: 116, 1871 (hereafter, *Vis. Notts.*); *List of Sheriffs*, 104; *M. of P.* 1: 470, 482.

[620] Bodleian Clarendon MSS, 129, fol. 2.

[621] The officials of Magdalen College were reproached in 1623 for refusing to admit young Hyde as a Demy upon the king's recommendation. *C.S.P. Dom.*, 1623–1625, 120.

[622] Bodleian Clarendon MSS, 129, fols. 19, 27.

[623] For this correction on the date of Hyde's marriage (1629, *D.N.B.*), see *E.H.R.* 32: 405–407, 1917.

[624] I.P.M., Henry Hyde, C. 142/519/100.

[625] C. 193/13; S.P. 16/405.

[626] *M. of P.* 1: 481, 484; *C.S.P. Dom., 1640*, 42.

[627] Courtney, *Parl. Rep. Corn.*, 150.

[628] *C.J.* 2: 302.

[629] Falkland wrote to Hyde on 23 March 1642 to say that the latter had been named one of the group to proceed against Laud and the judges, but that the House had begun to take exception to his non-attendance. *Calendar of the Clarendon State Papers* 1: 226–227.

[630] Bodleian Clarendon MSS, 129, fol. 2; *E.H.R.* 32: 407, 1917.

[631] Clarendon MSS, 129, fols. 14–15.

[632] I.P.M. cited above.

[633] D'Ewes (N), 438, n.

[634] *English Baronetage* 4: 377, 1741.

[635] *M. of P.* 1: 496; *C.J.* 2: 703.

[636] *Al. Oxon.*

[637] *Mid. Temp. Rec.* 2: 530.

[638] *Acts P.C., 1625–1626*, 111.

[639] S.P. 16, 78/47; C. 181/4, fol. 17v.

[640] C. 193/13; S.P. 16/405.

[641] *C.S.P. Dom., 1637–1638*, 480.

[642] *Ibid., 1639–1640*, 604; D'Ewes (N), 83, 98–99, 544–545; *M. of P.* 1: 484. Cf. Salisbury election.

[643] *C.S.P. Dom., 1638–1639*, 186.

[644] D'Ewes (N), 438.

[645] *C.J.* 2: 703; Bodleian Rawl. MSS, D. 141, fol. 31.

was living. He had been allowed by his father £50 a year while he was a law student,[646] and when he compounded he declared that his several Wiltshire properties had a combined rent of something over £100 yearly. He asserted, however, that his debts of £1100 amounted to more than the sale value of the land. His fine was set at a tenth, £233, with a subsequent addition of £10.[647] Presumably his main income before 1640 was from his practice of law. His will reflects the decided improvement which the Restoration brought to his fortunes.[648]

* Sir Arthur Ingram (c. 1570–1642), of York, was M.P. for Callington, Cornwall, from 1640 until his death in 1642. The son of Hugh Ingram of Yorkshire and London, he was born about 1570,[1] was for a time a merchant's factor in Italy,[2] and became a wealthy merchant in London himself and the owner of extensive properties in the northern counties.[3] He aspired also to a career at court and acquired several lucrative posts in the royal administration as well as aid for his business projects.[4] For some time he had a pension of £200 a year.[5] Ingram held local offices also, serving in Yorkshire as sheriff, J.P., and member of numerous commissions,[6] and he was an alderman in the city of York.[7] The magnificence of his house in York was reported by various writers, 1635–1639,[8] and when his daughter married Lord Holland in 1641 he was reported to have given her £10,000 and £1000 a year for seven years.[9] Beginning with his election in 1609 to fill a vacancy for Stafford, Sir Arthur sat in each successive parliament, usually for northern constituencies, until his death.[10]

Ingram was among the first to pledge his bond for £1000 to support the loan in 1640,[11] and later subscribed £1000 with Penington for reducing Ireland.[12] He was named to various committees of importance and seems to have gone along with the popular party.[13] The king stopped at his house in Yorkshire in November, 1641, while Ingram was attending parliament.[14] He was named as late as 22 March 1642 to a committee,[15] but died a few months afterwards, before 10 September 1642.[16]

Sir Arthur was the father of Sir Thomas Ingram, M.P. for Thirsk, and by the marriage of his elder son, Sir Arthur Ingram, junior, was connected with Sir Henry Slingsby.

Sir Thomas Ingram (d. 1672), of Sheriff Hutton, Yorkshire, was M.P. for Thirsk in that county, 1640–6 September 1642. He was the younger son of Sir Arthur Ingram (q.v.),[17] being the son of his second wife, Alice Ferrers (married 1613), but nothing further is known of him before he was knighted at Newmarket on 16 October 1636.[18] The following year he married Frances Belasyse, daughter of Lord Fauconberg,[19] and sister of Henry and John Belasyse (q.v.). Sir Thomas had no political experience, it seems, before 1640, and his election for Thirsk with John Belasyse suggests that his wife's relatives aided him there. He was named but rarely to committees in the parliament, though he was apparently sent into Yorkshire in May, 1641, with the younger Cholmley on a mission to the army.[20] He

[646] E.H.R. 32: 407, 1917.
[647] S.P. 23/192/814; Cal. Com. Comp., 1562.
[648] Dated 6 April 1664. P.C.C., 49 Hyde.
[1] Wedgwood, Staff. Parl. Hist. 2: 7.
[2] Fairfax correspondence 1: 34, n. (35).
[3] He was interested in the East India and Virginia companies, and in numerous projects in England. His own riches he increased in 1613 by marrying Alice Ferrers, the widow Holyday (or Halliday), who was reputedly worth £3000; and he was said to have offered for his third wife and for some large tracts of her family's lands some £22,000. The personal goods lost in the fire at his home in 1636 were worth £4000. Brown, Genesis of the U. S., 930; Strafford letters 1: 525; C.S.P. Dom., 1639, 245; Yorks. Arch. Jour. 2: 95–96, 1873; Add. MSS, 6666, fol. 159.
[4] Many references to Ingram's business projects and to his relations with Lionel Cranfield have been published in H.M.C., Cal. of MSS of Lord Buckhurst at Knole, 49, 86, passim.
[5] S.P. 16, 180/18/69.
[6] C. 193/12, 13; S.P. 16/405; C. 181/3, fol. 121; 181/5, fols. 76, 105, 73.
[7] Bean, Northern Counties, 1128.
[8] Six North Country Diaries, Surtees Society, 118: 4, 1910; C.S.P. Dom., 1639, 48.
[9] Add. MSS, 29,974, fol. 326; Kensington parish register, Harleian Society, Register Series, 16: 71, 1890.
[10] Sir Arthur was elected to the Short Parliament for Windsor upon the recommendation of the Earl of Holland

(H.M.C., Various collections 8, MSS of the Hon. F. L. Wood, 53), and probably owed his election at Callington to the same auspices. It has been suggested (D.N.B. and elsewhere) that the member of the two 1640 parliaments may have been Sir Arthur's eldest son who bore his name. But D'Ewes referred to the member specifically in August, 1641, as "Sir Arthur Ingram the elder" (D'Ewes [B], 471–472). The "young Sir Arthur Ingram" named on one occasion in the Journals (C.J. 2: 138) probably was Sir Arthur's other son, Sir Thomas (q.v.). Sir Arthur was referred to as deceased at the time that a writ for choosing his successor was ordered in 1646 (M. of P. 3: xliv), but his son, Sir Arthur, was living after that time (H.M.C., Various collections 8: 64; Al. Cant.).
[11] D'Ewes (N), 51.
[12] C.S.P. Ireland, Adventurers, 160–161.
[13] He was named to more than twenty committees, 1640–1642, including those on recusants, on breaches of privilege, on Star Chamber, and others of a reforming nature. C.J. 2: 21, 24, 53, passim; Pink MSS, 305, fol. 7.
[14] H.M.C., Various collections 8: vii. The visit was in 1641, not in 1642, as stated in D.N.B.
[15] C.J. 2: 491.
[16] His will of 15 August 1640 was proved on 10 September 1642. P.C.C., 107 Cambell.
[17] Yorks. Arch. Jour. 23: 364, 1915.
[18] Shaw, K. of E. 2: 204.
[19] The license was issued in 1637 (Y.A.S. Rec. Ser. 40: 114, 1909), and their daughter, Mary, was baptized at York, 21 December 1638. Register of St. Michael le Belfrey, York (Yorkshire Parish Register Society Publications, 1, 11) 1: 193, 1899–1901.
[20] C.J. 2: 138, 151, 423. The man sent to Yorkshire on army matters was designated in the Journals as "young Sir

followed the lead of his brothers-in-law, rather than of his father, in deserting parliament for the king. He was absent on 16 June 1642,[21] helped to execute the Commission of Array,[22] and was disabled, 6 September 1642.[23] After serving under Newcastle,[24] he petitioned in 1646 to compound, and paid his fine in 1649. He lived to gain prominence in the service of Charles II, and, when he died on 13 February 1671/2, was buried in Westminster Abbey.[25]

Although Sir Thomas was a younger son and his father was living in 1640, he seems to have been amply provided for even then. His "particular" presented to the compounding commissioners in 1646 listed four manors with additional lands in Yorkshire and Suffolk, with a yearly net income of at least £1000. His fine, at a half, £3649, or a third, £2933, was set in 1649 at the lower figure.[26]

Sir Anthony Irby (1605–1682), of Whaplode and Boston, served as M.P. for Boston, 1640–1648. His family had long been associated with Boston, and almost regularly represented the town in parliament between 1588 and 1681.[27] Sir Anthony's grandfather, a distinguished lawyer of Lincoln's Inn, a Master of Chancery, and Recorder of Boston, was Anthony Irby, Esq., of Whaplode (d. 1625), who multiplied the family holdings in the vicinity of Boston.[28] The lawyer's son, Sir Anthony Irby, married Elizabeth, daughter of Sir John Peyton of Iselham, Cambridgeshire, and died in June, 1610, leaving a five-year-old son, Anthony.[29] The latter was admitted to Lincoln's Inn, 15 May 1620, and to Emmanuel College, Cambridge, the following month. He was knighted in June, 1624,[30] and on his grandfather's death in 1625 succeeded to an inheritance rumored to be worth four or five thousand pounds a year. Irby married four times, (1) in 1623, Frances, daughter of Sir William Wray of Glentworth; (2) Margaret, daughter of Sir Richard Smith, privy councillor, of Ostenhanger, Kent; (3) Margaret, daughter of Sir

Edward Barkham of Southacre, Norfolk, and Lord Mayor of London, who died soon after the Long Parliament opened; and (4) in 1647, Catherine, daughter of William Lord Paget and granddaughter of the Earl of Holland.

From his early manhood Irby was a leader in Boston and county affairs. He was appointed recorder at Boston in May, 1624, while he was still an "apprentice in the law," [31] possibly as an assistant to his aged grandfather. He was a J.P. for Boston and the county, and a member of the sewers commission and others during most of the reign of Charles.[32] With his brother-in-law, Sir John Wray, Irby opposed the forced loan of 1627, but apparently made his peace by appearing before Council without arrest.[33] The next year he was returned to parliament for Boston.[34] He was a D.L. in Lincolnshire by 1636,[35] and as sheriff, 1637–1638, was responsible for ship money. He met with difficulty in trying to change the assessments to favor some poorer areas, and ended his term considerably in arrears. His correspondence with Council sets forth the usual excuses of the hardness of the times, and the refractoriness of local constables, as well as his own illness and his preoccupation with his military responsibilities, as 1639 arrived and his collections were still incomplete. He may have appeared before Council in March, 1639, but postponed further rendering of accounts, and owed more than £1700 of his quota in July. Early in January, 1640, he was in custody, apparently in London, and was kept in daily attendance upon Council until, by the middle of the month, he had paid in the final £200 of what he owed.[36]

Returned for Boston to both of the 1640 parliaments, Irby was an active member of the reform element. He offered his bond for £500 for securing the loan in March, 1641, promised his support again in August,[37] and was named to many committees, including those on privileges, Leighton's grievances, and the problem of the lords lieutenant and the trained band levies.[38] He was interested in ecclesiastical matters, too, and seems to have gained license from the House in 1641 for the publishing of a manuscript in his possession concerning reforms attempted in the twelfth century.[39] At the

Arthur Ingram," the clerk evidently using this means to distinguish him from his father, but confusing the names. A companion, "young Mr. John Mallory," was distinguished similarly from his father.

[21] C.J. 2: 626.

[22] Yorks. Arch. Jour. 1: 95, 1870.

[23] C.J. 2: 754.

[24] H.M.C., Various collections 8, MSS of the Hon. F. L. Wood, viii, 59.

[25] The date appears as 1671 in Yorks. Arch. Jour. (23: 364, 1915), but 1672 seems to be correct (Pink MSS, 305, fol. 9). Plans for the filling of his seat in the 1661 parliament were begun even before his death (H.M.C., Fifth Report, MSS of the Duke of Sutherland, 197), and his successor was returned, 18 February 1672/3. M. of P. 1: 532.

[26] Cal. Com. Comp., 1342–1343; Y.A.S. Rec. Ser. 18: 124–126, 1895; Pink MSS, 305, fol. 9.

[27] M. of P. 1: 423, 428, passim.

[28] Add. MSS, 24,121 (Collections by Thomas Wotton), fol. 2.

[29] I.P.M., Sir Anthony Irby, 1611, C. 142/325/185.

[30] Al. Cant.; Linc. Inn Rec. Adm. 1: 185.

[31] Lincs. N. and Q. 13: 81, 1914–1915.

[32] C. 193/12, 13; S.P. 16/405; C. 181/3; 181/4, fol. 30; 181/5, fols. 19, 27, 83, 361.

[33] S.P. 16, 56/39, fol. 73v. A memorial to Irby from Boston in 1648 recalled his carriage "against the Loan money and other projects tending to publick detriment." Thompson, Boston, 394, n.

[34] M. of P. 1: 476.

[35] C.S.P. Dom., 1636–1637, 149; 1639, 49.

[36] Ibid., 1637, 526; 1637–1638, 28, 197, 211–212, passim; 1638–1639, 16, 29, 503, passim; 1639 and 1639–1640, passim.

[37] D'Ewes (N), 439, n.; C.J. 2: 238.

[38] C.J. 2: 21, 28, 50, passim. Pink estimated that Irby served on 103 committees, 1640–1648. Pink MSS, 305, fols. 11–12.

[39] B. M. Stowe MSS, 107, as described in the Catalogue of Stowe MSS 1: 61.

outbreak of war, Sir Anthony took up arms against the king, and was among those of his shire proclaimed "traitors" in 1643.[40] He was secluded in 1648,[41] but sat again in 1656 and 1659 and in the parliaments of Charles II. He died on 2 January 1682, and was buried in St. Margaret's, Westminster.

Irby's wealth had already been indicated. His properties in the Holland area of Lincolnshire were extensive, and his family had been interested in the drainage projects of that region.[42] His grandfather was a member of the Virginia Company,[43] and he was in 1633 himself a member of the new fisheries venture.[44]

Relatives of Irby in the 1640 House were his first wife's brother and half-brother, the Wrays, and his second wife's cousin, Sir Thomas Fanshawe, K.B.[45]

Sir John Jacob (*c.* 1598–1666), of London and of Bromley, Middlesex, farmer of the customs, was a member for Rye from November, 1640, until he was expelled, 21 January 1641.[1] He was the eldest surviving son of Abraham Jacob of Gamlingay, Cambridgeshire, and of Bromley, one of the customs farmers (d. 1629), by Mary, daughter of Francis Rogers of Dartford, Kent, and was born about 1598 at Gamlingay.[2] He matriculated at Oxford (Merton) in January, 1617, was awarded his B.A. the next month, and for the next few years may have been abroad as Sir Isaac Wake's secretary at Turin.[3] But before his father's death in 1629 he had returned to England to enter upon a career in the customs office. A life interest in the collecting of tobacco duties had been granted in 1618 to Abraham Jacob and his son, an office several times afterwards confirmed, and enjoyed by John until about 1638. And sometime before 1629 they received a joint grant of the office of collector of pretermitted customs in the port of London, a grant which, with the farm of the tobacco duties, was confirmed to John for life after his father died.[4] He was possibly the John Jacobs, Esquire, who was sworn by the king's wish to be clerk of the

council in extraordinary, 13 June 1627,[5] and he was admitted with a group of others attached to the court to Gray's Inn in 1631.[6] In May of 1633 he was knighted at Whitehall, being then of Stanstead, Essex, and having an estate of £3000 a year. By that time he had married twice, his first wife (about 1628) being Elizabeth, daughter of John Hallyday (Holliday), and his second (1632), Alice (Clowes), widow of John Eaglesfield, a London merchant.[7]

Sir John probably spent most of the decade before 1640 in London. He was named to several commissions on city and trade matters,[8] and had a pretentious residence near the customs house in 1638.[9] With his fellow customers he advanced £30,000 for the king's use in 1631 and was asked with them for £10,000 as part of the 1640 loan.[10] He ventured some £50 in the Irish fisheries, was interested also in the East India Company,[11] and was said in 1641 to have made from his office a net gain of £16,175.[12] His real estate in 1640 included inherited and purchased manors in the counties of Cambridge, Essex, Middlesex, and Kent.[13]

Sir John was elected to his first parliament in the spring of 1640 for Harwich,[14] and probably owed his return for Rye [15] to the Lord Warden, with whom he had long been acquainted.[16] But he was not to sit long in the House, for on 21 November he was attacked by Trelawney of Plymouth as a monopolist, especially for the control over the tobacco trade resulting from his customs offices, and for his attempt to make London the only port handling the commodity. After a preliminary defense, Jacob withdrew until his case could be determined, and on 21 January 1641 was formally expelled as a monopolist of tobacco.[17] With the other customs farmers he sought later in the year to clear himself of the charges by submitting and paying a fine,[18] but he did not regain his seat. He was a zealous royalist during the war, lending money to the king, being imprisoned for a time, and being heavily assessed for his delinquency. He does not seem to have compounded, how-

---

[40] *Lincs. N. and Q.* **8**: 148, 1904–1905.

[41] *O.P.H.* **9**: *32.

[42] *Lincs. N. and Q.* **13**: 83, 1914–1915; S.P. 16, 378/1; *H.M.C., Sixth Report*, House of Lords MSS, 130.

[43] Kingsbury, *Records of the Virginia Company* **3**: 328.

[44] S.P. 16, 231/15/i and 325/43/i.

[45] Other authorities used for this sketch: Thompson, *Boston*, 392–395; Maddison, *Lincs. Ped.* **2**: 542; T. Allen, *The history of the county of Lincoln* **1**: 331, London, 1834.

[1] *M. of P.* **1**: 497; *C.J.* **2**: 71.

[2] I.P.M., Abraham Jacob, C. 142/451/100.

[3] One John Jacob received in October, 1617, a pass for travel for three years (*Acts P.C., 1616–1617*, 340) and one of the name, as Wake's secretary, was travelling between England, Tunis, and Berne, 1620–1621 (*C.S.P., Venetian, 1619–1621*, 250, 332, n., 576); Eg. MSS, 2594, fols. 60–62. Wake in 1627 referred to Abraham Jacob as one who knew the "quintessence" of the Exchequer. Add. MSS, 33,935, fol. 177.

[4] *C.S.P. Dom., 1611–1618*, 535; *1619–1623*, 175, 179; *1628–1629*, 596, 597; *1638–1639*, 253; Stowe MSS, 326, fols. 81v–82.

[5] *Acts P.C., 1627*, 342.

[6] *Gray's Inn Adm. Reg.*, 191.

[7] *Complete Baronetage* **4**: 3; I.P.M., cited above. His third wife, probably much later, was a daughter of Sir John Ashburnham. Add. MSS, 33,923, fol. 87.

[8] *C.S.P. Dom., 1635–1636*, 241; *1636–1637*, 404; *1639*, 219.

[9] Dale, *Inhabitants of London, 1638*, 18.

[10] The rent of their farm was in 1631 £150,000 a year. *C.S.P. Dom., 1629–1631*, 512, 518; S.P. 16, 453/74.

[11] S.P. 16, 231/15/i; India Office MSS, Home Series Misc., **1**: fol. 17.

[12] Verney, 79.

[13] I.P.M. cited above; Morant, *Essex* **2**: 222; Hasted, *Kent* **2**: 503; Lysons, *Mag Brit.* **2** (1): 200–201.

[14] *M. of P.* **1**: 481.

[15] Sir John was probably not the John Jacobs, Serjeant of the Admiralty in the Cinque Ports, 1627–1637, who does not seem to have been knighted. *C.S.P. Dom., 1627–1628* and *1637, passim*.

[16] *Ibid., 1623–1625*, 135; *Cal. Com. Comp.*, 680.

[17] *C.J.* **2**: 33, 71; D'Ewes (N), 50, 224, 267, 268.

[18] Stowe MSS, 326, fol. 91v; Verney, 79; *C.J.* **2**: 167.

ever. He regained his place in the customs house under Charles II, was created a baronet in 1665, and died the following year. He was buried at Bromley, 13 March 1666.[19]

* Joseph Jane (c. 1600–c. 1660), of Liskeard, Cornwall, was M.P. for his borough, 1640–22 January 1644. He was the son of a former mayor and deputy steward of Liskeard, Thomas Jane, who had had some education in the law.[20] He married (1) at St. Andrew's, Plymouth, 29 June 1629, Jane Sparker of Plymouth; and (2) at St. Germans, 15 August 1633, Loveday, daughter of William Kekewich of Calchfrench, Cornwall.[21] He was M.P. for Liskeard in 1626,[22] and was twice mayor, 1631 and 1635–1636.[23]

Jane was named to a few committees of the Long Parliament, including those on the judges and tonnage and poundage, but he was absent at call on 16 June 1642.[24] His fears for the established church had led him to royalism, and he was disabled in 1644.[25] He died shortly before 26 August 1660, when the lease of Liskeard Park was granted to his children.[26] His estate was probably a modest one, consisting chiefly of houses in and near Liskeard.[27]

Robert Jenner (c. 1584–1651), of Widhill, Wiltshire, a goldsmith of London, was M.P. for Cricklade, 1640–1651. His parentage is unknown, but he had close relatives in both Gloucestershire and Wiltshire, and probably came from the region near Cricklade originally.[28] He was born about 1584, presumably passed his apprenticeship in London, and by 1622 had made enough name for himself in his trade to be acting as one of the trustees for property that had been left to the Goldsmiths' Company.[29] He was named in 1623 in the

patent issued to the "Company of Goldwiredrawers of the City of London."[30] Some silver was confiscated at his place of business that year by a searcher who thought Jenner intended to use it in a fashion contrary to the new proclamation regarding silver thread, but it was restored to him by Council order.[31] His company complained of him in the London Aldermen's Court in 1630 because he and his fellow "rentor" for the year, both men of ability and worth, had declined to furnish the customary dinner for the warden and livery. In the court Jenner remained "willful and obstinate," but a sojourn of a few hours in Newgate jail brought a change of mind, and he agreed to provide the dinner that was expected of him.[32] Because he had taken up residence in Wiltshire, he paid a fine so as to be excused from serving as warden of the company in 1639, but he took his turn as warden three years later while his duties as an M.P. were keeping him in town. He was reported in 1641 and 1642, however, as not having paid his part of the poll tax that had been required of company members.[33]

Sometime before 1617 Jenner married Elizabeth, daughter of Thomas Longstone, a London grocer, and from her family obtained in 1625 ownership of an inn in Dartford, Kent. Two years later he secured a clear title for some property in Widhill, Wiltshire, of which he already had possession, and in the next few years bought and sold the manor of Eysey.[34] He was still described as of his London parish of St. Leonard's, Foster Lane, in 1632, when his fifteen-year-old daughter, Anne, was licensed to marry the only son of Sir Thomas Trevor, Baron of the Exchequer.[35] But his Wiltshire connections were evident in his election by Cricklade to the parliament of 1628. He was a sewers commissioner for Wilts and Gloucestershire in 1635, and was for some years a Wiltshire J.P.[36] He was reported in 1638 as a London resident,[37] but he was probably spending much of his time at Widhill. He was elected by Cricklade to both parliaments of 1640.[38]

Jenner worked with the popular party in the Long Parliament. Having made some of his money earlier by investment in mortgages,[39] he was one member who ventured to speak out against the proposed act condemning usury;[40] but he was named to several com-

[19] Cal. Com. Adv. Money, 234, 1096. See also Pink MSS, 305, fol. 7; Al. Oxon.

[20] Western Antiquary 5: 135, 1885–1886; Pink MSS, 307, fol. 216. The elder Jane was involved in a factional quarrel among his fellow townsmen for some years and on one occasion was deprived of his posts as capital burgess and steward of the borough court. St. Ch. 8/15/11; 168/23; 181/6.

[21] S. Baring-Gould, Cornish characters and strange events, 206, London, J. Lane, 1909; Pink MSS, 307, fol. 216.

[22] M. of P. 1: 468. The year is given as 1625 in D.N.B.

[23] Pink MSS, loc. cit. D.N.B. gives 1625 as the date of his mayoralty. Courtney (Parl. Rep. Corn., 252) says Jane was twice mayor.

[24] C.J. 2: 47, 107, 626.

[25] C.J. 3: 374; Coate, Cornwall in the great Civil War, 28.

[26] Pink MSS, 307, fol. 216.

[27] Cal. Com. Comp., 3062.

[28] A John Jenner of Creedwell, Wilts, yeoman, was a party with him in transfers of property in 1628 and 1630. His will mentioned several kinsmen of the name of Jenner, and he was himself named overseer and guardian in the will of William Jenner of Keniesford, Gloucestershire (1638). Wilts. Arch. Mag. 42: 13–15, 1922–1924; Wilts. Arch. Soc. MSS, Sadler's "Wiltshire Genealogy," Cricklade Parish.

[29] Ibid. Sadler was informed by the company officials that their records do not show the date of Jenner's admission or indicate his origin.

[30] Carr, Select charters of trading companies, 124.

[31] Acts P.C., 1623–1625, 143.

[32] London Corporation MSS, Rep. 44, fols. 157–158, 160.

[33] Sadler's notes cited above; Sir Walter S. Prideaux, Memorials of the Goldsmiths' Company 1: 204, 341, 353, London, 1891–1896.

[34] Wilts. Arch. Mag. 42: 13–15, 1922–1924; Sadler's notes.

[35] Thomas Trevor (q.v.). Marriage licenses, London (Harleian Society, 26) 2: 206, 1887.

[36] M. of P. 1: 478; C. 181/5, fol. 42; C. 193/13; S.P. 16/405.

[37] Dale, Inhabitants of London, 91.

[38] M. of P. 1: 484, 495.

[39] Indentures of 1624 and 1634 cited by Sadler.

[40] D'Ewes (N), 486, n. The name is written as Mr. Jenings, but the speaker was more probably Jenner than Sir John Jennings.

mittees concerned with trade or with the reform of abuses, particularly in affairs of the church.[41] He promised to furnish two horses for the defense in 1642,[42] and was a parliamentary committeeman in Wiltshire during the war. Probably his most important work for the cause, however, was his appointment to various finance committees of the House in 1644, and especially to the Committee for Compounding that met in Goldsmiths' Hall.[43] He seems to have made use of the opportunity to increase his own estates, as in his purchase for £1100 of another Wiltshire manor, once church property, in 1648.[44] Although he supposedly was secluded in December, 1648,[45] he signed a letter as a member of the Goldsmiths' Hall committee on 19 February 1648/9.[46] He died, aged sixty-seven, on 7 December 1651.[47]

It is evident from his relationship with the Goldsmiths' Company, from his purchases of lands, and from his matching his daughter with Sir Thomas Trevor's son that Jenner was a man of considerable wealth. By his will of 1651 he left numerous endowments to Wiltshire and London parishes, provided a gift for a school at Cricklade, and turned over his great house in Foster Lane, for which he had once paid £1400, to the Goldsmiths' Company for charitable purposes.[48]

Sir John Jennings, K.B. (1596–1642), of Sandridge, near St. Albans, Hertfordshire, was M.P. for St. Albans from 1640 until his death in August, 1642. He came of a family connected with both London and Somersetshire, and was the eldest son of Sir John Jennings (d. 1609) of Sandridge and of Churchill, Somerset, by his first wife, Anne, daughter of Sir William Brounker of Wiltshire. He was born in 1596,[49] and was possibly the "John Jennings, gent," described as a servant in ordinary to the queen, who in 1614 and 1617 received passes for three years of foreign travel to learn the languages.[50] He seems to have been living in Somerset, however, in 1622 and was a J.P. there. That year he was engaged in several suits in Star Chamber as a result of a quarrel with a neighboring justice, and was already giving evidence of the turbulent disposition and impetuous conduct which in later years were to bring him into further conflict with authority.[51] By this time he had married Alice, daughter of Sir Richard Spencer of Hertfordshire, and before 1624 had taken up residence at the Sandridge estate there.[52] He was created K.B. at the coronation of King Charles in 1626,[53] but no later connections with the court are known.

Jennings was named sheriff for Hertfordshire late in 1626,[54] but was soon afterwards arrested with other well-to-do men for resisting the loan, and yielded only after he had been brought before Council.[55] The next year he was chosen for parliament by St. Albans,[56] and for most of his life thereafter was a member of the commission of the peace and other local commissions for both that town and the county.[57] During the interval between parliaments, Sir John resisted the crown again, declining in 1636 and 1637 to pay what he regarded as an excessive rate of ship money in St. Albans, and taking up residence in London so as to remove his goods from the danger of seizure. When he was compelled to answer before Council in 1638, he protested that he had paid what was assessed on other lands, but refused at St. Albans because the rate had been set unduly high in proportion to the value of his holdings there.[58] At the same time, however, he was reported in arrears for one of the Somerset properties,[59] and in 1639 he declined to contribute toward the king's northern journey.[60]

In the spring of 1640 Jennings was elected to the Short Parliament for St. Albans.[61] He offended the authorities at Westminster once more during the following summer by failing to deal vigorously as a justice with unruly soldiers who had broken down chancel rails

[41] *C.J.* **2**: 48, 129, *passim.*

[42] *N. and Q.*, 1st Ser., **12**: 359, 1855.

[43] *Wilts. Arch. Mag.* **39**: 445, 1915–1917; Pink MSS, 305, fol. 39; *C.J.* **3**: 457; *Cal. Com. Comp.*, 951, 1013, *passim.*

[44] *Wilts. Arch. Mag.* **42**: 13, 1922–1924.

[45] *O.P.H.* **9**: 8.

[46] *The royalist composition papers . . . Lancaster*, Rec. Soc. Lancs. and Cheshire **29**: 173, 1896.

[47] *Wilts. Arch. Mag.* **42**: 14, 1922–1924.

[48] *Ibid.* **38**: 132, 1913–1914; Prideaux, *op. cit.* **1**: 257; W. Herbert, *The history of the twelve great livery companies of London* **2**: 277–278, 1836–1837.

[49] *The visitations of Hertfordshire*, Harleian Society, **22**: 147–148, 1886 (hereafter, *Vis. Herts.*); Clutterbuck, *Herts* **1**: 216–217; *Somerset Arch. Proc.* **31** (ii): 43, 1885; I.P.M., Sir John Jennings, 1610, C. 142/318/156 (1). According to one pedigree his great-grandfather, Bernard Jennings, was of Somerset, but according to other authorities his grandfather, Ralph Jennings of Islington, was the first of the line to own the Somerset properties. Ralph, who died in 1572, owned properties in London and Hertfordshire (*Somerset Arch. Proc.* **84**: 123–126, 1938.

[50] *Acts P.C., 1613–1614*, 392; *1618–1619*, 214.

[51] St. Ch. 8, 34/6; 186/21. A John Jennings, Esq. was on the sewers commission in Somerset in 1629 (C. 181/4, fol. 21v), but Sir John still held the manor of Churchill, and it remained in the hands of his widow and son until 1652. *Somerset Arch. Proc.* **31** (ii): 34, 1885.

[52] Burke, *Landed gentry* **1**: 648, 1850. Three of his sons were enrolled in St. Albans Grammar School in 1624. *Middlesex and Hertfordshire Notes and Queries* **1**: 42, 1895.

[53] Shaw, *K. of E.* **1**: 163.

[54] *H.M.C., Eighth Report*, MSS of the Duke of Marlborough, 2.

[55] S.P. 16, 44/14; *C.S.P. Dom., 1627–1628*, 9.

[56] *M. of P.* **1**: 475.

[57] *C.S.P. Dom., 1637–1638*, 448; C. 181/4, fols. 77v, 78, 268, 272; C. 181/5, fols. 23, 24, 44, 45, 169, *passim;* C. 193/12.

[58] The mayor acknowledged that Jennings had been more heavily rated because he was one of the wealthier men, and protested that the town would have been unable to collect its quota by a levy simply on property values. S.P. 16, 376/128, 143; 389/140; 400/108; *C.S.P. Dom., 1635–1636*, 282; *1636–1637*, 288.

[59] S.P. 16, 537/49/i.

[60] Rushworth, **3**: 914.

[61] Willis, **3**: 232.

in several churches in his county. He was possibly not averse himself to some "purifying" of the churches. Summoned before Council to explain his action, Jennings was committed to the Fleet for a few days in September and then was released on bond of £500 for appearing later in Star Chamber. Having participated in the autumn elections and been returned again for St. Albans, he was present in the House in November, but the next month was again committed to the Fleet.[62] No charge was specified in the warrant in order that habeas corpus proceedings might be avoided, but Sir John was back in parliament again by 29 January. When his case was discussed by his colleagues on 6 February, it was referred to the committee dealing with the jurisdiction of the Council.[63]

As a member of the Long Parliament Jennings's sympathies were naturally with the party of Pym. He gave his security for £1000 for the 1640 loan, and was named to various committees during the first year, including the Committee of Privileges and two others concerning elections.[64] He died, however, just as the war began, and on 5 August 1642 the House ordered a writ for the electing of his successor.[65]

The critics of Jennings referred more than once to his wealth,[66] and the list of his possessions as well as his offer for parliament are further indications that he was very well-to-do.[67] One report had it that his income was at least £1000 a year, and that he was six times richer than his neighbors; another report suggests that his estate was worth nearer £4000 annually. His twenty-two children, however, must indeed have been a "great charge" upon his income, as he himself complained.[68] His eldest son, Richard, who succeeded him, was the father of Sarah Jennings, afterwards Duchess of Marlborough.

William Jephson (1615?–1658), of Froyle, Hampshire, and of Ireland, was a member for Stockbridge, Hants, 1640–1648.[69] His father, Sir John Jephson,

had gone to Ireland with the army under Essex, had married there, and had been a member of the Irish Privy Council as late as 1628.[70] Sir John married as his second wife the widow of Sir Francis Rush, whose daughter's marriage with Lord Wentworth's brother, Sir George Wentworth (q.v.) was a forerunner of the famous lawsuits of the Lord Deputy and the Lord Chancellor. Although Sir John was a D.L. in Hampshire in 1627,[71] his son, William, seems to have held no offices there before 1640. Jephson, the son, was listed among the Hampshire men who ignored the loan request of 1639.[72] He served in parliament first when chosen by Stockbridge for the Short Parliament.[73] His subsequent career in Ireland and as a parliamentary officer in England are well known. He died at Borestall, Bucks, in December, 1658. His will, dated 6 December, was proved on 23 December 1658.[74]

Clarendon commented that Jephson had a "good fortune," [75] and his inclusion among those asked for a loan in 1639 indicates that he was a man of means. His will referred to a settlement of £5000 to provide for his family and £600 a year for his wife's maintenance. Part of it was to come from Irish lands. How much was based upon acquisitions after 1640 cannot be stated.

Jephson once referred to John Pym as a cousin,[76] and he wrote to Arthur Goodwin in 1642 as a kinsman.[77] Richard Whitehead also seems to have been a relative.[78]

Sir Thomas Jermyn (1573–1645), of Rushbrook, Suffolk, Comptroller of the Household and privy councillor, was M.P. for Bury St. Edmunds, 1640–1644. The eldest son and heir of a well known Suffolk gentleman,[79] Sir Robert Jermyn (d. 1614), by his wife, Judith, he was baptized at Rushbrook, 12 February 1573. He matriculated at Emmanuel College, Cambridge, in 1585, and entered the Middle Temple in 1590,[80] but soon afterwards went into the service of Essex. He was knighted while with Essex at Rouen in 1591, may have gone with him to Cadiz in 1596, and the next year was with him in Ireland and in the British attack on the Spanish fleet. He had some post at court by 1599, was a colonel under Essex in Ireland at the time of the "plot," but returned after that to live in England.[81] He married about this time Catherine, daughter of the

[62] C.S.P. Dom., 1640, 634; 1640–1641, 12, 32, 297; Kingston, Herts. during the Civil War, 7. Jennings was present at Hertford for the shire election on 22 October (C. 219/43/part 1). One of his fellow justices, a member of the Short Parliament for St. Albans, who was anxious to be re-elected, was his accuser (C.J. 2: 79–80, 88), and it may be suspected that there was politics in the case.

[63] C.J. 2: 75, 79; D'Ewes (N), 330, 370.

[64] Ibid., 52; C.J. 2: 21, 29, 75, 114, 219.

[65] Ibid. 2: 704. His will was proved 9 August 1642. P.C.C., 105 Cambell.

[66] St. Ch. 8, 34/6; C.S.P. Dom., 1638–1639, 78.

[67] His father had held at least four manors in Somerset, one in Hertfordshire, and various lands in Wiltshire (inquest of lunacy, Sir John Jennings, 1607, C. 142/297/160), and most of them passed to his son.

[68] He is said to have been able to grant a portion of only £500 to one of his daughters (Add. MSS, 15,931, fol. 149) but if the others fared as well, the portions must have come from a large estate. In his will, dated 21 March, 1638/9, he directed the arranging of a £500 portion for his youngest son.

[69] M. of P. 1: 493; O.P.H. 9: 1.

[70] C.S.P. Ireland, 1600, 527; 1600–1601, 418; 1647–1660, 128.

[71] Add. MSS, 21,922, fol. 92v.

[72] Rushworth, 3: 914.

[73] M. of P. 1: 483.

[74] P.C.C., 694 Wootton.

[75] Cited in Godwin, The Civil War in Hampshire, 3.

[76] H.M.C., Tenth Report 6, MSS of P. P. Bouverie, 88.

[77] Bodleian Carte MSS, 103, fol. 96.

[78] Vis. Hants., 90.

[79] Suff. Inst. Arch. 8: 173; Robert Reyce, The breviary of Suffolk, 90, 92, 95.

[80] Al. Cant.; Mid. Temp. Rec. 1: 312.

[81] For biographical details I have drawn heavily upon the section of "Jermyn Annals," Rushbrook parish registers, The Suffolk Green Books, 224–239, Woodbridge, G. Booth, 1903.

courtier, Sir William Killegrew,[82] and divided his time afterwards between Suffolk and the court. He was M.P. for Andover in 1604 and for Suffolk in 1614.[83] He went to France in 1616 with an embassy concerning the marriage of Prince Charles, suffering there an accident which may have lamed him permanently.

From 1620 until 1640 Sir Thomas was constantly in office. He sat for Bury St. Edmunds in the parliaments of 1621–1628 and in the Short Parliament,[84] was a J.P. in Suffolk and Norfolk,[85] a member of a variety of local commissions in that area and London,[86] a D.L. in Cambridge and Suffolk by 1623 and for many years after that, and colonel in command of troops in Suffolk in 1625.[87] Meanwhile he climbed to higher offices at court, although he never seems to have been regarded as of great ability and as a court favorite was before 1640 outshone by his younger son, Henry. He attached himself to Buckingham, possibly joined the prince in Spain in 1623, defended the royal policies in parliament, and in 1628 became vice-chamberlain to the queen.[88] He was disappointed when Sir Henry Vane was named in 1629 to be Comptroller of the Household, a post which he had sought, and in which he finally succeeded Vane in 1639,[89] but continued in the office of vice-chamberlain and acted, 1631–1638, as Governor of Jersey.[90] As a privy councillor Jermyn attended various Star Chamber sessions and was an advocate of severe treatment in the cases of Prynne and others.[91] He was among the councillors left in charge of royal affairs in 1639 and 1640 while the king went to the Scottish border,[92] and in the latter year shared the lieutenancy of Suffolk with the Earl of Suffolk, and acted as Pembroke's agent for the corresponding office

in Cornwall. He worked energetically to press troops in those counties and others,[93] and was reported willing to have the levies used in 1640 to overawe parliament.[94]

As in previous parliaments, Comptroller Jermyn was a spokesman for the king. In the debates of 1640 and 1641, he repeatedly urged deference to the crown,[95] and argued against the London petition on episcopacy. He was among the witnesses requested by Strafford,[96] but not listed among those voting against his attainder. After his surrender of his office in the household in August, 1641, however, Jermyn was less constant in his attendance in the Commons. His age and weakness kept him away frequently during the remainder of 1641 [97] and in 1642. He was summoned on 12 August 1642 to attend, and was brought up in custody, but released in December upon his promise to pay his assessment. A levy of £1000 was set upon him the following year, reduced later by half, and he was disabled on 5 February 1644.[98] He was not declared a delinquent, however, as was his son, Thomas (q.v.).[99] He died on 4 January 1645, and was buried three days later at Rushbrook.

Jermyn had inherited many manors from his father,[100] and his various sources of revenue open to him as a courtier [101] made him a man of considerable wealth. He had been required, however, to lend heavily to the king,[102] and by 1640 was said to have sold the greater part of his Suffolk lands and settled the rest on his heir. His properties had probably been worth over £1500 a year before the war, but he seems to have died in debt.[103]

Sir Thomas was a cousin of Sir Robert Crane and was related by marriage to Henry Killegrew.

[82] Ibid.; Copinger, The manors of Suffolk 6: 333. Jermyn married in March, 1641/2, Mary, daughter of Edmund Barber and widow of Thomas Newton. Ibid.; Suff. Inst. Arch. 7: 360, 1891.
[83] M. of P. 1: 445; 3: App., xl. It was probably a cousin of the same name who sat for Sudbury in 1588. Ibid. 1: 425; Rushbrook parish registers, 229.
[84] M. of P. 1: 453, passim.
[85] C. 193/12.
[86] C. 181/4, fol. 190v; 181/5, fols. 201, 243, 308, 337; C.S.P. Dom., 1631–1633, 6; 1633–1634, 326.
[87] Rushbrook parish registers, 231; Add. MSS, 39,245, fols. 72, 114, Bodleian Tanner MSS, 67, fol. 48v; C.S.P. Dom., 1628–1629, 143.
[88] Ibid., 1619–1623, 554; 1628–1629, 218; S.P. 16, 29/13; Harl. MSS, 1581, fols. 352, 383; Common Debates for 629, 236, 243, 266.
[89] S.P. 16, 139/68; C.S.P. Dom., 1628–1629, 508. Jermyn resigned the office to Sir Peter Wich in 1641 for the sum of £5000 to £7000. Ibid., 1639–1640, 589; 1641–1643, 73, 77.
[90] Ibid., 1629–1631, 523; 1637–1638, 324.
[91] S. R. Gardiner, ed., Documents relating to proceedings against William Prynne, 22–23, Camden Society, 1877, and Reports of cases in the courts of Star Chamber and High Commission, 1, 23, 103, Camden Society, 1886; C.S.P. Dom., 1640–1641, 123.
[92] Ibid., 1638–1639, 389; 1640, 590; 1640–1641, 3.

[93] Ibid., 1640, 336, 372, 471, 627, 659; Add. MSS, 15,084, fols. 25–28.
[94] V.C.H. Suffolk 2: 190.
[95] D'Ewes (N), 4, 41, 324; Gardiner, History of England 9: 273. He was thought by some to have damaged the king's cause in the Short Parliament by not opposing Vane in explaining the king's position on the subsidy. Lipscomb, Buckingham 3: 184.
[96] D'Ewes (N), 338, 515 and n.
[97] C.S.P. Dom., 1641–1643, 77; D'Ewes (B), 368, 377; Pink MSS, 305, fol. 59.
[98] C.J. 2: 716, 850, 871, 902; 3: 389. Jermyn once complained of the lies told about him by "that knave Gurdon." Ibid. 2: 907.
[99] Petition of Jermyn's widow in 1648. Bodleian Carte MSS, 74, fol. 476.
[100] Add. MSS, 33,858 (Muskett's collection), fol. 75; Suff. Inst. Arch. 8: 174, 1894; 11: 2–14, 1903; East Anglian, N.S., 6: 142, 1895–1896; 7: 270, 1897–1898.
[101] These included a lease of some royal lands in Huntingdonshire, certain game rights in Suffolk, £1500 as a free gift in 1637, and a grant up to £5000 from certain arrearages. C.S.P. Dom. 1625–1626, 578; 1637, 359, 552; 1638–1639, 627.
[102] £2000 was the contribution he made in 1639. S.P. 16, 453/74.
[103] Add. MSS, 15,520, fol. 58; Bodleian Tanner MSS, 98, fols. 16–17; Carte MSS, 74, fol. 476; Cal. Com. Comp., 38.

Thomas Jermyn (*c.* 1602–1659), of Rushbrook, Suffolk, son of Sir Thomas Jermyn, Comptroller of the Household (*q.v.*), sat for Bury St. Edmunds, 1640–1644 (?). The second but eldest surviving son of Sir Thomas, he was born about 1602,[104] and grew up in the atmosphere of the court. He was elected M.P. for Beeralston in 1624, and in 1625 for Leicester to fill a seat vacated by his kinsman, Sir Humphrey May.[105] It was doubtless the latter's influence as Chancellor of the Duchy of Lancaster which procured for Jermyn his elections at Lancaster in 1626 and Clitheroe in 1628.[106] About February, 1628/9, Jermyn married Rebecca, the heiress of a wealthy London merchant, William Rodway.[107] He had some office at court by this time and in the following December was granted a reversion of the governorship of Jersey after his father and two others. He received a small fee as keeper of the hare-warren at Hampton in 1635, was mentioned as one of the king's servants in 1637 and 1638 and as a groom of the bedchamber to Prince Charles when, in 1639, he was granted £2000 from the queen's income and one of the reversions of the office of Clerk of the Pipe.[108] He was active in the Suffolk musters of 1629 and was one of the D.L.'s a decade later.[109]

Jermyn was not a member of the Short Parliament, but from his place at court watched what he regarded as the king's magnanimity "in these tempestuous times." [110] In the Long Parliament he worked with his father for the king, but was named to no committees, and was absent by 16 June 1642.[111] He joined the king at Oxford and in the field, and followed the queen and prince into exile in 1646.[112] He compounded for his estates, 1648–1650, naming lands in Lincoln, Norfolk and Suffolk, with a net income of some £1420, and was

fined at least £2750 for his delinquency.[113] He died on 11 November 1659, aged fifty-eight, and was buried at Rushbrook.[114]

Richard Jervoise (*c.* 1604–1645), of Freefolk, Hants, M.P. for Whitchurch, 1640–1645,[115] was the eldest son of his colleague, Sir Thomas Jervoise (*q.v.*). Born about 1604,[116] he possibly served in 1625 as a lieutenant under Conway for the Cadiz expedition.[117] He was afterwards (1633, 1635, 1637) a captain in his father's regiment of Hampshire militia.[118] On 8 May 1637 he married Frances, daughter of Sir George Croke of Waterstoke, Oxfordshire, the judge. His father settled on him then the manor of Freefolk, part of his mother's inheritance.[119] He probably acquired the manor of Eastington, Bucks, by right of his wife.[120] Through his wife he was connected with Harbottle Grimston, who married another daughter of Justice Croke, and with Robert Croke (*q.v.*).

Jervoise was elected with his father to both parliaments of 1640 for Whitchurch.[121] He seems to have followed Sir Thomas's lead in politics, although he was not named to committee work in the Commons. He was a parliamentary committeeman in Hampshire, and on 3 June 1645, was granted a weekly allowance.[122] He died the following fall, a writ for a new election being ordered on 31 October 1645.[123] He left only daughters, and his younger brother, Thomas, became his father's heir.[124]

Sir Thomas Jervoise (1587–1654), of Herriard Park, Hampshire, was M.P. for Whitchurch, 1640–1653.[125] He had long been active in Hampshire affairs, having established his contact with the county by marrying one of its heiresses. He was the grandson of a London mercer and alderman of the early sixteenth century,

[104] Henry Jermyn, Henrietta Maria's favorite, is often called the second son (*D.N.B.*), but he was actually the third. Sir Thomas's first son was Robert (1601–1623). *Rushbrook parish registers*, 237. A Thomas Jermy, who entered Emmanuel College, Cambridge, in 1622 (B.A. 1626, and M.A. 1629), has been identified as Jermyn (*Al. Cant.*), but it seems improbable that he continued to be a student while serving as an M.P. The Jermy family of Suffolk has sometimes been confused with that of Jermyn.

[105] *M. of P.* **1**: 457, 464; Thompson, *Leicester*, 351.

[106] *M. of P.* **1**: 470, 476. The member for those boroughs is confused with his father in Pink and Beaven, *Parl. Rep. Lanc.* (117), and Bean, *Northern Counties*, 293.

[107] His father's deed of settlement at the time of his marriage was dated 4 February 1628/9 (S.P. 23/217/759), and on 12 February Jermyn and his wife acknowledged in the London Aldermen's Court the receipt from her father's trustees of her inheritance of some £4990. London Corp. MSS, Rep. 43, fol. 105.

[108] *C.S.P. Dom.*, *1635*, 576; *1637*, 479, 480; *1637–1638*, 158; *1639*, 1; *1639–1640*, 198.

[109] Add. MSS, 15,084, fol. 4; 39,245, fol. 157v.

[110] Letters of Jermyn to his cousin, Sir Robert Crane (*q.v.*), Bodleian Tanner MSS, 65, fols. 100, 112, 128v–129.

[111] Pink MSS, 305, fol. 60.

[112] *Rushbrook parish registers*, 240; *Suff. Inst. Arch.* **8**: 173, 1894.

[113] He declared that one manor was heavily mortgaged and that the debts of his father, his brother and himself totalled £7750–£8450. S.P. 23/217/759–761, 789–791. A sum of £1500 a year, to come from the proceeds of not over two-thirds of the estates of Thomas Jermyn and his father, was assigned to the Earl of Stamford during the war, but with the provision that the sum should be made up from other estates if the Jermyn lands did not yield so much. *Cal. Com. Comp.*, 38, 1869–1870.

[114] Jermyn has sometimes been referred to as Sir Thomas, but there is no record of his being knighted, and the register at Rushbrook records the burial on 13 November 1659 of "the Honble Mr. Thomas Jermine." *East Anglian*, N.S., **6**: 160, 1895–1896; *Suff. Inst. Arch.* **7**: 361, 1891.

[115] *M. of P.* **1**: 493.

[116] Pink MSS, 305, fol. 64.

[117] S.P. 16, 522/16.

[118] Add. MSS, 26,781, fols. 25, 35v; 21,922, fol. 201.

[119] *The Ancestor* **3**: 5, 1902.

[120] Lipscomb, *Buckingham* **1**: 132, 155.

[121] *M. of P.* **1**: 483.

[122] Godwin, *The Civil War in Hampshire*, 104; *C.J.* **4**: 161.

[123] *C.J.* **4**: 327; *O.P.H.* **9**: 1.

[124] *The Ancestor* **3**: 5, 1902.

[125] *M. of P.* **1**: 493; *O.P.H.* **9**: 1.

Richard Jervoise, who purchased lands in various midland and western counties, and was the only surviving son and heir of Thomas Jervoise of Britford, Wilts (d. 1588), by Cicely Ridley, a Shropshire heiress. The younger Thomas was born on 11 June 1587,[126] and was the ward for a time of Rowland Lacon and Francis Newport, and later of Sir George Wrottesley, who became his stepfather. In 1601 the wardship was sold for £1000 to Sir Richard Powlett of Herriard and Freefolk, Hants. Powlett's daughter and coheiress, Lucy, was married to the young ward by a license dated 17 July 1601. Jervoise was knighted at Salisbury in 1611, and in 1614 came into possession of his wife's inheritance in Hampshire.[127] He served as sheriff of Shropshire, 1612–1613,[128] but afterwards was more concerned with affairs in Hampshire than in Wilts, Salop, or other counties where he owned land.

Sir Thomas was engaged in a dispute, 1614–1615, with a clergyman, Thomas Williams, about the control of the living at Herriard vicarage, a dispute which led to suits in Chancery and the Star Chamber. By this time he was already a captain in the local trained bands,[129] and for many years afterwards he was active in military matters in the county. By 1625 he was a D.L.,[130] and in 1626–1627 he was a commissioner for the billeting of soldiers at Southampton and one of the commission for martial law.[131] He was a loan collector in 1625 and a commissioner for the loan of 1626–1627, contributing £30 with some reluctance himself.[132] He was a knighthood commissioner in 1630, too,[133] and served on various other local commissions.[134] His service as a J.P. had begun not later than 1617, and he worked as a magistrate during the next three decades.[135] In the years just before 1640 he was active in his work as a D.L. and as colonel of a regiment, and was engaged in arranging for troops to go to the Scottish border in 1639 and 1640.[136] He excused himself, however, from contributing money toward the king's journey north in 1639.[137] He sat in parliament for the Hampshire borough of Whitchurch six times before November, 1640 (1621–1640),[138] and in 1624 kept notes of the debates.[139] He procured one of the seats of another borough of the county, Andover, for the son of Secretary Conway in 1628,[140] and his power at Whitchurch was such that even a relative of Secretary Windebank feared to challenge it.[141]

Sir Thomas was a puritan, and showed himself eventually an Independent. James Sanborne, the puritan divine, was his friend and tutor.[142] In 1632 Jervoise was subpoenaed by Star Chamber for eating flesh on Fridays.[143] It it not surprising to find him and his son, Richard, his colleague for Whitchurch, working with the opposition forces in 1640.

Jervoise was named to several committees in the early months of the Long Parliament, but his activity in the House was greater in the period of 1648–1653.[144] He promised two horses for the defense in 1642,[145] and was active during the war years both as a military commander and as a parliamentary committeeman in Hampshire.[146] He died on 20 October 1654. His will, dated 19 October, was proved on 5 December 1654.[147] His first wife died in 1641, and he was survived by his second wife, Frances, daughter of Thomas Jay, Commissary General of Cavalry under Charles I.[148]

From his own and his first wife's family Jervoise inherited numerous properties in Wilts, Salop, Worcester, and Hants. One Wiltshire manor alone rented for £122 a year at one time.[149] Concerning three of his father's Worcestershire manors he was engaged in lawsuits, 1611–1624, but his title regarding them seems to have been cleared.[150] By 1636, however, he was financially embarrassed, and in 1639 was reported as hiding his head for debt.[151] He declared that the war cost him losses of £15,000,[152] but he gained some new sources of income by it also.[153] By the time of his death he could promise £1125 for one daughter and £500 for another, and as well make provision for his widow and his sons.

Cousins by marriage of Jervoise in the 1640 House were Sir Henry and Robert Wallop.[154]

[126] I.P.M., Thomas Jervoise, 1588, C. 142/216/64.
[127] F. H. T. Jervoise, "The Jervoises of Herriard and Britford," *The Ancestor* 3: 1–3, 1902.
[128] *List of Sheriffs*, 119.
[129] St. Ch. 8/189/4; H.M.C., *Various collections* 4, MSS of F. H. T. Jervoise, Esq., 171.
[130] *Acts. P.C., 1625–1626*, 290; Bodleian Rawl. MSS, D 666, fol. 77v; Add. MSS, 21,922, fol. 4v.
[131] C.S.P. Dom., 1625–1626, 360; Add. MSS, 21,922, fols. 88, 123, 145.
[132] S.P. 16, 521/77; Rawl. MSS, D 666, fols. 41–46, 78v; C.S.P. Dom., 1627–1628, 64, 92.
[133] Add. MSS, 21,922, fol. 174.
[134] C. 181/4 and 5, *passim*.
[135] Rawl. MSS, D 666, fols. 50v, 62v, 81, 85v; C. 193/12, 13.
[136] Add. MSS, 21,922, fols. 188, 201; Add. MSS, 26,781, fols. 4, 17, *passim*.
[137] Rushworth, 3: 912.

[138] *M. of P.* 1: 453, 460, *passim*.
[139] Wallace Notestein, manuscript in preparation on the Commons debates of 1624.
[140] C.S.P. Dom., 1627–1628, 477, 541, 566.
[141] Ibid., 1640–1641, 179.
[142] *Devon and Cornwall Notes and Queries* 9 (1): 220, 1916–1917.
[143] Add. MSS, 11,056, fol. 64.
[144] C.J. 2: 146, 161; Pink MSS, 305, fol. 65v.
[145] N. and Q., 1st Ser., 12: 360, 1855.
[146] Add. MSS, 24,860, fol. 145; Godwin, *The Civil War in Hampshire*, 104.
[147] P.C.C., 415 Alchin.
[148] Pink MSS, 305, fols. 65–65v.
[149] *The Ancestor* 3: 1–3, 1902; Jervoise's will.
[150] Birmingham Reference Library MSS, 357,396; 375,123.
[151] C.S.P. Dom., 1635–1636, 258; 1637–1638, 311; 1639, 265.
[152] Godwin, *op. cit.*, 371.
[153] Pink MSS, *loc. cit.*
[154] *The Ancestor* 3: 3, 1902.

William Jesson (d. 1651), alderman and dyer of Coventry, was a member for Coventry from 20 July 1641 until 1648. He was probably a candidate at the original election, when he was apparently defeated,[155] and entered the House after Norton's death. He was the third son of Richard Jesson of Coventry by his wife, Elizabeth Hill,[156] and was probably a brother of the Thomas Jesson who left £2000 for the city charities in 1634.[157] The family may originally have come from Hampshire.[158] William Jesson was active in the affairs of Coventry by 1620, and in the next twelve years passed through the various municipal offices, becoming mayor, 1631-1632, and alderman thereafter.[159] He married Elizabeth, daughter of John Barker, alderman, probably a sister or a cousin of the 1640 M.P. of that name,[160] and had a son old enough to enter the Inner Temple in 1635.[161] By 1640 Jesson was one of the masters of the Mercers' Company of Coventry.[162]

During the 1630's Jesson became entangled more than once with royal and church officials. In 1632, while he was mayor, he was summoned before Council for having failed to pay the musters fee due on some lands he owned in Leicestershire, but he excused himself satisfactorily.[163] He had subscribed with others of the local government to the 1627 loan,[164] but in 1635 he was one of the leaders in the city's protests against its ship money assessment. It was in his house in Little Park Street that the committee of townsmen met with the bishop, the sheriff, and members of the gentry to confer about the rates.[165] In 1638 he went with a committee to call upon their recorder, the Lord Keeper, in London regarding the city's suit against the minister of St. Michael's church, and another errand took him to Lambeth that year.[166] He was a member of the Short Parliament, but failed in the autumn elections, possibly because his religious views were more extreme than Norton's. During the interval between the parliaments

he was summoned to appear before Council, apparently for having delayed paying his coat and conduct money and his ship money assessment in Coventry. One of his answering arguments was that he had already paid ship money in six places in Warwickshire and Northamptonshire.[167]

In the Long Parliament Jesson took little part before 1642. He was appointed in December, 1641, however, to a committee to investigate the ship money and coat and conduct money still in the hands of sheriffs.[168] He promised in April, 1642, to lend £300, but was suspended for a short time the following September because he hesitated about supporting Essex. The next month he was asked by parliament to advance £1000 in money for preparing Coventry's defenses, and he remained loyal to parliament and a member until Pride's Purge.[169] He seems to have been removed from his aldermanship by parliament's order of 20 March 1651,[170] and died on 29 August 1651.[171] He was probably buried at St. Michael's in Coventry. His will, dated 13 October 1650 and sealed 25 March 1651, was proved 7 November 1651.[172]

Alderman Jesson owned, besides his business as a dyer and his town house, a country residence at Nuthurst. He was among those interested in developing the city's coal mines in 1622, and he held leases on various city properties as well as on some in the county and in neighboring shires.[173] He had purchased for £2000 in 1628 one of the Leicestershire properties of the Temple family.[174] In his will he wrote of his "plentiful" blessings in lands and goods, assigned properties worth at least £300 a year for the use of his widow, and others totalling £860 a year, some of them of recent purchase, to two of his sons. He provided also a marriage portion of over £500 for a recently married daughter and listed bequests amounting to over £1600. It is not to be wondered that parliament asked Jesson to advance cash for his city's defenses.

Arthur Jones, afterwards Lord Ranelagh (d. 1670), M.P. for Weobly, Herefordshire, 1640–5 February 1644, was the eldest son and heir apparent of Roger, first Viscount Ranelagh of Ireland (d. 1643), by his wife, Frances, daughter of Gerald (Moore), first Viscount Drogheda. Before 1630 he married Katherine, talented daughter of the Earl of Cork, gaining with her

---

[155] *C.J.* **2**: 78; *M. of P.* **1**: 495.

[156] Pink MSS, 305, fol. 68.

[157] *History, gazetteer and directory of Warwickshire,* 519. William Jesson referred in his will to the will of his brother, Thomas, and he had both a son and a grandson of that name (P.C.C., 215 Grey).

[158] W. H. Rylands, ed., *The visitation of the county of Warwick, 1682–3,* Harleian Society, **62**: 138, 1911 (hereafter, *Vis. Warwicks.*). Thomas Jesson, however, was born in Coventry. Add. MSS, 11,364, fol. 16.

[159] Coventry Corporation MSS, A 14 a, fols. 448, 465, 530, 535, 594–610, *passim.*

[160] Pink (*loc. cit.*) thought that Jesson's wife was a daughter of John Barker, the M.P., but it seems more probable that she was a daughter of the other alderman of that name who died in 1634.

[161] *Students admitted to the Inner Temple,* 287.

[162] Coventry Corporation MSS, A 100, Minutes of the Mercers' Company.

[163] *C.S.P. Dom., 1631–1633,* 374.

[164] Coventry Corporation MSS, F 5 e, Subscription List, fol. 1.

[165] *Ibid.,* A 35, Ship Money Accounts, 1635–1677.

[166] *Ibid.,* A 22, fol. 304.

[167] *C.S.P. Dom., 1640,* 473.

[168] *C.J.* **2**: 357. Jesson was present in Coventry council meetings on 14 July and throughout October, 1641. Coventry Corporation MSS, A 14 b, fols. 19–22.

[169] Pink MSS, 305, fol. 68; *C.J.* **2**: 811.

[170] The Coventry Council voted on 16 July to obey the order and choose his successor. Coventry Corporation MSS, A 14 b, fol. 99v.

[171] Pink, *loc. cit.*

[172] P.C.C., 215 Grey.

[173] Whitley, *Parl. Rep. Coventry,* 79; Coventry Corporation MSS, A 14 a, fols. 472, 629, 692; A 14 b, fol. 88v; A 22, fol. 320.

[174] Birmingham Reference Library MSS, 277,347.

a portion of £3000. He seems in his youth to have had an unenviable reputation as a drunkard and a gambler, but by 1639 he had become somewhat more discreet in his habits.[175] He was a member of the Irish parliament, 1634–1635, but has not served in England before 1640. His election at Weobly was doubtless secured for him by influential friends. After he entered the parliament he was admitted to Gray's Inn (March, 1641).[176]

Jones was a fairly active member of the Long Parliament in 1641. He was named to several committees, particularly those concerned with Irish affairs.[177] And in the debates on Irish matters, especially those in which his father was attacked, he was a vehement speaker. Strafford, writing of the charge against Ranelagh, remarked that "his [Ranelagh's] Sonne keeps such a Rackett as never was, Slavers and Railes as if he were mad, and all the while Speaks not a wise or a true word."[178] His loyalty came under suspicion after the war started. In 1642 he was granted leave to go to Ireland, where he was in May a captain in the army. His disablement as a royalist was considered in January, 1644, and voted on 5 February.[179] Afterwards he lived chiefly in Ireland, having in 1643 succeeded to his father's title, and he died there on 7 January 1670.

Jones was in 1640 a young man of ample means, although he had not come into his own estate and his dissolute habits had doubtless been expensive. He had married well and his wife later declared that he had surrendered to the parliamentary commissioners an estate in Ireland worth £1200 a year. He compounded, however, for nothing but a small personal estate.

Three brothers-in-law of widely different character and politics were fellow parliament men with Jones. Sir John Clotworthy, the parliamentarian, was his sister's husband; Lord Dungarvan was his wife's brother, and Colonel Goring, the royalist soldier, had married another of the daughters of the Earl of Cork.[180]

Henry Killigrew (c. 1598–1646), of Lanrack, Cornwall, was a member for West Looe, 1640–22 January 1644. He came of a family of courtiers, and was the second son of Sir Henry Killigrew of Cornwall and London, M.P., and ambassador to France (d. 1603), by his French second wife, Jael de Peigne. At the death of his elder brother, Sir Joseph, in 1616, Henry inherited several Cornish manors of the family.[1] His

cousin, Sir Robert Killigrew, (1579–1633),[2] the courtier, son of his father's brother, Sir William Killigrew, may have been his guardian. Sir Robert brought suit in Chancery in February, 1619, on behalf of Henry and a younger brother, Robert, concerning the mishandling of some of their properties by a trustee during their minority.[3] Henry matriculated at Queen's College, Oxford, 28 April 1615, aged seventeen, and entered Gray's Inn in 1617 as "of London, esquire."[4] He married a kinswoman of his cousin's wife, Jemimah, daughter of Sir Nicholas Bacon of Redgrove, Suffolk, and widow of Sir William Waldegrave (d. 1613), and had by her a son, Henry, who was living in 1620.[5] He seems to have resided thereafter partly at one of his wife's properties in Essex,[6] but he was reported by the loan collectors of that shire in 1627 as in default because he had gone out of the county.[7] Although his cousins, Sir Robert and his sons, were prominent at court, and another cousin was the wife of Sir Thomas Jermyn (q.v.), Killigrew seems not to have sought court life himself. He was well known, however, in court circles.[8] Apparently it was another cousin, probably the son of John Killigrew of Arwennack, aged thirty in 1630, who, as Captain Henry Killigrew, was active with Sir Ralph Hopton in army matters in 1624, served in several expeditions to the continent, and was knighted in 1625. He seems to have died during the Cadiz expedition.[9] Henry Killigrew "of Wormingford," Essex, was still "esquire" in 1627, and he was styled in the same fashion when, five years later, he was living in Cornwall. By that time he seems to have taken up residence on some of the estates which had come to him as his brother's heir male, but he was being sued in Chancery by his brother's daughter, and her husband, William Bassett (q.v.), for having taken more than his proper share of Sir Joseph's lands. Their claim seems to have won recognition to the extent of at least £200.[10]

Of Killigrew's role in Cornwall nothing is known. He was concerned in June, 1640, as to the effects of piracy on the town of Looe,[11] but his election to par-

---

[175] D. Townshend, *The life and letters of the great Earl of Cork*, 158, 234, 339.

[176] *Gray's Inn Adm. Reg.*, 229.

[177] *C.J.* 2: 72, 357, *passim*; Pink MSS, 305, fol. 94.

[178] Bodleian Tanner MSS, 65, fol. 266.

[179] *C.J.* 3: 374, 389; Pink MSS, *loc. cit.*; *H.M.C., MSS of the Earl of Egmont* 1 (1): 176.

[180] In addition to the authorities cited above see *Complete Peerage*, Gibbs ed. **10**: 731–732; *M. of P.*; Williams, *Hereford*, 157.

[1] Vivian, *Vis. Cornwall*, 268–269; I.P.M.'s of Sir Henry Killigrew (C. 142/281/40) and Sir Joseph Killigrew (C. 142/356/100).

[2] *D.N.B.* Sir Robert was the father of the dramatists, Sir William and Thomas Killigrew and of Henry Killigrew, D.D.

[3] C. 3/315/4.

[4] *Al. Oxon.*; *Gray's Inn Adm. Reg.*, 146.

[5] Pink MSS, 307, fol. 230v; will of Dame Jemimah Waldegrave, alias Killigrew, P.C.C., 47 Essex. Her surname appears by error as Bael in Vivian's *Vis. Cornwall* (loc cit.). As to the son, see *Al. Oxon.*

[6] His son was born in Essex.

[7] S.P. 16, 54/47; 76/12/ii. The estate of Wormingford, by which he was then identified, was mentioned by his widow in her will.

[8] Clarendon, *Rebellion* **4**: 216.

[9] Vivian, *op. cit.*, 269; St. Ch. 8/124/4; S.P. 16, 522/16; 68/79; 526/50; Add. MSS, 11,056, fol. 165; *C.S.P. Dom., 1623–1625*, 404; *1625–1626*, 352; *Western Antiquary* **11**: 46, 1891–1892.

[10] C. 3/395/103; *Cal. Com. Comp.*, 1984.

[11] *The Buller Papers*, 24.

liament that fall for West Looe brought him his first experience as a member.[12] He took no prominent part in the affairs of the House until 1642, when the sentiment against the king was running so strong that he could no longer restrain his sharp tongue. He then became "most zealous and passionate in the opposing all the extravagant proceedings of the Parliament,"[13] was sharply reprimanded by the Speaker for his remarks on the militia bill in April,[14] and when the members were pledging their support to Essex and promising to furnish horses and men, "he stood up and said, 'He would provide a good horse, and a good buff-coat, and a good pair of pistols, and then he doubted not he should find a good cause,' and so went out of the House, and rode post into Cornwall."[15] There he joined his good friends, Sir Ralph Hopton, the Arundells, and the other Cornish royalists, in raising forces for the king. His only son, Henry, fought for the king, too, and was killed at Bridgwater.[16] Killigrew was suspended by parliament on account of his absence, 2 September 1642, and disabled, 22 January 1644.[17] He escaped from England after the surrender of Pendennis Castle in 1646, but died at St. Malo in Brittany on September 27 of that year, and was buried in Jersey.[18]

Clarendon described Killigrew as "a very gallant gentleman, of a noble extraction, and a fair revenue in land; of excellent parts and great courage," and a man whom his countrymen "infinitely loved" for his spirit and sincerity. His holdings in Cornwall consisted chiefly of the manor of Lanrack (Lawarick) and its rectory and two other manors.[19] He owned also "Ince

House" in St. Stephen's, Saltash.[20] Values of over £265 a year are indicated by the compounding papers, but according to one source, Killigrew was said to be worth before the war some £800 yearly.[21]

Several of the parliament men of 1640 were connections of Killigrew. Edward Seymour was the son of his stepsister, Stawell was the husband of his brother's widow, and Bassett, of his niece. With the latter, however, Killigrew was probably on ill terms because of their disputes about property. The Jermyns were the husband and son of one of Killigrew's cousins.

Richard King (1590–1645), of the Inner Temple and of Sherborne, Dorset, Recorder of Weymouth and Melcombe Regis, was a member for Melcombe Regis from 1640 until his disablement, 27 February 1643.[22] Baptized at Castle Cary, Somerset, on 30 August 1590, he was the son and heir of William King of that place. He matriculated at Oriel College, Oxford, in 1610, and by November, 1611, was studying at the Inner Temple. He became a barrister in 1620, a bencher in 1638, and in May, 1641, was reader there.[23] His connections with Dorset were confirmed with his marriage on 25 December 1623 to Edith, daughter of Sir Robert Seymour of Hanford. He acquired with her property in several Dorset parishes representing a proposed dower of over £520. Between 1625 and 1627 King purchased several other properties in the county, some near Sherborne, and there his first wife was buried in 1634. He married again before July, 1639, his second wife being Margaret, daughter of Robert Harbin of Mudford. He mingled both professionally and socially with the gentry, one of his clients being the Earl of Cork. In 1641 he received a grant of arms.

King became recorder for Weymouth and Melcombe Regis in 1629.[24] He was a J.P. for the county and a member of the commissions of oyer and terminer and of piracy.[25] He was chosen for both parliaments of 1640 by Melcombe Regis, and during the early months was an active member of the reforming faction. He was named to the Committee of Privileges, was chairman of that on monopolies, and was appointed to those on the Bishop of Bath and Wells and on the customs, and a number of others.[26] He opposed abuses of power, whether by royal agents or by church officials, as he did in a speech in February, 1641, objecting to the new canons.[27] But he eventually came to feel, apparently, that parliament itself might abuse its powers, and he

---

[12] Some confusion about the identity of Killigrew has risen from the fact that in the records he has sometimes been referred to as "Sir Henry." Buller (loc. cit.) called him Mr. Killigrew, and he was styled "Esquire" in Walkley's list of members, 1640 (Thomasòn Tracts, E. 1091, 2). His name appears in C.J. without any indication of knighthood, but his friend, Clarendon, who always refers to him as a knight, states, that "Sir Henry" was the member (Rebellion 4: 216). He is referred to both with and without the title of "Sir" in the compounding papers (Cal. Com. Comp., 1181, 1984, 3290). Pink once suggested (Western Antiquary 11: 46, 1891–1892) that the member was "Sir" Henry's son, but since the son was killed in 1644 (Clarendon, op. cit. 3: 402; 4: 216) that suggestion must be discarded. Killigrew was perhaps knighted after he had withdrawn from Westminster at the coming of war.

[13] Clarendon, loc. cit.

[14] By a vote of 131 to 97 a measure to expel him at once was defeated. C.J. 2: 507; Verney, 171.

[15] Clarendon, op. cit. 4: 217.

[16] In Hopton's narrative of his campaign in the west, Somerset Record Society, 18: 11, 18, 1902, "Mr. Henry Killigrew" is mentioned as one of the officers serving under Lundsford in 1642. The officer may have been the M.P.'s son, since Clarendon states that Killigrew was consulted but never took command. Rebellion 4: 216–217; 3: 402; W. H. Tregellas, Cornish Worthies 2: 153, London, 1884.

[17] C.J. 2: 750; 4: 374. A writ was ordered for replacing Henry Killigrew, Esquire, on 21 December 1646. C.J. 5: 21.

[18] Clarendon, loc. cit.; Vivian, loc. cit.

[19] C. 3/395/103; Notes and Gleanings 3: 159, 1890.

[20] Cal. Com. Comp., 3290–3291.

[21] Tregellas, loc. cit.

[22] M. of P. 1: 488; C.J. 2: 982.

[23] Al. Oxon.; Cal. Inner Temp. Rec. 2: 120, 244, 260.

[24] Moule, Catalogue of the . . . documents of the borough of Weymouth and Melcombe Regis, 112.

[25] C. 193/13; C. 181/5, fol. 305.

[26] C.J. 2: 21, 50, 92, passim; D'Ewes (C), 55, 203.

[27] D'Ewes (N), 127.

was probably absent much of the time after January, 1642. He appeared in the House in April, 1642, following an absence of some time without leave, was suspended on account of absences in September, and was finally deprived of his seat in 1643.[28] He sat in the Oxford parliament. Dying in 1645, he was buried on 27 August at Sherborne.

Almost nothing is known of King's finances, except that he was evidently a successful lawyer and had before 1640 been buying lands in Dorset. The parliamentarians assessed him £1000 in 1644, but he probably never paid it.[29]

Roger Kirkby (c. 1601–1643), of Kirkby Ireleth, Lancashire, M.P. for his county, 1640–29 August 1642, was the descendant of an old county family. He was the son and heir of Roger Kirkby of Kirkby, H.S., D.L. (d. 1627), by his wife, Jane, daughter of Edward Rigby of Burgh, and was born about 1601. Sometime before 1625 he married Agnes, daughter of Sir John Lowther of Lowther.[30] Kirkby served as a J.P. and a sewers commissioner in Lancashire,[31] was sheriff, 1637–1638, and a collector of ship money.[32] He sat for Lancaster borough in the Short Parliament.[33]

In first period of the Long Parliament Kirkby was named to a number of important committees, several concerning grievances and breaches of privilege, and others, the "popish hierarchy," ecclesiastical innovations, and the Sabbath. As one of the county knights he was sent in August, 1641, to supervise the disarming of recusants in Lancashire.[34] He was evidently interested in the reform of abuses and inclined toward puritanism, but with the onset of war he followed his mother's family and the Earl of Derby, Lancashire's chief nobleman, in supporting the king. He was summoned on 22 July 1642 to attend the House, and ordered to be removed from the Lancashire commission of the peace.[35] Avoiding capture at Lancaster, he fled to Ireland and died there in August, 1643.[36]

The compounding papers of Kirkby's son and heir mention family holdings in Lancashire and Cumberland, but probably their estimated value of slightly under £400 a year does not represent all of Kirkby's income. The fine was set at a sixth, or £750, to be reduced to

£250, with £50 a year settled on a minister, but in 1660 the son's estate was said to be worth £1500 yearly.[37]

Edward Kirton, or **Kyrton** (c. 1580–1654), of Castle Cary, Somerset, was M.P. for Milbourne Port, 1640–11 August 1642. He was the son of Daniel Kirton of Castle Cary (d. 1594) by his wife, Frances, who afterwards married Sir Robert Vernon of Mitcham and of the court. He was a nephew of Sir James Kirton of Almsford, Somerset (d. 1620), who was several times M.P. for Wiltshire boroughs, and who was on the royal pension lists in 1614 and 1616.[38] This uncle and his mother's second husband influenced Kirton's early years. He was born about 1580,[39] and about the time of the accession of King James entered the royal household in some post under his stepfather. But his friendship with the younger members of the family of Seymour, in whose affairs his uncle was legal adviser,[40] brought him presently to grief. He was involved in the disgrace of Sir William Seymour on account of his marriage with Lady Arabella Stuart in 1610, and although he was permitted to be one of her attendants while she was in the custody of Sir Thomas Parry, he was dismissed from his employment in the king's household.[41] Kirton was a prisoner at various times between 1610 and 1614 in connection with that matter, was released occasionally on bail, and was among those examined by Council in 1617 regarding the Lady Arabella.[42] He probably retired to the country soon afterwards, embittered by his experience, but he apparently did not lose all his taste for court intrigue, for as late as 1641 he was interested in a new place at court.[43] And his relationship with the family of Seymour continued, for he was their agent for many years afterwards, and his politics strongly resembled theirs. They owned Castle Cary manor, which he held on lease from them, and they probably assisted him more than once to a seat in parliament.

Kirton entered parliament first in 1621, sitting for Newcastle, Staffordshire. He was returned for Lud-

[28] C.J. 2: 545, 750, 845, 966, 982.
[29] Pink MSS, 305, fol. 63. Other authorities are: *Somerset and Dorset N. and Q.* 3: 143, 145, 259, 260, 1892–1893; 4: 41, 1894–1895; 7: 299, 301, 1900–1901; *M. of P.*
[30] Pink and Beaven, *Parl. Rep. Lanc.,* 72; Cumberland and Westmoreland A. and A. Soc., *Trans.,* N.S., 6: opp. 97, 1906; S.P. 16, 8/15, i.
[31] C. 193/12; C. 181/4, fol. 130v.
[32] C.S.P. Dom., 1637–1638, 146, 149.
[33] M. of P. 1: 482.
[34] C.J. 2: 40, 52, 53, 61, 105, 197, 267, 438.
[35] Ibid. 2: 685, 742, 821.
[36] Pink MSS, 305, fol. 76; Bean, *Northern Counties,* 293.

[37] *The royalist composition papers . . . of Lancaster,* Part 4, Rec. Soc. Lancs. and Cheshire, 36: 43–44, 1898; Cumberland and Westmoreland A. and A. Soc., *Trans.,* N.S., 6: 115, 117, 1906.
[38] Brown, *Somerset Wills* 1: 43, 44; *M. of P.* 1: 430, *passim;* S.P. 14, 78/6; 94/125. Edward Kirton in 1606 attested the marriage license of one of his sisters, to which assent was given by their mother, Lady Vernon (spelled Vernam). *Marriage licenses, London,* Harleian Society, 25: 300, 1887.
[39] Wedgwood, *Staff. Parl. Hist.* 2: 25.
[40] Add. MSS, 32,324, fol. 6; B. C. Hardy, *Arabella Stuart,* 96, London, Constable, 1913.
[41] C.S.P. Dom., 1603–1610, 613.
[42] *Acts P.C., 1613–1614,* 106, 142, 539, 618; *1616–1617,* 134; Hardy, *op. cit.,* 242–243, 269, 296. The latter author is unreliable on some details.
[43] He seems to have secured some post in connection with the household of the prince. H.M.C., *Thirteenth Report* 2, MSS of the Duke of Portland, 133; *Somerset and Dorset N. and Q.* 3: 48, 1892–1893.

gershall in 1624, for Marlborough in 1625, for both Marlborough and Ilchester in 1626, when he chose the former, for Great Bedwin in 1628, and for Milborne Port in the spring of 1640.[44] He was among the anti-Buckingham group and by 1626 had become prominent in the faction. He helped manage the duke's impeachment in 1626, and attacked Carleton for yielding in the matter of the subsidy.[45] He was removed with Sir Robert Phelipps from the commission of the peace of Somerset that year.[46] In 1627 Kirton opposed the loan and suffered imprisonment once more in the Gatehouse.[47] He was active against Buckingham again in the parliament of 1628, and in 1629 spoke frequently against popery and Arminianism and against the collectors of tonnage and poundage.[48] During the period of personal rule he was one of the commissioners on depopulation in Somerset,[49] and probably continued to act as the Seymours' agent for their property in that county.[50]

Kirton returned to the parliaments of 1640 as one of the anti-court element, and was named to the committees of privilege of both the Short and the Long Parliament. Other important committees were those on the state of the kingdom and of the army, on monopolists and on several other grievances, and that for preparing the charges against Strafford.[51] But, as in the case of Sir Francis Seymour, Kirton presently showed that his views had moderated. He was more cautious than previously on the matter of the subsidy, incurred the displeasure of the House during the proceedings against Strafford, and voted against the earl's attainder.[52] He was a defender of episcopacy, joined the Hyde-Strangways element in deploring the increasing trend toward violence in London, and opposed the forming of the Guildhall Committee on 5 January 1642.[53] Kirton seems to have re-established himself in some position connected with the royal household in the summer of 1641, and when war came he quickly deserted parliament. Absent at call on 16 June 1642, he was disabled on 11 August, and on 30 August was charged with treason.[54] He compounded for his estates in 1646 and survived the war, but died early in 1654. He was buried on 30 January at Easton, near Pewsey, Wilts.

At some time before 1646 he married, but the name of his wife is unknown.[55]

When he compounded Kirton reported his holdings as three leases in the Castle Cary region, whose yearly value to him was £176. His fine at a third, £504, was changed afterwards to £102 or £112, with £30 to be settled on a rectory.[56]

Somewhat indirectly connected with Kirton by marriage were two fellow M.P.'s of 1640, Sir Edward Rodney and John Trenchard.[57]

* **Norton Knatchbull** (1602–1685), of Mersham Hatch, Kent, M.P. for New Romney, 1640–1648, was the son of Thomas Knatchbull (d. 1623) and the nephew and heir of Sir Norton Knatchbull (H.S., J.P., M.P., d. 1636).[58] He studied at the Middle Temple after leaving Cambridge,[59] and may have been in Ireland in 1629.[60] The next year he was licensed at Canterbury to marry Dorothy Westrow, daughter of a London alderman, and by that time had begun to serve on local commissions. He was a J.P. by 1634,[61] and in the heated contest of March, 1640, for knights of the shire, seems to have had no difficulty in getting the first place.[62] His uncle's reputation as a loan resister, at least in 1621,[63] perhaps helped.

Knatchbull was elected for New Romney on 18 October 1640, apparently without undue effort.[64] He offered his bond for the loans of 1640 and 1641,[65] but eventually lost some of his interest in the cause. He was created a baronet in August, 1641, was not named to many of the parliamentary committees for Kent in 1642, and was frequently absent. He was summoned in 1643 to pay a fine to be discharged from "sequestration," but did not lose his seat in the House until the purge of 1648.[66]

Knatchbull owned various properties near Maidstone and at other places in Kent.[67] His penalty of 1000 marks indicates that he was accounted well-to-do.

---

[44] M. of P.

[45] S.P. 16, 29/13; C.S.P. Dom., 1625–1626, 316; Forster, Eliot 1: 534.

[46] Somerset Arch. Proc. 16 (ii): 26, 1870.

[47] Forster, Eliot 2: 84. His name is missing from Rushworth's list.

[48] Forster, Eliot 2: 114; Commons Debates for 1629, 14–15, 37, 113, passim; Harl. MSS, 2217, fol. 85.

[49] S.P. 16, 229/112/252; C. 181/5, fols. 1, 43.

[50] Somerset Arch. Proc. 16 (ii): 5, 1870.

[51] C.J. 2: 4, 20, 25, 30, 34, passim.

[52] D'Ewes (N), 319, 380; C.J. 2: 119, 120; Verney, 58.

[53] D'Ewes (N), 337; D'Ewes (C), 166, 176, 215, 386.

[54] C.J. 2: 626, 715, 745.

[55] Wedgwood, loc. cit. The register at Easton described him as "Officer to the Lord Marquesse of Hertford." Wilts. Arch. Mag. 6: 299, 1860. His wife was referred to in his compounding papers.

[56] S.P. 23/194/491; Cal. Com. Comp., 1286. Lloyd's statement (Memoires, 694) that his fine was £1464 seems wholly wrong.

[57] His uncle, James Kirton, married Rodney's sister. Add. MSS, 34,239, fol. 14.

[58] M. of P. 1: 497; C. 193/13; D.N.B.

[59] Mid. Temp. Rec. 2: 690.

[60] C.S.P. Dom., 1628–1629, 532.

[61] C. 181/4, fols. 18v, 38v; 181/5, fols. 81, 288, 292; C. 193/13.

[62] Larking, Proceedings in Kent, 2, 5–8; Bodleian Rawl. MSS, D. 141, 4.

[63] S.P. 14, 127/82.

[64] New Romney Borough MSS, Common Assembly Book, 1622–1701, fols. 282–283.

[65] D'Ewes (N), 52, n.; 451, n.

[66] C.J. 2: 845; 3: 390; Arch. Cant. 2: 181–184, 1859; O.P.H. 9: 13.

[67] I.P.M., Thomas Knatchbull, C. 142/543/7; Hasted, Kent 5: 429; 7: 596, 598; 8: 403; Complete Baronetage 2: 118.

* Richard Knightley (1610 ?–1661), of Fawsley, Northamptonshire, M.P. for Northampton, 1640–1648, was the son of Richard Knightley, "senior," of Fawsley (1580–1650), and a cousin of Eliot's friend of the same name, the puritan who championed the liberties of the subject until his death in 1639. He was a son-in-law of John Hampden and a cousin of Sir Edward Littleton, the Staffordshire member.[68] Knightley was educated at Lincoln College, Oxford, and at Gray's Inn.[69] He had probably held no public office before his election to the Short Parliament, but was named with his father to the forest commission for their county in 1641.[70] Although he probably held little property in his own name in 1640, his father owned several manors in Northamptonshire,[71] and his pledge for the defense in June, 1642, was one of the larger offers.[72]

Sir Francis Knollys, or **Knolles** (c. 1550–1648), of Battel, near Reading, was M.P. for Reading, 1640–1648. He was the sixth son of Sir Francis Knollys, K.G., Treasurer of the Household to Queen Elizabeth (d. 1596), by his wife, Catherine Carey, Elizabeth's cousin and Lord Hunsdon's sister.[73] Incredible as it seems that a man of ninety should be elected to parliament, there can be no doubt about his identity. A contemporary writer, commenting on the action of some soldiers about Reading, remarked that "old Sir Francis Knolles, the ancientest Parliament man in England, had much prejudice done to his houses and their tenants in January, 1643,"[74] and Fuller noted that he was ninety-nine years old when he died.[75]

Born about 1550, Francis Knollys was a commoner at Magdalen College, Oxford, about 1564, and the next year was a student at Gray's Inn. His Oxford degree of M.A. was conferred in 1598.[76] He was elected to his first parliament for Oxford in 1575, filling a vacancy caused by the death of his brother, Edward, and was returned for Oxford to the parliaments of 1584, 1586, and 1588.[77] He probably spent much time at court during his father's life, but was engaged also in a naval career. His eldest brother, Henry (d. 1582), was one of Elizabeth's captains who preyed on ships of Spain,

part of the time acting in the service of Don Antonio of Crato, and in 1578 Francis commanded a ship in one of Henry's private ventures in the Channel, in the course of which they captured a French vessel. When the fate of that ship was the subject of inquiry four years later, Francis was his brother's intermediary with Secretary Walsingham.[78] Some years afterwards Francis wrote, "I have passed my tyme not obscurely, havinge tasted as many waters as most have donne."[79] As Captain Francis Knollys he sailed with Drake and Frobisher of 1585 on their raiding voyage to the West Indies. He commanded the *Leicester* and was rear-admiral of the expedition at the start. A disagreement about authority occurred during the voyage, Knollys objecting to some of Drake's orders and coming near to court martial himself, but they eventually reached an understanding and Knollys apparently stayed with the expedition until its return to England in July, 1586.[80] He was knighted in December, 1587, by his brother-in-law, the Earl of Leicester, on his embarking for Flushing,[81] and was back in England for the parliament the next year. About the end of 1588 (license dated 21 December), Knollys married Lettice, daughter of John Barrett of Hanham, Gloucester. He was then described as of London,[82] and was known at court as "young Sir Francis," but presently took up residence in Berkshire. He seems to have been living there in 1592, and in 1595 he obtained from the queen the lease of Battel manor.[83] Although he retained some connections with the court after his father's death,[84] he concerned himself more after that event with local affairs.

He was named to the Berkshire commission of the peace in 1592, and in 1596 became a D.L. there under the lieutenancy of his brother, Sir William.[85] In both of these offices he served for many years, apparently functioning in the latter capacity in 1625 and 1626, possibly as late as 1639.[86] He was a J.P. in Oxford-

---

[68] Knightley's mother was a daughter of Sir Edward Littleton of Pillaton, Staffordshire.

[69] He matriculated at Oxford, 24 October 1628, aged eighteen (*Al. Oxon.*). *D.N.B.* gives 1617 as the date of his birth.

[70] C. 181/5, fol. 417.

[71] Baker, *Northampton* 1: 255, 369, 380.

[72] Two horses and £100. *N. and Q.*, 1st Ser., 12: 359, 1855.

[73] Knollys is mentioned briefly in the *D.N.B.* article on his father, and in Williams, *Oxford*, 110.

[74] Cited in Cooper King, *A history of Berkshire*, 162, London, 1887.

[75] *Worthies of England* (Nuttall) 3: 16, London, 1840. His elder brother, William Earl of Banbury (1547–1632), is said to have hunted at the age of eighty-four (*D.N.B.*), and their sister, Lettice, Countess of Leicester, died in her ninety-fifth year (*Berks. Arch. Jour.* 39: 82, 1935).

[76] *Al. Oxon.*

[77] *M. of P.* 1: 410, 415, 419, 424.

[78] *C.S.P. Foreign, 1579–1580*, 464; *1581–1582*, 418, 433–434; *1582*, 42, 271–272, 467, 514.

[79] Knollys to Drake, 6 January [1685/6]. Harl. MSS, 2202, fol. 54.

[80] A copy of Knollys's letter to his commander at the time of their disagreement and a log of part of the voyage as kept by his servant are found in Harl. MSS, 2202, fols. 54–70. For other accounts of the voyage, see "A Summarie and true discourse of sir Francis Drakes West Indian Voyage," in *Hakluyt's Voyages*, Hakluyt Society, Extra Series, 10: 97–134, 1904; *Papers relating to the Navy during the Spanish War, 1585–1587*, J. S. Corbett, ed., The Navy Records Society 11: 1–96, 1898; and *Sir William Monson's Naval Tracts*, The Navy Records Society 22: 121–135, 1902.

[81] Shaw, *K. of E.* 2: 86.

[82] *Marriage licenses, London* (Harleian Society, 25) 1: 174, 1887.

[83] *C.S.P. Dom., 1595–1597*, 11.

[84] A letter from him to Lord Zouch in August, 1600, implies that he was still in touch with court circles. Eg. MSS, 2812, fol. 9.

[85] *C.S.P. Dom., 1591–1594*, 186; *1595–1597*, 297.

[86] S.P. 16, 15/7; 44/40; Add. MSS, 21,922, fol. 86. He or his son, Sir Francis, was a D.L. in 1639. *C.S.P. Dom., 1639–1640*, 230.

shire, also, and for the town of Reading, and a member of various local commissions,[87] and was appointed one of the keepers of Windsor Forest in 1613.[88] As a J.P. Knollys assisted in at least one recusant hunt near Reading in 1599.[89] He was returned to parliament for Berkshire in 1597.[90] He was being held in custody by the queen's orders early in 1601, probably because of the treason of Essex, whose uncle he was, but was back in service as a magistrate within a few months' time.[91] He was a Berkshire M.P. also in 1604, and was one of the parliamentary commissioners for the Scottish union, and was chosen again for the 1625 parliament.[92]

During the reign of King Charles, although Sir Francis was now advanced in years, he was still a man of importance, and more than once opposed the policies of Buckingham and of the crown. Named a loan commissioner in 1626, he was absent himself from meetings and was even charged with recovering the £20 he himself had lent. He opposed the ship money levies, as did his brother, the Earl of Banbury. In a speech at a county meeting he argued from his experience in the navy that the levy was not needed each year, and attacked the rates of assessment. He was said also to have refused to help secure the timber for ships as required of Reading residents, and to have been in arrears in certain other obligations he owed there.[93] He, his son-in-law, and a servant were warned in May, 1637, to answer to Council for the charges so preferred against them.[94] When he was asked to lend money for the king's expenses in 1639, he sent excuses instead.[95] At the 1640 elections, therefore, it was not surprising that Knollys joined his son as a candidate at Reading against the court nominees. They were not chosen in the original Short Parliament election, but in the by-election of April 30 defeated a court candidate.[96] And they won in the autumn, being elected unanimously over three local opponents.[97].

Neither Sir Francis, senior nor junior, was a conspicuous member of the Long Parliament, and age was very probably the explanation in the case of the father.

They joined in offering to be bound for £1000 to secure the loan in 1640,[98] and their attachment to the parliamentary cause was doubtless strengthened by the marriage in 1641 of John Hampden with the elder Knollys's widowed daughter, Lettice.[99] Both father and son were named to parliamentary committees during the war,[100] but neither lived to see it end. The elder Knollys outlived his son and died early in 1648.[101]

Although a younger son, Knollys seems to have had considerable wealth. He leased various properties in Reading after he took up residence near there,[102] and was at one time interested in the Virginia Company.[103] His pledge for the 1640 loan and his offer for the defense in 1642 of four horses for himself and his son [104] are indications that he was at least moderately wealthy.

Sir Francis Knollys, or **Knolles** (1592–1643), member for Reading, 1640–1643, was the second but eldest surviving son [105] of his colleague, Sir Francis Knollys (c. 1550–1648). Born in 1592, he was graduated B.A. from Oxford (Queen's College) in 1607 and entered the Middle Temple three years later.[106] On 26 December 1611 he married Helena (Elinor), daughter and heiress of Richard Milles of Nether-Winchenden, and apparently settled down to live with his father at Reading.[107] His wife died in 1629, and in 1633, then aged forty-one, he married at St. Anne's, Blackfriars, London, Cicely, widow of Robert Edolph of Hinxhill, Kent.[108] He was knighted before 1624,[109] was a J.P. for Reading or Berkshire in 1627, and served in later years both on the commission of the peace and on other

---

[87] *Acts P.C., 1618–1619,* 4; C. 193/13; Guilding, *Reading Records* 2: 59, 117, 245; 3: 417; C. 181/3, fol. 6v, *passim;* C. 181/5, fols. 198, 353. In the later years it is impossible to say whether father or son was intended; sometimes, however, both the older and the younger Sir Francis (*q.v.*) were named.

[88] St. Ch. 8/20/22; *C.S.P. Dom., 1611–1618,* 209.

[89] *Berks Archaeological and Architectural Society Quart. Jour.* 3: 34–39, 1893; Sloane MSS, 2251, fols. 75, 80. Knollys's daughter afterwards married the victim's nephew.

[90] *M. of P.* 1: 432.

[91] *Acts P. C., 1600–1601,* 171; *1601–1604,* 194.

[92] *M. of P.* 1: 432, 462; Pink MSS, 307, fol. 30.

[93] S.P. 16, 40/39, fol. 90; 341/50.

[94] *C.S.P. Dom., 1637,* 60.

[95] Rushworth 3: 912.

[96] The original members decided to sit for other constituencies. The other candidate defeated by Knollys and his son was Sir Robert Heath. Guilding, *Reading records* 3: 492–493; *M. of P.* 1: 480, 484.

[97] Guilding, *op. cit.* 3: 507–508.

[98] D'Ewes (N), 52.

[99] *V.C.H. Berks* 3: 364. The elder Knollys was a great-uncle of the Earl of Warwick.

[100] *Berks. Arch. Jour.* 31: 177, 186, 1927; *Cal. Com. Comp.,* 805.

[101] He was excused for being absent, 9 October 1647 (*C.J.* 5: 329). His will, dated 6 December 1646, was proved on 5 May 1648. He described himself in his will as weak in body because of old age. P.C.C., 90 and 94 Essex.

[102] Guilding, *op. cit.* 2: 50; 3: 196, 316, 404; *Berkshire Notes and Queries* 1 (iv): 110, 1891. He probably held also some of his family's lands in Oxfordshire. *Berks. Arch. Jour.* 31: 186, 1927.

[103] Brown, *Genesis of the U. S.,* 935. Through his sister, Anne, he was a brother-in-law of Lord De la Warre and a relative of various members of the Pelham family of both Virginia and New England fame. *Ibid.,* 1045.

[104] *N. and Q.,* 1st Ser., 12: 338, 1855.

[105] His older brother, Robert, living in 1623, died without issue and probably before their father. *Vis. Berks.* 1: 103; Lipscomb, *Buckingham* 1: 528.

[106] *Al. Oxon.; Mid. Temp. Rec.* 2: 525.

[107] Charles Coates, *The history and antiquities of Reading,* 230, London, 1802; Lipscomb, *loc. cit.*

[108] Coates, *loc. cit.;* Hasted, *Kent* 7: 561; *Marriage licenses, London* (Harleian Society, 26) 2: 213, 1887.

[109] He was a knight by the time of his first election to parliament, and may have been so earlier, for his father was referred to in March, 1622/3, as Sir Francis Knollys, the elder (Guilding, *Reading records* 2: 117).

local commissions.[110] He may have assisted his aged father in the deputy-lieutenancy, one of their name being active in the work of that office in 1640,[111] and he was present at the shire election in October of that year.[112]

Sir Francis, junior, was elected M.P. for Reading in 1624, upon the nomination of his uncle, Lord Wallingford, then High Steward of the borough, and was re-elected under the same auspices for the next three parliaments.[113] Chosen again with his father on 30 April 1640, he was re-elected with him in the autumn, and sat in the Long Parliament until his death. He bore various messages to the Upper House in the summer of 1641,[114] but does not seem to have been named often to committees. He was buried at Reading, 17 May 1643.[115] Surviving him were his father, his widow, a son, Richard, and a daughter, Elizabeth.[116]

The younger Knollys probably had little control of his family's estate, since his father was still alive and apparently kept it in his own hands, as their joint pledges for the parliamentary cause indicate. He doubtless held some property through his first wife during her lifetime. His second wife lost part of her holdings in Kent by abandoning her widowhood, but retained some interests there.[117]

Walter Kyrle or **Kirle** (*c.* 1600–1650), a lawyer of the Middle Temple and of Ross, Herefordshire, was M.P. for Leominster, 1640–1650. The second son of Robert Kyrle of Walford Court, Herefordshire, by his wife, Jane, daughter of E. Evans *alias* Bithell, he was born about 1600 [118] and was educated at Oxford and the Middle Temple. He was a defendant in cases in the Star Chamber in 1623 and 1635, probably as legal adviser to the principals,[119] but he seems to have gained no great reputation as a lawyer. He was a J.P. in his county.

Kyrle was elected to both parliaments of 1640 for Leominster, and worked with the popular party. He was named to some early committees,[120] but he was not an outstanding member. He promised in 1642 to supply one horse for the defense,[121] and during the war was named to several parliamentary committees for his county. His absence for some time in 1643 and 1644 led to a suspicion that he was leaning toward royalism,

and his disablement was considered early in 1644, but late in 1646 he was permitted to explain his actions and return to the House.[122] He was still a member at the time of his death, 10 February 1650.

Kyrle's estate was said to be worth £500 or £600 a year when it passed at his death to his son, John Kyrle (1637–1724),[123] who became known as "the Man of Ross." Kyrle's income from his legal practice no doubt made his annual income somewhat higher than that figure.[124]

Thomas Lane (d. 1652), of Perivale, Middlesex, and Recorder of Wycombe (Chipping Wycombe, High Wycombe), Bucks, sat for that borough, 1640–1648. He was the son of Robert Lane of Hughenden, near Wycombe, by Alice, daughter of Robert Saunders of Hambledon, and descended from the Lanes of Northamptonshire.[1] He entered the Inner Temple in 1601, became a barrister there in 1610, bencher (1627), reader (1629), and treasurer (1645–1646).[2] By March, 1623, he was recorder at Wycombe, a post which he continued to hold until 1650,[3] and in 1629 he was one of the feodaries of the county.[4] He was a J.P. there for many years and a member of various local commissions.[5] He seems to have resided, however, in the neighboring county of Middlesex, being identified variously as of Perivale, his country seat, or of the Temple, and he owned several properties in Southwark.[6] He married twice, his first wife being known only by her first name, Frances, and his second being Jane, daughter of John Duncombe of East Claydon, Bucks.[7]

Lane sat for Wycombe in the parliaments of 1625 and 1628 and in both of 1640.[8] He gained some unpopularity in the county because he urged the collecting of ship money and complained to the Council about a sheriff's negligence in the matter. A petition presented to parliament on this subject in 1641 stated further that

---

[110] *Ibid.* **2**: 353, 355; **3**: 458; C. 181/5, fols. 198, 270, 354.

[111] *C.S.P. Dom., 1640,* 489.

[112] Berkshire indenture, C. 219/43/Part 1.

[113] Guilding, *op. cit.* **2**: 169, 231, 270, 271, 273, 386–387; *M. of P.* **1**: 456, 462, 468, 474.

[114] D'Ewes (B), 535, 581.

[115] Coates, *op. cit.,* 230.

[116] These are referred to in his father's will. P.C.C., 90 Essex.

[117] Hasted, *Kent* **7**: 561, 565.

[118] His elder brother was born in 1596. I.P.M., Robert Kyrle, C. 142/354/117.

[119] St. Ch. 8/156/26; S.P. 16, 302/22, 82.

[120] *C.J.* **2**: 160, *passim.*

[121] *N. and Q.,* 1st Ser., **12**: 359, 1855.

[122] *C.J.* **3**: 374; Pink MSS, 305, fol. 145. A number of Kyrle's letters to a cousin, written in Herefordshire, 1645–1646, are among the Scudamore papers, Add. MSS, 11,047, fols. 130–143.

[123] W. H. Cooke, *Collections towards the history and antiquities of the county of Hereford, in continuation of Duncombe's History* **3**: 109, London, 1882; *D.N.B.,* "John Kyrle."

[124] In addition to the above authorities see Williams, *Hereford,* 127.

[1] *Vis. Bucks.,* 80; Burke, *Landed gentry,* 1851; *Middlesex pedigrees,* 149.

[2] *Students admitted to the Inner Temple,* 161; *Cal. Inner Temp. Rec.* **2**: 54, 271, 273.

[3] *Recs. Bucks.* **7**: 306, 1897; Pink MSS, 307, fol. 107.

[4] He was so named in an I.P.M., C. 142/451/107.

[5] C. 193/12, 13; S.P. 16/405; C. 181/5, fols. 338, 352.

[6] *Vis. Bucks.,* 80; S.P. 16, 359/23/ii, iii.

[7] A son by his wife, Frances, was buried at Hughenden in 1621 (*Recs. Bucks.* **5**: 227, 1878). By his wife, Jane, who was named in his will, he seems to have had no children. P.C.C., 219 Brent.

[8] *M. of P.* **1**: 462, 474, 480.

he had encouraged the profanation of the Sabbath by sports and games.[9] One Thomas Lane was an assessor of ship money for Great Kimble, Hampden's region, but he was listed in January, 1636, with Hampden, as delinquent in his payment,[10] and could hardly have been accused later of attempting to advance the collection. Possibly some of the bitterness aroused at Wycombe during Lane's recordership by the taking away of funds subscribed for a puritan vicar [11] accounts for the petition against him. It was referred to a committee and seems to have died there. Lane's conduct during the Long Parliament indicates no sympathy for the royal administration. He was named to such important early committees as those on recusants and ship money, and joined in the attack on Lord Keeper Finch as an evil counselor.[12] He promised one horse for the defense,[13] helped to manage the trials of Berkeley and Laud, and served on the county committees for Bucks and Middlesex during the war. Lane was secluded in December, 1648,[14] and died 31 December 1652.

Almost nothing is known of Lane's financial standing. He probably inherited several manors near Wycombe which belonged to his family,[15] and he owned some properties near London. He was evidently a successful lawyer, and in his will referred to his worldly blessings as greater than he deserved. Annuities amounting to £120 and legacies of over £800 enumerated therein suggest that he had an income of some size in addition to that from his practice.[16] The tone of the will suggests also that by 1652 he was strongly puritanical.

Sir Richard Lee, Bart. (1600–1660), of Langley and Acton Burnell, Salop, was a member for his county, 1640–6 September 1642. He was the son and heir of Sir Humphrey Lee, Bart. (H.S. 1599, d. 1632), by his wife, Margaret, daughter of Reginald Corbet of Stoke.[17] Richard was born at Lee Hall in Preston Gobalds parish, 6 September 1600, and was educated at Shrewsbury School and at Queen's, Oxford, where he matriculated in 1616. About ten years later he married Elizabeth, daughter of Edward Allen, a London alderman,[18]

and on his father's death succeeded to the baronetcy. He was a J.P. in Shropshire,[19] a member of the commission of oyer and terminer,[20] and was sheriff, 1638–1639. He probably spent a good deal of his time at Stone House, the Shrewsbury mansion built by his father, and was said to belong to a "knot of company keepers" who met as a club at one of the town inns.[21] His father left him an estate numbering seven manors with various rectories, mills and farms, the total value of which was over £1000 a year.[22] His wealth enabled him in the Long Parliament to pledge £1000 to support the 1640 loan,[23] and his fine for being a royalist was heavy.

Although he was a newcomer to Westminster in November, 1640, Lee was soon sharing in the work of the House. His royalist views showed as early as the vote on Strafford's attainder,[24] however, and when war broke out he was among the first to join the king. He was disabled on 6 September 1642,[25] was taken prisoner at Shrewsbury early in 1645.[26] After some time Lee compounded for his estate, securing its discharge in 1652 by paying a fine of over £2800.[27] Sir Richard outlived his sons and died in 1660. He may have become a Roman Catholic before his death.[28]

Richard Lee, Esquire (fl. 1640–1648), of Great Delce, near Rochester, Kent, was M.P. for Rochester, 1640–1648.[29] His identity has not been absolutely established, for there is some confusion between a father and a son of the same name. He was probably Richard Lee, senior (c. 1591–1653), but possibly was the son, Richard (born c. 1617). Descended from Sir Richard Lee, Lord Mayor of London (1470), Richard Lee, senior, was the son and heir of Richard Lee of Great Delce (d. 1618) and his wife, Anna, daughter of William

---

[9] C.J. 2: 108; D'Ewes (N), 513.

[10] Stowe MSS, 142, fol. 44.

[11] V.C.H. Buckingham 4: 532.

[12] C.J. 2: 42, 45; The note book of Sir John Northcote, 95.

[13] N. and Q., 1st Ser., 12: 359, 1855.

[14] O.P.H. 9: *16; Pink MSS, 307, fol. 107; Berks. Arch. Jour. 31: 178, 1927.

[15] V.C.H. Buckingham 3: 59; Lysons, Mag. Brit. 1: 580, 581, 653. Burke states that Lane had an older brother, but the 1634 pedigree (Vis. Bucks.) indicates that Thomas was his father's heir.

[16] The will, dated 17 March 1651/2, was proved 10 May 1653. P.C.C., 219 Brent.

[17] Complete Baronetage 1: 143; Shrops. Arch. Soc., Trans., 2nd Ser., 6: 22, 1894; I.P.M. of Sir Humphrey Lee, C. 142/531/189. Lee and Sir John Corbet were first cousins.

[18] The date of marriage is given as 1626 in Complete Baronetage, but according to some notes from the registers of

Acton Burnell, their first child was baptized in May, 1625. Bodleian Blakeway MSS, 2, fol. 5.

[19] C. 193/13; S.P. 16/405.

[20] C. 181/5, fols. 12, 65, passim.

[21] Shrops. Arch. Soc., Trans., 3rd Ser., 9: 256, 1909.

[22] I.P.M. cited above; S.P. 23/207/151, 173–174.

[23] D'Ewes (N), 52, n.

[24] Verney, 58.

[25] C.J. 2: 755.

[26] Stowe MSS, 190, fol. 145.

[27] Various figures regarding his estates and fines appear among the compounding papers, owing to omissions and reviews. The earliest amount set for his fine was at ½, £6288, changed later to ⅓, £4193, or £2866 with £122 a year settled (Cal. Com. Comp., 1005–1006). A catalogue of fines printed in 1655 lists him as having compounded at £3719 with £169 a year settled (Shrops. Arch. Soc., Trans., 1st Ser., 4: 157, 1881).

[28] A sketch of Lee's life by H. T. Weyman is printed in Shrops. Arch. Soc., Trans., 4th Ser., 11: 171–172, 1927–1928.

[29] M. of P. 1: 490; Pink MSS, 306, fol. 80. He was perhaps the Colonel Leigh who was secluded in 1648 (Rushworth 7: 1355), but according to O.P.H. (9: *30), he seems to have sat longer.

Clarke of Ford, and was born about 1591.[30] He may have been a student at the Inner Temple in 1607.[31] He married in 1614 at St. Stephen's, Coleman Street, London, Mary, daughter of John Shirley of Lewes, Sussex, Serjeant-at-Law.[32] He seems to have been a legal consultant in a case involving Hythe in 1621,[33] was in the same year a captain in the Kentish trained bands, and still held his command in 1637.[34] He was a sewers commissioner and a J.P.[35] Before 1629 he married a second time, his wife being Sybel Wenland, widow of Sir George Newman. To Lee, her husband, was granted administration of her estate in June, 1629.[36] A third wife may have been Joan Lewknor, who died before 23 February 1646.[37] Since Richard Lee, the elder, survived until 1652 or 1653,[38] he could easily have been the Long Parliament member, and the naming of Lee with other Kent members, chiefly J.P.'s, to go to the Kent assizes in July, 1642, to forestall action against parliament [39] seems to indicate a man experienced as a justice, as the elder Lee was. The Mr. Lee who was a member, moreover, was named to more committees in the House than was usual for so young a man as the son.[40] It is not clear whether the Captain Lee who, with various young men of Kent, reported to parliament in April, 1642, on events at the assizes was a member, or whether the Captain Lee of Rochester who was authorized on 23 August to muster and command troops there was the M.P., but the member was apparently the Captain Lee who on 9 September was granted leave to go to Kent to take charge of Upnor Castle. He seems to have been acting as mayor of Rochester that year, also,[41] and was named a D.L. by parliament and appointed to the various parliamentary committees for the county.[42]. He was still a captain in March, 1648, when he presented an account of ex-pense money owing to him.[43] If, however, as Colonel Lee he returned with the Rump in 1660,[44] he could not have been the elder Richard, who had died before that year. The will of the elder Richard, dated 13 July 1652, was proved at Westminster, 16 May 1653.[45]

Richard Lee, junior (born c. 1617), only son of the elder Richard by his first wife, Mary Shirley, matriculated at University College, Oxford, in 1636 and the same year was a student at the Inner Temple.[46] He married, date unknown, Elizabeth, daughter of Sir John Honywood of Elmested, Kent.[47] He was concerned with the trained bands, as was his father, was perhaps a captain with him in 1642,[48] and was certainly so before 1645. In that year his loyalty was suspected. He took the oath on 13 November 1645 as Captain Richard Lee, junior, and on 9 March 1647, as "Richard Lee, junior, gent.," begged to compound for delinquency in arms, pleading that he had been in the service of parliament since August, 1645. His fine was set in July at a tenth, slightly over £34.[49] He may have been the Colonel Leigh who was implicated in the 1648 royalist uprising, for Richard Lee, junior, of Rochester was among the delinquents reported in 1651 as having recently compounded, and as late as 1656 Lee was having to report his movements.[50] He seems to have been dead by 1663, for the family property was then in the hands of a female heir.[51]

Whether the father or the son sat in the 1640 House, neither had had previous experience as an M.P. Nor were they men of great wealth. Their estates consisted chiefly of two manors and appurtenances in and near Rochester and Chatham. A sister of the elder Lee had been promised a dowry of £500, but there was doubt as to whether the full sum could be paid.[52] The Lee who sat in the House pledged a horse and maintenance for the defense in 1642.[53] When the son compounded

[30] He was aged twenty-seven and more at his father's death (I.P.M., Richard Lee, 1619, C. 142/395/115) ; *Vis. Kent, 1619*, 56.

[31] As Richard Lee of Seal, Kent. *Students admitted to the Inner Temple*, 181.

[32] I.P.M. cited above; Challen's Transcripts of Parish Registers (Guildhall Library), **25**, St. Stephen's, Coleman Street.

[33] "Mr. Lee of Rochester, being of Counsel with Mrs. Cranmer," Hythe Borough MSS, Assembly Book, 1624–1635, fol. 143.

[34] *H.M.C., MSS of A. G. Finch* **1**: 42; *C.S.P. Dom., 1637*, 572.

[35] C. 181/3; 181/5, fol. 258; C. 193/13; S.P. 16/405.

[36] *Arch. Cant.* **20**: 19, 1893; Add. MSS, 16,279, fol. 163v.

[37] *Arch. Cant.* **20**: 37, 1893. Joan may, however, have been a (second?) wife of Ρ'chard's son.

[38] His will, dated 13 July 1652, was proved 16 May 1653. P.C.C., 116 Brent.

[39] *C.J.* **2**: 686.

[40] *C.J.* **2**: 44, 61, 87.

[41] *C.J.* **2**: 549–550, 733, 760; *Arch. Cant.* **10**: 212, 1876; **17**: 363, n., 1887.

[42] *Arch. Cant.* **9**: 33, 1874; Add. MSS, 33,512, fol. 78; *C.J.* **2**: 724.

[43] *C.J.* **5**: 499.

[44] According to Pink (Pink MSS, 306, fol. 81), Colonel Lee returned in 1660 and was named to several committees. His name does not appear in the list of returned Rumpers in Thomason Tracts, 669. f. 24, p. 37. F. F. Smith (*Rochester in Parliament, 1295–1933*, 112–113, London, Simpkin, Marshall, 1933) thought the Richard Lee who was living in 1656 was a son of the M.P.

[45] P.C.C., 116 Brent.

[46] *Al. Oxon.*

[47] Add. MSS, 16,279, fol. 164. Honywood was named one of the executors of the elder Lee's will. P.C.C., 116 Brent. Joan Lewknor (see note 37 above) was a wife of either the father or the son.

[48] See the Captain Lee who reported to parliament in April, 1642. *C.J.* **2**: 549–550.

[49] The composition papers contain no reference, as was customary with M.P.'s, to his having been a member. *Cal Com. Comp.*, 1686; S.P. 23/203/65, 71.

[50] *Cal. Com. Comp.*, 460; *Arch. Cant.* **9**: 38, n., 1874; **23**: 75, 1898.

[51] *Vis. Kent., 1663–1668*, 102.

[52] I.P.M., C. 142/395/115; Chancery suit, C. 3/318/34; Hasted, *Kent* **4**: 170, 209, 212, 214.

[53] *N. and Q.*, 1st Ser., **12**: 360, 1855.

he mentioned lands worth but £26 a year.[54] But the father's will in 1652 referred to plans for at least £300 in portions for a daughter and a grandchild.

Thomas Leedes (d. 1645), of Wappingthorne near Steyning, Sussex, was a member for Steyning, 1640 (recognized 15 February 1641) to 1642.[55] He came of an old family associated with both Sussex and Yorkshire and noted in Elizabeth's day for its recusant members. Sir Thomas Leedes, K.B., grandfather of the M.P., was a voluntary exile for his religion for a time, and at least two uncles of the M.P. were stanch Catholics who lived in France. His father, however, Sir John Leedes of Wappingthorne (J.P., M.P., d. 1656), married Bridget, eldest daughter of the anti-Catholic Sir Thomas Monson, and in the time of King James was prominent in court circles. He and his wife were imprisoned for some remarks about the king at the time of the Overbury case, and in parliament Sir John was more than once a critic of the crown. As late as 1639 he refused a loan.[56] Thomas Leedes, second son but by 1637 heir apparent of Sir John, was born sometime after 1611,[57] and was admitted in 1637 to the Middle Temple. There he was bound with Christopher Lewknor (q.v.). He had surrendered his chamber by May, 1640,[58] and appeared next as a candidate for Steyning in the Long Parliament elections. His father had sat for the borough in the spring,[59] and possibly felt that his heir should now succeed him there, although he might be less sure of election. The return was protested, but on 15 February 1641 Leedes was granted permission to sit until the election should be determined, and no further record of the case appears. Not until after he had been a member nearly a year did Leedes marry Anne, daughter of his colleague, Sir Ambrose Browne of Bettsworth (q.v.). An indenture of 6 December 1641 cited in his father's will was apparently made for the marriage settlement.[60]

Leedes was never a conspicuous member of the House. But with the approach of war, although his father had earlier opposed the king and his father-in-law was a parliamentarian, he became an active royalist. With Christopher Lewknor, he was one of the group of Sussex men expelled on 23 November 1642 for attempting to secure Chichester for the king.[61] And in 1645 Leedes was killed in the king's service near Oxford.[62]

The family fortunes of Leedes were somewhat clouded in 1640, for his father was then considerably in debt and his lands were encumbered by annuities and mortgages. Their Sussex estates reputedly brought in £950 a year in rents, and they had some interests also in Yorkshire.[63] The father's assessment in 1644 was £500, and his own was possibly £1000, but he died without making a payment, and his father was discharged upon paying a tenth of his original rate.[64]

Peter Legh, or **Leigh** (1623–1642), of Lyme Hall, Cheshire, sat for Newton, Lancashire, a borough frequently influenced by his family, from 1640 until his death, 2 February 1642.[65] He was the only son and heir of Piers Legh (d. 1624), by Anne, daughter of Sir John Savile of Howley, Yorkshire, first Lord Savile, and grandson and heir of Sir Peter Legh of Lyme. The latter, a man of distinction in Lancashire and Cheshire, a J.P., D.L. and M.P., had disinherited his eldest son because of his marriage, but young Peter was recognized as his heir at his death in 1636.[66] He had been born on 12 August 1623 and was in wardship most of the time before 1640, among his guardians having been his relative, Richard Lord Molyneux, Receiver General of the Duchy of Lancaster under Charles I.[67] He was too young to have held public office before 1640, and doubtless for the same reason was named to no committees in the Long Parliament. He is generally listed as a royalist, probably because the Legh family was traditionally loyal, but no evidence remains of his personal views. Young Legh died on 1 or 2 February 1642 after being wounded in a duel.[68]

Legh's family was one of great wealth, its head in 1660 being reputedly worth £4000 a year.[69] Among his relatives in the 1640 Commons were Peter Venables and probably the Ashtons.[70]

Sir Charles Le Groos, or **Le Grosse** (c. 1596–1650), of Crostwight, Norfolk, sat for Orford, Suffolk, 1640–1648.[71] He was the eldest son and heir of Sir Thomas Le Groos (d. before 1621) of Crostwight, by his wife,

---

[54] S.P. 23/203/65, 67.

[55] *M. of P.* 1: 495; *C.J.* 2: 86; D'Ewes (N), 361.

[56] Pink MSS, 306, fol. 84; E. Lloyd, Leedes of Wappingthorne, *Sussex Arch. Coll.* 54: 37–39, 44–52, 1911; *Acts P.C., 1615–1616,* 323; S.P. 16/405.

[57] Sir John's marriage license was dated 30 May 1610. *Marriage licenses, London* (Harleian Society, 25) 1: 321, 1887; *Sussex Arch. Coll.* 54: 50, 1911.

[58] *Mid. Temp. Rec.* 2: 857, 892. He was not the Thomas Leedes, who entered Oxford in 1609, although he has been so identified. *Al. Oxon.*

[59] *M. of P.* 1: 483.

[60] P.C.C., 623 Wootton.

[61] *C.J.* 2: 860.

[62] Pink MSS, 306, fol. 85; *Sussex Arch. Coll.* 54: 51, 1911.

[63] *Ibid.* 54: 50, 1911; Sir John Leedes's will (note 60).

[64] Pink, *loc. cit.; Cal. Com. Adv. Money,* 436.

[65] Pink and Beaven, *Parl. Rep. Lanc.,* 280. Legh's name is missing from the official list of members, but the House ordered the election of a new burgess in his place, 4 February 1642. *C.J.* 2: 414.

[66] Pink and Beaven, *op. cit.,* 222; Earwaker, *East Cheshire* 2: 298–299 and n.; C. 193/12, 13.

[67] H.M.C., *Twelfth Report* 1, Coke MSS, 159; *C.S.P. Dom., 1635,* 123.

[68] Earwaker, *loc. cit.*

[69] Wotton, *English Baronetage* 4: 365, 1741 ed.

[70] Will of Sir Peter Legh of Lyme, 1636, Chester Probate Registry. Ralph Ashton and Roger Mostyn witnessed the M.P.'s will made after he was wounded. Earwaker 2: 299, n.

[71] *M. of P.* 1: 494; Thomason Tracts, E. 454, 17.

Elizabeth, daughter of Sir Charles Cornwallis of Brome, Suffolk, and of Beeston, Norfolk. The Le Groos family was of ancient lineage, and his paternal grandmother was one of the Norfolk Pastons.[72] Charles was born in Norwich about 1596,[73] was educated at Aylsham and Wymondham, entered Caius College, Cambridge, in 1611, aged fifteen, and in November, 1614, was admitted to Gray's Inn. He was knighted at Newmarket in 1616,[74] and before 27 March 1621 married Muriel, daughter of Sir Thomas Knyvet of Ashwellthorpe, Norfolk. He became head of his family upon the death of his grandfather, Thomas Le Groos, Esq., in 1622,[75] and seems to have spent most of his life in the country, although his mother was a first cousin of Sir Frederick Cornwallis (q.v.), and he could probably have had a career at court had he so desired.[76] He may have lived part of the time in Norwich.[77]

Le Groos was a J.P. in Norfolk before the end of the reign of James,[78] was a member of other local commissions,[79] was sheriff in 1627,[80] and may have been a vice admiral or a special commissioner for the Admiralty in 1635.[81] He was a strong candidate in the Norfolk shire elections of 1625, but was defeated,[82] and turned afterwards to the Suffolk borough of Orford, which elected him to the parliaments of 1626 and 1628 and both times in 1640.[83]

At Westminster, though, Sir Charles was never prominent. He was a kinsman not only of Cornwallis, but of such opposition workers as Heveningham and Sir John Holland,[84] and seems to have been willing neither to go the full way with his Norfolk relatives nor to break completely with parliament as did Cornwallis. He gave his bond for £1000 for the loan in

1640, promised afterwards £50 for the state,[85] but was probably absent much of the time after the first year. He was granted leave to go into the country for his health in August, 1641, was summoned to attend on 12 September 1642 and again the next spring, and was fined £200 for failing to comply. An assessment of £1500 was charged against him in 1645, of which he had paid £250 by 1647, but he was never disabled or declared a delinquent, and as late as April, 1648, made excuses for his absence. He was probably secluded by Pride's Purge,[86] and died about 1650.[87]

Sir Charles was evidently one of the well-to-do members of the House. He owned several manors and rectories in Norfolk,[88] and his younger brothers and sisters were well provided for by their grandfather's will.[89] His wartime assessment of £1500 indicates that he was considered to have ample means.

Sir John Leigh (c. 1598–1666), of North Court in Shorwell, Isle of Wight, sat for the island's borough of Yarmouth, 1640–1648. He was a grandson of Sir John Leigh (d. 1630), who built the North Court house and was long a J.P.[90] His old friend, Sir John Oglander, wrote that the elder Sir John Leigh started with a small fortune but that he improved it to a good estate by good husbandry and frugality, and his son increased it much by the same means and by favorable marriages.[91] The son, Barnaby Leigh, married as his first wife Elizabeth, daughter of Hugh Bamfield of Somerset (d. 1615–1616).[92] Their eldest son, John, probably matriculated at Christ Church, Oxford, on 25 October 1616, aged eighteen.[93] He was knighted during the king's visit to the Isle of Wight in September, 1628, at the request of the Chancellor of Scotland, whose son had been billeted in the Leigh home.[94] Leigh was probably serving then as a lieutenant or a captain in one of the Hampshire regiments,[95] and about this time he mar-

---

[72] W. Rye, *Norfolk families*, 273 Norwich, Goose, 1913; Blomefield, *Norfolk* 11: 9–10; *East Anglian*, 1st Ser., 4: 65, 1869.

[73] Pink MSS, 302, fol. 468.

[74] *Al. Cant.*

[75] The will of Thomas Le Groos, dated 27 March 1621, and proved 25 November 1622. P.C.C., 101 Savile.

[76] One of his sisters married a Nathaniel Bacon, probably related to the Sir Nathaniel Bacon who was Cornwallis's stepfather (Blomefield, *op. cit.* 11: 11), and his wife, Muriel, was closely related to that family. *The correspondence of Lady Katherine Paston*, ed. by Ruth Hughey, Norfolk Record Society 14: 37–38, 1941.

[77] Several of his children were named in the parish registers of St. Stephen's, Norwich, 1631–1636. Norwich Public Library MSS, 56 (Jessop's extracts from parish registers), 3: 174, 180; the original registers of the parish, used with the permission of the pastor in 1935, fols. 6, 7.

[78] *Acts P.C., 1621*, 194; C. 193/12, 13; Norfolk County MSS, Sessions Rolls, 1626, 1632.

[79] C. 181/5, fols. 205, 291.

[80] *List of Sheriffs*, 88.

[81] *C.S.P. Dom., 1635*, 248, 291.

[82] *The correspondence of Lady Katherine Paston*, 82.

[83] *M. of P.* 1: 471, 477, 483, 494.

[84] Holland was a cousin of his wife's and Heveningham was related through the Pastons. Pedigrees in *The correspondence of Lady Katherine Paston*, 37–38, and in Bodleian Add. MSS, E. 13.

[85] D'Ewes (N), 52; Pink MSS, 302, fol. 468.

[86] *C.J.* 2: 233, 763; Pink MSS, 302, fol. 468; *Cal. Com. Adv. Money*, 634; Mason, *The history of Norfolk*, 289. I have been unable to discover a date or a statement about the disabling of Le Groos, and *O.P.H.* (9: 3) makes it appear that he was still a member after the purge.

[87] His son Thomas on 31 May 1650 petitioned the Committee of Compounding about a sequestered estate for which his father had once been a trustee (*Cal. Com. Comp.*, 2322), and on 29 July succeeded Sir Charles, "deceased," as the executor of the will of Sir Charles's grandfather. P.C.C., 101 Savile.

[88] Blomefield, *Norfolk* 10: 287; 11: 13, 66, 197; *Norf. Arch.* 3: 90 and n., 1852.

[89] £3000 went to a brother, 2000 marks and £1000 to unmarried sisters, and Sir Charles was residuary legatee.

[90] *C.S.P. Dom., 1611–1618*, 243; Add. MSS, 5752, fol. 328; C. 193/12.

[91] *The Oglander memoirs* (ed. Long), 145–146.

[92] Berry, *Ped. Hants.*, 122.

[93] *Al. Oxon.*

[94] *The Oglander memoirs*, 41.

[95] S.P. 16, 111/62; 116/85.

ried Elizabeth, sister of John Bulkley of Burgate.[96]

Leigh seems not to have taken much part in county affairs during the next decade, but to have lived as a country gentleman in his father's home, making occasional trips for amusement to Yarmouth.[97] He was elected to his first parliament when Yarmouth chose him on 27 October 1640. But Leigh seems to have been as little energetic as an M.P. as he had been about county affairs. He was frequently absent in 1641 and 1642, but in September of the latter year promised £50 for the cause of parliament.[98] He was soon afterwards granted leave to go to the Isle of Wight as a colonel under the new governor, the Earl of Pembroke.[99] Several times later he was summoned to attend, was granted repeated respites, and was finally secluded in December, 1648.[100] He was re-elected by Yarmouth in 1660.[101] He died about 1666, and was succeeded by his son, John.[102]

Sir John, according to the comment of his grandfather's friend, inherited a good estate, but its extent and value are not known. His chief properties were in the Isle of Wight.[103]

* **William Lenthall** (1591–1662), of Oxfordshire and London, Speaker of the House, was M.P. for Woodstock, Oxfordshire, 1640–1653. A successful lawyer, owner of estates in Oxford and Berks counties, he had been a J.P. in the former,[104] member of several local commissions in that region and in London,[105] and was recorder for both Gloucester and Woodstock. Lenthall excused himself in 1639 from contributing toward the king's expenses.[106] He was a candidate at Gloucester for both of the 1640 parliamentary elections, but in each case found the Woodstock seat easier to secure.[107]

Lenthall was wealthy at the time of his election, having a practice of some £2500 a year, and lands as well. One of his friends assured him in 1641, when he was complaining of the expense of the Speakership, that his great estate would help him bear it.[108] He offered his bond for £1000 for the loan in 1640, and for £500 in March, 1641. His pledge for the defense in 1642 was £50 and the maintenance of one horse.[109]

Sir Richard Leveson, K.B. (1598–1661), of Trentham, Staffordshire and Lilleshull, Salop, was M.P. for Newcastle-under-Lyme, 13 October 1640–24 November 1642. He was the son of a Kentish father and through his mother was related to the Mildmays and the Fanes.[110] He succeeded his father in 1615, inheriting lands in Kent, Essex and Shropshire,[111] and as the heir of a kinsman (d. 1605), he acquired vast holdings in both Shropshire and Staffordshire. Through his wife he gained interests also in Warwickshire.[112] Leveson was reported a musters defaulter in 1625,[113] but otherwise conformed to rules, serving as a J.P. in two counties, and as a member of various local commissions [114] and of the Council of Wales.[115] He was steward of Newcastle, a royal manor, in 1639.[116]

Sir Richard offered his bond for £1000 to support the loans in November, 1640, and March, 1641,[117] but was disabled early as a royalist. His fine was £6000, with nearly £4000 settled.[118] It was probably his heir, Francis Leveson, who was nominated for the Knights of the Royal Oak in 1660 with an estate of £2000 a year.[119] According to Lloyd, Sir Richard was a man highly regarded by his fellows, serving the king with wisdom and integrity.[120]

Sir William Lewis, Bart. (1598–1677), of Llangorse, Brecknockshire, and of Borden, Hampshire, was a member for Petersfield in the latter county, 1640–1648. He was the grandson of a Brecon mercer and the son and heir of Lodowick Lewis of Trewalter, Brecon (H.S. 1606, d. 1614), by Eleanor, daughter and coheiress of William Watkins of Llangorse. He was born in March, 1598,[121] may have entered University College, Oxford, in 1613 (B.A. 1616), and was admitted to Lincoln's Inn in November, 1616.[122] He was sheriff in his native county in 1619–1620. In or after 1622 he married Mary, widow of Sir Thomas Neale of Warneford, Hants, a daughter of Robert Calton of Goring, Oxfordshire, and seems to have

---

[96] Berry, *loc. cit.* Their eldest child died at less than a year in January, 1629/30. *The Oglander memoirs*, 147, n.

[97] *A royalist's notebook*, ed. Bamford, 73.

[98] *C.J.* **2**: 120, 178, 626, 772.

[99] *C.J.* **2**: 775; *A royalist's notebook*, 110.

[100] Pink MSS, 306, fol. 110; Thomason Tracts, 669. f. 24, p. 37.

[101] *M. of P.* **1**: 516.

[102] Berry, *loc. cit.*

[103] *V.C.H. Hampshire* **5**: 278, 280.

[104] C. 191/13; S.P. 16/405.

[105] C. 181/4, fol. 179v; 181/5, fol. 42; S.P. 16, 171/3/4.

[106] Rushworth **3**: 912.

[107] *C.S.P. Dom., 1639–1640*, 582; Williams, *Oxford*, 60.

[108] Sir Thomas Tempest to Lenthall, August, 1641. Bodleian Tanner MSS, 66, fol. 166.

[109] D'Ewes (N), 52, 439, n.; *N. and Q.*, 1st Ser., **12**: 358, 1855.

[110] Other relatives of Leveson in the 1640 parliament were Francis Newport, whose mother was a Leveson, and Sir Peter Temple (*q.v.*).

[111] His elder brother, Sir John, died in 1613, and his father in 1615. I.P.M., Sir John Leveson, C. 142/349/174; Add. MSS, 14,311, fol. 8v; *The letters of John Chamberlain* **1**: 326, 491; Hasted, *Kent* **3**: 447.

[112] *C.S.P. Dom., 1637–1638*, 77.

[113] *Ibid., 1625–1626*, 143.

[114] C. 181/5, fols. 65, 95, 124.

[115] *Arch. Camb.*, 6th Ser., **17**: 195, 1917.

[116] *H.M.C., Fifth Report*, MSS of the Duke of Sutherland, 141.

[117] D'Ewes (N), 52, 439, n., 452, n.

[118] *Cal. Com. Comp.*, 990.

[119] *English Baronetage* **4**: 375, 1741.

[120] *Memoires*, 667. For Leveson's career, see Wedgwood, *Staff. Parl. Hist.* **2**: 31–33.

[121] I.P.M., Lodowick Lewis, 1616, C. 142/356/125; *Complete Baronetage* **2**: 59; Williams, *Parl. Hist. Wales*, 17.

[122] *Al. Oxon.*; *Linc. Inn Rec. Adm.* **1**: 175.

resided thereafter chiefly at Borden in Hampshire. He was created a baronet, 14 September 1628.[123] When the 1627 loan was being collected, Lewis first attempted to be excused and then paid £16.[124] He was reported by the knighthood commissioners in 1630 as refusing to compound, his excuse being that he had not been particularly named in the summons to take up knighthood at the coronation. He was described then as "of Westbury." [125]

Although Lewis was now living chiefly in southern England, serving there as a J.P.,[126] and contributing for the militia,[127] his properties in Wales continued to bring him responsibilities. He was sheriff of Brecknockshire for the second time, 1635–1636, and had then the thankless job of assessing and collecting ship money.[128] He afterwards complained of the hardship of having to maintain residence in the county during his term of office, since he had been living in Hampshire when he was named sheriff, and of the expense of travelling to the south and to London from Wales.[129] His wife died in February of that year (1636). Lewis was proposed for the shrievalty of Carnarvonshire in 1638,[130] but was spared on that occasion. By 1640 he was back in Hampshire, occupied with duties as a D.L.,[131] and he was elected to parliament in the spring and in the fall of that year for Petersfield.[132]

Lewis was a prominent member of the Presbyterian group in the Commons, working closely with Holles, Glyn, Harley, and Stapleton much of the time.[133] He was named to numerous committees, including those on monopolies and idolatry, serving on more than a hundred between 1640 and 1648. He was one of the eight men chosen in March, 1642, to present the declaration to the king, and in September was sent to be governor of Portsmouth for parliament.[134] There were times when he favored making peace, but he was an early advocate of the sequestration ordinance and he served on the parliamentary committees of Hampshire during the war.[135] He was one of "the eleven" against whom the army brought charges in 1647, was out of the House from January to June, 1648, and was finally secluded by the purge of the following December.[136] He sat for

Brecon in 1660 and for Lymington in 1661. He died in 1677, his will, dated 4 March 1675, being proved 28 November 1677.[137]

Lewis was a man of means as well as of influence. He inherited from his parents numerous properties in Wales, chiefly in Brecknockshire, which were declared in the charges brought against him in 1647 to be worth over £600 a year.[138] He held others in Hampshire.[139] His name does not appear in the lists of loan and security offers of 1640–1641, but Clarendon included him with Holles and the others of the eleven in stating that they "were all men of parts, interest, and signal courage." [140]

Christopher Lewknor (1598?–c. 1653), Recorder of Chichester, was M.P. for that town from 1640 until he was disabled for royalism, 2 September and 23 November 1642.[141] He came of an ancient knightly family of Sussex, being a younger son of Richard Lewknor of West Dean (d. 1602), a grandson of Sir Richard Lewknor, Chief Justice of Chester (d. 1616), and brother of a third Richard (d. 1635, aet. 46),[142] who was active in county affairs and several times an M.P.[143] His mother was Eleanor, daughter of Christopher Brome of Halton, Oxfordshire. He was probably baptized at Chichester on 5 March 1597/8.[144] He entered the Middle Temple (10 November 1617), where his brother, Richard, was a fellow, and was called to the bar in 1625. Numbered among his close associates at the Temple were six future colleagues in the Long Parliament.[145] With some of his fellow students Lewknor was in 1620 hauled before Star Chamber by an older lawyer on account of some "riotous" pranks, but no serious results ensued; and once Lewknor was fined by the Temple authorities for mishandling some expense funds for a feast,[146] but all other evidences of his life portray him as a dignified member of his profession. About 1619 he married a young widow, Mary, relict of William

---

[123] *Complete Baronetage* 2: 59–60.

[124] Bodleian Rawl. MSS, D 666, fol. 103v.

[125] Add. MSS, 21,922, fols. 178v, 183.

[126] S.P. 16, 191/27/51; S.P. 16/405; C. 193/13.

[127] Add. MSS, 26,781, fol. 39.

[128] *C.S.P. Dom., 1635*, 524; *1636–1637*, 567; *1637*, 103, 549.

[129] *C.S.P. Dom., 1638–1639*, 235–236.

[130] S.P. 16, 401/11.

[131] *C.S.P. Dom., 1640*, 438.

[132] *M. of P.* 1: 483, 493.

[133] Williams, *loc. cit.;* Clarendon, *Rebellion* 4: 238; Add. MSS, 37,343, fol. 239v.

[134] *C.J.* 2: 31, 84, 115, 129; Pink MSS, 306, fols. 175–177.

[135] Hexter, *The reign of King Pym*, 39, 65; Godwin, *The Civil War in Hampshire*, 104; Add. MSS, 24,860, fol. 145.

[136] Pink, *loc. cit.; Memoirs of Denzil Holles*, 154; *C.J.* 5: 445, 589.

[137] Williams, *loc. cit.; Complete Baronetage* 2: 60. The return of his successor for Lymington was dated 11 February 1678. *M. of P.* 1: 528.

[138] I.P.M. cited above; Brit. Mus. Bibl. Eg. 1048, fols. 70–77.

[139] *V.C.H. Hampshire* 3: 101.

[140] *Rebellion* 4: 238.

[141] *M. of P.* 1: 494, n.; *C.J.* 2: 750, 860.

[142] Because of the series of Richards, genealogists have sometimes confused the generation to which Christopher belonged. E.g., Comber, *Sussex Genealogies* 3: 155; *Sussex Arch. Coll.* 3: 99, 1850; Pink MSS, 306, fol. 179. The statement of relationships given above is based upon the M.I. to the three Richards at West Dean church (Add. MSS, 5699, fol. 203), upon *Vis. Sussex, 1633–4*, 27, *The visitation of Sussex, 1662*, Harleian Society 89: 72, 1937 (hereafter, *Vis. Sussex, 1662*), and upon the description of Christopher when he entered the Middle Temple.

[143] Add. MSS, 5699, fol. 203; Pink MSS, 306, fol. 187.

[144] Notes from the parish register of St. Peter the Great, Chichester. Add. MSS, 5699, fol. 183.

[145] *Mid. Temp. Rec.* 2: 622, 637, 700, 730, 738, 848, 857.

[146] St. Ch. 8/130/16; *Mid. Temp. Rec.* 2: 695.

Smyth of the Temple and of Binderton, daughter of John May of Rawmere.[147] She was a sister of Thomas May, M.P. (q.v.).

Lewknor represented Midhurst in the parliament of 1628, and not only kept notes of the proceedings [148] but wrote some reports of them for the Earl of Northumberland.[149] He was named at various times during the next decade to local commissions in Sussex,[150] and by 1631 was a J.P. there [151] and also Recorder of Chichester.[152] In 1636 he was a legal adviser and also J.P. for Guildford.[153] Although his brother, Richard, had opposed the 1621 loan and been summoned before Council,[154] Christopher by the 1630's at least seems to have been inclining toward the court. He was active with his "cousin," John Ashburnham, in one of his financial ventures,[155] and in 1636 was named a royal commissioner for investigating damages to timberland in Sussex caused by the growth of the iron industry.[156] About this time also Council referred to him the investigation of the case of a man jailed for non-payment of ship money, and in the summer of 1640 he reported to the lord lieutenant of the county the case of a man he had had imprisoned for language liberal "on matters above him." He became in 1640 counsellor for the enterprise of the New Corporation, after serving for some time as a chamberlain.[157] Elected to the Short Parliament for Chichester,[158] he was returned apparently without trouble in the fall.

Lewknor's prestige at the opening of the parliament is indicated by his being named to the Committee of Privileges. But since he was named to no others, and does not appear to have spoken in debate, it must be concluded that he did not often attend.[159] Perhaps the early attacks on king and court antagonized him. He was engaged actively for the king in 1642, especially in the attempt to secure the Chichester magazine, and he was associated with Goring in the defense of Portsmouth. He was disabled by the House on 2 September 1642 and again on 23 November,[160] became a colonel in the royalist army, and sat in the Oxford parliament. He was created D.C.L. at Oxford late in 1642 and was knighted there in 1644.[161] His lands were sequestered

and in 1651 were ordered to be sold. Various claims were made against his estates, including those by two daughters who petitioned in 1650 and 1651 as being greatly in want.[162] On 1 July 1653 Lewknor made his will, describing himself then as of the Middle Temple, "Esquire," and as ill in body,[163] and he probably died soon afterwards. The will was proved at London in 1660 by his daughter Elizabeth.

Lewknor's estate included some Chichester properties leased from the corporation and at least one other property which he seems to have purchased by borrowing £2000 in 1640.[164] His income from his practice was probably his chief source of wealth.

* John Lisle (c. 1610–1664), lawyer of the Middle Temple and Recorder of Winchester, represented that borough, 1640–1653. An Isle of Wight man and a younger son, he was said to have secured for himself most of his father's estate and to have gained by his marriage with Mary Elizabeth, daughter of Chief Justice Hobart, a fortune of £4000 in gold.[165] His first wife died in 1633. His marriage with Alice Beckenshaw occurred in 1636, and he acquired then the inheritance of two manors in Ellingham, the Isle of Wight.[166] Lisle was a sewers commissioner for Hampshire in 1638.[167] He was elected to the Short Parliament for Winchester in March, 1640, and by the autumn was Recorder there.[168] He was excused from attending the House in the summer of 1641 because he was in the north on army business,[169] but his career seems to have followed civil rather than military lines.

Apparently Lisle was at least moderately well-to-do, but not wealthy. His associates and relatives of both of his wives were opponents of the court. His first wife's brother had been active in the 1628 parliament and was imprisoned afterwards,[170] and his second wife's father paid a heavy knighthood composition.[171] Among his kinsmen in the 1640 parliament were the Hungerfords, relatives through his mother. Sir Robert Crane was a connection by marriage.

Sir John Lister (1587–1640), of Hull, elected M.P. by Hull on 26 October 1640, died in London just before Christmas, 1640. He had probably worked in the

---

[147] Comber, *Sussex Genealogies* 3: 155; *Vis. Sussex, 1662,* 73.
[148] *M. of P.* 1: 478; *C.J.* 2: 7.
[149] *H.M.C., Third Report,* MSS of the Duke of Northumberland, 69–70.
[150] C. 181/4, fol. 47; 181/5, fols. 136, 138, 230.
[151] C. 193/13; S.P. 16, 19/138v.
[152] *C.S.P. Dom., 1631–1633,* 39.
[153] Add. MSS, 6167, fol. 206v.
[154] S.P. 14, 127/79.
[155] *C.S.P. Dom., 1631–1633,* 378.
[156] *Sussex Arch. Coll.* 2: 195, 1849.
[157] *C.S.P. Dom., 1635–1636,* 460; *1640,* 290, 583.
[158] *M. of P.* 1: 483.
[159] *C.J.* 2: 21; Pink MSS, 306, fol. 179. He was not even listed among those taking the 1641 Protestation.
[160] *C.J.* 2: 750, 860; Thomas-Stanford, *Sussex in the great Civil War,* 39, 40.
[161] Pink MSS, *loc. cit.;* Wood, *Fasti Oxon.* 2: 39.

[162] *Sussex Arch. Coll.* 5: 48, n., 1852; *Cal. Com. Comp.,* 216, 2573.
[163] P.C.C., 287 Nabbs.
[164] *Cal. Com. Comp.,* 216, 2574.
[165] Lipscomb, *Buckingham* 2: 276; *A royalist's notebook,* ed. Bamford, 72, 86–87, 125. Sir John Oglander, the author, speaks in very uncomplimentary fashion of Mrs. Lisle and of John's treatment of his aging father.
[166] Richard Warner, *Collections for the history of Hampshire* 1 (i): 212, London, 1795; *V.C.H. Hampshire* 4: 563, 565.
[167] C. 181/5, fol. 230.
[168] *M. of P.* 1: 483, 493.
[169] *C.J.* 2: 263.
[170] Lipscomb, *Buckingham* 2: 276.
[171] Add. MSS, 21,922, fol. 176v.

House for a short time, and his death deprived it of an experienced and able member. Lister was the grandson of John Lister of Hull (d. 1555), and eldest son of John Lister (d. 1617), merchant, alderman and M.P. for Hull. His mother was Anne, daughter of Robert Geyton of that city, and he was baptized on 7 June 1587.[172] He matriculated at University College, Oxford, in 1604, and was admitted to the Middle Temple on 30 June 1606. He does not seem to have become a barrister, but his later employment about many legal matters in Hull and his retention of a chamber as late as 1628[173] indicate that he drew his livelihood from a profession as well as from his father's business. Lister returned to Hull to marry Elizabeth, daughter and heiress of Hugh Armyn, draper and former mayor,[174] and the first of their sixteen children, a son, John, was born about March, 1608/9.[175] He lived at a house in High Street, afterwards known as the Wilberforce Museum, where he transacted his business and where, in 1639, he entertained King Charles.[176] Shortly after his father's death in 1617, the town governors summoned Lister to fill his chair in the corporation. He agreed to do so and, on 18 March 1617, having paid a fine in lieu of serving as chamberlain and sheriff, was elected an alderman.[177] He was mayor in 1618,[178] and from that time on was greatly occupied in the town's service.

During the period of 1620 to 1630 Lister was employed much in London both as an M.P. and as an agent for special matters. He sat in the five parliaments of the decade, although his election was deferred in 1624 until a member who had been elected in response to patronage decided to sit for another place.[179] Instructed to work for improvements in trade, concerning which there was much anxiety in Hull at this time,[180] Lister spoke several times during the 1621 debates on trade regulations.[181] He wrote letters home to his constituents on several occasions, and in the parliament

of 1628 was so much interested in the arguments on the liberties of the subject that he had copies made of them for taking back to Hull.[182] He was knighted at Whitehall, 23 May 1628,[183] perhaps in recognition of his work in 1627–1628 in organizing the shipping at Hull for transporting troops to the continent.[184] He was a loan commissioner, 1625–1626,[185] and served a second time as mayor, 1629–1630. The trend of both mayor and town toward puritanism is revealed by his vigorous enforcement of the ordinances against alehouses and players, and the revival of those on Sabbath observance.[186]

During the next decade Lister continued to be a useful citizen. At the start he was assessed the heavy sum of £50 for knighthood composition, despite his recently acquired title.[187] He journeyed several times to London in connection with a lawsuit involving the town charter and the management of the castle, and for a trade agreement with London merchants.[188] He was a J.P. of Hull in 1637,[189] as he had probably been for some time. When the king visited Hull in 1639 not only did Lister entertain him at his house, but when the town was embarrassed about the expenses he offered to lend £620, albeit at a good interest rate, so that the town could meet its bills.[190] When he returned to London for the Short Parliament he secured the documents marking the end of Hull's long suit in Exchequer.[191] He was possibly not well when he went to London again in the autumn. He wrote his will on 21 December, directing that if he died there his body should be taken to Hull for burial. His death occurred on December 23, and he was buried on 19 January 1641 in Hull's church of Holy Trinity, near his parents.[192] His friend, Andrew Marvel, at whose election to the ministry there in 1624 he had been present,[193] probably preached the sermon.

Lister must have been wealthy. He lent ready money several times to Hull,[194] and owned properties nearby in Yorkshire and Lincolnshire.[195] He left a substantial

[172] Pink MSS, 319; Dugdale, *Vis. York*, 128; *Yorks. Arch. Jour.* 14: 199, 1898; Wildridge, *Old and new Hull*, 146.

[173] *Al. Oxon.; Mid. Temp. Rec.* 2: 467, 732.

[174] Dugdale, *loc. cit.*; Thomas Gent, *Annales Regioduni Hullini*, 23, London, 1735; reprint, Hull, 1869 (hereafter, Gent, *Hull*).

[175] Wildridge, *Old and new Hull*, 147 and notes. Some of Wildridge's statements are ambiguous. This son and his son, John, in turn were identified by Dugdale as of Linton, Yorkshire.

[176] Wildridge, *op. cit.*, 146. Lister's portrait was hanging in the house in 1935.

[177] He seems to have refused a similar election earlier. Hull Corporation MSS, Bench Book 5, fols. 25, 25v.

[178] Hull Corporation MSS, Bench Book 5, fol. 30.

[179] *M. of P.* 1: 454, 461, *passim*; Hull Corporation MSS, Bench Book 5, fols. 60v, 61. Sentiment against outsiders as M.P.'s was developing at Hull now. *Ibid.*, fols. 70v, 91.

[180] *Ibid.*, fols. 41, 45–48; J. Malet Lambert, *Two thousand years of gild life*, 169–170, Hull, 1871.

[181] *Commons Debates 1621* 2: 178, n., 365; 3: 194, 247, n., 298, n.; 6: 60.

[182] Hull Corporation MSS, Guildhall Letters, 1621 and 1625; Bench Book 5, fols. 93, 94.

[183] Shaw, *K. of E.* 2: 194.

[184] Hull Corporation MSS, Bench Book 5, fols. 80, 89v, 92v; Wildridge, *Hull letters*, 9.

[185] *Acts. P.C., 1625–1626*, 424.

[186] Hull Corporation MSS, Bench Book 5, fols. 98v, 100–104, 112.

[187] Several other Yorkshire knights were so fined. *Y.A.S. Rec. Ser.* 61: 89, 106, 1920.

[188] Hull Corporation MSS, Bench Book 5, fols. 162, 172v, 182, 185v, 187v, 195–197.

[189] C. 181/5, fol. 159.

[190] Hull Corporation MSS, Bench Book 5, fols. 250–251; Gent, *Hull*, 139.

[191] Hull Corporation MSS, Bench Book 5, 260, 262.

[192] Wildridge, *Old and new Hull*, 147; *Yorks. Arch. Jour.* 14: 203, 1898.

[193] Hull Corporation MSS, Bench Book 5, fol. 63.

[194] *Ibid.*, fol. 204, and instances cited earlier.

[195] *Y.A.S. Rec. Ser.* 53: 106, 1915; 58: 159, 162, 1917; abstract of Lister's will (*ibid.* 9: 165, n., 1890).

sum for a city charity,[196] and his eldest son was able, when he made his will two years afterwards, to plan £1000 portions for his two daughters.[197]

Sir Martin Lister (c. 1602–1670), of Radcliffe, Bucks, Thorpe Ernald, Leicestershire, and Burwell, Lincolnshire, sat for Brackley, Northants, 1640–1648. He came of a Yorkshire family connected with many of the midland counties, being apparently the only son of Michael Lister of Frearhead in Craven, Yorkshire, by his wife, Mary Kebell, and the nephew of Sir Matthew Lister, M.D., physician to Queen Anne and to Charles I. He was born about 1602, entered Trinity College, Oxford, in 1619, aged seventeen, and in October, 1621, was admitted to Lincoln's Inn. Probably through the intercession of his uncle he was knighted at Hampton Court in July, 1625. He resided chiefly at Radcliffe, Bucks, or at Thorpe Ernald, although he probably held some lands in Northamptonshire.[198] He married twice, (1) Mary, daughter of Richard Lord Wenman of Oxfordshire, who died about 1635, and (2) Susanna, daughter of Sir Alexander Temple of St. Mary's Hoo, Kent, widow of Sir Geoffrey Thornhurst. His son by his second wife, Martin, became a physician and scientist of note.

Apparently Lister had held no county offices before 1640, but he was elected by Brackley to both of the 1640 parliaments.[199] He was not often named to committees before 1643, but supported the popular party and was a county committeeman during the war. Lister was secluded in 1648, survived the Restoration, and was buried at Burwell, Lincolnshire, in August, 1670, aged sixty-seven.[200]

By his first marriage Lister was a brother-in-law of Lord Wenman and of Arthur Goodwin.

Sir Edward Littleton, Bart. (1599–1657), of Pillaton, Staffordshire, was M.P. for his county, 1640–4 March 1644. He was a J.P. and member of several lesser commissions.[201] As sheriff, he tried to collect ship money, 1636–1637, but was in trouble about arrears in 1637 and as late as 1640.[202] He probably sympa-thized with the nonconformists in religion,[203] and was involved in 1635 with several others of his county in a High Commission case.[204] He was a cousin of Richard Knightley and of Humphrey Salway (q.v.), and was active in the cause of parliament until 1643, afterwards turning to the side of the king.

Sir Edward inherited a good estate, numbering five manors and other properties in Staffordshire and Worcestershire, and his marriage about 1625 with a daughter of Sir William Courteen,[205] the wealthy merchant, enriched him further. He purchased a baronetcy for himself, but the war practically ruined him. The value of half of his Staffordshire lands was quoted in 1646 as only £254 a year.[206]

Thomas Littleton (c. 1620–1681), of Stoke Milburgh, Salop, was M.P. for Great Wenlock, 1640–5 February 1644.[207] He was the son and heir of Adam Littleton of Stoke Milburgh (baronet, 1642; d. 1647) and his wife, Ethelred, daughter and heiress of Thomas Poyntz of North Ockenden, Essex. Thomas was born about 1620 or 1622, was admitted to the Inner Temple in 1636, and matriculated at Jesus College, Oxford, 15 June 1638, "aged sixteen." [208] On 6 October 1637 he had been licensed to marry his cousin, Anne, only child of Sir Edward Littleton, the Solicitor General and later Lord Keeper. The bride and groom were, according to the license, aged twelve and seventeen. Their fathers drew up a marriage settlement in September, 1638, agreeing that £2000 should be settled by the wife's father as soon as she had issue and that an income of £200 a year should be guaranteed them by Thomas's father.[209] Upon his father-in-law's request, Thomas was called to the bar at the Temple on 22 May 1642.[210]

Young Littleton was elected to both of the 1640 parliaments by Wenlock borough, where his father was recorder,[211] but he was never an important member of the House. He was disabled as a royalist, 5 February 1644, and succeeded his father as a baronet in 1647. He compounded in time for his estates, with a fine of £295,[212] and lived for many years afterwards. He died on 12 April 1681.[213]

---

[196] Lansd. MSS, 891 (De la Pryme's "Annals of Hull"), fols. 303–304.

[197] Y.A.S. Rec. Ser. **9**: 165–166, 1890.

[198] Northamptonshire Notes and Queries **3**: 120, 1890.

[199] Willis **2**: 234; M. of P. **1**: 491. Bean (Northern Counties, 270, 1197) points out the discrepancies in the pedigrees, some of which identify him as the son rather than the nephew of Martin Lister, M.P. Clitheroe, 1604, another brother of Dr. Matthew Lister.

[200] Other references used for this sketch are Al. Oxon.; Foster, Pedigrees of the county families of Yorkshire **1**, pedigree of Lister of Gisburne; Yorks. Arch. Jour. **2**: 297–298, 1873; Pink MSS, 306, fol. 221.

[201] S.P. 16/405; C. 181/5, fols. 12, 65, passim; C.S.P. Dom., 1639–1640, 172.

[202] Ibid., 1636–1637, 439, 493; 1637–1638, 90; 1640, 250.

[203] His father sued in the Star Chamber in 1622 a neighbor who accused him, among other things, of maintaining a nonconformist minister in one of his churches. St. Ch. 8/198/12.

[204] C.S.P. Dom., 1635–1636, 107, 114, 116, 123.

[205] I.P.M., Sir Edward Littleton (d. 1629), C. 142/456/76.

[206] Cal. Com. Comp., 2082. His fine as a royalist was £1134. For other details on Littleton's career, see Wedgwood, Staff. Parl. Hist. **2**: 58–61.

[207] M. of P. **1**: 492; C.J. **2**: 389.

[208] Al. Oxon.

[209] S.P. 17, Case E, No. 6.

[210] Cal. Inner Temp. Rec. **2**: 266.

[211] Shrops. Arch. Soc., Trans., 3rd Ser., **2**: 327, 1902.

[212] Cal. Com. Comp., 2030.

[213] Complete Baronetage **2**: 204.

Francis Lloyd (d. 1699), of Maesyfelin, Cardiganshire, was M.P. for Carmarthen borough, 1640–5 February 1644.[214] The son and heir of the Welsh judge, Sir Marmaduke Lloyd, member of the Council of Wales,[215] by Mary, daughter of John Gwyn Stedman of Strata Florida,[216] he entered the Middle Temple in the summer of 1628.[217] He probably served under Sir Ralph Hopton in the Scottish war (1639).[218] He was by that time a J.P. in Carmarthenshire,[219] and he sat in parliament for the first time in the spring of 1640.

A courtier and a royalist, Lloyd voted against Strafford's attainder,[220] and he was disabled in 1644. When he compounded in 1646 for his estates his "particular" reported lands in the shires of Cardigan and Carmarthen of which he had some £150 a year in possession, with slightly over £200 to come in reversion after his parents. He was fined at a third, £1275, afterwards increased to £1320, and then lowered again by £267.[221]

Lloyd's wife was a niece of Henry Vaughan, the Carmarthenshire member (q.v.), and he was related through his mother to another fellow M.P., John Vaughan.[222]

Walter Lloyd (born 1599), of Llanfair Clydogan and Llanney, Cardiganshire, was M.P. for his county, 1640–5 February 1644.[223] The son and heir of John Lloyd of Llanfair (d. 1606), by his wife, Jane, daughter of Sir Walter Rice of Newton,[224] he was born on 24 November 1599.[225] He was admitted to the Inner Temple in 1615, the same year as his future colleagues of the Long Parliament, Parry and Prideaux.[226] After serving as sheriff of county Cardigan in 1621 he was J.P. there for many years.[227] He was one of the loan commissioners for that county in 1627,[228] too, but he had not been an M.P. before the Long Parliament.

Lloyd was named to a few early committees, 1640–1641, one of them on a Welsh election.[229] He was a teller with Digby for the Noes in the vote on Strafford's

attainder,[230] and of course was listed as a "Straffordian."[231] He is said to have withdrawn soon afterwards.[232]

An assessment of £1000 levied against him in 1644[233] was probably based upon an overassessment of Lloyd's wealth. His composition papers three years later, although apparently incomplete, reveal properties in Carmarthen and Cardigan counties worth slightly under £90 a year.[234] His fine, set at a third, £1033, with another £261 representing a sixth on another property, was largely unpaid in 1652. At the latter date Lloyd declared himself very aged, heavily indebted, and burdened with eighteen living children.[235]

Richard Long (d. 1648), alderman of Bristol, sat for his town, 1640–12 May 1642. He was the son of an Axminster merchant, Thomas Long, and after serving an apprenticeship to John Merrick, a Bristol merchant, was admitted as a burgess there on 29 September 1608. He was a member of the town council ten years later, and passed through the municipal offices in turn, becoming alderman in 1636 and serving as mayor, 1636–1637.[236] He was concerned not only with matters of trade and with the upkeep of streets and wharves, but took an active interest for many years in the city charities.[237] During the year of Long's mayoralty, as in the year before and the year afterwards, the Bristol government voted to pay only a part of its ship money rate.[238]

An active merchant and ship owner, Long was a partner in 1627 in a vessel that was licensed as a privateer,[239] and the next year he assisted in fitting out ships for guarding the Irish coast.[240] He had an interest in 1637 in a ship in the Newfoundland trade and in 1639 was granted permission with two partners to employ another ship for taking emigrants and supplies to New England.[241] Shortly before May, 1640, he sent his eldest son to live for a time in Massachusetts, perhaps in the interest of his trade.[242] Long's name appears regularly in the annals of the Bristol Merchant Venturers from 1613, when he subscribed £25 toward outfitting ships against the pirates, until the Civil War.

[214] M. of P. 1: 498; C.J. 3: 389.
[215] Arch. Camb., 6th Ser., 17: 195, 1917.
[216] Ibid., 3rd Ser., 6: 177, 1860.
[217] Mid. Temp. Rec. 2: 736.
[218] S.P. 16, 427/38/v.
[219] S.P. 16/405; C. 193/13.
[220] Verney, 58. His name appears as "Floyde."
[221] Cal. Com. Comp., 1084–1085; S.P. 23/184/317–335.
[222] In addition to the above authorities see Williams, Parl. Hist. Wales, 53.
[223] M. of P. 1: 498 and n.; C.J. 3: 389.
[224] She was a granddaughter of the Stedmans of Strata Florida. Arch. Camb., 3rd Ser., 7: 156, 1861. Cf. Francis Lloyd.
[225] I.P.M., John Vaughan of "Llanvairgledagey," C. 142/305/120. Williams (Parl. Hist. Wales., 29) wrongly identifies him with the Walter Lloyd who entered Oxford in 1595, aged fifteen.
[226] Students admitted to the Inner Temple, 213.
[227] C. 193/12, 13; S.P. 16/405.
[228] S.P. 16, 54/74.
[229] C.J. 2: 62, 99; D'Ewes (N), 455.

[230] Lord Nugent calls attention to the error in the listing of the tellers in the Journals, 16 April 1641. Some memorials of John Hampden, 4, n., 4th ed.; London, 1860.
[231] Verney, 58.
[232] Cal. Com. Comp., 600.
[233] Cal. Com. Adv. Money, 435.
[234] S.P. 23/219/161.
[235] Cal. Com. Comp., 572, 1751–1752.
[236] Nott, The deposition books of Bristol, 252.
[237] Bristol Corp. MSS, Common Council Book 3, 15 September 1628, passim.
[238] Ibid., 3 November 1635, 13 December 1636, 19 December 1637.
[239] C.S.P. Dom., 1628–1629, 302.
[240] Bristol Corp. MSS, Common Council Book 3, 3 July 1628.
[241] Bristol Municipal Library MSS, Bristol Collection, 7077, fols. 3, 20, 23; Latimer, Annals of Bristol, 146–147.
[242] Winthrop Papers 4: 263, 1929.

He held various offices in the Society, and was master twice in succession, 1636–1638. With Humphrey Hooke (*q.v.*), with whom Long was associated in most of his official work in Bristol and in the Merchant Venturers, he joined in the Society's agreements for exporting Welsh butter and for collecting the wine tax for the London vintners.[243] During his second year as master Long worked with the town clerk in opposing the royal commissioners who came to examine the company books under a patent for searching out excessive duties, and he had the backing of Hooke and the mayor in devising various ruses by which the efforts of the commissioners were frustrated.[244] The charges against the Society were not proved, but the company planned in the spring of 1640 to ask parliament for action against the abusive proceedings, and in January, 1641, the city government instructed the two Bristol M.P.'s who had played so active a part in the affair to work for that redress.[245]

The autumn of 1640 found Long attending his first parliament. He pledged £1000 jointly with Hooke for the loan in November,[246] but was otherwise not conspicuous as a member. He was named, as was Hooke, to an occasional committee on matters of shipping, but after the House undertook early in 1642 to review the contracts of the Merchant Venturers he and Hooke were expelled from the House as monopolists in May.[247] During the war Long subscribed £200 for the royal war chest, was turned out of his municipal office by House order in 1645, and in 1646 compounded as a delinquent,[248] suffering the heaviest fine in the city. He died before the proceedings were finished, and was buried on 11 February 1648 at St. Stephen's Church.[249]

Of Long's family little is known. His widow, Mary, who survived him, was possibly a daughter of the John Barker who was co-owner of a ship with Long in 1627.[250] Their two elder sons, John and Richard, became members of the Merchant Venturers in 1639.[251] Long's religious and charitable nature are revealed by his will, for he left remembrances to numerous school-masters, ministers, and parishes, and provided especially a charity for the merchants' almshouse.[252]

Long was described in 1640 as "of great estate."[253] He declared to the compounding commissioners property in Bristol and in nearby parts of Somerset and Gloucestershire worth £300–£350 a year, but his principal income doubtless came from his business ventures. His compounding papers refer to £3200 due him from doubtful ventures, £1500 in business losses by reason of the war, and debts of £2600.[254] His fine at a tenth was £800.[255]

Walter Long (d. 1672), of Whaddon, Wiltshire, one of the Presbyterian leaders of the Long Parliament, was chosen for Ludgershall, Wilts, after the disabling of William Ashburnham on 9 December 1641. He was present in debate on 27 December,[256] and remained a member until the attack on the Presbyterians, 1647–1648. He was one of several Walter Longs of Wiltshire, being the son of a family which had been seated at Whaddon at least from the time of Henry III. His father, Henry Long (d. 1612), had in Elizabeth's time been interested in voyages to the West Indies and in privateering. His mother, Rebecca, daughter of Christopher Bailey, married Henry Sherfield of Berkshire after her first husband's death.[257] Walter's elder brother, Henry, aged twenty-two in 1612, succeeded to the estates, but Walter is said to have inherited them eventually.[258] Walter entered Lincoln's Inn in 1611,[259] and by 1622 was seated at Whaddon.[260] In or before 1627 he married Mary, daughter of Joseph Cocks or Coxe.[261]

Long was a member of the city council of Salisbury in 1625 and as such was elected to the parliament that year for the city.[262] He sat for the county in 1626, and although he was sheriff of Wiltshire, 1627–1628, was returned for Bath in the neighboring county of Somerset to the parliament of 1628.[263] Since Long had spoken

---

[243] MSS of the Society of Merchant Venturers of Bristol, Book of Trade, 1598–1693, accounts for 1613–1614, and fols. 65, 244–249; Book of Ordinances, fols. 55, 89, 109, 125, *passim*; Hall Book of Proceedings, fols. 25, 32.

[244] S.P. 16, 378/4.

[245] Latimer, *Merchant Venturers, Bristol*, 111; Bristol Corp. MSS, Common Council Book 3, 15 January 1640/1; MSS of the Society of Merchant Venturers, Hall Book of Proceedings, 1: 23.

[246] D'Ewes (N), 52.

[247] *C.J.* 2: 375, 401, 415, 567–568.

[248] Latimer, *Merchant Venturers, Bristol*, 161, 163.

[249] Nott, *op. cit.*, 253. Pink dates his death as 4 February 1648. Pink MSS, 306, fol. 290.

[250] *C.S.P. Dom., 1628–1629*, 302. Long mentioned in his will a sister Barker and a brother, Thomas Barker (P.C.C., 91 Essex).

[251] MSS of the Society of Merchant Venturers of Bristol, Hall Book of Proceedings 1, fols. 6, 10.

[252] His will bears several dates between 10 June 1646 and 26 January 1648, and was proved on 20 June 1648. The legacies mentioned in it total nearly £850.

[253] *Winthrop Papers* 4: 263, 1929.

[254] S.P. 23/193/661–666. A deed of settlement of 1645 is among the Bristol Corp. MSS, 00906 (3) C.

[255] *Cal. Com. Comp.*, 1556.

[256] D'Ewes (C), 352; *C.J.* 2: 358.

[257] Add. MSS, 15,561 (Long Family Papers), fols. 1–12, 48, 49, 101, 183; Add. MSS, 11,757, fols. 24, 27, *passim; Complete Baronetage* 3: 181.

[258] *Ibid.*; I.P.M., Henry Long, 1612, C. 142/331/111.

[259] *Complete Baronetage, loc. cit.*

[260] Add. MSS, 11,757, fol. 66.

[261] *Complete Baronetage, loc. cit.*

[262] *M. of P.* 1: 466. Walter Long of Draycot, afterwards Sir Walter Long, sat in the same parliament for Westbury, a borough which he represented several times. *Ibid.* 1: 454, 466, 472. This was the Walter Long who was a Wiltshire J.P. C. 193/12, 13.

[263] *M. of P.* 1: 472, 477; *List of Sheriffs*, 154.

in the 1626 parliament against granting the supply,[264] and had in 1627 declined to lend to the king,[265] it may be suspected that his appointment to the shrievalty had been planned so that he could not sit in the next parliament. He evaded the well known rule that sheriffs could not return themselves to parliament by getting himself chosen for a constituency in Somerset, where he owned some property,[266] and in the 1628 session was "one of the hottest men" against Buckingham. A Star Chamber suit was brought against him after that session, charging him with violating his sheriff's oath by absenting himself from the county, and in February, 1629, the court sentenced him with a fine of 2000 marks and imprisonment until he submitted. Since his properties were then in the hands of trustees, allegedly for the purpose of settling debts amounting to £4000, the court ordered that John Ashburnham, the courtier (q.v.), should be allowed to collect £200 of the fine each year until the full amount had been paid.[267] Meanwhile Long attended the 1629 session of the parliament, took part in the famous proceedings of 25 February and 2 March, and with Strode was made the object of a special proclamation on 27 March for their arrest. In the subsequent Star Chamber trial, the old charge concerning his conduct as sheriff was linked with another based upon his words in parliament.[268] Sent to the Tower and that summer denied a writ of habeas corpus as in the case of the other members who were held, he was out for a few days in the fall, and again in 1631 on the occasion of his wife's illness, but he was not finally released until the summer of 1633. During the course of his imprisonment his wife and six children suffered severely, as he afterwards declared, and his wife died. He asserted that the confiscation of the income from his lands for the purpose of collecting his fine had nearly ruined him.[269]

Long lived in Shropshire for a time after his release, and by absence from his Wiltshire house laid himself open to the charge of defaulting from the Wiltshire musters.[270] He was probably the Walter Long who in 1639 complained of an overassessment of ship money.

[264] S.P. 16, 29/13.

[265] S.P. 16, 80/33/i, fol. 142.

[266] S.P. 16, 89/30; C. 142/331/111.

[267] C.S.P. Dom., 1628–1629, 183; D'Ewes (N), 495–496; Birch, The court and times of Charles the First 2: 55. See also Jour. Modern Hist. 1: 370–372, 1930.

[268] Long had criticized, among other matters, the king's counsellors, the trend toward popery, and tonnage and poundage. Commons Debates for 1629, 22, 41, 171, 205.

[269] S.P. 16, 142/36; Add. MSS, 12,511, fol. 80v; H.M.C., Twelfth Report 2: Coke MSS, 8; Gardiner, H. of E. 7: 87–96, 110–111, 120; Birch, The court and times of Charles the First 2: 162; C.S.P. Dom., 1628–1629, 504, 587; 1631–1633, 29; D'Ewes (N), 496. Although not until May, 1638, was his fine fully discharged (C.S.P. Dom., 1637–1638, 409), Long seems to have been present to defend himself in a case in Chancery in July, 1633. Wilts. Arch. Soc. MSS, Taylor's Notes on the Brounker Family, 2.

[270] C.S.P. Dom., 1636–1637, 395, 469.

He secured the arrest of the offending constable and went to London to press the charge.[271] He was not elected originally to the Long Parliament, but was in London in December, 1640, to follow his petition concerning the earlier breach of his parliamentary privilege. He wrote to a friend from there that "there is an expectation that I shall bee chosen to serve for this parliament."[272] When the opportunity arose, it was symbolic of the times that Ashburnham of the army plot, brother of the courtier who had collected Long's fines, should be replaced by the critic and victim of the king's policies.

Since Long entered the parliament so near to the end of 1641 his influence in the House during the period here studied was not great. He was an important leader for the parliamentarians during the war years, however, both within the House and in managing military and local affairs in Wiltshire and Shropshire. He was one of the Presbyterian "eleven" who were expelled by the army in 1647. He returned in the summer of 1648, and then was finally secluded in December. Reversing his politics after that, he joined the royalist exiles, and after the Restoration was made a baronet. He died in 1672.[273]

Long's financial standing in 1640 is difficult to estimate. His father owned four or five manors in Wilts and Somerset, arranged for dowries of 1000 marks apiece for each of three daughters, and provided £500 each for his two younger sons.[274] Since Walter apparently succeeded as the head of his family, he must have owned an estate that was fairly good. However, his arrests and trials, his fine and long imprisonment, must by 1640 have reduced his fortune greatly. Parliament voted in 1645 to reimburse him for his fine, and afterwards to pay him £5000 more. He declared in 1660 that the latter sum was never paid.[275] His pledge for the defense in June, 1642, however, was a large one, four horses and £200, and by 1643 he was said to have advanced £1000 for the cause.[276]

George Lowe (born c. 1600), of Calne, Wiltshire, was a member for Calne, 1640–1644. He has sometimes been confused with his uncle, the London merchant who was associated in several of Sir Arthur Ingram's undertakings,[277] but he was explicitly identified as of Calne

[271] Ibid., 1639, 22, 238.

[272] Bodleian Tanner MSS, 65, fol. 228. Long's case was discussed in December, 1640, and in October, 1641. D'Ewes (N), 495–496; C.J. 2: 298.

[273] Brit. Mus. Bibl. Eg., 1048, fols. 78–80; O.P.H. 9: 8; C.J. 5: 589; H.M.C., Seventh Report, House of Lords MSS, 79; Pink MSS, loc. cit.; Complete Baronetage, loc. cit.

[274] I.P.M., Henry Long, C. 142/331/111.

[275] Pink MSS, 306, fol. 298; H.M.C., Seventh Report, loc. cit.

[276] N. and Q., 1st Ser., 12: 338, 1855; Pink MSS, loc. cit.

[277] George Lowe, the London merchant, was an associate of Ingram's in connection with the tobacco farm and the Irish customs, and was one of the alum contractors for some years (Commons Debates 1621 7: 453; Add. MSS, 4794, fol. 298;

on various occasions, notably at the time he was compounding for his desertion of parliament.[278] He was identified in the return as George Lowe, senior,[279] possibly to distinguish him from his younger London cousin of the same name, or perhaps from someone nearer him in Calne, for George was a popular name in in the family. He was apparently a grandson of William Lowe of Shrewsbury and of Calne, and the fourth son of Richard Lowe of Calne by his second wife, Mary, daughter of Charles Wotton. His age was given as twenty-three at the heralds' visitation of 1623.[280] Whether he or his uncle was Calne's M.P. in 1625, 1626, and 1628 it is impossible to state with certainty.[281] And there is no evidence to indicate that he was active in county affairs. In 1636, however, he was assisting in relief work for the plague sufferers in Calne, and the next year he reported to the county justices on the disposal of the relief funds.[282] Other men represented Calne in the Short Parliament, but George Lowe of Calne was the borough's member in the second parliament of 1640.

Lowe was not prominent in the Long Parliament. He took the Protestation on 3 May 1641, and in June of 1642 promised to lend £50 for the defense.[283] But he joined the king at Oxford after the war began, and was consequently disabled, 5 February 1644.[284] He was a prisoner of parliament for several months in 1645, and when he was released he promptly petitioned to compound. He declared that he left parliament to go into Wiltshire on business connected with a large estate for which he was trustee, that he had been persuaded to go to Oxford, but that he had withdrawn before the vote against parliament. Lowe apparently served again for Calne in the parliament of 1661, and died sometime after its close, possibly in 1682.[285]

Lowe seems to have been connected by marriage with

Edward Hyde. The latter had a sister, Mrs. Lowe, who not long after 1635 had three young children. She was probably the Elizabeth Hyde, daughter of Henry Hyde of Pyrton who married about 1625 Lowe's brother Richard.[286] Lowe's career in parliament seems to have followed the pattern of Hyde's, and it was quite possibly the latter who persuaded him to join the royalists at Oxford.

George Lowe, according to the assessments for the 1642 subsidy, paid the highest rate in Calne borough and hundred.[287] When he compounded he declared as his principal estate the manor and parsonage of Calne, which had a clear income before the war of £200 or £300 a year, the lower figure being his estimate. By 1645 he said his debts overbalanced what his creditors owed him. He was fined first at a third, but managed by 1649 to get the fine reduced to a tenth, £336.[288]

Thomas Lower (1615–1661), of St. Winnow, Cornwall, was M.P. for East Looe, 1640–22 January 1644. He was the posthumous son and heir of Sir William Lower of St. Winnow and of Treventy, Carmarthenshire (M.P., Virginia Company stockholder, d. 1615).[289] His mother was the Welsh heiress, Penelope, daughter of Sir Thomas Perrott and granddaughter of Walter, Earl of Essex. She married as her second husband in 1618 Sir Robert Naunton, Secretary of State, and her son, Thomas, who was born in Wales in November, 1615,[290] probably grew up in the atmosphere of the court under his stepfather's care. His only sister, Dorothy, married in time an usher of the king's chamber, but Thomas seems never to have married. Nothing appears of him in the local records of Cornwall, although his uncle, Nicholas Lower, whose properties he inherited in time, was a J.P. there in 1638.[291] Lower's election to his first parliament in October, 1640, probably represents a court nomination.

Lower was named to a few committees in the Long Parliament, one being that on scandalous ministers.[292] But he deserted the House with the outbreak of war. He was created M.A. at Oxford by the king's command early in 1643 and sat in the parliament there.[293] He

C.S.P. Dom., 1611–1618, 457; H.M.C., Various Collections 8, MSS of the Hon. F. L. Wood, 14–16). He was an officer in the Merchant Adventurers of London (C.S.P. Dom., 1635, 524; 1637–1638, 176), but may have died about 1639. One George Lowe who was of the Drapers' Company died then (P. Boyd, The roll of the Drapers' Company of London, 118). W. D. Pink thought the merchant was the M.P. in 1640 as well as in earlier parliaments (Pink MSS, 311, fols. 466b, 496c).

[278] Cal. Com. Comp., 959; S.P. 23/177/335.
[279] M. of P. 1: 495.
[280] Marshall, Vis. Wilts, 38.
[281] M. of P. 1: 466, 472, 478. George Lowe, senior, was the name given each time. Since a break in continuity of service came with the Short Parliament, it is possible that the member of the three earlier ones was the Londoner and that his nephew entered the House for the first time in November, 1640.
[282] Marsh, Hist. of Calne, 107, 108.
[283] C.J. 2: 133; Bodleian Tanner MSS, 63, fol. 59v ("Mr. G. Lowe of Calne").
[284] C.J. 3: 389.
[285] M. of P. 1: 530; Wilts. Arch Mag. 24: 309–312, 1889. The death date was suggested by Basil Henning of Yale University on the basis of his study of the personnel of the 1661 parliament.

[286] Will of Henry, brother of Edward Hyde (Bodleian Clarendon MSS, 129, fol. 14); Wilts Arch. Soc. MSS, Kite's Salisbury Licenses (1621–1628); Marshall, Vis. Wilts., 38.
[287] Marsh, Hist. of Calne, 337.
[288] Cal. Com. Comp., 959; S.P. 23/177/335; Wilts. Arch. Mag. 24: 309–312, 1889.
[289] Vivian, Vis. Cornwall, 300; Brown, Genesis of the U. S., 940.
[290] I.P.M., Sir William Lower, Wards 7/58/198; Misc. Geneal. et Herald., 5th Ser., 8: 252, 1932–1934; Sir John Maclean, Parochial and family history of the parish of St. Tudy, 77, Exeter, 1879.
[291] S.P. 16/405. This uncle was a brother-in-law of Henry Killigrew (q.v.). Maclean, op. cit., 78.
[292] C.J. 2: 54, passim.
[293] Wood, Fasti Oxon. 2: 33; Al. Oxon.; Pink MSS, 307, fol. 223.

was disabled in January, 1644,[294] and compounded for his estates, 1646–1649. He died in London shortly after the Restoration, and was buried at St. Clement Danes in March, 1661.[295] His will, having a codicil of 5 February 1661, was proved on 13 April following by his designated heir, Sir William Lower.[296]

The Lower family seems to have been well-to-do. At the time of his parents' marriage in 1605 a yearly income of £310 from St. Winnow alone was mentioned in provision for his mother, and her dowry, besides her lands, was £1400.[297] The Committee for the Advance of Money assessed Lower £2500, designating him then as Lady Naunton's son, but they reduced the figure afterwards to £600, and may have excused him from the rate entirely in 1647. When he compounded he listed his property values as slightly more than £610 a year, but declared that annuities of £490 were payable out of them and that most of his holdings had been mortgaged to enable him to meet his obligations. His fine, set at two years' value after Fairfax had included him in an order for lenience, was £1174, but it was eventually settled upon payment of half of that amount.[298]

John Lowry (d. 1669), chandler and Common Councillor of Cambridge, sat for his borough, 1640–1653. His parentage is unknown, but he gained his freedom of the borough after having served an apprenticeship to a chandler, and set up his own business.[299] He had some minor municipal responsibilities in 1624, and from July, 1626, was a member of the Common Council of the borough. He was on a committee to improve the rules for the town government in 1629, assisted afterwards with the removing of some undesirables from the borough council, and was elevated to an aldermanship in May, 1641.[300] Lowry owned some land within the borough, leased others for business purposes, and seems to have been prosperous.[301] He married before 1639, but his wife's name is not known.

National affairs claimed Lowry's interests by 1640. He was probably a friend of the Cambridge chandler who in August reported some pamphlets regarding the Scottish war,[302] but his name was not connected with the incident. His election to his first parliament in October was not unopposed, and he seems not to have been entirely popular with his fellow townsmen, for in August, 1641, a Cambridge man was sent for by the House to answer for his terming Lowry an ass and a fool.[303] Inconspicuous in the early period of the Long Parliament, except for his possible pledge in support of the loan in November, 1640,[304] Lowry became more active with the war. He served in the parliamentary army and on numerous local committees, and was mayor of Cambridge in 1645, though retaining his seat in the House. He was named a justice for the king's trial, but did not act, was returned to parliament again in 1658 and sat with the Rump in 1659 and 1660. After the Restoration he was called to account for his deeds and was removed from his aldermanship for his conduct during the war and for refusing to take the oath under the Corporation Act.[305] Lowry was buried at St. Sepulchre's in Cambridge, 18 July 1669.[306]

* Henry Lucas (d. 1663), member for Cambridge University, 1640–1648, came of a Suffolk family, but his father seems to have died in Cambridgeshire, and Lucas, besides being a graduate of the University, was secretary to its Chancellor, the Earl of Holland, and doubtless his nominee for both of the 1640 elections. He entered the Middle Temple, 24 January 1606, as the son and heir of Edward Lucas, late of Thriplow, Cambridgeshire,[307] and was by 1629 secretary to the Earl of Dorchester,[308] afterwards entering the service of the Earl of Holland. Although Lucas is remembered chiefly for the bequests he left at his death in 1663,[309] he does not appear to have been particularly wealthy in 1640. His name is not in the lists of loan subscribers, 1640–1641, and his pledge for the defense in 1642 was not larger than the average.[310]

* Sir Thomas Lucy (1586–1640), of Charlecote, Warwickshire, was M.P. for Warwick borough a little more than a month, for he died on 8 December 1640. It is doubtful whether he was ever present in the Long Parliament, for he was quite ill in the spring, just

[294] C.J. 3 : 374.
[295] Wood, Fasti Oxon. 2 : 33; Athenae Oxon. 3 : 57.
[296] P.C.C., 54 and 59 May.
[297] I.P.M. cited above.
[298] Cal. Com. Adv. Money, 423; S.P. 23/204/821–822; Cal. Com. Comp., 57, 1083; Pink MSS, 307, fol. 209.
[299] Cooper, Annals of Cambridge 3 : 304, n., 542; Cambridge Corp. MSS, Day Book, 1610–1646, fol. 191.
[300] Ibid., fols. 130, 133, 151v, passim.
[301] Ibid., fols. 187v, 225v. He was one of the larger rate payers in Bridge Ward in 1640–1641 (Cambridge Antiquarian Society, Proceedings 17 : 135, 1914), and afterwards sent his son, John, born about 1639, to Eton and Cambridge. Al. Cant.
[302] C.S.P. Dom., 1640, 614. That chandler, Robert Ibbot, was the one named in the discounted story of Oliver Cromwell's first Cambridge election as one of his sponsors. Sanford, St. and ill., 265.

[303] C.J. 2 : 252.
[304] Lowry's name appears in one list (D'Ewes [N], 52, n.), but possibly in error for another member. His pledge of one horse for the defense in June, 1642 (N. and Q., 1st Ser., 12 : 360, 1855), seems small by comparison, and later the House voted him £300 for his losses during the war. Add. MSS, 5803, fol. 53v.
[305] Cambridge Antiquarian Society, Proceedings 17 : 77–84, 106, 1914; Cooper, Annals of Cambridge 3 : 342, 392, 459, passim; Pink MSS, 307, fols. 125–126.
[306] Add. MSS, 5803 (Cole's collections), fol. 55.
[307] Mid. Temp. Rec. 2 : 462.
[308] C.S.P. Dom., 1629–1631, 28, 476.
[309] Berks Archaeological and Architectural Society Quart. Jour. 2 : 95, 1892; Cooper, Annals of Cambridge 3 : 510–511.
[310] N. and Q., 1st Ser., 12 : 359, 1855.

before he should have gone to the Short Parliament,[311] and there is no indication from the records that he was able to attend in November. He had been a member of seven earlier parliaments, and had been active in his county as a J.P., H.S., and D.L.[312] He was a member of the Council of Wales in 1633, and was named to numerous commissions for the border and midland counties.[313] Sir Thomas was probably considered one of the opposition group in 1640. He had been somewhat interested in reforms as early as the 1621 parliament,[314] and in 1637 was a ship money defaulter for one of his Herefordshire estates.[315]

Sir Thomas's estates, including considerable land he inherited from his mother, lay in the counties of Hereford, Worcester, Warwick, and in Hampshire.[316] It was said of him that "his tables were ever open to the learned, and his gates never fast to the poor." [317]

Sir Henry Ludlow (1592–1643), of Maiden Bradley, Wilts, was a member for his county, 1640–1643. He was one of the extremists of the popular party and was father of Edmund Ludlow, the regicide.[318] His family had settled in Wiltshire in the fourteenth century, and held numerous estates there and in Hampshire.[319] His father was Sir Edmund Ludlow of Hill Deverill (M.P. 1603, J.P., H.S.; d. 1624), and his mother, Sir Edmund's second wife, was Margaret, daughter of Sir Henry Manning, a courtier (Viscountess Bindon by her first marriage). An elder stepbrother, Sir Edmund's son by his first wife, was Henry Ludlow of Hill Deverill and later of Tadley, Hants (d. 1639).[320]

Born at Maiden Bradley in 1592, Ludlow studied at Brasenose College, Oxford (matriculated 1607; B.A. 1610), and in 1609 entered the Inner Temple.[321] Two years later he married Elizabeth, daughter of Richard Phelipps of Whitchurch, Dorset, a niece of Sir Edward Phelipps of Montacute, Master of the Rolls and Speaker.

Association with his wife's relatives doubtless encouraged Ludlow in his opposition views in later years. About the time of his marriage his father settled on him three manors and other properties in Wiltshire and Hampshire. By 1621 he was a knight.[322]

Ludlow entered parliament in 1614, sitting for Heytesbury and being identified as of the Inner Temple. He sat for the same borough in 1621 and 1624, being styled Sir Henry Ludlow of Horningsham.[323] He was from about this time a J.P. in Wiltshire.[324] He served on the commission concerning depopulation in 1632 and 1635, and was sheriff, 1633–1634.[325] Meanwhile his half-brother, Henry Ludlow, Esquire, of Hampshire, was a loan refuser in 1627, and in 1637 and 1638 was called before Council and held in custody pending a hearing on some unstated charge.[326] Sir Henry, the Wiltshire Ludlow, was a defaulter from the 1636 musters,[327] and with other J.P.'s was reproached in 1637 for neglecting to assist the royal purveyors of timber for the navy and was threatened with summons before the Lords for contempt.[328] He was threatened also by Laud for sending in so little money for the repair of St. Paul's.[329] He ignored the king's loan request of 1639.[330] He was not a member of the Short Parliament, but his election in October, 1640, was apparently unopposed.[331]

Sir Henry now allied himself openly with Pym's faction. He was a friend of Henry Marten, and although he did not speak frequently in the early months or serve on many committees,[332] he became bolder by the time of the attempted arrest of the five members. He even ventured in May, 1642, to challenge the king's worthiness to rule.[333] And in June he promised to furnish three horses for the defense, and three more if needed.[334] But he died a few months before John Pym, in October, 1643, and was buried on 1 November at St. Andrew's, Holborn.[335]

Ludlow came of a wealthy family and, although he was a younger son, seems to have been himself a man of

[311] He wrote in March, 1640, asking to be excused from appearing before Council, pleading ill health for the previous ten weeks. *C.S.P. Dom., 1639–1640,* 584.

[312] C. 193/12, 13; S.P. 16/405; *C.S.P. Dom., 1639,* 19; *List of Sheriffs,* 147.

[313] *Arch. Camb.,* 6th Ser., **17**: 195, 1917; C. 181/3, fols. 5v, 26; 181/4, fols. 162v, 199v; 181/5, fols. 68, 126.

[314] *Commons Debates 1621* **6**: 258, 262.

[315] S.P. 16, 365/73.

[316] William Dugdale, *The antiquities of Warwickshire,* 368–370, *passim,* later ed.; London, 1765; Lipscomb, *Buckingham* **4**: 188; *V.C.H. Hampshire* **4**: 278. Various properties are mentioned in Lucy's will, dated 22 September 1639, and proved 18 February 1640/1. P.C.C., 20 Evelyn.

[317] Burke, *Landed gentry,* 1850. See also *D.N.B.,* "Sir Thomas Lucy (1532–1600)."

[318] Ludlow is mentioned briefly in *D.N.B.,* "Edmund Ludlow (1617?–1692)."

[319] *Wilts. Arch. Mag.* **28**: 246, 1894–1896; Hoare, *Wilts.* **1** (2): 14–15; Noble, *Regicides* **2**: 10.

[320] *Wilts. Arch. Mag.* **26**: 173, 1892; *C.S.P. Dom., 1639–1640,* 335.

[321] *Al. Oxon.; Students admitted to the Inner Temple,* 189; *Cal. Inner Temp. Rec.* **2**: cix.

[322] I.P.M., Sir Edmund Ludlow, 1625, C. 142/457/86; *Wilts. Arch. Mag.* **26**: 173, 1892.

[323] *M. of P.* **1**: 454, 461; **3**: xl. His stepbrother, Henry, was M.P. in 1601 and 1604.

[324] C. 193/13; S.P. 16/405.

[325] S.P. 16, 229/112/252; C. 181/5, fol. 44; *Wilts. Arch. Mag.* **3**: 220, 1857; **26**: 173, 1892.

[326] S.P. 16, 52/67; *C.S.P. Dom., 1636–1637,* 395; *1637–1638,* 433, 443. Council ordered an inquiry about his estate in 1640. *Ibid., 1639–1640,* 335.

[327] S.P. 16, 345/99.

[328] *C.S.P. Dom., 1637,* 137.

[329] Add. MSS, 33,324, fol. 12.

[330] Rushworth **3**: 915.

[331] *Calendar of Clarendon State Papers* **1**: 209.

[332] One of his earliest committees was that on assessments for the new subsidy, 30 April 1641. *C.J.* **2**: 130.

[333] D'Ewes (C), 398; Clarendon, *Rebellion* **2**: 149 and n.; May, 230.

[334] *N. and Q., 1st Ser.,* **12**: 360, 1855.

[335] *Wilts. Arch. Mag.* **26**: 173, 1892.

means. He was not among the subscribers for the parliamentary loans of 1640 and 1641, but his offer for the defense in 1642 suggests that he had funds as well as zeal to devote to the cause.

Among Ludlow's relatives in the 1640 House were his wife's cousin, Sir Edward Phelipps, and possibly Sir John and Giles Strangways.[336]

Sir Oliver Luke (1574–c. 1650), of Haynes and Woodend in Cople, Bedfordshire, one of the knights for his county, 1640–1648, was one of the most experienced "parliament men" of the House, for, beginning with the parliament of 1597, he served either for his county or for Bedford borough in each successive parliament, except those of 1601 and 1603, until his seclusion in 1648.[337]

The descendant of an old county family, and the son and heir of Nicholas Luke of Woodend, Esq., by his wife, Margaret, daughter of Oliver, first Lord St. John of Bletsoe, he was baptized at Cople, 26 October 1574.[338] He probably matriculated at King's College, Cambridge, in 1588, and on 24 April 1592 was admitted to the Middle Temple, where he still had a chamber in 1595.[339] On 5 August 1599 he married Elizabeth, daughter and coheiress of Sir Valentine Knightley of Fawsley, Northamptonshire, so establishing a connection of importance in his political career. He was knighted at the Charter-House in 1603,[340] shortly after the birth of his eldest son Samuel (q.v.). He was a widower for some time after Lady Luke died in 1607, but had married his second wife, Maud, before June, 1616.[341]

Luke succeeded upon his father's death in 1613 to several manors and advowsons in Bedfordshire, to which he added other properties by purchase there and in Huntingdonshire, and some interests in Somerset.[342] Since the portion of one of his sisters was set at £1000, his was evidently a family of means, and he seems to have been careful, if not parsimonious, in managing his affairs.[343] His sale of some of his properties before

1640[344] may lend some color to the royalist jibe that he was "decayed in his estate,"[345] as does the absence of his name from the lists of those offering security for the loans in 1640–1641, but the comment may have been provoked by the acquiring of some "malignants'" goods by Sir Oliver and his son during the war.[346]

Luke's experience in office was extensive. Besides being often a member of parliament, he was named on various commissions in Bedfordshire and the neighboring counties,[347] and was a J.P. for both Bedford and the county throughout the reign of Charles I.[348] He was sheriff, 1617–1618,[349] and may for a time have had the stewardship of Grafton Park in Northamptonshire,[350] but was among the early members of the developing country party. His connection with the Knightleys, his friendship with Sir John Eliot, which began in the 1614 parliament and continued until Eliot's death,[351] and the family alliances with the Hampdens all illustrate the circles in which he moved. With others of his county he was threatened by Council for resisting the loan of 1621,[352] and in 1627, though named a loan commissioner, he refused to lend, and was committed to the Gate-House until shortly before the next election.[353] A decade later, although he apparently paid his ship money rates, Luke asked for lower assessments on some of his lands and seemed in no way ready to help the sheriff with his collections.[354]

In both parliaments of 1640 Sir Oliver was an active member. He was named to the committees of privilege for both, and to committees dealing with policies and grievances, including those on subsidies, ship money, the lords lieutenant, Archbishop Laud, and the breach of parliamentary privilege.[355] He undertook various types of local committee work during the war, but in 1645 supported the efforts to secure a treaty with the king.[356] He was among the Presbyterians secluded in 1648, and probably died shortly after a dangerous illness of November, 1650, certainly before 20 March 1656.[357]

Sir Oliver had numerous relatives in the 1640 House besides his son, Samuel. They included his brother-

[336] The will of Ludlow's widow, Lady Elizabeth, dated 18 May 1660, mentioned a number of Strangways grandchildren. Brown, *Somerset Wills* 5: 29.

[337] *M. of P.* 1: 432, 450, *passim*; 3: xxxvii. Sir Oliver Luke is mentioned briefly in the *D.N.B.* article on his son, Sir Samuel Luke.

[338] *Vis. Beds.*, 179–180; Blaydes, *Genealogia Bedfordiensis*, 84–85.

[339] *Al. Cant.; Mid. Temp. Rec.* 1: 327, 353.

[340] *Beds. N. and Q.* 1: 210, 1886.

[341] Dame Maud, his wife, was named in an indenture dated 22 June 1616. *Beds. Hist. Rec.* 2: 99, 1914. Her will, dated 20 March 1655/6, directed that she be buried beside her husband, already buried at Cople. Brown, *Somerset Wills* 5: 41.

[342] Lysons, *Mag. Brit.* 1: 71–72, 92–93; *V.C.H. Bedford* 2: 262, 282, 339–340; 3: 29, 193, 239; *Beds. Hist. Rec.* 2: 99, 1914; *H.M.C., Seventh Report*, House of Lords MSS, 5.

[343] His watchfulness for a sister's welfare was said to have prevented her marriage (St. Ch. 8/197/3). Various letters to his son Samuel during the war illustrate his care for his properties. Stowe MSS, 190, fols. 154v, 162, 194v, *passim*.

[344] *V.C.H. Huntingdonshire* 2: 273, 333, 335, 375.

[345] Bankes, *The story of Corfe Castle*, 227.

[346] Stowe MSS, 190, fol. 141v.

[347] C. 181/3, fols. 4v, 117; 181/4, fol. 10; 181/5, *passim*; Add. MSS, 25,302, fol. 41; *C.S.P. Dom., 1619–1623*, 463.

[348] C. 193/12, 13; C. 181/4 and 5; S.P. 16/405.

[349] *List of Sheriffs*, 3.

[350] The stewardship was vacant in 1623 (*C.S.P. Dom., 1619–1623*, 602), and Luke seems to have been in possession of Grafton Lodge in 1645. Stowe MSS, 190, fols. 154v, 162, 296.

[351] Forster, *Eliot* 1: 22; 2: 334, 690; *C.S.P. Dom., 1628–1629*, 543.

[352] S.P. 14, 127/82.

[353] S.P. 16, 89/1 and 5; *C.S.P. Dom., 1627–1628*, 44, 246, 306; Rushworth 1: 473.

[354] *Beds. Hist. Rec.* 18: 56, 59, 61, 1936.

[355] *C.J.* 2: 4, 20, 31, 45, 50, 52, 53, *passim*.

[356] Pink MSS, 307, fol. 3; *V.C.H. Bedford* 2: 44; Stowe MSS, 190, fol. 112v.

[357] Pink MSS, *loc. cit.*; Brown, *Somerset Wills* 5: 41.

in-law, Sir Miles Fleetwood, his first cousins, Sir Beauchamp St. John and Sir William Lytton, cousins by marriage, Sir Henry Wallop and Sir Thomas Barrington, and only slightly further removed, Robert Wallop, Oliver St. John, and Richard Knightley, and various others of the Barrington connection.

* Sir Samuel Luke (1603–1670), of Woodend in Cople, near Bedford, sat for that borough, 1641–1648. He was the eldest son of Sir Oliver Luke, the county member (*q.v.*), and was baptized at Southill, 27 March 1603.[358] He and a brother were granted a pass in April, 1623, for travelling in Europe for six months,[359] and in 1625 both he and his father were listed in the burgess rolls of Bedford.[360] Sir Samuel was a member of the Bedfordshire sewers commission in 1636, and a J.P. of the borough in 1640.[361] He was named in a double return from that town for the Short Parliament, but as late as four days before the end of the session had not been allowed to sit, the case still being undetermined. A similar condition followed the autumn elections, Luke's rival again being William Boteler, and Luke apparently did not begin his work in the House before August, 1641.[362]

Sir Samuel's wartime correspondence contains a few hints as to his personal character, in addition to the aspects already familiar, such as his fatherly concern for the education of his son in Italy and in the Netherlands armies, and an interest in falconry which he shared with his powerful kinsman, Lord Say and Sele.[363]

Sir Martin Lumley, Bart. (*c.* 1596–1651), of Great Bardfield, Essex, was returned to parliament, 16 February 1641 for Essex, replacing Robert Lord Rich who was called to the House of Lords, and sat until the purge of 1648. He was a Londoner in his early life, his father being Sir Martin Lumley, a wealthy draper,[364] who was Lord Mayor, 1623–1624 (d. 1634). His mother, Mary, was the daughter and heiress of Robert Withorne or Witham, citizen and upholsterer of London. Martin was born about 1596,[365] but nothing is known of his early life. He married (1) at St. Andrew's Undershaft, 15 January 1620/1, Jane, daughter

and heiress of John Meredith of Denbighshire; and (2) at St. Andrew's, 29 May 1627, Mary, daughter of Edward Allen of Finchley, a London alderman.

Meanwhile Lumley's father acquired various lands in Essex and built a fine house at Great Bardfield;[366] and in 1625 and regularly after 1631, the son was a J.P. of that county.[367] Succeeding his father in his numerous possessions in 1634, Lumley seems to have kept his residence in Essex, renting his great city house. A tenant in 1638 was the ambassador from Morocco.[368] In Essex he was on terms of neighborliness, even intimacy, with the family of Rich, Earls of Warwick,[369] and his politics and his religion attached him to the opponents of the crown. He was listed in 1636 as one of the men of quality seeking to evade the payment of ship money, but by the following spring had paid more than £19 on two of his properties.[370] Appointed sheriff in 1639, Lumley faced a Star Chamber suit in May, 1640, on the charge of negligence in collecting ship money and refusal to turn in what he had collected, a charge with some justification, it seems, for Lumley had turned in less than £174 of the £8000 assessment by May, and more than £7668 apparently remained uncollected at the end of the year.[371] He was probably confined to the Fleet in June, 1640,[372] and seems to have planned to have Oliver St. John act as his attorney.[373] As late as December, 1640, with two other sheriffs similarly accused, Lumley appealed to parliament for protection.[374] Possibly the conferring upon him of a baronetcy and knighthood in January, 1641, was intended as a peace offer, but it did not change his sentiments.

Sent to parliament for the first time the following month, Lumley was named to committee work in March,[375] and joined heartily in the work of his fellow Presbyterians. He offered his bond for £1000 on 4 March and in July lent £1000 outright. The next year he pledged four horses for the defense,[376] and during the war was a parliamentary committeeman in Essex.[377] He was a Presbyterian elder there, also,[378] and was

---

[358] *Beds. N. and Q.* 1: 353, 1886. *D.N.B.* gives no date of birth.

[359] *Acts P.C., 1621–1623,* 468.

[360] *Beds. N. and Q.* 3: 94, 1893.

[361] C. 181/5, fols. 74, 373.

[362] *M. of P.* 1: 480, 485, and notes. By error the note which refers to the Short Parliament return states that Luke was recognized on 6 August 1641. See *C.J.* 2: 239.

[363] Stowe MSS, 190, fols. 21, 44, 197v, 232v.

[364] The elder Lumley was among those assessed heavily for the 1614 subsidy, and in 1615 was the king's creditor for the sum of £692 (Lansd. MSS, 165, fol. 228v; Add. MSS, 12,498, fol. 295). He was buried magnificiently at Great St. Helen's in 1634. *Essex Review* 9: 9, 1900.

[365] He was aged twenty-three at his mother's death in 1619, and over thirty at his father's death. *Complete Baronetage* 2: 80; I.P.M., Sir Martin Lumley, C. 142/523/58.

[366] *Essex Review* 9: 8–9, 1900; Wright, *Essex* 2: 63, 543.

[367] *H.M.C., Tenth Report* 4, County of Essex MSS, 502–507; Harl. MSS, 2240, fol. 2v; C. 181/4, fol. 174.

[368] *C.S.P. Dom., 1637–1638,* 476.

[369] Miss C. Fell-Smith, Bardfield Great Lodge and the Lumleys, *Essex Review* 9: 2–19, 1900.

[370] S.P. 16, 335/67/i; 358/4, 55.

[371] *C.S.P. Dom., 1640,* 126; Add. MSS, 25,277, fols. 21–48; Royal Hist. Soc., *Trans.,* 3rd Ser., 4: 157, 1910.

[372] Bodleian Tanner MSS, 65, fol. 89.

[373] Some notes identified as St. John's are in Add. MSS, 25,277, fols. 40–43v.

[374] *H.M.C., Fourth Report,* House of Lords MSS, 30. *Cf.* Yelverton.

[375] Early appointments were concerned with Strafford's trial and with the "popish hierarchy." *C.J.* 2: 98, 105.

[376] D'Ewes (N), 438, n.; *C.J.* 2: 228–229; *N. and Q.,* 1st Ser., 12: 360, 1855.

[377] Stowe MSS, 189, fol. 5.

[378] *A.H.R.* 44: 36, n., 1938–1939.

secluded from parliament by Pride's Purge in 1648. Lumley died in October, 1651, and was buried at Great Bardfield.[379]

Having inherited the wealth his father and his maternal grandfather had made in trade, and having made good marriages, Lumley seems to have been a rich man. His properties, which included several in London and Essex, one in Huntingdonshire and some lands in Kent, amounted to over 3500 acres.[380] His contributions for the cause, 1641–1642, indicate ample means, as do the provisions of his will. Although his estate seems to have been settled by 1651, his will provided £1000 for his widow and £6000 for a younger son.[381]

Alexander Luttrell (1622–1642), of Dunster Castle, Somerset, was M.P. for Minehead, 1640–1642. His colleague for the borough was his grandfather, Sir Francis Popham (*q.v.*). He was the eldest son of Thomas Luttrell of Dunster (M.P., H.S., J.P., d. 1644), by his wife, Jane, daughter of Sir Francis Popham,[382] and was the namesake of his uncle, Alexander Popham, M.P. for Bath in 1640. He was born about 1622 and matriculated at Lincoln's College, Oxford, 24 November 1637, aged fifteen.[383] Apparently his return to parliament in 1640 was his first experience in public office, and was the result of his family's influence at Minehead.[384] He took the Protestation in May, 1641,[385] but was otherwise an unnoticed member of the House. If he followed the guidance of the Pophams, he should be considered a parliamentarian, but he was perhaps not more than a lukewarm follower, for his father surrendered Dunster Castle without much resistance to the royalist forces,[386] and a younger brother, Francis, was listed in 1660 for the Order of the Royal Oak.[387] Luttrell died in the spring of 1642, the writ for choosing his successor being ordered on 3 June of that year.[388]

Luttrell was not in possession of his paternal estate, but was the heir apparent to considerable wealth. His family owned many lands in Somerset,[389] and the estate value in 1660 was estimated to be £1500 a year.

---

[379] His will, dated 9 October, was proved 22 October 1651. P.C.C., 196 Grey.

[380] I.P.M. cited above.

[381] These sums were assigned from his personal estate and from his Kentish properties.

[382] H. C. Maxwell Lyte, *A history of Dunster and the families of Mohun and Luttrell* 1, 179, 183, 184; S.P. 16/405.

[383] *Al. Oxon.*

[384] His father had sat for Minehead in 1625 and his uncle had been elected there as well as at Bath for the Short Parliament. *M. of P.*

[385] *C.J.* 2: 133.

[386] Clarendon, *Rebellion* 3: 78. Thomas Luttrell named as one of the executors of his will the royalist, Sir William Portman, Bart. Brown, *Somerset Wills* 6: 17.

[387] *Western Antiquary* 7: 39, 1887–1888.

[388] *C.J.* 2: 604.

[389] Collinson, *Somerset* 2: 12–13; Gerard, *Partic. Descr. Somerset*, 20. His grandfather's assessments for loans and subsidies had been among the heaviest in the county. Add. MSS, 5496, fol. 100; Lansd. MSS, 165, fol. 233.

Sir William Lytton (1586–1660), of Knebworth, Hertfordshire, knight for his shire, 1640–1648, was the descendant of a family that had moved from Derbyshire into Hertfordshire in the time of Elizabeth.[390] His father, Sir Rowland Lytton (d. 1616), had been M.P., H.S., and Lord Lieutenant for Herts, and captain of the band of gentlemen pensioners; and his mother was Anne, daughter of Oliver, first Lord St. John of Bletsoe.[391] William, their eldest surviving son, was born on 29 September 1586,[392] attended Westminster School, 1601–1602, and was admitted in 1603 to Emmanuel College, Cambridge. He was still a student there in 1607.[393] He had become by that time an intimate of the Earl of Salisbury's eldest son, with whom he went on hunting trips, and whose friendship he enjoyed for many years.[394] In the summer of 1607 he journeyed into Cornwall with Sir Henry Wallop (*q.v.*), husband of his stepsister, Elizabeth, and during much of the next year was travelling abroad. He considered joining the army for Cleves in 1610, and his father hoped a year or two later to have him go with his friend, Sir Dudley Carleton, on one of his embassies,[395] but most of his career was carried out in England. He married (1) in 1612 Anne, daughter and heiress of Stephen Slaney of Norton, Salop, and (2) after 1626, Ruth, daughter of Sir Francis Barrington of Essex, and sister of Sir Thomas Barrington (*q.v.*).[396] Lytton was knighted at his mother's family home of Bletsoe in 1624, at the end of the honors list which included also his kinsmen, Sir Oliver Luke and Sir Miles Fleetwood (*q.v.*).[397]

Before his father's death Lytton had begun to perform his public services, for he was training one of the militia companies in 1615.[398] By 1620 he was a J.P. in St. Albans and in the county, an office which he long held.[399] He was among those of his county who were warned in 1622 to attend Council regarding the 1621 loan,[400] and in 1624 was chosen for Hertfordshire for his first parliament. He was sheriff the next year, 1625–1626, but was returned again for the county as

---

[390] Add. MSS, 6669, fols. 97–99.

[391] Clutterbuck, *Herts* 2: 375–377; Burke, *Landed gentry* 1: 782, 1850.

[392] The date is based upon the I.P.M. of Sir Rowland Lytton (C. 142/359/114). According to the M.I. mentioned by Clutterbuck (*Herts* 2: 384), he was aged seventy-one in 1660.

[393] Barker and Stenning, *The record of old Westminsters* 2: 602; *Al. Cant.*; *C.S.P. Dom., 1603–1610*, 375.

[394] *The letters of John Chamberlain* 1: 232, 309; Eg. MSS, 2646, fol. 84.

[395] *C.S.P. Dom., 1603–1610*, 368, 505, 629; *The letters of John Chamberlain* 1: 272, 281, 400.

[396] *Ibid.* 1: 337; I.P.M. cited above; Barker and Stenning, *loc. cit.*

[397] *The letters of John Chamberlain* 2: 574–575.

[398] *Ibid.* 1: 614.

[399] C. 181/3, fols. 1, 17; 181/5, fols. 45, 110; C. 193/12, 13; S.P. 16/405.

[400] S.P. 14, 127/77.

M.P. in 1628.[401]   Later he became a D.L., and was named to various local commissions.[402]   His politics by this time were clearly in agreement with those of his kinsmen of the Barrington clan, with whom he continued to be intimate.   In 1636 he was reported as much in arrears in ship money, but that he was so powerful a man that the bailiffs dared not collect from him by distraint.[403]   And in 1639 he declined to send a contribution to the king.[404]

In 1640 Lytton was M.P. for Herts in the Short Parliament and during the summer his house at Knebworth was probably one of the meeting places of the opposition leaders.[405]   That September he went with Capel to York to deliver personally to the king their county's petition of grievance.[406]   As a member of the Long Parliament, his place with the opposition was assured.   He was named to the Committee of Privileges and numerous others of importance, including that of the 1641 recess.[407]   In June, 1642, he promised two horses for the defense,[408] and he worked actively with Hampden in the early part of the war.   He was among those secluded in 1648, however.[409]   Lytton died on 14 August 1660, and was buried at Knebworth.   His will, dated 29 June 1660, was proved 11 May 1661.[410]

Sir William had inherited wealth from his father and in 1623 had a "windfall" of several thousand pounds and some lands from a London mayor's widow who was a relative of his wife.[411]   He owned several manors in Hertfordshire and other properties in Bedfordshire, and had enjoyed handsome dowries by his marriages.[412]   He had once bought some Virginia Company stock, but had done so at the persuasion of a friend and had quickly parted with it.[413]   He seems to have been less concerned than many of his friends and relatives with colonization schemes.   One of his sports was hawking.[414]

Through his mother Lytton was a relative of Sir Beauchamp St. John, the Lukes, and Fleetwood, and was a kinsman by marriage of the Wallops, Barrington, and the latter's numerous connection.

---

[401] M. of P. 1: 458, 475; List of Sheriffs, 64.
[402] Clutterbuck, Herts 2: 376; C. 181/5, fols. 268, 269.
[403] S.P. 16, 376/106.
[404] Rushworth 3: 912.
[405] Kingston, Herts. during the Civil War, 28, 37.
[406] Add. MSS, 11,045, fol. 121v; D'Ewes, Autobiography 2: 242.
[407] C.J. 2: 20, 24, 25, 29, 288, passim.
[408] N. and Q., 1st Ser., 12: 338, 1855.
[409] A vindication of the imprisoned and secluded members of the House of Commons, 29, London, 1649.
[410] P.C.C., 75 May.
[411] The letters of John Chamberlain 2: 498.
[412] I.P.M. (C. 142/359/114); Middlesex and Hertfordshire Notes and Queries 4: 118, 1898; H. Chauncy, The historical antiquities of Hertfordshire, 318, London, 1700; Add. MSS, 25,302, fol. 43; Stowe MSS, 744, fol. 118.
[413] Brown, Genesis of the U. S., 655–656, 938.
[414] Eg. MSS, 2646, fols. 84, 113.

John Mallory (c. 1611–1656), of Studley, was a member for Ripon, Yorkshire, from 1640 until he was disabled, 16 January 1643.[1]   The second but eldest surviving son of William Mallory (q.v.), he was born about 1611,[2] and went to school at Heversham, Westmorland.   He matriculated at Caius College, Cambridge, in 1625, was readmitted in February, 1627, and in November of that year entered the Middle Temple.[3]   Possibly he was intended for the law, but after the death of his elder brother, William, in 1636, he returned to York to learn the responsibilities of heir apparent of his family.   He married (York license, 1638) Mary, daughter and coheir of John Moseley of York.[4]   Probably he had some share in the military affairs of his county during the next two years, possibly under his father's command, but he seems to have had no political experience before 1640.

It is noted in the Ripon town records that on 8 October 1640 John Mallory, gentleman, was admitted a freeman of the borough,[5] and on the following day he was elected with his father as M.P.   He divided his time, however, between attendance at Westminster and business in Yorkshire, apparently with the army.   On 12 December he was granted leave of absence on employment for the king's business and his own.[6]   He was probably present to vote against Strafford's attainder,[7] and seems to have been in the House on 7 May, although his name is missing from the lists of those who took the Protestation that month; and when his father left for Yorkshire at the end of July he was instructed to send up his son to the service of the House.[8]   After the recess he spoke against the militia bill, 7 December 1641, and on December 23 he was knighted.[9]   In the late winter of 1642 he was reported to be back in his county.[10]   He was absent at the call, 16 June 1642, and on the date of his father's disablement in September was ordered to put in an appearance within three weeks.   His own disablement for appearing in arms for the king followed on 16 January 1643.[11]

Mallory began his compounding proceedings in 1646 after his father's death.   He declared he had had but a small allowance during his father's lifetime, though he held in his wife's right some properties worth £100 a year and the value of his inherited properties was about £376 a year, with the expectation of another £200.   Later reports accused him of considerably underestimating the values, and his fine was set first at a half,

---

[1] He was disabled again, 22 January 1644. C.J. 2: 929; 3: 374.
[2] Visitation of Yorkshire in 1584/5 and 1612, 157.
[3] Al. Cant.
[4] Y.A.S. Rec. Ser. 40: 119 and n., 1909.
[5] Ripon MSS, Old Towne Book, 1607–1666, fol. 362.
[6] C.J. 2: 49.
[7] Verney, 58. See also William Mallory.
[8] C.J. 2: 138, 231, 265.
[9] D'Ewes (C), 246–247 and n.
[10] Fairfax correspondence 2: 376, 384.
[11] C.J. 2: 626, 754, 929.

£3323, and then changed in 1649 to a third, £2210.[12] He and his father had each been assessed £1000 for the "twentieth" and "fifth" in 1644.[13] Having paid his heavy fine, Sir John died on 23 January 1655/6, and was buried in Ripon Minster.[14]

William Mallory (c. 1579–1646), of Studley, Ripon, Yorkshire, was M.P. for Ripon, 1640–6 September 1642. His family had been prominent in Yorkshire during the previous century, and held part of their lands under the Archbishop of York, for whom they acted sometimes as stewards of Ripon.[15] Mallory's grandfather, Sir William Mallory (d. 1603), was sheriff and M.P., and in his later years, although he had been favorable to Catholicism, took an active part officially against recusants.[16] Sir William's son, Sir John Mallory (d. about 1620), was a J.P., M.P., and member of the Council of the North.[17] William Mallory, eldest son of Sir John by his first wife, Anne, daughter of William Lord Eure,[18] was born about 1579 or 1580.[19] He was admitted pensioner at Caius College, Cambridge, in 1594, after having attended school at Thirsk, and was readmitted in 1595.[20] In 1599 he married Alice, daughter of Sir James Bellingham of Over Levens, Westmorland, sister of Sir Henry Bellingham (q.v.).[21] By her he had three children, William (d. 1636),[22] John (q.v.), and Alice, who married Richard Aldborough (q.v.).[23]

The matter of recusancy within the family and the stand which the head of the house should take toward recusants officially continued to be a problem for the Mallorys.[24] For some years after 1603 William Mallory and his father were involved in quarrels with a neighboring J.P., Stephen Proctor of Fountains Abbey, who had quarrelled with Sir William before them, and now brought suits in Star Chamber accusing them of hindering him in his investigations concerning the gunpowder conspiracy. On the second occasion, 1614, when William was named one of the defendants with his father, they raised the plea of parliamentary privilege, and Proctor's imprisonment in the Tower for violating it was cited in the debates of 1621.[25] As late as 1625 hints of William's insincerity, apparently in religious matters, were still considered good campaign material at elections.[26]

Whatever may have been Mallory's personal religious views, he was by 1621 a full fledged member of the growing country group. He had served his parliamentary apprenticeship in 1614 for Ripon,[27] had begun his long service as a J.P. by 1618,[28] and with his election for Ripon again in 1621 came into national prominence. He spoke frequently and vigorously in the debates, attacking the evils in the commonwealth, the hindrances to free elections, and the abuses of parliamentary privileges. And though he affirmed his loyalty to the king, he did not hesitate on one occasion (9 March) to declare that he feared not those who sat in thrones or chairs.[29] His reward, which he seems to have anticipated, was several months' imprisonment in the Tower and then at home after the parliament, along with Coke and Sir Robert Phelipps.[30] In the succeeding parliaments, 1624, 1625, 1628, in which he sat for Ripon, Mallory worked with the reform party.[31]

In spite of his anti-court attitude in parliament, Mallory served as a commissioner for the loans on privy seals in 1626,[32] and was named a commissioner in 1629 for raising the subsidy.[33] He paid a heavy fine of £50 to the knighthood commissioners about 1630.[34] During the following decade he concerned himself with affairs at Ripon and with his duties as a country magistrate.[35] He had a command in the trained bands, also,[36] and

[12] *Cal. Com. Comp.*, 1008; *Y.A.S. Rec. Ser.* **18**: 135–137, 1895.
[13] *Cal. Com. Adv. Money*, 436.
[14] T. D. Whitaker, *The history and antiquities of the deanery of Craven*, 412 and n., 3rd ed., Morant, London, 1878.
[15] *Ripon Millenary Record* **2**: 37, Ripon, 1886–1891.
[16] Gooder, *Parl. Rep. York* **2**: 30–31.
[17] *V.C.H. York, North Riding* **1**: 403–404; Sir John Mallory's I.P.M. (1621), C. 142/708/102; *Ripon Millenary Record* **2**: xiii.
[18] Brown, *Genesis of the U. S.*, 940.
[19] He was aged five at the 1585 visitation (*Ripon Millenary Record* **2**: xiii), but was sixteen when he entered college in 1594. He was over forty at the time of his father's death.
[20] *Al. Cant.*
[21] Alice was buried in her father's parish church in May, 1611. *Yorks. Arch. Jour.* **10**: 169 and n., 1889.
[22] Administration of the younger William's estate was recorded at York on 17 September 1636 (*Y.A.S. Rec. Ser.* **35**: 205, 1905). W. D. Pink, who missed this fact, identified the 1640 M.P. as the son (Pink MSS, 319 and 322).
[23] Two other children died early. *Ripon Millenary Record* **2**: xiii–xiv.
[24] His father's brother, Robert, was said to be turning papist in 1594 (Lansd. MSS, 77, fol. 48), and one Christopher Mallory, gent., of Ripon, who had been living abroad for two decades, was examined in 1628 as to his conformity (*C.S.P. Dom., 1628–1629*, 343). A religious survey of the Ripon area in 1604, however, lists no Mallory as a recusant or non-communicant. Bodleian Rawl. MSS, B 452, fols. 18–21.

[25] Star Chamber bills, 1604 and 1614 (St. Ch. 8/227/1, 37); *Commons Debates 1621* **6**: 352.
[26] *Fairfax correspondence* **1**: 6–7.
[27] *M. of P.* **3**: xli.
[28] S.P. 14, 97/51; C. 181/3, fols. 11, 125; C. 193/12, 13.
[29] *M. of P.* **3**: iii, n.; *Commons Debates 1621* **2**: 484; **3**: 436–437; **5**: 283, *passim*.
[30] *Acts P.C., 1621–1623*, 119, 308, 396; *C.S.P. Dom., 1619–1623*, 336, 339; *The diary of Walter Yonge, Esq.*, 49, Camden Society, 1848.
[31] *M. of P.*; Forster, *Eliot* **1**: 153; Add. MSS, 32,324, fol. 8; *Commons Debates in 1625*, v, 7, Camden Society, 1873.
[32] S.P. 16, 45/12/ii. His own assessment was 13 *l.* 6 *s.* 8 *d. Acts P.C., 1625–1626*, 429.
[33] *Fairfax correspondence* **1**: 210, n.
[34] *Y.A.S. Rec. Ser.* **61**: 98, 1920.
[35] Ripon Borough MSS, Ripon Old Towne Book, 1607–1666, fols. 262, 263; *Y.A.S. Rec. Ser.* **27**: 229, 1899; *C.S.P. Dom., 1635–1636*, 418; *Yorks. Arch. Jour.* **5**: 378, 1879.
[36] Bean, *Northern Counties*, 1038.

joined in the request of 1639 that at least some of the forces be left in the county for its defense.[37]

Mallory attended both parliaments of 1640, having as his colleague in November his son and heir, John. But his old fire had left him. While he was named to several early committees, and spoke against Finch,[38] he seems to have been more concerned with the plight of his county than with matters of liberty.[39] The "Mr. Mallory" named in the list of "Straffordians" was more probably his son than he;[40] John seems to have taken a distaste for the way things were going earlier than did his father. On 31 July 1641 William Mallory was granted leave of absence, with the instruction that he should send his son back to the House; and it seems likely that it was the impetuous son rather than the father who spoke against the militia bill on December 7.[41] William Mallory was disabled before his son, however, for aiding the king in Yorkshire, 6 September 1642.[42] But he probably left to his son the role of fighting for the king, for when he began his compounding proceedings on 28 November 1645 he declared that he had not borne arms, and had been living quietly for the past two years. He was weak from illness then and he died on 13 March 1646 before he had completed his composition.[43] He was buried in Ripon Minster.

Mallory and his son were assessed £1000 each by the Committee for Advance of Money in 1644.[44] But his once good estate, which had included three or parts of three manors near Ripon,[45] had so declined by the time he made his will, 9 January 1645, that he feared his personal estate would not cover his obligations. Most of his lands by that time, of course, had been settled on his son,[46] and it was Sir John Mallory who arranged for the heavy fine imposed on their estates for their royalism.

Mallory was related by blood and by marriage, particularly through his wife's family, with a number of his fellow M.P.'s of 1640.

Ambrose Manaton (d. 1651), Recorder of Launceston, Cornwall, was M.P. for that borough, 1640–22 January 1644. Identified sometimes as of Trecarrel and South Petherwyn, Manaton was the second son of Peter Manaton of Manaton (Manington), by his wife,

Frances, daughter and coheiress of Edward Couch of Houghton. An uncle, Ambrose Manaton, commanded a merchant ship serving under Sir Francis Drake.[47] The date of Manaton's birth is uncertain, but it was probably between 1590 and 1600, for he was admitted to Lincoln's Inn on 7 November 1612. He was eventually called to the bar in February, 1637, and the next month was made an Associate of the Bench, his friend, John Glanville, backing the move. He was by this time a Master of Chancery Extraordinary.[48] About the same period he succeeded Glanville as recorder at Launceston.[49]

But Manaton had not spent all his time at the law courts. He was M.P. for Bossiney in 1621 and for Tregony in 1624,[50] and from about the same period served as a J.P. in Cornwall.[51] He was one of the loan commissioners in 1626 who joined with Sir Richard Buller and others in protesting against the loan, and was threatened at the time with removal from the commission of the peace, although he escaped being called before Council for a reprimand.[52] He was a loan refuser again in 1639,[53] sat for Launceston in the Short Parliament,[54] and was still on terms of intimacy with the popular party leader, Buller, the following summer.[55] As mayor of Camelford he signed the election indenture of that borough in October.[56]

In the Long Parliament Manaton was at the start an active member, working with the reform group. He was named to various committees, including those on the Stannaries, the Court of Wards, and the act for barring the clergy from lay offices.[57] But he was frequently absent in 1642, since he opposed war, and he tried as late as September of that year to avert hostilities in Cornwall.[58] He was eventually disabled in 1644 for having deserted the House, and was present at Oxford that year to be created D.C.L.[59] He was host at his house at Trecarrel to the king that year, too.[60]

[37] H.M.C., Twelfth Report 2, Coke MSS, 208.
[38] C.J. 2: 42, 48; Note book of Sir John Northcote, 94–95.
[39] Two of the three remarks D'Ewes recorded in the early months were of this nature. D'Ewes (N), 67, 432.
[40] Verney, 58. His son-in-law, Aldborough, was listed also. John Mallory, however, was absent frequently and this vote may have been his father's.
[41] C.J. 2: 231; D'Ewes (C), 246–247 and n.
[42] C.J. 2: 754.
[43] Cal. Com. Comp., 1008; S.P. 23/193/624.
[44] Cal. Com. Adv. Money, 436.
[45] Yorks. Arch. Jour. 32: 65, 79, n., 1935; Y.A.S. Rec. Ser. 58: 233, 1917.
[46] Mallory's will, proved at York, 23 January 1667. York Probate Registry 48, fol. 161.

[47] Vivian, Vis. Cornwall, 305; Western Antiquary 9: 88, 1889–1890.
[48] Linc. Inn Rec. Adm. 1: 160; Black Books 2: 342, 343.
[49] Glanville was recorder there as late as 1630, and the first appearance of Manaton as recorder among the borough manuscripts was in March, 1637/8. Since some of the manuscripts for the years immediately preceding 1638 are missing, it is possible that Manaton was serving as recorder before that, or possibly as Glanville's deputy. Launceston Borough MSS, Stewards' Accounts, 1621–1622; Mayors' Court Books, 1624–1630, 1638–1639, 1641–1642.
[50] Willis 3: 177, 188.
[51] C. 193/12, 13; S.P. 14, 144/10/i; S.P. 16, 190/6, 7, 89; S.P. 16/405.
[52] S.P. 16, 54/20; C.S.P. Dom., 1627–1628, 232, 254.
[53] Rushworth 3: 913.
[54] Willis 3: 230.
[55] The Buller Papers, 26.
[56] C. 219/43/Part 1.
[57] C.J. 2: 29, 87, 99, passim.
[58] Coate, Cornwall in the great Civil War, 36, 37.
[59] C.J. 3: 374; Wood, Fasti Oxon. 2: 66.
[60] Courtney, Parl. Rep. Corn., 364.

Eventually Manaton compounded for his delinquency. He died on 1 June 1651 and was buried at South Petherwyn.[61] He appears to have been a pious man and a genuine lover of peace. He closed his will with a prayer for "more patience and peace and truth here on Earth."[62]

Manaton married twice. His first wife, who died in 1638, was Anne, daughter of Piers Edgcombe of Mount Edgcombe, and widow of Richard Trefusis. Through her Manaton was an uncle of Piers and Richard Edgcombe, the young Cornish royalists who were M.P.'s in 1640. Piers Manaton described in his will as a "truly noble and good gentleman." Manaton's second wife, Jane, who proved Manaton's will is otherwise unknown.

In addition to his income from his practice, Manaton seems to have enjoyed at least a moderate income from lands. His holdings in Devon and Cornwall before the war brought him about £550 a year, and his assessment by the Committee for the Advance of Money was £800. His fine as a delinquent, set at a tenth of two years' value, £700, was increased by £38 before his estates were discharged.[63] But when Manaton wrote his will in 1650, he planned portions of £1000 and £900 for his two young daughters, somewhat larger sums than the estimated value of his lands would seem to warrant.

William Marlott (1574–1646), of Shoreham, was M.P. for New Shoreham from 1640 until his death in 1646.[64] He probably came of the family seated at Mundham in Itchingfield, Sussex, from the fourteenth century, but should not be confused with his contemporaries of the same name who are commonly identified as of that place. These were William Marlott, "the elder" (1590–1652), and his son, William Marlott (1620–1657). The M.P. was probably an uncle of the first named, and the third son of Thomas Marlott of Itchingfield, gentleman (d. 1601), by his first wife. He was baptized on 30 May 1574, and was married in 1612 or earlier,[65] but nothing more is known of him until 1624. He was elected that year to parliament for Shoreham and was regularly chosen thereafter, serving in five parliaments before the autumn of 1640.[66] In 1630 and 1637 as "William Marlott of Shoreham, Esq.," he was named on the Sussex sewers commission.[67] The William Marlott who reported on admiralty matters in 1628 and was a deputy vice admiral in 1637 was possibly his nephew;[68] for either the nephew or his son was acting in that capacity in 1652.[69]

Although the Marlotts of Itchingfield seem to have been royalists, the Shoreham M.P. worked with parliament until his death[70] He was not prominent in the House, and was absent on parliamentary business in February, 1644, but he took the Covenant on 27 March,[71] and on 11 September 1645 was voted £4 a week for maintenance.[72] He was buried at Shoreham, 8 February 1646, leaving a widow, Mary, to whom administration of his estate was granted the following July.[73]

Nothing definite can be said of Marlott's occupation or financial condition. The Marlotts of Itchingfield owned in 1649 some malthouses in Shoreham,[74] which may once have been his. And a daughter of the Itchingfield family married around 1650 a Shoreham merchant.[75] Very possibly the M.P. was a tradesman of some kind, but he apparently was not wealthy.

* Henry Marten (1602–1680), of Beckett in Shrivenham, Berkshire, and of London, member for Berkshire, 1640–1653, was the heir of Sir Henry Marten (d. 1641), M.P., J.P., judge and member of the Court of High Commission. He was educated at Oxford and the Inner Temple,[76] and by foreign travel. He seems to have married twice, his first (?) wife being Elizabeth, daughter of of Sir Richard Lovelace of Hurley, and sister of the wife of Sir George Stonehouse (q.v.).[77] His marriage with Margaret Staunton, widow of a wealthy London grocer, occurred apparently between 1631 and 1635.[78]

---

[61] Vivian, loc. cit.

[62] His will was dated 26 October 1650 and was proved in 1651. P.C.C., 161 Grey.

[63] Cal. Com. Adv. Money, 423; S.P. 23/199/475–477, 485–487; Cal. Com. Comp., 1084.

[64] M. of P. 1: 495 and n.; O.P.H. 9: 5.

[65] Sussex Arch. Coll. 40: 126–129, 1896; 41: 108–109, 114–115, 1897; Berry, Sussex Genealogies, 122. The M.P. is referred to once in the Journals (3: 173, 18 July 1643) as "senior," a title by which the elder Marlott of Itchingfield has sometimes been distinguished from his own son. However, that adjective in 1643 was appropriate for Marlott of Shoreham, since he was a generation older than William of Itchingfield. The death dates seem to make it clear that the Shoreham man was the M.P.

[66] M. of P. 1: 460, 466, 472, 478, 483.

[67] C. 181/4, fol. 47; 181/5, fol. 139.

[68] C.S.P. Dom., 1627–1628, 572; 1637, 112, 314.

[69] Sussex Arch. Coll. 41: 96, 97, 1897.

[70] Ibid. 41: 95–96, 1897.

[71] C.J. 3: 389; Sussex Arch. Coll. 5: 102, 1852.

[72] C.J. 4: 272.

[73] Sussex Arch. Coll. 41: 113, 1897.

[74] Ibid. 40: 128, 1896; I.P.M.'s, C. 142/242/24 and 254/85; will of William Marlott of Itchingfield (1652), P.C.C., 149 Brent.

[75] Vis. Sussex, 1662, 91.

[76] Al. Oxon. The Henry Marten who entered Gray's Inn in 1618 (D.N.B.) was styled the son of Henry Marten of Blackfriars, Esq. (Gray's Inn Adm. Reg., 142). The M.P.'s father, however, had been knighted in 1617, and Henry himself was still at Oxford in 1619.

[77] Elias Ashmole, The history and antiquities of Berkshire, 207, Reading, 1736. Stonehouse, whose marriage occurred in 1633, was addressed as his cousin by Marten in an undated letter mentioned by John Aubrey (Brief lives [Clark] 2: 46, Oxford, 1890). More distant connections by this marriage were Thomas Lord Wentworth and Henry Coke.

[78] Mrs. Staunton's first husband's estate was valued at £10,500 in 1637, one-third of it being payable to a daughter. London Corporation MSS, Rep. 49, fol. 352; Rep. 51, fols. 92–93.

Marten served as a J.P. in Berkshire for some years,[79] and was a member of the sewers commission there and in Wiltshire and Gloucestershire.[80] The Short Parliament was his first. Even in the Long Parliament, according to Aubrey, he was wont to sleep much in the House.[81]

Marten was the heir apparent to a rich patrimony, said to be worth £3000 a year,[82] and had married well, but was reputedly costing his father £1000 a year in 1639. He declined to advance money to the king that year,[83] but his father lent to the crown £3000 about that time.[84] In 1641 Henry Marten pledged £2000 for the use of the state, on behalf of his father, himself, and the other Berkshire burgesses,[85] and in 1642 promised the maintenance of six horses for the defense.[86] Eventually he sold various properties in Berkshire for the payment of his debts.[87]

Sir William Masham, Bart. (1592–1656), of Otes in High Laver, Essex, was M.P. for his county, 1640–1653. He was the descendant of an old Yorkshire family, the grandson of a prominent London merchant and alderman, William Masham (d. 1575), and the son of William Masham of London (d. 1605), purchaser of the Otes estate, by Alice Calton.[88] He was born in 1592,[89] matriculated at Magdalen College, Oxford, in 1607, as "of London," and entered the Inner Temple in 1610 as "of Creetingham, Suffolk." [90] Before 1616 he married into the wealthy puritan family of Barrington, his wife being Elizabeth, daughter of Sir Francis Barrington, and widow of Sir James Altham.[91] By this marriage Masham was linked with many prominent east county families, including that of Hampden and others who in 1640 were of the opposi-

tion group. He was created a baronet in December, 1621.

By this time Masham had begun to show his political views. He was summoned with his father-in-law that year to attend Council for having resisted the loan, and in 1625 was again warned to appear.[92] He was elected M.P. for Maldon, 1624, 1625, and 1626, and was now a J.P. in Essex and a member of the commission of oyer and terminer.[93] In October, 1626, he and his father-in-law, having recently been removed from the commission of the peace, declined to serve as commissioners for the new loan, and were imprisoned with other obstructors of the measure. Masham was committed to the Fleet,[94] but was released before the next parliament. He was elected M.P. for Colchester in 1628, having the support of the common burgesses rather than the corporation, and as such was recognized by the Committee of Privileges.[95] By 1631 Sir William had become a J.P. once more, and he served regularly thereafter, and on other local commissions.[96] He seems to have escaped the office of sheriff in 1631, however.[97] He and his brother-in-law, Sir Thomas Barrington (q.v.), were called before the Admiralty officials in 1633 for having failed as justices to assist the saltpetre men in their work in the county, and Masham's case was referred to Council, but was dropped in February, 1634.[98] It is not surprising to find that he was distrained for refusing to pay ship money on the 1636 writ, but he was credited in March, 1637, with having paid nearly £16 on two properties.[99] Masham was naturally among those selected as county spokesmen in 1640, being returned to parliament for Colchester in March and for the county in the autumn.

Besides being active in Essex, Masham was concerned also in colonial affairs before 1640. He had an interest in the Virginia Company in 1623,[100] and was a friend of John Winthrop. And two men who had been chaplains in his home gained prominence in New England, Roger Williams and John Norton.[101] It is not known whether he was connected with the Providence

[79] C. 193/13; S.P. 16/405; C.S.P. Dom., 1634–1635, 444.
[80] C. 181/5, fols. 42, 270.
[81] Quoted in Lipscomb, Buckingham 4: 557, n.
[82] Noble, Regicides 2: 45–46.
[83] Rushworth 3: 912.
[84] S.P. 16, 453/74.
[85] C.J. 2: 273.
[86] N. and Q., 1st Ser., 12: 338, 1855.
[87] V.C.H. Berks. 3: 175; 4: 464, 533, 535, passim. His entire remaining estate at the time of his attainder was estimated as worth about £1000 a year, of which £400 were his wife's jointure, but the whole was so heavily burdened with obligations of some £30,000 that the encumbrances were said to be twice as great as the price that could be got by sale. H.M.C., Thirteenth Report 4, MSS of Captain Loder-Symonds, 399–400.
[88] Morant, Essex 1: 141; Essex Review 5: 198, 1896; Add. MSS, 19,079, fol. 37v. His father was possibly the William Masham who was imprisoned in connection with Essex's treason, paid a heavy fine, and petitioned early in James's reign for redress. Bodleian Tanner MSS, 76, fols. 98v–99v.
[89] I.P.M., William Masham, Esq., C. 142/294/112; Wright, Essex 2: 346 and n.
[90] Al. Oxon. Creetingham was one of his father's properties (I.P.M. cited above).
[91] Their eldest son was aged eighteen in 1634. Vis. Essex 1: 445.

[92] C.S.P. Dom., 1619–1623, 349; S.P. 14, 127/82; S.P. 16, 522/120.
[93] C. 193/13; C. 181/3, fol. 120; H.M.C., Tenth Report 4, County of Essex MSS, 502.
[94] Birch, The court and times of Charles the First 1: 161–162; Acts P.C., 1626, 328.
[95] The corporation had returned Cheeke and Edward Alford (M. of P. 1: 475), but Masham was recognized on the basis of the broader franchise (transcription of a report by the committee, Bristol Public Library MSS, Bristol Collection, 10160, fol. 102).
[96] H.M.C., Tenth Report 4, County of Essex MSS, 503, 504; C. 193/13; C. 181/4, fols. 23, 72; 181/5, fols. 16, 55, passim.
[97] Eg. MSS, 2645, fol. 319.
[98] C.S.P. Dom., 1633–1634, 281, 289, passim.
[99] S.P. 16, 335/67/i, 358/16, 134.
[100] Kingsbury, Records of the Virginia Company 4: 214.
[101] Royal Hist. Soc., Trans., 1st Ser., 10: 269–270, 1882; Winthrop Papers 1: 367 and n.; 2: 33, n., 1929; Eg. MSS, 2643, fol. 3.

Island Company with which so many of his friends and relatives were associated, but he no doubt watched it, too, with interest.

In the Long Parliament Masham was named on the Committee of Privileges and on others of importance, working regularly with Pym's party. He presented his county's petition against the hierarchy in January, 1641,[102] and as war drew near, paid £600 for reducing the Irish rebellion, and pledged four horses for the defense.[103] He was a committeeman during the war, was taken as a hostage by the royalists in 1648 and was apparently exchanged for John Ashburnham, an honor which indicates the important place Masham had in the puritan faction.[104] Although he had been an elder in the Essex presbytery, he remained in parliament after 1648. He was named a commissioner for the trial of the king and, though he did not act as one of the judges, afterwards served his kinsman, Cromwell, in several high posts.[105] He made his will on 18 March 1656, and died before 1 July of that year.[106]

Masham's estate included properties in Suffolk, Middlesex, and Essex,[107] and he was able, in spite of the expenses his resistance to royal pressure must have involved, to offer substantial monetary support to the popular cause. He may not have been so wealthy as his wife's family, the Barringtons, but his means were undoubtedly ample.

Sir William's relatives in the 1640 parliament were numerous. Besides his wife's brother, brothers-in-law, cousins and nephews,[108] there was Oliver St. John, whose first wife was Masham's stepdaughter and who was living with her in the Masham home in 1630.[109] Another intimate friend was Sir John Trevor, whose daughter, Elizabeth,[110] was the wife of Masham's elder son, William.[111]

Sir Edward Master, or Masters (1574–1648), of Ospringe, East Langdon, and Canterbury, was M.P. for Canterbury from 1640 until his death. The descendant of a line of Sandwich citizens, he was the eldest son of James Master (d. 1631) of East Langdon, near Dover, who obtained a grant of arms in 1608. His mother was Martha Norton of London. Born

about 1574,[112] he probably matriculated at Clare, Cambridge, about 1593. He entered Gray's Inn in 1595 and was called to the bar there in 1603.[113] The preceding year he married Ethelreda, or Audrey, Streynsham, daughter and coheiress of Robert Streynsham of Ospringe, secretary to the Earl of Pembroke, and received with her the estate of Ospringe where he took up his residence.[114] He was knighted on 7 June 1630.[115]

Sir Edward's father, James Master, seems to have opposed the loans of 1621 and 1627 to the extent of being summoned before Council,[116] but of the son little was heard until after his father's death. From 1631 to 1639 he served on some local commissions for highways and sewers, and in 1637 he was a warden for a hospital at Sandwich.[117] He was sheriff for his county in 1639, and though he collected some ship money, failed with a considerable portion of his allotment.[118] That year he was commander of a company of trained bands from Canterbury.[119] With his son-in-law, John Nutt (q.v.), he carried the Short Parliament election there amidst some tumult, winning over candidates proposed by the Archbishop and the Lord Chamberlain.[120] Doubtless the city's preference for local men of popular views accounts for their return again in the autumn.

In the Long Parliament Master was not frequently named to committees, possibly because of his age, but he was named to at least one.[121] In July, 1641, he promised to lend £500 for the public service, and in June, 1642, he pledged £100 for the defense at once and another £100 within a month.[122] He was sent into Kent to the assizes that year and was named to the parliamentary wartime committees for the county. He seems to have kept his place in the House until he died, 3 August 1648. He was buried in St. Michael's Chapel, Canterbury Cathedral.[123] His will, dated 18 May, was proved by his widow, 21 August 1648.[124] Numerous children, including his heir, Edward, and James, D.C.L., survived.

Master's estates included chiefly lands near Sandwich and Romney inherited from his father, and those he

[102] C.J. 2: 21, passim; D'Ewes (N), 249.

[103] C.S.P. Ireland, Adventurers, 105; N. and Q., 1st Ser., 12: 360, 1855.

[104] Add. MSS, 19,398, fol. 174; Essex Review 34: 210, 1925; D.N.B. article on Ashburnham.

[105] A.H.R. 44: 31, n. (32), 1938–1939; Sanford, St. and ill., 257; Bodleian Carte MSS, 74, fol. 416; Noble, Regicides 2: 62.

[106] Letters of administration were issued 1 July 1656. P.C.C., 255 Berkeley.

[107] I.P.M., C. 142/294/112; Add. MSS, 19,079, fols. 25v, 37v.

[108] For their names, see Sir Thomas Barrington.

[109] Eg. MSS, 2645, fols. 120, 154, 196.

[110] Arch. Camb., 6th Ser., 5: opp. 100, 1905. Marsham's will mentioned this daughter-in-law and named Trevor one of his executors.

[111] Additional references: Complete Baronetage 1: 182; M. of P. 1: 457, 463, passim.

[112] Arch. Cant. 5: 238–241, 1863; Boys, Sandwich, 358.

[113] Al. Cant.; Gray's Inn Adm. Reg., 88. He was probably not the Edward Master of Kent who matriculated at Oxford, 1604, aged seventeen, although that has been suggested. Al. Oxon.

[114] Arch. Cant. 5: 239, 241, 1863; Hasted, Kent 6: 526.

[115] Al. Cant.

[116] S.P. 14, 127/82; S.P. 16, 89/1.

[117] C. 181/4, fol. 88v; 181/5, fols. 135, 292; Boys, Sandwich, 167.

[118] Sandwich Borough MSS, S/N/1; List of Sheriffs, 69; Royal Hist. Soc., Trans., 3rd Ser., 4: 158, 1910.

[119] Canterbury City MSS, Burghmote, 1630–1658, fol. 156 c.

[120] Ibid., fol. 151v; Add. MSS, 11,045, fol. 99v; C.S.P. Dom., 1639–1640, 562; Willis 3: 232.

[121] C.J. 2: 75.

[122] C.J. 2: 222; N. and Q., 1st Ser., 12: 359, 1855.

[123] Arch. Cant. 2: 182, 1859; 5: 241, 1863; 9: 33, 1874.

[124] P.C.C., 128 Essex.

acquired near Canterbury by marriage.[125] His contribution for the defense in 1642 was not small, and his will reveals plans for portions of £1000 each for three unmarried daughters. It mentions also a joint venture with Sir Edward Partridge (q.v.) of £300 for Irish lands.[126]

Sir Thomas Walsingham had a slight family connection with Master, having married the widow of Master's brother, Nathaniel.[127]

Roger Matthew (d. 1646), merchant of Dartmouth, Devon, sat for his borough from 1640 until he was disabled, 5 February 1644. He was probably a native of Dartmouth, was possibly the Roger Matthew who married in 1599 a widow named Joan Carnes,[128] and was certainly the one who married Joan Martin at St. Saviour's Church, Dartmouth, on 16 November 1607.[129] In 1615-1616 Matthew was Receiver for his borough,[130] and he represented it in every parliament from 1621 to 1629.[131] He was possibly mayor of Dartmouth in 1624,[132] and was holding that office, 1639-1640.[133] He was a shipowner and was interested in overseas trade. In 1628 with others he secured letters of marque for two ships, and in 1634 he spent several weeks in London attending Council hearings requested by Trinity House concerning vessels used in the fish trade from Newfoundland, and finally asked to be allowed to return to Dartmouth because he had fishing ships then bound for sea.[134]

In politics Matthew seems to have supported the country party in the 1620's. He spoke in the 1621 parliament against the excessive fees exacted by the customs officials,[135] and in 1629, with the Reverend John White of Dorchester, he sought access to Eliot and the others imprisoned in the Tower.[136] He was

named a commissioner on exacted fees in Devon in 1638.[137] Matthew was named to several committees touching commercial matters in the Long Parliament, and was outspoken where the merchants' interests were involved.[138] At the outbreak of the war he promised to supply a horse and £50 for the defense, and advanced over £300 toward the reducing of Ireland.[139] By 1644, however, he had deserted Westminster, and although he was granted a respite to explain his absence on 22 January, he was disabled on 5 February, and was afterwards committed to the Tower for his disloyalty.[140] Released on bail, he petitioned to compound in March, 1646, declaring that he had gone to the Oxford parliament as a move for peace, but had maintained six soldiers and two sons in the service of parliament.[141] He died a few weeks afterwards, being buried at St. Margaret's, Westminster, in July[142] His will, dated 4 November 1645, was proved by his widow on 10 August 1646.[143]

Matthew seems to have been an enterprising merchant, investing his money in lands as well as in ships and goods. His compounding papers, which reveal only his real estate, including his chief residence in Townstal parish near Dartmouth and other Devon properties, record values of nearly £180 a year. His fine, reckoned at a half, £1000, or a third, £666, was greatly reduced upon review.[144]

He was probably elected to the 1640 parliament as a man able to speak for his fellow merchants and shipowners, and one unafraid of the royal administration, even though he turned later, as did his neighbor, Edward Seymour of Berry Pomeroy, to the support of the king.

* Thomas Mauleverer (1599–c. 1655), of Allerton Mauleverer, Yorkshire (created baronet, 1641), the regicide, was M.P. for Boroughbridge, 1640-1653. Born in April, 1599,[145] he matriculated at St. John's, Cambridge, in 1616, and went from there to Gray's Inn.[146] He was a J.P. in Yorkshire by 1630, possibly before,[147] but had sat in no parliament before his election in the autumn of 1640.

Mauleverer inherited from his father three Yorkshire

---

[125] I.P.M., James Master, C. 142/480/115; Hasted, *Kent* **6**: 526; **8**: 100.

[126] His £300 was included in Partridge's pledge of £600. *C.S.P. Ireland, Adventurers*, 73.

[127] *Arch. Cant.* **5**: 239, 1863.

[128] Transcript of Townstal Parish (Dartmouth) Register (Devon and Cornwall Record Society MSS at the Exeter City Library).

[129] Transcript of St. Saviour's Parish Register (Devon and Cornwall Record Society MSS). Matthew mentions his wife Joan in his will, as well as his son's grandfather, Martin (P.C.C. 123 Twisse). With one possible exception the children of Roger Matthew, M.P., were born after 1607 (St. Saviour's Register and Townstal Register). Another Roger Matthew was living in Dartmouth in 1597, but had died by 1616 (St. Saviour's Register).

[130] E. Windeatt, The Borough of Clifton-Dartmouth-Hardness and Its Mayors and Mayoralties, Devon *Trans.* **44**: 652, 1912.

[131] *M. of P.*

[132] His son, Robert, was baptized on 19 September 1624 as the son of Roger "maior." St. Saviour's Register.

[133] Devon *Trans.* **44**: 661, 1912.

[134] *C.S.P. Dom., 1628-1629*, 439; *1633-1634*, 532-533.

[135] *Commons Debates 1621* **3**: 186.

[136] *C.S.P. Dom., 1628-1629*, 543.

[137] C. 181/5, fol. 218.

[138] *C.J.* **2**: 75, 82, 750; D'Ewes (C), 114, n., 117.

[139] *N. and Q.*, 1st Ser., **12**: 359, 1855; Matthew's will. He subscribed £400 in 1642, afterwards assigning his share of the sum to a son. *C.S.P. Ireland, Adventurers*, 329.

[140] *C.J.* **3**: 374, 389; *Western Antiquary* **10**: 85, 1890-1891.

[141] *Cal. Com. Comp.*, 1131-1132.

[142] *Cal. Com. Adv. Money*, 788.

[143] P.C.C., 123 Twisse.

[144] S.P. 23/181/37-38, 44, 49-51; *Cal. Com. Comp.*, 1132; Matthew's will.

[145] He was aged a little over four in May, 1603 (Sir Richard Mauleverer's I.P.M., C. 142/294/80), and was baptized on 9 April 1599 (*Complete Baronetage* **2**: 117). No birth date is given in *D.N.B.*

[146] *Al. Cant.*

[147] *Y.A.S. Rec. Ser.* **54**: 21 and n., *passim*, 1915; C. 193/13.

manors with over 3000 acres of land,[148] and when his royalist son, Sir Richard, declared his property values to the compounding commissioners, he stated that Sir Thomas's income was £1500 a year.[149]

Through his first wife Mauleverer was a brother-in-law of Sir Philip Musgrave (q.v.).

Thomas May (c. 1604–1655), of Rawmere in Mid-Lavant, Sussex, M.P. for Midhurst, 1640–23 November 1642, came of a family well known in the county, in London, and at court. His grandfather, Richard May (d. 1588), had made his wealth in the city, two of his daughters married aldermen, and one son, Sir Humphrey May, became chancellor of the duchy of Lancaster. Richard's younger son, John (d. 1631), married Elizabeth Hill, daughter of a London merchant, and settled at Rawmere, where Richard had built a mansion. John's eldest son was Thomas, the M.P., and another son, Adrian, became a groom of the bedchamber to King Charles. Thomas May (1595–1650), the poet and historian, was a third cousin.[150] Born about 1604, Thomas of Rawmere matriculated at St. John's, Oxford, on 8 April 1620, aged sixteen,[151] and was admitted the same year to the Middle Temple. Two of his uncles, Humphrey and Thomas, were members there then.[152] By 1634 May had married Margaret, daughter of John Austin of Shalford, Surrey, and he was then serving as captain of a troop of horse for the rape of Chichester.[153] The baptisms of five children of this marriage are recorded in the Mid-Lavant registers from December, 1634, until June, 1642.[154] One Thomas May was a J.P. in Sussex in 1634,[155] but this was possibly the uncle of the same name who seems to have made his home at Rawmere, too. In 1637 both "the elder" and "the younger" Thomas May of Rawmere were sewers commissioners for the county,[156] and in 1640 one of them, probably the M.P., was on the commission for the subsidy.[157]

May's experience in parliament began with the first one of 1640, when he served for Midhurst, a borough not far from his residence.[158] Although one of that borough's seats was contested in the autumn election by the parliamentarian, Cawley, May's position there

seems not to have been challenged, and he was instructed to take his place in the House even before a decision about the other seat had been reached.[159] He was never an active member, however. In spite of his court connections, he was placed in command of a troop of horse for parliament in 1642, but on 23 November 1642 he was among those disabled for having seized Chichester for the king.[160] Thereafter his zeal for royalism seems to have waned, for he returned to his home after Waller took Chichester in December, and stayed on as a tenant on his sequestered estate. In attempting to escape the heavy £900 penalty imposed for his delinquency May in 1646 declared that his presence in Chichester with his troop in 1642 had been against his will, and that he never bore arms against parliament. The compounding commissioners confirmed the fine, but in February, 1646/7, parliament granted a pardon which extended to all except his rights of advowson and patronage.[161] May lived until 1655, and was buried 29 December 1655 at Mid-Lavant.[162] His will, dated 16 January 1649/50, was proved 26 January 1655/6.[163]

May's estate had before the war brought him a yearly income of at least £429 according to his own reckoning, or £500 according to that of the commissioners. Several of his properties were mortgaged. He declared that he lost £3000 in personal estate during the war through fines and plundering.[164] But when he made his will early in 1649 May expressed the desire, if the settlement of his debts permitted, that a £500 portion be allowed each of his two daughters, £1000, if possible, for the elder.

May was a brother-in-law of Christopher Lewknor, and was possibly related to others of the 1640 House through his London connections.

* John Maynard (1602–1690), of Devon and London, the well known Presbyterian leader, was elected for both Totness and Newport, Cornwall, but decided on 8 December 1640 to serve for Totness.[165] He stayed until 1648.

The son of a Devon lawyer and J.P.,[166] Maynard practiced law himself at Westminster and in the west, and was elected legal counsellor for Exeter in 1638 and for Plymouth in 1640.[167] In both 1640 elections he was chosen for Newport as well as for Totness.[168]

No estimate of Maynard's wealth in 1640 has been

[148] I.P.M. cited above.
[149] Y.A.S. Rec. Ser. 3: 5–6, 1896.
[150] Vis. Sussex, 1633–4, 105; Berry, Sussex Genealogies, 21; D.N.B., "Thomas May (1595–1650)."
[151] I.P.M. of John May, C. 142/470/47; Al. Oxon.
[152] Mid. Temp. Rec. 2: 649, 650.
[153] Vis. Sussex, 1633–4, 105.
[154] Add. MSS, 5699, fol. 265.
[155] C. 193/13.
[156] C. 181/5, fol. 139. Both Thomas Mays of Rawmere were parties to a marriage settlement for a sister of the younger Thomas in 1638. Sussex Rec. Soc. 29: 22, 1924.
[157] Sussex Arch. Coll. 9: 105, 1857.
[158] M. of P. 1: 483. He was probably not the member for Liverpool in 1621. Pink and Beaven, Parl. Rep. Lanc., 186.

[159] C.J. 2: 63, 86.
[160] C.J. 2: 860.
[161] Cal. Com. Comp., 834; C.J. 5: 81; L.J. 9: 15.
[162] Add. MSS, 5699, fol. 265.
[163] P.C.C., 4 Berkeley.
[164] C.J. 5: 81; S.P. 23/176/215, 217, 223.
[165] C.J. 2: 47.
[166] C. 193/13.
[167] Exeter Corporation MSS, Act Book 8, fols. 165, 166; Plymouth Corporation MSS, No. 359.
[168] C.J. 2: 4; M. of P. 1: 481.

found.[169] He had already gained a large practice, however, and later became wealthy.[170]

Among his colleagues in the Long Parliament were Henry Garton and Bulstrode Whitelocke, who had been called to the bar with him at the Temple in 1626.[171]

* **Sir John Melton** (d. 1640), of York, Secretary of the Council of the North, was named in a double return for Newcastle, Northumberland, but apparently never took his seat, for he died on 16 December 1640 before the case had been determined.[172] He was born in Bampton parish, Devonshire, and was a kinsman of Hugh Potter (q.v.), who was later associated with him in his relations with the Earl of Northumberland.[173] He may have studied at Sidney Sussex, Cambridge, entering in 1608,[174] and was admitted to Gray's Inn in 1634[175] after he had already made his reputation as a politician and writer. He married (1), in 1624, Elizabeth, widow of Sir Ferdinando Heborne of Tottenham High Cross, a daughter of Francis Moore of Sussex,[176] and (2) Katherine, daughter of Allan Currance of London.[177] He was a J.P. in Yorkshire in 1638.[178]

At the time of his election and of his death, Melton had houses in Northumberland, York, and London. He owned coal mines and collieries in the north and had other lands in Kent and Middlesex. By his will he made provision for large portions for his children.[179]

John Meux, or **Mewes** (c. 1612–1657), of Kingston in the Isle of Wight, was M.P. for Newtown, 1640–5 February 1644.[180] The only son of Sir William Meux of Kingston (d. 1638) by his first wife, Winifred, daughter of Sir Francis Barrington of Essex, he was born about 1612. He was admitted to Gray's Inn on 11 February 1630,[181] and was under the guidance of his uncle, Sir Thomas Barrington (q.v.), late in 1631.[182] About 1633 he married Elizabeth, daughter of Sir

Richard Worsley, Bart., and sister of Sir Henry Worsley (q.v.).[183] He seems to have distinguished himself before 1640 principally by being a disappointment to his family. Sir John Oglander, a friend of his father, wrote, "He has a wild son, John, and to prevent future dangers has married him betimes to a most religious family." The inefficacy of the cure is indicated by the same writer's comments in 1639, when he told of an event during the visit of the Earl of Portland to the island. Young Meux with Goring, Nicholas Weston, and other gay blades staged a drinking party at the gallows after having been entertained at Meux's house with no want of wine.[184]

Mewes was elected to parliament for Newtown in the spring and the fall of 1640,[185] but took little part in the work of the House in spite of his relationship to distinguished leaders of the popular side.[186] He was apparently influenced rather by his gayer royalist friends. One evidence of this may have been his creation as a baronet on 11 December 1641. He was disabled for deserting parliament in 1644 and sat in the assemblage at Oxford.[187] He petitioned to compound in 1646, but was still pleading his case with the committee ten years later.[188] He died in 1657 and was buried at Kingston on 12 February.[189]

Meux's inheritance from his father consisted of several manors and properties in numerous towns in the Isle of Wight, including Newtown, which were worth at least £420 a year. And he received with his wife a portion of £2000.[190] His mode of life was such, however, that by 1641 he was forced to mortgage most of his possessions, retaining for himself £100 a year, for his wife and children £200 a year, and assigning the rest for the paying of debts and arranging portions for his younger children. In spite of debts amounting to some £3000, he planned portions of £1500 for each of his two daughters.[191] His fine was set in 1646 at a moiety, £375, but by 1656 he had not been able to arrange a settlement to his satisfaction.[192]

* **Sir John Meyrick**, or **Merrick** (c. 1600–1659), of Monkton, Pembrokeshire, army colonel, was M.P. for Newcastle-under-Lyme, Staffordshire, 1640–1648. Having served earlier as a lieutenant in the Palatinate, he was recommended to a captaincy in Mansfeld's ex-

169 The absence of his name from the lists of those contributing at various times to the uses of parliament seems inconsistent with Maynard's devotion to the cause, unless his income was small.
170 Lipscomb, Buckingham 4: 107.
171 Mid. Temp. Rec. 2: 714.
172 C.J. 2: 53; Yorkshire County Magazine 1: 312, 1891–1892.
173 Melton's will (P.C.C., 29 Evelyn) refers to these matters.
174 Al. Cant.
175 Gray's Inn Adm. Reg., 204.
176 The letters of John Chamberlain 2: 544, n.
177 Yorkshire County Magazine 1: 312, 1891–1892.
178 S.P. 16/405.
179 The will mentions £1500 for each of Melton's two elder children, £1300 for another, and £1000 each for the three younger ones, parts of the portions being assigned from legacies left by other relatives.
180 C.J. 3: 389.
181 Complete Baronetage 2: 146; I.P.M., Sir William Meux, C. 142/786/58.
182 Eg. MSS, 2645, fol. 331.

183 A marriage settlement was dated 28 June 1633. I.P.M. cited above.
184 A royalist's notebook (ed. Bamford, London, Constable, 1936), 98, 99, 160.
185 M. of P. 1: 483, 493 and n.
186 Not only was Meux a nephew of Barrington and of Sir Gilbert Gerard and related to others of their family group, but he was a brother-in-law of Worsley, John Button was a cousin of his father's, and the Wallops were intimates of his family.
187 O.P.H. 9: 1.
188 Cal. Com. Comp., 1243–1244.
189 Complete Baronetage 2: 146.
190 I.P.M. cited above; S.P. 23/188/768–770.
191 S.P. 23/188/766–770; V.C.H. Hampshire 5: 147.
192 Cal. Com. Comp., 1243–1244.

pedition, 1624,[193] and his later experiences under the Earl of Essex probably account for his election to the 1640 parliaments for a borough in the earl's county.[194] Sir John was in command of a regiment on the Scottish border in June and October, 1640, and was occupied during the spring months of 1641 more with his military than with his parliamentary duties.[195] He was named, however, to several committees on army affairs, 1640–1641.[196] He pledged two horses for the defense in June, 1642.[197]

Although he was included in Richard Baxter's list of army men who were moderate Episcopal conformants, Meyrick was rather a Presbyterian with a leaning toward Independency.[198] He was the owner of lands in various parts of Pembrokeshire, and when he made his will in 1653 he planned portions of £500 for each of his two young daughters.[199]

* Sir Thomas Middleton, or Myddleton (1586–1666), of Chirk Castle, Denbighshire, was M.P. for county Denbigh, 1640–1648. The son and heir of a rich London grocer, Lord Mayor, and adventurer in overseas projects, he had over 5000 acres of property in Wales settled on him at his first marriage in 1612, and in 1631 he succeeded his father in the possession of most of his more than 13,000 acres in Denbighshire and other Welsh counties.[200] He lived part of the time in Bedfordshire after marrying as his second wife in February, 1616 (1616/17?), Mary, daughter of Sir Robert Napier. Several of their children were baptized at the Napier parish church of Luton Hoo.[201] And he probably owed his first seat in parliament (Weymouth, 1624) to his wife's Dorset relatives. From the latter part of the reign of King James, however, Middleton was a J.P. in Denbighshire,[202] and during the 1630's he was a member of the Council of Wales[203] and of the commission of oyer and terminer for Wales and the Marches.[204] He seems to have inherited his father's interest in overseas affairs and ventured £100 in the fisheries project of 1633.[205] In November, 1640, he declared that he had been prevented from attending a trial in the Court of Wards in which he was interested

because he had been employed abroad in his Majesty's service.[206]

Sir Thomas was certainly one of the wealthier members of the 1640 House. His father had been considered able to provide £3000 for a daughter's dowry,[207] and in 1640 Sir Thomas pledged £1000 to back the loan.[208] Even after losing heavily during the war and spending "most of his estate," he was reckoned to be worth £600 a year in 1660.[209]

Middleton was a friend of the Wynns of Gwydir, including Sir Richard Wynn,[210] and was a brother-in-law of Sir Robert Napier, M.P. for Peterborough.[211]

Thomas Middleton (1589–c. 1662), of Horsham, Sussex, was a member for that borough, 1640–1648. The eldest son and heir of John Middleton of Horsham (J.P., H.S., six times M.P. for Horsham, d. 1636),[212] by his wife, Frances, daughter of Nicholas Fowle of Rotherfield,[213] Thomas was baptized at the latter place on 1 March 1588/9.[214] He may have matriculated at Trinity College, Cambridge, in 1606, and was admitted to the Inner Temple in 1607.[215] On 29 May 1610 he married Barbara, daughter of Henry Shelley of Worminghurst.[216] The entries of the Horsham parish register indicate that he lived chiefly at Horsham,[217] where he succeeded to his father's estate in 1636.

Middleton was a captain at the Sussex musters in 1618,[218] was for some years escheator,[219] and served as a J.P. and member of various commissions.[220] In 1638 he was reported 15 s. in arrears in ship money payments,[221] and was probably counted by the opposition group in his shire as one of their number. He was chosen at both 1640 elections to fill the Horsham seat which his father had occupied earlier.[222]

Although he was never conspicuous as a member of the Commons, Middleton was named a committeeman for parliament and a D.L. in Sussex during the war.

---

[193] S.P. 14, 174/49.

[194] He was admitted to the liberty of Newcastle in March, 1640, and was promptly chosen M.P. Newcastle Corporation MSS, Order Book 1 (1368–1684).

[195] *C.S.P. Dom., 1640,* 286; *1640–1641,* 129, *passim.*

[196] *C.J.* 2: 34, 66, 188.

[197] *N. and Q.,* 1st Ser., 12: 359, 1855.

[198] *Arch. Camb.,* 6th Ser., 15: 15, 16, 1915; *A.H.R.* 17: 485, 1911–1912.

[199] P.C.C., 309 Pell. A sketch of Meyrick's life appears in Wedgwood, *Staff. Parl. Hist.* 2: 63–64.

[200] I.P.M., Sir Thomas Middleton, 1634, C. 142/501/48.

[201] Transcript of the parish register of Luton, Bedfordshire, baptisms, 17, 23.

[202] C. 193/12, 13; S.P. 16/405.

[203] *Arch. Camb.,* 6th Ser., 17: 195, 1917.

[204] C. 181/4, fol. 162v; 181/5, fol. 369.

[205] S.P. 16, 231/15/31.

[206] *C.S.P. Dom., 1640–1641,* 220.

[207] *Cal. Wynn Papers,* 57.

[208] D'Ewes (N), 51.

[209] *English Baronetage* 4: 379, 1741. In 1659 Sir Thomas and his son were reported to hold 264 estates in most of the counties of north Wales and to have holdings also in Cheshire, Yorkshire, Worcestershire and Salop. *Cal. Com. Comp.,* 3246–3247.

[210] Frequent references to the Middletons appear in *Cal. Wynn Papers.*

[211] In addition to the authorities already cited see Williams, *Parl. Hist. Wales,* 72–73.

[212] Pink MSS, 319; S.P. 16, 189/16; I.P.M., C. 142/595/103.

[213] *Vis. Sussex, 1633–4,* 56.

[214] Add. MSS, 5697, fol. 294.

[215] *Al. Cant.; Students admitted to the Inner Temple,* 181.

[216] *Sussex Rec. Soc.* 9: 43, 1909; Add. MSS, 5698, fol. 268.

[217] *Sussex Rec. Soc.* 21: 233, *passim,* 1915.

[218] *Sussex Arch. Coll.* 59: 119, 1918.

[219] C. 142/379/56; 380/124; *Sussex Arch. Coll.* 69: 125, 1928.

[220] C. 193/13; C. 181/3; 181/4, fol. 47; 181/5, fol. 137.

[221] S.P. 16, 379/131.

[222] *M. of P.* 1: 483, 494.

He was suspected of lukewarmness toward the cause in 1644, however, and in 1648, with his royalist son, John, was arrested for an alleged part in the Horsham uprising. They both spent some time afterwards attempting to prove they had not been "delinquents," [223] but the purge of 1648 had already removed Middleton from parliament.[224] He was listed among the restored members in 1660, though he was absent.[225] He died about 1661 or 1662. His will, dated 16 October 1661, was proved in October, 1662.[226]

Middleton possessed considerable means. He inherited a half dozen or more sizable properties in or near Horsham,[227] and when he settled his estate in 1640 at the time of his son's marriage he retained the use for himself, but guaranteed the son £400 a year.[228] He held by lease also some timberlands, and may have been interested in the iron industry. His income seems to have been well over £700 a year, and he mortgaged one manor about 1647 to raise £600 for a daughter's portion.[229]

By his son's marriage Middleton became a distant connection of Sir Edward Rodney, a fellow M.P. Another colleague, Hall Ravenscrofte, was a neighbor and life-long associate.

* **Sir Henry Mildmay** (d. 1664?), of Wanstead, Essex, Master of the Jewels, sat for Maldon, 1640–1653. A younger son of Humphrey Mildmay of Danbury, Essex, he was born sometime after 1592,[230] entered Emmanuel College, Cambridge, in 1610, and was graduated B.A. in 1612.[231] He was said to be a young man of small means and experience at the time of his appointment to the Jewel House about January, 1618,[232] but his close association with the court from that time until 1640 brought him a rich marriage and gave him his share of the grants and annuities available to courtiers.[233] The steward of Maldon from 1620, he was

elected by that town to the parliaments of 1621, 1625, 1628, and April, 1640,[234] being preferred in 1625 to Sir Julius Caesar, and sat for Westbury, Wiltshire, in 1624. Possibly the influence of his brother-in-law, Sir Edward Hungerford (q.v.), helped him there.[235] Mildmay was generally ready to defend the policies of the king and his favorites in his early parliaments,[236] but his ability to adjust himself to circumstances, which his Long Parliament career demonstrated, is indicated by his letter to Secretary Conway in June, 1624, when he protested that he had done the king no disservice in the House, but rather served him truly, at the same time so preserving his reputation with the House as to be able to serve his master again.[237]

Mildmay was perhaps a member of the Virginia Company in 1622 and one of the committee to plan for governing the colony when its charter was voided.[238] He was a J.P. in Essex and Hampshire,[239] and served on many commissions, both local and special and ranging in subject from sewers to the gold and silver thread business and the investigation of exacted fees.[240] He was also a D.L. and was an officer in the north in 1639.[241]

Mildmay owned lands in Hertfordshire, Hampshire and Essex, his estate of Wanstead alone being reckoned as worth about £1000 a year.[242] In March, 1641, he promised to be bound for the loan.[243] He was undoubtedly well-to-do, a fact which, as Clarendon suggested, made him useful to the opposition faction. He acted as an elder in the Essex presbytery during the war.[244]

Among Mildmay's relatives in the 1640 House, besides his brother-in-law, Hungerford, were his cousins, George Fane and William Fitzwilliam, all being grandsons of Sir Walter Mildmay, and his mother's kinsman, Arthur Capel.

* **Gilbert Millington** (1598?–1666), of Felley Abbey, Notts, the regicide, was a member for Nottingham, 1640–1653. The eldest son of Anthony Millington of

[223] Thomas-Stanford, *Sussex in the great Civil War*, 80, 202–203; W. Albery, *A parliamentary history of Horsham*, 515. John was sequestered and fined (*Sussex Arch. Coll.* 19: 109, 1867), and Thomas himself seems to have been proposed for the Knights of the Royal Oak in 1660 (*ibid.* 23: 210, 1871).

[224] *O.P.H.* 9: 5.

[225] Thomason Tracts, 669. f. 24, p. 37.

[226] P.C.C., 129 Laud.

[227] C. 142/595/103.

[228] The son's bride had a portion of £3000. *Sussex Arch. Coll.* 19: 109, 1867.

[229] The estimate is based upon the lands John was holding in 1648. The part Middleton retained for himself may have been worth £488 a year. *Sussex Arch. Coll.* 19: 108–109, 1867; *Cal. Com. Comp.*, 339, 406.

[230] His elder brother, Humphrey, was born in 1592. I.P.M., Humphrey Mildmay, 1613. C. 142/335/4.

[231] *Al. Cant.*

[232] *The letters of John Chamberlain* 2: 125.

[233] *Ibid.* 2: 203, 228. He was listed among the receivers of annuities, £75 having been paid him in February, 1639. S.P. 16, 412/149. Clarendon, commenting on the Long Parliament's

attacks on monopolists, pointed out that Mildmay, "who had been most scandalously engaged in those pressures," was never questioned. The gold and silver thread project was one of his interests. *Rebellion* 1: 228–229 and n. See also *The mystery of the good old cause*, 32.

[234] *M. of P.* 1: 451, 463, 475, 481; Add. MSS, 12,496, fol. 106.

[235] Both had married daughters of Alderman Halliday.

[236] E.g., 1629, when he urged moderation in the attacks on the king's officials. *Commons Debates for 1629*, 176, 188.

[237] *C.S.P. Dom., 1623–1625*, 271.

[238] Brown, *Genesis of the U. S.*, 950; Kingsbury, *Records of the Virginia Company* 3: 65; 4: 491.

[239] S.P. 16, 59/52; 405; C. 191/13.

[240] *C.S.P. Dom., 1633–1634*, 176; *1635–1636*, 178; *1637–1638*, 77; C. 181/4, fols. 72, 76; 181/5, fols. 10, 92, *passim*.

[241] S.P. 16, 57/1; 62/93; 427/38/ii.

[242] Morant, *Essex* 1: 30; Chancery Proceedings, C. 3/318/21; Kingston, *Hertfordshire during the great Civil War*, 153; *Hampshire N. and Q.* 2: 79, 1884.

[243] Either £500 or £1000. D'Ewes (N), 439, 451, n.

[244] *A.H.R.* 44: 31, n. (32), 1938–1939.

the same and of London (d. 1620), he was born in or shortly before 1598,[245] studied at Peterhouse, Cambridge (B.A. 1616), and became a barrister at Lincoln's Inn in 1621.[246] About 1618 he married Alatheie, probably of the Lawley family of Shropshire.[247] He spent much of his time in Nottinghamshire thereafter, where he was a sewers commissioner in 1629,[248] a J.P. by 1631,[249] and a D.L. in 1638,[250] but he was also a Master of Chancery by May, 1639, and doubtless retained his London connections. In the latter year Lord Chaworth asked permission for Millington to deputize for him as county sheriff and ship money collector.[251] His first election to parliament, though, was in October, 1640.[252]

Millington inherited from his father the Felley Abbey property of some 800 acres, to which a yearly value of £200, possibly an underestimate, was assigned in 1621.[253] His assessment for the privy seals in 1626 was £20, the same as that of the well-to-do Robert Sutton,[254] and his income was no doubt considerably larger than the income from Felley. His pledge of £50 for the defense in June, 1642, indicates circumstances not below moderate.[255]

* **Sir William Monson, Viscount Monson of Castlemain** (d. 1672?), was a member for Reigate, 1640–1653. Although there was a double return for Reigate, Monson seems to have established title to his seat without difficulty.[256] A younger son of the courtier, Sir Thomas Monson (d. 1641) of the Lincolnshire family, he was born sometime after 1600,[257] and probably soon after 1624 married Margaret Stuart, widow of the Earl of Nottingham (d. 1624). Partly by this marriage and partly by purchase in 1628 Monson became the owner of the manor and town of Reigate.[258] He was described as of Reigate in the privy seals list of 1625, the amount required of him then being £60, an unusually large sum.[259] The next year he was elected to parliament for Reigate.[260] He was reported a defaulter at the Surrey musters in 1626,[261] and a ship money refuser later. He served as one of the county J.P.'s.[262] Although Monson was frequently in debt, he promised in the Long Parliament £1000 as security for the loan proposed in 1641.[263] He belonged with the Independents in matters of religion.[264]

* **Edward Montagu** (1616–1684), of Northamptonshire, the son and heir apparent of Edward, first Baron Montagu of Boughton (d. 1644), was M.P. for Huntingdon borough, 1640–1644, his place being vacated only when he joined the Upper House after his father's death.[265] Entering Cambridge in 1631, he was created M.A. the next year.[266] In 1633 the settlement was made for his marriage with Anne, daughter of Sir Ralph Winwood, the Secretary of State,[267] and sister of Richard Winwood, M.P. for Windsor, 1640. He was the prospective heir to great wealth and by 1641 much of his father's estate had been settled on him.[268] Apparently he held no local offices before 1640, nor had he sat in parliament, but he or his cousin George, the other "Mr. Montagu" of the House, was named to several early committees.[269] He promised £100 for the defense in 1642.[270]

Relatives of Montagu in the Long Parliament, besides the above named cousin and brother-in-law, were his uncle, Sir Sydney Montagu, and at least two other cousins, Sir John Wray and Arthur Capel.[271]

[245] He was aged twenty-two and more in 1620, according to the I.P.M. of Anthony Millington. C. 142/382/9.

[246] Al. Cant.

[247] She is mentioned only by her given name in Anthony Millington's I.P.M., which cites a settlement of 10 October 1618 affecting her, one of the trustees of which was Edward Lawley of the Inner Temple, son of Thomas Lawley of Shropshire.

[248] C. 181/4, fol. 17.

[249] S.P. 16, 193, fol. 187v; Nottingham Quarter Sessions Minute Books, 10, 11, passim.

[250] S.P. 16, 381/73.

[251] C.S.P.Dom., 1639, 151. The Earl of Clare named Millington his deputy for the recordership of Nottingham in 1643, Nottingham Corporation MSS, Hall Book 3416, fols. 56, 60; 3419, fol. 1. One of his committee appointments in parliament, however, was for London and Middlesex matters. C.J. 2: 884.

[252] His brother John, who had secured a minor place at court in 1626 (Al. Cant), wrote to him several times about developments in the parliaments of 1626 and 1628. C.S.P. Dom., 1625–1626, 316, 331, 348; 1628–1629, 43, 172, 175.

[253] This is the value mentioned in the I.P.M. of his father, but documents of this sort usually record only a nominal value.

[254] S.P. 16, 19/21, vii.

[255] N. and Q., 1st Ser., 12: 359, 1855.

[256] M. of P. 1: 494.

[257] His elder brother, John, was born in 1600. D.N.B., "Sir Thomas Monson."

[258] Manning and Bray, Surrey 1: 278, 281; Aubrey, Surrey 4: 189–190.

[259] Brayley, Surrey 5: App. 2, 25.

[260] M. of P. 1: 472.

[261] Acts P.C., 1626, 172.

[262] C. 193/13.

[263] D'Ewes (N), 439, n.

[264] A.H.R. 44: 36, n., 1938–1939.

[265] M. of P. 1: 490. Disablement on account of absences was considered in 1644, but Montagu was respited instead, 22 January. C.J. 3: 374.

[266] Al. Cant.

[267] Complete Peerage 5: 342. The marriage occurred before August, 1633 (H.M.C., MSS of the Duke of Buccleugh and Queensbury 1: 273). When Edward's marriage was discussed in 1631, his father said he wished his son to see a little of the world before he settled down (H.M.C., MSS of Lord Montagu of Beaulieu, 115, 116), but I have found no other indication of plans for travel.

[268] His father was described in 1631 as rich in lands, houses, and stock, and as a bountiful housekeeper (ibid.), and when he made his will, 12 November 1641, he had already settled much of his landed estate on his son. P.C.C., 99 Twisse.

[269] C.J. 2: 51, 60, 62.

[270] His pledge was for the defense of king and parliament "conjunctively" and not divided. N. and Q., 1st Ser., 12: 359, 1855.

[271] For Montagu's life, see D.N.B., "Edward Montagu (1562–1644)."

George Montagu (*c.* 1624–1681), of Northampton-shire, member for Huntingdon borough, 1640–1648,[272] was a newcomer to parliament and the youngest member of his family to have a place there in 1640. He was a cousin of his colleague, Edward Montagu, and a half-brother of Lord Mandeville, being the fifth son of Henry, Earl of Manchester, his eldest son by his third wife, Margaret, daughter of John Crouch of Corn-bury (married, 26 April 1620). George was born at Westminster, attended school at Amersham under Dr. Croke, and at the age of fifteen entered Christ's College, Cambridge, 21 March 1639. He matriculated that year and was granted the M.A. degree in 1640. Three days after his election to the Long Parliament, 26 October 1640, he was admitted to the Middle Temple, and he was still associated there in February, 1644.[273] Montagu's marriage with a daughter of his colleague, Sir Anthony Irby (*q.v.*), did not occur until 1645, but in 1642 his father settled on him the manor of Horton, Northamptonshire, with which he is commonly identi-fied.[274] He was but a minor member of the 1640 House. He lived until 1681, having been for the last years of his life Master of the Hospital of St. Katherine-by-the-Tower in London.

Among his sons were Charles, Earl of Halifax (1661–1715), and Sir James Montagu (1666–1723).[275]

Sir Sydney Montagu (*c.* 1571–1644), of Hinchin-brooke, Huntingdonshire, was knight for his shire from 1640 until he was disabled, 3 December 1642, for re-fusing to take the oath to support the Earl of Essex against the king. One of a family powerful in his county, he was the sixth surviving son of Sir Edward Montagu of Boughton, Northamptonshire (d. 1602), by his wife, Elizabeth, daughter of Sir James Harring-ton, and was born about 1571.[276] He matriculated at Christ's College, Cambridge, in 1588, entered the Mid-dle Temple in 1593, and was called to the bar there in 1601 and to the bench in 1616.[277] He was an aspirant for some post at court in 1606,[278] and with the help of his elder brother, James, then Bishop of Bath and Wells, secured in 1616 an appointment as a Master of Re-

quests.[279] He was knighted in July of that year, and for some time was a groom of the bedchamber to King James.[280] About 1617 he married Paulina, daughter of John Pepys of Cottenham, Cambridgeshire, who lived until 1638.[281] Sir Sydney divided his time between London and one of his family's estates, such as Hen-nington or Barnwell, until 1627,[282] when he established his residence at Hinchinbrooke, one of the Cromwell properties he purchased with his brother, the Earl of Manchester.[283] He was host to the king there in 1634.[284]

Montagu was not only prominent in his profession and at court, but shared in local responsibilities. In 1601 he was appointed one of the receivers of coat and conduct money in Northamptonshire,[285] was a J.P. in Huntingdonshire from the reign of King James, and a member of numerous commissions for the midland and East Anglian counties as well as London.[286] He was a commissioner for the knighthood compositions in Huntingdonshire, 1630–1632.[287] As a member of par-liament also Montagu had some experience, having been elected for Brackley, 1593, Malmesbury, 1601, and Wells, 1614.[288] He was defeated in the 1621 elections for Huntingdonshire, however,[289] and did not sit again until the autumn of 1640.

Throughout most of his career, Sir Sydney was a loyal servant of the crown, but in the summer of 1640 he lost his office as Master of Requests, the rumor run-ning that it was because he had declined to lend the king £2000,[290] and his election as M.P. for Huntingdon-shire in October was possibly helped by that fact.[291] He was a fairly active member during the early months of the Long Parliament, being named on various com-mittees,[292] and probably cooperating with the reform element, to which his son-in-law, Pickering, and his

---

[272] *M. of P.* 1: 490; Thomason Tracts, E. 454, 17.

[273] *Al. Cant.; Mid. Temp. Rec.* 2: 898, 933.

[274] Thompson, *Boston*, 395; *V.C.H., Huntingdonshire* 2: 64. In addition to Horton, Montagu's father bequeathed to him £50 a year during his mother's lifetime, a grange worth £110 yearly, and 1000 marks for purchasing some property adjoin-ing Horton. The will of Henry, Earl of Manchester, dated 22 March 1642, and proved in 1644. P.C.C., 47 Rivers.

[275] *D.N.B.* Montagu is mentioned in the *D.N.B.* article on his father.

[276] F. R. Harris, *The life of Edward Montagu, K.G., first Earl of Sandwich* 1: 10, 18, London, J. Murray, 1912 (here-after, Harris, *Earl of Sandwich*); *V.C.H. Huntingdonshire* 2: 62; *D.N.B.*, articles on Sir Edward Montagu (1532–1602) and Edward Montagu, first Earl of Sandwich (1625–1672).

[277] *Al. Cant.; Mid. Temp. Rec.* 1: 333, 413; 2: 602.

[278] Bodleian Carte MSS, 74, fols. 361, 377, 379.

[279] *Ibid.*, fols. 339, 383; *Acts P.C., 1615–1616*, 388, 400; *The letters of John Chamberlain* 2: 99, 131.

[280] Shaw, *K. of E.* 2: 159; Burke, *Peerage*, 2186, 1938.

[281] Carte MSS, 74, fol. 371v; *Complete Peerage* 7: 49. Early in 1644 he married Anne Isham, widow of John Pey of Westminster. Harris, *Earl of Sandwich* 1: 18; Baker, *North-ampton* 1: 264.

[282] Carte MSS, 1, fol. 141; 74, fols. 369, 390; *V.C.H. Northamptonshire* 3: 175. He seems to have disagreed with his brother, Edward Lord Montagu, about lands during this period, their dispute finally reaching the law courts. *H.M.C., MSS of the Duke of Buccleugh and Queensbury* 3: 214, 226, *passim.*

[283] *Ibid.* 1: 266; *V.C.H. Huntingdonshire* 2: 273, 339.

[284] Carte MSS, 74, fol. 177.

[285] *Acts P.C., 1601–1604*, 317.

[286] C. 193/12, 13; S.P. 16, 189/94, fol. 251; C. 181/4, fols. 9v, 153v; 181/5, fols. 18, 59, 62, *passim.*

[287] Carte MSS, 103, fol. 31; 74, fols. 174, 208.

[288] *M. of P.* 1: 429, 440; 3: App., xxxix.

[289] One of his supporters brought suit in Star Chamber against the sheriff afterwards. St. Ch. 8/47/7.

[290] *H.M.C., Twelfth Report* 4, *MSS of the Duke of Rutland* 1: 521.

[291] Bodleian Tanner MSS, 65, fol. 175.

[292] Most of them concerned matters of secondary importance, however. *C.J.* 2: 73, 75, 164, 195.

nephews in both chambers belonged. He was absent in Huntingdonshire in February, 1642, and in May was collecting funds there by order of parliament,[293] but when the war came he refused to pledge his support to Essex, pleading his old age and his unwillingness to share in treasonable action. He was therefore expelled, 3 December 1642, and sent to the Tower for a time, but was presently allowed to retire to his home in the country.[294] He seems to have retained a considerable interest in the cause of parliament, although not participating in it himself.[295] He died on 25 September 1644.

Although a younger son, Sir Sydney seems to have been a man of ample means. His income from his office as Master of Requests probably was more than the £100 a year annuity allotted him,[296] and his real estate investments included mines in Somersetshire as well as lands and mortgages in Bedfordshire and Huntingdonshire.[297] The king's request of £2000 from him in 1639–1640 and parliament's for £1000 in 1642[298] indicate that he was regarded as well to do. Most of his property by the time of his death, however, had already been settled on his son Edward, the future Earl of Sandwich.[299]

Sir Sydney was a devoutly religious man, delighting in religious exercises and in writing long commentaries on texts.[300] Antiquarianism, too, at least as it touched his own family, seems to have been one of his interests.[301]

He was related to various members of the 1640 parliament, having a brother and a nephew in the House of Lords, and in the Commons, besides his son-in-law, Pickering, and the Montagu nephews who represented Huntingdon borough, two other nephews, Sir John Wray and Arthur Capel.

John Moore (c. 1599–1650), of Banks Hall, in or near Liverpool, sat for Liverpool, 1640–1650. His was an old family and his father, Edward Moore of Banks Hall (d. 1633), had been a strongly Protestant magistrate for Derbyshire, M.P. for Liverpool, and H.S. of Lancashire. John, his eldest son by his wife, Katherine Hockenhall, was born about 1599, became bailiff and later mayor of Liverpool, and a J.P. in the county.[302]

In 1633 he married Mary, daughter of Alexander Rigby of the royalist line of Burgh.[303] He was admitted to Lincoln's Inn in 1638 at the request of Hugh Rigby, reader,[304] but he drew his income from real estate and from shipping interests at Liverpool.[305]

Elected to parliament for the first time in the fall of 1640, Moore was a vigorous parliamentarian, and kept notes of the proceedings.[306] He was named to such important committees as those on monopolies and the Star Chamber, was active against recusancy, and pledged £1500 for the loan in 1640 and £500 in March, 1641.[307] When war came, he promised two horses for the defense,[308] served on the parliamentary committees in Lancashire, was a colonel in the army, and fitted out ships at his own expense for the war in Ireland. He was an elder in the Lancashire presbytery, but was evidently an Independent.[309] Moore was one of the regicides. He died while he was in Ireland as a parliamentary commissioner in 1650.[310]

Moore was probably prosperous in 1640. After his father's death he had contracted to buy out his mother's interests in the estate for £10,000, and he owned several properties in and near Liverpool, and at least one ship. He incurred losses during the war, however, and was said to have left debts of £10,000 when he died.[311] One of his relatives was Colonel Ashton, the county member,[312] and through his wife he was related to Roger Kirkby.

Poynings Moore, or **More** (1606–1649), of Loseley, Surrey, was M.P. for Haslemere, 1640–1649.[313] He was the son and heir of Sir Robert Moore (d. 1626), M.P., D.L., and gentleman pensioner,[314] by his wife, Frances, daughter of Sampson Lennard and Margaret, Baroness Dacre. His family had been seated at Loseley near Guildford, from the time of Henry VIII, and had held numerous offices at court and in the county. Sir

---

[293] Carte MSS, 74, fol. 392; Add. MSS, 34,401, fol. 66v.

[294] Warwick, *Memoires,* 221; Carte MSS, 74, fols. 349, 375; *C.J.* 2: 874, 891.

[295] Carte MSS, 74, fol. 155; 223, fol. 143.

[296] Stowe MSS, 575, fol. 13v; *C.S.P. Dom.,* 1625–1626, 542.

[297] Carte MSS, 74, fols. 335, 337, 400; 223, fol. 145; Add. MSS, 34,401, fols. 56, 64v, 82; *C.S.P. Dom.,* 1625–1626, 197; *V.C.H. Huntingdonshire* 2: 27, 273, 339; 3: 37.

[298] See note 290 above; *C.J.* 2: 891.

[299] In his will, dated 18 March 1644, Montagu requested his son to pay £1000 or £100 a year to the wife he had recently married. P.C.C., 31 Rivers.

[300] Harris, *Earl of Sandwich* 1: 11; Tanner MSS, 74, fol. 14.

[301] Carte MSS, 74, fol. 424.

[302] Pink and Beaven, *Parl. Rep. Lanc.,* 186, 188; *The Moore Rental* (ed. by T. Heywood, Chetham Society, 1st Ser., 12:

v–ix, 1847); *Lancashire funeral certificates,* Chetham Society, 1st Ser., 75: 56, 61, 1869; R. Stewart-Brown, Moore of Bankhall, *Historic Society of Lancashire and Cheshire Transactions* 63: 92–119, 1911.

[303] *The Moore Rental, loc. cit.;* H.M.C., *Tenth Report* 4, Capt. Stewart's MSS, 63.

[304] *Linc. Inn Rec. Adm.* 1: 236.

[305] *Moore Papers,* Rec. Soc. Lancs. and Cheshire, 67: 49, 50. Moore "and the merchants" of the House were added to the committee on monopolies (*C.J.* 2: 45). His difficulties with the Navy Commissioners about payment for his ships are revealed in his correspondence with his wife during the war. H.M.C., *Tenth Report* 4: 97–98.

[306] D'Ewes (N), xii.

[307] *C.J.* 2: 45, 75, 267; D'Ewes (N), 52, 438, n. (439).

[308] *N. and Q.,* 1st Ser., 12: 359, 1855.

[309] *A.H.R.* 44: 31, n. (32), 1938–1939.

[310] Bean, *Northern Counties,* 345–346; H.M.C., *Tenth Report* 4, Captain Stewart's MSS, 83, 99.

[311] *Moore Papers,* 49, 50; *The Moore Rental,* xlvii.

[312] *Moore Papers,* 51.

[313] *M. of P.* 1: 494; *C.J.* 6: 239.

[314] *Surrey Arch. Coll.* 24: 180, 1911; 39: 54, 1931; Manning and Bray, *Surrey* 1: 96.

George Moore (1553–1632), grandfather of Poynings, was sheriff, J.P., and M.P., treasurer to Henry, Prince of Wales, Lieutenant of the Tower, and Chancellor of the Order of the Garter. He had invested in the Virginia Company, had given manuscripts and money to Oxford University, and was noted for his lavish hospitality until, as a son-in-law reported, with the death of Prince Henry, "then fell all his fortunes." [315] Poynings, who was named for his paternal grandmother, a Dorsetshire heiress, was born on 13 February 1606,[316] was a student at Trinity College, Oxford, in 1622,[317] and late that year was admitted to the Inner Temple.[318] He was in lodgings in Fleet Street in 1629. His grandfather then was planning a marriage for him, partly to gain relief for the family's finances and partly, perhaps, to lead the young heir to more sober habits than gossip attributed to him. The marriage, however, did not occur,[319] and in 1630 Moore and a cousin, Francis Carew, made a trip to France, seemingly to evade some creditors.[320] Again in 1632 Moore planned to travel, for he was granted a license to do so for three years for cultural purposes.[321] His grandfather's death soon afterwards doubtless brought him back to England to take over the estates. He married, probably by 1641, Elizabeth, daughter of Sir John Fytch of Essex and widow of Christopher Rous of Suffolk. She was a kinswoman of the courtly family of Cornwallis.[322]

In the meantime Moore was elected four times to parliament, in 1624, 1625, and 1626 for Haslemere, virtually a family borough of the Moores, and in 1628 for Guildford.[323] He was a J.P. in Surrey,[324] a commissioner for surveying the River Wey,[325] and possibly a D.L.[326] He did not sit in the Short Parliament, and was named in a double return in the autumn of 1640, but seems to have had no trouble gaining recognition.[327] Although he had sent no answer in 1639 to the king's

request for a loan,[328] Moore was no conspicuous member of the popular party. The tradition of his family and his wife's was with the court, and he seems to have steered a course between the two extremes, keeping his place until his death. He accepted a baronetcy in May, 1642, and was under suspicion on account of absence in January, 1644, but was respited.[329] Because he was not among those secluded by Colonel Pride, he has been accounted an Independent in religion,[330] but it is doubtful whether he was fervently so. He died at Loseley, 11 April 1649, and was buried in the family chapel at St. Nicholas, Guildford.

The fortune of the Moore family was on the wane by the time Poynings succeeded his grandfather, and it seems unlikely that he had either the ability or the wisdom to rebuild it. In Sir George's day the extent of their lands, the chief of which lay near Guildford and Haslemere, was greatest. His assessment for the subsidy in 1613 was among the highest in England, but the loss of his patron at court and probably the extravagances of his grandson and heir afterwards brought difficulties.[331] Enough remained of the fortune, however, for Poynings Moore to be listed among those asked for a benevolence in 1639. It may have been lack of interest rather than of means which accounts for the absence of his name from the lists of pledges for the parliamentary cause, 1640–1642.

Moore was connected by marriage with two of his fellow M.P.'s, Sir Frederick Cornwallis and Sir Thomas Parker.

Thomas Moore (1618–1695), of Heytesbury, Wiltshire, of Spargrove, Somerset, and of Hawkchurch, Dorset, was M.P. for Heytesbury, 1640–1648 (1653 ?).[332] He was the son of Thomas Moore of Heytesbury (H.S. Wilts.; d. 1626), and the heir through him to estates of both the older and younger lines of Moores, descendants of Thomas Moore of the Priory, Taunton (d. 1575). The family were large landowners in three counties and were connected through marriage with such important families as the Pakingtons of Worcestershire and Bucks and the Windhams of Somerset. Through his mother, Rachel, daughter of Sir John Windham of Orchard, Somerset, the M.P. was related to the royalist, Edmund Windham

---

315 *Ibid.* 1: 66–67, 94–95; *The Oglander memoirs* (Long), 139–141; Kingsbury, *Records of the Virginia Company* 3: 329; 4: 157.

316 Berry, *Surrey families*, 86–87; *Complete Baronetage* 2: 175.

317 *H.M.C., Seventh Report*, MSS of W. M. Molyneux, Esq., 674.

318 *Students admitted to the Inner Temple*, 236.

319 *H.M.C., Seventh Report*, 677, 678.

320 The latter's father was concerned about the influence of his companion on Carew as well as by the expenses they were likely to incur. Add. MSS, 29,599 (Carew Papers), fols. 36, 38, 39.

321 *H.M.C., Seventh Report*, 677.

322 She was a granddaughter of Sir Charles Cornwallis of Suffolk. Their second child was born in August, 1643. Manning and Bray, *Surrey* 1: 67; *Complete Baronetage* 2: 175; Add. MSS, 14,311, fol. 68. *Cf.* Sir Frederick Cornwallis.

323 *M. of P.* 1: 460, *passim; Surrey Arch. Coll.* 39: 61, 1931.

324 C. 191/13; S.P. 16/405.

325 Manning and Bray, *Surrey* 1: Intro., ii.

326 *H.M.C., Seventh Report*, 677; *Surrey Arch. Coll.* 40: 42, 1932.

327 Pink MSS, 311, fol. 495b.

328 Rushworth 3: 914.

329 *C.J.* 3: 374. It is stated in *V.C.H. Surrey* (1: 406) that Moore forsook his party before the execution of the king.

330 Hexter, *The reign of King Pym*, 98, n.; *A.H.R.* 44: 36, n., 1938–1939.

331 Lansd. MSS, 165, fol. 233; Manning and Bray, *Surrey* 1: 86, 91; *Surrey Arch. Coll.* 18: 26, 28, 1903; Surrey Deeds, Guildford Muniment Room MSS, nos. 5/2/273, 294, 335; 5/3/110, 112.

332 *M. of P.* 1: 496. According to Pink (Pink MSS, 311, fol. 496d), Moore was secluded in 1648. The list in *O.P.H.* (9: 7), however, indicates that he remained a member until the end.

(*q.v.*).[333] Born on 14 April 1618, Moore was only eight when his father died, leaving him heir to six or seven manors and their appurtenances. The assignment of £1500 portions for three of his sisters and £750 each for two others indicates that the family was one of wealth.[334] Young Thomas entered Lincoln's Inn in 1635.[335] He was elected by Heytesbury to the first parliament after his coming of age, the Short Parliament.[336] His ownership of the manor of Heytesbury—until he sold it in 1641 to his colleague, Edward Ashe—doubtless insured his election both times in 1640.

In the early period of the Long Parliament, Moore was never a conspicuous member. He was inexperienced, his first appointment even in county administrative work apparently being that of 1641 to the commission for the subsidy.[337] In June, 1642, he promised two horses for the defense,[338] and he worked with the parliamentarians during the war. He is said to have been assigned by them to some office in the customs house.[339] About 1651 he married Bridget, daughter of Sir Thomas Trenchard of Wolveton, Dorset, a niece of John Trenchard, another opposition M.P.[340] He survived the Restoration, sat in several later parliaments,[341] and died on 6 August 1695. His epitaph at Hawkchurch, Dorset, described him as of calm and moderate habits, pious, upright, and serene.[342]

* **Richard More** (*c.* 1576–1643), of Linley, near Bishop's Castle, Shropshire, was M.P. for that borough from 1640 until he died in 1643. He was born in 1576 or earlier,[343] and was married probably before 1600.[344] He was chosen a member for Bishop's Castle at a by-election in 1610,[345] but did not sit again until the Short Parliament. Meanwhile he was a J.P. for the county,[346] a member of the corporation of Bishop's Castle in

1632, and bailiff there in 1637.[347] More was known for his learning and for his writing in defense of puritanism.

Little is known of More's wealth, although he seems to have owned one or two manors. He was a connection by marriage of Pierrepont.

William Morgan (d. 1649), lawyer, of Ddrew, or Therrow, Brecknockshire, was M.P. for his county, with some interruptions, from 1640 until 1649. As the son and heir of Llewellyn Morgan of Ystradvelltrey, Brecon, gentleman, he was admitted to the Middle Temple on 17 March 1616. He shared a chamber there with Walter Kyrle and was called to the bar in 1623 in company with others who were to be his colleagues of the Long Parliament, D'Ewes, Davies, and John George.[348] His marriage with Elizabeth, daughter of Sir William Morgan of Tredegar (d. 1653), probably accounts for his sitting in the 1628 parliament for Monmouth borough.[349] He was a J.P. in county Brecon in 1634 and 1638, being styled in the lists as King's Attorney for the county.[350] And in March, 1639, he received a grant for life of the office of Solicitor General before the President and Council of Wales.[351] As such he was among the official candidates nominated for the Long Parliament.[352] He had probably owed his Short Parliament election to the same influence.

Morgan was not prominent in the House, but was named to occasional committees.[353] It was reported to Hyde in 1643 that Mr. Morgan might be won over to help the royalist cause in Monmouthshire,[354] and Morgan was absent from the House for some time in 1644. He was assessed as if he were a royalist,[355] and seems even to have been present at the Oxford parliament for a time, although he declared it was against his will. He was temporarily barred from the House in 1647, but he escaped disablement.[356] He died between 27 May and 27 June 1649, the writ for the election of his successor being ordered on the latter date.[357]

Morgan owned the manor of Brecon and had at least one other nearby.[358] He was reputed to be worth £800

[333] Marshall, *Vis. Wilts.*, 9–10; Hoare, *Wilts.* 1 (2): 118; Wilts. Arch. Soc. MSS, Taylor's Notes on the Brouncker, Smith, and Moore Families.

[334] I.P.M., Thomas Moore, 1627, C. 142/423/69; will of Thomas Moore, senior, in Taylor's notes cited above.

[335] *Linc. Inn Rec. Adm.* 1: 226.

[336] *M. of P.* 1: 484.

[337] *Wilts. Arch. Mag.* 38: 593, 1913–1914.

[338] *N. and Q.*, 1st Ser., 12: 359, 1855.

[339] *The mystery of the good old cause*, 28.

[340] She died in 1653 after two years of marriage. Moore's second wife, Elizabeth Bampfield, survived him. Hutchins, *Dorset* 4: 53; Brown, *Somerset Wills* 4: 52.

[341] *M. of P.* 1: 517, 541, 547.

[342] Hutchins, *loc. cit.*

[343] According to the I.P.M. of his father, Richard was twenty-eight "and more" in March, 1603/4. C. 142/284/71.

[344] The baptisms and burials of several children of Richard More of Linley, 1601–1613, are recorded in *Shropshire Parish Registers*, Shropshire Parish Register Society, Hereford, 2, More, 6–11, 1901. He had two grandchildren by the time of the 1623 visitation. *The visitation of Shropshire* (Harleian Society, 28–29) 1: 172, 1889 (hereafter, *Vis. Shropshire*).

[345] Shrops. Arch. Soc., *Trans.*, 1st Ser., 10: 133, 1887.

[346] C. 193/12, 13.

[347] Shrops. Arch. Soc., *Trans.*, 2nd Ser., 10: 46, 1897–1898.

[348] *Mid. Temp. Rec.* 2: 604, 668, 682, 920.

[349] As William Morgan of the Middle Temple. Sir William Morgan had sat for Monmouthshire in 1624 and 1625. *M. of P.* 1: 458, 464, 476; *Al. Oxon.*

[350] C. 193/13; S.P. 16/405.

[351] *C.S.P. Dom., 1638–1639*, 617.

[352] Kershaw, The elections for the Long Parliament, *E.H.R.* 38: 497 and n., 1923.

[353] *C.J.* 2: 161, 191.

[354] *Calendar of Clarendon State Papers* 1: 238.

[355] *Cal. Com. Adv. Money*, 434; *C.J.* 3: 390.

[356] *Cal. Com. Adv. Money*, 588. Morgan's petition stating his war activities appears in *H.M.C., Sixth Report*, House of Lords MSS, 173.

[357] *M. of P.* 1: 498. His will of 27 May 1649 was proved the following 14 November. P.C.C., 169 Fairfax.

[358] British Museum Add. Charters, 24,458, 24,462, 24,470.

a year in 1644,[359] and when he made his will in 1649 he mentioned lands which he had purchased and desired that a portion of not over £2000 be set aside for his only daughter, Blanche. His son, William, was his heir.[360]

* **Herbert Morley** (1616–1667), of Glynde, Sussex, the parliamentary colonel, was M.P. for Lewes, 1640–1653. He was educated at Emmanuel College, Cambridge (admitted 1632),[361] was a sewers commissioner in Sussex in 1637,[362] and seems to have been elected for Lewes, *vice* Stapeley, a few days before the Short Parliament ended.[363] Morley's father before him had opposed the 1621 loan and the knighthood composition, but had probably assisted as a J.P. with the enforcing of martial law in the county in 1627.[364] Before he reached his majority Morley had the experience of being a royal ward.[365]

Morley was present at the county election in October, 1640,[366] and in the months before war came was named to several important committees in the parliament. They included those on Emmanuel College, on recusancy, and the recess committee.[367]

Morley's inherited estate consisted of at least four manors and other properties, one being an iron mill.[368] He pledged two horses for the defense in 1642.[369] The historian, May, described him as "a gentleman of good rank."[370] He seems not to have been related to Sir William Morley, his royalist colleague, but William Hay was a kinsman.

Sir William Morley (1606–1658 ?), of Halnaker near Chichester, Sussex, was M.P. for Chichester, 1640–23 November 1642. He was the son and heir of Sir John Morley of Halnaker (d. 1622) by his wife, Cicely, daughter of Sir Edward Carrell of Harting, and the grandson of the John Morley of Saxham (d. 1587), who became rich in his office in the Exchequer under Elizabeth and purchased both the Halnaker estate and the family arms.[371] Born early in 1606,[372] William in-

herited his father's estate in 1622 and probably soon afterwards married Mary, daughter of Sir Robert Heath, the Chief Justice of Common Pleas. One of their children was baptized at Boxgrove, the family parish, in December, 1624.[373] Morley was probably knighted on 4 September 1625, and seems to have begun to emulate the careers of his father and grandfather as M.P.'s [374] at the Guildford by-election in 1626.[375]

Sir William was probably a member of the commission for martial law in Sussex in 1627 [376] and during the 1630's was a J.P. and member of the commissions on sewers and piracy.[377] As sheriff of Surrey and Sussex in 1636 he had some trouble collecting the arrears of ship money but seems to have tried to obey orders regarding them.[378] For a few years after 1631 Morley enjoyed a share of the profits of the clerkship of the court of Star Chamber, being associated in the grant with Sir William Uvedale, but he seems not to have performed his duties in the post and about 1635 was offered satisfaction for relinquishing it.[379] An allowance of £2000 seems to have been set aside for him from the royal revenues in 1639, but he apparently lent a like amount the following year.[380] In 1640 he was one of the subsidy commissioners in Sussex.[381]

Morley did not sit in the Short Parliament, but his election at Chichester in the fall was a repetition of the successes his father had several times enjoyed there. As one of the wealthier members Sir William offered his bond for £1000 for the November loan. He was named to a committee regarding one of the London churches,[382] but was not heard often in debate. In April, 1642, he subscribed for the reducing of Ireland, but was absent later that spring. In September, having incurred suspicion of inclining toward royalism, he promised for the defense six horses and £200, changing his offer later to £400 and two horses. Soon, however, his participation in the attempt to gain Chichester for the king revealed his loyalties, and on 23 November

[359] *Cal. Com. Adv. Money*, 434.

[360] In addition to the authorities cited above see Williams, *Parl. Hist. Wales*, 16.

[361] *Al. Cant.*

[362] C. 181/5, fol. 139.

[363] Notes in the files of the Committee on the History of Parliament, memoranda on additional M.P.'s.

[364] S.P. 14, 127/79; *Sussex Arch. Coll.* **16**: 48, 1864; *C.S.P. Dom.*, *1627–1628*, 461.

[365] *Vis. Sussex*, *1633–4*, 48.

[366] Sussex indenture, C. 219/43/Part 2.

[367] *C.J.* **2**: 52, 113, 288.

[368] I.P.M., Robert Morley, C. 142/488/92.

[369] *N. and Q.*, 1st Ser., **12**: 360, 1855.

[370] May, 310.

[371] *Vis. Sussex*, *1633–4*, 140–141; *Sussex Arch. Coll.* **5**: 45, 1852. The member has frequently been identified as a younger son of John Morley of Saxham (*Al. Oxon.*; Pink MSS, 319; and elsewhere), but that son never seems to have been knighted and as early as 1605 was identified as of Chichester (*cf.* his marriage license [*Sussex Rec. Soc.* **12**: 182, 1911]

and the note of his wife's burial in 1628 [Add. MSS, 5699, fol. 183]). Sir John Morley mentioned his younger brother, William Morley, Esquire, in his will (*Sussex Rec. Soc.* **14**: 166, 1912), and both William Morley, Esquire, and William Morley, Knight, were members of the Sussex sewers commission in 1630 and 1637 (C. 181/4, fols. 46v–47; 181/5, fols. 138–139). The apparent wealth of the M.P. indicates that he was the head of his house rather than a younger brother. The member has been confused occasionally also with Sir William Morley, K.B. (*c.* 1639–1701), who was his son.

[372] *Sussex Rec. Soc.* **14**: 166, 1912.

[373] Add. MSS, 5699, fol. 154v.

[374] Pink MSS, 319.

[375] Pink MSS, 311, fol. 471c; *M. of P.* **1**: 472, n.

[376] *C.S.P. Dom.*, *1627–1628*, 461.

[377] C. 193/13; S.P. 16/405; C. 181/4, fol. 46v; 181/5, *passim*.

[378] *C.S.P. Dom.*, *1636–1637*, 74.

[379] *Ibid.*, *1631–1633*, 68; *1635–1636*, 57.

[380] S.P. 16, 450/30; 453/74.

[381] *Sussex Arch. Coll.* **9**: 104, 1857.

[382] D'Ewes (N), 52; *C.J.* **2**: 191.

1642 he was disabled.[383]   He recovered his sequestered estates within a year by paying a fine of £1000,[384] and apparently maintained an inactive role thereafter until his death.   He was buried at Boxgrove in June, 1658, or January, 1658/9,[385] and his will, dated 14 June 1658, was proved 16 February 1659.[386]

From his father Sir William inherited four Sussex manors, and he seems to have acquired two or three others by purchase before 1640.[387] His sister who married Sir Thomas Puckering in 1616 was said to have had a portion of £5000,[388] and in his will Sir William planned a portion of £3000 for his elder daughter and £2000 for a younger one.   His pledges in parliament, 1640–1642, are further indications that he was a man of wealth.

Sir William Morley does not seem to have been related to his fellow M.P. of the same surname, the parliamentarian,[389] but he was distantly connected with the family of Edward Kirton and through his wife with Henry Shelley.

John Mostyn (*c.* 1603–1675), of the Inner Temple and of Tregarneth, Anglesey, was M.P. for county Flint, 1640–5 February 1644.[390] He was the second son of Sir Roger Mostyn of Mostyn in Flint (M.P., H.S., Member of the Council of Wales, d. 1642) [391] by his wife, Mary, daughter of Sir John Wynn, Bart., of Gwydir, and was a nephew of the courtier, Sir Richard Wynn (*q.v.*).[392] His eldest brother, Thomas (d. 1641), married in 1623 a sister of Bulstrode Whitelocke.[393] John Mostyn was born about 1603, and was reared at both Gwydir and Mostyn under tutors,[394] and matriculated in 1619 at Queen's, Cambridge.[395] In the summer of 1621 he entered the service of a great friend of the Wynn family, John Williams, Dean of Westminster, who had just become Bishop of Lincoln and Lord Keeper,[396] and the following year, by the

special request of William Noye, was admitted to Lincoln's Inn.[397] He was M.P. for Anglesey in 1624, having been elected doubtless through the influence of his relatives,[398] and spent most of his time for the next decade or more in the service of Williams. When the latter withdrew to his bishopric after being removed from the Council, Mostyn divided his time principally between Northamptonshire and London.[399] He was admitted to the Inner Temple in 1637, perhaps choosing to live there as a companion to his elder brother's son, Roger, who was admitted that year.[400]

A member of both parliaments of 1640 for his family's county of Flint, Mostyn was called upon in November, 1640, to testify regarding some words of Dr. Cosins. He offered his bond for £1000 to support the loan that month,[401] and was named to a committee as late as 1 September 1641. But he had leave of absence granted him on 14 December,[402] and when war came he abandoned parliament for the king. In so doing he joined forces with his cousin, John Bodvel (*q.v.*), rather than following their uncle, Sir Richard Wynn. He was assessed at £1000 by the parliamentarians, his estate being considered worth £1000 a year,[403] and in 1654 he was dealing with the compounding commissioners regarding his properties.[404] He retired afterwards to Maesmynan, an estate his father had granted him, and died unmarried on 26 December 1675 in his seventy-third year.[405]

Sir Edmund Moundeford (*c.* 1595–1643), of Feltwell, Norfolk, sat for his county, 1640–1653.[406] Descended from an ancient family of Norfolk gentlemen, he was the only son and heir of Sir Edmund Moundeford of Feltwell (d. 1617), by his first wife, Frances, daughter of Sir Thomas Gawdy of Claxton.[407] He was born about 1595, and was educated at Wymondham and at

[383] *C.J.* 2: 757, 765, 860; *Sussex Arch. Coll.* 5: 46, 1852; Thomas-Stanford, *Sussex in the great Civil War*, 45.

[384] G. N. Godwin, *The Civil War in Hampshire*, 103.

[385] The date in the parish register has been read as 23 Jan. 1658 in *Sussex Arch. Coll.* 5: 46, n., but as 23 June 1658 in Add. MSS, 154v. The January entry would of course be 1658/9, new style.

[386] P.C.C., 45 Pell.

[387] *Sussex Rec. Soc.* 14: 166, 1912; 19: 4, 22, 1914; *Sussex Arch. Coll* 5: 46, 1852.

[388] *The letters of John Chamberlain* 2: 15.

[389] Thomas-Stanford, *op. cit.*, 15.

[390] *M. of P.* 1: 498; *C.J.* 3: 389.

[391] *Arch. Camb.*, 6th Ser., 17: 195, 1917; S.P. 14, 135/41.

[392] *Cal. Wynn Papers*, 38, 479; The Right Hon. Lord Mostyn and T. A. Glenn, *History of the family of Mostyn of Mostyn*, 196, London, Harrison, 1925. The sketch of Mostyn given by Williams (*Parl. Hist. Wales*, 86) contains so many errors that I have rewritten it.

[393] Whitelocke, *Memorials of the English affairs* 1: 144, 1853; *Cal. Wynn Papers*, 177.

[394] *Cal. Wynn Papers*, 79, 96, 101.

[395] *Al. Cant.*

[396] *Cal. Wynn Papers*, 151.

[397] *Linc. Inn Rec. Adm.* 1: 191.

[398] *M. of P.* 1: 462; *Cal. Wynn Papers*, 199, 205.

[399] *Ibid.*, 156, 157, 178, 221, 237, 243, 251.

[400] *Students admitted to the Inner Temple*, 292, 295. The article in *D.N.B.* on this Roger Mostyn errs as to his parents.

[401] D'Ewes (N), 52, n., 541.

[402] *C.J.* 2: 279, 342.

[403] *Cal. Com. Adv. Money*, 434. His family's lands, including properties at Chester and important coal lands and collieries in the Dee estuary (Nef, *The rise of the British coal industry* 2: 7; Harl. MSS, 1991, fol. 132), were probably worth £1500 or more a year in his father's day. *Cal. Wynn Papers*, 132.

[404] He petitioned as of county Flint, of the Inner Temple, and of Tregarneth, Anglesey, and was especially concerned about his Temple chamber which had been seized in 1643 and about his books. *Cal. Com. Comp.*, 1200; *Cal. Wynn Papers*, 299, 327.

[405] Lord Mostyn and T. A. Glenn, *loc. cit.*; *Flintshire Historical Society Journal*, 1916–1917: 89; *Cal. Wynn Papers*, 415.

[406] *M. of P.* 1: 491. Moundeford's name appears sometimes as Edward, but Edmund was the form he used.

[407] W. Rye, ed., *The visitations of Norfolk, 1563, 1589, 1613*, Harleian Society 32: 202, 1891; *Norfolk Archaeology* 5: 55, 57, 1859.

Caius College, Cambridge, where he was admitted in 1612.[408] On 2 September 1614 he married Penelope, daughter of William or Thomas Brews of Wenham, Suffolk,[409] and in 1617 succeeded his father. He was knighted on 9 September 1629 and seems to have taken as his second wife, possibly by 1632, a member of the Heveningham family, probably a daughter of Sir John Heveningham of Ketteringham and sister of William Heveningham, the regicide (q.v.).[410]

Moundeford was active in county affairs by Charles's reign. He was one of the 1627 loan commissioners, a J.P. at the same period and regularly thereafter,[411] and a member of various other commissions.[412] He was elected to parliament for Thetford in 1628 and for the county in the spring of 1640.[413] While he was in London attending parliament, and at frequent intervals in the period between 1626 and 1635, Moundeford corresponded with his cousin and intimate friend, Framlingham Gawdy (q.v.).[414] He was a stanch puritan and was one of those interested in the Providence Island Company.[415] Among his close friends he counted Tobias Frere of Harleston,[416] who was later active as a sequestrator and was viewed in more conservative circles as a schismatic and a promoter of factionalism in the county,[417] and probably had his support in the 1640 elections.

As a member of the Long Parliament Moundeford worked with Pym's party, was one of the Committee of Privileges and of those dealing with the monopolists and the Jesuits. He urged debate on the Book of Common Prayer in November, upheld the London petition against episcopacy, and seems to have been one of the extreme group in matters of religion. His wealth he offered without hesitation for the cause, as his pledges of £1000 and £500 for the loans, 1640–1641, testify,[418] and his offer of £600 jointly with Harman for reducing Ireland, and his promise to supply and maintain two horses for the defense in 1642.[419] With the outbreak of war, Moundeford prepared to take an active part in military matters, but he died on 5 May 1643, apparently after a short illness, and was buried at Feltwell.[420]

Moundeford's properties in Norfolk were extensive, including at least four or five manors,[421] and enabling him to provide annuities of over £245 for his stepmother and other relatives, but the amount of his own income is not known. His interest in religious matters, as indicated by his role in parliament, is evident in the directions he made in his will for turning over to a cleric his Greek lexicon and his books on religion. His law books he assigned to a cousin.[422]

John Moyle (c. 1614–1658), of Bake, Cornwall, returned for St. Germans in that county, was temporarily barred from his seat pending a decision on his election, but was sitting in the House by May, 1641. He kept his seat probably until 1648.[423] He was the eldest son and heir apparent of John Moyle of Bake (1592 ?–1661), the chief squire in the district of St. Germans and Sir John Eliot's friend. His mother was Admonition, daughter of Edmund Prideaux of Netherton, Devon, and half-sister of the 1640 M.P. of that name.[424] Moyle was born about 1614 and seems to have been inactive in public life before 1640. His father was the family's representative on the commission of the peace,[425] and was the one who protested having been charged too much for his knighthood composition.[426] The younger

---

[408] *Al. Cant.* Edmund was aged twenty-two and more when his father died in May, 1617. I.P.M., Sir Edmund Moundeford, C. 142/369/166.

[409] Her father's name appears as William in the I.P.M. cited above, but as Thomas in Blomefield, *Norfolk* 2: 193 and *Norfolk Archaeology* 5: 55, 1859.

[410] Most of the printed sources mention no second marriage, although Rye (*Norfolk families,* 580) confuses the two wives, writing Penelope Brews as the daughter of a Heveningham. Moundeford referred in his will, however, to his first wife and mentioned as brothers-in-law William and Arthur Heveningham, as an uncle, Thomas Heveningham, and as an aunt, Lady Pettus. The latter was probably Abigail, a sister of Sir John Heveningham (*Vis Norfolk,* 221). In a letter of 1632 Moundeford addressed William Heveningham as "brother" (*H.M.C., Tenth Report* 2, Gawdy MSS, 141), and Heveningham was a trustee in an estate settlement which Moundeford made in December, 1634. I.P.M., Sir Edmund Moundeford, 1643, C. 142/710/33.

[411] C. 193/12 and 13; S.P. 16, 60/65; Norfolk County MSS, Sessions Rolls, 1626, 1631–1632, 1636–1637, 1639–1640.

[412] C. 181/4, fols. 21v, 31v; 181/5, fols. 19, 284, 361.

[413] *M. of P.* 1: 476; *Willis* 3: 233.

[414] *H.M.C., Tenth Report* 2, Gawdy MSS, 123, 129, 135, 155; *Norfolk Archaeology* 5: 53–73, 1859.

[415] He tried once to interest his kinsman and friend, Sir Simonds D'Ewes, in the project. Harl. MSS, 287, fol. 265.

[416] In his will Moundeford called Frere "my honest friend," and he was godfather to one of Frere's sons. P.C.C., 45 Rivers.

[417] W. Rye, *History of Norfolk,* 98, London, 1885; Rye, *Norfolk families,* 231.

[418] *C.J.* 2: 21, 30, 73; D'Ewes (N), 52, 63, 337, 439.

[419] *C.S.P. Ireland, Adventurers,* 314; *N. and Q.,* 1st Ser., 12: 358, 1855.

[420] Cooper, *Annals of Cambridge* 3: 331. His will was dated 18 April 1643, less than a month before his death.

[421] I.P.M.'s of Sir Edmund Moundeford and his father as cited above, notes 408 and 410.

[422] Among the friends to whom he left mourning rings were eight fellow members of the 1640 parliament, including, besides those mentioned above, Sir Thomas Wodehouse, Sir Thomas Barrington, Sir Roger North, and Sir John Potts.

[423] *C.J.* 2: 63, 133; D'Ewes (N), 107, 222. Moyle's father wrote on 19 December 1640 to thank Sir Richard Buller and his sons for speaking against the proposal to oust his son, John, from the Commons, declaring it foolish for Mr. Scawen (William Scawen, M.P. for the borough in the spring) to try to challenge the election (*The Buller Papers,* 30). That letter clearly establishes the identity of the member, concerning which some doubts have existed (e.g., *Western Antiquary* 5: 86, 1885–1886; 7: 40, 1887–1888). See below for the origin of the doubts.

[424] Vivian, *Vis. Cornwall,* 334–335; *Western Antiquary* 5: 86, 1885–1886.

[425] C. 193/12, 13; S.P. 16/405.

[426] S.P. 16, 238/83. For other details of the elder Moyle's career see *D.N.B.*

Moyle owed his election chiefly to the influence of the Eliot family and to his father,[427] and in the Long Parliament supported the popular cause. He was never prominent in the House,[428] however, and on one day in 1646, apparently through some error and in his absence, the Commons ordered a new election for replacing him as "sithence deceased."[429] But the election does not seem to have occurred,[430] and Moyle was still listed as a member in July, 1648. His father also was by that time a member, having entered the House from East Looe.[431] The son was probably secluded by Pride's Purge.[432] But he lived until 1658, and was buried at St. Germans, 4 February 1658.[433]

John Moyle, junior, married probably after 1645, and he and his wife, Martha, had four children baptized at St. Germans, 1648–1657.[434] Of his financial standing almost nothing is known except that his family's estate in the early part of the century included seven manors in Cornwall and Devon.[435]

* **Sir Philip Musgrave, Bart.** (1607–1678), of Hartley in Westmorland and Edenhall in Cumberland, was M.P. for Westmorland, 1640–15 March 1643.[436] His father, Sir Richard Musgrave, K.B., who had been a J.P., D.L., and M.P., died while travelling in Italy in 1615. Philip lived for a time thereafter with his grandfather, Lord Wharton, who was his guardian, and then in the home of Judge Hutton of Yorkshire, one of whose daughters he married in 1625. His health was poor in his early years, and he was said to be of a somewhat melancholy disposition and not inclined toward an active life. He became a J.P. in both Cumberland and Westmorland, however,[437] was a commissioner of oyer and terminer,[438] and a D.L.,[439] and in 1639 was colonel of a regiment of foot.[440]

Musgrave's family, one of the oldest in the region,[441] held several manors in the border counties.[442] His estates were said to be much disordered during his minority, but he improved their condition, and was one of the wealthy M.P.'s who offered £500 as security for a loan in 1641.[443]

Sir Philip was a cousin of Sir Patrick Curwen and Sir William Widdrington, and a brother-in-law of Sir Thomas Mauleverer.[444]

* **Gerard Napier** (1606–1673), of More Crichel and Middlemarsh Hall, Dorset, was M.P. for Melcombe Regis, 1640–22 January 1644.[1] He was the eldest son of Nathaniel Napier of More Crichel (H.S., M.P., d. 1635).[2] Gerard entered the Middle Temple on 8 November 1627,[3] and the following February was chosen to serve for Wareham in parliament.[4] He was afterwards a J.P. and member of several local commissions in Dorset, Hampshire, and Wilts,[5] and in 1637 was a deputy vice admiral.[6] He was a D.L. in 1640, the year in which he was called before Council for laxity in the raising of troops.[7] He had declined to contribute toward the royal expenses by loan in 1639.[8] Napier was made a freeman of Weymouth and Melcombe Regis on 16 October 1640,[9] doubtless in preparation for his election to parliament a few days later. Before the first session of the parliament was over, however, Napier was won over by the court faction. He became a baronet and a knight in June, 1641, and was eventually disabled as a royalist. After the Restoration he was prominent at court.

Napier owned considerable land in Dorset and Hampshire. Some of his properties in the latter county he sold shortly before the war for £3000. As "Mr. Napper" in November, 1640, he pledged his security for £1000 for the loan.[10] Both the assessment of £3500 laid on him later and the fine levied for his delinquency (a tenth, £3514, with allowance to be made of £1250 lent

427 *The Buller Papers*, 30–31.
428 He was named to a few minor committees. Pink MSS, 307, fol. 263.
429 *C.J.* 4: 719. The idea that Moyle was dead perhaps developed from his prolonged absence, or from some confusion of identities. One royalist officer named Moyle had been killed in 1643 (Add. MSS, 18,980, fol. 115). Or the wording in the *Journal* may simply have resulted from a clerk's error, as in the case of Jonathan Rashleigh (*q.v.*).
430 It is suggested in *M. of P.* (1: 487, n.) that Scawen succeeded to Moyle's seat in 1646, but I have found no return at the Public Record Office to bear out that suggestion.
431 Thomason Tracts, E. 454, 17.
432 Pink MSS, 307, fol. 263.
433 Vivian, *loc. cit.*
434 *Ibid.*
435 A suit in Chancery concerning their holdings was in progress in 1620. C. 3/318/3.
436 *M. of P.* 1: 495; *C.J.* 3: 1.
437 C. 193/13; *C.S.P. Dom.*, 1638–1639, 312.
438 C. 181/5, fols. 255, 274, 323.
439 *H.M.C., Third Report*, MSS of the Duke of Devonshire, 40.
440 Samuel Jefferson, *The history and antiquities of Cumberland* 1: 473, Carlisle, 1840–1842.

441 *Ibid.* 1: 405; Ferguson, *Cumberland and Westmorland M.P.'s*, 417.
442 J. F. Curwen, ed., *The later records of North Westmorland*, Cumb. and Westm. A. and A. Soc., Record Series, 8 (Kendal): 111, 130, 179, 181, 1932; D. Fleming, *A description of Cumberland and Westmorland*, Cumb. and Westm. A. and A. Soc., Tract Series, 1: 22, 1882; *Cal. Com. Comp.*, 2308.
443 D'Ewes (N), 435, n.
444 In addition to the above authorities, see G. Burton, *Life of Sir Philip Musgrave*, ed. by S. Jefferson, Carlisle, 1839.
1 *M. of P.* 1: 488; *C.J.* 3: 374.
2 *Complete Baronetage* 2: 91; Hutchins, *Dorset* 3: 126.
3 *Mid. Temp. Rec.* 2: 726.
4 *Complete Baronetage* 2: 91; *M. of P.* 1: 475.
5 C. 193/13; C. 181/5, fols. 210, 226, *passim*.
6 *C.S.P. Dom.*, 1636–1637, 527.
7 *Ibid.*, 1640, 55; *D.N.B.*
8 Rushworth 3: 913.
9 Moule, *Catalogue of the . . . documents of the borough of Weymouth and Melcombe Regis*, 113.
10 D'Ewes (N), 52.

to the Weymouth garrison) [11] indicate that he was a man of wealth.

Gerard Napier was related distantly to Sir Robert Napier, the M.P. for Peterborough. Through his wife he was a kinsman of John Coventry and Sir William Portman, since they had all married daughters of John Colles of Barton, Somerset. Possibly the influence of his royalist brothers-in-law affected his politics in 1641.

Sir Robert Napier, Bart. (1602–1661), of Luton Hoo, Bedfordshire, returned for Peterborough, Northamptonshire, and seated by vote of the House, 4 February 1641, after some doubt as to his election, served until December, 1648.[12] Of Scottish descent, he was related to the Napiers of Dorset and Devon. His father, Sir Robert Napier, the first baronet, known as of Luton Hoo at his death in 1637, had been a London grocer and had been associated with the victuallers of the navy.[13] Sir Robert's son and heir by his third wife, Mary (or Margaret), daughter of John Robinson of London, merchant of the Staple, Robert was born in August, 1602,[14] matriculated at Exeter College, Oxford, 17 December 1619, aged sixteen, and was admitted to Gray's Inn in 1620. He was knighted at Whitehall on 20 April 1623, and that year he married at court a niece of the Duchess of Lenox, Frances, daughter of Sir William Thornhurst of Agincourt, Kent. She died in 1626, and about seven years later Napier married well again, his second wife being Penelope, a daughter of the first Earl of Bridgewater.[15]

Sir Robert may have lived part of the time in Dorset, with his own or his wife's relatives,[16] and was M.P. for Corfe Castle in 1626 and Weymouth and Melcombe Regis in 1628.[17] He was a J.P. in Bedfordshire, however, from 1634, as well as a commissioner for other local matters there and in nearby counties, and in 1635 was a D.L.[18] He was an unsuccessful candidate for the Short Parliament at Ludlow, despite his father-in-law's support,[19] and did not win his election at Peterborough in October without a contest. In politics,

though he supported parliament enough to keep his seat until 1648, he was lukewarm. He was asked in January, 1643, to advance £1000, and a year later, having been for some time suspect, barely escaped disablement.[20] He lived until 1661, and was buried at Luton, 7 March 1661. His will, dated 29 January, was proved 26 April 1661.[21]

Napier was evidently well-to-do, and owned properties in Northants in addition to his principal ones in Bedfordshire.[22] One of his relatives in the House was his wealthy brother-in-law, Sir Thomas Middleton of Denbighshire. Another kinsman was Gerard Napier of his Dorset connections.

John Nash (1590–1662), clothier and alderman of Worcester, was M.P. for Worcester, 1640–1648. He was probably the second son of Richard Nash, Worcester clothier, bailiff (1581), and M.P. (1584), who died in 1605, by his wife, Margaret, daughter of Thomas Fleet, and a nephew by marriage of John Cowcher (q.v.).[23] He was a relative of Thomas Nash, the linguist and lawyer of the Inner Temple.[24] John was born in 1590,[25] and was probably a member of the lower chamber of Worcester's municipal government when he was reported in 1627 as a partial defaulter from the loan.[26] He was a collector for the city charities in 1628, was chosen one of the "Four-and-Twenty" in 1630, and reluctantly paid a fine instead of serving also as chamberlain that year. He was sheriff in 1632, mayor, 1633, and alderman afterwards.[27]

Nash was not often named to committees in the Long Parliament, but he promised to supply £40 for the defense in September, 1642,[28] and remained a member until 1648. At his death in 1662 he established various charities, including £300 for loans to young tradesmen.[29]

* **Francis Newport** (1620–1708), of High Ercall, near Shrewsbury, Salop, was M.P. for Shrewsbury, 1640–22

[11] Cal. Com. Adv. Money, 429; Cal. Com. Comp., 1062.

[12] M. of P. 1: 491, n.; D'Ewes (N), 222–223; C.J. 2: 63, 78.

[13] MSS of the Grocers' Company of London, Index of Freemen, 1345–1645, and Quire of Warden's Accounts, 1622–1623, fols. 186, 233v; C.S.P. Dom., 1611–1618, 538, 545; D.N.B., "Richard Napier."

[14] Notes on the life of Napier. Sloane MSS, 1708, fol. 118.

[15] The letters of John Chamberlain 2: 495. In 1621, when plans were being made for the marriage of the earl's eldest daughter, her portion was rumored to be £2000 in lands and £4000 in money, with additions if the earl should die without male issue. Ibid. 2: 364.

[16] His son Robert was born there. Somerset and Dorset N. and Q. 1: 267, 1889–1890.

[17] M. of P. 1: 469, 475. The 1626 M.P. has sometimes been indentified as his father, but the return designates him as "knight," not "baronet."

[18] C. 193/13; S.P. 16/405; C. 181/5, fols. 6, 62, 91, 120; C.S.P. Dom., 1635, 159.

[19] Shrops. Arch Soc., Trans., 2nd Ser., 7: 26, 1894–1895.

[20] C.J. 2: 916; 3: 374.

[21] P.C.C., 60 May.

[22] C.S.P. Dom., 1619–1623, 92; 1623–1625, 112. See also Complete Baronetage 1: 80; Vis. Beds., 184.

[23] The will of Richard Nash (P.C.C., 70 Hayes); I.P.M. of Richard Nash (C. 142/311/95); Wilson, ed., The parish book of St. Helen's Church in Worcester 2: 7, 101, 108, 137. T. R. Nash, in his Collections for the history of Worcestershire (2 v., London, 1781–1782), places John Nash (1590–1662) in the pedigree of the Ombersley-Droitwich branch of the family instead of with his kinsmen of Tappenhall in Claynes, and omits his father, Richard, entirely (1: 327).

[24] D.N.B., "Thomas Nash."

[25] His portrait, dated 1658, in his sixty-eighth year, is printed in Nash, op. cit. 1: opp. 326.

[26] C.S.P. Dom., 1627–1628, 267.

[27] Worcester Corporation MSS, Order Book 2, fols. 117v, 145, 150, 164; Audit Book 2, fols. 118v, 121v.

[28] C.J. 2: 772.

[29] Nash, loc. cit. The M.I. to him at St. Helen's Church does not mention a wife or children but refers to his benevolences. See also Williams, Worcester, 96.

January 1644.[30] He was born in March, 1620,[31] and was the heir apparent to "the best estate of any gentleman in that country." [32] His father, Sir Richard Newport (d. 1651), held many county offices and was a member of the Council of Wales.[33] Like him, Francis was a royalist and together they were heavily fined. Even during his father's lifetime Francis seems to have enjoyed an income of between £800 and £1000 a year. His fine as a delinquent, apparently in combination with his father's, was set first at over £16,000, and later changed to some £10,000.[34] Clarendon described him as "a young gentleman of great expectation and of excellent parts." [35]

* **Robert Nicholas** (1595–1667), of the Middle Temple, Recorder of Devizes, Wiltshire, sat for that borough, 1640–1653. Descended from a family long settled in All Cannings and Bishops Cannings parishes near Devizes, he was the son and heir of John Nicholas of Roundway and Devizes, and his wife, Mary. He was baptized at Devizes in 1595 and probably was graduated B.A. from Queen's College, Oxford, in 1613. In the fall of the same year he was admitted to the Middle Temple.[36] He was called to the bar in 1621, helped to provide the Readers' feast in 1639, and by May, 1646, was a Bencher.[37] But he retained his connections with Wiltshire, seems to have been living at Devizes by 1636, and was acting in legal matters for the borough.[38] In 1639 he was both town clerk and recorder. That the borough appreciated his efforts in the Long Parliament, his first, is indicated by its special vote in September, 1641, of £40 for his great pains and expenses for attending parliament.[39] He was outspoken against ship money and against the judges who had upheld it, and was an active parliamentarian during

the war and the commonwealth. He became a Serjeant-at-law in 1648 [40] and a judge under Cromwell.

Nicholas apparently married twice, although the names of his wives are not known. By his will of 6 May 1667 he made provision for two daughters, one already married, and for his "present wife." He is said to have died that year. His will was proved early in 1669.[41] He does not seem to have held extensive lands or to have been particularly wealthy. His subscription of £20 for the defense in 1642 was made as a gift rather than as a loan, but was one of the smaller sums in the list of contributions.[42]

* **Anthony Nicoll**, or **Nichols** (1611–1659), of Penvose in St. Tudy, Cornwall, was M.P. for Bodmin, 1640–1647. His return was disputed by John Bramston, son of the judge,[43] but through the influence of his uncle, John Pym, Nicoll retained the seat. He was present as a member by 3 May 1641.[44] The son and heir apparent of Humphrey Nicoll (d. 1642), he seems to have made his first appearance in public office as M.P. in the Short Parliament for Bossiney. His family properties included some houses in the latter borough as well as three manors in St. Tudy parish and elsewhere.[45] He was related to the Lower family of that parish, whose representative in the Long Parliament was Thomas Lower, and was a nephew not only of Pym but of Francis Rouse.

Michael Noble (c. 1591–1649), of the Close in Lichfield, was M.P. for Lichfield, 1640–1649. The son and heir of Edward Noble, also of the Close, who was probably a lawyer or agent of some sort for the cathedral,[46] Michael Noble was apparently a lawyer, too.[47] He became coroner and town clerk of Lichfield, and in 1631 compounded for not being a knight.[48] Noble's wife was reported to the Court of High Commission in 1638 for misconduct in the cathedral, for venturing to dispute with the wives of the canons for a seat of honor, and for other unseemly behavior.[49]

---

[30] C.J. 3: 374.

[31] The correction of his birth date from that given in D.N.B. is based on Shrops. Arch. Soc., Trans., 2nd Ser., 12: 7 and n., 1899–1900; Vis. Shrops. 2: 374. He was aged twenty-two in April, 1642, when he married. Marriage licenses, London (Harleian Society, 26) 2: 265, 1887.

[32] His father was said to have presented £6000 to the king on being created Baron Newport of High Ercall (Clarendon, Rebellion 2: 339–340); one of his daughters had a dowry of £5000 (C.S.P. Dom., 1637, 118).

[33] S.P. 14, 104/99; S.P. 16/405; 408/73.

[34] Cal. Com. Comp., 924–926; Shrops. Arch. Soc., Trans., 2nd Ser., 12: 17–20, 27–29, 1899–1900.

[35] Rebellion 2: 339.

[36] Wilts. Arch. Mag. 32: 248, 1901–1902; 41: 315, 1920–1922; Mid. Temp. Rec. 2: 572. Some authorities have confused him with a cousin, Robert, son of Edward Nicholas of All Cannings, born in 1597 and a student at the Inner Temple in 1614. Al. Oxon.; D.N.B.; Students admitted to the Inner Temple, 206.

[37] He was referred to in the Middle Temple records of 1644 specifically as of the House of Commons. Mid. Temp. Rec. 2: 669, 878, 932, 940. See also D'Ewes (N), 353–354; Cal. Com. Comp., 991.

[38] Add. MSS, 34,008, fols. 31–38.

[39] Wilts. Arch. Mag. 41: 315, 1920–1922; B. H. Cunnington, Some annals of the borough of Devizes 1: 98, Devizes, G. Simpson, 1925–1926.

[40] Wilts. Arch. Mag. 41: 315, 1920–1922.

[41] He described himself in his will as of "Seende Rewe" or Row, Wiltshire, and named his kinsman, Robert Nicholas of Roundway, among his executors. Ibid.; P.C.C., 20 Coke. The will of Robert Nicholas of Roundway was proved in 1670. P.C.C., 179 Penn.

[42] N. and Q., 1st Ser., 12: 360, 1855.

[43] His rival was not the judge himself as is suggested in the D.N.B. article on Nicoll. See M. of P. 1: 486, n.; 3: li.

[44] C.J. 2: 133, 155.

[45] Maclean, Parochial and family history of the parish of St. Tudy, 47.

[46] A Lichfield attorney in 1613 made notes of some memoranda of rentals of a prebend that Edward Noble had discovered. Birmingham Reference Library MSS, 381,201, fol. 53.

[47] On 7 November 1640 John, son of Michael Noble of Lichfield, was admitted to the Middle Temple and bound with his father. Mid. Temp. Rec. 2: 900.

[48] Staff. Hist. Coll. 2 (2): 20, 1881.

[49] C.S.P. Dom., 1637–1638, 219.

Noble was named in the Long Parliament to two early committees dealing with church reform, to one on enclosures, and one concerned with University College, Oxford.[50] He promised £100 for the defense in June, 1642,[51] and remained a member until his death.[52]

Noble was purchasing land in the county by 1617.[53] When he made his will in 1648, he owned several properties in Lichfield and the county and provided portions of £600 and £500 for two younger daughters.[54]

* **Baptist Noel** (1611–1682), of Exton, Rutlandshire, was M.P. for his county from 1640 until he succeeded his father as Viscount Camden in March, 1643,[55] but had probably been absent from the House for some time before the latter date. The eldest son of Edward Noel, second Viscount Camden, he was the heir apparent to a great fortune.[56] He was granted the degree of M.A. at Cambridge in 1628,[57] and probably lived at court much of the time thereafter. He offered his bond for £1000 for the loan in November, 1640, and was named to committees dealing with the army and with Sir Henry Spiller,[58] but he voted against Strafford's attainder [59] and from that time played a diminishing role. With his colleague, Palmes, he was summoned to be brought up in custody, 17 December 1642,[60] and was an active royalist.

* **Sir Dudley North**, K.B. (1602–1677), of Kirtling, Cambridgeshire, sat for the county from 12 November 1640 until he was secluded in 1648. The son and heir apparent of Dudley, third Baron North, he was a cousin of Sir Roger North, M.P. for Eye.[61] North was admitted to Gray's Inn in August, 1619, probably after his brief stay at Cambridge, and in 1622, after two years of service on the continent, he entered the Inner Temple for a short time.[62] Returning again from his

travels, he was M.P. for Horsham in 1628, was named on a committee on buildings in London in 1630, and during the next decade was a J.P. and member of other local commissions in the counties of Cambridge, Hunts, Lincoln, Suffolk, and others.[63]

Continuing his family's interest in the ventures of their times, Sir Dudley was concerned with the fen drainage program in Lincolnshire, 1637–1638.[64] He married well in 1632, and even during his father's lifetime owned various properties in Cambridgeshire and other parts of East Anglia.[65] He pledged £1000 to back the proposed loan in November, 1640, and in June, 1642, gave £60 outright for the defense.[66]

Sir Roger North (1588–1651), of Great Finborough and Mildenhall, Suffolk, was a member for Eye, 1640–1648. A grandson of Roger Lord North of Kirtling, he was the eldest son and heir of Sir Henry North (d. 1620) of Mildenhall, by his wife, Mary, daughter and coheiress of Richard Knyvet.[67] Born 12 March and baptized 17 March 1587/8 at Mildenhall,[68] Roger was trained in the armies, serving for a time in Ireland under Lord Deputy St. John, and in the Palatinate in a subordinate command in 1619.[69] He married (1) at Mildenhall, 29 December 1607, Elizabeth, daughter and coheiress of Sir John Gilbert of Great Finborough, a distant relative of Sir Walter Raleigh; and (2) Thomasine, daughter of Thomas Clenche of Holbrooke.[70] On 16 June 1618 North was knighted by the king at Theobalds.[71]

Sir Roger sat for Eye in the parliament of 1621, for Suffolk in 1624, and for Eye in each succeeding parliament thereafter until the end of the reign of Charles I.[72] He served also as a J.P.,[73] as a member of numerous

---

[50] C.J. **2**: 54, 92, 101, 195.

[51] N. and Q., 1st Ser., **12**: 359, 1855.

[52] Wedgwood, Staff. Parl. Hist. **2**: 83–84.

[53] Staff. Hist. Coll., N.S., **6** (1): 39, 1903.

[54] His will, dated 14 March 1647/8, was proved 12 March 1649 (1649/50?). P.C.C., 43 Pembroke.

[55] M. of P. **1**: 492 and n.

[56] The story of his losing £2500 of his wife's portion at a tennis match is well known. When his fine for royalism was first set in 1646 at over £19,500, he declared that his estate would not bring that amount if sold, and stated his income to be £1537 a year, with some £5000 more in reversion. His properties, inherited from his father and from his maternal grandfather, lay in Rutland, Lincoln, Middlesex, Kent, and Gloucestershire. H.M.C., Sixth Report, House of Lords MSS, 130; Cal. Com. Comp., 63, 939.

[57] Al. Cant. His father had studied at Sidney College, but no record of Baptist's admission has been found.

[58] D'Ewes (N), 52; C.J. **2**: 34, 48.

[59] Verney, 58.

[60] C.J. **2**: 893.

[61] Baker, Northampton **1**: 527. North was related through his wife to the Montagus, also M.P.'s, and to Sir Christopher Hatton.

[62] Cal. Inner Temple Recs. **2**: 130.

[63] S.P. 16, 171/3, 4; C. 193/13; C. 181/5, fols. 18, 201, 283, 317, passim.

[64] C.S.P. Dom., 1637, 184; S.P. 16, 378/49.

[65] Suffolk ship money returns, 1639–1640, V. B. Redstone, ed., 59, 60, 178, Suff. Inst. Arch., Ipswich, 1904; East Anglian, N.S., **9**: 285, 1901–1902.

[66] D'Ewes (N), 52; N. and Q., 1st Ser., **12**: 358, 1855.
In addition to the above references, see also Al. Cant., in which one error in D.N.B. is corrected, and M. of P. **1**: 478.

[67] Copinger, The manors of Suffolk **4**: 178; Baker, Northampton **1**: 526–527. Sir Roger was a first cousin of the father of Dudley Lord North (q.v.). He should not be confused with Roger North, the latter's uncle, who was a captain and explorer of note.

[68] Add. MSS, 19,095 (Davy collection), fols. 204, 205; Mildenhall Parish Register, Baptisms (transcript at Ipswich City Library), **1**: 34.

[69] Copinger, loc. cit. He was possibly a gentleman of the privy chamber about 1611 and in 1624, when one of the name and position obtained a license to travel (S.P. 14, 67/147; C.S.P. Dom., 1623–1625, 243), although his parliament service at the latter period makes the travel plans unlikely.

[70] Copinger, loc. cit.; Marriages in Lackford Hundred (transcript in Ipswich City Library), **1**: 48.

[71] Shaw, K. of E. **2**: 168.

[72] M. of P. **1**: 453, 460, passim.

[73] C. 193/12, 13; S.P. 16/405; Suff. Inst. Arch. **15**: 159, 1913–1915.

other commissions, including that on knighthood,[74] and was active as a D.L. from his appointment in 1623 until the time of the Long Parliament.[75]

Sir Roger had been a supporter of Buckingham at the beginning of Charles's reign,[76] and in the county elections of 1640 worked for his son Henry, the court party candidate,[77] but he made his peace with the country party men before the Long Parliament had gone far with its work.[78] In January, 1641, he joined in the attack on "superstitious idolatry"[79] in the churches, and in June, 1642, promised to bring in £100 in plate as a gift for the defense.[80] He took the covenant, became an elder in the Suffolk presbytery and remained a member of the House until December 1648.[81] North died on 7 June 1651 and was buried at Mildenhall.[82]

North's estate included manors in Suffolk, Norfolk, and Cambridgeshire which he inherited, and others which he bought or acquired by marriage.[83] His income was reputed to be some £2000 a year.[84]

* John Northcote (*c.* 1599–1676) of Hayne, Devon, sat for Ashburton, 1640–1653.[85] Born about 1599,[86] the eldest surviving son and heir of John Northcote of

---

[74] C. 181/3, fol. 126v; 181/4, fols. 30, 186v; 181/5, fols. 19, 55, 121, 165; Suckling, *The history and antiquities of the county of Suffolk* 2: 116.

[75] H.M.C., *Thirteenth Report* 4, MSS of E. R. Wodehouse, 441, 457; Add. MSS, 39,245, fols. 71, 157v, 185; S.P. 16, 60/2 and 421/136; *C.S.P. Dom., 1629–1631*, 93.

[76] Forster, *Eliot* 1: 407.

[77] Henry North was a follower of Buckingham and a royalist during the war (Copinger, *The manors of Suffolk* 4: 178). For his father's part in the 1640 elections, see T. Carlyle, *Critical and miscellaneous essays* 4: 400–426, 1860; D'Ewes, *Autobiography* 2: 255.

[78] D'Ewes, who had been sheriff at the time of the elections, wrote to his wife in December that North, far from complaining of the sheriff's conduct, had come to him with excuses and offers of appeasement, and "promising all neighbourhood and friendshipp." *Ibid.*

[79] D'Ewes (N), 270. Copinger surely is mistaken when he writes that Sir Roger was a stanch supporter of church and king (*op. cit.* 4: 178).

[80] *N. and Q.*, 1st ser., 12: 358, 1855.

[81] *O.P.H.* 9: 3; *A.H.R.* 44: 31, n. (32), 1938–1939. He is styled an Independent in the latter reference, apparently on the assumption that he was a member of the Rump.

[82] His will, dated 14 January 1650/1, was proved 10 May 1652. P.C.C., 86 Bowyer.

[83] *Suff. Inst. Arch.* 8: 185, 1894; I.P.M. of Sir Henry North, 1621, C. 142/387/111; abstract of Sir Henry North's will, Add. MSS, 33,858, fol. 143v.

[84] Add. MSS, 15,520, fol. 43v. The renaissance wall paintings at the Mildenhall Manor House are indicative of the wealth and taste of his family. *Suff. Inst. Arch.* 22: 108, 1936.

[85] The official list gives his title as baronet (*M. of P.* 1: 487), but he was not given that rank until the summer of 1641. Ashburton was restored by vote of the House, 26 November 1640 (*C.J.* 2: 37), but Northcote's first notes on the proceedings are dated 24 November (*Note book of Sir John Northcote*, xvii). His first committee appointment was 16 February 1641 (*C.J.* 2: 87).

[86] *D.N.B.* gives 1599. He was buried in June, 1676, aged seventy-seven (*Complete Baronetage* 2: 106).

Upton and Hayne (d. 1632), he was through his mother a first cousin of Hugh Pollard, M.P. After his years at Oxford and the Middle Temple,[87] Northcote in 1626 married the heiress of Hugh Halswell of Somerset, and had part of his father's estate settled on him.[88] He was captain of a foot company at the Devon musters in 1629. Another of the name, possibly his father, was a musters defaulter that year, being then absent in London,[89] perhaps because of a Star Chamber suit in which he was engaged.[90] In 1633 Northcote was a J.P for Devon, and a captain in Colonel John Bampfield's regiment of trained bands.[91] He defaulted his ship money payment under the 1637 writ,[92] and was named a commissioner for exacted fees in his county the following year.[93]

His duties with the Earl of Northumberland and the army in the north may have prevented his serving in the Short Parliament, but in the autumn he helped elect the shire knights[94] as well as to win his own place. Soon afterwards his neighbor, Bamfield, wrote to another member that Northcote "will prove an excellent member of your house, if you can keep him silent."[95] Northcote's work in the House, however, seems to have been more of action than of speech. In March, 1641, he subscribed £500 with Upton for securing the loan.[96] Late in 1641 he was particularly interested in Irish affairs,[97] and afterwards contributed liberally for that cause and for the popular side against the king.

Northcote enjoyed an ample inheritance[98] and doubtless his marriage added to his wealth. His subscriptions of £450 for reducing the Irish rebels and of £100 in addition to a pledge of six horses for the defense are indicative of his means as well as of his sympathies. His estate was valued in 1660 at £1500 a year.[99]

---

[87] At the Temple he was bound with George Peard, the M.P., from 1618 to 1623, or longer. *Mid. Temp. Rec.* 2: 633, 681.

[88] The indentures of settlement are cited in his father's I.P.M., C. 142/509/27.

[89] S.P., 16, 150/76/i, ii.

[90] Several authorities state that the younger Northcote was Sheriff of Devon, 1626–1627, but Hamilton (*Note book of Sir John Northcote*, xiii) attributes the office to the father and suggests that his Star Chamber case may have developed from his handling of the post. Since the elder Northcote did not die until 1632, it seems more probable that he, rather than his son not yet thirty, was sheriff. One of them was a loan commissioner, 1626–1627. S.P. 16, 53/96.

[91] Exeter City Library MSS, Lane's Collections for Devonshire, fols. 118, 120.

[92] S.P. 16, 435/33/i.

[93] C. 181/5, fol. 218.

[94] His name appears on the county indenture, C. 219/43/Part 1.

[95] H.M.C., *Fifteenth Report*, 7, MSS of the Duke of Somerset, 64.

[96] D'Ewes (N), 438, n. (439).

[97] D'Ewes (C), 189, 289, 372.

[98] His father's I.P.M. enumerated various manors and other holdings in Devon and cited the provision for £1000 for another son at the time of John's marriage settlement.

[99] *Devon and Cornwall N. & Q.* 18: 316, 1934–1935.

Simon Norton (1578–1641), dyer and alderman of Coventry, was M.P. for his city from 1640 until his death in July, 1641. He was the second son of John Norton of Allesley, near Coventry, by his wife, Elizabeth Pitsford. His father, a younger son, had come into the county from Yorkshire and died about 1580. Simon was baptized at Allesley, 26 November 1578.[100] He became a dyer and developed a large business at Coventry, accumulating enough wealth to buy land in the surrounding region.[101] He married (1) Prudence Jesson of Coventry, probably a kinswoman of William Jesson (q.v.), and (2) Ellen—.[102] Norton was one of the sheriffs of Coventry in 1623, a council member by 1629, mayor in 1633 to 1634, and alderman from the latter year until his death.[103] In 1635, with his son-in-law, Humfry Burton, clerk of the city council, Mayor John Barker and alderman William Jesson, Norton was a leader in the effort to secure a lower ship money rate for Coventry, going several times to interview the sheriff on the matter.[104] He was elected Coventry's representative to both of the 1640 parliaments.[105]

Norton joined with John Barker in offering £1000 as security for the loan in November, 1640.[106] He was interested in the debates on religion, and was named to several committees dealing with the church.[107] But Norton does not seem to have been an extremist, for he wrote in his will in 1641 that certain funds should go to a Coventry church having an "able and orthodox preaching minister conformable to the Church of England." He was ill at the time he made his will, 2 July 1641, and died two days later.

Norton was living in 1613 in a modest house at Smythford Bridge, but he afterwards had a house on Little Park Street, leased various properties from the city, and shortly before his death purchased several outlying lands, including a country place called Harnall. His will, with its references to his silver plate and legacies of over £2000, in addition to 300 marks for city charities, indicates that he had prospered.[108]

One of Norton's sons became an ardent royalist and another was created a baronet at the Restoration.

John Nutt (c. 1605–c. 1668), of Nackington in Canterbury, was M.P. for that city, 1640–1653. He came of a family for some generations established at Canterbury,[109] his father having been William Nutt, a lawyer (d. 1607).[110] His mother, Anne, daughter of John Polhill of Otford, married as her second husband Thomas Milles of Norton Court.[111] John, who was about two and a half years of age when his father died, was the heir not only of his father but in part of his stepfather.[112] He was sent to Oxford, matriculating at Exeter College in 1621, and in May, 1623, he entered the Middle Temple, where he was bound with Thomas Hodges (q.v.).[113] In 1628 Nutt married Anne, daughter of Edward Master (afterwards Sir Edward) of Ospringe, Kent,[114] his future colleague in local and national affairs. His second marriage at an unknown date was with Anne, daughter of John Aldrich of Norfolk.[115]

Nutt concerned himself with local matters before 1640. He was a sewers commissioner for northern Kent in 1639,[116] but seems to have been especially interested in military activities. By November, 1636, he was captain of a select band of soldiers from Canterbury, and as such was admitted to the freedom of the city without the usual fine.[117] He and his father-in-law, Master, were captains of companies from the city pressed for service in the border war in April, 1639. Together they were elected to the Short Parliament, winning over candidates proposed by patrons.[118]

Captain Nutt, like Master, was a parliamentarian, but he was not a conspicuous member during the early months of the Long Parliament.[119] He was sent into Kent at the outbreak of war, was a member of various parliamentary committees for the county, and a D.L.[120] He kept his seat until the end, but declined to act as a judge at the trial of the king.[121] He was named in 1651 to a committee for the sale of traitors' estates,[122] and returned with the Rumpers in 1660.[123] He survived until about 1668.[124]

Nutt does not seem to have been wealthy, but his

[100] *Vis. Warwicks.,* 138.

[101] Whitley, *Parl. Rep. Coventry,* 79–80; Poole, *Hist. Coventry,* 212.

[102] *Vis. Warwicks.,* 138. His second wife, Ellen, is mentioned in his will. P.C.C., 114 Evelyn.

[103] Coventry Corporation MSS, A 14 a, fols. 377, 383, 574, 619–631; Add. MSS, 11,364, fol. 15.

[104] Coventry Corporation MSS, A 35.

[105] *M. of P.* **1**: 484, 495.

[106] D'Ewes (N), 52.

[107] *C.J.* **2**: 75, 84.

[108] Coventry Corporation MSS, A 14 a, fols. 543, 572, 689; A 14 b, fols. 22, 28; Norton's will, P.C.C., 114 Evelyn.

[109] Several mayors came from his family in the sixteenth century. Hasted, *Kent* **12**: 606, 607.

[110] *Vis. Kent, 1663–1668,* 122; *Mid. Temp. Rec.* **1**: 262, 327; I.P.M., William Nutt, C. 142/317/111.

[111] *Vis. Kent, 1619,* 88, 150.

[112] I.P.M. cited above; Canterbury City MSS, Chamberlains' Accounts **21**: 1648–1649; Hasted, *Kent* **11**: 225, n.

[113] *Al. Oxon.; Mid. Temp. Rec.* **2**: 682.

[114] *Arch. Cant.* **5**: 239, 241, 1863.

[115] *Vis. Kent, 1663–1668,* 122.

[116] C. 181/5, fol. 293.

[117] Canterbury City MSS, Chamberlains' Accounts, **20**, 1636–1637; Burghmote, 1630–1658, fol. 121v.

[118] *Ibid.,* Burghmote, 1630–1658, fol. 156c; Willis, **3**: 232. See Master.

[119] *C.J.* **2**: 65, 159.

[120] Bodleian Rawl. MSS, D. 141, fol. 31; *Arch. Cant.* **2**: 182, 1859; **9**: 33, 1874; Add. MSS, 33,512, fol. 78.

[121] *O.P.H.* **9**: *30.

[122] *C.J.* **7**: 23.

[123] Thomason Tracts, 669. f. 24, p. 37.

[124] He seems to have paid his usual rents, 1666–1667, but they were paid by his heirs the next year. Canterbury City MSS, Chamberlains' Accounts **23**.

father had owned a dozen or more properties in Canterbury, including an inn, and he himself held at least four properties there in the period before 1640.[125] His name is missing from the various lists of contributors for the parliamentary cause.

Sir William Ogle (*c.* 1600–1682), later Viscount Ogle of Catherlough, a soldier, was M.P. for Winchester, Hants, 1640–24 June 1643.[1] Descended from the north country Ogles, and possibly related to the renowned soldier, Sir John Ogle (1569–1640) of Lincolnshire,[2] he was the grandson and eventual heir of George Ogle of Hirst and North Seaton, Northumberland. The son and heir of the latter's third son, Cuthbert (died before 15 March 1628), William was born about 1600. He brought suit in Chancery in 1628, as Sir William Ogle of Winchester, to recover possession of his inheritance.[3] Ogle may have graduated B.A. from Jesus College, Cambridge, 1619–1620,[4] but he embarked early upon his career as a soldier. In 1622 and later he saw service for the Crown in the Low Countries.[5] In 1625 he was probably a member of the Cadiz expedition, serving under Sir Edward Conway and having as a fellow officer George Goring,[6] with whom he was frequently associated afterwards. He was billeted in Hampshire in 1626, at Waltham and later at Winchester, and was summoned before the commission for martial law there because he and his men had defied the civil authorities of the county and town. A decision to reduce his rank as the Cadiz troops were reorganized was reversed after friends interceded with Buckingham on his behalf.[7] He was one of Conway's captains listed for the Rochelle expedition, may have been a prisoner in Flanders for a short time in the summer of 1627, and by 1628 was a knight.[8] He married about May, 1627, Charity, daughter and coheiress of William Waller of Oldstoke and Stoke Charity, Hampshire. She was the widow of Sir Thomas Phelipps, Bart., of Barrington, Somerset, who died in 1626.[9] Ogle now became the guardian of his young stepson and controlled by right of his wife various Hampshire properties, including the castle at Winchester. He is said to have enjoyed £1000 a year which he lost with her death during the siege of Winchester in 1645.[10] He had a house in Winchester, but was described in 1635 as of Stoke Charity.[11]

During the lull between wars Ogle was captain of Winchester's militia company (1631–1637).[12] He was a member also of the local commission for gaol delivery.[13] He probably had a command in Ireland during this period, also. He raised his own regiment for the war with the Scots, and although he was elected by Winchester for the Short Parliament, was commanding his men as colonel in skirmishes that summer.[14] He attended Conway in October, 1640, during the negotiations for the treaty at Ripon,[15] and was elected again that month as Winchester's M.P.

Ogle was one of the witnesses sworn by the House of Lords in Strafford's cause on 22 December 1640,[16] but his name is not in the list of those who voted against the earl's attainder. During the first half of 1641 Ogle was named to several committees dealing with the army.[17] In the summer of 1642 he was sent to Ireland to help quell the rebellion.[18] He was in London in September of that year, however, when he was named to the committee on Irish affairs and on that to consider the judges in Ireland. He promised then to contribute £100 for the defense.[19] In 1643, however, he joined the royalists and on 24 June was discharged from his seat in the House and from his command in Ireland.[20] He commanded Winchester for the king, 1643–1645, and in December, 1645, was created Viscount Ogle of Catherlough (Ireland).[21] He compounded for his estate in 1646, declaring then that most of his estates had been held for his lady's life, and that outside of them he could claim only £28 a year and some £431 owing to him. He estimated his wartime losses at £8000. He was fined at a tenth, £240.[22]

Ogle married well a second time before 25 August,

[125] *Ibid.* **20, 21**; I.P.M. cited above.

[1] *M. of P.* **1**: 493; *C.J.* **3**: 142.

[2] Lloyd, *Memoires*, 675. Although I have found no close relationship indicated in the family pedigrees, there is a marked similarity in the military careers of William and Sir John Ogle. *D.N.B.,* "Sir John Ogle"; Maddison, *Lincs. Ped.* **2**: 732; *The Genealogist,* 1st Ser., **1**: 321, 1877. Sir John Ogle's will, dated in 1628 and proved in 1640, does not, however, mention William Ogle among his relatives. P.C.C., 105 Coventry.

[3] *Complete Peerage,* Gibbs ed. **10**: 39 and n.

[4] *Al. Cant.* He was probably not the Oxford B.A. of 1628 as suggested in *Al. Oxon.*

[5] *C.S.P. Dom.,* 1627–1628, 139; *Complete Peerage, loc. cit.*

[6] S.P. 16, 61/102, 103; 522/16.

[7] Add. MSS, 21,922, fols. 79v, 88; *C.S.P. Dom., 1627–1628,* 139, 143.

[8] *Acts P.C., 1627,* 189, 299, 473; S.P. 16, 116/85.

[9] Charity proved her first husband's will on 26 May 1627 after she had married Ogle. Her first husband died in April, 1627, according to *Complete Baronetage* (**1**: 137). The date should be 1626. *V.C.H. Hampshire* **3**: 449.

[10] Godwin, *The Civil War in Hampshire,* **4**, 336.

[11] Add. MSS, 26,781, fol. 39; F. R. Goodman, ed., *The diary of John Young, S.T.P.,* 152, n., London, Macmillan, 1928.

[12] Add. MSS, 26,781, fols. 26, 36v; 21,922, fols. 188v, 201v.

[13] C. 181/4, fol. 104v.

[14] *C.S.P. Dom., 1640,* 366, 462; B. H. Cunnington, ed., *Records of the county of Wilts, Extracts from the quarter sessions great rolls,* 322, 323, Devizes, G. Simpson, 1932; *M. of P.* **1**: 483.

[15] *C.S.P. Dom., 1640–1641,* 190.

[16] *L.J.* **4**: 115.

[17] *C.J.* **2**: 66, 75, 172, 188.

[18] Townshend, *The life and letters of the great Earl of Cork,* 421.

[19] *C.J.* **2**: 750, 759, 772.

[20] *C.J.* **3**: 142.

[21] *V.C.H. Hampshire* **3**: 449; *Complete Baronetage* **1**: 137.

[22] S.P. 23/192/139; *Cal. Com. Comp.,* 1563. The fine was presumably two years' value.

1648,[23] and is said to have lived until 14 July 1682. He died then without male heirs, and was buried at Michelmarsh.[24] He was described by a contemporary royalist, Sir John Oglander, in an unflattering manner, being grouped with Goring and Prince Rupert in a list of officers who were "debased with drinking, whoring and swearing." [25]

* **Michael Oldisworth** (1591–1660?), secretary to Philip, Earl of Pembroke and Montgomery, was M.P. for Salisbury, 1640–1653.[26] He had sat regularly in parliament, beginning in 1624, usually owing his seat to his patron. As secretary to the earl, who was captain general of the king's bodyguard, Oldisworth was listed among the officers of the army in the north in 1639.[27] Elected by two boroughs in the autumn of 1640, he chose to serve for Salisbury rather than for Plympton in Devon, even though there was a contest at Salisbury. The decision of the House in his favor in the latter instance seems not to have been without bias.[28] He seems to have had no particular connections in Wiltshire beyond the influence of his employer there.

Oldisworth used his court connections to acquire some leases of royal lands, such as a manor in Kent, for the lease of which he paid £1200 before 1629, some lands later claimed by the Duke of Lenox, and the right to certain income from the western stannaries.[29] Apparently, however, he was not in a financial position to offer substantial loans to parliament. His pledge in 1642 for the defense was one horse and £50.[30]

The date of Oldisworth's death, sometimes suggested as 1654, is uncertain. He seems to have been among the Rumpers who returned in 1659–1660.[31]

Arthur Onslow (1622–1688), of Cranley, Surrey, was named for Bramber, Sussex, in a double return in October, 1640.[32] The House declared the election void on 16 December, but he was re-elected soon afterwards, and was present in the House by 3 May 1641. He was a member until the purge of 1648.[33]

The eldest son of Sir Richard Onslow (*q.v.*) by his wife, Elizabeth Strangways, Arthur was born in 1622,[34] and matriculated at Oxford in 1639, aged seventeen. He was neither of age nor married at the time of his election to the Long Parliament,[35] and had held no office before. His father's influence, since he owned property in Sussex [36] as well as in Surrey, no doubt secured his election.

Young Onslow, like his father, was a parliamentarian, but during the period of this study played an unimportant part. He served in later parliaments both before and after the Restoration,[37] although he seems to have opposed the return of the Stuarts more strenuously than did his father. He died on 21 July 1688.[38]

* **Sir Richard Onslow** (1601–1664), of Knoll in Cranley, Surrey, M.P. for his county, 1640–1648, had represented it also in 1628 and in the Short Parliament. He served as a J.P. there during most of the reign of Charles I, and as a D.L. and a member of various special commissions.[39] He was educated at Cambridge (Jesus College) and Lincoln's Inn.[40] He does not seem to have opposed the 1625 loan,[41] and in 1639 contributed £20 toward the king's trip to the north,[42] but he disliked the extension of the forests in Surrey.[43] His activities for the cause of parliament and Presbyterianism after 1640 are well known.

Onslow was one of the wealthier parliament men. He inherited a number of Surrey estates and purchased more.[44] He pledged £1000 for securing the loan in 1640,[45] and in 1642 promised to maintain four horses for himself and son.[46] A descendant described him as "of large fortune" and of wide influence in his county.[47]

Arthur Onslow (*q.v.*) was his son. He was probably related to several Sussex members through his mother's family, the Shirleys.

Hugh Owen (1604–1670), of Orielton, county Pembroke, and of Bodowen, Anglesey, was M.P. for Pem-

---

[23] His second wife was Sarah (Dauntsey), widowed daughter-in-law of Sir Thomas Stewkley of Hampshire. Abstract of the will of Dame Elizabeth Stewkley in F. Brown's *Somerset Wills* 1: 82.

[24] *Complete Baronetage* 1: 137; *Complete Peerage*, Gibbs ed. 10: 41 and n. Burke's earlier identification of Viscount Ogle as Richard Ogle (*Extinct Peerage*) was incorrect.

[25] *A royalist's notebook*, 118 and n.

[26] *M. of P.* 1: 496.

[27] S.P. 16, 538/91/1.

[28] *C.J.* 2: 95–96; D'Ewes (N), 83, 98–99, *passim; E.H.R.* 50: 250, 252, 1935. See account of the Salisbury election.

[29] *C.S.P. Dom., 1629–1631*, 133; *1637*, 300; *Cal. Com. Comp.*, 1531–1533.

[30] *N. and Q.*, 1st Ser., 12: 359, 1855.

[31] Pink MSS, 311, fol. 496e; Thomason Tracts, 669. f. 24, p. 37.

[32] Bramber indenture, C. 219/43/Part 2.

[33] *C.J.* 2: 51, 133; *O.P.H.* 9: 5.

[34] He was baptized at Cranley, 23 April 1622, according to Symmes's notes (Add. MSS, 6167, fol. 123), but the date, also said to be based on the registers, appears as 22 May 1624 in *Sussex Arch. Coll.* 6: 54, 1853. In the brief reference to Arthur Onslow in the *D.N.B.* article on his father, 1621 appears as the year of his birth.

[35] He married for the first time in 1647. *Al. Oxon.;* Brayley, *Surrey* 1: 446.

[36] *Sussex Rec. Soc.* 19: 123, 1914.

[37] *M. of P., passim.*

[38] Manning and Bray, *Surrey* 3: 55, cxxvii.

[39] C. 193/12, 13; S.P. 16/405; Manning and Bray, *Surrey* 1: Intro., ii; 3: 670; *C.S.P. Dom., 1640*, 287; C. 181/5, fol. 347.

[40] *Al. Cant.; Linc. Inn Rec. Adm.* 1: 181.

[41] *Surrey Arch. Coll.* 17: 80, 1902–1903.

[42] Rushworth 3: 911.

[43] Manning and Bray, *Surrey* 1: Intro., xiii, n.

[44] *Ibid.* 1: 134, 538, 539; *Sussex Rec. Soc.* 19: 123, 282, 1914.

[45] D'Ewes (N), 52.

[46] *N. and Q.*, 1st Ser., 12: 359, 1855.

[47] *H.M.C., Fourteenth Report* 9, Onslow MSS, 476.

broke borough, 1640–1648. He was born in 1604, the elder son of John Owen (d. 1612) by his wife, Dorothy, daughter of John Laugharne of St. Brides, Pembrokeshire. He was the heir in 1614 of his grandfather, Sir Hugh Owen of Bodowen, whose wife, Elizabeth, daughter of George Merriott, had brought the Orielton estate into the family.[48] And he was a cousin of John Wogan (q.v.). Owen was admitted to Lincoln's Inn in 1622.[49]

Besides serving as M.P. in 1626, 1628, and both times in 1640,[50] Owen seems as early as 1622 to have been named a J.P. in Pembrokeshire.[51] He was acting as such by 1631 and during the following decade, and was probably a justice in Anglesey also.[52] He was sheriff for county Pembroke, 1633–1634,[53] and was mayor of Pembroke borough, 1632, 1633, and 1639.[54]

Owen was not active in the early period of the Long Parliament, but he was named to several committees concerned with war supplies late in 1641, and was interested particularly in raising forces for Ireland.[55] In June, 1642, he offered to provide two horses for the defense.[56]

The estate Owen inherited at his grandfather's death consisted of five manors, with numerous houses and five mills and over 6800 acres of land in various parts of Pembrokeshire, including some in Pembroke borough, and he held the advowson of two churches.[57] His estate was reckoned to be worth £1000 a year at least.[58]

Samuel Owfield, or **Oldfield** (c. 1595–1643), of Gatton, Surrey, and of Elsham, Lincolnshire, was M.P. for Gatton from 1640 until his death in 1643. There was a contest at Gatton but Owfield's place does not seem to have been questioned,[59] and he was active in the House from the start. He was the son and heir of Roger Owfield, a well-to-do citizen and fishmonger of London (d. 1608), by his wife, Thomasine [Moore] (d. 1639). The family probably came from Derbyshire and shortly before his death Roger was buying lands in the counties of Stafford, York, and Lincoln.[60] Samuel was

born about 1595,[61] matriculated in 1612 at Emmanuel College, Cambridge, in which his father had been interested,[62] and in 1613 entered the Middle Temple. He retained a chamber there as late as 1631 but seems to have given it up soon after that.[63] He was admitted by patrimony to the Fishmongers' Company of London in 1618,[64] but there is no indication that he followed his father's trade. The business seems to have passed either to a younger brother or to a cousin.[65] Sometime before 1626 Owfield married, but only his wife's first name, Katherine, is known.[66]

Owfield acquired his country place at Gatton by 1624, and was elected M.P. for the borough that year as "of Gatton." He was re-elected there in 1626, 1628, and at both elections of 1640. In 1625 he sat for Midhurst.[67] But his chief residence was in Lincolnshire. In 1626 Owfield was arrested as a musters defaulter in Surrey, but was able to satisfy Council that he had been overassessed there, his principal estate being in Lincolnshire.[68] He was a sewers commissioner in the latter county, 1634, 1635, and 1642,[69] and his estate of Elsham made him a neighbor of the Pelham family of Brocklesby.[70] Two of his children were baptized at Gatton, however, in 1636 and 1642, and he described himself in his will of 1636 as of Gatton.[71] Several of Owfield's close relatives were active in the Massachusetts Bay Company,[72] but he does not appear to have subscribed.

Belonging to the popular party, Owfield was fairly active in the Long Parliament. His most important committee was that on privileges, but he was named also to some concerned with the grievances of individuals, such as Chambers and Bastwick. He offered £1000 as security for the 1640 loan,[73] and in 1642 promised for the defense maintenance of four horses and more if needed.[74] He was knighted at Whitehall, 13 May 1641, as of Lincolnshire,[75] and his war activities as a committeeman were with that county rather than with

---

[48] I.P.M. of John Owen (C. 142/337/104) and of Sir Hugh Owen (C. 142/346/166); *Complete Baronetage* 2: 131; *West Wales historical records* 5: 127, 1915; *Trans. of the Hon. Soc. of Cymmrodorion* 1901–1902, 142.

[49] *Linc. Inn Rec. Adm.* 1: 191.

[50] He sat in the Short Parliament for Haverfordwest. Willis 3: 239.

[51] *Cal. Wynn Papers*, 159.

[52] C. 193/13; S.P. 16, 185/19/32; S.P. 16/405.

[53] *List of Sheriffs*, 266.

[54] *West Wales historical records* 5: 121, 127, 1915.

[55] *C.J.* 2: 331, 347, 352, 357.

[56] *N. and Q.*, 1st Ser., 12: 360, 1855.

[57] I.P.M. of Sir Hugh Owen cited above.

[58] Williams, *Parl. Hist. Wales*, 161.

[59] *C.J.* 2: 303.

[60] Will of Roger Owfield (P.C.C., 111 Windebanck); I.P.M.'s of Roger Owfield and his widow, C. 142/660/30; C. 142/588/63.

[61] I.P.M., C. 142/660/30.

[62] *Al. Cant.* Roger Owfield by his will left £100 for a divinity student at Cambridge or Oxford or for scholarships at Sidney and Emmanuel Colleges, Cambridge.

[63] *Mid. Temp. Rec.* 2: 575, 787, 797, 798.

[64] W. P. Haskett-Smith, *The Worshipful Company of Fishmongers . . . apprentices and freemen*, 32, London, privately printed, 1916.

[65] Roger Owfield's will; London Corporation MSS, Rep. 54, fols. 26, 83–84.

[66] His daughter, Thomasine, died in 1711 in her eighty-sixth year. Add. MSS, 5698, fol. 166v.

[67] *M. of P.* 1: 460, passim.

[68] He declared he had less than £100 a year in Surrey lands. *Acts P.C., 1626*, 172, 182, 184, 189, 210–211.

[69] C. 181/4, fols. 170, 201; 181/5, fol. 445.

[70] *C.S.P. Dom., 1638–1639*, 322; will of Sir William Pelham, P.C.C., 32 Essex. Cf. Henry Pelham.

[71] Manning and Bray, *Surrey* 2: 238; P.C.C., 46 Rivers.

[72] F. Rose-Troup, *The Massachusetts Bay Company and its predecessors*, 149.

[73] *C.J.* 2: 21, 43, 52, passim; D'Ewes (N), 52.

[74] *N. and Q.*, 1st Ser., 12: 359, 1855.

[75] Shaw, *K. of E.* 2: 208.

Surrey.[76] He was at Hull in May, 1642,[77] and died there on 4 May 1643.[78] His will, dated 6 December 1636, was proved by his widow on 10 February 1644/5.

Owfield was apparently a rich man. His father's estate in 1611 amounted to well over £22,000 after all debts had been paid, and one of his sisters had a portion of £3000. Samuel received a special legacy of £1000 in addition to his share of the inheritance and lands in several of the northern counties.[79] He later bought his mother's interest in some of the London and Lincolnshire properties,[80] and in Surrey purchased several manors in Gatton parish.[81] His pledges of 1640 and 1642 are indicative of his financial well-being.

Among Owfield's friends in the 1640 parliament were undoubtedly the Surrey Goodwins, into whose family one of his daughters married.[82] Among his Lincolnshire neighbors were the Pelhams and John Broxholme.

Edward Owner (1575–1650), merchant and alderman of Yarmouth, Norfolk, was M.P. for his town, 1640–1648(?).[83] He was the younger son of Ralph Owner, a Yarmouth merchant, by his wife, Grace, was baptized on 16 October 1575, and on 13 November 1589 married Elizabeth, daughter of Hisea Harrison.[84] He became a freeman of Yarmouth in 1597, and had a shop near the market place. Passing through the routine offices of the town, Owner became one of the "eight and forty" in 1606, was chamberlain in 1610, and four times bailiff, 1616, 1625, 1634, 1646.[85] He was one of the Yarmouth aldermen appointed in 1630 to the Norfolk commission on piracy, and in 1636 was president of his town's artillery corps.[86] He was Yarmouth's representative in parliament in 1621 and 1625, and in both sessions of 1640.[87]

Owner was a leader not only in municipal affairs, but in the controversies of his period. Described as "a man of turbulent spirit" by the Cinque Port barons whose interests in the Yarmouth fair he opposed,[88] Owner was bold in the support of his convictions, a leader in the two decades before 1640 in his town's resistance to king, bishop, and other influences from without. With his fellow bailiff he protested in 1625 against the burden of the privy seals,[89] and was so "factious" in opposing, 1625–1629, a plan for reorganizing the democratic government of Yarmouth that he was called before Council at least once to explain his conduct.[90] In 1628 he defended the Reverend John Brinsley of Yarmouth, who had married Owner's only daughter, in a dispute with the Bishop of Norwich, and procured for him a certificate of good conduct under the corporate seal.[91] He was called before the Earl of Arundel, Marshall of England, in 1635 for having affronted the Cinque Port men while he was bailiff, and was Yarmouth's representative in the consultations among the Norfolk towns regarding ship money.[92] Although he opposed the levy, he was named one of the assessors in Yarmouth for the collections in January, 1640.[93] Owner's interest in the welfare of his town, and a different side of his character, appear in his gift of £1500 for the "Children's Hospital," and his efforts to get a workhouse established and a public library. As a member of the Long Parliament Owner was never conspicuous, but he supported the attack on ship money and in 1645 was one of the navy committee.[94] His subscription of £600 for reducing Ireland in 1642 was as the agent of Yarmouth, but his pledge of £50 for the defense shortly afterwards was probably his own.[95] He was absent several times in 1647 and 1648, may have been secluded with the Presbyterians, and died in 1650. He was buried in the Church House of St. Nicholas's, of which he was an elder, in August.

According to his will, dated 10 August 1650, Owner possessed various properties within the limits of Yarmouth, partly his wife's inheritance, and a house in Norwich and some lands in Suffolk.[96]

* Sir John Pakington, Bart. (1620–1680), of Westwood, Worcestershire, was M.P. for Aylesbury, Bucks,

[76] *Lincolnshire Notes & Queries* **8**: 104, 1904–1905; Abbott, *Cromwell* **1**: 228, n.

[77] *H.M.C., Thirteenth Report*, MSS of the Duke of Portland, **1**: 38.

[78] Register of St. Mary's, Hull, *Yorks. Arch. Jour.* **12**: 468, 1893.

[79] London Corporation MSS, Common Serjeants' Book **1**: fols. 287v, 384v, 404.

[80] Will and I.P.M.'s as in note 60.

[81] *Surrey Arch. Coll.* **39**: 61, 1931; Manning and Bray, *Surrey* **2**: 235, 243, 245.

[82] Add. MSS, 5698, fol. 166v.

[83] *M. of P.* **1**: 491. He may have been secluded in 1648, or have continued to be a member until his death. *East Anglian*, N.S., **3**: 196, 1889–1890.

[84] Pink MSS, 321.

[85] Yarmouth Corporation MSS, Calendar of Freemen, 1429–1800, fol. 49; Assembly Book **5**, fols. 44, 52; *East Anglian*, N.S., **3**: 216, 1889–1890; Manship's *Yarmouth* **1**: 131.

[86] C. 181/4, fol. 50; Pink MSS, 321.

[87] *M. of P.* **1**: 452, 464, 482.

[88] C. J. Palmer, *The perlustration of Great Yarmouth* **2**: 258–259, Great Yarmouth, 1872–1875.

[89] *H.M.C., Ninth Report* **1**, MSS of Yarmouth Corp., 309.

[90] Palmer, *The perlustration of Great Yarmouth* **1**: 122–123; H. Swinden, *The history and antiquities of Great Yarmouth*, 477 ff., Norwich, 1772; *Acts P.C., 1625–1626*, 376.

[91] Manship's *Yarmouth* **2**: 307, n.; Pink MSS, 321.

[92] Swinden, *Yarmouth*, 531–532.

[93] Yarmouth Corp. MSS, Assembly Book, 1625–1642, fols. 451, 452.

[94] Pink MSS, 321.

[95] *C.S.P. Ireland, Adventurers*, 14; *N and Q.*, 1st Ser., **12**: 360, 1855.

[96] He enumerated some £175 in legacies to be paid to relatives and friends, two being children of another so-called "father-in-law," Edward Fisher. P.C.C., 193 Gray. His widow, Elizabeth, died in 1672 (*East Anglian*, N.S., **3**: 216, 1889–1890).

1640–20 August 1642.[1] The heir of a well known and wealthy family and the ward of Thomas Lord Coventry, the Lord Keeper, he owned considerable property in Aylesbury. His education and travel had made him an accomplished gentleman.[2] He was living at Westwood in 1636.[3] He preferred Worcestershire to Aylesbury as his constituency for the Short Parliament, though returned by both,[4] but the strength of the parliamentarians in that county in the next elections may have made him content to serve then for the Buckinghamshire borough. In spite of his youth, Pakington ventured early in the Long Parliament to attack Secretary Windebank.[5] He seems to have acquiesced to Strafford's attainder, but by 1642 had joined the king's party.

Although he probably did not have control over his inheritance at the time of his election, young Pakington was the heir to a large estate. It included three Worcestershire manors, and several more in Bucks, with adjoining lands. Their annual value before the war was estimated by Pakington at £1520, but by the sequestration agents at £1947. His sister's dowry was some £4000.[6] Pakington's losses during the war were heavy, being estimated at from £10,000 to £20,000,[7] and his fine at compounding was one of the highest assessed among the parliament men. Set originally at one-half, £13,395, it was reduced to one-third, £7670, and paid by 1650.[8]

Pakington's marriage with Dorothy Coventry, his guardian's daughter, sister of Savile's wife, probably did not occur until after 1640.[9]

* **Geoffrey Palmer** (1598–1670), of Carlton, Northamptonshire, and of the Middle Temple, sat for Stamford, Lincolnshire, 1640–7 September 1642. The son and heir of Thomas Palmer of Carlton (d. 1628), he was educated at Christ's College, Cambridge (B.A. 1616, M.A. 1619), and at the Middle Temple, and was University Counsel in 1635.[10] He was a sewers commissioner in Lincoln and Northants in 1638 and 1640,[11] and was one of the lawyers asked for an opinion regarding the franchise of Higham Ferrers in 1640.[12]

Besides having a well established legal reputation and practice,[13] Palmer owned various properties in Northamptonshire and Lincolnshire, and had married a wife with a portion of over £1000.[14] His fine as a royalist, set at a tenth in 1646, was £580,[15] but his son's estate was reported to be worth £800 a year in 1660, while Sir Geoffrey was still alive.[16]

Palmer was a cousin of his fellow members of 1640, Whitelocke and Edward Montagu, and a friend of the Hydes and Maynard from his law school days.[17]

Sir Roger Palmer, K.B. (1577–1657), of Westminster and of Kent, master of the royal household, was M.P. for Newton, Lancashire, 1640–22 January 1644.[18] The second son of Sir Thomas Palmer, Bart. (d. 1626), of Wingham, Kent, by his wife, Margaret, daughter of Edmond Poley of Badley, Suffolk, he was baptized at Wingham, 9 July 1577.[19] After studying at Staple Inn he was admitted in 1597 to Gray's Inn,[20] where he was said to have attracted the attention of Sir Francis Bacon. Soon afterwards he was introduced at court, where his accomplishments in languages, music, horsemanship, and especially in dancing won recognition. One of a family of courtiers,[21] Roger became cupbearer to the princes Henry and Charles, master of the household for Charles I, and K.B. at his coronation, and by 1632 was his cofferer. He used his connections to gain a great estate, and was said to be "as rich a younger brother as any in his time."[22] He received pensions from the court, but lent generously to the king.[23] About 1620 he married Katherine, daughter of Sir Thomas Porter of Gloucestershire, widow of Sir Richard Welsh, and with her acquired an additional pension.[24]

Sir Roger lived chiefly at Westminster and what local

---

[1] M. of P. 1: 485; C.J. 2: 729.

[2] English Baronetage 1: 187, 1771; C.S.P. Dom., 1637–1638, 427, 428.

[3] Worcestershire Archaeological Society, Transactions, N.S., 13: 38, 1936.

[4] His father had been M.P. for Aylesbury in 1624. M. of P. 1: 456, 480, 484.

[5] D'Ewes (N), 26–27.

[6] S.P. 23/189/851–858.

[7] Ibid.; English Baronetage, loc. cit.

[8] Cal. Com. Comp., 1194–1196.

[9] A sketch of Pakington's life occurs in Williams, Worcester, 41–42. See also Complete Baronetage 1: 148.

[10] Al. Cant.

[11] C. 181/5, fols. 202, 362.

[12] Palmer upheld the liberal interpretation of the borough charter. Northants MSS, F.H., 3467.

[13] In the discussion of Palmer's conduct regarding the Remonstrance in November, 1641, both critics and defenders spoke of his ability in his profession and his "temperateness of nature." D'Ewes (C), 197–198.

[14] I.P.M. of Thomas Palmer, C. 142/446/83.

[15] Cal. Com. Comp., 1433.

[16] English Baronetage 4: 370, 1741.

[17] H.M.C., MSS of the Duke of Buccleugh and Queensbury 1: 286; R. H. Whitelocke, Memoirs of Bulstrode Whitelocke, 14.

[18] Palmer's return for 1640 is missing, but he was named to a committee on 15 February 1641 (C.J. 2: 86), and was therefore a colleague of Legh, rather than his successor, as some authors have assumed.

[19] Wotton, English Baronetage 1: 207–208, 1771.

[20] Foster, Gray's Inn Adm. Reg., 94.

[21] His father was a Gentleman of the Privy Chamber to King James, and a younger brother had a similar post under Charles. One of his nieces married Lord Cottington.

[22] H.M.C., Sixth Report, MSS of the Earl of Moray, 672; C.S.P. Dom., 1635, 48; C. 181/4, fol. 115v.

[23] C.S.P. Dom., 1611–1618, 248; S.P. 16, 186/90, fol. 184; 453/74.

[24] C.S.P. Dom., 1619–1623, 178; S.P. 16, 180/16, fol. 36v.

administrative work he did was there,[25] but he sat for Queenborough, Kent, in the 1614 parliament, and four later ones, having at least once been nominated by the Earl of Montgomery.[26] He sought election at Canterbury early in 1640,[27] but was rejected, and doubtless found Lancaster borough with duchy control easier to win in the autumn. In the Long Parliament Palmer was not active, possibly because of his advancing age. He was one of the first, however, to offer his bond for £1000 to support the loan,[28] and is not named in the list of "Straffordians." His loyalty to the king led to the sequestration of his estates on 28 September 1643, and his "disablement," 22 January 1644.[29] Sir Roger died a widower and without children on 8 October 1657, and was buried at his estate in Dorney, Bucks.

Palmer's wealth, aside from royal pensions, included income from lands in Kent, Bucks, Middlesex, Suffolk, Wiltshire, and several of the Welsh counties. His yearly income, according to his compounding papers, was over £1,850, and his fine, set at a tenth, was £3,377. Despite heavy losses brought by the war,[30] he listed in his will in 1656 legacies for his brothers' children of over £2800.[31]

Sir Guy Palmes (1580–1653), of Ashwell, Rutlandshire, and of Lindley, Yorkshire, was M.P. for Rutland, 1640–28 September 1643.[32] The descendant of an old north country family, Palmes was born in 1580, the son and heir of Sir Francis Palmes of Lindley, a Yorkshire magistrate, by his wife, Mary, daughter and coheiress of Stephen Hadnall of Lauslevy, Northamptonshire.[33] He was admitted to the Inner Temple in 1597,[34] and not long afterward married Anne, daughter and coheiress of Sir Edward Stafford.[35] He was knighted on 11 May 1603,[36] succeeded his father in 1613,[37] and in 1626 married a second time, his wife being Elizabeth, daughter of John Doyley and widow of Francis Harley of Northamptonshire. They were married at Barnack in that county and probably lived there much of the time until Lady Palmes died in 1635.[38]

Palmes was active in public affairs for many years. He served as J.P. in Rutland and York counties,[39] was a member of numerous special commissions there and in Northamptonshire,[40] was three times sheriff for Rutlandshire (1607, 1617, 1625) and once for Yorkshire (1622),[41] and in Northamptonshire was a D.L.[42] He sat for Rutland in every parliament from 1614 to 1643,[43] with the exception of that of 1626, and gained distinction in the 1620's as a foe of abuses. He spoke in 1621 against corruption in office, against monopolists, against recusants, and urged the enacting of laws before voting on subsidies;[44] in 1624 he was on a committee concerning the abuses of heralds;[45] and in 1625 he was so outspoken in the debates on supply that he was singled out with Wentworth and four others to be pricked sheriff so that they would be ineligible for the next session.[46] He was among the loan refusers in Rutland and Northamptonshire in 1627,[47] and the next year was reported a musters defaulter for some properties he owned in Hampshire.[48]

In the Long Parliament Palmes worked at first with his old associates of the opposition, to which several of his kinsmen, such as the Wallops, belonged, and was named to the Committee of Privileges and others of importance.[49] But he did not become the leader he had earlier dared to be. Once he urged moderation in the proceedings against Strafford, but he was not among those listed as opposing his attainder, and was present in the House as late as December, 1641.[50] He was absent in the early summer of 1642 when pledges were being made for the defense, but late in September promised to supply four horses. He was ordered to be brought up in custody, however, on 17 December 1642, and on 28 September 1643 was disabled for his absences.[51] Afterwards he compounded for his estates

[25] Overseers Accounts, St. Margaret's Parish, Westminster **153**, 1630–1633; C. 181/4, fols. 5v, 115v, 158; 181/5, fol. 243.

[26] *M. of P.* **1**: 458, 464, 469, 476; **3**: App., xxxviii; *Arch. Cant.* **22**: 183, 1897.

[27] Canterbury City MSS, Chamberlains' Accounts, **20**, 1639–1640; Burghmote, 1630–1658, fol. 151v; Add. MSS, 11,045, fol. 99v.

[28] D'Ewes (N), 51.

[29] *C.J.* **3**: 256, 374.

[30] S.P. 23/190, pp. 260–269; *Cal. Com. Comp.*, 1394.

[31] P.C.C., 453 Ruthen.

In addition to the references cited above, see *Complete Baronetage* **1**: 166; *Misc. Geneal. et Herald.*, 1st Ser., **1**: 109, 1868; *D.N.B.*, "Sir Thomas Palmer (1540–1626)."

[32] *M. of P.* **1**: 492 and n.; *C.J.* **3**: 256.

[33] Foster, *Pedigrees of the county families of Yorkshire* **3**, Palmes of Naburn; J. Wright, *The history and antiquities of the county of Rutland* 17, London, 1684 (hereafter, Wright, *Rutland*).

[34] *Students admitted to the Inner Temple*, 148.

[35] Foster, *loc. cit.*; Add. MSS, 5531, fol. 16v. Their son Bryan entered Oxford in 1615, aged sixteen. *Al. Oxon.*

[36] Shaw, *K. of E.* **2**: 108.

[37] I.P.M. of Sir Francis Palmes, C. 142/333/43.

[38] Notes from the Barnack parish register in Bishop Kennett's Collections, Lansd. MSS, 991, fols. 148v, 149; *Fenland N. and Q.* **2**: 54, 1892–1894.

[39] C. 181/3, fols. 11, 24, 125; 193/13; S.P. 16, 185/55, fol. 107v; S.P. 16/405.

[40] C. 181/3, fols. 5, 118; 191/4, fols. 159, 161; 181/5, fols. 8, 68, *passim*; *C.S.P. Dom.*, **1**: *1639–1640*, 498; *Fairfax correspondence* **1**: 210, n.; *H.M.C., Twelfth Report* **4**, The Duke of Rutland's MSS, **1**: 494.

[41] *List of Sheriffs*, 114, 163.

[42] *H.M.C., Tenth Report* **6**, MSS of Lord Braye, 116.

[43] *M. of P.* **1**: 459, 465, *passim*; **3**: iii, n., xxxix.

[44] *Commons Debates 1621* **2**: 38, 459; **3**: 71, 163, 387, 472; **5**: 26, n.

[45] Add. MSS, 32,324, fol. 8.

[46] *Commons Debates in 1625*, 112, Camden Society, 1873; *Strafford letters* **1**: 29.

[47] S.P. 16, 79/72/i.

[48] Add. MSS, 21,922, fol. 152v.

[49] *C.J.* **2**: 20, 24, *passim*.

[50] D'Ewes (N), 303; D'Ewes (C), 296.

[51] *C.J.* **2**: 787, 893; **3**: 256. When Palmes petitioned to compound in 1646 he asserted that he went into Yorkshire in

and died in 1653, being buried 25 March at Ashwell.[52]

Palmes was a man of means and high social position. He was a friend of the Fairfaxes, the Wentworths, and other prominent families of Yorkshire,[53] and was a kinsman of the Wallops of Hampshire and other M.P.'s of their connection.[54] He inherited from his father four manors and other holdings in Yorkshire, one manor in Rutland, and at least three in Hampshire.[55] He was a stockholder in the Virginia Company in 1612,[56] and increased his landed possessions by purchases and leases.[57] Before 1640, however, he had settled a considerable part of his estate upon his heir at his marriage, retaining for himself a yearly income of some £900.[58]

Sir Philip Parker (1602–1675), of Erwarton, Suffolk, was a knight for his county, 1640–1648. He was the son and heir of Sir Calthorp Parker (d. 1618) by his wife, Mercy, daughter of Sir Stephen Soame, Lord Mayor of London. His grandfather, Sir Philip Parker, and his father had both been sheriffs of Suffolk.[59] Philip was born in 1602,[60] was admitted to Queen's College, Cambridge, 18 April 1618, and to the Inner Temple in 1622. He was knighted on 19 November 1624 and about that time married Dorothy (d. 1639), daughter and heiress of Sir Robert Gawdy of Claxton in Norfolk.[61] He had succeeded to his family estates in 1618, inheriting Erwarton and four other manors in Norfolk and Suffolk.[62] He acquired others by marriage, but does not seem to have been considered so wealthy as many of his colleagues of the 1640 parliament.

Parker was a J.P. in Suffolk and Norfolk,[63] was

active in the Suffolk militia,[64] and in 1637 was sheriff of that county. He collected more of his quota of ship money than had his predecessor in office, the judges' decision in Hampden's case no doubt furnishing the incentive.[65] He was a Presbyterian,[66] as was his uncle, Barnardiston (q.v.), with whom he was elected to both parliaments of 1640. At each election Parker defeated the royalist aspirant, Henry North, and in the October voting polled the largest vote, 2240, more than 800 above North's tally.[67]

Parker was not a leader, however, in the work of parliament. He was named to committee service as early as December, 1640, and in January, 1641, presented a petition from some of the Suffolk clergy asking relief from the burdens of the hierarchy,[68] but he took no great part in debates. He was reluctant about taking the covenant in November, 1643, and was absent part of the following winter,[69] but eventually he took it, and continued to be a member until Pride's Purge of 1648.[70] He died 22 June 1675.[71]

Sir Thomas Parker (c. 1596–1663), of Ratton in Willingdon, Sussex, was a member for Seaford from the time of its restoration in February, 1641, until 1648.[72] Born early in 1596, he was the son and heir of Sir Nicholas Parker of Ratton (d. 1620), by his third wife, Katherine, daughter of John Temple of Stowe, Bucks.[73] The family had been prominent in the southern counties for some generations, and Sir Nicholas, besides serving as sheriff, D.L., and M.P. for Sussex, had been governor of Plymouth for a time, and also of Pendennis Castle and D.L. for Cornwall.[74] Thomas entered Gray's Inn in 1614,[75] was knighted at Theobalds in 1617, and late in the following year married in London Philadelphia Lennard, daughter of Henry Lord Dacres.[76] Soon after his father's death, Sir Thomas began his long years of service as a J.P. in Sussex and member of other commissions.[77] He

---

May, 1643, on estate business but without permission of the House, that he avoided the royalist garrisons, and that illness had prevented his return before the vote on his disablement. S.P. 23/198/42.

[52] *Fenland N. and Q.* **2**: 54, 1892–1894.

[53] *Fairfax correspondence* **1**: 318, n.; Bodleian Firth MSS, b. 2, fols. 236, 243v.

[54] Add. MSS, 5531, fol. 16v.

[55] I.P.M. cited above.

[56] Brown, *Genesis of the U. S.*, 545.

[57] East Riding Antiq. Soc., *Transactions* **7**: 5, 1899; *Yorkshire fines*, Y.A.S. Rec. Ser., **58**: 27, 42, *passim* 1917.

[58] Two particulars, varying somewhat in detail, remain among Sir Guy's composition papers. The yearly values in one, omitting the son's settlement, total nearly £900; in the other, where his life interest in part of the son's lands seems to be included, the total income appears as about £1050 clear. S.P. 23/198/34, 42–44. See also *Cal. Com. Comp.*, 1316; *V.C.H. Rutland* **2**: 109.

[59] Copinger, *The manors of Suffolk* **6**: 37; Suckling, *The history and antiquities of the county of Suffolk* **1**: xlii; *The visitation of London* (Harleian Society, 17) **2**: 251, 1883. Parker was a nephew of Sir Thomas Soame and of Nathaniel Barnardiston. John Gurdon was a brother-in-law.

[60] I.P.M. of Sir Calthorp Parker, 1618/9, C. 142/369/134.

[61] *Al. Cant.; Cal. Inner Temp. Rec.* **2**: 130.

[62] I.P.M. cited above. £500 portions were provided for two of Parker's sisters by their father's will. Add. MSS, 33,858, fol. 147.

[63] S.P. 16, 193/59; S.P. 16/405.

[64] Add. MSS, 39,245, fols. 157v, 189.

[65] *C.S.P. Dom., 1637*, 401, 408; *1637–1638*, 200; *V.C.H. Suffolk* **2**: 189.

[66] *A.H.R.* **44**: 36, n., 1938–1939.

[67] Raven, *The history of Suffolk*, 205–206; *M. of P.* **1**: 483, 494.

[68] *C.J.* **2**: 44, 52; D'Ewes (N), 249.

[69] *H.M.C., Seventh Report*, MSS of Sir Henry Verney, Bart., 445; *C.J.* **3**: 389.

[70] *O.P.H.* **9**: 3.

[71] Copinger, *op. cit.* **6**: 37.

[72] *M. of P.* **1**: 497 and n.; Pink MSS, 311, fol. 498 d.

[73] *Vis. Sussex, 1633–4*, 22; Add. MSS, 5697, fol. 332. Thomas was aged a little over 24 years and 6 months in August, 1620. I.P.M., Sir Nicholas Parker, C. 142/380/124.

[74] *Sussex Arch. Coll.* **59**: 118, 122, 1918; Horsfield, *Hist. Sussex* **1**: 86; Pink MSS, cited above.

[75] *Gray's Inn Adm. Reg.*, 133.

[76] *Vis. Sussex*, 22; I.P.M. cited above. The baptisms of twelve children of this union between 1619 and 1639 appear in the Willingdon registers. Add. MSS, 5697, fol. 336.

[77] C. 193/13; S.P. 16, 405; C. 181/3 (1624, 1627); 181/4, fols. 18v, 38; 181/5, fol. 288.

was a D.L. by 1624, and in 1627 was one of the commissioners for martial law for the soldiers billeted in his county.[78] The religious and political views of the Parkers are indicated by his father's signing the petition for reforms in the church early in James's reign, and by Sir Thomas's being warned in 1622 and 1623 to attend Council regarding the forced loan.[79]

Sir Thomas had not sat in parliament before 1640, but considered challenging the spring elections at Hastings that year when the rumor of bribery was abroad.[80] No doubt he was urged by his puritan friends to seek the place for Seaford when that borough was "restored" early in the next session. He served on various committees during 1641, went into Sussex as a parliamentary deputy lieutenant in 1642, and was absent in service early in 1644.[81] There were some suspicions regarding his loyalty in October, 1644,[82] but he retained his place in the House until 1648.[83] Parker died on 31 May 1663, and was buried 3 June at Willingdon.[84]

The Parker family held numerous estates in Sussex, at least six manors with rectories and other appurtenances having been theirs in 1620, and others added later. They held also some interest in the Virginia plantation. The generous provisions which Sir Thomas made in his will, 1654–1656, for his younger children are further indications of ample means.[85]

Relatives of Parker in the 1640 House were his cousins, Sir Peter Temple, Denton, and the brothers Fiennes, and their kinsmen by marriage, the Verneys. Through his wife, Parker was connected also with Sir Francis Barnham.

Sir Robert Parkhurst (c. 1603–1651), of London and of Pirford, Surrey, was M.P. for Guildford, 1640–1651. His grandfather was Henry Parkhurst, a mercer of Guildford and a relative of John Parkhurst, Bishop of Norwich (d. 1575), who had been inclined toward nonconformity. One uncle, Thomas, was several times mayor of Guildford, and another, John Parkhurst (1564–1639), was a master of Balliol, Oxford.[86] The member's father, Sir Robert Parkhurst (d. 1636), was

a London clothworker and Lord Mayor (1634–1635), who was active in the affairs of his guild and the year before his death was governor of the London companies' plantation in Ireland.[87] The younger Robert, son of the clothworker by his wife, Eleanor, daughter of William Babington of Chorley, Cheshire,[88] was born about 1603. He matriculated at Balliol, Oxford, in 1619, and was graduated B.A. in 1622. He may have been admitted to the Inner Temple in 1620.[89] In 1628 he married Elizabeth, daughter of Sir Henry Baker, Bart., of Sissinghurst, Kent, who died young.[90] His second wife was Anne or Silena, a daughter of Sir Thomas Crew of Stene, Northamptonshire, sister of John Crew (q.v.).[91]

Parkhurst was M.P. for Guildford, 1625, 1626, 1628 and both times in 1640.[92] He was a J.P. in Surrey,[93] and in 1635 was on the commission concerning the navigability of the Wey.[94] He went to Ireland, doubtless to look after the interests of his estate there after his father's death, and was knighted in Dublin in 1638.[95] The next year he ignored the request for a contribution to the king.[96] He seems to have agreed in political and religious views with William Spurstow (q.v.), the London merchant who was his uncle by marriage and was a trustee for some of his estates.[97] In 1641 Parkhurst was named with the group to investigate the extension of the forests in Surrey.[98]

Parkhurst supported the reformers in parliament, but he was not prominent in debate or in committee work on constitutional matters. He was named to the committee on the Virginia plantation, in which his father had been interested,[99] and pledged £1000 as security for the first loan.[100] He was named a parliamentary D.L. for Surrey,[101] and apparently held his seat after the purge of the Presbyterians in 1648.[102] He made his will early in 1650, referring then to his "long infirmity of body," and died the following year. He was

---

[78] *Sussex Arch. Coll.* **40**: 2, 1896; *C.S.P. Dom., 1627–1628,* 461.

[79] *Sussex Arch. Coll.* **9**: 47, 1857; S.P. 14, 127/79. He was reported in 1623 to be £30 in arrears. S.P. 14, 148/29.

[80] *C.S.P. Dom., 1639–1640,* 607.

[81] *C.J.* **2**: 105, 164; **3**: 390; Thomas-Stanford, *Sussex in the great Civil War,* 42.

[82] *Sussex Arch. Coll.* **5**: 72, 1852.

[83] *O.P.H.* **9**: 14.

[84] Add. MSS, 5697, fol. 336. His will, dated 1654–1656, was proved 17 July 1663 by his son, George. P.C.C., 100 Juxon.

[85] I.P.M. and will cited above; *Sussex manors* (Sussex Record Society 20) **2**: 493, 1915; Kingsbury, *Records of the Virginia Company* **3**: 331. According to his will, Sir Thomas assigned £1000 each to two younger sons and £1500 for a younger daughter's portion.

[86] *Vis. London* **2**: 144; Manning and Bray, *Surrey* **1**: 39; *D.N.B.,* "John Parkhurst (1512?–1575)" and "John Parkhurst (1564–1639)."

[87] Brown, *Genesis of the U. S.,* 961; W. Herbert, *The history of the twelve great livery companies of London* **2**: 658; *C.S.P. Dom., 1634–1635,* 287, 295, 345; *C.S.P. Ireland, 1647–1660,* 192.

[88] *Vis. Surrey, 1623,* 97.

[89] *Al. Oxon.; Students admitted to the Inner Temple,* 229. The Temple student was described as the son of Robert Parkhurst of Catesby, Northants, a place with which Sir Robert was associated in his later years. Baker, *Northampton* **1**: 287.

[90] I.P.M., Sir Robert Parkhurst, senior, C. 142/543/21.

[91] Baker, *op. cit.* **1**: 287, 288.

[92] *M. of P.* **1**: 466, *passim.*

[93] C. 193/13; S.P. 16/405.

[94] Manning and Bray, *Surrey* **1**: Intro., ii.

[95] Pink MSS, 322.

[96] Rushworth **3**: 914.

[97] *Vis. Surrey, 1623,* 97; C. 142/543/21.

[98] Manning and Bray, *Surrey* **1**: Intro., xiii, n.

[99] *C.J.* **2**: 54; Brown, *Genesis of the U. S.,* 961. The elder Parkhurst had been interested also in the East India Company. India Office MSS, Home Ser., Misc., 1, fol. 29.

[100] D'Ewes (N), 52, n.

[101] *Surrey Arch. Coll.* **40**: 42, 1932.

[102] *O.P.H.* **9**: 4; *A.H.R.* **44**: 36, n., 1938–1939.

buried at Guildford, 21 August 1651, and his will was proved on 5 February 1651/2.[103]

Sir Robert's estates, parts of which he had purchased with his father, included, besides the manor of Pirford near Guildford and two others nearby, some lands in Devon and Cornwall and two manors in Gloucestershire.[104] His will referred to a mansion house in Exeter and to large portions for two daughters and a younger son which were based upon his lands and some legacies left by his mother.[105] Parkhurst seems to have been one of the wealthier men of the 1640 Commons.

George Parry, LL.D. (c. 1601–c. 1660), of Exeter, was M.P. for St. Mawes, Cornwall, 1640–22 January 1644. A younger son of Henry Parry, D.D., Bishop of Worcester (d. 1616),[106] he was born about 1601, and was admitted to the Inner Temple in 1616. He matriculated at Merton College, Oxford, in March, 1617, was graduated B.A. in 1619, and went thence to Cambridge (Magdalene College), where he became a fellow and where in 1628 he received his degree of LL.D. In the same year he was admitted an advocate at the Inner Temple.[107] Two years earlier he became attached to the diocese of Exeter as chancellor to the bishop, an office which he held until 1653, possibly until 1660.[108] Before 1638 he married Dorothy, daughter of Sir Ralph Hossey (Honey?) of Dorset and widow of Sir Nicholas Smith of Larkbeax, Devon. About 1638 Dr. Parry and his wife were petitioning about the wardship of her grandchild, but she died either late that year or early in 1639.[109] Parry married again before 30 June 1642, and by his second wife, Mary, had four children before 1649.[110]

Dr. Parry was accused about 1629, with some other officials of Exeter diocese, of having exacted unusual fees and of having abused his power of excommunication for the sake of fees. He denied the charges both as to himself and as to his subordinates.[111] From 1635 to 1639 he served with the Court of High Commission.[112] In local matters, he was named a member of the Devon piracy commission in 1639.[113] He was somewhat embarrassed that year by being reported a defaulter from the county musters, although he was Judge Marshal of the field. The chief county officials soon exonerated him. His neighbor, John Bampfield, in particular, who was one of the D.L.'s, wrote that the list of defaulters seemed to have been compiled more on the idea of the ability to pay than on the nature of the offense, and that Dr. Parry ought to be excused for any default not only because he held a military office but because the recent death of his wife had resulted in a diminution of his estate. And Council discharged his case upon Parry's promise to conform thereafter.[114]

The chancellor was elected, possibly through royal influence, to both parliaments of 1640 for St. Mawes.[115] Distrust of him appeared in the House as early as December, 1640, on the ground that he had been a promoter of the new canons, and in February he and other church officials in the House were objected to because they had taken the oaths.[116] Parry voted against Strafford's attainder.[117] Although he was employed as a messenger to Doctors' Commons in the early summer, he probably was absent much of the time afterwards. He was summoned to be brought up in custody in November, 1642, and early in 1644 he was disabled.[118] He was knighted while attending the king's parliament at Oxford, and served in legal work in Devon and Cornwall during the war.[119] After compounding for his estates, 1646–1649, Dr. Parry was surrogate to the master of the prerogative court of Canterbury (1652),[120] and he died in Ireland about 1660. Letters of administration were granted to his son, Suetonius, in 1670.[121]

While he lived in Exeter Dr. Parry resided in the Close and was one of the heavier rate payers of the city.[122] At the time of his compounding he listed properties in and near Exeter worth £50 a year and named certain manors in Devon and Cornwall which he was holding in trusteeship. He planned in 1642 to provide portions of £500 to £1000 for any daughter he might have, but when his compounding fine was set at a tenth in 1649, it was only £200.[123]

[103] Manning and Bray, *Surrey* 1: 50, n.; will, P.C.C., 41 Bowyer.

[104] Aubrey, *Surrey* 3: 197; Manning and Bray, *Surrey* 1: 17–18; 3: 119; Exeter City Library MSS, Exeter Deeds and Documents, Nos. 1559, 1858; Exeter Cathedral Library MSS, No. 3499, Letter No. 171.

[105] An unmarried daughter's portion, for example, was to be £2000.

[106] G. S. Parry, *Genealogical abstracts of Parry wills*, 95–96, London, G. Sherwood, 1911. It is incorrectly stated in *D.N.B.*, "Henry Parry (1561–1616)," that the bishop never married. His wife, Elizabeth, proved his will, and he mentioned therein three sons and a daughter.

[107] *Al. Oxon.; Al. Cant.*

[108] Manuscripts of the Exeter Diocesan Registry, List of Chancellors of the Diocese of Exeter. I have found no evidence in the Exeter Corporation MSS that Parry was ever recorder of the city, as is stated in *Al. Cant.*

[109] Pink MSS, 307, fol. 276; *C.S.P. Dom., 1638–1639*, 256, 496.

[110] S.P. 23/208/60.

[111] S.P. 16, 530/131; 185/136.

[112] *C.S.P. Dom., 1634–1635*, 545; *1635*, 100; *1639*, 69.

[113] C. 181/5, fol. 264.

[114] S.P. 16, 409/46; *C.S.P. Dom., 1638–1639*, 365, 496.

[115] *M. of P.* 1: 480, 487.

[116] D'Ewes (N), 163, 307.

[117] Verney, 58.

[118] *C.J.* 2: 199, 845; 3: 374.

[119] Pink MSS, 307, fol. 276; Coate, *Cornwall in the great Civil War*, 185.

[120] A will was proved before him on 14 January 1651/2. P.C.C., 15 Bowyer.

[121] Pink, *loc. cit.;* Parry, *op. cit.,* 17. The dates are confused in *Al. Cant.*

[122] Exeter Corporation MSS, Subsidy Rolls, Section II, No. 15; Act Book 8, fol. 55.

[123] S.P. 23/208/60–61; *Cal. Com. Comp.,* 1381.

Parry was a first cousin of his fellow M.P., Dr. Samuel Turner (*q.v.*). He was a friend of the poet, Herrick, who addressed to him one of his shorter poems.[124]

Edward Partridge or **Partherich** (born 1602), of Greenaway Court and of Bridge, near Canterbury, was a member for Sandwich, 1640–1648. The grandson of William Partridge (d. 1598), who settled at Bridge in Elizabeth's reign,[125] he was the eldest son and heir of Edward Partridge of that place (d. 1612), and was born in November, 1602.[126] His mother was Susanna, daughter of William Steede of Harrietsham and step-daughter of Francis Colepeper of Greenaway Court (d. 1591).[127] Partridge matriculated at Hart Hall, Oxford, in 1618, entered the Middle Temple in 1621, but left there before 10 May 1623,[128] and retired to a quiet life in the country. He married (1) Mary, elder daughter and coheir of Edward Fogg (Fagge) of Ewell, near Faversham, and (2), in 1627, Catherine, daughter and coheir of Sir Arthur Throgmorton.[129]

Partridge was a member of the sewers commissions in Kent and Sussex from 1629 to 1639,[130] but otherwise seems to have been little active in local affairs before 1640. He maintained a very religious household, observing the puritan sabbath, but he attended religious services that conformed with the Common Prayer, and frowned upon the efforts of some of his household to attend services conducted by a puritan minister.[131]

Early in 1640 Partridge wrote to the town of Sandwich announcing his candidacy for the coming parliament, and particularly stating that he had avoided seeking the patronage of a lord. But there were five other candidates on this occasion, several with backing such as he had disdained, and he and two other hapless ones were denied the freedom of the town and declared incapable of serving. An attempt by the commonalty to override the decision of the corporation and after-

wards to have parliament declare the election void came to nothing, but Partridge's work with the nonconformist faction in the town was credited in part for the defeat of Edward Nicholas, clerk of the Council, on the same occasion.[132] In the interval before the next election, however, Partridge so worked with the common people that his place was practically assured even before the writ reached the town, and the officials were powerless to prevent it. He was granted the freedom of the town on 28 October and was promptly chosen to be one of the M.P.'s, although he was not even present to observe the proceedings and was described by an official as a stranger. When, in keeping with the town customs, a commissioner was sent to administer his oaths as freeman and baron, he excused himself from taking them, probably from puritanical scruples, and entered upon his service in parliament unsworn.[133]

Although a newcomer to parliament, Partridge was named in the early months to several committees, and worked actively with the reform element.[134] He was knighted at Whitehall on 31 July 1641,[135] but continued to work with the parliamentarians. In 1642 he pledged £600 for the Irish venture, half of the sum being his own.[136] That summer he was a member of the committee sent to the Kent assizes[137] and in September he promised £50 in plate for the cause.[138] He was on the committee to help remove the queen's Capuchin works from Somerset House,[139] and seems to have worked more in London than in his county during the war. He was secluded by Pride's Purge, and when he rejoined the Rump[140] in 1660 voted for the king's return. He offered himself for the 1660 elections at Sandwich, but nothing later is known of him.[141]

Partridge inherited two manors and other properties in Kent, a part of which he seems to have alienated before 1640,[142] and had some interests in Sussex[143]

---

[124] *The poetical works of Robert Herrick* (Moorman ed.), 322, 1915.

[125] Hasted, *Kent* **9**: 287. This was probably the Mr. Partridge who was a commissioner for Dover harbor in 1585. *Arch. Cant.* **10**: cxiv, n., 1876.

[126] I.P.M. of Edward Partridge, C. 142/328/152.

[127] *Sussex Arch. Coll.* **47**: 73, 1904; *Vis. Kent, 1619,* 71. Francis Colepeper was a brother of John Colepeper of Wigsell, grandfather of Sir John Colepeper, 1640 M.P.

[128] *Al. Oxon.; Mid. Temp. Rec.* **2**: 669, 681. His father had studied at the Inner Temple. *Students admitted to the Inner Temple,* 136.

[129] Pink MSS, 322; Hasted, *Kent* **6**: 551.

[130] C. 181/4, fols. 19, 38v, 75v, 101v; 181/5, fols. 288, 293.

[131] His sister, Katherine, who lived with him after her husband's death, was strongly puritanical, and her son, Sir William Springate (Springett), afterwards co-commander of Arundel Castle, was an Independent. Springate's wife, a niece of Partridge's first wife, described the household later for her grandson, Springett Penn. *Gentlemen's Magazine,* part 2: 365–374, 585–593, 1851; Thomas-Stanford, *Sussex in the great Civil War,* 110–118.

[132] Sandwich Borough MSS, 5.N.5 (Letters, 1639–1644), fols. 11–14; 5.M.7 (Year Book C and D), fols. 364v–367v; *C.S.P. Dom., 1639–1640,* 561, 568.

[133] The Lord Warden wrote on 3 October to commend Lord Grandison to the town, but the officials replied on 13 October that it would be impossible to secure his election. The royal writ arrived on the 23rd and the election was held on the 28th. Sandwich Borough MSS, 5.N.5, fols. 37v–38; 5.M.7, fols. 376, 377.

[134] *C.J.* **2**: 44, 51, 64, 146, 235. He urged his constituents in April, 1641, to be mindful of the public peace and the advancement of "our" religion. Sandwich Borough MSS, S.N. 1, fol. 120.

[135] Shaw, *K. of E.* **2**: 210. He was styled Sir Edward on 14 May 1641 (*C.J.* **2**: 146), however.

[136] *C.S.P. Ireland, Adventurers,* 73–74.

[137] *Arch. Cant.* **2**: 181, 1859.

[138] *C.J.* **2**: 772.

[139] *Sussex Arch. Coll.* **5**: 68, n., 1852.

[140] Sandwich Borough MSS, S.N. 1, fol. 146; *O.P.H.* **9**: 13; Thomason Tracts, 669. f. 24, p. 37.

[141] Boys, *Sandwich,* 716.

[142] I.P.M. cited above; S.P. 14, 79/142; Hasted, *Kent* **9**: 288.

[143] *Sussex manors* (Sussex Record Society **19**) **1**: 171, 1914.

and possibly some in Lincolnshire and Cambridge.[144] He was probably a man of moderate estate at the time of his election to the Long Parliament,[145] but he was related to several prominent M.P.'s. Colepeper was connected by the half-blood through Partridge's mother, and Sir Peter Temple was a kinsman by marriage.[146]

* **George Peard** (c. 1594–1644), of Barnstaple, M.P. for that borough, 1640–1644, came of a local family which had been active in Barnstaple affairs for several generations. His parents were John Peard, a barrister, and Gillian Beaple.[147] His father was frequently a trustee for the town, and was possibly alderman (1616–24) and mayor (1622–23).[148] His father's brother, George (d. 1621),[149] served for many years as legal adviser for Barnstaple, and represented it in several parliaments.[150] The younger George, heir of both father and uncle, was a student at the Middle Temple from 1613 to 1620, and while there was "bound" with John Northcote (q.v.).[151] After being called to the bar in 1620 he was employed by Barnstaple in legal matters, was regularly one of the "learned counsell" from 1628,[152] and became deputy recorder in 1637.[153] His business sometimes took him to London.[154] In 1634 both he and one Mrs. Peard, probably his mother, were listed as defaulters for the military rates. His mother was afterwards a ship money defaulter.[155]

The Short Parliament was his first, but Peard seems to have been re-elected in the autumn without difficulty, although three other candidates were standing.[156] Possibly his bold speech against ship money in the spring won votes; certainly his vigorous support of Pym's program afterwards was in keeping with Barnstaple sentiment.[157]

Peard was a property owner, having inherited from his father and uncle various lands and houses in and near Barnstaple,[158] and having leased others there himself.[159] He was attempting to collect several sums of money owing to him, possibly fees, 1638–1640.[160] Peard's contributions toward the popular cause in 1642 are indicative of considerable substance as well as sympathy.[161] Peard and Dering were friends.[162]

Henry Pelham (b. 1597), of Belvoir, Lincolnshire, and of Gray's Inn, sat for Grantham, 1640–1648. A grandson of Sir William Pelham (d. 1587), Elizabeth's Lord Justice of Ireland, he was the third son of Sir William Pelham (d. 1629) of Brocklesby, Lincolnshire, by his wife, Anne, daughter of Charles Lord Willoughby of Parham.[163] He was baptized at Brocklesby, 9 June 1597,[164] matriculated at Trinity College, Cambridge, in 1615, and entered Gray's Inn, 6 November 1616.[165] His inn remained his chief residence afterwards, but in 1621 he was "beyond the seas" in the company of one of the royal ambassadors, and he maintained his Lincolnshire connections. During his absence from England he was returned for one of Grimsby's seats in the 1621 parliament, but the House rejected him as a member because his absence, both at the time of the election and afterwards, was not on state business.[166] He was elected by Grimsby, however, to the sessions of 1624, 1625, 1626 and 1628.[167] He spoke in favor of parliamenetary privileges during the debate on tonnage and poundage in January, 1629.[168]

During the 1630's Pelham divided his time between his home county and London. He had become a business adviser of the Earl of Lindsey and of his own powerful kinsman, the Earl of Rutland, and by 1634

---

[144] Edward Partridge, Esq. in June, 1641, and Sir Edward Partridge in December, 1641, were named to the Lincolnshire sewers commission (C. 181/5, fols. 393, 429), and in 1645 Sir Edward was named to a committee regarding drainage problems in Cambridgeshire (C.J. 4: 229). An Edward Partridge, Esq., possibly a relative, was M.P. for Cambridgeshire in 1679. M. of P. 1: 534.

[145] The jointure of his sister, Katherine Springate, was £240 a year. Thomas-Stanford, Sussex in the great Civil War, 112.

[146] Partridge's second wife was a sister of Temple's first wife (d. 1620).

[147] Devon Trans. 72: 259, 1940. Oliver Peard, merchant and alderman (Barnstaple Corporation MSS, Nos. 349, 958, 960), was his grandfather.

[148] Barnstaple MSS, Nos. 109–111, 126, 128, 153–164; Barnstaple Receivers' Accounts, 1389–1643, membrane 200.

[149] I.P.M., George Peard, gent., 25 April 1622, C. 142/766/77.

[150] Barnstaple MSS, Receivers' Accounts, 1389–1643, membranes 80, 164, 177, 189, 192; Cotton, Barnstaple during the great Civil War, 35–36.

[151] Mid. Temp. Rec. 2: 567, 633, 653.

[152] Barnstaple MSS, Receivers' Accounts, 1389–1643, membranes 200, 211, 214, 217, passim.

[153] Barnstaple MSS, Sessions Court Book, 1631–1642, 9 and 23 October 1637, 1 and 15 January 1638, passim.

[154] Barnstaple MSS, No. 1722; Receivers' Accounts, 1389–1643, membrane 229. Peard was doubtless active in the case of his borough in Star Chamber in 1640, as well as in securing the remission of the fine then imposed. C.S.P. Dom., 1640, 542.

[155] Barnstaple MSS, Nos. 607, 608. Mrs. "Julian Peard" of Barnstaple refused to pay 10 s. for ship money in 1637 and was reported to Council in 1639. S.P. 16, 376/137/i; C.S.P. Dom., 1639, 512.

[156] Gribble, Memorials of Barnstaple, 346–350.

[157] He had a personal quarrel with at least one royalist, Carnaby, in March, 1641 (C.J. 2: 111–112), and was one of the most active members in the latter part of that year. D'Ewes (C), 186, 295, passim.

[158] I.P.M., cited above; Barnstaple MSS, Nos. 204, 349, 989.

[159] Barnstaple MSS, Nos. 195, 339, 385.

[160] Barnstaple MSS, Sessions Court Book, 1631–1642.

[161] He promised £100 at no interest in June, 1642 (N. and Q., 1st Ser., 12: 359, 1855), and pledged a smaller sum annually for the duration of the Irish war. Cotton, op. cit., 38.

[162] Add. MS. 34,195, fol. 30.

[163] Maddison, Lincs. Ped. 3: 765–766; Lincs. N. and Q. 1: 155, 1888–1889; D.N.B., "Sir William Pelham (d. 1587)."

[164] The parish register of Brocklesby, ed. by C. W. Foster, 49, privately printed, 1912.

[165] Al. Cant.; Gray's Inn Adm. Reg., 145.

[166] M. of P. 1: 452; S.P. 14, 119/81; Bodleian Firth MSS, b.2, fol. 37.

[167] M. of P.

[168] Commons Debates for 1629, 109.

was serving as deputy recorder for Grantham under the latter.[169] He was named to some commissions dealing with his county and Rutland, 1634–1635,[170] was living at Freeston, near Belvoir Castle, in 1637,[171] and was identified as "of Belvoir" when he was returned for Grantham to the Short Parliament.[172] He kept his chambers at Gray's Inn, however,[173] and was probably a not infrequent visitor at the home of his Sussex relative, Sir Thomas Pelham of Laughton (q.v.).[174]

In the parliaments of 1640 Pelham, as well as both of his kinsmen of the name, worked with the popular group, although his brother, Sir William, head of the Lincolnshire branch, was a royalist. Henry was probably the "Mr. Pelham" named to the December, 1640 committees on recusants and the charges to be brought against Laud,[175] but the presence of his cousin, Peregrine, also "Mr. Pelham," makes the distinction between the two difficult after the opening weeks. Henry Pelham, however, pledged £100 for the defense in 1642,[176] and continued high in the favor of the House. By parliament order he served for a brief time during the war as Lincoln's recorder,[177] and in the summer of 1647 was for a few days in the chair as Speaker of the House. He was chosen in Lenthall's absence on 30 July, at the time of the contest with the army, but lost the honor when the army reached London a week later.[178] Pelham was secluded with the less extreme members in December, 1648, and, when the parliament was recalled in 1659–1660, was listed among those "returned," although illness or some other reason prevented him from actually attending.[179] He is said to have died after the Restoration.[180]

Pelham, who came of a wealthy family, enjoyed an annuity of £60 which had been left him by his father,[181] and seems to have had a legal practice which must have brought him considerably more than that a year. No figures regarding his wealth, however, are available.

Peregrine Pelham (1602–1650), merchant of Hull, was elected for Hull, 18 January 1641, following Sir John Lister's death, and sat until 1650. He was a descendant of the Pelhams of Laughton, Sussex, through his grandfather, Sir William Pelham (d. 1587), Elizabeth's Lord Justice of Ireland. The Pelhams of Brocklesby, Lincolnshire (see Henry Pelham), were the judge's descendants by his first marriage. To a younger son, Peregrine, said by most authorities to have been his son by his second wife, the judge left parts of the manor of Wickham and other lands in Lincolnshire. This Peregrine was the father of the Hull M.P. The younger Peregrine Pelham, his father's eldest son,[182] was baptized at Bosham, Sussex, on 27 September 1602,[183] and a younger brother and sister were baptized in that county in 1611 and 1613.[184] But in their later years the members of this branch of the Pelham family were associated more with the region of their Lincolnshire kinsmen.[185] Peregrine was apprenticed to a Hull merchant, Thomas Aslaby, and was thereafter principally a resident of that town. He was admitted to the freedom of Hull by virtue of his apprenticeship, 3 August 1626,[186] and was engaged soon afterwards in trade with the continent. He was importing French wine about 1627, and the next year petitioned Council for permission to export two thousand pigs of lead which had been held up by the new trade restrictions.[187] In the meantime he had married — Bowes, probably a daughter of one of the local families, and his son, John, was baptized at St. Mary's, Hull, on 25 April 1628.[188]

---

[169] Grantham Corporation MSS, Court Minute Book, I, fols. 6, 44v, 60v, 68v; Add. MSS, 37,343 (Whitelocke's Annals), fols. 134, 137; *Abstracts of Sussex Deeds,* Sussex Rec. Soc., **29**: 136, 1924.

[170] C. 181/4, fol. 159; 181/5, fol. 29.

[171] *H.M.C., MSS of the Duke of Rutland* **4**: 529.

[172] *M. of P.* **1**: 482.

[173] *C.S.P. Dom., 1635–1636,* 230; *H.M.C., Twelfth Report* **4**, MSS of the Duke of Rutland (I), 520.

[174] He was a guest at Sir Thomas's third wedding (*ibid.*), and was named a trustee in his will (P.C.C., 461 Alchin). According to some authors, Henry Pelham married Sir Thomas's daughter, Elizabeth (A. Collins, *History of the family of Pelham,* 560, London, 1755; Berry, *Sussex Geneal.,* 315; *Lincs. N. and Q.* **1**: 155, 1888–1889), but if so it was not until after 1648, for that daughter, younger than Henry by some twenty-five years, was still unmarried then, according to the wording of her father's will. She seems to have married by 1654 (Pelham accounts, Add. MSS, 33,148, fol. 60v), but I have not discovered her husband's name in the family papers.

[175] *C.J.* **2**: 42, 52.

[176] Bodleian Tanner MSS, 53, fol. 56.

[177] *C.J.* **2**: 890; *Lincs. N. and Q.* **8**: 137, 1904–1905.

[178] *C.J.* **5**: 259, 268–269; *Memoirs of Denzil, Lord Holles,* 156; Rushworth **7**: 737; A. Collins, *An historical and genealogical history of the family of Pelham,* 559–560, London, 1755. Some letters addressed by Pelham as Speaker to army officers are in B.M. Sloane MSS, 1519, fol. 162; *H.M.C., Sixth Report,* House of Lords MSS, 190.

[179] Thomason Tracts, 669. f. 24, p. 37.

[180] Notes of J. B. King.

[181] Will of Sir William Pelham, 1628, Lincoln Probate Registry, D. 70. His brother's heir was fined in 1646 at a tenth, £3000, later reduced to £2250. *Cal. Com. Comp.,* 1049.

[182] Collins, *History of the family of Pelham,* 553; Wildridge, *Hull letters,* 186; Maddison, *Lincolnshire pedigrees* **3**: 765. The seal attached to various letters of Peregrine Pelham among the Hull Corporation MSS bears the familiar pelicans and buckles of the Sussex Pelhams' arms. Even Noble (*Regicides* **2**: 118–119) admits that Peregrine belonged to that illustrious family.

[183] *Sussex Arch. Coll.* **54**: 57, 1911.

[184] Notes from Cocking parish register, Add. MSS, 5699, fol. 193. Peregrine, senior, made a fine concerning some land in Cocking in 1611 (*Sussex Notes and Queries* **2**: 88, 1928–1929).

[185] A sister, Eleanor, was married in 1629 at the Brocklesby parish church to the rector there. *The parish register of Brocklesby,* 16.

[186] Hull Corporation MSS, Bench Book 1, fol. 254.

[187] *C.S.P. Dom., 1625–1649,* 249; *1628–1629,* 313.

[188] Maddison, *Lincolnshire pedigrees* **3**: 765; *Yorks. Arch. Jour.* **12**: 467, 1893. This was the son who after Pelham's

Pelham married again, sometime between 1630 and 1649, a woman who must have been older than he, her wealth possibly being one of her attractions. She was Dame Jacoba Van Lore, widow of Sir Peter Van Lore, the wealthy merchant and money-lender, who owned lands in the Tunbridge area of Kent.[189]

Pelham began his civic responsibilities by being elected chamberlain at Hull in September, 1630, just as his good friend, Sir John Lister, was ending his second term as mayor. He was sheriff of Hull in 1636, but did not reach an aldermanship until after 1640. His next election was to Lister's vacant seat in parliament. Not until nine years later (September, 1649), with the special consent of the House, did he become mayor of Hull.[190]

The role of Peregrine Pelham in the early period of the Long Parliament is not easy to discover because of the possibility of his being confused with his cousin Henry, who was more experienced as a member and whose views, like Peregrine's, were of the "opposition." But with the approach of war and the preparations for defending Hull, Peregrine's importance grew.[191] His letters to Hull, 1643–1645, reveal impatience with the attempts to deal with the king, and approval of the execution of traitors to the parliamentary cause.[192] He served on several important committees, being particularly interested in naval affairs, and was one of the most zealous of the regicides.[193] He died near the close of 1650.[194]

Almost nothing definite is known of Pelham's financial standing, but presumably he was before 1640 a merchant of some local importance. Certainly neither he nor members of his family were reluctant to collect

what they felt the public owed for his services in parliament and at Hull.[195]

Sir Thomas Pelham, Bart. (1597–1654), of Halland in Laughton, Sussex, was M.P. for his county, 1640–1648.[196] He came of a family connected with east Sussex for many years and owning extensive lands in the area, being the only son of Sir Thomas Pelham, the first baronet (M.P., H.S., J.P., d. 1624), by his wife, Mary, daughter of Sir Thomas Walsingham of Scadbury, Kent. He was baptized at East Hoathley, Sussex, 22 September 1597, and in 1615 both matriculated at Emmanuel College, Cambridge, and was admitted to Gray's Inn.[197] He married not long afterwards.[198] His first wife was Mary, daughter and coheir of Sir Roger Wilbraham, Master of Requests, and after her death in 1635 [199] Pelham was considered by his friends as quite distracted and unsettled. He married (2) in 1637 Judith, widow of John Shurley of Lewes, and daughter of Sir Robert Honeywood, but she died the following year. His third marriage in the spring of 1640 with Margaret, daughter of Sir Henry Vane, senior, Treasurer of the Household (q.v.), was an occasion for great entertainment.[200] Pelham inherited his father's title and estates in 1624 and became a man of wide influence.

Pelham sat for East Grinstead in the 1621 parliament, and for Sussex in 1624 and 1625 and in the Short Parliament.[201] His service as a J.P in Sussex had begun before his father's death, and he was regularly a member of the commission of the peace,[202] as well as of numerous other commissions in the county.[203] He was also a D.L.[204] In his politics Pelham showed early that he belonged to the party working for the rights of the subject, but he favored a peaceful settlement of the question.[205] His father had opposed the 1621 loan and in 1627 Pelham was warned to attend Council for re-

---

death collected from Hull his arrears of salary as an M.P. Pelham's wife was doubtless a sister of the John Bowes who in 1650 called himself a brother-in-law of the M.P. (C.J. 6: 516).

[189] Sir Peter Van Lore's wife, still a widow in 1630, was petitioning the Crown regarding the rights of herself, her children and her grandchildren (C.S.P. Dom., 1629–1631, 49, 293; S.P. 16, 169/59). In 1651 parliament allotted £100 to Lady Van Lore, late wife of its deceased member, Pelham (C.J. 7: 22), and in 1653 she petitioned concerning some royalists' lands formerly granted to her (Cal. Com. Comp., 1645).

[190] Hull Corporation MSS, Bench Book 5, fols. 116v, 209v, 407–407v. I have found no substantiation of Bean's statement (Northern Counties, 875) that Pelham was recorder of Hull.

[191] Sanford, St. and ill., 474.

[192] Wildridge, Hull letters, 48–52, 54.

[193] Pelham attended 21 sessions of the trial, being surpassed by few in regularity of attendance. Abbott, Cromwell 1: 728, n.

[194] He was alive in August, probably in November, 1650, as indicated by the minutes of the city's affairs (Hull Corporation MSS, Bench Book 5, fols. 416v, 417; 6, fol. 4). A petition about his estate, however, reached parliament on 27 December (C.J. 6: 516), and in January, 1651, the Hull council considered the salary owing to Pelham as M.P. from June, 1649, until Christmas, 1650 (Hull Bench Book 6, fol. 6).

[195] Hull Corporation MSS cited above; Yorkshire County Magazine 1: 252–253, 1891. The notes by W. D. Pink (Yorkshire Genealogist 1: 219, 1888) confuse the M.P. with his father.

[196] M. of P. 1: 494; O.P.H. 9: 4.

[197] Al. Cant.; Gray's Inn Adm. Reg., 137.

[198] His father's will, dated 4 October 1616, referred to the marriage settlement made for his son on 23 June 1615. A previous will had directed the rearing of his son "in virtue and good learning" until he reached eighteen. Pelham family papers, Add. MSS, 33,137, fols. 54, 60.

[199] Add. MSS, 5697, fol. 265.

[200] One of the guests was Pelham's kinsman, Henry Pelham (q.v.). H.M.C., Twelfth Report 4, MSS of the Duke of Rutland (I), 520.

[201] M. of P. 1: 453, 460, 466, 483.

[202] C. 193/12, 13; S.P. 16/405; Sussex Arch. Coll. 16: 30, 1864.

[203] C. 181/3, fol. 120; 181/4 and 181/5, passim; C.S.P. Dom., 1627–1628, 461; Sussex Arch. Coll. 9: 104, 1857.

[204] Thomas-Stanford, Sussex in the great Civil War, 42.

[205] A. Collins, History of the family of Pelham, 558.

sisting likewise.[206] He ignored the king's request for funds again in 1639.[207]

The years before 1640 were marked for Pelham also by a feud with his neighbors and kinsmen, the Lunsfords, a quarrel dating from his father's day. It led in the 1630's from deer poaching to an attack on Pelham's life and to suits in the Star Chamber and fines for the Lunsfords.[208] The younger Lunsford afterwards became a colonel in the army, and when his nomination by the king for the lieutenancy of the Tower in December, 1641, was protested in London and in the House, his conduct toward Pelham was cited.[209]

Sir Thomas was a prominent member of the opposition group in the Long Parliament. A puritan, he was named to such committees as that on London papists and on the preaching ministry. He was appointed to consider matters for the defense of Sussex, and in the summer of 1641 was sent into his county to assist with the disarming of recusants. He offered his bond for £1000 for the loan in 1640, and in September, 1642, promised to provide £200.[210] He was a parliamentary committeeman in Sussex during the war, but was suspected in 1643 and 1644 of becoming somewhat lukewarm.[211] After his seclusion with the Presbyterians in 1648 Pelham lived in retirement until his death. He was buried at Laughton 28 August 1654.

The Pelham family was one of the wealthiest in Sussex, their lands including besides the entire rape of Hastings and three hundreds nearly twenty manors and other smaller properties.[212] Sir Thomas's assessment for the 1626 loan on privy seals was large, £60, though originally set at £100.[213] Among his Sussex holdings were timberlands and iron works which contributed substantially to his income in the 1630's and 1640's. According to the family accounts his income from Sussex rents and the sale of iron was £2698 in 1636, £2724 in 1640, and nearly £4000 in 1641. There were various smaller receipts besides, and in 1640 came £1000 as the first payment on his third wife's portion.[214] When he made his will in 1653 he provided £1000 each for two younger sons and £5000 for an unmarried daughter, two older children having been previously arranged for.[215]

Pelham's colleagues in the 1640 parliament included numerous relatives and intimate friends. Among them were the Vanes, his father-in-law and brother-in-law, Henry Pelham, a cousin and good friend, Peregrine Pelham of Hull, and Sir Thomas Walsingham. Intimate friends and kinsmen were Anthony Stapley, James Rivers, and Henry Shelley.[216]

* **Isaac Penington** (*c.* 1587–1661), puritan merchant and alderman of London, sat for his city, 1640–1653. He had learned the drapers' trade and, although he afterwards entered the fishmongers' company by patrimony and served as one of its wardens,[217] he seems to have been interested in the cloth trade in 1634.[218] He was interested also in the East India Company before 1635,[219] and was afterwards (1644) a governor of the Levant Company.[220]

One of the wealthiest residents of Coleman Street Ward,[221] Penington offered to advance £2000 personally for the loan in March, 1641, after the city had failed to meet the request made of it by parliament.[222] He subscribed £1000 for the Irish adventure in 1642, about half of the sum being his own,[223] and in June of that year pledged £200 for the defense.[224] He held several properties in Buckinghamshire, some by inheritance and some by purchase, and owned real estate also in London.[225]

Penington died a prisoner in the Tower shortly before 19 December 1661, when a warrant was issued for the delivery of his body to relatives.[226]

* **Sir William Pennyman, Bart.** (1607–1643), of Marske, Yorkshire, was M.P. for Richmond, 1640–11 August 1642. The son of William Pennyman, an official in London, by Anne, daughter of Richard Tottle,[227] he attended Westminster School before going to Oxford

---

[206] S.P. 14, 127/79; S.P. 16, 89/5.

[207] Rushworth 3: 914.

[208] *C.S.P. Dom., 1631–1633*, 410; *1635*, 39, 99; *1637*, 472; Birch, *The court and times of Charles the First* 2: 182; *Sussex Arch. Coll.* 3: 223–224, 1850.

[209] *C.J.* 2: 355; Thomas-Stanford, *op. cit.,* 19–20; D'Ewes (C), 340.

[210] *C.J.* 2: 24, 54, 146, 267, 787; D'Ewes (N), 52.

[211] Thomas-Stanford, *op. cit.,* 156; *Sussex Arch. Coll.* 5: 72 and n., 101, 1852; 31: 171, 1881.

[212] Add. MSS, 6344, fol. 172v.

[213] *Acts P. C., 1625–1626,* 371.

[214] Pelham family papers, Add. MSS, 33,144, fols. 55v–61, 84v–97, 230–263. The accounts show that the profit from his iron works constituted a sizable percentage of his income.

[215] P.C.C., 461 Alchin.

[216] Stapley and Rivers were with Pelham when Lunsford sought to kill him (S.P. 16, 369/58); Stapley and Shelley were made trustees for part of his estate in 1652. P.C.C., 461 Alchin.
In addition to the above sources, see *Complete Baronetage* 1: 8, 9.

[217] London Corporation MSS, Rep. 29, fol. 32v; *Members of the city companies, 1641* (Society of Genealogists) 3, 200.

[218] "Mr. Pennington" was among those so interested who were called to appear before Council in January, 1634. S.P. 16, 259/75, fol. 163.

[219] The company minutes of 27 November 1635 record the transfer of Penington's £ 1625 stock to another. Sainsbury, *A calendar of the court minutes, &c. of the East India Company, 1635–1639,* 121.

[220] Beaven, *The aldermen of the city of London* 2: 64. Beaven makes several corrections to the article on Penington in *D.N.B.*

[221] He was listed among those most able to lend money to the king in May, 1640. S.P. 16, 453/75.

[222] D'Ewes (N), 433 and n.

[223] *C.S.P. Ireland, Adventurers,* 160–161.

[224] *N. and Q.,* 1st Ser., 12: 358, 1855.

[225] Lipscomb, *Buckingham* 3: 240; 4: 587; S.P. 16, 378/93.

[226] *C.S.P. Dom., 1661–1662,* 184.

[227] *Complete Baronetage* 2: 36.

and the inns of court.[228]   He was once removed from the Yorkshire commission of the peace (1634) for derogatory remarks he was reported to have made about Wentworth,[229] but was soon back serving the crown loyally. He was sheriff of his county, 1635–1636,[230] and collected his ship money in full.[231] His actions in this respect as well as his conduct as a D.L., 1639–1640, which was openly complained of by some of his fellow parliament men in December, 1640, made him more than one enemy.[232] But though Pennyman was now Strafford's friend and loyal to the king, he was a friend also of Sir Thomas Hutchinson, a relative of his wife's.[233]

Besides an office worth £2000 a year which he bought in 1639, Pennyman owned lands in several Yorkshire parishes worth at least £600 a year. They included alum mines in Skelton.[234]

John Percival (d. 1644), merchant and alderman of King's Lynn, Norfolk, sat for his borough from 1640 until his death in 1644. Probably the son of Timothy Percival and Mary Gap, who were married at Swaffam on 26 December 1576, and grandson of John Percival, "clerk," [235] he was apprenticed in turn to alderman Thomas Boston and Thomas Clayborn, Lynn merchants, and was admitted a freeman to "exercise merchandize" there in 1608.[236] He married twice, (1) on 13 November 1617, Margery, daughter of John Atkin, merchant and alderman of Lynn; [237] and (2) on 25 September 1633, Judith St. John, probably a sister of Oliver St. John, the puritan lawyer, and a kinswoman of Cromwell.[238] Percival embarked upon a civic career with

reluctance, twice requesting a fine of £50 to avoid entering upon an office to which he had been elected, but consenting in 1618, probably with the encouragement of his wife's family, to become a council member. He was an alderman in 1623, mayor in 1630–1631, and in 1639 filled out the term of a mayor who had died in office.[239] Not before 1640, however, was he elected to parliament.

Percival seems to have been entrusted with many of the town's fiscal affairs. He handled its funds for various purposes, was almost regularly an auditor of its accounts, worked for improvements in its buildings and defenses, and during his second mayoralty had to account for the ship money turned in by the collectors.[240] His mercantile interests probably carried him often to Cambridge, for he was made a freeman there in 1626, and was active in raising funds for the Cambridge plague victims in 1630.[241] He was a man of serious outlook and piety. He donated several pieces of church plate to St. Margaret's in Lynn, helped pay the expenses of a visiting minister, 1620–1621,[242] and acquired as a son-in-law one minister of the town, Mr. John Arrowsmith.[243]

Percival was named to an occasional committee of the Long Parliament,[244] promised £50 for the defense in 1642,[245] and with the outbreak of war supported parliament actively, although a royalist faction controlled Lynn in 1643.[246] He was in Lynn during most of the winter of 1643–1644, and died about the middle of August, 1644.[247]

The chief indications of Percival's wealth are found in his will, which was dated 9 July 1644, with a codicil of 23 July, and was proved in 1656. It refers to the sum of £600 which he had agreed to settle upon his second wife, and to an additional £100 for her, as well as portions of £350 and £210 for two younger daughters. Besides a mansion and a country house near Lynn he owned some land and buildings in Boston. The will reveals in numerous ways the puritanical views of the testator, and directs the rearing of his younger children in the true nurture and fear of God, with "sufficient" learning.[248]

* Henry Percy (1605–1659), younger brother of the Earl of Northumberland, a courtier and soldier, was

[228] Barker and Stenning, *The record of old Westminsters* 2: 732.
[229] Pennyman to Wentworth, 16 April 1634, Bodleian Firth MSS, b.2, fol. 241.
[230] S.P. 16, 311/89; *List of Sheriffs*, 163.
[231] Royal Hist. Soc., *Trans.*, 3rd Ser., 4: 161, 1910.
[232] D'Ewes (N), 104–105, 151–152; *Note book of Sir John Northcote*, 63–64.
[233] *Memoirs of the life of Colonel Hutchinson*, ed. Firth, 1: 96–97, London, 1885.
[234] *Cal. Com. Comp.*, 2529–2530; *Y.A.S. Rec. Ser.* 15: 189–190, 1893; 20: 140, 1896.
[235] Norwich Public Library MSS, 56, Jessop's Extracts from Norfolk Parish Registers 2: 191. Percival's only son was named Timothy.
[236] *A calendar of the freeman of Lynn, 1292–1836*, 135, **144**, Norwich, printed for the Norfolk & Norwich Archaeological Society by Goose & Son, 1913; H.J. Hillen, *History of the borough of King's Lynn* 1: 356, n., Norwich, E. of Eng. Newspaper Co., 1907.
[237] Norwich Public Library MSS, 70, Cokayne's Norfolk Parish Registers 1: 219; Lynn Corporation MSS, Hall Book 7, fols. 78v, 99.
[238] Norwich Public Library MSS, 56, Jessop's Extracts 2: 99. Percival mentioned in his will the contract at the time of his second marriage, with Oliver St. John of Lincoln's Inn representing his wife's family. Cromwell, in a letter to the governor of Lynn in 1644, sent his regards to "my cousin Percevall." Abbott, *The writings and speeches of Oliver Cromwell* 1: 288.

[239] King's Lynn MSS, Hall Book 7, fols. 91v, 94v, 126v, 128, 201v, 327v; 8, fols. 34v, 42v.
[240] *Ibid.*, Hall Book 7, fols. 303v, 341; 8, fols. 35v, 36v, 42v.
[241] Cambridge Corp. MSS, Day Book, 1610–1646, fols. 143v, 151; King's Lynn MSS, Hall Book 7, fol. 325.
[242] *Ibid.*, Hall Book 7, fol. 169v; B. Mackerell, *The history and antiquities of King's Lynn*, 16–18, London, 1738.
[243] Will of John Percival, P.C.C., 40 Berkeley.
[244] *C.J.* 2: 166.
[245] *N. and Q.*, 1st Ser., 12: 360, 1855.
[246] Mackerell, *op. cit.*, 187; Hillen, *op. cit.*, 356.
[247] He was present at a Lynn Council meeting on 1 August, but died before the end of the month (King's Lynn MSS, Hall Book 8, fols. 127–130).
[248] P.C.C., 40 Berkeley.

elected for both Portsmouth, Hampshire, and the county of Northumberland. Having chosen to serve for the latter, he was expelled on 9 December 1641 for his part in the "army plot." [249] Percy was born in 1605,[250] and was the heir apparent to what D'Ewes described as one of the greatest families in Christendom.[251] In 1641 he was granted a pension of £1000 for life in lieu of payment of a debt of £6420 that he had advanced at court.[252] When he offered his bond for the loan in parliament in November, 1640, he promised "as much as his security will be taken for." [253] He was named to the committee on the bill against usury, and was ordered by Pym to be present during Strafford's trial.[254] His usefulness in the House ended with the army plot.

Percy was an uncle of Lord Lisle (q.v.).

Sir Thomas Peyton, Bart. (1613–1684), of Knowlton, Kent, was a member for Sandwich, 1640–5 February 1644, and was one of the diarists of the parliament. Descended from an old Cambridgeshire family, he was the eldest son and heir of Sir Samuel Peyton of Knowlton, the first baronet (J.P., M.P., d. 1623), and his wife, Mary, daughter and coheiress of Sir Roger Aston, Master of the Wardrobe to King James.[255] He was born in December, 1613,[256] and received a good education, although apparently at neither university nor inn of court.[257] On 21 May 1636 at St. Bride's in London he married Elizabeth, daughter of Sir Peter Osborne of Chicksand, Bedfordshire. She was a sister of Dorothy Osborne, from whose pen have come some pithy comments on Peyton's habits and character.[258] He had suffered somewhat in fortune by 1639 but, by arranging loans in London, was attempting to pay off his "high & mighty debts honestly & truly." [259]

Sir Thomas had been little involved in politics or in public affairs of any sort before 1640. He had been named to the sewers commission for Kent in 1639,[260] but had probably not found it necessary to commit himself on questions of national policy. With the summoning

of the first parliament of 1640, however, Peyton offered himself at Sandwich, a borough for which his father had once served and in which he owned some property. Although his decision was made almost on the eve of the election, and only after it was reported that one of the several candidates had withdrawn, he felt that the support of the commonalty might bring him success. The town officials ruled in his case as in that of Partridge (q.v.), however, that he should not be granted the freedom of the town and was therefore ineligible; and the shouts of the populace for Peyton and Partridge and a later appeal to parliament brought no results.[261] Peyton seems to have been kindly disposed toward the king himself at this period, but viewed Pym also with some favor, and was sufficiently interested in the matter of taxation to borrow a book on the ship money arguments.[262] He won the October election at Sandwich by the largest number of voices,[263] but was so uncertain of the outcome until the last that he had not dared to attend the shire elections to help Dering, his relative and friend.[264] His victory was probably accounted one for the popular side, with some of whom, such as Sir Edward Boys, he was on terms of intimacy then,[265] but his loyalty to King Charles eventually triumphed.

Peyton was not often named to committees in the parliament, but kept careful notes of the proceedings,[266] and recognized the need to consider general rather than local problems.[267] Although absent occasionally, he was quite regular in his attendance most of the time before January, 1642, possibly until the following autumn;[268] and he subscribed part of £400 for reducing Ireland that year,[269] and on 17 August was named one of the parliamentary D.L.'s for Kent.[270] The strengthening of the opposition, however, and his own inclination to avoid violence led him to break with the parliamentary leaders

---

[249] C.J. 2: 26, 337.

[250] Arch. Ael., 4th Ser., 23: 113, 1945.

[251] D'Ewes (C), 259.

[252] C.S.P. Dom., 1640–1641, 570.

[253] D'Ewes (N), 52.

[254] C.J. 2: 108, 115.

[255] Complete Baronetage 1: 70–71; Vis. Kent, 1619, 66–67; C. 193/13.

[256] I.P.M., Sir Samuel Peyton, C. 142/398/116.

[257] His correspondence reveals a considerable interest in books. In a letter of 1634, written in Latin, he mentioned a proposed trip to Oxford (Add. MSS, 27,999, fol. 190). One of his letters was dated from the Inner Temple in 1665 (Add. MSS, 28,005, fol. 21). For a comment on Peyton's literary interests, see W. H. Coates's introduction (D'Ewes [C], xxxix–xl).

[258] The first Lady Peyton died in September, 1642, and Peyton married twice afterwards. Complete Baronetage, loc. cit.

[259] Add. MSS, 27,999, fols. 300, 304, 306.

[260] C. 181/5, fol. 292.

[261] Hasted, Kent 10: 150; Sandwich Borough MSS, 5.N.5 (Letters), fol. 13v; 5.M.7 (Year Book), fols. 364v–367v; Peyton Letter Book (Add. MSS, 44,846), letters of Peyton in March, 1640, to Sandwich, to Foster, and to Palmer. Peyton's letter book, formerly in the possession of Lady Capel Cure, now Add. MSS, 44,846, had no pagination at the time I used it. My attention was called to it by Mrs. Dorothy Gardiner.

[262] Ibid., Peyton to Sir James Oxenden, 4 April 1640. Mr. Coates feels that Peyton was willing to accept the extreme royalist argument regarding taxation (D'Ewes [C], xli).

[263] Sandwich Borough MSS, 5.N.5, fols. 37v–38; 5.M.7 (Year Book C and D), fols. 376v–377. His vote was larger than Partridge's, although he seems not to have waged so active a campaign.

[264] Stowe MSS, 743, fol. 159; Add. MSS, 44,846, Peyton to Dering, October, 1640.

[265] Dorothy Gardiner, The Oxinden and Peyton letters, 29–30, London, Macmillan, 1937. Henry Heyman was another friend (ibid., 32).

[266] Peyton's diary is frequently cited by the editors of the journals of D'Ewes (cf. D'Ewes [N], xii–xiii).

[267] Letters to Sandwich, 14 January 1641 and 23 December 1641. Add. MSS, 44,846.

[268] D'Ewes (N), 497, n.; D'Ewes (C), passim; C.J. 2: 724.

[269] C.S.P. Ireland, Adventurers, 229.

[270] C.J. 2: 724.

in 1643.[271] He was disabled on 5 February 1644,[272] and was a prisoner for several periods during the war. During one interval he was allowed to compound for his estates, his fine being set at £1000.[273] He survived to be rewarded for his loyalty by Charles II,[274] died on 11 February 1684, and was buried four days later in Westminster Abbey.

Although Peyton was somewhat embarrassed financially in 1639, he admitted that his lands, embracing five Kentish manors at least, with marsh lands near Sandwich, and others in Berkshire, were worth £1000 a year.[275] His personal tastes were those of a country gentleman who preferred the sport of coursing or the quieter pleasures of reading to the rigors of a public career. His interest in books ranged from family history to Hebrew treatises or books on coins. In religion he strongly opposed the papists, and during the interregnum condemned a godson's gaming in quite puritanical vein.[276] His sister-in-law, Dorothy Osborne, once wrote of him, "He is an honest gentleman, in earnest, has understanding enough, and was an excellent husband to two very different wives," getting along equally well with one who was quiet and inclined to melancholy and with one who loved humor and company.[277]

Edward Phelipps, or **Philips** (1613–1680), of Montacute, Somerset, was elected for Ilchester early in 1641, following the voiding of the original election.[278] He was disabled as a royalist, 5 February 1644. He was the grandson of Sir Edward Phelipps, Master of the Rolls and Speaker of the House (d. 1614), and the son and heir of Sir Robert Phelipps (d. 1638), who had distinguished himself for his defense of the rights of the subject in earlier Stuart parliament.[279] Through his mother, Bridget, daughter of Sir Thomas Gorges, Edward Phelipps was a nephew of Sir Theobald Gorges

(q.v.). He was born in 1613,[280] matriculated at Wadham College, Oxford, 30 October 1629,[281] and on 21 February 1632 married Anne, daughter of Sir Robert Pye, Auditor of the Exchequer (q.v.). She brought him a jointure of £3000.[282] Before 1640 Phelipps was a J.P. in his county.[283] He joined his father in resisting ship money, engaging at the time in a spirited conflict with the sheriff, William Bassett (q.v.), and the latter's stepfather, Sir John Stawell (q.v.).[284] Family quarrels as well as national issues seem to have been involved,[285] and the king himself in 1637 ordered the heads of the families to lay aside their ways and cooperate in the service of king and country.[286] Edward Phelipps was still in arrears in 1638 and 1639.[287]

Elected M.P. for Ilchester for the Short Parliament,[288] Edward was perhaps Sir Henry Berkeley's opponent in the contest of the fall. His family had earlier quarrelled with the Berkeleys and the Pouletts.[289] In the Long Parliament, it might have been expected that Phelipps would be a leader in the ranks of the opposition, but instead he was a quite inconspicuous member. Possibly he attended infrequently, and in time he joined the king.[290] He was accordingly disabled in 1644.[291] He survived the war and the Restoration to sit again in parliament, and died in 1680. He was buried on 17 February 1679/80 at Montacute. His will, dated 16 January 1679/80, was proved on the following 28 June.[292]

The Phelipps family was well-to-do, and their residence at Montacute was described in 1633 as far surpassing any near it.[293] Although Sir Edward, the Master of the Rolls, was said to have left at his death an estate smaller than had been expected,[294] his grandson had had settled on him at the time of his marriage an

---

[271] Letters to various correspondents, 1642-1643, Add. MSS, 44,846; Gardiner, *The Oxinden and Peyton letters*, 12–13, *passim*.

[272] *C.J.* 3: 389.

[273] *Arch. Cant.* 9: 38, n., 44, 1874; *Cal. Com. Comp.*, 864; *Complete Baronetage* 1: 71.

[274] *Arch. Cant.* 21: 238, 1895; *Flagellum Parliamentarium*, Aungerville Society Reprints, 1st Ser., 14, Edinburgh, 1881.

[275] I.P.M. cited above; Hasted, *Kent* 10: 106, 150; Add. MSS, 28,008, fols. 6, 11–12; *Cal. Com. Comp.*, 864. His father had planned dowries of £1200–£1500 for each of his three daughters.

[276] *Arch. Cant.* 25: 257, 1902; Add. MSS, 28,001, fols. 12, 13; 28,002, fol. 293; 28,003, fols. 337, 339, 417, 446; 28,005, fol. 56; 44,846 (Peyton to Oxinden, August, 1640).

[277] *The letters of Dorothy Osborne to William Temple*, ed. G. C. Moore Smith, 89–90, Oxford, Clarendon Press, 1928.

[278] He was present to take the Protestation on 4 May 1641. *C.J.* 2: 134.

[279] Edward is but briefly mentioned in *D.N.B.*, "Sir Robert Phelipps." A sketch of his life, principally for the period after 1640, appears in Bates Harbin, *Members of Parliament, Somerset*, 173–174.

[280] *Vis. Somerset*, 85; I.P.M., Sir Robert Phelipps, C. 142/571/151.

[281] *Al. Oxon.*

[282] I.P.M. cited above.

[283] *Somerset and Dorset N. and Q.* 9: 175–176, 1904–1905; C. 193/13.

[284] *V.C.H. Somerset* 2: 201–202.

[285] Stawell had been fined £500 in Star Chamber for certain wrongs to Sir Robert Phelipps in 1629 (*H.M.C., Seventh Report*, MSS. of G. A. Lowndes, 545), and was active in publicizing the Phelipps' stand on ship money now. See Stawell.

[286] *C.S.P. Dom., 1635*, 120, 409, 502; *1637*, 18–19, 98, 133.

[287] *Ibid., 1637–1638*, 314; *1639–1640*, 141.

[288] *M. of P.* 1: 482.

[289] *E.H.R.* 44: 579–599, 1929.

[290] Phelipps may have sought at first to avoid the issue, for one "Edward Phillips" in April, 1643, applied for a pass to go to Spa with his household (*H.M.C., Fifth Report*, House of Lords MSS, 81), but by October of that year Phelipps was raising funds for the king. (*H.M.C., First Report*, MSS at Montacute House, 58).

[291] *C.J.* 3: 389.

[292] *Al. Oxon.*; Brown, *Somerset Wills* 1: 78.

[293] Gerard, *Partic. Descr. Somerset*, 99.

[294] *The letters of John Chamberlain* 1: 556.

estate of £500 a year,[295] and his wife's jointure was large. The declaration that Phelipps made to the compounding commissioners showed the value of that earlier settled portion of his estate as only £400 a year and his full inheritance as worth £793 yearly,[296] but he was said in 1660 to be worth £1500 a year.[297]

* Sir Gilbert Pickering, Bart. (1611–1668), of Titchmarsh, Northamptonshire, was M.P. for his shire, 1640–1653. A nephew of his colleague, Dryden (*q.v.*), and son of Sir John Pickering (d. 1628), who had been imprisoned for resisting the 1627 loan,[298] Pickering was a follower of their principles. He was baptized at Titchmarsh, 10 March 1611, was admitted to Emmanuel College, Cambridge, at Easter, 1625, and was graduated B.A. in 1629.[299] He was created a baronet in 1638,[300] but seems not to have been active in public life before 1640. He was connected by marriage with all the Montagus who were in the 1640 parliament, for his first wife was Sir Sydney Montagu's daughter.

Pickering was described by a contemporary as a knight "of the old stamp, and of considerable revenue in Northamptonshire." He owned lands in Huntingdonshire also,[301] and his pledge for the defense in 1642 was among the larger offers.[302]

* William Pierrepont (1607 ?–1678), of Thoresby, Nottinghamshire, and Tong Castle, Salop, was M.P. for Great Wenlock in the latter county, 1640–1648. The second son of the wealthy Earl of Kingston, and a resident usually of the Thoresby estate settled on him by his father, he had married a Shropshire heiress and was the holder of various offices in that county, too. He was born in 1607 or 1608,[303] and was educated at Emmanuel College, Cambridge (matric. 1624), and Lincoln's Inn (entered 14 April 1627).[304] After serving as sheriff in Shropshire in 1638 and collecting ship money, he was among those who petitioned in 1639 for a change in the rates.[305] He was a candidate at the Shropshire county

election in March, 1640, and seems to have won, although there was a close contest.[306] One of the moderate men of the popular faction, Pierrepont was a Presbyterian elder.[307]

Pierrepont was wealthy enough in his own right to pledge his bond for £1000 in November, 1640, and March, 1641.[308] His possessions probably included some lands in Lincolnshire as well as in the western counties.[309] He was a kinsman of several of his fellow parliament men, notably Savile and Armine, and by his marriage had a connection with Richard More.

Sir William Playters, or **Platers, Bart.** (1590–1668), of Sotterley, Suffolk, sat for Orford, 1640–1648. He came of an old and wealthy family, being the son and heir of Sir Thomas Playters, Bart. (J.P., H.S., d. 1638), by his first wife, Anne, daughter of Sir William Swan of Southfleet, Kent. He was baptized at Sotterley 17 January 1590,[310] was educated as a gentleman and travelled long enough on the continent to become something of a linguist.[311] He married in 1615 Frances, daughter and heiress of Sir Charles Le Grys of Billingford, Norfolk, acquiring with her lands in that county. His family estates in his father's lifetime were reputed to be worth £2000 a year,[312] and an estimate of £3000 was put on Playter's own income afterwards.[313] He was knighted in 1623 and lived part of the time in London, ostensibly on account of his wife's ill health,[314] but also, if Aubrey is to be trusted, because he was attracted by the handsome women of the city and cronies such as Henry Marten.

Accounted sober and thrifty in other matters, Playters was active in the country as a J.P. and member of local commissions, was a vice admiral for Suffolk, and diligent about its military affairs, serving as colonel of a regiment and as a D.L. for many years.[315] He was especially vigorous in executing the orders for pressing men and collecting money in 1640, imprisoning several

---

[295] *C.S.P. Dom., 1637*, 19.

[296] S.P. 23/181/315. Perhaps his father-in-law, Pye, helped to get his fine eased from the original £3191, reckoned at a third, to £276. *Cal. Com. Comp.*, 1252.

[297] *Western Antiquary* **7**: 39, 1887–1888.

[298] Rushworth **1**: 473.

[299] *Al. Cant. D.N.B.* dates his birth in 1613, and mentions only his Gray's Inn training.

[300] *Complete Baronetage* **2**: 433.

[301] J. H. Hill, *The history of the parish of Langton*, 28, Leicester, 1867; *V.C.H. Northampton* **3**: 144, 145–146; I.P.M. of Sir John Pickering, C. 142/446/84.

[302] Four horses and £150. *N. and Q.*, 1st Ser., **12**: 359, 1855.

[303] *D.N.B.* gives 1607 as the approximate date. He was said to be six years old, however, in 1614 (*Vis. Notts.*, 51). Confirmation of his death date as 1678 rather than 1679 comes from the fact that his will, dated 2 July 1677, was proved 17 August 1678. Shrops. Arch. Soc., *Trans.*, 3rd Ser., **2**: 330, 1902.

[304] *Al. Cant.; Linc. Inn Rec. Adm.* **1**: 202.

[305] *C.S.P. Dom., 1639*, 252.

[306] Shrops. Arch. Soc., *Trans.*, 4th Ser., **11**: 168, 1927–1928. He was a member of the Committee of Privileges of the Short Parliament. *C.J.* **2**: 4.

[307] *A.H.R.* **44**: 36, n., 1938–1939.

[308] D'Ewes (N), 51, 439, n.

[309] Some of his eastern land he inherited from his mother's family, the Talbots (*Fenland N. and Q.* **2**: 104, 1892–1894). He was listed as a musters defaulter in Lincolnshire in 1639. *C.S.P. Dom., 1638–1639*, 510.

[310] *Complete Baronetage* **1**: 220; Suckling, *The history and antiquities of the county of Suffolk* **1**: 83, 86; Reyce, *The breviary of Suffolk*, 90.

[311] Aubrey, *Brief lives* (Clark) **2**: 156.

[312] Blomefield, *Norfolk* **5**: 321; Suckling, *op. cit.* **1**: 83; *Suff. Inst. Arch.* **8**: 188–189, 1894. Sir William Playters, Master for the Earl of Arundel, asserted in 1649 that he had been an adventurer in the drainage projects of the Earl of Bedford. *Fenland Notes and Queries* **1**: 124, 1889–1891.

[313] Aubrey, *loc. cit.* £5000 a year is stated once by Aubrey.

[314] *C.S.P. Dom., 1631–1633*, 380; *1640–1641*, 280.

[315] Blomefield, *Norfolk* **1**: 198; C. 181/3; 181/5, fols. 350, 379; S.P. 16, 65/43; *C.S.P. Dom., 1629–1631*, 67.

mutinous soldiers who attacked him,[316] but was nevertheless elected in the following October to his first parliament.[317]

Sir William's reputation and his activities in his county that year had probably not endeared him to the opposition leaders of the House, for he was not named before the following summer to committee work. He was, however, among the first to offer his bond for the loan in November, 1640,[318] and when war threatened promised to supply two horses for the defense.[319] He apparently kept his place in the House until Pride's Purge,[320] and has been classified among the Presbyterians of his county;[321] but his son was an active royalist and Sir William was said in time to have been turned out of all of his offices.[322] He was under suspicion as a possible delinquent in 1650 and 1652, but seems to have cleared himself.[323] He died in April, 1668, and was buried 24 April at Sotterley.

William Pleydell (born *c.* 1602), of Mudgehall in Lydiard Tregoze, Wiltshire, lawyer and royalist, was M.P. for Wootton Bassett, 1640–5 February 1644.[324] He was a younger son of Sir Charles Pleydell (H.S. Wilts, 1621; d. 1642), of Mudgehall and of county Middlesex, by his first wife, Catherine, daughter and heir of Thomas Bouchier, Esquire.[325] Through his father's second wife, Jane, daughter of Sir John St. John, he was connected with the Hungerfords (*q.v.*).[326] His family, branches of which lived also in Berks and Gloucestershire, seem to have held the manor or farm of Mudgehall, once part of the lands of Stanley Abbey near Calne and Wootton Bassett, from the time of Henry VIII.[327] His father was listed for the 1611 loan in Wiltshire,[328] but between 1617 and 1620 was evidently living at Westminster, where he was a rate payer in St. Margaret's parish.[329] He was described as of Kilburn, Middlesex, when his sons were admitted to Oxford in 1618. Possibly his second wife's connection

with the Villiers family had opened for him some place at court.[330]

William Pleydell was born about 1602, and in 1618, with his elder brother, John, entered Trinity College, Oxford.[331] Where he studied afterwards is not known,[332] but by 1640 he appears to have become a lawyer of some note. D'Ewes referred to him as a lawyer,[333] and he was created D.C.L. at Oxford in 1644.[334] His reputation for learning was strong enough in Wiltshire for an acquaintance, Lady Lee, to write to Edward Hyde in November, 1640, inquiring whether Pleydell had made any learned speeches in parliament. She added that, "He would have done well to have bin chose Speaker."[335] Pleydell had served, however, in no previous parliament, and seems to have had no part in local administration. He was not listed in the Long Parliament as a Straffordian, but he early showed his willingness to support the established church.[336] He was disabled in 1644 for having joined the king at Oxford.[337]

Pleydell's name appears in none of the lists of loan subscribers during the parliament, but he perhaps had little income at his disposal for such purposes. His father, who survived until 1642, seems not to have had great wealth, and most of his estate went to the elder son.[338] No record of Pleydell, the M.P., has been found in the royalist composition papers,[339] although he was possibly living as late as 1659.[340]

William Pole or **Poole** (1614–1619) of Colyton and Colcombe, Devon, was M.P. for Honiton from its restoration as a parliamentary borough until he was disabled, 24 June 1643, for having taken up arms against parliament.[341] He was the grandson of Sir William Pole (d. 1636), the Devonshire antiquary and J.P., and the son and heir apparent of Sir John Pole, Bart. (M.P. Devon, 1628; H.S. 1639; d. 1658), by his wife, Elizabeth, only daughter of Roger How, a London mer-

---

[316] Bodleian Tanner MSS, 69, fol. 47; *C.S.P. Dom., 1640,* 336, 471.

[317] *M. of P.* **1**: 494. He became a freeman of Dunwich on 17 October 1640, doubtless with an eye on the elections. Dunwich Borough MSS, Minute Books, 1627–1653, fol. 118.

[318] *C.J.* **2**: 200; D'Ewes (N), 52.

[319] *N. and Q.,* 1st Ser., **12**: 360, 1855.

[320] His name appears in a list of members printed in 1648. Thomason Tracts, E. 454, 17.

[321] *A.H.R.* **44**: 36, n., 1938–1939.

[322] Suckling, *op. cit.* **1**: 83–84; *O.P.H.* **9**: 3.

[323] *Cal. Com. Comp.,* 2228.

[324] *M. of P.* **1**: 496; *C.J.* **3**: 389.

[325] Pink MSS, 311, fol. 496e; *List of Sheriffs,* 154.

[236] Add. MSS, 33,412, fols. 24, 67, 104, 117v. Sir Edward Hungerford, M.P., was her half-brother.

[327] *Vis. Glouc.,* 124; Marshall, *Vis. Wilts.,* 100–101; *Vis. Berks.* **1**: 122; Marsh, *Hist. of Calne,* 232, 235; Wilts. Arch. Soc. MSS, Sadler's "Wiltshire Genealogy," Lydiard Tregoze.

[328] Add. MSS, 5496, fol. 96.

[329] Records of St. Margaret's Parish, Overseers' Accounts, 151.

[330] Her sister, Barbara St. John, was the wife of Sir Edward Villiers. Add. MSS, 33,412, fol. 67.

[331] *Al. Oxon.*

[332] His elder brother, John, may have studied at the Middle Temple. *Ibid.*

[333] D'Ewes (N), 459.

[334] *Al. Oxon.;* Wood, *Fasti Oxon.* **2**: 72.

[335] Bodleian Clarendon MSS, 19, No. 1457.

[336] D'Ewes (N), 459.

[337] *O.P.H.* **9**: 9.

[338] Sir Charles Pleydell's will of 1640 (proved 1642, P.C.C., 68 Cambell) mentioned a proposed dowry of £500 for one daughter and an annuity of £200 to be paid by his wife's son-in-law. His manor house at Mudgehall was the only property specifically named. Probably most of his lands had been settled previously on his elder son, John, who was the executor.

[339] The William Pleydell, gent., of Akeley, Bucks, who compounded in 1651 with a fine at a sixth, 1 *l.* 13 *s.* 4 *d.,* was hardly the M.P. *Cal. Com. Comp.,* 2712; S.P. 23/221/139.

[340] Pink MSS, 311, fol. 496e.

[341] *M. of P.* **1**: 487; *C.J.* **3**: 142.

chant.[342] William was baptized at Colyton, 1 December 1614, and married (1) on 30 September 1633 Grace, daughter of Sir Thomas Trenchard of Wolveton, Dorset, and niece of John Trenchard (q.v.), and (2), about 1635, Catherine, only daughter of Henry St. Barb of Ashenton, Somerset, and Broadlands, Hants.[343] Although his father was long active as a J.P.,[344] was captain of the trained bands,[345] sheriff (1638–1639), and D.L.,[346] William seems to have filled no local office. Nor, while the father was a backer of the colonization plans of the Reverend John White, Erle, and the Dorchester group,[347] and delayed in paying ship money on his properties and in collecting it as sheriff,[348] does the son seem to have shared actively in his father's interests and views.

Pole no doubt owed his election at Honiton to his father, who had worked for its restoration as a borough,[349] but in this, his first parliament, he was a quiet member. He was knighted at Whitehall, 19 April 1641,[350] and took the Protestation on 3 May following,[351] but probably absented himself soon afterwards. During the war he opposed his father and his first wife's family in taking up arms for the king, and was disabled in 1643. He began compounding proceedings in June, 1646, but died before they were completed. He was buried at Colyton, 20 January 1649.[352]

---

[342] English Baronetage (Kimber ed.) 1: 333–334, 1771; A. J. P. Skinner, ed., Colyton parish register 2: 635, Exeter, The Devon and Cornwall Record Society, 1928; Vis. Devon, 1620, 214. A brief note on Pole appears in Major W. H. Wilkins's Notes on the members for Honiton, 1640–1868, Devon Trans. 66: 260, 1934.

[343] Colyton parish register 1: 97, 142 and n.; English Baronetage, loc. cit. Pole had no children by his first marriage (S.P. 23/109/191), but his eldest son, John, was buried at Colyton, 8 December 1635, and a second son, William, lived 1636–1638. Colyton parish register 1: 142; 2: 634, 638.

[344] S.P. 16, 189/5/10; Devonshire MSS, Quarter Sessions Minute Book 1633–1640, passim.

[345] Exeter City Library MSS, Lane's Collections for Devonshire, fol. 119.

[346] C.S.P. Dom., 1639, 20–21.

[347] Devon and Cornwall N. and Q. 18: 88, 1934–1935. A brother and sister of Sir John went to New England. New England Historical and Genealogical Register 48: 490–491, 1894.

[348] S.P. 16, 435/33/i; C.S.P. Dom., 1639, 20–21, 229; 1639–1640, 105–106.

[349] A. Farquharson, The history of Honiton, 38, 43–44, Exeter, 1868. The author, however, strangely confuses father and son.

[350] He is identified as of Wiltshire by Metcalfe (Book of knights, 196) and Shaw (K. of E. 2: 208), but I have found no Sir William Pole or Poole from that country who could have served as M.P. for Honiton. The member was described as Sir William Poole at the time of the Protestation in May, 1641, but was simply styled "esquire" in the indenture from Honiton on 25 June 1646 which named his successor. Perhaps his knighthood was not recognized locally. Sir William Poole of Colyton was assessed £1500 by the parliamentarians in 1645. Cal. Com. Adv. Money, 667.

[351] C.J. 2: 133.

[352] Cal. Com. Comp., 537, 1314; Colyton parish register 2: 657.

Although his father was then living, Pole was enjoying in 1640 a life interest in various family estates in Devon, Gloucestershire and Dorset, having an income of several hundred pounds a year.[353] He was assessed £1500 in 1645. At his compounding, however, he declared that his first wife's jointure of £2500 had never been paid. His fine, reckoned at a third, £2855, or a tenth, £1142, seems to have been remitted after his death.[354] In 1660 the estate of his brother, the family heir, was valued at £1000 a year.[355]

* Hugh Pollard (c. 1610–1666), of King's Nympton, Devon, elected for Beeralston on 19 November 1640 to fill the place vacated by Cheeke, was expelled on 9 December 1641 for his part in the army plot.

The son and heir apparent of Sir Lewis Pollard, Bart. (d. 1641), by Margaret Berkeley, and born about 1610, Hugh was a lieutenant in a Devonshire foot regiment at the musters in July, 1629.[356] His father served as a J.P.,[357] but Hugh seems to have preferred military life, and as a captain joined the army in the north in 1640.[358] He was never a prominent member of the Long Parliament, but he voted against Strafford's attainder,[359] and his involvement a few months afterwards in the army plot terminated his service in the House.

Pollard came of an apparently well-to-do family. Although at compounding he declared a pre-war income of only £320 a year, with debts of £3000,[360] he was described by his fellow countryman, Prince, as "a gentleman of noble mind, . . . magnificently hospitable to all persons who came to his house." [361]

Relatives of Pollard in the 1640 House were his first cousin, John Northcote, a cousin by marriage, Francis Godolphin (Helston M.P.), and an uncle, Sir Henry Berkeley.[362]

John Polwhele, or **Polewheele** (c. 1607–1672), of Lincoln's Inn and of Polwhele and Treworgan, Cornwall, was a member for Tregony, 1640–22 January 1644. He was the son and heir of Thomas Polwhele by Dionis, daughter of Judge John Glanville of Tavistock (married

---

[353] Several annuities were payable out of his lands, and he was in 1646 considerably in debt. His declaration is further confused by his undervaluing several of his properties considerably.

[354] Cal. Com. Comp., 1314–15, 2307; S.P. 23/185/187–191, 293–297.

[355] English Baronetage 4: 366, 1741.

[356] S.P. 16, 150/76/i. His colonel was another Hugh Pollard, possibly the one who as Captain Pollard had served in the Cadiz expedition of 1625. S.P. 16, 522/16.

[357] C. 193/12; S.P. 16, 405.

[358] C.S.P. Dom., 1640, 122, 182, 441.

[359] Verney, 58. Pollard took the Protestation on 3 May 1641. C.J. 2: 133.

[360] His fine, set first at a sixth, £495, later raised to £558, was paid in 1653 at £518. Cal. Com. Comp., 1287; S.P. 23/210/143.

[361] John Prince, The worthies of Devon, 642, London, 1810.

[362] In addition to the authorities cited above, see Complete Baronetage 2: 23.

3 March 1606), and sister of the Speaker of the Short Parliament. He was "aged fourteen" in 1620, was admitted to Lincoln's Inn in 1623, and was called to the bar there early in 1631.[363] He married Anne, daughter of Thomas Baskerville of Richardston, Wiltshire. He owned various properties in Cornwall, some of which lay near Truro,[364] but he probably spent most of his time in London. He was described as of Lincoln's Inn when he was handling a legal matter for a Devon man in 1637.[365] In addition to being a lawyer, Polwhele was something of a poet. He wrote several odes, and made some translations from Horace and Boethius.[366]

Polewhele's first venture in politics or public office was apparently his election by Tregony to the Long Parliament. He had earlier written some lines in praise of Sir John Eliot,[367] but he never became prominent in parliament himself. He was named to a few minor committees in the early months, but was probably absent much of the time after the summer of 1641, as were his cousins, William Glanville and Piers Edgcombe, and his friends, the Godolphins. He supported the king when war came, was suspended for absences in September, 1642, and ordered to be brought up in custody afterwards. But he sat in the Oxford parliament and was "disabled" in 1644.[368] After being held a prisoner for a time, he was permitted to compound for his estates, 1646–1648. He died on 6 July 1672.[369] His will, dated in 1667, was proved on 30 March 1678.

Polwhele's declaration to the compounding commissioners regarding his estate is probably not a correct index to his full income. It sets forth only the return from his real estate and that he was reported to have undervalued. On a declared valuation of about £90 his fine was reckoned at a tenth, 192 l. 3 s. 4 d. The assessment of £500 charged against him by the Commission for the Advance of Money was, however, greatly reduced [370] because he declared that he had debts equal to the assessment.[371]

Edward Poole (c. 1617–1673), of Oaksey and Kemble, Wiltshire, M.P. for Wootton Bassett, 1640–1648,[372] was the eldest son of Sir Neville Poole (q.v.), by his wife, Frances. He matriculated at Magdalen Hall, Oxford, in 1635, aged eighteen, and was admitted to Lincoln's Inn in February, 1636.[373] About two years later he

married Dorothy, daughter of Sir Robert Pye of Farringdon, Berkshire (q.v.). The marriage settlement was dated 29 May 1638.[374]

The Long Parliament was Edward Poole's first, and he was not prominent there, but he served several times after 1658. He followed his father's politics, and was inactive in the period between 1648 and 1659.[375] He was knighted sometime before June, 1661,[376] and died in 1673.[377]

Sir Neville Poole (c. 1592–c. 1661), of Oaksey, Wiltshire, M.P. for Malmesbury, Wilts, 1640–1648, was a man well known in his county. He was the eldest son of Sir Henry Poole of Kemble and Oaksey (J.P., M.P.; d. 1632),[378] by his wife, Griselda (Neville ?), and was born about 1592.[379] He entered Gray's Inn in February, 1611. Shortly afterwards, before 8 December 1612, he married Frances, daughter of Sir Henry Poole of Sapperton, Gloucestershire, a distant relative, and in January, 1613, was knighted at Newmarket.[380] He was elected M.P. for Malmesbury in 1614, for Cricklade in 1624, and for Cirencester in 1626.[381] He succeeded in 1632 to his father's estate, which included at least six manors in Wiltshire and Gloucestershire.

County offices had been Poole's responsibilities for some years before that. He was a J.P before the end of James's reign and continuously thereafter,[382] and a member of various local commissions.[383] By 1631 he was a D.L. for Wiltshire.[384] As sheriff six years later he was responsible for ship money collections under the 1636 writ. During the year of his shrievalty he turned in only £5800 of the £7000 required, and from the fall of 1637 until the spring of 1639 received from Council sharp reminders about the arrears.[385] He seems to have been one of the officials most behind in his returns during his year in office,[386] and a considerable part of his quota was never collected.[387] Although part of the fault

---

[363] *Linc. Inn Rec. Adm.* 1: 194; *Black Books* 2: 299.

[364] Carew, *Survey of Cornwall*, 338 and n.

[365] Exeter City Library MSS, Exeter Deeds and Documents, No. 30,308.

[366] Gilbert, *Hist. survey of Cornwall* 2: 239.

[367] Courtney, *Parl. Rep. Corn.*, 170.

[368] *C.J.* 2: 29, 130, 750, 845; 3: 374.

[369] Pink MSS, 307, fol. 296.

[370] S.P. 23/207/511; *Cal. Com. Comp.*, 336, 1252; *Cal. Com. Adv. Money*, 1329.

[371] In addition to the authorities cited above see Burke, *Landed gentry* 2: 1055, 1851; Vivian, *Vis. Cornwall*, 377; *Vis. Devon, 1620*, 130.

[372] *M. of P.* 1: 496; *O.P.H.* 9: 9.

[373] *Al. Oxon.*; *Linc. Inn Rec. Adm.* 1: 229.

[374] *Vis. Berks.* 1: 270; Wilts. Arch. Soc. MSS, Sadler's "Wiltshire Genealogy," Kemble.

[375] *M. of P.* 1: 510, 517, 531.

[376] He was styled "esquire" in the return of 10 April 1660 (*M. of P.*), but was a knight when he proved his father's will in June, 1661. P.C.C., 100 May.

[377] The election of his successor as M.P. occurred on 3 November 1673. *M. of P.* 1: 531.

[378] Williams, *Oxford*, 51.

[379] I.P.M., Sir Henry Poole, C. 142/489/144. At the time of Poole's marriage one of the parties to the deed of settlement was Francis Neville of Kynor, Sussex, probably a relative on his mother's side. Wilts. Arch. Soc. MSS, Sadler's "Wiltshire Genealogy," Kemble.

[380] *Ibid.*; Williams, *Gloucester*, 156.

[381] *M. of P.* 1: 461, 469; 3: xl.

[382] C. 193/13; S.P. 16/405.

[383] C. 181/5, fols. 42, 187, *passim*.

[384] *C.S.P. Dom., 1631–1633*, 67.

[385] *Ibid., 1637*, 122, 574; *1638–1639*, 369; *1639*, 246.

[386] S.P. 16, 367/37; 370/74.

[387] Royal Hist. Soc., *Trans.*, 3rd Ser., 4: 161, 1910.

lay with the constables, Sir Neville doubtless condoned it. He was one of the loan refusers in 1639.[388]

Agreeing with his colleagues and neighbors, Sir Edward Bayntun and Walter Long (q.v.), Poole was clearly a foe of court policies at the time of his election to the parliaments of 1640. He was returned both times for Malmesbury,[389] and became an active member of the popular party. He advocated the abolition of monopolies, and offered his bond for £1000 to secure the loan in November, 1640, and in March, 1641.[390] He disliked the tone of the London petition against episcopacy, however.[391] When the war approached he promised to supply four horses on behalf of his son, Edward (q.v.), and himself.[392] He participated in some of the military events of the war in Wiltshire, being present at the defense of Marlborough,[393] and was later granted by parliament an allowance for some special service.[394] He was secluded by the purge of 1648.[395] Poole was probably still living in the spring of 1660,[396] but must have died soon afterwards, for his will, dated 24 January 1654, was proved on 29 June 1661.[397]

Poole's estate seems to have been ample, and when his son was holding it later his income was reckoned at £1000 a year. This was after the losses resulting from the war had forced the sale of some of their lands.[398]

* **Alexander Popham** (1605–1669), of Littlecote, Wiltshire, and of Wellington, was M.P. for Bath, Somerset, 1640–1653. He was the second son but heir of Sir Francis Popham (q.v.), and was educated at Oxford and the Middle Temple. He was "bound" there in 1622 with John Pyne, a kinsman and future colleague of the Long Parliament, and seems to have kept his chamber at least until 1628. In the latter year he was associated at the Temple with Christopher Lewknor.[399] He was apparently outlawed for debts in 1627, however, with a brother, Edward.[400] Part of the debts had been jointly incurred with their elder brother, John (d. 1638).[401] In 1630–1631 Popham was travelling in

Spain.[402] He may have been a sewers commissioner in Somerset,[403] and a grand juror at Bath in 1637, but there were others of his name in the county who may have performed those duties.[404]

Popham was with the army in the north in 1639.[405] He was elected to the Short Parliament at both Bath and Minehead, and chose to serve for the former.[406] He was a Presbyterian elder for a time,[407] but continued to sit with the Independents after 1648.[408]

* **Sir Francis Popham** (1573–1644), of Littlecote, Wiltshire, and of Wellington, Somerset, was M.P. for Minehead, 1640–1644. He owned lands in Wilts, Devon, and Somerset, and held other properties in Middlesex,[409] his estate being worth at one time, according to John Aubrey, £10,000 a year. He had settled much of it, however, on his spendthrift son, John (d. 1638), retaining for himself perhaps a fifth of the income,[410] and he was involved in 1636 in arranging in some fashion for the debts of his sons.[411] He still had enough wealth to offer his security for £1000 for the loan of November, 1640.[412] Popham's interest in the American colonies and in numerous projects is well known. To the list should be added the company for the mines royal, of which he was a charter undertaker early in the reign of James.[413]

Sir Francis had filled many local offices, J.P., sheriff, D.L., commissioner for numerous special functions, and others.[414] And he was a parliament man of experience since 1597. His election for Chippenham in 1624 had been challenged by John Pym,[415] and in the Long Parliament elections he unsuccessfully challenged Sir Edward Bayntun there.[416] His seat for Minehead was

---

[388] Rushworth 3: 915.

[389] M. of P. 1: 484, 496.

[390] D'Ewes (N), 51, 451, n., 533.

[391] Ibid., 337; Note book of Sir John Northcote, 51.

[392] N. and Q., 1st Ser., 12: 360, 1855.

[393] Waylen, Hist. of Marlborough, 157.

[394] Brit. Mus. Bibl. Eg., 806, fol. 57.

[395] O.P.H. 9: 8.

[396] Thomason Tracts, 669. f. 24, p. 37.

[397] P.C.C., 100 May.

[398] John Aubrey, Wiltshire, ed. J. E. Jackson, 277 and n., Devizes, 1862.

[399] Mid. Temp. Rec. 2: 677, 730.

[400] C.S.P. Dom., 1627–1628, 104. The identity of the Popham so outlawed with the M.P. seems probable to me, although some doubt is expressed in D.N.B.

[401] It was rumored when John died in 1638 that his debts, for which his brothers, but not their father, were "jointly engaged," totalled £38,000. C.S.P. Dom., 1637–1638, 176.

[402] Ibid., 1629–1631, 250; 1631–1633, 11.

[403] C. 181/4, fols. 21v, 173.

[404] Add. MSS, 28,273, fol. 83; Vis. Somerset, 87–88; Somerset and Dorset N. and Q. 4: 111, 1894–1895.

[405] S.P. 16, 427/38/iii.

[406] M. of P. 1: 483.

[407] A.H.R. 44: 31, n. (32), 1938–1939.

[408] For several additional facts, including those on his wives, which are not complete in D.N.B., see Bates Harbin, Members of Parliament, Somerset, 167–168.

[409] Collinson, Somerset 2: 482–483; Gerard, Partic. Descr. Somerset, 40; Pole, Description of Devonshire, 78, 202–204; C.S.P. Dom., 1637–1638, 461.

[410] John Aubrey, Brief lives (Clarke) 2: 159–160. An estate of £8000 a year was said to have been guaranteed to his eldest son at the time of his marriage in 1621. C. 3/358/17.

[411] C.S.P. Dom., 1635–1636, 163.

[412] D'Ewes (N), 52, n.

[413] Carr, Select charters of trading companies, 15, n.

[414] C. 193/12; S.P. 16/405; C. 181/3, 4, 5, passim; Add. MSS, 5496, fol. 92; List of Sheriffs, 194. For other offices see Bates Harbin, Members of Parliament, Somerset, 133.

[415] The reports on the 1624 case are conflicting, but Pym, whose choice was by the closed corporation, seems to have sat for Tavistock, leaving Chippenham for Popham. C.J. 1: 735; Harl. MSS, 6806, fol. 262; M. of P. 1: 461, n.; John Glanville, Reports of certain cases, 47–62.

[416] C.J. 2: 68, 81.

perhaps gained through his son-in-law, Luttrell, the father of his young colleague, Alexander Luttrell (*q.v.*).

Sir Francis was involved in 1637 in a quarrel with the Bishop of Bath and Wells regarding the patronage of a Somerset rectory, and appealed to Laud for recognition of his rights. In 1639 he was called before Council for being a musters defaulter in Devon, but was released upon promise to conform in the future.[417]

Popham had with him in the 1640 House one son, Alexander, two grandsons, Luttrell and John Borlase, and two grand-nephews, John Pyne and Hugh Rogers.

* Endymion Porter (1587–1649), courtier, Gentleman of the Bedchamber, was M.P. for Droitwich, Worcestershire, 1640–10 March 1643. The heir of a Gloucestershire family and attached to the court from his youth, Porter had spent much of his life abroad and at London, and seems to have had little connection with Worcestershire.[418] He was a J.P for Middlesex,[419] but was known chiefly because of his position near the king and the personal advantages which he had derived from that intimacy. He enjoyed a royal pension of £500 a year for a time, and the office of postmaster was said to have been worth at the start £5000 a year and afterwards much more.[420] His surveyorship of petty customs in London was worth £700 a year, and he had other sources of income from Ireland as well as from his "projects." Furthermore he owned lands in the counties of Gloucester, Lincoln, Herts, Bedford, Middlesex, and Surrey which were worth before the war about £800 or more annually. But his expenses were heavy, too, his favors from the king had had to be returned by such gestures as a £1000 loan in 1640, and even before 1640 Porter had mortgaged his most valuable manors.[421]

Sir William Portman, Bart. (1608–1645), of Orchard Portman, near Taunton, Somerset, was a member for Taunton, 1640–5 February 1644. The fourth son of Sir John Portman, first baronet (d. 1612), by his wife, Anne, daughter of Sir Henry Gifford of Hampshire, he outlived his three elder brothers and in 1629 came into possession of the family estate and title. He was born in 1608,[422] matriculated at Wadham College, Oxford, in June, 1626, and was admitted in 1628 to the Middle Temple. He surrendered his chamber there before the end of 1632.[423] Sometime before November,

1633, Portman married Anne, one of the daughters and coheiresses of John Colles of Barton in Somerset.[424] By this marriage he became a brother-in-law of John Coventry, who lived nearby, and of Gerard Napier, and a connection of Thomas Smith, all of whom were fellow parliament men in 1640. Another brother-in-law, husband of Portman's sister, Anne, was Edward Seymour (*q.v.*).

In Somerset Portman was treasurer of the county hospitals, an active J.P.,[425] and a member of various local commissions.[426] He supported in 1637 Taunton's petition for a lower ship money rate, but as sheriff the following year was himself complained against for some of the rates he set. He attempted to expedite collections but met with criticism from Council because of some delays. One complainant against his rates was John Ashe (*q.v.*).[427] Portman ignored, however, the king's loan request of 1639.[428]

Sir William was elected to parliament for the first time in 1640, sitting for Taunton in the spring. In the following parliament Portman displayed his royalist sympathies, for he was a Straffordian.[429] He offered his wealth for the public cause, however, pledging his bond for £1000 for the November loan, and agreeing to lend £500 for the army's needs in July, 1641.[430] Joining the king when the war started, Portman was disabled in 1644.[431] He was taken prisoner at Naseby and died in the Tower in September, 1645. On the sixteenth of that month the House ordered that his body should be carried to his home in Somerset for burial.[432] His will of 1643 was proved on 17 October 1648.[433]

Portman was one of the wealthiest men in his county. His father's estate was described as great and flourishing, and his elder brother, Sir Henry (d. 1621), had owned what was called "a great living." [434] The family lands that were enumerated at the death of Sir William's immediate predecessor in 1629 included more than twenty manors in Somerset, Devon, Hants, and Middlesex, with additional holdings on those counties and in four others.[435] The estates listed in the compounding

[417] *C.S.P. Dom., 1637*, 263; *1638–1639*, 297, 542; S.P. 16, 409/46.
[418] Williams, *Worcester*, 121–123.
[419] C. 193/13; S.P. 16/405.
[420] D. Townshend, *Life and letters of Mr. Endymion Porter* 152–156, London, 1897.
[421] *C.S.P. Dom., 1637–1638*, 492; *1637*, 457; *1639*, 497; *C.S.P. Ireland, 1647–1660, Addenda, 1625–1669*, 90, 91; S.P. 16, 447/37; *Cal. Com. Comp.*, 1804–1805; S.P. 23/214/771–773.
[422] He was aged twenty-one years and six months when his brother, Hugh, died in October, 1629. I.P.M., Sir Hugh Portman, C. 142/469/91.
[423] *Complete Baronetage* 1: 90; *Mid. Temp. Rec.* 2: 729, 803.

[424] She was Portman's wife at the time of her mother's will of that date. Brown, *Somerset Wills* 1: 34.
[425] *Quarter sessions records for the county of Somerset* 2: 162, 178, *passim*; C. 193/13.
[426] C. 181/4, fol. 172v; 181/5, fols. 10, 64, 197.
[427] *C.S.P. Dom., 1636–1637*, 536; *1637–1638*, 222, 354; *1639–1640*, 588.
[428] Rushworth 3: 914.
[429] Verney, 58.
[430] D'Ewes, 52; *C.J.* 2: 222. D'Ewes confused Portman with his elder brother, Sir Hugh, whose name he noted as a loan subscriber.
[431] *C.J.* 3: 389.
[432] *Complete Baronetage* 1: 90. The brief reference to Portman in the article on his son, Sir William Portman, in *D.N.B.* errs in the matter of dates.
[433] P.C.C., 146 Essex.
[434] Fuller, *Worthies of England* 3: 97, 1840; *The letters of John Chamberlain* 2: 347.
[435] I.P.M. cited above.

papers filed in the name of Portman's infant son were declared to be worth over £2200 yearly, and were considered to have a sale value of more than £20,000.[436]

Hugh Potter (1596–1662), of Lincoln's Inn, was M.P. for Plympton, Devon, from 20 November 1640 [437] until 1648. The eldest son and heir of Tobias Potter of Iddersleigh, Devon, and his wife, Susan, daughter of Hugh Osborne, and baptized there on 1 August 1596,[438] he entered Lincoln's Inn on 10 June 1615.[439] By July, 1626, he had secured employment as secretary to the earl of Northumberland, and was described by an acquaintance as a "marvellous honest civil young man." [440] His life thereafter was devoted to his patron's interests, and the scenes of his activities were the north country, Sussex and London, rather than his native county. In 1630 and 1637 he was named on the sewers commission for Sussex,[441] and as the earl's solicitor and secretary he was busy in 1639 and 1640 with army affairs in the north.[442] Through the earl's influence Potter was elected to the Short Parliament for Berwick-on-Tweed, but his re-election there in the autumn was prevented by the tardiness of his patron's letter and by the strength of a Strafford nominee for the place.[443] The earl's influence, as well as that of the Potter family, probably secured his election to the open seat at Plympton soon after the session started.

Potter's interests in the Long Parliament, to judge by his recorded speeches and committee appointments, were the affairs of the admiralty, the customs, and the seaports.[444] He was among the witnesses requested by Strafford to testify in his behalf on 20 March 1641,[445] but he seems not to have voted against the earl's attainder.[446] On 27 June 1642 he was granted leave to go into the country on his employer's business, and was granted a similar leave in the winter of 1645–

1646.[447] He was hardly a royalist and a member of the Oxford parliament, as has sometimes been stated,[448] but was secluded in December, 1648. He returned to the House in 1660,[449] was elected M.P. for Cockermouth in 1661,[450] and died about 12 February 1662.[451]

Potter never married, and at his death he assigned his personal estate to various relatives. He probably owned some land in Devon in 1640, and leased more later. When he wrote his will, 1659–1662, he had profited enough to plan annuities of some £60 and legacies of over £4200, but in the early 1640's he does not seem to have felt prosperous enough to make pledges for the popular cause.

Potter was a kinsman of Trelawney, the Plymouth M.P.,[452] and of Sir John Melton, and was possibly connected by marriage with John Northcote.[453]

John Potts (1593?–1673), of Mannington, Norfolk, was one of his county's knights, 1640–1648. The son of John Potts of Lincoln's Inn (d. 1598), by his wife, Anne, daughter and coheiress of John Dodge of Mannington, he was born about 1593,[454] and a few months after his father's death became the ward of Sir Charles Heydon of Baconsthorp, his mother's second husband.[455] Of his education nothing is known,[456] but he is said to have been required during his wardship to marry the daughter of a court favorite, Goodsill, with small fortune. Later he married Ursula, the widow of Sir Clement Spelman of Narborough, and daughter of Sir Henry (John?) Willoughby of Risley, Derbyshire, and was living with her at Mannington in 1632.[457] As a young man Potts lived for a time at Norwich,[458] and was active in county affairs during the decade of 1620–1630, serving as a J.P.[459] and a member of other com-

---

[436] In addition to the lands valued at £2200 a year, others worth £1000 yearly were listed as claimed but not in possession. S.P. 23/206/623–631. The compounding fine set at a tenth, £5,414, was reduced afterwards to £857. *Cal. Com. Comp.*, 900–901.

[437] He was elected after Slanning chose to sit for Penryn.

[438] *Vis. Devon, 1620*, 218; *Genealogist*, 1st Ser., **7**: 83, 1883; Pink MSS, 321.

[439] *Linc. Inn Rec. Adm.* **1**: 170.

[440] Ferguson, *Cumberland and Westmorland M.P.'s*, 431. Potter may have owed his place with the earl to his kinsman, Sir John Melton, the secretary of the Council of the North, who afterwards named Potter one of the executors of his will.

[441] C. 181/4, fols. 47v, 54v; 181/5, fol. 140.

[442] *Fairfax correspondence* **1**: 359; *C.S.P. Dom., 1640*, 268; *1640–41*, 510, 532, 570.

[443] *C.S.P. Dom., 1640–41*, 258, 404; *M. of P.* **1**: 482.

[444] D'Ewes (N), 429; *C.J.* **2**: 82, 157, 591, *passim*.

[445] D'Ewes (N), 515, n.

[446] Unless "Mr. Porter" in the list of Straffordians is intended for this member instead of for Endymion Porter (Verney, 58). Northumberland's other agent, Scawen, voted against the attainder but afterwards served parliament well.

[447] *C.J.* **2**: 641; *History of Northumberland* **5**: 74, Northumberland County History Committee.

[448] *O.P.H.* **9**: *24.

[449] Pink MSS, 321.

[450] *M. of P.* **1**: 521.

[451] He wrote a codicil to his will on that date, shortly before he died (P.C.C., 53 Laud). A new election was ordered, 14 February. Pink MSS, 311, fol. 521.

[452] The latter left legacies to "my cousin Hugh Potter" and his brother George in 1643. J. P. Baxter ed., *The Trelawny Papers*, Collections of the Maine Historical Society, 2nd Ser., **3**: 454, 1884.

[453] Northcote noted in 1640 the purchase of some lands from "my brother George Potter." *Note book of John Northcote*, 120 and n.

[454] I.P.M. of John Potts, Gent., C. 142/256/40.

[455] Blomefield, *Norfolk* **6**: 464.

[456] The John Potts who entered Gray's Inn and Cambridge in 1634 (*Al. Cant.*) was probably his son, not the member, as suggested in *Complete Baronetage* **2**: 138.

[457] *Ibid.; The visitation of Norfolk, 1664*, Norfolk Record Society **5**: 170, 204, 1934; Norwich Public Library MSS, 55, Jessop's Extracts from Norfolk Parish Registers **2**: 178.

[458] Bodleian Tanner MSS, 283, fol. 170.

[459] C. 193/12 and 13; Norfolk County MSS, Sessions Rolls, 1620–1621, 1626, 1631.

missions, including those for the 1621 and 1627 loans.[460] He was not a seeker of office, however, and probably preferred a quiet life in the country to such activities.

In March, 1640, however, yielding to the pleadings of his friends for his moderating influence, Potts became a candidate for the shire parliamentary election, although his poor health and his distaste for publicity and the scorn of his opponents made him reluctant,[461] and he was prepared beforehand for the defeat that came. He succeeded in the autumn elections, possibly through the decision of Sir John Holland (q.v.) to withdraw from the shire contest. Potts worked quietly with the reform group in the House, being named to several committees on religious matters, such as the one on pluralities,[462] and although he accepted knighthood and a baronetcy in August, 1641, was not turned by his titles from his course. He offered his bond for £1000 for the November loan, £500 for that of March, 1641, subscribed £600, of which at least a fourth was his own, for the Irish venture in 1642, and later that year promised to provide £100 for the defense.[463] He was an active committeeman in Norfolk during the war,[464] but was secluded in the purge of 1648. He died in 1673, having by that time, with his characteristic tolerance, reaffirmed his loyalties to the established church. His will, dated 6 January, was proved 6 October 1673.[465]

Presumably Potts was a man of considerable wealth at the time the Long Parliament opened, for his loan subscriptions so indicate. He inherited from his father's family a score or more of houses in the London area and from both sides of his house lands in Norfolk.[466] When he died more than thirty years after 1640, however, administration of his estate was granted to a creditor. Fellow M.P.'s of 1640 who were his friends were Sir Thomas Wodehouse and Sir Simonds D'Ewes.[467]

* Sir John Poulett (1615–1665), of Courtaweek in Yalton, Somerset, was M.P. for his county, 1640–August, 1642. The eldest son and heir apparent of John, first Baron Poulett (M.P., J.P., D.L., d. 1649),[468] he was educated at Oxford and travelled for a time on the continent.[469] He was with his father in Northumberland's fleet in the Channel in 1636 when he was knighted, and was described then as a young gentleman who "is like to succeed his father in fortune and vir-

tue." [470] In February, 1640, Sir John secured a command under Conway and was with the army in the north the following summer.[471] His principal occupation in the country, since his father was alive and holding offices, was probably that of hunting.[472]

Poulett's family was one of the most influential in the shire, a complainant in a suit about lands once declaring that they were so potent that no man dared displease them.[473] Their estate was said in 1638 to be worth some £2500 a year, of which at least £2100 was clear above rents and other charges.[474] Sir John's portion which was settled for his use during his father's lifetime included properties in Somerset, Dorset, Berks, and Essex, having the value of over £1500 yearly.[475] Although they were sympathizers with the popular party before 1640, both he and his father paid heavy fines for their subsequent delinquency.

Among his fellow parliament men of 1640 were Poulett's brother-in-law, Thomas Smith, and his father's "near relative," Fairfax.[476]

Charles Price (fl. 1616–1642), soldier, of Pilleth, county Radnor, was M.P. for his county, 1640–4 October 1642. He was probably the son of James Price of Pilleth, sheriff and several times M.P. for Radnor,[477] and was Radnor's member in the five parliaments of the 1620's and in both of 1640.[478] But his profession was that of soldier. He had probably trained under the Veres in the Netherlands, for he referred in his will to a sword he owned that was once "my Lord of Oxford's." And he had been muster-master for Shropshire for at least three years before September, 1619, when his pension of £50 was reported to have gone for that length of time unpaid.[479] He was succeeded shortly afterwards by Ralph Goodwin (q.v.), and early in 1625 was captain of a company being organized for Ireland from the Welsh counties.[480] But he was elected to parliament that spring. Between the sessions of the 1628–1629 parliament he may have been the messenger who carried to King Charles the news

---

[460] C. 181/3, fols. 115v, 205; Tanner MSS, 243, fol. 33; S.P. 1., 74/60.

[461] Bodleian Tanner MSS, 67, fols. 176–178, 189; D'Ewes (N), 364.

[462] C.J. 2: 36; Tanner MSS, 69, fol. 198.

[463] D'Ewes (N), 52, 439; C.S.P. Ireland, Adventurers, 41; N. & Q., 1st Ser., 12: 360, 1855.

[464] Stowe MSS, 190, fol. 213; Egerton MSS, 2943, fol. 19.

[465] Norwich Consistory Court, 1670–1673, fols. 504–505.

[466] I.P.M. cited above.

[467] D'Ewes, Autobiography 2: 295, 297.

[468] S.P. 16, 10/48; S.P. 16/405.

[469] H.M.C., Twelfth Report 2: Coke MSS, 76.

[470] The naval tracts of Sir William Monson, ed. M. Oppenheim, 3: 264–265, London, The Navy Record Society, 1902–1914.

[471] C.S.P. Dom., 1639–1640, 461; 1640, 314; 1640–1641, 190.

[472] Dorset N. H. Proceedings 13: 73, 1892.

[473] C. 3/334/10.

[474] Verney Papers, 199.

[475] Other properties which were to revert to him at his father's death were valued at about £1800 annually. S.P. 23/184/777–780.

[476] Cal. Com. Comp. 5: xvi. A sketch of Poulett's life, with some additions to D.N.B., appears in Bates Harbin, Members of Parliament, Somerset, 151–152.

[477] Williams, Parl. Hist. Wales, 173. In his will Charles Price of Pilleth mentioned a brother James, then living, and two nephews and a cousin of that name. P.C.C., 101 Twisse.

[478] Williams, loc. cit.

[479] H.M.C., Tenth Report 4, Earl of Kilmorey's MSS, 367.

[480] Acts P.C., 1623–1625, 441; C.S.P. Dom., 1623–1625, 483.

of Buckingham's death.[481] And in the closing months of that parliament he spoke more than once in defense of the king and in opposition to the faction of Eliot.[482] He probably spent much of the next decade in Ireland, where he became intimate with Lord Deputy Wentworth.[483] The war on the Scottish border found him again in Britain and he was involved in the first skirmishes near Newcastle in 1639.[484]

A lieutenant-colonel by the end of 1640, Price was present at both parliaments of that year.[485] He seems to have approved in part of the early attack in Windebank,[486] and was named to several committees, 1640–1641, including one on grievances and one on a part of the charges against Strafford.[487] He voted against the earl's attainder,[488] and opposed the abolishing of episcopacy,[489] but as late as 12 November 1641 was especially recommended by the House for a military command in Ireland that would be worthy of his merit.[490] He supported the king in 1642, was a prisoner by November,[491] and died before 16 June 1646. His will, dated 3 September 1640, was proved by his executor, a niece, on 16 June 1646.

Before 1640 Price was attempting to recover, for the benefit of his heirs, his nieces and nephews, the family inheritance of a kinsman, John Price of Manachty, an effort which brought him into some conflict with Sir Robert Harley (q.v.), who had been an executor of that estate.[492] His own lands in Radnor passed, according to his will, to various nephews, and he assigned by it annuities of over £150 and money amounting to over £3300. Close friends who were named in the will included Lord Craven, Lord and Lady Coventry, and the Earl of Strafford, who had bestowed 1000 acres of Irish lands on Price.[493] It may have been his heir who was nominated for the Knights of the Royal Oak in 1660 with an estimated estate of £1000 a year.[494]

Herbert Price (d. 1678), of the Priory, Brecon, was named in a double return from Brecon borough with one Robert Williams. On 6 January 1641 Price was ordered to sit until the election was voided, and Williams was instructed not to sit. And Price remained a member until his disablement, 3 May 1643.[495]

The second son of Thomas Price of the Priory, doubtless H.S. for Brecknockshire in 1615,[496] he was admitted to the Middle Temple in 1622 and bound there with William Morgan.[497] Both Price and his wife held posts in the household of Queen Henrietta Maria,[498] and in 1633 Price was reported to have been dangerously wounded in a duel with one of the king's pages.[499]

Price was named to a few committees of the Long Parliament, such as one on the queen's properties, and the group of Commoners who were to attend at Strafford's trial.[500] He apparently voted against the attainder.[501] With Sir William Widdrington Price was ordered to the Tower in June, 1641, for having offended the House during debate,[502] but he was still an active member as late as 6 January 1642.[503] He was absent at the call on 16 June 1642,[504] and was a royalist during the war.

Price's estates included some Warwickshire property held in right of his wife and others in Worcestershire, in addition to his chief holdings in county Brecon. The Welsh ones had an estimated value, according to a 1648 report, of some £300 a year.[505]

Sir John Price, Bart. (d. 1657), of Newtown, Montgomeryshire, was M.P. for his county, 1640–20 October 1645. He was the son and heir of Edward Price of Newtown (H.S., 1615) and was related to the Herberts of Cherbury.[506] The Prices and the Herberts were at various times the principal rivals for the political plums in their shire.[507] John Price spent a short time at the Inner Temple and he probably travelled abroad for a period, starting in 1616.[508] He may have become a courtier afterwards or a soldier. About 1631, having married and been created a baronet, Price was involved in several lawsuits. For some previous offense he was then seeking the king's pardon, and one petitioner,

---

[481] Sir John Oglander, *A royalist's notebook*, 38 and n. The bearer of the news, according to Clarendon, was Sir John Hippisley (q.v.).

[482] *Commons Debates for 1629*, 6, n., 169, 238.

[483] *C.S.P. Ireland, 1625–1632*, 601; *1633–1647*, 122–123; *C.S.P. Dom.*, *1637*, 391; *1638–1639*, 264.

[484] *C.S.P. Dom., 1639*, 201; *Verney Papers* (Camden Society), 240.

[485] *C.J.* **2**: 17, *passim*; Bodleian Carte MSS, 1, fol. 183v; *C.S.P. Dom., 1640–1641*, 303.

[486] D'Ewes (N), 26 and n., 30 and n.

[487] *C.J.* **2**: 52, 64, 79.

[488] Verney, 58.

[489] He was a teller for the negative (misprinted for the Yeas) at a division on that subject on 27 May 1641. *C.J.* **2**: 159. *Cf.* Sanford, *St. and ill.*, 364.

[490] *C.J.* **2**: 313; D'Ewes (C), 127.

[491] *C.J.* **2**: 837.

[492] *C.S.P. Dom., 1638–1639*, 264.

[493] P.C.C., 101 Twisse. The niece, a widow, who proved Price's will, was erroneously referred to as Price's widow in *Cal. Com. Comp.* (1387) and Williams (*loc. cit.*).

[494] *English Baronetage* **4**: 380, 1741.

[495] *C.J.* **2**: 63; D'Ewes (N), 223; *O.P.H.* **9**: 14.

[496] *List of Sheriffs*, 239.

[497] *Mid. Temp. Rec.* **2**: 676.

[498] Bibl. Eg., 1048, fols. 186v, 187.

[499] Add. MSS, 29,974, fol. 214.

[500] *C.J.* **2**: 87, 115.

[501] The name appears as Pirce in Verney's list (58), but as Price in Rushworth **4**: 249.

[502] *C.J.* **2**: 171.

[503] D'Ewes (C), 386.

[504] *C.J.* **2**: 626.

[505] *Cal. Com. Comp.*, 1203–1204, 2042–2043; Bibl. Eg., 1048, fols. 74–75. In addition to the authorities cited above see Williams, *Parl. Hist. Wales*, 23.

[506] *Montgomeryshire Collections* **31**: 66, 1899.

[507] *E.H.R.* **46**: 227–228, 1931.

[508] *Acts P.C., 1615–1616*, 539.

declaring he had been suing Price in Star Chamber for about five years, asked that the pardon be stayed. He mentioned that Price had but recently returned from overseas.[509] In 1631 also Richard Steele, a gentleman of the privy chamber, petitioned Council for a hearing of his complaints against Price and others, and as late as 1639 Price complained of being continually molested by pursuivants and of the nuisance of having to send witnesses to London instead of to a court nearer to Wales.[510] Price was a candidate for the county seat for the Short Parliament, but was defeated by Richard Herbert (q.v.).[511]

In the Long Parliament Price worked at first with the popular party. He informed against Sir Percy Herbert, one of his opponents in his lawsuits, and about the control of the magazine in Wales under the Earl of Worcester. In January, 1641, he was added to a subcommittee on Strafford's case.[512] He informed also against a Welsh J.P. for leniency toward recusants,[513] and seems to have been quite constant in his attendance throughout 1641.[514] In June, 1642, he pledged two horses for the defense,[515] but was under suspicion because of absence by 1644. He was granted a respite in February, was welcomed back to the parliamentary fold by Thelwall in October, but a year later, 20 October 1645, was disabled for going over to the king.[516] He was assessed £2000 the following December,[517] and began compounding proceedings in 1650. The amount of his fine does not appear in the records. His estate valuations, as he declared them, were probably incomplete or were underestimates, for they showed an income of not quite £250 a year.[518] Price died on 18 June 1657.[519]

William Price (born 1619), of Rhiwlas, county Merioneth, was a member for Merioneth, 1640–5 February 1644.[520] The eldest son of John Price (1601–1629) of Rhiwlas, by Eleanor Jones, he was a grandson of John Price of Rhiwlas (d. 1613), who had been H.S.

of Merioneth, 1608–1609.[521] Through his mother he was related to the Griffiths of Carnarvonshire (q.v.), and his mother's father, Sir William Jones (d. December, 1640), was a justice of King's Bench and a member of the Council of the Marches.[522] Price had barely reached his majority when he was elected to the Long Parliament, his first.

From his father Price inherited lands in the counties of Merioneth, Flint, and Denbigh of a thousand acres or more, on which were located mills of various kinds.[523] In 1660 he was reported to have an estate of £1500 a year.[524] But when he compounded for his royalism in 1649 he enumerated properties worth only £200 a year, and his fine was set at £200.[525]

* Edmund Prideaux (1601–1659), of Ottery St. Mary, Devon,[526] and of the Inner Temple, represented Lyme Regis in Dorset, 1640–1653. Born in September, 1601, and baptized at Farway, Devon, 27 February 1602, he was the second surviving son of the distinguished lawyer, Sir Edmund Prideaux, Bart., of Netherton and of the Inner Temple, by his second wife, Katherine, daughter of Piers Edgcombe of Mount Edgcombe.[527] His stepmother, his father's third wife, was Mary (Reynell), widow of Arthur Fowell and mother of Sir Edmund Fowell (q.v.).[528] He seems to have attended neither Oxford nor Cambridge,[529] but was admitted to the Inner Temple in 1615 and called to the bar there in 1623.[530]

Prideaux was active in the 1630's in Devon, where he made his residence. He was a J.P. and a sewers commissioner for some years.[531] Some charge against him was before the Court of High Commission in 1635,

[509] S.P. 16, 533/83. The nature of the charges is not clear, but quarrels involving Price's wife entered into the case.

[510] C.S.P. Dom., 1631–1633, 110; 1638–1639, 431. Price was at London at various times during this period, and in 1638 had a lawyer searching for documents pertaining to his legal difficulties with Steele, Sir Percy Herbert, and others. Montgomeryshire Collections 31: 79–80, 292, 1899.

[511] Ibid. 31: 303, 1899.

[512] C.J. 2: 75; D'Ewes (N), 301.

[513] D'Ewes (C), 142, 181–182.

[514] Montgomeryshire Collections 31: 83–106, 1899.

[515] N. and Q., 1st Ser., 12: 360, 1855.

[516] C.J. 3: 390; 4: 316; Montgomeryshire Collections 31: 108–109, 1899.

[517] Cal. Com. Adv. Money, 664.

[518] S.P. 23/109/673; Cal. Com. Comp., 2552.

[519] Montgomeryshire Collections 16: 38, 1883. In addition to the authorities cited see Complete Baronetage 2: 50; Williams, Parl. Hist. Wales, 143.

[520] M. of P. 1: 498; C.J. 3: 389.

[521] The above details and dates are based upon the I.P.M.'s of John Price, Esq., son of Cadwalader Price (1613, C. 142/335/ 22) and John Price, Esq. (1629, C. 142/453/97). See also Edward Breese, Kalendars of Gwynedd, 73, London, 1873.

[522] Williams, Parl. Hist. Wales, 9, 116. Although Price's mother seems to have been Eleanor Jones, in his compounding papers he mentioned properties he was to receive in reversion after his mother, Mrs. Katherine Lloyd (S.P. 23/213/829). The latter may have been his mother-in-law. If so, his wife was perhaps Mary Lloyd, rather than Mary Holland, as Williams gives her name.

[523] C. 142/453/97.

[524] English Baronetage 4: 380, 1741.

[525] The petition and "particular" are of William Price, "of Rhulas," late M.P. (S.P. 23/213/827, 829), but they appear in the Cal. Com. Comp. (2090) as of Henry Price, M.P.

[526] Western Antiquary 1: 97, 1881–1882; C.S.P. Dom., 1635–1636, 88. The Ford Abbey estate became his after 1640. Complete Baronetage 3: 6.

[527] Ibid. 1: 200, n.; 3: 6; Vis. Devon, 1620, 229. Prideaux's parentage and birth date are not given in D.N.B.

[528] Cf. Fowell.

[529] The Edmund Prideaux who attended the universities and has been by various authorities identified as the M.P. was a cousin. Al. Cant.

[530] Students admitted to the Inner Temple, 212.

[531] C. 193/13; S.P. 16/405; Devonshire MSS, Quarter Sessions Minute Book, 1633–1640; C. 181/4, fol. 164.

but was dismissed upon his denial of the charge and the lack of prosecution against him.[532] In the spring of 1640 he was chosen by Lyme Regis for his first parliament.[533] His official connections with Exeter came after that, for he became a legal counsellor there in 1642 and recorder in 1643.[534]

Little evidence has been discovered as to Prideaux's financial standing when he entered the Long Parliament. His two marriages had probably brought him properties in Devon and Somerset,[535] but he was not among the wealthy M.P.'s who pledged security for the loans of 1640–1641. His promise of £100 for the defense in 1642 shows that he was not a poor man.[536] His great fortune, though, came later.

Prideaux was a kinsman through his mother of the Edgcombe brothers, who were fellow M.P.'s in 1640. Unlike them, he served as an elder in his presbytery, and worked afterwards with the Independents.[537]

* William Purefoy (1580?–1659), of Caldecote, Warwickshire, the regicide, sat for Warwick, 1640–1653. Although some writers have stated that he came from an obscure family without fortune, he was actually the descendant of an old family of the counties of Lincoln and Warwick and was the holder of "a good landed estate."[538] He probably spent some time at Emmanuel College, Cambridge, before going to study at Gray's Inn, and may have been graduated B.A. from Pembroke.[539]

Purefoy sat for Coventry in the 1628 parliament, winning the election by vote of the freemen in a contest with the city residents who had been chosen by the corporation,[540] and he sat for Warwick in both parliaments of 1640.[541] He was a J.P. in the county and a member of minor commissions there.[542] He was one of the loan commissioners who were summoned in 1627 to appear before Council for having themselves refused to lend.[543] And in 1635 he was called to the conference concerning the ship money rates of Coventry.[544] Although his place at Warwick was already assured, Purefoy was a candidate at the shire election, too, in

November, 1640, but the sheriff refused to take the poll for him because he had been chosen elsewhere. Purefoy's friends petitioned, but he does not seem to have tried further to win the place.[545]

Thomas Pury (c. 1590–1666), alderman of Gloucester, was M.P. for his city, 1640–1653. The son of Walter Pury, a Gloucester clothier, and probably a descendant of Thomas Pury, mercer and alderman (d. 1579), he was apprenticed in 1606, after his father's death, to Lawrence Wilsheire, another clothier of the city.[546] He married, probably about 1618,[547] and in that year began his services as a city official. He was a common councillor (1618–1638), was steward (1619–1620), and sheriff (1626), and in 1638 became an alderman.[548] But before 1630 he had turned for his livelihood from trade to the law, becoming apparently without formal training a country solicitor.[549] Much of his practice came to him from the city itself, and through it he gained considerable experience with the London courts, for he was appointed in 1630 as attorney and deputy to the mayor and other officials in handling their yearly accounting to the Exchequer, and he served them in this capacity and as legal adviser during the next decade.[550] He became in 1632 solicitor for part of the sheriff's business, and during the period between 1635 and 1640 was occupied with numerous city suits in the local courts and in London.[551] Locally he served on committees on trade, on property, and on interceding with the county sheriff regarding ship money.[552]

A nonconformist in belief, Pury was active in matters affecting the church also. With several other Gloucester officials he was involved in a case before High Commission, 1633–1635, regarding a stipend the city government had voted to a nonconformist preacher who had been removed from his lectureship. And he was a member of the committee whose revision of the ordinances for the city hospital was challenged by the same court, 1636–1638.[553] Pury was active, 1639–1641, in the matter of placing a nonconformist master in Christ's School, in spite of the king's support of the incum-

[532] *C.S.P. Dom., 1635–1636,* 88.
[533] *M. of P.* 1: 481.
[534] Exeter Corporation MSS, Act Book **8** (3 Nov. 1642, 13 April and 2 May 1643).
[535] He lived part of the time at the Ottery St. Mary estate to which his first wife was heir. In 1631 he seems to have been party to the sale of a manor of more than 11,000 acres in Dorset. *Somerset and Dorset N. and Q.* 7: 339, 1898–1899.
[536] *N. and Q.,* 1st Ser., **12** : 359, 1855.
[537] *A.H.R.* **44**: 31, n. (32), 1938–1939.
[538] F. L. Colvile, *The worthies of Warwickshire,* 599–603, Warwick, 1870; Noble, *Regicides* 2: 134, 137.
[539] *Al. Cant.*
[540] *C.J.* **1**: 880; Whitley, *Parl. Rep. Coventry,* 75.
[541] *M. of P.* **1**: 495; Willis 3: 237.
[542] C. 191/13; S.P. 16/405; C. 181/4, fol. 199v; 181/5, fol. 181.
[543] S.P. 16, 50/54; 56/70.
[544] Coventry Corporation MSS, A 35.

[545] *C.J.* **2**: 23, 43; D'Ewes (N), 95–96, 302, 306.
[546] Gloucester Corp. MSS, Minute Book, 1486–c. 1600, fol. 37v; Roll of Apprentices, 1598–1646, fol. 129.
[547] Williams, *Gloucester,* 194, 198.
[548] Gloucester Corp. MSS, Minute Book, 1565–1632, fols. 457v, 459, *passim;* Minute Book, 1632–1656, *passim.*
[549] He was called an "ignorant country solicitor" in *The mystery of the good old cause* (36), and was described in 1640 in a letter among the State Papers as "sometimes a weaver, now an attorney." *C.S.P. Dom., 1639–1640,* 582.
[550] Gloucester Corp. MSS, Minute Book, 1565–1632, fol. 540; 1632–1656, fols. 18, 24, 56, 79; Accounts, 1635–1653, *passim.*
[551] *Ibid.,* Minute Book, 1565–1632, fol. 558; 1632–1656, fols. 21, 90; Accounts, 1635–1653, fols. 26, 45, 69, 84v, *passim.*
[552] *Ibid.,* Minute Book, 1632–1656, fols. 58, 125, 139, 140, 156.
[553] *Ibid.,* fols., 12, 18, 22, 121–122, 227, *passim;* Willcox, *Gloucestershire,* 216–217; S.P. 16, 383/47.

bent.[554] And when he was a candidate for election to the Short Parliament, it was said that his custom of sitting in church with his head covered had greatly endeared him to the puritan element.[555] But that was not enough to win the election.

The Long Parliament was Alderman Pury's first. His religious views and his customary vigor made him an active member of the reforming group. Beginning in January, 1641, he was named to various committees, including several on legal and ecclesiastical matters.[556] And during the war he became increasingly prominent, and assumed an office under the puritan regime. He died, aged about seventy-six, in 1666.[557]

Of Pury's financial standing little evidence remains. His legal practice seems to have been considerable, and he held several leases in Gloucester.[558] That he was not unduly wealthy is suggested by his promise of only one horse for the defense in 1642,[559] but he and his son were both said to have profited in purse by the opportunities brought by the war.[560]

* Sir Robert Pye (1585–1662), of Farringdon, Berkshire, Auditor of the Exchequer, was elected for New Woodstock at a by-election, 2 December 1640, and retained his seat until 1648.[561] A younger son of Roger Pye of the Mind, Herefordshire, and Bridget, daughter of Thomas Kirke (Kyrle?) of Walford,[562] he was a brother of Sir Walter Pye, Attorney-General of the Court of Wards. He was admitted to the Middle Temple in 1607.[563] Under the patronage of Buckingham, he began a career at court, becoming Auditor of the Exchequer, and receiving various grants and honors. He was a navy commissioner in 1626, but asked to be excused from reappointment because of his many other employments in the king's service.[564] Pye resided chiefly at Westminster,[565] but he bought an estate in Berkshire in 1622. He was a J.P. in Westminster,

Middlesex, and Surrey, and a sewers commissioner for Oxfordshire and Berkshire in 1634.[566] He was M.P. for Bath in 1621 and 1624, for Ludgershall in 1625, and Westminster in 1626. Buckingham was then steward of the latter city and doubtless secured Pye's election, but his support failed to win it for him there again in 1628, and Pye sat that year for Grampound.[567] He was not returned again until his belated election to the Long Parliament, but was still active in his duties at the Exchequer in 1640.[568]

Sir Robert seems to have been useful to the House in its early period largely because of his experience in administrative matters and his familiarity with Westminster.[569] He was among the witnesses requested by Strafford for his trial and his testimony tended to clear Strafford of the charge of mishandling funds in Ireland for his personal gain.[570] But Pye was not listed as voting against the attainder, and he was named to the important recess committee of 1641. He pledged his bond for £1000 for the loan in March, 1641, was a guarantor again in July,[571] and the next year pledged the maintenance of four horses and £200 for the defense, one of the largest offers.[572] He was named in October, 1642, to the Committee for the Advance of Money. He was under some suspicion in 1643, but aided perhaps by his son, who by that time had married Hampden's daughter, managed to retain both his place in the Exchequer and his seat in parliament for five more years.

Pye was undoubtedly a wealthy man. He had some interests in Ireland from 1622,[573] was listed in 1639 as lending £2000 to the king,[574] and was apparently quite able to back up his large pledges made in parliament, 1640–1642. He held land in several counties besides Berkshire.[575]

Edward Phelipps, another 1640 M.P., was Pye's son-in-law.

Charles Pym (c. 1620–1671), of Brymore, Somerset, elected for Beeralston, Devon, after Pollard's expulsion on 9 December 1641, sat until the purge in 1648. The second son of the celebrated John Pym by his wife, Anna Hooker, Charles was born about 1620.[576] He matricu-

[554] Gloucester Corp. MSS, Minute Book, 1632–1656, fols. 132–134, 143–144, 148, 150, 176–179; Willcox, Gloucestershire, 218–220.

[555] C.S.P. Dom., 1639–1640, 582.

[556] C.J. 2: 73, 75, 115, passim; D'Ewes (C), 212, 232.

[557] Williams, Gloucester, 194.

[558] Gloucester Corp. MSS, Minute Book, 1565–1632, fols. 463v, 487, 558v; 1632–1656, fols. 188, 191.

[559] N. and Q., 1st Ser., 12: 359, 1855. Pury contributed personally part of the £1350 he subscribed for Gloucester toward the Irish venture in 1642. C.S.P. Ireland, Adventurers, 38.

[560] The mystery of the good old cause, 36, 37.

[561] M. of P. 1: 492; Williams, Oxford, 203–204. Pye is mentioned briefly in the article on his son, Sir Robert (d. 1701), in D.N.B.

[562] Vis. Berks. 1: 270; Misc. Geneal. et Herald., 5th Ser., 8: 252, 1932–1934. Williams errs in calling his father William Pye.

[563] Mid. Temp. Rec. 2: 479, 513, 619.

[564] C.S.P. Dom., 1619–1623, 170; 1628–1629, 310; S.P. 16, 525/59.

[565] St. Margaret's Parish Records, Overseers' Accounts, 1620–1642.

[566] C. 181/3, fol. 16; C. 193/12, 13; S.P. 16/405; C. 181/4, fol. 179v.

[567] S.P. 14, 119/28; Commons Debates 1621 2: 208, n.; M. of P. 1: 459, 466, 470, 474; Birch, The court and times of Charles the First 1: 327.

[568] C.S.P. Dom., 1640, 59, passim; 1640–1641, 114, passim.

[569] C.J. 2: 57, 107, 316, 341, 348.

[570] D'Ewes (N), 515 and n.; Verney, 31.

[571] C.J. 2: 222, 288, 825; D'Ewes (N), 438, n., 451, n.

[572] N. and Q., 1st Ser., 12: 338, 1855.

[573] Add. MSS, 4794, fol. 672.

[574] S.P. 16, 453/74.

[575] Somerset and Dorset N. and Q. 11: 153, 1908–1909; will of Sir Robert Pye (1662), P.C.C., 70 Laud.

[576] According to Complete Baronetage (3: 281), his marriage license of 1663 gives his age as 35, so setting his birth about 1628. According to D.N.B., however, his mother died in 1620,

lated at Cambridge (St. Catherine's) in 1632, entered Lincoln's Inn in 1635, and was called to the bar there in 1644.[577] He seems to have had no connection with Beeralston and must have owed his seat to the influence of his father's friends. Arriving too late to have a part in the early work of the Long Parliament, young Pym captained a troop of horse in the army on his father's side during the war. He was secluded in 1648.[578] He succeeded his elder brother, Alexander, about 1660, sat for Minehead in the 1660 parliament, was created a baronet in 1663, and died in 1671. He did not marry until 1663.[579]

* **John Pym** (1584?–1643), of Brymore, Somerset, M.P. for Tavistock from 1640 until his death, came of a family which owned considerable land in Somerset.[580] A man of legal training, though not a barrister, Pym was Receiver General of Wiltshire, Hampshire, and Gloucestershire from about 1607,[581] until 1636 or later.[582] To the list of Pym's well known activities in the royal administration and in colonization schemes should be added a record of his part in local administration. He was probably a J.P. in Hampshire in 1626,[583] a member of the commission for surveying and dividing Braydon forest, Wilts, in 1627,[584] a sewers commissioner for the Isle of Wight (1631) and for Middlesex (1639),[585] and for several years he was on the commission on depopulation for Wilts and Gloucestershire.[586] His contacts at court probably account for his signing a receipt with the courtier, Verney, for letters patent of the Frith in 1629.[587] His official experience and his work with the Providence Island Company had made him familiar with the problems of revenue and finance, with economic conditions in the counties, and with a group of puritan leaders. The latter he had met also in parliament. His constituencies were Calne (1621),[588] Tavistock (1624), although he tried also for Chippenham that year,[589] and Tavistock

in the next five parliaments. His seat there was no doubt secured for him by the Russell family, earls of Bedford, and their agent, St. John, for Pym seems to have had no direct dealings with the borough.

The details of Pym's political career need not be repeated. His early leadership in 1621 led to a brief imprisonment after the parliament.[590] He was possibly the John Pym of Wherwell, Esquire, who was reported by the Hampshire D.L.'s as capable of lending £10 in 1625. Two years later the same John Pym was reported as not subscribing for the loan, but as paying in £10 voluntarily.[591] He was apparently not among the ardent loan resisters of that period. But the record of his activities between 1636 and 1640 leaves little doubt that Pym helped to organize the resistance movement of the years immediately preceding 1640 as well as to work for the calling of the parliaments of that year.[592]

Although Pym has been regarded by some as a man who had not profited either in position or in goods from the opportunities open to him,[593] he was the owner of large and scattered holdings in Somerset before 1635. Some of these he may have sold or mortgaged in order to make his investment in the Providence Island Company.[594] He perhaps had some interest in coal properties near Coventry, too.[595] He seems to have maintained also a house in St. Andrew's, Holborn, at least until the summer of 1638, although he had probably disposed of his office as Receiver General by that time.[596] He had sufficient means to offer his bond as security for the loan in March, 1641,[597] and in 1642 he promised £600 for reducing Ireland, and two horses and £100 for

---

and the dates of his education make it appear that he was born about that time, or a little before.

[577] *Al. Cant.; Linc. Inn Rec., Black Books* 2: 363.

[578] *O.P.H.* 9: *25.

[579] *Complete Baronetage, loc. cit.;* Brown, *Somerset Wills* 6: 22; Harl. MSS, 6861, fol. 12; *M. of P.* 1: 515.

[580] S. R. Brett, *John Pym,* xvii, xviii.

[581] *Bull. Institute of Historical Research* 3: 67, 1925–1926; *C.S.P. Dom., 1611–1618,* 205, 578.

[582] His servant collected the payments from Bristol in 1636. Bristol Corporation MSS, Audit Book 20: 1636.

[583] C. 193/12.

[584] *C.S.P. Dom., 1627–1628,* 84.

[585] C. 181/4, fol. 89; 181/5, fol. 285.

[586] C. 181/5, fol. 44; S.P. 16, 229/112/252.

[587] *C.S.P. Dom., 1628–1629,* 482.

[588] *M. of P.* 1: 454. The statement in *D.N.B.* that Pym served for Calne in 1614 seems to be erroneous (Brett, *op. cit.,* 23, n.). Pym had some dealings with Calne while he was supervising Bowood Forest. (Marsh, *Hist. of Calne,* 43).

[589] *M. of P.* 1: 457, 461 and n. See also Sir Francis Popham.

[590] Gardiner, *H. of E.* 4: 267.

[591] S.P. 16, 521/177/i; Add. MSS, 21,922, fol. 16v; Bodleian Rawl. MSS, D 666, fol. 103v. Wherwell manor was in this period the property of Thomas West, third Lord De La Warr (*V.C.H. Hampshire* 4: 412).

[592] *Cf.* Brett, *op. cit.,* 126–127, 154; Hexter, *The reign of King Pym,* 74–81, *passim.*

[593] E.g., Abbott, *Cromwell* 1: 57; *Note book of Sir John Northcote,* lxiii.

[594] Brett, *op. cit.,* xxiii, xxvi–xxvii; Collinson, *Somerset* 1: 234; 3: 82; *Somerset and Dorset N. and Q.* 11: 152, 1908–1909.

[595] "Pymmes' house" is referred to in a list of city properties under lease in 1613 (Coventry Corporation MSS, A 29, Leases and Rentals, 1613–1808, fol. 5). "Pym the collier" was mentioned in a royalist speech before the 1640 elections there, according to T. W. Whitley, *Parliamentary representation of the city of Coventry* (79, 86). The references to early projects and lands in a notebook once thought to have been Pym's (*H.M.C., Tenth Report* 6, Bouverie MSS, 83) are to be avoided, since Gardiner has shown that the notes were not Pym's (*E.H.R.* 10: 105, 1895).

[596] Pym defied the order against keeping Christmas in London in 1637 (S.P. 16, 378/94), but he told a friend in a letter dated at London, 20 July 1638, that he had spent most of the previous two years in the country (*C.S.P. Dom., 1637–1638,* 571). See also Dale, *Inhabitants of London,* 193.

[597] D'Ewes (N), 451, n. (452).

the defense.[598] He was by no means a poor man in 1640.

Relatives of Pym in the Commons with him were his stepbrother, Francis Rous, a brother-in-law and friend, John Upton, a nephew, Antony Nicoll, and later, Pym's son, Charles. William Whitaker was an intimate friend and sometime a trustee for Pym's estates,[599] and Sir William Masham once wrote of him as "my brother Pyme."[600]

John Pyne (1600–1678), of Curry Mallet, Somerset, a lawyer, was M.P. for Poole in Dorset, 1640–1653. He was the son and heir of Thomas Pyne of Merriott, Somerset (d. 1609), who was the eldest son of John Pyne of Curry Mallett (d. 1609). Through his mother, Amy, daughter of Thomas Hanham of Wimborne Minster, Dorset, Pyne was a great-grandson of Sir John Popham, the Chief Justice. He was born on 26 March 1600.[601] He may have matriculated at Hart Hall, Oxford, in February, 1610 (B.A. 1612),[602] but not until January, 1619, did he enter the Middle Temple. There he was "bound" for part of the time with his cousin, Alexander Popham, and with Bulstrode White-locke, who became an intimate friend. Pyne was called to the bar on 19 June 1629, and kept his chamber at the Temple until 1637.[603] It was probably shortly after his admission to the bar that, aided by his friend, White-locke, Pyne managed to elope with his cousin, Eleanor Hanham, daughter and heiress of Sir John Hanham of London and Dorset (d. 1625). Her uncle and guardian, Thomas Hanham, had disapproved of the match. In October, 1629, Pyne and his wife became administrators of her father's estate.[604]

Already Pyne had started his political career. He was M.P. for Poole in 1625, 1626, and 1628.[605] His mother's relatives perhaps helped him gain his seat, but his political mentor more probably was his uncle, Hugh Pyne, a Lincoln's Inn lawyer, who was a J.P. in both Somerset and Dorset. The latter's opposition to the 1626 loan and his criticism of Buckingham and the king, followed by imprisonment and examination, brought him great notoriety in 1627–1628.[606] His death in November, 1628, possibly saved his family from difficulties.[607] Of John Pyne's role in his early parliaments nothing is known, but he doubtless worked with the opposition and must have followed with sympathy his uncle's experience. By 1634 John Pyne was a sewers commissioner in Somerset and by 1636, a J.P. and treasurer of the hospitals in the western part of that county.[608] He was an active opponent of ship money, 1636–1638.[609]

Returned again to parliament for Poole both times in 1640, Pyne became one of what his former friend, Whitelocke, called the "more rigid party."[610] His committee appointments included that on the Bishop of Bath and Wells,[611] and he became very active with the war.[612] Although he functioned as an elder in his presbytery,[613] he heartily sanctioned the purge of parliament by the army in 1648,[614] and remained a member until 1653. He survived the Restoration, and died in 1678. He was survived then by his second wife, Amy, and two sons.[615]

Clarendon wrote of Pyne as a gentleman "well known, and of a fair estate."[616] His properties, besides his Somerset inheritance from his father and grandfather, lay in Dorset and some in Devon.[617] His uncle, Hugh Pyne, was supposed to have had an income of at least £2000 a year,[618] and John, the family heir, perhaps had as much. He asserted in 1660 that his own purse in 1640 contained above £1000 and that the war reduced the value of his estate by more than that amount.[619]

Pyne, like his uncle, seems to have been a man of strong convictions, whose words and deeds brought him

---

[598] *C.S.P. Ireland, Adventurers*, 188; *N. and Q.*, 1st Ser., **12**: 338, 1855. The subscription for Ireland appears to have been entirely Pym's.

[599] Brett, *op. cit.*, xxv.

[600] Eg. MSS, 2645, fol. 293.

[601] I.P.M., Thomas Pyne, C. 142/307/8; Brown, *Somerset Wills* **1**: 3–4; **2**: 71, 73; **5**: 108; Hutchins, *Dorset* **3**: 231. A sketch of Pyne's life, chiefly for the period after 1642, appears in Bates Harbin, *Members of Parliament, Somerset*, 156–157.

[602] As "of Somerset, gent.," aged thirteen. *Al. Oxon.* Another John Pyne, who studied at Cambridge, became rector at Bere Ferris in Devon. *Al. Cant.; Western Antiquary* **4**: 54, 1884–1885.

[603] *Mid. Temp. Rec.* **2**: 634, 677, 726, 752, 855.

[604] Eleanor Hanham, aged sixteen in 1625, was her father's heir, but Thomas Hanham was the successor to the estates. Hutchins, *Dorset* **3**: 231; *Somerset and Dorset N. and Q.* **3**: 166, 1892–1893; R. H. Whitelocke, *Memoirs of Bulstrode Whitelocke*, 40.

[605] *M. of P.*

[606] The case involved petty local jealousies as well as questions of state, and it seems to have been still undetermined in February, 1628. *C.S.P. Dom., 1625–1626*, 436, 480; *1627–1628*, 213, 461, 498; Bodleian Clarendon MSS, 4, Nos. 254–257; Birch, *The court and times of Charles the First* **1**: 292, 295.

[607] Brown, *Somerset Wills* **2**: 71–72.

[608] C. 181/4, fol. 172v; Bates Harbin, *loc. cit.*

[609] *C.S.P. Dom., 1637–1638*, 407, 486.

[610] R. H. Whitelocke, *loc. cit.*

[611] *C.J.* **2**: 75.

[612] For his wartime career, see Bates Harbin, *loc. cit.*

[613] *Somerset and Dorset N. and Q.* **10**: 83, 1906–1907.

[614] Sloane MSS, 1519, fol. 188.

[615] Pyne's will is abstracted in Brown, *Somerset Wills* **2**: 73.

[616] *Rebellion* **3**: 491.

[617] I.P.M. cited above; Brown, *Somerset Wills* **1**: 3–4; **2**: 73; *Somerset and Dorset N. and Q.* **7**: 203, 1900–1901; Exeter City Library, Exeter Deeds and Documents, No. 30349. The presence of other John Pynes in the same region makes identification of property owners difficult.

[618] Birch, *op. cit.* **1**: 295. Hugh's will (Brown, *op. cit.* **2**: 71–72) mentioned £1000 as the dowry of a younger daughter. Doubtless his income came from a lucrative practice as well as from real estate.

[619] *H.M.C., Ninth Report* **2**, MSS of the Rev. W. Pyne, 494.

into violent disagreement with his fellows. He once wrote in disapproval of that "very firebrand," Prynne, and his "fellows in evil." [620] But of Pyne his erstwhile colleague, John Ashe, said in 1650 that he was a man "subject to passion and misinformation." [621] There was probably some ground for the royalists' conclusions that as colonel and committeeman he ruled the committee and the county by inspirations. [622]

Pyne had various relatives in the 1640 Commons. Among them were his great-uncle, Sir Francis Popham, his cousins, Alexander Popham and Hugh Rogers, and two cousins by marriage, William Constantine and Edmund Windham.

* William Rainborow or Rainsborough (1587–1642),

of Wapping, navy captain, sat for Aldeburgh, Suffolk, from 1640 until his death in 1642. He was the eldest son of Thomas Rainborow, mariner, of Greenwich (d. 1622), by his wife, Martha or Margaret (d. 1626),[1] and was baptized at Whitechapel, 11 June 1587. Before 1624 he married Judith, daughter of Renold Huxton, and was living at Wapping at the time of her death in 1638. He declined the honor of knighthood in 1637, following his expedition against the Salee pirates, accepting a medal instead. He was interested in all matters of trade, especially in the American colonies, to which one of his daughters migrated before 1638.

Elected to both 1640 parliaments for Aldeburgh,[2] perhaps with the aid of the mercantile family of Bence, his colleague, Rainborow was named to most of the committees of the Long Parliament dealing with the navy and with trade, and to the recess committee of 1641.[3] He died early in February, 1642.[4]

Besides being the co-owner of several ships, Rainborow owned various properties in and near London. His will of 1638 specified portions ranging from £700 to £1200 for each of his five younger children, as well as legacies totalling over £600,[5] and he was one of the residents of Billingsgate Ward listed in 1640 as most able to lend to the treasury.[6]

Sir Henry Rainsford (1599–1641), of Clifford,

Gloucestershire, and of Combe, Hants, was M.P. for Andover in the latter county from 1640 until his death

early in 1641.[7] He was the eldest surviving son of Sir Henry Rainsford of Clifford (d. 1622) by Anne, daughter and coheir of Sir Henry Goodere of Polesworth in Warwickshire. He was born in 1599.[8] In his early years he had contact with such literary figures as Ben Jonson and Shakespeare, who were said to have visited his father's home, and with Drayton, who had served his maternal grandfather and often spent his summers with the Rainsfords. His father was reported to be a learned man and interested in poetry and Henry himself wrote some verse.[9] The latter studied at Oxford (subscribed 1613) and at the Middle Temple (1616–1619).[10] About 1620 he married Eleanor, daughter and coheir of Robert Boswell of Eastwicke and Combe, Hants, and in 1622 he succeeded his father.[11] He was knighted about that time or in 1624.[12]

Rainsford probably divided his time between his own and his wife's estates in Gloucestershire and Hants. He was a J.P. in his native county in 1626.[13] That year he was named also to the loan commission, but was among those who absented themselves from the meeting in 1627 at which many of the commissioners protested against the loan.[14] Probably he wished to avoid involvement in the heated controversy. He seems to have taken little part in political matters, preferring rather to consort with the learned men whom Lord Falkland drew to his home at Great Tew.[15] His wife died in October, 1640.[16] Almost immediately afterwards the town of Andover elected Rainsford to parliament. A friend of the family wrote that the action was quite unexpected, being without suit by either Rainsford or his friends.[17] He had served in no previous parliament.

Sir Henry was probably considered a follower of his friend, Lord Falkland, and seems to have been interested in the reform movement of the opening weeks. He was named to several committees, including that on the courts of High Commission and Star Chamber and on limiting the temporal powers of the clergy,[18] and

[620] Sloane MSS, 1519, fol. 188.

[621] Cal. Com. Comp., 222.

[622] Bayley, The great Civil War in Dorset, 22 and n.

[1] Archaeologia 46: 10–11, 1881; John Rylands Library English MSS, Peacock MSS, 235, fols. 218, 240.

[2] M. of P. 1: 483, 494.

[3] C.J. 2: 34, 43, 54, 288, passim.

[4] On 1 February 1642 Rainborow added a codicil to his will, and on 14 February the House ordered that his successor be elected. C.J. 2: 429.

[5] The principal sources of material supplementing D.N.B. are Archaeologia, loc. cit., and New England Historical and Genealogical Register 40: 161, 163–168, 170, 1886.

[6] S.P. 16, 453/75.

[7] M. of P. 1: 493; C.J. 2: 114.

[8] I.P.M., Sir Henry Rainsford, C. 142/402/145; Transactions of the Bristol and Gloucestershire Archaeological Society 14: 68–69, 1889–1890.

[9] Emily A. Buckland, The Rainsford family, 106, 108, 151, Worcester, Caxton Press, 1932. The younger Rainsford wrote some lines in commendation of George Sandys's Divine Poems. K. Weber, Lucius Cary, second Viscount Falkland, 61.

[10] Al. Oxon.; Mid. Temp. Rec. 2: 611, 638.

[11] I.P.M. cited above.

[12] He was referred to as a knight in his father's I.P.M. (1622), possibly by error. Henry Rainsford of Clifford Chambers, Gloucestershire, was knighted at Tutbury, 17 August 1624. Shaw, K. of E. 2: 186.

[13] C. 193/12.

[14] S.P. 16, 44/5; 54/28/i.

[15] Weber, op. cit., 60–61; John Aubrey, Brief lives (Clark) 1: 151.

[16] C.S.P. Dom., 1640–1641, 179.

[17] Ibid., 198.

[18] C.J. 2: 44, 54, 64, 99.

on 4 March 1641 he offered his bond for £500 for the loan.[19] But later that month he fell a victim of smallpox and died quickly. The House on 31 March ordered an election to fill his place.[20]

Rainsford probably enjoyed a comfortable estate. His mother's portion was said to have been £1500,[21] and his own marriage brought him the expectation of Hampshire lands. When he died he owned a manor in Gloucestershire and part of one in Warwickshire, with some smaller properties.[22] These were stated by his royalist son at compounding to be worth only £340 a year,[23] but Rainsford's pledge for the loan in 1641 suggests that the statement may have been an underestimate.

Jonathan Rashleigh (1591–1675), of Fowey and Menabilly, Cornwall, was M.P. for Fowey, 1640–22 January 1644. He came of a merchant family of Devonshire stock which had settled in Fowey two generations earlier and by their wealth and enterprise had improved the town and their own fortunes. His father, Jonathan (d. 1624), had gone to Virginia in 1585, had fought against the Armada, and had been a county J.P. and M.P. for Fowey. He allied himself with the gentry of the shire by marrying Alice, daughter of Richard Boniton of Kerteleowe, and, while "daily bettering his estate" by trade, adapted his mode of life to that of a gentleman.[24] His second son, Jonathan, was baptized at Fowey on 4 July 1591 and in 1624, upon the deaths of his father and elder brother, inherited all of his father's estate, including the new seat at Menabilly. He had before that been educated as a gentleman at Oxford (matriculated at Exeter, 1607), and at the Middle Temple (admitted 1610).[25] But he continued with his father's business as a merchant, traded with Londoners,[26] and was able to increase his land holdings by further purchases.[27] About 1614 he married Anne, daughter of Sir Robert Bassett of Umberleigh, Devon. Sometime after her death (1631), possibly before 1640, he married Mary, daughter of John Harris of Lanrest, a sister of John Harris, M.P. for Liskeard (q.v.).[28]

Rashleigh went to parliament for Fowey in 1614, 1621, and 1625, and to both the parliaments of 1640.[29] He was inclined in his earlier years toward the opposition group, although he seems to have paid the £10 required of him for the forced loan in 1626.[30] He was sheriff of Cornwall, 1627–1628, and afterwards a member of the piracy commission.[31] The knighthood commissioners reported him as refusing to pay the required fine, and he was among those listed for Council proceedings in 1633 for the offense.[32] A few years later he had a quarrel, involving a challenge, with Sir Reginald Mohun, and took the case to Star Chamber. It was scheduled for a hearing in January, 1638,[33] but nothing further of the case is known.

In the Long Parliament Rashleigh seems to have taken little part. He had had two leaves of absence in 1641, was absent at call on 16 June 1642, and was disabled for his deserting the cause, 22 January 1644.[34] Although he attended the Oxford parliament, he declared when he compounded, 1646–1650, that illness had been the chief reason for his earlier absences and that he had never voted against parliament. He survived to sit as M.P. again in 1661,[35] and died on 1 May 1675.[36]

The "great wealth" of Rashleigh's family was referred to in a lawsuit as early as 1616, and according to his own statements Rashleigh improved upon the income from his inheritance.[37] His 1644 assessment by parliament, £1200, was one of the higher figures,[38] and he afterwards estimated his losses for the period of 1640–1660 as over £16,400.[39] Although his "particular" listed real estate to the value of only £415 a year, his compounding fine was set, after revision because of undervaluations, at £1105.[40]

The Godolphins of Godolphin were among Rashleigh's kinsmen.[41]

Hall Ravenscroft (born c. 1600), of Horsham, was a member for that Sussex borough, 1640–1648.[42] The grandson of Peter Ravenscroft of Cheshire, who had come to Sussex as gentleman of the horse to the Duke

---

[19] D'Ewes (N), 439, n.

[20] C.J. 2: 114. His death was after that of Wise on 18 March (Buckland, op. cit., 113). According to his I.P.M. held at Cirencester on 3 May 1641, however, he was said to have died on 10 April. C. 142/615/105.

[21] Buckland, op. cit., 151.

[22] I.P.M., C. 142/615/105.

[23] S.P. 23/194/195. The son's fine at a sixth was £900. Cal. Com. Comp., 1202.

[24] Carew, Survey of Cornwall, 317; Lawrance, Parl. Rep. Corn., 269; Vivian, Vis. Cornwall, 391–392; Coate, Cornwall in the great Civil War, 2.

[25] Al. Oxon.; Mid. Temp. Rec. 2: 529.

[26] Devon Notes and Queries 4 (i): 145–146, 1906–1907.

[27] Exeter City Library MSS, Exeter Deeds and Documents, no. 3983.

[28] Although Pink gives 1666 as the marriage date (Pink MSS, 307, fol. 190), Rashleigh and his son were named as trustees by Harris, the M.P., in his will of 1648 (P.C.C., 175

Fairfax), and Rashleigh's wife handled some of his business matters during the war (Coate, op. cit., 358).

[29] M. of P. 1: 450, 463, 480, 486; 3: xxxvii.

[30] Coate, op. cit., 20.

[31] List of Sheriffs, 23; C. 181/5, fol. 166.

[32] S.P. 16, 242/64/124.

[33] S.P. 16, 379/77.

[34] C.J. 2: 332, 626; 3: 374; Pink MSS, 307, fol. 190. The ordering of a new election in place of Rashleigh, "deceased" (C.J. 5: 21), represents a clerical error.

[35] M. of P. 1: 520.

[36] Vivian, loc. cit.

[37] St. Ch. 8/75/16; Royal Hist. Soc., Trans., 4th Ser., 10: 150, 1927.

[38] Cal. Com. Adv. Money, 431.

[39] Coate, op. cit., 357–359.

[40] S.P. 23/206/649–650; Cal. Com. Comp., 336, 1327.

[41] Coate, op. cit., 20.

[42] His name is printed as "Cavenscrofte" in M. of P. 1: 494.

of Norfolk and settled at Horsham, he was the only surviving son of John Ravenscroft, gentleman (d. 1615), by his wife, Judith, daughter of George Ferne. He was named for his great-grandfather, John Hall of Horsham, whose estates passed to the Ravenscrofts.[43] Born about 1600,[44] he matriculated at Christ's Church, Oxford, 8 November 1616, and was admitted to Lincoln's Inn in March, 1618.[45] In or before 1621 he married Elizabeth, daughter of John Stapley of Hickstead and widow of Henry Colthurst, citizen and haberdasher of London.[46]

Ravenscroft compounded for knighthood in 1629 with a fine of £10. Although he was listed among the Sussex gentry in 1634,[47] he does not seem to have been active in public affairs outside of Horsham before 1640. In that year he was one of the commissioners for a subsidy,[48] and was chosen Horsham's member for both parliaments.[49]

In the Long Parliament Ravenscroft was of the popular party but was not prominent. He was named a Sussex committeemen during the war, but was secluded from the House by Pride's Purge of 1648.[50] He survived the Restoration and died sometime after 1672. His will, dated 7 May 1673, was proved 29 July 1681.[51]

The estate Ravenscroft inherited from his father included several messuages and the rectory of Horsham, a manor known as Hewells, and some other lands outside the borough.[52] The marriage of his only daughter and heir with a knightly family of Cheshire indicates that he was a man of some means.

* **Robert Reynolds** (c. 1601–1661?), of the Middle Temple, was M.P. for Hindon in Wiltshire, 1640–1653. He came of a Cambridgeshire family, studied at Queen's College, Cambridge, and entered the Middle Temple in 1620. He was called to the bar in 1628 and to the bench in 1648.[53] Most of his connections were with the eastern counties. His father, Sir James Reynolds, was still serving on local commissions in Cambridgeshire in 1638 and 1640,[54] and the families of his mother (Margaret Milbourne) and of his first wife were both of Dunmow, Essex.[55] Reynolds probably kept his

chambers at the Temple most of the time until his first marriage in 1635,[56] and may have had a London house in 1638.[57] But he may have been the one of his name who was appointed to the Suffolk commission of oyer and terminer in 1640.[58] He was described in 1655 as an attorney of the Court of Wards.[59] If his practice there began before 1640, his election for Hindon as the colleague of Sir Miles Fleetwood, the Receiver General of the court, may be traceable to that fact. He must have owed his return primarily, however, to the influence of the borough's patron, possibly the Earl of Pembroke.[60] He seems to have had no direct association with Wiltshire.

Reynold's financial position in 1640 was probably good. In July, 1641, he promised to continue, with four other members, a loan of £2000 for the use of parliament, and in June, 1642, he offered to furnish two horses and £100 in plate for the cause.[61] Reynolds served as a Presbyterian elder before 1648, but sat with the Independents afterwards.[62] He survived the Restoration and died probably about 1661.[63]

Robert Lord Rich (1611–1659), of Leighs, Essex, son and heir apparent of the second Earl of Warwick (d. 1658), was returned for Essex in October, 1640, but left the Commons when he was called to the Lords on 27 January 1641 as Baron Rich.[64] Born 28 June and baptized 13 July 1611 at Hackney, he was styled Lord Rich after 1619 and was made K.B. in February, 1626.[65] He was admitted to Gray's Inn in 1619, was created M.A. at Cambridge in 1629 and afterwards (at Oxford, 1642), D.C.L.[66] He was elected to parliament for Essex in January, 1629, to fill a vacancy,[67] travelled afterwards in France, and upon his return married, 9 April 1632, Anne (d. 1638), daughter of William Cavendish, second Earl of Devonshire. The report was that her portion was eleven or twelve thousand pounds, with a jointure of £2000 a year, and that Lord Rich was to have a portion, after his father's death, of £6000 a year, and until then an allowance of £1500 annually.[68]

Lord Rich seems to have been named to no local commissions, and in 1639 was listed among the gentlemen who, having promised to attend the king, possibly for

[43] *Vis. Sussex, 1633–4*, 171; Comber, *Sussex Genealogies*, Horsham, 313–314.
[44] I.P.M., John Ravenscroft, C. 142/351/114.
[45] *Al. Oxon.; Linc. Inn Rec. Adm.* 1: 179.
[46] A son, John, was baptized in October, 1621. Comber, *loc. cit.*
[47] *Sussex Arch. Coll.* **16**: 49, 1864; **39**: 113, 1894.
[48] *Ibid.* **9**: 105, 1857.
[49] *M. of P.* 1: 483.
[50] Thomas-Stanford, *Sussex in the great Civil War*, 120; *Western Antiquary* **9**: 133, 1889–1890.
[51] Comber, *loc. cit.*
[52] C. 142/351/114; Albery, *A parliamentary history of Horsham*, 21, 27.
[53] *Mid. Temp. Rec.* **2**: 646, 733, 971; *Al. Cant.*
[54] S.P. 16/405; C. 181/5, fol. 353.
[55] *Al. Cant.; D.N.B.*

[56] *Mid. Temp. Rec.* **2**: 792.
[57] Dale, *Inhabitants of London*, 141.
[58] C. 181/5, fol. 350.
[59] Add. MSS, 15,520, fol. 57v.
[60] See Hindon election.
[61] *C.J.* **2**: 222; *N. and Q.*, 1st Ser., **12**: 359, 1855.
[62] *A.H.R.* **44**: 31, n. (32), 1938–1939.
[63] *Al. Cant.*
[64] *M. of P.* 1: 488; *C.J.* **2**: 74.
[65] *Complete Peerage* **8**: 66, 67. Lord Rich is mentioned briefly in the *D.N.B.* article on his father.
[66] *Gray's Inn Adm. Reg.*, 154; *Al. Cant.; Al. Oxon.*
[67] *M. of P.* 1: 475.
[68] *Complete Peerage, loc. cit.*; Birch, *The court and times of Charles the First* **2**: 170.

army service in the north, had failed to do so.[69] He was not a member of the Short Parliament, and sat in the next one for little more than two months, taking no prominent part while there. He left his father's party during the war to join the king at York, possibly being influenced by his in-laws, the Cavendishes, but he never bore arms and when the Committee for Compounding laid on him a fine, at a tenth, of over £2300, his father intervened to arrange for his estate to be spared.[70]

A widower at the time he entered the Long Parliament, Lord Rich married twice afterwards, his second wife (1645) being his cousin, the "fair Mrs. Rogers," daughter of Sir Thomas Cheeke (q.v.) and widow of Richard Rogers (q.v.).[71] Although the heir apparent to one of the wealthiest puritan earls,[72] and supplied with a generous allowance, Lord Rich had before 1640 had to borrow money to keep up his mode of life.[73]

Two uncles by marriage were fellow members with Rich in the 1640 parliament, Sir Gervase Clifton and Sir Thomas Cheeke. Young Lord Mansfield was a relative of his first wife.

* Alexander Rigby (1594–1650), of Gray's Inn and of Wigan and Middleton, Lancashire, was M.P. for Wigan, 1640–1650. He had been educated at St. John's, Cambridge (B.A. 1614, M.A. 1615), and at Gray's Inn,[74] inherited lands in several Lancashire parishes at his father's death (1632),[75] and was probably a J.P. in the county in 1638, and possibly a D.L.[76] He was elected by easy margins at Wigan for both parliaments of 1640.[77] He became an elder in the Lancashire presbytery, although he was actually an Independent,[78] and was known as a man who was both wealthy and religious.[79] His pledge for the defense in 1642, however, was only one horse.[80]

Rigby was a friend of Ralph Ashton of Middleton, and a personal as well as a political foe of some of the royalists in his county.[81]

James Rivers (1603–1641), of Combe in Hamsey parish, Sussex, and of Kent, sat for Lewes from the opening of the parliament until his death in June, 1641.[82] His father's family seat was at Chafford, Kent, but his wife was of a Sussex family and he seems to have lived after his marriage chiefly in the latter county. He was the eldest surviving son of Sir John Rivers, Bart. (J.P. Kent, d. about 1651), by Dorothy, daughter and coheir of Thomas Potter of Westerham. He was baptized at Westerham on 15 December 1603,[83] matriculated at Corpus Christi, Oxford, in 1616, and was graduated B.A. on 3 July 1620.[84] Four years later (22 July 1624) he married Charity, daughter and coheiress of Sir John Shirley of Isfield, Sussex. Their elder children were baptized at that parish, but those born after 1636 were baptized at Hamsey.[85] A former resident of Hamsey complained to Archbishop Laud in 1638 that Rivers had let the chapel at Combe fall into ruin and was preventing her from recovering a bell she had sent for use there. Sir John Lambe was appointed to examine the matter, but no other details appear.[86]

Rivers was a Sussex J.P.[87] and was in 1639 reported with Stapley and Hay as ringleaders among the puritan justices who were attempting to settle in the civil courts such church matters as the placement of communion tables.[88] He delayed paying his ship money on some Kentish estates in 1636,[89] and in 1639 joined his friends, Stapley and Sir Thomas Pelham, in declining to supply the king with funds for his northern journey.[90] He was a commissioner for the subsidy in 1640,[91] and was elected by Lewes to both parliaments of that year.[92] He won his seat despite the influence of Lord Goring and the Earl of Dorset in favor of less puritanical candidates.[93]

Taking his place with the reform group during the early months of the Long Parliament, Rivers was named to several committees, including one on the ministry,[94] and would perhaps have become a leader in opposition circles had death not cut short his career. He took the Protestation in May, but died at London, probably of

---

[69] S.P. 16, 427/38/vi.

[70] Cal. Com. Comp., 1729.

[71] H.M.C., Seventh Report, MSS of Sir H. Verney, Bart., 454.

[72] Clarendon, Rebellion 1: 78, 242. His Essex holdings included 75 manors, the majority of the advowsons, and control over three hundreds (Morant, Essex 2: 75, 84–85, passim; Wright, Essex 2: 55; Lansd. MSS, 459, fols. 114v–140); and by his first marriage, of which Lord Rich was the issue, he held an interest in various Hatton properties in the midlands (Northants MSS, Finch Hatton 1235).

[73] A London creditor asked recognition of his claim, dating back to about 1638, when Rich's composition case was being considered. Cal. Com. Comp., 1729, 1730.

[74] Al. Cant.

[75] Palatine notebook 3: 137–138, 1883.

[76] S.P. 16, 370/87; 383/56.

[77] Pink and Beaven, Parl. Rep. Lanc., 351, 352.

[78] A.H.R. 44: 31, n. (32), 1938–1939.

[79] Winthrop, Journal 2: 157.

[80] N. and Q., 1st Ser., 12: 359, 1855. A royalist writer doubted Rigby's statement that he advanced £2000 of his own money to help pay his soldiers. Harl. MSS, 2043 (Holme's collections), fol. 5.

[81] Sanford, St. and ill., 481.

[82] M. of P. 1: 494.

[83] Complete Baronetage 1: 169–170; S.P. 16/405.

[84] Al. Oxon.

[85] Add. MSS, 5697, fol. 261; 5698, fol. 57.

[86] C.S.P. Dom., 1638–1639, 53.

[87] C. 193/13; S.P. 16/405.

[88] C.S.P. Dom., 1639–1640, 386.

[89] S.P. 16, 319/90.

[90] Rushworth 3: 914. Rivers's father-in-law, Shirley, had opposed the 1627 loan. S.P. 16, 89/5.

[91] Sussex Arch. Coll. 9: 105, 1857.

[92] M. of P. 1: 483.

[93] C.S.P. Dom., 1639–1640, 387.

[94] C.J. 2: 54, 73.

the plague, on 8 June 1641.[95] He was buried at St. Bartholomew the Great. His will was dated on 2 June and was proved by his widow on 14 July 1641.[96]

Although Rivers's father was still living in 1640, he had had settled on him two manors and several farms in Kent which were worth several hundred pounds a year, and he held also a number of Sussex properties.[97] According to his will, his eldest daughter was to have a portion of £1000, including a legacy from her grandmother, his six younger daughters were to have £500 each, and his two younger sons, £300 each. He was evidently a man of considerable wealth and the heir apparent to even more.

Rivers's wife was a cousin of Henry Garton [98] (q.v.) and a relative by marriage of Sir Thomas Pelham. A sister of Rivers was the wife of Robert Goodwin, another puritan M.P.

Sir Edward Rodney (1590–1657), of Stoke Rodney and Pilton, Somerset, sat for Wells in 1640 but he was disabled, 12 August 1642. He was the eldest son and heir of Sir John Rodney (d. 1612) by his wife, Jane, daughter of Sir Henry Seymour.[99] His was an old family and his father, who was sheriff in Somerset in 1612, had inherited a large estate and married well, but the size of his family and the number of his lawsuits had reduced the family fortunes by the time Edward succeeded him. The latter was born at Pilton on 29 June 1590, attended Trowbridge Grammar School for six years with the younger generation of his mother's kinsmen, the Seymours, spent four years at Magdalen College, Oxford, and a short time at the Middle Temple. There, he recalled afterwards, "he only saluted the Law afar off and misspent his time." [100] He went to France with his cousin, William Seymour, after the latter's secret marriage with Arabella Stuart, but Seymour's grandfather seemed to disapprove of Rodney's influence and current lack of money, and he returned soon afterwards to England.[101] His father's death the next year brought him heavy responsibilities. In 1614 Rodney married at Denmark House one of the queen's ladies, Frances, daughter of Sir Robert Southwell of Woodrising, Norfolk. The king and queen were present, and the wedding was expensive to the bridegroom, but the bride's dower of £2000 and her social position and family connection with the Howards probably eased

his worries. King James knighted Rodney on this occasion,[102] and he returned presently to Somerset to take up a long career in public life.

From as early as 1617 Rodney was a J.P. in his shire,[103] and he served on numerous commissions, including that for the benevolence of 1626. In that work and in his duties as D.L. afterwards, Rodney defended the king's program on the grounds of necessity and defended his own actions in helping to execute the royal commands.[104] For many years also Rodney was a vice admiral.[105] He sat for Wells in the parliament of 1621 and regularly thereafter, except in 1628, when he served for the county.[106] He was apparently loyal to the crown, although he recognized the growing criticism of the Stuart policies. And in 1639 he was sufficiently out of sympathy with the court, influenced, perhaps, by his Seymour cousins, to excuse himself from contributing again toward the king's expenses.[107]

In the Long Parliament Rodney was named to some early committees of importance, such as those on monopolists and on Chamber's petition,[108] and he may have worked for some of the administrative reforms. But he disapproved of the attack on the king and at the outbreak of the war joined his cousin, the Marquis of Hertford, and was consequently disabled.[109] After enduring several periods of imprisonment he seems to have lived in retirement in Somerset, writing his memoirs and perhaps some essays on theological subjects.[110] He died at Stoke, 25 May 1657, having outlived his

---

[95] His epitaph refers to his death by "a disease malignant as the time." W. H. Beable, *Epitaphs, graveyard humor & eulogy*, 69, New York, Crowell, 1925.

[96] P.C.C., 86 Evelyn.

[97] I.P.M., James Rivers, C. 142/612/36.

[98] *Vis. Sussex, 1633–4*, 65.

[99] *Vis. Somerset*, 94.

[100] Rodney's memoir of his family, Add. MSS, 34,329, fol. 2–16. A considerable portion, if not all, of the memoir is printed in *Genealogist*, N.S., **16**: 207–214, 1900 and **17**: 6–12, 100–106, 1901. The date of his admission to the Temple was 1608. *Mid. Temp. Rec.* 2: 492.

[101] Add. MSS, 34,329, fol. 15; S.P. 14, 67/3.

[102] Add. MSS, 34,329, fols. 15v–16; *The letters of John Chamberlain* 1: 512. Chamberlain referred to Rodney at this time as having a good living, and Rodney noted in his memoirs that his inheritance was about £1000 a year. He was able later to increase his income (Add. MSS, 34,329, fol. 18). The dowry of one of his sisters was £1200 (*Ibid.*, fol. 14). The particular of Rodney's estate at the time of his compounding, showing only lands in Somerset worth some £355 a year, is apparently incomplete or an underestimate. The same properties were valued by Rodney in his memoirs at some £700 yearly (S.P. 23/177/578–585; Add. MSS, 34,239, fol. 4v). His assessment of £1200 in 1644 was reduced to £600 in 1645 (*Cal. Com. Adv. Money*, 432), but his compounding fine was £1200 (*Cal. Com. Comp.*, 916).

[103] *Quarter sessions records for the county of Somerset* 1: 195, *passim*.

[104] *C.S.P. Dom., 1625–1626*, 445; Add. MSS, 34,239, fols. 45–51; S.P. 16, 10/48. In the 1628 parliament Rodney defended against attacks by opposition leaders such as Phelipps the work of the D.L.'s. Rodney's speech of 28 March 1628 appears in a collection of speeches of this year in the John Rylands Library MSS, 522, fols. 59–60.

[105] *C.S.P. Dom., 1628–1629*, 501; Bates Harbin, *Members of Parliament, Somerset*, 146–147.

[106] *M. of P.* Rodney's speeches in his first parliament were unimportant. *Commons Debates 1621* 3: 217, 356.

[107] Rushworth 3: 912.

[108] *C.J.* 2: 31, 43.

[109] May, 226; *C.J.* 2: 716.

[110] In the volume with his memoirs are several essays on theology, possibly his own, which display a moderate Protestant outlook. Add. MSS, 34,329, fols. 21–79.

five sons.[111] His will, dated 24 May, was proved on 31 June 1657 by his widow.[112]

Rodney was a cousin of Sir Francis Seymour (*q.v.*) and a brother-in-law of John Trenchard, the Dorset puritan.

* **Sir Thomas Roe** (1581 ?–1644), of Gloucestershire and of Cranford, Middlesex, the ambassador and privy councillor, was M.P. for Oxford University, 1640–1644. He was greatly interested in matters of trade, not only as an official of the government, but as a private individual, and invested large sums in several trading and colonizing projects.[113] He was working in 1637 on plans for a development in the West Indies.[114] Roe was a J.P. in Middlesex in 1634.[115]

Sir Thomas offered his bond for £1000 for the November loan,[116] but was absent most of the time after May, 1641.[117] He seems to have been required as a royalist sympathizer to pay £300 to the parliamentary committees before his death,[118] but was still a member of parliament in January, 1644.[119]

Hugh Rogers (1622–1654 ?), of Cannington, Somerset, was a member for Calne in Wiltshire, 1640–1653. He was the only son of Sir Francis Rogers of Cannington (d. 1638) by his wife, Helena, daughter of Sir Hugh Smith of Long Ashton, and was born on 1 February 1622.[120] He matriculated at Hart Hall, Oxford, in 1637,[121] and in 1640 married Anne, daughter of Sir Edward Bayntun of Bromham (*q.v.*).[122] It was doubtless through the influence of the Bayntuns that he was elected for Calne to his first parliament in the autumn of 1640, when he was only eighteen. In his politics he apparently was guided by his father-in-law, for in 1643, after both had served with the parliamentary army, the elder Bayntun included his "son Rogers" in the overture he made to the king for pardon.[123] But Rogers

returned sooner than Bayntun to his early loyalties, taking the Covenant in September, 1643, and serving as a colonel for parliament and as a committeeman in Somerset. He may have been secluded in 1648, but was readmitted to the House in November, 1650, and kept his seat from then until the end.[124] He probably died shortly before March, 1654.[125] His wife, Anne Bayntun, seems to have died during the war, and sometime between 1646 and 1651 he married (Dorothy ?) the widow of his wealthy royalist cousin, Sir John Hele. He petitioned the compounding commissioners in the winter of 1651–1652 regarding the Devonshire manors which he claimed by right of that wife.[126]

Rogers inherited his father's ten manors in Somerset, two in Cornwall, and one in Wiltshire, in addition to other lands in Hampshire and Dorset. From an uncle who died in 1638 he inherited three other Somerset manors.[127] He may have been the "Mr. Rogers" who proffered security of £1000 for the loans of 1640 and 1641,[128] but the fact that he was not yet of age then makes it improbable.

Young Rogers was related to many families of note and to several of his fellow members in the Long Parliament besides the Bayntuns. On his mother's side were his uncle, Thomas Smith, an uncle by marriage, Sir Thomas Smith of Chester, and a great uncle, Theobald Gorges. Sir Francis Popham was a relative of the latter degree on his father's side. Alexander Popham was a cousin, and John Pyne, a second cousin. More distant connections by marriage included Phelipps and Poulett.

Richard Rogers (1611–1643), of Brianston, Dorset, was knight for his county, 1640–12 September 1642. He came of a family that had been active in the county for some generations and had intermarried with prominent western families. He was a grandson of Sir Richard Rogers of Brianston (d. 1604), and the second son of Sir John Rogers (M.P., d. 1613) by his second wife, Margaret, daughter of Sir Arthur Hopton, K.B., of Witham, Somerset. His father's sister, Honora, married Edward Seymour, Lord Beauchamp. Richard

---

[111] Collinson, *Somerset* 3 : 607.

[112] P.C.C., 282 Ruthen; Brown, *Somerset Wills* 6 : 67.

[113] Birch, *The court and times of Charles the First* 2 : 181; Brown, *Genesis of the U. S.*, 984–986.

[114] *C.S.P. Dom., 1637*, 429, 553.

[115] C. 193/13.

[116] D'Ewes (N), 51.

[117] R. B. Mowatt, The mission of Sir Thomas Roe to Vienna, 1641–2, *E.H.R.* **25** : 266–274, 1910.

[118] *Cal. Com. Adv. Money*, 302.

[119] *C.J.* **3** : 374.

[120] I.P.M., Sir Francis Rogers, C. 142/568/114; *Wilts. Arch. Mag.* **5** : 367, 1859; *Vis. Somerset*, 101.

[121] *Al. Oxon.*

[122] Some doubt has been expressed as to whether this marriage occurred so early. W. D. Pink suggested once that Rogers may have married Bayntun's daughter only after a royalist first husband, Sir John Hele, died (*Western Antiquary* **12** : 34, 1893). There is no evidence, however, that Lady Hele, who by 1652 was Rogers's wife, was a Bayntun. And in August, 1643, Sir Edward Bayntun mentioned his "son Rogers" in a letter (see below).

[123] *Calendar of Clarendon State Papers* 1 : 244; Wilts. Arch. Soc. MSS, Bayntun Commonplace Book, opp. fol. 1.

---

[124] *O.P.H.* **9** : 7; *Western Antiquary* **12** : 34, 1893; Thomason Tracts, E 454, 17; C. E. H. Chadwyck Healey, ed., *Hopton's narrative of the campaign in the west*, 5, n.; Pink MSS, 311, fol. 496c.

[125] Hugh Rogers acted as lord of one Somerset manor in 1651 and 1653, but another of the family performed the function in October, 1654 (Chadwyck Healey, *West Somerset*, 293). The estate of Hugh Rogers, deceased, is listed among the Dorset administrations granted in March, 1654. *Somerset and Dorset N. and Q.* **4** : 251, 1894–1895. See also *Western Antiquary* **12** : 34, 1893.

[126] *Ibid.; Cal. Com. Comp.*, 542, 2894. Occasional references to Rogers's wife as Dorothy (e.g. Pink MSS, 319) rather than Anne suggest that Dorothy may have been the name of his second wife.

[127] I.P.M. cited above; Chadwyck Healey, *West Somerset*, 293; Brown, *Somerset Wills* 2 : 91–92.

[128] D'Ewes (N), 52, 451, n.

was born about 6 August 1611 and in 1623, upon the death of his half-brother, Edward, became heir to the family estates.[129] He probably entered the Middle Temple in 1629.[130] About 1630 he paid £10 as composition for knighthood.[131] He married twice, his first wife being Elizabeth, only daughter and heir of Sir Justinian Lewin (d. 1620) of Otterden, Kent.[132] Her mother had married as her second husband in 1623 Rogers's kinsman, Sir Ralph Hopton of Somerset (q.v.).[133] His second wife, whom he married probably a short time before 1640, was Anne, daughter of Sir Thomas Cheeke of Essex (q.v.).[134]

After he came of age Rogers entered upon the responsibilities which his position in the county required. He was a J.P. and a member of various local commissions,[135] and was sheriff, 1636–1637. He showed himself diligent in carrying out the duties of the latter office, especially in the troublesome matter of ship money. By the end of his term, in spite of considerable resistance by such leaders as Sir Walter Erle and John Browne of Frampton, he had turned in all but some £400 of the £5000 levy, winning Lord Cottington's commendation as "a very good sheriff, and heartily affected to his Majesty's service." [136] But his marriage with a daughter of an eastern puritan who was a leader in the movement against the king perhaps explains the appearance of Rogers's name in the list of those who sent excuses instead of funds in reply to the king's loan request of 1639.[137] He may have been a D.L. by 1640.[138] Chosen by his county for the Short Parliament, he was possibly uncertain of re-election in the autumn, for he had himself made a freeman of Weymouth and Melcombe Regis on 29 September. However, he seems to have been re-elected by Dorset without difficulty.[139]

The role of Richard Rogers in the Long Parliament is difficult to follow, inasmuch as Hugh Rogers also was present. Since the latter was some ten years younger, however, and lacking in the experience in public office that the Dorset M.P. had had, it may be assumed that the "Mr. Rogers" of the Journals was usually Richard Rogers. He was probably the one who gave his bond for £1000 for the loan in November, 1640. And he may have been named to some of the early committees, such as that to consider the new canons, and that of May, 1641, regarding the disbanding of the army.[140] His later course seems to have been shaped less, however, by his wife's relatives of the Warwick faction, than by the example of his own first cousins, Sir Francis Seymour and the Marquis of Hertford,[141] or that other kinsman, Sir Ralph Hopton. In August, 1641, he fought a duel for some cause with Sir Edward Bayntun, one of the Wiltshire parliamentarians, in which he wounded Bayntun severely.[142] He was absent during the summer of 1642, and was suspended therefore on 2 September. Ten days later he was disabled for helping to raise forces to defend Sherborne Castle against parliament.[143] Rogers died in 1643 and was buried at Blandford near Brianston. His will, dated 2 and 29 May 1643, was proved on 23 September 1645 by his widow.[144] The latter afterward married her cousin, Robert Lord Rich, the third Earl of Warwick.[145]

Rogers was a man of wealth and influence. His inheritance included at least five manors and other holdings in Dorset and Somerset.[146] Besides some Kentish lands which he acquired through his first marriage, he probably had some in Hampshire and Essex with his second wife, and he owned at least one house in or near London. His lands in Somerset alone were worth over £200 a year, and his second wife's jointure was intended to be £800 a year.[147] That his estate was worth well over £1000 annually appears from a reference in his will to certain lands to be enjoyed by a male cousin, unless he managed to secure by entail land worth £1000 a year.[148] His legacy of £250 to the poor of Blandford indicates both his wealth and his generosity. Clarendon pictured him as "a gentleman of rare

---

[129] I.P.M., Sir John Rogers (1614), Wards 7/49/253; Brown, Somerset Wills 6: 20; Somerset and Dorset N. and Q. 2: 313, 1891; 8: 338–341, 1902–1903. Rogers must be distinguished from an uncle of the same name.

[130] The admission entry identifies him as the son and heir of Sir Richard Rogers of Brianston, Gloucestershire, deceased (Mid. Temp. Rec. 2: 759). By this time, Richard, son of Sir John, was heir to the estates of his grandfather, Sir Richard (d. 1604).

[131] Somerset and Dorset N. and Q. 4: 21, 1894–1895.

[132] This wife is not mentioned in the Dorset accounts of Rogers, but the descent of the manor of Otterden to Rogers and then to his daughter, Elizabeth, afterwards wife of the Duke of Lenox and Richmond, is attested by the list of Rogers's estates (S.P. 23/240/47–48) and by some of the family portraits. Hasted, Kent 5: 537; 6: 184; Arch. Cant. 11: 253, 1877.

[133] D.N.B., "Sir Ralph Hopton."

[134] Somerset and Dorset N. and Q. 8: 341, 1902–1903.

[135] C. 193/13; S.P. 16/405; C. 181/5, fols. 226, 304.

[136] C.S.P. Dom., 1636–1637, 419, 547; 1637, 400, 426.

[137] Rushworth 3: 912.

[138] The name appears perhaps by error as Sir Richard Rogers. C.S.P. Dom., 1640, 453.

[139] M. of P. 1: 481, 488; Moule, Catalogue of the . . . documents of the borough of Weymouth and Melcombe Regis, 113.

[140] D'Ewes (N), 52; C.J. 2: 52, 152.

[141] Clarendon referred to the intimacy between Rogers and Hertford. Rebellion 3: 77.

[142] The Nicholas papers, 5, Camden Society, 1886; Wilts. Arch. Soc. MSS, Bayntun Commonplace Book, cover.

[143] C.J. 2: 750, 762.

[144] P.C.C., 115 Rivers; Somerset and Dorset N. and Q. 8: 341, 1902–1903.

[145] Rogers's daughter, Elizabeth, married Charles, Viscount Mansfield (q.v.), and his other daughter, Rogersa, married the eldest son of John Belasyse (q.v.). Ibid.; Hasted, Kent 5: 537.

[146] I.P.M. cited above.

[147] Hasted, Kent 5: 537; 6: 184; Cal. Com. Comp., 2873–2874; S.P. 23/240/47–50; Rogers's will.

[148] The cousin afterwards declared that Richard had tried to deprive him of his title as rightful heir male to their grandfather's estates. Cal. Com. Comp., 2874.

temper and excellent understanding; . . . passionately inclined to advance the [king's] service," and one who "had a wonderful great influence upon the county of Dorset." [149]

Besides the relatives of Rogers already mentioned who sat with him in the 1640 parliament there was Sir John Strangways, whose daughter married Rogers's half-brother, Arthur Capel, a kinsman of his first wife, and the numerous members of the Cheeke connection.

* **John Rolle** (1598–1657), of London, merchant, was M.P. for Truro, Cornwall, 1640–1648 (?).[150] A Devonshire man by birth and a Londoner by residence, Rolle had sat for Cornish boroughs in three earlier parliaments. He had won considerable notice by his stand against tonnage and poundage, having had £5000 worth of goods taken by the collectors when he refused to pay.[151] He married, possibly after 1640, Alice, daughter of Sir George Chudleigh, Bart., of Ashton, Devon, and had by her two sons who were not of age in 1657.[152] He was a brother of Sir Samuel Rolle, a brother-in-law of Alexander Carew, and a cousin of Sir Thomas Hele, all fellow M.P.'s in 1640.

In the Long Parliament John Rolle was named to various committees dealing with ecclesiastical reforms, as well as to ones concerned with grievances such as his own.[153] He pledged £100 for the defense in June, 1642.[154] He was probably secluded from parliament by Colonel Pride.[155] By the time he made his will in 1657 he owned a mansion at Widdecombe in Devon and had recovered sufficient wealth to plan portions of £2600 for each of his two sons and other legacies of over £750. He possessed also some lands in Ireland and merchandise "beyond the seas." He died probably late in 1657, for his will, dated 21 November of that year, was proved by his executors on 13 January 1657/8.

Sir Samuel Rolle (c. 1588–1647), of Heanton Sackville in Petrockstow, Devon, sat for Devon from the spring of 1641 until his death in 1647.[156] He was the eldest son and heir of Robert Rolle of Heanton (d. 1633), by Joan, daughter of Thomas Hele of Fleet, and was the brother of John Rolle, the merchant and M.P., and of Henry Rolle, the judge. He was a cousin of Sir Thomas Hele (q.v.). Samuel was born about 1588,[157] matriculated at Exeter College, Oxford, in 1605, and entered the Inner Temple in 1609.[158] His first wife is said to have been Mary, daughter and coheir of Sir Edward Stradling of Somerset.[159] In 1620, following a settlement arranged in 1618, Rolle married Margaret, daughter of Sir Thomas Wise, K.B., who brought him a marriage portion of £2500.[160] He was knighted at Wimbledon the following year. He and his father-in-law were called before Council in 1622, but were released when it was found there was no case against them.[161] He lived at Insworth in Cornwall for a time,[162] and in 1633 succeeded to the large estates of his family. He was a J.P. in both Devon and Cornwall,[163] and a member of the piracy commisssion of both shires.[164]

Sir Samuel was M.P. for Grampound in 1625, but did not sit again until 1640. In the meantime occurred his brother Henry's work in parliament against Buckingham and his brother John's celebrated tonnage and poundage case. Samuel was concerned in the interim with restoring the prosperity of his borough of Callington, a market town for the yarn trade, and was reported by a contemporary to have brought it back to a thriving condition.[165] He was one of the 1639 loan refusers,[166] and was elected to the Short Parliament for Callington. Rolle joined with other Devon leaders in drawing up the petition against Coryton and the Stannaries shortly before the Long Parliament was summoned,[167] and helped to elect his brother-in-law, Thomas Wise, as one of the county knights in October.[168] Why he himself

---

[149] *Rebellion* **3**: 77.

[150] Rolle did not die in 1648, as is stated in *D.N.B.* and elsewhere. The authority for that statement is the reference of J. L. Vivian (*The visitations of the county of Devon*, 654, Exeter, 1895) to an entry in the parish register of Petrockstowe recording the burial on 18 November 1648 of John Rolle. Whether the entry referred to another of the name or whether Vivian made a mistake in recording the date, it is impossible to say. The will of John Rolle of London, merchant, which, on the basis of internal evidence, must be that of the M.P., was not written until 21 November 1657 (P.C.C., 3 Wotton). Petrockstowe parish was mentioned therein for one of Rolle's charitable bequests. Possibly the John Rolle buried in 1648 was a son. His surviving sons, George and Robert, were the only children named in his will, and none of them appears in the printed pedigrees.

[151] *Commons Debates for 1629*, 9, n.

[152] Harl. MSS, 6861, fol. 10; *Western Antiquary* **1**: 97, 1881–1882; Rolle's will. This corrects the statement in *D.N.B.* that Rolle died unmarried.

[153] Pink counted 73 committee appointments for Rolle, 1640–1648, the last occurring on 20 July 1648. Pink MSS, 307, fol. 300.

[154] *N. and Q.*, 1st Ser., **12**: 358, 1855.

[155] The list of members in *O.P.H.* (**9**: *19), however, gives no indication that Rolle did not sit until the end of the parliament.

[156] He was elected after Wise's death and was named to a committee on 27 April. *C.J.* **2**: 128.

[157] He was aged 15 when he entered Oxford (*Al. Oxon.*), but was said to be forty-five and more in 1633. I.P.M., Robert Rolle, C. 142/502/65.

[158] *Students admitted to the Inner Temple*, 183.

[159] Pink MSS, 307, fol. 338.

[160] I.P.M. cited above.

[161] *Acts. P.C., 1621–1623*, 349, 357.

[162] Plymouth Inst. *Trans.* **9**: 65, 1884–1887; *H.M.C., Ninth Report* **1**: MSS of the Corporation of Plymouth, 283; *Note book of Tristram Risdon*, 183.

[163] C. 193/13; S.P. 16/405; Devonshire MSS, Quarter Sessions Minute Books, 1633–1640.

[164] C. 181/3, fols. 113, 130; 181/4, fol. 52v; 181/5, fol. 264.

[165] C. S. Gilbert, *A historical survey of Cornwall* **2**: 469.

[166] Rushworth **3**: 913.

[167] *The Buller papers*, 137, 139.

[168] Devon indenture, C. 219/43/Part 1.

was not returned in the original elections of the fall is not clear. He apparently sought the Beeralston seat that was vacated in November, but was defeated by Pollard.[169] He hoped next for a vacancy to occur at some other Devon or Cornwall borough,[170] and finally stepped into the county seat vacated by his brother-in-law's death.

Rolle entered into action immediately with the reform group. Among the committees to which he was appointed were those on the disarming of recusants, the impeaching of the bishops, and the Remonstrance. He was named in 1642 to the Guildhall Committee of Safety and to the Devonshire committee on scandalous ministers.[171] In June of that year he made one of the largest offers by an individual member in promising to maintain twelve horses for the defense.[172] He advanced £1000, his personal subscription, for reducing Ireland,[173] and worked vigorously for the cause of parliament in his county until illness incapacitated him. He died in December, 1647. His will, dated 2 March and 10 May 1647, was proved by his brothers, John and Henry, on 10 April 1648.[174]

Rolle inherited extensive lands in Devon, Cornwall, and Somerset, including some dozen manors and interests in such towns as Saltash, Liskeard, Callington, and St. Germans.[175] His wife, Margaret, brought him a handsome dowry and he purchased additional lands, including three more manors in Devon. When he made his will he planned portions of £1000 each for five younger children, and larger amounts for an elder daughter and for his heir, Robert Rolle.[176] His generous subscriptions for the cause of parliament were not out of proportion to his means.

Relatives of Sir Samuel who were his fellows in the Long Parliament, besides his brother, John, were the Bullers, who were connections by marriage. His cousin, Hele, and his brother-in-law, Alexander Carew, were his kinsmen who turned to the king.[177]

Richard Rose (d. 1655 ?), of Lyme Regis and of Wotton Fitzpaine, Dorset, a merchant, represented

Lyme Regis, 1640–1648 (?).[178] He was the son and heir of John Rose, who came from Jersey and was mayor of Lyme in 1611, by his wife, Faith Ellesdon.[179] He may have been graduated M.A. from Exeter College, Oxford, in 1621, and have entered the Middle Temple in 1622.[180] But before 1626 he married Elizabeth, daughter of Henry Henley of Leigh, Somerset. His eldest son, John, one of ten children, was born at Leigh that year.[181] Rose seems to have taken over his father's business in Lyme, gaining some prominence as a merchant and a town official. On 22 August 1631 he was sworn a freeman and made a capital burgess, or council member, and in 1633–1634 he served as mayor.[182] In business he was associated with his wife's brother-in-law, John Hayne, an Exeter merchant.[183] He was summoned before the commissioners for knighthood in 1632,[184] and presumably paid his composition. Several years later it was reported to Council that Rose, a J.P. of Lyme, had been outspoken against the heavy taxation for maintaining the king's titles and honors, declaring that he himself was already £10 the worse for it. It was decided, however, not to press action against Rose for his words.[185]

Rose was possibly a candidate for one of Lyme's places in the Short Parliament, but it is doubtful whether he sat.[186] After his election in the autumn, however, he became an active member. He was named to such early committees as the subcommittee on religion, those on customs and patents and on the Bishop of Ely.[187] He apparently did not contribute heavily in money for the cause of parliament, but after the war began he was active in the west, especially in the siege of Lyme, and won the approval of both borough and parliament.[188] The last reference to him in the House occurred within a month of Pride's Purge, and he was

---

[169] Among the Buller papers is an indenture dated 19 November 1640, the date of Pollard's election, which states that Rolle was that day elected for Beeralston; but the indenture was never signed by the sheriff or sent in. It was probably one of the "blanks" prepared ahead of time and not used. *The Buller Papers*, 28–29.

[170] He hoped particularly for "Lidford" (Liskeard?), Newport, or Okehampton. *Ibid.*, 31, 34.

[171] *C.J.* 2: 128, 136, 230, 235, 349, 369; Pink MSS, 307, fols. 337–338.

[172] *N. and Q.*, 1st Ser., 12: 338, 1855.

[173] *C.S.P. Ireland, Adventurers*, 30; Rolle's will.

[174] P.C.C., 58 Essex. See also a brief sketch of Rolle in Devon *Trans.*, 48: 332, 1916.

[175] I.P.M. cited above.

[176] Rolle's will.

[177] In addition to the above authorities see *M. of P.*

[178] *M. of P.* 1: 488; *Somerset and Dorset N. and Q.* 3: 112, 1892–1893.

[179] *Ibid.* 10: 280, 1906–1907.

[180] *Al. Oxon.* I have been able to find no reference to his admission to the Middle Temple or to the Inner Temple in the published records of the inns. His own son, Richard, entered Lincoln's Inn in 1659. *Linc. Inn Rec. Adm.* 1: 280.

[181] *Somerset and Dorset N. and Q.* 10: 280, 1906–1907; G. Roberts, *The history of Lyme Regis*, 157, Sherborne, 1823.

[182] Notes from Lyme Borough MSS supplied by Mr. Cyril Wanklyn of Overton, Lyme Regis.

[183] Hayne possibly acted as Rose's agent. Devon *Trans.* 33: 198–199, 253, 1901; Exeter City MSS, Hayne's Account Book, fol. 2.

[184] *Somerset and Dorset N. and Q.* 4: 19, 1894–1895.

[185] S.P. 16, 370/1; *C.S.P. Dom.*, 1637, 481.

[186] There seems to have been a double return, Rose being named in one of them (Hutchins, *Dorset* 2: 52; Willis 3: 231). This may have been one of the cases of blank indentures referred to in connection with Sir Walter Erle's return (*C.J.* 2: 14), but no record of a decision remains.

[187] *C.J.* 2: 54, 55, 56.

[188] Notes supplied by Mr. Wanklyn; *Somerset and Dorset N. and Q.* 3: 112, 1892–1893. Rose was absent at the time of the subscriptions of June, 1642. *C.J.* 2: 626.

perhaps secluded then.[189] He returned to Dorset, where he was living in January, 1652.[190] He was ill at the time he wrote his will, 31 October 1655, and it was proved on 19 February 1658.[191]

Although Rose was charged by the royalist writers with plundering the malignants to round out his own estates,[192] he was probably a prosperous merchant in 1640. Various houses in Lyme and Ware, a fulling mill, and possibly the estate of Wotton Fitzpaine were presumably his before the war. His plan in 1655 to provide dowries of £1000 each for his three younger daughters and £1100 for the eldest shows a considerable accumulation of wealth either before 1640 or during the war.[193]

* Francis Rous (1579–1659), of Landrake, Cornwall, M.P. for Truro, 1640–1653, was the puritan writer, already known for his attacks on leading churchmen in the parliament of 1628–1629.[194] He was a half-brother of John Pym and was related by the half-blood and by marriage to John Upton and Anthony Nicoll. Rous seems to have been not particularly active in county affairs, although he sat in three parliaments before the Long Parliament.

* Sir Benjamin Rudyard (1572–1658), lawyer and royal official, was M.P. for Wilton, 1640–1648. He probably owed his election to the Earl of Pembroke, having been elected to six previous parliaments under the Herbert patronage.[195] The younger son of a Hampshire family, he lived in Berkshire and at the court most of his life. He was educated at the New Inn and the Middle Temple.[196] His attainments in letters and politics are well known.

Besides serving as Surveyor of the Court of Wards from 1618 to 1647, Rudyard tried unsuccessfully to secure the mastership of that court in 1624.[197] In 1619 he was granted an annuity of £200, a pension which was still being paid, apparently, at the time of the Long Parliament.[198] He received other grants, also, by virtue of his connections, but in turn contributed from his pocket to the king's accounts. The loan required of him and which he paid in 1640, for example, was £500.[199] This was five times the figure of his offer for the cause of parliament two years later.[200] Sir Benjamin served in

humbler posts as well as in greater ones, being named several times as a J.P. and a commissioner for other functions in Surrey, London, Middlesex, and the Isle of Wight.[201]

John Russell (c. 1620–1687), of London and Cambridgeshire, succeeded his elder brother, William Lord Russell, as M.P. for the family borough of Tavistock, Devon, on 17 June 1641. He was disabled for royalism, 22 January 1644.[202] The third son of Francis, fourth Earl of Bedford (d. 1641), he matriculated at Magdalen Hall, Oxford, on 6 July 1634, aged fourteen.[203] Perhaps he travelled abroad as his older brother did and as his younger brother was licensed to do in 1640.[204] Nothing else of his early life is known. He seems to have done little to distinguish himself in the Long Parliament except to act as teller for the "Noes" for a division during the debate on printing the Remonstrance, 15 December 1641.[205] He opposed parliament during the war, serving as a colonel in the king's forces, but was permitted in 1646 to compound for his estates. He died unmarried in 1687.[206]

Russell came into his share of his father's ample estate shortly after his election to parliament, the bill for the settling of the estate being passed by the House in July, 1641.[207] His part, consisting of lands in Cambridgeshire and Bedfordshire and some of the Covent Garden houses, was worth at least £970 a year. Russell's fine, set first at a moiety, £7000, was reduced to a tenth, £2204.[208] For his relatives in the House, see William Lord Russell.

* William Lord Russell, K.B. (1613–1700), heir apparent of Francis, Earl of Bedford, was M.P. for Tavistock, 1640–9 May 1641. His service in the Commons ended when his father's death brought his succession to the earldom and to a seat in the Upper House.[209] He was educated at Oxford and at Lincoln's Inn, but left each without a degree.[210] He travelled abroad for a time, returning in 1634 "much bettered by his travels," as his Oxford friend, Ralph Verney, noted. He was disappointed two years later by the refusal of the Earl of Arundel to take him on his mission to the emperor.[211] His marriage with the daughter of the Earl of Somerset occurred in 1637, and from 1638 until

[189] *Somerset and Dorset N. and Q.* **3**: 112, 1892–1893.

[190] *Cal. Com. Comp.*, 523, 581.

[191] P.C.C., 82 Wotton.

[192] Noble, *Regicides* **2**: 281; Mayo, *The minute books of the Dorset standing committee*, 125.

[193] Rose's will cited above.

[194] *Commons Debates for 1629*, 12–14, 37, 109; *D.N.B.*

[195] *E.H.R.* **50**: 242, 1935; *D.N.B.*

[196] Ingpen, *The Middle Temple bench book*, 181. *D.N.B.* gives the Inner Temple as his inn.

[197] *C.S.P. Dom., 1623–1625*, 292.

[198] *C.S.P. Dom., 1619–1623*, 63; S.P. 16, 180/17/54; 478/4.

[199] *C.S.P. Dom., 1603–1610*, 491; S.P. 16, 446/42; 453/74.

[200] *N. and Q.*, 1st Ser., **12**: 338, 1855.

[201] C. 193/12, 13; S.P. 16/405; C. 181/4, fol. 89.

[202] *M. of P.* **1**: 488; *C.J.* **3**: 374.

[203] *Al. Oxon.*

[204] *C.S.P. Dom., 1639–1640*, 493.

[205] *C.J.* **2**: 344; D'Ewes (C), 295.

[206] 1681 is given as the date of Russell's death in *Al. Oxon.* and in Pink MSS, 311, but 1687 is the date in Lipscomb, *Buckingham* (3: 249), and the brief reference to John Russell in the article on his father in *D.N.B.*

[207] *C.J.* **2**: 204, 211, 217.

[208] S.P. 23/188/135, 155–159; *Cal. Com. Comp.*, 1208–1209.

[209] A new election was ordered on 24 May 1641. *C.J.* **2**: 155.

[210] *Verney Papers*, 150; *Linc. Inn Rec. Adm.* **1**: 210.

[211] *Verney Papers*, 159, 170.

1640 Lord Russell shared with his father the lord lieutenancy of Devon.[212]   He was elected to both of the 1640 parliaments for Tavistock, a borough of which his father held the barony.[213]   His chief work during his brief service in the Commons of the Long Parliament was with one of the grievance committees and in conferences with the Lords.[214]   He worked with the faction of the parliamentarians until the summer of 1643.

Russell's father was described by Clarendon as the man of best estate and best understanding in the popular party,[215] and the family's lands were distributed in the Midlands and in Wilts and Devon.[216]   After his marriage his father allowed him £2000 a year, and his income from the family properties for the first year after his accession to the earldom was £8500.[217]

Lord Russell had several kinsmen in the 1640 House, the closest being his brother-in-law, Lord Digby. His brother, John, succeeded to his seat for Tavistock. Newport became his brother-in-law later.

Sir Beauchamp St. John (fl. 1610–1667), of Tillbrook, Bedfordshire, member for Bedford borough, 1640–1648, was a brother of the first Earl of Bolingbroke, being the seventh born son of Oliver, third Baron St. John of Bletsoe (d. 1618), by his wife, Dorothy, daughter of John Read of Bodington, Gloucestershire. His family owned extensive lands in the counties of Bedford and Huntingdon, but were in somewhat straightened circumstances by 1640. Beauchamp, who was named for the ancestress who had brought the Bletsoe estate into the family,[1] was born probably about 1590 or 1595, was admitted to Queen's College, Cambridge, 9 March 1610, and made M.A. there on the occasion of the king's visit in 1613. In May of that year he was admitted to Lincoln's Inn,[2] and about five months later he married Rebecca, daughter of William Hawkins of Tillbrook. The latter estate passed to St. John in 1625 and remained in his hands even after his lady's death in 1631. He was knighted, with his brother, Henry, at Bletsoe on 24 July 1619,[3] and be-

fore 1640 acquired in his own name interest in several properties in Bedfordshire and Huntingdonshire.[4]

Sir Beauchamp sat for Bedfordshire in the Parliament of 1621, and for Bedford borough in 1626, 1628, and in the Short Parliament.[5]   He served as a J.P. for both county and borough, and in Huntingdonshire, also, and was a sewers commissioner in both shires.[6]   With his cousin, Sir Oliver Luke (q.v.), he was named a commissioner for the enforced loan, and imprisoned in 1627 for refusing to lend.[7]   No doubt he approved the stand of his brother, Bolingbroke, against paying ship money in 1637,[8] and of the arguments of his kinsman, Oliver St. John (q.v.), in Hampden's case, for he belonged to the forces of the opposition.

St. John's local popularity is attested by his return for Bedford to both parliaments of 1640, apparently without a rival, although the second place was contested each time. He was named to several committees dealing with grievances and with the church,[9] promised two horses for the defense in 1642,[10] and was a parliamentary committeeman during the war, but was secluded by Pride's Purge. He returned with the secluded members in February, 1660, and lived for some years thereafter.[11]   His will was dated at Leicester in 1667, and he probably died about that time.[12]

* Oliver St. John (c. 1598–1673), of Lincoln's Inn, Solicitor to the King (1641), was M.P. for Totness in Devon, 1640–1653. He had sat for the borough in the Short Parliament, owing his elections probably to the Earl of Bedford, his client and relative.[13]   A descendant of the Bedfordshire St. Johns, he seems to have had no other connection with Devon.

St. John was related to the Cromwell-Barrington clan through both of his wives. After his first marriage in 1630 with Sir Thomas Barrington's niece, a stepdaughter of Sir William Masham (q.v.), he lived for a time in the Masham household in Essex.[14]   The Earl of Bedford had interceded with the Barrington family in arranging for the match, but there was some hesitation on the part of the lady's relatives because St. John's estate was so small, possibly being as low as £200 a

---

[212] C.S.P. Dom., 1638–1639, 365; 1640, 202, passim.
[213] M. of P. 1: 481, 488; Devon Trans. 43: 371, 1911; Pole, Descr. of Devon, 33.
[214] C.J. 2: 43, 60, 90; D'Ewes (N), 387.
[215] Rebellion 1: 333.
[216] Lysons, Mag. Brit. 1: 14, 152–154, 584–585; Lipscomb, Buckingham 3: 250; Exeter City Library MSS, Exeter Deeds and Documents, No. 1876.
[217] Gladys Scott Thomson, Life in a noble household, 30–31, 45–46, London, J. Cope, 1936.
[1] Lysons, Mag. Brit. 1: 58, 69, 83, 102, passim. Clarendon referred to the Earl of Bolingbroke's family as "decayed" (Rebellion 2: 369), and in 1639 a group of his son's creditors declared he owed them £5900. C.S.P. Dom., 1639–1640, 40.
[2] Al. Cant.; Linc. Inn Rec. Adm. 1: 162.
[3] Beds. N. and Q. 1: 211, 216, 1886; Blaydes, Genealogia Bedfordiensis, 291; V.C.H. Bedford 3: 172. It is pointed out in Al. Cant. that some writers have confused the date of Sir Beauchamp's death with that of his wife.

[4] V.C.H. Bedford 3: 163; Add. MSS, 34,401, fol. 73. His father had been Lord Lieutenant of Huntingdonshire, 1596–1618 (V.C.H. Huntingdonshire 2: 23).
[5] M. of P. 1: 450, 468, 474, 480.
[6] C. 193/12 and 13; S.P. 16, 186/92/i, fol. 189; C. 181/5, fols. 18, 74.
[7] C.S.P. Dom., 1627–1628, 44; Rushworth 1: 473.
[8] Eg. MSS, 807, fol. 67v.
[9] C.J. 2: 43, 129; Pink MSS, 307, fol. 7.
[10] N. and Q., 1st Ser., 12: 359, 1855.
[11] Pink MSS, 307, fol. 7; H.M.C., Seventh Report, MSS of G. A. Lowndes, Esq., 554.
[12] References in addition to those cited above are: Burke, Extinct Peerage, 467; Vis. Beds., 194.
[13] The Earl termed him a cousin in 1630. Eg. MSS, 2645, fol. 186.
[14] Ibid., fols. 154, 186, 196, 237; Sanford, St. and ill., 220, 257, 258; Abbott, Cromwell 1: 96 and n.

year, and because he was then involved in heavy expenses of possibly £500 a year.[15] The latter were the result, presumably, of his difficulties in Star Chamber and his imprisonment the year before in connection with the "seditious" document he found in Sir Robert Cotton's library.[16] Although his practice increased after his part in Hampden's ship money case,[17] he was described by the royalist writers as of slender fortune,[18] and certainly he was not one of the wealthy parliament men. He is said to have been a man of great reserve, "of a dark and clouded countenance, very proud, and conversant with few but those of his own humour and inclination."[19]

* **Richard Sackville, Lord Buckhurst** (1622–1677) was returned for two Sussex boroughs in October, 1640. The House seems to have been willing to recognize Steyning as his borough in February, 1641, but Farnefold and Leedes were the men who served for that town; and Buckhurst had already been recognized on 16 November 1640, for East Grinstead,[20] a borough where his family long had influence. His successor in parliament was returned for the latter town in 1645.[21] Buckhurst was disabled for royalism, 5 February 1643/4.[22]

The eldest son of Edward, fourth Earl of Dorset (d. 1652), young Lord Buckhurst seems to have had no political experience before the 1640 elections. His most conspicuous act in the Long Parliament probably was his vote against the attainder of Strafford,[23] and his arrest in 1642 for royalist activity no doubt marked the end of his connection with the House, even though the vote for his disablement had not occurred.

Buckhurst was the heir apparent to large estates in Kent, Surrey, and Sussex, although the family fortunes had been considered impaired by his uncle, the third earl.[24] His mother's portion was said to have brought £1000 a year to the family, however,[25] and his own marriage in 1637 with the daughter of the Earl of Middlesex improved his fortunes.[26] His father was assessed £5000 by the parliamentarians in 1644,[27] and his own fine for royalism was £1500.

Peter Sainthill (1593–1648), of Bradninch, Devon, was M.P. for Tiverton, 1640–22 January 1644. The

third of his name in as many generations, he was the eldest son of Peter Sainthill (d. 1618) and Elizabeth, daughter of Thomas Martin, D.C.L., of Steeple Morden, Cambridgeshire. He was born at Bradninch in July, 1593, was educated at Blundell's School in Tiverton and at Oriel College, Oxford, and in December, 1611, entered the Middle Temple. He kept a chamber there at least until 1615,[28] and, though he apparently was not called to the bar, built up a legal practice in his native county. In 1614 he married Dorothy, daughter and heiress of Robert Packer (Parker?) of Foldhay in Devon.[29] Four years later he succeeded to his family estates.

Sainthill was commissioned by the city of Exeter in 1631 to represent it in a case in Chancery,[30] and he was listed in 1634 as a Master in Chancery.[31] He seems to have occupied a London house in 1638.[32] He was recorder for Bradninch borough, 1632–1637, and served faithfully as a J.P. in the county for some years before 1640.[33] He was a member of the commission on exacted fees in 1638.[34] Sainthill was by this time an opponent of some of the Stuart policies as they affected his county. He or his agent was accused of encouraging some Exeter soap manufacturers to resist the collecting of increased duties on their soap about 1638, although £300 had recently been awarded to Sainthill for his efforts to make the heavier duties effective.[35] He was reported in 1639 to be in arrears for a small amount of ship money under the 1637 writ,[36] and in the same year he ignored the king's loan request.[37]

Elected to both parliaments of 1640 for Tiverton, Sainthill was at first inclined toward the popular side. But he was never a prominent member and probably withdrew from the House as the more radical element gained strength. He sat in the king's parliament at Oxford, supported the king actively in Devon, was disabled early in 1644,[38] and later in the year was particularly disabled by parliament's orders from further office holding. He joined his merchant brother, Robert, in Tuscany in 1646, and from there petitioned about his sequestered estates. He died abroad, however, on 12 August 1648 at Leghorn, and was buried afterwards at Bradninch.[39]

A family document states that Sainthill was possessed of large property and that he lent liberally to the royal

[15] Eg. MSS, 2645, fols. 120, 126, 154, 170, 186.

[16] Gardiner, H. of E. 7: 139–140; D.N.B.

[17] D.N.B.; Clarendon, Rebellion 1: 246.

[18] The mystery of the good old cause, 23.

[19] Sir John Percival's description. Add. MSS, 27,990, fol. 46.

[20] C.J. 2: 30, 86; D'Ewes (N), 361; D'Ewes (C), 60, n.

[21] M. of P. 1: 494, 495 and notes; C.J. 4: 272.

[22] C.J. 3: 389.

[23] Verney, 58.

[24] Hasted, Kent 3: 43, 71, 291; Sussex Arch. Coll. 4: 57–58, 1851; Sussex Rec. Soc. 4: 12–16, 1905.

[25] The letters of John Chamberlain 2: 466.

[26] H.M.C., Cal. of MSS of Lord Sackville at Knole 1: xiv.

[27] Cal. Com. Adv. Money, 398.

[28] Al. Oxon.; Mid. Temp. Rec. 2: 544, 597.

[29] I.P.M., Peter Sainthill (1618), C. 142/370/75.

[30] Exeter Corporation MSS, Act Book 7, fol. 785.

[31] He was so listed in one of the Devonshire commissions of the peace. C. 193/13.

[32] Dale, Inhabitants of London, 19.

[33] C. 193/13; S.P. 16/405; Devonshire MSS, Quarter Sessions Minute Books, 1633–1640.

[34] C. 181/5, fol. 218.

[35] C.S.P. Dom., 1637–1638, 203; 1638–1639, 240.

[36] S.P. 16, 435/33/i.

[37] Rushworth 3: 913.

[38] C.J. 3: 374; O.P.H. 9: *25.

[39] Harding MSS (North Devon Athenaeum, Barnstaple), No. 91, Part 17, notes on Bradninch parish.

cause. According to his compounding papers he enjoyed before the war an annual net income of some £513 from lands in Devon, Warwickshire and Yorkshire, but he asked for allowance for nearly £1200 in debts. In addition to his income from lands, of course, were his lawyer's fees. His fine for royalism, reduced from £749 to £584, was paid by his son.[40]

Sainthill was said to be "of a courteous and affable disposition; charitable, and of such unaffected simplicity of manners, that he secured the esteem of all, and gained universal confidence by his integrity." [41]

John Salisbury, or **Salusbury** (fl. 1640–1644), "junior, Esquire," was M.P. for Flint borough from 1640 until 5 February 1644.[42] He was one of a family which had been active in Denbighshire politics for several generations,[43] and came from a cadet branch of the Llewenny line of the family, being a cousin of the baronets.[44] The 1640 M.P. has been identified by Williams with the one who sat for Flint in 1626. The latter was John, son of Roger Salisbury of Bachegraig, county Flint, by his wife, Catherine, daughter of Sir Richard Clough, and was said to have died at a great age in 1685.[45] The appellation of "junior," however, suggests that the Long Parliament member was rather the son of the 1626 M.P. by his wife, Elizabeth, daughter of Thomas Ravenscroft.[46] The son was admitted to Gray's Inn on 14 August 1640.[47]

John Salisbury, junior, represented Denbigh borough in the Short Parliament, his cousin, Sir Thomas Salisbury, Bart., the poet, sitting for Denbighshire.[48] In the Long Parliament John Salisbury was not an important member. He was present to take the Protestation in May, 1641,[49] but he joined the king during the war. In October, 1644, Simon Thelwell was attempting to moderate the feeling of the House toward "Jack Salisburie," who had been put out.[50] He may have been the

one of his name who in 1660 was nominated for the Knights of the Royal Oak.[51]

The younger John Salisbury of Bachegraig married (1) Elizabeth, daughter of Sir William Norreys of Speke; and (2) Judith, daughter of Thomas Whichcote and relict of Henry Bowes.[52] His family seem to have been on terms of intimacy with the Wynns of Gwydir and the Middletons of Chirk Castle.[53]

* Humphrey Salway (1575 ?–1652), of Stanford, Worcestershire, was chosen by a strong majority as M.P. for his county, 21 October 1640, and sat until his death.[54] The eldest son and heir of Arthur Salway of Stanford, an official of the Exchequer, he was himself prominent in the county. He was a J.P.[55] and had served on several special commissions concerned with shire affairs and with the River Avon.[56] He was a man of some means, and joined with another member in March, 1641, to pledge £1000 for the loan.[57] He promised a horse and maintenance for the defense in June, 1642,[58] and was a strong parliamentarian.[59]

Salway was an uncle of Sir Edward Littleton, M.P. for Staffordshire, and was related also to Richard Knightley (q.v.).

Samuel Sandys (1615–1685), of Ombersley, Worcestershire, was M.P. for Droitwich, 1640–20 August 1642. He was a great-grandson of Edwin Sandys, Bishop of Worcester and Archbishop of York and a grandnephew of Sir Edwin Sandys of Virginia Company fame and of others of that illustrious family.[60] His grandfather, Sir Samuel Sandys (d. 1623), was twice M.P. for the county, opposed the jurisdiction of the Council of the Marches, and in the 1621 parliament worked with the country party.[61] Samuel, the 1640 M.P., was the son of Sir Edwin Sandys of Ombersley (M.P., d. 1623) by his wife, Penelope, daughter of Sir Richard Bulkeley of Beaumaris. He was born in June, 1615,[62] and was probably married by 1640,[63] but of his early life nothing else is known. He sat for Droitwich in the Short Parliament, his first. Sandys was probably the "Mr. Sandes" who pledged £1000 for the loan in

---

[40] S.P. 23/222/797–799; *Cal. Com. Comp.*, 1391–1392.

[41] Devon *Trans.* **21**: 402–403, 1889. Other authorities in addition to those previously cited are Devon *Trans.* **67**: 322–323, 1935; *M. of P.; Vis Devon, 1620*, 249.

[42] *M. of P.* **1**: 498; *C.J.* **3**: 389.

[43] *E.H.R.* **46**: 212, 218–220, 1931.

[44] The John Salisbury who afterwards was a baronet in that line was too young to have been the M.P. His elder brother, Thomas, the third baronet, was born in 1634. *D.N.B.,* "Sir Thomas Salisbury."

[45] Williams, *Parl. Hist. Wales,* 81.

[46] This seems to be the identification accepted by J. Y. W. Lloyd in his pedigree of the family. *The history of Powys Fadog* **4**: 336–338, London, 1881–1887.

[47] *Gray's Inn Adm. Reg.,* 227.

[48] Willis **3**: 239. Only the name of the county member appears in *M. of P.* (**1**: 484). By error Sir Thomas Salisbury is said in *D.N.B.* to have remained a member until 1643.

[49] The name appears in the list (*C.J.* **2**: 133) as Sir John Salisbury, perhaps because the clerk confused him with his kinsman of the Short Parliament, or with the knight whose name proceeded his in the list.

[50] *Montgomeryshire Collections* **31**: 110, 1899.

[51] Williams, *loc. cit.*

[52] Lloyd, *The history of Powys Fadog* **4**: 338.

[53] *Cal. Wynn Papers,* 19, 37, 63, 114–115, 347, 388, *passim.*

[54] D'Ewes (N), 440–442, 461–463, 492.

[55] C. 193/12, 13.

[56] C. 181/3, fol. 114; 181/4, fol. 18.

[57] D'Ewes (N), 438, n.

[58] *N. and Q.,* 1st Ser., **12**: 360, 1855.

[59] Williams, *Worcester,* 42–43.

[60] Brown, *Genesis of the U. S.,* 992–996; *The visitation of the county of Cumberland, 1615,* Harleian Society, **7**: 17–18, 1872.

[61] Williams, *Worcester,* 37, 52–53; *C.S.P. Dom., 1603–1610,* 539; *Commons Debates 1621, passim.*

[62] I.P.M., Sir Edwin Sandys, C. 142/405/154.

[63] His son, Samuel, was an M.P. in 1661. Pink MSS, 320.

November, 1640,[64] but he was disabled as a royalist soon after the war began.

Sandys was the head of a family of "power and greatness" in his county,[65] and when he compounded for his estates he listed holdings in Essex, Hunts, Notts and London, as well as those of Worcestershire. Their yearly value, beyond annuities of £350, was some £1000,[66] and his fine was heavy.

William Sandys, M.P. for Evesham, was either a cousin or an uncle of the Droitwich member, and some of the members from Wales were probably kinsmen on his mother's side.

Thomas Sandys, member for Gatton, Surrey, was returned in October, 1640, but was not definitely seated until 3 November 1641, when the House recognized him rather than Edmund Saunder, who had sat for the borough in the spring. He appears not to have taken his seat before that time, but he sat from then until at least 1648.[67] He probably was of the Sandys family of Little Pattensham (Pachevesham), Leatherhead, Surrey,[68] although two members of the Sandys family of Northborne, Kent, who were living in 1640 might possibly have been this Thomas Sandys. The elder of them, a younger son of Edwin, Archbishop of York, and brother of Sir Edwin Sandys, lived from 1568 to 1649, being styled in 1634 as of London.[69] The younger Thomas Sandys of Kent was a nephew of the above, a son of Sir Edwin Sandys of Northborne. He was a student at Oxford in 1635, aged seventeen, and at Gray's Inn in 1639.[70] He was said to have been knighted later and may have been living in 1663.[71] The circumstances of the Gatton election, however, with Sandys winning because he received more votes from burgesses resident in the town, point to one who had been living longer within the neighborhood of Gatton and more probably, therefore, to the Sandys of Leatherhead.

Thomas Sandys (c. 1601–c. 1659) of that line was the son and heir of John Sandys of Little Pattensham (d. 1632), by his wife, Mary, daughter of Richard Hatton of Long Ditton. He was born about 1601,[72] and in 1629 married Katherine, daughter of Edward Michell of Sunmerham in Horsham, Sussex, widow of Law-

rence Pierce of Westhill.[73] He may have studied at Oxford (Christ's Church) and at the Middle Temple,[74] but no further details of his career are known. He seems not to have been active in county affairs before the war and had belonged to no previous parliament. He was, however, a parliamentarian, pledged one horse for the defense in 1642,[75] and kept his seat until 1648, possibly later.[76] Letters of administration for his estate were granted on 12 January 1658/9 to a daughter.[77]

In 1625 John Sandys of Little Pattensham settled his estate, most of it passing to his son, Thomas. It consisted chiefly of the manor of Little Pattensham and several other parcels of land in and near Leatherhead, and two houses in the city of Coventry.[78]

William Sandys (c. 1607–1669), of Fladbury, near Evesham, sat for Evesham from 1640 until he was expelled as a monopolist, 21 January 1641.[79] He may have been a younger son of Sir Samuel Sandys of Ombersley (d. 1623) and uncle of Samuel Sandys, the Droitwich member (q.v.); [80] but it seems more probable that he was a son of Sir William Sandys of Fladbury (d. 1639 or 1640), who was a first cousin of the elder Sir Samuel Sandys,[81] and was a member of the Council of Wales in 1633 and a J.P. for Worcestershire and Gloucestershire.[82] Sir William's wife was Margaret, daughter and coheir of Walter Colepeper of Hamborough, Oxfordshire,[83] cousin of Sir John Colepeper (q.v.). Sandys was born about 1607,[84] was bailiff of Fladbury in 1635,[85] and was eventually J.P. and alder-

---

[64] D'Ewes (N), 52.

[65] So it was characterized in a lawsuit in the time of King James. C. 3/369/1.

[66] S.P. 23/181/267. The estate was similarly valued in 1661. *English Baronetage* **4**: 377, 1741.

[67] *M. of P.* **1**: 483, 494; *C.J.* **2**: 303; *O.P.H.* **9**: 4.

[68] *Surrey Arch. Coll.* **39**: 61, 1931; *V.C.H. Surrey* **3**: 296.

[69] *Vis. London* **2**: 228; Browne, *Genesis of the U. S.*, 996; will of Thomas Sandys, P.C.C., 31 Pembroke.

[70] *Al. Oxon.; Vis. Kent, 1619,* 148.

[71] Pink MSS, 320. One Sir Thomas Sandys of Kent had a warrant for a baronetcy in March, 1663/4, but is otherwise unknown. *Complete Baronetage,* Appendix, 87.

[72] I.P.M., John Sandys, C. 142/496/127; Manning and Bray, *Surrey* **2**: 671.

[73] *Vis. Surrey, 1623,* 35; C. 142/496/127; will of Katherine Sandys, P.C.C., 91 Twisse.

[74] Pink MSS, 322.

[75] Bodleian Tanner MSS, 63, fol. 59.

[76] His name appears in a list of secluded members (*A vindication of the imprisoned and secluded members of the House of Commons,* 28, London, 1649) but elsewhere he is said to have belonged to the Rump and to have had no known connection with the Presbyterians. *A.H.R.* **44**: 37, n., 1938–1939.

[77] P.C.C., Act Book 1659, fol. 3v.

[78] I.P.M. cited above.

[79] *C.J.* **2**: 71.

[80] This identification was accepted by Pink (MS 311, fol. 484, but not MS 320), and also by Williams, though the latter states that he was Captain William Sandys of Askham, Notts, as well as of Fladbury (*Worcester,* 143). The William Sandys of Askham who compounded at the same time as Samuel Sandys of Ombersley, declaring an estate of £100 a year (*Cal. Com. Comp.,* 1296–1297), does not appear, however, to have had Worcestershire connections comparable with those of the M.P., the monopolist.

[81] J. Haviland, *A history of Fladbury,* 20, Worcester, 1872. Sir William of Fladbury was a son of Miles Sandys of Latimers, Bucks. Add. MSS, 34,307, fol. 4v.

[82] *Arch. Camb.,* 6th Ser., **17**: 195, 1917; S.P. 16/405.

[83] Add. MSS, 34,307, fol. 4v. They were married in 1599. *Sussex Arch. Coll.* **47**: opp. 72, 1904.

[84] He died in 1669, aged sixty-two (Pink MSS, 320). If he was the William Sandys who attended Oxford (identified in *Al. Oxon.* as the M.P., but of Askham and son of Sir Samuel), he was aged fourteen in 1623.

[85] Haviland, *loc. cit.*

man of Evesham. By 1640 he was a D.L. for Worcestershire.[86] He was best known before 1640, however, for the undertaking he began in 1635 to make the Avon navigable from the Severn up to Coventry, a project which involved him in quarrels with Sir William Russell that brought both men before Council in 1637,[87] but seemed to win him favor in Gloucester and Bristol, if not in the city of Worcester.[88] The venture was finally abandoned after he had lost heavily. A royalist in politics, Sandys lost his place in parliament because he had been granted a royal patent for a percentage of the tax on sea coals, the charge of monopoly being pressed against him particularly by John Coventry, a rival for his seat in the House.[89]

Sir William Savile, Bart. (1612–1644), of Thornhill, Yorkshire, was M.P. for Old Sarum from the end of January, 1641, succeeding Edward Herbert, until 6 September 1642.[90] He owned some lands in Wiltshire, but probably owed his election to the Earl of Pembroke, with whose family he was distantly connected, and whose northern estates he helped to manage.[91] The second son of Sir George Savile (d. 1614), by his second wife, Anne, daughter of Sir William Wentworth, Bart., he was born in June, 1612, and succeeded his elder brother, Sir George Savile, Bart., in 1626.[92] He was educated at University College, Oxford, and at Gray's Inn,[93] and in 1629 married Anne, daughter of Thomas Lord Coventry. He may have held some place in the royal household, for he was in London part of the time in 1638 and 1639 and in the latter year was listed among the king's servants "above stairs." [94]

But Savile was active also in the affairs of his native county and others where he held estates. He was a member of the commissions of oyer and terminer of several counties of the Midlands and the north, and was a conscientious J.P. in Derbyshire, Lincolnshire, and the West Riding.[95] He was made a D.L. and colonel through the influence of his uncle, Lord Wentworth, in 1633,[96] and was later made a member of the Council of the North. His regiment was participating in the border defense in 1639.

In national politics Savile was apparently groomed to follow his uncle's leadership. An older relative occupied Wentworth's seat in parliament after his elevation to the peerage in 1628, although young Savile was considered for it,[97] but in the Short Parliament Savile sat for Yorkshire. By this time, however, the nephew was somewhat restive under Strafford's authority. Sir Edward Osborne, Vice President of the Council of the North, complained as early as 1638 of Savile's disdainful bearing and his attempt to arouse criticism of his administration, and Strafford himself warned his nephew in March, 1640, that his impetuous challenge to his authority was likely to have but little effect.[98] That same month Savile delayed his reply to Council's request for a loan for the king,[99] and during the Short Parliament he expressed himself on his county's grievances. He went less far, however, than Hotham and Belasyse, whose speeches led to their imprisonment after the session. Savile's testimony regarding Belasyse and his friends before Council, even though he signed the Yorkshire petition of July, was probably the reason for his defeat at the county election in the autumn. His uncle's power and the sheriff's management could not win him the place.[100] And the consideration of his conduct by the Long Parliament prevented his taking his seat for Old Sarum until on 29 June 1641 he acknowledged his fault.[101] He shared in the work of the House but a few months, and then withdrew to the north to prepare for war. Savile died on 19 or 20 January 1644, while he was governor at York, and was buried at Thornhill.[102] His eldest son, George, became the first Marquis of Halifax.[103]

---

[86] Worcester Corporation MSS, Audit Book 3, 1639–1640; Williams, *loc. cit.* He was an alderman and J.P. when he was returned for Evesham in 1661. *M. of P.* 1: 531.

[87] Haviland, *op. cit.,* 20–21; *C.S.P. Dom., 1635–1636,* 449, 522–523; *1636–1637,* 203, *passim;* Add. MSS, 15,857, fol. 211; Birch, *The court and times of Charles the First* 2: 283.

[88] He was made a freeman of Gloucester in 1639 because he expected to bring in trade there (Gloucester Corporation MSS, Minute Book, 1632–1656, fol. 113), and seems to have won Bristol's approval in 1636 and 1641 (Bristol Corporation MSS, Common Council Book 3, 4 February 1635/6, 15 January 1640/1). Worcester, however, had some objections to his program (Worcester Corporation MSS, Order Book 2, fol 176). The Avon project was reported worthless in 1641, and Sandys was in debt to the king. *C.S.P. Dom., 1641–1643, 174.*

[89] D'Ewes (N), 23, n., 267; *C.J.* 2: 27, 71.

[90] *M. of P.* 1: 496; D'Ewes (N), 323; *C.J.* 2: 754.

[91] *Yorks. Arch. Jour.* 34: 329–341, 1939; Eg. MSS, 2623, fol. 41.

[92] I.P.M.'s of Sir George Savile, knight, and Sir George Savile, Bart., C. 142/380/128; C. 142/424/90.

[93] *Gray's Inn Adm. Reg.,* 186.

[94] Eg. MSS, 2623, fol. 41; S.P. 16, 427/38/v; 447/36, 94. In 1637 he acted on one occasion as agent for his father-in-law, the Lord Keeper. Sainsbury, *A calendar of the court minutes, &c. of the East India Company, 1635–1639, 285.*

[95] C. 181/4, fol. 184; 181/5, fols. 8, 32, 67, *passim;* C. 193/13; S.P. 16/405; *Y.A.S. Rec. Ser.* 54: 27, *passim,* 1915.

[96] Bodleian Firth MSS, b.2, fol. 233.

[97] J. J. Cartwright, *Chapters in Yorkshire history,* 245, Wakefield, 1872; *M. of P.* 1: 479.

[98] *H.M.C., Twelfth Report* 2, Coke MSS, 204; Bodleian Firth MSS, b.2, fol. 191; *Strafford letters* 2: 311–312.

[99] S.P. 16, 447/36, 37, 94.

[100] *C.S.P. Dom., 1640–1641,* 158; *H.M.C., Various Collections* 8, MSS of the Hon. F. L. Wood, 54.

[101] D'Ewes (N), 323; *C.J.* 2: 78, 192, *passim.*

[102] The last letter in Savile's military correspondence was dated 19 January (Bodleian Add. MSS, C. 259, fols. 86, 87); his successor was functioning at York on 20 January (Sloane MSS, 1519, fol. 24); and his will was proved on 21 January (*Yorks. Arch. Jour.* 25: 24, 1920). There has been some disagreement among authors as to the date of Savile's death, probably because in his I.P.M., taken more than a year later (C. 142/774/17), it was stated that he died on 24 January.

[103] A few facts about Savile's life are mentioned in the *D.N.B.* article on his son.

Savile was a wealthy man. From his Savile and Talbot ancestors he inherited over a dozen manors and more than twenty thousand acres of land in the counties of York, Derby, Lincoln and Nottingham. One manor alone was worth £200 a year in 1642.[104] The list of estates he held at the time of his death included properties also in Straffordshire, Shropshire and Wilts. By the terms of his will, which he wrote at the start of the war, his two daughters were to have dowries of £5000 each, and his sons were well provided for.[105] His ownership of numerous cloth mills in the Wakefield area of Yorkshire had made him interested in the problems of the clothiers.[106] And in 1638 he was proposing to utilize his property in York city as the site for a fair.[107] He could probably well afford to lend the king the £1000 that was asked of him in 1639.

Many acquaintances and kinsmen of Savile were in the 1640 Commons. Danby and Selden were friends he mentioned in his will. The two Sir George Wentworths were an uncle and a cousin. Pakington and John Coventry were brothers-in-law. And among the parliamentarians were his father's first cousins, Pierrpont and Armine. Several others were more distantly related.[108]

Robert Scawen (1602–1670), of Cornwall and London, was M.P. for Berwick, Northumberland, from 21 December 1640 until 1653. He was elected after the House had disallowed the return naming Sir Edward Osborne, Vice President of the Council of the North, on December 7,[109] and doubtless owed his election to his employer, the Earl of Northumberland.

Scawen came of a Cornish family, being the second son of Robert Scawen of Molenick, St. Germans (d. 1628),[110] by his wife, Isabella, daughter of Humphrey Nicholls (Nicoll), and a brother of William Scawen (c. 1601–1689), antiquary, M.P. (Short Parliament), and Vice Warden of the Stannaries. Through his mother he was a kinsman of Anthony Nicoll (q.v.). Robert was baptized at St. Germans, 16 May 1602,[111] and probably gained his early experience as a clerk or secretary in the western counties. He may have had some connection with the Stannaries, since he was nominated by Coryton in 1631 to receive a royal grant of part ownership of some lands in Cornwall.[112] And he was

possibly employed at some time by Francis, Earl of Bedford, for his will mentions an annuity of £40 formerly granted him by the earl.[113] Before 1640, however, he entered the service of the Earl of Northumberland, and in that year was living in his house and acting as his secretary and financial agent. He was concerned especially with the army and its finances, 1640–1641.[114] Scawen married Catherine, daughter of Cavendish Alsop of London, and purchased, probably after 1640, an estate at Horton, Bucks, by which he was identified in his later years.[115]

Although Scawen was a newcomer to parliament in 1640, he quickly gained prominence. His familiarity with army matters and his kinship with Anthony Nicoll, Pym's nephew, no doubt account in part for the roles assigned him. He was named to various early committees on army matters, as well as for local problems in the north and the west, and although he voted against Strafford's attainder, he became a strong supporter of parliament as well as of his patron, Northumberland. He was one of the committee for the recess,[116] was chairman of the army committee during much of the war, and was voted £2000 in 1646 in recognition of his extraordinary efforts in that capacity.[117] Scawen served again in parliament after the Restoration, and died early in 1670.[118] His will, dated 5 January 1667/8, was proved 21 March 1669/70.

Scawen was probably not well-to-do in 1640, although his family owned considerable property in Cornwall.[119] His pledge for the defense in 1642 was £30, somewhat below the average.[120] His fortunes apparently improved, possibly as a result of the opportunities the war afforded him, for he was able to provide generously for his children,[121] but even a royalist commented that he "hath the esteem of an honest man." [122]

Richard Seaborne (born c. 1590), of Hereford, was M.P. for his town, 1640–3 January 1646. He was born about 1590,[123] being the second son of Edward Seaborne of Felton, Herefordshire, and was educated at the New Inn and the Middle Temple. He was called to the bar at the Temple and in 1642 was Lent Reader. For a time he shared a chamber with Christopher Lewknor (q.v.), and in 1632 was with Walter Kyrle (q.v.).[124]

---

[104] I.P.M., C. 142/424/90; *Y.A.S. Rec. Ser.* **18**: 9, 1895.

[105] I.P.M., C. 142/774/17; Hoare, *Wilts.* **1** (2) : 226; *Yorks. Arch. Jour.* **25**: 24–26, 1920.

[106] *Ibid.*; C.S.P. Dom., 1640, 296.

[107] York Corporation MSS, House Book 35, fols. 349b, 351; House Book 36, fols. 1, 3, 32.

[108] A sketch of Savile's life in its fuller political aspects appears in Gooder, *Parl. Rep. York*, 49–51. See also *Complete Baronetage* **1**: 50.

[109] Berwick indenture, C. 219/43/Part 2; *M. of P.* **1**: 491; *O.P.H.* **9**: *35.

[110] I.P.M. of Robert Scawen, C. 142/755/65.

[111] Vivian, *Vis. Cornwall*, 422; Pink MSS, 307, fol. 259.

[112] C.S.P. Dom., 1631–1633, 125.

[113] P.C.C., 41 Penn.

[114] *C.S.P. Dom., 1640*, 137; *1640–1641*, 125, 241, *passim*.

[115] Scawen's will; Lysons, *Mag. Brit.* **1**: 582.

[116] *C.J.* **2** : 61, 88, 140, 215, 288; Verney, 58.

[117] Bean, *Northern Counties,* 504, n.; *H.M.C., Sixth Report,* House of Lords MSS, 117, 210; Add. MSS, 19,398, fol. 179.

[118] Bean, *Northern Counties,* 64; *M. of P.* **1**: 521.

[119] One William Scawen, possibly Robert's royalist elder brother, was accounted as worth £800 a year in 1660. *English Baronetage* **4**: 364, 1741.

[120] *C.J.* **2**: 772.

[121] Scawen's will cited above.

[122] *The mystery of the good old cause,* 42.

[123] He stated in 1646 that his age was about 56. S.P. 23/179/356, 366.

[124] *Mid. Temp. Rec.* **2**: 535, 629, 636, 794, 912.

Seaborne was in Herefordshire in 1635, serving as a collector for the contributions toward the repair of St. Paul's,[125] and he was by this time married.[126] His residence was at Hereford. During the war Seaborne was reported to be a Papist.[127]

A member of both of the 1640 parliaments, Seaborne was used for some committee work requiring a knowledge of the law,[128] but he was not often active. Nor does he seem to have contributed financially for the cause of parliament in the early period. He apparently went to the parliament at Oxford, but for some reason he was not disabled in 1644. He was taken prisoner at Hereford late in 1645, was finally disabled on 3 January 1646, and, after being held a prisoner for several more months, was permitted to compound for his estate.[129] He was living on 2 July 1649,[130] but the date of his death is unknown.

Seaborne's real estate consisted of some farm land in Herefordshire and some buildings in Hereford, the clear income from which was less than £200 a year. His fine, reckoned in 1646 at a half, £1009, or a third, £673, was set in 1649 at £290, with £29 a year settled on the ministry.[131]

George Searle (d. 1658), of Taunton, Somerset, sat for that borough, 1640–1653. His parentage is uncertain. The suggestion that he was a Lincoln's Inn barrister who came of the family of Searle at St. Cruce on the Isle of Wight [132] seems less probable than that he came from the west country originally. Perhaps he was the George Searle, merchant, of Honiton, Devon, who was named in a deed of 8 May 1615 regarding the marriage of a daughter of John Searle of Heathfield in Honiton, a yeoman.[133] The fact that the M.P. had Honiton connections afterwards and died there (see below) suggests that he may have been the merchant of the 1615 deed, perhaps a son of the yeoman, John. He must have lived at Taunton for some years before 1640, for he seems to have been serving his second term as mayor there that year.[134] And some time before April, 1640, Searle had been sued in the Earl Marshal's court for disparaging remarks on the lowly ancestry

of Robert Brown, a grandson of the Portmans, an important family in the neighborhood of Taunton.[135] The suit had cost him £140 in damages and costs and £100 in personal expense, and he had been required afterwards "to make an unworthy submission before various Taunton persons." During his mayoralty of 1640 Searle petitioned against this verdict,[136] and in the Long Parliament it was referred to the committee on the Court of Honor and Heralds.[137] The summer of Searle's mayoralty was troubled by an epidemic of the plague,[138] and there was some hesitancy about admitting him to the House in November because of that condition.[139]

The Long Parliament was Searle's first, and he seems to have played a quiet part in the House. He pledged £50 for the defense in 1642,[140] and during the war was a J.P. in Somerset, and an elder in the presbytery.[141] He was voted £2500 in 1646 as recompense for losses, was mayor of Taunton again in 1649, and kept his seat in parliament until the end.[142] He died on 28 September 1658 at Honiton, Devon, and letters of administration were granted to his widow, Welthian Searle, on 6 December 1658. At that time Searle was referred to as "late of Taunton." [143] A brass inscribed to his memory, removed afterwards from his burial place, stated that he was thrice mayor of Taunton, and described him as a humble and pious Christian and a faithful and vigilant magistrate.[144]

* John Selden (1584–1654), of the Inner Temple, the distinguished lawyer, scholar, and defender of parliament, sat for Oxford University, 1640–1653.[145] His many interests included membership in the Virginia Company.[146]

---

[125] *C.S.P. Dom., 1635–1636*, 173.

[126] By 1646 he had nine children, eight of whom were small. S.P. 23/179/366.

[127] *Cal. Com. Adv. Money*, 722.

[128] E.g., *C.J.* 2: 160.

[129] *C.J.* 3: 374; 4: 396. He admitted deserting Westminster, but declared he had not voted at Oxford to declare the parliamentarians traitors. *Cal. Com. Comp.*, 1125.

[130] *Ibid*.

[131] *Ibid*. See also Williams, *Hereford*, 90.

[132] Pink MSS, 321; *Al. Oxon.*; *Somerset and Dorset N. and Q.* 4: 78, 1894–1895.

[133] Exeter City Library MSS, Exeter Deeds and Documents, No. 1810.

[134] He was mayor three times, according to his M.I. (see below).

[135] This Brown or Browne was apparently a younger brother of John Browne of Frampton, Dorset (*q.v.*).

[136] *H.M.C., Fourth Report, House of Lords MSS*, 25.

[137] D'Ewes (N), 226–227.

[138] He appealed to Exeter for relief for Taunton. Exeter Corporation MSS, Act Book 8, fol. 213; MS 60 F, Letters, No. 384.

[139] *C.J.* 2: 21.

[140] *N. and Q.*, 1st Ser., 12: 360, 1855.

[141] *A.H.R.* 44: 31, n. (32), 1938–1939.

[142] *Somerset and Dorset N. and Q.* 4: 78, 1894–1895.

[143] P.C.C., Act Book for 1658, fol. 347v. Searle wrote a letter to the Committee for Advance of Money from Werrington in Honiton on 22 January 1648 (*Cal. Com. Adv. Money*, 845), and one to the compounding committee from Taunton on 12 September 1651 (*Cal. Com. Comp.*, 481).

[144] *Somerset Arch. Proc.* 50 (i): 70, 1904. Mr. A. Vivian-Neal of Taunton, who called my attention to this note, suggests that the brass, now in the Taunton Castle museum, may have come from Ottery St. Mary, or possibly from Honiton, where All Saints Chapel was taken down in the eighteenth century. A search of the published registers of Ottery St. Mary has revealed no reference to a George Searle of his approximate dates, although his family name occurs frequently.

[145] Williams, *Oxford*, 150.

[146] Kingsbury, *Records of the Virginia Company* 4: 157.

Edward Seymour (1610–1688), of Berry Pomeroy Castle, Devon, was one of his county's knights, 1640–16 January 1643. The son and heir of Sir Edward Seymour, second baronet (d. 1659), by Dorothy, daughter of Sir Henry Killigrew of Laroch (Lanrack), Cornwall, Seymour was baptized at Bury Pomeroy on 10 September 1610. He was a descendant of the Duke of Somerset, Edward VI's Lord Protector, and his grandfather and his father had served in various parliaments. His father was once ambassador to Denmark [147] and in his own county was a member of various local commissions, a J.P., D.L., vice admiral, and colonel in the trained bands.[148] About 1630 Edward Seymour married Anne, daughter of Sir John Portman, Bart., of Somerset, a sister of Sir William Portman (*q.v.*). With his marriage came control of the manor of Maiden Bradley, Wiltshire.[149] Seymour quarrelled in 1638 with Sir Henry Ludlow, the puritan M.P. of 1640, regarding the taxes there, and the next year he petitioned the king for permission to change the dates of the markets.[150] He was named in 1637 to the Devonshire commission on piracy and served thereafter with his father in that work.[151] He was elected to his first parliament as a county member in the spring of 1640,[152] owing his election then and in the fall probably to family influence and possibly to some backing from the court.

Seymour was not a prominent member of the Long Parliament. He offered his bond for £1000 for the loan in November, 1640,[153] but was named to no committee, and on 2 September 1642 was suspended for non-attendance. His disablement followed early in 1643.[154] With his father he joined the king's forces, was captured and imprisoned, and was forced to compound for his estate. He afterwards sat in the parliaments of 1660 and 1661, and died on 7 December 1688.[155] His son, Sir Edward Seymour (1633–1708), Speaker of the House of Commons, succeeded him.

Throughout the Long Parliament Seymour's aged father was still living, but the M.P. was already in possession of much of the family property. When he compounded he reported his net income from two Devon manors as nearly £600 a year, but asked allowance for the portions of £1500 which had been planned for each of his three sisters and for annuities of £297 and other heavy charges upon the estate. The Wiltshire property was said to have been worth £200 a year before

the war, and there were other Devon lands whose values must have increased his income considerably above the stated figure. His fine, reckoned at a third, £3133, or £2700 if the portions and other charges were to be allowed, was reduced eventually to £1200.[156]

Seymour's kinsmen in the 1640 Commons, among others, were Sir Francis Seymour, Henry Killigrew, an uncle, the Jermyns and the Godolphin brothers, who were cousins,[157] his brother-in-law, Portman, and another connection by marriage, Sir Nicholas Slanning.[158]

* Sir Francis Seymour (1590?–1664), M.P. for Marlborough, Wilts, from 1640 until his call to the House of Lords in 1641 as Baron Seymour of Trowbridge, had sat in five previous parliaments either for that borough or for his county. He had served also as sheriff and as J.P., having been restored to the commission of the peace after his removal in 1626, and was a member of various other commissions in the county.[159] He was a D.L., also,[160] and appears for a time to have been connected with the office of the receiver general of the Duchy of Cornwall.[161]

Seymour was admitted to the Middle Temple in January, 1626,[162] doubtless an honorary admission, for he was then serving as sheriff. For the latter office he had been pricked deliberately that year so that he would be ineligible to sit in the coming parliament. Although he was chosen by several places as M.P., the king refused to release him from his sheriff's oath.[163]

In his own county Seymour was on good terms with the town of Marlborough, where he resided part of the time.[164] He was interested also in the county's clothing industry and in 1634 led the opposition of the local justices against a special commission sent in to reform the industry. He encouraged ship money resistance in 1638, refused to pay his own share in 1639, and when parliament met attacked one of the sheriffs, Bayntun, for his severity.[165] He ignored the king's loan request of 1639,[166] but he seems to have been with the king in the north in September, 1640.[167] He won his election as county knight for the Short Parliament without

---

[147] *Complete Baronetage* 1: 33–34; *M. of P.* 1: 428, 437, *passim.*

[148] C. 181/4 and 5, *passim;* C. 193/12, 13; S.P. 16, 410/163; *Acts P.C., 1613–1614,* 428; *C.S.P. Dom.,* 1637, 487.

[149] S.P. 23/179/330; *Western Antiquary* 1: 97, 1881–1882.

[150] *C.S.P. Dom., 1637–1638,* 385; *1639–1640,* 143.

[151] C. 181/5, fols. 168, 264, 265.

[152] Willis 3: 231.

[153] D'Ewes (N), 52.

[154] *C.J.* 2: 750, 929.

[155] *Complete Baronetage* 1: 34; Pink MSS, 307, fol. 336. His death occurred in December, 1685, according to the brief reference to him in the article on his son in *D.N.B.*

[156] S.P. 23/179/298–300, 330, 338; *Cal. Com. Comp.,* 77, 1126; *H.M.C., Fifteenth Report 7,* MSS of the Duke of Somerset, 90–91. The assessment listed for him in 1644 by parliament was £2000. *Cal. Com. Adv. Money,* 432.

[157] Vivian, *Vis. Cornwall,* 268–270.

[158] Stowe MSS, 651, pedigree.

[159] C. 193/13; S.P. 16/405; C. 181/5, fols. 44, 270.

[160] S.P. 16, 15/14; 160/11.

[161] S.P. 16, 528/32.

[162] *Mid. Temp. Rec.* 2: 703.

[163] Bodleian Firth MSS, b.2, fol. 190v; *The letters of John Chamberlain* 2: 628.

[164] Marlborough MSS, Chamberlains' Accounts, 1572–1771; Waylen, *Hist of Marlborough,* 147–148.

[165] *C.S.P. Dom., 1634–1635,* 3–4, 306; *1638–1639,* 232; D'Ewes (N), 141–142.

[166] Rushworth 3: 915.

[167] *C.S.P. Dom., 1640–1641,* 46.

opposition,[168] and doubtless met with as little difficulty at Marlborough on the next occasion.

When Seymour compounded in 1646 for having turned to the king, he listed possessions in Wiltshire and Somerset which were worth nearly £1350 a year. He declared, however, that they had been heavily mortgaged in 1641. His fine, set originally at a tenth, £3725, was later reduced to £2725.[169]

Seymour's relatives in the 1640 House included Richard Rogers, a first cousin on his mother's side, and Edward Seymour, a more distant kinsman.

Henry Shelley (1599–1654), of Southover, near Lewes, Sussex, sat for Lewes from June, 1641,[170] until 1648 or 1653. He belonged to a widespread Sussex family that stemmed from John Shelley of Michelgrove, *temp*. Henry VIII, being the second but eldest surviving son of Henry Shelley of Patcham, later of Southover (d. between 1630 and 1634), by his wife, Jane, daughter of Richard Bellingham of Hangleton. He was baptized at Patcham on 13 December 1599.[171] Nothing is known of his education, although his older brother, Thomas, who died in 1620, and a younger brother, Richard, attended Emmanuel College, Cambridge.[172] His father was living at Southover in 1621, having apparently sold Patcham,[173] and Henry was described as of Southover in the license (12 September 1626) for his marriage with Martha, daughter and heiress of William Heath of Deans, Sussex.[174]

Shelley was a member of the county sewers commission in 1637 and was one of the subsidy commissioners in 1640.[175] He had not served in parliament, however, before he was elected to fill the seat for Lewes that was vacated by the death of James Rivers in June, 1641.[176] He was named on 25 June to a committee on an Irish manor and on 2 July to one on money due for army expenses. He collaborated with his neighbor, Stapley, and the other puritans of the House, and was sent to Sussex in August, 1641, to help with the disarming of recusants.[177] With the coming of war Shelley was made a D.L. and a member of the sequestrating committee for the county.[178] He pledged £50 for the defense in June, 1642,[179] and was absent in service in February, 1644.[180] He retained his seat at least until 1648, probably until 1653.[181] Re-elected for Lewes in 1654, he died soon afterwards.[182] His will, dated 10 May 1653, with a codicil of 24 May 1654, was proved by his brother-in-law, Robert Heath, 22 August 1654.[183]

Shelley owned a splendid mansion near Lewes and his marriage with an heiress increased his fortunes.[184] In the introduction to his will, however, he admitted that, because of their many children, his estate could not well bear all of his wife's jointure or additional bequests. He directed, however, that £550 be provided for a younger son and £550 for each of three younger daughters, portions that were by no means meagre.

Through his wife Shelley was distantly related to Sir William Morley.[185] He was a kinsman and friend of Sir Thomas Pelham and probably of Stapley, also.

* Richard Shuckburgh (1596–1656), of Over Shuckburgh, Warwickshire, was M.P. for his county from a by-election in December, 1640, until he was disabled on 14 January 1644.[186] He was the second son but eventual heir of John Shuckburgh of that place (d. 1631/2). His estate, said by one author to be worth about £200 a year, but probably yielding in its entirety considerably more than that, embraced three manors in Warwickshire and two in Northamptonshire.[187] When he made his will in 1655, he had six sons living, but wished provision of £500 to be made for any child that he might have afterwards.[188]

Shuckburgh was a J.P. in Warwickshire.[189] Through his first wife he was related to Ralph Sneyd, the royalist M.P. for Stafford.

Richard Shuttleworth (1587–1669), of Gawthorpe Hall near Burnely, Lancashire, sat for Preston from 1640 until 1648 or 1653. The eldest son of Thomas Shuttleworth (d. 1593) by his wife, Anne, daughter of Richard Lever, he was the nephew and eventual heir of Sir Richard Shuttleworth, Justice of Chester, *temp*.

---

[168] *Ibid., 1639–1640*, 604.

[169] *Cal. Com. Comp.*, 1507; S.P. 23/191/785–786; *Wilts. Arch. Mag.* **4**: 150, 1858; Waylen, *op. cit.*, 236.

[170] *M. of P.* **1**: 494 and n.; Pink MSS, 320.

[171] T. W. Horsfield, *History and antiquities of Lewes* **2**: 178–179, 1824–1827; Comber, *Sussex Genealogies* **3**: 249.

[172] *Al. Cant.*

[173] *V.C.H. Sussex* **7**: 217; *Sussex Arch. Coll.* **9**: 73, 1857.

[174] *Sussex Rec. Soc.* **1**: 155, 1902; Horsfield, *op. cit.* **2**: opp. 180.

[175] C. 181/5, fol. 139; *Sussex Arch. Coll.* **9**: 105, 1857.

[176] The Henry Shelley, junior, M.P. for Bramber, 1614 (*M. of P.*), was a lawyer of Gray's Inn and of the Worminghurst branch of the family (1582–1644 or 1645). *Al. Oxon.;* I.P.M. of Henry Shelley, sen., of Worminghurst, 1624 (C. 142/438/121).

[177] *C.J.* **2**: 186, 196, 267.

[178] Thomas-Stanford, *Sussex in the great Civil War*, 120, 156.

[179] *N. and Q.*, 1st Ser., **12**: 360, 1855.

[180] *C.J.* **3**: 389.

[181] Pink (Pink MSS, 320) thought he was secluded in 1648, but the list in *O.P.H.* (**9**: 5) indicates that he sat until 1653.

[182] The return of his successor was dated 2 November 1654. *M. of P.* **1**: 502.

[183] P.C.C., 455 Alchin.

[184] Horsfield, *op. cit.* **2**: 179.

[185] She was a kinswoman of Sir Robert Heath, the Chief Justice. *Vis. Sussex, 1633–4*, 134.

[186] *M. of P.* **1**: 495 and notes.

[187] Colvile, *The worthies of Warwickshire*, 689–690; Dugdale, *The antiquities of Warwickshire*, 217–219, 235, 373, 1765; Baker, *Northampton* **1**: 211, 371; Birmingham Reference Library MSS, 412,977.

[188] P.C.C., 372 Berkeley.

[189] C. 193/13.

Elizabeth, and succeeded to his family's estates in 1608 or 1609, aged about nineteen.[190] He studied at Brasenose, Oxford, and at Gray's Inn,[191] and before 1613 married Fleetwood, daughter and heiress of Richard Barton of Barton, acquiring with her additional lands in the county. He was a J.P. in Lancashire by 1616, a member of other local commissions,[192] probably served twice as sheriff, 1620 and 1636–1637, and accounted in full for the ship money assessment in the latter term.[193] He was a Presbyterian in belief.[194]

A member for Preston in both parliaments of 1640, Shuttleworth worked with the popular party, and during the war served both as an army officer and as a vigorous sequestrator and magistrate. He died in 1669, having outlived his son Richard, M.P. for Clitheroe. Other fellow members who had family connections with him were Ralph Ashton of Whalley and Thomas Standish.

Shuttleworth's properties lay in Yorkshire as well as in Lancashire. Two of his sisters' portions of £620 and £406 give some indication of his family's standing.[195] His pledge for the defense in 1642 on behalf of his son and himself, however, was only £100.[196]

Richard Shuttleworth (1613–1650), "gentleman," of Gawthorpe Hall, Lancashire, M.P. for Clitheroe, 1640–1648?,[197] was the eldest son of Richard Shuttleworth, the member for Preston. He was baptized at Padiham, 13 October 1613,[198] was graduated B.A. from Oxford (Brasenose) in 1633, and was a student at the Inner Temple that year. He was elected by Clitheroe for the Short Parliament, and kept his seat in the Long Parliament at least until the purge of 1648,[199] for he was a

Presbyterian as was his father.[200] He fought in the parliamentary army and died on 21 January 1650. His wife was Jane or Joan, daughter of John Kirke of London.[201]

* Philip Sidney, Lord Lisle (1619–1698), eldest surviving son of Robert, second Earl of Leicester, was a member for Yarmouth, Isle of Wight, 1640–1653. He preferred that borough to St. Ives, for which also he had been returned.[202] He was educated at Gray's Inn (admitted 1633)[203] and at Oxford, as well as by travel abroad during his father's embassies. Unmarried and scarcely of age at the time of his election to parliament in 1640, Lord Lisle was still largely dependent upon his father. It had been proposed in 1639 that £5000 a year be settled on him when he should marry.[204]

Lord Lisle was a nephew of Henry Percy (q.v.) and of the Earl of Northumberland.

* Sir Nicholas Slanning (1606?–1643), of Maristow, Devon, was M.P. for Penryn, Cornwall, 1640–9 August 1642.[205] He was born probably in 1606.[206] According to Prince, Slanning studied sometime at Oxford, probably before he was admitted to the Inner Temple. He was interested in experiments, but afterwards went to the Netherlands to learn the art of war. "He was able to attend as well the crucible as the gun, and knew how to improve his time to advantage in his study, and in the field also."[207] Besides being governor of Pendennis Castle from 1635, Slanning was a J.P. in both Devon and Cornwall,[208] a member of the commission on piracy for both counties, and a vice admiral.[209] He was elected for Plympton, where he was recorder, in the spring of 1640,[210] and was elected for both Plympton and Penryn in the autumn.[211] The secret

[190] *Vis. Lanc., 1664–1665*, 271–272; Burke, *Landed gentry*, 1850; *The house and farm accounts of the Shuttleworths of Gawthorpe Hall*, ed. by John Harland (Chetham Society, 35, 41, 43, 46) 2: 271–272, 298, 1856–1858 (hereafter, *The Shuttleworth accounts*).

[191] *Al. Oxon.*

[192] C. 193/12; *Lancaster Quarter Sessions, Manchester* (Rec. Soc. Lancs. and Cheshire, 42) 1: vi, 113, 152, 1901; C. 181/4, fol. 130v.

[193] *C.S.P. Dom., 1636–1637*, 208; *1637*, 504, 525. His terms as sheriff are misdated in Pink and Beaven, *Parl. Rep. Lanc.* (151), and the name given for the 1620 term in the *List of Sheriffs* (73) is Thomas Shuttleworth. His father had died before that, however, and Richard was the logical one of his family to be in the office.

[194] Bean, *Northern Counties*, 425; *The Shuttleworth accounts* 2: 298.

[195] *V.C.H. York, North Riding* 1: 66; *The Shuttleworth accounts* 2: 302, 305–308.

[196] *N. and Q.*, 1st Ser., 12: 360, 1855.

[197] According to various authors, Shuttleworth died early in 1648, but he was still listed as a member in July, 1648. Thomason Tracts, E. 454, 17.

[198] *Lancashire deeds* (Chetham Society, N.S., 91) 1: 33, 1934.

[199] He attracted attention one day in 1641 by refusing to go out for a division, possibly for fear of losing his seat, whereupon one diarist noted the danger of admitting "infants" into the House. D'Ewes (N), 420 and n. *O.P.H.* (9: *31) does not list him as secluded.

[200] *A.H.R.* 44: 36, n., 1938–1939.

[201] Pink and Beaven, *Parl. Rep. Lanc.*, 253; *Al. Oxon.*; *The Shuttleworth accounts* 2: 273. Most of the authorities cited his death in 1648, but the year was 1650, according to *Vis. Lanc., 1664–1665* (272).

[202] *M. of P.* 1: 493; *C.J.* 2: 25.

[203] *Gray's Inn Adm. Reg.*, 201.

[204] *H.M.C., Third Report*, MSS of the Duke of Northumberland, 79. A marriage portion of £4000 went to Lisle's elder sister, Lucy, and £3000 was intended for each of his younger sisters. Add. MSS, 32,683, fols. 55–70.

[205] *C.J.* 2: 711.

[206] For the question of whether Slanning was born about 1611 or in 1606, see Devon *Trans.* 19: 459, 1887. Although the later date would make Slanning's age come nearer to the youthfulness mentioned by Clarendon, the reliance on the I.P.M. of 1612 which gave his age as six years seems justifiable. 1606 is the date accepted by *D.N.B.* Other authorities (e.g., *Complete Baronetage* 3: 270; Coate, *Cornwall in the great Civil War*, 99, n.) follow the statement in *Vis. Devon, 1620* (262), that he was aged nine in 1620.

[207] John Prince, *Worthies of Devon*, 713, 1810.

[208] C. 193/13; S.P. 16/405.

[209] C. 181/5, fols. 165, 167, 264, 374.

[210] Devon *Trans.* 17: 262, 1885; *M. of P.* 1: 481.

[211] *M. of P.* 1: 487, 488; *C.J.* 2: 22.

business upon which he was summoned post from Plymouth to attend the king about October, 1640,[212] was possibly election matters, for his wife was a daughter of Buckingham's former agent, Sir James Bagge, and Slanning was undoubtedly regarded as a king's man in the west before the war.

Slanning, who was described by Clarendon as of good fortune,[213] owned several Devonshire manors near Plymouth and others in Cornwall.[214] The "particular" of his estate which was presented after his death to the compounding commissioners declared a yearly income of some £419, but some omissions were afterwards reported. The final fine required of his heir was slightly over £1197.[215]

Slanning was connected by marriage with Edward Seymour. He was a friend of Grenville and Trevanion, with whose names his is linked in the royalist couplet on Cornish heroes.[216]

* Sir Henry Slingsby, Bart (1602–1658), of Scriven, near Knaresborough, and of the Redhouse near York, was a member for Knaresborough, 1640–6 September 1642. His father had been a deputy steward for the liberty of Knaresborough, owning numerous houses in the town,[217] and Sir Henry held the post for a time also.[218] He was well educated, and sat in the parliament of 1625 for Knaresborough.[219] In March, 1626, he was granted a license to travel abroad for three years.[220] He was a candidate for Knaresborough again in 1628, but was defeated.[221]

After Slingsby's succession to his father's ample estate and his marriage, he was a J.P. and a member of the commission of oyer and terminer,[222] and in 1638 he performed the duties of a D.L., though without a formal commission.[223] Yet he was a man more inclined to studies than to war. A contemporary declared that he had "a greater influence upon the people than they who talked more and louder." [224]

Slingsby's estates were numerous, and he spent fully £500 a year in 1638 on household expenses for his family and their twenty-four servants.[225] He was a

kinsman of Henry Percy and of the Mallorys,[226] and was a brother-in-law of two other fellow M.P.,'s the Belasyse brothers, and was closely connected by marriage with the Ingrams.

John Smith (1609?–1657), "gentleman" of Oxford, was elected in Lord Andover's place for Oxford, 30 November 1640, and was disabled probably early in 1644. He was a younger son of Oliver Smith (d. 1637), alderman and twice mayor of Oxford, and a grandson of Thomas Smith, brewer and one-time mayor (d. 1601).[227] John probably matriculated at Wadham College, Oxford, in 1624, aged fifteen (B.A., New College, 1627?),[228] and in 1627 married at St. Addes, Oxford, Eleanor, daughter of an Oxford brewer, Henry Bosworth.[229] He became a freeman and a bailiff of his town in March, 1630, and served with his brother, Thomas, as bailiff in charge of the city funds during their father's final term as mayor, 1631–1632. He continued to be an active member of the local government during the next decade, becoming a member of the Upper Council in 1638 and mayor in 1639. He was a candidate for election to the Long Parliament in October, 1640, but was defeated by or deferred to Lord Andover, son of the city's steward.[230] When that young man moved to the House of Lords, Smith, the local magistrate, replaced him.

Because of the confusion occasioned by the presence in the House of more than one "Mr. Smith," practically nothing is known of John Smith's role in the Long Parliament. He probably withdrew from Westminster some time before taking his seat in the king's parliament in Oxford. Having compounded afterwards for his delinquency, he died in 1657.

Smith's landed estate was not large, his income from lands in Oxfordshire and Berkshire being but slightly more than £100 a year.[231] The assessment of £100 on him in 1651 [232] indicates that he was not wealthy, and even in his will, dated 28 October, and proved 25 November 1657, he referred to his estate as small.[233] No doubt he had sources of income from some kind of business in 1640 which the estate figures do not reveal.

[212] C.S.P. Dom., 1640–1641, 209.
[213] Rebellion 3: 113.
[214] Devon Trans. 19: 455–456, 459, 1887; Lysons, Mag. Brit. 4: 47, 221; Plymouth City Library MSS, Nos. B 21, B 31a; Exeter City Library MSS, No. 75.
[215] S.P. 23/117/813–818; Cal. Com. Comp., 2210.
[216] See Sidney Godolphin.
[217] Bodleian MSS Top. Yorks. C 4, fols. 4–26.
[218] Fairfax correspondence 2: 266.
[219] M. of P. 1: 467.
[220] Acts P.C., 1625–1626, 376.
[221] Yorks. Arch. Jour. 34: 213–221, 1939.
[222] York Corporation MSS, House Book 35, fol. 207; C. 181/4, fols. 36, 61.
[223] The diary of Sir Henry Slingsby, of Scriven, Bart., 14.
[224] Add. MSS, 27,990, fol. 36.
[225] The diary of Sir Henry Slingsby, of Scriven, Bart., 26, 349–352. Besides his Yorkshire lands he owned an estate in Hertfordshire. Kingston, Herts. during the Civil War, 5.

[226] E. Hargrove, The history of the castle, town and forest of Knaresborough, 149, 150, 6th ed., Knaresborough, 1809.
[227] Williams, Oxford, 117; Compton Reade, The Smith family, 169, London, E. Stock, 1902. Smith was often referred to in the Oxford City documents as John Smith, junior, since there was another of the name, possibly his uncle, who also was a member of the city government in the 1630's. Reade seems to confuse them in his pedigree.
[228] Al. Oxon.
[229] Pink MSS, 321.
[230] Oxford Corporation MSS, A.5.7, Council Book, 1629–1663, fols. 12, 26, 28, 38, 90v, 95, 110, 111v; P.5.2, Audit Book, 1592–1682, fols. 215, 220v.
[231] S.P. 23/192/481, 483.
[232] Cal. Com. Adv. Money, 1308.
[233] P.C.C., 472 Ruthen.

Philip Smith (d. 1664), M.P. for Marlborough, Wilts, from March, 1641, following Seymour's elevation to the peerage, served until 1653.[234] A barrister of the Inner Temple,[235] he was the son of Henry Smith of Baydon or Haydon, Wiltshire. He was probably a descendant of the yeoman clothier family which produced Sir Thomas Smith of East India and Virginia Company fame and held courtly offices in the times of Elizabeth and James.[236] One Henry Smith of Baydon, gentleman, probably Philip's father or stepbrother, was associated in 1628 with his Wiltshire neighbors, Sir Edward Hungerford and Sir Francis Seymour (q.v.), in work of the office of Receiver General of the Duchy of Cornwall.[237] And one of that name was a trustee for Baydon church in 1627.[238]

Philip was born sometime after 1592, and was admitted to the Inner Temple in 1618, and called to the bar in 1628. He assisted his mother in proving his father's will in 1632. The home at Baydon with other properties was assigned to him.[239] He was presumably the "Mr. Smith of Baydon" to whom Marlborough paid interest on a loan of £40, 1631–1635.[240] Smith apparently married three times. His first wife seems to have been Cicely, daughter of Henry Bulstrode (married 1633, he aged twenty-eight),[241] but she must have died early and childless. The wife mentioned in Smith's will (1664) as his "late" wife was Elizabeth, who seems to have belonged to the Goddard family of Okebourne St. George and other places near Marlborough.[242] The wife who survived him can be identified only by her first name, Theodosia. One child of Smith's by his wife, Elizabeth, was married when he made his will.

Elected to his first parliament in 1641, Smith joined his colleague, Franklin of Marlborough, in the opposi-tion: On 20 March 1641, for instance, he was added to the committee considering the ship money judges and knighthood compositions. When the war came he promised to lend £40 for the cause, and in September, 1642, he was appointed to the committee on absent members.[243] He was a committeeman in Wiltshire during the war.[244] Smith held his place in parliament until 1653, and took part in the final work when the members reassembled in 1659.[245]

By the latter date Smith had moved to Kensington. The births of three of the four children he had by his wife Theodosia are recorded in the Kensington parish registers, 1658–1662,[246] and in his will, dated 2 August 1664 (proved 25 October), he described himself as "Philip Smith of Kensington, Middlesex, Esquire." The identity of the properties and names referred to in this will with those mentioned in the will and pedigree of Henry Smith of Baydon makes it certain that the testator was the former Philip Smith of Baydon.

Smith was probably not wealthy in 1640. By his father's will he received a legacy of £50, the home at Baydon, and certain lands which his father had purchased. His offer for the defense was among the smaller ones. But by 1664 he owned properties in Hammersmith as well as in Wiltshire and felt able to plan dowries of £1000 each for his two younger daughters. He had possibly taken advantage of the losses of the royalists after 1642.

Sir Thomas Smith (c. 1595–1668), of Hatherton and Hough, Cheshire, was a member for Chester, 1640–22 January 1644. He came of a merchant family which had for some generations supplied city magistrates and philanthropists, and had purchased large estates in the county. Among them were his great-grandfather, Sir Lawrence Smith (d. 1582), four times mayor, and his grandfather, Sir Thomas (d. 1614), whose chief heir he was. Smith's parents were Lawrence Smith of Hough (d. 1621) and Anne, daughter of Sir Randle Mainwaring of Chester and Over Peover. Born about 1595,[247] Thomas was admitted to Lincoln's Inn, 14 February 1614,[248] and was knighted at Whitehall, 21 July 1615.[249] Six months before, immediately after his grandfather's death and upon his own request, Smith had been admitted a freeman of Chester and chosen to succeed his grandfather as alderman.[250] He succeeded

[234] M. of P. 1: 496; C.J. 2: 109.

[235] D'Ewes (B), 390.

[236] His admission to the Temple was as the son and heir of Henry Smith of Haydon in Rodbourne Cheyney parish (Students admitted to the Inner Temple, 223). The Wiltshire pedigrees of the family of Corsham and Baydon, however, show a Philip, seventh son of Henry Smith of Baydon (d. 1631), but eldest son of Henry's second wife, Jane Angers (Marshall, Vis. Wilts., 67; Arch. Cant. 20: 77–78, 1893). W. D. Pink (Pink MSS, 320, 322) thought that Philip Smith of the Baydon line was more probably the M.P. than others of the name who were contemporaries, and who lived farther from Marlborough.

[237] S.P. 16, 528/32. The pedigree of the Wiltshire visitation was signed in 1623 by Henry Smith of Baydon, junior, then aged 31.

[238] Wilts Arch. Soc. MSS, Sadler's "Wiltshire Genealogy," Aldbourne.

[239] P.C.C., 18 Audley.

[240] Marlborough MSS, Chamberlains' Accounts, 1572–1771.

[241] London marriage licenses, 1521–1869, ed. Joseph Foster, 1247, London, 1887.

[242] His will referred to lands worth £140 a year which his eldest son John inherited in Cricklade and "Ogburne," by right of his mother, Elizabeth, but title to which was contested by "my uncle Mr. Thomas Goddard." It mentioned also legacies for the children from Thomas and Edward Goddard. P.C.C., 113 Bruce.

[243] C.J. 2: 109, 756; N. and Q., 1st Ser., 12: 360, 1855.

[244] Wilts. Arch. Mag. 26: 344, 1892.

[245] Thomason Tracts, 669. f. 21, p. 43; 669. f. 24, p. 37.

[246] Kensington parish registers, Harleian Society, Register Series, 16: 44, 45, 46, 1890.

[247] Morriss, The siege of Chester, 8; Pedigrees made at the visitation of Cheshire, 1613, Harleian Society, 59: 212–214, 1909 (hereafter, Vis. Cheshire, 1613); Ormerod, Chester 1: 341.

[248] Linc. Inn Rec. Adm. 1: 165.

[249] Shaw, K. of E. 2: 156.

[250] Chester Corporation MSS, Assembly Book, 1539–1624, fol. 332.

also to his grandfather's extensive properties then, although his father lived until 1621.[251] In 1616 Sir Thomas married Mary, daughter of Sir Hugh Smith of Long Ashton, Somerset, and sister of Thomas Smith, M.P. (*q.v.*), and afterwards visited often with his wife's family.[252] His younger brother, Stephen, went into the service of the Marquess of Ormonde and married a sister of the wife of the first Earl of Portland, Lord Treasurer.[253]

Smith became increasingly active in civic affairs, was Mayor of Chester, 1622–1623, and afterwards an alderman.[254] He was county sheriff in 1623, a J.P., and member of various commissions for the county.[255] In 1626 he lent £20 on a privy seal, one of the larger sums collected in the county, and the next year was one of the loan commissioners for Chester,[256] but in 1635 he objected with the support of the city officials to being assessed for ship money in more than one place, his protest bringing a reprimand from Council.[257] In 1638 Sir Thomas signed the letter from Chester to Council about the controversy between the city and the county on the ship money rates.[258]

Smith seems to have been a very popular and strong candidate for one of the city's seats for the Short Parliament, several other men withdrawing when it was learned that he was willing to stand, and the elections occurring before he returned from a visit with his Somerset relatives.[259] He was active in plans for the city's defense in the summer of 1640 and was being considered for mayor once more in October, but was chosen instead to return to Westminster.[260] On the national scene Smith was less prominent, but he was named to a few committees of the Long Parliament, including that on superstition and idolatry.[261] Pleading poor health, he obtained leave of absence in June, 1642, and apparently did not go back. He promised to advance some funds for the king in Chester that year,[262] and was disabled as a royalist, 22 January 1644,[263] but afterwards asserted that only military developments had thwarted his plans for returning to Westminster.[264] With his son he compounded for his estates in 1646, his fine being £6700 at two-thirds, later reduced to a third, or £3350.[265] Sir Thomas made his will in the summer of 1666, and died at Aston, near Birmingham, in 1668.[266]

Although Smith was intimately associated with Chester and had a town residence there, he was also something of a country gentleman, owning at least five manors and numerous other properties. He declared in 1646 that their annual value, above rents and annuities, was some £589, but he planned a £2000 marriage portion for at least one of his children, and even after his properties had been damaged by the war,[267] his will proposed a £1000 portion for another child.

Sir Thomas was a man respected and beloved by his neighbors and fellow townsmen, one whose "good Christmas jests" made his absences noted.[268] He was proud of his family, but asked to be buried as privately as decency and civility would permit.

Thomas Smith, or **Smyth** (1610–1642), of Long Ashton, Somerset, was elected M.P. for Bridgwater early in 1641, following the removal of Windham as a monopolist (21 January), but he was himself discharged for royalism on 5 August 1642.[269] He was the only son and heir of Sir Hugh Smith of Long Ashton (H.S., D.L., d. 1627),[270] by his wife, daughter of Sir Thomas Gorges of Langford, Wilts. Lady Smith was a sister of Lord Gorges and of Sir Theobald Gorges (*q.v.*), and after her husband's death married her kinsman, Sir Ferdinando Gorges.[271] Thomas was born in the summer of 1610, matriculated at St. John's College, Oxford, in 1624,[272] and on 12 April 1627, when he was not yet seventeen, married Florence, daughter of John Poulett, afterwards Baron Poulett of Hinton St. George. Three days after the wedding his father died,[273] and Thomas completed his education partly under the tutelage of his father-in-law. In April, 1629, Lord Poulett wrote to Dorchester regarding arrangements for Smith

[251] I.P.M. of Sir Thomas Smith, Public Record Office, Chester 3/97/12; will of Sir Thomas Smith at the Chester Probate Registry, an abstract of which is in *Palatine note-book* 2: 83–84, 1882.

[252] H. Hobhouse's MSS Genealogical Notes on the Smith Pedigree, Somerset Record Office, Taunton; *C.S.P. Dom., 1629–1631*, 412; *1639–1640*, 353.

[253] *Palatine note-book* 2: 83, 1882.

[254] Chester Corporation MSS, Assembly Book, 1539–1624, fols. 350, 363–369; 1624–1684, fols. 26v, *passim;* A9, Mayor's Court File, 1622.

[255] *C.S.P. Dom., 1619–1623*, 542; C. 193/12, 13; S.P. 16/405; C. 181/3; 181/4, fol. 192v.

[256] S.P. 16, 20/41 and 53/28.

[257] *C.S.P. Dom., 1634–1635*, 504; Harl. MSS, 2093, fol. 135.

[258] S.P. 16, 388/31.

[259] *C.S.P. Dom., 1639–1640*, 168, 341, *passim.*

[260] Chester Corporation MSS, Assembly Book, 1624–1684, fol. 52v; A2, Assembly Orders, 1639–1642, October 1640.

[261] Pink MSS, 307, fol. 145; *C.J.* 2: 84.

[262] Chester Corporation MSS, Assembly Book, 1624–1684, fol. 57.

[263] *C.J.* 3: 374.

[264] *Cheshire Sheaf*, 3rd Ser., 1: 90–91, 1896; *Cal. Com. Adv. Money*, 738–739.

[265] *Cheshire Sheaf*, 3rd Ser., 1: 70–72, 1896; *Cal. Com. Comp.*, 1319–1320.

[266] His place as alderman was filled at Chester on 15 May 1668 (Chester Assembly Book, 1624–1684, fol. 160v), and his will was proved the following November (P.C.C., 146 Hene). For the place of Smith's death, see J. H. Morrison, *Prerogative court of Canterbury, wills, sentences and probate acts,* 226, London, Mrs. F. E. Poulton, 1935.

[267] S.P. 23/187/75–76.

[268] *C.S.P. Dom., 1639–1640*, 353. See also *Complete Baronetage* 3: 112.

[269] Smith was present by 3 May, possibly as early as 25 February 1641. *C.J.* 2: 71, 92, 133; *M. of P.* 1: 492 and n.

[270] Collinson, *Somerset* 1: xxxviii; Add. MSS, 5496, fol. 7v.

[271] *Vis. Somerset*, 101; Collinson, *Somerset* 2: 293; *Somerset Arch. Proc.* 14 (ii): 58, 1867.

[272] *Al. Oxon.*

[273] I.P.M., Sir Hugh Smith, 1627. C. 142/438/130.

and another son-in-law to accompany the Earl of Danby on his mission to France.[274]

Meanwhile Smith had sat for Bridgwater in the 1628 parliament.[275] During the period of personal rule he assumed many responsibilities in his county. He was named to various local commissions,[276] was treasurer of the county hospitals in 1633, and was a J.P.[277] He was recommended for appointment as sheriff one year because of his wealth, ability, and social position,[278] but escaped being pricked. In 1639 Smith sent no reply to the request for a loan to the king.[279] In his election to parliament for the county in the spring of 1640 he was probably considered one of the popular party to which his wife's family, the Pouletts, still adhered. He may have been a candidate for the shire again in the autumn, coupled with Poulett, for a petition against the return of the more certain royalist, Stawell, was referred on 9 November to the Committee of Privileges.[280] Perhaps the prospect that Windham's seat for Bridgwater would soon be vacant offered Smith an easier entry, however, for nothing further appears concerning the county petition.

It is practically impossible to trace Smith's course in the daily work of the Long Parliament because of the number of "Mr. Smith"s who were present. With the coming of war, however, he joined with his brother-in-law, Sir John Poulett, in executing the Commission of Array, declined to attend upon summons, and was therefore disabled, 5 August 1642.[281] He went into Wales with the royalist army that year and died at Cardiff, 2 October 1642. His body was brought back to Long Ashton for burial.[282]

Smith was known in his lifetime as a man of good estate, having at least £2000 a year.[283] The land his family had been accumulating since one of them had been mayor of Bristol a century before included eight manors in Somerset and three in Gloucestershire.[284] He had a large town house in Bristol,[285] and in 1634 employed Inigo Jones to remodel the Long Ashton mansion.[286] When he made his will in 1638 Smith gave directions for raising portions of £2000 for each of his four young daughters, and assigned £300 for the deserving poor of three parishes.[287]

Thomas Smith's relatives in the 1640 Commons included his uncle, Sir Theobald Gorges, his brother-in-law, Poulett, and another brother-in-law, Sir Thomas Smith of Chester, his nephew, Hugh Rogers, and his cousin, Edward Phelipps.[288]

Sir Walter Smith (d. 1648), of Shalborne and Great Bedwin, was a member for the latter borough, 1640–5 February 1644.[289] His parentage is not definitely known, but he was a Londoner in his early years and perhaps did not take up residence in Wiltshire until about 1618. He was related, probably through his mother, to the Stonehouse family of Berkshire, Kent, and London. A cousin, Duke Stonehouse of Bexley, Kent, was the executor of Smith's will, and Smith was referred to in the will of the latter's uncles, Sir William Stonehouse of Radley (d. 1632) and Sir James Stonehouse of Islington (d. 1638 ?), as cousin and nephew.[290] He may have been the Walter Smith "of London" who matriculated at Queen's College, Oxford, in 1605, aged nineteen (B.A. 1608), and possibly was admitted to the Middle Temple in March, 1609, as the son and heir of Humphrey Smith of Charlton, Devon, deceased.[291] It was doubtless his connection with the courtly family of Stonehouse that led to his being knighted at Theobalds in 1616.[292] About two years later Smith made a settlement of his estates, including properties in Surrey, Islington, London, and other places in Middlesex, as if he were preparing for some major event in his life. Since the trustees of the settlement were Sir Francis Dowse of Hampshire and a brother,[293] whose family had Wiltshire connections (cf. Edward Dowse), it may be suggested that it concerned Smith's marriage with some relative of their family. And since Smith was at Great Bedwin by 1622,[294] at an estate in which he never had more than a life interest, it may be surmised that he moved from London to Wiltshire about the time of the settlement. In the 1630's Sir Walter Smith was a J.P in Wiltshire. He was among those rebuked in

beneficiaries of his charity be only those who had honestly contracted their poverty.

[288] Phelipps was mentioned as such in Smith's will. Their mothers were sisters.

[289] *M. of P.* **1**: 495; *C.J.* **3**: 389.

[290] Smith's will, P.C.C., 90 Essex; the Stonehouse wills in Brown, *Somerset Wills* **5**: 46–47. For the identification of Duke Stonehouse see *Vis. Kent, 1619,* 71; *Students admitted to the Inner Temple,* 229.

[291] *Al. Oxon.; Mid. Temp. Rec.* **2**: 504, 533. Possibly Smith's mother was a daughter of George Stonehouse of Radley, a household official under Elizabeth, who married the daughter of a London alderman. Several of his children married into western families (*Vis. Berks.* **1**: 132; *Vis. Kent, 1619,* 71). If Smith's father, a Devon man, died early Walter might have been reared in the home of one of his mother's kinsmen.

[292] Pink MSS, 311, fol. 496c. Sir James Stonehouse was of the king's privy chamber in 1614. Add. MSS, 24,934, fols. 113, 115.

[293] The settlement is referred to in Smith's will cited above.

[294] The celebrated Dr. Thomas Willis, son of Smith's steward, was born at Bedwin in January, 1621/2. John Aubrey, *Brief lives* (Clark) **2**: 302–303.

[274] *C.S.P. Dom., 1628–1629,* 530, 532.

[275] *M. of P.* **1**: 477.

[276] C. 181/4, fols. 3v, 172v; 181/5, fols. 11, 94, 317.

[277] Bates Harbin, *Members of Parliament, Somerset,* 149.

[278] *Somerset Arch. Proc.* **13** (ii): 11, 1865–1866.

[279] Rushworth **3**: 914.

[280] *C.J.* **2**: 22, 23.

[281] May, 226; *C.J.* **2**: 704.

[282] Collinson, *Somerset* **2**: 293; *Al. Oxon.*

[283] *Somerset Arch. Proc.* **13** (ii): 11, 1865–1866.

[284] Collinson, *Somerset* **2**: 81, 292, 296, 422, 425, 441; I.P.M. cited above.

[285] Bristol Corporation MSS, Audit Book **16** (1610), **20** (1630), **21** (1640, 1641); Common Council Book **3** (1642).

[286] Collinson, *Somerset* **2**: 294.

[287] P.C.C., 44 Pembroke. He directed that his children be given a complete and religious education, and asked that the

1637 for their negligence about providing timber for ships.[295] And in 1639 he ignored the king's request for a loan.[296]

The Long Parliament was Smith's first, and in it he took no prominent part. He withdrew from London before 1644, probably about the time the war began. He made the excuse afterwards that he left because of old age and infirmities, that he was forced by the royalists to go to Oxford in 1644 even while he was ill, and that he was not present in the Oxford assembly when it took its vote denouncing the parliament at Westminster.[297] He died in 1648 and was buried, a widower and childless, at Great Bedwin on 28 April 1648.[298]

According to his compounding particular and his will, Smith's property consisted of a lifetime lease at Great Bedwin and other holdings in and near London. Their value he estimated at slightly above £400 a year. His fine, reckoned at a third, £1600, or a tenth, £750, was finally adjusted to £1085, or £685, if he would settle £40 a year on a rectory at Islington.[299]

Smith was a kinsman, possibly a first cousin, of Sir George Stonehouse, his fellow M.P.

William Smith (c. 1616–1696), of the Middle Temple and of Akeley, Buckinghamshire, was elected for Winchelsea in February, 1641, after the ousting of Crispe as a monopolist, and was himself disabled, 16 January 1644.[300] He was the eldest son and heir of Robert Smith of Buckingham and London, Principal of New Inn (d. 1645), by his wife, Martha, and grandson of William Smith, a distinguished lawyer. Born about 1616, he matriculated at Trinity College, Oxford, 13 March 1635,[301] and fourteen months later entered the Middle Temple as William Smith of New Inn. He was fined for absences in 1639, but was called to the bar, 9 July 1641.[302] Possibly he had already gained some connection with the household of the dowager Duchess of Richmond and Lenox, one of the name being among the witnesses and executors of her will in 1639;[303] if so, his election for Winchelsea in 1641 may have been upon the nomination of her son, the Lord Warden of the Cinque Ports. No other connection with the port or even with Kent is known. Smith's first wife, whom he married probably after 1641, was Margaret, daughter of Sir Alexander Denton (q.v.).[304]

During the early months of the Long Parliament young Smith was not an active member. He was excused for being absent, 19 August 1641, but on 28 October made "a long confused yet well-penned speech," pleading for liberties but also for understanding among all parties, both in religious matters and on the question of the royal prerogative.[305] His politics perhaps resembled those of his father-in-law, Denton, who turned to royalism only when armed conflict approached. On 4 January 1642 Smith was named to go to the Middle Temple when four lawyer M.P.'s were sent as messengers to their respective inns to check an attempt to arouse the inns against parliament, and on 19 September of that year, having failed previously to subscribe for the defense, he announced that he would make a declaration of a considerable amount to the committee.[306] He was created D.C.L. at Oxford in November, 1642, and may have taken the Covenant, but probably withdrew soon afterwards from the House. He took up arms for the king, being for some time at Oxford,[307] and was accordingly disabled in 1644. He compounded for his delinquency, 1647–1649, was created a baronet in 1661, served again in parliament, and died at Stepney, Middlesex, in 1696, aged about eighty.

Since Smith's father was living in 1641 and he himself was not yet twenty-five, his income was probably not large then. When he compounded, he declared an interest of £110–£120 a year in some lands of his mother's, and declared his own income from lands in Bucks and tenements in Bristol to be about £218. His fine, set first at two-thirds, £108, was afterwards reduced by half, and, although there were reports of undervaluations, seems to have remained at the lower figure.[308]

Ralph Sneyd (c. 1612–1650), of Keele, Staffordshire, M.P. for Stafford, 1640–1643, was the heir apparent of a well known Staffordshire family. His father, Ralph (d. 1643), had long been a J.P.,[309] and had served as sheriff.[310] Ralph, junior, after he abandoned parliament to fight for the king, succeeded to estates in Staffordshire worth at least £800 a year, but they were somewhat encumbered by debts even before the outbreak of the war.[311] His brother stated in 1661 that lands worth £1000 a year were sold to pay Colonel Sneyd's debts.[312]

Simon Snow (c. 1590–c. 1668), of Exeter, merchant, was M.P. for his city, 1640–1648. He was the eldest

---

[295] C. 193/13; S.P. 16/405; C.S.P. Dom., 1637, 137.

[296] Rushworth 3: 915.

[297] Cal. Com. Comp., 948; S.P. 23/174/669.

[298] Wilts. Arch. Mag. 6: 300, 1860.

[299] Cal. Com. Comp., 948–949; S.P. 23/174/654, 659.

[300] M. of P. 1: 497; C.J. 3: 369.

[301] Complete Baronetage 3: 191; Al. Oxon.

[302] Mid. Temp. Rec. 2: 848, 885, 911.

[303] Arch. Cant. 11: 250, 1877.

[304] Margaret Denton was baptized in 1625. Complete Baronetage.

[305] D'Ewes (C), 44–45; Diurnal occurrences, 1640, 1641, 395–399.

[306] D'Ewes (C), 378, 379; C.J. 2: 772.

[307] Cal. Com. Adv. Money, 1150; Pink MSS, 311, fol. 498d.

[308] Cal. Com. Comp., 68, 1770–1771; S.P. 23/203/491, 495, 497, 503.

[309] C. 193/12, 13.

[310] Burke, Landed gentry, 1853.

[311] S.P. 23/190/341–343. The family seems to have managed to pay some £2000 in fines for royalism. Cal. Com. Comp., 1032–1034.

[312] Wedgwood, Staff. Parl. Hist. 2: 61–62, 113.

son of Thomas Snow, merchant and bailiff of Exeter (d. 1609), by Grace, daughter of Peter Vilvayne (bailiff, 1579), and was the nephew and eventual heir of Dr. Robert Vilvayne, Exeter's physician and benefactor. He was born probably about 1590, and was admitted as a merchant to the freedom of Exeter on 24 January 1624.[313] He married (1) a daughter of Peter and Joan Taylor, and (2) on 7 May 1626 at Allhallows, Elinor Chappell.[314] He seems to have lived in Allhallows parish.[315]

Snow was handling some of the city's funds in 1631, and in 1635 he was elected to the city council of twenty-four.[316] He was employed thereafter for many civic functions, ranging from supervision of the streets, waterworks, and charities, to the preparation of new regulations for the city's wool business. He was sent in 1636 to interview the bishop about a complaint the cathedral authorities had made to the king against the city government.[317] And in 1639, having been concerned about a new lease for the farm of the city's quay and haven, Snow acquired the farm of the haven for a year himself, apparently as the financial backer of the new lessees. He was frequently responsible for the administering of the city money,[318] a foreshadowing of the important part he was to play in later years as financier for the town.[319] In many of his civic actions Snow was affiliated wtih Robert Walker, his colleague in parliament in 1640. One of his intimates was the wealthy merchant of Plymouth, Robert Trelawney (q.v.), in whose will Snow was named.[320] Snow was probably a man known by many of the west country merchants outside of Exeter.

Snow is said to have been chosen for the Short Parliament to replace James Tucker, but if so, it was so late that he probably did not serve before the dissolution.[321] He attended the meetings of the Long Parliament regularly during its first year, and gave his bond jointly with Walker for £1000 for the 1640 loan.[322] He was not active on committees, however, and seems to have been hesitant about his course as the crisis approached. During part of the autumn of 1641 and in 1642 Snow was in Exeter while parliament was sitting, and although on 30 August 1642 his wages for attending parliament 265 days were voted,[323] both he and his colleague, Walker, were summoned several times that year to attend the House. Eventually Snow resumed his seat and maintained at least the fiction of loyalty to parliament until the purge of 1648.[324] Afterwards he served as mayor of Exeter, and was returned again to parliament in 1660. He died about 1668. His will, dated 24 January 1667/8, was proved on 31 March 1669.[325]

Simon Snow was a well-to-do merchant. He was among the biggest ratepayers in his parish before the war, and he had real estate in other parishes and outside the city.[326] His backing of the 1640 loan and his bonds and legacies for Exeter afterwards are further indications of his prosperity.[327]

Thomas Soame (c. 1584–1671), grocer and alderman of London, was one of the London M.P.'s, 1640–1648. Descended from a Norfolk family, he was the third son of Sir Stephen Soame (d. 1619), grocer, alderman, Lord Mayor, and M.P. for London, by his wife, Anne, daughter of William Stone of London. Sir Stephen had been active in the East India, Virginia, and other trading companies,[328] and at the time of his death was said to be worth £6000 in lands and £40,000 in goods.[329] Thomas was born about 1584,[330] and with his brother, John, was admitted by patrimony to the Grocers' Company in 1615 and to the livery in 1617. He was one of the active members of the company between 1630 and 1650.[331] By that time he had become a great merchant

---

[313] Although some authorities have called Snow his father's second son, he was styled "senior" son when he was admitted to the freedom of Exeter (Exeter Corporation MSS, Mayor's Court Book 83, fol. 297). His father had seven children, of whom three were sons. The eldest child was born on 21 September 1590, and the youngest in 1607 (H.M.C., Report on the records of the city of Exeter, 81). Thomas, probably the second son, was baptized at Allhallows in 1592; a daughter was baptized there in 1594 (H. Tapley-Soper, ed., Exeter parish registers 2, Allhallows, 21, Devon and Cornwall Record Society, 1933). See also Devon Trans. 61: 211, 1929.

[314] Exeter parish registers 2: 8; Western Antiquary 6: 15, 1886–1887.

[315] Exeter Corporation MSS, Subsidy Rolls, Sect. II, nos. 15, 17, 18.

[316] Exeter Corporation MSS, Act Book 7, fol. 790; 8, fols. 48, 49; Devon Trans. 33: 260, 1901.

[317] Exeter Corporation MSS, Act Book 8, fols. 55–150, passim.

[318] Ibid. 8, fols. 156–193; Receivers' Accounts, 1635–1638.

[319] He gave his bond for the city not less than seven times between 1648 and 1661, for sums ranging from £90 to £3000. For this fact I am indebted to Mr. W. A. Gay, who was curator of the city manuscripts at the time I used them.

[320] J. P. Baxter, ed., The Trelawny papers (Collections of the Maine Historical Society), 448, 455.

[321] Devon Trans. 61: 203, 1929.

[322] D'Ewes (N), 52.

[323] Exeter Corporation MSS, Act Book 8, fols. 236–247, 266, 275–287.

[324] C.J. 2: 699, 845, 888; Exeter Act Book 8, fols. 304, 380, 393; W. Cotton and H. Woolcombe, Gleanings from the municipal . . . records of Exeter, 137, Exeter, 1877; O.P.H. 9: *23.

[325] Devon Trans. 61: 211, 1929; P.C.C., 37 Coke.

[326] Exeter Corporation MSS, Subsidy Rolls cited above; Exeter Cathedral Library MSS, 3499, letter 223; Exeter City Library MSS, Exeter Deeds and Documents, Nos. 1859, 2912.

[327] Devon Trans. 61: 211, 1929; H.M.C., Report on the records of the city of Exeter, 332, 335.

[328] Brown, Genesis of the U. S., 1018; Carr, Select charters of trading companies, 64, 80; Add. MSS, 24,934, fol. 3.

[329] C.S.P. Dom., 1619–1623, 49. His annual income was elsewhere estimated at £4000. Norwich Library MSS, 6183.

[330] He died in January, 1671, "aged" eighty-eight. Pink MSS, 308, fol. 14.

[331] MSS of the Grocers' Company of London, Quire of Wardens' Accounts, 1611–1622, fol. 147; Calendar of Orders

in his own right, being interested in the Russia Company, the East India Company, of which he was a prominent member, and in trade in the Adriatic. He was part owner in 1634 of at least one ship.[332]

Early in 1629 Soame served in the London Court of Requests, and he was named later to special royal commissions for the London area.[333] He was an alderman in 1635 and also sheriff of Middlesex, and in the latter capacity collected ship money, but was warned by Council regarding his arrears.[334] Besides serving regularly thereafter as alderman, Soame became colonel of one of the city regiments in 1638, and continued as such until 1642.[335]

Soame and his family were closely connected with the puritan circles of the eastern counties. He was acquainted with the Winthrops [336] and was a brother-in-law of Sir Nathaniel Barnardiston. His religious views were possibly on the borders of Independency, although he has usually been accounted a Presbyterian.[337] Even before his own delays in the matter of ship money collections, the name of Soame had occurred in instances of opposition to royal policies. His father had been a musters defaulter for one of his estates in 1619, and his elder brother, Sir William, had been summoned before Council for failing to contribute his assessment for the Palatinate wars.[338] Thomas himself was delinquent about the £130 asked of him in 1626–1627, but does not appear to have been arrested.[339] He attained greater notoriety, however, in 1640. After having served for London in the Short Parliament, Soame was one of the four aldermen who were imprisoned in the Fleet by Council order of May 10 for their refusal to list the men in their wards able to advance money for the loan the king demanded from the city. When they were examined in the Star Chamber Soame offended the king further by bluntly declaring that he considered the duty required of him dishonest.[340] Again, in the mayoralty elections at the end of September, when the loan was once more an issue, Soame, though by seniority not yet near to the office, was the leading candidate. He might have been declared elected had the Lord

Mayor not managed the election so as to have the choice fall on one more pleasing to the king.[341]

Re-elected a few weeks later to parliament, Soame was a member of Pym's party. He was named to the committee on grievances and to that for the recess, as well as to several lesser ones,[342] and though he was knighted at Hampton Court with four other aldermen in December, 1641,[343] his loyalty to parliament was unshaken. He was especially helpful in financial matters, not only pledging two horses himself for the defense in June, 1642, but being instrumental in securing a substantial loan from the Grocers' Company for the same purpose.[344] In 1647 it was ordered that £1440 be repaid to him.[345] Soame was a member also of the committee on maimed soldiers.[346] He was secluded by the purge of 1648 and removed from his aldermanship a few months later, but returned with the Rump and to his municipal office in 1660. He died on 1 January 1671 and was buried at Throcking in Hertfordshire.

He had married Joan, daughter of William Freeman of Alpenden, Herts, and had a residence at Throcking. Besides his chief property there and his business in London, Soame owned other lands. Some of his neighbors in Enfield complained in 1637 that his tax rates were too low, since he was "a man of a greate estate besides his lands of inheritance." [347] His London house in Soper Lane was listed among the finest in a 1638 catalogue of rents.[348] More distant properties were in Carlton, Northamptonshire.[349]

Soame was no doubt well known by many of his fellow members of the 1640 parliament, and he was related to two of them, Barnardiston, his brother-in-law, and Sir Philip Parker, their nephew. Another kinsman, the poet Herrick, eulogized Soame as one not wearing his civic purple only for show, but for true service, worthy of the gown.[350]

William Spurstow (d. 1646 ?), a London merchant, was M.P. for his native town of Shrewsbury from 1640 until his death shortly before 19 January 1646. He

---

of the Court of Assistants, **3**: 48, 227, *passim; ***4**: 220, *passim;* Index of Freemen, 1345–1645.

[332] W. S. Page, *The Russia Company from 1553–1660,* 80, London, W. Brown, 1912; Sainsbury, *A calendar of court minutes, &c. of the East India Company, 1635–1639,* 39; *1640–1643,* 61, 177, *passim; C.S.P. Dom., 1634–1635,* 234; *C.S.P. Venetian, 1640–1642,* 233.

[333] C. 181/4, fol. 157v; 181/5, fol. 285; London Corporation MSS, Rep. 43, fol. 81v.

[334] *Ibid.,* Rep. 49, fols. 202, 282v; Rep. 50, fols. 3, 159v; *C.S.P. Dom., 1635–1636,* 419, 549, 559.

[335] London Corporation MSS, Rep. 52, fol. 264v.

[336] *Winthrop Papers* **1**: 407, 411, 1929.

[337] *A.H.R.* **44**: 37, n., 1938–1939.

[338] *C.S.P. Dom., 1619–1623,* 48; S.P. 14, 148/29.

[339] S.P. 16, 44/13; 73/13.

[340] *C.S.P. Dom., 1640,* 142, 155, 168, 170; Add. MSS, 11,045 (Scudamore Papers), fol. 116.

[341] *Ibid.,* fol. 122; *C.S.P. Dom., 1640–1641,* 115; *Calendar of Clarendon State Papers* **1**: 207–208; Gardiner, *H. of E.* **9**: 211, 214.

[342] *C.J.* **2**: 82, 288.

[343] Shaw, *K. of E.* **2**: 211.

[344] *N. and Q.,* 1st Ser., **12**: 359, 1855; *C.J.* **2**: 612.

[345] *H.M.C., Sixth Report,* App., House of Lords MSS, 174.

[346] Add. MSS, 22,619, fol. 181.

[347] S.P. 16, 376/101.

[348] T. C. Dale, *The inhabitants of London in 1638,* 173.

[349] He was reported to Star Chamber for offences resulting in depopulation there in 1639 (*C.S.P. Dom., 1639–1640,* 144), and in Cromwell's time was listed as the patron of Carlton rectory (Lansd. MSS, 459, fol. 179v).

[350] *The poetical works of Robert Herrick,* 176, Moorman ed., Oxford, 1915.

Additional references: *M. of P.;* Pink MSS, 308, fol. 14; 311, fol. 482v; *Vis. London* (Harleian Society, **17**) **2**: 251, 1883; Beaven, *The aldermen of the city of London* **1**: 102, 103; **2**: 63.

was the eldest son of Thomas Spurstow of Shrewsbury and his wife, Catherine, and a grandson of Roger Spurstow,[351] who was an active member of the Company of Sheremen in that city. The family had been engaged in the woolen industry of Shrewsbury since the late fifteenth century.[352] By 1594 William Spurstow was a member of the local Drapers' Company and by 1602 had become one of the company's London brethren. He was still listed as a member of the Shrewsbury company in 1624, but was probably in London most of the time after 1602. He continued to work for his old company's interests for at least a decade,[353] but his own affairs prospered at London and his interests widened. About 1604 Spurstow married Damaris, daughter of Henry Parkhurst of Guildford,[354] and sister of Robert Parkhurst, also of the cloth trade, who became Lord Mayor of London. He was admitted in 1606 to the Mercers' Company of London by redemption,[355] and to London citizenship.[356] Eventually he took up residence on Coleman Street, was a member of the London Court of Requests in 1624 and 1633,[357] and one of the commission to deal with policies of assurance on the royal exchange in 1630 and 1631.[358]

Spurstow was an associate of Thomas Soame (q.v.) and others of the East India adventurers in 1624.[359] He was among the Londoners who refused to contribute to the forced loan and in 1627 was sent in custody to Lancashire for a time.[360] He was a member of the Massachusetts Bay Company in 1629,[361] and by 1635 was one of the inner group of wealthy merchants and a director of the East India Company.[362] He was named in 1636 as an examiner of the city's tables of package, scavage, balliage and portage.[363] In the year of the Long Parliament Spurstow was listed as one of the wealthy men of his ward and able to advance money to the crown.[364]

Although Spurstow had not sat in parliament before, Shrewsbury, in whose affairs he had continued to take an interest, elected him in the autumn of 1640, and he soon became an active member. He was named with the Londoners on most of the delegations sent to deal with the city, and served on numerous committees, including that for the recess.[365] He pledged £200 for the defense in June, 1642,[366] and showed himself strongly in favor of reforms in both church and state, as was his son and namesake, the Presbyterian chaplain of the parliamentary army. Spurstow died shortly before 19 January 1646 and, if the directions in his will were followed, was buried in St. Stephen's, Coleman Street.[367]

Spurstow's will gives evidence not only of its author's Calvinistic views but of his worldly possessions. He assigned some lands in Shropshire and Montgomeryshire to his elder son, having apparently arranged for his business interests to be shared by his younger children. To them he assigned legacies of £6000, and to friends and relatives sums of over £630, and left more than £600 to charities in Shrewsbury and London and for Cambridge scholars.

Spurstow's second son, Henry, was a mercer, a member of the East India and Levant companies, and a London alderman (1661).[368]

Thomas Standish (c. 1594–1642), of Duxbury Hall near Chorley, Lancashire, sat for Preston-in-Amounderness, 1640–1642. The son and heir of Alexander Standish of Duxbury (d. 1623), by his wife Alice (or Margaret), daughter of Ralph Ashton of Great Lever, and a first cousin of Ralph Ashton, M.P. for Clitheroe (q.v.), Standish was born about 1594.[369] He probably studied at Queen's, Cambridge, was admitted to Gray's Inn in 1614, and succeeded his father in 1623, having by that time married and lost a wife. He married (1) Anne, daughter of Sir Thomas Wingfield of Letheringham, Suffolk, and (2) Anne, daughter of Christopher Whittingham of Suffolk.[370]

Standish was a J.P. in his county in 1626, a sewers commissioner in 1627,[371] M.P. for Liverpool, 1626, and for Preston in the Short Parliament.[372] He was a parliamentarian in views, went into Lancashire early in 1642 to assist with the Protestation,[373] and was probably

[351] Vis. London, Harleian Society, 2: 259.
[352] H. E. Forrest, Shrewsbury burgess roll, 272, Shrewsbury, Shrops. Arch. & Par. Reg. Soc., 1924.
[353] Information supplied by T. C. Mendenhall of Yale University from his study of the records of the Shrewsbury Drapers' Company.
[354] Vis. London 2: 259. His son, William, the Presbyterian divine, was born probably in 1605 (D.N.B.). Robert Parkhurst, M.P. for Guildford in 1640, was a nephew of Damaris.
[355] Note supplied by Mr. Frank D. Watney, Clerk of the Mercers' Company.
[356] London Corporation MSS, Rep. 27, fol. 225v.
[357] Ibid., Rep. 38, fol. 205; Rep. 47, fol. 130.
[358] Ibid., Rep. 44, fol. 326; C. 181/4, fol. 102.
[359] C.S.P. Colonial, East Indies, 1622–1624, 491, 492.
[360] S.P. 16, 72/63; 89/2; Rushworth 1: 473.
[361] F. Rose-Troup, The Massachusetts Bay Company and its predecessors, 74, 155.
[362] Sainsbury, A calendar of the court minutes, &c. of the East India Company, 1635–1639, vi, 73, 185; 1640–1643, 177.
[363] C.S.P. Dom., 1635–1636, 241.
[364] S.P. 16, 453/75.

[365] C.J. 2: 24, 44, 288, 294, passim.
[366] N. and Q., 1st Ser., 12: 360, 1855.
[367] His will, dated 20 September 1644, was proved 4 February 1645/6 (P.C.C., 26 Twisse). A new election to fill his seat in parliament was ordered on 19 January 1646. M. of P. 1: 492, n.; 3: xliv.
[368] Beaven, The aldermen of London 2: 92.
[369] He was aged twenty-nine and more in September, 1623. I.P.M. of Alexander Standish, Public Record Office, D.L., 7/24/56.
[370] Ibid.; Al. Cant.; Vis. Lanc., 1613, 46; Pink and Beaven, Parl. Rep. Lanc., 151–152.
[371] C. 193/12; C. 181/3.
[372] M. of P. 1: 470, 482.
[373] A letter from the Lancashire commissioners to the Speaker was dated at Chorley, 2 March 1641/2. Bodleian Tanner MSS, 66, fol. 284.

absent from the House much of the time thereafter. His name does not appear among those subscribing for the defense funds in the summer of 1642, and he died sometime between 4 October and 11 November 1642.[374]

At least three manors in Lancashire were included in Standish's inheritance,[375] and he was of sufficient importance to find a bride with £2000 portion for his heir.[376] Besides being a cousin of Ralph Ashton, the Clitheroe member, Standish was a connection by marriage of the Shuttleworths.

Ferdinando Stanhope (c. 1615–1643), fourth son of Philip, first Earl of Chesterfield,[377] was M.P. for Tamworth, Staffordshire, from 1640 until he was disabled, 27 March 1643. He was admitted to Sidney Sussex, Cambridge, in January, 1636, and awarded the degree of M.A. that year.[378] He probably owed his election at Tamworth in 1640 to his father's second wife, Anne, widow of Sir Humphrey Ferrers of Tamworth Castle.[379] Late in 1641 Ferdinando married her daughter, Lettice, and had settled on him by his father two manors in Nottinghamshire.[380]

Stanhope was a nephew by the half-blood of William Stanhope, Nottingham M.P., and had connections by marriage with Noel, Tufton, Hales, and Pakington.[381] A royalist comment praised his virtues of gentleness and affability as well as his courage.[382]

William Stanhope (born c. 1591), of Linbey, Notts, was M.P. for Nottingham, 1640–1644. Born about 1591, he was a younger son of Sir John Stanhope of Elvaston, Derbyshire (d. 1609 ?), by his second wife, Catherine, daughter of Thomas Trentham of Staffordshire, and a half-brother of Philip, first Earl of Chesterfield. He was admitted to the Inner Temple in 1612,[383] and probably visited at times with his kinsman, Sir Michael Stanhope of Sudbury, Suffolk,[384] for on 10 July 1622 he married at Wordwell in that county Anne,

a younger daughter of Sir Bassingborne Gawdy.[385] She was a half-sister of Framlingham Gawdy (q.v.), who provided her with a modest portion of £200.[386] Stanhope owned some Derbyshire properties settled on him by his father in 1609, and was variously described as of Elvaston or of Highedge in Derbyshire, and as of Edmondsbury, Suffolk, but he seems to have lived in or near Nottingham most of the time after 1629, and in 1639 described himself as of Linbey, Notts.[387] Although his brother, Sir John, was a ship money refuser of some note in 1635, William seems to have been little in the public eye, and to have held no office before 1640. He was one of the sponsors of a petition sent by the millers and fullers of his county to Council in July, 1640, however, and was named in 1641 a commissioner for Sherwood forest.[388] He was made a freeman of Nottingham, 12 October 1640.[389]

The Long Parliament was Stanhope's first, and he was inconspicious there. Although he was a brother-in-law of such popular party men as Sir Thomas Hutchinson and Gawdy, and a cousin of Denzil Holles, he went with the Stanhopes to the support of the king, and was disabled as a royalist, 22 January 1644.[390] He is said to have lived to a great age,[391] at least until 1672.

Little is known of Stanhope's wealth. He invested £100 in stock in the Irish fisheries venture in 1633,[392] and before 1648 owned a number of properties in Nottingham as well as in the county.[393]

Ferdinando Stanhope, M.P. for Tamworth, was a half-nephew.[394]

* Sir Philip Stapleton (1603–1647), of Warter, Yorkshire, and of London, M.P. for Boroughbridge, 1640–1647, soldier and Presbyterian leader, was of the Wighill family. He was admitted to the Inner Temple in 1620,[395] and his first marriage with Sir John Hotham's widowed daughter, Frances Gee, occurred in 1629.[396]

---

[374] His will, dated 4 October and proved 2 December, was filed at Chester with an inventory taken 11 November 1642. Chester Probate Registry.

[375] I.P.M. cited above.

[376] List of debts due Standish, filed with his will.

[377] Wedgwood, *Staff. Parl. Hist.* **2**: 87. Ferdinando Stanhope is mentioned in *D.N.B.*, "Philip Stanhope, first Earl of Chesterfield," but the date of his death appears there as 1644.

[378] *Al. Cant.*

[379] Lipscomb, *Buckingham* **1**: 479–480. The town was a closed corporation (Add. MSS, 28,175, fol. 109). Ferdinando was captured at the fall of Tamworth Castle to the parliamentarians in June, 1643. Bodleian Rawl. MSS, D 141, "England's Memorable Accidents," 116.

[380] British Museum Add. Charters, 58525.

[381] Hasted, *Kent* **5**: 403; Lipscomb, *loc. cit.*

[382] Harl. MSS, 2043, fol. 179v.

[383] *Students admitted to the Inner Temple,* 199.

[384] Add. MSS, 6673 (A. Wolley's Derbyshire Collections), fol. 233v; Add. MSS, 15,520, fol. 126v; Eg. MSS, 2410, fol. 4.

[385] *West Stow and Wordwell parish registers,* S. H. A. Hervey, ed., Suffolk Green Books, **7**: 100, Woodbridge, G. Booth, 1903.

[386] Chancery suit regarding Sir Bassingborne's younger children, 1625, C. 2/352/4.

[387] Add. MSS, 6670, fols. 355–359; Nottingham Corporation MSS, Hall Book 3413, fol. 20. Several of Stanhope's children were baptized at St. Mary's, Nottingham, 1630–1637 (MSS Parish Registers), and he was a rate payer in that parish in 1637 (Thoroton Soc., *Trans.* **33**: 16, 1929).

[388] *C.S.P. Dom.,* 1635, 558; 1636–1637, 338, 365; 1640, 532; C. 181/5, fol. 420.

[389] Nottingham Corp. MSS, Hall Book 3415, fol. 91.

[390] *C.J.* **3**: 374.

[391] *Notts and Derbys. N. and Q.* **2**: 47, 1894.

[392] S.P. 16, 231/16; *C.S.P. Dom.,* 1635–1636, 532.

[393] Nottingham Public Library MSS, Clement's collection of deeds, No. 17.

[394] Other references are: *Vis. Notts.,* 8; Thoroton, *Notts.* **1**: 288; **2**: 234; Add. MSS, 6674 (Wolley's collection), fol. 186; *M. of P.*

[395] *Al. Cant.*

[396] Marriage license cited in *Yorks. Arch. Jour.* **20**: 83, 1909. The date given in *D.N.B.* is 1627.

He was a member of the East Riding sewers commission for some years,[397] and was also a J.P. there.[398] In the Short Parliament he sat for Hedon.[399]

Although Clarendon states that, as a younger son, Stapleton enjoyed but a moderate estate of about £500 a year, he pledged £500 to support the proposed loan in March, 1641,[400] and afterwards directed in his will that his three daughters should have portions of £1000 each.[401]

Besides being related by his first marriage with Sir John Hotham and his son, Stapleton was a brother-in-law of Henry Cholmley and was connected through his mother's family with the Fenwicks. He was described by one of his friends, probably Denzil Holles, as not strong of body, but full of spirit, "quick of apprehension, sound of judgment, of clear and good elocution," one who overspent his energies for the cause.[402]

*Anthony Stapley (1590–1655), of Patcham, Sussex, M.P. for his county, 1640–1653, was the regicide. His father, Anthony, died in 1606, and he was for a time a ward of the crown, his manors in Sussex and Somersetshire being managed for him by trustees. One of them was Thomas Pelham,[403] father of Sir Thomas Pelham, the 1640 M.P., and Stapley may have lived for a time in his home, for he was identified as of East Hoathley, one of the Pelham residences, when he was admitted to Gray's Inn on 5 January 1608/9.[404] He was described as of Lewes in 1614 at the time of his marriage to his first wife, Ann Goring.[405]

Stapley was listed as a possibility for sheriff of Sussex in 1625, but he was not pricked.[406] He was named to various local commissions between 1624 and 1640,[407] and had served some years as a J.P. before the well known report to Laud's chaplain that Stapley was a ringleader in the attempt to bring ecclesiastical innovations before the justices.[408] He was named a D.L. for the county in 1642,[409] and may have acted as such before. His experience in four parliaments before the Long Parliament had prepared him for an active role under the leadership of Pym.

Stapley was sufficiently well-to-do to be asked for a loan to the crown in 1639, a request which he ignored.[410] In 1642 he promised to furnish two horses for the defense.[411] He owned lands in several parts of Sussex, but his brief will late in 1654 gives little indication of what his financial standing was.

James Rivers and Sir Thomas Pelham were among Stapley's relatives and close friends. Henry Shelley was a neighbor.

* Sir John Stawell, K.B. (1600–1662), of Cothelstone, near Taunton, was M.P. for Somerset, 1640–8 August 1642. He was born in August, 1600.[412] By his mother's second marriage he acquired a stepbrother, who, as Sir Edward Griffin (q.v.), sat with him afterwards in parliament. Stawell married Elizabeth (Hext), widow of Sir Joseph Killigrew, on 9 December 1617.[413] In his county he was active as sheriff, D.L., and J.P.[414] His service on many commissions included that for the 1626 benevolence, for which he was said to have worked heartily.[415] His official zeal, however, brought some complaints, for in the 1628 parliament Stawell was accused of having billeted a soldier in a parliament member's house and of attempting to use the military to influence elections.[416] He was afterwards sued in Star Chamber by Sir Robert Phelipps for allegedly assaulting and using abusive language toward the sheriff at a county election. Stawell was fined £200 but the fine had been "respited" by 1633. The occasion of the attack was probably the 1625 shire election, for Stawell was chosen for the county then and Phelipps was sheriff that year. Stawell was said to have returned from the Star Chamber hearings pleased with the king's gracious usage of him.[417] A later critic of Stawell, Sir Edward Bayntun (q.v.), once described him as "a lofty proud man." [418]

In 1639 Stawell contributed £100 toward the king's expenses in the north.[419] His emerging as a candidate for the county election in October, 1640, after having sat but once before (1625), may have resulted from urging by friends of the king. In becoming a candidate in his shire he possibly upset plans of the Poulett family to occupy both county seats instead of one as in the spring,

[397] C. 181/4, fol. 189v; 181/5, fols. 82, 331.
[398] C. 193/13; S.P. 16/405.
[399] Willis 3: 238.
[400] D'Ewes (N), 439, n.
[401] Yorks. Arch. Jour. 8: 459, 1884.
[402] Ibid.
[403] Sussex Rec. Soc. 14: 216, 1912; C.S.P. Dom., 1628–1629, 11; MSS of the Sussex Archaeological Society at Lewes, Calendar of Deeds, H 83 (notes supplied by Mildred Campbell).
[404] Gray's Inn Adm. Reg., 120.
[405] The license was dated 11 May 1614 (Sussex Rec. Soc. 1: 89, 1902), and the wedding occurred on 19 May. Add. MSS, 5698, fol. 93v.
[406] S.P. 16, 9/43.
[407] C. 181/3; 181/4, fol. 47; 181/5, fols. 136, 138; Sussex Arch. Coll. 9: 105, 1857.
[408] C. 193/15; S.P. 16/405; C.S.P. Dom., 1639–1640, 386.
[409] Thomas-Stanford, Sussex in the great Civil War, 42.

[410] Rushworth 3: 914.
[411] N. and Q., 1st Ser., 12: 360, 1855.
[412] The date of his birth is based upon the statement of his age at the time of his father's I.P.M. (Calendar of Sherborne muniments, 189–190). The date in D.N.B., 1599, was apparently based on the statement of his age at the time he entered Oxford.
[413] G. D. Stawell, The Stawells of Cothelstone, 83.
[414] Collinson, Somerset 3: 251; Bates Harbin, Members of Parliament, Somerset, 143; S.P. 16, 10/48.
[415] C. 181/4, fol. 172v; 181/5, fols. 316, 339; C.S.P. Dom., 1625–1626, 445.
[416] Diary of Walter Yonge, Esq., 115, Camden Society, 1848; Acts P.C., 1627, 270, 453–454; S.P. 16, 102/57.
[417] S.P. 16, 232/43/107; Bates Harbin, loc. cit.
[418] Stawell, op. cit., 395.
[419] Rushworth 3: 911.

and at least one protest about his election was presented to parliament.[420]

Sir John was one of the members of the House who offered their bonds for £1000 to secure the 1640 loan.[421] That he was very wealthy all writers agree. The yearly value of his lands which lay in four of the southwestern counties was at least £3200, probably more.[422] Clarendon said that his estate was one of the greatest in those parts,[423] and when his son was listed for the Order of the Royal Oak, his income was estimated to be £5000 a year.[424] Collinson described Stawell as "one of the most eminent persons in this county for estate, wisdom, and prudence."[425] To these attributes might be added his scientific knowledge, for he was much interested in chemistry.

Among Stawell's kinsmen in the 1640 Commons were his stepbrother, Griffin, and his stepdaughter's husband, William Bassett. Through his wife he was a connection of Sir George Stonehouse of Berkshire.

Edward Stephens (1597–c. 1670), of Little Sodbury, Gloucestershire, was M.P. for Tewkesbury. He was returned first in October, 1640, but the election was voided the following August because of a contest. Another double return followed in October, 1641. Stephens probably took his place then, although a final decision on the case was not reached until the end of 1643. He sat until 1648.[426] A first cousin of the county member, Nathaniel Stephens, Edward was the son of a prominent lawyer, Thomas Stephens (d. 1613), and his London wife, Elizabeth Stone. He was born on 23 April 1597,[427] studied at Oxford and the Middle Temple, and retained his connections at the Temple at least until 1636.[428] In or before 1619 he married Anne, daughter of Sir Thomas Crew of Stene, Northamptonshire, a sister of John Crew (q.v.).[429]

Stephens was active in Gloucestershire affairs, being a J.P., a member of the commission of oyer and ter-

miner,[430] and a captain in the trained bands.[431] As sheriff of the county, 1635–1636, he collected ship money with some difficulty and expense, ending the year somewhat in arrears, and about £150 out of pocket.[432] He supported the candidacy of his puritan cousin, Nathaniel Stephens, in the county election of the spring of 1640, thereby incurring the wrath of the more conservative groups and damaging the "fair esteem" in which he had previously been held.[433] His own election at Tewkesbury was his first experience of the kind, and he seems to have been elected there because the broader group of voters preferred him to Alford, the candidate of royalist tendencies. The delay in the deciding of the case prevented his being an active member in the House during the first year of the Long Parliament, and even afterwards he was overshadowed by his more vigorous cousin, Nathaniel. He supported parliament during the war, and survived until about 1670.[434]

Edward Stephens inherited from his father two Gloucestershire manors,[435] and he probably inherited some of the wealth of his maternal grandfather, but there are few indications of the extent of his estate. He may have owned some East India Company stock,[436] and in December, 1642, he was one of a group who gave their bonds for £6000 for repaying a loan advanced by the Bristol merchants for the cause.[437]

Nathaniel Stephens (1589–1660), of Eastington, Gloucestershire, represented his county, 1640–1648. Born in 1589, he was the only surviving son of Richard Stephens of Eastington (d. 1599) by his first wife, Margaret, daughter of Edward Seintloe of Kingston, Wilts,[438] and a first cousin of Edward Stephens (q.v.). He was admitted in 1604 to the Middle Temple and maintained his connections there long afterwards without being called to the bar.[439] In or before 1617 he married Catherine Beale.[440] He was a J.P. by 1623.[441] He was appointed a loan commissioner for his county in 1627 and was one of those who refused to serve or to advance money himself. The resulting summons before Council brought him into greater prominence. He failed to appear, but was not imprisoned.[442] His elec-

[420] See Thomas Smith.

[421] D'Ewes (N), 52.

[422] The "particular" among Sir John's compounding papers on which the above figure is based does not include his Devonshire properties (Pole, *Description of Devonshire*, 78); but a statement of the rents collected from his estate at one time during the war indicates a somewhat lower value then. S.P. 23/226/339–346; S.P. 23/119/863–867. An allowance of £500 yearly, or one-fifth of his estate, was made for the use of his family (*D.N.B.*).

[423] *Rebellion* 3: 78.

[424] *English Baronetage* 4: 374, 1741.

[425] *Somerset* 3: 251.

[426] *M. of P.* 1: 489 and n.; Williams, *Gloucester*, 59, 237–238. See Tewkesbury election.

[427] Williams, *op. cit.*, 52; I.P.M., Thomas Stephens, C. 142/335/30; I.P.M., Richard Stephens, C. 142/256/39; *Vis. Glouc.*, 151–152.

[428] He was admitted to the Middle Temple in 1613 while his father was treasurer, but was studying at Oxford when his father died that year. I.P.M. cited above; *Mid. Temp. Rec.* 2: 559, 848.

[429] Their eldest son was aged four in 1623. *Vis. Glouc.*, 151.

[430] Gloucester Corp. MSS, Letter Book, 1640–1660, fol. 3; C. 181/4, fol. 81v.

[431] Gloucester Corp. MSS, Letter Book, 1619–1639, fol. 202.

[432] *C.S.P. Dom., 1635*, 556, 577; *1635–1636*, 154, 168, 170; Royal Hist. Soc., *Trans.*, 3rd Ser., 4: 158, 1910.

[433] *C.S.P. Dom., 1639–1640*, 581.

[434] Williams, *op. cit.*, 59; Pink MSS, 320.

[435] I.P.M. of Thomas Stephens cited above.

[436] India Office MSS, Home Series, Misc., 1, fol. 35.

[437] Bristol Museum and Art Gallery, Ellacombe MSS, 216.

[438] I.P.M., Richard Stephens, C. 142/256/39; *Vis. Glouc.*, 152.

[439] *Mid. Temp. Rec.* 2: 447, 848.

[440] Their eldest son was aged six in 1623, according to the visitation.

[441] A neighbor accused Stephens in Star Chamber that year of misusing his authority. St. Ch. 8/161/26.

[442] S.P. 16, 54/28/i, vi; S.P. 16, 56/70; Willcox, *Gloucestershire*, 119.

tion for the shire to the 1628 parliament was doubtless one result of his conduct.

During the 1630's Stephens was active as a local official, and his course in opposing the royal administration and in favoring puritanism brought him further into the public view. He was a member of the commission of oyer and terminer, a J.P., and a militia captain.[443] As a justice he opposed the commissioners sent into the county by the Merchant Adventurers to examine the cloth trade, interfered with the appointment of searchers, and persuaded other J.P.'s to obstruct the work. A summons and a rebuke by Council finally wrung from him a promise to end such tactics.[444] Perhaps he was the Mr. Stephens who carried a plea against the knighthood composition to the Exchequer court, and was defended there by Littleton of the Inner Temple.[445] In 1637 Stephens was reported as one of the Gloucestershire J.P.'s who refused to pay ship money,[446] and he was removed from the commission for his recalcitrancy. Because of his stand at this time and because his puritanism made him a man "of much zeal toward the zealous,"[447] it is not astonishing that his name was presented once more for the shire in the elections of the spring of 1640. He was not favored by the less puritanical reformers such as John Dutton (q.v.), and he declared himself that his nomination was unexpected, although one of the principal candidates, Sir Robert Cooke, was a brother-in-law of Thomas Hodges (q.v.), one of Stephens' intimate friends. The support of the puritan laymen and various dispossessed clergymen was not sufficient to win him a seat that time,[448] but Stephens was elected in the autumn with Dutton as his colleague.

In the Long Parliament Stephens was an active member. He was named to various committees, of which the most important was that on ship money,[449] and he spoke once of the danger of an attack by armed recusants from Ireland.[450] He was probably the Mr. Stephens who in 1642 pledged two completely furnished horses for the defense,[451] and with his good friend, Hodges, he advanced £720 toward the defense of Gloucester before 18 February 1643.[452] He served as a colonel in the parliamentary army, was captured by the royalists in

1645,[453] and in 1648 was secluded from parliament by Pride's Purge. He died in the spring of 1660, and was buried on 30 May at Eastington.[454] His will of 27 December 1658 was proved on 6 June 1661.[455]

As his father's only son Stephens inherited at an early age five manors and numerous other properties in Gloucestershire.[456] He added others by purchase, and may have bought also some stock in the East India Company.[457] He seems to have been able to provide well for his children, for he mentioned in his will plans for a portion of £2000 for an unmarried daughter and had at that time already given dowries to three others.

Sir John Stepney, Bart. (born c. 1608), of Prendergast, Pembrokeshire, was M.P. for Haverfordwest in his county, 1640–19 April 1643.[458] He was the second son of Sir John Stepney, Bart. (H.S., d. 1624), by his wife, Jane, daughter of Sir Francis Mansel, Bart., of Muddlescombe, and in July, 1628, then aged nineteen or twenty, succeeded his elder brother, Alban, as the third baronet.[459] His father set aside by his will certain lands for the educating of John and his younger brothers in grammar school, university, and inn of court,[460] but where John studied is not known.

Stepney was a J.P. for Pembrokeshire and for Haverfordwest, and a commissioner for exacted fees in his county.[461] As sheriff in 1636–1637 he collected ship money carefully, intending to leave no arrears for his successor's responsibility.[462] Although Haverfordwest had been reluctant about ship money and afterwards showed its parliamentarian sympathies,[463] it elected Stepney to both of the 1640 parliaments. He was not an active member in the Commons, but he seems to have been considered willing to support parliament as late as August, 1642, when he was named in the ordinance for the militia.[464] Stepney was living in 1655,[465] but the date of his death is unknown.

Stepney was probably not a man of enormous wealth. Although his family inheritance consisted of some 1400 acres in two counties, and buildings in the boroughs of Haverfordwest and Carmarthen,[466] he had borrowed money from the corporation of Haverfordwest before

---

[443] C. 181/4, fol. 81v; Gloucester Corp. MSS, Letter Book, 1619–1639, fol. 201.

[444] *Wilts. Arch. Mag.* 42: 539, 1922–1924; *C.S.P. Dom., 1631–1633,* 312, 434, 449; Willcox, *op. cit.,* 165–166.

[445] Add. MSS, 12,511, fols. 1–31.

[446] S.P. 16, 345/66; Willcox, *op. cit.,* 128.

[447] *C.S.P. Dom., 1639–1640,* 581.

[448] *Ibid.;* Willcox, *op. cit.,* 35–36.

[449] *C.J.* 2: 45, 51, 64, 219.

[450] D'Ewes (N), 532.

[451] *N. and Q.,* 1st Ser., 12: 359, 1855. The name appears in the list only as "Mr. Stevens," but it was more probably Nathaniel than Edward who made the offer. His was the senior branch of the family.

[452] *H.M.C., Fifth Report,* House of Lords MSS, 73. Stephens referred to Hodges in his will.

[453] Sanford, *St. and ill.,* 527–528; Stowe MSS, 190, fol. 198.

[454] Williams, *op. cit.,* 53.

[455] P.C.C., 100 May.

[456] I.P.M. cited above.

[457] India Office MSS, Home Ser., Misc., **39**, fol. 69v.

[458] *M. of P.* 1: 498; *C.J.* 3: 52.

[459] I.P.M.'s of Sir John Stepney, Bart., 1626 (C. 142/429/145) and Sir Alban Stepney, Bart., 1629 (C. 142/441/17); *Complete Baronetage* 1: 178–179. There are errors in the sketch of Stepney in Williams, *Parl. Hist. Wales,* 162.

[460] I.P.M. cited above.

[461] C. 193/13; S.P. 16/405; C. 181/5, fols. 31, 41, 198.

[462] *C.S.P. Dom., 1637,* 389, 469.

[463] *Arch. Camb.,* 6th Ser., **15**: 1–4, 1915.

[464] *Idem.*

[465] *West Wales Historical Records* 6: 167, 1916.

[466] I.P.M., C. 142/429/145.

1642.[467]   His composition papers reveal that, although his rents amounted to some £618 a year, he was bound for £1200 in dowries for his sisters and £100 in annuities to his brothers, had mortgaged several parts of his properties between 1628 and 1642, and by the latter year had debts of £1200.   His fine, set at a third, was £1230, afterwards reduced to £530, with £70 settled on his rectories.[468]

Sir George Stonehouse, Bart. (c. 1604–1675), of Radley, Berkshire

was Abingdon's sole burgess from 1640 to 22 January 1644.   He came of a family with various court connections.   His grandfather, George Stonehouse, was a clerk of the Green Cloth under Elizabeth; an uncle, Sir James Stonehouse, was in the privy chamber of James I; and his elder brother, John, began a similar career at the court of Charles.   George was the second son of Sir William Stonehouse, Bart. (d. 1632), by Elizabeth, daughter and heiress of John Powell of Pengethley, Hereford, and Fulham, Middlesex, and became the head of his family when his brother, John, died a few months after their father in 1632.[469]   He was born about 1604,[470] and on 20 October 1619 entered Gray's Inn with his elder brother.   While the latter travelled abroad and then began his court career, George seems to have led a quieter life until in 1632 he became head of his house.   The next year he married Margaret, daughter of Richard Lord Lovelace of Hurley, a sister-in-law of Thomas Lord Wentworth (q.v.), and probably of Henry Marten (q.v.).[471]

Entering now upon his role of squire, Sir George served as a J.P. in Berkshire as had his father,[472] and on various local commissions.[473]   As sheriff, 1637–1638, he collected ship money conscientiously but with concern for a fair distribution of rates.[474]   For some reason he did not reply to the request for a loan to the crown in 1639,[475] although his father nine years before had paid his knighthood composition apparently without protest.[476]   In 1640, however, Stonehouse diligently pressed his work as a D.L., in contrast, as he declared, with his negligent fellow deputies.[477]   He stood for election that spring at Abingdon, the town for which his brother had been M.P. in 1628, and in which he was well known and esteemed.   He was opposed by Bulstrode Whitelocke (q.v.), the borough's recorder, who had been induced to enter the race against the court faction.   According to Whitelocke, Stonehouse so used the tradespeople who enjoyed his patronage that "he prevayled by his beefe, bacon & bag pudding, & by permitting as many of them as would, to be drunke at his charge," and by appeals outside of the usual electorate.   Only the abrupt ending of the parliament prevented Whitelocke from challenging the election.[478]   Sir George was returned again for Abingdon in the fall, and was present at the shire election which was held there, too.[479]

In the Long Parliament Stonehouse served on a few committees, offered his bond for £1000 for the 1640 loan, and apparently did not vote against Strafford's attainder.[480]   He promised four horses for the defense in September, 1642,[481] and in the spring and summer of 1643 was named on the parliamentary committee for Berkshire.[482]   He was absent in October, however, joined the king at Oxford shortly afterwards, and was disabled, 22 January 1644.[483]   He recovered his sequestered estates in 1649, sat in the parliaments of 1660 and 1661, and died in 1675.[484]

Stonehouse was reputed to be a man of wealth.   He owned at least four manors, two in Berkshire and the others in Kent and Oxfordshire, which were worth, above rent charges, £1000 to £1100 annually, according to his statement to the compounding commissioners.   He had accumulated some debts, especially between 1638 and 1640, totalling £2760 or more, and his fine, set first at a third, £2705, was reduced in 1649 to a tenth, £1460.[485]

Giles Strangways (1615–1675), of Abbotsbury, Dorset

M.P. for Bridport, 1640–22 January 1644,[486] was the second but eldest surviving son of Sir John Strangways (q.v.), and his wife, Grace Trenchard.   He was born on 3 June and baptized on 18 June 1615 at Melbury Sampford, and in 1629 matriculated at Wadham College, Oxford.   His only degree seems to have been the D.C.L. awarded him in 1665.[487]   He was probably travelling abroad in 1633.[488]   Sometime before 1636 he married Susanna, daughter and coheiress of Thomas Edwards, a London merchant who was described as of

[467] Arch. Camb., 6th Ser., 15: 4, 1915.
[468] S.P. 23/194/355–357, 373–375; Cal. Com. Comp., 1036.
[469] Complete Baronetage 1: 36–37; Vis. Berks. 1: 132; Add. MSS, 24,943, fols. 113, 115.
[470] His age was sixty-one at the 1665 visitation (Vis. Berks. 2: 217), and he was aged twenty-six and over in June, 1632 (I.P.M., Sir John Stonehouse C. 142/489/110).
[471] Ashmole, The history and antiquities of Berkshire, 67; Berks. Arch. Jour. 35: 54, 1931; Gray's Inn Adm. Reg., 157.
[472] C. 193/13; S.P. 16/405.
[473] C. 181/4, fol. 179; 181/5, fols. 280, 321, 353.
[474] Add. MSS, 25,040, fol. 116; C.S.P. Dom., 1637–1638, 89, 348.
[475] Rushworth 3: 913.
[476] S.P. 16, 180/24/fol. 93v.
[477] C.S.P. Dom., 1640, 476.

[478] Add. MSS, 37,343, fols. 198–199, 200v.
[479] Berkshire indenture, C. 219/43/Part 1; M. of P.
[480] D'Ewes (N), 52; C.J. 2: 105, 152.
[481] Ibid. 2: 772.
[482] Berks. Arch. Jour. 31: 174, 1927.
[483] C.J. 3: 374; Pink MSS, 307, fol. 23.
[484] M. of P. 1: 512, 519; Complete Baronetage.   His successor to parliament was elected on 19 April 1675, and his will was proved that year.
[485] I.P.M.'s of his father and brother, C. 142/488/72, 489/110; Hasted, Kent 8: 395; Cal. Com. Comp., 1629; S.P. 23/195/203–205.
[486] M. of P. 1: 488.
[487] Al. Oxon.
[488] Dorset N.H. Proceedings 13: 73, 1892.

Fayre Crooch.[489] After his election to parliament, in 1641 and in 1642, Strangways was named to the commission of oyer and terminer for Hants and Dorset.[490]

Strangways was returned with his father in March, 1640, as burgess for Weymouth and Melcombe Regis.[491] As Bridport's member in the Long Parliament, although he was young in years and experience, he was named to several important committees, including that on privileges.[492] He joined his father in defending Lord Digby in debate,[493] and with him was suspended for absences on 2 September 1642. Finally disabled on 22 January 1644,[494] he fought as a colonel for the king, was captured at Sherborne in 1645, and was released from a long imprisonment only upon the paying of a heavy fine. He survived the Restoration to sit as Sir Giles Strangways in the parliament of 1661,[495] and died on 20 July 1675.

Probably a part of the family inheritance was settled upon Giles at the time of his marriage. Even though his father was still living in 1661, his income then was reckoned at £5000 a year.[496] With his father he shares Lloyd's praise as a man of learning, honor, courage, and tolerance.

Sir John Strangways (1584–1666), of Chirk Castle and Melbury Sampford, Dorset, was a member for Weymouth, 1640–6 September 1642. He came of an old family and had for many years played a prominent role both in his county and in parliament. He was born in 1584, a younger son but eventual successor of John Strangways of Melbury (d. 1593) by Dorothy, daughter of Sir John Thynne of Longleat, Wilts. He was a collateral descendant of the founder of Wadham College, Oxford.[497] He matriculated at Queen's, Oxford, in 1601, and about ten years later (4 January 1611), already a knight, was granted special admission to the Middle Temple.[498] For many years he was a trustee of Wadham College and concerned himself with learning there and in other fields. He gained some little reputation as a patron of the arts,[499] and wrote at least one poem which appeared in the introduction to Thomas Coryate's *Crudities*.[500] Antiquarianism, too, was one of his avocations, and the damage his manuscript collection suffered during the Civil War was one of his later trib-

ulations.[501] Before 1607 Strangways married Grace, daughter of Sir George Trenchard of Dorset, and sister of John Trenchard (*q.v.*). One of his daughters married first the heir of the Rogers family of Brianston and afterwards (1624) Sir Lewis Dives, stepson of the Earl of Bristol. With the latter Strangways was long on terms of intimacy. In 1623 Sir John succeeded his elder brother in the possession of the family estates.[502]

Before that date, however, Strangways became a public figure. He was sheriff of Dorset, 1612–1613,[503] represented his county in parliament the next year, and was long a J.P. and a member of various local commissions.[504] He accompanied Lord Digby on one of his journeys to Spain, possibly about 1618, and was afterwards reported to have exported some gold illegally then.[505] He was named one of the collectors of funds for the Palatinate in 1620, but was listed in 1623 for a Council summons because he was £50 in arrears in his contribution.[506] As M.P. for Dorset again in 1621 Strangways worked actively with the group opposed to Buckingham. He advocated reforms in regard to Fleet prison, monopolies, and trade, and censured Shepherd's denunciation of puritanism.[507] He sat for the county in 1624, and for Weymouth and Melcombe Regis in 1625 and 1626. In the latter instance a complaint was made that he and his powerful faction had bought up borough seats.[508] He spoke in 1626 on the mismanagement of defense moneys, defended the Earl of Bristol, and worked for the impeachment of Buckingham.[509] His removal from the Dorset commission of the peace the following July, as in the case of Sir Walter Erle (*q.v.*), was the result. The next year he refused the loan and was imprisoned in Bedfordshire.[510] Upon his release he was promptly re-elected M.P. for Dorset. His position in the debates of 1629 on Rolle's case that the customs officials, not the king, were to blame in the matter,[511] suggests the line he was to follow later.

During the following decade Sir John's activities were chiefly in his county. He probably disapproved of the ship money levies, although he is not known to

[489] His eldest son was born in 1636. Hutchins, *Dorset* 2: 663.

[490] C. 181/5, fols. 404, 442.

[491] *M. of P.* 1: 481.

[492] *C.J.* 2: 21, *passim*.

[493] D'Ewes (N), 421.

[494] *C.J.* 2: 750; 3: 374.

[495] *M. of P.* 1: 522.

[496] Many of the biographical details above appear in *Somerset and Dorset N. and Q.* 12: 97, 170, 1910–1911.

[497] *Vis. Dorset, 1623*, 87; Hutchins, *Dorset* 2: 662.

[498] *Al. Oxon.*; *Mid. Temp. Rec.* 2: 531.

[499] Lloyd, *Memoires*, 691; Hutchins, *op. cit.* 2: 664.

[500] Thomas Coryate, *Coryat's crudities* 1: 34–35, Glasgow, MacLehose, 1905.

[501] D'Ewes, *Autobiography* 2: 317.

[502] Hutchins, *op. cit.* 2: 662–663.

[503] *List of Sheriffs* 9: 39.

[504] C. 193/13; C. 181/3, fols. 6, 118v; C. 181/4 and 181/5, *passim*.

[505] Strangways, Dives, and another were named as defendants in a Star Chamber case in this matter in 1637 (S.P. 16, 361/92). A case involving some merchants for a similar charge was started in 1618 and adjourned in 1619. Gardiner, *H. of E.* 3: 323. Digby held the title of Lord Digby between 1618 and 1622.

[506] S.P. 14, 148/29.

[507] *Commons Debates 1621* 2: 80, 82, 263, n.; 5: 500, 516, *passim*.

[508] *H.M.C., Twelfth Report* 1: Coke MSS, 305.

[509] *E.H.R.* 17: 735, 1902; Forster, *Eliot* 1: 514, 534; S.P. 16, 29/13; 453/24.

[510] *Somerset Arch. Proc.* 16 (ii): 26, 1870; S.P. 16, 89/2; Rushworth 1: 473.

[511] *Commons Debates for 1629*, 90, 164.

have been a defaulter himself, for he was anxious to have an early debate on them when parliament met once more.[512] He was being examined in the Star Chamber in 1637 on the old charge of having transported gold out of the kingdom (see above), and it was rumored that heavy fines would probably fall on some of the defendants, but that Sir John "does very much slight it."[513] Two years later he ignored the request for a loan to the king.[514] He was elected by Weymouth to both of the 1640 parliaments.

During the opening months of the Long Parliament Strangways worked, as did Bristol's son, Lord Digby, with the reformers. He was prominent in debate and was named to numerous committees. He objected, however, to the trend of the extremists in matters of the church and the authority of parliament.[515] Apparently he acquiesced in the attainder of Strafford,[516] but demurred at being required to take the May Protestation, taking it only after a week's delay.[517] By the following October his course had so veered that Nicholas listed him as one of the king's champions in the House.[518] And in November he was threatened with violence by the crowd gathered outside the House demanding a vote against the bishops. He spoke on 29 December in defense of the Earl of Bristol, and when war came was among the earliest to be disabled for royalism.[519] He sat in the Oxford parliament and was especially exempted from pardon. With his son, Giles (q.v.), Strangways was taken prisoner in 1645, and after being imprisoned for over a year, was at length permitted to compound for his delinquency. He survived to sit in 1661 for Weymouth, but died on 30 December 1666.[520]

Strangways owned great estates in Dorset and Somerset. His father's property included seven manors and other properties, besides over 2100 acres of former church property, of which one farm alone was worth £180 a year in 1651. To these Sir John added others, such as a farm worth £330 a year in 1641.[521] He was the patron of at least four churches in Dorset.[522] The fine levied on him and his son was £10,000,[523] and their loyalty to the king is said to have cost them to-

gether £35,000. Lloyd's tribute to Strangways and his son mentions their ability as orators, their veneration of schools and learning, and their great services in their county. "They were stout men that flattered none, but boast[ed] themselves more true, just, and faithful than any thing but their own memories: Memories that forget nothing but their own Injuries."[524]

Sir John Strangways had numerous kinsmen among the parliament men. Among them, besides his son, were Trenchard, a brother-in-law, Thynne, a first cousin, Lord Digby and his brother and John Browne, who were connections by marriage. And D'Ewes, who was distantly related, was drawn to him by a mutual interest in antiquarianism.[525]

Robert Strickland (d. 1670), of Sizergh, Westmorland, and of Thornton Bridge, Yorkshire, was M.P. for Aldborough, Yorkshire, 1640–21 January 1642/3. He came of an old Catholic family of Westmorland, being the grandson of Walter Strickland of Sizergh, M.P. 1563, and son and heir of Sir Thomas Strickland, K.B., sheriff of Yorkshire and twice M.P. for Westmorland (d. before 1619). His mother, who was Margaret, daughter of Sir Nicholas Curwen of Workington and kinswoman of the Musgraves,[526] was a recusant as late as 1629, and it is not improbable that her son leaned toward her faith. He is not known to have espoused it openly, but his son did so after the Restoration.[527] Of Strickland's education nothing is known. He married at Kilnwick on 10 January 1619 Margaret, daughter and coheir of Sir William Alford of Bylton and Kilnwick in the East Riding.[528] They probably divided their time between his family's place at Sizergh, of which he was the owner when Dodsworth visited Kendall parish in 1628 (1629?),[529] and the East Riding, where his marriage had brought him some interests.[530] He was residing at Thornton Bridge in 1636 and 1641.[531] He was described in 1644 as of Kilnsea, Yorkshire.[532] He sat for Westmorland in the 1624 parliament,[533] and was a J.P. and a sewers commissioner in the East Riding in the 1630's.[534]

Strickland served as colonel in command of some of the North Riding troops in 1638 and in 1640 was or-

---

[512] D'Ewes (N), 541, 542.

[513] S.P. 16, 361/92; 362/31.

[514] Rushworth 3: 913.

[515] Add. MSS, 11,045, fol. 145; D'Ewes (N), 313, 315, n., 318, n., 339–340.

[516] He was indignant that his name appeared by mistake on one list of Straffordians. Sanford, St. and ill., 388, 355. His name is not in Verney's list.

[517] C.J. 2: 141.

[518] The diary and correspondence of John Evelyn, ed. W. Bray, 4: 116, rev. ed., London, Bickers, 1906.

[519] D'Ewes (C), 213–214, 361; C.J. 2: 750, 754.

[520] Hutchins, Dorset 2: 662.

[521] Ibid. 2: 544, 620, 664; Somerset and Dorset N. and Q. 7: 252, 1900–1901; 8: 128, 1902–1903; 15: 136, 1916–1917; T. Gerard, Partic. Descr. Somerset, 83, 84, 87.

[522] Lansd. MSS, 459, fols. 23v, 24v, 26, 31v.

[523] Cal. Com. Comp., 1828.

[524] Memoires, 690–691.

[525] D'Ewes, Autobiography 1: 21, n.; 2: 316–318. Additional references: Harl. MSS, 158, fol. 270; M. of P.

[526] See Sir Philip Musgrave and Sir Patrick Curwen.

[527] Nicolson and Burn, Hist. of Westmorland and Cumberland 1: 100–101; Cumb. and Westm. Trans., 1st Ser., 10: 49, opp. 74, 85, 89, 1889.

[528] Ibid. 10: opp. 74, 1889. According to the marriage license (Yorks. Arch. Jour. 14: 480, 1898), Robert was styled "Esquire" and "of Brafferton."

[529] Y.A.S. Rec. Ser. 34: 160, 1904.

[530] Ibid. 58: 172, 1917.

[531] Add. MSS, 11,323, fol. 21; Gray's Inn Adm. Reg., 230.

[532] Y.A.S. Rec. Ser. 40: 196, 1909.

[533] M. of P. 1: 460.

[534] C. 193/13; S.P. 16/405; C. 181/4, fol. 189v; 181/5, fols. 82, 331.

dered to take his regiment to Newcastle.[535] He was present at the Yorkshire election on 5 October 1640,[536] and was chosen two days later to sit for Aldborough. He never became prominent in the House. As Sir Robert Strickland, he was absent at the call, 16 June 1642.[537] He led a command for the king at Edgehill and was disabled, 21 January 1643.[538] He seems not to have compounded for his estate, having settled most of it on his son. Surviving the war and the Restoration, he wrote to his son, Sir Thomas, M.P. in the 1661 parliament, advising him to let the king "play Rex to God's glory, his own preservation, and the kingdom's good."[539] He died in 1670.[540]

When Strickland's son, Sir Thomas, dealt with the commissioners for compounding, he complained that his family's estate had been much impaired by his grandfather's gambling, and that, whereas it was reputed to be worth £1000 a year, it was so encumbered when he came into ownership that he had had to use most of his income to pay annuities and debts, and had had to live on what his wife brought him.[541]

* **Sir William Strickland** (1596?–1673), of Boynton, Yorkshire, member for Hedon, 1640–1653, was a strong parliamentarian. He attended Queen's College, Cambridge, as well as Gray's Inn, as did his father and his brother, Walter.[542] Before his first term as an M.P., sitting for Hedon in the Long Parliament, Strickland was a J.P. in the East and North Ridings,[543] and a member of other local commissions.[544] He signed the Yorkshire petition of July, 1640.[545]

Strickland was somewhat distantly related to Robert Strickland, the royalist M.P. for Aldborough,[546] was a brother-in-law by his first marriage of the Cholmley brothers, and was connected through his second marriage with John Finch, the Winchelsea member. During the interim between his marriages, acquaintances of his in the Barrington clan, Sir William Masham and Oliver St. John (q.v.), considered him eligible to marry one of their young cousins, since he had an estate in Yorkshire of £1500 to £2000 a year.[547] His first wife's

portion was said to have been £2000,[548] and his father's fairly high rate of £20 in the 1626 loan on privy seals [549] seems to have been in keeping with the nine manors and other Yorkshire properties mentioned as Strickland's patrimony.[550] Sir William's pledge of £1000 jointly with Sir Hugh Cholmley for the 1641 loan [551] was certainly within his means.

* **William Strode** (1599?–1645), of Newnham, Devon, sat for Beeralston, which he preferred to Tamworth,[552] from 1640 until 1645. He was the second son of Sir William Strode of Newnham who had served as J.P. and D.L. in Devon, was for a time Recorder of Plymouth, several times an M.P., and was one of those interested in the Dorchester plan for New England settlement.[553] William Strode the younger was M.P. for Beeralston in 1624, and in each parliament thereafter until his death.[554] In 1627 he or his father was on the Devonshire loan commission,[555] but his conduct in the 1628–1629 parliament with the subsequent imprisonment and Star Chamber proceedings kept the son out of further political action until January, 1640. His prominent role in the Long Parliament in attacking the king's counselors and the trend toward popery, his impulsive nature and his sometimes violent language, are well known.[556] He was the last of the Five Members to leave the House on 4 January 1642, resisting the efforts to send him away, and was virtually dragged out by Sir Walter Erle.[557] He died unmarried in 1645.[558]

There are few indications of Strode's financial standing beyond his promise in June, 1642, of two horses, £50 and some plate for the defense,[559] a not inconsiderable contribution for a younger son. He owned some Devonshire lands in 1640.[560] His pledge of £600 for reducing Ireland, however, was for others as well as for himself.[561]

---

[535] Nicholson and Burn, *op. cit.* 1: 101.

[536] Indenture, C. 219/43/Part 3.

[537] *C.J.* 2: 626.

[538] *C.J.* 2: 938.

[539] *H.M.C., Fifth Report,* MSS of W. C. Strickland, Esq., 330.

[540] Pink MSS, 320.

[541] Cumb. and Westm. *Trans.,* 1st Ser., 10: 85, 89, 91, 1889. The particulars he presented show income from properties once his father's worth some £254 a year (*Y.A.S. Rec. Ser.* 15: 160–161, 1893). Sir Robert's assessment of £1500 for his twentieth had not been paid by 1645 (*Cal. Com. Adv. Money,* 931).

[542] *Al. Cant.*

[543] C. 193/13; S.P. 16/405.

[544] C. 181/3; 181/4, fols. 114, 189v, 331; 181/5, fols. 128, 255.

[545] *C.S.P. Dom.,* 1640, 524.

[546] Ferguson, *Cumberland and Westmorland M.P.'s,* 442.

[547] Letters to Lady Barrington in February, 1631. Eg. MSS, 2645, fols. 241, 243.

[548] *Memoirs of Sir Hugh Cholmley,* 23, 1787.

[549] *Acts P.C., 1625–1626,* 430.

[550] I.P.M. of Walter Strickland (1636), C. 142/553/45.

[551] D'Ewes (N), 439, n.

[552] *M. of P.* 1: 487, 494.

[553] *M. of P.* 1: 433, 438, *passim;* S.P. 16, 193/71; 405; *Notes and Gleanings* 2: 35–36, 1889; *Devon and Cornwall N. and Q.* 18: 88, 1934–1935; Plymouth Inst. *Trans.* 9: 90, 1884–1887.

[554] *M. of P.* 1: 457, *passim;* *C.J.* 2: 14. The Beeralston M.P. is to be distinguished from the "recruiter" for Ilchester (1646), who was of Barrington, Somerset, and of the Middle Temple (*D.N.B.; Mid. Temp. Rec.* 2: 553, 623, 933; *Somerset Arch. Proc.* 30 [ii]: 32–65, 1884).

[555] S.P. 16, 53–96.

[556] D'Ewes (N) and (C), *passim;* Hexter, *The reign of King Pym,* 51.

[557] D'Ewes (C), 381, 384.

[558] The date of Strode's will appears as 4 July 1654 (*sic*), perhaps a misprint for 1645, in *C.S.P. Ireland, Adventurers,* 82.

[559] *N. and Q.,* 1st Ser., 12: 338, 1855.

[560] Exeter City Library MSS, Exeter Deeds and Documents, Nos. 12, 114.

[561] *C.S.P. Ireland, loc. cit.*

Strode was connected by marriages in his family with both Sir Walter Erle and Walter Yonge.[562]

* Robert Sutton (1594–1668), of Aram or Averham, Notts, was knight for his shire, 1640–1642. The son and heir of Sir William Sutton of Aram, he probably studied at Trinity College, Cambridge.[563] He was a J.P. in Notts in 1618 and regularly thereafter, was named to a variety of local commissions for that county and Lincolnshire,[564] was a loan commissioner in 1627, sheriff in 1630–1631, and by 1638 was a D.L.[565] He served in parliament twice before November, 1640, and in the Long Parliament was named to several important early committees, including those on ship money and the lords lieutenant. He joined with his colleague, Hutchinson, in pledging £1000 toward the November loan, and similarly in March, 1641, and in the following August was sent to his county to help execute the order for disarming recusants.[566] He was evidently anxious for administrative reforms, but was personally loyal to the crown, was probably absent much of the time after the 1641 recess, and was suspended by the House, 2 September 1642.[567]

Of Sutton Thoroton wrote in 1674 that "he very much increased his patrimony, [and] ever kept a plentiful sober house."[568] He owned in 1640 five manors and other properties, the principal one comprising 2000 acres, and had a yearly income of about £1700 clear. His fine for royalism was set at a third, £4861, or a half, £7291, and he had paid it at the lower figure by March, 1649.[569]

Sutton was a son-in-law of Sir Guy Palmes (*q.v.*).

Sir Ralph Sydenham (d. 1671), of Youlston in north Devon, and of the court, was M.P. for Bossiney, Cornwall, having been named three successive times in disputed returns, October, 1640–February, 1641. He was disabled as a royalist, 29 September 1642.[570] Descended from an old Somerset family, he was the second son of Sir John Sydenham of Brympton (d. 1625) by his first wife, Mary (d. 1596), daughter and heiress of John Buckland of West Harptree, and was born probably

after 1589.[571] Following his father's second marriage with Mary, widow of John Baker of Kent, a lady known for her recusancy, the family lived part of the time at London,[572] and Ralph evidently secured some place at court. He was knighted in Scotland, 17 July 1617, being then one of the band of gentlemen pensioners,[573] and about that time or soon afterwards he became a gentleman of the privy chamber.[574] In 1630 he received a grant of the reversion of the office of surveyor of the ordnance of the Tower, a grant he had been seeking for some years on the basis of a promise made to him by King James.[575] Sydenham had married in March, 1629, Mary, daughter of Robert Hill of Shilston, Devon, and widow of Sir Robert Chichester, K.B., of Raleigh and Youlston, Devon;[576] and two years later his wife was granted letters patent for an annual pension of £200 for life.[577]

Following his marriage Sir Ralph probably spent more time than before in Devon. His father had settled on him several Somerset properties,[578] but his wife's first husband had owned lands in and near Barnstaple, and Sydenham established his country residence at Youlston in Sherwell parish nearby.[579] During the 1630's Sir Ralph was J.P. for Devonshire.[580] and a member of various special commissions.[581] He was concerned with some military matters in Exeter in 1637 and may have been with the army on the northern border in 1639.[582]

Sydenham had not been in parliament before 1640, but his repeated elections at Bossiney, 1640–1641, indicate that he had powerful backing there. He was never an active member of the Commons, however, had frequent leaves of absence, and was named to no committees. He accompanied the king to York in 1642 and then went to Devon to help execute the Commission of Array. Suspended for non-attendance, 2 September

---

[562] Erle was a brother-in-law of Strode's elder brother, and Yonge's son married one of Strode's sisters. *Western Antiquary* 1: 56, 1881–1882; *Complete Baronetage* 3: 232.

[563] *Al. Cant.*

[564] Thoroton, *Notts.* 2: 141; C. 193/13; 181/3, fols. 10v, 23v, 103; S.P. 16, 405; C. 181/4, fols. 23v, 84, 159; 181/5, fols. 28, 320.

[565] S.P. 16, 78/64; 381/73; *List of Sheriffs,* 105.

[566] *C.J.* 2: 45, 50, 101, 267; D'Ewes (N), 52, n.; 435, n.

[567] *C.J.* 2: 750.

[568] *Notts.* 3: 111.

[569] *Ibid.* 3: 112; S.P. 23/201/703–705, 713, 715; *Cal. Com. Comp.*, 1336–1337; *C.J.* 5: 429.

[570] His colleague in the third election, Yelverton, was in the House on 27 April and both were there on 3 May 1641. *C.J.* 2: 29, 46–47, 66, 86, 129, 133, 788.

[571] Chadwyck Healey, *West Somerset*, 311–312. Ralph's next older brother, John, was born about 1589, according to their father's I.P.M., C. 142/716/61.

[572] Dr. G. F. Sydenham, *The history of the Sydenham family*, ed. A. T. Cameron, 138–139, privately printed, 1928; *Acts P.C., 1625–1626*, 482.

[573] Sydenham, *op. cit.*, 140; *Somerset and Dorset N. and Q.* 2: 288, 1891.

[574] He declared in 1646 that he had served the king in that capacity for many years, and in 1660 he stated that he had served two kings for forty years. *Cal. Com. Comp.*, 1535; Pink MSS, 307, fol. 170.

[575] *C.S.P. Dom., 1623–1625*, 251, 397; *1629–1631*, 555.

[576] *Kensington parish registers*, Harleian Society Publications, Register Series, **16**: 69; Sydenham, *op. cit.*, 140.

[577] S.P. 16, 187/46/104.

[578] Chadwyck Healey, *op. cit.*, 311–312; I.P.M. cited above.

[579] Sydenham, *op. cit.*, 140; Barnstaple Corporation MSS, Receivers' Accounts, 1389–1643; Sessions Court Book, 1631–1642.

[580] Devonshire MSS, Quarter Sessions Minute Books, 1633–1640, *passim;* C. 193/13.

[581] C. 181/4, fols. 52v, 163v; 181/5, fols. 167, 183, 204.

[582] *C.S.P. Dom., 1636–1637*, 509; S.P. 16, 427/38/iii.

1642, he was disabled before the end of the month.[583] He crossed to France before April, 1645, but returned to England to start his composition proceedings in October, 1646.[584] Later he was said to have been instrumental in persuading General Monk to restore the king,[585] and was rewarded by Charles II with the appointment to the mastership of the Charter House.[586] Sydenham died in the autumn of 1671 and was buried in St. Martin's in the Fields. His will was dated 10 October and proved 20 November 1671.[587]

Sir Ralph probably enjoyed no large estate, since he was a younger son, nor does he seem to have been adept at lining his purse at court. His assessment by the parliamentarians in 1644 was £500, a comparatively low figure for a parliament man.[588] Much of his income before the war had been from lands enjoyed in his wife's right, and it is small wonder that he complained that his compounding fine, set in 1647 at a half, £1310, was heavy and extreme. He managed to get it abated to £500.[589]

* **Zouch Tate** (1606–1650), of Delapré, Northamptonshire, M.P. for Northampton borough, 1640–1648, was the son and heir of Sir William Tate of Delapré and of Whitley, Warwickshire, J.P., M.P., D.L. (d. 1617), by his wife Elizabeth (Eleanor?), daughter and coheiress of Edward Lord Zouch.[1] He was born in March, 1606,[2] was Lord Zouch's ward after 1617, studied at Trinity College, Oxford, and, before entering the Middle Temple in 1625, travelled in France[3] He married Catherine, daughter of Sir Giles Allington of Horseheath, Cambridgeshire, becoming through her a brother-in-law of Sir Robert Crane and Sir Thomas Fanshawe, K.B. (q.v.).

Tate was reported a musters defaulter in 1635, but his excuse of infirmity saved him from penalty, as did his plea of "sore eyes" in 1637 from charges of not attending properly to some payments on inclosures.[4] He was elected to the first as well as the second parliament of 1640 for Northampton,[5] and was an active par-

liamentarian. He died late in 1650, his will, dated 23 December 1650, being proved by his widow, 5 February 1651.[6]

Tate inherited from his father two manors in Northamptonshire, one in Warwickshire, and other properties. He was the coheir also to three Hampshire manors and other holdings of Lord Zouch, but in 1627 sold at least part of these interests to a cousin.[7] His offer for the defense in 1642 was not much above the average,[8] but the estate of William Tate of Delapré, probably his son, was estimated to be worth £1500 annually in 1660.[9]

William Taylor, returned for Windsor, Berkshire, 22 October 1640 (void, 8 December 1640), and M.P. 16 December 1640–27 May 1641, presents some confusion as to identity. It seems probable that the Taylor named with Cornelius Holland in a double return in October died in November before he had entered the House and that his son of the same name was elected in his place. It is possible, however, that the son was elected on both occasions and that the statement about the original candidate's death resulted from the confusing of son and father.[10] It was the son who was actually present in the parliament.

William Taylor (d. 1640), the father, was the son of William Taylor, alias Danvill, of Essex, by Joan, daughter of Sir John Aubrey of Glamorganshire. At least as early as January, 1623/4, he was paymaster of the works of Windsor Castle.[11] He may have been in the employ of Sir Robert Pye, then auditor of the Exchequer. He seems to have resisted the knighthood composition in 1630,[12] and in 1638 he promised to pay ship money only after he had been brought before Council.[13] He died soon after the Windsor elections of October, 1640, for his will was proved on 27 November. His widow, Mary, daughter of Nicholas William of Llanfoist, Monmouthshire, died shortly afterward.[14]

William Taylor (born c. 1612), elder son of the above, was a member of the House certainly from 16 December 1640 until the following May. Born about 1612, he was admitted to the Middle Temple on 5 June 1633 upon the special request of Sir Walter Pye. During part of his stay Taylor was "bound" with Pye's son, James, and was possibly being groomed for a career

[583] *C.J.* **2**: 750, 788; Pink MSS, *loc. cit.*

[584] *H.M.C., Seventh Report,* MSS of Sir H. Verney, Bart., 450, 456; *Cal. Com. Comp.,* 1535.

[585] John Aubrey, *Brief lives* (Clark ed.) **2**: 74.

[586] Cotton, *Barnstaple during the great Civil War,* 67, n.

[587] Sydenham, *op. cit.,* 142, 438.

[588] *Cal. Com. Adv. Money,* 792.

[589] *Cal. Com. Comp.,* 1535.

[1] *Northamptonshire Notes and Queries* **4**: 9, 1892; Burke, *Landed gentry* **2**: 1352, 1850; W. C. Metcalfe, *The visitations of Northamptonshire,* 199, London, 1887; Northants MSS, F.H. 1077; *The Montagu musters book,* ed. J. Wake and H. I. Longden, Northamptonshire Record Society Publications, **7**: lii, 27, *passim,* 1935. Tate is mentioned briefly in the article on his uncle, Francis Tate, the antiquary, in *D.N.B.*

[2] I.P.M. of Sir William Tate, C. 142/365/149.

[3] *C.S.P. Dom., 1623–1625,* 105, 211; S.P. 14, 161/40 and and 164/77; *Al. Oxon.*

[4] *C.S.P. Dom., 1635,* 517, 546, 583; *1636–1637,* 465.

[5] *Records of Northampton* **2**: 496.

[6] P.C.C., 41 Grey.

[7] I.P.M. of Sir William Tate, cited above, and of Edward Lord Zouch (C. 142/447/28); *V.C.H. Hampshire* **4**: 80.

[8] *N. and Q.,* 1st Ser., **12**: 359, 1855.

[9] *Northamptonshire Notes and Queries* **2**: 208, 1888.

[10] Tighe and Davis, *Annals of Windsor* **2**: 149–150; Pink MSS, 307, fol. 43; *M. of P.* **1**: 485; *C.J.* **2**: 47.

[11] Tighe and Davis, *op. cit.* **2**: 88.

[12] S.P. 16, 180/24, fol. 88.

[13] *C.S.P. Dom., 1638–1639,* 2, 9.

[14] Her will was proved on 5 January 1641. Pink MSS, 307, fol. 52; *Vis. Berks.* **1**: 292.

under the guidance of that family. He was called to the bar, 19 June 1640,[15] and was still busy with his studies when elected to parliament.[16] His royalist leanings, perhaps the result of his association with Sir Walter Pye, soon came into evidence. He voted against Strafford's attainder,[17] and although he took the Protestation of May, he was expelled on the twenty-seventh of that month and committed to the Tower for a few weeks for words he had spoken at Windsor regarding the treatment of Strafford.[18] He served as colonel with the royalist forces, and after the Restoration was Surveyor of the Works at Windsor Castle and Steward of Windsor Forest. He was alive in October, 1667, possibly in 1673.[19]

Taylor was probably not a wealthy man, but is said to have been a great sufferer for the king. His fine for his delinquency was set at £700 in 1646.[20] It was probably about this time that he married Frances, daughter and coheiress of Sir William Parkhurst.[21]

* Sir Peter Temple, Bart. (1592–1653), of Stowe, near Buckingham borough, was M.P. for that town, 1640–1653. He was the heir of a family whose fortunes were built upon lands and sheep-farming in the counties of Leicester, Warwick, and Bucks, but in his father's day and his, partly through their own extravagances, financial difficulties beset them. Their debts increased, lawsuits, even among themselves, multiplied, and by 1639, although Sir Peter was still well-to-do, he was being embarrassed by the demands of his creditors.[22]

Sir Peter was the eldest son of Sir Thomas Temple of Stowe, the first baronet, H.S. Oxfordshire, Warwickshire, and Bucks (d. 1637), by his wife, Hester, daughter of Miles Sandys of Latimers.[23] He married on 5 July 1614 Anne, daughter and coheir of Sir Arthur Throckmorton, whose dowry lands in Bucks and Northamptonshire were valued at £700 a year. His father promised then to settle on him most of the family estates, and an estimated income of £800 a year. But

his wife's death in 1620 and disagreements with his father about provisions for the younger children and about his own "unthriftiness" and rumored extravagances and gambling led to much bickering within the family. Peter's second marriage in 1630 with Christian, daughter and coheir of Sir John Leveson, whose ample dower was £3000, improved his fortunes only temporarily. He was borrowing regularly and heavily, especially in 1634 and 1640.[24]

In spite of his financial problems, Sir Peter continued to play the role of a leading country gentleman, served as J.P. in the county and the borough of Buckingham,[25] and in 1634–1635 was sheriff of Bucks. As such he was involved in the ship money resistance of Hampden and others, and during part of the summer of 1636 was in the custody of a messenger for appearing before Council on account of his alleged negligence and delays in collecting the arrears.[26] A few years later he was complained of to Laud and Coventry by the vicar of Thornborough because Temple allowed him only a bare stipend of £40 a year,[27] but what the outcome was does not appear.

Elected to both 1640 parliaments by Buckingham borough, Sir Peter worked with the parliamentarians, but served on relatively few committees and was somewhat irregular in his attendance.[28] He may have been swayed somewhat by his wife, who seems to have had Romanist leanings,[29] and whose brother, Sir Richard Leveson (q.v.), was a royalist, or by his cousin and close friend, Sir Alexander Denton (q.v.). He promised his security for £1000 for the 1640 loan,[30] but does not seem to have subscribed for the defense in June, 1642. He cast his lot, however, with his parliamentarian kinsmen, who included his other cousins, Sir Thomas Parker and the Fiennes brothers, and was named to various county committees for the war. He was named a king's judge, but did not act,[31] and died in 1653.

Temple's finances, precarious in 1640, were complicated further by the war. He eventually turned over to his creditors his properties which, in 1653, were valued at £3500 a year, and administration of his estate was granted at his death to a creditor.[32]

---

[15] Mid. Temp. Rec. 2: 808, 895.

[16] In February, 1641, the House gravely ordered that Mr. Taylor be excused by the Temple from doing his exercises until after the parliament, without losing his seniority. D'Ewes (N), 346; C.J. 2: 82.

[17] Verney, 58.

[18] C.J. 2: 137, 158–159, 173. He was said to have declared in Windsor that in condemning Strafford the House had "committed murder with the sword of justice."

[19] Tighe and Davis, op. cit. 2: 297–298, 333–336, 349, 363.

[20] Cal. Com. Comp., 1369.

[21] Vis. Berks. 1: 292. Their eldest son, William, was seventeen in 1665.

[22] The financial history of the family during this period, based upon their family papers, has been written by E. F. Gay in a series of articles in the Huntington Library Quarterly 1: 367–390, 1937–1938; 2: 404–437, 1938–1939; 6: 255–291, 1942–1943.

[23] Complete Baronetage 1: 82; Lipscomb, Buckingham 3: 86. Sir Peter is mentioned very briefly in D.N.B., "Sir Richard Temple."

[24] Huntington Library Quarterly 2: 409–433, 1938–1939; V.C.H. Buckingham 4: 198; C.J. 2: 201, 204.

[25] C. 181/4, fol. 68; 181/5, fol. 240; C. 193/12.

[26] Stowe MSS, 142, fol. 45.

[27] C.S.P. Dom., 1638–1639, 211.

[28] Pink MSS, 307, fol. 81.

[29] Life of Marmaduke Rawdon, 81 and n., Camden Society, 1863.

[30] D'Ewes (N), 452.

[31] Pink MSS, loc. cit. Temple is to be distinguished from his nephew, Sir Peter Temple of Stanton Bury, and from Peter Temple (1600–1663), the regicide, who was a cousin.

[32] Pink MSS, loc. cit.; Huntington Library Quarterly 2: 434–437, 1938–1939; 6: 256–257, 1942–1943. The estates had been worth £2700–£3000 a year about 1630 (ibid. 2: 421–433, 1938–1939).

Simon Thelwall (fl. 1637–1654), "junior," of Plas-y-Ward, county Denbigh, was M.P. for Denbigh borough, 1640–1648.[33] His grandfather was Simon Thelwall (d. 1655), a lawyer and official in the courts of Wales and England, who was M.P. 1593–1614, and H.S. Denbighshire 1612.[34] He was the eldest son of Edward Thelwall of Plas-y-Ward, also a lawyer,[35] by his wife, Margaret, daughter and heiress of Andrew Maredydd of Glantanad.[36] He was not the Simon Thelwall who entered Oxford in 1616, aged fifteen.[37] He was probably considerably younger than the Oxonian, and he entered the Inner Temple in November, 1637.[38] His first experience in office came with his election to the Long Parliament in October, 1640. He was then unmarried, his match with Lady Margaret Sheffield, daughter of Edward, Earl of Musgrave, not occurring until June, 1645.[39]

Thelwall's name occurs but rarely in the records of the early period of the parliament, but he pledged £500 in ready money for the loan of March, 1641.[40] He served as an officer in the parliamentary army during the war, as did his brother, Edward,[41] and he remained a member of the House until 1648. He was elected for Denbighshire in 1654, and may have gone to Ireland afterwards.[42] But he had died before 9 June 1660.[43]

Edward Thomas (fl. 1625–1648), M.P. for Okehampton in Devon, 1641–1648, has not been identified completely. He owed his election, as did his colleague, Whitaker, to Lord Mohun, Baron of Okehampton, who helped to secure the restoration of the borough that year, and whose nominees were promptly chosen by the voters. The vote for Thomas was without protest.[44] Since Thomas had sat in three earlier parliaments for Cornish boroughs in which Lord Mohun had influence (West Looe in 1625 and 1628, Grampound in 1626),[45] it seems probable that he was an employee, possibly secretary or solicitor, for Mohun. The Thomas families of Cornwall and Glamorganshire seem to have had none of the name of Edward who could have been the M.P.[46] There was, however, an Edward Thomas who entered Gray's Inn in 1617 as of Astwood, Worcestershire, gentleman, and who described himself in the year of his death (1656) as "of Gray's Inn, gent."[47] He was a relative of both of the M.P.'s for the city of Worcester,[48] and does not seem to have married. That he was a parliamentarian is suggested by the fact that during the war he purchased lands from the trustees for the sale of church properties in his native county.[49] Since Edward Thomas, the parliament member, was named in 1641 to a committee concerned with the parish of St. Andrew's, Holborn, a committee consisting chiefly of men connected with the inns of court and property owners in and near London,[50] it may be surmised at least that he had London associations. There is no proof, however, that he and the Gray's Inn lawyer were identical.

Probably Edward Thomas supported his patron's royalist program while Buckingham lived, but in the 1640 parliament he worked with the opposition. In departing thus from Mohun's politics he had Whitaker's company. Whether he or William Thomas was the Mr. Thomas who spoke against bishops in 1641[51] it is impossible to say. The Okehampton man in no other way gained prominence during the first year of the parliament. He promised a free loan of £50 for the defense

---

[33] *O.P.H.* **9**: 15. He was active with the parliamentarians in the autumn of 1644 (*cf.* Sir John Price), although in the list of members disabled on 5 February 1644 (*C.J.* **3**: 389) one "Giles Thelwall" was named. There was no such member. Simon Thelwall was still an M.P. in 1648. Thomason Tracts, E. 454, 18.

[34] Williams, *Parl. Hist. Wales*, 72; *Al. Oxon.*; *Cal. Wynn Papers*, 83, 345; Lloyd, *The history of Powys Fadog* **4**: 308–310.

[35] *Cal. Wynn Papers*, 358, 470. The office of recorder of Ruthin, county Denbigh, was granted for life to Edward and Simon Thelwall in 1615. *C.S.P. Dom., 1611–1618*, 275.

[36] Lloyd, *op. cit.* **4**: 310.

[37] He is so identified, however, by Williams, and it is suggested in *Al. Oxon.*, although the editor of the latter work points out that apparently the same Simon entered Gray's Inn as the son of Richard Thelwall. There were at least two other Simon Thelwalls, kinsmen of the Plas-y-Ward line, both of them related to Sir Eubule Thelwall of Jesus College, and one of them was the Gray's Inn man. Lloyd, *op. cit.* **4**: 312–320.

[38] *Students admitted to the Inner Temple*, 294.

[39] *Kensington parish register*, Harleian Society, Register Series, **16**: 73. Williams states that Thelwall married a second time, but he has in that fact confused the M.P. with the elder Simon, his grandfather (Lloyd, *op. cit.* **4**: 309). Lady Margaret Thelwall outlived her husband and afterwards had difficulties with his relatives about the inheritance. *Cal. Wynn Papers*, 357, 358, 364.

[40] D'Ewes (N), 439, n.

[41] Captain Edward Thelwall was killed in Ireland. Lloyd, *op. cit.* **4**: 310.

[42] His grandfather, Simon, in a letter of July, 1656, mentioned his grandchildren in Ireland. *Cal. Wynn Papers*, 346.

[43] By this time his widow's disagreements with his family had begun.

[44] Bridges, *Okehampton*, 29, 92–93.

[45] *M. of P.* **1**: 463, 468, 474; *Western Antiquary* **9**: 198, 1889–1890; **10**: 85, 1890–1891.

[46] The Edward Thomas of the family seated at Curry in Cornwall was too young to have been the M.P. in 1625 (Pink MSS, 311, fol. 462c). The possibility from the Thomas family named Wenvoe Castle, Glamorganshire, seems to have been named Edmund rather than Edward (Burke, *Peerage*, 2406, 1940). This family were parliamentarians (Wood, *Athenae Oxon.* **3**: 105). The Edward Thomas of Glamorganshire who became a baronet in 1641 and was a royalist (*Complete Baronetage* **2**: 159; *Cal. Com. Comp.*, 42) could not have been the M.P.

[47] *Gray's Inn Adm. Reg.*, 148; will, P.C.C., 416 Berkeley.

[48] Both John Nash and John Cowcher of Worcester were mentioned in his will. Other Worcestershire relatives named therein appear in the pedigree of Porter of Tapenhall. *Vis. Worcester* (ed. Metcalfe), 77–78.

[49] According to his will Thomas left, in addition to some real estate, bequests totalling about £1700. His trustees for the purchase of lands in 1650 were a London merchant taylor and a resident of Holborn, Middlesex.

[50] *C.J.* **2**: 177, 203.

[51] Whitelocke, *Memorials of the English affairs* **1**: 135, 1853.

in 1642,[52] and remained a member until Pride's Purge.[53] Although it has been stated that he was living in 1659,[54] Thomas's name is missing from the list of members of 1659–1660.[55]

William Thomas (fl. 1618–1653), of Aber, Carnarvonshire, was returned M.P. for Carnarvon, 3 December 1640, but his election was challenged by Thomas Glyn, who had been elected for the county in the spring. Although the election had not been determined as late as May, 1641, and there was a report in July that the decision would probably be against him,[56] William Thomas took the Protestation of the spring of 1641 and was not turned out of parliament until he was disabled for royalism, 5 February 1644.[57]

Thomas was the second son but heir of Sir William Thomas of Aber (d. 1635) by his wife, Gaynora, daughter of Sir William Maurice. His father, a great friend of the Wynns of Gwydir, was active in public affairs, and was sheriff in 1607.[58] The younger William, born probably after 1595,[59] may have attended Jesus College, Oxford,[60] and was admitted in 1618 to Gray's Inn.[61] Shortly afterwards, probably the same year, he married Catherine, daughter of Richard Parry, Bishop of St. Asaph (d. 1623). He had two sons living in 1635.[62] He seems to have spent most of his time after his marriage in Wales, was a J.P. in Anglesey and Carnarvon,[63] and sheriff of the latter county, 1637–1638.[64] He collected ship money then, apparently without hesitation.[65]

William Thomas was not a prominent member of the Long Parliament. He may have been the Mr. Thomas who spoke in 1641 against corruption in the church government and against the authority of bishops and deans.[66] And in 1642 he joined with John Moore in pledging £600 for the Irish venture,[67] and promised

later one horse for the cause.[68] But he was disabled afterwards for joining the king, and was assessed £800 by parliament, his estate being supposedly worth that sum per year. As Sir William Thomas, Bart., recently M.P., he petitioned in 1651 to compound for his estates, and was still engaged in the process in 1653.[69] He may have died in the latter year.[70] The William Thomas who was involved in a lawsuit regarding Aber in 1656 was possibly his son.[71]

Sir James Thynne (c. 1605–1670), of Longleat, Wiltshire, was a member for his county from 1640 until about 1644. He was the eldest surviving son of Sir Thomas Thynne of Longleat (d. 1639) by his first wife, Mary, daughter of Lord Audley, and was one of the wealthiest members of the House. He was born about 1605, studied at Magdalen College, Oxford (matriculated 1620, aged fifteen; B.A. 1622),[72] and may possibly have served as an ensign with the Rochelle expedition in 1628.[73] He was away from his home most of the time between his going to Oxford and his father's death, because of disagreements with his father's second wife,[74] and probably spent considerable time at court. He was with the army in the north in the summer of 1639, and was knighted at Berwick on 23 June.[75] The following August his father died and there began a prolonged lawsuit in the Star Chamber and the Court of Wards with his stepmother and her eldest son, Henry Frederick Thynne, regarding the division of the property and the administration of the estate. Early in 1640 both Sir James and his stepbrother became gentlemen of the privy chamber, and both soon lent generously for the royal expenses.[76] At some time before August, 1640, Thynne married Isabel, daughter of Henry Rich, Earl of Holland. He and his wife were then granted permission to have an oratory in their chapel at Longleat.[77] Although Sir James's father had served as a J.P. and sheriff in Wiltshire and other counties where he held land,[78] and had sat in most of the parliaments from

[52] Mr. William Thomas made a different offer. *N. and Q.,* 1st Ser., **12**: 360, 1855.
[53] *A vindication of the imprisoned and secluded members of the House of Commons,* 28, 1649; *O.P.H.* **9**: *25.
[54] Pink in *Western Antiquary* **10**: 85, 1890–1891; Pink MSS, 311, fol. 462c.
[55] Thomason Tracts, 669. f. 21, p. 43; 669. f. 24, p. 37.
[56] *Cal. Wynn Papers,* 271, 274; *C.J.* **2**: 66, 123, 144; D'Ewes (N), 455–456, n., 475–476, n.
[57] *C.J.* **2**: 133; **3**: 389.
[58] I.P.M. of Sir William Thomas, 1635, C. 142/534/112; *Cal. Wynn Papers,* 81, 97, *passim; List of Sheriffs,* 248. Williams (*Parl. Hist. Wales,* 66) has confused the father and son.
[59] His elder brother, who was probably defective in some way, was aged forty in 1635.
[60] Wood, *Athenae Oxon.* **3**: 104–105.
[61] *Gray's Inn Adm. Reg.,* 151.
[62] I.P.M. cited above; *D.N.B.,* "Richard Parry (1560–1623)."
[63] C. 193/13; S.P. 16/405.
[64] *List of Sheriffs,* 249.
[65] *C.S.P. Dom., 1637–1638,* 220.
[66] The speech is attributed to this Thomas by Wood (*loc. cit.*). He defended his stand on 11 June 1641. *Diurnal occurrences,* 128–137. *Cf.* Edward Thomas.
[67] Rushworth **4**: 565.

[68] *N. and Q.,* 1st Ser., **12**: 360, 1855.
[69] *Cal. Com. Adv. Money,* 434; *Cal. Com. Comp.,* 2740–2741. The valuation of the estates Thomas declared in his "particular" was only £260 a year, and he asserted various sums were payable out of that income to sisters. S.P. 23/222/258–259. His fine, set originally at a third, £780, was reduced to £713.
[70] Williams, *Parl. Hist. Wales,* 66.
[71] Another lawsuit was in progress in 1676. *Cal. Wynn Papers,* 347, 416.
[72] *Al. Oxon.* Thynne's age was simply given in his father's I.P.M. as "thirty" at his father's death in 1639 (C. 142/765/47).
[73] Ensign Thynne was named in several lists. E.g., S.P. 16, 111/62.
[74] *H.M.C., Sixth Report,* House of Lords MSS, 175.
[75] S.P. 16, 427/38/ii, iv; *C.S.P. Dom., 1639,* 384.
[76] Sir James lent £3000 and his brother, £2000. Add. MSS, 11,045, fol. 97; S.P. 16, 447/36, 37.
[77] Hoare, *Wilts.* **1** (2): 60; *H.M.C., Third Report,* MSS of the Marquis of Bath, 201.
[78] *C.S.P. Dom., 1619–1623,* 311; *1629–1631,* 105; *Wilts. Arch. Mag.* **1**: 223, 1854; S.P. 16/405.

1601 to 1628,[79] Thynne himself seems to have engaged in no political activities beyond those of the court until after his father's death.

In the autumn elections of 1640 Sir James was a candidate in two places. His father-in-law, who was steward of Reading, backed him unsuccessfully for that town.[80] But he stood without contest with Sir Henry Ludlow for Wiltshire and was accordingly returned.[81] In the parliament he took no great part. His name occurred in the records chiefly, in fact, in connection with the lawsuit then current against his stepbrother and with his use of his parliamentary privilege to further his own interests in the disputed properties. Although Hyde and Falkland helped him to get his case before a committee, the decision in August, 1641, was that he had abused his privilege.[82] It was rumored about this time that Thynne was in line for a peerage, but that parliament's plan to bar the sale of titles stood in the way.[83] He apparently was not courtier enough to vote against Strafford's attainder, but neither did he offer his great wealth to back the loans parliament proposed. Early in 1643 he was suspected of disloyalty, but Pym's intercession, possibly because of his connection with Holland, averted action against him then.[84] He joined the king at Oxford, however, in 1644 and was subsequently disabled. The writ for the choosing of his successor was ordered on 30 December 1645.[85]

Thynne later arranged to compound for his estate. He survived the Restoration to serve as sheriff of his county, 1660–1661, and to sit in the parliament of 1661. He died at Richmond, Surrey, on 12 October 1670.[86]

The wealth of the Thynnes, which had greatly increased in his father's lifetime and had become almost legendary by the next generation, was exemplified by their splendid mansion at Longleat near Bath. Begun by Sir James's grandfather and completed by Sir James, it was described by Aubrey as "the most august building in the Kingdom."[87] When Sir Thomas Thynne died in 1639 he owned more than a dozen manors and even more scattered properties lying in Wilts, Gloucester, and Somerset, and in five other counties.[88] Although Sir James later protested the terms of his father's will because it assigned an undue proportion of the estate to the younger children, he was said to have inherited

himself £6000 a year.[89] Even after the ravages of war he acknowledged in his compounding papers an annual income of nearly £2000. His fine at a tenth, after some adjustments to cover omissions, totalled between £3100 and £3500.[90]

Thomas Toll (d. 1653), merchant and alderman of King's Lynn, Norfolk, served for his borough, 1640–1653. He was probably a native of Lynn, for he was admitted a freeman there in 1615 after serving his apprenticeship under Joshua Green, linen draper,[91] and his brother, Nicholas, was minister of the parish of St. Nicholas there.[92] Before 1623 he married Alice, daughter of Thomas Soame, three times mayor of the town,[93] and relative of the Atkin family into which John Percival (q.v.) married about the same period. As a merchant Toll supplied the town with such varying commodities as gunpowder and rye, and was concerned with numerous problems of its trade.

Toll became a member of the Common Council in 1624, served as his father-in-law's deputy alderman the next year, was frequently one of the town's auditors, and in 1632 became an alderman. He went to Norwich in 1629 and 1630 with messages regarding the ministry at Lynn, represented his borough before the royal council in 1630 for an inquiry about the sea coal imported from Newcastle, and travelled to London again in 1634 to meet with other Norfolk men in protesting the ship money rates set upon their towns.[94] He was an assessor for the ship money levy in 1635 and 1637, one of the town coroners in the latter year, and was mayor, 1639–1640.[95] He was active also in church affairs at Lynn, serving as a churchwarden of St. Margaret's parish, and being one of the committee sent to Norwich in 1637 to negotiate about the lease of the Lynn parsonage and to warn the diocesan officials that the corporation intended to keep the right to name their own ministers.[96]

The Long Parliament was Toll's first, and he was not a prominent member in the early period, either in

[79] M. of P.
[80] Guilding, Reading records 3: 505.
[81] Calendar of Clarendon State Papers 1: 209.
[82] C.S.P. Dom., 1640–1641, 404; Sanford, St. and ill., 371, n.; C.J. 2: 162, 191, 200, 210, 217.
[83] C.S.P. Dom., 1641–1643, 41.
[84] Sanford, op. cit., 546.
[85] C.J. 4: 391.
[86] M. of P. 1: 530; Wilts. Arch. Mag. 24: 332–334, 1889; 27: 114, 1893–1894; H.M.C., Seventh Report, MSS of Sir H. Verney, Bart., 488.
[87] J. Stratford, Wiltshire and Its Worthies, 68, Salisbury, 1882.
[88] I.P.M. cited above.

[89] A daughter's dowry was set at £20,000, with £6000 more in jewels and plate, and the younger son, Sir James's stepbrother, was to have £4000 a year. Ibid.; H.M.C., Various collections 8, MSS of the Hon. F. L. Wood, 51. One writer declared that £10,000 had been "given from" the heir. Add. MSS, 11,045, fol. 44v.
[90] Cal. Com. Comp., 913; Wilts. Arch. Mag. 24: 330–331, 1889.
[91] King's Lynn MSS, Hall Book 7, fol. 71v.
[92] Mackerell, The history and antiquities of King's Lynn, 132. Toll mentions this brother in his will. P.C.C., 266 Alchin.
[93] Their son Thomas died in 1682, aged fifty-nine. East Anglian, N.S., 3: 296, 1889–1890.
[94] King's Lynn MSS, Hall Book 7, fols. 223, 239, 248, 261v, 298, 306v, 402–403, passim.
[95] Ibid., fol. 418; Hall Book 8, fols. 4, 8, 41, 43.
[96] Ibid., Hall Book 7, fol. 292v; 8, fols. 6v, 7v.

debate or in committees.[97] He was a parliamentarian, pledged £50 for the defense in June, 1642,[98] but as late as September of that year was blaming the king's "delinckquants and cavelers" rather than the monarch himself for the continuing differences with parliament.[99] He worked for parliament during the war and continued his leadership in town affairs as well as his membership in the Commons until 1653.[100] He died on 29 October 1653 and was buried in St. Nicholas's Chapel at Lynn.[101]

Toll was probably not rich, but he owned some properties and leases in Lynn.[102] According to his will, proved in 1654, most of his estates had been settled earlier, but he arranged for £100 a year as a jointure for his son's wife, and listed bequests of over £650, part of which were to come from lands once belonging to the church.[103]

Thomas Tomkins (d. 1674), of Monnington and Garnstone, Herefordshire, was M.P. for Weobly from 15 January 1641, succeeding his brother, William (*q.v.*), until 22 January 1644.[104] He was the fourth but second surviving son of James Tomkins of Monnington and of the Middle Temple (1569–1636), and was called to the bar at the Middle Temple in 1631.[105] In 1633 he married Mary, sixth daughter of Sir Walter Pye, and niece of Sir Robert Pye of the Exchequer (*q.v.*). Her jointure was £1000.[106] Tomkins was elected in the spring of 1640 [107] to his first parliament, sitting with his brother for Weobly, the borough where his family's interest was strong. He seems to have yielded his seat in the autumn to Arthur Jones, but was chosen again early in 1641 after his brother died.

Thomas Tomkins was named to several committees in 1641, including those on Emmanuel College, on one of the charges against Strafford, and on the jurisdiction of the Council of the Marches of Wales.[108] He was among the border county gentlemen who signed the petition advocating the abolition of the Marches Court,[109] and apparently worked for a time with the

reform element. In June, 1642, he promised a free gift of two horses for the parliamentary cause.[110] Eventually, however, Tomkins went to the Oxford parliament, was disabled in January, 1644, and was afterwards imprisoned and compelled to compound for his estates. He was in high royal favor at the Restoration, sat again for Weobly in 1660 and 1661, and died in 1674.

As the heir of his brother, William, Tomkins inherited an estate, chiefly in Herefordshire, valued at more than £1000, possibly £1200, a year. But because it was somewhat encumbered by the annuities payable to his brother's widow and by his own debts, some lenience was shown in the matter of Tomkins's fine. Set first at a third, £2110, it was reduced to £1443.[111] In 1660, however, Tomkins was said to be worth £2000 a year.[112]

Tomkins has been confused by some writers with Nathaniel Tomkins, Clerk of the Queen's Council, who was hanged for his part in the royalist plot of his brother-in-law, Edmund Waller.[113] Thomas Tomkins had a son, Nathaniel, for whose delinquency some properties in Worcestershire were sequestered,[114] but that son was too young to have been involved in Waller's plot.

William Tomkins (*c.* 1600–1640), of Monnington, Herefordshire, was M.P. for Weobly in 1640, but he died before the year ended and a new election was ordered on 2 January 1641.[115] He was a grandson of Richard Tomkins (d. 1603), escheator and sheriff of Herefordshire, and the second but eldest surviving son of James Tomkins (1569–1636) of Monnington (M.P., H.S.), by his wife, Anne, elder daughter and coheiress of James Boyle of Hereford. He was born about 1600 and when about nineteen married Mary Morton, sister of Sir George Morton, Bart., of Clenston, Dorset. The marriage settlement of 1 April 1619 specified her portion as £1600.[116] In 1628 James Tomkins, then M.P. for Leominster, secured the restoration of Weobly, of the manor of which he was lord, as a parliamentary borough, and his son, William, was promptly elected as one of its M.P.'s. William succeeded his father in 1636, was a J.P. in the county,[117] and was elected to both 1640 parliaments for Weobly. He was present at

---

[97] Almost the only reference to him in the early period is his claim of parliamentary privilege to stay a process started against him in Exchequer. *C.J.* **2**: 56–57.

[98] *N. and Q.,* 1st Ser., **12**: 360, 1855.

[99] Toll to the mayor of Norwich, 10 September 1642. Add. MSS, 22,619, fol. 38.

[100] He was granted leave of absence to be mayor of Lynn in 1646. Hillen, *History of the borough of King's Lynn* **1**: 348, 356, 363. Toll is charged in *The mystery of the good old cause* (43) with procuring the office of customer of Lynn for himself under his son's name.

[101] *East Anglian,* N.S., **3**: 296, 1889–1890.

[102] King's Lynn MSS, Hall Book, **7**, fols. 326, 395v; **8**, fol. 36v.

[103] P.C.C., 266 Alchin.

[104] *M. of P.* **1**: 489; *C.J.* **3**: 374.

[105] *Mid. Temp. Rec.* **2**: 675, 781, 838.

[106] I.P.M., James Tomkins, C. 142/556/101.

[107] *M. of P.* **1**: 481.

[108] *C.J.* **2**: 79, 95, 191.

[109] Add. MSS, 11,053, fols. 180–181.

[110] *N. and Q.,* 1st Ser., **12**: 338, 1855.

[111] S.P. 23/210/315, 333–334; *Cal. Com. Comp.,* 1036–1037. £1200 a year was the valuation noted by Richard Symonds in his *Diary* (Camden Society), 196.

[112] *English Baronetage* **4**: 367, 1741.

[113] Sanford, *St. and ill.,* 373. By Williams (*Hereford,* 126) James Tomkins, father of the M.P., is confused with the Tomkins of the plot. But see Clarendon, *Rebellion* **3**: 39, 64, n. (65); John Aubrey, *Brief lives* (Clark ed.) **2**: 275; *C.S.P. Dom., 1640–1641,* 539.

[114] *Cal. Com. Comp.,* 1036.

[115] *M. of P.* **1**: 489; *C.J.* **2**: 62.

[116] I.P.M., James Tomkins, C. 142/556/101.

[117] S.P. 16/405.

the county election on 24 October, too.[118] He died, however, before the role he might have played in the new parliament became clear. His will, dated 10 October 1639, was proved by his widow, 10 March 1641.[119] He had no children, and his estate of at least five manors worth £1000 or more a year passed to his brother, his successor for Weobly, Thomas Tomkins (*q.v.*).[120]

Robert Trelawney, or **Trelawny** (1598–1644), merchant of Plymouth, sat for his town, 1640–9 March 1642. He came of Cornish stock and of a line of Plymouth merchants and magistrates. His great-uncle, John, or Sir John Trelawney, was twice mayor of Plymouth (1597, 1611), and his father, Robert Trelawney (d. 1627), who was associated with a London company trading to France and with the fishmongers' company of the metropolis, was three times mayor of Plymouth and a great benefactor of the city.[121] During his second mayoralty (1616–1617) he was host to the company of Sir Walter Raleigh as they prepared for their final voyage.[122] Robert, the son of the mayor by his first wife, Elizabeth, daughter of Alexander Mayne of Exeter, was born on 25 March and baptized on 1 April 1598 at St. Andrew's, Plymouth. Since he was not admitted to the freedom of the town until 1626,[123] it is possible that he was sent away from Plymouth, perhaps to London or even abroad, for his apprenticeship in trade. He married in Cornwall, however, in 1623, his wife being Anne Voga (or Coga or Crooke) of St. Michael Caerhayes.[124] Following his admission as a freeman of Plymouth, Trelawney became active in civic affairs. He was one of the "Four and Twenty," 1626–1627, was one of the receivers the following year, and was mayor, 1633–1634. At this time he was active in a controversy which had developed between the corporation on one side and the royal and episcopal officials on the other concerning the appointment by the corporation of a puritan vicar for St. Andrew's. Although Trelawney showed an interest in the erecting of a new church, a form of protest decided upon by the noncomformists, he was instrumental also in arranging for a compromise and the accepting of a new royalist appointee in 1635.[125]

The spirit of compromise is indicated by Trelawney's bequests in his will for money for the new church and for the preachers in both the old and the new buildings.

Meanwhile Trelawney, watchful of business opportunities, took out letters of marque for some of his ships, 1625–1629,[126] and spent large sums to encourage the exploration and settlement of the coast of Maine. He was rewarded in 1631 with a grant of land there under the Council of New England.[127] Early in 1640 he joined with a dozen Plymouth men in asking Laud's intervention against Kirke's plantation patent which might interfere with the interests of Plymouth fishermen in Newfoundland.[128] At home he was appointed in 1638 to the Devonshire commission on exacted fees.[129] He was reported the next year as a defaulter from the Devonshire musters and required to make a personal appearance before Council, but the accusation seems to have been made by mistake, and Trelawney afterwards declared that he was always prepared to furnish ten men's arms and twice the levy required of him.[130] He was indeed, as Clarendon described him, "a merchant of great reputation." He was sent by Plymouth to both parliaments of 1640.

In the Commons Trelawney worked vigorously against abuses that affected trade. His complaint against Sir John Jacobs as a monopolist led to that member's dismissal, and he urged an investigation of the whole customs service.[131] He opposed a bill for reducing usury rates, however, as liable to damage English trade by discouraging the inflow of foreign capital.[132] With his Plymouth colleague he offered security for £1000 for the loan of November, 1640,[133] and there is no evidence that he opposed the administrative reforms of the first year of the parliament. In the spring of 1642, however, he disapproved the defying of the king, and, because he had voiced his disapproval in a private conversation, was on 9 March peremptorily dismissed from his seat in the House and imprisoned. He was afterwards permitted to subscribe for the Irish venture and to go to Plymouth, but was brought back to London in the autumn, probably because of his activities in supplying royalist garrisons, and was kept a prisoner at Winchester House [134] until his death early in 1644. He is said to have been buried on 2 March 1644 at St. Mary,

[118] Herefordshire indenture, C. 219/43/Part 1.

[119] P.C.C., 38 Evelyn.

[120] In addition to the above authorities see Williams, *Hereford*, 126, 156.

[121] Devon *Trans.* **14**: 360, 361, 1882; Plymouth Inst. *Trans.* **9**: 50, 63, 1884–1887; Carr, *Select charters of trading companies*, 65.

[122] *H.M.C., Tenth Report* 4, MSS of the Corporation of Plymouth, 541.

[123] Plymouth Corporation MSS, 46, Black Book, fol. 311.

[124] Plymouth Inst. *Trans.* **8**: 98, 1881–1884.

[125] Plymouth Corporation MSS, 132, Widey Court Book, fols. 212–220, 233, 250; MS 48, White Book, fols. 95, 98; Plymouth Inst. *Trans.* **6**: 49–50, 1876–1878. The new preacher, although he was accepted in 1635, was jailed for a time because one of his sermons offended the puritans. H. F. Whitfeld, *Plymouth and Devonport in times of war and peace*, 98–99, Plymouth, E. Chapple, 1900.

[126] *C.S.P. Dom., 1629–1631*, 153, 155; Devon *Trans.* **14**: 360–361, 1882.

[127] Plymouth Inst. *Trans.* **8**: 101, 106–108, 1881–1884.

[128] S.P. 16, 442/77.

[129] C. 181/5, fol. 218.

[130] S.P. 16, 403/46; *C.S.P. Dom., 1638–1639*, 338–339.

[131] Lansd. MSS, 491, fol. 56; *C.J.* **2**: 33; *Note book of Sir John Northcote*, 88.

[132] D'Ewes (N), 511, n.

[133] *Ibid.*, 52.

[134] *C.J.* **2**: 473, 811, 859; Plymouth Inst. *Trans.* **5**: 251–252, 1873–1876; *H.M.C., Fifteenth Report* 7, MSS of the Duke of Somerset, 66; *C.S.P. Ireland, Adventurers*, 226.

Woolchurch.[135] His will, dated 24 August 1643, was proved on 19 November 1644.[136]

Trelawney was unquestionably a well-to-do merchant. From his father he inherited lands in Devon and Cornwall as well as his business,[137] and by 1640 he had accumulated more properties in Plymouth, and had erected a country house nearby at Ham.[138] His "very good" estate enabled him to plan bequests in his original will (1640) of £7700 for his seven children and £1500 for his wife, in addition to real estate, and some £400 in other gifts. His final will (1643) provided for the distributing of over £9500, including £450 which he had ventured for Irish lands during the Long Parliament.[139]

Trelawney was a friend of Simon Snow, the Exeter M.P., although they differed in politics. Hugh Potter was a cousin.[140]

John Trenchard (1586–1662), of Warmwell, Dorset, sat for Wareham, 1640–1653. He came of a distinguished family long seated at Wolveton near Dorchester, and was the second surviving son of Sir George Trenchard (M.P., H.S.) by his first wife, Anne, daughter of Sir George Speke of Whitlackington, Somerset. His elder brother, Sir Thomas Trenchard, was M.P. in 1621 and 1645, and was sheriff of Dorset, 1634–1635. John was baptized at Charminster in 1586, matriculated at St. Alban's Hall, Oxford, in 1602, and was graduated B.A. in 1605. The next year he was studying at the Middle Temple.[141] Before 1617 he married Jane, daughter of Sir John Rodney of Stoke, Somerset, a sister of Sir Edward Rodney (q.v.), receiving with her £1200 as dowry.[142] His Dorset residence was at Warmwell, but he does not seem to have shared with his brother the local responsibilities of serving as J.P. or on other commissions there.[143] He compounded with the knighthood commissioners of the county for £10 in 1630.[144] But he may have spent a good deal of time in London, too.

Trenchard was M.P. for Wareham in the parliaments of 1621, 1624, and 1625, and again in the spring of 1640. In the elections of 1624, perhaps on other occasions, he had the support of the powerful Sir Francis Ashley.[145] He was at his town house in Covent Garden in 1635 and may have been questioned by Council regarding his brother's delays in ship money collection as sheriff in Dorset that year.[146]

Throughout the Long Parliament Trenchard worked with the popular party. His numerous committee appointments included those on Sir Henry Spiller, on ship money, and on the Bishop of Bath and Wells. He was a member also of the Committee for the Advance of Money (1642), the Committee of Goldsmiths' Hall (1643) and of the wartime committees for his county.[147] He brought in as recruiters for the vacant seats of royalists not only his brother but two sons-in-law.[148] Trenchard was named a commissioner for the king's trial, but he took no part in it. He did not refrain, however, from securing for himself and his family much sequestered property.[149] He sat again in the parliament of 1654, and probably in 1656 and 1659, and died in 1662.

The second son of a wealthy family and allied with others of prominence, Trenchard was wealthy enough in 1640 to propose a dowry of £1000 for one of his five daughters. He owned before the war at least two manors which contained more than 3000 acres of land.[150] His contribution toward the defense in 1642, however, was the moderate one of one horse.[151]

Three brothers-in-law of Trenchard's were returned as M.P.'s in 1640, Rodney, Sir John Strangways, and John Browne of Frampton. And there were other relatives by marriage, such as William Pole.[152]

John Trevanion (c. 1613–1643), of Carhayes, Cornwall, was M.P. for Lostwithiel from 1640 until the war began.[153] He was among the Cavaliers of the county who were commemorated as "the four wheels of Charles's wain."[154] Born about 1613, he was the eldest son of Charles (later Sir Charles) Trevanion (d. 1644), by Amye, daughter of Sir John Mallet of Enmore, Somerset, and was the heir apparent to a great fortune.[155] His father was a J.P., M.P., sheriff, and D.L.

[135] Exeter City Library, Clipping Collection, Family History, Trelawney.
[136] P.C.C., 6 Rivers.
[137] I.P.M., Robert Trelawney, 1628, C. 142/751/167.
[138] Plymouth Inst. *Trans.* 8: 99–102, 1881–1884; Plymouth Corporation MSS, 132, Widey Court Book, fols. 233v, 236; MSS 181, 185, 187 (Rentals, 1633–1639), *passim.*
[139] P.C.C., 6 Rivers.
[140] Both were named in Trelawney's will. Authorities in addition to those cited above are: Baxter, J. P., ed., *The Trelawny Papers* (Collections of the Maine Historical Society), xvii–xxv, 445–456; Clarendon, *Rebellion* 1: 587; *M. of P.; Western Antiquary* 4: 153–154, 1884–1885.
[141] *Al. Oxon.*
[142] Brit. Mus. Birch MSS, 4224, fol. 3; Add. MSS, 34,329, fol. 14.
[143] C. 193/13.
[144] *Somerset and Dorset N. and Q.* 4: 18, 1894–1895.

[145] Add. MSS, 29,974, fol. 76.
[146] *C.S.P. Dom., 1635,* 502. In 1639 a "Mr. Trencher" was assessed for some improvements about Whitehall Palace. S.P. 16, 432/48.
[147] *C.J.* 2: 33, 45, 50, 825; Prideaux, *Memorials of the Goldsmiths' Company* 1: 212; *Somerset and Dorset N. and Q.* 13: 267, 1912–1913.
[148] John Bingham and William Sydenham, *The mystery of the good old cause,* 42–43.
[149] Noble, *Regicides* 2: 281.
[150] *Somerset and Dorset N. and Q.* 7: 340, 1900–1901; 8: 55, 1902–1903.
[151] *N. and Q.,* 1st Ser., 12: 360, 1855.
[152] References in addition to those cited above are: Burke, *Landed gentry* 2: Addenda, 385, 1851; Hutchins, *Dorset* 3: 326, 329; *M. of P.*
[153] I have found no date of disablement, but Trevanion was probably absent after 1641.
[154] See Sidney Godolphin.
[155] Vivian, *Vis. Cornwall,* 502; Clarendon, *Rebellion* 2: 452.

for Cornwall.[156] About the time he went to London to enter Lincoln's Inn in 1633,[157] John was recommended to Secretary Coke by Charles Lord Lambert, who described him as a proper young gentleman, the best seated of any man in Cornwall, and heir apparent to an estate of about £2000 a year.[158] Trevanion had married while still a minor (8 November 1630) Anne, daughter of John Arundell of Trerice,[159] and he was presently joined at his inn by her brothers, John and Richard, later his colleagues in parliament.

Trevanion was elected to his first parliament in March, 1640, serving for Grampound.[160] His father had paid an overassessment some years earlier to avoid knighthood, and had ignored the request for a contribution to the king in 1639.[161] Probably the politics of the Trevanions were much like those of the Arundells of Trerice, with whom John intermarried. Both families became strong royalists by 1642. Young Trevanion early showed the trend by voting against Strafford's attainder.[162] He obtained leaves of absence for his health on 8 May and 17 December 1641, and was named to no committees of the House. He may not have been present after his second leave of absence. He was missing at the call on 16 June 1642,[163] took up arms for the king as soon as the fighting started, and before the summer of 1643 was colonel of a volunteer regiment. He died at Bristol in July of that year.[164] Clarendon wrote of him as follows: "He was a steady young man, of a good understanding, great courage, but of few words, yet what he said was always to the purpose." [165]

* **Sir John Trevor** (d. 1673), of Trevalyn and Plas Teg, Denbighshire, and of Oatlands, Surrey, was a member for Grampound, Cornwall, 1640–1653.[166] He was the son and heir of Sir John Trevor of Oatlands and of Denbighshire (d. 1630), Surveyor of the Navy and keeper of several royal parks,[167] by his wife, Margaret, daughter of Hugh Trevanion of Cornwall. He was a nephew of Sir Thomas Trevor, Baron of the

Exchequer, and first cousin of Thomas Trevor (q.v.).[168] He was admitted to Queen's College, Cambridge, on 13 May 1612, and entered the Inner Temple the next year.[169] In 1617 he received with Thomas Trevor the grant of an office, or the reversion thereof, as auditor of part of the Duchy of Lancaster.[170] And in 1619 he was knighted.[171] In February of the latter year he married Anne, eldest daughter of Edmund Hampden of Wendover, Bucks, one of the coheiresses of her uncle, Sir Alexander Hampden of Hartwell, and received with her a substantial portion.[172]

As Sir John Trevor, junior, he was elected M.P. for Denbighshire, 1621, for Flintshire, 1624 and 1625, and for Great Bedwin, 1628.[173] He succeeded his father in the surveyorship of Windsor and the keeping of the house and park at Oatlands, and in part ownership of the monopoly of farming sea-coal at Newcastle.[174] From his father and from one of his uncles he inherited several Denbighshire estates.[175] But he was probably in the neighborhood of the court much of the time before 1640, living in St. Margaret's parish, Westminster.[176] He was in 1635 one of the commissioners to compound with violators of the statutes on the wool trade.[177] And he was among the "king's servants" who were expected to go with the king to the north in 1639 and to lend generously the next year. Trevor evinced some reluctance about performing both of these duties.[178]

Trevor perhaps gained his seat for the Long Parliament through his mother's Cornish relatives. But he was linked by marriage with a number of the reforming group from the Midlands. He was a brother-in-law of Lord Wenman and of Sir Alexander Denton,[179] and a connection of Winwood and Hampden. Among his Welsh kinsmen was Roger Mostyn.[180] With the faction of Hampden and Cromwell his later career lay.

---

[156] Vivian, loc. cit.; C.S.P. Dom., 1639, 333.

[157] Linc. Inn Rec. Adm. 1: 220.

[158] C.S.P. Dom., 1633–1634, 59. Richard Symonds noted that the estate was worth £1500 a year (Symonds, Diary, 61, Camden Society). A considerably smaller valuation, perhaps because the estate had already been settled, was reported by Trevanion's father to the compounding commissioners. S.P. 23/206/811; Cal. Com. Comp., 1258.

[159] Vivian, loc. cit. Clarendon was evidently mistaken in referring to him as newly married at the time of his death. He also thought him several years younger than he actually was. Rebellion 3: 103, n. (104).

[160] M. of P. 1: 480; Courtney, Parl. Rep. Corn., 188.

[161] S.P. 16, 239/59; Rushworth 3: 913.

[162] Verney, 58.

[163] C.J. 2: 139, 346, 626; Pink MSS, 307, fol. 237.

[164] Vivian, loc. cit.; Clarendon, Rebellion 2: 452.

[165] Rebellion 3: 103, n. (104).

[166] M. of P. 1: 486 and notes.

[167] C.S.P. Dom., 1603–1610, 13, 22, 52; E.H.R. 7: 477, 1892.

[168] Trevor pedigree in Arch. Camb., 6th Ser., 5: opp. 100, 1905; Williams, Parl. Hist. Wales, 72. There is some confusing of the generations, particularly of Trevor and his father, in D.N.B. For some of the corrections, see Bull. Institute of Historical Research 18: 136, 1940–1941.

[169] Al. Cant.

[170] W. R. Williams, Official lists of the duchy and county palatine of Lancaster, 57.

[171] Williams, Parl. Hist. Wales, 72.

[172] Her uncle originally planned for her to have lands worth £1200 a year, but when she married Trevor her dower was reported to be £10,000 less. The letters of John Chamberlain 2: 86, 210.

[173] M. of P. 1: 455, 462, 467, 478.

[174] Pink MSS, 307, fol. 198; C.S.P. Dom., 1637, 502.

[175] Williams, Parl. Hist. Wales, 72. From his father he received also some Virginia Company stock. Brown, Genesis of the U. S. 2: 1033.

[176] Records of St. Margaret's Parish, Overseers' Accounts, 153, 154.

[177] C.S.P. Dom., 1635, 514.

[178] S.P. 16, 427/38/vi; 447/36, 37.

[179] Lipscomb, Buckingham 2: 302.

[180] R. H. Whitelocke, The memoirs of Bulstrode Whitelocke, 51.

Thomas Trevor (*c.* 1612–1676), of Enfield, Middlesex, was one of the two men returned for the single place allotted to Monmouth borough, in October, 1640, but the election was not voided until 29 November 1644, and he may have attended some of the meetings of the parliament.[181] He was the only son of Sir Thomas Trevor, Baron of the Exchequer (d. 1656), by Prudence, daughter of Henry Butler, and was born about 1612. He was admitted to the Inner Temple in 1625 and was called to the bar in 1634.[182] Two years before he became a barrister he married Anne, daughter of Robert Jenner of London (*q.v.*). He was granted one of the auditorships of the Duchy of Lancaster in 1637.[183] He seems to have been proposed by his father as a candidate for the Short Parliament, but was not elected.[184]

Trevor's role in the Long Parliament, if he sat at all, is obscure. His opponent for election, William Watkins, was reproved on 16 November for being present and was ordered to withdraw.[185] But no references to Thomas Trevor appear. Consideration of the election was ordered in January, 1644, but the voiding did not occur until late in the year.[186]

Trevor was a cousin of Sir John Trevor and son-in-law of Robert Jenner, M.P.'s of 1640.[187]

Sir Humphrey Tufton (1584–1659), of Le Mote in Maidstone and of Bobbing Court, Kent, was M.P. for Maidstone from 1640 until the purge of 1648.[188] He was the second surviving son of Sir John Tufton of Hothfield, Bart. (H.S. Kent, d. 1624), by his second wife, Christian, daughter and coheiress of Sir Humphrey Brown, Justice of Common Pleas, and was a younger brother of Nicholas, first Earl of Thanet. Born in 1584, he was educated at Oxford (University College) and the Inner Temple.[189] He may have aspired early to a court career. He was granted a lease of some royal lands in 1611,[190] was knighted in 1614, and for some years seems to have maintained a residence not far from the court.[191] He was recommended by the Countess of Rutland in the parliamentary election at Chippenham in 1614, but without success.[192] Late in

1615 Sir Humphrey married Margaret, first daughter and coheir of Herbert Morley of Glynde, Sussex, her portion being rumored to be £6000. The following year, while they were living near Lincoln's Inn Fields, Tufton became involved in a Star Chamber suit for having beaten his wife's cousin, Christopher Nevill, son of Lord Abergavenny, for his attentions to Lady Tufton, and was fined almost £4000 for his violence.[193] He seems to have had a town house in Westminster in 1631, but probably lived much of the time in Kent, where he now owned Bobbing Court and the Mote.[194]

Sir Humphrey apparently opposed the 1621 loan, for he was among the sixty Kentish men who were summoned to attend Council regarding the matter in 1622.[195] About this time he became a J.P. for the county, and served as such for many years.[196] He was a member also of numerous local commissions on a variety of subjects.[197] He was active, too, in military affairs, being one of the county D.L.'s from as early as 1630.[198] His "wary and cheerful" management of the reluctant militia being summoned for the Scottish expedition was noted in May, 1640.[199] He had not served in parliament before that year, but was a vigorous candidate for the Maidstone election in October. He defeated one candidate easily and contested, even to the point of blows, Sir Francis Barnham's efforts for the first place.[200]

Tufton was a member of the popular party in the 1640 Commons, and was named in the early months to at least one committee of some importance, that on pluralities.[201] He was created a baronet in December, 1641, but continued his work against the crown. He was sent into Kent to oppose the commission of array, was named a parliamentary D.L. and committeeman there,[202] remained a member of the House until 1648. He had some difficulties, 1651–1654, with the compounding commissioners regarding certain properties which had been sequestered as belonging to his wife's relatives.[203] He died at the age of seventy-six in 1659, administration of his estate being granted, 8 October 1659, to his son, Sir John.[204]

Although Tufton's family had wealth and his wife's portion had been large, he does not appear to have been a man of great means in 1640. His estate had quite possibly been settled on his heirs before that time. It

---

[181] *M. of P.* **1**: 491.

[182] *Students admitted to the Inner Temple*, 246.

[183] Williams, *Official lists of the duchy and county Palatine of Lancaster*, 57.

[184] S.P. 16, 450/15.

[185] D'Ewes (N), 537.

[186] *C.J.* **3**: 374, 708.

[187] In addition to the authorities cited above see *Complete Baronetage* **2**: 130; Williams, *Parl. Hist. Wales*, 135.

[188] *M. of P.* **1**: 490; *O.P.H.* **9**: *30.

[189] *Complete Baronetage* **2**: 151; *Vis. Kent, 1619*, 119; Hasted, *Kent* **7**: 518; *Students admitted to the Inner Temple*, 157.

[190] *C.S.P. Dom., 1611–1618*, 29.

[191] St. Ch. 8/223/2; Records of St. Margaret's Parish, Overseers' Accounts, **153**, 1631–1632.

[192] F. H. Goldney, *Records of Chippenham*, 328, Chippenham, 1889.

[193] St. Ch. 8/223/2; *C.S.P. Dom., 1611–1618*, 414; *The letters of John Chamberlain* **2**: 179.

[194] Hasted, *Kent* **4**: 294; **6**: 199.

[195] S.P. 14, 127/82.

[196] C. 193/13; S.P. 16/405.

[197] *C.S.P. Dom., 1627–1628*, 449; C. 181/3; 181/4, fols. 18v, 38; 181/5, *passim*; Boys, *Sandwich*, 216.

[198] S.P. 16, 160/10; 409/7.

[199] *C.S.P. Dom., 1640*, 148.

[200] Bodleian Rawl. MSS. D. 141, fol. 7.

[201] *C.J.* **2**: 93, 100.

[202] Rawl. MSS. D. 141, fol. 31; *Arch. Cant.* **2**: 181, 1859; **9**: 32, n., 1874; *C.J.* **2**: 724.

[203] *Cal. Com. Comp.* 2282, 2766.

[204] *Complete Baronetage* **2**: 151; P.C.C., Act Book, 1659, fol. 331v.

seems to have consisted principally of the two manors by which he was identified, other holdings near Maidstone, and certain others in Wilts and Sussex.[205] He must have had some knowledge of colonial affairs, whether he was financially interested or not, for his brother, Nicholas, had been active in the Virginia Company, and his brother, William, was for some time governor of Barbados.[206]

Among the 1640 M.P.'s with whom Tufton was related were Herbert Morley, the parliamentarian, a kinsmen of his wife, and Sir Edward Dering, a nephew by marriage (q.v.).

Henry Tulse (fl. 1607–1642), of Hinton in Christchurch parish, Hampshire, was M.P. for Christchurch from 1640 until his death in 1642.[207] He was probably a descendant of the Tulse family of Avon and a son of the William Tulse who in 1603 purchased several manors in Christchurch parish.[208] The latter was probably the son and heir of William Tulse of Avon (d. 1587) and his wife, Agnes (will proved 1609).[209] Henry Tulse was probably the child of that name who was referred to in the will (25 December 1607) of Agnes Tulse. In 1625 William Tulse of Hinton, Esquire, presumably Henry's father, was reported as capable of lending £15 on a privy seal.[210] Five years later Henry Tulse of Hinton and William Tulse of Avon made excuses for not becoming knights, declaring that they had had no freehold land worth £40 a year at the time of the king's coronation, but each paid £17 as composition the following year.[211] In April, 1630, at the quarter sessions at Winchester, Henry Tulse was named one of the two treasurers for the Marshalsea.[212] He was a J.P., 1634–1639, at least,[213] and a sewers commissioner also.[214] And for the same period, probably longer, he was one of the farmers of Christchurch rectory.[215] His

wife, Elizabeth, who died on 27 April 1632, was buried in the chancel of Christchurch Priory church.[216]

Tulse was one of the J.P.'s who protested in 1639 against contributing further for St. Paul's,[217] and was elected to both 1640 parliaments for Christchurch. He seems to have been chosen each time as the local man to balance the outsider who was elected upon the nomination of the borough lord.[218] Tulse, however, took little part in debate or committee. He may have been absent at the time of the Protestation of May, 1641, for he did not take it until June 18.[219] But he promised a free gift of £20 for the defense in June, 1642,[220] and was evidently a parliamentarian in his sympathies. He died before 21 September 1642.[221]

Of Tulse's financial standing little can be said. His position in county affairs indicates a growing prestige, but he was apparently not a man of great wealth or influence. The Henry Tulse of Hinton who represented Christchurch in several later parliaments[222] was probably his son.

* Samuel Turner, M.D. (d. 1647 ?), of London, was M.P. for Shaftesbury, Dorset, 1640–24 January 1644. He seems to have little or no connection with either Shaftesbury or the county beyond the fact that he had sat for that borough in 1626 and that his father had served several times for Bridport. Wood speculates, however, that he may have practiced medicine in Dorset for a time after his foreign study.[223]

Aside from his attack on Buckingham in the 1626 parliament Turner seems to have been known chiefly as a physician attendant at court.[224] He was paid £220 for attendance on Queen Anne in 1619.[225] He may have travelled to Vienna with the Earl of Arundel in 1636.[226] Before 1633 he formed some connection with the earls of Pembroke and became in that year with Rudyard a tenant of the earl's son-in-law. In 1639 Turner named as executors of his will the earl's son and son-in-law. And he doubtless owed his seat in the Long Parliament to the Herberts' influence.[227] Dr.

[205] Hasted, *Kent* 7 : 16 ; *Cal. Com. Comp.* 2282, 2766.
[206] Brown, *Genesis of the U. S.*, 1034.
[207] He died in 1642, but a writ for replacing him was not ordered until 25 November 1645. *Hampshire Notes and Queries* 5 : 123, 1890.
[208] *V.C.H. Hampshire* 5 : 96, 99. One William Tulse contributed £25 to the Armada fund in 1588. *Hampshire Notes and Queries* 2 : 41, 1884.
[209] According to the I.P.M. (C. 142/277/127) of the elder William Tulse, his heir, William, was aged 22 in 1587. Agnes Tulse's will of 1607 was proved by her son, William, in 1609. P.C.C., 12 Dorset.
[210] S.P. 16, 521/177/i ; Add. MSS, 21,922, fol. 17.
[211] Henry Tulse was termed "esquire" in the 1630 report and "gentleman" in 1631 ; William was styled "gentleman" each time. Add. MSS, 21,922, fols. 178v, 182v. William may have been a brother of Henry.
[212] Bodleian Rawl. MSS, D 666, fol. 79v.
[213] *Ibid.*, fols. 85v, 87 ; C. 193/13 ; Add. MSS, 21,922, fol. 199 ; S.P. 16/405.
[214] C. 181/5, fol. 230.
[215] F. R. Goodman, ed., *The diary of John Young, S.T.P.*, 173.

[216] Woodward, Wilks, and Lockhart, *A general history of Hampshire* 3 : 127, n.
[217] Bodleian Rawl. MSS, D 666, fol. 85v.
[218] *M. of P.* 1 : 483, 493. The mayor wrote on 26 October 1640 to one nobleman, announcing the election of Mr. Tulse, the town's neighbor. Note supplied from Christchurch MSS by Mr. Herbert Druitt.
[219] *C.J.* 2 : 178.
[220] *N. and Q.*, 1st Ser., 12 : 360, 1855.
[221] *Hampshire Notes and Queries* 5 : 123, 1890.
[222] *M. of P.* 1 : 509, 515, 527.
[223] *Fasti. Oxon.* 1 : 303.
[224] Sir Philip Warwick (*Memoires*, 16) dismissed Turner as an inconsiderable courtier-dependant. But Wotton called him "a travelled doctor of physic, of bold spirit and able elocution." *Fairfax correspondence* 1 : 39, n.
[225] *C.S.P. Dom., 1619–1623*, 66.
[226] Birch, *The court and times of Charles the First* 2 : 238.
[227] *E.H.R.* 50 : 243, 248, 251, 252, 1935.

Turner was listed in 1639 as one of the London doctors who excused themselves from the loan, declaring they had contributed in another way.[228] Except for his vote against Strafford's attainder, Turner's role in the Long Parliament was undistinguished. He was absent at call on 16 June 1642,[229] and probably attended little after that.

When Turner compounded for his royalism he declared as his estate only a house in Whitehall and an income of £250 a year arising from his professional connection at court.[230] No reference to gains from a private practice appears.

Dr. Turner had at least one relative in the 1640 Commons, a first cousin, Dr. George Parry.[231] And he was evidently a friend of Selden, whom he named as one of his executors.[232]

John Upton (1590–1641), of Lupton in Brixham, Devon, represented Clifton-Dartmouth-Hardness from 1640 [1] until his death in September, 1641. He was born on 7 April 1590, the son and heir of Arthur Upton (d. 1618),[2] by Gertrude, daughter of Hugh Fortescue of Filleigh (Tilley).[3] He studied at Lincoln College, Oxford (B.A. 1608), and at the Inner Temple (admitted 1609),[4] and in February, 1613, married Dorothy, daughter of Sir Anthony Rous of Halton, Cornwall. The marriage brought him not only a settlement of some of his father's lands and his wife's dowry of £1000,[5] but provided for him an important political connection, for his wife was a half-sister of both Francis Rous, the puritan writer and M.P., and John Pym.[6]

After his father's death Upton became active in affairs in his county. He was a J.P. as early as 1626 and for many years afterwards.[7] He served too as a foefee

of his parish.[8] He was a loan commissioner in 1626–1627,[9] and was named to the commissions on piracy, sewers, western affairs, and exacted fees.[10] He defaulted from the musters of 1629, possibly through a messenger's mistake,[11] and in 1638 was among the Devon justices who supported the protest of the local manufacturers against a London project for engrossing Spanish cloth.[12] He was M.P. for Dartmouth, regularly, 1625–1640.[13] His puritan connections led Upton to work with the Providence Island Company. In 1632 he bought a quarter of Pym's share of the stock and became afterwards the company's agent in western England. He did considerable work for the project and subscribed several later times to its capital.[14]

Although he was not a prominent speaker, Upton was one of the mainstays of Pym's group in the Long Parliament. Within the first month he was named to five committees, including that on privileges, and he was named to various later ones. He was present as late as 17 July 1641.[15] He joined with John Northcote in March, 1641, in pledging £500 for the loan,[16] but died during the recess, 11 September 1641.[17] When the Commons reassembled the Speaker and other members openly expressed their sorrow "for the losse of soe worthie and usefull a member." [18]

Upton inherited from his father at least three manors and other properties in Brixham and nearby parishes, and he owned at his death such additional property as two grain mills.[19] But before 1640 he had made a settlement of his estate upon the occasion of his eldest son's marriage (1638), and had provided portions for two daughters. Although his family was large, seven sons and eight daughters, he planned by his will for portions of £400 and £300 for his unmarried daughters, annuities of £100 for his second and third sons, and portions of £220 each for the younger ones to start them in business.[20] His means seem to have been ample.

John Upton's will reveals a typical puritan's concern for the rearing of his children so that they should be God-fearing and not given to idleness and pleasure.

---

[228] Rushworth **3**: 912.

[229] *C.J.* **2**: 626.

[230] S.P. 23/125/441.

[231] Turner's mother was a sister of Henry Parry, Bishop of Worcester.

[232] *E.H.R.* **50**: 248, 1935.

[1] John Upton's name is missing from the official list, and the Dartmouth member is listed by error as Arthur Upton in *O.P.H.* (**9**: *24) and Carlyle (*Cromwell* **3**: 338). The latter was either the brother or the son of John. It was John Upton who took the Protestation in May, 1641 (*C.J.* **2**: 133), and whose death in September necessitated a new election. The John Upton who has been listed sometimes as a "recruiter" for Fowey (Carlyle, *loc. cit.*; *O.P.H.* **9**: *21) and confused with the Dartmouth M.P., was possibly his son (Pink MSS, 307, fol. 193; *Western Antiquary* **5**: 268–269, 1885–1886; **6**: 16, 1886–1887).

[2] Devon *Trans.* **18**: 212, 1886; I.P.M., Arthur Upton, 1618, C. 142/650/140.

[3] Burke, *Landed gentry* **2**: 1458, 1851; *Vis. Devon, 1620*, 293.

[4] *Al. Oxon.; Students admitted to the Inner Temple*, 188.

[5] I.P.M. cited above.

[6] In 1641 Upton was named a trustee for the marriage settlement of Pym's daughter, Dorothy. Devon *Trans.* **43**: 352, 1911.

[7] C. 193/12, 13; Devonshire MSS, Quarter Sessions Minute Books, 1625–1633, 1633–1640.

[8] Exeter City Library MSS, Exeter Deeds and Documents, Nos. 4534, 4536, 4537, 4542.

[9] S.P. 16, 53/96.

[10] C. 181/4, fols. 52v, 164; 181/5, fols. 183, 218.

[11] S.P. 16, 150/76/iii.

[12] S.P. 16, 380/88.

[13] *M. of P., passim.*

[14] Newton, *The colonising activities of the English puritans*, 126.

[15] *C.J.* **2**: 21, 29, 31, 34, 40, *passim.*

[16] D'Ewes (N), 438, n. (439).

[17] I.P.M., 28 October 1641 (C. 142/701/11); Devon *Trans.* **18**: 212, 1886.

[18] D'Ewes (C), 16.

[19] I.P.M.'s of Arthur Upton and John Upton cited above. An annuity of 200 marks out of one of the manors was guaranteed for his son's wife.

[20] Upton's will, P.C.C., 153 Evelyn.

It stated also his hope that his cherished books would be used by his son.[21]

Not only was Upton closely related to Rous and Pym, but he was a connection by marriage of Sir John Clotworthy. The latter's sister was the wife of Upton's brother, Henry Upton of county Antrim.[22]

Sir William Uvedale (c. 1587–1652), of Wickham, Hampshire, a courtier, was M.P. for Petersfield from 1640 until 1648 (?).[23] He was a prominent man both at court and in his county, being the last in the line of a family that had been settled at Wickham in the fourteenth century. One ancestor had been treasurer of the king's chamber under Henry VIII, and the same office was held by Sir William Uvedale of Wickham (H.S. Hampshire, 1594; d. 1616). The latter, by his wife, Mary, daughter of Sir Richard Norton, was father of the 1640 M.P.[24] The member should be distinguished from a kinsman of the same name, Sir William Uvedale of Horton, Dorset (d. 1645), who, too, had court connections. The latter was sheriff of Dorset, 1640–1641.[25] William Uvedale of Wickham, the second but eldest surviving son of his parents, was born about 1587.[26] He entered Queen's College, Oxford, in 1598, and was admitted to the Middle Temple in 1601.[27] He was knighted before 1607,[28] and before 1608 he married Anne, daughter of Sir Edmund Carey, a younger son of Henry Lord Hunsdon.[29] Early in 1640 he married a young second wife, Victoria Cary, daughter of Henry Lord Falkland, and sister of Lucius Lord Falkland (q.v.).[30]

Uvedale's career at court was launched under King James. He may have been granted with Sir Humphrey May the reversion of the office of clerk of the Council of Star Chamber in 1609, an office shared with Sir William Morley (q.v.) in 1635, apparently as a trustee.[31] He came into favor with the Earl of Somerset, and probably through him was granted in 1615 the reversion of the treasurership of the Chamber. He entered into the office in 1618 and was still holding it in 1640.[32] From 1615 until 1623 he held a lease on certain fines collected in Ireland, which his father had once enjoyed, and which was worth £300 to £800 a year.[33] He was popular at court and seems to have remained in royal favor throughout the reign of King Charles. He may have been the "Will Udall" who was involved in the scandal of Lord Essex's separation from his wife in 1636, but if so, his career was not adversely affected thereby.[34] In 1639 he became Treasurer for the Army, accompanying it to the north, and in 1640, as Treasurer at Wars, was a member of the Council.[35]

In Hampshire, meanwhile, Uvedale was not inactive. Aided by Somerset, whose favorite he then was, he defeated Sir Henry Wallop in the heated parliamentary election for the shire in 1614.[36] He was M.P. for Newport (1621), for Portsmouth (1624), and for Petersfield, 1625, 1626, 1628, and both times in 1640.[37] He was a J.P. at least as early as 1625, serving afterwards in Westminster, too,[38] and was a D.L. in Hampshire[39] and a member in 1627 of the commission on martial law.[40] He was on the knighthood commission in 1630 and was named to various others of a local nature.[41] Uvedale was widely known in his county for his influence and his hospitality.[42] When the Duchess of Chevreux landed at Portsmouth in 1638, she was entertained at his home.[43] And at Westminster Sir William was known as one of the outstanding courtiers. Lloyd described him as handsome and "most accomplished,"

---

[21] *Ibid.* Upton's eldest son, Arthur, was M.P. for Devon, 1654 and 1656 (*Al. Oxon.*). His second son, John, became a brother-in-law of Cromwell's secretary, Thurlow, and a commissioner of the customs. Another son, Anthony, was a merchant in Spain. Royal Hist. Soc., *Trans.*, 2d Ser., **6**: 147, 149, 1892.

[22] Burke, *Landed gentry* **2**: 1458, 1851. Henry Upton, John's younger brother, could scarcely have gone to Ireland as early as the time of Essex, however, as is stated by Burke. His son, Arthur, the Irish Presbyterian leader, was born in 1623 (*D.N.B.*).

[23] *M. of P.* **1**: 493. On 5 February 1644, Uvedale was granted a respite until April, and seems to have been readmitted to the House by October (*C.J.* **3**: 389; B. Whitelocke, *Memorials of the English affairs* **1**: 324, 1853). He was apparently still a member in 1648. Pink MSS, 311, fol. 494 a.

[24] Berry, *Ped. Hants.*, 74–75; Pink MSS, 311, fol. 453 c.

[25] Berry, *loc. cit.*; *Surrey Arch. Coll.* **3**: 126, 1865; *List of Sheriffs*, 39.

[26] *Surrey Arch. Coll.* **3**: 122, 125, 1865; I.P.M., Sir William Uvedale, 1616, C. 142/354/122.

[27] *Al. Oxon.*; *Mid. Temp. Rec.* **1**: 410.

[28] I.P.M. cited above.

[29] A daughter was born in June, 1608. *Surrey Arch. Coll.* **3**: 125, 128, 1865.

[30] *C.S.P. Dom., 1639–1640*, 474; *Surrey Arch. Coll.* **3**: 130, 1865.

[31] *C.S.P. Dom., 1603–1610*, 530; *1631–1633*, 68; *1635–1636*, 57. Possibly the Dorset Uvedale, however, was the holder of this office, since no title follows Uvedale's name in the grant. The Dorset Uvedale seems to have followed more closely the career of May. *Surrey Arch. Coll.* **3**: 126, 1865.

[32] *The letters of John Chamberlain* **1**: 606; *C.S.P. Dom., 1611–1618*, 291, 513; *1639–1640*, 389.

[33] *C.S.P. Ireland, 1611–1614*, 305, 448; *1615–1625*, 400, 572; Bodleian Clarendon MSS, 2, No. 101; *H.M.C., Fourth Report*, MSS of Earl De la Warr, 314.

[34] *Verney Papers*, 168–169 and n., Camden Society, 1853.

[35] *C.S.P. Dom., 1638–1639*, 539; *1639–1640*, 364, 458; *Verney Papers*, 242; S.P. 16, 442/143.

[36] *M. of P.* **3**: App., xxxix; *The letters of John Chamberlain* **1**: 518. A Star Chamber case ensued. St. Ch. 8/293/11.

[37] *M. of P., passim.*

[38] C. 193/12, 13; Add. MSS, 21,922, fol. 38; S.P. 16/405.

[39] Add. MSS, 21,922, fols. 8v, 11; 26,781, fol. 4, *passim*.

[40] *C.S.P. Dom., 1627–1628*, 440.

[41] Add. MSS, 21,922, fol. 174; C. 181/4, fol. 89; 181/5, *passim*.

[42] See the lines written about him by his brother-in-law, the poet, Patrick Cary. George Saintsbury, ed., *Minor poets of the Caroline period* **2**: 458–460, Oxford, Clarendon Press, 1906.

[43] *Strafford letters* **2**: 166.

and "as knowing as much Learning, long Travels, and great Observations could make him." [44]

As a parliament man and as Treasurer of the Chamber and for the war Uvedale was exceedingly busy in 1640 and 1641. He was named to several of the committees of the parliament during the early months, [45] but was frequently absent, both because of his other affairs and because of his health. [46] He was present to pledge £1000 as security for the loan in November, 1640, and £500 in the following March. [47] He was at York on army business in August. [48] When the war began he seems to have been with the king at Nottingham, and was one of the bearers of the king's propositions to London in August, 1642. [49] He was apparently present at a royalist meeting in Hampshire in November, 1643. [50] But he did not lose all favor with parliament, for he was named to some of the parliamentary committees for the county, and in 1644, instead of being disabled in February, was respited until April, and eventually allowed in October to resume his place. He remained a member until 1647 or 1648. [51] As in his youth when he was said to be popular with all sides, he managed now in courtly fashion to straddle the issues of the day. He died in 1652 and was buried on 3 December at Wickham. [52]

Sir William was wealthy, holding lands in Hampshire and Surrey which, when he inherited them, totalled about 5000 acres belonging to eight manors. [53] Other lands he acquired through royal favor, [54] and in his life at court he looked after his own purse as well as that of the king. Commenting in 1640 about the possibility of recovering a personal loan of £1000 to the crown from funds collected for the army, he declared, "It is the rule that we ought to look to ourselves in the first place." [55] In April, 1641, he put in a claim for £1000 as a creditor of the Earl of Strafford. [56] When he made his will in 1651 he planned portions of £1500 for each of his two younger daughters. [57]

Uvedale had several relatives and close friends in the 1640 Commons. The Verneys, particularly Sir Edmund, were intimate friends. [58] Ogle was a neighbor. [59] Falkland was a brother-in-law, and Sir Edward Griffin was a son-in-law. Sir Francis Knollys and his son were second cousins of Uvedale's first wife.

* **Benjamin Valentine** (d. 1652 ?), of Cheshire (?), was M.P. for St. Germans, Cornwall, 1640–1652. Sir John Eliot's friend and co-sufferer, released from his long imprisonment only in January, 1640, Valentine was welcomed into the House. There seems to have been no inclination to question his election although he was one of three men returned for St. Germans. [1] His previous connection with Cornwall had been as a member for the same borough in the notable session of 1628–1629, but he was probably a Cheshire man himself, and his family seem to have been living in Lincolnshire while he was in prison. [2] Valentine's wealth was probably not great. His pledge of two horses for the defense in June, 1642, [3] indicates at least a fair income, if a comparison with the offers of other members is to be trusted.

* **Sir Henry Vane** (1589–1655), Treasurer of the Household and Secretary of State, sat for Wilton, 1640–1653. He had been returned for Wilton after failing to be elected for Kent in the spring, [4] and the Long Parliament was his eighth. [5] A courtier and royal official of long experience, Vane had used opportunities to increase his estate. He was on the pension list of 1630 for £900, [6] and by 1640 had accumulated lands, especially in his native Kent and in the north, worth £3000 a year. [7] He was able to advance the king £2000 as a loan or gift in May, 1640, and to offer his bond for £2000 for the loan in November. [8] Sir Henry had earlier been interested in the Virginia Company, [9] and in 1640, with Windebank, was hoping to make some profit out of the postal service. [10]

Among Vane's official duties was membership in the Council's group to study the fisheries, and in the commission for the ecclesiastical jurisdiction of England and Wales in 1633. [11] In 1634 and 1637 he attended the Star Chamber proceedings against Prynne and ac-

[44] *Memoires*, 655.

[45] *C.J.* **2**: 34 (2), 115.

[46] *C.S.P. Dom., 1640*, 415, 570; *1640–1641*, 292.

[47] D'Ewes (N), 52, 438, n.

[48] Bodleian Tanner MSS, 66, fol. 146.

[49] Clarendon, *Rebellion* **2**: 304; Whitelocke, *Memorials of the English affairs* **1**: 179, 1853.

[50] Add. MSS, 26,781, fol. 115.

[51] *C.J.* **3**: 389; Whitelocke, *op. cit.* **1**: 324; Woodward, Wilks, and Lockhart, *A general history of Hampshire* **3**: 146, n.; Pink MSS, 311, fol. 494 a. His readmission to the House was mentioned in the charges against A. Nicoll in 1647. Brit. Mus. Bibl. Eg., 1048, fol. 78.

[52] *Surrey Arch. Coll.* **3**: 127, 1865.

[53] I.P.M., C. 142/354/122; Manning and Bray, *Surrey* **2**: 409, 424.

[54] *V.C.H. Hampshire* **3**: 159; *C.S.P. Dom., 1619–1623*, 607.

[55] Several letters of his in this vein appear in *C.S.P. Dom., 1640–1641*, 324, 431–432, *passim*.

[56] *H.M.C., Fourth Report*, House of Lords MSS, 60.

[57] P.C.C., 414 Alchin. The will is abstracted in *Surrey Arch. Coll.* **3**: 179–180, 1865.

[58] *C.S.P. Dom., 1640–1641*, 554; *Verney Papers*, 188.

[59] *C.S.P. Dom., 1640–1641*, 432.

[1] *C.J.* **2**: 63; D'Ewes (N), 107, 222.

[2] His son, Matthew, of Newton, Lincolnshire, was admitted to the Inner Temple in 1633. *Students admitted to the Inner Temple*, 277.

[3] *N. and Q.*, 1st Ser., **12**: 338, 1855.

[4] See Kent election.

[5] *M. of P., passim; D.N.B.* His constituency in 1628 was Thetford, not Retford, as in *D.N.B.*

[6] S.P. 16, 180/18/71v.

[7] Hasted, *Kent* **5**: 47–48; *D.N.B.*

[8] S.P. 16, 453/74; D'Ewes (N), 52. His salary as Secretary of State in 1639 was only £100, but with £700 allowed for certain expenses. *C.S.P. Dom., 1639–1640*, 419.

[9] Brown, *Genesis of the U. S.*, 1036.

[10] *C.S.P. Dom., 1640–1641*, 315.

[11] S.P. 16, 241/80/188; *C.S.P. Dom., 1633–1634*, 326.

quiesced in the decisions about the penalties. With another councillor, Jermyn, therefore, Vane advised caution when parliament proposed reopening that case in 1640.[12] Less important assignments were numerous commissions on special or local matters, chiefly in London and the southeastern counties.[13] And he was a J.P. at one time or another in Essex, Durham, Kent, Middlesex, and Westminster.[14]

Vane was one of the carpetbaggers of the 1640 Commons. His name was on the list of court candidates for the Short Parliament,[15] and the Herbert influence at Wilton no doubt helped him to secure his seat at that time, and also in the autumn.[16] He was related to various M.P.'s, including his second cousin, Dering, and his son, Sir Henry Vane, junior.

* **Sir Henry Vane** (1613–1662), Treasurer of the Navy, and son of Secretary Vane, was M.P. for Hull, 1640–1653. He had spent most of his life south of the Humber or beyond the seas. But he married a Lincolnshire wife in the summer of 1640 and his office in the navy had doubtless made him somewhat known in northern ports. His election for Hull for the Short Parliament, however, was accomplished only through the intercession of the Earl of Northumberland, using his influence as Lord Admiral, and of his father, the Secretary.[17] No doubt his re-election in October was accomplished by similar means.

Vane was entered at Gray's Inn in 1633 [18] after his travels on the continent. When he married Sir Christopher Wray's daughter in 1640 his navy office was worth £800 a year and his wife's jointure was to be £600 a year; [19] and the Vane family lands of some £3000 a year value were settled on him.

Fellow members of Vane's in the Long Parliament were his father, his father-in-law, the latter's brother, and his own brother-in-law, Sir Thomas Pelham.

* **Samuel Vassall** (1586–1667), London clothier, merchant, and colonizer, sat for London, 1640–1648.[20] A member and official of the drapers' company,[21] he was interested in the East Indies and the Levant, as well as in the development of North America, and for some time before 1637 was a leading distributor of English textiles in the regions dominated by Turkey and Venice.[22] In London affairs, he was named to the Court of Requests in 1629 [23] and was probably sometime an alderman. He was among those imprisoned for refusing the 1627 loan,[24] afterwards for his stand regarding tonnage and poundage, and in September, 1639, a search of his house by agents of the crown produced papers dealing with matters in which the puritan leaders were notoriously interested, Scottish affairs, ship money, and Catholicism at the court.[25] When parliament was considering in December, 1640, the case of Richard Chambers, a fellow sufferer, Vassall reminded the House that his own grievances were but little less, that he had been "committed" sixteen times within seven years, and had lost well over £10,000. But though his financial penalties had been heavy, Vassall was still wealthy. He subscribed for the loan in November, 1640,[26] promised one horse, and more if needed, for the defense in 1642,[27] and pledged a considerable sum for the reducing of Ireland.

* **Henry Vaughan** (1587 ?–c. 1660), of Derwydd, Carmarthen, was M.P. for his shire, 1640–5 February 1644.[28] A younger son of Walter Vaughan, several times M.P. for the county, he probably sat for the town of Carmarthen in 1614,[29] as he did for the parliaments of 1621–1628. He was returned for the county for the first time in the spring of 1640.[30] Besides being M.P. and sheriff, Vaughan was a J.P. in Carmarthenshire.[31] He died probably not long before January, 1661, when his will [32] was proved.[33]

[12] *Documents relating to the proceedings against William Prynne*, ed. J. Bruce and S. R. Gardiner, 16, Camden Society, 1877; S.P. 16, 361/77; D'Ewes (N), 4.

[13] S.P. 16, 171/3/4; C. 181/4 and 5, *passim*.

[14] C. 193/13; S.P. 16/405; *H.M.C., Tenth Report* **4**, County of Essex MSS, 502–507.

[15] S.P. 16, 450/15.

[16] *E.H.R.* **50**: 252, 1935.

[17] Hull Corporation MSS, letter of December, 1639, from the Earl of Northumberland; *C.S.P. Dom., 1639–1640*, 568.

[18] *Gray's Inn Adm. Reg.*, 202.

[19] Charles Dalton, *History of the Wrays of Glentworth, 1523–1852* **2**: 102–104, London, 1880–1881 (hereafter, Dalton, *The Wrays of Glentworth*).

[20] *A vindication of the imprisoned and secluded members of the House of Commons*, 29, London, printed for Michael Spark, 1649. He is numbered by Hexter, however, with the Independents. *A.H.R.* **44**: 37, n., 1938–1939.

[21] A. H. Johnson, *The history of the worshipful company of drapers of London* **4**: 140, Oxford, Clarendon Press, 1914–1922.

[22] S.P. 16, 147/41; *C.S.P. Dom., 1637–1638*, 104; *C.S.P. Venetian, 1636–1639*, 329–330, 374; *1640–1642*, 156, 233.

[23] London Corporation MSS, Rep. 43, fol. 302.

[24] Rushworth **1**: 473.

[25] Windebank's notes on the seized papers. *C.S.P. Dom., 1639*, 525.

[26] D'Ewes (N), 94 and n., 539.

[27] *N. and Q.*, 1st Ser., **12**: 359, 1855.

Other references: Beaven, *The aldermen of the city of London* **1**: 276; *Western Antiquary* **8**: 45, 1888–1889.

[28] *M. of P.* **1**: 498; *C.J.* **3**: 389.

[29] No names appear for the borough in *M. of P.* His name is given in a list of 1614 M.P.'s, based upon a manuscript at Kimbolton Castle, among the Pink MSS.

[30] His return for 1625 was voided. *M. of P.* **1**: 467, n.

[31] S.P. 16/405.

[32] The will of Sir Henry Vaughan, Derwith, Carmarthen, knight. J. H. Morrison, *Prerogative court of Canterbury, wills, sentences, and probate acts, 1661–1670*, 250.

[33] *D.N.B.* corrects the account of Vaughan's life as it appears in Williams, *Parl. Hist. Wales*, 45.

* John Vaughan (1603–1674), lawyer of the Inner Temple, and of Trawscoed, Cardigan, was M.P. for Cardigan borough from December, 1640,[34] until 1 September 1645.[35] Already recognized in his profession, and a friend of John Selden, he was probably the "Mr. Vaughan" who was named to several early committees, such as those to consider points of law in connection with the trial of Strafford.[36] His career afterwards is well known.[37]

Peter Venables (1604–1669), "Baron of Kinderton," represented Cheshire, 1640–22 January 1644. Twenty-first in the line of owners of the old barony of Kinderton in Cheshire, he was born on 22 April 1604,[38] the only surviving son of Thomas Venables (d. 1605) by his second wife, Anne, daughter of Sir Cotton Gargreave of Nostoll, Yorkshire. He entered Lincoln's Inn in 1620,[39] but seems shortly afterwards to have married and settled down to manage his estates. His first wife, Mary Wilbraham, whom he married about 1622, died early,[40] and about September, 1628, Venables married Frances, daughter of Sir Hugh Cholmondeley of Cheshire, and sister of Robert Lord Cholmondeley, afterwards Earl of Leinster.[41]

Venables was a J.P. in Cheshire during most of the reign of Charles I, and a member of other commissions in 1628 and 1635.[42] He was H.S., Cheshire, 1633–1634,[43] and in 1638 joined with other officials and gentlemen of the county in their controversy with Chester city regarding ship money assessments.[44] Some of his tenants in the summer of 1640 resisted ship money collections with violence,[45] and possibly when Venables was elected to the Long Parliament, his first, it was as a foe of such abuses, although he was doubtless aided by his brother-in-law, Lord Cholmondeley, whose powers had been felt in the spring election.[46]

In the 1640 House, however, Venables distinguished himself chiefly by voting against Strafford's attainder,[47] but he took the Protestation of May, 1641, and on 21 August was named with Brereton to assist with the disarming of recusants in their county. He was suspended for non-attendance, 2 September 1642, disabled 22 January 1644,[48] and was loyal to the king through the war. He sat again in the 1661 parliament,[49] and died on 13 November 1669.

Venables inherited from his father more than eight manors in Cheshire, some saltworks at Nantwich and various Staffordshire properties. His mother's and sisters' portions had been £1000 or more,[50] and his own net income was over £1660, possibly £2000, a year. Among his most valuable holdings were new salt works at Middlewich which he stated to be worth some £200 yearly, but which the compounding commissioners valued at £550 a year.[51] His fine at compounding, reckoned at two-thirds, was £9800, with a large assessment for his son, but the family seems to have secured a reduction by half, paying a combined fine of £6150.[52]

A traveller in Cheshire about the time Peter Venables came of age described him as a "towardly young gentleman." He was sufficiently interested in history to contribute toward the expense of producing the first topographical work on Cheshire.[53]

* John Venn (1586–1650), merchant tailor of London, was a member for the city from 1 June 1641, when he replaced Cradock, until his death in 1650.[54] The son of a Somerset yeoman family, Venn kept his contacts with the west country through trade,[55] and was probably the Captain Venn whose advice about a new muster master was sought in 1626 by the citizens of Exeter,[56] for he was an officer in the London artillery company.[57] He was a member of the common council of London and an

---

[34] The return was dated 14 December (*M. of P.* **1**: 498), the election probably having been delayed as in some other places in Wales because of the late arrival of the writs.
[35] His absence was respited on 5 February 1644, but he was disabled in 1645. *C.J.* **3**: 390; **4**: 260.
[36] *C.J.* **2**: 64, 88. "Mr. John Vaughan" was added to the elections committee for the case of Carnarvonshire. *C.J.* **2**: 99.
[37] In addition to *D.N.B.* see Williams, *Parl. Hist. Wales*, 31.
[38] *Cheshire inquisitions post mortem, 1603–1660*, Rec. Soc. Lancs. and Cheshire, **91**: 127, 1938.
[39] *Linc. Inn Rec. Adm.* **1**: 186.
[40] She was a daughter of Sir Richard Wilbraham of Woodhey. *Cheshire Sheaf*, 1st Ser., **3**: 24, 1885; Ormerod, *Chester* **3**: 200; *Vis. Cheshire, 1613*, 241. In Hunter's pedigrees (Add. MSS, 24,444, fol. 82), however, her father is named as Sir Peter Warburton of Woodhey.
[41] A deed of settlement, with powers to reserve £250 a year for his wife, was made on 28 September 1625; a marriage settlement of 11 September 1628 anticipated his second wedding, and a deed of 26 September that year made provision for his first wife's child, Robert. S.P. 23/196/502–505.
[42] C. 193/12, 13; S.P. 16/405; C. 181/3; 181/4, fol. 192v.
[43] *List of Sheriffs*, 18.
[44] S.P. 16, 390/10.
[45] The sheriff of that year, writing of his general troubles with ship money, as well as of this incident, remarked that there was danger that "these great ones will trample us and his Majesty's business down." *C.S.P. Dom., 1640–1641*, 17–18.

[46] *Ibid., 1639–1640*, 564, 591.
[47] Verney, 58.
[48] *C.J.* **2**: 133, 267, 750; **3**: 374.
[49] *M. of P.* **1**: 520.
[50] Will of Thomas Venables, *Lancashire and Cheshire wills and inventories*, ed. J. P. Earwaker (Chetham Society, *N.S.*, **28**) **2**: 166–167, 1893.
[51] The figures presented by Venables differ more than once from those of the commissioners. His papers show that his second wife's jointure of £600 a year was covered by lands worth £350 yearly and a £250 annuity. S.P. 23/196/473–475, 483–486, 489–491, 498–505.
[52] *Ibid.; Cal. Com. Comp.*, 107, 1183, 1184.
[53] Ormerod, *Chester* **3**: 196 and n.; Pink MSS, 307, fol. 135.
[54] *M. of P.* **1**: 491. He was not the original member, as implied by *D.N.B.*, but was present in the House by 4 June 1641. *C.J.* **2**: 168.
[55] *C.S.P. Dom., 1637*, 51, 59.
[56] Exeter Corporation MSS, Act Book **7**: 640.
[57] He was a captain in 1633 (London Corporation MSS, Rep. 47, fol. 154), earlier than the date suggested in *D.N.B.*

auditor in 1640,[58] but had not served in any earlier parliament. He was among the wealthier citizens listed that year as able to advance money for the loan,[59] and in June, 1642, promised to provide £100 for the defense, as well as to "have a horse ready for himselfe to serve allwayes uppon." [60]

* Sir Edmund Verney (1590–1642), of Claydon, Bucks, Marshal of the Household for Charles I, sat for Wycombe, 1640–1642. He was educated at Oxford and by travel, and had long experience at court. But he was familiar, too, with local affairs, for he was a J.P. of Buckinghamshire and of Middlesex, and a member of various commissions. He was one of the loan commissioners in 1627,[61] and for many years was a D.L. in Bucks.[62] Verney served in four parliaments before the Long Parliament.[63]

Although Verney's lands were worth about £1000 a year,[64] and he received £200 or more in pensions,[65] in addition to the profits from his offices and his patents for a variety of projects,[66] he was not in a sound financial state in 1640. His lands, in which by 1639 he retained but a life interest, were under many obligations.[67] His offices were expensive, requiring him to advance money to the king, such as £1000 for a loan in 1640, and his Covent Garden house cost him £160 a year in rent alone.[68] And some of his enterprises had brought him heavy losses rather than profits.

Among Verney's fellow members were his son, Ralph, his brother-in-law, Denton, various other kinsmen by marriage, and many men whom he had known at court.

* Ralph Verney (1613–1696), eldest son of Sir Edmund (q.v.), represented Aylesbury, 1640–1645, though he was in voluntary exile from 1643. He had been a member for the same borough in the Short Parliament.

Verney had had considerable experience in managing his father's estates in Buckinghamshire while Sir Edmund attended to his affairs at court, and other properties which he acquired through his wife.[69] It is not known that he travelled before 1640, as did his brothers, or that he filled any office in county administration before 1640. Although he described himself in 1633 as a country clown, he seems by 1639 to have been residing in London much of the time.[70]

Henry Vernon sat in the parliament for a short time, having been returned for Andover, Hampshire, after a new election to replace Rainsford had been ordered on 31 March 1641. He was present in the House in April to vote against the attainder of Strafford, and took the Protestation on 3 May. His election was contested by Sir William Waller, whose petition was presented on 30 April 1641, and his name does not occur in the *Journals* after early May. Not until 3 May 1642, however, did the Commons' decision against Vernon enable Waller to take the seat.[71]

He was probably Henry Vernon (c. 1606–1676) of Hodnet, Shropshire,[72] and of the court, a first cousin of Thomas, fourth Earl of Southampton. His parents were Sir Robert Vernon of Hodnet, K.B., Comptroller of the Household to Queen Elizabeth (d. 1625), and Mary, daughter of Sir Robert Needham. Through his father he was a kinsman of the Earl of Essex, and through the marriage of his father's sister, Elizabeth, with Henry, third Earl of Southampton (1573–1624), he was linked with the noble house whose politics he followed. He was aged seventeen at the herald's visitation in 1623.[73] Apparently he entered the service of the fourth earl and went with him to France in 1634.[74]

---

[58] London MSS, Journal 39, fols. 65, 68, 99.

[59] S.P. 16, 453/75.

[60] Bodleian Tanner MSS, 63, fol. 56. The passage is misquoted in the version printed in *N. and Q.*, 1st Ser., **12**: 359, 1855.

[61] C. 193/12, 13; C. 181/4, fol. 191; 181/5, fols. 2, 62, *passim*; S.P. 16, 70/71.

[62] *Verney Papers*, 128; *C.S.P. Dom., 1637*, 101; *1640*, 537.

[63] Only three parliaments are mentioned in *D.N.B.*, but he was doubtless the Sir Edmund "Varney" who sat for New Romney in 1625. *M. of P.* **1**: 467.

[64] The family properties held by his son were evaluated at £1002 in 1647 (*Cal. Com. Comp.*, 3243), a total which seems not to include a small estate which was in 1612 worth something under £200 a year (*Verney Papers*, 104).

[65] *C.S.P. Dom., 1625–1626*, 159, 281; S.P. 16, 180/16/39, 45.

[66] The projects ranged from those dealing with tobacco or wool to hackney coaches and Irish lands. *Verney Papers*, 154–156, 165–167, 185–186, 224–225; *C.S.P. Dom., 1637–1638*, 97.

[67] *Verney Papers*, 104, 135, 206; *Recs. Bucks.* **5**: 422, 1878; will of Sir Edmund Verney, dated 26 March 1639. P.C.C., 129 Cambell.

[68] *Verney Papers*, 172; S.P. 16, 446/42.

[69] His wife was the heiress to several manors and other properties in Bucks and Oxfordshire. *Verney Papers*, 138–139, 170, 231. For the condition of the Verney estate, see Sir Edmund Verney.

[70] *Verney Papers*, 157, 274.

[71] *O.P.H.* **9**: 1; Carlyle, **3**: 334; Verney, 59; *C.J.* **2**: 130, 133, 554.

[72] Two other Henry Vernons were living at the period and were royalists, but the close association with the Earl of Southampton seems most clearly to establish the identity of the Andover M.P. Henry Vernon of Farnham, Surrey (c. 1589–1657), was descended from the Shropshire family, but nothing has been discovered to indicate that he served in parliament (Manning and Bray, *Surrey* **3**: 159; Wotton, *English Baronetage* **4**: 376, 1741). A descendant of the older line of Vernon of Haddon was Henry Vernon (1615–1659) of the Temple and of Haslington, Cheshire, who married a daughter of Sir George Vernon, the judge, and was the ancestor of Lord Vernon. His compounding papers in 1645–1646 do not indicate that he was ever an M.P. (Burke, *Landed gentry* **2**: 1478, 1851; *Students admitted to the Inner Temple*, 278, 346; I.P.M., Sir George Vernon, Wards 7/94/212; Chancery suit, C. 3/420/41; *Cal. Com. Comp.*, 922; *Vis. Shropshire*, 472–473).

[73] *Vis. Shropshire*, 473; *Complete Baronetage* **3**: 93; *D.N.B.*, "Henry Wriothesley, Earl of Southampton," and "Thomas Wriothesley, Earl of Southampton."

[74] *C.S.P. Dom., 1634–1635*, 166.

Through the earl Vernon was connected with the influential Wallop family of Hampshire. The earl had been Sir Henry Wallop's ward and his sister, Anne, Vernon's cousin, married Robert Wallop (q.v.),[75] who occupied one of the Andover seats in the Long Parliament. To the Wallops or more probably to Southampton, who was now opposed to the radical trend in the parliament, Vernon doubtless owed his return for Andover in 1641. Having been supplanted in 1642 by the parliamentarian, Sir William Waller, Vernon joined his patron in supporting the king in the war. He was created a baronet in 1660 and was staying in 1666 in Southampton's London house.[76] When Robert Wallop's estates were confiscated, Vernon shared with the earl and others in the enjoyment of them.[77] He was M.P. for Shropshire in 1660 and for West Looe in 1661. He died in April, 1676. Vernon's wife (married 1636) was Elizabeth, daughter and heiress of Sir Richard White of Anglesey.[78]

Sir Richard Vivian, or **Vyvyan** (1613–1665), of Trelowarren, near Helston, Cornwall, was M.P. for Tregony, 1640–1644. He came of a very old Cornish family, being the son and heir of Sir Francis Vivian (d. 1635) by his second wife, Loveday, daughter of John Connock of Treworgy, and was born in 1613.[79] His father was sheriff of the county, 1617–1618, M.P. and J.P., and was captain of St. Mawes castle from 1603 until he was removed in 1632 for mismanaging his office.[80] Richard matriculated at Exeter College, 20 June 1631, received his B.A. the same day,[81] and in November of that year entered the Middle Temple. He reigned as prince at the Christmas revels there in 1635, an honor which was said to have cost him £2000 or even more.[82] He left the Temple without having been called to the bar, but was knighted, 1 March 1636. In October of the same year he married at Barnstaple Mary, daughter of James Bulteel.[83] Sir Richard was named to the commission on piracy for Cornwall in 1637,[84] but he seems to have lived a rather quiet life at

Trelowarren. He was interested in theology and the arts, perhaps, more than he was in politics.[85] In 1639 he sent excuses instead of a contribution to the king when asked for a loan,[86] but there is no indication that he was counted upon by the popular leaders as an ally.

Vivian sat for Penryn in the Short Parliament. He distinguished himself as a statesman, however, neither in that meeting nor in the next, although he was named to the Committee of Privileges in November, 1640.[87] He obtained several leaves of absence and when war came won fame for himself as an active royalist. He commanded a regiment for the king in 1642, and the next year was appointed Master of the Mint at Exeter. Disabled from sitting at Westminster, 22 January 1644,[88] Vivian sat in the king's parliament at Oxford. He was created D.C.L. by the university in February, 1644, and the next year became a baronet.[89] He sat again in parliament after the Restoration, and died in October or November, 1665. He was buried at Mawgan in Meneage.[90]

The Vivians were a family of wealth, and Richard inherited from his father eight Cornish manors and parts of others, as well as portions of the boroughs of Okehampton, Plympton, Tiverton, and Exminster.[91] His father's debts, however, were large, and much of the property had to be put into trusteeship to pay the debts and raise the generous portions allotted to five younger children. According to Sir Richard's declaration to the compounding commissioners, which was afterwards reported as undervaluing his income by a third or even two-thirds, his annual income before 1640 was under £400. His fine at a tenth, £600,[92] was but a small part of the expense and loss he incurred during the war, for it was estimated that his total losses, including contributions to the royal cause, amounted to nearly £10,000.[93]

John Waddon, or **Whaddon** (1590–1653), merchant of Plymouth, was M.P. for his town, 1640–1648.[1] He

---

[75] Richard Warner, *Collections for the history of Hampshire* 3: 129–130.

[76] Brit. Mus. Birch MSS, 4165, fols. 23–24.

[77] *V.C.H. Hampshire* 4: 358. Vernon's father, Sir Robert, had a lawsuit against Sir Henry Wallop and his wife in 1622 regarding the boundaries of some of their Shropshire lands. C. 3/387/18.

[78] *Complete Baronetage* 3: 93.

[79] Coate, *Cornwall in the great Civil War,* 3–4; Sir Francis Vivian's I.P.M., C. 142/550/99.

[80] *M. of P.* 1: 442; 3: xxxvii; C. 193/13; *C.S.P. Dom., 1629–1631,* 450; *1631–1633,* 62, 439, 536; Vivian, *Vis Cornwall,* 530.

[81] *Al. Oxon.*

[82] *Mid. Temp. Rec.* 2: 787, 830; *Strafford letters* 1: 506–507. Gervase Holles noted with some disapproval that he heard Vivian's expenses were £6000. *Memorials of the Holles family,* 236, Camden Society, 1937.

[83] Wainwright, ed., *Barnstaple parish register,* 25.

[84] C. 181/5, fol. 165.

[85] Coate, *op. cit.,* 4.

[86] Rushworth 3: 912.

[87] *M. of P.* 1: 480; *C.J.* 2: 21.

[88] Coate, *op. cit.,* 36, 108; *C.J.* 3: 374.

[89] *Al. Oxon.*

[90] The month was October, according to *Complete Baronetage* (2: 229), but November, according to Vivian, *Vis. Cornwall* (530). The latter date is said to have been based upon the parish register.

[91] I.P.M. cited above; Coate, *op. cit.,* 3–4; *C.S.P. Dom., 1631–1633,* 337.

[92] S.P. 23/188/798–799; *Cal. Com. Comp.,* 336, 1190. An assessment by parliament of £1500 in 1644 was reduced two years later to £1000. *Cal. Com. Adv. Money,* 434.

[93] Coate, *op. cit.,* 368.

[1] He was not a "recruiter" chosen to fill Trelawney's place in 1642, as implied in Sanford (*St. and ill.,* 273) and *M. of P.* (1: 488, n.). He was present in the House in May, 1641 (*C.J.* 2: 151), and in 1641 was paid by Plymouth for 298 days of attendance as an M.P. Plymouth Corporation MSS, 132, fol. 250.

was the eldest son of John Waddon (d. 1620) and his wife, Alice, and was baptized at St. Andrew's, 23 January 1590.[2] His father, a prominent cloth merchant, and owner of a fulling mill, was mayor of Plymouth, 1612–1613. John's younger brother, Peter, went to the West Indies for a time,[3] but John and the second son of the family, James, stayed in Plymouth and took an active part in civic affairs. John was admitted to the freedom of the town in 1612 during his father's mayoralty, and the next year he married Prudence, the daughter of another substantial citizen, Thomas Fownes (mayor, 1619–1620). By the time of his father's death four of their fifteen children had been born.[4]

By 1630 John and James Waddon were members of the lower body of the town government; and in 1631–1632 John was mayor and James was receiver. Several events of Waddon's mayoralty illustrate his puritanical views. He restrained from travelling a scholar who could show no other reason for going abroad than to gain preferment at Rome; he bargained with the vintners to restrict gaming and drinking at their establishments, as well as to sell at reasonable prices. And at the close of his mayoralty he and his brother participated in the plan for ousting the incumbent in the parish church so that a new puritanical vicar might come in. This precipitated the controversy involving corporation, church, and crown that continued into the mayoralty of Robert Trelawney (q.v.). After his term as mayor Waddon continued to serve the town, frequently auditing its accounts and travelling in 1635 and 1636 to Exeter on matters of shipping and ship money.[5]

Waddon was sent by Plymouth to both parliaments of 1640. He worked quietly with the puritan group there, playing a much less conspicuous role than did his colleague, Trelawney. He joined the latter in offering to be bound for £1000 for the 1640 loan[6] and in working for the bill to secure Plymouth's new parish. In that matter he was probably more zealous than Trelawney.[7] He kept his seat until the purge of 1648,[8] and lived until 1653. His will, dated 7 March 1652/3, was proved at Westminster, 21 May 1653.[9]

Little is known of Waddon's wealth beyond the fact that he received from his father various properties in

Plymouth and in two Cornish parishes and that he added to these by his own purchases.[10] He had already settled his estate by the time he made his will in 1653, and his legacies named at that time were small. He was probably a man of ample means at the time he was elected to parliament, however.

He was no doubt acquainted with the Exeter members, as well as with his fellow townsman, Trelawney. And Richard Long of Bristol had once been a co-trustee with Waddon for the affairs of another party.[11]

Robert Walker (c. 1597–1673), merchant of Exeter, was M.P. for Exeter, 1640–6 March 1643. He came of a family long prominent in his city. His father, Thomas Walker (d. 1629), was three times mayor, was an active member and governor of the guild of Merchant Adventurers,[12] and was reported in 1625 to be worth £70,-000, and one of the "greatest men of wealth" in the region.[13] Thomas's elder son, James, became a freeman of Exeter in 1632,[14] but his second son, Robert, was the one who inherited the father's talents for civic leadership. Born about 1597,[15] he served his apprenticeship under another prominent merchant, Thomas Amye, and on 3 June 1622 gained his admission to the freedom of Exeter by redemption.[16] Sometime before 1629 he married, but his wife, Margaret, died that year.[17] And on 19 May 1630 he took as his second wife Mary, daughter of William Cotton, rector of Silverton, and granddaughter of Bishop Cotton. Her father seems to have been of the resident clergy of Exeter Cathedral in 1641.[18]

Robert Walker was a bailiff of Exeter in 1626, became a councilman in 1628, and served in turn as receiver (1633–1634), as sheriff (1634–1635), and as mayor (1639–1640).[19] His duties included trusteeship for the school his father had endowed, and an active part in improving the city's trade, whether by improving the harbor and the management of the quay, or asserting the city's rights in dealings with other ports and with the king's Council. He was frequently a negotiator with the cathedral authorities, too, possibly because of

---

[2] *Western Antiquary* 7: 243, 1887–1888; *Vis. Devon, 1620*, 304; Plymouth Inst. *Trans.* 9: 101–102, 1884–1887.

[3] *Ibid.* 9: 101, n., 1884–1887; Plymouth Corporation MSS, 132, fol. 171v; R. N. Worth, *Calendar of the Plymouth municipal records*, 284, Plymouth, 1893; Carr, *Select charters of English trading companies*, 65.

[4] *Western Antiquary* 7: 243, 1887–1888; *Vis. Devon, 1620*, 304; Plymouth Corporation MSS. 46, Black Book, fol. 308.

[5] Plymouth Corporation MSS, 132, Widey Court Book, fols. 220v–243; MS 46, fol. 312v; MS 48, White Book, fol. 93; H.M.C., *Twelfth Report* 1, Coke MSS, 451.

[6] *M. of P.* 1: 481, 488; D'Ewes (N), 52.

[7] He advanced £80 to secure the passage of the bill. Plymouth Corporation MSS, 132, fol. 250.

[8] *Western Antiquary* 7: 187, 243, 1887–1888; *O.P.H.* 9: *23.

[9] P.C.C., 351 Brent.

[10] I.P.M., C. 142/650/116; Plymouth Inst. *Trans.* 9: 101, n., 1884–1887; Exeter City Library MSS, Exeter Deeds and Documents, No. 90.

[11] *Ibid.*, No. 12,041.

[12] *Western Antiquary* 6: 15, 1928–1929; W. Cotton, *An Elizabethan guild of the city of Exeter*, 37, 43, Exeter, 1873.

[13] *Devon and Cornwall N. and Q.* 15: 94, 1928–1929.

[14] Exeter Corporation MSS, Act Book 7, fol. 805.

[15] He died in his seventy-seventh year in 1673. M.I. at St. Mary Arches, Exeter.

[16] Exeter Corporation MSS, Mayor's Court Book 83, fol. 109v; Book 55A, List of Freemen, 1621–1818, fol. 241.

[17] Memorials at St. Mary Arches.

[18] *The register of baptisms, marriages & burials of the city of Exeter*, ed. W. W. Reynell-Upham and H. Tapley-Soper, 23, Exeter, Devon and Cornwall Record Society, 1910; Exeter Corporation MSS, Subsidy Rolls, Sect. II, No. 17.

[19] Exeter Corporation MSS, Act Book 7, fols. 695, 856; 8: 25, 186.

his wife's family connections, dealing with common interests such as the school or with questions in which lay and clerical authorities were rivals. He was one of the city councillors sent in 1638 to London to reply to charges made by the bishop against the local government.[20] He collected ship money while he was sheriff,[21] negotiated with the county D.L.'s for supplies for the city's defense, and was concerned with matters of poor relief. During his mayoralty he consented to the broadening of the powers of the council at the expense of the mayor's prerogatives, but worked to prevent encroachments on the city's authority by the judges of assize.[22]

So popular was Walker in Exeter that he was elected to the Short Parliament while he was still mayor, and was sent to Westminster armed with copies of the official oaths and the assurance that the charters would be available for his use should parliament challenge his eligibility to serve. The Committee of Privileges seems to have reached no decision on his case before the parliament ended.[23] Walker's re-election in the autumn was therefore to be expected. But he did not attain the prominence in St. Stephen's Hall that he had enjoyed in Exeter. With his fellow member, Snow, he pledged £1000 for the November loan,[24] but seldom appeared afterwards in the records. He returned to Devon before time for the recess,[25] and by the summer of 1642 seems to have absented himself frequently. After having been summoned several times in the autumn of 1642, Walker was disabled on account of his absences, 6 March 1643.[26] In 1644 he joined the king at Oxford, convincing the Exeter council that he should receive wages just as much as if he attended at Westminster.[27] He compounded for his delinquency, 1646–1647. He was returned again as M.P. in 1661, and died in his seventy-seventh year, 23 August 1673. His epitaph described him as faithful to God, to church, and to king.

Walker seems to have been a prosperous merchant. Although he was not the heir to his father's large estate, he was rated among the highest in his city for the ship money collection of 1638–1639, and he owned numerous properties there.[28] His compounding papers show that he held land also outside the city in Devon and in Cornwall, having a net income from real estate alone of more

than £376 a year. His total income must have been well beyond that figure. His fine, figured at a third, £2333, was finally set at a tenth, £889.[29]

Walker's acquaintances in parliament included not only his colleague, Simon Snow, but Dr. George Parry, with whom as chancellor to the Bishop of Exeter he had had frequent contact. Not all of them had been pleasant meetings, but Parry seems to have been a friend[30] of Walker's brother, Thomas.[31]

* Edmund Waller (1606–1687), of Beaconsfield, Bucks, the poet, was elected M.P. for St. Ives, Cornwall, in November, 1640, replacing Lord Lisle,[32] and was disabled in 1643. He was possibly the Mr. Waller who held some post with the Court of Common Pleas in 1627 and was that year listed as able to lend the king £1000 because he had a great estate and had enjoyed royal favor in the avoidance of certain lawsuits.[33] The king was influential in the matter of Waller's marriage a few years later. Waller served in several parliaments before 1640 for Bucks or Somerset boroughs, and was named in that year to the commission of oyer and terminer in Bucks.[34] But he probably owed his election for St. Ives less to his experience or his politics than to his friendship with a dominant family there, the Godolphins, with whom his literary tastes had made him intimate.[35] Although he was related to both Hampden and Cromwell and was named as late as September, 1641, to the important recess committee,[36] Waller's disagreement with the popular party had already begun to show.

Waller was said to be very wealthy, his inheritance from his father having been worth £2500 to £3500 a year, and his marriage had added to his fortune. Waller was a friend of many of Falkland's literary circle who were members of the 1640 parliament.[37]

Sir Henry Wallop (1568–1642), of Farleigh Wallop, Hampshire, was M.P. for his county from 1640 until his death in November, 1642. He was the son and heir of Sir Henry Wallop (d. 1599), M.P., lord justice of Ireland and treasurer of wars there, by his wife, Cather-

[20] *Ibid.*, Act Book 7, fols. 788, 791, 792, 796, 839, 846, 860, 865; 8, fols. 27, 60, 64, 70, 137–140, *passim*; *C.S.P. Dom., 1631–1633*, 337.

[21] *Ibid., 1636–1637*, 521; Exeter Act Book 8, fol. 121.

[22] Exeter Act Book 8, fols. 164, 179, 180, 191, 202, 204.

[23] *Ibid.*, fols. 203, 204; *C.J.* 2: 3.

[24] D'Ewes (N), 52.

[25] He was present at city council meetings several times during the summer. Exeter Act Book 8, fols. 234–246.

[26] *Ibid.*, fols. 275–286; *C.J.* 2: 699, 845, 888, 991.

[27] Exeter Act Book 8, fol. 315.

[28] Exeter Corporation MSS, Act Book 8, fol. 764; Receivers' Accounts, 1639–1640; Subsidy Rolls 2, No. 18; Exeter City Library MSS, Exeter Deeds and Documents, No. 4355.

[29] S.P. 23/183/660–662; *Cal. Com. Comp.*, 1259.

[30] *Cf.* Parry.

[31] In addition to the authorities cited above see Devon *Trans.* 33: 265, 1901; 61: 211, 1929; *M. of P.*

[32] Lisle decided on 9 November to serve instead for Yarmouth. *C.J.* 2: 25.

[33] S.P. 16, 52/61.

[34] C. 181/5, fol. 352. It was probably his kinsman, Edmund Waller of Gregories (*ibid.*), who was one of the county's D.L.'s. *Recs. Bucks.* 7: 97, 1897; *C.S.P. Dom., 1640*, 498; *V.C.H. Buckingham* 3: 161.

[35] Waller completed and published Sidney Godolphin's translation of Virgil, according to Wood (*Athenae Oxon.* 3: 46).

[36] *C.J.* 2: 288.

[37] Sanford, *St. and ill.*, 560; K. Weber, *Lucius Cary, second Viscount Falkland*, 111–120.

ine, daughter of Richard Gifford of Hampshire.[38] He was born on 18 October 1568,[39] and was educated at Oxford (B.A., St. John's, 1588) and at Lincoln's Inn.[40] He married the Shropshire heiress, Elizabeth, daughter of Robert Corbet of Morton Corbet, who was a stepsister of Sir William Lytton (q.v.). At the Lytton's parish in Hertfordshire Wallop's daughter, Anne, was baptized on 22 July 1597.[41] He joined his father in Ireland that summer, acted as his deputy for a time in 1598, and went over again in 1599, when his father died. He was knighted at Dublin that year.[42] He seems to have been in Ireland often until 1601, being engaged particularly in winding up his father's affairs and clearing his official accounts. Wallop did not care for life in Ireland,[43] however, and returned soon to his Hampshire estates.

Sir Henry had entered parliament for the first time before his father's death, serving for Lymington in 1597. He sat for Hampshire in 1601.[44] He was sheriff for that county in 1603 and for Shropshire in 1606.[45] Afterwards he was a member of the Council of the Marches of Wales.[46] He was a J.P. for both Hampshire and Shropshire for many years,[47] and a member of numerous special commissions in those counties and Wales.[48] He was one of the commissioners for martial law in Hampshire in 1627, and was listed as one of the militia officers of that period.[49] Wallop was sheriff of Hampshire again, 1629-1630, and was reported among those fined £200 for having summoned fewer persons for knighthood composition than the commissioners had discovered.[50] He narrowly avoided having to be sheriff in Shropshire the following year.[51]

Meanwhile Sir Henry had continued his career in parliament. He failed in 1614 to secure a place either for the shire or for Stockbridge, being defeated in the former contest by Sir William Uvedale (q.v.).[52] But he sat for Hampshire in 1621, for Whitchurch in 1624, for Andover in 1625, and for the county in 1626, 1628, and both parliaments of 1640.[53] His knowledge of Irish affairs was utilized in the 1621 meeting;[54] in 1624 he was named to at least one committee dealing with abuses;[55] and in 1628 he was one of the committee of twelve sent to the king to learn whether he planned a recess or prorogation of the parliament. A fellow member described him then as one of the richest members.[56] That Wallop was ready to oppose the court had already become apparent. Listed in 1625 as able to lend the largest sum of any in Hampshire,[57] he contributed £50 the following year only after some protest.[58] He was lenient regarding knighthood compositions, and in 1633 was summoned before Star Chamber for having stayed in London contrary to the proclamation, and for eating meat on Fridays.[59] In 1640, having the previous year ignored a request for a new contribution to the crown, he was called before Council for a repetition of the demand, but he was firm in his refusal.[60]

In the Long Parliament Wallop's place was assured by his experience, his wealth, and his influence, and by his family connections with various puritan leaders. He was among those who presented petitions on personal grounds regarding Strafford's administration in Ireland, and he offered his wealth to secure the loan in November, 1640. He served on various committees, especially on matters of the church,[61] but his advancing age may have made him less active than in previous parliaments. He seems to have been absent at the time of the Protestation in May, 1641. In June of the next year he and his son, Robert (q.v.), offered to provide eight horses for the defense.[62] He died on 15 November 1642, and was buried at Farleigh.[63]

Sir Henry was said to be one of the wealthiest commoners of his day, keeping a hospitable house as was suitable with his fortune.[64] In addition to his father's ten manors in Hampshire, Wilts, Devon, and Somerset,[65] Wallop owned Irish lands and numerous manors in Shropshire and other counties which came to him by

[38] Wallop is mentioned briefly in the D.N.B. articles on his father, Sir Henry Wallop (1540?-1599), and his son, Robert Wallop.

[39] Warner, Collections for the history of Hampshire 3: 127.

[40] Al. Oxon.; Linc. Inn Rec. Adm. 1: 110.

[41] Royal Hist. Soc., Trans., 1st Ser., 8: 231, 1880. Sir Henry's wife died in 1623. The letters of John Chamberlain 2: 527.

[42] The letters of John Chamberlain 1: 32; C.S.P. Ireland, 1598-1599, 379; D.N.B.

[43] The letters of John Chamberlain 1: 82, 105; C.S.P. Ireland, 1599-1600, 23, 368; Acts P.C., 1601-1604, 222, 351.

[44] M. of P. 1: 434, 439.

[45] List of Sheriffs, 56, 119.

[46] Cal. Wynn Papers, 130.

[47] C. 193/12, 13; S.P. 16/405; Bodleian Rawl. MSS, D 666, fols. 50v, 62v; Add. MSS, 21,922, fol. 223.

[48] C. 181/3, fols. 26, 129v; 181/4 and 181/5, passim.

[49] Add. MSS, 21,922, fols. 5, 123; C.S.P. Dom., 1627-1628, 440.

[50] Ibid., 1629-1631, 172, 184, 193; List of Sheriffs, 56; Birch, The court and times of Charles the First 2: 96.

[51] S.P. 16, 533/52.

[52] M. of P. 3: App., xxxix; C.S.P. Dom., 1611-1618, 233, 234; Commons Debates 1621 7: 635, 637. Wallop attributed his defeat in the county election to foul play by the sheriff and planned to take his case to Star Chamber. The letters of John Chamberlain 1: 518, 521, 523.

[53] M. of P. 1: passim.

[54] Commons Debates 1621 6: 102.

[55] Add. MSS, 32,324, fol. 8.

[56] H.M.C., Twelfth Report, Coke MSS (I), 351.

[57] £100 as compared with figures of £10 to £50 for men of his title. S.P. 16, 521/177; Add. MSS, 21,922, fol. 16.

[58] His was again the largest sum listed for his county. Rawl. MSS, D 666, fol. 42v. He seems to have failed to pay an allotment in London that year. S.P. 16, 61/100.

[59] Add. MSS, 11,056, fol. 64.

[60] Rushworth 3: 914; Add. MSS, 11,045, fol. 116.

[61] C.J. 2: 54, 67, 129, passim; D'Ewes (N), 52, 244.

[62] N. and Q., 1st Ser., 12: 360, 1855.

[63] Warner, op. cit. 3: 130.

[64] Idem.

[65] I.P.M., Sir Henry Wallop, 1599, C. 142/256/6.

marriage. He purchased others afterwards. He was interested in some iron works on his Shropshire lands, and doubtless his familiarity with the wool trade there led to his appointment on a commission for improving the Welsh woolen manufacturing in 1622.[66] One of his daughters had a portion of £4000.[67]

Wallop's numerous relatives among the 1640 parliament men included such other strong opposition members as his son, Robert, his brothers-in-law, Lytton and Barrington, and his sons-in-law, Sir Henry Worsley and William Heveningham. His influence probably explains the election of the latter for a Hampshire borough. He was more distantly connected with Harley, Palmes, Gervase Holles,[68] the Jervoises, and others.

* **Robert Wallop** (1601–1667), the regicide, was M.P. for Andover, Hampshire, 1640–1653. He was the only son and heir apparent of Sir Henry Wallop (q.v.). Not only had he sat in parliament six times previously, starting in 1621 and serving for either Andover or the county, but he had from an early age been a J.P. in Hampshire.[69] He was a member of the commission for martial law in 1627 [70] and was named to various other local commissions.[71] From as early as 1626 he was a colonel in the county militia.[72] Wallop was listed for the loan in 1627 and promised after urging to make a payment.[73] He refused, however, to compound for knighthood, declaring that he had not possessed the required income at the time of the coronation.[74] By 1640 Wallop seems to have had settled on him the Northamptonshire lands inherited from his mother, but to have disposed of most of them.[75] For his family's wealth, see Sir Henry Wallop. By 1649 he declared that he had lost through the war £50,000.[76]

Sir Thomas Walsingham (1594–1669) of Scadbury in Chislehurst, Kent, was M.P. for Rochester, 1640–1653, as he had been six times previously. A great-grandson of Sir Edmund Walsingham (d. 1550), Lieutenant of the Tower, he was the son and heir of Sir Thomas Walsingham of Scadbury, courtier (d. 1630), by his wife, Ethelred, daughter of Sir Ralph Shelton of

Norfolk, a favorite of Queen Anne's.[77] He was born in 1594,[78] was probably a student at King's, Cambridge, in 1606, and was knighted on 26 November 1613.[79] He married (1) in 1616 Elizabeth, eldest daughter of Sir Peter Manwood of Hackington; [80] (2) in 1634 Elizabeth, daughter of Richard Bourne of London, widow of Nathaniel Master, a well-to-do London merchant and brother of Sir Edward Master (q.v.).[81]

Sir Thomas does not seem to have sought a court career like his father's, but in 1625 a grant of a £200 a year pension was proposed for him on condition that he remit all arrears due on the pension previously granted to his mother.[82] He seems to have contented himself with the duties of a country gentleman and M.P. Beginning in his father's lifetime he served on various local commissons, including that for the loan of 1626–1627,[83] and for knighthood compositions.[84] He was a vice admiral for Kent from 1626 at least until 1639,[85] was a D.L. from as early as 1630,[86] and for many years was a J.P.[87] In parliament he sat for Poole in 1614, and in 1621 stepped into his father's old constituency of Rochester, and was elected there regularly thereafter.[88] He had sat in seven parliaments before the Long Parliament.

Walsingham had been in disagreement with royal policies for some time before 1640. He was summoned before Council early in 1637 for alleged support of a plan to defy an ordinance against grubbing wood without license on some of his property, but was released when he denied the charge.[89] In the spring of 1640, when he was asked to lend £500 to the king, he excused himself repeatedly.[90] He was one of the earliest in the field for the county election that year, persuaded, perhaps, by a friend's views that those who had been sheriffs and deputy lieutenants might need to be present to justify themselves in parliament for their actions.[91] But he withdrew from the contest to allow Sir Henry Vane, senior, a better chance, his own old place for Rochester being secure.[92] And he apparently did not

[66] Warner, op. cit. **3**: 125–130; V.C.H. Hampshire **4**: 289; Bodleian Tanner MSS, 66, fol. 166; Chancery suit, C. 3/389/33; Acts P.C., 1619–1621, 374.

[67] This was the daughter who married Sir Henry Worsley. A royalist's notebook, 73.

[68] Add. MSS, 5531, fol. 16v; H.M.C., Fourteenth Report **2**, MSS of the Duke of Portland (III), 15.

[69] C. 193/12, 13; S.P. 16/405; Bodleian Rawl. MSS, D 666, fol. 81; Add. MSS, 21,922, fols. 38, 223.

[70] Add. MSS, 21,922, fol. 123; C.S.P. Dom., 1627–1628, 440.

[71] C. 181/4, fols. 3, 17v; 181/5, fols. 47, 116.

[72] Add. MSS, 21,922, fols. 59v, 108, passim.

[73] S.P. 16, 52/69.

[74] Add. MSS, 21,922, fols. 178, 183.

[75] Baker, Northamptonshire **1**: 130.

[76] Godwin, The Civil War in Hampshire, 371.

[77] The 1640 M.P. and his father are mentioned briefly in D.N.B., "Sir Edmund Walsingham." See also Arch. Cant. **17**: 391, 1887.

[78] F. F. Smith, Rochester in Parliament, 108.

[79] Al. Cant.

[80] I.P.M., Thomas Walsingham, senior, C. 142/467/71.

[81] Arch. Cant. **15**: 152–153, 1883; London Corporation MSS, Rep. 49, fols. 14v, 15.

[82] C.S.P. Dom., 1623–1625, 444.

[83] S.P. 16, 42/120/234; C. 181/3; 181/4, fols. 48v, 88; 181/5, passim; C.S.P. Dom., 1627–1628, 449.

[84] Stowe MSS, 743, fol. 85.

[85] C.S.P. Dom., 1625–1626, 427, 475; 1628–1629, 517; 1629–1631 and succeeding volumes, passim.

[86] S.P. 16, 160/10; 409/7; C.S.P. Dom., 1635, 429.

[87] C. 193/12, 13; S.P. 16/405; C.S.P. Dom., 1639–1640, 520.

[88] M. of P., passim.

[89] S.P. 16, 343/17; C.S.P. Dom., 1636–1637, 389–390, 401.

[90] S.P. 16, 447/36, 37, 94.

[91] Sondes to Walsingham, 9 December 1639. Stowe MSS, 743, fol. 136.

[92] Ibid.; Larking, Proceedings in Kent, 6.

try for a seat with greater prestige in the autumn. That he was not entirely popular with his neighbors is suggested by Twysden's comment on references to Walsingham as a "coxcombe colonel" at a time when it was proposed to make all D.L.'s colonels.[93]

Walsingham worked with the opposition in the 1640 parliaments. He gave his bond for £1000 for the loan in 1640,[94] and in 1642 promised two horses promptly and £100.[95] He was a parliamentary D.L. and committeeman in Kent during the war, was a prisoner of the royalists for a short time, and remained in parliament until 1653.[96] Surviving the Restoration, he died in 1669 and was buried at Chislehurst.

That he was well-to-do is indicated by Walsingham's advances for the cause and by the sum requested of him for a loan in 1640. From his father he inherited four manors in Kent, one in Surrey, and one in Essex, with other small holdings in Kent and London.[97] Both of his marriages seem to have been advantageous.

Sir Thomas, though of puritan leanings, was not averse to sports. In 1650 he and his stepson invested £5 in an imported flying goshawke.[98] Walsingham was a first cousin of Sir Thomas Pelham (q.v.).

* **Valentine Walton** (c. 1594–1661 ?), of Great Staughton, Huntingdonshire, M.P. for his county, 1640–1653, and regicide, was the son of Nicholas Walton, of the younger branch of an old county family, and was once the ward of Sir Oliver Cromwell.[99] In 1606, aged twelve, Valentine inherited from his grandfather's cousin, Sir George Walton, the family manor of Great Staughton, but he had a vigorous dispute with a kinsman concerning his title to it when he came of age.[100] In 1617 he married Margaret, sister of Oliver Cromwell,[101] a step which doubtless strongly influenced his subsequent career.

Walton was present at the Huntingdonshire musters of January, 1630, as captain,[102] but seems to have been appointed to no civil offices before 1640. Summoned in September, 1630, to compound for knighthood, he asked a respite for a time, but probably paid his fine later.[103] He opposed ship money also, and was imprisoned for paying a half crown short of his full assessment, an

action which was said to account for his election to the Long Parliament, his first. Although described then as "a private obscure gentleman" of about £400 a year, which had come to him from a relative, he was elected in preference to the candidate of Sir Oliver Cromwell, his former guardian.[104] His pledge for the defense in 1642, two horses and £100, was higher than the average.[105]

Michael Warton, or **Wharton** (1593–1645), of Beverley, Yorkshire, was M.P. for Beverley, 1640–22 January 1644. The third in line of his name in as many generations, he was the only son and heir apparent of Sir Michael Warton of Beverley (d. 1655), sheriff of Yorkshire, 1616, by Elizabeth, daughter and coheiress of Ralph Hansby of Beverley.[106] He was baptized 23 October 1593 at Beverley, matriculated at St. John's, Cambridge, in 1610, and was admitted to Gray's Inn, 25 November 1611.[107] His father married Everilda, widow of Christopher Maltby, in 1619,[108] and by 1621 her daughter, Catherine, a coheiress, married Michael, the younger.[109] Their eldest son, the fourth Michael, later to figure as a royalist, was baptized in 1623.[110]

Warton's father appears to have been an active man. He was a J.P. for Beverley and for Hull and a sewers commissioner for Lincolnshire.[111] He was penalized by Council in 1617 for having been unduly severe toward recusants while he was sheriff,[112] and in 1635 he was reported by his neighbor and kinsman, Sir John Hotham, for refusing to pay what he considered an overcharge of ship money.[113] But the son's name is missing from the lists of officials. He very probably acted as business manager or legal adviser for his father, for theirs were large estates, lying in Yorkshire, Lincolnshire, and Middlesex. Michael, "Esquire," received in 1628 a confirmation from the royal trustees of the lease of the manor of Beverley at a rent of some £274 a year.[114] He emerged from his father's shadow with his election to

[93] *Arch. Cant.* 3: 176, 1860.
[94] D'Ewes (N), 52.
[95] *N. and Q.,* 1st Ser., 12: 359, 1855.
[96] *C.J.* 2: 724; *Arch. Cant.* 2: 181, 1859; 9: 32, n., 1874; 17: 365, 1887; *H.M.C., Seventh Report,* MSS of G. A. Lowndes, 561.
[97] I.P.M., C. 142/467/71; *Arch. Cant.* 13: 388, 389, 1880; Hasted, *Kent* 5: 60; Lansd. MSS, 459, fol. 114. One property he sold for £8000 in 1650. *Arch. Cant.* 18: 161, 1889.
[98] *Ibid.* 15: 153, 188, 1883.
[99] Bodleian Tanner MSS, 65, fol. 164.
[100] *Acts P.C., 1623–1625,* 218, 227; *V.C.H. Huntingdonshire* 2: 358 and n.
[101] Sanford, *St. and ill.,* 209. This marriage made Walton a relative of many of his fellow M.P.'s in 1640.
[102] *C.S.P. Dom., 1629–1631,* 159.
[103] Bodleian Carte MSS, 74, fols. 191, 193v.

[104] Henry Smyth to Isaac Appleton, Tanner MSS, 65, fol. 164.
[105] "Mr. Wauton" (Tanner MSS, 63, fol. 54) was read as "Warten" for the printed list appearing in *N. and Q.,* 1st Ser., 12: 333, 1855.
[106] Dugdale, *Vis. York,* 331. J. W. Clay's notes on the various Michael Wartons of five generations (*Yorks. Arch. Jour.* 23: 379, 1915) contain several errors of dates. Many genealogical notes collected about the family are now in the Wharton MSS at the Bodleian.
[107] *Al. Cant.*
[108] *Yorks. Arch. Jour.* 14: 489, 1898; *Y.A.S. Rec. Ser.* 18: 93, 1895.
[109] *Y.A.S. Rec. Ser.* 58: 176, 1917; Dugdale, *loc. cit.* Catherine Maltby's sister, Averil, became the second wife of Sir George Wentworth of Woolley (q.v.).
[110] Yorkshire Archaeological Society MSS at Leeds, Dade MSS, M 80.
[111] C. 181/5, fols. 133, 159, 176, 287.
[112] *Acts P.C., 1616–1617,* 255, 273, 280–282.
[113] *C.S.P. Dom., 1635,* 290, 479.
[114] The Wartons paid to the trustees at this time some £3593. *C.S.P. Dom., 1627–1628,* 557.

the Short Parliament for Beverley,[115] and he won the next election in October with Sir John Hotham against a third candidate, Sir Thomas Metham, a royalist.[116]

Warton did not distinguish himself in the 1640 House. Besides the note of a leave of absence in March, 1641, so that he might attend the York assizes on a matter concerning his estate,[117] his name is almost absent from the records. He apparently did not leave with the first group of Yorkshire royalists in 1642, and may even have followed the Hothams' example for a time, but he pledged his estate for the king's service in 1643,[118] attended the king at Oxford,[119] and was secluded in January, 1644.[120] He was killed in 1645 during the siege of Scarborough.[121] After his death his father and his son dealt with the compounding commissions, beginning their negotiations on 11 November 1645. The father's estates, according to his own admission, were worth over £2000 a year before the war.[122]

Warton was a brother-in-law of Sir George Wentworth of Woolley and a kinsman of the Hothams. He was a cousin also of the royalist commander, Sir Marmaduke Langdale.[123]

* **Philip Warwick** (1609–1683), of Westminster, clerk of the signet, was elected in 1640 for both New Romney in Kent and Radnor borough, but he chose to serve for the latter. He was disabled for his royalism, 5 February 1644.[124] The son of Thomas Warwick, Westminster organist, he may have attended Pembroke College, Cambridge, after leaving Eton,[125] but his degree of B.C.L. was from Oxford. His travels on the continent in 1634 included not only study but also some practice with the pike in the Netherlands.[126] He was already a friend of Windebank then and on his way to posts at court, and in 1636 he was seeking a pension of £50.[127] By 1640 he was expecting to receive £500 a year from the "copperas farm."[128]

Warwick's first marriage, arranged in 1634,[129] was with Dorothy, daughter of Matthew Hutton, Esquire.[130] Warwick was a commissioner for sewers in Lincolnshire in 1639, and for Kent the next year. He owned property in the latter county.[131] Although Warwick was one of the court nominees for the Short Parliament,[132] he was not elected. He owed both of his successes in the autumn to court pressure. The New Romney place was won for him through the intercession of the Lord Warden.[133]

When Warwick compounded for his sequestered estates he listed some property in Westminster, some in Gloucestershire, and an interest in a Kentish manor belonging partly to his friend, William Watkins (q.v.). He declared his revenue from his lands was not more than £275 a year, and that he had debts amounting to £700. His fine, set first at a tenth, £477, was afterwards reduced to £241.[134]

John Wastell (c. 1593–1659), of Scorton, Yorkshire, a lawyer, sat for North Allerton from his election, 15 January 1641, following the borough's restoration, until 1653.[135] He was the eldest son of Leonard Wastell of Scorton, "gentleman" (d. c. 1629), by his wife, Anne, daughter of Edmund Danby of Kirkby-Knole, and was born about 1593.[136] He was admitted pensioner at Sidney Sussex College, Cambridge, in February, 1611, entered Gray's Inn in 1613, and eventually became a Master in Chancery.[137] He married, probably before his father's death, Anne, daughter of John Robinson of Hackforth.[138] As "John Wastell, Esquire, Counsellor at Law," he was elected recorder at Ripon, 5 May 1626, and he held the office until his death.[139] Although a deputy seems to have handled the routine business, Wastell attended meetings of the council about once a year. He was present in January, 1638, when the town chose to keep the old rates for ship money rather than risk expensive trials by making changes.[140] He was recorder of Richmond, also, by April, 1631,[141] and served on the sewers commission and as a J.P. in the North

115 M. of P. 1 : 484.
116 Beverley Borough MSS, Minute Book C, fol. 66; Bean, Northern Counties, 763.
117 C.J. 2 : 99.
118 Add. MSS, 15,858, fol. 237.
119 H.M.C., Seventh Report, House of Lords MSS, 122.
120 C.J. 3 : 374.
121 Dugdale, loc. cit.; Bodleian Wharton MSS, 14, fol. 43.
122 Cal. Com. Comp., 955. The manor of Beverley alone, which had apparently been settled on Michael, the M.P., was valued, above the rents of £284 due the crown and the borough, at £1197 a year. Y.A.S. Rec. Ser. 18 : 55–57, 93–94, 1895.
123 Bodleian Wharton MSS, 14, fol. 31v.
124 M. of P. 1 : 497, 498; C.J. 3 : 389.
125 Al. Cant.
126 C.S.P. Dom., 1634–1635, 189.
127 Ibid., 1636–1637, 309.
128 S.P. 16, 450/30.
129 He was travelling abroad that summer, but a deed connected with the marriage settlement was dated 2 April 1634. S.P. 23/192/722.

130 Ibid. Her father's name appears as Thomas Hutton in D.N.B.
131 S.P. 16, 437/13; C. 181/5, fol. 336.
132 S.P. 16, 450/15.
133 New Romney Borough MSS, Common Assembly Book, 1622–1701, fols. 282–283.
134 Cal. Com. Comp., 1447; S.P. 23/192/722–726. In addition to the authorities cited above and D.N.B., see Williams, Parl. Hist. Wales, 179.
135 M. of P. 1 : 497 and n.; O.P.H. 9 : 13.
136 Dugdale, Vis. York, 227.
137 Al. Cant.
138 Dugdale, loc. cit. His father's will, dated 4 March 1628/9, indicates that most of his lands had already been settled. Will of Leonard Wastell, proved 26 April 1659, P.C.C. 209 Pell.
139 Ripon Borough MSS, Old Towne Book, 1607–1666, fols. 220, 269, 332, 351, 516.
140 Ibid., fols. 343–344.
141 C.S.P. Dom., 1631–1633, 26.

Riding.[142] He was present at the shire election in October, 1640.[143]

Although Wastell had not been a parliament man before 1641, he was named to several early committees,[144] and worked with the reform group. He became a colonel in the parliamentary army and remained a member of the parliament until the end. When he died shortly before 2 December 1659, the tribute, "that eminent one," was penned after his name in the burial register at Bolton upon Swale.[145]

Wastell probably inherited only a modest estate consisting chiefly of the manor of Scorton, for his father seems not to have been wealthy and could plan for his two younger sons and a daughter portions of but £100 each and for his second son chiefly the proceeds of a mill at Scorton.[146] Wastell's success in his profession probably enabled him to improve his position, for his widow married a knight as her second husband.[147] The choice of apostolic names for John and his three brothers suggests that he came of an earnestly religious, possibly a puritan, family.

William Watkins (fl. 1628–1650), of Westminster, was named in a double return for Monmouth borough in October, 1640, and was present in the House soon after the session opened. He was ordered to withdraw on 16 November, however, and the election was voided on 29 November 1644.[148] His parentage is unknown, but if he came from one of the border counties, he may have been the William Watkin[s] (born 1591) whose parents were William Watkin, gentleman, formerly styled yeoman, of Hugh Cople, Herefordshire (d. 1600), and Mary Cocks.[149] He seems to have gained employment of various sorts in the administrative offices at Westminster, however, and to have spent most of his time, at least during the reign of King Charles I, in the shadow of the court. He probably had a minor clerkship concerned with privy seals in 1626 [150] and was referred to in 1629 as a clerk of the privy seal.[151] In 1636 he had the reversion of one of the clerkships,[152] and in his work apparently became an intimate of Philip Warwick (q.v.), who held a similar office.[153] He was

doubtless the William Watkins who was a sealer of playing cards in 1628 and who was a commissioner afterwards for investigating violations of the various regulations on trade.[154] At least from 1634 he was a resident in the parish of St. Margaret's, Westminster,[155] and by March, 1639, he was probably one of the two receivers of the king's revenue for South Wales.[156] As William Watkins of Westminster he was returned as Monmouth's representative to the Short Parliament,[157] but he does not seem to have held other offices for that shire.

Watkins was evidently present in the Long Parliament, although his election was in doubt. On 16 November, however, he was censured for having disobeyed the orders regarding undetermined elections and for disregarding the order against monopolists. A special committee was named to consider his delinquency in the latter respect, and he is said to have narrowly escaped imprisonment and a heavy fine.[158] According to one authority Watkins changed sides afterwards and became a parliamentary official in South Wales in 1650, and was alive in 1681.[159] But he clearly took no further part in the work of the House during the period of this study, and he was at one time under sequestration as a delinquent.

No indications of Watkins's wealth have been found except that he was said to be much in arrears with the crown for his receivership in South Wales in 1641, and that he mortgaged in 1639 and 1642 some land he owned in Kent that was worth £200 a year.[160]

Richard Weaver (1575–1642), magistrate of Hereford, was M.P. for his city, 1640–16 May 1642. The descendant of a family of Welsh ancestry, Richard was the son of Edmund Weaver of Aymestrey,[161] and apparently became a successful business man in Hereford. He was a member of the city government from 1620, serving as councillor, mayor, and alderman, and was interested in many city charities. He was a member of parliament for Hereford five times before the autumn of 1640.[162]

[142] C. 181/4, fol. 114v; C. 193/13; S.P. 16/405.
[143] Indenture, C. 219/43/Part 3.
[144] C.J. 2: 100, 151, 196.
[145] Yorks. Arch. Jour. 1: 131 and n., 1870. The burial date here given was 2 December, but according to Al. Cant., where his M.I. is cited, Wastell died on 4 December 1659, aged sixty-six.
[146] Will cited above.
[147] Cumb. and Westm. Trans., N.S., 1: 148, 1901.
[148] M. of P. 1: 491 and n.; C.J. 2: 29.
[149] I.P.M., William Watkin, C. 142/783/3.
[150] C.S.P. Dom., 1625–1626, 286.
[151] Commons Debates for 1629, 130, 174.
[152] Bodleian Carte MSS, 74, fol. 385.
[153] Watkins was a party to a settlement of some of Warwick's lands on one occasion (S.P. 23/192/725), and in 1649 he was occupying some of Warwick's property. Cal. Com. Adv. Money, 1144.

[154] C.S.P. Dom., 1628–1629, 354; 1635–1636, 4; 1639–1640, 39.
[155] Records of St. Margaret's Parish, Overseers' Accounts, 153, 154.
[156] C.S.P. Dom., 1638–1639, 540.
[157] M. of P. 1: 482. This was a double return which had not been decided before the parliament ended. Williams, Parl. Hist. Wales, 135.
[158] D'Ewes (N), 36, 537; C.J. 2: 30; Lansd. MSS, 491, fol. 55.
[159] Williams, loc. cit. It is difficult, however, to reconcile Watkins, the monopolist of Westminster, with the "active partizan and principal agent of the Propagators" (quoted by Williams from an unstated source), who lived at Penyworlodd House, county Brecon, from 1651 until his death.
[160] Particular of the estate of Philip Warwick. S.P. 23/192/727–778.
[161] Lucius E. Weaver, History and genealogy of a branch of the Weaver family, 23, Rochester, N. Y., privately printed, 1928; Williams, Hereford, 89.
[162] M. of P.

He was a widower and the father of seven children by the latter date. Weaver was not an active member, 1640–1642, possibly because of his health, and he died on 16 May 1642 before events reached their crisis. He was probably a parliamentarian in views.[163]

Most of Weaver's possessions lay in or near Hereford, but he owned also some lands in Shropshire. His provision by his will of £600 portions for each of his elder daughters and £400 for a third indicates considerable means, as do his references to various pieces of plate among his household goods.[164] His heir was his son, Edmund, a barrister of the Inner Temple, and afterwards M.P.[165]

Thomas Webb (c. 1600–1649), of Westminster, secretary to the Duke of Lenox, was M.P. for New Romney from 13 November 1640, when he was elected to fill a vacancy, until he was expelled as a monopolist, 21 January 1641.[166] His ancestry has not been established definitely. Hasted identified him as one of the Webbs of Frittenden parish, Kent, probably the third son of William Webb, by Martha, daughter of William Shakelton and heiress of Sir Rowland Hayward of London.[167] His career at court, however, suggests that he may have been one of the royalist Webbs of Odstock, Wiltshire, possibly Sir John Webb's son who entered Gray's Inn in 1619 and was a brother of William, the royalist general.[168] Probably he was the Thomas Webb who was for some years in the service of the Earl of Carlisle, being with him on his embassy in France as Lord Doncaster in 1621[169] and carrying dispatches while the earl was ambassador to Savoy in 1628.[170] Before June of 1632, however, he had become the secretary of the Duke of Lenox, and had travelled abroad with him also.[171] The following year he was looking after his master's interests in Irish lands so zealously that he drew a comment from none other than the Lord Deputy, who wrote

to Cottington that "care should be had that Webb do not possess the Duke too far, for I take him to be a very nimble young gentleman, and one, I mistake not, that will notably work his own Ends out of the Duke."[172]

Webb's continuous association with the court gave him opportunities not only to help friends who aspired to places in the king's service[173] but to line his own pocket. He may have been an officer of the Court of Delegates in 1634, with certain powers over the importing of goods, and the Webb who in 1635 was seeking an interest in certain projects in the Thames.[174] Since his master was the holder of more than one patent affecting imported goods,[175] his sharp-witted secretary was no doubt interested too. He was in the north on his master's business in 1639, and with him and the king in 1640, and in the latter year sent out the duke's letters recommending candidates for the parliamentary elections.[176] He had probably written the duke's letter commending Philip Warwick to New Romney, and when Warwick chose to sit for Radnor instead, the nomination of Webb to fill the vacancy was scarcely strange. The town acquiesced quickly on 13 November, although Webb was neither present nor a freeman of the town,[177] and had sat in no previous parliament.

But Lenox's secretary was not to be an active member of the parliament. On 31 January 1641, when Peard reported on monopolies, Webb was listed as a monopolizer of bone-lace and was ordered to be expelled from the House. Before his successor was chosen on 26 April Webb was called in to explain why he had detained the writ for the new election,[178] but appeared no more in parliament. His career followed afterwards that of his master, with whom he was in Scotland in 1641, and in attendance upon the king at Oxford.[179] He petitioned in 1646 for permission to compound for his delinquency in being at the king's quarters during

[163] Pink MSS, 311, fols. 451c, 489c.

[164] P.C.C., 78 Campbell.

[165] *Students admitted to the Inner Temple*, 257.

[166] *M. of P.* 1: 497; D'Ewes (N), 267–268; New Romney Borough MSS, Common Assembly Book, 1622–1701, fol. 287.

[167] *Kent* 7: 114; *Vis. Kent, 1619*, 123–124. There were other Webbs in Kent at this period, however, and no evidence proves positively that the M.P. was of the Frittenden line or even of the county.

[168] *Gray's Inn Adm. Reg.*, 156; Wilts. Arch. Soc. Library MSS, Kite's Pedigrees, 1: 296. If he was of the Wiltshire family, he was probably related to the Sir William Webb who was in the household of Prince Henry in 1613 and afterwards lived in Westmorland and Yorkshire. *C.S.P. Dom., 1611–1618*, 199; *The letters of John Chamberlain* 1: 476; Nicolson and Burn, *History and antiquities of Westmorland and Cumberland* 1: 100.

[169] Thomas Webb was an intimate of Peregrine Fairfax when he was in France with Doncaster in 1621. *Fairfax correspondence* 1, "Memoir," li–lvi.

[170] *C.S.P. Dom., 1625–1626*, 208; *1628–1629*, 164.

[171] He was proposing to leave the duke's service in 1632, but later abandoned the idea. Add. MSS, 33,936 (Moreton correspondence), fols. 32–34, 36, 45.

[172] *Arch. Cant.* 12: 66, 1878. Webb seems to have been using for the advantage of his new master some information he had gained in the service of Carlisle, whose plantation in Connaught was here involved. *Verney Papers*, 154, 156, Camden Society, 1853.

[173] Webb was an intimate of the Moreton family of Cheshire, and between 1632 and 1641 was advising Peter Moreton about his career. Add. MSS, 33,936, fols. 45, 102, 123, *passim*.

[174] *C.S.P. Dom., 1631–1633*, 473; *1634–1635*, 85–86, 135; *1635–1636*, 55. There was apparently another Thomas Webb in some minor post at the court at this time (*ibid., 1637–1638*, 190), and a barrister of Lincoln's Inn (*Linc. Inn Rec. Adm.* 1: 168; *Black Books* 2: 236, 368), from whom it is difficult to distinguish the duke's secretary.

[175] *Arch. Cant.* 12: 80–81, 1878; *C.S.P. Dom., 1639–1640*, 599.

[176] *Verney Papers*, 234, Camden Society; *C.S.P. Dom., 1640–1641*, 121–122.

[177] New Romney Borough MSS, Common Assembly Book, 1622–1701, fols. 287–289; Add. MSS, 24,798, fols. 379v–382.

[178] *C.J.* 2: 71, 99, 123; D'Ewes (N), 267–268, 357; New Romney Borough MSS, Common Assembly Book, 1622–1701, fol. 293.

[179] Bodleian Tanner MSS, 66, fols. 191–193; D'Ewes (C), 85–86; Nicholas Papers 1: 11, *passim*, Camden Society, 1886; *Arch. Cant.* 12: 90, 1878.

the war, acknowledging but a small personal estate and some Irish lands, but he was still listed as sequestered in 1648.[180] He died in his forty-ninth year, 7 October 1649, and was buried at Cobham church in Kent.[181]

Webb married, probably before 1632, Elizabeth Wodehouse, of the Norfolk family. She died during the siege of Oxford, leaving two children, James and Lucy.[182]

* **Thomas, Viscount Wenman** (1596–1665), of Thame Park, Oxfordshire, sat for his county, 1640–1648. Besides serving in six earlier parliaments, he was for some years a member of several local commissions and a J.P. for Oxfordshire.[183]

Whitelocke described him in 1640 as a nobleman of great fortune.[184] He pledged £1000 to support the loan in November, 1640.[185] He had married the coheiress to an ample fortune,[186] and when he made his will in 1658 he provided an annuity of £1000 for a brother and legacies of over £8000 to various children and grandchildren, those sums apparently being additions to portions and settlements previously arranged.[187]

Lord Wenman was a brother-in-law of four fellow parliament men, Denton, Arthur Goodwin, Sir Martin Lister, and Trevor, and was a relative of John Hampden.

Sir George Wentworth (c. 1600–1660), of Woolley, Yorkshire, M.P. for Pontefract, 1640–6 September 1642, was a third cousin of his fellow member, Sir George Wentworth (1609–1666 ?), and of the Earl of Strafford, and his father and he were on terms of intimacy with the elder branch of the family at Wentworth Woodhouse.[188] George was the third son but by 1640 the heir apparent of Michael Wentworth of Woolley (d. 1641), by his wife, Frances, daughter and heir of George Downes of Herefordshire.[189] He was born about 1600

and was admitted to the Inner Temple in 1617.[190] He was named that year as his father's legal heir, an elder brother, Michael, being for some reason cut off from the succession.[191] In 1621 Wentworth married Anne, daughter of Thomas Lord Fairfax of Denton.[192] By this step, if by no other, it must have been made clear that George was no recusant, although his aging father paid fines regularly for recusancy and his mother never renounced her Catholicism.[193] Two years after Anne's death in 1624 Wentworth married Averil (Everild) Maltby, daughter of Christopher Maltby of York, who lived until 1639.[194] In 1630 Michael Wentworth made a final settlement of his estates and George became head of his branch of the family.[195] That year he was knighted.[196]

As early as 1625 Wentworth was interested in politics, working for the shire candidates, his wife's father and his cousin, Fairfax and Sir Thomas Wentworth,[197] but he seems to have had no aspirations to serve in parliament himself until 1640. He was a J.P. in the West Riding and Treasurer for Lame Soldiers in 1634,[198] and a sewers commissioner.[199] While his kinsman, Sir Thomas Wentworth, was in Ireland, he managed some of his personal affairs.[200] He was a colonel in the Yorkshire militia, possibly a D.L., in 1639 and 1640, and was ordered in March, 1640, to the Berwick garrison, although he had signed the letter of January, 1639, asking that some of the troops be left in Yorkshire. He signed the Yorkshire petition of July, 1640,[201] also, but certainly intended thereby no attack on Strafford personally. He was a newcomer to parliament when he was chosen with his cousin for Pontefract.

It was probably this Sir George Wentworth who was named to a committee of the House in March, 1641,[202] for, aside from his opposing Strafford's attainder,[203] he seems to have been willing to cooperate in the work of the parliament. He was listed as late as 1642 in the army being raised by Essex as Quarter Master for Artillery under Fairfax, but at the end of the summer he joined the king, and was disabled, 6 September 1642.[204]

---

[180] His personalty was valued at only £100, and his fine at a tenth was only £35. *Cal. Com. Comp.*, 94, 1572; S.P. 23/195/155.

[181] A stone near the chancel describes him as the faithful secretary of the Duke of Richmond and Lenox. A copy of the inscription, made by Mrs. Marsh, was sent me by the Rev. C. P. G. Rose, vicar.

[182] M.I. at Cobham; Hasted, *Kent* 2: 17. An Elizabeth Webb was a contributor in St. Margaret's, Westminster, in 1632–1633. Records of the Parish of St. Margaret's, Churchwardens' Accounts, **18**.

[183] C. 181/4, fol. 179; 181/5, fols. 65, 123, 321; S.P. 16/405.

[184] Add. MSS, 37,343, fol. 206v.

[185] D'Ewes (N), 52.

[186] His wife's portion was reported to be £500 a year in land. *The letters of John Chamberlain* 2: 56.

[187] P.C.C., 20 Hyde.

[188] Foster, *Yorkshire Families* 2, Wentworth; G. E. Wentworth, History of the Wentworths of Woolley, *Yorks. Arch. Jour.* **12**: 1–35, 159–194, 1893.

[189] Dugdale, *Vis. York*, 10. His father's second son, Michael, was living in 1646, but the family estates were settled on George. See below.

[190] *Students admitted to the Inner Temple*, 217.

[191] *Yorks. Arch. Jour.* **12**: 10, 20, 1893.

[192] *Ibid.* Her portion was £1500 (Bodleian Fairfax MSS, 30, fol. 150).

[193] *H.M.C., Various collections* 2, MSS of Mrs. Wentworth of Woolley Park, 371, 373; *Yorks. Arch. Jour.* **12**: 6–9, 160, 1893.

[194] Averil was a sister of Michael Warton's wife (*q.v.*).

[195] *Yorks. Arch. Jour.* **12**: 20, 1893.

[196] Shaw, *K. of E.* 2: 197.

[197] *Yorks. Arch. Jour.* **12**: 23–24, 1893.

[198] C. 193/13; *Yorks. Arch. Jour.* **5**: 373, *passim*, 1877; Add. MSS, 26,739, fol. 425v.

[199] C. 181/5, fols. 106, 173.

[200] *H.M.C., Various collections* 2: 371–372.

[201] *H.M.C., Twelfth Report* 2, Coke MSS, 208; *Y.A.S. Rec. Ser.* **54**: 207, 1915; *C.S.P. Dom., 1639–1640*, 567; *1640*, 524; S.P. 16, 409/53.

[202] *C.J.* 2: 95.

[203] Verney, 58.

[204] *C.J.* 2: 754; *Yorks. Arch. Jour.* **12**: 27, 1893.

He pledged his fortunes as well as his services to King Charles and suffered heavy losses during the war. He died on 19 October 1660, in his sixty-first year, and was buried at Woolley.[205]

Wentworth's large family estates included several manors in Yorkshire with coal works near Woolley, and some property in Suffolk. These were valued at the time of his father's death on the eve of the war at 1136 *l*. 13 *s*. 4 *d*. a year. Sir George increased his income by his marriages, and added more lands by purchase. His compounding papers show an income of about £935 a year, from which about £200 in annuities were payable. His fine, set first at a third, £4302, was reduced in 1649 to £3188.[206]

Sir George had various relatives in the Long Parliament. Besides his cousin of the same name, he was a cousin of Savile, and a brother-in-law by his two marriages of Michael Warton and Lord Fairfax. The latter remembered one of Wentworth's sons in his will.[207]

Sir George Wentworth (1609–1666 ?), of Wentworth Woodhouse, Yorkshire, and of Ireland,

was M.P. for Pontefract, 1640–22 January 1644. He was a third cousin of his colleague of the same name, and was about sixteen years younger than his brother, Thomas Wentworth, Earl of Strafford, with whose fortunes his own were closely linked. The youngest son of Sir William Wentworth of Wentworth Woodhouse, Bart. (d. 1614), by Anne, daughter of Robert Atkinson of Stowell, Gloucestershire, he was baptized at Wentworth on 20 July 1609,[208] and was left with three other young brothers to the care of their brother Thomas when their father died. The father had instructed that they be reared in God's fear and service and in good manners and learning,[209] and George matriculated at University College, Oxford, in December, 1626.[210] He joined his brother, then Lord Deputy in Ireland, in 1633, and was knighted by him there in July, along with Sir Thomas Danby (*q.v.*).[211] The following winter he spent a few months in England on business for his brother.[212] Nominated by the Lord Deputy, he sat in the Irish parliament of 1634 for Bandonbridge.[213] He attended the Council of War in December, 1635, and in March, 1640, was sworn a member of the Irish Privy Council.[214]

But George's presence in Ireland was not always helpful to his brother. Within a year after his arrival he fell in love with Anne Rush or Ruishe, whose father, Sir Francis Rush, had reputedly left her £1000 a year in revenue, and whose mother had by 1634 married as her second husband Sir John Jephson of Ireland and of Froyle, Hampshire.[215] Anne's marriage with young Wentworth was opposed, however, by the Lord Chancellor, Loftus, whose son, Sir Robert, had married Anne's sister and who had hoped to control the major part of the inheritance. It was somewhat opposed also by the Lord Deputy, who seemed to realize more than George the problems that were involved; and somewhat, it was said, by Anne's mother, because Sir George's fortune was not large. By the end of 1634, however, all seemed to be arranged, the Lord Deputy guaranteeing his brother £500 a year, besides an annuity and "company," and Lady Jephson planning to petition the king for permission to refer to the Lord Deputy the disagreement with the Loftus family about Anne's inheritance.[216] But it was not until 18 January 1635/6 that Lord Wentworth wrote to his wife of the end of this "weary business," and declared his acceptance into the family of his new sister-in-law.[217] The weary business, however, had not ended. Sir George by his marriage not only acquired right to some manors in Kent,[218] but became involved in a prolonged lawsuit with Lord Chancellor Loftus regarding Irish lands worth £800 to £1200, the right to which was claimed by his wife and by the Lord Chancellor's daughter-in-law. This case, through the Lord Deputy's arbitrary handling of it in 1638, became a political issue between him and the Lord Chancellor and the basis of one of the charges against him in 1640.[219] Even after Strafford's downfall and a decision by the House of Lords in May, 1642, reversing the Lord Deputy's decree that favored his brother and Robert Loftus, it was alleged that Sir George was still holding more than £4000 not legally his, and the case was being argued by heirs of the families as late as 1678.[220]

[205] *Ibid*. **12**: 27–29, 32, 159, 1893.

[206] Wentworth's second wife's property was supposed to be worth £133 a year. *Yorks. Arch. Jour.* **12**: 16–30, 159, 1893; *Y.A.S. Rec. Ser.* **18**: 154–155, 1895; S.P. 23/199/151–153.

[207] *Y.A.S. Rec. Ser.* **9**: 7, 1890.

[208] *Complete Baronetage* **1**: 30; Foster, *Yorkshire families* **2**, Wentworth of Wentworth Woodhouse.

[209] Will of Sir William Wentworth, Bart., 1614, York Probate Registry, **33**, fols. 329–332.

[210] His age was then given as fifteen (*Al. Oxon*.). He is confused somewhat here with his cousin, Sir George Wentworth of Woolley, but it was probably Strafford's brother who was created M.A. in 1642.

[211] Shaw, *K. of E.* **2**: 202.

[212] *Strafford letters* **1**: 194; *Verney Papers*, 158, Camden Society, 1853; C. V. Wedgwood, *Strafford*, 122, *passim*, London, Cape, 1935.

[213] *C.S.P. Ireland, 1633–1647*, 63; Townshend, *The life and letters of the great Earl of Cork*, 244.

[214] *C.S.P. Ireland, 1633–1647*, 117, 236.

[215] This was the father of William Jephson, 1640 M.P. (*q.v.*).

[216] Bodleian Firth MSS, b. 2, fol. 244v.

[217] *Yorks. Arch. Jour.* **6**: 377, 1881. See also *C.S.P. Ireland, 1633–1647*, 76, 121; Firth MSS, b. 2, fol. 182; Lady Burghclere, *Strafford*, **2**: 1–6, London, Macmillan, 1931.

[218] Hasted, *Kent* **10**: 251, 257.

[219] *H.M.C., Various collections* **3**, MSS of Sir Thomas Barrett-Lennard, Bart., lvii–lxvi, 158–164, 169–200, *passim; Fourth Report*, House of Lords MSS, 101.

[220] *H.M.C., Ninth Report* **2**, MSS of the Marquis of Drogheda, 315–318, 327–328; Add. MSS, 15,903, fol. 65; Firth MSS, b. 2, fol. 201. His brother's connection with the Loftus affair has been overlooked by some of Strafford's biographers. *Cf*. Birkenhead's *Strafford*, 194–195, London, 1938.

Meanwhile, Sir George was pushed by his brother into military as well as political experience. He requested Secretary Coke in 1638 that George be given a troop of carbineers,[221] and in the Irish army lists of 1640 Sir George was included as serjeant major and captain in the Lord General's regiment.[222] He was in Bristol in July, 1639, possibly on his way to the Scottish border.[223] He sat in his first English parliament the following spring for Pontefract,[224] but returned to Ireland that summer.[225]

In the Long Parliament Sir George was important chiefly as Strafford's brother. Strafford requested his witness on his behalf, and he of course voted against the earl's attainder.[226] He may have gone to Ireland in the summer of 1641,[227] and he finally left for there again in February, 1642, having the permission of the House to attend to his military duties against the rebellion.[228] He was disabled as a royalist, 22 January 1644.[229] An assessment of £2000 charged to him in 1644 was written off in 1649, upon payment of £50, because he was much in debt.[230] He lived to see the Restoration, but died before 1667. His will was proved in Ireland in 1666.[231]

* **Sir Peter Wentworth**, K.B. (1592–1675), of Lillingston Lovell, Bucks (then Oxfordshire),[232] and of Wolston, Warwickshire, was elected a member for Tamworth, Staffordshire, 18 December 1641, replacing Wilmot, and sat until 1653. He was a J.P. in Oxfordshire [233] and was sheriff during the ship money period. His difficulties in collecting the levy and arrears led to his being examined by Council in 1638.[234] He was listed in 1639 as having been summoned to attend the army in the north but as failing to go.[235] After he entered the parliament late in 1641 Wentworth became a leader in the opposition group.

At the time Wentworth was making excuses about his ship money collecting, he complained of losses he had recently incurred in his estates, of having sold a large part, and of being burdened with debts. He mentioned also that he had performed some earlier expensive tasks for the king, including an embassy for the Duke of

Buckingham.[236] But in June, 1642, Wentworth made one of the larger subscriptions for the defense, three horses and £100.[237]

Wentworth was a cousin of Sir Edward Boys and of Sir William Strickland.[238]

* **Thomas Lord Wentworth**, K.B. (1613–1665), of Toddington, Bedfordshire, member for his county until he was called to the upper house as Baron Wentworth of Nettlestead on 25 November 1640, was a royalist. He was the eldest surviving son of Thomas, fourth Baron Wentworth and first Earl of Cleveland, and was unmarried as late as July, 1639.[239] With his father he was named as a J.P. in Bedfordshire in 1634 and 1638, was a commissioner of oyer and terminer for that and neighboring counties several times between 1635 and 1640,[240] was a vice admiral in 1638, and was acting the next year as his father's deputy for the joint lieutenancy of Bedfordshire.[241]

The family held numerous possessions in the counties of Bedford, Suffolk, and Middlesex, one of which alone was worth £600 a year,[242] and when in 1636 a marriage was proposed between Sir Thomas and a daughter of Sir John Lambe, £1000 a year was to have been her jointure, and £1200 a year the maintenance allowance for the couple. But the marriage did not occur,[243] and the debts of the earl and his son were so heavy by 1640 that various portions of their property had been mortgaged or sold to satisfy their creditors.[244]

Benjamin Weston (fl. 1640–1659), of Walton-on-Thames, was a member for Dover from about February, 1641, when he was chosen to replace Sir Peter Heyman, until 1653.[245] He was the fourth son of Richard, first Earl of Portland (d. 1635), by his second wife, Frances Waldegrave, the Catholic, and was a brother of Nicholas Weston, a fellow member.[246] He may have been travelling abroad with a brother about 1632,[247] and sometime before 1640 married Elizabeth, daughter of William Sheldon of Hornby, Leicestershire, widow of Bucking-

[221] Bodleian Firth MSS, b. 2, fol. 205v.
[222] Bodleian Carte MSS, 1, fol. 184v.
[223] C.S.P. Dom., 1639, 410.
[224] M. of P. 1: 484.
[225] C.S.P. Dom., 1640, 306.
[226] D'Ewes (N), 515 and n.; Verney, 58.
[227] C.S.P. Ireland, 1633–1647, 301.
[228] H.M.C., Various collections 3: 212–213; MSS of the Earl of Egmont 1 (i): 180.
[229] C.J. 3: 374. His cousin, the other Sir George, had been disabled earlier for being in arms in England.
[230] Cal. Com. Adv. Money, 434–435.
[231] Pink MSS, 320.
[232] V.C.H. Buckingham 4: 191.
[233] C. 193/12.
[234] C.S.P. Dom., 1635–1636, viii–xiv, 224; 1637–1638, 234; S.P. 16/381/33, 41, 42.
[235] S.P. 16, 427/38/vi.

[236] C.S.P. Dom., 1635–1636, 224. His Warwickshire estate of Wolston was a part of his inheritance. Dugdale, The antiquities of Warwickshire, 27, 1765.
[237] N. and Q., 1st Ser., 12: 338, 1855.
[238] A sketch of Wentworth's life appears in Wedgwood, Staff. Parl. Hist. 2: 88–89.
[239] C.S.P. Dom., 1639, 426.
[240] C. 193/13; S.P. 16/405; C. 181/5, fols. 6, 62, 120, 186, 358.
[241] C.S.P. Dom., 1637–1638, 501; 1639, 259.
[242] Lysons, Mag. Brit. 1: 66, 143–144; C.J. 2: 278; H.M.C., Fourth Report, House of Lords MSS, 30; Beds. Hist. Rec. 11: 129–136, 1927.
[243] S.P. 16, 342/21 and 408/62; V.C.H. Bedford 3: 440.
[244] Debts of £19,200 to two creditors were listed in 1637. S.P. 16, 377/169.
[245] M. of P. 1: 497; O.P.H. 9: 13.
[246] D.N.B., "Richard Weston, 1577–1635."
[247] C.S.P. Dom., 1629–1631, 150; 1631–1633, 383.

ham's brother, the Earl of Anglesey.[248] He probably resided at one of his father's estates in Surrey, and in 1654 was described as of Walton-on-Thames.[249] He seems, however, to have had no connection with the Cinque Ports, or with local affairs before 1640, and may have owed his seat for Dover to the Lord Warden, the Duke of Lenox, whose sister in 1632 married Weston's elder brother, Jerome.[250]

Weston's activities in the parliament can scarcely be traced because of the presence there of his brother and another "Mr. Weston." With his brother he was among those voting against Strafford's attainder,[251] but their ways parted afterwards, Benjamin casting his lot with the parliamentarians, and adapting himself to the changing currents of the times. He was listed as an elder in his county presbytery, but was afterwards a Rumper and, though he did not act, was named one of the king's judges. Holles intimates that his loyalty to parliament was purchased by the reviving of arrears of a pension which his wife had once held, some £4000.[252]

Weston may have sat for Midhurst, Sussex, in 1658,[253] and in 1659 he returned with the Rump, although he was not listed among those present in March, 1660.[254] The date of his death is unknown.

Nicholas Weston (1611–1656), M.P. for Newtown, Isle of Wight, 1640–16 August 1642,[255] was the third son of Richard, first Earl of Portland (d. 1635), by his second wife, Frances, daughter of Nicholas Waldegrave of Borley, Essex.[256] He was baptized at Roxwell, Essex, 10 May 1611, and was made M.A. at Cambridge in 1629 as the son of a nobleman.[257] He may have travelled abroad for a time,[258] and was possibly the "Mr. Weston" who in 1638 held some court post near the king.[259] With his younger brother, Benjamin (q.v.), he was made a burgess of Yarmouth in the Isle of Wight in August, 1634.[260] After his elder brother, the second earl, became captain of the island, Nicholas visited there,

too. In 1639 the conduct of such revellers as George Goring and John Meux (q.v.) and young "Nick Weston" scandalized the Newport people.[261] He was elected, doubtless through his brother's influence in the island's elections, as M.P. for Newtown in March and in October, 1640,[262] although he seems to have served in no local post before.

Weston's royalist leaning showed soon in the Long Parliament. He voted against the attainder of Strafford [263] and in the summer of 1642 worked to secure Portsmouth for the king. For his part in that affair he was disabled by vote of the House, 16 August 1642.[264] He had never been active in the work of the parliament.

Weston is said to have married, but to have left no surviving issue. He died in 1656, administration of his estate being granted, 12 January 1656/7, to a creditor.[265] His brother, Benjamin, a fellow M.P. in 1640, sided with parliament.

Richard Weston (c. 1609–1652), of Rugeley, Staffordshire, was M.P. for Stafford, 1640–30 October 1642. He was the son and heir apparent of Sir Richard Weston, Baron of the Exchequer, who was impeached with the other judges in 1641 for their stand on ship money.[266] The younger Weston was a barrister of the Inner Temple, having been called to the bar at the same time as Orlando Bridgeman (q.v.).[267] He seems to have held no public office before 1640, although his father had for years been a J.P in Staffordshire.[268] Weston probably voted against the attainder of Strafford,[269] and was disabled as a royalist in 1642. He was killed in 1652, before his father's death.[270]

William Wheeler, or **Wheler** (c. 1601–1666), of Westminster, sat for Westbury, Wiltshire, 1640–1648.[271] He came of a London family. His grandfather, Henry Wheeler (d. 1565), was a grocer. Henry's eldest son, John, was a merchant, possibly the John Wheeler who in 1606 was secretary to the Merchant Adventurers.[272] William, who was John's son and heir by his first wife, Anne, daughter of Henry Harvey of Chessington, Surrey, a sister of William Lord Harvey, may have been born in Holland. He was there during some of his early years, for his father was living at Middleburgh in 1612,

---

[248] Their daughter Elizabeth was married in 1652. *Complete Baronetage* **1**: 25–26; Burke, *Dormant and extinct Peerages*, 580.

[249] Manning and Bray, *Hist. Surrey* **3**: 290; *Surrey Arch. Coll.* **3**: 203, 1865.

[250] *Arch. Cant.* **12**: 62, 1878.

[251] Verney, 58.

[252] *A.H.R.* **44**: 31, n. (32), 1938–1939; *O.P.H.* **9**: 13; Noble, *Regicides* **2**: 326; *Memoirs of Denzil Holles*, 137.

[253] Pink MSS, 311, fol. 498c.

[254] Thomason Tracts, 669. f. 21, p. 43; 669. f. 24, p. 37.

[255] Because the writ for replacing "Mr. Nicholas" (1645) did not specify that it was Nicholas Weston, the latter has occasionally been listed as a "recruiter" and Edward Nicholas, the Council secretary, as the original member. Sanford, *St. and ill.*, 278; *O.P.H.* **9**: 1, *40. The latter, however, was not a member.

[256] *D.N.B.*, "Richard Weston, first Earl of Portland."

[257] *Al. Cant.*

[258] Two sons of the Lord Treasurer were licensed to travel, 1629–1632. *C.S.P. Dom., 1629–1631*, 150.

[259] *Ibid., 1637–1638*, 467; S.P. 16, 427/38/v.

[260] Add. MSS, 5669, fol. **97v.**

[261] *A royalist's notebook*, 98–99; *The Oglander memoirs* (Long), xxiii–xxiv.

[262] *M. of P.* **1**: 483, 493, n.

[263] Verney, 58.

[264] *C.J.* **2**: 723; Godwin, *The Civil War in Hampshire*, 21, 25.

[265] *Al. Cant.; D.N.B.*

[266] *D.N.B.*

[267] *Students admitted to the Inner Temple*, 243.

[268] C. 193/12, 13; S.P. 16/405.

[269] "Mr. Weston" and the "brothers Weston" appear in the list of Straffordians. Verney, 58, 59.

[270] Wedgwood, *Staff. Parl. Hist.* **2**: 26, 62. The father died in 1656 or 1659, rather than in 1652, as it appears in *D.N.B.*

[271] *M. of P.* **1**: 496; *O.P.H.* **9**: 7.

[272] London Corporation MSS, Rep. 27, fol. 262v.

and John's second wife, who survived him, was living at Dort in 1619.[273] William was born about 1601 [274] and succeeded his father about 1617 or 1618. Nothing is known of his education, but since he left at his death a collection of books of Greek, Latin, French, Spanish, "and some divinity," [275] it must be assumed that it followed classical lines, perhaps at one of the universities of the continent. His later interest in Presbyterianism was doubtless influenced by these early years. Instead of following a trade Wheeler turned to a career in official life, aided, perhaps, by the influence of his mother's family.

In July, 1630, one William Wheeler, possibly the M.P., was associated in some fashion with the Dean of Westminster.[276] The member was described by a relative in 1636 as "William Wheeler of Westminster, Esquire," [277] and it is known that at some time he was connected with the First Fruits Office.[278] Since Wheeler was regarded in the Long Parliament as something of an authority on ecclesiastical questions, and was often assigned, furthermore, with the Exchequer official, Sir Robert Pye, to handle funds, it may be assumed that he had had considerable experience with such matters before 1640. Nor was he without connection with the royal household itself. His wife, Elizabeth, who was the daughter and heiress of Michael Cole of Kensington, and whom he married before 1636,[279] was said to have been of the household, and the laundress for King Charles I. To her the king entrusted some of his valuables, it was said, early in the Civil War.[280]

Wheeler owned some lands in Wiltshire, including some in Westbury parish, at the time of his death, and he may have acquired them before 1640, but whether he ever resided in that county is doubtful. His first official connection with it seems to have been his return to the Long Parliament. Soon after the parliament began, however, a Westbury man tried to serve him with a subpoena,[281] and during the war he was named to the parliamentary committees for Wiltshire.[282] He was primarily a Londoner, though, was a J.P. for Middlesex in 1641, and was several times employed by parliament in work concerned with Westminster.[283]

In spite of his wife's connections, Wheeler's sympathies seem from the start to have been with the anti-court and anti-Laud groups. To him was attributed the list of "Straffordians" that was posted in Westminster.[284] He was named to the recess committee of 1641. Having earlier showed himself opposed to pluralities and favoring reforms in the church, he was active in the attack in the autumn of 1641 on the bishops who had voted for the new canons.[285] He served with Pye in handling the poll money for the use of parliament and in auditing the accounts of some of the northern garrisons and of the contributions of members toward Irish relief.[286] A Presbyterian in religion, Wheeler was a lay member of the Westminster Assembly, and was secluded from the House in 1648. He seems to have been knighted by Cromwell in 1657, and to have returned to the parliaments of 1659 and 1660. But he made his peace with Charles II before the Restoration, perhaps through the influence of his wife or of the future Earl of Sandwich, and was rewarded with a baronetcy. He died on 6 August 1666.[287]

Wheeler was probably a man of considerable wealth. He offered his bond as security for £1000 for the loan in November, 1640,[288] and at the time of his death his estate was estimated to be worth at least £1000 a year. In his will of 1665 he stated that he had been bountifully blessed in worldly estate, and the list of properties he held then ranged from his home in fashionable Canon Row, Westminster, and over thirty houses in or near London, to manors in Hants and Bucks, and two manors and other properties in Wiltshire.[289] Some he doubtless acquired after 1640, but he probably owned many of his London possessions at the time he was elected to parliament.

John Whistler (1580–1646), of Gray's Inn, Recorder of Oxford, was M.P. for Oxford, 1640–1644.[290] The son and heir of Hugh Whistler, gentleman, of Milton Parva, Oxfordshire, and of Little Haseley, Berks, he was educated at Oxford and at Gray's Inn. Two of his brothers were clergymen.[291] He seems to have divided his time between Oxford and London after he became a barrister,[292] and was called by D'Ewes a common lawyer.[293] He was deputy recorder and then recorder of Oxford, M.P. for that city in the parliaments of

---

[273] The confusion about Wheeler's parentage (e.g., *Complete Baronetage* **3**: 106) was cleared up by Bower Marsh in 1909. *Genealogist*, N.S., **25**: 209–215, 1909.

[274] He died in his sixty-sixth year in 1666. *Complete Baronetage.*

[275] *Genealogist*, N.S., **2**: 206, 1885.

[276] In a letter to Sir Edward Dering that month Wheeler expressed his desire to have the continuing favor of "Mr. Dean" and of Dering, writing as if he were in the former's employ. Add. MSS, 34,195, fol. 20.

[277] *Genealogist*, N.S., **25**: 212, 1909.

[278] *Ibid.*, N.S., **2**: 206, 1885.

[279] *Ibid.*, N.S., **25**: 212, 1909; *Complete Baronetage* **3**: 106.

[280] L. Echard, *The history of England* **2**: 639, London, 1707–1718; *Genealogist*, N.S., **3**: 42, 1886.

[281] *C.J.* **2**: 58.

[282] *Wilts. Arch. Mag.* **26**: 344, 1892.

[283] *C.J.* **2**: 317, 340, 361; D'Ewes (C), 148, 219.

[284] Sanford, *St. and ill.*, 346.

[285] D'Ewes (N), 464; D'Ewes (C), 49, n., 282, *passim; C.J.* **2**: 288, 329.

[286] *C.J.* **2**: 298, 310, 344, 352, 360; D'Ewes (C), 47, 340, 359.

[287] *Complete Baronetage* **3**: 106; *Genealogist*, N.S., **25**: 213–214, 1909.

[288] D'Ewes (N), 52.

[289] P.C.C., 96 Carr. See also *Genealogist*, N.S., **25**: 213–214, 1909.

[290] Williams, *Oxford*, 115.

[291] R. F. Whistler, The annals of an English family, *Sussex Arch. Coll.* **35**: 61–88, 1887.

[292] In 1617 he had residences at both places. St. Ch. 8/32/17.

[293] D'Ewes (N), 179.

1624–1628, and was a J.P. and a member of other commissions in the county.[294]   He received a gift of money from Oxford in 1630 in honor of his being reader at his inn, and performed many of the legal duties of his office from London.[295]   He was not a member of the Short Parliament, but was elected in preference to Lord Andover for the town's first seat in October, 1640.[296]

Whistler was particularly interested in questions of the subsidy, and was an advocate of reforms.   In the parliament of 1625 he favored delay in granting funds to the king,[297] and in the Long Parliament was frequently in the chair for the debates on supply.   He was a member also of the Committee of Privileges, and of several on grievances, and spoke frequently on matters ecclesiastical, attacking the new canons.   He was somewhat interested also in military affairs,[298] but after the war started withdrew to Oxford and sat in the king's parliament there.   He was a prisoner several times, and declared later that his absence from Westminster was involuntary.   He died about 1646 and was buried at Haseley, Berkshire.   His will, dated 11 September 1646, was proved 14 May 1647.[299]   He never married.

Whistler does not seem to have been a wealthy man. He listed for the compounding commissioners properties in Oxford, Berks, and Hampshire worth £143 a year,[300] and the bequests made in his will to relatives and friends and one to Trinity College, Oxford, were not large.

Lawrence Whitaker (*c.* 1579–1654), of Drury Lane, Middlesex, poet, clerk of the Council, and diarist, was M.P. for Okehampton, Devon, 1641–1653.[301]   He is said to have been a native of Somerset and was born about 1579.[302]   He matriculated a sizar at St. John's, Cambridge, in 1593, was graduated B.A. in 1597 and M.A. in 1600, and was incorporated at Oxford in 1603. Eleven years later, when he was especially admitted to the Middle Temple, he was described as of London.[303] He had probably gone there under the auspices of Sir Edward Phelipps, of Somerset, Master of the Rolls,

whose secretary he was for a time.[304]   By then he had made a name for himself as "an ingenious poet" and man of learning.   One of his friends was Thomas Coryate, for the introduction to whose *Crudities* (1611) he wrote verses in four languages.[305]   After the death of Phelipps he apparently entered the services of the Earl of Somerset, and was among those questioned in 1615 regarding the Overbury case.[306]   The disgrace of Somerset meant only that Whitaker formed new attachments at the court, for between 1619 and 1623 he received "for divers good causes" a share in numerous grants of fee farm rents from crown lands in more than a dozen counties.[307]   He had probably married by this time.   His first wife (d. before 1638) seems to have been a widow, Margaret, daughter of Sir John Egerton of Egerton in Cheshire and of Farthingo, Northamptonshire.[308]   Whitaker married again in 1638, declaring his age at that time as fifty.   His second wife was Dorothy, daughter of Charles Hoskins of St. Andrew's, Holborn,[309] and through her Whitaker became a connection of the Bedingfield family of Suffolk and London.[310]

Whitaker was an M.P. for the parliaments of 1624–1629 for Peterborough in Northamptonshire.   He kept notes of the 1626 debates, some of which were designed as memoranda for Lord Carleton,[311] who was perhaps Whitaker's new patron.   And after the parliament of 1628–1629 he helped to search Eliot's study, acting as a J.P. on the command of king and council.[312]

At this period and during the following decade Whitaker was clearly in the service of the court.   He had become one of the clerks extraordinary of the Privy Council in September, 1624,[313] and seems to have func-

---

[294] Williams, *loc. cit.;* C. 181/3, fol. 115; 181/4, fol. 57; 181/5, fols. 136, 157.

[295] Oxford Corporation MSS, P.5.2, Audit Book, 1592–1682, fols. 211, 226, 253.

[296] Oxford Corporation MSS, A.5.7, Council Book, 1629–1663, fol. 110.

[297] *Commons Debates in 1625,* 77, 122, 146.

[298] *C.J.* **2**: 20, 39, 41; D'Ewes (N), 12 and n., 17 and n., 146–148, 179, 184–185, *passim;* D'Ewes (C), 139, 207, 258.

[299] P.C.C., 90 Fines.

[300] S.P. 23/129/611.

[301] Okehampton was one of the "restored" boroughs.

[302] He died in 1654 at the age of seventy-six or in his seventy-sixth year (Wood, *Fasti Oxon.* **1**: 300).   Whether Whitaker was connected with the Whitakers of Lancashire I have been unable to discover.   Lawrence was a not uncommon name in that family, and the M.P.'s connection by marriage (see below) with families of Cheshire and Northamptonshire suggests that his roots were not all in Somerset.

[303] *Al. Cant.; Mid. Temp. Rec.* **2**: 578.

[304] Wood, *loc. cit.*

[305] Thomas Coryate, *Coryat's crudities* **1**: 40–43, Glasgow, MacLehose, 1905.

[306] A Mr. Whitaker was a messenger sent several times by the countess to Mrs. Turner in 1615 (*C.S.P. Dom., 1611–1618,* 314).   Lawrence Whitaker wrote various times from his Drury Lane residence to the Earl of Somerset at Chiswick in 1624.   *H.M.C., Sixth Report,* MSS of the Earl of Moray, 635.

[307] Chancery proceedings, C. 3/418/147; Add. MSS, 6673, fol. 169; *C.S.P. Dom., 1623–1625,* 36, 180; Lipscomb, *Buckingham* **2**: 376, 475; **3**: 546.

[308] His first wife, Margaret, was mentioned in Whitaker's will.   That she was Margaret Egerton is suggested by the Egerton pedigree in Baker's *Northampton* (**1**: 621), and by the letters Whitaker received in 1640 from his "brother," Sir Thomas Powell of Cheshire (*C.S.P. Dom., 1640,* 8, 444). Powell's wife was Katherine, daughter of Sir John Egerton of Egerton (Ormerod, *Chester* **2**: 461).

[309] *Marriage licenses, London,* Harleian Society, **2**: 233. His wife's age was given as twenty-eight.

[310] Another daughter of Hoskins was the wife of Sir Thomas Bedingfield of Darsham, Attorney General for the Duchy of Lancaster (Add. MSS, 19,080, fols. 257–258).   To the latter's brother, Anthony Bedingfield, the London merchant (*q.v.*), Whitaker referred one of his problems as a local magistrate in 1638.   S.P. 16, 390/167.

[311] *M. of P.;* S.P. 16, 29/13.

[312] *C.J.* **2**: 202, 203.

[313] *Acts P.C., 1623–1625,* 310.

tioned as such even after a disappointment in 1635 when Nicholas and not he succeeded to the regular clerkship. As late as 1640 he was still one of the clerks in the employ of Council.[314] Much of his time seems to have gone into work as a J.P. in Middlesex and Westminster,[315] and as a commissioner for such local problems as the buildings in the Drury Lane region or the sewers.[316] But other appointments smacked of the prying and the fee-seeking common to courtiers, such as commissions to investigate the execution of various trade regulations, abuses in the manufacture of brick and tile, violations of the soap manufacturing patent or of the rules about the gold thread business.[317] Probably it was such activities that led to the later comment that Whitaker was as much a monopolist as some of the members expelled from the Long Parliament on that ground. His connection with the royal Council doubtless explains his work with Sir Richard Wynn (q.v.) and others in 1635 in a report on the functioning of the Court of Wards, and in suggesting a plan for advancing the king's service in the matter of knighthood compositions.[318] Perhaps his failure to win the clerkship of the Council that year accounts for the shift in Whitaker's loyalties afterwards. Or possibly the change came with his second marriage in 1638 which tied him in with one of the eastern groups of puritans. His appointment in 1639 to a body set up to report weekly to Council on the dullness of London trade, especially in western woolens, and to propose remedies [319] suggests that he was still a trusted agent of the crown, but also that his knowledge of economic matters was such as to make him useful to friends or foes of the Stuart program.

Whitaker was not a member of the first parliament of 1640. He apparently owed his place in the Long Parliament to the influence of Lord Mohun, who presented his name at Okehampton after helping to reinstate it as a parliamentary borough. Whitaker acknowledged his gratitude for his election by sending forty shillings for the poor of the town.[320] In view of his actions in earlier parliaments it is not surprising that there was some doubt that he would be accepted as a member of the reforming House of 1641.[321] Clarendon and King Charles complained afterwards that Whitaker, like Mildmay, had not been expelled with the monopolists, for he "had been most scandalously engaged in those pressures, though since more scanda-

lously in all enterprises against his majesty." [322] Whitaker apparently convinced the leaders of the House that he was to be trusted. Not only did he not vote to save Strafford, but he was named to several committees of the spring of 1641.[323] His part in connection with Eliot's arrest and the search of his papers was brought up in July, but he was permitted, after sojourning about a week in the Tower, to make his submission and to resume an active role in the parliament.[324] He was named a member of the important recess committee in September,[325] promised £20 as a gift for the defense in 1642,[326] and continued to work with parliament during the war. His diary of proceedings in parliament began after the war broke out.[327] Whitaker was a member of the committee of December, 1648, which decided that the king should be tried. But he did not sit with the commission for the trial, trimmer though he was.[328] He seems to have kept his seat until parliament ended,[329] and died the following year. He died, "aged seventy-six," on 15 April 1654, and was buried at St. Giles-in-the-Fields. His will, dated 21 September 1646, was proved by his widow on 9 May 1654.[330] He died without direct heirs.

Little is known of Whitaker's financial position. His ambitions had no doubt gained for him lucrative rewards both in lands and in fees. His country place at Chiswick, where he was living part of the time before 1640, was said in 1653 to be worth £60 a year.[331] His will mentioned holdings in London, Lambeth, Chiswick, rents from a rectory in Lincoln, and three manors in Somerset. From the lands in the latter county he enjoyed an income of about £240 a year.[332]

William Whitaker (d. 1646), recorder of Shaftesbury, Dorset, sat for that borough from 1640 until his death. The grandson of a well-to-do clothier of Westbury, Wilts, he was the eldest surviving son of Henry Whitaker (M.P. 1586), secretary to Sir Christopher Hatton. His mother was Judith, daughter of William Hawkins of Plymouth. He entered the Middle Temple on 23 April 1602 as the son of Henry Whitaker, deceased. John Pym entered at the same time and was at once "bound" with Whitaker. Several of Pym's relatives in the Rouse family were bound with Whitaker

[314] C.S.P. Dom., 1635, 385; 1640, 238, 256–257; Verney, 28.
[315] C. 193/12, 13.
[316] C.S.P. Dom., 1629–1631, 55; 1631–1633, 60, passim; 1635–1636, 157, 301; C. 181/4, fol. 191.
[317] C.S.P. Dom., 1635–1636, 162, 178; 1637, 164; 1638–1639, 36, 132; C. 181/4, fol. 186v; 181/5, fol. 296.
[318] Strafford letters 1: 372; C.S.P. Dom., 1635, 483.
[319] Ibid., 1629–1640, 244.
[320] Bridges, Okehampton, 92–93.
[321] The Buller Papers, 34.

[322] Clarendon, Rebellion 1: 228–229 and n.
[323] C.J. 2: 107, 113, 128.
[324] C.J. 2: 202–203, 211; Bodleian Tanner MSS, 66, fol. 110; Diurnal occurences, 267.
[325] C.J. 2: 288.
[326] N. and Q., 1st Ser., 12: 359, 1855.
[327] D'Ewes (C), xv.
[328] Western Antiquary 10: 16, 1890–1891.
[329] O.P.H. 9: *25.
[330] Wood, loc. cit.; will, P.C.C., 44 Alchin.
[331] Bodleian Rawl. MSS, D. 715, fol. 21. When compared with the £70 a year value assigned in the same survey to Lord Poulett's house and 30 acres in the same suburb, Whitaker's property seems to have been fairly pretentious.
[332] Whitaker's will; S.P. 16, 359/25/2, 6.

afterwards,[333] and the closeness of their friendship is indicated by Pym's naming Whitaker as one of the trustees for his estate (1614–1635).[334] Whitaker was called to the bar in 1611, was Reader in 1627, a Master of the Bench in 1636, Treasurer, 1635–1637, and he kept his relations with the Temple for the rest of his life.[335] But he retained his western connections, too. He married Honora, daughter of Edward Hooper of Boveridge, Dorset, and by 1623 had settled at Shaftesbury.[336] He was acting in some official capacity for the town in 1626, and by December, 1634, was its recorder.[337] He was steward for some of the Dorset properties of the Earl of Elgin also.[338] In 1632 he compounded with the county knighthood commissioners.[339] He was appointed a J.P. and a member of the sewers commission,[340] and he sat in five parliaments for Shaftesbury (1624, 1625, 1626, 1640[2]).

Although he was less conspicuous in the Long Parliament than Lawrence Whitaker of London, he was doubtless one of the trusted supporters of his old friends, Pym and Rous. He was possibly the "Mr. Whitaker" who was named to the Committee of Privileges, and he was appointed to the committee on ecclesiastical reforms in April, 1641. He spoke later that year against papists. With King, another Dorset lawyer, Whitaker was reported several times for absence in 1642 and 1643,[341] but he was still a member of the House at his death, 3 October 1646. His will, dated 23 March 1642, was re-read and published on 10 September 1646.[342]

Whitaker may not have had a large landed estate, although he probably inherited the Wiltshire properties of his grandfather and he had with his wife a portion of £1000. He seems to have purchased other lands afterwards[343] and in his will in 1642 he referred to several that he held by leasehold and copyhold. He was not a subscriber to the loans in 1640 and 1641, however, and even in June, 1642, his name was absent from the subscribers' list.

Whitaker's will indicates a nature religious and retiring, a man who did not desire ostentation and who was concerned for the spiritual and material welfare of his children.[344]

* **John White** (1590–1645), of the Middle Temple, member for Southwark, 1640–1645, was the well known puritan of Welsh descent who had experienced the censure of Laud and the Star Chamber for his activities on behalf of the preaching ministry. He was perhaps one of Coryton's lawyers when the charges were preferred against him in 1629 for his conduct in parliament,[345] but he was not a parliament man himself before 1640. Nor does White seem to have had any connections with county administration in Surrey. He may have had a house in St. Andrew's, Holborn, in 1638,[346] and was possibly the John White who was named to the sewers commission for Middlesex in 1629 and 1630.[347] Little evidence of his financial standing remains beyond his offer of £100 without interest for the defense in 1642, a larger sum than was offered by many, but perhaps more indicative of zeal than of wealth.[348] White had been interested in both the Virginia and the Massachusetts Bay Companies.[349] Among his close associates at the Temple before 1640 were William Drake, D'Ewes, Bagshaw, and Seaborne,[350] all fellow M.P.'s in 1640.

According to the pedigree at the visitation of London, White's mother was a daughter of Thomas Fletcher of Bangor, and his wives were (1) Katherine Barfoote of Essex and (2) Mary Style of Bucks.[351] These points disagree with the corresponding details in *D.N.B.*

John White (fl. 1599–1655), secretary to the Earl of Dorset, was M.P. for Rye, 1640–5 February 1644. He probably came of the Sussex family seated at Nordiam, not far from Rye, being apparently the son of John White, gentleman, of that place (d. 1599), by his second wife, Mary, daughter of John Spencer of London. An elder half-brother, William (born *c.* 1593),[352] was a J.P., 1632–1639, quite possibly the one who protested against the attempts of the puritan justices to deal with religious matters at the sessions.[353] John was named in his father's will, 22 October 1599,[354] and was probably reared by his mother and her second husband, Thomas Ballard. He may have been the "John White, gent."

---

[333] *Mid. Temp. Rec.* 1: 421; 2: 587, 667.
[334] Brett, *John Pym*, xxiii–xxv.
[335] *Mid. Temp. Rec.* 2: 542, 712, 839, 858, 942.
[336] *Vis. Dorset, 1623*, 97.
[337] Mayo, *The municipal records of the borough of Shaftesbury*, 56–57, 82.
[338] Hutchins, *Dorset* 3: 629.
[339] *Somerset and Dorset N. and Q.* 4: 19, 1894–1895.
[340] *C.S.P. Dom., 1631–1633*, 74; S.P. 16/405; C. 181/5, fol. 226.
[341] *C.J.* 2: 21, 128, 545, 966; D'Ewes (C), 23–24.
[342] P.C.C., 169 Twisse.
[343] *Somerset and Dorset N. and Q.* 7: 303, 1900–1901; 8: 128, 1902–1903.
[344] References in addition to those above are: Hoare, *Wilts.* 3 (1): 42–43; Hutchins, *Dorset* 3: 628; *M. of P.*

[345] *C.S.P. Dom., 1628–1629*, 555.
[346] Dale, *Inhabitants of London*, 189.
[347] C. 181/4, fols. 23v, 64.
[348] *N. and Q.*, 1st Ser., 12: 359, 1855.
[349] Brown, *Genesis of the U. S.*, 1051; *Winthrop Papers* 2: 82, n., 1929. He is of course to be distinguished from the Reverend John White of Dorchester (F. Rose-Troup, *The Massachusetts Bay Company and its predecessors*, 159).
[350] *Mid. Temp. Rec.* 2: 703, 777, 882.
[351] *Vis. London* 2: 346. Katherine Barfoote was a daughter of Edward Barfoote of Lamburne Hall, Essex, according to White's M.I. at the Temple as recorded by Dugdale. *East Anglian*, N.S., 12: 99, 1907–1908.
[352] *Vis. Sussex, 1530, 1633–4*, 130; I.P.M. of John White of Nordiam, C. 142/260/149.
[353] *Sussex Arch. Coll.* 16: 43, 1864; C. 193/13; *C.S.P. Dom., 1639–1640*, 386.
[354] I.P.M. cited above. He was probably then an infant, his mother's marriage settlement having been dated about two years before.

who was admitted to Gray's Inn, 30 January 1627.[355] He married about 1630, or earlier, Joan, the youngest daughter of John Sackville of Selscombe. She was a sister of William White's wife and of Sir Thomas Sackville, K.B., and a kinswoman of the earls of Dorset.[356] It was probably about this time also that White entered the service of Dorset, living part of the time thereafter at Westminster.[357]

In the elections for the Short Parliament, White was commended by his patron to Rye,[358] and he sought a place also in the Sackville borough of East Grinstead, where the bailiff gave him strong support. His return for the latter borough was ruled out by the Commons in April, 1640, but his seat for Rye went unchallenged.[359] White had worked in the same elections to win a place at Hastings for one court candidate against another, and was charged with attempting bribery.[360] His return for Rye in the autumn of 1640 was probably again the result of patronage.

White seems to have been a consistent royalist in the Long Parliament, although his activities were somewhat obscured by the presence of the other John White, M.P. for Southwark. He voted against Strafford's attainder,[361] and offered in August to be bail for a French priest in the queen's service who was under arrest. On 11 June 1642 he opposed censuring the lords who had joined the king at York.[362] He probably deserted the House soon afterwards to join his patron and was disabled on the same day as the latter's son, Lord Buckhurst, 5 February 1644.[363] He petitioned to compound in 1646, describing himself then as of Eltham, Kent, and admitting that he had sat in the parliament at Oxford. He seems to have been alive in August, 1655.[364]

Of White's worldly estate little is known. His father's will mentioned some lands in Sussex and Kent which were to be his,[365] but most of the family property had gone to his brother. His compounding fine of £165 implies but a small income from land.

Richard Whitehead (c. 1594–1664 ?), of Norman's Court in West Tytherley, Hants, was M.P. for Hampshire, 1640–1648. He was the son and heir of Sir Henry Whitehead of Norman's Court (d. 1629) by his first wife, Anne, daughter of James Weston of Lichfield,

Staffordshire. His father was a J.P. and sheriff in Hampshire,[366] an M.P., and a critic of the royal administration in 1626.[367] Richard, born about 1594,[368] entered Brasenose College, Oxford, in 1610, was graduated B.A. in 1612, and in the latter year was admitted a student at the Inner Temple.[369] He was licensed in 1614 to travel for three years,[370] and perhaps gained some military experience overseas, for he was interested in military affairs for many years afterwards. He may have been the Lieutenant Whitehead who was listed as a member of the Cadiz expedition in 1625. He was captain of a Hampshire regiment in the musters of 1625–1629. Possibly he was the Captain Whitehead who was taken prisoner at the Isle of Rhé in 1627, and who was on the rolls of the Rochelle expedition in 1628. After 1631 he was regularly reported as colonel of the Andover regiment of his county militia.[371] About 1621 Whitehead married Margery, daughter of John Culliford of Purbeck, Dorset.[372] He seems to have married twice afterwards, his second wife (d. 1632) being a daughter of Robert Love,[373] and the wife who survived him being described in his will as Lady Cecilia Knollis.[374]

Whitehead was concerned with civil as well as with military affairs in his county. He was a J.P during most of the reign of Charles I,[375] and a member of other commissions in Hampshire and neighboring counties.[376] He was sheriff of Hampshire in 1636 and had considerable difficulty with collecting his predecessor's ship money arrears in addition to his own assignment. He was rebuked for being one of the officers most in arrears in December, 1636. Early in 1638 he professed to be still trying to make collections, but declared he would have to pay nearly £30 out of his own pocket to make up the amount.[377] But his performance as sheriff was not the first indication of his attitude toward the policies of the crown. In 1627, following his father's attacks on the administration, Whitehead opposed the forced

[355] *Gray's Inn Adm. Reg.,* 180.

[356] Berry, *Sussex Genealogies,* 181, 300–301; *Vis. Sussex, 1530, 1633–4,* 183. John and Joan White had three children by the time of the visitation of 1633–1634 (*ibid.,* 130).

[357] One Mr. John White was a parishioner at St. Margaret's, 1637–1639 (Parish Records, Overseers' Accounts, 1638–1642).

[358] *H.M.C., Thirteenth Report* 4, Rye MSS, 209–210.

[359] *M. of P.* 1: 483 and n.; 3: App., xliii; *Sussex Arch. Coll.* **20:** 153–154, 1868.

[360] *C.S.P. Dom., 1639–1640,* 565, 607; *1640,* 3, 12.

[361] Verney, 58.

[362] *C.J.* 2: 620; Sanford, *St. and ill.,* 493, 495; D'Ewes (B), 397.

[363] *C.J.* 3: 389.

[364] *Cal. Com. Comp.,* 728, 1512.

[365] I.P.M. cited above.

[366] *Vis. Hants.,* 90; Berry, *Ped. Hants.,* ix; C. 193/12, 13.

[367] *M. of P.* 1: 465; *E.H.R.* 17: 736, 1902.

[368] I.P.M., Sir Henry Whitehead, C. 142/448/92.

[369] *Al. Oxon.; Students admitted to the Inner Temple,* 202.

[370] *Acts P.C., 1613–1614,* 585.

[371] S.P. 16, 522/16; 116/85; Add. MSS, 21,922, fols. 5, 61v, *passim;* Add. MSS, 26,781, fols. 17, 21v, *passim.*

[372] *Vis. Hants.,* 90; I.P.M. cited above.

[373] *V.C.H. Hampshire* 4: 523. The date and inscription on her memorial (1632) make it seem more probable that she was the wife of this Richard Whitehead than the widow of his grandfather (d. 1593).

[374] P.C.C., 24 Bruce. Several authors have stated that Whitehead was a son-in-law also of Colonel Richard Norton, perhaps confusing him with the Richard of a later generation, possibly his second son. Berry, *Ped. Hants.,* 194; Whitehead's will.

[375] C. 193/12, 13; S.P. 16/405; Bodleian Rawl. MSS, D 666, fol. 81.

[376] C. 181/4, fols. 2v, 147v; 181/5, fols. 230, 378.

[377] *C.S.P. Dom., 1635–1636,* 392; *1636–1637, 1637,* and *1637–1638, passim.* He was nearly fifty per cent in arrears in 1637. S.P. 16, 367/37.

loan. He finally agreed to pay £3 to the commissioners.[378] And he refused to be knighted in 1630, paying instead the large composition of £25.[379] He joined with Jervoise, Tulse, and five other J.P.'s in protesting to Council in 1639 against having to make further contributions toward the repair of St. Paul's.[380] He agreed, however, to contribute £20 that year toward the king's journey north.[381] He had sat in the 1628 parliament for Lymington, and was returned to both of 1640 for the county.[382] Among his intimates were such Hampshire puritans as Jervoise, Button, and Tulse.

Whitehead supported Pym's group in the Long Parliament. He served on several early committees,[383] offered his bond for £1000 for the November loan,[384] and in 1642 pledged two horses for the defense.[385] He was an active committeeman in his county during the war, and was especially severe in his dealings with royalists. He was quoted as saying that cruelty to them was work acceptable to God.[386] He was apparently secluded by Pride's Purge in 1648, but returned to his seat in 1660.[387] He survived until about 1664. His will, dated 22 December 1659, when he was in perfect health, was proved on 17 May 1664.[388]

The Whitehead family had held estates in Hampshire from the fifteenth century, and Richard was apparently one of the wealthy men of his region.[389] His paternal inheritance included at least five manors in Hampshire and Wiltshire,[390] and his listing for the several loans and assessments are indicative of his wealth. In his will he referred to the "plentiful" blessing of worldly goods which he had enjoyed, to the £1500 which had already been paid for a daughter's portion, and £500 for a son, and arranged for over £4600 more to be provided for his wife and younger children.

Whitehead was related to several of his fellow parliament men of 1640, including Jephson and the Jervoises.[391] One of his daughters, sometime before he wrote his will, became the second wife of Nathaniel Fiennes.

* **Bulstrode Whitelocke** (1605–1676 ?), of Phillis Court and Fawley, Bucks, was M.P. for Great Marlow,

1640–1653. The son of Sir James Whitelocke, the judge, he was a lawyer and a J.P. of some repute by 1640. He had travelled both on the continent and in England. He took seriously his first experience in parliament, when he represented Stafford in 1626, keeping for himself a record of the proceedings. He somewhat begrudged the time he had to spend as a J.P. and member of various commissions in his county,[392] but in that service gained his first distinction. Not only did he oppose the extension of the forests and of the jurisdiction of ecclesiastical courts, but Whitelocke was consulted by Hampden and his lawyers on the ship money test case. He disapproved of traffic with the Scots, however, and of their opposition to the king.[393] He yielded to the urging of friends in challenging the court faction for a place in the Short Parliament for Abingdon, where he was recorder, but was defeated by Sir George Stonehouse (q.v.). His election for Marlow in the autumn came only after he had decided not to try for Oxfordshire and after he had become involved, without previous knowledge of the plans, in a heated contest and a by-election at Marlow. The presence of a number of his friends on the Committee of Privileges facilitated his efforts.[394]

Whitelocke was among friends and relatives in the 1640 House. There were the future royalists, such as his kinsman, Robert Croke, and his intimates of days at the Temple, Bridgeman, Edward Hyde, and Palmer. And among his friends of the opposition, besides those from his own county, were Maynard, Glyn, Selden, Sir Arthur Ingram, and the younger Grimston.[395] John Mostyn was a relative by marriage.

Whitelocke was a man of means, having inherited in three counties lands on which his ancestors had lived "plentifully and generously," and others which his father had purchased. The inherited lands were worth at least £1000 a year,[396] and the dowries of his wives were, respectively, £3000 and £2500. Whitelocke did not receive the latter amount in full, but he seems to have used those portions to buy more lands. One investment in trade was so disappointing that he advised his children to avoid such ventures.[397] He once described his own estate as small,[398] but he was wealthy enough to pledge £500 in support of the loan of March,

---

[378] Rawl. MSS, D 666, fol. 103v.

[379] Add. MSS, 21,922, fol. 177.

[380] Rawl. MSS, D 666, fol. 85v.

[381] Rushworth **3**: 911.

[382] M. of P. **1**: 477, 483, 493.

[383] C.J. **2**: 37, 62, 75.

[384] D'Ewes (N), 52, where the name appears as "Mr. Whiting."

[385] N. and Q., 1st Ser., **12**: 360, 1855.

[386] Godwin, The Civil War in Hampshire, 97, 104; Add. MSS, 24,860, fols. 53, 134, 145.

[387] Thomason Tracts, 669. f. 24, p. 17.

[388] P.C.C., 24 Bruce. He was removed in September, 1662, from the burgess roll of Portsmouth corporation. Robert East, Extracts from records . . . of Portsmouth, 169.

[389] V.C.H. Hampshire **3**: 429, 430; **4**: 148.

[390] I.P.M., C. 142/448/92.

[391] Vis. Hants., 90; Rawl. MSS, D 666, fol. 87.

[392] R. H. Whitelocke, Memoirs of Bulstrode Whitelocke, 18, 29–30, 43–52, 101–107, London, 1860; Add. MSS, 37,343 (Whitelocke's "Annals"), fols. 13, 132, 140; C. 193/13; C. 181/4, fol. 179v; 181/5, fols. 270, 380.

[393] Add. MSS, 37,343, fols. 142–143, 160.

[394] Ibid., fols. 197–198, 206–212, 229.

[395] Whitelocke tried in vain to dissuade Palmer from his actions which brought on him the displeasure of the House in December, 1641. Ibid., fols. 139v, 152, 234–235, 237, 249, 258.

[396] Add. MSS, 37,341, fol. 3v; J. Bruce, ed., Liber Familicus of Sir James Whitelocke, xiv, 15, 53, Camden Society, 1858.

[397] R. H. Whitelocke, op. cit., 65; Add. MSS, 37,343, fols. 137, 145v, 146v, 150, 153v, 161–162.

[398] R. H. Whitelocke, op. cit., 453.

1641, and he promised two horses for the defense in 1642.[399]

The account of his life which Whitelocke left for his children reveals his human qualities, his enjoyment of visiting and entertaining, his fondness of card playing and music, of hunting and fishing. A friend wrote of him about the time of his second marriage that he was of a "fair, great and full fortune," and was of "as good parts as any gentleman in England of his rank, & of a nature and disposition as good as his parts."[400]

Thomas Whitmore (1612–1653), of Apley, Shropshire, M.P. for Bridgnorth, 1640–5 February 1644, was the eldest surviving son of the principal landlord and owner of the markets of that borough, Sir William Whitmore (d. 1648). The latter, a lawyer and formerly of the London Haberdashers' Company, was sheriff of Shropshire in 1620, a J.P., and three times M.P. for Bridgnorth.[401] Thomas's mother was Sir William's second wife, Dorothy, daughter of William Weld of London. He was born in London in 1612 and matriculated at Trinity College, Oxford, in 1630 (B.A. 1631). He was admitted also in 1630 to the Middle Temple, where he was called to the bar in 1639.[402] He married at Leyton, Essex, on 16 April 1635 Elizabeth, daughter and heiress of Sir William Acton, alderman and later mayor of London. He seems to have held no public office before his election to the Short Parliament for Bridgnorth.[403]

Whitmore was named to several committees in the early period of the Long Parliament,[404] but was possibly leaning toward royalism then, for he was created a baronet on 28 June 1641. He was disabled with his colleague and kinsman, Acton, on 5 February 1644, and was taken prisoner by the parliamentarians early in 1645.[405] He and his father had suffered heavy damages from the war, and when he compounded for his delinquency, he was fined £5000. He died in 1653 and was buried, 18 May, at Stockton.[406]

Because both his father and his father-in-law were still living during the period that Whitmore was a parliament man, his personal wealth then was not great. He paid an assessment of some £500 in 1643, but did not petition to compound in full until after his father's death in 1648 and declared then that his own estate before that was inconsiderable.[407] His father's possessions, including manors in the counties of Worcester, Somerset, and Salop, were worth about £900 a year, however,[408] and that income, in addition to his wife's expected inheritance, enabled him when he drew up his will in 1652 to plan large portions for their children.[409]

* Sir Thomas Widdrington (*c*. 1600–1664), of Cheesebourne Grange in Stamfordham, Northumberland, sat for Berwick, 1640–1653. He was a distinguished lawyer and recorder of both Berwick and York. Widdrington was born about 1600,[410] and became recorder at Berwick in 1631. He presided for Lord Howard at his borough court in Morpeth in 1632,[411] and was appointed York's recorder in April, 1637. He was recommended to that office by Justice Hutton, who described Widdrington as "exceedingly well learned and well esteemed . . . and generally beloved by all that know him."[412] His house in York served as a temporary prison for Lord Say or Lord Brooke in the spring of 1639, when those lords were ordered held for refusing to fight in the army or take the military oath.[413] He continued meanwhile to be recorder of Berwick, and was a J.P. there in 1640.[414] He hoped to be elected by York to the Long Parliament, but Strafford's support of his candidacy apparently worked against him.[415]

Widdrington's interest in York led him to compile a history of that city upon which later historians have drawn.[416] His studies were also in the field of di-

---

[399] D'Ewes (N), 439; *N. and Q.*, 1st Ser., **12**: 359, 1855.

[400] Add. MSS, 37,343, fols. 1–2, 5v, 9, 10, 139v, 152.

[401] Shrops. Arch. Soc., *Trans.*, 4th Ser., **4**: 272–273, 1914; **5**: 54, 1915; *Complete Baronetage* **2**: 92; Burke, *Landed gentry*, 1850.

[402] *Al. Oxon.*

[403] *M. of P.* **1**: 482. Because he was described in the October return (*ibid.* **1**: 492) as the son of Sir John Whitmore, it has been suggested by H. T. Weyman (Shrops. Arch. Soc., *Trans.*, 4th Ser., **5**: 57, 1915) that the Long Parliament member was the son of John Whitmore of Ludstone, Esq. That Thomas Whitmore, however, also a lawyer of the Middle Temple, was possibly living in Southwark in 1637 and was still without knighthood in 1648 (A. R. Ingpen, *The Middle Temple bench book*, 198; *C.S.P. Dom., 1637–1638*, 505; London Corporation MSS, Rep. 52, fol. 41v; Shrops. Arch. Soc., *Trans.*, 3rd Ser., **2**: 331, 1902). Thomas Whitmore, the M.P., after the date of the baronetcy, was referred to in the *Journals* and later in the compounding proceedings as Sir Thomas Whitmore, or Sir Thomas Whitmore, Baronet (*C.J.* **3**: 389; **4**: 543; *Cal. Com. Comp.*, 1483).

[404] *C.J.* **2**: 55, 107.

[405] *C.J.* **3**: 389; Stowe MSS, 190, fols. 161, 187.

[406] Shrops. Arch. Soc., *Trans.*, 4th Ser., **4**: 272–274, 1914.

[407] He owned before the war a group of houses in Bridgnorth valued at some £198 yearly (*ibid.; Cal. Com. Comp.*, 1483).

[408] Shrops. Arch. Soc., *Trans.*, *loc. cit.*; S.P. 23/209/453–457, 465–469.

[409] He referred in his will to his wife's "good estate" of her own, but desired her to have also £200 a year from his estate; and he wished each of their four younger children to have a portion, including what their grandfather Acton had provided, of £5000. The will, dated 11 November 1652, codicil 24 February 1652/3, was proved 20 September 1654. P.C.C., 222 Alchin. An abstract of the will (410 Alchin) is printed in Shrops. Arch. Soc., *Trans.*, 4th Ser., **4**: 274–275, 1914.

[410] He was aged thirty at his father's death in 1630. I.P.M. of Lewis Widdrington, C. 142/475/104.

[411] *Arch. Ael.*, 2nd Ser., **16**: 62, 1894.

[412] York Corporation MSS, City House Book 35, fol. 326.

[413] *C.S.P. Dom., 1639*, 98.

[414] C. 181/5, fol. 330.

[415] *C.S.P. Dom., 1640–1641*, 158.

[416] Drake, *York*, preface; *The life of Marmaduke Rawdon*, xxxvi, n., Camden Society, 1863.

vinity.[417] And he was a man of means as well as of attainments. His Northumberland properties which, when he inherited them, included over five hundred acres, were worth by 1663 more than £799 a year.[418] His wife's marriage portion was over £1000, probably £1500.[419]

Sir Thomas was a son-in-law of Ferdinando Lord Fairfax, M.P. for Yorkshire, and a kinsman of Sir William Widdrington and Sir William Carnaby (q.v.).

* Sir William Widdrington (1610–1651), of Widdrington, Northumberland, was M.P. for his county from 1640 until he was disabled for royalism, 26 August 1642. After the death of his father, Sir Henry, who had been sheriff and three times knight for his shire,[420] William was for a time the ward of an uncle.[421] In 1627 the king granted the wardship to Lord Mansfield, with the understanding that the ward was to marry a daughter of John Steward of Coldingham,[422] but the marriage probably did not take place, for he married Mary Thorold in 1629. He was knighted in 1632,[423] and served as a J.P. and member of various local commissions for his county and others in the north.[424] He collected most of Northumberland's ship money levy during his term as sheriff, 1636–1637, but in spite of his pains was called before Council late in 1637. He promised to attend as early as he could, but no other details are known.[425] He was living at that time at his Lincolnshire estate of Blankney, but was a D.L. in Northumberland in 1640.[426] He may at some time have been attached to the court, possibly during his minority,[427] but seems to have concerned himself after he came of age with north country affairs.

Widdrington offered his bond for the unusually large sum of £2000 when loan pledges were offered in March, 1641,[428] and he served on a number of committees dealing with secondary matters.[429] His royalist zeal was early in evidence, however, and his membership terminated soon after the war began.

His father's only son, Widdrington inherited at least five Northumberland manors,[430] and he increased his holdings by marriage. His loan promise of 1641 indicates that he was wealthy. The list of his estates that were sold by the sequestration committees is long, including mills and mines in addition to other properties.[431]

Widdrington was a cousin of Sir Patrick Curwen and was related more distantly to Sir Thomas Widdrington and Sir William Carnaby.

* John Wilde, or Wylde (1590–1669), Serjeant-at-Law, was M.P. for Worcestershire, 1640–1648, having won the election in a contest with the royalist, Sir Thomas Littleton. He was born of a Worcestershire family, and was a J.P. there during much of the reign of King Charles,[432] and a member of various local commissions and of the Council of Wales.[433] He was one of the legal advisers of the city of Worcester in 1627 and in March, 1640, was elected its recorder.[434] He sat for Droitwich in six parliaments, including that of the spring of 1640, and had been an outspoken critic of abuses in administration and of the king's foreign policy as early as 1621.[435]

Wilde inherited from his father a number of houses and other properties in Droitwich, about thirty buildings in Worcester, and various others in the county,[436] and he married a coheiress. But his income from his legal practice may have been larger than that from his lands. He pledged some £66 for the king's expenses in 1640.[437] In the Long Parliament he offered his bond for £1000 to secure the first loan,[438] and was a member of numerous important committees, including that of the recess in 1641.[439]

Serjeant Wilde was a brother-in-law of William Pierrepont (q.v.), since they married sisters.

Sir Charles Williams (1590–1642), of Llangibby, Monmouthshire, was M.P. for his county, 1640–1642. An election for filling his seat following his death was ordered on 19 March 1642.[440] The son of Rowland Williams of Llangibby (H.S., d. 1612), he was born in 1590,[441] and became a man of prominence in his county.

[417] Widdrington's will refers to his books on divinity, history, and other subjects. *Arch. Ael.*, 3rd Ser., **6**: 36, 1909.
[418] I.P.M. cited above; John Hodgson, *A history of Northumberland*, Part 3, **1**: 332, Newcastle, 1820–1858.
[419] Bodleian Fairfax MSS, 31, fols. 66, 70.
[420] Bean, *Northern Counties*, 500–501.
[421] *Acts P.C.*, 1626, 375.
[422] *C.S.P. Ireland*, 1625–1632, 205.
[423] *Complete Baronetage*. The date appears in *D.N.B.* as 1642.
[424] C. 193/13; S.P. 16/405; C. 181/5, fols. 15, 70, *passim; C.S.P. Dom.*, 1635, 510.
[425] *Ibid.*, 1636–1637, 413, 490; 1637, 103, 139, 383; 1637–1638, 15, 213.
[426] *Ibid.*, 1637–1638, 16; 1639–1640, 312.
[427] Bean, *op. cit.*, 501.
[428] D'Ewes (N), 439, n.
[429] *C.J.* **2**: 77, 99, 152.
[430] I.P.M. of Henry Widdrington, C. 142/404/139.

[431] *Cal. Com. Comp.*, 2416–2418, 2671.
[432] C. 193/12; S.P. 16/405.
[433] C. 181/3, fol. 114; 181/4, fol. 18; 181/5, fols. 124, 199, 280, 322; *Arch. Camb.*, 6th Ser., **17**: 196, 1917.
[434] Worcester Corporation MSS, Audit Book **2**, fols. 108d, 193; Order Book **2**, fol. 195v.
[435] *Commons Debates 1621* **3**: 80, n., 113, 459, n., *passim.*
[436] I.P.M. of George Wilde, Serjeant-at-Law, C. 142/356/104; Worcester Corporation MSS, Audit Book **2**, fols. 3, 11, *passim.*
[437] S.P. 16, 538/84.
[438] D'Ewes (N), 52.
[439] *C.J.* **2**: 288. A sketch of Wilde's life appears in Williams, *Worcester*, 42.
[440] *M. of P.* **1**: 491; *C.J.* **2**: 489.
[441] I.P.M. of Rowland Williams, C. 142/327/101. "Esquire" was the rank of his father, but he was referred to as a knight in *Complete Baronetage* (**2**: 173) and Williams, *Parl. Hist. Wales* (122).

He represented it in parliament in 1621,[442] and was a J.P. during most of the reign of King Charles, and a member of various local commissions.[443] In 1627 he was one of the county's D.L.'s [444] as well as sheriff.

In the Long Parliament Sir Charles was not a leader. He was so outspoken, however, on 27 May 1641 when he opposed the bill abolishing episcopacy, that he had to apologize for his words.[445] He probably inclined toward royalism, too, for his son and heir governed Monmouth for the king in 1645.[446] Williams was ill at the time he made his will on 5 March 1641/2, and died soon afterwards. He was evidently a man of some means, for by his will he arranged for sums of £500 each for two younger sons and £800 for an unmarried daughter.[447]

By his first marriage Williams was connected with William Morgan, M.P. for county Brecon, their wives being sisters. And by his second marriage, he was apparently a brother-in-law of Sir John Trevor (q.v.).

* Henry Wilmot (1612–1658), army captain and the king's commissary general of horse in 1640, was M.P. for Tamworth, Staffordshire, from 12 November 1640, when Strode (q.v.) decided to serve for a Devon borough, until his expulsion for his part in the army plot, 9 December 1641.[448] He was the only surviving son of Charles, first Viscount Wilmot (d. 1644), and was educated at Oxford and trained in the wars on the continent. Wilmot owned some properties in Oxfordshire.[449]

* Sir Francis Windebank (1582–1646), the well known Secretary of State of Charles I, was M.P. for Corfe Castle from November, 1640, until he fled to France in December.[450] He had failed to be re-elected by Oxford University, his constituency of the spring, and doubtless owed his seat for the Dorset borough to Sir John Banks. He is not known to have had any connection with Dorset before, although his appointment to various commissions of the peace and for piracy and other matters had not been limited to Westminster and Berkshire, his chief fields of activity.[451] Windebank's

association with Laud's program [452] and his harsh condemnation of Prynne in the Star Chamber actions of 1633 and 1637 [453] were perhaps in part responsible for his failure to secure the Short Parliament election for Berkshire, and for his difficulties in the autumn.[454]

The owner of property in Berkshire and Wiltshire, Windebank had been accounted among those able in 1611 to lend money to the king.[455] His offices at court shortly before 1640 yielded him fees in return for favors done for individuals,[456] in addition to his salary of £800 or £900.[457] But his expenses and the obligations to the king which his position imposed had by 1638 impaired his finances.[458] On the eve of the Long Parliament not only was his own salary much in arrears, but a loan of £3000 to the king brought him to serious straights, for he presently declared that his private revenue was insufficient to maintain him and his family.[459] The first month of the Long Parliament brought Windebank political and financial ruin.

Edmund Windham, or Wyndham (1601–1682), of Westminster and of Kentsford in St. Decumens, Somerset, was M.P. for Bridgwater from 1640 until his disablement as a monopolist, 21 January 1641. He was the eldest son and heir of Sir Thomas Windham (d. 1635) by his wife, Elizabeth, daughter of Richard Coningsby of Hampton Court, Hereford, and was born in 1601. He matriculated at Wadham College, Oxford, 16 April 1619,[460] and was admitted to Lincoln's Inn in 1620.[461] He saw service in the Low Countries,[462] but was back in England by 1623. In August of that year he married Christabella, daughter and coheiress of Hugh Pyne of Lincoln's Inn and of Cathanger, Somerset.[463] For the next five years Windham was probably influenced in his politics by Pyne. As Minehead's M.P. in 1625 and 1628 [464] he attacked Buckingham and helped to expose his schemes against parliament.[465]

[442] M. of P. 1: 452. Whether he was an M.P. in the Short Parliament, too, is not known, since his county's return is missing.
[443] C. 193/12, 13; S.P. 16/405; C. 181/4, fols. 44, 186v; 181/5, fols. 13, 66, 189, 321.
[444] S.P. 16, 76/30.
[445] Sanford, St. and ill., 364.
[446] Complete Baronetage 2: 173.
[447] P.C.C., 55 Cambell.
[448] Wedgwood, Staff. Parl. Hist. 2: 87–88. The date of his death is given by Wedgwood as 19 February 1657, rather than 1658, as in D.N.B.
[449] Cal. Com. Comp., 2235.
[450] M. of P. 1: 488; C.J. 2: 53.
[451] Some of his commissions were for Devon and Cornwall. C. 193/12, 13; C. 181/3, fol. 16; C. 181/4 and 181/5, passim; S.P. 16, 24/94v.

[452] D.N.B.; C.S.P. Dom., 1633–1634, 326.
[453] Documents relating to the proceedings against William Prynne, 21, Camden Society, 1877; S.P. 16, 361/77.
[454] C.S.P. Dom., 1639–1640, 161–162; 1640–1641, 107.
[455] Berks. Arch. Jour. 19: 122, 1913; C.S.P. Dom., 1640–1641, 546; Add. MSS, 5496, fol. 94.
[456] A list of Windebank's gifts for six months in 1637 appears in S.P. 16, 371/60.
[457] S.P. 16, 301/9; D'Ewes (B), 136.
[458] The king in 1638 assured the proposed father-in-law of Windebank's son that Windebank's fortune could not but be improved daily by his nearness to the king. C.S.P. Dom., 1638–1639, 139.
[459] Exchequer Receipts, 1640 (S.P. 453/74); C.S.P. Dom., 1640–1641, 313, 315, 435, 436.
[460] Somerset and Dorset N. and Q. 11: 157, 1908–1909; Al. Oxon.
[461] Linc. Inn Rec. Adm. 1: 185.
[462] Collinson, Somerset 3: 492.
[463] I.P.M., Sir Thomas Windham, 1637, C. 142/568/120.
[464] M. of P. 1: 465, 477.
[465] Forster, Eliot 2: 268. For the bolder politics of Pyne, see his nephew, John Pyne.

But after his father-in-law's sufferings on account of his politics, and his death in 1628, Windham turned to the court. His wife became the nurse of the baby prince, Charles, in 1630, and remained an intimate of the court thereafter.[466] They were residents of St. Margaret's parish in Westminster,[467] and by 1635 Windham was a gentleman of the king's privy chamber.[468] Both he and his wife sought to improve their fortunes by the means customary to courtiers. He secured, in spite of the judges' opposition to such a political appointment, a clerkship in one of the Exchequer offices in 1632.[469] Between that year and 1640 he was associated with the soap monopoly, with mining operations in county Flint, and with a variety of other projects, and with the founts of the royal revenue. Endymion Porter was an associate in one enterprise. Windham lost money in the Earl of Bedford's Great Level,[470] but those losses were partially covered by his other gains, and he was reputed to be a gentleman of fortune in his county.[471] He was a member of several of the royal commissions on depopulation in the 1630's,[472] but was apparently more concerned with his court connections that he was with county affairs. He accompanied the king to York in 1639 and agreed with some reluctance to lend him £500 in 1640.[473]

Elected to both of the 1640 parliaments for Bridgwater,[474] Windham was allowed to keep his seat but a short time, for he was quickly attacked and expelled as a monopolist.[475] He fought with the royalists during the war, compounded eventually for his estate, and went to France after the execution of the king. He returned with the Restoration, sat again in parliament, and died in 1682.[476]

Wyndham inherited from his father numerous manors and parts of manors in Somerset and Devon, and received with his wife a dowry of £1500. Their combined income from lands and from his principal office at court seems to have brought them a total gross income of £3000 a year before the war. However, because of annuities payable from his lands, and because about two-fifths of them were mortgaged in 1638, perhaps to cover losses in the Great Level venture, his available income from his lands and his office amounted to about £1500 a year.[477] His compounding fine, at a sixth, was about £692.[478]

Edward Wingate (1606–1685), of Lockley, Hertfordshire, M.P. for St. Albans, 1640–1648,[479] was inexperienced in earlier parliaments, but his sympathy with the popular side led to his taking an active part within a few weeks of the opening of the session. He was the eldest son of Edward Wingate of Lockley, and of Harlington, Bedfordshire (d. 1654), by his wife, Margaret, daughter of Peter Tavener of Hexton.[480] He was baptized at Harlington on 20 July 1606,[481] and matriculated at Trinity College, Cambridge, at Easter, 1623. He was admitted to Gray's Inn in 1626.[482] Probably not long after that he married Mary, daughter and coheiress of Ralph Alwey of Canons in Shenley, Herts, and thereby became the possessor of the manor of Holmes, alias Canons.[483]

Wingate seems not to have served in local offices before 1640, unless possibly with the militia,[484] and his election in October of that year was vigorously opposed by Thomas Coningsby, who had occupied the seat in the Short Parliament.[485] Wingate was appointed to several committees in the early months, including those on the judges, the Bishop of Ely, and the breach of parliamentary privilege,[486] and with the outbreak of war took up arms against the king. He served as a committeeman and an army officer, was a prisoner of war for a while, and was among the members to whom parliament voted money for expenses. He was secluded in 1648 and seems to have lived in retirement afterwards, until Charles II appointed him one of the Commissioners of the Excise. He died at the age of seventy-nine, and was buried at Welwyn, 10 August 1685.[487]

[466] C.S.P. Dom., 1629–1631, 334; 1631–1633, 277; 1639, 509. Windham was sometimes referred to as the nurse's husband. Add. MSS, 33,935, fol. 355. His wife was described as one of the most beautiful women of her time (Collinson, op. cit. 3: 492), but Clarendon pictured her as "a woman of great rudeness" and "country pride." Rebellion 4: 22–23.

[467] Records of St. Margaret's Parish, Overseers' Accounts, 153–154.

[468] C. 181/5, fol. 1.

[469] C.S.P. Dom., 1625–1626, 198; S.P. 16, 533/69; H.M.C., Fourth Report, House of Lords MSS, 22.

[470] C.S.P. Dom., 1635, 1635–1636, 1637, 1638–1639, 1640–1641, passim. For an account of Windham's offices and projects see H. A. Wyndham, A family history, 1410–1688, The Wyndhams of Norfolk and Somerset, 176, 179–183, London, Oxford Univ. Press, 1939.

[471] Clarendon, Rebellion 3: 79.

[472] S.P. 16, 229/112/252; C. 181/5, fols. 1, 172, 183.

[473] S.P. 16, 427/21, 38/ii; 447/36, 37, 94.

[474] M. of P. 1: 483, 492.

[475] C.J. 2: 71.

[476] Collinson, Somerset 3: 492; Somerset and Dorset N. and Q. 11: 157, 1908–1909.

[477] I.P.M. cited above; H. A. Wyndham, op. cit., 223–225, 230.

[478] Cal. Com. Comp., 964.

[479] M. of P. 1: 489, O.P.H. 9: *29.

[480] Clutterbuck, Herts 2: 496; Vis. Beds., 152, 203. He was a cousin of Edmund Wingate, the mathematician (Wood, Athenae Oxon. 3: 423).

[481] Blaydes, Genealogia Bedfordiensis, 127, 386. His father did not purchase Lockley until 1624. V.C.H. Hertford 3: 167.

[482] Al. Cant.

[483] Clutterbuck, Herts 1: 484.

[484] His father was probably a J.P. in 1637 (C.S.P. Dom., 1637–1638, 448), and the son may have had some experience with the trained bands, for he was called a captain as early as 14 July 1642 (C.J. 2: 671).

[485] D'Ewes (N), 370, 496, 508.

[486] C.J. 2: 50, 59, 91.

[487] Kingston, Herts. during the Civil War, 28, 59, 143–145; Al. Cant.

Very little is known of Wingate's financial standing in 1640. Since his father survived until 1654, he probably did not have a large estate at the time of his election, and his wife's request for assistance during his imprisonment suggests that the war may have impaired the value of what he held.[488]

Richard Winwood (1609–1688), of Denham and Ditton, Buckinghamshire, was M.P. for Windsor, Berkshire, from the summer of 1641 until 1648. His election in place of Taylor, who was expelled on 27 May 1641, was in some question, but on 5 July he was permitted to take the Protestation and was named on 24 July to a committee, even though as late as 28 June 1642, the matter of his election had not been entirely settled.[489] His family connections and parliamentarian view doubtless explain the situation.

Winwood was the eldest surviving son and heir of Sir Ralph Winwood, the diplomat and Secretary of State (d. 1617), by his wife, Elizabeth, daughter and coheiress of Nicholas Ball of Totnes, Devon. He was born on 15 April 1609.[490] Of his education nothing is known. One of his brothers went to Eton, and his younger brothers to the Middle Temple,[491] but the family responsibilities which became his after the death of his father doubtless required Richard to spend much of the time after he came of age in the country. In 1633 his sister, Anne, married Edward, heir apparent of Lord Montagu of Boughton (q.v.), and probably not long afterward Winwood married Anne, daughter of Sir Thomas Read of Berkshire.[492] This connection probably accounts for the grant to him in 1636 of the keepership of pheasants in the honor of Windsor.[493]

Winwood's mother, who seems to have managed the estates competently during her son's minority, followed somewhat the example of her puritan kinsmen of the region in regard to loans and taxes. She was listed as a musters defaulter in 1626,[494] and in 1627, having made a payment for the loan at one place, carefully avoided paying elsewhere.[495] She protested in 1636 against the ship money rates set on one of her Bucks properties, declaring it was seventeen times too high, but made her payments on the others.[496] Richard meanwhile was interested in adding to the family estates.[497] In 1638 he was named to local commissions in Bucks and other counties,[498] though he was probably not yet a J.P.

Winwod was without experience in national politics when he was chosen to fill the Windsor vacancy in the late spring of 1641, but he quickly joined the parliamentarians. He was named to the recess committee that summer.[499] In June, 1642, he promised to supply six horses for the defense at once and to furnish six more if they were needed,[500] a large contribution. He worked then with Hampden and Goodwin to gather forces in his county for the parliamentary army and was named a D.L. for Bucks.[501] But he was interested in keeping the peace if possible, and went in January, 1643, as one of the commissioners to negotiate with the king.[502] He was secluded by the purge of 1648.[503] Winwood sat again for Windsor after the Restoration,[504] and died on 28 June 1688. He was buried at Quainton, Bucks.[505]

Winwood's financial position was good. His father was said to have owned lands in Buckinghamshire worth £1000 annually in 1614, and shortly before his death he purchased for £6100 several other manors there.[506] He owned lands in Norfolk and Suffolk, also, and planned portions of £4000 for his daughters. When Sir Ralph died it was considered that he left "a very good estate," with £1500 a year in Bucks for his heir, in addition to the manor and park of Ditton.[507] Part of the property was enjoyed by his widow until her death in 1659, but she assisted her son in adding to the family possessions in the county.[508] He enjoyed, furthermore, a pension which the republic of Holland had granted for life to his father and him,[509] and was doubtless one of the wealthy men of the region. At his death Winwood endowed the almshouses at Quainton, not far from Aylesbury.

[488] He owned in 1661 some lands in Diggeswell parish, Hertfordshire. W. Le Hardy, ed., *Calendar to the Sessions Books, 1658–1700*, Hertfordshire County Records, **6**: 41, Hertford, 1930.

[489] *M. of P.* **1**: 485 and notes; *C.J.* **2**: 199, 223, 643.

[490] *Vis. Bucks.*, 131. An elder brother was born in 1605 (*The letters of John Chamberlain* **1**: 214). The date of Richard's birth has been reckoned from data in the I.P.M. of Sir Ralph Winwood, C. 142/376/99. The date given in *D.N.B.* (*sub* Sir Ralph Winwood) is incorrect.

[491] *Liber Familicus of Sir James Whitelocke*, 47; *Mid. Temp. Rec.* **2**: 813.

[492] Lipscomb, *Buckingham* **1**: 427. At the time of the heralds' visitation in 1634 he was not married.

[493] *C.S.P. Dom., 1635–1636*, 269.

[494] S.P. 16, 36/55.

[495] She had paid on a privy seal in Bucks in 1626, and was assessed both in London and in the country in 1627. *Verney Papers*, 286, Camden Society, 1853; S.P. 16, 61/100; 76/21/i.

[496] *C.S.P. Dom., 1635–1636*, 539–540.

[497] *V.C.H. Buckingham* **3**: 308, 319; **4**: 94.

[498] C. 181/5, fols. 244, 272, 352. He was named on a commission in Norfolk and Suffolk in 1641. *Ibid.*, fol. 380.

[499] *C.J.* **2**: 288.

[500] *N. and Q.*, 1st Ser., **12**: 338, 1855.

[501] Lipscomb, *op. cit.* **1**: 597.

[502] May, 277.

[503] *O.P.H.* **9**: *15; Pink MSS, 307, fol. 53v.

[504] *M. of P.* **1**: 512, 534, 540, 546.

[505] Lipscomb, *op. cit.* **1**: 427.

[506] *C.S.P. Dom., 1611–1618*, 260; I.P.M., C. 142/376/99. One Bucks manor was worth £150 a year in 1614 (*V.C.H. Buckingham* **3**: 308), and another, between £450 and £500 yearly in 1620 (Bodleian Willis MSS, 30, fols. 6v, 10).

[507] *The letters of John Chamberlain* **2**: 109.

[508] Winwood's purchase of Ditton manor, where his father had held only a lease on the park there, is an example. See note 497 above, and Lysons, *Mag. Brit.* **1**: 639; Lipscomb, *op. cit.* **1**: 274, 397, 597.

[509] He was said to be enjoying the pension in 1631. Birch, *The court and times of Charles the First* **2**: 94.

Among Winwood's fellow parliament men of 1640, besides his kinsman and neighbor, Hampden, were his cousins by marriage, Denton and Wenman,[510] and his brother-in-law, Edward Montagu.

Thomas Wise, or **Wyse** (*c*. 1605–1641), of Sydenham and Mount Wise, near Plymouth, was one of the knights for Devonshire from 1640 until his death in March, 1641. He was the son and heir of the wealthy Sir Thomas Wise, K.B. (M.P., J.P., D.L., d. *c*. 1630),[511] by his wife, Margery, daughter and sole heir of Robert Stafford of Stowford. Through his paternal grandmother, one of the Bullers of Shillingham, Wise was related to the three gentlemen of that family who were fellow parliament men. He seems to have been guided by them frequently in his politics. Born about 1605,[512] Wise was educated at Cambridge (matric. Sidney Sussex, 1619; B.A. 1622; incorporated at Oxford 1622).[513] He entered his first parliament in 1625, sitting for Callington, Cornwall, and in the next two he represented Beeralston, a town his father had earlier served and where the family appear to have had considerable influence. In 1629 he married Mary, daughter of Edward Lord Chichester, and shortly afterwards succeeded his father as the owner of large estates in Devon and Cornwall.

Wise lived much of the time in a mansion near Plymouth which had been settled on his wife at their marriage, and he exchanged courtesies with the Plymouth officials.[514] Several of his children were baptized, however, in the parish church of Stoke Damerell.[515] In 1637 and 1638 he was living at Sydenham.[516] He probably lived and entertained expensively, for his wardrobe included many handsome suits, and his debts by 1641 amounted to some £3000.

The first public office Wise held after his father's death seems to have been that of sheriff of his county, 1637–1638. One experience of his shrievalty was being fined £10 by the Quarter Sessions for not attending court at its first session for returning writs and orders.[517] But his principal difficulty was with ship money. In May, 1638, nearly a third of the £9000 expected of Devon was still uncollected, and although Wise had various excuses to explain the delay, it must be suspected that his shortcomings were not entirely unintentional. As late as December, 1639, he was still explaining to Council about arrears and making excuses for not attending the lords in person to give satisfaction.

His kinsmen, the Bullers, were sometimes the bearers of his messages, and he doubtless had the backing of others of their belief.[518] One high church vicar was reported in 1640 as prepared to denounce Wise from his pulpit as a factious man and one who did not levy ship money.[519]

In the elections for the Short Parliament Wise stood both for Beeralston and for the county, but with the understanding that, if he succeeded in the shire, the Beeralston place should go to William Strode. His influence with the county was strong enough to secure him the knightship both then and in the autumn election.[520] And his brother-in-law, Sir Samuel Rolle, sought his aid in getting a place for some Devon or Cornwall borough in a by-election.[521] Wise was definitely one of the opposition.[522] He offered his security for the 1640 loan,[523] but his death in London on 18 March 1641 [524] cut short a career that promised to be interesting. Wise was buried in St. Margaret's, Westminster, and his will was proved on 24 March by his cousin, Francis Buller (*q.v.*), whom he called his best friend. Wise's widow afterwards married another of her husband's friends, John Harris of Radford, M.P. for Liskeard. Other fellow parliament men who were mentioned in his will as friends were the Rolle brothers and Jonathan Rashleigh.[525]

Although his debts were accumulating by 1641, Wise must have been wealthy. His family's real estate included six manors in Devon and three in Cornwall, in addition to numerous other holdings, and one of his sisters had a dowry of £2500.[526] In 1629 he was part owner of some privateers sailing under letters of marque from Plymouth.[527] When he made his will he planned portions of £1000 each for his younger children.[528]

Sir Thomas Wodehouse, or **Woodhouse, Bart.** (1585–1658), of Kimberley, member for Thetford, 1640–1653, came of a family seated near Thetford for centuries and active in county affairs. His father, Sir Philip Wodehouse, the first baronet, (d. 1623), had seen service at Cadiz, and had been sheriff, J.P. and M.P., and his mother was Grisell, daughter of William

---

[510] Edmund Hampden's daughters, who married Denton and Wenman, were nieces of Lady Winwood. *The letters of John Chamberlain* **2**: 56.

[511] C. 193/12, 13; S.P. 16, 15/4.

[512] His parents were married in 1604.

[513] *Al. Cant.*

[514] Plymouth Corporation MSS, 132, fol. 222.

[515] Plymouth Inst. *Trans.* **9**: 93, 1884–1887.

[516] *C.S.P. Dom., 1637*, 500; *1637–1638*, 456.

[517] Devonshire MSS, Quarter Sessions Minute Books, 1633–1640, Easter, 1638.

[518] *C.S.P. Dom., 1637*, 500; *1637–1638*, 456; *1639*, 94–95; *1639–1640*, 147.

[519] *The Buller Papers*, 33–34.

[520] *C.J.* **2**: 14; Willis **3**: 231.

[521] *The Buller Papers*, 33.

[522] For some reason Pink thought Wise was of the court party. Pink MSS, 307, fol. 335.

[523] D'Ewes (N), 52, n.

[524] I.P.M., C. 142/607/103. Wise's will was dated in January, 1640/1 and attested by witnesses on 15 March. According to various authors he died of smallpox or of the plague.

[525] P.C.C., 35 Evelyn.

[526] I.P.M. cited above and I.P.M. of Robert Rolle, C. 142/502/65.

[527] *C.S.P. Dom., 1629–1631*, 156.

[528] In addition to the authorities cited above are the following: Burke, *Landed gentry* **2**: 1618, 1851; Devon *Trans.* **41**: 131–136, 1909; *M. of P.* **1**: 451, 475.

Yelverton of Rougham, Norfolk, and widow of Hamon (Thomas ?) LeStrange. Lady Wodehouse was a Catholic, although Sir Philip was not, and her son may have been trained in his early years in that faith.[529] Thomas was born about 1585, was "bred gallantly," entering Caius College, Cambridge, in 1598 and Lincoln's Inn in 1601.[530] He was knighted in 1603 when King James stopped in Northamptonshire on his way to London to be crowned, and became a gentleman of the bedchamber to Prince Henry. Under the prince's auspices, as a preparation for higher functions at court, Wodehouse was sent in 1611 to France, Spain and Italy,[531] but his career in that direction ended with the death of the prince, and he retired to country life. He married in 1605 Blanche, daughter of John Carey, Baron Hunsdon, and widow of Christopher Peyton, and succeeded his father in 1623. He lived at Kimberley in ease and plenty, for his estate was said to be worth £2000 a year, taking his pleasure in hounds and horses, with "musick and his book" for home entertainment. He performed his gentleman's duties by being a J.P. in both Norfolk and Thetford for many years, county sheriff, 1624–1625, one of the loan commissioners in 1627, and a member of other commissions for his region.[532]

Sir Thomas's first parliament was that of the spring of 1640. He seems to have been stirred into action then by fear of the factionalism he saw developing around him, and urged others, such as his kinsman, John Potts (q.v.), to seek election likewise in the cause of moderation.[533] He stood for the same principles in the autumn,[534] and in the Long Parliament, though working with the majority for the rights of the subject, let others take the lead.[535] He was not named often to committees,[536] and in the spring of 1641 was absent for a time, possibly on account of illness. He wrote that April to Potts, commenting on the need for defense of church and commonwealth, "especially in this hereticall age, wherein there lives so many sublapsarians (sic)," but regretting the delay in the execution of Strafford, whom he regarded as a principal "artifficer of mischiefe" in the kingdom, and hoping that other measures against arbitrary rule might be adopted before more serious trouble developed.[537] When war finally approached Wodehouse promised to supply two horses and £200 for the defense,[538] and soon afterwards went into Norfolk to oppose the execution of the commission of array.[539] He remained a member of the House until its dissolution, but was absent most of the time after the radical element assumed power, and limited himself to his county responsibilities. He died on 18 March 1658, and his will, dated 2 March 1657,[540] was proved 17 May 1658.[541]

John Wogan (1588–1644), of Wiston, Pembrokeshire, was M.P. for his county, 1640–1644.[542] His family were engaged in some of the feuds that were still typical of the Welsh counties, and in his young manhood he was accused with his parents and brothers in Star Chamber suits of riotous dealings with their neighbors in the county and town of Pembroke. John himself was said to have gained and used illegally the captaincy of the trained bands.[543] Wogan married Jane, daughter of Sir Thomas Colclough of Tintern, Ireland.[544] He was a J.P. in his county by 1626 and long afterwards,[545] was a commissioner on exacted fees in 1635,[546] and a D.L.,[547] and was sheriff in 1636.[548] He was M.P. for Pembroke county in every parliament from 1614 to 1640, except that of 1624.

Wogan did not take an active part in the Commons of the Long Parliament, but he supported the popular side, and in June, 1642, he promised to supply one horse for the defense.[549] He died sometime in 1644.[550]

Wogan was a first cousin of Hugh Owen, a fellow member, and was the father of Thomas Wogan (M.P. 1646), the regicide.[551]

Sir Henry Worsley, Bart. (1613–1666), of Apuldercombe, Isle of Wight, was M.P. for Newport, one of the island's boroughs, 1640–1648. He was the son

---

[529] Testimony of her nephew, Charles Yelverton, a recusant, in 1601, and of a priest who in 1608 attributed his conversion largely to his residence in the Wodehouse household. Norwich Public Library MSS, 37–51, Norfolk Collections, **3**: 103; **5**: 43–44.

[530] Al. Cant.; Linc. Inn Rec. Adm. **1**: 131.

[531] Blomefield, Norfolk **2**: 554; C.S.P. Dom., 1611–1618, 100.

[532] C. 193/12 and 13; S.P. 16/405; LeStrange, Norfolk official lists, 21; C. 181/3; 181/4, fol. 68v; 181/5, fol. 205; C.S.P. Dom., 1627–1628, 320.

[533] Bodleian Tanner MSS, 67, fols. 176, 178, 189.

[534] V.C.H. Norfolk **2**: 507.

[535] Blomefield, Norfolk **2**: 556.

[536] C.J. **2**: 44, 200.

[537] Tanner MSS, 66, fol. 65.

[538] N. and Q., 1st Ser., **12**: 358, 1855.

[539] Mason, Norfolk, 281.

[540] P.C.C., 354 Wootton. Further indications of Wodehouse's wealth and interests appear in his will, such as his references to jewelry of diamond and pearl, his "organ, harpsecall and chest of vyolls," and his "herballs & a book called the dispensatorie."

[541] References in addition to those cited above are M. of P. **1**: 482, 491; Complete Baronetage **1**: 51–52; The visitation of Norfolk, 1664, Norfolk Record Society, **5**: 240–241, 1934.

[542] M. of P. **1**: 498. He was styled "senior" in the return, doubtless to distinguish him from his son, John, who died about 1642. F. Green, "The Wogans of Pembrokeshire," West Wales Historical Records **6**: 214–215, 1916.

[543] St. Ch. 8/75/1; 239/20.

[544] West Wales Historical Records **6**: 208, 1916.

[545] C.S.P. Dom., 1625–1626, 387; C. 193/12, 13; S.P. 16/405.

[546] C. 181/5, fol. 31.

[547] C.S.P. Dom., 1634–1635, 169.

[548] Ibid., 1636–1637, 153; S.P. 16, 311/89.

[549] N. and Q., 1st Ser., **12**: 360, 1855.

[550] O.P.H. **9**: 16.

[551] West Wales Historical Records **6**: 208–209, 1916. In addition to the authorities previously cited see Williams, Parl. Hist. Wales, 155.

and heir of Sir Richard Worsley, first baronet (H.S. Hampshire, 1617; M.P. for Newport, 1614, 1621; d. 1621), by his wife, Frances, daughter of Sir Henry Neville of Billingbeare, Berkshire, and was born in 1613.[552] His father, who was educated at Oxford, was known as a very scholarly gentleman, a wise magistrate, and keeper of a bountiful house, and the family was considered very religious. The son, however, seems not to have enjoyed the same kind of education, nor to have inherited all of his father's admirable qualities. He does not appear to have been named to local office before 1640. He married about 1632 or 1634, his wife being Bridget, a daughter of Sir Henry Wallop (q.v.), with a portion, it was said, of £4000.[553] Worsley showed some reluctance about paying his ship money in 1637.[554] And in 1639, following his father-in-law's example, he ignored the request for a loan to the king.[555] He had a personal grievance against one aspect of the royal administration, too, for he was a royal ward for twelve years after his father's death, and from 1636 to 1641 he was engaged in lawsuits seeking to avoid a levy under authority of the Court of Wards which he declared was based on a great overestimate of the value of his property.[556] With his mother he was a party to another lawsuit during the same period brought by Sir Bevis Thelwell for losses he declared his drainage project in the Isle of Wight had suffered from their negligence.[557] When he was returned to parliament for Newport in the spring and in the autumn of 1640,[558] Sir Henry was still involved in the legal proceedings.

As a young member Worsley was not conspicuous in the House. He offered his security for £1000 for the 1640 loan, however,[559] and was named to several committees, including two that interested him personally. One was concerned with the authority of the Court of Wards and the other dealt with a local matter in the Isle of Wight. On 29 September 1642 he promised to support the Earl of Essex and to bring in £100 for the cause,[560] and he served on several parliamentary committees in his county, 1643–1645.[561] He was secluded from the House in December, 1648, but was sheriff of Hampshire in 1658 and M.P. again in 1660 and 1661. He died at Compton, Hants, on 11 September 1666.[562]

Worsley's family inheritance consisted of more than a dozen manors lying in the Isle of Wight, including

Newport, and in other parts of Hampshire, Wilts, Dorset, and Sussex.[563] A single one of them he declared worth over £144 yearly, but it may have been worth as much as £300 a year.[564] With his wife's handsome portion added to his wealth he was certainly qualified to be on the loan lists for both king and parliament.

Relatives of Worsley's in the 1640 parliament, besides his father-in-law, Wallop, were three brothers-in-law, Robert Wallop, William Hevingham, and John Meux. With the latter he probably had little in common in the matter of habits and politics. More distant relatives through his mother were Henry Killigrew and Sir Henry Berkeley.

* Sir Christopher Wray (1601–1646), of Ashby and Barlings, Lincolnshire, sat for Grimsby from 1640 until his death in 1646. He had served for the same borough in the parliaments of 1621, 1624, 1625, and 1628, as well as in the Short Parliament.[565] He was a D.L. in his county as early as 1627,[566] a member of several commissions on local matters,[567] and a J.P. for many years.[568] Having inherited through his mother properties of the Drury family in Suffolk and near Grimsby, and increased his fortune by his marriage with Albinia Cecil, coheiress of Viscount Wimbledon,[569] Sir Christopher was in 1640 a well-to-do member. He gave his bond for £1000 for securing the loan in November,[570] and when he made his will in 1645 planned handsome portions for his younger daughters.[571]

Wray was a half-brother of Sir John Wray, the county member, a brother-in-law of Sir Anthony Irby and Sir Edward Ayscough and, by 1640, the father-in-law of the younger Vane. Several other members were more distantly related.[572]

* Sir John Wray, Bart. (1586–1655), of Glentworth, county Lincoln, was knight for his shire, 1640–1653. The eldest son of Sir William Wray of Glentworth, Bart. (d. 1617), by his first wife, Lucy, daughter of Sir Edward Montagu of Boughton, he was a nephew of

[552] I.P.M., Sir Richard Worsley, 1622, C. 142/389/126; *Complete Baronetage* 1: 66.
[553] *The Oglander memoirs* (Long), 148–151; *A royalist's notebook*, 73, 160–161, 188.
[554] *The Oglander memoirs* (Long), xxii.
[555] Rushworth 3: 914.
[556] *C.S.P. Dom., 1640–1641*, 494–495.
[557] Ibid., *1637–1638*, 128; *1640*, 151; *The Oglander memoirs* (Long), 116–117.
[558] *M. of P.* 1: 483, 493.
[559] D'Ewes (N), 52.
[560] *C.J.* 2: 87, 155, 787.
[561] Add. MSS, 24,860, fol. 145; Godwin, *The Civil War in Hampshire*, 104.
[562] *Complete Baronetage* 1: 66.

[563] I.P.M. cited above; *V.C.H. Hampshire* 5: 171, 172, 194, 202, 237.
[564] The higher figure was what Worsley called an overestimate by the Court of Wards. *C.S.P. Dom., 1640–1641*, 494–495.
[565] *M. of P.* 1: 452, 458, 464, 476, 482. Only Wray's Long Parliament service is mentioned in *D.N.B.*
[566] S.P. 16, 78/8/i.
[567] C. 181/3; 181/4, fols. 30, 158v; 181/5, fols. 176, 202.
[568] C. 193/13; S.P. 16/405; *Lincs. N. and Q.* 4: 182, 1894–1895.
[569] Dalton, *The Wrays of Glentworth* 1: 70, 76, 220–222; *Lincs. N. and Q.* 7: 123, 1902–1903.
[570] D'Ewes (N), 52.
[571] Portions of £3000 and £2500 were mentioned for two unmarried daughters, and to Vane's wife, the elder daughter, whose portion had been settled earlier, at least £200 a year had gone, as well as certain properties. P.C.C., 36 Twisse.
[572] For Wray's life see *D.N.B.*, "Sir Christopher Wray (1524–1592)."

his fellow member, Sir Sidney Montagu, and a cousin of Edward and George Montagu and of Arthur Capel, as well as half-brother of Sir Christopher Wray. He was probably a student at Sidney Sussex College, Cambridge, in 1600,[573] and was elected to the parliament of 1614 for Grimsby,[574] as well as to three sessions early in the reign of Charles. He may have been prevented deliberately from serving in the 1626 parliament, for he was sheriff of his county that year,[575] and in 1627 was one of the leaders in resisting the forced loan. He was a J.P. for many years.[576]

Wray was undoubtedly a man of wealth. He offered his bond for £1000 to secure the loan in November, 1640, and when subscribing for the defense in 1642 he pledged £100 and 200 marks in plate, in addition to five horses.[577] He owned lands in Yorkshire, probably through his wife, a family heiress,[578] and even in his father's lifetime had the enjoyment of eight manors in his own county.[579]

Sir Peter Wroth (d. 1644), of Blendon Hall in Bexley, Kent, was M.P. for Bridgwater, Somerset, 1640–April, 1644. He was a younger son of Thomas Wroth, a lawyer of the Inner Temple (d. 1610), by his wife, Joan, daughter and heiress of Thomas Bulmer of London. His grandfather, Sir Thomas Wroth (1516–1573), was a politician of the sixteenth century who married into the family of Rich. Peter's elder brother, Sir Thomas Wroth (1584–1672),[580] resided at Petherton in Somerset, was recorder for Bridgwater and its M.P. in 1628, and was a J.P. in the county and sheriff (1640).[581] Peter was born sometime after 1584 while his parents were residents of St. Stephen's Coleman Street, London,[582] and with his brother, Thomas, was admitted to the Inner Temple in February, 1607.[583] He was knighted at Theobalds in 1619,[584] and made his residence at the place in Kent which his father had bought, while the older brother occupied the Somerset properties of the family. He shared with Sir Thomas

in purchasing and selling lands in the west, however,[585] and since the brother had no sons, Peter was his heir apparent. In February, 1625, Wroth married Margaret, eldest daughter of Sir Anthony Dering of Kent, a sister of Sir Edward Dering (q.v.).[586] Sir Peter resembled that brother-in-law in some respects, for he was something of an antiquary and has been described as "a gentleman of great learning."[587] He was a member of the Kent sewers commissions of 1639 and 1640,[588] but seems to have been generally inactive in public affairs before 1640.

Wroth's brother was a puritan and one of his letters to the clergyman, Dr. Stoughton, in 1635, in which he bemoaned the sadness of the times, had been called "dangerous and seditious."[589] Peter was present in Somerset for the shire election at Ilchester on 12 October,[590] and his election as one of Bridgwater's members five days later was no doubt managed with his brother's assistance. The latter could not well serve because his term as sheriff was not over. But before the end of the month, Sir Peter was in prison for some unknown cause, possibly a political one. He was released about 30 October,[591] in time for him to take his seat in parliament. Wroth was named to several minor committees that dealt with legal papers, and was appointed in the summer of 1641 to the committee for the recess.[592] He apparently supported the party favoring moderate reforms, his views probably resembling Dering's more than his brother's. He was probably the author of two letters to the elder Vane in October, urging Vane, for the sake of his political future, to give up his attempt to deal with the Scots. His letters referred to the puritans as factious people, and he spoke unfavorably of Pym and of "those that study the great change of all places."[593] Certainly Wroth was provoked to an unusual degree by the more violent members at the time of Dering's expulsion from the House.[594] He promised in June, 1642, to provide a horse for the

---

[573] *Al. Cant.*

[574] *M. of P.* 3: xxxviii. *D.N.B.* omits this fact.

[575] *List of Sheriffs*, 80; S.P. 16, 9/43. His term is misdated in *D.N.B.*

[576] C. 193/12 and 13; *Lincs. N. and Q.* 1: 137, 1888–1889.

[577] D'Ewes (N), 52; *C.J.* 2: 772.

[578] St. Ch. 8/55/7.

[579] Several of the more important of these manors were sold in trust in 1617 for the sum of £8000. I.P.M. of Sir William Wray, 1618. C. 142/386/87.

[580] *Vis. Kent, 1619,* 214; *D.N.B.,* "Sir Thomas Wroth"; Brown, *Somerset Wills* 2: 86.

[581] *C.S.P. Dom., 1639,* 191, 200; *1640,* 62. Sir Thomas came into the Long Parliament later, probably after his brother's death in 1644. He was not the original member, as is stated in *D.N.B.*

[582] Wills of Sir Peter Wroth (P.C.C., 85 Rivers) and Sir Thomas Wroth (Brown, *op. cit.* 2: 84).

[583] *Cal. Inner Temp. Rec.* 2: 28.

[584] Shaw, *K. of E.* 2: 171.

[585] *C.S.P. Dom., 1638–1639,* 203; *Somerset and Dorset N. and Q.* 6: 68, 1898–1899.

[586] *Vis. Kent, 1663–1668,* 185; Larking, *Proceedings in Kent,* 20, n.

[587] Collinson based his account of the Wroth family largely on Sir Peter's materials. *Somerset* 3: 69.

[588] C. 181/5, fols. 302, 335.

[589] *C.S.P. Dom., 1635,* 377.

[590] He signed the return that was sent in by his brother for the shire. C. 219/43/Part 2.

[591] Dering wrote to his wife on 31 October telling of Wroth's release. Larking, *op. cit.,* 20.

[592] *C.J.* 2: 129, 221, 288.

[593] He was probably the writer, since the letters were signed by "P.W.," and Wroth was the only member of those initials who was on the recess committee, the work of which is mentioned, too (*C.S.P. Dom., 1641–1643,* 132, 135). Vane was a neighbor in Kent and a connection of Wroth's by marriage.

[594] Wroth's view was then said to be that "We shall never be at peace, until five or six of this house be hanged." Larking, *op. cit.,* 74.

defense,[595] but he probably took no part in the war. He died on 18 April 1644,[596] and was buried on 12 May at Bexley.[597]

Wroth does not seem to have been wealthy, but he owned several properties in Kent and the London house in Coleman Street.[598] His family was larger than he could provide for as he wished, but he expected his brother to arrange for their portions. His will expressed religious beliefs that leaned somewhat toward puritanism, but in it he urged that his children be educated in the Church of England, which he hoped would "continue to us and our posterity." [599]

Sir Richard Wynn, or **Winne, Bart.** (1588–1649), of the royal court and of Gwydir, county Carnarvon, was M.P. for Liverpool, 1640–1649. He came of a wealthy and influential family of north Wales, being the second but eldest surviving son of Sir John Wynn of Gwydir (d. 1627), who had been M.P., J.P., D.L., several times sheriff, and member of the Council of the Marches, and whose interests ranged from the compiling of a Welsh dictionary to local politics and the development of lead mines. Through his mother, Sidney, daughter of Sir William Gerrard, Chancellor of Ireland, Richard was connected with another family of wide influence both locally and at court. Richard was born about 1588, studied at Lincoln's Inn, 1606–1608, at the end of that time entering the service of the Earl of Suffolk, Lord Chamberlain, and so, under the auspices of the Howards, beginning his career at court.[600] He was knighted in 1616 and in 1618, after a prolonged search for a bride suitable in person and portion, he married Anne, daughter and coheiress of Sir Francis Darcy of Isleworth, Middlesex.[601] From this time forth, except for occasional trips to Wales, Wynn's associations were chiefly with the court, and he was nimble enough to switch to the patronage of the new Lord Chamberlain, the Earl of Pembroke, upon the fall of Suffolk.[602] His intimacy with the royal family dates from 1617, when he became a gentleman of the privy chamber to Prince Charles, and he was one of the prince's company on the journey to Spain in 1623, and assisted at his corona-

tion.[603] His court connections, as well as his family's friendship with Lord Keeper Williams, enabled him to help his brothers and nephews find jobs, but he was prevented in 1624 by another group of Welshmen from getting for himself the grant of some of the legal revenues accruing to the prince from Wales.[604] After the accession of Charles to the throne, Wynn was granted in 1626 the reversion to the post of receiver general and treasurer to the queen, and entered upon his functions in 1629.[605]

Wynn's position at court inevitably brought him other assignments, although the extent of his activities in them is questionable. He was a member of the Council of Wales in 1633,[606] and before 1640 had been named to the commission of the peace and other local commissions for Middlesex and London as well as for Carnarvonshire.[607] He was one of the collectors of the knighthood fines in Middlesex about 1632.[608] In parliament also he had experience. He had won for Carnarvonshire under his father's influence in 1614, but was defeated there in 1621, partly, perhaps, because of the fall of his patron, Suffolk. Doubtless through the influence of his new chief in the household, Pembroke, he got a seat for Ilchester, 1621, 1624 and 1625.[609] One of the royal nominees for the Short Parliament, he was returned for three places, Newton, Bodmin, and Andover, and chose to sit for the last.[610] His election for Liverpool in October, 1640, was probably gained in a similar fashion.

Although his career lay with the court, and Wynn showed his loyalty by voting against Strafford's attainder,[611] he managed as a politician to adjust himself to the trend of the majority. He pledged £2000 to support the loan in November, 1640, and £1000 in March,[612] and was named to the committee on the Council of the Marches and that on Strafford's alleged plans for raising armed forces in Wales.[613] He and his brothers were laying in their private store of arms in the spring of 1641, for use if the times proved bad,[614] but in De-

---

[595] N. and Q., 1st Ser., **12**: 360, 1855.

[596] I.P.M., London, 1644. C. 142/745/57.

[597] Brown, *Somerset Wills* **2**: 87.

[598] Some Romney Marsh lands produced at least £77 yearly, and the London house had a rental value of £50 a year, according to Wroth's will. The nominal assessments in his I.P.M. suggest that the other Kentish properties were worth probably fifty per cent more than the marsh holdings. If so, the value of his lands may have been £225–250 a year.

[599] Will of Sir Peter Wroth, proved 20 June 1645. P.C.C., 85 Rivers.

[600] Williams, *Parl. Hist. Wales*, 59; *Complete Baronetage* **1**: 64; C. 193/13 (Merioneth); *Cal. Wynn Papers,* xv, xvi, 68, 79, 86, 113, 128, *passim.*

[601] *Ibid.,* 109–111, 124–129, 134–136. £5000 was the portion at which the Wynns originally aimed.

[602] A. H. Dodd, Wales's Parliamentary Apprenticeship (1536–1625), *Trans. of the Hon. Soc. of Cymmrodorion,* 68, 1942.

[603] *Cal. Wynn Papers,* 127, 173, 176, 179, 223. Wynn's narrative of the Spanish journey is printed in the second volume of *The autobiography and correspondence of Sir Simonds D'Ewes* **2**: 415–458.

[604] *Cal. Wynn Papers,* 152, 155, 195, 197, 199, 201; *Trans. of the Hon. Soc. of Cymmrodorion,* 60–61, 1942.

[605] *Cal. Wynn Papers,* 231, 245; *C.S.P. Dom., 1628–1629,* 507; *1629–1631,* 324.

[606] *Arch. Camb.,* 6th Ser., **17**: 195, 1917.

[607] C. 193/13; S.P. 16, 405; C. 181/3, fol. 112v; 181/4, fols. 16, 105; 181/5, fols. 3, 117, 368; *C.S.P. Dom., 1627–1628,* 567.

[608] *C.S.P. Dom., 1635,* 483.

[609] *Cal. Wynn Papers,* 102, 144–148; *M. of P.* **1**: 453, *passim;* **3**: xli; *Trans. of the Hon. Soc. of Cymmrodorion,* 68, n., 1942. The feud between Wynn's family and the Griffiths (*q.v.*) appears plainly in the correspondence about the 1621 election.

[610] S.P. 16, 450/15; *C.S.P. Dom., 1640,* 42; Pink MSS, 307, fol. 155; *M. of P.* **1**: 480, 482, 483.

[611] Verney, 58.

[612] D'Ewes (N), 52, 451, n. (452).

[613] *C.J.* **2**: 57, 75.

[614] *Cal. Wynn Papers,* 272.

cember Sir Richard was trusted sufficiently to be named to the committee sent with the Grand Remonstrance to the king.[615] He was suspended on account of absences, 2 September 1642,[616] but was able to regain his place, and continued as a member until his death, 19 July 1649. He was buried at Wimbledon.[617]

Wynn came of a wealthy family, and found opportunities to add to his fortunes. £3000 a year in lands was the inheritance his father planned for him at the time of his marriage, and though the son omitted "giving mourning" when his father died because that was too costly,[618] he purchased additional properties and interests in Wales and Lincolnshire. He was reported at one period to have been a heavy loser at gaming,[619] but was deemed capable of lending the king £3000 in 1640,[620] and his pledges for the loans in parliament the following winter were large. He kept a town house and a country place near London, and so steered his course during the war as to avoid sequestration and to list cash legacies of £1800 in his will.[621]

Colleagues of the 1640 Commons, besides his family's arch foes of Carnarvonshire, the two John Griffiths, were two nephews of Wynn's, John Bodvel and John Mostyn.

Sir Christopher Yelverton (*c.* 1602–1654), of Easton Mauduit, Northamptonshire, was returned for Bossiney, Cornwall, in two successive by-elections, 1640–1641. He took his seat after being returned on 22 December 1640, was suspended because of further doubts about the election on 12 January, but was re-elected soon after 15 February. He kept his place until 1648.[1] He was a grandson of Sir Christopher Yelverton, Justice of the King's Bench under Elizabeth and James, and the son and heir of Sir Henry Yelverton of Easton Mauduit, the judge (d. 1630), by his wife, Margaret, daughter of Robert Beale, Elizabeth's clerk of the Council.[2] He was born about 1602,[3] was granted admission to Gray's Inn in February, 1607,[4] probably in compliment to his father, and matriculated at Queen's College, Cambridge, in 1619. He was knighted on 6 May 1623,[5]

and probably married about this time or shortly before. But in December, 1624, John Chamberlain wrote of the death of Anne, young Lady Yelverton, who had brought her husband over £1000 a year,[6] and at the end of that month his father secured for him a pass for three years of travel abroad.[7] He sat in the parliaments of 1626 and 1628 for Newport in the Isle of Wight,[8] and succeeded his father in 1630. In April of that year, a few months after his father's death, Yelverton married at St. Giles Cripplegate Anne, the youngest daughter of Sir William Twysden of Royden Hall, Kent.[9]

Yelverton seems to have been living in London during the early part of the reign of King Charles. He was listed in March, 1627, as one who had refused the loan in Cripplegate Ward, declaring that he had been overassessed.[10] He was not, however, among those imprisoned for refusing. In the winter of 1630–1631 he and his wife were the London hosts of Lady Yelverton's brother-in-law and sister, Sir Hugh Cholmley of Yorkshire (*q.v.*) and his wife.[11] The authorities of Clerkenwell parish reported Yelverton for failing to give relief for the plague sufferers in 1636 and for having kept Christmas in London in 1637.[12] And he was still listed as a resident of the ward of Cripplegate Without in 1640.[13] But in the decade of the 1630's he was active also in Northamptonshire affairs and resided at least part of the time at his seat in that county. He was a J.P. and a member of the commission of oyer and terminer there,[14] and eventually was sheriff. But Yelverton was a man who interpreted in his own fashion the rules and regulations of the day. He was on the Star Chamber schedule of 1633 to appear for having eaten flesh on Fridays.[15] He was reported to Council as a musters defaulter in 1635, but made his submission and promised to conform.[16] Apparently he paid his ship money rates in Easton Mauduit,[17] although his friend, Cholmley, helped lead the opposition to the levy in Yorkshire. But when Yelverton became sheriff of Northamptonshire for the year, 1639–1640, his position on the subject became clear. He protested to Council in February, 1640, against being expected to collect the arrears for three earlier years as well as his own year's rate, calling attention to the stiffening opposition in the whole county, and in May he was ordered

[615] D'Ewes (C), 219–220.
[616] *C.J.* 2: 750.
[617] Bean, *Northern Counties*, 299, n.; *Cal. Wynn Papers*, 297, 306, 344. Aubrey, *Surrey* 1: 107, 1718.
[618] *Cal. Wynn Papers*, 242, 243.
[619] *Ibid.*, 148, 233, 277; *C.S.P. Dom., 1627–1628*, 75.
[620] *Fairfax correspondence* 1: 402.
[621] His will, dated in 1648 and proved, P.C.C. (157 Fairfax), in 1649, differs slightly from that dated in 1642 (*Cal. Wynn Papers*, 276–277). A brief sketch of Wynn's life appears in *D.N.B.*, "Sir John Wynn."
[1] *M. of P.* 1: 486 and n.; *C.J.* 2: 60, 66, 86; D'Ewes (N), 242, 256, 362; Pink MSS, 307, fol. 168.
[2] *Complete Baronetage* 2: 95. Yelverton is mentioned briefly in the *D.N.B.* article on his father.
[3] I.P.M., Sir Henry Yelverton, C. 142/467/68.
[4] *Gray's Inn Adm. Reg.*, 114.
[5] *Al. Cant.* The date of his knighting appears as 1630 in *Complete Baronetage*, but he was a knight before December, 1624.

[6] *The letters of John Chamberlain* 2: 590 and n. Yelverton had an uncle, also Sir Christopher Yelverton, who was mentioned in Sir Henry's I.P.M., but the circumstances suggest that the lady mentioned by Chamberlain was the wife of the heir of the family. Her identity is not otherwise known.
[7] *Acts P.C., 1623–1625*, 416.
[8] *M. of P.* 1: 471, 477.
[9] *Complete Baronetage* 2: 96.
[10] S.P. 16, 58/109.
[11] *The memoirs of Sir Hugh Cholmley*, 51, 1787.
[12] *C.S.P. Dom., 1635–1636*, 421; S.P. 16, 378/94.
[13] S.P. 16, 453/75.
[14] C. 193/13; S.P. 16/405; C. 181/5, fols. 9, 68, *passim*.
[15] Add. MSS, 11,056, fol. 64v.
[16] *C.S.P. Dom., 1635*, 470.
[17] S.P. 16, 314/97/i.

to appear before the Lords to answer for his negligence.[18] The records indicate that a large part of his county's assessment went uncollected that year.[19] His position as sheriff made him ineligible for election to the Short Parliament, and may explain why he was not a candidate for the original elections in the autumn. Yelverton joined with Martin Lumley (q.v.) and another sheriff on 1 December to ask the House of Lords for protection from the proceedings begun against them for their failure to levy their ship money rates.[20]

Yelverton doubtless had many friends among the popular party leaders in the west. Nathaniel Stephens of Gloucestershire was an uncle,[21] and there must have been others who worked for his return in the by-elections for the borough of Bossiney. He was permitted on 30 December 1640 to take his oath as a member of the House, and was that day named to a committee.[22] He was presumably absent from mid-January until about March, but was named again for committee work on 27 April, and from that time until 1648 was a working member. He was made a baronet in June, 1641, out of consideration, it was said, of his having maintained thirty foot soldiers in Ireland for three years,[23] but the honor wrought no change in his politics. Yelverton promised four horses for the defense in 1642,[24] and served as a parliamentary committeeman in his own county and in Warwickshire and Yorkshire.[25] He was apparently secluded from parliament by Pride's Purge and retired to Northamptonshire. There he died on 4 December 1654.[26] His will, dated 24 November 1654, was proved by his son, Sir Henry, on 23 February 1655.[27]

Sir Christopher seems to have been very well-to-do. He inherited land in the counties of Northampton, Warwick, Bedford, and Gloucester, and in London.[28] Even when he settled his estate for his married son shortly before his death he was able to retain an income of £310 a year from his chief estate in Northamptonshire, to arrange for a dowry of £8000 for his daughter, and legacies of more than £500. His will reflects not only his wealth but his puritan views, his piety mingled with pride of family, and his fondness for books.[29]

* **Walter Yonge** (1579–1649), of Upton Helions and of Colyton, Devon, the puritan diarist, represented Honiton from its restoration as a parliamentary borough until 1648 or 1649. He was baptized at Colyton, 16 April 1579,[30] and was educated at Oxford and the Middle Temple. The second son but eventual heir of a prominent merchant and landowner, Walter became a J.P. and served in that capacity for many years.[31] He was sheriff in 1628, and was on the commissions for sewers and for exacted fees.[32] He was appointed in 1635 to be Quartermaster General of the Devonshire militia.[33] As his father before him had been interested in matters of overseas development, such as the trade to Africa,[34] Walter invested some money in the Dorchester Company.[35] In his project he was perhaps interested as much for religious reasons as for financial gain.

Yonge inherited from his father several manors and rectories in Devon, one manor lying in Honiton parish, and he added other properties by purchase.[36] He was assessed in Exeter for the 1642 subsidy.[37] By 1640, however, he had probably settled most of his possessions on his heir, Sir John Yonge.[38] He was not a loan subscriber, 1640–1641, but in 1642 he promised £100 for the defense, and his son, by that time a member, promised £200.[39]

Walter Yonge was related to at least two fellow parliament men of 1640. Roger Hill was a nephew and William Strode was a brother-in-law of Yonge's son.[40] With others of his county he had long been acquainted.[41]

[18] S.P. 16, 445/54, 54/i; C.S.P. Dom., 1639–1640, 185; 1640, 126, 147.

[19] Royal Hist. Soc., Trans., 3rd Ser., 4: 159, 1910.

[20] H.M.C., Fourth Report, House of Lords MSS, 30.

[21] Yelverton so referred to Stephens in his will. The latter's wife, Catherine Beale, was doubtless a sister of Yelverton's mother.

[22] C.S.P. Dom., 1640–1641, 328; C.J. 2: 60.

[23] C.S.P. Dom., 1641–1643, 30.

[24] N. and Q., 1st Ser., 12: 360, 1855. He may have offered £200 in money besides. Bodleian Tanner MSS, 63, fol. 60. Yelverton was not in the House at the time of the 1640–1641 loan subscriptions.

[25] Northamptonshire Notes and Queries 4: 250, 1892; H.M.C., Sixth Report, House of Lords MSS, 85.

[26] Pink MSS, 307, fol. 169. The date of Yelverton's death is confused in Complete Baronetage with that of his wife (Add. MSS, 34, 177 [Twysden papers], fol. 33).

[27] P.C.C., 217 Aylett.

[28] I.P.M. cited above; Add. MSS, 14,030 (Yelverton Papers), fols. 181v–194. One Judge Yelverton, probably his grandfather, was declared by a relative to be worth £1000 a year in 1601 (Norwich Library MSS, 37–51, Norfolk Collection, 3: 103), and their income had doubtless increased after that date.

[29] Some of Yelverton's personal letters attest further his interest in books and in affairs outside of England. Add. MSS, 14,030, fol. 164.

[30] The register of the parish of Colyton, Devon, ed. A. J. P. Skinner, 40, Devon and Cornwall Record Society, 1928.

[31] C. 193/12, 13; Devonshire MSS, Quarter Sessions Minute Books, 1625–1633, 1633–1640, passim.

[32] C. 181/4, fol. 164; 181/5, fol. 218; Devon Trans. 10: 320, 1878.

[33] S.P. 16, 291/14/ii.

[34] N. and Q., 1st Ser., 11: 330–331, 1855.

[35] F. Rose-Troup, John White, the patriarch of Dorchester, 458, New York, Putnam, 1930. His son, Sir John, was actively interested in the Massachusetts settlements. F. Rose-Troup, The Massachusetts Bay Company and its predecessors, 161.

[36] I.P.M., John Yonge, gent., 1613 (C. 142/328/164); Pole, Descr. of Devon, 134, 176, 200, 221, 224; Exeter City Library MSS, Exeter Deeds and Documents, Nos. 651, 1274, 1801, 2095.

[37] Exeter Corporation MSS, Subsidy Rolls, 2: No. 18.

[38] Walter Yonge's will, P.C.C., 29 Pembroke.

[39] N. and Q., 1st Ser., 12: 360, 1855.

[40] Brown, Somerset Wills 1: 35–36; Vis. Devon, 1620, 325; Complete Baronetage 3: 232.

[41] A brief note on Yonge appears in Devon Trans. 66: 260, 1934.

INDEX

Parts II and III, because their arrangement is alphabetical, have not been indexed. The index includes, however, a number of variations in the spelling of names, and designates by bold face type (**83**) the page references to the biographies of members of the parliament whose names appear in the Introduction or Part I.